The Oxford Handbook of Personality and
Social Psychology

OXFORD LIBRARY OF PSYCHOLOGY

Editor-in-Chief PETER E. NATHAN

The Oxford Handbook of Personality and Social Psychology

Edited by

Kay Deaux

Mark Snyder

OXFORD
UNIVERSITY PRESS

OXFORD
UNIVERSITY PRESS

Oxford University Press, Inc., publishes works that further Oxford University's
objective of excellence in research, scholarship, and education

Oxford New York
Auckland   Cape Town   Dar es Salaam   Hong Kong   Karachi
Kuala Lumpur   Madrid   Melbourne   Mexico City   Nairobi
New Delhi   Shanghai   Taipei   Toronto

With offices in
Argentina   Austria   Brazil   Chile   Czech Republic   France   Greece
Guatemala   Hungary   Italy   Japan   Poland   Portugal   Singapore
South Korea   Switzerland   Thailand   Turkey   Ukraine   Vietnam

Copyright © 2012 by Oxford University Press, Inc.

Published by Oxford University Press, Inc.
198 Madison Avenue, New York, New York 10016
www.oup.com

Library of Congress Cataloging-in-Publication Data
The Oxford handbook of personality and social psychology / edited by
Kay Deaux, Mark Snyder.
    p. cm. — (Oxford library of psychology)
ISBN 978-0-19-539899-1
1. Psychology—Handbooks, manuals, etc. 2. Social psychology—Handbooks,
manuals, etc. I. Deaux, Kay. II. Snyder, Mark.
BF131.O94 2012
155.2—dc22
                              2011016640

9 8 7 6 5 4 3 2
Printed in the United States of America on acid-free paper

SHORT CONTENTS

Oxford Library of Psychology   vii

About the Editors   ix

Contributors   xi

Table of Contents   xv

Chapters   3–836

Index   837

OXFORD LIBRARY OF PSYCHOLOGY

The *Oxford Library of Psychology,* a landmark series of handbooks, is published by Oxford University Press, one of the world's oldest and most highly respected publishers, with a tradition of publishing significant books in psychology. The ambitious goal of the *Oxford Library of Psychology* is nothing less than to span a vibrant, wide-ranging field and, in so doing, to fill a clear market need.

Encompassing a comprehensive set of handbooks, organized hierarchically, the *Library* incorporates volumes at different levels, each designed to meet a distinct need. At one level are a set of handbooks designed broadly to survey the major subfields of psychology; at another are numerous handbooks that cover important current focal research and scholarly areas of psychology in depth and detail. Planned as a reflection of the dynamism of psychology, the *Library* will grow and expand as psychology itself develops, thereby highlighting significant new research that will impact on the field. Adding to its accessibility and ease of use, the *Library* will be published in print and, later on, electronically.

The *Library* surveys psychology's principal subfields with a set of handbooks that capture the current status and future prospects of those major subdisciplines. This initial set includes handbooks of social and personality psychology, clinical psychology, counseling psychology, school psychology, educational psychology, industrial and organizational psychology, cognitive psychology, cognitive neuroscience, methods and measurements, history, neuropsychology, personality assessment, developmental psychology, and more. Each handbook undertakes to review one of psychology's major subdisciplines with breadth, comprehensiveness, and exemplary scholarship. In addition to these broadly conceived volumes, the *Library* also includes a large number of handbooks designed to explore in depth more specialized areas of scholarship and research, such as stress, health and coping, anxiety and related disorders, cognitive development, and child and adolescent assessment. In contrast to the broad coverage of the subfield handbooks, each of these latter volumes focuses on an especially productive, more highly focused line of scholarship and research. Whether at the broadest or most specific level, however, all of the *Library* handbooks offer synthetic coverage that reviews and evaluates the relevant past and present research and anticipates research in the future. Each handbook in the *Library* includes introductory and concluding chapters written by its editor to provide a roadmap to the handbook's table of contents and to offer informed anticipations of significant future developments in that field.

An undertaking of this scope calls for handbook editors and chapter authors who are established scholars in the areas about which they write. Many of the nation's and world's most productive and best-respected psychologists have agreed to edit *Library* handbooks or write authoritative chapters in their areas of expertise.

For whom has the *Oxford Library of Psychology* been written? Because of its breadth, depth, and accessibility, the *Library* serves a diverse audience, including graduate students in psychology and their faculty mentors, scholars, researchers, and practitioners in psychology and related fields. Each will find in the *Library* the information they seek on the subfield or focal area of psychology in which they work or are interested.

Befitting its commitment to accessibility, each handbook includes a comprehensive index, as well as extensive references to help guide research. And because the *Library* was designed from its inception as an online as well as a print resource, its structure and contents will be readily and rationally searchable online. Further, once the *Library* is released online, the handbooks will be regularly and thoroughly updated.

In summary, the *Oxford Library of Psychology* will grow organically to provide a thoroughly informed perspective on the field of psychology, one that reflects both psychology's dynamism and its increasing interdisciplinarity. Once published electronically, the *Library* is also destined to become a uniquely valuable interactive tool, with extended search and browsing capabilities. As you begin to consult this handbook, we sincerely hope you will share our enthusiasm for the more than five-hundred-year tradition of Oxford University Press for excellence, innovation, and quality, as exemplified by the *Oxford Library of Psychology*.

Peter E. Nathan
Editor-in-Chief
Oxford Library of Psychology

ABOUT THE EDITORS

Kay Deaux

Kay Deaux is Distinguished Professor Emerita at the Graduate Center of the City University of New York and a Visiting Research Scholar at New York University. Topics of scholarly interest include social identity, gender, and immigration, and her theoretical and empirical work often combines levels of analysis from the macro (e.g., social conditions) to the micro (individual psychological processes). She is the author of several books, including most recently *To Be an Immigrant*. She has served as president of the Society for Personality and Social Psychology and of the Association for Psychological Science.

Mark Snyder

Mark Snyder is Professor of Psychology at the University of Minnesota, where he holds the McKnight Presidential Chair in Psychology and is the Director of the Center for the Study of the Individual and Society. His research interests focus on the interplay of personality, motivation, and social behavior. He is the author of the book *Public Appearances/Private Realities: The Psychology of Self-Monitoring*. He has served as president of the Society for Personality and Social Psychology and of the Foundation for Personality and Social Psychology.

CONTRIBUTORS

Glenn Adams
Department of Psychology
University of Kansas
Lawrence, KS

Christopher R. Agnew
Department of Psychological Sciences
Purdue University
West Lafayette, IN

Icek Ajzen
Department of Psychology
University of Massachusetts
Amherst, MA

David M. Amodio
Department of Psychology and
Center for Neural Science
New York University
New York, NY

Özlem Ayduk
Department of Psychology
University of California, Berkeley
Berkeley, CA

Austin S. Baldwin
Department of Psychology
Southern Methodist University
Dallas, TX

Verónica Benet-Martínez
ICREA and Universitat
Pompeu Fabra
Barcelona, Spain

Amy Canevello
Department of Psychology
University of North Carolina
Charlotte, NC

Emanuele Castano
New School for Social Research
New York, NY

Frances Cherry
Department of Psychology
Carleton University
Ottawa, Ontario, Canada

Oliver Christ
Department of Psychology
University of Marburg
Marburg, Germany

Gerald L. Clore
Department of Psychology
University of Virginia
Charlottesville, VA

Philip R. Costanzo
Department of Psychology and
Neuroscience
Duke University
Durham, NC

Jennifer Crocker
Department of Psychology
The Ohio State University
Columbus, OH

David V. Day
Management and Organisations
University of Western Australia
Perth, Australia

Kay Deaux
New York University
New York, NY

M. Brent Donnellan
Department of Psychology
Michigan State University
East Lansing, MI

Lauren E. Duncan
Department of Psychology
Smith College
Northampton, MA

William Fleeson
Department of Psychology
Wake Forest University
Winston-Salem, NC

Steven W. Gangestad
Department of Psychology
University of New Mexico
Albuquerque, NM

Eddie Harmon-Jones
Department of Psychology
Texas A&M University
College Station, TX

John G. Holmes
Department of Psychology
University of Waterloo
Waterloo, Ontario, Canada

Rick H. Hoyle
Department of Psychology and
Neuroscience
Duke University
Durham, NC

Deborah A. Kashy
Department of Psychology
Michigan State University
East Lansing, MI

Saul Kassin
John Jay College of Criminal Justice
City University of New York
New York, NY

Janice R. Kelly
Department of Psychological Sciences
Purdue University
West Lafayette, IN

Margaret Bull Kovera
John Jay College of Criminal Justice
City University of New York
New York, NY

Mark R. Leary
Department of Psychology and
Neuroscience
Duke University
Durham, NC

Rodolfo Mendoza-Denton
Department of Psychology
University of California, Berkeley
Berkeley, CA

Mario Mikulincer
Interdisciplinary Center (IDC)
Herzliya, Israel

Ludwin E. Molina
Department of Psychology
University of Kansas
Lawrence, KS

Arie Nadler
Department of Psychology
Tel Aviv University
Tel Aviv, Israel

Julie K. Norem
Department of Psychology
Wellesley College
Wellesley, MA

Shigehiro Oishi
Department of Psychology
University of Virginia
Charlottesville, VA

Allen M. Omoto
School of Behavioral and
Organizational Sciences
Claremont Graduate University
Claremont, CA

Craig D. Parks
Department of Psychology
Washington State University
Pullman, WA

Thomas F. Pettigrew
Department of Psychology
University of California,
Santa Cruz
Santa Cruz, CA

Harry T. Reis
Department of Clinical and Social
Sciences in Psychology
University of Rochester
Rochester, NY

Michael D. Robinson
Department of Psychology
North Dakota State University
Fargo, ND

Alexander J. Rothman
Department of Psychology
University of Minnesota
Minneapolis, MN

S. Adil Saribay
Bremen International Graduate
School of Social Sciences
Bremen, Germany
Assistant Professor of
Psychology
Bogazici University
Istanbul, Turkey

Deidra J. Schleicher
Krannert Graduate School of
Management
Purdue University
West Lafayette, IN

Phillip R. Shaver
Department of Psychology
University of California, Davis
Davis, CA

Chris G. Sibley
Department of Psychology
University of Auckland
Auckland, New Zealand

Jeffry A. Simpson
Department of Psychology
University of Minnesota
Minneapolis, MN

Mark Snyder
Department of Psychology
University of Minnesota
Minneapolis, MN

Abigail J. Stewart
Departments of Psychology and
Women's Studies
University of Michigan
Ann Arbor, MI

Linda R. Tropp
Department of Psychology
University of Massachusetts Amherst
Amherst, MA

James S. Uleman
Department of Psychology
New York University
New York, NY

Daan van Knippenberg
Rotterdam School of Management
Erasmus University Rotterdam
Rotterdam, The Netherlands

Ulrich Wagner
Department of Psychology
University of Marburg
Marburg, Germany

Heike A. Winterheld
Department of Psychology
California State University,
East Bay
Hayward, CA

CONTENTS

1. Personality and Social Psychology: Crossing Boundaries and Integrating Perspectives   3
   Mark Snyder and *Kay Deaux*

Part One • Foundations of Personality and Social Psychology: Historical, Conceptual, and Methodological Perspectives

2. The Intertwined Histories of Personality and Social Psychology   13
   Thomas F. Pettigrew and *Frances Cherry*
3. Perspectives on the Person: Rapid Growth and Opportunities for Integration   33
   William Fleeson
4. Perspectives on the Situation   64
   Harry T. Reis and *John G. Holmes*
5. Behavior and Behavior Assessment   93
   Janice R. Kelly and *Christopher R. Agnew*
6. Neuroscience Approaches in Social and Personality Psychology   111
   David M. Amodio and *Eddie Harmon-Jones*
7. Evolutionary Perspectives   151
   Steven W. Gangestad
8. Context in Person, Person in Context: A Cultural Psychology Approach to Social-Personality Psychology   182
   Glenn Adams
9. Conceptual and Methodological Issues in the Analysis of Data from Dyads and Groups   209
   Deborah A. Kashy and *M. Brent Donnellan*
10. Multilevel Modeling in Personality and Social Psychology   239
    Oliver Christ, Chris G. Sibley, and *Ulrich Wagner*

Part Two • Substantive Areas Approached from Personality and Social Psychology Perspectives

11. Self and Identity: Dynamics of Persons and Their Situations   263
    Jennifer Crocker and *Amy Canevello*
12. Motivation and Goal Pursuit: Integration Across the Social/Personality Divide   287
    Julie K. Norem

13. Five New Ideas About Emotion and Their Implications for
    Social-Personality Psychology 315
    Gerald L. Clore and *Michael D. Robinson*
14. Initial Impressions of Others 337
    James S. Uleman and *S. Adil Saribay*
15. Attitudes and Persuasion 367
    Icek Ajzen
16. From Help-Giving to Helping Relations: Belongingness and
    Independence in Social Interaction 394
    Arie Nadler
17. Antisocial Behavior in Individuals and Groups:
    An Empathy-Focused Approach 419
    Emanuele Castano
18. Personality and Social Interaction: Interpenetrating Processes 446
    Rodolfo Mendoza-Denton and *Özlem Ayduk*
19. Attachment Theory Expanded: A Behavioral Systems Approach 467
    Mario Mikulincer and *Phillip R. Shaver*
20. Person-by-Situation Perspectives on Close Relationships 493
    Jeffry A. Simpson and *Heike A. Winterheld*
21. Personality Influences on Group Processes:
    The Past, Present, and Future 517
    Craig D. Parks
22. Intergroup Processes: From Prejudice to Positive
    Relations Between Groups 545
    Linda R. Tropp and *Ludwin E. Molina*

Part Three • Life Domains
23. Personality, Social Psychology, and Psychopathology:
    Reflections on a Lewinian Vision 573
    Philip R. Costanzo, Rick H. Hoyle, and *Mark R. Leary*
24. Individual and Societal Well-Being 597
    Shigehiro Oishi
25. Multiculturalism: Cultural, Social, and Personality Processes 623
    Verónica Benet-Martínez
26. Personality and Social Contexts as Sources of Change and
    Continuity Across the Life Span 649
    Abigail J. Stewart and *Kay Deaux*
27. Leadership: A Person-in-Situation Perspective 673
    Daan van Knippenberg
28. Work and Organizations: Contextualizing Personality and
    Social Psychology 701
    David V. Day and *Deidra J. Schleicher*
29. A Person x Intervention Strategy Approach to Understanding
    Health Behavior 729
    Alexander J. Rothman and *Austin S. Baldwin*

30. Forensic Personality and Social Psychology   753
    Saul Kassin and *Margaret Bull Kovera*
31. The Psychology of Collective Action   781
    Lauren E. Duncan
32. Social Policy: Barriers and Opportunities for Personality and
    Social Psychology   804
    Allen M. Omoto
33. Personality and Social Psychology: The State of the Union   830
    Kay Deaux and *Mark Snyder*

Index   837

behavior (by Kelly and Agnew, in chapter 5). The point of departure for each of these chapters is distinctive, but areas of convergence become evident in each account. Indeed, the wisdom of Lewin's tripartite formula seems unquestionable, in that all three pieces are necessary for a comprehensive analysis of human behavior and, despite different emphases and historical traditions, the interrelationships among the components are clear. Thus, for example, although conceptions of the person are most fully developed in personality psychology, there is nonetheless much to be offered by social psychology (as Fleeson notes in chapter 3), with the contributions of each side of the equation complementing and enhancing each other. By the same token, although conceptions of the situation are most fully articulated in social psychology, valuable perspectives are also provided by personality psychology (as Reis and Holmes point out in chapter 4), with considerable mutual benefit afforded by their integration. And, in like fashion, both personality psychology and social psychology offer valued and valuable perspectives on just how to think about and measure behavior, with much added value from bringing together the perspectives.

As further foundation for establishing common ground for personality and social psychology, Part One of the *Handbook* continues with a consideration of the larger contexts in which persons, situations, and behaviors operate. Specifically, Amodio and Harmon-Jones probe the neuroscientific foundations of personality-social psychology (in chapter 6). Gangestad analyzes the evolutionary context for personality and social psychology (in chapter 7), and Adams considers the cultural context (in chapter 8). Then, to complement these considerations of conceptual foundations of personality and social psychology, the *Handbook* turns its attention to examples of some of the methodological considerations involved in bridging social and personality psychology, with discussions of the analysis of data from dyads and groups (by Kashy and Donnellan, in chapter 9) and multilevel modeling in personality and social psychology (by Christ, Sibley, and Wagner, in chapter 10).

With the conceptual and methodological foundations established, the *Handbook* next turns, in Part Two, to considerations of substantive areas that have been, and that can be, approached from integrated personality and social psychology perspectives. Although the substantive areas that are considered are by no means exhaustive of the substantive areas that have been examined within social psychology

and personality, they do represent ones where researchers have attempted to bring together perspectives and methods drawn from both personality and social psychology, doing so in domains that range from the individual to the dyadic to the group levels of analysis. Thus, this section includes chapters on: self and identity (by Crocker and Canevello, chapter 11), motivation and goal pursuit (by Norem, chapter 12), emotion (by Clore and Robinson, chapter 13), initial impressions of others (by Uleman and Saribay, chapter 14), attitudes and persuasion (by Ajzen, chapter 15), help-giving and helping relations (by Nadler, chapter 16), antisocial behavior (by Castano, chapter 17), social interaction processes (by Mendoza-Denton and Ayduk, chapter 18), attachment processes (by Mikulincer and Shaver, chapter 19), close relationships (by Simpson and Winterheld, chapter 20), group processes (by Parks, chapter 21), and intergroup processes (by Tropp and Molina, chapter 22). As will become evident upon reading the chapters, these authors approach their subject matter from a variety of perspectives, sometimes with personality more in the foreground and sometimes with social psychology more in the foreground, sometimes with the joint influences of social and personality being considered in additive fashion and sometimes in interactive fashion, sometimes focusing on the actual bringing together of personality and social perspective and sometimes pointing to the potential of bridges to be built between social and personality perspectives. Whatever their starting points, authors were encouraged to move beyond their normal "comfort zones" and to analyze the topic from a multifaceted perspective.

Next, in Part Three of the *Handbook*, the focus of the analysis shifts to domains in which the benefits of bringing together the perspectives of personality and social psychology are seen in addressing issues that confront and challenge individuals, groups, communities, and society at large. Thus, this section includes chapters on psychopathology (by Costanzo, Hoyle, and Leary, chapter 23), individual and societal well-being (by Oishi, chapter 24), multiculturalism (by Benet-Martínez, chapter 25), change and continuity across the lifespan (by Stewart and Deaux, chapter 26), leadership (by van Knippenberg, chapter 27), work and organizations (by Day and Schleicher, chapter 28), health behavior (by Rothman and Baldwin, chapter 29), forensic psychology (by Kassin and Kovera, chapter 30), collective action (by Duncan, chapter 31), and matters of social and public policy (by Omoto, chapter 32).

As diverse as the life domains and practical problems considered in these chapters are, the chapters illustrate the range and diversity of ways in which social psychology and personality can be brought to bear on addressing them.

We close the *Handbook* with a brief epilogue that reflects on how the chapters of this *Handbook* have illustrated the ways in which personality and social psychology can and do relate to and contribute to each other. We look forward to prospects for the continuing growth and development of an integrated personality and social psychology, including the ways in which integrated perspectives can be facilitated through the activities of professional associations, scientific journals and edited collections, departmental structures, funding agencies, and the design of educational and training programs.

With this preview of what is to come, we invite you to turn to the chapters of the *Handbook of Personality and Social Psychology*. We hope that you will be as impressed as we have been with the ways that the chapter authors have thought deeply and generatively, and have pushed beyond traditional boundaries and "business as usual" ways of thinking, to identify and explore the combined and interlocking contributions of personality and social psychology.

References

Allport, G. (1937). *Personality: A psychological interpretation.* New York: Holt.

Allport, G. (1968). The historical background of modern social psychology. In G. Lindzey & E. Aronson (Eds.), *The handbook of social psychology: Vol. 1. Historical introduction and systematic positions* (2nd ed., pp. 1–80). Reading, MA: Addison-Wesley.

Baumeister, R. F. (1999). On the interface between personality and social psychology. In L. A. Pervin & O. P. John (Eds.), *Handbook of personality: Theory and research* (2nd ed., pp. 367–377). New York: Guilford.

Crocker, J. (2010). The blurry line between social and personality. *Dialogue, 25*(1), 4–5.

Cronbach, L. J. (1957). The two disciplines of scientific psychology. *American Psychologist, 12,* 671–684.

Ekehammar, B. (1974). Interactionism in personality from a historical perspective. *Psychological Bulletin, 81,* 1026–1048.

Endler, N. S., & Magnusson, D. (1976). Toward an interactional psychology of personality. *Psychological Bulletin, 83,* 956–974.

Fenigstein, A., Scheier, M. F., & Buss, A. H. (1975). Public and private self-consciousness: Assessment and theory. *Journal of Consulting and Clinical Psychology, 43,* 522–527.

Fleeson, W. (2004). Moving personality beyond the person-situation debate: The challenge and the opportunity of within-person variability. *Current Directions in Psychological Science, 13,* 83–87.

Funder, D. C. (2008). Persons, situations, and person-situation interactions. In O. P. John, R. W. Robins, & L. A. Pervin (Eds.), *Handbook of personality: Theory and research* (3rd ed., pp. 568–581). New York: Guilford.

Funder, D. C., & Fast, L. A. (2010). Personality in social psychology. In S. T. Fiske, D. T. Gilbert, & G. Lindzey (Eds.), *Handbook of social psychology* (5th ed., Vol. 1, pp. 668–697). Hoboken, NJ: Wiley.

Goldberg, L. R. (1990). An alternative description of personality: The big-five factor structure. *Journal of Personality and Social Psychology, 59,* 1216–1229.

Higgins, E. T. (1990). Personality, social psychology, and person-situation relations: Standards and knowledge activation as a common language. In L. A. Pervin (Ed.), *Handbook of personality: Theory and research* (pp. 301–338). New York: Guilford.

Hogan, R., & Roberts, B. W. (2000). A socioanalytic perspective on person-environment interaction. In W. B. Walsh, K. H. Craik, & R. H. Price (Eds.), *Person-environment psychology: New directions and perspectives* (2nd ed., pp. 1–23). Mahwah, NJ: Erlbaum.

Ickes, W., Snyder, M., & Garcia, S. (1997). Personality influences on the choice of situations. In R. Hogan, J. Johnson, & S. Briggs (Eds.), *Handbook of personality psychology* (pp. 165–195). New York: Academic Press.

Kelley, H. H., Holmes, J. W., Kerr, N. L., Reis, H. T., Rusbult, C. E., & Van Lange, P. A. M. (2003). *An atlas of interpersonal situations.* New York: Cambridge.

Leary, M. R., & Hoyle, R. H. (2009). *Individual differences in social behavior.* New York: Guilford.

Lewin, K. (1936). *A dynamic theory of personality.* New York: McGraw-Hill.

Macrae, R. R., & Costa, P. T., Jr. (1987). Validation of the five-factor model of personality across instruments and observers. *Journal of Personality and Social Psychology, 52,* 81–90.

Marlowe, D., & Gergen, K. J. (1969). Personality and social interaction. In G. Lindzey & E. Aronson (Eds.), *Handbook of social psychology: Vol. 3. The individual in a social context* (2nd ed., pp. 590–665). Reading, MA: Addison-Wesley.

Mischel, W. (2011). Most cited, least read. In Arkin, R. M. (Ed.), *Most underappreciated: 50 prominent social psychologists describe their most unloved work* (pp. 5–9). New York: Oxford University Press.

Mischel, W., & Shoda, Y. (1995). A cognitive-affective system theory of personality: Reconceptualizing situations, dispositions, dynamics, and invariance in personality structure. *Psychological Review, 102,* 246–268.

Pettigrew, T. F. (1997). Personality and social structure: Social and psychological considerations. In R. Hogan, J. Johnson, & S. Briggs (Eds.), *Handbook of personality psychology* (pp. 417–439). New York: Academic Press.

Reynolds, K. J., Turner, J. C., Branscombe, N. R., Mavor, K. I., Bizumic, B., & Subasic, E. (2010). Interactionism in personality and social psychology: An integrated approach to understanding the mind and behavior. *European Journal of Personality, 24,* 458–482.

Snyder, M. (1987). *Public appearances/Private realities: The psychology of self-monitoring.* New York: W. H. Freeman.

Snyder, M. (2006). Building bridges between personality and social psychology: Understanding the ties that bind persons and situations. In P. A. M. Van Lange (Ed.), *Bridging social psychology: The benefits of transdisciplinary approaches* (pp. 187–191). Mahwah, NJ: Erlbaum.

Snyder, M. (2011). Products of their personalities, or creatures of their situations? Personality and social behavior has the answer. In M. A. Gernsbacher, R. W. Pew, L. Hough, & J. R. Pomerantz (Eds.), *Psychology and the real world: Essays illustrating fundamental contributions to society* (pp. 173–180). New York: Worth Publishers.

Snyder, M., & Cantor, N. (1998). Understanding personality and social behavior: A functionalist strategy. In D. T. Gilbert, S. T. Fiske, & G. Lindzey (Eds.), *The handbook of social psychology* (4th ed, Vol. 1, pp. 635–679). Boston: McGraw-Hill.

Snyder, M., & Ickes, W. (1985). Personality and social behavior. In G. Lindzey & E. Aronson (Eds.), *Handbook of social psychology: Vol. 2. Special fields and applications* (3rd ed., pp. 883–948). New York: Random House.

Tracy, J. L., Robins, R. W., & Sherman, J. W. (2009). The practice of psychological science: Searching for Cronbach's two streams in social-personality psychology. *Journal of Personality and Social Psychology, 96,* 1206–1225.

Triandis, H. C. (1997). Cross cultural perspectives on psychology. In R. Hogan, J. Johnson, & S. Briggs (Eds.), *Handbook of personality psychology* (pp. 440–465). New York: Academic Press.

Foundations of Personality and Social Psychology: Historical, Conceptual, and Methodological Perspectives

The Intertwined Histories of Personality and Social Psychology

Thomas F. Pettigrew *and* Frances Cherry

Abstract

The histories of personality and social psychology have been closely intertwined for more than a century. But there have been several critical differences that have at times acted to separate the two fields. One such divergence involved their models of humans—whether largely irrational (the personality emphasis) or largely rational (the social emphasis). This difference has now subsided with their joint acceptance of a "bounded rationality." More important has been their difference in focus—the microlevel of the person versus the mesolevel of the group and situation. But now both fields largely agree on interaction models that include both the person and the situation. We trace these tensions between the two fields across six diverse eras: (1) Origins through World War I (1890–1919); (2) Early Developments (1920–1935); (3) War Influences (1936–1950); (4) Structural Differentiation and Slow Acceptance (1951–1965); (5) Dual Crises (1966–1985); and (6) Coming Back Together Again (1986–present).

Keywords: Gordon Allport, Kurt Lewin, Henry Murray, situation, interaction, dual crises

Gordon Allport (1898–1967) and Kurt Lewin (1890–1947) would have heartily approved of this *Oxford Handbook*. Working in the 1930s before the structural differentiation of personality and social psychology, they helped to shape both disciplines.

Allport (1935) fashioned "attitudes" as a basic concept in social psychology and then wrote the definitive text on personality that established the field as an integral part of academic psychology (Allport, 1937; Pettigrew, 1990). He followed up his famous *Personality: A Psychological Interpretation* with a series of influential works—another text (Allport, 1961) and numerous books and articles focused on traits, motivation, the self, and the use of personal documents (Allport, 1943, 1950, 1955, 1960, 1968a). Later, he wrote a social psychological classic—*The Nature of Prejudice* (Allport, 1954)—which according to Google Scholar has been cited more than 12,000 times by social psychologists and others interested in this central topic of the field. Significantly, this famous volume combines Allport's

two sides; 9 of the book's 31 chapters are devoted to personality topics and how they relate to prejudice.

Lewin also importantly contributed to both fields. He invigorated experimental research in social psychology with his high-impact approach. And his ideas were institutionalized in social psychology by the efforts of the remarkable cohort of talented students whom he trained (Patnoe, 1988). But he is also a major figure in the development of personality psychology. Following his *Dynamic Theory of Personality* (Lewin, 1935), translated and published just a few years after his arrival in the United States from Germany, Lewin continued to utilize his field theory to stress viewing the person within a social context (e.g., Lewin, 1951).

Allport and Lewin were not alone. Gardner Murphy was another influential exemplar of one who effectively joined personality and social psychological concerns. With his developmental psychologist wife, Lois, he wrote the text *Experimental Social Psychology* (Murphy & Murphy, 1937). Later he published the widely adopted *Personality: A Biosocial Approach to Origins and Structure* (Murphy, 1947).

Though these giants of psychology combined work in the two fields with ease, there is a fundamental tension between the two disciplines that soon led them to follow somewhat different paths. Personality psychology focuses on the dynamic and organized set of characteristics that individuals possess that uniquely influences their cognitions, affects, motivations, and behaviors. The field is interested in both intra-individual and inter-individual differences (Rhodewalt, 2008, pp. 16–18).

By contrast, social psychology has come to emphasize several broad phenomena: the power of situational forces to shape behavior (situationalism) and the importance of how people construe their environment (subjectivism) (Pettigrew, 1991; Ross & Nisbett, 1991). The second of these emphases obviously fits well with personality interests. But the situational stance of social psychology has often led to strong disagreements between the two fields. And it is this cyclical history of the relationship between the personality and social psychology disciplines—sometimes together in agreement, sometimes apart in disagreement—that we shall trace in this chapter.

First, a few caveats are in order. Like all such histories, our account of how personality and social psychology have been intertwined over a century must of necessity be selective and interpretive. Moreover, neither the notion of "personality" nor of "social situation" has remained constant across time and place. Persons and social situations are not natural entities; rather they are social entities, constructed within social, economic, and cultural contexts (Danziger, 1997). The premodern subject of scientific analysis of the 19th century is neither the modern subject of the 1920s nor the potentially postmodern subject of the 21st century (Smith, 2005).

In addition, even the nature of what constitutes a science of personality and social psychology has changed over time. At times, throughout the development of both fields, debates have raged over the nature of what kind of science is possible, relevant, and even ethical. The distinction is frequently articulated in terms of human and natural science alternatives (Dilthey, 1976). Wilhelm Dilthey (1833–1911) saw the former as descriptive and interpretive sciences concerned with understanding the meaning of human experience in the context of history and culture, and the latter as explanatory empirical sciences concerned with explanations of human activity.

Dilthey's contemporary, Wilhelm Windelband (1848–1915), put the dichotomy in terms of the methodological goals of scientific work. Nomothetic sciences sought to establish general laws whereas idiographic sciences sought to establish the uniqueness of a phenomenon (Windelband, 1904). The former suggests experimental methods, the latter case study methods. In the natural science framework, scores on a personality inventory or attitudinal measurements in a laboratory are the products of a predictive science of the person in social situations. Knowledge claims are made primarily from the researcher's perspective. In the human science framework, narrative accounts of people's understanding of their social situation are the products of an interpretive science, and knowledge claims arise largely from the point of view of the researched.

These two approaches are not antithetical. But they are quite different vantage points that, over the course of the past century, bear on notions of what is sound, ethical, and socially useful science. It is tempting to infer from current practices that the nomothetic is more likely to be closely associated with social psychology and the idiographic with personality psychology. However, historically each has found its way into the other's domain.

With these general caveats in place, we structure our discussion of the intertwining of social and personality psychology across six specific chronological eras—each with its distinctive foci, understandings, and controversies: (1) Origins through World War I (1890–1919); (2) Early Developments (1920–1935); (3) War Influences (1936–1950); (4) Structural Differentiation and Slow Acceptance (1951–1965); (5) Dual Crises (1966–1985); and (6) Coming Back Together Again (1986–present).

Origins through World War I (1890–1919)

The roots of both personality and social psychology are to be found in European traditions where a science of persons and social situations was emerging by the middle of the 19th century. But the precise origins of the two fields are difficult to pinpoint.

With respect to social psychology, the traditions that found their way to North America were those developed by Wilhelm Wundt (1832–1920) and the many students who visited and studied in his Leipzig laboratory and then established their own laboratories all over the world. For Wundt, there was a sharp dichotomy between a natural science–oriented experimental psychology intended to discover laws of basic sensory, cognitive, and memory the founders aged, the university's administration grew less supportive and the Social Relations template was not copied by other universities. Harvard closed its unique department in 1972 over the strenuous objections of Parsons, Bales, Kelman, Vogel, and the first author.

Despite such joint programs, the post–World War II period marked an era of growing separation between personality and social psychology. The attention to issues of socialization and personality by social psychologists diminished as they turned increasingly to a primarily laboratory-based investigation of situational factors influencing attitudes and groups. Personality specialists focused on individual differences that clashed with the growing situational emphasis of social psychologists. Furthermore, in keeping with distinctions made at the outset of this chapter, the eclecticism in personality and social psychology had solidified into a natural science framework with a narrowing of investigative practices as well.

Structural Differentiation and Slow Acceptance (1950–1965)

By 1950, personality and social psychology programs were established in only a minority of universities in North America and Europe. The fields were generally viewed as marginal at best to psychology's primary concerns. Not even Lewin held tenured academic appointments at Cornell, Iowa, and the Massachusetts Institute of Technology. Despite the flourishing programs at Berkeley, Harvard, and Michigan, most psychology departments, even at prominent universities, still had neither program. At the University of Virginia (U.Va.), for example, the psychology department, highly regarded for its work in learning and physiological psychology, resisted having specialists in either personality or social psychology on its staff. From his undergraduate days at U.Va. (1949–1952), the first author recalls well the general sentiment that the two fields were simply too "soft" to meet truly scientific standards.

The dominant view of "science" in the Virginia department and elsewhere in experimental psychology at the time was shaped largely by a rigid interpretation of Vienna-circle positivism flavored with Percy Bridgman's (1959) view of operational definitions. The working model to be emulated was classical physics. Physiological instruments, memory drums for nonsense syllables and activity wheels for rats comprised the research laboratories. Personality was represented by just one undergraduate course—labeled abnormal psychology; and it was in the curriculum primarily for premedical students rather than psychology majors. Social psychology was also represented by just one undergraduate course taught by an assistant professor who was a leading expert on hearing but who nevertheless taught an excellent course. Neither course was required for the major in psychology.

Years later, after the first author had become a social psychologist, old U.Va. friends would tease him at conventions by repeatedly asking, "How are things going in *social work*?" There was in such jovial taunts a touch of political bias. Experimentalists tend to be more politically conservative than other psychologists, and this feeds into the "soft, do-gooder" view of both personality and social psychology. From her early career days, Ellen Berscheid (1992) recalls in an insightful and candid article similar views being expressed even at the University of Minnesota, where strong personality and social programs were already in place.

Zimbardo (1992, pp. xiv) summed it up when he noted that social psychology was "long relegated to a subordinate position within psychology's status hierarchy." Nor was this low status limited to North America. When the first author taught at the University of Amsterdam, an experimental psychologist asserted in a faculty meeting that he thought of social psychology as simply an applied field without any "fundamental work." Widespread acceptance by experimental psychologists of both personality and social psychology was only slowly being achieved during this period.

Together with the excitement generated by Kurt Lewin's high-impact style of laboratory experiments, this status differential explains in part why psychological social psychology in the 1950s turned away from field studies, surveys, and interest in the work of the other social sciences. White laboratory coats and full-scale laboratory experiments became the order of the day as both personality and social psychologists strove to win acceptance and status within the experimentally dominated departments.

Another factor of importance in the United States in the early 1950s entailed extreme right-wing political pressure led by the Republican Senator Joseph McCarthy from Wisconsin. McCarthy's sustained attack on what he considered communism in higher education made research on politically sensitive topics a dangerous endeavor (Schrecker, 1986). This problem persisted even after the senator's death in 1957. Indeed, this factor together with the related scarcity of research funding led to social psychology largely failing to study the exciting and historic Civil Rights Movement (Pettigrew, 2011a).

After his untimely death in 1947, Kurt Lewin's inspiration was institutionalized in social psychology by the efforts of the extraordinary cohort of talented students whom he had trained (Patnoe, 1988). Their names read today like a who's who of the leading social psychologists of the period: Kurt Back (1920-1999), Roger Barker (1903-1990), Alex Bavelas (1913-1993), Morton Deutsch (1920–), Leon Festinger (1919–1989), Harold Kelley (1921-2003), Ronald Lippitt (1914-1986), Albert Pepitone (1923-), John Thibaut (1917-1986), Alvin Zander (1913-1908), and others. Their contributions have been wide ranging. Festinger's cognitive dissonance (1957) and social comparison (1954) theories and Deutsch's conflict resolution theory (1977) enriched a theory-starved field. In research, they perfected the high-impact laboratory experiments on central issues that reoriented the field's empirical work. And the influence of their teacher is clearly apparent in all their work. But they failed to perpetuate Lewin's interest in personality.

These first-generation Lewinians encountered and overcame the low status that social psychology occupied during the 1950s in psychology departments dominated by experimental psychologists. Thus, it is not surprising that they typically followed the basic theory and research side of the Lewinian tradition rather than its applied side. Laboratory studies replaced cross-disciplinary and applied research. Consequently, applied work received far less attention as social psychologists of the period struggled to acquire full acceptance within academic psychology (Jones, 1985; Berscheid, 1992).

The Authoritarian Personality (Adorno et al., 1950) is a major contribution of personality psychology in this period. This work had early roots in Germany. The Marxists at the Frankfurt School needed to explain Hitler's popularity among lower-middle-class German voters in the ill-fated election of 1933, in which the Nazi vote rose to 43%. Marx's concept of "false consciousness" offered an insufficient explanation. The early formulations of authoritarianism found in Horkheimer (1936) and Fromm (1941), however, provided a more direct explanation. The Berkeley study, led in part by two Europeans—Theodor Adorno (1903–1969) of the Frankfurt School and Else Frenkel-Brunswik (1908–1958)—began during World War II and carried this work further. But the two American contributors—Daniel Levinson (1920–1994) and Nevitt Sanford (1909–1996)—added scale measures for the key concepts. Befitting the gross stereotype of the difference between European and North American social science, the two Europeans largely provided the theory and the two Americans largely provided the measurement.

Authoritarianism continues to attract the interest of social psychologists, particularly in Canada and Germany, because of its consistent prediction of a variety of dependent variables—especially intergroup prejudices of many types in countries around the globe. The theory has been repeatedly battered with a multitude of both theoretical and methodological criticisms from all directions, many of which have merit. One of the most serious criticisms is that the original work ignored influences of the meso- and macrolevels of situations, institutions, and cultures (Pettigrew, 1958, 1959, 1999b). For instance, *The Authoritarian Personality* (pp. 130, 171, 267, 817ff) recorded its highest F score average in an infamously harsh prison without considering the authoritarian context in which the inmates were taking the measure. For these imprisoned respondents, some of the items were literally true. Later work, however, has repeatedly demonstrated the ubiquitous interaction between such personality syndromes as authoritarianism and the social context (e.g., Peterson, 2011; Baier, Hadjar, & Boehnke, 2011).

The study of authoritarianism has also been hampered by poor measurement in numerous scales in various languages, and typically tested around the world with extremely limited and biased samples of convenience. Yet authoritarian theory has proven indestructible (Pettigrew, 2011b). Despite its many problems, it remains a major theory in both personality and social psychology. However, the two fields have employed the theory in different ways. Social psychologists tend to use it as a mediating and moderating variable in intergroup relations analyses. Personality and developmental psychologists have used it for such tasks as distinguishing between "authoritarian parenting" and "authoritative parenting" (e.g., Baumrind, 1968).

Advances concerning achievement motivation, anxiety, and field independence also evolved at this time. So, too, did the test analyses by Raymond Cattell (1905–1998) emerge that led to the 16 Principle Factors personality inventory (16 PF) and a reinvigoration of the psychometric tradition in personality psychology (Cattell, 1984; Cattell & Cattell, 1995). For good reason, Cattell remains a highly controversial figure in the history of American personality psychology for his racist writings (Tucker, 2009). But his tireless seeking of the basic dimensions of personality and temperament is

Separate organizations have also formed in Europe and North America: the European Association of Social Psychology, the European Association of Personality, the Society of Experimental Social Psychology, and the Association for Research in Personality. These groups, too, now publish leading journals. But these separate groups have come together to publish yet another joint publication—*Social Psychology and Personality Science*. In the United States, some of the motivation to form new groups was estrangement from the clinically dominated American Psychological Association. This disaffection spread to other parts of psychology as well and led to the founding of the Association for Psychological Science (APS). This group publishes four journals, none of which is dedicated to specific domains of psychology.

Another reason for the coming together of the two psychologies concerns their growing agreement on a semirational model of human beings. Contrasting models in the past acted to separate the fields. Marcus and Zajonc (1985, p. 176) noted the remarkable "cyclical series of swings peculiar to social psychology." Irrationality was an early emphasis with demonstrations of the power of norms (Sherif, 1936) and prestige and halo effects (Lorge, 1936). Later the field swung to a more rational model, with Asch (1946) explaining prestige effects as a search for meaning. Indeed, Asch (1952) published a highly original textbook for social psychology that is one of the most explicit defenses of the rational model of human beings ever advanced in the discipline. But the field's primary perspective turned again with Festinger's (1957) cognitive dissonance theory. This influential theory viewed humans as surrendering their commitment to objective reality to obtain psychological comfort. For instance, Elliot Aronson and Merrill Carlsmith (1962), following dissonance theory, showed the extremes people will go to preserve a consistent self-concept even when the self-concept is negative.

Next came Harold Kelley's (1967) highly rational "ANOVA model" of attribution that assumed the individual is "motivated to attain a cognitive mastery of the causal structure of his environment." This model of human beings as ANOVA calculators is among the most rational ones ever advanced in the field. By the 1970s and 1980s, however, the focus on biases and heuristics (Kahneman & Tversky, 1972, 1973, 1982; Nisbett & Ross, 1980) swung the pendulum back by exposing serious flaws in the rational model. From then, a "bounded rationality model" has generally prevailed in social psychology.

Such swings are less discernible in personality psychology. Influenced initially by Freudian theory, the field began with a strongly irrational model. But over the years, this stance has softened. First, it was countered by Allport's focus on largely rational, adult human beings. More recently, the growing acceptance of dynamic interactionism and the acceptance of individuals authoring and coauthoring their own identities have moved the field toward the center of the rational-irrational continuum (e.g., Thorne, 2000; Pasupathi, 2001). Consequently, both fields' eventual acceptance of a bounded rationality stance represents yet another reason for the rapprochement of the two fields.

Another deterrence to the unity of the two psychologies is the continued dominance of experimental social psychology within social psychology. This dominance disunites social psychology as well as restrains the link between personality and social psychology. History chapters in various editions of the *Handbook of Social Psychology* (Jones, 1985; Ross, Lepper, & Ward, 2010) provide illuminating and insightful accounts of the history of *North American experimental psychology*. But they fail to present social psychology as an international and multimethod discipline—those parts of the discipline closest to personality psychology. Apart from these limited history chapters, however, recent editions of the *Handbook* offer broad general coverage of the field—boasting non-American authors and careful attention to a great variety of methods.

This dominance of one branch has led to some alienation of social psychologists who specialize in field work (Cialdini, 2009) and survey research—both of which have had close ties with personality psychology. Take, for example, the rule of major social psychological journals requiring multiple studies in a single paper. To be sure, replication is important, and this rule makes complete sense for laboratory experiments with small samples of subjects which can usually be easily repeated. Not so, as Cialdini points out, for much applied work. Likewise, expensive probability surveys with thousands of subjects are not easily repeated. One technique tried by survey specialists to meet the requirement is to split their large samples randomly and test for replication. But even this obvious method has been flatly rejected by some social psychological reviewers.

A comparable problem arises in personality psychology (e.g., Bruner, 1986, 1990; Josselson, Lieblich, & McAdams, 2003). Holistic researchers complain that their qualitative data are often valued by journal editors and reviewers only if they have been reduced to numbers. The leading journals in personality frequently view holistic narratives as merely anecdotal—not "real science." Judging from the absence of articles with only qualitative data in their pages, editors of social psychological journals appear to have a similar perspective.

Despite these twists and turns in their separate histories, personality psychology and social psychology find themselves both institutionally and intellectually close today. Like Allport, Lewin, and Murphy in the past, many psychologists today work in both fields—appropriately, the two editors of this *Handbook* are prime examples. And in small psychology departments, one person often represents both fields.

We can trace this growing together by the stances taken in the three chapters written on the two fields in the *Handbook of Social Psychology* over the years. In the 1969 edition, Marlowe and Gergen (1969) were on the defensive. They found it necessary to focus on the many instances in which there were substantial associations between personality and behavior. In the 1985 edition, Snyder and Ickes (1985) dared to hope for the emergence of a "hybrid discipline of personality and social behavior." But by the 1998 edition, Snyder and Cantor (1998, pp. 636–637) could confidently declare that the boundary between the two fields had grown "rather indistinct." With relief, they wrote: "Gone are the days, it would seem, when one was greeted with skepticism, polite or otherwise, for working to understand the nature of personality or to chart the linkages between personality and social behavior." This new confidence was bolstered by the array of personality-oriented chapters in the 1998 edition of the *Handbook of Social Psychology* (Gilbert, Fiske, & Lindzey, 1998)—on the self, personal relationships, health, culture, altruism, and aggression.

Baumeister (1999) emphasizes how the two fields need one another. With a broad brush, he points out that personality psychology tends to focus on independent variables (e.g., the Big Five), while social psychology tends to focus on dependent variables (e.g., prejudice reduction). Their common interests are reflected organizationally, in their many joint publications, and in this *Oxford Handbook* itself.

There are many reasons to believe that the two fields will continue to come together with increasingly mutual interests. One principal reason for this optimistic prediction is the similarity of the needed theory and research trends in the future for both personality and social psychology. We would emphasize three such needed trends for the future that are discussed in greater detail in the following chapters of this *Handbook*.

[1] Theory needs to broaden to include multilevel models. Such models would help join the microindividual and mesosituational levels of the two fields (see Christ, Sibley & Wagner, chapter 10, this volume). But they could also ideally reach out to the macrostructural and macrocultural levels of analyses as well and help to combine psychological phenomena with those of the other social sciences. New software now makes multilevel research far easier to execute. There is also reason to believe that the macrolevel social sciences are now more amenable to including psychological phenomena in their work. Note how modern economics now boasts a growing "microeconomics" branch that finally tests the many psychological assumptions made by their sweeping models. This trend in economics was in part inspired by the Nobel Memorial Prize in Economics in 2002 awarded to Daniel Kahneman for his work on prospect theory in collaboration with his long-time colleague, the late Amos Tversky.

[2] As noted earlier, much more longitudinal research is needed to nail down causal connections and expand theory in both personality and social psychology (see Stewart & Deaux, chapter 26, this volume). To be sure, such work is expensive and time-consuming; but its importance is underlined by the fact that many of the most influential studies in both fields have been longitudinal in design. Here ties with developmental psychology and new analytic software will be highly useful.

[3] Integrating the cognitive advances with the more recent advances in emotion is a third needed step for the future that would also tie personality and social psychology closer together (see Clore & Robinson, chapter 13, this volume). Work during the 1970s, as we noted earlier, came close to ignoring affect. More recent decades have witnessed exciting advances on emotion. Some integrative work has already begun this task; but we predict that it will emerge as a major emphasis in the future.

Acknowledgment

The authors wish to thank Professor Avril Thorne of the University of California, Santa Cruz, for her invaluable help in the writing of this chapter.

References

Adorno, T. W., Frenkel-Brunswik, E., Levinson, D. J., & Sanford, R. N. (1950). *The authoritarian personality*. New York: Harper.

Allport, F. H. (1924). *Social psychology*. New York: Houghton Mifflin.

Allport, F. H., & Allport, G. W. (1928). A test for ascendance-submission. *Journal of Abnormal and Social Psychology, 23,* 118–136.

Allport, G. W. (1935). Attitudes. In C. C. Murchison (Ed.), *A handbook of social psychology* (Chapter 17). Worcester, MA: Clark University Press.

Allport, G. W. (1937). *Personality: A psychological interpretation.* New York: Holt.

Allport, G. W. (1943). The ego in contemporary psychology. *Psychological Review, 50,* 451–478.

Allport, G. W. (1950). *The nature of personality: Selected papers.* Cambridge, MA: Addison-Wesley.

Allport, G. W. (1954). *The nature of prejudice.* Reading, MA: Addison-Wesley.

Allport, G. W. (1955). *Becoming: Basic considerations for a psychology of personality.* New Haven, CT: Yale University Press.

Allport, G. W. (1960). *Personality and social encounter: Selected essays.* Boston: Beacon Press.

Allport, G. W. (1961). *Pattern and growth in personality.* New York: Holt, Rinehart, and Winston.

Allport, G. W. (1968a). *The person in psychology: Selected essays.* Boston: Beacon Press.

Allport, G. W. (1968b). The historical background of modern social psychology. In G. Lindzey & E. Aronson (Eds.), *The handbook of social psychology* (2nd ed., Vol. 1, pp. 1–80). Reading, MA: Addison-Wesley.

Allport, G. W., & Boring, E. G. (1946). Psychology and social relations at Harvard University. *American Psychologist, 1,* 119–122.

Allport, G. W., & Postman, L. (1947). *The psychology of rumor.* New York: Holt.

Angell, R. C. (1968). Charles H. Cooley. In D. Sills (Ed.), *International encyclopedia of the social sciences* (Vol. 3., pp. 367–382). New York: Macmillan and Free Press.

Aronson, E., & Carlsmith, J. M. (1962). Performance expectancy as a determinant of actual performance. *Journal of Abnormal and Social Psychology, 65,* 178–182.

Asch, S. E. (1946). Forming impressions of personality. *Journal of Abnormal and Social Psychology, 41,* 258–290.

Asch, S. E. (1952). *Social psychology.* Englewood Cliffs, NJ: Prentice-Hall.

Asendorpf, J. B., & Motti-Stefanidi, F. (2010). European Association of Personality Psychology. *Observer, 23*(7), 16.

Baier, D., Hadjar, A., & Boehnke, K. (2011). Authoritarianism in everyday context—dispositional, situational, or what? In F. Funke, T. Petzel, C. Cohrs, & J. Duckitt (Eds.), *Perspectives on authoritarianism* (pp. 211–241). Wiesbaden, Germany: Verlag fuer Sozialwissenschaften.

Bales, R. F. (1950). *Interaction process analysis.* Cambridge, MA: Addison-Wesley.

Bales, R. F. (1970). *Personality and interpersonal behavior.* New York: Holt, Rinehart, and Winston.

Bales, R. F. (1999). *Social interaction systems: Theory and measurement.* New Brunswick, NJ: Transition Publishers.

Bales, R. F., & Cohen, S. (1950). *SYMLOG.* New York: Free Press, 1979.

Barenbaum, N. (2000). How social was personality? The Allports' "connection" of personality and social psychology. *Journal of the History of the Behavioral Sciences, 36,* 471–287.

Barenbaum, N., & Winter, D. (2003). Personality. In I. B. Weiner (Ed) *Handbook of psychology* (Vol. 1, pp. 177–203). New York: Wiley.

Baron, R. M., & Boudreau, L. A. (1987). An ecological perspective on integrating personality and social psychology. *Journal of Personality and Social Psychology, 53,* 1222–1228.

Baron, R. M., & Kenny, D. A. (1986). The moderator-mediator variable distinction in social psychological research: Conceptual, strategic, and statistical considerations. *Journal of Personality and Social Psychology, 51*(6), 1173–1182.

Baumeister, R. F. (1999). On the interface between personality and social psychology. In L. A. Pervin & O. P. John (Eds.), *Handbook of personality: Theory and research* (2nd ed., pp. 367–377). New York: Guilford.

Baumrind, D. (1968). Authoritarian vs. authoritative parental control. *Adolescence, 3*(11), 255–272.

Bem, D. J., & Allen, A. (1974). Predicting some of the people some of the time: The search for cross-situational consistencies in behavior. *Psychological Review, 81,* 506–520.

Benjamin, L. T., Jr., & Baker, D. B. (2004). *From séance to science: A history of the profession of psychology in America.* Belmont, CA: Wadsworth.

Bernreuter, R. G. (1931). *The personality inventory.* Stanford, CA: Stanford University Press.

Berscheid, E. (1992). A glance back at a quarter century of social psychology. *Journal of Personality and Social Psychology, 61*(4), 525–533.

Blass, T. (1984). Social psychology and personality: Toward a convergence. *Journal of Personality and Social Psychology, 47*(5), 1013–1027.

Brewer, M. B. (1979). In-group bias in the minimal intergroup situation: A cognitive-motivational analysis. *Psychological Bulletin, 86,* 307–324.

Bridgman, P. W. (1959). *The way things are.* Cambridge, MA: Harvard University Press.

Brooks, M. L., Buhrmester, M., & Swann, W. B. (2010). Interactionism spoken like a true situationist. *European Journal of Personality, 24*(5), 483–487.

Bruner, J. (1986). *Actual minds, possible worlds.* Cambridge, MA: Harvard University Press.

Bruner, J. (1990). *Acts of meaning.* Cambridge, MA: Harvard University Press.

Capshew, J. H. (1992). Psychologists on site: A reconnaissance of the historiography of the laboratory. *American Psychologist, 47,* 132–142.

Carlson, R. (1971). Where is the *person* in personality research? *Psychological Bulletin, 75*(3), 203–219.

Cartwright, D. (1979). Contemporary social psychology in historical perspective. *Social Psychology Quarterly, 42,* 82–93.

Caspi, A., Bem, D. J., & Elder, G. H. (1989). Continuities and consequences of interactional styles across the life course. *Journal of Personality, 57*(2), 375–406.

Cattell, R. B. (1984). The voyage of a laboratory, 1928–1984. *Multivariate Behavioral Research, 19*(2–3), 121–174.

Cattell, R. B., & Cattell, H. E. P. (1995). Personality structure and the new fifth edition of the 16 PF. *Educational and Psychological Measurement, 55*(6), 926–937.

Cervone, D., Caldwell, T. L., & Orom, H. (2008). Beyond person and situation effects: Intraindividual personality architecture and its implications for the study of personality and social behavior. In F. Rhodewait (Ed.), *Personality and social behavior* (pp. 2–48). New York: Psychology Press.

Cherry, F., & Borshuk, C. (1998). Social action research and the Commission on Community Interrelations. *Journal of Social Issues, 54,* 119–142.

Cialdini, R. B. (2009). We have to break up. *Perspectives on Psychological Science, 1,* 5–6.

Collier, G., Minton, H. L., & Reynolds, G. (1991). *Currents of thought in American social psychology*. New York: Oxford University Press.

Cooley, C. H. (1897). Genius, fame, and the comparison of races. *Annals of the American Academy of Political and Social Sciences, 9*, 1–4.

Coser, L. A. (1971). *Masters of sociological thought: Ideas in historical and social context*. New York: Harcourt Brace Jovanovich.

Danziger, K. (1997). *Naming the mind: How psychology found its language*. Thousand Oaks, CA: Sage Publications.

Deutsch, M. (1977). *The resolution of conflict: Constructive and destructive processes*. New Haven, CT: Yale University Press.

Dijker, A. J. M. (1987). Emotional reactions to ethnic minorities. *European Journal of Social Psychology, 17*, 305–325.

Dillehay, R. C. (1973). On the irrelevance of the classical negative evidence concerning the effects of attitudes on behavior. *American Psychologist, 28*, 887–891.

Dilthey, W. (1976). *Selected writings* (H. P. Rickman, Trans.). Cambridge: Cambridge University Press.

Dovidio, J. F., Glick, P., & Rudman, L. P. (Eds.). (2005). *On the nature of prejudice: Fifty years after Allport*. Oxford, UK: Blackwell.

Durkheim, E. (1938). *The rules of sociological method*. New York: Free Press.

Durkheim, E. (1951). *Suicide* (J. A. Spaulding & G. Simpson, Trans.). New York: Free Press.

Durkheim, E. (1984). *The division of labor in society* (W. D. Halls, Trans.). New York: Free Press.

Edwards, K., & von Hippel, W. (1995). Hearts and minds: The priority of affective versus cognitive factors in person perception. *Personality and Social Psychology Bulletin, 21*, 996–1011.

Elms, A. C. (1975). The crisis of confidence in social psychology. *American Psychologist, 30*, 967–976.

Epstein, S. (1979). The stability of behavior: I. On predicting most of the people much of the time. *Journal of Personality and Social Psychology, 37*, 1097–1126.

Epstein, S. (1980). The stability of behavior: II. Implications for psychological research. *American Psychologist, 35*(9), 790–806.

Erikson, E. (1950). *Childhood and society*. New York: Norton.

Erikson, E. (1962). *Young man Luther*. New York: Norton.

Erikson, E. (1968). *Identity: Youth and crisis*. New York: Norton.

Esses, V. M., Haddock, G., & Zanna, M. P. (1993). Values, stereotypes, and emotions as determinants of intergroup attitudes. In D. M. Mackie & D. L. Hamilton (Eds.), *Affect, cognition, and stereotyping*. San Diego, CA: Academic.

Festinger, L. (1954). A theory of social comparison processes. *Human Relations, 7*, 117–140.

Festinger, L. (1957). *A theory of cognitive dissonance*. Evanston, IL: Row, Peterson.

Finison, L. J. (1976). Unemployment, politics, and the history of organized psychology. *American Psychologist, 31*, 747–755.

Finison, L. J. (1986). The psychological insurgency: 1936–1945. *Journal of Social Issues, 42*, 21–33.

Frijda, N. (1986). *The emotions*. New York: Cambridge University Press.

Fromm, E. (1941). *Escape from freedom*. New York: Rinehart.

Funder, D. C., & Ozer, D. J. (1983). Behavior as a function of the situation. *Journal of Personality and Social Psychology, 44*(1), 107–112.

Gergen, K. J. (1973). Social psychology as history. *Journal of Personality and Social Psychology, 26*, 309–320.

Gilbert, D. T., Fiske, S. T., & Lindzey, G. (Eds.). (1998). *The handbook of social psychology* (4th ed.). New York: McGraw-Hill.

Graumann, C. F. (2001). Introducing social psychology historically. In M. Hewstone & W. Stroebe (Eds.), *Introduction to social psychology: A European perspective* (3rd ed., pp. 3–22). Oxford, UK: Blackwell.

Greenwood, J. D. (2004). The *disappearance of the social in American social psychology*. Cambridge, UK: Cambridge University Press.

Guilford, J. P., Fruchter, B., & Zimmerman, W. S. (1952). Factor analysis of the Army Air Forces Shepard Field battery of experimental aptitude tests. *Psychometrika, 17*, 45–68.

Hamilton, D. L. (Ed.). (1981). *Cognitive processes in stereotyping and intergroup behavior*. Hillsdale, NJ: Erlbaum.

Helmreich, R. (1975). Applied social psychology: The unfulfilled promise. *Personality and Social Psychology Bulletin, 1*, 548–560.

Hilgard, E. R. (1987). *Psychology in America: A historical survey*. New York: Harcourt Brace Jovanovich.

Hogan, R., Johnson, J. A., & Briggs, S. (Eds.), *Handbook of personality*. San Diego, CA: Academic.

Horkheimer, M. (Ed.). (1936). *Studien über Autorität und Familie* [Studies on authority and the family]. Paris: Felix Alcan.

Ickes, W., Snyder, M., & Garcia, S. (1997). Personality influences on the choice of situations. In R. Hogan, J. A. Johnson, & S. R. Briggs (Eds.), *Handbook of personality psychology* (pp. 165–195). San Diego, CA: Academic.

Igo, S.E. (2007). *The averaged American: Surveys, citizens, and the making of a mass public*. Cambridge, MA: Harvard University Press.

Institute for Social Research (2010). *Institute for Social Research*. http://www.isr.umich.edu/home/about/ Retrieved Sept. 15, 2010.

Israel, J., & Tajfel, H. (1972). *The context of social psychology: A critical assessment*. New York: Academic.

James, W. (1890). *The principles of psychology*. New York: Holt.

John, O. P., & Srivastava, S. (1999). The Big Five taxonomy: History, measurement, and theoretical perspectives. In L. A. Pervin & O. P. John (Eds.), *Handbook of personality: Theory and research* (2nd ed., pp. 102–138). New York: Guilford.

Jones, E. E. (1985). Major developments in social psychology during the past five decades. In G. Lindzey & E. Aronson (Eds.), *The handbook of social psychology* (3rd ed., Vol. 1, pp. 47–107). Reading, MA: Addison-Wesley.

Josselson, R., Lieblich, A., & McAdams, D. P. (Eds.). (2003). *Up close and personal: The teaching and learning of narrative research*. Washington, DC: American Psychological Association Press.

Jost, J. T., & Kruglanski, A. W. (2002). The estrangement of social constructionism and experimental social psychology: History of the rift and prospects for reconciliation. *Personality and Social Psychology Review, 6*, 168–187.

Kahneman, D., & Tversky, A. (1972). Subjective probability: A judgment of representativeness. *Cognitive Psychology, 3*, 430–454.

Kahneman, D., & Tversky, A. (1973). On the psychology of prediction. *Psychological Review, 80*, 237–251.

Kahneman, D., & Tversky, A. (1982). On the study of statistical intuitions. *Cognition, 11*, 123–141.

Kelley, H. H. (1967). Attribution theory in social psychology. *Nebraska Symposium on Motivation, 14*, 192–241.

Kelman, H. C. (1974). Attitudes are alive and well and gainfully employed in the sphere of action. *American Psychologist, 29*(5), 310–324.

Kihlstrom, J. F. (1987). Introduction to the special issue: Integrating personality and social psychology. *Journal of Personality and Social Psychology, 53*(6), 989–992.

Kihlstrom, J. F., & Hastie, R. (1997). Mental representations of persons and personality. In R. Hogan, J. Johnson, &

S. Briggs (Eds.), *Handbook of personality psychology* (pp. 711–735). San Diego, CA: Academic.

Klineberg, O. (1935a). *Negro intelligence and selective migration.* New York: Columbia University Press.

Klineberg, O. (1935b). *Race differences.* New York: Harper & Row.

Kluckhohn, C., & Murray, H. A. (1953). *Personality in nature, society, and culture.* New York: Knopf.

Lamiell, J. (1997). Individuals and the differences between them. In R. Hogan, J. Johnson, & S. Briggs (Eds.)., *Handbook of personality psychology* (pp. 117–141). San Diego, CA: Academic.

Lesser, A. (1968). Franz Boas. In D. Sills (Ed.), *International encyclopedia of the social sciences* (Vol. 2, pp. 99–110). New York: Macmillan and Free Press.

Lewin, K. (1935). *A dynamic theory of personality: Selected papers.* (D. K. Adams & K. E. Zener, Trans.). New York: McGraw-Hill.

Lewin, K. (1940). Review of *Explorations in Personality. Journal of Abnormal and Social Psychology, 35*(2), 283–285.

Lewin, K. (1951). *Field theory in social science.* New York: Harper.

Lorge, I. (1936). Prestige, suggestion, and attitudes. *Journal of Social Psychology, 7,* 386–402.

Mackie, D. M., & Hamilton, D. L. (1993). *Affect, cognition, and stereotyping.* San Diego, CA: Academic.

Marcus, H., & Zajonc, R. B. (1985). The cognitive perspective in social psychology. In G. Lindzey & E. Aronson (Eds.), *The handbook of social psychology* (3rd ed., Vol. 1, pp. 137–230). New York: Random House.

Marlowe, D., & Gergen, K. J. (1969). Personality and social interaction. In G. Lindzey & E. Aronson (Eds.), *The handbook of social psychology,* (2nd ed., Vol. 3, pp. 590–665). Reading, MA: Addison-Wesley.

McAdams, D. P. (1990). *The person: An introduction to personality psychology.* San Diego, CA: Harcourt Brace Jovanovich.

McAdams, D. P. (1997). A conceptual history of personality psychology. In R. Hogan, J. Johnson, & S. Briggs (Eds.), *Handbook of personality psychology* (pp. 3–39). San Diego, CA: Academic.

McClelland, D. C. (1953). *The achievement motive.* New York: Appleton-Century-Crofts.

McCrae, R. R., & Costa, P. T., Jr. (2008). The five-factor theory of personality. In O. P. John, R. W. Robins, & L. A. Pervin (Eds.), *Handbook of personality: Theory and research* (3rd ed., pp. 159–181). New York: Guilford.

McDougall, W. (1908/1963). *An introduction to social psychology.* London, UK: Methuen.

McGuire, W. J. (1973). The yin and yang of progress in social psychology. *Journal of Personality and Social Psychology, 26,* 446–456.

Mednick, M. S., & Tangri, S. S. (Eds.). (1972). New perspectives on women. *Journal of Social Issues, 28*(2), 1–190.

Milgram, S. (1974). *Obedience to authority: An experimental view.* New York: Harper & Row.

Mischel, W. (1968). *Personality and assessment.* New York: Wiley.

Mischel, W., & Shoda, Y. (1995). A cognitive-affective system theory of personality: Reconceptualizing situations, dispositions, dynamics, and invariance in personality structure. *Psychological Review, 102,* 246–268.

Morawski, J. G., & Bayer, B. M. (2003). *Social psychology.* In I. B. Weiner, I. B. (Ed.), *Handbook of psychology* (Vol. 1, pp. 223–247). New York: Wiley.

Moscovici, S. (1985). *The age of the crowd: A historical treatise on mass psychology* (J. C. Whitehouse, Trans.). New York: Cambridge University Press.

Moscovici, S. (1993). *The invention of society: Psychological explanations for social phenomena* (W. D. Halls, Trans.). Cambridge, UK: Polity Press.

Moscovici, S. (2000). *Social representations: Explorations in social psychology.* Cambridge, UK: Polity Press.

Murphy, G. (1947). *Personality: A biosocial approach to origins and structure.* New York: Harper.

Murphy, G., & Murphy, L. B. (1937). *Experimental social psychology.* New York: Harper.

Murray, H. (1938). *Explorations in personality.* New York: Oxford University Press.

Myrdal, G. (1944). *An American dilemma.* New York: Harper & Row.

Newcomb, T. M. (1965). Attitude development as a function of reference groups: The Bennington Study. In E. Maccoby, T. Newcomb, & E. Hartley (Eds.), *Readings in social psychology* (pp. 265–275). New York: Holt, Rinehart, and Winston.

Nicholson, I. A. M. (2003). *Inventing personality: Gordon Allport and the science of selfhood.* Washington, DC: American Psychological Association.

Nisbett, R., & Ross, L. (1980). *Human inference: Strategies and shortcomings of social judgment.* Englewood Cliffs, NJ: Prentice-Hall.

Office of Strategic Services (1948). *Assessment of men: Selection of personnel for the Office of Strategic Service.* New York: Rinehart.

Pasupathi, M. (2001). The social construction of the personal past and its implications for adult development. *Psychological Bulletin, 127,* 651–672.

Patnoe, S. (1988). *A narrative history of experimental social psychology: The Lewin tradition.* New York: Springer-Verlag.

Peterson, B. E. (2011). Social influences: The implications of threat and culture for the expression of authoritarianism. In F. Funke, T. Petzel, C. Cohrs, & J. Duckitt (Eds.), *Perspectives on authoritarianism* (pp. 211–241). Wiesbaden, Germany: Verlag fuer Sozialwissenschaften.

Pettigrew, T. F. (1958). Personality and socio-cultural factors in intergroup attitudes: A cross-national comparison. *Journal of Conflict Resolution, 2,* 29-42.

Pettigrew, T. F. (1959). Regional differences in anti-Negro prejudice. *Journal of Abnormal and Social Psychology, 59,* 28–36.

Pettigrew, T. F. (1990). A bold stroke for personality a half-century ago: A retrospective review of Gordon Allport's *Personality: A psychological interpretation. Contemporary Psychology, 35,* 533–536.

Pettigrew, T. F. (1991). Is unity possible? A summary. In C. Stephan, W. Stephan, & T. F. Pettigrew (Eds.), *The future of social psychology* (pp. 99–121). New York: Springer-Verlag.

Pettigrew, T. F. (1997). The emotional component of prejudice: Results from Western Europe. In S. A. Tuch & J. K. Martin (Eds.), *Racial attitudes in the 1990s: Continuity and change* (pp. 76–90). Westport, CT: Praeger, 1997.

Pettigrew, T. F. (1999a). Gordon Willard Allport: A tribute. *Journal of Social Issues, 55*(3), 415–427.

Pettigrew, T. F. (1999b). Placing authoritarianism in social context. *Politics, Groups, and the Individual, 8,* 5–20.

Pettigrew, T. F. (2005). The social science study of American race relations in the 20th century. In C. S. Crandall & M. Schaller (Eds.), *The social psychology of prejudice: Historical and contemporary issues* (pp. 1–32). Seattle, WA: Lewinian Press.

Pettigrew, T. F. (2011a). SPSSI and racial research. *Journal of Social Issues, 67*(1),137–149.

Pettigrew, T. F. (2011b). The indestructible theory. In F. Funke, T. Petzel, C. Cohrs & J. Duckitt (Eds.), *Perspectives on authoritarianism.* Wiesbaden, Germany: Verlag fuer Sozialwissenschaften.

Reynolds, K. J., Turner, J. C., Branscomb, L. R., Mavor, K. I., Bizumic, B., & Subasic, E. (2010). Interactionism in personality and social psychology: An integrated approach to understanding the mind and behaviour. *European Journal of Personality, 24*(5), 458–482.

Rhodewalt, F. (Ed.) (2008). *Personality and social behavior*. New York: Psychology Press.

Ring, K. (1967). Experimental social psychology: Some sober questions about some frivolous values. *Journal of Experimental Social Psychology, 3,* 113–123.

Ross, E. A. (1908). *Social psychology: An outline and source book*. New York: Macmillan.

Ross, L. (1977). The intuitive psychologist and his shortcomings: Distortions in the attribution process. In L. Berkowitz (Ed.), *Advances in experimental social psychology* (Vol. 10). New York: Academic.

Ross, L., Lepper M., & Ward, A. (2010). A history of social psychology: Insights, challenges, and contributions to theory and application. In Fiske, S. T., Gilbert, D. T., & Lindzey, G. (Eds.), *Handbook of social psychology*, Vol. 1 (5th ed.) (pp. 3-50). New York: Wiley.

Ross, L., & Nisbett, R. E. (1991). *The person and the situation: Perspectives of social psychology*. New York: McGraw-Hill.

Scherer, K. R. (Ed.). (1988). *Facets of emotion: Recent research*. Hillsdale, NJ: Erlbaum.

Schrecker, E. W. (1986). *No ivory tower: McCarthyism and the universities*. New York: Oxford University Press.

Sechrest, L. (1976). Personality. *Annual Review of Psychology, 27,* 1–27.

Sherif, M. (1936). *The psychology of social norms*. New York: Harper.

Sherif, M. (1977). Crisis in social psychology: Some remarks towards breaking through the crisis. *Personality and Social Psychology Bulletin, 3,* 368–382.

Sloan, T. (2009). Theories of personality. In D. Fox, I. Prilleltensky, & S. Austin (Eds.), *Critical psychology: An introduction* (2nd ed., pp. 57–74). Thousand Oaks, CA: Sage.

Smith, E. R. (1993). Social identity and social emotions: Toward new conceptions of prejudice. In D. M. Mackie & D. L. Hamilton (Eds.), *Affect, cognition, and stereotyping* (pp. 297–315). San Diego, CA: Academic.

Smith, M. B. (2002). Robert W. White (1904–2001): Humanistic psychologist. *Journal of Humanistic Psychology, 42,* 9–12.

Smith, M. B. (2005). Personality and social psychology: Retrospections and aspirations. *Personality and Social Psychology Review, 9,* 334–340.

Smith, R. (1997). *The Norton history of the human sciences*. New York: Norton.

Snyder, M., & Ickes, W. (1985). Personality and social behavior. In G. Lindzey & E. Aronson (Eds.), *The handbook of social psychology* (3rd ed., Vol. 2, pp. 833–948). New York: Random House.

Snyder, M., & Carter, N. (1998). Personality and social behavior. In D. T. Gilbert, S. T. Fiske, & G. Lindzey (Eds.), *The handbook of social psychology* (4th ed., Vol. 1, Pp. 635–679). New York: McGraw-Hill.

Stagner, R. (1937). *Psychology of personality*. New York: McGraw-Hill.

Stagner, R. (1986). Reminiscences about the founding of SPSSI. *Journal of Social Issues, 42,* 35–42.

Stangor, C. L., Sullivan, A., & Ford, T. E. (1991). Affective and cognitive determinants of prejudice. *Social Cognition, 9,* 359–380.

Steiner, I. (1974). Whatever happened to the group in *social* psychology? *Journal of Experimental Social Psychology, 10*(1), 94–108.

Stouffer, S. A., Suchman, E. A., DeVinney, L. C., Starr, S. A. & Williams, R. M. (1949). *The American soldier: Adjustment to army life* (Vol. 1). Princeton, NJ: Princeton University Press.

Strickland, L. H., Aboud, F. E., & Gergen, K. J. (Eds.). (1974). *Social psychology in transition*. New York: Plenum Press.

Tajfel, H. (Ed.) (1982). *Social identity and intergroup relations*. Cambridge, UK: Cambridge University Press.

Thomas, W. I. (1904). The psychology of race-prejudice. *American Journal of Sociology, 9,* 593–611.

Thomas, W. I. (1907). The mind of woman and the lower races. *American Journal of Sociology, 12,* 435–469.

Thomas, W. I., & Thomas, D. S. (1928). *The child in America: Behavior problems and programs*. New York: Knopf.

Thorne, A. (2000). Personal memory telling and personality development. *Personality and Social Psychology Review, 4,* 45–56.

Tropp, L. R., & Pettigrew, T. F. (2004). Intergroup contact and the central role of affect in intergroup prejudice. In L. Tiedens & C. W. Leach (Eds.), *The social life of emotion: Studies in emotion and social interaction* (pp. 246–269). New York: Cambridge University Press, 2004.

Tropp, L. R., & Pettigrew, T. F. (2005). Differential relationships between intergroup contact and affective and cognitive dimensions of prejudice. *Personality and Social Psychology Bulletin, 31*(8), 1145–1158.

Tucker, W. H. (1994). *The science and politics of racial research*. Urbana: University of Illinois Press.

Tucker, W. H. (2009). *The Cattell controversy*. Urbana: University of Illinois Press.

Turner, J. C., Hogg, M. A., Oakes, P. J., Reicher, S. D., & Wetherell, M. S. (1987). *Rediscovering the social group: A self-categorization theory*. Cambridge, MA: Blackwell.

Watson, G. (Ed.). (1942). *Civilian morale: Second yearbook of the Society for the Psychological Study of Social Issues*. Boston: Houghton Mifflin.

West, S. G. (1986). Methodological developments in personality research: An introduction. *Journal of Personality, 54*(1), 1–17.

White, R. W. (1948). *The abnormal personality*. New York: Ronald Press.

White, R. W. (1959). Motivation reconsidered: The concept of competence. *Psychological Review. 66*(5), 297–333.

White, R. W. (1966). *Lives in progress: A study of the natural growth of personality*. New York: Holt, Rinehart, and Winston.

Wicker, A. W. (1969). Attitudes versus actions: The relationship of verbal and overt behavioral responses to *attitude* objects. *Journal of Social Issues, 25*(4), 41–78.

Wilder, D. A., & Shapiro, P. N. (1984). Role of out-group cues in determining identity. *Journal of Personality and Social Psychology, 47*(2), 342–348.

Windelband, W. (1904). *Geschichte und Naturwissenschaft* [History and natural science]. Strassbourg, France: Heitz.

Winter, D. G. (1973). *The power motive*. New York: Free Press.

Woodworth, R. S. (1919). Examination of emotional fitness for warfare. *Psychological Bulletin, 15,* 59–60.

Zanna, M., M. P., Haddock, G., & Esses, V. M. (1990). *The determinants of prejudice*. Paper presented at the annual meeting of the Society for Experimental Social Psychology, Buffalo, NY.

Zimbardo, P. G. (1992). Foreword. In S. S. Brehm (Ed.), *Intimate relationships* (pp. xiv–xvi). New York: McGraw-Hill.

Zuroff, D. C. (1986). Was Gordon Allport a trait theorist? *Journal of Personality and Social Psychology, 51*(5), 993–1000.

Perspectives on the Person
Rapid Growth and Opportunities for Integration

William Fleeson

Abstract

This chapter addresses the P of the Lewinian equation, $B = f(P, E)$, by providing a conceptual map of perspectives on how to characterize the P, that is, how to characterize persons. Because most of these perspectives operate within personality psychology, this chapter emphasizes those perspectives within personality, but because several perspectives on the person operate within social psychology, this chapter describes those perspectives as well. When Lewin wrote his equation, he intended that the P and E (environment) parts would be considered in tandem. Thus, this chapter also considers from a personality perspective the prospects and potential routes of integration between personality and social psychology; the chapter argues that although integration has proceeded a great deal, the two fields still hold each other at a kind of arm's-length mutual acceptance. The final section of the chapter describes a theory of personality, whole trait theory, which includes both P and E in its formulation as one possible way to close that last arm's-length distance. In this theory, traits become both explanatory and descriptive concepts, require both persons and situations to be described, and become investigated with both correlational and experimental methods.

Keywords: personality, social, Lewin, Allport, traits, integration, overview, person-situation debate, behavior, whole traits

Perspectives on the Person: Rapid Growth and Opportunities for Integration

The Lewinian equation, $B = f(P, E)$, sets the context for this handbook (Snyder & Deaux, chapter 1, this volume), and argues that *Behavior* is a *function* of the *Person* and of the *Environment*. Thus, Lewin argues, the field needs to characterize P's and E's, and to do so in ways that are concrete and usefully entered into the equation to allow the prediction of B's. With his equation, Lewin (1936) is suggesting that the prediction of behavior requires ways to characterize the person concretely, to serve as input to how he or she will behave: "it is impossible to derive the psychological processes in the life space without including changes both of person and of environment in the representation" (Lewin, 1936, p. 167). Reis and Holmes (chapter 4, this volume) emphasize the E; this chapter's purpose is to characterize the P.

The call for the inclusion of P can be taken in at least three ways: (1) it is not possible to detail environmental factors alone when explaining psychology, because it is also necessary to know the factors internal to the person that are responsive to those environmental factors; (2) people differ dramatically from each other, so it is necessary to know how to characterize such differences between people if behavior is to be predicted; and/or (3) psychological factors that are internal to the person act on each other and interact with each other, so it will be impossible to predict behavior without knowing how the factors internal to persons work together to characterize the person as a whole.

This chapter focuses on the latter two meanings, partly because the traditional split between social and personality psychology has been along those two lines. In particular, its purpose is to provide an overview conceptual map of the currently productive perspectives on individual differences between persons and on the interaction of factors internal to persons. This purpose is in the service of providing the current characterization of the *P* factor, because of the *P* factor's input to the prediction of behavior. I hope that this chapter will help a professional in the field apprehend the space within which perspectives on the person are organized, which will allow him or her to understand how the perspectives relate to and differ from each other. But I hope even more that a reader who reads through the chapter will witness the exciting developments going on in personality psychology and will be tempted to find out more.

The other context of this *Handbook* is the integration of personality and social psychology. The input to the equation, $f(P, E)$, implies that the *P* and *E* parts are required to be considered in tandem. Of course, this does not have to be the case throughout the whole process—substantial gains can be achieved by studying the *P* or the *E* separately, and in fact, some research programs may be better off doing so. But eventually they will have to be integrated. Furthermore, Lewin argues that it would be most productive to characterize *P*'s and *E*'s in a common language and set of terms, so that prediction and explanation could take into account whole situations, not just *P*'s or just *E*'s in parallel. Thus, a second purpose of this chapter is to consider from a personality perspective the prospects and potential routes of integration. The chapter also considers whether a theory of personality that includes both *P* and *E* in its formulation may be one effective way to get past paying lip service to integration and get past the very real barrier of limited researcher time, and proposes such a theory, one that I and my lab have been working on for many years precisely to address the integration of *P* with *E*.

Perspectives on the Person

Perspectives on persons are investigated primarily but not exclusively within personality psychology. Personality psychology is an explosive field, with a huge amount of new and exciting research, and a wide diversity of topics.

Personality psychology, like most fields, started with a collection of purposes and questions. At the beginning, the scientists who constituted the field were trying to understand something or to solve a set of loosely associated problems, and these efforts eventually coalesced into a field. The goals of personality psychology have been diverse, but have

included at least the following four goals. The first goal is to determine how to characterize the person. This includes determining the basic ways people differ from each other and helping people figure out who they are and where they fit in. A second goal is also to determine how to characterize the person, but this goal is to identify the internal processes and structures that link various parts of the person together. This is an ambitious goal, and pursuit of this goal means that personality psychology draws on all other psychology fields. A third goal is to explain why people differ from each other. This goal means that personality psychologists are trying to identify mechanisms and processes that underlie differences between people, and that explain why people are different, how those differences become manifest in their behavior, and what consequences personality differences have for people's lives. That is, like other psychologists, personality psychologists are interested in determining how the mind works, but they have a fundamental conviction that stable variables are an integral part of the way the mind works. The fourth goal is to provide a foundation for interventions to improve people's lives. Personality appears to make a difference in people's lives, which means that one way to improve one's own life may be to adjust one's personality—not an uncontroversial or light undertaking, but at least a potentially liberating opportunity.

The pursuit of these goals has led to a wide and rich variety of perspectives on persons. Like social, developmental, or other fields of psychology, personality consists of a diverse but relatively unconnected multitude of "miniperspectives." To go through them all would take more than one chapter and would be hard to process for the reader. There are so many, that even describing a portion of them requires an organizing scheme.

In the case of personality psychology, multiple schemes have been proposed for organizing the perspectives on the person. Whether it is McAdams's (1995) three levels of personality, Snyder and Ickes's (1985) three strategies for identifying and explaining consistency, or Pervin's (2003) three types of units, such schemes help to convey what would otherwise be a hard-to-comprehend vastness of research. Fortunately, it is possible to remain true to the goals of personality psychology and also provide an organizing map of perspectives at the same time. This is because most research on personality has tried to accomplish the first goal, identifying how to characterize persons. The different answers arrived at have usually emphasized a particular type of variable, and these types of variables have generally fallen into one of four types. Thus, the many perspectives on persons can be organized into four groups, based on the primary type of variable they use to characterize persons (based on Pervin, 2003). The four perspectives are trait-based, cognitive, motivational, and disorder-based.

Trait-based perspectives try to characterize persons by descriptions of them, usually focused on describing persons' styles of behavior. Cognitive perspectives try to characterize persons by how and what they think. Motivational perspectives try to characterize persons by the goals they pursue. Disorder-based perspectives try to characterize persons by their problems in living (McCrae, Loeckenhoff, & Costa, 2005).

For each perspective group, I will first provide a brief overview of the major features of the perspective, as an introduction to the type of perspective. Within each group, some of the perspectives tend to focus more on differences between persons, and others tend to focus more on processes describing how factors internal to the person work and interrelate. I will describe both subtypes for each perspective. In all cases, I will highlight concrete examples to illustrate the perspectives and their major features. However, it will not be possible to be comprehensive.

I will devote some attention to developments in the last 10–20 years. Oftentimes, such a focus might date a chapter or reduces its longevity. In the case of personality, however, a focus on the last 10–20 years may be warranted. It was an exciting, productive, and busy time for personality psychologists; the 1990s represent the first decade of solid quantities of research after the decline that occurred in the 1970s and 1980s, and it set the field up for a highly productive 21st century. All this exciting research going on means I will have to be selective, leaving out many important developments, which I regret. When one keeps an eye on the past 10–20 years, one really sees the way personality perspectives have blossomed to reveal fascinating conclusions about how the mind works.

Finally, there are a surprising number of research programs that try to characterize the person, either in terms of individual differences between persons or in terms of how the factors within the person fit together, but that are based within the field of social psychology (conducted by social psychologists who are trained in social psychology programs, occupy social psychology departments, and publish in social psychology journals). Given the goal of these research programs to characterize the person, it is

unclear why they are not based within personality psychology, but the reasons are most likely historical. The positive implication of this fact is that productive integration between the two fields is surely within reach—it is already happening without intentionality or perhaps even explicit recognition. Because of the personality-social integrative nature of this *Handbook* and chapter, I will take some time to highlight these perspectives. I will have to be selective here as well.

Traits Perspectives on the Person

The variables most commonly associated with personality are traits. Trait perspectives try to characterize persons by descriptions of them, usually focused on describing persons' styles of behavior, but also on describing how people act, feel, and think, and possibly also how they are motivated (Revelle, Wilt, & Rosenthal, 2010).

Current Knowledge About Traits

Despite, or perhaps because of, people's intuitive grasp of the trait concept, there is surprisingly little certainty about the nature of traits. Most trait theories agree on the following five points. First, traits describe individuals and emphasize the style or manner in which individuals act, think, and feel. For example, bolder individuals act, think, and feel in a bolder manner. Second, traits are characteristics on which people differ from each other. For example, some individuals are bolder than others. Third, individuals most likely do not differ in whether or not they have a trait but rather in the degree to which they have a trait. For example, although it may be convenient to speak of bold people and timid people, it is more likely that individuals differ all along a continuous dimension of boldness.

Fourth, traits endure for at least some extended time. For example, describing someone as a bold individual is more accurate if that individual is bold for more than just a moment. Finally, traits are broad descriptions of some kind of regularity, generality, or coherence in behavior, thought, and feeling. This generality may refer to the way the individuals act across different situations, to the way they act in significant, defining situations, or to a wide range of ways they act. For example, bolder individuals engage in a variety of bold actions, such as stating opinions, taking risks, and making decisions.

Four Types of Trait Perspectives

Two types of trait perspectives characterize persons largely in terms of the differences between them (cf. Zuroff, 1986). The first of these two perspectives focuses on the behavior patterns that result from traits. For example, the Density Distributions and Act-Frequency approaches (Buss & Craik, 1983; Fleeson, 2001) characterize persons by the frequency with which they perform acts representative of a trait.

The second of these two perspectives investigates the patterns of relationships among individual differences in traits, in order to identify the traits that should be used to characterize persons. The idea is that the patterns of individual differences will reveal the systematic organization of traits as well as the traits that are most important and that capture the nature of the person. The pool of traits to systematize is large. For example, just considering trait words that start with the letter a, there are at least: artistic, arresting, alert, attentive, argumentative, antsy, antisocial, asinine, alluring, aloof, assertive, aggressive, ardent, anal, arrogant, active, and so on. In fact, there are over 17,000 such trait words in the English language (Allport & Odbert, 1936).

This state of affairs creates two main problems. First, identifying the important traits requires comprehensiveness, that is, a system that includes all the important traits. Second, the potential traits are not organized, creating an unwieldy collection of traits, in which it is unknown how the different traits relate to each other, whether they are redundant or unique, and which ones are central or most important.

John, Naumann, and Soto (2008) describe the brilliant two-step development of the Big 5. It started with the lexical hypothesis, which claimed that a separate word existed in the language for each and every important difference between individuals' behavior (Allport & Odbert, 1936). Thus, to obtain a comprehensive system, the only requirement was to include all the trait words in a given language's dictionary; every important difference, in fact every difference, between people in their behavior would be included on such a list. But such a list turned out to be too large and too disorganized. The second stage of the solution was to use factor analysis to reduce redundancy in the list. What was especially creative about this step was that it allowed people, as their personalities actually were, to determine what the redundancies were—factor analysis designates redundancy precisely in those cases where levels of two traits co-occur naturally in people, as people are naturally. Participants rated themselves on the traits, and if individuals' scores on one trait were similar to their scores on another trait, then those two traits were designated as redundant with each other.

It turned out that redundancies were large among the 17,000 words, and only became small when the 17,000 traits were reduced to about 5, a remarkably small number. Suddenly the problems had a viable solution: all important traits were included, there was little redundancy, and traits were organized relative to each other. The five traits were the-by-now-familiar extraversion, agreeableness, conscientiousness, emotional stability, and intellect. Extraversion, for example, was one trait, because people were such that any person who was relatively talkative was likely to be also relatively energetic, relatively assertive, and relatively bold (among other related characteristics).

The third type of trait perspective characterizes persons in terms of the causal forces underlying traits, in order to explain trait-relevant behavior. For example, Gordon W. Allport proposed one of the early and prominent theories of the causal forces underlying traits. He claimed that traits are neurocognitive structures that lead individuals to interpret a range of situations as being equivalent to each other and relevant to the trait. Although subsequent theories have proposed other causal forces, there has not been enough research yet to explain how traits cause behavior. Unresolved issues include how many causes underlie traits and what the causes' relative strengths are. The fourth trait perspective characterizers persons by conditional traits (Ryle, 1949; Mischel & Shoda, 1995); this perspective tends to use the word "disposition" rather than the word "trait," because it emphasizes the potentiality of the trait. According to these theories, the trait is a readiness to act in a certain way when certain conditions arise. Just as a glass has the disposition of brittleness, making it likely to break if and only if a sharp force is applied to it, a courageous person might have the disposition to take risks if and only if an opportunity to accomplish something valuable is both present and hindered by clear dangers.

Developments This Decade

The research on traits in the past 10–20 years has been astounding. Not only has the research been voluminous, but it has also been persuasive and it has been innovative. In the following, I review developments of several particularly active topics.

FILLING OUT THE TRAIT HIERARCHY
Personality psychologists have not been content with the simple five-trait view of personality, but rather have created a hierarchical tree structure with levels both higher and lower than the Big Five. Even the

middle level has been revised, as it now appears that adding a sixth trait, honesty, may create a better representation (Lee & Ashton, 2008; Saucier, 2009). Moving up the hierarchy eliminates even the slight redundancies among the Big Five, and results in two supertraits: growth (extraversion/openness) and citizenship (agreeableness, conscientiousness, and emotional stability) (Anusic, Schimmack, Pinkus, & Lockwood, 2009). Moving down the hierarchy results in smaller, subcomponent traits. For example, reliability, orderliness, impulse control, decisiveness, punctuality, formalness, conventionality, and industriousness may be subcomponents or facets of conscientiousness (Roberts & Pomerantz, 2004). It is not clear yet whether there are 10 (DeYoung, Quilty, & Peterson, 2007) or 30 (Costa & McCrae, 1992), or another number of these smaller traits (Soto & John, 2009). Filling out this hierarchy not only adds sophistication and subtlety to traits, but it provides additional organization and characterization to the various traits. In particular, as one moves higher in the organization, traits become broader and more widely predictive. Redundancy within a trait as well as redundancy between traits goes down. As one moves down the hierarchy, traits become more narrow and more specific, although perhaps stronger, in their predictions (Paunonen & Ashton, 2001). Furthermore, redundancy within a trait and between traits increases.

EVIDENCE FOR THE CROSS-CULTURAL VALIDITY OF THE BIG FIVE

Because the lexical hypothesis claims that language reveals the structure of personality, the best test of the lexical hypothesis is whether the same structure emerges in different languages. Testing the structure across cultures also can be used to refine the hierarchy of the Big Five (de Fruyt, de Bolle, McCrae, Terracciano, & Costa, 2009; Saucier, 2008). Many studies revealed replicated Big Five structures across many diverse cultures (Saucier, 2008; Church, 2009), providing strong evidence for the validity of the Big Five as a structure of individual differences in personality. This research was followed by investigations of cultural differences in personality. Although some mean level differences exist, patterns of adult development are rather reliable (McCrae et al., 2000). With some excitement, researchers were even able to find some evidence for the legitimacy of the Big Five in other species, including dogs (Hirayoshi & Nakajima, 2009), horses (Morris, Gale, & Duffy, 2002), and chimpanzees (King, Weiss, & Farmer, 2005), by discovering the Big Five

structure in observer ratings of animals, demonstrating agreement between distinct observer ratings of the same animals, and by finding validity correlations with other variables.

IMPROVING MEASUREMENT

Measurement continued to be an important topic among trait perspectives, as investigators focused on the features that affect the quality of the data, such as biases, error, and response formats. New developments included recording ambient sounds in everyday life (Mehl, Gosling, & Pennebaker, 2006) and taking advantage of the Internet to collect massive samples (Gosling & Johnson, 2010; Srivastava, Gosling, John, & Potter, 2003), in turn allowing very precise estimates of important relationships (Soto, John, Gosling, & Potter, 2008). The use of large samples may have encouraged the development of short questionnaires (Ashton & Lee, 2009; Gosling, Rentfrow, & Swan, 2003). Finally, researchers began exploring the usefulness of implicit tests of personality (Back, Schmuckle, & Egloff, 2009; Shnabel, Asendorpf, & Greenwald, 2008).

EMERGENCE OF SUBJECTIVE WELL-BEING AS A MAJOR TOPIC OF STUDY

Reaching back into the 90s and even 80s, subjective well-being (SWB) became an important topic of study in personality (see Oishi, chapter 24, this volume). Most personality psychologists believe that quality of life is best defined subjectively, as the individual's own evaluation of the quality of his or her life. A prominent model of well-being breaks this evaluation into three components. Two affective components describe the amount of excitement in the individual's life ("positive affect," PA), and the amount of peace and contentment in the individual's life (lack of "negative affect," NA). The remaining component is a cognitive judgment, evaluating the life as a whole, and is known as life satisfaction (see also Ryff's conception of psychological well-being, 1989). Admittedly, such subjective accounts of SWB have problems. Specifically, when the evaluation is left up to the individual, the measure may mean something different for each subject, and furthermore, subjective accounts are open to bias, such as a social desirability bias or repression. Nonetheless, the subjective school has three main arguments in its favor. First, it argues that all of the objective indicators of quality of life, such as money and relationships, are good only because they feed into happiness and satisfaction. Therefore, happiness and satisfaction appear to be the ultimate definition of the good life. Second, who should decide whether a life is good or not? Researchers are not necessarily better equipped than other individuals for deciding what makes a life good. Finally, objective indicators do not predict subjective indicators nearly as strongly as they should, if they really mattered to individuals. Thus, apparent objective indicators of life quality may not be as important as they appear.

PREDICTING IMPORTANT LIFE OUTCOMES

One of the most startling findings to emerge this decade was that traits powerfully predict important life outcomes, both concurrently and predictively over decades (Ozer & Benet-Martinez, 2006; Roberts, Kuncel, Shiner, Caspi, & Goldberg, 2007). Extraversion and neuroticism have been known to predict positive affect and negative affect at about the .3 to .4 level for some time (Lucas & Fujita, 2000; Costa & McCrae, 1980). This prediction level is greater than any other variable's ability to predict affect, and has now been replicated across multiple labs, age groups, and cultures (Lucas & Fujita, 2000). It is even true within introverts, as Fleeson, Malanos, and Achille (2002) showed that both extraverts and introverts were happier when they acted extraverted, and McNiel and Fleeson (2006) verified that even manipulating state extraversion induced state positive affect.

Although happiness may be a subjective phenomenon, conscientiousness predicts work and school performance about equally as strongly as does intelligence (Noftle & Robins, 2007; Ones, Viswesvaran, & Schmidt 1993), regardless of type of measure of work performance. Even physical health and death are influenced by personality: tens of studies have now demonstrated that personality traits are important predictors of mortality (Roberts et al., 2007). People higher in conscientiousness, extraversion, emotional stability, and agreeableness live longer lives, on the order of years. These associations are at least as strong as those connecting SES and IQ to mortality, and these associations are present even when controlling for SES, gender, education, cognitive ability, cardiovascular disease, smoking, disease severity, and other similar variables (Roberts et al., 2007). Personality traits are also directly related to both Axis 1 and Axis 2 mental disorders, an empirical finding likely to be reflected in a dimensional personality trait model revision to the upcoming *Diagnostic and Statistical Manual, 5th edition (DSM-V)* from the American Psychiatric Association (Skodol et al., 2011). It may be that a dimensional model is appropriate because personality psychopathology is a variant or manifestation of extreme personality traits, or because personality factors lead to mental illness via mechanisms such as physiological reactions to stressful events or dysfunctional coping styles (Tackett, Silberschmidt, Krueger, & Sponheim, 2009).

At the same time, one of the biggest questions in SWB research was whether events create lasting effects on SWB, or in contrast people eventually adapt and return to their starting levels of SWB. There is strong evidence for the ability of people to adapt to adverse situations (Mancini & Bonanno, 2009), as well as strong evidence that some events leave long-lasting consequences on well-being, such as high-quality marriages (Lucas et al., 2003), divorce (Lucas, 2005), and long-term disability (Lucas, 2007). Although income appears to matter to SWB, it matters much more at lower levels than at medium or high levels (Lucas & Schimmack, 2009).

PREDICTION OF GENERAL OUTCOMES

There were a wide variety of unrelated studies predicting a variety of outcomes from traits. Some of this research focused on predicting validation criteria, such as behavior, to demonstrate that traits really do exist (Fleeson & Gallagher, 2009; Back et al., 2009). Other research focused on what it is like to be someone with a given trait: what their living spaces look like (Gosling, Ko, Mannarelli, & Morris, 2002), how likable and normal they are considered to be (Wood, Gosling, & Potter, 2007; Wortman & Wood, 2010), what sort of e-mail names (Heisler & Crabhill, 2006) or Web pages they have (Vazire & Gosling, 2004), their music preferences (Rentfrow & Gosling, 2003), and their relationship behaviors (Asendorpf, 1998). One creative development in this research was honing in on cultural trends, such as speed dating (Luo & Zhang, 2009), the Internet, and Web and e-mail presences.

BEHAVIORAL GENETICS AND GENETICS

It is important to note that traits are not necessarily biological in origin. Traits could be the result of early childhood experience, and traits could be the lasting legacy of powerful situation effects. In fact, if situations have any effects beyond the immediate moment, these effects would be encoded as personality. Nonetheless, some important work in personality investigates behavioral genetics, and the main conclusions in behavioral genetics were solidified

(Turkheimer, 2000). The most important conclusion from behavioral genetics is that heritability is never 0. No matter what the characteristic is, it has some component that is due to genetics: intelligence, personality, mental disorders, attitudes, or anything else. However, the size of that component is not known (Krueger, South, Johnson, & Iacono, 2008). It could be anywhere from 1 to 50%: different studies give different results, different methods give different results, and, most importantly, the size depends on the existing variation and on the existing degree to which—and effectiveness with which—people try to change the characteristic. Finally, shared environment appears to have very little effect on personality. However, this result could be due to restriction of range resulting from adoption agency policies; correcting for that restriction may increase estimates of shared environment to as high as 50% (Stoolmiller, 1999; but see Loehlin & Horn, 2000).

Turkheimer (2000) argued that genetics may not be the route to explaining personality. The pathway from genes to behavior is long and complex. For example, whether people vote Democratic versus Republican is heritable, despite the unlikelihood of a gene for party preference. Genes influence proteins, which in turn influence cells; cells in turn create structures, which create organs, which ultimately influence personality, which needs one more step to influence voting. This chain is very complex and intricate, likely to involve many multivariable interactions, including epigenetic effects (Champagne, 2009). Turkheimer (2000) argues that starting at the genetic level therefore may not be fruitful.

ADULTHOOD PERSONALITY CHANGE

Part of the interest in personality change arises from the importance of personality to valued life outcomes. Part of the interest arises from scientific curiosity about the role of life experience in personality, the continuity between childhood and adulthood, the definition of maturity, and the endurance of identity. Adult development was a very productive topic this decade (Stewart & Deaux, chapter 1, this volume). When it comes to the mean level of questionnaire scores, it appears that the average person becomes more agreeable, conscientious, and emotionally stable over adulthood, does not change in openness, and increases in some parts of extraversion but decreases in other parts (McCrae et al., 2000; Roberts et al., 2006). Noftle and Fleeson (2010) suggest that these trends might be even

stronger when actual manifestation of traits in behavior is investigated.

However, averages mask interindividual differences in direction of change (Bleidorn, Kandler, Reimann, Angleitner, & Spinath, 2009; Mroczek, 2003). Longitudinal correlations reveal that individuals shift their relative position to a fair degree (Caspi, Roberts, & Shiner, 2005), because individuals change in different directions in adulthood. It is also becoming clear that more of this change occurs earlier in adulthood (Caspi et al., 2005; Terracciano, McCrae, & Costa, 2006).

TARGET AND OBSERVER AGREEMENT

The accuracy of personality impressions returned to favor in the last 10–20 years. Results show that targets and observers agree in their judgments about the targets' personalities, including both close others and brand new acquaintances (Hall, Andrzejewski, Murphy, Mast, & Feinstein, 2008). Even people who have never interacted with the participant agree about his or her personality: "thin slices" of the targets depicted in photographs or very brief video clips can lead to agreement about personality impressions (Ambady, Bernieri, & Richeson, 2000).

SPECIFIC, IMPORTANT TRAITS

As befits a maturing science, much of the research in personality began to focus more narrowly on specific, important traits. Identifying potentially important traits requires special insight into people, so it is not easy. Identified traits include at least dominance, aggression, leadership, narcissism, and ego-control and ego-resiliency. The circumplex is an important model of traits that highlights agency and communion (Wiggins, 1996). Another set of specific traits are the character-related traits or virtues (Chang & Sanna, 2003; Lapsley & Power, 2005; Peterson & Seligman, 2004). Research on individual traits aims to explain the individual trait or to investigate its correlates. Sometimes the researchers explore more narrow subtraits of the Big Five, and at other times they approach the study of a given trait with carefree, benign, or perhaps competitive neglect of the Big Five. Although acceptance of the Big Five is widespread, there is still some reasoned skepticism of its validity, completeness, and universality (e.g., Block, 2010).

THE PERSON-SITUATION DEBATE

Finally, much headway was made in moving toward a resolution of the person-situation debate

(Donnellan et al., 2009). There is no universal agreement about the central issue of the debate (Fleeson, 2004), but one key issue was whether—and how much—individual differences in behavior are consistent. Consistency is not only necessary for the existence of traits, it is sufficient as well: if there are repeatable individual differences between individuals in their behavior, then there are traits (Allport, 1937; Eysenck & Eysenck, 1980). These traits will vary in their centrality to the notion of personality, with some traits outside or barely inside the domain of personality, such as handedness, and other traits very central in the domain of personality, such as extraversion. The key point is that the consistency is what makes the behavior a trait rather than an accident, a fluke, or the sole consequence of circumstances.

The trait thesis is the naturalistic position that different people have different ways of acting, that these are consistent, and that people generally act in their typical ways (e.g., Allport, 1937; McCrae & Costa, 2003). The opposing thesis, the situationist position, is that when actual behavior is examined, rather than retrospective, summary questionnaires, consistency is difficult to find. That is, what people do, think, and feel when in real situations with real pressures and real consequences is not consistent from moment to moment. When Mischel (1968) reviewed the evidence, he concluded that the correlations between behavior in one situation and behavior in another situation were only about .1 to.3. One crux of the debate was that broad traits appeared to have validity, because they had consequences for life, were stable across the lifespan, and were observable to observers, yet they apparently could not have validity, because they had to work their effects through behavior, and the data showed that behavior was not consistent. One force preventing the debate from ending was the inability to reconcile these apparently contradictory facts (Fleeson & Noftle, 2008).

Based on the writings of personality psychologists (e.g., Epstein, 1983; Hogan, DeSoto, & Solano, 1977; Mischel, 2004; Ozer, 1986), Fleeson and Noftle (2008) proposed that the person-situation debate is ending in a synthesis, a new thesis that combines the two formerly opposing sides in a unitary idea. The synthesis is that there is not only one kind of important behavioral consistency, and traits produce different kinds of consistency to different degrees. Most importantly, traits produce consistency of aggregates to a greater degree than they produce consistency of single behaviors. The

synthesis that several types of behavior consistency exist has several advantages in resolving the debate. First, it removes the competition from both sides on who is correct about the consistency of behavior. In some ways, behavior is consistent and in some ways it is inconsistent, so both sides are correct. Second, gains on one side are not achieved at the expense of the other. Third, research can be conducted on several types of consistency within the same study. Finally, and perhaps most importantly, the synthesis takes seriously the valid, legitimate points of both sides of the debate.

Social psychology went through a very similar debate about attitudes, remarkably with almost no interchange between the two fields about the overlapping issues. Attitudes make up perhaps the most well-known perspective on the person that is based within social psychology, and the debate about attitudes concerned whether behavior was consistent with attitudes, just like the debate about whether behavior was consistent with traits. Because the two debates proceeded independently of each other, every insight was required to occur twice, once in each field. Eventually the debate about attitudes was resolved with clear evidence that attitudes do indeed predict behavior at a reasonably strong level (Ajzen, chapter 15, this volume). Research on attitudes is a massive topic, and covers a wide variety of issues within attitudes, including the measurement of attitudes, the characteristics of attitudes, change in attitudes, and the consistency of behavior with attitudes. The similarities between this research and the research on traits are strong.

PROCESSES AND MECHANISMS UNDERLYING TRAITS

Although the majority of trait perspectives have tried to characterize differences between people, a small and growing number of researchers have tried to characterize the trait-related processes characterizing the person. Robinson and colleagues have produced an impressive volume of findings showing individual differences in cognitive reaction times related to traits (e.g., Robinson & Wilkowski, 2010). However, biological explanations have received the most attention. Much of this research has taken a neurobiological approach and has focused on avoidance systems as fundamental to personality (Carver & Conner-Smith, 2010). The hormonal and neurotransmitter influences on traits have also begun to be studied (DePue, 2006).

Much research has tried to explain why extraversion leads to happiness, and researchers have proposed dopamine, sociability, hedonic level, reactivity, and behavioral enactment explanations (DePue, 2006; Lucas, Le, & Dyrenforth, 2008; Wilt, Noftle, Fleeson, and Spain, 2011). Another focus has been on explaining why personality leads to health. Personality traits appear to affect mortality through at least four mechanisms: (1) cognitive and physiological responses to stressful life events; (2) health-promoting and health-threatening behaviors, such as smoking, exercise, and risk-taking; (3) contribution to other social risk factors for illness such as social relationships and career attainment; and (4) behaviors involved in illness, such as coping and treatment adherence (Roberts et al., 2007).

Trait Perspectives Based in Social Psychology

Not surprisingly traits are not studied much in social psychology. When traits are studied, they tend to be studied as contributors to social processes (which is an important form of integration, as I will discuss later), but not as entities themselves. One type of this research examines the effects of traits on relationships (Mendoza-Denton & Ayduk, chapter 18, this volume; Knippenberg, chapter 27, this volume; Sadler, Ethier, Gunn, Duong, & Woody, 2009) and group processes (Anderson & Kilduff, 2009). Another type of this research examines the processes by which individuals perceive persons' traits (Uleman & Saribay, chapter 14, this volume), including automatic trait inferences (Uleman, Saribay, & Gonzalez, 2008), and the ability to judge persons based on "thin slices" of perception of them, as short as a few seconds of videotape (Ambady et al., 2000).

Attachment is an exception, and is a trait-like concept studied for its own sake in all three fields of personality, social, and developmental psychology (Mikulciner & Shaver, chapter 19, this volume; Sroufe, Egeland, Carlson, & Collins, 2005). Attachment perspectives have demonstrated that persons differ in their general orientations to relationships (secure, anxious, or avoidant), and that orientations are visible in behaviors, in romantic relationships, and in beliefs about others.

Probably the research in social psychology that is closest to trait perspectives is the work of Wood and colleagues on habits (Wood, Quinn, & Kashy, 2002), which characterizes stable differences between persons in how they behave, but at a more narrow level of behavior characterization than the broad traits of the Big Five. Habits are defined as learned dispositions to repeat past responses (Wood & Neal, 2007). Thus, they are trait-like in their central emphasis on individual differences in regularities of behavior; nonetheless they inherently refer to situations, in that habits are considered to be automatic responses to situational cues. In fact, habits are in part the long-term consequences of situations. Thus, the theory of habits represents a potential trailhead for investigating the person and the situation together.

Cognitive Perspectives on the Person

Cognitive perspectives try to characterize persons by how and what they think. People think in different ways from each other, and these ways of thinking have consequences for who the people are and for the things that happen in their lives. There are two types of cognitive perspectives: characterizing persons by individual differences in single or groups of variables; and characterizing the cognitive processes that link different factors in persons together. The first perspective requires some insight into people and some understanding of them. Researchers following this perspective create a questionnaire to measure the way of thinking, and find out its importance and impact. One of the most successful of these variables is locus of control. Some 40–50 years ago, Rotter (1966) had the insight that an important factor in thinking was an individual's belief about whether he or she has control over the events that happen in his or her life. Since then, over 15,000 articles have been published about locus of control, covering topics such as athletics, multiple sclerosis, parenting, and diabetes.

Many important variables have been identified this way. A short sampling includes need for cognition (Cacioppo & Petty, 1982; Epstein, 1996), dogmatism (Rokeach, 1954), procrastination (Lay, 1986), hope (Snyder et al., 1991), disgust sensitivity (Haidt, McCauley, & Rozin, 1994), self-monitoring (Snyder, 1974), belief in a just world (Lipkus, 1991), moral identity (Aquino & Reed, 2002), and defenses (Cramer, 1988). Note that some of these differences describe individual differences in the content of thought, whereas others focus on individual differences in the process of thought. For example, self-esteem and the self-concept describe the content of thought—the specific thoughts an individual has. Need for cognition describes the processes of thought—how people think, regardless of the material about which they are thinking.

Some of these variables are assessed with qualitative measures. One very important example is the life story, and Dan McAdams has led a large group of researchers investigating the types of stories people tell about their lives, as well as the consequences of those stories. Significant memories make up another important type of narrative for understanding people (Woike & Polo, 2001; Blagov & Singer, 2004). Finally, scripts are elaborate beliefs about how events proceed, and scripts about emotions can be powerful in affecting behavior (Demorest, 2008).

The second cognitive perspective attempts to characterize the cognitive structures and processes that are important for all people and for which there may be individual differences (Pervin, 2003). This approach is closely tied to social psychology, often even referred to as the social-cognitive perspective. It grew in part from the writings of Allport and Kelly and their emphasis on construal and alternativism (Cantor & Fleeson, 1994). Allport (1937) and Kelly (1963) emphasized the power of interpretation to change the meaning of a situation, which meant that the same situation could lead to different behaviors from different individuals. This interpretative process was called "construal," and it led naturally to alternativism. Given that construal changes the meaning of the situation, and even though interpretations have a subjective certainty to them, construal suggests that each individual may have alternative ways he or she can construe a situation. People may be able to use the power of alternative construals in their own adaptive self-regulation (Cantor & Fleeson, 1994).

Mischel and Shoda (1995) argued that researchers need to look to construal and alternativism to explain personality. People are not automatons, but rather are perceptive and discriminative; as a result they end up acting differently in different situations. Thus, simple consistency in behavior is not likely. They argued that explaining behavior will require looking for mechanisms underlying inconsistency, and the place to look for such mechanisms is in cognitions, including specifically encodings, expectancies and beliefs, affects, goals and values, competencies, and self-regulatory plans (Mischel, 1973). Updating Allport's (1937) arguments, Mischel and Shoda proposed that once these mechanisms are understood, apparently inconsistent behavior will appear to be the logical consequence of individuals' construals. Persons differ reliably in the chronic activation levels of thoughts underlying construals, and thus differ reliably in how they act in specific situations. These differences in activation are enduring, and therefore, the resulting differences

in behavior patterns will be enduring. However, these differences are closely tied to the triggering situations, which means that they produce "dispositions," or "behavioral signatures" that are like mini-traits, which consistently link specific behavioral reactions to specific situational features.

Mischel and Shoda's theory, known as the cognitive-affective processing system (CAPS), is a persuasive and compelling suggestion of where to look for mechanisms of personality, and a call for looking for such mechanisms, although it is not itself a theory of specific mechanisms. It is what Mischel and Shoda call a "metatheory."

Developments This Decade
Researchers continue to make insightful observations about individual differences in thought patterns, and these observations turn into productive units. Many of these units have character (virtue), humanistic, or positive psychology themes, such as gratitude (Emmons, 2009), mindfulness (Lau et al., 2006), meaning in life (Steger, Frazier, Oishi, & Kaler, 2006), forgiveness (Hargrave & Sells, 1997), authenticity (Kernis & Goldman, 2005), and inspiration (Thrash & Elliot 2003).

Another trend was continued emphasis on classic cognitive variables. Identifying a viable cognitive difference between persons requires creativity and insight. Perhaps the best evidence for the veridicality of that insight is the amount of research generated by identification of these variables. Through out the past 10–20 years, many studies have continued to investigate previously discovered cognitive variables.

Finally, CAPS provided a metatheory of places to look for explanations of processes underlying personality, and this decade many researchers followed that call. Donnellan et al. (2009) produced a special issue highlighting that research, which included if-then patterns (Smith, Shoda, Cumming, & Smoll, 2009), profile analysis (Furr, 2009), interpersonal signatures (Fournier, Moskowitz, & Zuroff, 2009), and research about rejection sensitivity (Romero-Canyas, Anderson, Reddy, & Downey, 2009).

Cognitive Perspectives Based in Social Psychology
Most of the research characterizing the person in social psychology takes a cognitive perspective. This is not surprising given social psychology's emphasis on meaning-making and on explaining processes (Smith & Mackie, 1995). The amount of work

identifying important variables and the interrelationships among them. I believe a third contributor to separation was that social psychology required that situations be powerful for the legitimacy of their field, but effects of the person appeared to deny the importance of situations. A zero-sum game seemed to operate between the fields of social and personality psychology (Funder, 2006; Leising, 2007), which saw explicit expression in the person-situation debate. It also appears that, fourth, the development and growth of traits as a topic within personality psychology surprisingly deepened the split, as theory and research about traits increasingly ignored interpretation as an important part of trait constructs.

Tracy et al. (2009), surveyed active personality and social psychology researchers on a wide variety of topics concerning their theoretical bases and their methodological preferences. The main finding was of significant differences between personality and social psychologists on almost every assessed variable, such that personality and social psychologists used different methods, studied different topics, and differed in whether they believed the situation or the person was a more powerful force. At the same time, and perhaps more significantly, there was substantial overlap between the two groups: social psychologists occasionally used the methods of personality psychology, and vice versa, and social psychologists acknowledged that stable dispositions do have some influence on behavior, while personality psychologists acknowledged that situations do have some influence on behavior.

This is a new development, a development that both represents progress and presents a difficulty. Table 3.1 shows some possible depths of integration between the two fields. The left column depicts increasing depths of integration in the explanation of phenomena. Least integrated is when the two fields have contrasting explanations for phenomena that actually oppose each other. More integrated is when researchers have parallel explanations for the same phenomena, wasting efforts as the same discoveries are made twice. Still more integrated is when the explanations can be added together—there is still no intellectual interaction, but at least the two fields are both contributing to knowledge. Very integrated is when the theories and findings in the two fields interact with and influence each other, and most integrated is when basic phenomena are reconceptualized in a way that incorporates the interests, theories, and findings of both fields. This would create an exciting and fertile set of fields,

Table 3.1 Possible Levels of Integration Between Personality and Social Psychology

Explanatory Integration	Practical Integration
Opposing explanations	Mutual disdain
Parallel explanations	Acceptance of mutual value
Additive explanations	Shared methods
Interactive explanations	Attend to findings in other field
Joint reconceptualization	Collaboration

The left column depicts increasing levels of integration in the explanation of phenomena. The right column describes interaction in more mundane, practical terms, by what it means for the individual researcher.

because people across fields would be working together, on the same problems.

The right column depicts interaction in more mundane, practical terms, by what it means for the individual researcher. This is important to the state of integration, because it is only through the efforts of individual researchers that integration will happen. And researchers are busy—without compelling reasons, they are unlikely to invest the significant time and effort into integration. Least integrated practice is when researchers in the two fields do not believe the other field contributes anything of worth. A significant advance is when the researchers in the two fields accept the value of the other field, even when they have no interest in it personally. This does not create interaction, but at least it allows for it. A similar step is when the two fields begin to use similar methods, which allows individual researchers in the two fields to understand and have confidence in the findings of the other field. Two fields become much more integrated when individual researchers start to pay attention to the advances occurring in the other field. This is difficult, because researchers are busy, so it requires that the advances in the other field have importance for the individual researcher. This can happen only at the highest levels of conceptual integration. The highest level of practical integration occurs when researchers begin to collaborate across the two fields on research projects together.

The findings of Tracy et al. (2009) suggest that the two fields have reached some degree of mutual acceptance but are currently holding each other at arm's length. In terms of table 3.1, Tracy et al.'s (2009) findings mean that integration has advanced to the stages of accepting the mutual value of the other field and of conceptual development in parallel. But the significant differences also mean that the fields have not advanced past these stages, to the point where they are working together on the same problems.

Likely Routes of Integration

There is much to be gained for a given research project to take a personality- and social-psychology integrated approach. Such advantages include identifying the causal processes that lead to behavior, increasing the accuracy of prediction, improving the discovery of key variables, and demonstrating the long-term impacts of situations. Integration likely needs to be done in a way that overcomes the causes of separation, including the differences in goals between the two fields, differences in methods, the need to defend the role of situations, moving past the person-situation debate, and the need for personality to assert its independence. If these benefits are out there, and if the identified barriers are the ones reducing access to these benefits, what are the ways researchers attempt to overcome those barriers to enjoy those outcomes? What paths will and do researchers follow to reach those benefits and short-circuit those barriers?

I don't mean to impose a top-down approach, in which I list the primary or most valuable ways in which to integrate personality and social psychology. Rather, I mean to generate an abstract, loose collection of some possible paths I predict for getting to integration, as well as routes I see already well-trodden by researchers currently doing integration.

I divide the routes to integration into those from the personality side and those from the social side. I start with several ways personality psychologists may move more toward social psychology. First, personality psychologists may *incorporate interpretation and meaning* into their constructs more routinely. "Meaning" refers to the interpretations and conclusions individuals draw from the events around them. Meaning occupies a central role in some perspectives on personality, especially cognitive perspectives but also motivational perspectives. However, meaning is not central to many perspectives on the person, including trait perspectives most notably. By incorporating meaning, personality psychologists will embrace social psychologists' emphasis on interpretation.

In addition to incorporating meaning, personality psychologists will move toward social psychology by *incorporating situations* into their constructs.

Incorporating situations into their constructs means redefining constructs in a way such that situations are part of their very meaning, rather than something that comes after the trait, from the outside. It also means incorporating situations into the process models of how traits affect behavior, and in particular, the social processes aspects of situations. In an integrated approach, personality units might begin to be characterized in terms of their role in social processes, and their development might begin to be characterized as a consequence of social processes.

Personality psychologists may move toward social psychology by putting increased effort into *discovering the processes and mechanisms underlying personality* variables. Such a move would reduce the gap in underlying theoretical approaches (e.g., on explanation versus description) and reduce the gap in preferred methodological tools (experiments versus correlations).

Finally, moving even further into the methodological terrain of social psychology, personality psychologists may begin manipulating personality traits. I do not mean the manipulation of genetics to change traits, but rather the manipulation of states, of current manifestation of traits, in order to discover the consequences of those states (Fleeson et al., 2002). Once causal consequences of states are determined, careful efforts to generalize them to traits can be made. For example, Fleeson et al. (2002) manipulated participants' state extraversion—the degree to which they were extraverted in the moment—and demonstrated a causal effect of state extraversion on positive affect. Assuming that trait extraversion leads to state extraversion, this strategy demonstrates that the robust extraversion to positive affect correlation is in fact an extraversion to positive affect causation (Wilt, Noftle, Spain, & Fleeson, 2011).

Social psychology can also take some steps to integrate the two fields. One step is to *include person variables in the conceptualization of processes*. It is likely that characteristics of individuals contribute to the functioning of individuals—if so, a complete account of that functioning would have to refer to those characteristics of individuals. If so, then theoretical accounts of processes would be improved by considering such variables. That is, if it is true that behavior is influenced by the person, and that those influences are complex and interactive with the situation, then behavior can only be explained by including proper places for person variables. In addition, this would increase the predictive power of such models. Most controversially, if social psychologists locate these person characteristics within the space of the Big Five hierarchy, then they would be able to communicate with other researchers in an efficient and mutually productive manner.

Another route social psychologists might take to integrating is to begin to *chart the long-term consequences of situations*. If situations have long-term consequences, then those consequences are represented as personality. That is, the consequences are carried by an individual, based on his or her past history of situations. Ironically, by studying such long-term consequences (i.e., personality), social psychologists will be extending the power of the situations.

Finally, methodologically, social psychologists may begin to *pay closer attention to measurement*. Personality psychologists, because of their emphasis on correlational methodology, have developed sophisticated measurement techniques. If social psychologists were to adopt more of those techniques than they already do, the resulting findings may become more robust and powerful, and more subtle processes may be discovered.

Given the practical difficulties involved in paying attention to a second field, Roberts (2009) made the excellent point that one very powerful route to integration may be comprehensive theories, theories that incorporate both personalities and situations, allowing the researcher to be efficient when they act integratively. Indeed, a sudden increase in integrative models has appeared on the scene. In the past, integrative theories organized different perspectives by keeping them distinct but placing them in a structure that clarified their relationship to each other. In recent years, integrative theories have started connecting the different perspectives in a more integrated manner. Rick Hoyle has attempted to integrate traits and processes in the explanation of problem behavior (2000) and in the explanation of self-regulation (2006) (also see Constanzo et al., chapter 23, this volume). Read et al. (2010) have presented a connectionist model of personality that integrates connectionist processes with dispositions. Mischel and Shoda (2008) have presented the CAPS system as a process model underlying dispositions. Donnellan et al. (2009) presented an entire special issue of the *Journal of Research in Personality* on integrated perspectives in personality. Heller et al. (2009) have presented a model that describes how goals and social roles interact to create manifestations of traits. In each of these perspectives, the concerns of personality psychologists and social psychologists are folded together, so that integrated work is possible and efficient.

Whole Trait Theory

Because of the many persuasive calls for integration within personality psychology and between personality and social psychology (e.g., Fleeson, 2004; Kihlstrom, 1987), integration appears to have made great progress. The Donnellan et al. (2009) volume of integrative work in personality and this *Handbook of Personality and Social Psychology* are good evidence. Tracy et al. (2009) added empirical evidence that each of the various perspectives accepts the other perspective as a valid way to contribute to science. At the same time, integration appears to have reached a comfortable resting place. Although personality psychologists agree that situations provide powerful influences on behavior, and social psychologists admit that personality can impact behavior, the two fields continue their work independently, without crossing over to dabble in the other side's business. Personality psychologists continue to report correlations between individual differences, and social psychologists continue to report experimental tests of causal processes. There simply isn't *time* to keep abreast of a separate field that cares about different topics and that uses alternative methods (Roberts, 2009). Similarly, within personality itself, the trait and the social-cognitive perspectives share an arm's-length acceptance of each other, albeit a possibly more grudging acceptance than the one across fields between social and personality psychologists. They also share the differences in preferences for correlations among differences or experimental tests of universal processes. And the motivational perspective also continues to exist side by side with the trait and cognitive perspectives.

Lack of integration is not wholly bad. Researchers are addressing different questions, so their answers are not necessarily mutually relevant. The characterization of the *P* and of the *E* can occur in pieces. However, eventually they must be integrated, and along the way there are many benefits to be had by integrating, as elaborated by Snyder and Deaux in the introductory chapter to this *Handbook*. And as a result of this lack of integration, the characterization of Lewin's *P* and *E* is going to occur piecemeal rather than comprehensively.

The question is, if and when integration is to occur, how will this impasse be overcome? This is the question my lab and I have been working on for some time now, and it is the reason we have developed *Whole Trait Theory* (e.g., Fleeson, 2001; Fleeson, 2004; Fleeson, 2007; Fleeson and Jolley, 2006; McCabe & Fleeson, 2011.; Fleeson & Noftle, 2009; Fleeson & Wilt, 2010; McNiel & Fleeson,

2006; Noftle & Fleeson, 2010). Whole trait theory is a theory that tries to describe how the different parts or sides of traits fit together into wholes. Although space limitations require a short version in this chapter, please see Fleeson (2011) for the full whole trait theory.

There are two phases to integrating personality and social psychology in a way that facilitates overcoming this impasse. The first phase is to integrate the trait and social-cognitive perspectives within personality into a single theory. This is an arduous task, and requires several individual integrative steps.

Step 1. Recognizing the Complementary Strengths of the Trait Perspective and the Social-Cognitive Perspective

The trait perspective and the social-cognitive perspective have each produced important advances in understanding the person, by each clarifying one of the key parts or sides of traits. The trait perspective has clarified the descriptive side of traits, by organizing ways to describe people's personalities. It is widely agreed that differences between people can be organized into a hierarchical structure, with the five traits of extraversion, agreeableness, conscientiousness, emotional stability, and intellect (the "Big Five") at a middle level (John et al., 2008). Describing a person, then, involves indicating the person's level of these five traits. The Big Five clarify the descriptive side of traits, because the Big Five identify the main ways to describe what a person is like and how he or she is different from other people. Each of the Big Five traits is broad, and carries with it a fairly rich description of what a person is like. For example, describing a person as extraverted implies that the person is talkative, energetic, and verbal; that he or she is assertive, bold, and commanding; and that he or she is adventurous and daring. Describing a person as agreeable implies that he or she is friendly, kind, and warm, and that he or she is generous, giving, and respectful.

The social-cognitive perspective has made important theoretical advances in clarifying the explanatory side of traits, by proposing explanatory mechanisms underlying individual differences in behavior. In 1937, Allport described traits as made up of cognitive, motivational, and affective processes that produce trait-manifesting behavior. Mischel (1973) and Mischel and Shoda (1995, 2008) provided a specifically social-cognitive version of this explanatory account. They argued that various cognitive and affective (and motivational)

units are behind the situation-based tendencies in individuals' behavior. A given child may be aggressive when peers tease but compliant when adults approach because of various expectations the child has about the behavior of peers and adults. Although Mischel and Shoda did not provide concrete accounts of these processes, they made a persuasive argument in favor of identifying the processes, they provided an outline of what the processes would be like, they pointed to social-cognitive mechanisms as likely locations of these processes, and they provided a set of components likely to be involved in these processes. Included in these components were encodings, expectancies, affects, competencies, and self-regulatory plans (Mischel, 1973). For example, the social-cognitive approach has pointed to goals and beliefs as causes of personality-relevant behavior, so that when psychologists wish to explain personality-relevant behavior, they should look to goals and beliefs.

Step 2. Recognizing the Complementary Weaknesses of the Two Perspectives

Despite the impressive advances in identifying and validating the Big Five, the Big Five remain primarily descriptive variables. Although the field has witnessed a plethora of reasonable definitions of traits (Allport, 1937; McCrae & Costa, 2003; Funder, 2006; Matthews, Deary, & Whiteman, 2003), no scientifically accepted theory of traits goes much beyond the definitions (Fleeson, 2008; Matthews et al., 2003). As a result, very little is known about how traits produce behavior, why persons differ in their traits, what in behavior traits describe, or what traits consist of. The Big Five clarify only one side of traits, not the whole trait. The Big Five describe how people differ from each other, but they do not provide any knowledge about why people differ in those ways, how people became those different ways, or how those differences are manifest in behavior. For example, although it is known that some people are more extraverted than others, it is not known why some people are more extraverted than others, how people become extraverted, or how differences in extraversion become manifest in behavior. The Big Five are sorely in need of explanation.

Conversely, as useful and compelling as Allport's theory and Mischel and Shoda's CAPS model are as explanatory accounts, they lack a descriptive content to apply to. The theories can explain why people differ, but the theories have not yet explicitly identified how people differ or which individual differences the theories should be used to explain (with some notable exceptions, such as rejection sensitivity, Romero-Canyas et al., 2009, and narcissism, Morf & Rhodewalt, 2001). The implication is that social-cognitive theories do not have a ready pool of differences to explain. Rather, these theories claim that whatever ways people turn out to differ, the causes of those differences will be social-cognitive mechanisms such as encodings, expectancies, and self-regulatory plans. Social-cognitive approaches provide a strong account of the explanatory side of traits, but this is only part of traits. The weakness of each perspective is precisely the strength of the other.

Step 3. Fitting the Two Parts of Traits Together

It now becomes apparent that joining the two perspectives together would have great advantages: The strength of each perspective precisely covers the weakness of the other. Whole trait theory proposes fusing the explanatory social-cognitive side of traits to the descriptive Big Five side of traits, in order to create whole traits. Social-cognitive approaches provide the explanation of how traits work, and the Big Five provide the description of what traits are to be explained. For example, whole trait theory would use encodings, expectancies, and self-regulatory plans to explain why people differ in extraversion and how those differences become manifest in behavior.

The two sides are like two sides of a coin. With a coin, the existence of one side logically necessitates the existence of the other side of the coin. With traits, the existence of the descriptive side demands the existence of a causal side that led to the descriptive side. Whole trait theory designates the causal side as $Trait_{EXP}$ ("EXP" stands for "explanatory") and the descriptive side as $Trait_{DES}$ ("DES" stands for "descriptive"). Thus, for example, extraversion has two sides: one side is the causal factors that lead to extraverted behaviors ($Extra_{EXP}$), and the other side is the description of the individual as having enacted many extraverted behaviors ($Extra_{DES}$).

Joining the social-cognitive and the Big Five trait perspective in one theory is a big step. Like magnetic poles, the social-cognitive approaches of CAPS and the trait approach of the Big Five repel each other. Mischel and Shoda openly and conspicuously call their theory a theory of "dispositions," but equally conspicuously avoid the term "trait" and avoid the Big Five (Mischel, 2004). Big Five theorists rarely look inside the Big Five, placing all

social-cognitive mechanisms at a different level of analysis (McAdams & Olson, 2010), as correlates of traits (Roberts & Wood, 2006), or as translations of traits into patterns of behavior (McCrae & Costa, 2003). Historically, the two ideas that traits are causal forces or that they are descriptive labels have been considered opposed to each other, and the assumption has been that one or the other account will turn out to be true (Matthews, et al., 2003; Zuroff, 1986). The two perspectives have been conceptually opposed, whereas whole trait theory proposes that they be conceptually fused.

It appears as though the two aspects of personality have remained separate for many of the same reasons that social and personality psychology have remained separate. Social-cognitive personality psychologists have generally been more interested in process and in experimentation, whereas trait psychologists have generally been more interested in structure and in assessment. Social-cognitive theorists have emphasized the power of the situation (albeit as an elicitor of individual differences) whereas trait theorists have emphasized the across-situation regularities in behavior. Finally, the social-cognitive approach historically grew with the situation side of the person-situation debate, whereas the trait approach grew with the person side of the person-situation debate.

Some reasons for the opposition include conflictual assumptions or inferences. First, social-cognitive approaches are committed to dispositions smaller in size than are the Big Five traits (Mischel & Shoda, 2008). Stable dispositions to act in certain ways are believed to be highly localized to specific situations, with differences in situations as small as hair color making a difference to which disposition is activated (Shoda & LeeTiernan, 2002). Big Five proponents, in contrast, believe in broad, general tendencies to act in certain ways. If a person is generally friendly in some situations, he will tend to be generally kind and polite in other situations. Second, trait proponents often envision traits as caused by unified, single, isolated, likely biological, and independent causes of behavior (e.g., McCrae & Costa, 2003). For example, extraversion may be the result of a less arousable brain (Eysenck & Eysenck, 1985) or of stronger emotional processing centers (Canli et al., 2006; Matthews, et al., 2003). In contrast, social-cognitive perspectives propose multiple, divergent causes. Thus, applying social-cognitive explanatory perspectives to descriptive Big Five traits requires deviating from currently accepted views of both.

Step 4. Modifying the Descriptive Side to Make Room for the Dynamics of the Explanatory Side

The explanatory side brings dynamic processes to traits. However, the descriptive side does not appear to have room for dynamic processes. Explanatory processes are changing, situation-based, and activation-based, producing changes in behavior, whereas the descriptive side refers to stability, the way the person is in general; yes, the person might change his or her behavior in response to extreme situations such as funerals or weddings, but the person is presumed to act and be more or less the way he or she is most of the time. The changes inherent to the social-cognitive perspective are not consistent with the stability inherent to current conceptions of traits. Thus, the stability view of trait descriptions must be modified to allow room for the changing, responsive elements of the explanatory side, that is, to fit the dynamic into the stable. The Density Distributions approach (Fleeson, 2001), was designed to investigate just how much room for dynamics there was in the descriptive side of traits.

PERSONALITY STATES

The basic goal was to determine how much a person was manifesting a given trait at any moment, and to discover how much stability and variability was evident in those manifestations. To determine how much a person was manifesting a given trait at a given moment, my lab and I employed "personality state" assessment (Cattell, Cattell, & Rhymer, 1947; Fleeson, 2001; Fleeson et al., 2002; Fridhandler, 1986). A state is defined as having the same affective, behavioral, and cognitive content as a corresponding trait (Pytlik Zillig, Hemenover, & Dienstbier, 2002), but as applying for a shorter duration. For example, an extraverted state has the same content as extraversion (talkativeness, energy, boldness, assertiveness, etc.), but applies as an accurate description for only a few minutes to a few hours rather than for the months or years that a trait description applies.

The state concept is a familiar one, having been used to characterize emotions and anxiety for some time (e.g., Watson & Clark, 1988; Taylor, 1953). However, despite this familiarity of the state concept in the affect domain, the concept of state has almost never been applied to a non-emotion domain, such as the trait/personality domain. That is what was done in the Density Distributions approach.

Just as trait extraversion is assessed by self-reports of how talkative, bold, and assertive an individual is in general, e.g. from 1 to 7, state extraversion is assessed by self-reports of how talkative, bold, and assertive an individual is at the moment, from 1 to 7. This definition transfers the content of the trait as a whole to the state. Thus, states are directly commensurate with traits.

DENSITY DISTRIBUTIONS OF STATES

Over time, each individual's various states will form a distribution, indicating the frequency with which the individual is at each level of the state. It is possible to calculate a standard deviation of this distribution for each person, separately, describing the amount that his or her states differed across occasions. A large standard deviation means that the individual's state levels varied widely, such that on some occasions he or she behaved at a high level of the state, and on other occasions he or she behaved at a low level of the state. A low standard deviation, in contrast, indicates that the individual behaved the same or similar way on most occasions. The average of the standard deviations across all people is the typical individual's amount of variability. Results showed that the amount that one typical individual varied in his or her behavior across two weeks was (1) almost as much as the total amount that behavior varied in the entire sample, meaning that knowing who a person is does not much reduce the range of behaviors one can expect of the person; (2) about the same as the amount of within-person variation in affect, something that is commonly known to vary so much that it is hard to conceive of it as a trait; and (3) more than the amount of variability between individuals, meaning that individuals differ from themselves more than they differ from others (Fleeson, 2001; Noftle & Fleeson, 2010). This variability within the distributions is meaningful. When generally introverted individuals act extraverted, they are being extraverted in the moment, in a way that has affective consequences (McNiel & Fleeson, 2006), is responsive to situations (Fleeson, 2007), is designed to accomplish goals (McCabe & Fleeson, 2011), and that feels true to themselves (Fleeson & Wilt, 2010). It is not a hollow act, faking it, or an insincere forced behavior.

However, this high degree of variability did not deny that individuals differed strongly in the traits they manifested (Fleeson, 2001; Fleeson & Noftle, 2009). Persons' distributions were centered around personal averages, and persons differed from each other in these averages. Furthermore, these averages were highly stable from week to week, with correlations around .8 (Fleeson, 2001; Baird, Le, & Lucas, 2006). Thus, these distributions capture individual differences in trait manifestation in everyday behavior.

And it is the high variability (the width of the density distributions) that creates the descriptive space into which the dynamics of the explanatory account might be placed. Because the typical person's traits, as manifest, are shifting rapidly from occasion to occasion, this shifting may be the result of a dynamic process. Because this shifting of states is part and parcel of the distribution, and because the distribution makes up the individual differences in the descriptive side of traits, this shifting represents the potential location of the consequences of the explanatory side of traits within the descriptive side of traits.

For example, almost all people shift from being extraverted to introverted and all points in between during the course of just a few days, and this is the fact that allows for the dynamics of the explanatory account to apply to extraversion. These shifts in how extraverted or introverted a person is from moment to moment could very well be the result of social-cognitive mechanisms such as encodings, expectancies, and self-regulatory plans. And since the distribution of extraversion states is possibly the person's trait, then the person's trait has room for dynamic explanations.

Step 5. Setting the Explanatory Side as the Producer of the Descriptive Side Distribution

The next recognition is that explaining how traits work requires predicting states, that is, predicting the traits the person actually shows in his or her behavior. The predictors reveal the processes underlying trait manifestations in behavior, affect, and cognition. Because states vary so rapidly over time and within person, candidate predictors must be variables that similarly vary rapidly over time and within person; such candidate predictors include situations, cognitions, affects, and drives.

It is then an easy generalization to the trait level: if a given predictor demonstrably predicts a given state in the moment, then standing levels of the predictor may predict standing levels of the trait. For example, if pursuing the goal of connecting with others demonstrably predicts state extraversion in the moment, then standing levels of pursuit of connecting with others may predict standing levels of

trait extraversion (McCabe & Fleeson, 2011). Or, if interpreting another's behavior as hostile predicts low levels of state agreeableness in the moment, then chronic accessibility of hostility attributions may predict low levels of trait agreeableness in general.

Whole trait theory, incorporating the explanatory side of traits from Allport (1937) and CAPS (Mischel & Shoda, 1995), proposes that several processes, including social-cognitive ones, are the determinants of states (Fleeson & Jolley, 2006). These processes are not identical to those described in CAPS. They include interpretative processes, motivational processes, stability-inducing processes, temporal processes, and random error processes. These processes make up the explanatory side of traits, and as a set are designated $Trait_{EXP}$.

The *interpretative process* represents the cognitive aspects of the mind, specifically, the manner in which information is processed and which results in implications for behavior. The *motivational process* brings the representation of end-states into the model. Desired and feared end-states create the directional impetus in the individual. The *stability-inducing process* is present in order to account for any factors that guide the individual toward his or her typical trait manifestation, such as genetic, homeostatic, or habit forces. The *temporal process* is necessary to account for influences of past events on the present, such as inertia or cycles. Finally the *random error process* is needed to account for unpredictable trait manifestations. For example, extraversion state levels are proposed to be the result of interpreting the current situation as favorable toward extraversion, pursuing a goal that produces extraverted behavior, a homeostatic tendency toward extraverted behaviors, carrying out a trend that leads to extraverted behavior, and/or purely random processes.

PROCESSES IN TRAIT$_{EXP}$

The processes are similar to each other but differ in content and in some of their flows. As shown in the schematic of figure 3.1, all processes have structural elements and dynamic elements. The structural elements include inputs, intermediates, outputs, and links. The dynamic elements are flows. The outputs are always increases or decreases in at least one of the Big Five states. For example, the output of an interpretative process might be to increase an individual's state extraversion and to decrease his or her state conscientiousness. The input is some environmental or internal event, and the intermediates are other environmental or internal events influenced by those inputs. Links are connections between inputs, intermediates, and/or outputs; they are structural elements that allow other structural elements to influence each other. Finally, flows are the dynamic elements, and they describe the paths of influence among the structural elements.

Most importantly, individuals differ in these processes. Individuals differ in these processes because they differ in the links between the inputs, intermediates, and outputs. As a result, the same input to different individuals may lead to different outputs (trait manifestations), depending on the individuals' strengths of the links between those inputs and those outputs. For example, individuals who have a strong link between other people's conflict behavior and attributions to hostile intentions may manifest low levels of agreeableness in their states (Jensen-Campbell & Graziano, 2001); individuals with strong links between goals of connecting with others and extraverted behavior are likely to manifest high levels of extraversion in their behavior (McCabe & Fleeson, 2011).

The outputs of these processes are changes in current levels of states. Because states include affective, behavioral, and cognitive elements, states may influence each other. For example, the cognitive change in a state may then lead to a behavioral change in the same state. It is important to keep in mind that states have these dual roles as outputs and intermediates.

THE INTERPRETATIVE PROCESS

Detailing the interpretative process in terms of figure 3.1 will serve as an example. In an interpretative process, psychologically active elements of situations trigger cognitive-affective units that ultimately lead to behavior (Shoda & LeeTiernan, 2002; Fleeson, 2007). That is, trait manifestation partially represents flexible and discriminative changes in behavior due to interpretations of changing situations. For example, an individual in a relatively *structured* situation may expect it to be easy to concentrate and so may increase his or her level of *conscientiousness* (Fleeson, 2007). The inputted environmental or internal events flow via encoding of the events into interpretations, which flow via activation to other beliefs. These beliefs flow to implications for behavior, and the output of that flow is behavioral changes in manifestation of states. This step is the final step only in the schematic of the process. All outputs (interpretations, beliefs, and behaviors) count as internal or environmental events that feed back into the process, continuously adjusting the interpretative process (Mischel, 1973), and impacts of the outputs on the situation also change the environmental events, creating new situations (Snyder, 2006; Snyder & Stukas, 1999). Thus, the interpretative process is a continuous process, which includes changes in states on an ongoing basis—those changes in states influence other beliefs, which continue to influence other beliefs, other emotions, and other behaviors. For example, encoding of a partner's grimace as a threat already is a cognitive manifestation of neuroticism; activation of fear of future threats is a further, affective manifestation of neuroticism; and biting one's nails is a final, behavioral manifestation of neuroticism, which may in turn activate further thoughts about threat, continuing the process.

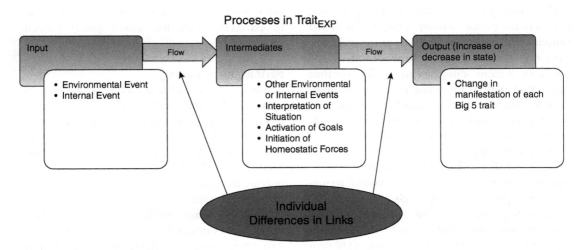

Fig. 3.1 Schematic for Processes Underlying Traits

WHOLE TRAITS

Because individuals differ in the links in the processes, they will differ in the outputs of the processes and ultimately will differ in the distribution of states they manifest in their behavior. In fact, the entire distribution of states—its whole range, its location, and its width—is produced by $Trait_{EXP}$. Variability in states is produced because the inputs to the links change from moment to moment, and when the inputs change, the outputs change. A stable mean and shape of the distribution are produced because the links are stable; over time, the same links will tend to produce similar output. Thus, the descriptive, manifesting side of traits is intimately linked to the explanatory, causal side of traits, and, individual differences in the descriptive, manifesting side of traits are intimately linked to individual differences in the explanatory, causal side of traits. Putting the two sides together results in what I am calling "whole traits".

Because both sides of traits are parts of whole traits, individual differences in traits refer to individual differences in both parts of traits. An individual's level of a $Trait_{DES}$ is the mean of his or her enacted states. For example, to say that someone is extraverted is to say that he or she acts more extraverted than others do on average. An individual's level on $Trait_{EXP}$ is the level of $Trait_{DES}$ that his or her processes would produce with typical or average input (e.g., how extraverted his or her processes would lead him or her to act in an average situation). For example, to say that someone is extraverted is also to say that in a given situation, he or she is more likely to interpret things in such a way or to pursue such goals that more extraverted behavior will be produced. Note that these levels will not always match up. Because the outputs of the processes are determined not only by the links in the processes, but also by the inputs to the processes (such as situations, moods, etc.), individuals with the same level of $Trait_{EXP}$ may have different levels of $Trait_{DES}$. When individuals complete personality questionnaires, they are probably referring to some combination of these two individual difference factors to report their level of the whole traits (Fleeson & Gallagher, 2009).

Step 6. Accretion of Processes Produces the Big Five

The complexity and multitude of links constituting the processes in $Trait_{EXP}$ raises the question whether there are thousands of minitraits or a small number of broad and general traits. If each link in the processes were independent of the other links, such that an individual could be bold in one kind of situation and timid in another, the resulting traits would have too specific and narrow in applicability. Traits would consist of thousands of unrelated, very narrow conditionals; a kind of Thorndikian behaviorism would result (Allport, 1937; Funder, 2001). In contrast, the Big Five are broad and general: if an individual is extraverted, he or she is expected to be bold in most situations, and also to be daring and assertive in most situations as well. If the social-cognitive processes are to explain the Big Five, and if the explanatory part of traits is to be fused to the descriptive side of traits into wholes, it is necessary for the links to be organized in such a way that they produce broad and general traits rather than minitraits.

Whole trait theory proposes three main accretion mechanisms to align links to each other to produce the Big Five. The first mechanism is generalization (Allport, 1937). As individuals develop, they begin to recognize similarities in situations, similarities in behaviors, and similarities in effects of behaviors, and this recognition leads to accreting generalized processes together. As they develop, individuals recognize for instance that bold behaviors and assertive behaviors tend to have similar effects on other people, and consequentially join those behaviors together. A second mechanism of trait accretion is that individuals learn abstract principles about situations and behavior, and apply these general principles broadly. These principles follow the same logical, cultural, and biological principles that produce the Big Five, and so themselves lead to systems of linkages that produce the Big Five. Individuals may learn, for example, that boldness has conceptual ties to assertiveness. The final accretion mechanism is that the links and outputs cause each other and interact with each other. That is, the positive correlations between subcomponents of a given trait are proposed to result from a network of bidirectionally related behavioral processes facilitating and benefiting each other during development (Cramer, Waldorp, van der Maas, & Borsboom, 2010; van der Maas et al., 2006). Energy and adventure, for instance, have bidirectional causal influences on each other.

Integrating Perspectives Within Personality

The study of traits as wholes is intended to provide some integration of the trait and social-cognitive perspectives and some integration of description with explanation, because it includes both the Big Five and the social-cognitive processes in one perspective.

Most importantly, it does so without doing damage to either perspective, by recognizing the way that the perspectives fit together as they stand. The study of traits as wholes does this not by laying the perspectives side by side, but by noting them being logically connected by necessity, as two parts of a whole. It is not accidental that these two perspectives fit together, but rather is an outcome of their separately demonstrated accuracy and their mutually fitting needs.

These steps also integrate the motivational and disorders perspectives together. Because of the motivational processes, motivational perspectives play an essential, causal role. Disorders are represented as inappropriate, rigid, or extreme outputs of these processes. Finally, following this set of steps also joins the four types of trait perspectives into one: traits are descriptive of behavior, traits follow the co-occurrence of individual differences, traits include causal forces, and traits show conditional properties.

Phase 2. Recognize the Included Concerns of Social Psychology

For the purposes of this chapter, the goal is that whole trait theory facilitate some degree of integration between personality and social psychology, because it is a theory that is sensitive to the concerns of both fields. First, it integrates the person with the environment into a common framework, thus integrating the main two topic areas of personality and social psychology. Second, it integrates process with structure, two topics loosely aligned with the two fields. Third, it integrates explanation with description, two goals loosely aligned with social and personality psychology. Fourth, it integrates experiments with correlations, the methods associated with the two fields. Fifth, it focuses on interpretation, which is a central commonality between the two fields. In sum, the experimental investigation of situation-based processes becomes essential to understanding the correlations among individual differences in traits. What this means is that social psychological research is relevant at each and every stage of the investigation of whole traits.

Most importantly, it does this in a single theory. Roberts (2009) argued that integration will never happen until a comprehensive theory is proposed that speaks to researchers in both fields. Otherwise, the undeniable practicalities will result in the two fields producing parallel but noninteractive theories. If whole trait theory is successful, it will be one way to move integration down the levels in table 3.1 to a more active and interactive level.

Conclusion: Emerging Opportunities for Integration

This chapter started with the Lewinian equation, $B = f(P, E)$, and noted that the P in the equation could be taken in at least three ways: (1) it could mean that there must be constructs within the person for the E to operate on, and these constructs must be known; (2) it could refer to the differences between persons that need to be known to predict behaviors; or (3) it could refer to the need to determine the relationships among the different constructs with the person, so that prediction can take into account the entire lifespace at once. The chapter took as its mission to provide an overview of the latter two meanings of the P, and moved into an overview of the many, diverse perspectives on the person. This overview revealed the productivity and variety of research on personality going on now and recently, and hopefully provided a conceptual map of many of the perspectives on the person. It also revealed the deep split in personality psychology between those who study structures of individual differences and those who study processes underlying individual differences. The chapter then described a parallel split between personality and social psychology in their interests, whereby personality psychologists are more interested in correlational studies of individual differences, and social psychologists are more interested in experimental studies of processes. This split has narrowed in recent decades, but remains at a level of arm's-length acceptance, whereby researchers in each field accept the work of the other field as valid, but generally don't participate in it or even keep up with it very closely. This set the stage for the final section of the chapter, which introduced whole trait theory, as the result of following a trail of increasingly integrative steps to fuse the two streams of research within personality psychology, and to provide a theory that incorporates the interests of both personality and social psychologists. In this vein, the number one opportunity I see for integration resides in theories that can push researchers past the current arm's-length acceptance and into working on the same problems in both personality and social psychology.

Prospects for Integration Within Each of the Four Perspectives on Persons

Given that perspectives on the person can be organized into four types of perspectives, I would like to close by evaluating each perspective type's potential for following some of the likely routes of integration between personality and social psychology. From the personality side, these routes might be incorporating interpretation and meaning into personality variables, incorporating situations into personality variables, and investigating the processes and mechanisms underlying personality variables. From the social side, these routes might be including person variables in the conceptualization of processes, charting the long-term consequences of situations, and paying closer attention to measurement.

Cognitive perspectives have always been promising perspectives for producing integration, because the nature of cognition naturally invokes these likely routes of integration. Cognitive perspectives on the person inherently describe meanings created by the person, and these meanings often are constructed out of cognitions about the environment. Personality psychologists who take a cognitive perspective on the person typically already study the processes leading from cognitions to other cognitions and to affects and behaviors. Social psychologists have also been more open to accepting person variables when the person variables have been cognitive, such as need for cognition (Cacioppo & Petty, 1982; Epstein et al., 1996), self-monitoring (Synder, 1974), and self-esteem (Rosenberg, Schooler, Schoenbach, & Rosenberg, 1995), and have paid close attention to measurement in such cases. In particular, variables related to the self and identity appear likely to lead to much integration between social and personality psychology.

Motivational perspectives have also been promising for integration, because the nature of motivation also naturally invokes the likely routes of integration. In most cases, the object of a given motivation is part of the environment; at the very least, the individual usually must operate on and respond to the environment to satisfy a motivation. Thus, process is typically part of any person-based perspective on motivation. Similarly, social psychologists will need to include person variables when investigating goals that individuals pursue for more than fleeting moments. Self-regulation in particular is a strong candidate for intense integration. Hoyle (2010) has already presented a personality- and social-psychology integrated perspective on self-regulation, and self-regulation is already a topic that has been studied in both fields. When personality psychologists have studied self-regulation, they have incorporated situations and processes (e.g., Cantor & Fleeson, 1994; Kuhl, 1992). Although social psychology has tended to focus on short-term goals, as social psychologists move toward incorporating longer-term goals and dispositional contributions to self-regulation, or when they begin to look at the long-term effects of situations on goal pursuit, then they will begin including persons in their study of self-regulation.

Finally, the group of perspectives that traditionally has been least promising for integration over the years may have jumped to the fore. Now that traits have near universal acceptance as viable ways to characterize persons, personality psychologists have begun to turn their attention to the processes underlying traits. I believe that it may be this investigation of the process underlying traits—including the meanings people make of situations and the goals people pursue—that has the most promise of becoming a prime locus of personality and social psychology integrated research.

Acknowledgment

I would like to thank Brent Roberts, Jess Tracy, and Mike Furr for discussions of the ideas in this chapter. Preparation of this article was supported by National Institute of Mental Health Grants R01 MH70571 and 2R01 MH070571 and by a Kirby Faculty Fellowship.

References

Allport, G. W. (1937). *Personality: A psychological interpretation.* New York: Holt.

Allport, G. W., & Odbert, H. S. (1936). *Trait-names: A psycholexical study.* Psychological Monographs, 47. Albany, NY: Psychological Review.

Ambady, N., Bernieri, F. J., & Richeson, J. A. (2000). Toward a histology of social behavior: Judgmental accuracy from thin slices of the behavioral stream. *Advances in Experimental Social Psychology, 32,* 201–271.

Anderson, C., & Kilduff, G. J. (2009). Why do dominant personalities attain influence in face-to-face groups? The competence-signaling effects of trait dominance. *Journal of Personality and Social Psychology, 96,* 491–503.

Anusic, I., Schimmack, U., Pinkus, R. T., & Lockwood, P. (2009). The nature and structure of correlations among Big Five ratings: The Halo-Alpha-Beta Model. *Journal of Personality and Social Psychology, 97,* 1142–1156.

Asendorpf, J. B. (1998). Personality effects on social relationships. *Journal of Personality and Social Psychology, 74,* 1531–1544.

Ashton, M. C., & Lee, K. (2009). The HEXACO-60: A short measure of the major dimensions of personality. *Journal of Personality Assessment, 9,* 340–345. doi:10.1080/00223890902935878.

Aquino, K., & Reed, A. (2002). The self-importance of moral identity. *Journal of Personality and Social Psychology, 83*(6), 1423–1440. doi:10.1037/0022-3514.83.6.1423.

Austin, J. T., & Vancouver, J. B. (1996). Goal constructs in psychology: Structure, process, and content. *Psychological Bulletin, 120,* 338–375. doi:10.1037/0033-2909.120.3.338.

Back, M. D., Schmukle, S. C., & Egloff, B. (2009). Predicting actual behavior from the explicit and implicit self-concept of personality. *Journal of Personality and Social Psychology, 97,* 533–548. doi:10.1037/a0016229.

Baird, B. M., Le, K., & Lucas, R. E. (2006). On the nature of intraindividual personality variability: Reliability, validity, and associations with well-being. *Journal of Personality and Social Psychology, 90*(3), 512–527. doi:10.1037/0022-3514.90.3.512.

Bardi, A., & Schwartz, S. H. (2003). Values and behavior: Strength and structure of relations. *Personality and Social Psychology Bulletin, 29*(10), 1207–1220. doi:10.1177/0146167203254602.

Baumeister, R. F. (2005). Self and volition. *Judeo-Christian perspectives on psychology: Human nature, motivation, and change* (pp. 57–72). Washington, DC: American Psychological Association. doi:10.1037/10859-003.

Blagov, P. S., & Singer, J. A. (2004). Four dimensions of self-defining memories (specificity, meaning, content, and affect) and their relationships to self-restraint, distress, and repressive defensiveness. *Journal of Personality, 72,* 481–511. doi:10.1111/j.0022-3506.2004.00270.x.

Bleidorn, W., Kandler, C., Riemann, R., Angleitner, A., & Spinath, F. M. (2009). Patterns and sources of adult personality development: Growth curve analyses of the NEO PI-R scales in a longitudinal twin study. *Journal of Personality and Social Psychology, 97,* 142–155.

Block, J. (2010). The five-factor framing of personality and beyond: Some ruminations. *Psychological Inquiry, 21,* 2–25.

Boschen, M. J, & Warner, J. C. (2009). Publication trends in individual DSM personality disorders: 1971–2015. *Australian Psychologist, 44*(2), 136–142. doi:10.1080/00050060802680598.

Buss, D. M., & Craik, K. H. (1983). The act frequency approach to personality. *Psychological Review, 90,* 105–126.

Cacioppo, J. T., & Petty, R. E. (1982). The need for cognition. *Journal of Personality and Social Psychology, 42*(1), 116–131. doi:10.1037/0022-3514.42.1.116.

Canli, T. (2006). Genomic imaging of extraversion. *Biology of personality and individual differences* (pp. 93–115). New York: Guilford.

Cantor, N., & Fleeson, W. (1991). Life tasks and self-regulatory processes. In M. L. Maehr & P. R. Pintrich (Eds.), *Advances in motivation and achievement* (Vol. 7, pp. 327–369). Greenwich, CT: JAI Press.

Cantor, N., & Fleeson, W. (1994). Social intelligence and intelligent goal pursuit: A cognitive slice of motivation. In R. Dienstbier (Series Ed.) & W. D. Spaulding (Volume Ed.), *Nebraska symposium on motivation: Vol. 41. Integrative views of motivation, cognition, and emotion* (pp. 125–179). Lincoln: University of Nebraska Press.

Carver, C. S. (2006). Approach, avoidance, and the self-regulation of affect and action. *Motivation and Emotion, 30*(2), 105–110. doi:10.1007/s11031-006-9044-7.

Carver, C. S., & Connor-Smith, J. (2010). Personality and coping. *Annual Review of Psychology, 61,* 679–704.

Caspi, A., Roberts, B. W., & Shiner, R. L. (2005). Personality development: Stability and change. *Annual Review of Psychology, 56,* 453–484. doi:10.1146/annurev.psych.55.090902.141913.

Cattell, R. B., Cattell, A. K. S., & Rhymer, R. M. (1947). P-technique demonstrated in determining psycho-physiological source traits in a normal individual. *Psychometrika, 12,* 267–288.

Champagne, F. A. (2009). Epigenetic influences of social experiences across the lifespan. *Developmental Psychology, 52,* 299–311.

Chang, E. C., & Sanna, L. J. (2003). *Virtue, vice, and personality: The complexity of behavior.* Washington, DC: American Psychological Association.

Church, A. (2009). Prospects for an integrated trait and cultural psychology. *European Journal of Personality, 23,* 153–182. doi:10.1002/per.700.

Costa, P. T., Jr., & McCrae, R. R. (1980). Influence of extraversion and neuroticism on subjective well-being: Happy and unhappy people. *Journal of Personality and Social Psychology, 38,* 668–678.

Costa, P. T., Jr., & McCrae, R. R. (1992). *NEO PI-R professional manual.* Odessa, FL: Psychological Assessment Resources, Inc.

Cramer, A. J., Waldorp, L. J., van der Maas, H. J., & Borsboom, D. (2010). Comorbidity: A network perspective. *Behavioral and Brain Sciences, 33*(2–3), 137–150. doi:10.1017/S0140525X09991567.

Cramer, P. (1988). The Defense Mechanism Inventory: A review of research and discussion of the scales. *Journal of Personality Assessment, 52,* 142–164. doi:10.1207/s15327752jpa5201_13.

Crocker, J. (2010). President's column: The blurry line between social and personality. *Dialogue: The Official Newsletter of the Society for Personality and Social Psychology, 25,* 4-5.

Crocker, J., & Wolfe, C. T. (2001). Contingencies of self-worth. *Psychological Review, 108*(3), 593–623. doi:10.1037/0033-295X.108.3.593.

Deci, E. L., & Ryan, R. M. (2008). Self-determination theory: A macrotheory of human motivation, development, and health. *Canadian Psychology/Psychologie canadienne, 49,* 182–185. doi:10.1037/a0012801.

De Fruyt, F., De Bolle, M., McCrae, R. R., Terracciano, A., & Costa, P. (2009). Assessing the universal structure of personality in early adolescence: The NEO-PI-R and NEO-PI-3 in 24 cultures. *Assessment, 16,* 301–311. doi:10.1177/1073191109333760.

Depue, R. A. (2006). Interpersonal behavior and the structure of personality: Neurobehavioral foundation of agentic extraversion and affiliation. In T. Canli (Ed.), *Biology of personality and individual differences* (pp. 60–92). New York: Guilford.

Demorest, A. P. (2008). A taxonomy for scenes. *Journal of Research in Personality, 42,* 239–246. doi:10.1016/j.jrp.2007.05.004

DeYoung, C. G., Quilty, L. C., & Peterson, J. (2007). Between facets and domains: 10 aspects of the Big Five. *Journal of Personality and Social Psychology, 93,* 880–896.

Donnellan, M. B., Lucas, R. E., & Fleeson, W. (Eds.). (2009). Personality and assessment at age 40: Reflections on the past person-situation debate and emerging directions of future person-situation integration [Special issue]. *Journal of Research in Personality, 43.*

Emmons, R. A. (2009). Greatest of the virtues? Gratitude and the grateful personality. In D. Narvaez & D. K. Lapsley (Eds.), *Personality, identity, and character: Explorations in moral psychology* (pp. 256–270). New York: Cambridge University Press.

Epstein, S. (1983). A research paradigm for the study of personality and emotions. *Nebraska Symposium on Motivation,* 91–154.

Epstein, S., Pacini, R., Denes-Raj, V., & Heier, H. (1996). Individual differences in intuitive-experiential and analytical-rational thinking styles. *Journal of Personality and Social Psychology, 71*(2), 390–405. doi:10.1037/0022-3514.71.2.390.

Eysenck, H. J., & Eysenck, M. W. (1985). *Personality and individual differences: A natural science approach.* New York: Plenum.

Eysenck, M. W., & Eysenck, H. J. (1980). Mischel and the concept of personality. *British Journal of Psychology, 71,* 191–204.

Fleeson, W. (2001). Towards a structure- and process-integrated view of personality: Traits as density distributions of states. *Journal of Personality and Social Psychology, 80,* 1011–1027.

Fleeson, W. (2004). Moving personality beyond the person-situation debate: The challenge and the opportunity of within-person variability. *Current Directions in Psychological Science, 13,* 83–87. doi:10.1111/j.0963-7214.2004.00280.x.

Fleeson, W. (2007). Situation-based contingencies underlying trait-content manifestation in behavior. *Journal of Personality, 75,* 825–862. doi:10.1111/j.1467-6494.2007.00458.x.

Fleeson, W. (2008). Personality theories, traits. In F. T. L. Leong, H. E. A. Tinsley, & S. H. Lease (Eds.), *Encyclopedia of Counseling: Vol. 2. Personal Counseling and Mental Health Problems* (pp. 327–330). Los Angeles: Sage.

Fleeson, W. (2011). *Whole trait theory.* Manuscript in preparation.

Fleeson, W., & Gallagher, P. (2009). The implications of Big Five standing for the distribution of trait manifestation in behavior: Fifteen experience-sampling studies and a meta-analysis. *Journal of Personality and Social Psychology, 97,* 1097–1114. doi:10.1037/a0016786.

Fleeson, W., & Jolley, S. (2006). A proposed theory of the adult development of intraindividual variability in trait-manifesting behavior. In D. Mroczek & T. D. Little (Eds.), *Handbook of personality development* (pp. 41–59). Mahwah, NJ: Erlbaum.

Fleeson, W., & Noftle, E. E. (2008). Where does personality have its influence? A supermatrix of consistency concepts. *Journal of Personality, 76,* 1355–1386. doi:10.1111/j.1467-6494.2008.00525.x.

Fleeson, W., & Noftle, E. E. (2009). In favor of the synthetic resolution to the person-situation debate. *Journal of Research in Personality, 43,* 150–154. doi:10.1016/j.jrp.2009.02.008.

Fleeson, W., Malanos, A. B., & Achille, N. M. (2002). An intraindividual process approach to the relationship between extraversion and positive affect: Is acting extraverted as "good" as being extraverted? *Journal of Personality and Social Psychology, 83,* 1409–1422.

Fleeson, W., & Wilt, J. (2010). The relevance of Big-Five trait content in behavior to subjective authenticity: Do high levels of within-person behavioral variability undermine or enable authenticity achievement? *Journal of Personality, 78,* 1353–1382.

Fournier, M. A., Moskowitz, D. S., & Zuroff, D. C. (2009). The interpersonal signature. *Journal of Research in Personality, 43*(2), 155–162. doi:10.1016/j.jrp.2009.01.023.

Fridhandler, B. M. (1986). Conceptual note on state, trait, and the state-trait distinction. *Journal of Personality and Social Psychology, 50,* 169–174.

Funder, D. C. (2001). Personality. *Annual Review of Psychology, 52,* 197–221. doi:10.1146/annurev.psych.52.1.197.

Funder, D. C. (2006). Towards a resolution of the personality triad: Persons, situations, and behaviors. *Journal of Research in Personality, 40,* 21–34.

Funder, D. C. (2007). *The personality puzzle* (4th ed.). New York: Norton.

Furr, R. M. (2009). Profile analysis in person-situation integration. *Journal of Research in Personality, 43*(2), 196–207. doi:10.1016/j.jrp.2008.08.002.

Gosling, S. D., & Johnson, J. A. (2010). *Advanced methods for conducting online behavioral research.* Washington, DC: American Psychological Association.

Gosling, S. D., Ko, S. J., Mannarelli, T., & Morris, M. E. (2002). A room with a cue: Personality judgments based on offices and bedrooms. *Journal of Personality and Social Psychology, 82,* 379–398.

Gosling, S. D., Rentfrow, P. J., & Swann, W. (2003). A very brief measure of the Big-Five personality domains. *Journal of Research in Personality, 37,* 504–528. doi:10.1016/S0092-6566(03)00046-1.

Graham, J., Haidt, J., & Nosek, B. (2009). Liberals and conservatives rely on different sets of moral foundations. *Journal of Personality & Social Psychology, 96,* 1029–1046.

Greenberg, J., Koole, S., & Pyszczynski, T. (2004). *Handbook of experimental existential psychology.* New York: Guilford.

Greenwald, A. G., Poehlman, T., Uhlmann, E., & Banaji, M. (2009). Understanding and using the Implicit Association Test: III. Meta-analysis of predictive validity. *Journal of Personality and Social Psychology, 97*(1), 17–41. doi:10.1037/a0015575.

Gross, J. J., & John, O. P. (2003). Individual differences in two emotion regulation processes: Implications for affect, relationships, and well-being. *Journal of Personality and Social Psychology, 85,* 348–362. doi:10.1037/0022-3514.85.2.348.

Haidt, J., McCauley, C., & Rozin, P. (1994). Individual differences in sensitivity to disgust: A scale sampling seven domains of disgust elicitors. *Personality and Individual Differences, 16,* 701–713. doi:10.1016/0191-8869(94)90212-7.

Hall, J. A., Andrzejewski, S. A., Murphy, N. A., Mast, M., & Feinstein, B. A. (2008). Accuracy of judging others' traits and states: Comparing mean levels across tests. *Journal of Research in Personality, 42,* 1476–1489. doi:10.1016/j.jrp.2008.06.013.

Hargrave, T. D., & Sells, J. N. (1997). The development of a forgiveness scale. *Journal of Marital and Family Therapy, 23*(1), 41–63. doi:10.1111/j.1752-0606.1997.tb00230.x.

Heisler, J. M., & Crabhill, S. L. (2006). Who are "stinkybug" and "Packerfan4'? Email pseudonyms and participants' perceptions of demography, productivity, and personality. *Journal of Computer-Mediated Communication, 12,* 114–135.

Heller, D., Perunovic, W., & Reichman, D. (2009). The future of person-situation integration in the interface between traits and goals: A bottom-up framework. *Journal of Research in Personality, 43*(2), 171–178. doi:10.1016/j.jrp.2008.12.011.

Higgins, E. (1987). Self-discrepancy: A theory relating self and affect. *Psychological Review, 94*(3), 319–340. doi:10.1037/0033-295X.94.3.319.

Higgins, E. (1990). Personality, social psychology, and person-situation relations: Standards and knowledge activation as a common language. *Handbook of personality: Theory and research* (pp. 301–338). New York: Guilford.

Higgins, E., & Brendl, C. (1995). Accessibility and applicability: Some 'activation rules' influencing judgment. *Journal of Experimental Social Psychology, 31*(3), 218–243. doi:10.1006/jesp.1995.1011.

Hirayoshi, S., & Nakajima, S. (2009). Analysis of personality-trait structure of dogs with personality-trait descriptors. *Japanese Journal of Animal Psychology, 59,* 57–75. doi:10.2502/janip.59.1.8.

Hogan, R., DeSoto, C. B., & Solano, C. (1977). Traits, tests, and personality research. *American Psychologist, 32,* 255–264.

Hoyle, R. H. (2000). Personality processes and problem behavior. *Journal of Personality, 68*, 953–966.

Hoyle, R. H. (2006). Personality and self-regulation: Trait and information-processing perspectives. *Journal of Personality, 74*(6), 1507–1525. doi:10.1111/j.1467-6494.2006.00418.x.

Hoyle, R. H. (2010). Personality and self-regulation. *Handbook of personality and self-regulation* (pp. 1–18). Chichester, UK: Wiley-Blackwell. doi:10.1002/9781444318111.ch1.

Jensen-Campbell, L. A., & Graziano, W. G. (2001). Agreeableness as a moderator of interpersonal conflict. *Journal of Personality, 69*, 323-362.

John, O. P., Naumann, L. P., & Soto, C. J. (2008). Paradigm shift to the integrative Big Five trait taxonomy. In O. P. John, R. W. Robins, & L. A. Pervin (Eds.), *Handbook of personality: Theory and research* (3rd ed., pp. 114–158). New York: Guilford.

Jost, J. T., Federico, C. M., & Napier, J. L. (2009). Political ideology: Its structure, functions, and elective affinities. *Annual Review of Psychology, 60*, 307–337. doi:10.1146/annurev.psych.60.110707.163600.

Kelly, G. A. (1963). *A theory of personality: The psychology of personal constructs.* Oxford, UK: Norton. Retrieved from PsycINFO database.

Kelley, H. H., Holmes, J. G., Kerr, N. L., Reis, H. T., Rusbult, C. E., & Van Lange, P. A. M. (2003). *An atlas of interpersonal situations.* Cambridge: Cambridge University Press.

Kernis, M. H., & Goldman, B. M. (2005). From thought and experience to behavior and interpersonal relationships: A multicomponent conceptualization of authenticity. *On building, defending, and regulating the self: A psychological perspective* (pp. 31–52). New York: Psychology Press.

Kihlstrom, J. F. (1987). Introduction to the special issue: Integrating personality and social psychology. *Journal of Personality and Social Psychology, 53*(6), 989–992. doi:10.1037/h0092817.

King, J. E., Weiss, A., & Farmer, K. H. (2005). A chimpanzee (Pan troglodytes) analogue of cross-national generalization of personality structure: Zoological parks and an African sanctuary. *Journal of Personality, 73*, 389–410. doi:10.1111/j.1467-6494.2005.00313.x.

Krueger, R. F., South, S., Johnson, W., & Iacono, W. (2008). The heritability of personality is not always 50%: Gene-environment interactions and correlations between personality and parenting. *Journal of Personality, 76*, 1485–1522. doi:10.1111/j.1467-6494.2008.00529.x.

Kuhl, J. (1992). A theory of self-regulation: Action versus state orientation, self-discrimination, and some applications. *Applied Psychology: An International Review, 41*(2), 97–129. doi:10.1111/j.1464-0597.1992.tb00688.x.

Lapsley, D. K., & Power, F. C. (2005). *Character psychology and character education.* Notre Dame, IN: University of Notre Dame Press.

Lau, M. A., Bishop, S. R., Segal, Z. V., Buis, T., Anderson, N. D., Carlson, L., et al. (2006). The Toronto Mindfulness Scale: Development and validation. *Journal of Clinical Psychology, 62*(12), 1445–1467. doi:10.1002/jclp.20326.

Lay, C. H. (1986). At last, my research article on procrastination. *Journal of Research in Personality, 20*(4), 474–495. doi:10.1016/0092-6566(86)90127-3.

Lee, K., & Ashton, M. C. (2008). The HEXACO personality factors in the indigenous personality lexicons of English and 11 other languages. *Journal of Personality, 76*, 1001–1054. doi:10.1111/j.1467-6494.2008.00512.x.

Leising, M. D., & Igl, W. (2007). Person and situation effects should be measured in the same terms. A comment on Funder (2006). *Journal of Research in Personality, 41*, 953-959.

Lewin, K. (1936). *Principles of topological psychology* (F. Heider, Trans.). New York: McGraw-Hill.

Lipkus, I. (1991). The construction and preliminary validation of a global belief in a just world scale and the exploratory analysis of the multidimensional belief in a just world scale. *Personality and Individual Differences, 12*(11), 1171–1178. doi:10.1016/0191-8869(91)90081-L.

Locke, E. A., & Latham, G. P. (2002). Building a practically useful theory of goal setting and task motivation: A 35-year odyssey. *American Psychologist, 57*(9), 705–717. doi:10.1037/0003-066X.57.9.705.

Loehlin, J. C., & Horn, J. M. (2000). Stoolmiller on restriction of range in adoption studies: A comment. *Behavior Genetics, 30*, 245.

Lucas, R. E. (2005). Time does not heal all wounds: A longitudinal study of reaction and adaptation to divorce. *Psychological Science, 16*, 945–950.

Lucas, R. E., (2007). Long-term disability is associated with lasting changes in subjective well-being: Evidence from two nationally representative longitudinal studies. *Journal of Personality and Social Psychology, 92*, 717–730.

Lucas, R. E., Clark, A. E., Georgellis, Y., & Diener, E. (2003). Reexamining adaptation and the set point model of happiness: Reactions to changes in marital status. *Journal of Personality and Social Psychology, 84*, 527–539.

Lucas, R. E., & Fujita, F. (2000). Factors influencing the relation between extraversion and pleasant affect. *Journal of Personality and Social Psychology, 79*, 1039–1056.

Lucas, R. E., & Donnellan, M. (2009). If the person-situation debate is really over, why does it still generate so much negative affect? *Journal of Research in Personality, 43*, 146–149. doi:10.1016/j.jrp.2009.02.009.

Lucas, R. E., Le, K., & Dyrenforth, P. (2008). Explaining the extraversion/positive affect relation: Sociability cannot account for extraverts' greater happiness. *Journal of Personality, 76*, 385–414. doi:10.1111/j.1467-6494.2008.00490.x.

Lucas, R. E., & Schimmack, U. (2009). Income and well-being: How big is the gap between the rich and the poor? *Journal of Research in Personality, 43*, 75–78.

Luo, S., & Zhang, G. (2009). What leads to romantic attraction: Similarity, reciprocity, security, or beauty? Evidence from a speed-dating study. *Journal of Personality, 77*, 933–964. doi:10.1111/j.1467-6494.2009.00570.x.

Mancini, A. D., & Bonanno, G. A. (2009). Predictors and parameters of resilience to loss: Toward an individual differences model. *Journal of Personality, 77*, 1805–1832. doi:10.1111/j.1467-6494.2009.00601.x.

Markus, H., & Nurius, P. (1986). Possible selves. *American Psychologist, 41*(9), 954–969. doi:10.1037/0003-066X.41.9.954.

Matthews, G., Deary, I., & Whiteman, M. C. (2003). *Personality traits* (2nd ed.). New York: Cambridge University Press.

Mayer, J. D. (1998). A systems framework for the field of personality. *Psychological Inquiry, 9*(2), 118–144. doi:10.1207/s15327965pli0902_10.

McAdams, D. P. (1995). What do we know when we know a person? *Journal of Personality, 63*, 365–396.

McAdams, D. P., & Olson, B. (2010). Personality development: Continuity and change over the life course. *Annual Review of*

Psychology, 61, 517–542. doi:10.1146/annurev.psych. 093008.100507.

McCabe, K. O., & Fleeson, W. (2011). *Momentary goals cause changes in personality states in everyday life.* Manuscript in preparation.

McClelland, D. C., Koestner, R., & Weinberger, J. (1992). How do self-attributed and implicit motives differ? *Motivation and personality: Handbook of thematic content analysis* (pp. 49–72). New York: Cambridge University Press.

McCrae, R. R., & Costa, P. T., Jr. (2003). Personality in adulthood: A five-factor theory perspective (2nd ed.). New York: Guilford.

McCrae, R. R., Costa, P. T., Ostendorf, F., Angleitner, A., Hrebickova, M., Avia, M. D., et al. (2000). Nature over nurture: Temperament, personality, and life span development. *Journal of Personality and Social Psychology, 78,* 173–186.

McCrae, R. R., Loeckenhoff, C. E., & Costa, P. T., Jr. (2005). A step toward DSM-V: Cataloguing personality-related problems in living. *European Journal of Personality, 19,* 269-286.

McNiel, J. M., & Fleeson, W. (2006). The causal effects of extraversion on positive affect and neuroticism on negative affect: Manipulating state extraversion and state neuroticism in an experimental approach. *Journal of Research in Personality, 40,* 529–550.

Mehl, M. R., Gosling, S. D., & Pennebaker, J. W. (2006). Personality in its natural habitat: Manifestations and implicit folk theories of personality in daily life. *Journal of Personality and Social Psychology, 90,* 862–877.

Mischel, W. (1968). *Personality and assessment.* New York: Wiley.

Mischel, W. (1973). Towards a cognitive social learning reconceptualization of personality. *Psychological Review, 80,* 252–283.

Mischel, W. (2004). Toward an integrative science of the person. *Annual Review of Psychology, 55,* 1–22.

Mischel, W., Cantor, N., & Feldman, S. (1996). Principles of self-regulation: The nature of willpower and self-control. *Social psychology: Handbook of basic principles* (pp. 329–360). New York: Guilford.

Mischel, W., & Shoda, Y. (1995). A cognitive-affective system theory of personality: Reconceptualizing situations, dispositions, dynamics, and invariance in personality structure. *Psychological Review, 102,* 246–268.

Mischel, W., & Shoda, Y. (2008). Toward a unified theory of personality: Integrating dispositions and processing dynamics within the cognitive-affective processing system. *Handbook of personality psychology: Theory and research* (3rd ed., pp. 208–241). New York: Guilford.

Morf, C. C., & Rhodewalt, F. (2001). Unraveling the paradoxes of narcissism: A dynamic self-regulatory processing model. *Psychological Inquiry, 12,* 177–196.

Morris, P. H., Gale, A., & Duffy, K. (2002). Can judges agree on the personality of horses? *Personality and Individual Differences, 33,* 67–81. doi:10.1016/S0191-8869(01)00136-2.

Mroczek, D. K., & Spiro III, A. (2003). Modeling intraindividual change in personality traits: Findings from the normative aging study. *Journals of Gerontology: Series B. Psychological Sciences and Social Sciences, 58,* P153.

Noftle, E. E., & Fleeson, W. (2010). Age differences in Big Five behavior averages and variabilities across the adult lifespan: Moving beyond retrospective, global summary accounts of personality. *Psychology and Aging, 25,* 95–107.

Noftle, E. E., & Robins, R. (2007). Personality predictors of academic outcomes: Big Five correlates of GPA and SAT scores. *Journal of Personality and Social Psychology, 93,* 116–130. doi:10.1037/0022-3514.93.1.116.

Ones, D. S., Viswesvaran, C., & Schmidt, F. L. (1993). Comprehensive meta-analysis of integrity test validities: Findings and implications for personnel selection and theories of job performance. *Journal of Applied Psychology, 78,* 679–703. doi:10.1037/0021-9010.78.4.679.

Ozer, D. J. (1986). *Consistency in personality: A methodological framework.* Berlin, Germany: Springer-Verlag.

Ozer, D. J., & Benet-Martinez, V. (2006). Personality and the prediction of consequential outcomes. *Annual Review of Psychology, 57,* 401–421.

Paunonen, S. V., Ashton, M. C. (2001). Big Five factors and facets and the prediction of behavior. *Journal of Personality and Social Psychology, 81,* 524–539.

Pervin, L. A. (2003). *The science of personality.* New York: Oxford University Press.

Peterson, C., & Seligman, E. P. (2004). *Character strengths and virtues: A handbook and classification.* Washington, DC: American Psychological Association.

Pytlik Zillig, L. M., Hemenover, S. H., & Dienstbier, R. A. (2002). What do we assess when we assess a Big 5 trait? A content analysis of the affective, behavioral, and cognitive processes represented in Big 5 personality inventories. *Personality and Social Psychology Bulletin, 28,* 847–858.

Read, S. J., Monroe, B. M., Brownstein, A. L., Yu, Y., Chopra, G., & Miller, L. C. (2010). A neural network model of the structure and dynamics of human personality. *Psychological Review, 117,* 61–92. doi:10.1037/a0018131.

Rentfrow, P. J., & Gosling, S. D. (2003). The do re mi's of everyday life: The structure and personality correlates of music preferences. *Journal of Personality and Social Psychology, 84,* 1236–1256. doi:10.1037/0022-3514.84.6.1236.

Revelle, W. Wilt, J., & Rosenthal, A. (2010). Personality and cognition: The personality-cognition link. In A. Gruszka, G. Matthews, & B. Szymura (Eds.), *Handbook of individual differences in cognition: Attention, memory and executive control* (pp. 27–49). New York: Springer.

Roberts, B. W. (2009). Back to the future: Personality and assessment and personality development. *Journal of Research in Personality, 43,* 137–145. doi:10.1016/j.jrp.2008.12.015.

Roberts, B. W., & Pomerantz, E. M. (2004). On traits, situations, and their integration: A developmental perspective. *Personality and Social Psychology Review, 8,* 402–416.

Roberts, B. W., Walton, K. E., & Viechtbauer, W. (2006). Patterns of mean-level change in personality traits across the life course: A meta-analysis of longitudinal studies. *Psychological Bulletin, 132,* 1–25.

Roberts, B. W. (2009). Ideology, method, and the seemingly intractable conflict between personality and social psychological worldviews. Presentation at the Meeting of the Society of Personality and Social Psychology, Tampa, FL.

Roberts, B. W., Kuncel, N. R., Shiner, R., Caspi, A., & Goldberg, L. R. (2007). The power of personality: The comparative validity of personality traits, socioeconomic status, and cognitive ability for predicting important life outcomes. *Perspectives on Psychological Science, 2,* 313–345.

Roberts, B. W., & Wood, D. (2006). Personality development in the context of the neo-socioanalytic model of personality. *Handbook of personality development* (pp. 11–39). Mahwah, NJ: Erlbaum.

Robinson, M. D., & Wilkowski, B. (2010). Personality processes in anger and reactive aggression: An introduction. *Journal of Personality*, 78, 1–8. doi:10.1111/j.1467-6494.2009.00606.x.

Rokeach, M. (1954). The nature and meaning of dogmatism. *Psychological Review*, 61(3), 194–204. doi:10.1037/h0060752.

Romero-Canyas, R., Anderson, V. T., Reddy, K. S., & Downey, G. (2009). Rejection sensitivity. In M. R. Leary & R. H. Hoyle (Eds.), *Handbook of individual differences in social behavior* (pp. 466–479). New York: Guilford.

Rosenberg, M., Schooler, C., Schoenbach, C., & Rosenberg, F. (1995). Global self-esteem and specific self-esteem: Different concepts, different outcomes. *American Sociological Review*, 60(1), 141–156. doi:10.2307/2096350.

Rotter, J. B. (1966). Generalized expectancies for internal versus external control of reinforcement. *Psychological Monographs: General and Applied*, 80(1), 1–28.

Ryff, C. D. (1989). Happiness is everything, or is it? Explorations on the meaning of psychological well-being. *Journal of Personality and Social Psychology*, 57, 1069–1081.

Ryle, G. (1949). *The concept of mind*. New York: Barnes & Noble.

Sadler, P., Ethier, N., Gunn, G. R., Duong, D., & Woody, E. (2009). Are we on the same wavelength? Interpersonal complementarity as shared cyclical patterns during interactions. *Journal of Personality and Social Psychology*, 97, 1005–1020.

Saucier, G. (2008). Measures of personality factors found recurrently in human lexicons. In G. J. Boyle, G. Matthews, & D. H. Saklofske (Eds.), *The SAGE handbook of personality theory and assessment, Vol. 2: Personality and measurement testing* (pp. 29–54). Thousand Oaks, CA: Sage Publications.

Saucier, G. (2009). Recurrent personality dimensions in inclusive lexical studies: Indications for a big six structure. *Journal of Personality*, 77, 1577–1614.

Schnabel, K., Asendorpf, J., & Greenwald, A. G. (2008). Using Implicit Association Tests for the assessment of implicit personality self-concept. In G. J. Boyle, G. Matthews, & D. H. Saklofske (Eds.), *The SAGE handbook of personality theory and assessment: Vol. 2. Personality measurement and testing* (pp. 508–528). Thousand Oaks, CA: Sage.

Shah, J., & Kruglanski, A. W. (2003). When opportunity knocks: Bottom-up priming of goals by means and its effects on self-regulation. *Journal of Personality and Social Psychology*, 84(6), 1109–1122. doi:10.1037/0022-3514.84.6.1109.

Sheldon, K. M., Elliot, A. J., Kim, Y., & Kasser, T. (2001). What is satisfying about satisfying events? Testing 10 candidate psychological needs. *Journal of Personality and Social Psychology*, 80(2), 325–339. doi:10.1037/0022-3514.80.2.325.

Sheldon, K. M., & Gunz, A. (2009). Psychological needs as basic motives, not just experiential requirements. *Journal of Personality*, 77(5), 1467–1492. doi:10.1111/j.1467-6494.2009.00589.x.

Shoda, Y., & LeeTiernan, S. (2002). What remains invariant? Finding order within a person's thoughts, feelings, and behaviors across situations. In D. Cervone & W. Mischel (Eds.), *Advances in personality science* (pp. 241–270). New York: Guilford.

Sidanius, J., Devereux, E., & Pratto, F. (1992). A comparison of symbolic racism theory and social dominance theory as explanations for racial policy attitudes. *Journal of Social Psychology*, 132(3), 377–395.

Skitka, L. J., Bauman, C. W., & Sargis, E. G. (2005). Moral conviction: Another contributor to attitude strength or something more? *Journal of Personality and Social Psychology*, 88(6), 895–917. doi:10.1037/0022-3514.88.6.895.

Skodol, A. E., Clark, L. A., Bender, D. S., Krueger, R. F., Morey, L. C., Verheul, R., Alarcon, R. D., Bell, C. C., Siever, L. J., and Oldham, J. M. (2011). Proposed changes in personality and personality disorder assessment and diagnosis for *DSM-5* Part 1: Description and rationale. *Personality Disorders: Theory, Research, and Treatment*, 2, 4-22.

Smith, E. R., & Mackie, D. M. (1995). *Social psychology*. New York: Worth Publishers.

Smith, R. E., Shoda, Y., Cumming, S. P., & Smoll, F. L. (2009). Behavioral signatures at the ballpark: Intraindividual consistency of adults' situation-behavior patterns and their interpersonal consequences. *Journal of Research in Personality*, 43(2), 187–195. doi:10.1016/j.jrp.2008.12.006.

Snyder, C. R., Harris, C., Anderson, J. R., Holleran, S. A., Irving, L. M., Sigmon, S. T., et al. (1991). The will and the ways: Development and validation of an individual-differences measure of hope. *Journal of Personality and Social Psychology*, 60(4), 570–585. doi:10.1037/0022-3514.60.4.570.

Snyder, M. (1974). Self-monitoring of expressive behavior. *Journal of Personality and Social Psychology*, 30(4), 526–537. doi:10.1037/h0037039.

Snyder, M. (2006). Building bridges between personality and social psychology: Understanding the ties that bind persons and situations. *Bridging social psychology: Benefits of transdisciplinary approaches* (pp. 187–191). Mahwah, NJ: Erlbaum.

Snyder, M., & Cantor, N. (1998). Understanding personality and social behavior: A functionalist strategy. In D. T. Gilbert, S. T. Fiske, & G. Lindzey (Eds.), *The handbook of social psychology* (2nd ed., pp. 635–679). New York: McGraw-Hill.

Snyder, M., & Ickes, W. (1985). Personality and social behavior. In G. Lindzey & E. Aronson (Eds.), *Handbook of social psychology: Vol. 2. Special fields and applications* (3rd ed., pp. 883–948). New York: Random House.

Snyder, M., & Stukas, A. (1999). Interpersonal processes: The interplay of cognitive, motivational, and behavioral activities in social interaction. *Annual Review of Psychology*, 50, 273–303. doi:10.1146/annurev.psych.50.1.273.

Soto, C. J., & John, O. P. (2009). Ten facet scales for the Big Five Inventory: Convergence with NEO PI-R facets, self-peer agreement, and discriminant validity. *Journal of Research in Personality*, 43, 84–90. doi:10.1016/j.jrp.2008.10.002.

Soto, C. J., John, O. P., Gosling, S. D., & Potter, J. (2008). The developmental psychometrics of Big Five self-reports: Acquiescence, factor structure, coherence, and differentiation from ages 10 to 20. *Journal of Personality and Social Psychology*, 94, 718–736.

Srivastava, S., John, O. P., Gosling, S. D., & Potter, J. (2003). Development of personality in early and middle adulthood: Set like plaster or persistent change? *Journal of Personality and Social Psychology*, 84, 1041–1053.

Sroufe, L. A., Egeland, B., Carlson, E. A., & Collins, W. A. (2005). *The development of the person: The Minnesota study of risk and adaptation from birth to adulthood*. New York: Guilford.

Steger, M. F., Frazier, P., Oishi, S., & Kaler, M. (2006). The meaning in life questionnaire: Assessing the presence of and search for meaning in life. *Journal of Counseling Psychology*, 53(1), 80–93. doi:10.1037/0022-0167.53.1.80.

Stoolmiller, M. (1999). Implications of the restricted range of family environments for estimates of heritability and non-shared environment in behavior-genetic adoption studies. *Psychological Bulletin*, 125, 392.

Tackett, J. L., Silberschmidt, A. L., Krueger, R. F., & Sponheim, S. R. (2009). A dimensional model of personality disorder: Incorporating DSM Cluster A characteristics. *Personality Disorders: Theory, Research, and Treatment, S*(1), 27–34. doi:10.1037/1949-2715.S.1.27.

Taylor, J. A. (1953). A personality scale of manifest anxiety. *Journal of Abnormal and Social Psychology, 48*(2), 285–290. doi:10.1037/h0056264.

Terracciano, A., McCrae, R. R>, & Costa, P. T., Jr. (2006). Longitudinal trajectories in Guilford Zimmerman temperament survey data: Results from the Baltimore longitudinal study of aging. *Journals of Gerontology: Series B. Psychological Sciences and Social Sciences, 61B*, 108–116.

Thrash, T. M., & Elliot, A. J. (2003). Inspiration as a psychological construct. *Journal of Personality and Social Psychology, 84*(4), 871–889. doi:10.1037/0022-3514.84.4.871.

Tracy, J. L., Robins, R. W., & Sherman, J. W. (2009). The practice of psychological science: Searching for Cronbach's two streams in social-personality psychology. *Journal of Personality and Social Psychology, 96*(6), 1206–1225. doi:10.1037/a0015173.

Turkheimer, E. (2000). Three laws of behavior genetics and what they mean. *Current Directions in Psychological Science, 9*, 160–164.

Turner, J. C., Hogg, M. A., Oakes, P. J., Reicher, S. D., & Wetherell, M. S. (1987). *Rediscovering the social group: A self-categorization theory.* Cambridge, MA: Basil Blackwell.

Uleman, J. S., Saribay, S. A., & Gonzalez, C. M. (2008). Spontaneous inferences, implicit impressions, and implicit theories. *Annual Review of Psychology, 59*, 329–360.

Van Der Maas, H. J., Dolan, C. V., Grasman, R. P., Wicherts, J. M., Huizenga, H. M., & Raijmakers, M. J. (2006). A dynamical model of general intelligence: The positive manifold of intelligence by mutualism. *Psychological Review, 113*(4), 842–861. doi:10.1037/0033-295X.113.4.842.

Vazire, S., & Gosling, S. D. (2004). e-Perceptions: Personality impressions based on personal websites. *Journal of Personality and Social Psychology, 87*, 123–132.

Watson, D., Clark, L. A., & Tellegen, A. (1988). Development and validation of brief measures of positive and negative affect: The PANAS scales. *Journal of Personality and Social Psychology, 54*(6), 1063–1070. doi:10.1037/0022-3514.54.6.1063.

Widiger, T., Livesley, W., & Clark, L. (2009). An integrative dimensional classification of personality disorder. *Psychological Assessment, 21*(3), 243–255. doi:10.1037/a0016606.

Wiggins, J. (1996). An informal history of the interpersonal circumplex tradition. *Journal of Personality Assessment, 66*(2), 217–233. doi:10.1207/s15327752jpa6602_2.

Wilt, J., Noftle, E. E., Fleeson, W., & Spain, J. S. (2011). *The dynamic role of personality states in mediating the relationship between extraversion and positive affect.* Manuscript submitted for publication.

Winter, D. G., John, O. P., Stewart, A. J., Klohnen, E. C., & Duncan, L. E. (1998). Traits and motives: Toward an integration of two traditions in personality research. *Psychological Review, 105*(2), 230–250. doi:10.1037/0033-295X.105.2.230.

Woike, B., & Polo, M. (2001). Motive-related memories: Content, structure, and affect. *Journal of Personality, 69*(3), 391–415. doi:10.1111/1467-6494.00150.

Wood, D., Gosling, S. D., & Potter, J. (2007). Normality evaluations and their relation to personality traits and well-being. *Journal of Personality and Social Psychology, 93*, 861–879.

Wood, W., & Neal, D. T. (2007). A new look at habits and the habit-goal interface. *Psychological Review, 114*, 843–863.

Wood, W., Quinn, J. M., & Kashy, D. A. (2002). Habits in everyday life: Thought, emotion, and action. *Journal of Personality and Social Psychology, 83*, 1281–1297.

Wortman, J., & Wood, D. (2010). *The personality traits of liked people.* Unpublished manuscript, Wake Forest University, Winston-Salem, NC.

Zanarini, M. C., Frankenburg, F. R., Reich, D., & Fitzmaurice, G. (2010). Time to attainment of recovery from borderline personality disorder and stability of recovery: A 10-year prospective follow-up study. *American Journal of Psychiatry, 167*(6), 663–667. doi:10.1176/appi.ajp.2009.09081130.

Zayas, V., & Shoda, Y. (2005). Do automatic reactions elicited by thoughts of romantic partner, mother, and self relate to adult romantic attachment? *Personality and Social Psychology Bulletin, 31*(8), 1011–1025. doi:10.1177/0146167204274100.

Zuroff, D. C. (1986). Was Gordon Allport a trait theorist? *Journal of Personality and Social Psychology, 51*, 993–1000.

Perspectives on the Situation

Harry T. Reis *and* John G. Holmes

Abstract

This chapter reviews major theoretical positions on the influence of situations and personality in social psychology. We review the history and current status of this debate and we describe in some detail two recent theories that seem particularly amenable toward resolving it. Broadly considered, our position is that personality and situations must be considered interacting factors, but in a theoretically specific way. The concept of affordance—that situations provide opportunities for the expression of certain personality traits—is central to our analysis. We also discuss several issues that social psychologists might profitably consider to provide better grounding for theories and research about the impact of situations on behavior.

Keywords: situation, personality, affordance, interdependence, interdependence theory, cognitive-affective personality system, taxonomies of situations, personality-situation interactionism.

Why Situations Matter in Social Psychology

Social psychologists take rightful pride in championing the importance of situations. Many important regularities in human behavior can be understood by identifying and appreciating the situations in which people find themselves, as well as by interpreting the characteristic ways in which people respond to those situations. Context, in other words, exerts potent influence on behavior. For many researchers, this simple principle defines social psychology's place in the hierarchy of sciences, falling somewhere between those disciplines that seek causal explanation within the individual (e.g., personality, neuroscience) and those that look to larger entities and systems (e.g., political science, economics, anthropology).

What do social psychologists mean when they refer to situations? Derived from the Latin *situs*, which means *place* or *position*, the term "situation" has come to have broad meaning, referring to any and all circumstances, conditions, states of affairs, and entities in the environment that have the potential to constrain or facilitate the individual's behavior.

An even more encompassing definition is offered by the popular Web site The Situationist, which states, somewhat vaguely, that "'The situation' refers to causally significant features around us and within us that we do not notice or believe are relevant in explaining human behavior." (The Situationist, 2011, para. 1). As the concept has come to be used in contemporary social psychology, situations include more or less everything that is not part of personality or other dispositional attributes of the person. On the favorable side, this breadth provides a wide umbrella for defining the field. Less helpfully, it has contributed to important ambiguities about how different kinds of situations should be categorized, and about how a general theoretical model of the influence of situations on behavior should be conceptualized. Some social psychologists limit their attention to *social* situations—that is, to those features of the situation that involve or refer to other people—but even casual inspection of social psychological journals suggests that this restriction is seldom heeded.

Sorting causal influences into two categories, one representing situations, the other representing personality and other person factors, is a common enterprise for which there is ample historical precedent. In 1936, Kurt Lewin wrote, "Every psychological event depends on the state of the person and at the same time on the environment, although their relative importance is different in different cases" (p. 12). As we explain later, relying on statements such as this to establish two separable and independent categories of causal influences on behavior is a substantial oversimplification of what Lewin meant (and, as we also explain, of reality); nonetheless, it set the stage for much of what was to follow. As Snyder and Ickes (1985; see also Snyder & Cantor, 1998) describe, most research on social behavior adopts one of three investigative strategies: the *dispositional strategy*, which "seeks to understand consistencies in social behavior in terms of relatively stable traits, enduring dispositions, and other propensities that are thought to reside 'within' individuals"; the *situational strategy*, which "seeks to identify the personal antecedents and the social consequences of regularities and consistencies in the settings and contexts in which individuals live their lives"; and the *interactional strategy*, which emphasizes "the interactive influence of dispositional features and situational features" (all quotes, 1985, p. 884).

Although these alternatives are often couched in terms of a "person-situation debate," we, like other commentators before us, see this debate as largely resolved in favor of the interactional approach (e.g., Fleeson & Noftle, 2008; Funder, 2009; Kenrick & Funder, 1988). Funder stated the case succinctly: "Nowadays, everybody is an interactionist" (2006, p. 22). In our view, the interactional strategy is the only one that provides an accurate, comprehensive, and generalizable foundation for the study of social behavior. This position—one that we believe is consistent with Lewin's intent—serves as a guiding perspective for this chapter. To be sure, the dispositional and situational strategies may be reasonable insofar as individual studies go—our sole reservation is that by oversimplifying the inherent complexity of social behavior, both approaches mask the ways in which dispositional effects are conditioned on contexts and, in turn, contextual effects depend on the expression of dispositions.

Our goal in writing this chapter is to review historical and contemporary approaches to research and theory about situations, as they have been utilized by both social and personality psychologists. We begin by discussing three broad ideas that will set the stage for our review: the "power of the

situation"; the need for a taxonomy of situations; and the importance of integrating situational and dispositional influences in models of social behavior. We then describe several different traditions for conceptualizing the most important features of situations, followed by a review of major theoretical models of situational effects. The chapter concludes with critical discussion of the future of the concept of situation within social and personality psychology. Throughout the chapter, our intent is to highlight those approaches and research trends that have helped advance the field's knowledge, and to foster further advances by drawing attention to concepts and principles that help integrate situational and dispositional influences on behavior. We also hope to show plainly that better understanding of situations ought to be a central enterprise for both social *and* personality psychologists (Funder, 2006).

The "Power of the Situation"

In their highly influential 1991 book *The Person and the Situation*, Ross and Nisbett articulated the oft-repeated principle of the "power of the situation":

> Often the situational variable makes quite a bit of difference. Occasionally, in fact, it makes nearly all the difference, and information about traits and individual differences that other people thought all-important proves all but trivial. . . . Such empirical [examples] are important because they illustrate the degree to which ordinary men and women are apt to be mistaken about the power of the situation—the power of particular situational features, and the power of situations in general. (p. 4)

Situations, in other words, influence behavior, and this influence is often underappreciated and underestimated, both in an absolute sense and in comparison to more dispositional explanations.

Evidence for the power of the situation is abundant, including just about every experiment demonstrating that manipulation of some property of the situation produces a significant change in some behavioral outcome. Four examples are commonly cited: the Sherif-Asch conformity experiments, which showed that modification of the social context can alter the expression of opinions and judgments (Asch, 1956; Sherif, 1936); Milgram's obedience studies, which revealed that situational pressure could lead ordinary people to enact brutal behaviors (Milgram, 1974); Latané and Darley's (1970) bystander intervention studies, which demonstrated that situational variations influence the likelihood of intervention in a putative emergency; and the Stanford prison study, which showed that an artificial environment could be constructed that would induce college students to behave like stereotypic prisoners and guards (Haney, Banks, & Zimbardo, 1973). Each of these examples manipulates different situational features in different ways, but all of them illustrate the power of situations to produce dramatic changes in behavior.

As the above quote indicates, advocates of the "power of the situation" often offer situational explanations in counterpoint to the presumed weakness of trait-based explanations. The argument that personality traits account at best for small portions of variance was introduced by Mischel (1968), who suggested that "the phrase 'personality coefficient' might be coined to describe the correlation between 0.20 and 0.30 which is found persistently when virtually any personality dimension inferred from a questionnaire is related to almost any conceivable external criterion involving responses sampled in a *different* medium" (p. 78, italics in the original). This estimate of the limited impact of personality variables was subsequently popularized by situationally oriented researchers. (Nisbett, 1980, later raised its upper bound to $r = 0.40$.) As a rationale for situational approaches, however, this argument falls short for several reasons, notably the observation (supported by meta-analyses) that standardized effect sizes for many situational variables turn out to be roughly equivalent in magnitude (e.g., Funder & Ozer, 1983; Richard, Bond, & Stokes-Zoota, 2003). Moreover, situational effects rarely describe the behavior of all subjects in an experiment. In most conformity and obedience research, even in high-pressure conditions, a sizable portion of subjects do not conform or obey. For example, about 40% of Milgram's subjects (1974) did not continue to give lethal shocks in the condition most commonly depicted as evidence of the power of situations. Although the 60% or so who did does provide evidence for the power of situations, some other explanation is needed for the 40% who did not, and it does not seem parsimonious to use one argument for some participants and a different argument for others. Similar reasoning applies to the considerable differences shown by individual guards and prisoners in the Stanford prison study (Carnahan & McFarland, 2007).

In the next section, we show how interactional strategies provide evidence about both personality and situational effects, by considering how each one moderates the effects of the other. We share Funder's (2009) belief that "main effects" research (that is,

research that examines only situations or personality) is a reasonable research strategy—there is no particular reason why every study should incorporate all sources of variance. However, conceptually, theoretical models should incorporate, or at least allow for, both situational and dispositional factors in order to properly represent the processes that lead to behavior in the social world.

Why Situations Matter to Personality Psychology: Interactions and Affordances

On the face of it, it would seem that the identification of situation effects would offer little benefit for personality psychology. After all, personality variables have traditionally been conceptualized as individual differences that transcend specific contexts (Alston, 1975). Even if the person-situation debate has come to an end, and even if it always was a "false dichotomy" (Funder, 2006, p. 32), to the extent that personality theories depend on identifying and making sense of cross-situational consistencies, contextual variances would appear to be largely irrelevant. Closer examination of this proposition suggests otherwise, however.

First, if the person-situation debate has concluded, it is because most behavior is best explained by Person × Situation (P × S) interactions (Funder, 2009; see also Fleeson, chapter 3, this volume). That is, and as reviewed later in this chapter, behavior depends on an interaction between properties of the person and properties of the situation (Magnusson & Endler, 1977). For example, persons high in the Big Five trait of neuroticism tend to be more reactive to stress and more distressed by recurrent problems than persons low in neuroticism (Suls, Green, & Hills, 1998). Of course, in any given study, a personality or a situation main effect may emerge, perhaps because one factor or the other has been experimentally or statistically held constant, has been minimized by the research design (e.g., limiting the study to a fixed context, such as high-achievement situations), or has been relegated to the error term (Krueger, 2009). Nevertheless, full explanations may depend on both personality and social variables in two ways: (1) because the findings of a given study require specifying not only what was found but also boundary conditions and limitations that contributed to the result; and (2) because valid theoretical accounts of a phenomenon must include contextual and dispositional factors that inhibit or facilitate its display in the real world (Brewer, 2000).

A second reason why personality research cannot ignore situations is that within-person, across-situation variability may in itself carry important information about individual differences. Although most trait-relevant behaviors vary across situations, the characteristics of these distributions (e.g., their mean, variance, and skew) tend to be stable and may reveal the impact of personality on social behavior (Fleeson, 2001). For example, trait extraversion is related to high levels of variability in extraversion-related behavior (Fleeson, 2001). Moreover, to the extent that within-person variability reflects "distinctions people make between situations . . . [it] would lead to a deep integration of the process and trait viewpoints" (Fleeson, 2004, p. 86; see also Shoda, Mischel, & Wright, 1994).

Third, rather than being isolated from each other, situational and personal causes are inextricably linked. The P × S perspective is commonly represented as if person and situation were separable and distinct factors, each moderating the other to yield a joint effect greater than the sum of their independent effects. (This may reflect the ANOVA-metaphor of orthogonal main effects and interactions.) A more nuanced view begins with the notion that person factors include all properties of the individual that come into play when he/she perceives and responds to a situation—motives, values, traits, habits, preferences, moods, and so on (Kelley et al., 2003). Situations present individuals with behavioral options, thereby making certain behaviors more likely, others less likely, and still others irrelevant. This occurs because situational features activate cognitive and affective processing systems within the individual that in turn lead to behavior (Mischel & Shoda, 1999).

Situations, in other words, offer a kind of social "affordance" (to use terminology introduced by Gibson, 1979, in a somewhat different context)— "opportunities for acting, interacting, and being acted upon" (Zebrowitz & Collins, 1997, p. 217) that inhere in every circumstance and context. To Kelley et al. (2003), and as described more fully later in this chapter, this analysis begins with the actual (objectively determined) properties of a situation. These properties afford certain responses and preclude others. For example, a friend in need is an occasion to assist, exploit, or ignore; a job that needs to be done is a chance to divide labor, delegate, or do it oneself; and a difficult test is an opportunity to study hard or self-handicap. Which of the available options is enacted reflects the individual's choice (made with or without deliberate awareness), depending on applicable person variables, such as those mentioned above. Thus, situations do not "cause" behavior, as other models suggest, but rather alter the likelihood of a given behavior by making certain alternatives more relevant and others irrelevant. This is depicted in Figure 4.1.

The affordance model suggests that neither person nor situation factors cause behavior independent of the other but rather that situations have properties that provide a context for the expression of person factors. The study of situations, then, becomes the study of what different constellations of features afford, and by which mechanisms people interpret and respond to those features. The study of person factors, on the other hand, becomes the study of "what the individual makes of the situation"

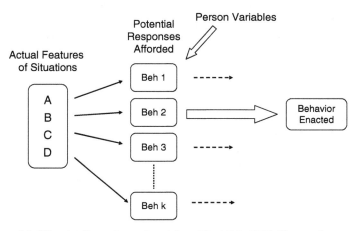

Fig. 4.1 The affordance model of Situation-Person interactions (adapted from Reis, 2008). The term "person variables" is broader than personality, referring to any properties of individuals that come into play when they are aware of situations, and choose between the various behavioral options available in that situation. Thus, person variables include standard personality traits, along with individual motives, values, preferences, goals, and habits. The dashed line represents the finite series of behavioral options from 3 to k.

(Kelley et al., 2003, p. 7)—that is, which of the available alternatives the individual values the most and thus accepts or rejects as behavioral options. (To ecological psychologists who work in the Gibsonian tradition, such as Baron and Boudreau, 1987, this step is sometimes called *feature utilization*.)

To illustrate the concept of affordance, we consider Milgram's well-known obedience experiments (Milgram, 1974), which, as mentioned above, are often used as a prototype for the "power of situations." Two key features of the standard Milgram situation were the aura of scientific legitimacy in which the research was conducted, and the experimenter's unrelenting demands that the participant continue delivering increasingly dangerous shocks to the confederate. This situation affords the participant with at least two behavioral options: to obey or to resist (which about 40% of participants did). In affordance terms, the participant's interaction with a domineering authority figure activates certain dispositionally linked motives and goals (e.g., to appease the experimenter, to avoid harming the learner, or to fulfill their role as an experimental participant), affording him or her an opportunity to select between the behavioral options of obedience or resistance. Both situation and person factors contribute to this causal analysis, but neither is causative of behavior independent of the other.

It follows from this logic that situations only afford certain possibilities; others are impossible. For example, the trait of benevolence cannot be displayed when the self and a partner both stand to benefit from one's actions, the trait of trust cannot be expressed when the self is dominant over a subordinate, and the trait of optimism cannot be shown when the most likely outcome is exceptionally good. Thus, in the language of affordance, it makes little sense to think in terms of main effects, inasmuch as that term implies that a given situation operates more or less universally across persons, and a given trait is expressed across all contexts. (Of course a study may obtain main effects, but it should be clear that those effects depend on the particular manipulation averaged across person factors. We refer here to the broader conceptualization of main effects and interactions.) Affordances thus are a special case of person × situation models, specifying that certain individual differences will be revealed only in certain situations.

Toward A Taxonomy of Situations

Social psychology's longstanding interest in situations notwithstanding, there is no consensually accepted framework for identifying, classifying, or conceptualizing what situations are (and, by implication, what they are not). Calling attention to this lacuna is something of a time-honored tradition. For example, Sells (1963) observed:

> The most obvious need in evaluating the manifold encounter of organism and environment is a more satisfactory and systematic conceptualization of the environment. This implies a taxonomic, dimensional analysis of stimulus variables comparable to the trait systems that have been developed for individual difference variables . . . . While work proceeds actively to extend the exploration of individual differences . . . the equally important frontier of situational dimensions is virtually ignored . . . Experimenters must have systematic information about relevant dimensions of the environment beyond the piecemeal, concrete, immediate variables customarily observed on the basis of experience. (p. 700)

Nearly 40 years later, Kenny, Mohr, and Levesque (2001) echoed this point:

> Although social psychologists have emphasized the importance of the situation, they have been less successful in its conceptualization . . . . [T]here is no universally accepted scheme for understanding what is meant by situation. It does not even appear that there are major competing schemes, and all too often the situation is undefined. (p. 129)

Others have commented on the same deficiency, including Swann and Seyle:

> Full implementation of Mischel and Shoda's (1999) innovative approach clearly requires the development of a comprehensive taxonomy of situations—a development that has been pursued with stunningly modest success since H. Wright and Barker's (1950) early attempt. (2005, p. 162)

Snyder and Cantor:

> The psychology of personality has long provided a considerably richer vocabulary and set of theoretical concepts for defining and assessing features of persons than social psychology has provided for conceptualizing and measuring features of situations. (1998, p. 662)

Fleeson and Noftle:

> The definition of a situation has been difficult to come by. (2008, p. 1677)

and finally Reis:

> Although descriptive taxonomies are common—and indeed fundamental—in the physical and biological sciences, and closer to home, in personality psychology . . . social psychology has no such catalog. (2008, p. 315).

In short, although the importance of situations to understanding behavior is beyond doubt, just how these situations should be conceptualized and organized remains at best ambiguous.

To some, the value of a taxonomy of situations seems self-evident. At the most elementary level, a taxonomy would help organize existing findings and theories, as we hope to illustrate in a later section of this chapter. "A taxonomy is a system for naming and organizing things into groups that share similar characteristics" (Montague Institute, 2009), which, much like the Periodic Table in chemistry or the *Diagnostic and Statistical Manual* (*DSM*) in psychopathology, would facilitate identification of conceptual similarities among situations, as well as ways in which situations differ from one another. This is similar to establishing convergent and discriminant validity among constructs. A good taxonomy establishes mutually exclusive categories, is sufficient to include all cases within its range, and can be applied unambiguously. Thus, taxonomies are more than classification schemes, in that they include a hierarchically structured order, encompassing superordinate (less differentiated) and subordinate (more differentiated) categories (Hull, 1998).

Another benefit is that taxonomies may contribute to theory development by describing the major and distinguishing features of the entities in question, thereby providing a scheme for hypothesizing about and investigating their causal characteristics and typical behavioral sequelae. For example, Darwin spent years observing and cataloging barnacles and finches, a process that eventually led him to formulate the theory of evolution (Quammen, 2007). Rozin (2001) made a related point, arguing that bottom-up, descriptive databases can be useful in highlighting for researchers what phenomena need to be understood, which constructs might be fruitful in this regard, and how they might integrate seemingly diverse phenomena.

Does social-personality psychology really need a taxonomy of situations? It might be argued that the study of situations has thrived for the past century without one. There is no apparent reason why researchers cannot study whichever situations offer the most valuable or intriguing insights without a systematic scheme for relating those situations to others already represented in the literature. Nonetheless, we believe that the continued lack of a taxonomy of situations will impair social psychology's movement toward becoming a cumulative science, a common criticism of the field (e.g., Mischel, 2006). In a cumulative science, findings build on prior findings, eventually creating a complex, dense, and coherent network of interrelated principles that together explain diverse, recurrent, and important phenomena (Kuhn, 1970). Reis (2007) likened this to a spider's web of theories and findings, rather than the current list-like structure evident in most textbooks. The potential of a good taxonomy for advancing cumulative knowledge can be seen in two fields with relatively recent taxonomies—psychopathology (the *DSM*) and personality (the Big Five)—albeit both not without significant controversy. Taxonomies help researchers "carve nature at its joints" (Meehl, 1992), a necessary step in fostering generalizable and useful theories.

The absence of even a hint of consensual agreement about a taxonomy of situations is particularly striking in view of the deep intuitive knowledge and rich conceptual language that people possess about everyday situations (Cantor, Mischel, & Schwartz, 1982; Kelley, 1997). Individuals and societies often rely on naive (informal) folk-taxonomies as an aid to understanding entities in their environment (e.g., plants, food sources; Atran, 1990), and this tendency to categorize likely applies to situations as well. For example, most people recognize fundamental differences in their relationships with kin and non-kin or their interactions with higher-status and lower-status others, or in cooperative and competitive situations. Later in this chapter we review some of the taxonomies and classification systems that have been proposed.

How Situations Are Defined: Major Distinctions

Following Lewin (1935), we use the term "situation" broadly to refer to any and all entities outside the individual that exert a causal influence on the individual's behavior. For example, the term "situation" has been used to describe the biochemical environment of single-cell organisms, the properties of physical spaces, activities being conducted, the person one is with at a given moment, appraisals of causally relevant stimuli, and personal goals. Several general distinctions may help clarify the various ways in which the term situation is used.

OBJECTIVE VERSUS PERCEIVED FEATURES OF SITUATIONS

One important distinction differentiates the actual, objective properties of situations from the ways in which they are perceived by individuals. Early on, Murray (1938) distinguished *alpha press*, the actual power of an external object to influence behavior, to the extent that it can be determined, from *beta press*, the person's interpretation of objects and phenomena. Similarly, Magnusson (1981) drew a distinction between "actual environments and situations" and "perceived environments and situations." Despite these and similar comments by other influential scholars, current research devotes little attention to this distinction.

Social psychology has long emphasized the latter over the former. Ross and Nisbett's (1991) principle of construal is often taken as axiomatic: that the causal analysis of situations should focus on the personal, subjective meaning of the situation to the actor. Bem and Allen observed similarly: "the classification of situations . . . will have to be in terms of the individual's phenomenology, not the investigator's" (1974, p. 518). This orientation follows from early theorists (e.g., Allport, 1924; Asch, 1952; Lewin, 1935) who argued that the most influential causes of behavior are the individual's personal interpretation of what is significant in the environment. As a result, many important models in social psychology begin with appraisals as independent variables, ignoring links between objective features and subjective construals. Examples of the appraisal approach include research on whether performance situations are perceived as threatening or challenging (Elliot & McGregor, 2001); on whether interaction partners' offer of help is experienced as controlling or supportive (Deci & Ryan, 1987); on whether relational events are perceived as signs of rejection (Downey & Feldman, 1996); and on whether certain words or pictures activate mental images of safety or anxiety, security or mortality (Mikulincer & Shaver, 2005).

Barker's descriptions of behavior settings were among the first to focus on the objective properties of situations (Barker, 1968; Barker & Wright, 1954). Barker believed that regularities in behavior settings could be described objectively, in much the same way that in the natural sciences regularities in atoms, molecules, and organisms are routinely described. Similarly, interdependence theory (Kelley & Thibaut, 1978) proposes that the properties defining outcome interdependence between interacting partners have an objective basis in reality that

can and should be identified. These general approaches aside, experimental manipulations (particularly those that are fixed rather than customized to individual participants) are designed to vary objective properties of the situation (Wilson, Aronson, & Carlsmith, 2010). Perhaps ironically, researchers often exclude participants whose subjective construal, assessed by manipulation checks, does not conform to the experimenter's intent. In our view, this practice is misguided; rather than treated as errors, discrepancies between objective circumstances and subjective construals ought to be the focus of research.

A new research program by Funder (2010; Sherman, Nave, & Funder, 2010) seems consistent with this idea. Funder has developed the Riverside Situational Q-Sort, which describes a series of commonly encountered situations (e.g., "a job needs to be done" and "situation might evoke warmth or compassion") in terms of their "mid-level properties"—that is, properties specific enough to evoke reasonable but not universal consensus. This allows the research to evaluate the impact of dispositions in construing and behaviorally responding to those situations (see also Furr & Funder, 2004).

A significant disadvantage of the emphasis on perceived situations is that it obscures the researcher's ability to determine how dispositions, goals, and other person variables influence construals (Reis, 2008). Suppose a researcher hypothesized that low-self-esteem persons were likely to interpret a close relationship partner's attempts to be supportive as patronizing. How would one know whether dispositional (low self-esteem) or situational (the partner's behavior) factors, or both, were responsible without some sort of objective characterization of the partner's behavior? (see Simpson, Rholes, & Philips, 1996, for a good example). The objective characterization of situations, in other words, makes it possible to identify "what the individual makes of the situation" (Kelley et al., 2003, p. 7), the centerpiece of construal approaches. It also circumvents the risk of circularity in defining situations according to the perceptions of persons in it (Funder, 2006).

A Gibsonian approach to the perception of situations, as described earlier, helps resolve this problem. This approach requires describing and explaining the configural cues of the social environment whose structure, after suitable processing by the individual, yields functionally useful perception (Zebrowitz & Collins, 1997). In other words, situations have objective properties that, once perceived, allow for the expression of individual goals and preferences. As shown in figure 4.1, conceptual analyses of the impact of situations would include both objective properties of the stimulus situation and individual construals of those properties. Rather than requiring researchers to choose one or the other orientation, and rather than confusing the issues, this approach allows for clear integration of both perspectives (Funder, 2006).

NOMINAL VERSUS PSYCHOLOGICAL SITUATIONS

This distinction, proposed by Mischel and Shoda (1995), distinguishes the physical ecology considered in its most basic, descriptive sense from its deeper impact on the individuals involved. According to Mischel and Shoda, "nominal situations refer to the particular places and activities in the setting, for example, woodworking activities in a summer camp, or arithmetic tests and dining halls, or playgrounds in a school setting" whereas psychological situations focus on "the active ingredients that impact on the person's behavior" (both quotes, 1999, p. 203).

One of the first (and, arguably, still most cited) social psychologists to describe nominal situations was Roger Barker (1968; Barker & Wright, 1954). Barker, who studied with Lewin at the University of Iowa, called attention to the ways in which ecological settings, such as homes, classrooms, medical offices, or roadways, evoked consistent patterns of behavior. Barker believed that to understand behavior, one had to first understand the physical context in which it occurs (that is, what sorts of behavior that context was likely to evoke). Barker's interest in settings has had less impact on social-personality psychology than on environmental psychology,[1] which he helped spawn and which includes studies of how the built and natural environment influence behavior (Proshansky, Ittelson, & Rivlin, 1976; Stokols & Altman, 1987). Environmental psychologists commonly study nominal situations, such as environmental stress (e.g., noise, crowding), personal space utilization, mental maps of places, and the impact of architectural and industrial design, as well as physical properties (e.g., temperature, odor, and color). Other examples of nominal situations include Argyle, Furnham, and Graham's (1981) account of social encounters that elicit familiar, consensually understood sequences of interaction (e.g., formal social events vs. intimate encounters with close friends or relations) and Schank and Abelson's (1977) model of scripts associated with common social episodes.

In contrast, by using the term "active ingredients," Mischel and Shoda refer to the manner in which situations activate "characteristic and relatively predictable patterns of cognitions and affects" (1999, p. 203). In other words, this category describes psychologically significant situations that can emerge in everyday activity. For example, rejection, criticism, thwarted goal attainment, and praise can occur in various settings but would be expected to have psychologically similar effects in all of them. Most contemporary social-psychological research falls into this category, in the sense that researchers tend to be interested in broad, generalizable patterns of behavior likely to transcend the particulars of a given setting. For example, interdependence theory (described later in this chapter) is concerned with the impact of interacting persons' interdependence with respect to outcomes on behavior. As might be expected, behavioral consistency tends to be greater when situations are defined psychologically rather than nominally (e.g., Mischel, Shoda, & Mendoza-Denton, 2002).

Psychological situations are often defined in terms of idiosyncratic perceptions or personal meaning. For example, Yang, Read, and Miller (2009) show how appraisal-based theories, which require that individuals interpret situational features according to goal relevance, exemplify the psychological approach to situations. In their view, the situation depends on interpretation of "what happened, is happening, or might happen to people's goals" (Yang et al., 2009, p. 19). Similarly, constructivist approaches to social cognition argue that the meaning ascribed to situations is what matters most (e.g., Bem & Allen, 1974; Krahé, 1990). However, models of psychological situations can also be based on objective properties of situations, such as their informational ambiguity or reward structure. Indeed, the very word "construct" implies that something exists to be built on, to have meaning ascribed to. This idea is discussed in more detail later in this chapter.

CONCRETE VERSUS ABSTRACT PROPERTIES OF SITUATIONS

As noted earlier, most researchers are interested in broad, generalizable patterns of behavior that transcend the particulars of a given setting. Concrete details of physical settings of the sort studied by Barker may help predict behavior, but to apply principles to novel contexts, features of the setting must be categorized into contextually based classes. For instance, theories extend their reach when such variables as noise, heat, and crowding are depicted in more abstract form, such as environmental stress. Similarly, there are many concrete ways to criticize someone, including blaming bad behavior on poor intentions, impugning personality, reminding someone that the current negative behavior is a repeat performance, and so on. Theoretical advances depend on grouping the various instantiations of criticism into a more general, abstract category, reflecting the possibility that their shared aspects produce a common, systematic, and predictable reaction, and it is these that lead to a theoretically valuable conclusion.

Shoda (2004) discusses this issue in terms of the trade-off between the accuracy of predictions (fidelity) and the generality of findings (bandwidth). For instance, keeping a narrow focus on blaming a person's intentions may result in somewhat more accurate predictions of a person's behavior, but having a theory tied only to instances of blame would require a large catalog of other offenses, each needing its own narrow interpretation. If criticism can be defined more broadly, a single proposition or two might reasonably (and more parsimoniously) describe reactions to a wide band of types of criticism. Similar logic is used in attitude theory. A very specific and proximal attitude, such as "I hate Rush Limbaugh" might lead to precise predictions about rating his radio show, but a more abstract, distal attitude, such as "I dislike conservative commentators," might predict a wide range of reactions to other people and entities.

DESCRIPTIVE VERSUS THEORY-DRIVEN APPROACHES

A bottom-up, descriptive approach is most commonly used in taxometric studies. Taxometric studies seek to identify a comprehensive scheme for categorizing situations (see Yang et al., 2009, for a review). Sometimes these categories are derived by logical analysis (e.g., Argyle, Furnham, & Graham, 1981), but empirical approaches have also been popular. Most such studies begin by generating a large pool of items, such as by asking people to record or retrospectively describe their everyday activity. These items are meant to represent as comprehensively as possible the many situations that occur in real life. Existing studies have focused on details of the behavior setting (e.g., place and activity; Price & Blashfield, 1975), categorical features of situations (e.g., emotional, dynamic, quiet, or rough; Edwards & Templeton, 2005), or literal descriptions of situations (e.g., chatting over coffee with friends, visiting the doctor; Forgas, 1976,

1979). In the next step, participants judge these items in any of several ways, for example, rating each possible pair for similarity, grouping them into clusters, or characterizing them along dimensions that can be used to assess similarity. Interrelations are then computed, with the goal of extracting and identifying commonalities or underlying dimensions. For example, Wish, Deutsch, and Kaplan (1976) used literal descriptions to derive four abstract dimensions of social interaction: cooperative/friendly versus competitive/hostile; equal versus unequal power, intense versus superficial; and socioemotional/informal versus task-oriented/formal. This is commonly done with factor analysis, cluster analysis, or multidimensional scaling.

One of the more structured methods for identifying item pools in descriptive-taxometric studies is based on language. This approach follows from the lexical hypothesis (Goldberg, 1981), which posits that if some aspect of the world matters, people will encode it into language—in other words, the more something matters, the more likely that there will be a word for it. In this approach, searches of dictionaries or verbal accounts of everyday activity are used to generate extensive lists, which are then reduced statistically to identify their most fundamental elements. For example, this approach has been used with Dutch nouns (Van Heck, 1984), English adjectives (Edwards & Templeton, 2005), and Chinese idioms (Yang, Read, & Miller, 2006).

In principle, descriptive approaches provide a useful foundation for theory development. As in the natural sciences, where descriptive taxonomies facilitate theories about structure and function, systematic observations can provide insights leading to models of causal characteristics and behavioral sequelae, as well as for conceptually integrating seemingly diverse phenomena. On the other hand, despite more than a dozen well-done studies (see Yang et al., 2009, for a review), no consensus has yet emerged as to the most appropriate dimensions for characterizing situations, and furthermore, this work has had little, if any, impact on social psychological theorizing. This is in marked contrast to personality psychology, where several typologies (notably, the well-known Big Five) have played a significant role in theory development (John & Srivastava, 1999; Snyder & Cantor, 1998, make a similar comparison). One reason may be that the descriptive approach depends on a comprehensive and generalizable sampling of situations or situational features, so that the obtained taxonomies are neither idiosyncratic nor skewed toward certain concepts. Current methods depend on self-reports (often constrained by sampling characteristics, recall bias, and the limits of self-awareness) and research participants' ability to articulate often-abstract distinctions. It may also be that situations vary along too many dimensions to be reducible by the sorts of methods that have been used thus far.

Top-down, theory-driven approaches begin with a phenomenon, process, or basic fact of social life and then infer from theory the dimensions most likely to contribute to them.[2] The only comprehensive example of a theory-driven taxonomy of situations is interdependence theory (Kelley & Thibaut, 1978; Kelley et al., 2003). Interdependence theory begins with the observation that most important outcomes depend on how interacting persons coordinate their activities, following which conceptually relevant dimensions that influence such coordination are articulated (as elaborated later in this chapter). Situations are thereby defined according to combinations of different points along these dimensions (e.g., one partner has relatively more control over the other's outcomes, and their goals conflict).

More commonly, and absent of attention to classification schemes, conceptually derived distinctions among situations serve as explanatory variables in social-psychological processes. For example, the theory of optimal distinctiveness distinguishes situations on the basis of inclusion and group distinctiveness (Brewer, 2003), whereas research on intrinsic and extrinsic motivation differentiates situations in terms of the locus and nature of salient rewards (Deci & Ryan, 1980). Such approaches neither claim comprehensiveness nor suggest links to taxonomies of situations, and are instead more typically limited to whichever situational features a theory happens to encompass.

Major Theoretical Perspectives on The Conceptualization of Situations
Early Concepts
In one of the earliest definitions to explicitly use the term "situation," Sherif (1948) defined social psychology as:

> the scientific study of the experience and behavior of individuals in relation to social stimulus situations. Interpersonal relationships, group interactions and their products, values or norms, language, art forms, institutions, and technology are certainly among the major social stimuli or stimulus situations. (p. 1)

In a later edition of this text, Sherif and Sherif refined the definition of social stimulus situations "as composed of people (individuals and groups) and items of the sociocultural setting" (1956, p. 4). By this description, Sherif helped formalize social psychology's interest in the impact of external conditions on behavior.

Earlier writings had been much more ambiguous about this focus. The earliest roots of social psychological thinking make little or no mention of situations (see Jahoda, 2007, for an enlightening review). It is equally difficult to find the concept of situation in either of the two 1908 volumes traditionally given credit for inaugurating social psychology. One of them, written by the sociologist Edward Alsworth Ross, defined social psychology's interest in "uniformities due to *social* causes, i.e., to *mental contacts* or *mental interactions* . . . . It is *social* only insofar as it arises out of the interplay of minds" (1908, p. 3; italics in the original). Ross explicitly excluded what he called "uniformities" attributable to the "conditions of life"—for example, the physical setting, culture, race, visual cues, and other features of the environment not subject to mental interplay between persons. In the other 1908 volume, the psychologist William McDougall emphasized instincts and their more behavioral manifestations. The closest he got to situations was to comment that "native tendencies . . . under the influence of the social environment . . . become gradually organised in systems of increasing complexity, while they remain unchanged as regards their essential attributes" (1908, p. 17).

To be sure, early social psychologists, like social scientists, philosophers, and scholars over the ages, recognized that external circumstances influence behavior. Notable examples include John Dewey's (1922) famous account of how the environment sustains or alters habits, one of the first acknowledgments of a situation × personality interaction; Floyd Allport's (1924) description of social psychology in terms of the individual's response to "the *social* portion of his environment" (p. 3, italics in the original), which helped shift the then-popular notion of a *group mind* to a more individual-centered focus; and Henry Murray's (1938) description of press, or the facilitating or obstructing effect that a *stimulus situation* can have on the individual. But in these writings, the concept of situation—what those external circumstances were, and how they differed systematically from other circumstances—tended to be imprecise and minimally defined (if at all), encompassing more or less anything situated outside of the individual actor's body. Perhaps for this reason, Yang et al., (2009) describe this early work as largely metatheoretical.

FIELD THEORY

No one did more to elevate the concept of situation to a formal topic of inquiry than Kurt Lewin, in his topological psychology of the 1930s and 1940s (e.g., Lewin, 1935; 1936; 1943; 1951). Lewin represented "the person in the life space" (that is, the behaving self) with topological diagrams that depicted relevant dispositional and environmental factors, using boundaries to differentiate them and arrows to symbolize facilitating or inhibiting forces. With these map-like diagrams, which he hoped would eventually lead to formal mathematical solutions, Lewin sought to express the dynamic interchange among the diverse factors that constitute the psychological "field" and that causally influence behavior.

In field theory, all behavior is the product of two sources, the person and the environment, hence the well-known equation $B = f (P, E)$. What Lewin meant by this equation is not as well known, however. This seminal equation is often interpreted in the statistical, analysis-of-variance sense, implying two independent effects, P and E, and a possible interaction between them, hence $B = f (P, E, and P \times E)$. In contrast, Lewin believed that P and E were fully interdependent and inseparable. For example, he also wrote, $E = f (P)$ and $P = f (E)$ (Lewin, 1946, p. 239). Thus, in describing himself as an interactionist, Lewin did so without isolating the effects of person from the effects of environment, a task he would have considered not only unhelpful but implausible. Rather, Lewin theorized about how each factor affected the other: "The person and his environment have to be considered as *one* constellation of interdependent factors" (Lewin, 1946, pp. 239–240). That person factors are always in a state of dynamic (i.e., mutually influential and constantly changing) interrelation with environmental factors, and that all psychological events are the result of these interacting forces is the major conceptual contribution of field theory.

Lewin did not offer propositions about which dimensions of situations were more or less relevant to field theory. Rather, his analysis began with the immediate situation as a whole, following which its most important components could be identified. This was necessary, he believed, to understand how various aspects of the field relate to one another, which "thereby avoids the danger of a 'wrong simplification' by abstraction" (Lewin, 1936, p. 17). Lewin further differentiated objective and subjective properties of situations, emphasizing the psychological significance of situations to the person: Psychological processes are "always to be derived from the relation of the concrete individual to the concrete situation" (Lewin, 1935, p. 41). In this respect, Lewin anticipated the prominence of subjective construal in later approaches.

As Deutsch (1954) and Jones (1985), among others, note, Lewin's field theory is more a metatheoretical approach than a formal theory. But this approach has been extraordinarily influential in social psychology, as researchers took and ran with the idea that situational factors could be conceptualized as the source of force fields that facilitate or inhibit certain behaviors. This idea was fundamental to the group dynamics research that dominated social psychology during the 1940s, 1950s, and 1960s, for example in the classic social-influence studies of Sherif, Asch, Festinger, Schachter, Deutsch, and Milgram (see Reis, 2010b, for elaboration). More generally, the force-field conception of situations provided a general model adopted by subsequent motivational constructs and theories in social psychology (Kruglanski, 1996).

PERSON × SITUATION INTERACTIONISM

In the 1960s and 1970s a number of theorists, such as Endler, Magnusson, Pervin, Argyle, and Epstein, developed what they described as an "interactional model of behavior," culminating in an influential edited volume, *Personality at the Crossroads* (Magnusson & Endler, 1977). The authors distinguished what they called a psychodynamic model from a trait model of behavior. As they explain, in interactional psychology, the term "interaction" has been used in two ways. First, in trait models, interaction has been used in the mechanistic, statistical sense, following a factorial analysis of variance logic by crossing person and situation variables and examining the shape of their interaction. Critics of this approach (e.g., Bowers, 1973) contend that many of experiments in this tradition have been atheoretical, simply creating any possible person-environment combinations. For instance, extraverts and introverts have been tested under conditions of high and low ambient stimulation. Extraverts performed well under high stimulation, introverts under low stimulation (Eysenck, 1981). Similarly, a wide variety of studies have examined how the behavior of high- and low-anxiety people differs in various situations that might engender stress (Magnusson & Endler, 1977). Partly to remedy this ambiguity,

Bem and Funder (1978) proposed a model of "template matching," in which templates describing persons expected to behave in particular ways are matched with the corresponding attributes of situations.

The second use of the term "interaction" is more *dynamic*, integrating person variables and situation features to describe the process by which behavior develops. Notwithstanding the perhaps unfortunate resemblance of this term to psychoanalytic perspectives, considerable progress was made on conceptualizing a dynamic link between situations and personality. Magnusson and Endler (1977) suggest that:

> Persons and situations are regarded as indispensably linked to one another during the process of interaction. Neither the person factors nor the situation factors per se determine behavior in isolation: it is determined by the inseparable person by situation interactions. (p. 4)

They made clear that they intended to go beyond the mechanistic statistical sense of the term "interaction," preferring instead the more dynamic idea of an interaction *process* in which persons and situations "form an inextricably interwoven structure" (p. 18).

Magnusson and Endler (1977) focused on the issue of consistency in behavior across *similar situations*. For instance, they reported correlations of 0.76, 0.73, and 0.69, respectively, for ratings of cooperative behavior, self-confidence, and leadership in two similar situations. Anticipating later formulations, they argued that "the psychological meaning of situations for the individual is the determining factor" (p. 9). In this regard, Magnusson and Endler noted that a trait is "a certain aspect of the mediating system's way of selecting, interpreting and treating information as a basis for coherent behavior across situations" (p. 17). As noted above, many studies in this period focused on anxiety, examining the effects of neuroticism in situations that are generally demanding, taxing and stressful. Such situations were seen as diagnostic of neurotic personality tendencies, in a stress-diathesis way, implying that a preexisting latent vulnerability is revealed (the diathesis) in the presence of particular events or contexts (the stress). Signs of rejection, for instance, may result in considerable anxiety for people who have an anxious attachment style (Simpson et al., 1996).

Shoda (2004) has pointed out that the rationale for most such studies was to logically connect personality to situational features that trigger the processing dynamics of persons with differing personality orientations. More recent examples of this perspective are easy to find. For instance, the diagnostic situations that engage the social-cognitive dynamics of individuals who are low on uncertainty orientation are likely to involve contexts that involve lack of control, nontraditional behavioral scripts, and an absence of full information (Sorrentino & Roney, 2000). Individuals with achievement-oriented processing dynamics tend to be more engaged and perform better in competitive contexts, especially with external rewards or performance markers (Barron & Harackiewicz, 2001). And, when opportunities for bolstering grandiose self-concepts are present, narcissists exert more effort toward providing evidence of their superiority, even if doing so may offend others (Morf & Rhodewalt, 2001). Another type of diagnostic situation for narcissists hinges on public versus private settings: Narcissists derogate others who outperform them most in public as compared to private settings (Morf & Rhodewalt, 2001).

Other theorists have developed frameworks that expand the Magnusson and Endler notion of dynamic processes in important ways. Snyder (1981) proposed that rather than being passive participants, individuals may often actively control and shape the type of situations they encounter. Buss (1987) suggested that individuals select environments by approaching or avoiding them, and further, can alter and shape the environment in ways that suit their goals. Similarly, Emmons, Diener, and Larsen (1986) developed two models of "reciprocal interactionism" (Bowers, 1973), a "choice of situation" model, in which individuals select certain situations and avoid others on the basis of underlying needs and dispositions, and a "congruence response" model, in which people experience more positive affect in situations congruent with their personality characteristics, and more negative affect in noncongruent situations.

MISCHEL AND SHODA'S BEHAVIORAL SIGNATURE MODEL

Though interactionist models continue to evolve, they have perhaps been largely integrated into a broader metatheory proposed by Mischel and Shoda (1995). Their cognitive-affective personality system (CAPS), which has had tremendous influence on personality psychology, incorporates a person-by-situation interactionist perspective (Cantor & Kihlstrom, 1987; Endler & Hunt, 1969), as described above, into a more social-cognitive interpretation of the meaning of personality (see also Mendoza-Denton & Ayduk, chapter 18, this volume; Simpson & Winterheld, chapter 20, this volume).

Mischel and Shoda (1995) present impressive evidence that an individual's behavioral signature is typically stable over time if behavior is examined within the context of *specific* categories of situations. They introduced the term *signature* to denote characteristic patterns of "if-then" associations between situations and behavior (see figure 4.2; note that the construal stage in the figure, the second from the left, was added by the current authors). The CAPS model contends that specific features of situations activate subsets of cognitive mediating units, which in turn generate responses to different situations. That is, individuals are seen to have a distinctive behavioral signature or style of adapting to features of their social environment.

Mischel and Shoda suggest that situations be considered in abstract terms, redefining them "to capture their basic psychological features, so that behavior can be predicted across a broad range of contexts that contain the same features" (1995, p. 248). Mischel (2009) regards the framework as a metatheory for building a cumulative, integrated science of persons interacting dynamically with their sociocultural life situations. The metatheory views the person as "a distinctive social-cognitive affective system. It is a system that dynamically interacts with situations and creates *contextualized* thoughts, feelings and behaviors" (Mischel, 2009; p, 286; emphasis ours). Mischel argues forcefully that personality should not be considered in an uncontextualized way; rather, the very definition of a

disposition should comprise stable if-then signatures, where the situation or context is integrally tied to the nature of the person.

The CAPS model distinguishes two subsystems, one a "hot" emotional system, the other a "cool" cognitive system. Balance between them is critical to self-regulatory efforts, including goal-directed delay of gratification (Metcalfe & Mischel, 1999). The hot emotional system is specialized for quick responding and is thus often under direct stimulus control. When 4-year-old children focus on the consummatory features of rewards (e.g., the taste of a cookie), they are more likely to succumb to temptation. The cool system of self-regulation changes the meaning of the objective situation by encoding it in a more cognitive, abstract way that diminishes the power of the external stimulus to control behavior. For instance, the child might consider how the cookie resembles a Frisbee. By focusing on certain selected mental representations and not others, children develop what we think of as "willpower" (Mischel, 2009).

Mischel's self-regulation research is a persuasive example of the logic of the CAPS model (see figure 4.2), and provides a strong argument for including construal as an explicit step in the model. In this delay of gratification example, personality displays itself in the context of an external temptation through the encoding process itself. Thus people are not considered as passive victims of situation forces or the stimuli that are imposed on them, but rather as having control over their environments. They do so both through cognitive strategies for construing and encoding external situations, and subsequently, the goal implementation strategies available in their CAPS system (e.g., Gollwitzer, 1996).

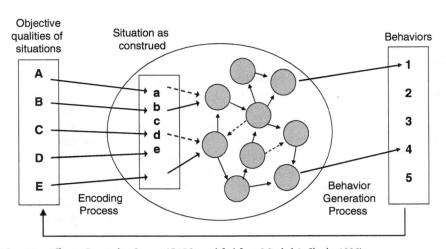

Fig. 4.2 The Cognitive-Affective Personality System (CAPS; modified from Mischel & Shoda, 1995).

Shoda and Mischel's (1996) definition of the situation, the *if* in their "if-then" model, has focused largely on other people's behavior as the context for the actor's behavior. For example, in their famous summer camp study, Mischel and Shoda (1995) videotaped a wide range of children's behavior, with the goal of identifying the "ifs" associated with aggressive behavior by each child—that is, their individual behavioral signatures for aggressive reactions. Most "ifs" or situations were comprised of behavior by others. Some boys reacted aggressively to teasing by peers (coded as, "child challenged by peers"), whereas others reacted negatively to authority figures (coded as "adult warned the child"). This perspective, centering on the situation as behavior enacted by others, seems consistent with many common usages of the term "situation" in social psychology (Ross & Nisbett, 1991). Similarly, Buss (1987) suggests that the displayed "personality of others may compose the central social environment that evokes modal human tendencies" (p. 1219).

Indeed, Mischel (2009) praises Fournier, Moscovich, and Zuroff's (2009) research on the interpersonal circle by commenting that it recognizes "that the most important and salient features of psychological situations are the behaviors of the people with whom the individual interacts" (p. 287). The interpersonal circle framework fits an if-then logic well by positing that a interaction partner's behavior (the if) invites a particular response in others (the then). Fournier et al. posit that the two key dimensions of interpersonal behavior are warm/cold and dominance/submissiveness, gradations of which can be arranged in a circular or circumplex pattern. Evidence suggests that one person's warm behavior pulls for others to reciprocate in kind. Similarly, cold behavior signals others to stay away and remain distant. In contrast, displays of dominance invite its inverse, submissiveness. A large literature supports the notion of behavioral invitations (the ifs) eliciting these particular complementary responses in others (the thens) (Sadler, Ethier, Gunn, Duong, & Woody, 2009; Sadler & Woody, 2003). This work highlights both the theoretical basis and long intellectual history (Leary, 1957) of constructs included in the CAPS model.

Mischel (2009) is less sanguine, however, when Fournier et al. (2009) appear to restrict the meaning of personality traits to aggregated measures or major dimensions without a situated context, such as describing someone as a "warm person." Mischel argues that personality should feature dispositions contextualized by the situations that elicit them, or "interpersonally situated persons" rather than broad, general dispositions.

The CAPS perspective is very compatible with one offered by McAdams and Pals (2006), as part of their "fundamental principles for an integrative science of personality." These authors argue that one critical aspect of personality involves "characteristic adaptations" to help the individual cope effectively with the ever-changing social environment. Such adaptations are more nearly implicated in situationally anchored personality processes and are more closely linked to motivation and cognition than are broad, general traits. McAdams and Pals note that their framework fits Cantor's distinction (1990) between the "having" side of personality—in the sense that people "have" their traits—and the "doing" side, which connects to the contextualized and contingent aspects of personality. McAdams and Pals consider characteristic adaptations as an important aspect of personality less studied than the Big Five, an aspect that relates directly to efforts to link personality to the processes of coping with everyday social problem-solving.

Mischel's (2009) emphasis on others' behavior in the behavioral signature approach is reflected in several research programs. For example, Downey and colleagues' research on rejection sensitivity (RS; Downey & Feldman, 1996; Downey, Freitas, Michaelis, & Khouri, 1998) indicates that people who are high on RS are quick to identify signs of possible rejection in their social environments, resulting in their experiencing a high number of false-positive identifications of rejection or lack of social responsiveness. A second example is Andersen and colleagues' research on transference (e.g., Andersen & Thorpe, 2009). Transference occurs when external social cues (e.g., a person with high standards, who is somewhat critical) trigger, often outside of awareness, a feeling of resemblance to a significant other (e.g., your mother). Once a mental representation of the significant other is activated in memory, cognitive and emotional elements of the self associated with that person are also activated; the self and relational representations are literally entangled. Thus one might feel anxious and immature around a new person who resembles one's judgmental and critical mother. Both programs show how cognitive and emotional elements of the CAPS model work together once the mental machinery has been activated by the appropriate construal.

At times, Mischel (1973, 2009) has focused not on the external stimulus, such as another's behavior, but on another aspect of figure 4.2, the "situation as construed." For example, "If we include the situation as it is perceived by the person, and analyze behavior *in this situational context*, the consistencies that characterize the person would be seen" (Mischel, 2009, p. 284, italics added). The CAPS model proposes a constructionist, dynamic view of the person as "a meaning-maker." Similarly, in Andersen's (e.g., Andersen & Thorpe, 2009) research, the resemblance process, linking external social cues to the activation of a significant other representation, is seldom studied. Instead, research typically focuses on the representation itself, the construal, as the "if" in the if-then sequence. So, "if mother representation is activated, then feel immature" is seen as the behavioral signature. In our view, this elision runs the risk of confusing situations and construals. As noted earlier, it is crucial to directly link construals to the stimulus features that activate them so that the CAPS model does not reside solely in the head. The encoding process itself is as much a part of personality as is the construal-behavior link, as the CAPS model clearly indicates. Mischel's research on delay of gratification and Downey's research on rejection sensitivity are two excellent cases in point.

We see much merit in Mischel's focus on other people's social behavior as a key external feature that triggers construal processes. However, an interesting issue to resolve is the extent to which it is also important to consider the overall context or social situation in which the social behavior of two persons occurs (a central theme in interdependence theory, examined in the next section). Partly, this issue is tied to Mischel's emphasis on the meaning people take from another's behavior. Interdependence theorists contend that the context of the behavior, the roles of the two persons in relation to each other, may be integral in predicting construals and attributions for what is happening. This is all the more true of the scientist's depiction of the nature of the "if" in the person's behavioral signature.

To borrow an example from Mischel and Shoda's (1995) camp study of aggression in young boys, the sequence "Adult warns the child" might actually represent any of several objective situations. For one, the counselor may be giving a command (with possible consequences) in a context in which the child's and adult's interests conflict; the child's aggressive response toward the adult might then be a negative reaction to authority figures. Or is the context one in which the counselor is criticizing the child's aggressive behavior toward another child? This might reflect a child's competitive tendencies with peers. Or finally, is it a context in which the counselor is simply trying to coordinate swimming activities by reminding the boy about relevant norms? An aggressive response might then reflect a lack of conscientiousness in the child, a negative reaction to following camp rules. As a further example, perhaps the boy who receives the warning has violated a rule to wait until later to go swimming. If the boy comes from a difficult background where one couldn't depend on adult promises, a behavioral violation would best be interpreted in a failure-to-delay-gratification context (Metcalfe & Mischel, 1999).

In this situation, we would not understand the child's interpretation of events without knowing more about the broader context in which it occurs. Similarly, scientists need to analyze context to identify the nature of the "if" triggering the behavioral signature. That is, from the simple depiction, "Adult warns the child," one may not be able to determine which of the four possibilities mentioned above is occurring and consequently it would be difficult to draw clear conclusions about the child's personality signature. On the other hand, if the social context is fully specified, it becomes possible to know which personality traits are relevant (and which are not) and therefore to better specify the child's personality signature.

Thus the CAPS model leaves open the issue of whether the situation, the "if," is described sufficiently by another person's actions, or whether the situational context for that behavior is also necessary for identifying the key psychological ingredients. Impressive as the CAPS framework is, if this argument is valid, it requires a theory of situations to create a model that starts by specifying abstract features of external situations and then predicts a priori which elements in the cognitive-affective system will be activated. That is, there would be considerable value in being able to predict how individual differences influence construals of the opportunities or challenges a particular social situation affords by its structure. The behavior of another person in this situation would then truly have a context in which his or her actions could be interpreted. We next turn to interdependence theory to explore how such a top-down theory of situations might provide a theoretical classification of situations and an analysis of the particular cognitive and motivational processes functionally related to the specific problems each situation entails.

INTERDEPENDENCE THEORY

This description of interdependence theory (IT) is adapted from *An Atlas of Interpersonal Situations* by Kelley et al. (2003). This book analyzes twenty of the most prototypical social situations in detail and presents propositions linking each to particular cognitive and goal processes, as well as to individual differences in personality. It expands on the long intellectual tradition of social exchange analysis first presented by Thibaut and Kelley (1959) and later elaborated by Kelley and Thibaut (1978) and Kelley (1979). Some implications of this general theory for social cognitive and personality processes were developed by Holmes (2002).

Generally speaking, IT expands the formula proposed by Lewin (1946), that behavior is a function of the person and the environment. In the context of social interaction, the behavioral interaction (I) that occurs between persons A and B is thought to be a function of both persons' respective goal tendencies in relation to each other *in the particular situation of interdependence* (S) in which the interaction occurs.

By the phrase "particular situation of interdependence," IT refers to the ways in which two persons depend on and influence each other with respect to their potential outcomes from an interaction (hence the term "interdependence"). The theory attempts to identify the kinds of interpersonal dispositions of persons A and B—their attitudes, motives, goals— that are functionally relevant to in each particular type of situation. The type of situation S, together with the relevant dispositions of persons A and B, determine the interaction, I (in symbols, the SABI elements; Holmes, 2000). As this model implies, interdependence theory adopts a person × situation interactionist approach with a strong social-psychological focus on the nature of situations. Each paradigmatic situation is viewed as presenting the two persons with a unique set of problems and opportunities, much as was shown in figure 4.1.

The Person and the Situation

To illustrate how situations are defined in interdependence theory terms, consider the well-known example of "Exchange with Mutual Profit" (also known as the Prisoner's Dilemma). In this type of exchange situation each person has the ability to reward or help the other, or not. If both individuals cooperate and conclude such a reciprocal exchange, they will both profit equally and benefit from "gains in trade" by dividing up a larger pie than is available by any other pair of choices. Such gains in trade are so ubiquitous in everyday social life that evolutionary psychologists have suggested that the rewards of reciprocal cooperation may have made cooperative, prosocial motives as heritable as aggressive, selfish motives (Tooby & Cosmides, 1996; Wilson, Van

Vugt, & O'Gorman, 2008; see also Gangestad, chapter 7, this volume).

However, in these exchange situations each person is tempted to defect from the cooperative exchange and to choose a different option, to be selfish and instead pursue their own interests. This would result in the greatest individual gain and a competitive advantage if the other person acts cooperatively. For example, a husband and wife may both dislike washing the dishes, but if both pitch in, the task is quickly accomplished and they reap the benefits of cooperation. Of course, each would be sorely tempted, if the other started the job, to just let the partner finish the unpleasant task. That way, the dishes are done and the dreaded task is avoided!

A central idea in IT is that because situations vary in the specific problems that they represent, different interpersonal dispositions are relevant to coping with different situations (Rusbult & Van Lange, 1996). Thus the linkages between the situation and person domains are ones of logical relevance or *affordance*. Essentially, interpersonal dispositions reflect people's preferences, or *valuation rules*, among the different interaction possibilities afforded by a particular situation. By distinguishing the valuation rules logically applicable in various situations, researchers obtain a summary of the attitudes, motives, and goals that potentially guide interpersonal behavior in each of them. For instance, the Exchange with Mutual Profit situation provides the opportunity through the choice of a rule for expressing certain dispositions but not others. This situation lets one convey cooperative or prosocial goals, because deciding to help or reward the other would follow valuation rules to "maximize joint profit" or "achieve equality." Alternatively, a person might have a valuation rule that specifies "maximize one's own competitive advantage" or "maximize own outcomes." However, this situation does *not* allow people to express various other possible interpersonal goals, such as being submissive, showing initiative, being loyal or dependable, and so on.

Thus, the situation and person domains exist in close, complementary relation to each other. One way to describe this relation is to say that each disposition can be defined abstractly as a tendency to psychologically transform one situation into another one, or using Lewin's (1946) concept, to "restructure the field." In the current example, a cooperative, agreeable person would be someone who turned this inherently ambiguous (i.e., mixed-motive) situation into a cooperative one by attaching particular value to the cooperative pair solution.

That is, the situation is mixed-motive in that it could be rewarding to either "cooperate for joint gain" or instead, to "look out for oneself." By choosing to cooperate, a person transforms the situation by acting as if cooperation is the rational choice, essentially disregarding the temptation to compete. From this perspective, one can only identify the *person* as a figure against the ground of the *situation*. More generally, it will often be the case that situational ambiguity affords the expression of dispositions that are activated to make sense of the situation (but see the discussion of strong versus weak situations later in this chapter).

Each actor's choice of rules does not occur in a vacuum. The goal person A pursues is likely to depend heavily on expectations about the other's goals and motives (B), especially the extent to which the other is expected to be responsive to one's needs (Reis, Clark, & Holmes, 2004). Indeed, Holmes (2002) has suggested that expectations about the other person's goals are the single-most important and basic consideration in interpersonal relations, one that probably has evolutionary roots. Thus, not only may two partners be behaviorally interdependent, but they will frequently be *rule interdependent* as well, especially in long-term close relationships. That is, one actor's rule choice may be contingent on the rule the other person is expected to choose.

Put another way, the type of person one can "be" is often constrained by the type of person a partner is expected to be: The expression of one's own personality may be contingent on expectations of the other's personality. In Kelley and Stahelski's (1970) pioneering research, cooperative individuals typically held contingent rules for the goal they would pursue (following a cooperative rule) only if they expected the other person to reciprocate. Faced with someone they believed had a competitive goal, they could not "be themselves" and instead engaged in more competitive behaviors. Competitive individuals, in contrast, rather uniformly expected others to be self-concerned and to look out for themselves. Their typical response was to react in kind to the *expected* competitive behavior of the other person, whether true or not. Thus responses are controlled both by the context depicted in this social dilemma, and inferences about the nature of the other person, a theme reminiscent of the CAPS framework (Mischel, 2009), discussed earlier.

A Taxonomy of Situations
The book *An Atlas of Interpersonal Situations* (Kelley et al., 2003) presents a systematic taxonomy of situations. Interdependence theory provides a top-down, abstract conceptual analysis of the fundamental dimensions of situations, relevant to the regulation and coordination of social behavior. The analysis is considered abstract because it is based on the interrelation of each person's goals and outcomes, rather than the persons themselves (e.g., their dispositions or physical features). This analysis can be highly complex. There is, however, an ironic difference between the complexity of IT and the intuitive ease with which people recognize interpersonal situations in everyday life and adjust their behavior accordingly (Kelley, 1997). For example, most of us readily appreciate that it is easier to trust someone with whom we share interests than to trust someone whose interests compete with our own. Similarly, most people worry more about offending others who hold power over them than they worry about offending subordinates. The significance of articulating abstract patterns of interdependence is in allowing researchers to describe the dimensions that underlie the organization of social life and the coordination of goal-directed activity.

These structural considerations describing the relation of the outcomes of two entities can be used to explore the dynamics of a dyad, but also can serve as a template for understanding the interdependence relation of groups and even organizations (see Parks, chapter 21, this volume, and Day & Schleicher, chapter 28, this volume). Considering the above examples of situational features, for instance, two organizations might be in a relationship where they primarily wish to coordinate their shared interests in a manufacturing supply line. Or instead, they might be competing for business or a scarce resource. Similarly, two groups might see themselves as having correspondent interests because of a shared membership in a large social network, as in the Sherif (1966) camp study on superordinate goals. In contrast, if the groups saw themselves as being differentiated as ingroup and outgroup, it is likely that they would see their goals as conflicting and be suspicious of the other group's motives. (This issue of interdependence theory as a template for considering levels of analysis other than dyads is discussed further in a later section).

It is beyond the purpose of this chapter to review IT. Nevertheless, it will be useful to briefly describe a few of its basic properties, and to illustrate their relevance for understanding social situations. IT characterizes social situations in terms of four dimensions of outcome interdependence that can be logically deduced from decisions in social dilemmas:

- The extent to which an individual's outcomes depend on the actions of the other person;
- The extent to which individuals have mutual power over each other's outcomes or whether power is asymmetric and one person is more dependent on the other's good will;
- The extent to which one person's outcomes correspond or conflict with the other's; and
- The extent to which partners must coordinate their activities to produce satisfactory outcomes from shared goals, or whether the goals are only partly shared and each one's actions in an exchange partly determine the other's outcomes.

Interdependence Theory also considers two additional elements of situations:

- Temporal structure: Whether the situation involves interaction over the longer term; and
- Information certainty: Whether partners have the information needed to make good decisions, or whether substantial uncertainty exists about the future.

To illustrate the fundamental importance of these dimensions to social psychology, a few brief examples of each dimension follow. These examples suggest that social psychology has long understood (though often more intuitively than explicitly) that these dimensions are important and that in everyday life people discriminate among them naturally and fluidly. For a more extended discussion and further examples, see Reis (2008). The dimensions are also logically central to understanding the dynamics of personality. Given the interdependence logic that each dimension of situations affords the expression of particular motives and adaptations, Holmes and Cameron (2005) have presented a meta-analytic framework linking the six dimensions to individual differences on the Big Five and attachment avoidance. In a sense, the synergy between situations and personality is most apparent when theorists explicitly consider in this way the relevance of personality features to the particular affordances of situations.

Outcome Interdependence

When outcome interdependence is low, partners exert little or no influence on each other's outcomes. When outcome interdependence is high, each person's outcomes are strongly influenced by the other's

actions. All other things being equal, when outcome interdependence is high, people think and act in ways that facilitate closeness and dependence. For instance, in such situations, people make more generous attributions for performance (Sedikides, Campbell, Reeder, & Elliot, 1998); make more individuated, less stereotypical judgments (Fiske, 1993); attend more and are more attracted to the other (Berscheid, Graziano, Monson, & Dermer, 1976); identify more closely with the other (Rabbie, Schot, & Visser, 1989); and engage in more prosocial actions toward the other person (Batson, 1998). Holmes and Cameron (2005) describe degree of interdependence as the spur to individual differences on the dimension of avoidance of attachment as compared to comfort with closeness and dependence.

Mutuality of Outcome Interdependence

When power in a dyad is unequal, the more dependent person, not surprisingly, attends more closely to the power holder's behavior (Berscheid et al., 1976); has better memory for the other's characteristics and forms more complex, nonstereotypic impressions (Dépret & Fiske, 1993); engages in more perspective-taking (Tjosvold & Sagaria, 1978); plays a lesser role in decision-making in close relationships (Safilios-Rothschild, 1976); and works harder at favorable self-presentation (Jones, Gergen, & Jones, 1963). On the other hand, asymmetric interdependence provides a diagnostic opportunity for the more powerful person to demonstrate empathic concern and altruism, by acting against his or her self-interest (Batson, 1998; Holmes, 1981). It also is likely to activate rejection concerns in people with anxious attachment who worry about the extent to which they will be valued and their needs responded to when they are dependent on others (Holmes & Cameron, 2005; Overall & Sibley, 2008).

Outcome Correspondence

The correspondence of two persons' outcomes reflects the extent to which their personal interests covary or conflict. Much research shows that high correspondence promotes cooperative processes and low correspondence competitive ones (Deutsch's, 1985, "crude law"). Further, individuals with a competitive personality are more inclined to interpret situations as competitive, partly to avoid being exploited, while cooperative people are more inclined to focus on opportunities to work together (Miller & Holmes, 1975). Corresponding interests not only foster cooperation but are associated with higher levels of trust (Simpson, 2007) and better social relations between partners (Sherif, 1966). Within-group cooperation is often fostered by between-group competition, as in the classic Sherif (1966) "Robbers Cave" study. That is, to achieve better outcomes in the face of outgroup competition, group members work together more cooperatively (Wildschut, Insko, & Gaertner, 2002).

In close relationships, partners typically presume reasonable accommodations to the other's preferences in the "mixed motive" aspects of exchange (competitive temptations and cooperative opportunities). Critically, then, conflict of interest situations put a premium on the other's goodwill, thereby revealing the partner's willingness to be responsive when it is costly. Because conflictual situations are diagnostic in this way (Holmes, 1981; Simpson, 2007), they afford the opportunity for people who lack of confidence or trust in their partner's caring to bring their concerns to the forefront. For example, people with an anxious attachment style or low self-esteem may react pessimistically in high-conflict situations, assuming (or preparing for) the worst in their partners' response (Simpson et al., 1996; Murray et al., 2003).

Basis of Interdependence

In *exchange situations*, each partner has meaningful control over the other's outcomes. This gives rise to the development of so-called moral norms (Turiel, 1983)—norms about responsibility, caregiving, and not hurting others—as well as to norms about reciprocity and equity over time and instances ("you benefit me now, I'll benefit you later") (e.g., Clark & Mills, 1979; Walster, Walster, & Berscheid, 1978). Because exchange situations involve fate control (absolute control over the other's outcomes) but confer advantage to those who can conceal their violations of fairness, they give rise to such phenomena as deception, freeloading (Kerr & Bruun, 1983), cheating in social dilemmas (Messick & Brewer, 1983), and suspicion (Holmes & Rempel, 1989). Tooby and Cosmides (1996) have suggested that such exchange dilemmas are so ubiquitous, and cheating so crucial to detect, that they may provide the evolved basis for mental mechanisms associated with trust and suspicion.

Coordination situations, on the other hand, require that partners synchronize behavior to achieve mutually desirable outcomes. Berscheid and Regan (2004) suggest that such situations may be very common, though they have received little empirical

attention. Coordination situations put a premium on processes such as communication and leadership, and other abilities that facilitate carrying out tasks with others. Indeed, coordination situations can be linked to individual differences in assertiveness and submissiveness (Holmes & Cameron, 2005). In an influential paper, Steiner (1972) distinguished two forms of process loss that occur in work groups, one concerned with motivational deficits, the other concerned with poor organization and deployment of resources. These problems reflect dysfunctional responses to exchange and coordination situations, respectively. More personal examples of coordination situations include responsive caregiving and sexual interaction.

Temporal Structure

Whereas many situations are one-time occurrences whose implications essentially end the moment behavior has been completed, others are extended in time. Within ongoing relationships, such interactions allow for the emergence and application of relationship-specific norms. For example, in multiple-trial games partners are more likely to develop cooperative norms to stabilize outcomes and to respond generously to their partners' noncooperative errors compared to single-trial games (Van Lange, Ouwerkerk, & Tazelaar, 2002). Similarly, in communal relationships, where the norm is to respond to another's needs as they occur, reciprocity may be evident only over time (e.g., Clark & Mills, 1979). Time-extended situations also allow persons to forego short-term rewards in anticipation of long-term gains. For example, more committed partners in close relationships, who tend to subscribe to communal norms, are more likely to make personal sacrifices or to respond prosocially by accommodating their partner's relationship-damaging actions (Rusbult, Olsen, Davis, & Hannon, 2001). Of course, sometimes these investments create social traps—circumstances in which people persist even as their outcomes deteriorate (e.g., Rubin & Brockner, 1975).

Time-extended sequences are intrinsic to delay-of-gratification situations, as mentioned earlier. Self-control in such situations is a self-regulatory strategy in which the less desirable of two available outcomes is chosen in anticipation of a later, larger reward (Mischel, Cantor, & Feldman, 1996). Further, the "strength model" of regulatory control posits that people's ability to accept poorer short-term outcomes in anticipation of greater long-term outcomes varies much as a muscle does—that is, willpower is depleted as a function of exertion and strengthened as a function of rest and training (Baumeister, Vohs & Tice, 2007). The ability to delay gratification depends on various factors, including dispositional ones (e.g., control strategies; Carver & Scheier, 1981), developmental considerations (Mischel & Mischel, 1983), and still others based on trust (i.e., expectations) that interaction partners will, over the long haul, "do the right thing" (e.g., Holmes & Rempel, 1989). Holmes and Cameron (2005) tie temporal structure to individual differences involving dependability and loyalty versus unreliability, that is, to conscientiousness.

Information Certainty

Situations differ in the availability and clarity of information relevant to behavioral choices. For example, uncertainty about future outcomes (i.e., risk) creates a situation in which individuals must choose between loss-avoidance or gain-seeking. Various situational (e.g., framing; Higgins, 1998; Kahneman & Tversky, 1984) and dispositional factors (e.g., optimism, need for closure, and uncertainty orientation; Kruglanski & Webster, 1996; Scheier & Carver, 1993; Sorrentino, Holmes, Hanna, & Sharp, 1995) influence this preference. Uncertainty is the essence of negotiations, in that each party is not fully aware of the other's contingencies and limits. Indeed, negotiators go to great lengths to conceal their "bottom line." Attributions associated with efforts to remove uncertainty about the other party's strategies tend to color the negotiation process (Pruitt & Carnevale, 1993). In everyday interaction, people try to overcome uncertainty "by going beyond the evidence" and developing a sense of trust. That is, when people must depend on each other for important outcomes but cannot know with certainty how the other will behave, repeated experiences of a responsive and dependable other often results in confidence in that person's good will (Holmes & Rempel, 1989; Simpson, 2007).

In summary, interdependence theory has expanded our understanding of the "P" and the "S" in both the P × S and CAPS frameworks. The situation, or S, refers to the particular pattern of outcome dependence faced by two persons in a social interaction, that is, how their respective goals and preferences fit with each other. The situation provides each person, or "P," with opportunities to act in certain ways and pursue certain goals, but not others. Thus the person-situation link is one of affordances to enact particular dispositions or preferences. The other person, the interaction partner, is not seen as the situation itself but rather is part of the "if" in the

Mischel CAPS framework, *along with* the situational context. Thus the "if" involves both the exchange situation context and the expected behavior of the other person in that situation, the "total environment" or life space that the person experiences, in Lewinian (1946) terminology. In short, IT both expands on the meaning of the concept of situation and describes a logical process linking the person to the social context or circumstances.

Final Issues
Strong Versus Weak Situations

At first glance, some of the material reviewed earlier in this chapter may remind readers of the distinction between so-called "strong" and "weak" situations, first suggested by sociological role theorists (e.g., Alexander & Knight, 1971), later codified by Mischel (1977), and then elaborated by Ickes (1982) and Snyder and Ickes (1985). These authors argued that situational factors will cause behavior to the extent that situations are "strong"—that is, to the extent that they present salient, unambiguous, and compelling cues about appropriate behavior in a relatively structured setting. Personality variables, in contrast, should be more influential in "weak" situations—that is, when situations are unstructured, offer little or no incentives, and have few or ambiguous cues to guide behavior. For example, in one study, reports of behavior in high constraint situations (e.g., a job interview) showed less behavioral variability than in low constraint situations (e.g., sitting in a park; Schutte, Kenrick, & Sadalla, 1985). Following this logic, Ickes (1982) developed the Unstructured Interaction Paradigm, in which participants are unobtrusively videotaped sitting on a couch, with nothing to do except wait for an experiment to begin, so that individual differences would be maximally influential. Over the years, this distinction has been accepted widely, and used for several purposes, notably to explain why the potency of situational and personality variables varies from one study to another.

Recently, Cooper and Withey (2009) have challenged this conclusion, asserting that its "transformation from hypothesis to dogma is based more on the plausibility of the hypothesis and sheer repetition than on any empirical evidence" (p. 64). Their argument derives directly from Mischel's four criteria for characterizing situational strength, namely whether or not:

• the situation would be construed similarly by most people;
• the situation induces uniform expectations regarding appropriate responses;

• the situation provides adequate incentives for the appropriate response;
• all participants possess the relevant skills for responding.

Cooper and Withey maintained that few studies have directly manipulated these four factors. Further, they concluded that among those that had and also among more indirect investigations, none had successfully demonstrated moderation of personality effect sizes as a function of situational strength. Thus, in their view, although the hypothesis may be correct, it has not yet been empirically validated.

In principle, we concur both with the plausibility of the strong situation hypothesis and with Cooper and Withey's proposal that endorsement be withheld pending empirical confirmation. At the same time, Kelley et al. (2003) describe how the concept of affordance suggests a broader conceptualization. That is, as reviewed earlier in this chapter, every situation makes possible the expression of certain dispositional variables and obviates others. (For example, situations involving conflicts of interest afford the expression of traits like generosity and concern for the well-being of others, which cannot be clearly displayed when one's own and another's interests correspond.) Situations afford the expression of particular traits if, among the various available behavioral options, there is a distinctive way in which that trait can be freely displayed by the individual. Thus, the defining characteristic of weakly structured situations (such as in the Ickes paradigm) may be that they afford opportunities for the expression of multiple traits—for example, gregariousness, awkwardness, openness, bookishness, and so on—rather than affording nothing at all.

If this reasoning is correct, it suggests that situational strength may simply be one of several (and perhaps many) situational variables that determines which dispositional variables are afforded in a given context. In turn, this idea suggests that we should be able to identify and evaluate the role of these variables in moderating the degree of association between personality and behavior (see Snyder & Ickes, 1985, for a similar suggestion). This logic points out, once again, that the study of situational factors is inextricably (and not merely additively) linked with the study of personality variables, as Lewin first suggested.

Which Aspects of Situations Should We Study?

If situations and their influence on behavior define social psychology's traditional home territory, one might further ask, which aspects of situations should social psychologists study? Following the Lewinian approach would suggest that any and all conditions and circumstances external to the individual would be relevant (a rather inclusive category, to say the least). Even a more limited definition, for example that social psychologists study those features of situations that give rise to basic psychological processes (Mischel & Shoda, 1995) may be overly broad. Instead, and consistent with nearly every formal definition of the field,[3] we believe that the most relevant situations for social psychology ought to involve the *social* context of behavior. This suggestion reflects G. Allport's classic definition of the field, "Social psychologists regard their discipline as an attempt to understand and explain how the thought, feeling, and behavior of individuals are influenced by the actual, imagined, or implied presence of *other human beings*" (1954, p. 5; italics added).

Although the models of situations presented in this chapter are readily adapted to most any kind of situation, the special (and, at least to us, sufficiently important) province of social psychology is social situations (Kelley, 2000). Abundant evidence demonstrates that social contexts—whom one is with or thinking about, one's history with this and similar persons and groups in related settings, and what one is trying to accomplish with this person or group—exert potent influence on behavior. It should be clear that social contexts matter across many traditional domains of social-psychological inquiry. For example, many important goals involve other people, either as the target of those goals (e.g., to influence the other in some way), or as an agent for assisting personal goal attainment (e.g., recruiting help). Because most human activity involves coordinating one's actions with the actions of others, success or failure in those processes of coordination are a principal determinant of achievement, productivity, and well-being (Bugental, 2000; Kelley et al., 2003). Much of everyday cognition is concerned with the social world (Higgins, 2000) and "emotions are brought into play most often by the actions of others, and, once aroused, emotions influence the course of interpersonal transactions" (Ekman & Davidson, 1994, p. 139). The ability to relate successfully to others is a principal determinant of success in nearly all domains of human activity and across all stages of the life cycle (Hartup & Stevens, 1997). Reflecting these and more reasons, evolutionary theorists increasingly acknowledge that social life provided the principal mechanisms for human adaptation, and that many of the human mind's most important processes evolved for the purposes of regulating social interactions and relationships (e.g., Buss & Kenrick, 1998; Cosmides & Tooby, 1992). In short, there is ample reason to focus our scientific mission on the social aspects of situations.

Smith and Semin (2004, 2007) offer a similar rationale for emphasizing social contexts in their model of socially situated cognition. Their analysis brings together two influential lines of research, that of situated cognition—that cognition emerges from the interaction of agents and their environment, rather than residing solely in the agent's mind—and of social cognition. They propose that social-cognitive processes "constitute an adaptive regulatory process that ultimately serves survival needs" (2004, p. 56)—that is, social cognition is the natural vehicle for the individual's attempts to interact effectively with the environment. Social cognition involves a dynamic process of continuous reciprocal influence between the self and the *social* environment. Because *social* coordination has been central to adaptive action throughout the evolutionary past, our species has evolved numerous mechanisms for solving the tasks of living, working, and reproducing with others (for example, but not limited to, empathy, synchrony, language, attachment, emotion regulation, face recognition, social categorization, love, sexual attraction, warmth and affection, affiliation and loneliness, trust, coping with stress, helping, cooperation, competition, dominance, and submission).

Because most interaction takes place with others with whom the actor has an ongoing association, emphasis on the social dimensions of situations leads naturally to consideration of relationship effects. Researchers increasingly recognize that the relationship context of behavior may moderate the expression of many important social psychological principles (see Reis, 2010a; Reis, Collins, & Berscheid, 2000, for reviews) but less well recognized is the idea that relationship effects may be understood as situation effects. That is, others who are present in a situation (either physically or mentally) play an often substantial role in determining which cognitions, affects, and goals are activated (Chen, Boucher, & Tapias, 2006; Fitzsimmons, 2006). (For example, a given request for help by a stranger is likely to activate different expectations, feelings, and goals than the same request by one's young child.) Furthermore, as reviewed earlier, the behavioral strategies that people enact to pursue their goals often depend on what they believe their partners will do, and how these expected actions are best coordinated with their own actions. Of course, much of this occurs outside of awareness (Fishbach & Ferguson, 2007), but the point is that specific "if-then" sequences activated in a given situation depend not only on the impersonal properties of that situation but also on the nature of ongoing relationships with relevant others. In other words, the operational definition of situations should consider not only what is going on at a given moment but also which persons are involved and the nature of their relationship. We refer readers interested in learning more about how relationship-specific dispositions fit into the situational affordance model to Holmes (2002) and to Reis, Capobianco, and Tsai (2002).

Beyond Dyads: Extending These Models to Groups, Organizations, and Cultures

Many of the illustrations used in this chapter focus on dyadic interactions, examining various ways in which the other person is an important feature of the situation. Situations can also encompass larger social entities, such as groups, organizations, and cultures. How would the various approaches reviewed in this chapter represent these larger social units?

At the simplest level, groups by definition have at least some (and often much) coherence in terms of their membership and ability to act as a unit, so that they may serve as a relatively unitary "other" for the individual in much the same way as another person does in the case of dyadic interaction. Individuals often act in ways that represent their groups or view individual group members as representations of the target group (Wildschut, Pinter, Vevea, Insko, & Schopler, 2003). For example, a university sending an offer of admission to a high-school senior affords certain outcomes, just as a dinner invitation from a casual acquaintance does. Groups differ in entativity, namely the extent to which they are perceived as coherent units (Lickel et al., 2000), which has implications for how they are responded to, but even a group relatively low in entativity can serve as the source of situational cues. Thus, in S × P models, the source of the S may be another person, some larger social entity, or, for that matter, something impersonal. (Of course, this generality again raises questions about the need for a taxonomy of situations, as discussed earlier.)

At a somewhat deeper level, both the CAPS model and IT allow for the influence of larger social groupings. In CAPS, situations refer to any features of the external environment (considered in abstract terms) that activate cognitive mediating units, which can readily apply to groups, organizations, or institutions. For example, in an impressive series of studies, Tyler (1990) has shown how procedures used by legal and governmental institutions affect perceived fairness, and in turn, behavior in legal settings. As for IT, the original presentation of this theory, *The Social Psychology of Groups*, proposed that the principles of interdependence in larger groups "should be derived, insofar as possible, from the concepts and theory developed to this point for dyads" (Thibaut & Kelley, 1959, p. 191). Thus, although analyses of situations involving larger groups add complexities—for example, the possibility of coalition formation—they retain the basic principle that the nature and structure of members' interdependence with respect to outcomes shapes possibilities for interaction.

Our analysis of situations also has implications for understanding the impact of culture on social behavior. Researchers who study culture often argue that the same objective situations may be construed differently in different cultures. For example, in a "culture of honor," an affront to personal or family honor is more likely to be seen as justifying a violent response than outside such cultures (Nisbett & Cohen, 1996). It is commonly stated, then, that situations have little or no objective meaning outside of the meaning that culture provides.

Many studies have documented differences in situation construal across diverse cultures (see also Adams, chapter 8, this volume). Rather than contradicting our insistence that situations have objective properties, however, these studies support the conceptual utility of distinguishing appraisals from the description of the objective properties of situations. How else could one determine that appraisal accounts for the difference? For example, in IT, culture-based learning through socialization and experience contributes to an individual's choices about which behavioral options to enact among the possibilities afforded by the objective properties of a situation. Kelley et al. (1970) demonstrated that competitive choices in bargaining games were seen as powerful by Americans but selfish and unfair by Europeans. In a similar vein, to individuals from a collective culture, the most salient aspect of a social influence attempt ("Please conform to the family's values") may be the opportunity to display harmony with one's group, whereas to individuals from an individualistic culture, the same request may highlight the opportunity to demonstrate autonomy (Iyengar & Lepper, 1999). The abstract structure of the objective situation (i.e., person with moderate amounts of outcome control requests compliance) is the same but the response activated for that individual differs. Culture-based responses are typically well learned and automatic.

Another way in which culture influences behavior is by making certain situations more or less common. For example, in collectivist cultures, in which persons are more likely to depend on the group for satisfaction of basic needs, situations involving high levels of interdependence and corresponding interests tend to be more common than in individualist cultures, where individuals are more apt to find themselves in situations requiring independent pursuit of outcomes (Markus & Kitayama, 1991).

Conclusion: The Future of the "Power of the Situation"

The phrase "the power of the situation" has become ubiquitous among social psychologists, rivaling use of the broad concept of "personality" among personality psychologists. In particular studies, focus on these two main effects may be appropriate, but at a broader theoretical level, as we have argued, they fall short of capturing the complexity required of a mature psychological science. Instead, the dynamic relation between the person and the situation is best captured by models that consider situations as *affordances*. Situations are best described in term of the opportunities they present, or the problems they pose for people, making certain motivations and goals relevant in that context and rendering others irrelevant. Framed from the personality side of things, particular values, goals, and dispositions can only achieve behavioral expression in certain contexts, not others.

If nothing else, then, it should be apparent that better understanding of situations has as much to offer to personality psychologists as it does to social psychologists. "A person cannot exist outside of a situation" (Funder, 2006, p. 32) and situations have no meaning without persons acting in them. More fully developed models of situations will allow personality psychologists to describe and explain variability in behavior from one person to another. In parallel, taking personality into account will allow social psychology to describe and explain how humans interpret and respond to the features of their environment. Perhaps it is finally time to do away with separate names for social and personality psychology, and instead to speak of a truly integrated model of persons acting within contexts.

The fundamentally symbiotic relation we describe between situation and personality has been captured in various models, including the Mischel and Shoda (1995) CAPS model, reviewed earlier. In our view, this latter model best summarizes the dynamics linking situations and persons when it depicts aspects of the objective environment that activate particular construals for a person (see figure 4.2), rather than focusing on social perceptions as the starting point. That is, when theorists working within the CAPS framework focus on the "key psychological ingredients" for a person, bypassing the issue of why and how certain features of an external situation trigger such construals for a person, they miss an important opportunity to elucidate one of the critical legs in the "personality triad" (Funder, 2006): How situations affect behavior. Indeed, appraisals of environmental or social features are so central to what constitutes personality, not to mention other individual differences such as motives, goals, and attitudes, that exploration of this link appears crucial for sophisticated models of predicting and understanding behavior. Similarly, the much-proclaimed "power of situations as construed" in social-psychological research and theory has encouraged some to start and end their analysis inside the person's head, and is subject to the same criticisms. As a result, and at considerable divergence from what we suspect Lewin would have hoped for, this perspective has resulted in a dearth of studies predicting behavioral expression (Holmes & Cavallo, 2010). Our perspective does not deny the importance of construal, but rather makes it part of what needs to be fleshed out theoretically and empirically. Construal of situations, in other words, rather than being an assumption becomes a focal point for research.

What progress has been made in identifying and categorizing the features of situations that might potentially activate the "psychological critical ingredients" of behavior, on theoretical grounds? Existing attempts at describing environmental features, reviewed earlier in this chapter, have been helpful in developing the logic of a more dynamic P × S interactive framework. On the other hand, as discussed earlier, most of those attempts were atheoretical and have yet to yield models adopted by the field. Nevertheless, the CAPS model, especially with its focus on the social behavior of others as the "situation," has the potential to interface effectively with such work (as well as other comparable approaches, such as circumplex theory; e.g., Sadler & Woody, 2003). The interdependence theory

perspective goes a step further and distinguishes the other person from the situational context itself, that is, the structure of interdependence that interacting people face. The added contribution of this framework is that an actor has a context available for appraising another person's behavior, so that construals of the other have a potential basis in a theoretically derived configuration of influences that help to "make sense" of the situation.

Theoretical developments in the past decade have thus made noticeable progress in conceptualizing the notion of the "situation." In doing so, they have largely abandoned perspectives that conceptualize the situation apart from the person. In a very real sense, then, to speak of "the power of the situation" absent of the person is to preclude identifying the causal processes that give situations their power. The logic of affordance demands that social and personality psychology be viewed as parts of the same puzzle, neither whole without the other.

Acknowledgments

We thank Peter Caprariello, David De Jong, and Michael Maniaci for helpful comments on an earlier draft of this chapter.

Notes

[1] But see Rentfrow, Gosling, and Potter (2008) for a novel application.

[2] The top-down versus bottom-up distinction is also evident in personality research. For example Cattell developed models of personality from the factors that emerged from analyses of large sets of items. Eysenck, on the other hand, wrote items to represent factors developed from theory.

[3] Nearly every contemporary social psychology textbook uses a variation of this definition.

References

Alexander, C. N., Jr., & Knight, G. W. (1971). Situated identities and social psychological experimentation. *Sociometry, 34*, 65-82.

Allport, F. H. (1924). *Social psychology*. Boston, MA: Houghton Mifflin.

Allport, G. W. (1954). The historical background of modern social psychology. In G. Lindzey (Ed.), *Handbook of social psychology* (Vol. 1, pp. 3–56). Reading, MA: Addison-Wesley.

Alston, W. P. (1975). Traits, consistency, and conceptual alternatives for personality theory. *Journal for the Theory of Social Behavior, 5*, 17–48.

Andersen, S., & Thorpe, J. (2009). An if-then theory of personality: Significant others and the relational self. *Journal of Research in Personality, 43*, 163–170.

Argyle, M., Furnham, A. & Graham, J. A. (1981). *Social situations*. Cambridge, UK: Cambridge University Press.

Asch, S. E. (1952). *Social Psychology*. New York: Prentice Hall.

Asch, S. E. (1956). *Studies of independence and conformity: A minority of one against a unanimous majority.* Psychological Monographs, 70, no. 9 (whole no. 416). Washington, DC: American Psychological Association.

Atran, S. (1990). Cognitive foundations of natural history: Towards an anthropology of science. New York: Cambridge University Press.

Barker, R. G., & Wright, H. F. (1954). *Midwest and its children: The psychological ecology of an American town.* New York: Row, Peterson and Company.

Barker, R. G. (1968). *Ecological psychology: Concepts and methods for studying the environment of human behavior.* Stanford, CA: Stanford University Press.

Baron, R. M., & Boudreau, L. A. (1987). An ecological perspective on integrating personality and social psychology. *Journal of Personality and Social Psychology, 53,* 1222-1228.

Barron, K., & Harackiewicz, J. (2001). Achievement goals and optimal motivation: Testing multiple goal models. *Journal of Personality and Social Psychology, 80,* 706–722.

Batson, C. D. (1998). Altruism and prosocial behavior. In D. Gilbert, S. T. Fiske, & G. Lindzey, (Eds.), *The handbook of social psychology* (4th ed., Vols. 1 & 2, pp. 282–316). New York: McGraw-Hill.

Baumeister, R. F., Vohs, K. D., & Tice, D. M. (2007). The strength model of self-control. *Current Directions in Psychological Science, 16,* 396–403.

Bem, D. J., & Allen, A. (1974). On predicting some of the people some of the time: The search for cross-situational consistencies in behavior. *Psychological Review, 81,* 506–520.

Bem, D. J., & Funder, D. C. (1978). Predicting more of the people more of the time: Assessing the personality of situations. *Psychological Review, 85,* 485–501.

Berscheid, E., Graziano, W., Monson, T., & Dermer, M. (1976). Outcome dependency: Attention, attribution, and attraction. *Journal of Personality and Social Psychology, 34,* 978–989.

Berscheid, E., & Regan, P. C. (2004). *The psychology of interpersonal relationships.* Upper Saddle River, NJ: Prentice Hall.

Bowers, K. (1973). Situationism in psychology. *Psychological Review, 17,* 307–336.

Brewer, M.B. (2000). Research design and issues of validity. In H. T. Reis & C. M. Judd (Eds.), *Handbook of research methods in social psychology* (pp. 3–16). New York: Cambridge University Press.

Brewer, M.B. (2003). Optimal distinctiveness, social identity, and the self. In M. Leary & J. Tangney (Eds.), *Handbook of self and identity* (pp. 480–491). New York: Guilford.

Bugental, D. B. (2000). Acquisition of the algorithms of social life: A domain-based approach. *Psychological Bulletin, 126,* 187–219.

Buss, D. (1987). Selection, evocation, and manipulation. *Journal of Personality and Social Psychology, 53,* 1214–1221.

Buss, D. M., & Kenrick, D. T. (1998). Evolutionary social psychology. In D. Gilbert & S. Fiske (Eds.), *The handbook of social psychology,* (4th ed., Vol. 2, pp. 982–1026). Boston: McGraw-Hill.

Cantor, N., & Kihlstrom, J. (1987). *Personality and social intelligence.* Englewood Cliffs, NJ: Prentice Hall.

Cantor, N. (1990). From thought to behavior: "Having" and "doing" in the study of personality and cognition. *American Psychologist, 45,* 735–750.

Cantor, N., Mischel, W., & Schwartz, J. C. (1982). A prototype analysis of psychological situations. *Cognitive Psychology, 14,* 45–77.

Carnahan, T., & McFarland, S. (2007). Revisiting the Stanford prison experiment: Could participant self-selection have led to the cruelty? *Personality and Social Psychology Bulletin, 33,* 603–614.

Carver, C. S., & Scheier, M. F. (1981). *Attention and self-regulation: A control-theory approach to human behavior.* New York: Springer.

Chen, S., Boucher, H. C., & Tapias, M. P. (2006). The relational self revealed: Integrative conceptualization and implications for interpersonal life. *Psychological Bulletin, 132,* 151–179.

Clark, M. S., & Mills, J. (1979). Interpersonal attraction in exchange and communal relationships. *Journal of Personality and Social Psychology, 37,* 12–24.

Cooper, W. H., & Withey, M. J. (2009). The strong situation hypothesis. *Personality and Social Psychology Review, 13,* 62–72.

Cosmides, L., & Tooby, J. (1992). Cognitive adaptations for social exchange. In J. H. Barkow, L. Cosmides, & J. Tooby (Eds.), *The adapted mind: Evolutionary psychology and the generation of culture* (pp. 163–228). New York: Oxford University Press.

Deci, E. L., & Ryan, R. M. (1980). The empirical exploration of intrinsic motivational processes. In L. Berkowitz (Ed.), *Advances in experimental social psychology* (pp. 39–80). New York: Academic Press.

Deci, E. L., & Ryan, R. M. (1987). The support of autonomy and the control of behavior. *Journal of Personality and Social Psychology, 53,* 1024–1037.

Dépret, E., & Fiske, S. T. (1993). Social cognition and power: Some cognitive consequences of social structure as a source of control deprivation. In G. Weary, F. Oleicher, & R. Marsh (Eds.), *Control motivation and social cognition* (pp. 176–202). New York: Springer-Verlag.

Deutsch, M. (1954). Field theory in social psychology. In G. Lindzey (Ed.), *The handbook of social psychology: Theory and method* (1st ed., Vol. 1, pp. 181–222). Reading, MA: Addison-Wesley.

Deutsch, M. (1985). *Distributive justice.* New Haven, CT: Yale University Press.

Dewey, J. (1922). *Human nature and conduct: An introduction to social psychology.* New York: Holt.

Downey, G., & Feldman, S. I. (1996). Implications of rejection sensitivity for intimate relationships. *Journal of Personality and Social Psychology, 70,* 1327–1341.

Downey, G., Freitas, A. L., Michaelis, B., & Khouri, H. (1998). The self-fulfilling prophecy in close relationships: Rejection sensitivity and rejection by romantic partners. *Journal of Personality and Social Psychology, 75,* 545–560.

Edwards, J. A., & Templeton, A. (2005). The structure of perceived qualities of situations. *European Journal of Social Psychology, 35,* 705–723.

Ekman, P., & Davidson, R. J. (1994). Afterword: How is evidence of universals in antecedents of emotion explained? In P. Ekman & R. J. Davidson (Eds.), *The nature of emotion: Fundamental questions* (pp. 176–177). New York: Oxford University Press.

Elliot A. J., & McGregor, H. A. (2001). A 2 x 2 achievement goal framework. *Journal of Personality and Social Psychology, 80,* 501–519.

Emmons, R., Diener, E., & Larsen, R. (1986). Choice and avoidance of everyday situations and affect congruence: Two models of reciprocal interactionism. *Journal of Personality and Social Psychology, 51,* 815–826.

Endler, N., & Hunt, J. (1969). Generalizability of contributions from sources of variance in the S-R inventories of anxiousness. *Journal of Personality, 37,* 1–24.

Eysenck, H.J. (1981). *A model for personality*. New York: Springer-Verlag.

Fishbach, A., & Ferguson, M. J. (2007). The goal construct in social psychology. In A. W. Kruglanski & E. T. Higgins (Eds.), *Social psychology: Handbook of basic principles* (pp. 490–515). New York: Guilford.

Fiske, A. P. (1993). Social errors in four cultures: Evidence about the elementary forms of social relations. *Journal of Cross-Cultural Psychology, 24*, 67–94.

Fitzsimons, G. M. (2006). Pursuing goals and perceiving others: A self-regulatory perspective on interpersonal relationships. In K. D. Vohs & E. J. Finkel (Eds.), *Intrapersonal and interpersonal processes* (pp. 32–53). New York: Guilford.

Fleeson, W. (2001). Toward a structure- and process-integrated view of personality: Traits as density distributions of states. *Journal of Personality and Social Psychology, 80*, 1011–1027.

Fleeson, W. (2004). Moving personality beyond the person-situation debate: The challenge and the opportunity of within-person variability. *Current Directions in Psychological Science, 13*, 83–87.

Fleeson, W., & Noftle, E. (2008). The end of the person-situation debate: An emerging synthesis in the answer to the consistency question. *Social and Personality Psychology Compass, 2*, 1667–1684.

Forgas, J. P. (1976). The perception of social episodes: Categorical and dimensional representations in two different social milieus. *Journal of Personality and Social Psychology, 34*, 199–209.

Forgas, J. P. (1979). *Social episodes: The study of interaction routines*. London: Academic.

Fournier, M., Moscovich, D., & Zuroff, D. (2009). The interpersonal signature. *Journal of Research in Personality, 43*, 155–162.

Funder, D.C. (2006). Towards a resolution of the personality triad: Persons, situations, and behaviors. *Journal of Research in Personality, 40*, 21–34.

Funder, D. C. (2009). Persons, behaviors, and situations: An agenda for personality psychology in the postwar era. *Journal of Research in Personality, 43*, 120–126.

Funder, D. C. (2010). The Riverside Situational Q-Sort. Unpublished manuscript, University of California, Riverside.

Funder, D. C., & Ozer, D. J. (1983). Behavior as a function of the situation. *Journal of Personality and Social Psychology, 44*, 107–112.

Furr, R. M., & Funder, D. C. (2004). Situational similarity and behavioral consistency: Subjective, objective, variable-centered, and person-centered approached. *Journal of Research in Personality, 38*, 421–447.

Gibson, J. J. (1979). *The ecological approach to visual perception*. Boston, MA: Houghton Mifflin.

Goldberg, L.R. (1981). Language and individual differences: The search for universals in personality lexicons. In L. Wheeler (Ed.), *Review of personality and social psychology* (Vol. 2, pp. 141–165). Beverly Hills, CA: Sage.

Gollwitzer, P. M. (1996). The volitional benefits of planning. In P. M. Gollwitzer & J. A. Bargh (Eds.), *The psychology of action: Linking cognition and motivation to behavior* (pp. 287–312). New York: Guilford.

Haney, C., Banks, C., & Zimbardo, P. (1973). Interpersonal dynamics in a simulated prison. *International Journal of Criminology and Penology, 1*, 69–97.

Hartup, W. W., & Stevens, N. (1997). Friendships and adaptation in the life course. *Psychological Bulletin, 121*, 355–370.

Higgins, E. T. (1998). Promotion and prevention: Regulatory focus as a motivational principle. In M. Zanna (Ed.), *Advances in experimental social psychology* (Vol. 30, pp. 1–46). San Diego, CA: Academic.

Higgins, E. T. (2000). Social cognition: Learning about what matters in the social world. *European Journal of Social Psychology, 30*, 3–40.

Holmes, J. G. (1981). The exchange process in close relationships: Microbehavior and macromotives. In M. J. Lerner & S. C. Lerner (Eds.), *The justice motive in social behavior* (pp. 261–284). New York: Plenum.

Holmes, J. G. (2000). Social relationships: The nature and function of relational schemas. *European Journal of Social Psychology, 30*, 447–496.

Holmes, J. G. (2002). Interpersonal expectations as the building blocks of social cognition: An interdependence theory perspective. *Personal Relationships, 9*, 1–26.

Holmes, J. G., & Cameron, J. (2005). An integrated review of theories of interpersonal cognition: An interdependence theory perspective. In M. Baldwin (Ed.), *Interpersonal cognition* (pp. 415–447). New York: Guilford.

Holmes, J. G., & Cavallo, J. V. (2010). The atlas of interpersonal situations: A theory-driven approach to behavioral signatures. In C. Agnew, D. Carlston, W. Graziano, & J. Kelly (Eds.), *Then a miracle occurs: Focusing on behavior in social psychological theory and research* (pp. 315–335). New York: Oxford University Press.

Holmes, J. G., & Rempel, J. K. (1989). Trust in close relationships. In C. Hendrick (Ed.), *Review of Personality and Social Psychology: Vol. 10. Close Relationships* (pp. 187–220). London: Sage.

Hull, D. L. (1998). Taxonomy. In E. Craig (Ed.), *Routledge Encyclopedia of Philosophy, Version 1.0* (pp. 876–877). London: Routledge.

Ickes, W. (1982). A basic paradigm for the study of personality, roles and social behavior. In: Ickes, W., Knowles, E.S. (Eds.), *Personality, roles and social behavior* (pp. 305-241). Springer-Verlag, New York.

Iyengar, S. S., & Lepper, M. R. (1999). Rethinking the value of choice: A cultural perspective on intrinsic motivation. *Journal of Personality and Social Psychology, 76*, 349–366.

Jahoda, G. (2007). *A history of social psychology: From the eighteenth-century Enlightenment to the Second World War*. New York: Cambridge University Press.

John, O. P. & Srivastava, S. (1999). The Big Five trait taxonomy: History, measurement, and theoretical perspectives. In L. A. Pervin & O. P. John (Eds.), *Handbook of personality* (2nd ed., pp. 102–138). New York: Guilford.

Jones, E. E. (1985). Major developments in social psychology during the past five decades. In G. Lindzey & E. Aronson (Eds.) *The handbook of social psychology* (3rd ed., Vol. 1, pp. 47–107). New York: Random House.

Jones, E. E., Gergen, K. J., & Jones, R. G. (1963). *Tactics of ingratiation among leaders and subordinates in a status hierarchy*. Psychological Monographs, 77, Whole number 566, no. 3. Washington, DC: American Psychological Association.

Kahneman, D., & Tversky, A. (1984). Choices, values, and frames. *American Psychologist, 39*, 341–350.

Kelley, H. H. (1979). *Personal relationships: Their structures and processes*. Hillsdale, NJ: Erlbaum.

Kelley, H. H. (1997). The "stimulus field" for interpersonal phenomena: The source of language and thought about interpersonal events. *Personality and Social Psychology Review, 1*, 140–169.

Kelley, H. H. (2000). The proper study of social psychology. *Social Psychology Quarterly, 63,* 3–15.

Kelley, H. H., Holmes, J. G., Kerr, N. L., Reis, H. T., Rusbult, C. E., & Van Lange, P. A. M. (2003). *An atlas of interpersonal situations.* Cambridge, UK: Cambridge University Press.

Kelley, H. H., & Stahelski, A. (1970). The social interaction basis of cooperators' and competitors' beliefs about others. *Journal of Personality and Social Psychology, 16,* 66–91.

Kelley, H. H., & Thibaut, J. W. (1978). *Interpersonal relations: A theory of interdependence.* New York: Wiley.

Kenny, D. A., Mohr, C. D., & Levesque, M. J. (2001). A social relations variance partitioning of dyadic behavior. *Psychological Bulletin, 127,* 128–141.

Kenrick, D. T., & Funder, D. C. (1988). Profiting from controversy: Lessons from the person-situation debate. *American Psychologist, 43,* 23–34.

Kerr, N. L., & Bruun, S. (1983). The dispensability of member effort and group motivation losses: Free rider effects. *Journal of Personality and Social Psychology, 44,* 78–94.

Krahé, B. (1990). *Situation cognition and coherence in personality: An individual-centered approach.* Cambridge, UK: Cambridge University Press.

Krueger, J. I. (2009). A componential model of situation effects, person effects, and situation-by-person interaction effects on social behavior. *Journal of Research in Personality, 43,* 127–136.

Kruglanski, A.W. (1996). Motivated social cognition: Principles of the interface. In E. T. Higgins & A. W. Kruglanski (Eds.), *Social psychology: Handbook of basic principles* (pp. 493–520). New York: Guilford.

Kruglanski, A. W., & Webster, D. M. (1996). Motivated closing of the mind: "Seizing" and "freezing." *Psychological Review, 103,* 263–283.

Kuhn, T. S. (1970). *The structure of scientific revolutions.* Chicago: Chicago University Press.

Latané, B., & Darley, J. (1970). *The unresponsive bystander: Why doesn't he help?* New York: Appleton-Century-Crofts.

Leary, T. (1957). *Interpersonal diagnosis of personality.* New York: Ronald.

Lewin, K. (1935). *Dynamic theory of personality.* New York: McGraw Hill.

Lewin, K. (1936). *Principles of topological psychology.* New York: McGraw Hill.

Lewin K. (1943). Defining the "field at a given time." *Psychological Review, 50,* 292–310.

Lewin, K. (1946). Behavior and development as a function of the total situation. In L. Carmichael (Ed.), *Manual of child psychology* (pp. 791–844). New York: Wiley.

Lewin, K. (1951). *Field theory in social science.* New York: Harper.

Lickel, B., Hamilton, D. L., Wieczorkowska, G., Lewis, A., Sherman, S. J., & Uhles, A. N. (2000). Varieties of groups and the perception of group entativity. *Journal of Personality and Social Psychology, 78,* 223–246.

Magnusson, D. (1981). *Toward a psychology of situations: An interactional perspective.* Hillsdale, N.J.: Erlbaum Associates.

Magnusson, D., & Endler, N. (1977). *Personality at the crossroads.* Hillsdale, NJ: Erlbaum.

Markus, H., & Kitiyama, S. (1991). Culture and the self: Implications for cognition, emotion, and motivation. *Psychological Review, 98,* 224–253.

McAdams, D. & Pals, J. (2006). A new big five: Fundamental principles for an integrative science of personality. *American Psychologist, 61,* 204–217.

McDougall, W. (1908). *Introduction to social psychology.* Boston: Luce.

Meehl, P. E. (1992). Factors and taxa, traits and types, differences of degree and differences in kind. *Journal of Personality, 60,* 117–174.

Messick, D. M., & Brewer, M. B. (1983). Solving social dilemmas: A review. *Review of Personality and Social Psychology, 4,* 11–44.

Metcalfe, J., & Mischel, W. (1999). A hot/cold system of delay of gratification: Dynamics of willpower. *Psychological Review, 106,* 3–19.

Mikulincer, M., & Shaver, P. R. (2005). Attachment theory and emotions in close relationships: Attachment-related dynamics of emotional reactions to relational events. *Personal Relationships, 12,* 149–168.

Milgram, S. (1974). *Obedience to authority.* New York: Harper & Row.

Miller, D. T., & Holmes, J. G. (1975). The role of situational restrictiveness on self-fulfilling prophecies: A theoretical and empirical extension of Kelley and Stahelski's triangle hypothesis. *Journal of Personality and Social Psychology, 31,* 661–673.

Mischel, W. (1968). *Personality and assessment.* New York: Wiley.

Mischel, W. (1973). Toward a cognitive social learning reconceptualization of personality. *Psychological Review, 80,* 252–283.

Mischel, W. (1977). The interaction of person and situation. In D. Magnusson and N.S. Endler (Eds.), *Personality at the crossroads* (pp. 332–352). Hillsdale, NJ: Erlbaum.

Mischel, W. (2006). Bridges toward a cumulative pscyhological science. In P. A. M. Van Lange (Ed.), *Bridging social psychology* (pp. 437–446). Mahwah, NJ: Erlbaum.

Mischel, W. (2009). From *Personality and assessment* (1968) to *Personality science* (2009). *Journal of Research in Personality, 43,* 282–290.

Mischel, W., Cantor, N., & Feldman, S. (1996). Principles of self-regulation: The nature of willpower and self-control. In E. T. Higgins & A. W. Kruglanski (Eds.), *Social psychology: Handbook of basic principles* (pp. 329–360). New York: Guilford.

Mischel, W, & Mischel, H. N. (1983). Development of children's knowledge of self-control strategies. *Child Development, 54,* 603–619.

Mischel, W., & Shoda, Y. (1995). A cognitive-affective system theory of personality: Reconceptualizing situations, dispositions, dynamics, and invariance in personality structure. *Psychological Review, 102,* 246–268.

Mischel, W., & Shoda, Y. (1999). Integrating dispositions and processing dynamics within a unified theory of personality: The cognitive-affective personality system. In L. A. Pervin & O. P. John (Eds.), *Handbook of Personality* (2nd ed., pp. 197–218). New York: Guilford.

Mischel, W., Shoda, Y., & Mendoza-Denton, R. (2002). Situation-behavior profiles as a locus of consistency in personality. *Current Directions in Psychological Science, 11,* 50–54.

Montague Institute (2009). *Ten taxonomy myths.* Retrieved February 10, 2010, from http://www.montague.com/review/myths.html

Morf, C. C., & Rhodewalt, F. (2001). Unraveling the paradoxes of narcissism: A dynamic self-regulatory processing model. *Psychological Inquiry, 12,* 177–196.

Murray, H.A. (1938). *Explorations in personality.* New York: Oxford University Press.

Murray, S. L., Griffin, D. W., Rose, P., & Bellavia, G. M. (2003). Calibrating the sociometer: The relational contingencies of self-esteem. *Journal of Personality and Social Psychology, 85,* 63–84.

Nisbett, R. E. (1980). The trait construct in lay and professional psychology. In L. Festinger (Ed.), *Retrospections on social psychology* (pp. 109-130). New York: Oxford University Press.

Nisbett, R. E., & Cohen, D. (1996). *Culture of honor: The psychology of violence in the South.* Boulder, CO: Westview Press.

Overall, N. C., & Sibley, C. G. (2008). When accommodation matters: Situational dependency within daily interactions with romantic partners. *Journal of Experimental Social Psychology, 44,* 95–104.

Price, R. H., & Blashfield, R. K. (1975). Explorations in the taxonomy of behavioral settings. *American Journal of Community Psychology, 3,* 335–351.

Proshansky, H. M., Ittelson, W. H., & Rivlin, L. G. (Eds.). (1976). *Environmental psychology: People and their physical settings* (2nd ed). Oxford, UK: Holt.

Pruitt, D. G., & Carnevale, P. J. (1993). *Negotiation in social conflict.* Buckingham, UK: Open University Press.

Quammen, D. (2007). *The reluctant Mr. Darwin: An intimate portrait of Charles Darwin and the making of his theory of evolution.* New York: W. W. Norton.

Rabbie, J. M., Schot, J. C., & Visser, L. (1989). Social identity theory: A conceptual and empirical critique from the perspective of a behavioural interaction model. *European Journal of Social Psychology, 19,* 171–202.

Reis, H. T. (2007). Steps toward the ripening of relationship science. *Personal Relationships, 14,* 1–23.

Reis, H. T. (2008). Reinvigorating the concept of situation in social psychology. *Personality and Social Psychology Review, 12,* 311–329.

Reis, H. T. (2010a). The relationship context of social behavior. In C. R. Agnew, D. E. Carlston, W. G. Graziano, & J. R. Kelly (Eds.), *Then a miracle occurs: Focusing on behavior in social psychological theory and research* (pp. 299–320). New York: Oxford University Press.

Reis, H. T. (2010b). How we got here from there: A brief history of social psychology. In R. Baumeister & E. Finkel (Eds.), *Advanced social psychology* (pp. 25-60). New York: Oxford University Press.

Reis, H. T., Capobianco, A., & Tsai, F. F. (2002). Finding the person in personal relationships. *Journal of Personality, 70,* 813–850.

Reis, H. T., Clark, M. S., & Holmes, J. G. (2004). Perceived partner responsiveness as an organizing construct in the study of intimacy and closeness. In D. Mashek & A. Aron (Eds.), *Handbook of closeness and intimacy* (pp. 201–225). Mahwah, NJ: Erlbaum.

Reis, H. T., Collins, W. A., & Berscheid, E. (2000). The relationship context of human behavior and development. *Psychological Bulletin, 126,* 844-872.

Rentfrow, P. J., Gosling, S. D., & Potter, J. (2008). A theory of the emergence, persistence, and expression of geographic variation in psychological characteristics. *Perspectives on Psychological Science, 3,* 339–369.

Richard, F. D., Bond, C. F., Jr., & Stokes-Zoota, J. J. (2003). One hundred years of social psychology quantitatively described. *Review of General Psychology, 7,* 331–363.

Ross, E.A. (1908). *Social psychology.* New York: McMillan.

Ross, L., & Nisbett, R.E. (1991). *The person and the situation: Perspectives of social psychology.* New York: McGraw-Hill.

Rozin, P. (2001). Social psychology and science: Some lessons from Solomon Asch. *Personality and Social Psychology Review, 5,* 2–14.

Rubin, J. Z., & Brockner, J. (1975). Factors affecting entrapment in waiting situations: The Rosencrantz and Guildenstein effect. *Journal of Personality and Social Psychology, 31,* 1054–1063.

Rusbult, C. E., Olsen, N., Davis, J. L., & Hannon, P. A. (2001). Commitment and relationship maintenance mechanisms. In J. H. Harvey & A. Wenzel (Eds.), *Close romantic relationships: Maintenance and enhancement* (pp. 87–113). Mahwah, NJ: Erlbaum.

Rusbult, C. E., & Van Lange, P. A. M. (1996). Interdependence processes. In E. T. Higgins & A. Kruglanski (Eds.), *Social psychology: Handbook of basic mechanisms and processes* (pp. 564–596). New York: Guilford.

Sadler, P., Ethier, N., Gunn, G. R., Duong, D., & Woody, E. (2009). Are we on the same wavelength? Interpersonal complementarity as shared cyclical patterns during interactions. *Journal of Personality and Social Psychology, 97,* 1005–1020.

Sadler, P., & Woody, E. (2003). Is who you are who you're talking to? Interpersonal style and complementarity in mixed-sex interactions. *Journal of Personality and Social Psychology, 84,* 80–96.

Safilios-Rothschild, C. (1976). A macro- and micro-examination of family power and love: An exchange model. *Journal of Marriage and the Family, 38,* 355–362.

Schank, R. C., & Abelson, R. P. (1977). *Scripts, plans, goals and understanding: An inquiry into human knowledge structures.* Hillsdale, NJ: Erlbaum.

Scheier, M. F., & Carver, C. S. (1993). On the power of positive thinking: The benefits of being optimistic. *Current Directions in Psychological Science, 2,* 26–30.

Schutte, N.S., Kenrick, D.T., & Sadalla, E.K. (1985). The search for predictable settings: Situational prototypes, constraint, and behavioral variation. *Journal of Personality and Social Psychology, 49,* 121-148.

Sedikides, C., Campbell, W. K., Reeder, G., & Elliot, A. J. (1998). The self-serving bias in relational context. *Journal of Personality and Social Psychology, 74,* 378-386.

Sells, S. B. (1963). An interactionist looks at the environment. *American Psychologist, 18,* 696–702.

Sherif, M. (1936). *The psychology of social norms.* New York: Harper Bros.

Sherif, M. (1948). *An outline of social psychology.* New York: Harper.

Sherif, M. (1966). *In common predicament: Social psychology of intergroup conflict and cooperation.* Boston, MA: Houghton Mifflin.

Sherif, M., & Sherif, C. W. (1956). *An outline of social psychology* (Rev. ed.) New York: Harper.

Sherman, R. A., Nave, C. S., & Funder, D. C. (2010). Situational similarity and personality predict behavioral consistency. *Journal of Personality and Social Psychology, 99,* 330–343.

Shoda, Y. (2004). Understanding situations to understand people, understanding people to understand situations. In C. Sansone, C. Morf, & A. Panter (Eds.), *Handbook of methods in social psychology* (pp. 117–141). Thousand Oaks, CA: Sage.

Shoda, Y., & Mischel, W. (1996). Toward a unified, intra-individual dynamic conception of personality. *Journal of Research in Personality, 30,* 414–428.

Shoda, Y., Mischel, W., & Wright, J. C. (1994). Intra-individual stability in the organization and patterning of behavior:

Incorporating psychological situations into the idiographic analysis of personality. *Journal of Personality and Social Psychology, 67,* 674–687.

Simpson, J. A. (2007). Foundations of interpersonal trust. In A. W. Kruglanski & E. T. Higgins (Eds.), *Social psychology: Handbook of basic principles* (2nd ed., pp. 587–607). New York: Guilford.

Simpson, J. A., Rholes, W. S., & Phillips, D. (1996). Conflict in close relationships: An attachment perspective. *Journal of Personality and Social Psychology, 71,* 899–914.

Smith, E. R., & Semin, G. R. (2004). Socially situated cognition: Cognition in its social context. *Advances in Experimental Social Psychology, 36,* 53–117.

Smith, E. R., & Semin, G. R. (2007). Situated social cognition. *Current Directions in Psychological Science, 16,* 132–135.

Snyder, M. (1981). On the influence of individuals on situations. In N. Cantor & J. Kihlstrom (Eds.), *Cognition, social interaction, and personality* (pp. 309–329). Hillsdale, NJ: Erlbaum.

Snyder, M., & Cantor, N. (1998). Understanding personality and social behavior. In D. Gilbert, S. T. Fiske, & G. Lindzey (Eds.), *The handbook of social psychology* (4th ed., Vol. 1, pp. 635–679). New York: McGraw-Hill.

Snyder, M., & Ickes, W. (1985). Personality and social behavior. In G. Lindzey & E. Aronson (Eds.), *The handbook of social psychology* (3rd ed., Vol. 2, pp. 883–947). New York: Random House.

Sorrentino, R. M., Holmes, J. G., Hanna, S. E., & Sharp A. (1995). Uncertainty orientation and trust in close relationships: Individual differences in cognitive styles. *Journal of Personality and Social Psychology, 68,* 314–327.

Sorrentino, R., & Roney, C. (2000). *The uncertain mind: Individual differences in facing the unknown.* London: Psychology Press.

Steiner, I. D. (1972). *Group process and productivity.* New York: Academic.

Stokols, D., & Altman, I. (1987). *Handbook of environmental psychology* (Vols. 1 & 2). New York: Wiley.

Suls, J., Green, P. & Hillis, S. (1998). Emotional reactivity to everyday problems, affective inertia, and neuroticism. *Personality and Social Psychology Bulletin, 24,* 127–136.

Swann, W. B., Jr., & Seyle, C. (2005). Personality psychology's comeback and its emerging symbiosis with social psychology. *Personality and Social Psychology Bulletin, 31,* 155–165.

The Situationist (2011). Retrieved from http://thesituationist. wordpress.com/about/.

Thibaut, J. W., & Kelley, H. H. (1959). *The social psychology of groups.* New York: Wiley.

Tjosvold, D., & Sagaria, S. (1978). Effects of relative power on cognitive perspective-taking. *Personality and Social Psychology Bulletin, 4,* 256–259.

Tooby, J., & Cosmides, L. (1996). Friendship and the banker's paradox: Other pathways to the evolution of adaptations for altruism. *Proceedings of the British Academy, 88,* 119–143.

Turiel, E. (1983). *The development of social knowledge: Morality and convention.* New York : Cambridge University Press.

Tyler, T. R. (1990). *Why people obey the law.* New Haven, CT: Yale University Press.

Van Heck, G. L. (1984). The construction of a general taxonomy of situations. In H. Bonarius, G. L. Van Heck, & N. Smid (Eds.), *Personality psychology in Europe: Theoretical and empirical developments* (pp. 149–164). Lisse: Swets and Zeitlinger.

Van Lange, P. A. M., Ouwerkerk, J. W., & Tazelaar, M. J. A. (2002). How to overcome the detrimental effects of noise in social interaction: The benefits of generosity. *Journal of Personality and Social Psychology, 82,* 768–780.

Walster, E., Walster, G. W., & Berscheid, E. (1978). *Equity: Theory and research.* Boston: Allyn and Bacon.

Wildschut, T., Insko, C. A., & Gaertner, L., (2002). Intragroup social influence and intergroup competition. *Journal of Personality and Social Psychology, 82,* 975–992.

Wildschut, T., Pinter, B., Vevea, J. L., Insko, C. A., & Schopler, J. (2003). Beyond the group mind: A quantitative review of the interindividual-intergroup discontinuity effect. *Psychological Bulletin, 129,* 698–722.

Wilson, T. D., Aronson, E., & Carlsmith, K. (2010). The art of laboratory experimentation. In S. T. Fiske, D. T. Gilbert, & G. Lindzey (Eds.), *Handbook of social psychology* (5th ed., Vol. 1, pp. 51–81). Hoboken, NJ: Wiley.

Wilson, D. S., Van Vugt, M., & O'Gorman, R. (2008). Multilevel selection theory and major evolutionary transitions: Implications for psychological science. *Current Directions in Psychological Science, 17,* 6–9.

Wish, M., Deutsch, M., & Kaplan, S. J. (1976). Perceived dimensions of interpersonal relations. *Journal of Personality and Social Psychology, 33,* 409–420.

Wright, H., & Barker, R. C. (1950). *Methods in psychological ecology: A progress report.* Oxford, UK: Oxford University Press.

Yang, Y., Read, S. J., & Miller, L. C. (2006). A taxonomy of situations from Chinese idioms. *Journal of Research in Personality, 40,* 750–778.

Yang, Y., Read, S. J., & Miller, L. C. (2009). The concept of situations. *Social and Personality Psychology Compass, 3,* 1018–1037.

Zebrowitz, L. A., & Collins, M.A. (1997). Accurate social perception at zero acquaintance: The affordances of a Gibsonian approach. *Personality and Social Psychology Review, 1,* 204–223.

Behavior and Behavior Assessment

Janice R. Kelly *and* Christopher R. Agnew

Abstract

This chapter addresses the questions (1) What do we mean by "behavior" in personality and social psychology? and (2) How can we best assess social behavior? We define behavior as being observable and socially meaningful, but also discuss the dimensions on which behavior varies (e.g., intentional vs. habitual, discrete vs. continuous). We also discuss important variabilities in behavior as they relate to issues of measurement (e.g., behavioral frequency or desirability). For behavior assessment, we focus on some of the practical issues involved (e.g., choosing a coding system, selecting an observational setting), as well as how behavior assessment might intersect with personality and social psychological theory (e.g., manipulating or assessing behavior as it serves as moderator, mediator, or outcome in a theory). We end by discussing some emerging technologies that might prove useful for behavioral assessment (e.g., virtual reality), as well as a call for more integration of behavioral measures into future research.

Keywords: behavior, behavioral assessment, behavioral observation, research methods

Behavior and Behavior Assessment

The past decades have featured a growing focus on cognition, affect, and motivation within personality and social psychology. With the rise of social cognition has come a reduction in focus on the behavioral consequences of it (Agnew, Carlston, Graziano, & Kelly, 2010). There has been a corresponding waning focus on direct observation of what people do (Baumeister, Vohs, & Funder, 2007). That is, data provided by independent observers who supply systematic descriptions of something they have actually seen someone else do has declined. Funder and colleagues have decried the decrease in behavioral focus among personality psychologists (Furr & Funder, 2007; Furr, Wagerman, & Funder, 2010), as have others, but the trend does not appear to be reversing. This is unfortunate, as behavior is obviously a critical ingredient—if not *the* critical ingredient—in understanding people.

Personality and social psychology have a long history of focusing on overt behavior. Some of the most well known studies in social psychology involve the enactment (or lack of enactment) of key social behaviors. For example, early studies of discrimination by LaPiere (1934) focused on observing the behavior of hotel and restaurant personnel in response to requests for accommodation by a Chinese couple. LaPiere's emphasis was on the discrepancy between expressed negative attitudes toward minority group members versus actions toward them, but his main interest (and one that he extolled psychologists to keep their eye on) was on what people actually did. Understanding the cognitive, affective, and/or motivational underpinnings of discriminatory behavior were certainly (and continue to be) of interest, but this interest was primarily in the service of understanding discriminatory actions themselves. Without the presence of overtly negative discriminatory behaviors, there would be little motivation to understand the underlying psychology.

Sherif et al.'s (1961) classic Robber's Cave experiments involved the observation of teams of boys who faced team vs. team competitions, as well as staged shared disasters that required interteam cooperative responding. The behaviors studied were real, with consequences for the participants and with clear parallels to situations beyond Robber's Cave. No questionnaire study could have had the same type of impact on generations of psychology students or on subsequent scholarly thinking regarding intergroup relations.

Darley and Latané's (1968) bystander intervention experiments also centered on actions (or inactions) of people in an emergency situation. Would bystanders offer help to someone in clear need of it? Although the focus was on the factors that increase or decrease likelihood of providing help, helping itself was of paramount concern. Similarly, Milgram's (1975) series of obedience experiments focused on how far participants would go in following the orders of an experimenter. What would people do when told to harm another, under the orders of an authority figure? Likewise, personality psychology has emphasized the actions of individuals from the inception of the field (e.g., Hartshorne & May's, 1928, research on children's character and "honesty" behaviors). However, with the shifting emphasis in social and personality psychology toward the psychological underpinnings of behavior, the focus on behavior itself and on its attendant measurement challenges has left the spotlight.

This situation is particularly ironic given the rise in the general public's interest in and appreciation for the kinds of behaviors social psychologists study. For example, witness the enormous success of the writer Malcolm Gladwell's books in recent years. *The Tipping Point* (2000), *Blink* (2005), and *Outliers* (2008) are replete with examples based on classic and current social psychological research. Moreover, television networks worldwide have a seemingly endless fascination with replicating or reenacting a number of classic social psychological studies featuring consequential behaviors (e.g., Milgram's obedience studies and Darley and Latané's bystander intervention studies). If there was ever a time when behavior should be at the forefront of social and personality psychology, it is now.

Of course, there are understandable barriers to maintaining a central focus on behavior. It certainly costs more to observe actions in situ than it does to collect self-reports of behavior. Beyond cost, there are also time demands that tend to favor methodologies that do not involve real-time behavior assessment. Moreover, there are many behaviors that are very difficult if not impossible to directly observe (e.g., illicit or low-frequency behaviors). However, as we hope to make clear, the importance of keeping social psychological and personality research grounded in actual behavior cannot be understated.

In this chapter, we consider the issues of what behavior is, what behavior is meaningful to examine from the perspective of social and personality psychologists, and how best to assess that behavior.

What is Behavior?

What is behavior? More specifically with respect to the focus of this volume, what might social and personality psychologists consider to be behavior? Even a cursory review of the literature provides a rich and varied answer to the question. For some, any action by a person constitutes a behavior of interest. At times, specific behaviors are of primary interest for either basic (e.g., the study of mimicry) or applied (e.g., the use of condoms to prevent HIV transmission) reasons. Moreover, some behaviors are more meaningful than others, either from the perspective of an actor or from the perspective of a researcher.

We take the position that behavior is what a person does overtly. Behavior is, thus, observable. We would not include as behavior unobservable internal processes, such as neural activity or the physiological machinations of brain components (Aron, 2010). We further assume that behavior must be meaningful, on some level, to be worthy of investigation in and of itself by social and personality psychologists. So, for example, although social psychologists who study social cognition may track the keyboard pressing of study participants, they are not ultimately interested in the overt behavior of keyboard pressing. Such behaviors are considered to be critical proxies for cognitive, affective, or motivational processes that are themselves of primary interest. *Thus, we define behavior as overt or observable actions that are socially meaningful.*

Obviously this is a very broad definition that encompasses many types of actions. Meaningful social actions may include nodding, talking, smoking, donating to charity, assembling an AM radio kit, smiling, walking on a treadmill, engaging in mutual eye gaze, or holding one's hand in freezing water. However, even within this general definition, important distinctions can be drawn regarding various dimensions of behavior (see table 5.1), including its intentionality, whether it is consciously guided, and whether it is relatively independent or interdependent. Such distinctions have implications for measurement.

Table 5.1 Important Dimensions of Behavior

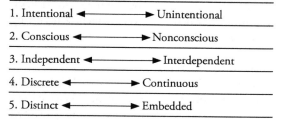

1. Intentional ←————→ Unintentional

2. Conscious ←————→ Nonconscious

3. Independent ←————→ Interdependent

4. Discrete ←————→ Continuous

5. Distinct ←————→ Embedded

Intentional behaviors, or behavior that follows from one's desire, have been the subject of investigation by social and personality psychologists for decades. Models of decision-making have as their core the assumption that most behaviors are enacted in line with the intentions of the decision-maker (e.g., theory of planned behavior; Ajzen, 1991; also Ajzen, chapter 15, this volume). In contrast, models of habitual behavior do not assume that intentions guide the enactment of habits (Verplanken, 2010). Although habits may have their origin as intentional behaviors (e.g., carefully buckling one's seat belt when first learning to drive), such behaviors may become increasingly unintentional over time (e.g., buckling up "automatically" upon getting in a car).

Behaviors also differ in the degree to which they may be considered guided by conscious awareness. Bargh and others have documented behavior that is not the result of conscious guidance (Bargh & Morsella, 2010). For example, work by Chartrand and Bargh on behavioral mimicry has shown that people copy (or "ape") the actions of others without conscious awareness of doing so (Chartrand & Bargh, 1999). The adequacy of self-reports to capture underlying reasons for such behavior is particularly suspect (Nisbett & Wilson, 1977). Indeed, how can one be expected to know what motivated an action that one had no awareness of enacting?

Some behaviors are conducted without the coaction of others (e.g., reading, eating alone). Such independent behaviors stand in contrast to the multiplicity of behaviors that are interdependent, requiring the coaction of another person for their enactment (Agnew, 1999). Interdependent behaviors simply could not be enacted independently (e.g., sexual intercourse). From an assessment perspective, such interdependence has both positive and negative implications. On the one hand, there are multiple reports available concerning interdependent behavioral enactment. On the other hand, multiple actors may not provide researchers with converging data regarding what did or did not occur. The lack of convergence, of course, may in

itself be of theoretical interest, but the assessment challenge remains (e.g., Bolger, Stadler, Paprocki, & DeLongis, 2010).

Behavior may also be said to differ based on the number of actions that compose the "behavior." Winking at a colleague is a discrete (and, perhaps, discreet) behavior. Driving an automobile, in contrast, is a series of interrelated actions that combine to form the behavior "driving." Depending on the research question, any number of the discrete actions that form the overall behavior "driving" may be of principle interest. Specificity with respect to the precise behavior of interest is, therefore, of critical importance from a measurement perspective (Ajzen & Fishbein, 1977). Assessing when a given behavior begins and ends (e.g., work on "break points" by Newtson & Engquist, 1976) can be a salient research consideration.

Behavior also differs in the degree to which it is discernable from other behaviors or whether it must be embedded in a context in order to be understood. The same collegial wink mentioned above might be interpreted as having vastly different meanings by the "winker" (who, for example, may have meant it to signify to a colleague the connection with matter discussed previously), the "winked at" (who may have completely missed a connection with the earlier discussion and is bewildered by the wink), and an outside observer (who wonders what is going on between the two). In this case, the behavior itself is discrete and easily described: closing one's eye quickly. But the meaning of the behavior is determined entirely by context, and not all participants in the setting featuring the wink are necessarily "in" on the context.

Dimensions Relevant to Measuring Behavior

Behavior is not unidimensional, and with each variation of behavior comes issues important to appropriate assessment of that behavior. Below we outline some of the major variations of types of behavior and discuss some of the associated measurement challenges. These distinctions are summarized in table 5.2.

Table 5.2 Variability in Behavior That Affects Measurement

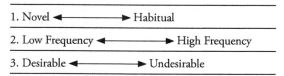

1. Novel ←————→ Habitual

2. Low Frequency ←————→ High Frequency

3. Desirable ←————→ Undesirable

NOVEL VERSUS HABITUAL BEHAVIORS

Initiating a behavior for the first time is different from initiating a behavior that one has enacted in the past. Different factors are likely considered before engaging in a behavior for the first time than are considered once the behavior is well practiced. For example, donating blood for the first time may give rise to a host of thoughts ("Will this really help someone?") and emotions ("Will it hurt?") that no longer cross the mind of a veteran donor. Moreover, repeated behaviors become habitual and decreasingly subject to cognitive input. Given its fleeting and transitory nature, truly novel behavior can be exceptionally challenging to capture either in the lab or the field.

LOW FREQUENCY BEHAVIORS

Some behaviors occur so infrequently that certain types of measurement procedures would be inappropriate. For example, for low frequency behaviors, direct observation of the behavior would be impractical given that it is unlikely that a low frequency behavior would actually occur during the timeframe of an observation period. However, some low frequency behaviors are extremely important to understanding human social life. For example, acts of heroism are important in furthering understanding of prosocial behavior. In order to gain knowledge about rare behavior, researchers often must rely on self-report measures of some type, certainly actor report, but perhaps also well-informed other reporters of a person's behavior as well. Biases of self-report, however, might be particularly threatening when the low frequency behavior is also socially undesirable (e.g., criminal behavior).

SOCIALLY UNDESIRABLE BEHAVIORS

Behaviors vary in the extent to which people wish to be associated with their enactment. Although researchers may be interested in learning about the cognitive or motivational underpinnings of littering, finding people who are willing to admit to, for example, littering can be challenging given the negative associations attending the behavior (e.g., inconsiderate of others, bad steward of the environment). Traditional approaches to detecting impression management tendencies include administration of social desirability inventories (such as Paulhus's, 1991, Balanced Inventory of Desirable Responding), the scores on which may be used as a covariate in statistical analyses. However, self-reporting behavior via an inventory is clearly a step removed from evidence of actually engaging in socially (un)desirable behaviors. Of course, researchers may be willing to "take what they can get," but refining approaches to capturing less desirable (yet frequently occurring) behavior remains important.

Assessing Behavior

The complexity of behavior is clear. It is therefore understandable that the assessment of behavior may be complex as well. There are four primary methods (physiological measures notwithstanding) for assessing outcome variables in social and personality psychology—self-report, informant report, direct observation, and trace measures (Webb, Campbell, Schwartz, Sechrest, & Grove, 1981). Some of these methods are particularly suited for assessing particular types of outcomes. For example, informants may be particularly good at providing behavior assessments within a specific context (e.g., teachers assessing behaviors in the school context) or sometimes across various contexts (e.g., a parent or romantic partner who interacts with the participant across a wide range of contexts). And self-reports are currently the only method that can be used for tapping internal cognitive and emotional states. Each of these methods has certain strengths and advantages, but each has weaknesses and disadvantages. For example, self-reports are relatively inexpensive to administer and can be used to assess a wide range of traits, attitudes, beliefs, and behaviors. But they are subject to various reporting biases, such as errors in retrospective memory, socially desirable responding, or response sets (Paulhus & Holden, 2010). Trace measures may be more immune to deliberate biases and distortions, especially given that the traces were not originally left for research purposes, but the number of trace measures that are meaningful for psychological research are somewhat few (see, however, our later discussion of Gosling et al., 2002).

All four methods potentially can be used to assess behavior. If you are interested in a person's behavior, or if you are interested in forming inferences about a person based on knowledge of their behavior, then you can ask the person themselves about their behavior (self-report), ask an informed other about the person's behavior (informant report), directly observe the person's behavior yourself (behavioral observation), or examine the evidence that is left behind from the behavior (trace measures). With respect to behavior assessment specifically, each method also has strengths and weaknesses. Self-reports of behavior are still subject to various memory and reporting biases. We may not be consciously aware of some of our behavior, such as normative or habitual behaviors, so that we cannot report their occurrence with accuracy. Other behaviors that we think may be associated with pejorative attitudes may be more deliberately underreported (e.g., use of swear words). Third-party informants may be able to provide estimates of behavior with somewhat more accuracy than self-reports, but their estimates may be based on knowledge of behavior within a limited context (Spain, Eaton, & Funder, 2000) and/or they may also be subject to some of the same biases affecting the actor (Sande, Goethals, & Radloff, 1988). So, for example, when a child is assessed for ADHD, their behavior must be reported within different and specific contexts, such as parent's report of behavior at home and teacher's report of behavior at school, in order to obtain a more accurate and global picture of the overall behavior (Achenbach, 1991). And some behaviors may be more private and less likely to be observable by a third party. Trace measures are somewhat specifically meant to unobtrusively measure behavior. For example, wear and tear of tiles may be used to assess foot traffic in a building (Webb et al., 1981). Cialdini's impressive body of work on norms also takes advantage of trace measures of behavior. For example, Cialdini counted the number of flyers that were discarded in various settings as an index of adherence to descriptive norms for disposing of trash (Cialdini, Reno, & Kallgren, 1990). However, many of the behaviors of interest to social and personality psychologists (e.g., conversations, emotional displays, interpersonal interaction) do not leave such observable traces. Direct observation of behavior, on the other hand, can be used to assess most types of important social behaviors, and this observation can be done over a range of contexts or within specific contexts. Because the behaviors are recorded as they happen, those reports are less likely to be distorted because of memory degradation or socially desirable responding.

In this chapter, we have therefore opted to focus on direct observation as the primary method of behavior assessment. We do so for a number of reasons. As described above, direct observation of behavior has a number of important strengths, particularly in terms of eliminating biases in respondent self-reports such as social desirability or errors of memory. But also, we want this chapter to serve as a call for researchers in the behavioral sciences to return to the assessment of actual behavior rather than the measurement proxies that have become so commonplace (Agnew, Carlton, Graziano, & Kelly, 2010; Agnew & Kelly, 2010; Baumeister, Vohs, &

Funder, 2007). As Furr and Funder (2007) argue, behavior itself is the ultimate source of knowledge for all psychological information. We have long known, at least since the classic studies by Nisbett and Wilson (1977), that people are often unaware of the factors that drive behavior. Therefore, without direct observation of behavior, the accuracy of such self-reports is in question. Without the ability to directly access another's thoughts, emotions, and motivations, behavior provides an important indication of another person's psychological state unfiltered by a person's possibly biased self-report regarding the behavior.

Behavioral Observation

We argue that direct observation of behavior is, in many cases, the most valid method we currently have for assessing behavior. If we are interested, for example, in the effects of some intervention on smoking behavior, we can assess those effects by directly observing smoking. If we are interested in how negotiators resolve a conflict, we can simply observe and code their negotiation behavior. Given that we are a social science and that social behaviors are for the most part directly observable, direct observation of behavior would seem to be the method of choice for assessing such social behaviors.

However, direct observation of behavior is less commonly used today than self-reports of behavior, and for obvious reasons. Behavioral observation can be difficult. Behavioral observation generally involves either selecting or designing a system for coding behavioral observations. That is, the behavior in question must be defined, and a system must be developed for systematically and reliably recording that behavior. The system must then be used in real time (whether live or from recordings) to assess the ongoing behaviors of choice and usually involves extensive training of coders in order to reliably implement the system. As opposed to self-reports of behavior, this sort of behavioral observation is generally time-intensive and resource-consuming, and those factors are undoubtedly primary reasons for the lack of direct behavioral observation in social and personality psychology. Behavioral observation can also simply be not practical for assessing some behaviors, especially when we are talking about behaviors that are low frequency, private, undesirable, or illegal.

There is some indication, however, that the use of direct behavioral observation is increasing. There have been a number of calls to arms concerning the field's overreliance on self-report and underreliance on behavioral observation (Baumeister, Vohs, & Funder, 2007; Furr & Funder, 2007; Moreland, Fetterman, Flagg, & Swanenburg, 2010). These calls stress the importance of studying actual behavior rather than behavioral substitutes (Furr & Funder, 2007). In addition, emerging technologies may be making direct observation of behavior more manageable (e.g., Mehl, 2009).

Furr and Funder (2007) argue that despite the difficulties of direct behavioral observation, behavioral data are fundamental to social and personality psychology. As stated earlier, they argue that behavior is essentially the end state or defining characteristic of all of scientific psychology. Funder (2006) argues that personality psychology involves the understanding of persons, situations, and behaviors and the links between them. However, lack of attention to the latter two elements has led to extensive knowledge about traits, but relatively little attention to the classification of behaviors and the situations in which they occur (also see Holmes & Cavallo, 2010). In fact, both social and personality psychology have suffered crises concerning the lack of empirical evidence linking important, proximal psychological constructs (e.g., attitudes and traits) to the behavioral outcomes they are meant to predict. We are well aware of the outcome of Wicker's (1969) classic review of the attitude-behavior relationship as well as Mischel's (1968) critique of the relationship between personality traits and behavior. Given those classic examples, as well as more recent critiques (e.g., Agnew et al., 2010), behavior must reemerge to serve a more central role in comprehensive frameworks of social and personality psychology.

The following sections focus on the mechanics of behavioral observation (see figure 5.1 for an overview),

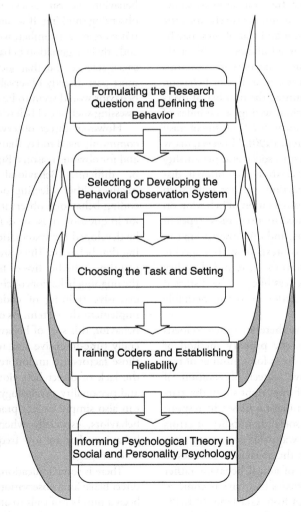

Fig. 5.1 Stages of Behavioral Observation.

given that lack of knowledge of the steps involved in behavior assessment could be a major impediment to utilizing this key research tool. What is important to understand is that the issues involved in the definition of behavior discussed at the beginning of this chapter are essential to keep in mind at each step of the assessment process. For example, as will be discussed more fully below, if we are interested in examining behaviors that are infrequent or novel, we may be more likely to choose to study these behaviors in a laboratory setting with a task that is designed to elicit those behaviors.

Formulating the Research Question and Defining the Behavior

While defining the research question might seem like an obvious step in the process of collecting behavioral data, it is an essential one. The research question that is generated has implications for all further steps in the assessment process. It does not matter whether behavioral measures are used in research if they do not address and inform the researcher's primary research question.

We argue, as do others (e.g., Aron, 2010; Weingart, 1997), that behavior can be included in research questions as mediators, as moderators, or as outcomes. That is, behavior can be assessed as an intervening step between inputs and outcomes; behavior can moderate the relationship between inputs and outcomes; or behavior can be assessed as the final outcome in a sequence of processes.

A number of theories exist in both social and personality psychology that include behavior as an intervening process. For example, in behavioral confirmation theory (Synder, 1984), the pattern of behavior elicited from a target mediates the relationship between the source's expectations concerning the target and the source's confirmation of those expectations. Bem's (1972) self-perception theory of attitude formation suggests that in the absence of knowledge about our attitude toward an object, we examine our behavior in order to infer our attitude. Too often, though, when behavior is assumed to be a mediating process, it is assessed through self-report, or sometimes merely assumed, rather than through behavioral observation.

Behavior can also serve as a moderator of other perceptions or behaviors. For example, in a powerful demonstration of the effects of behavior on participants' psychological and emotion states, Williams and Sommer (1997) had confederates engage in a ball-tossing game where they either included or excluded (ostracized) a naïve participant. Ostracized participants showed greatly depleted fundamental needs and negative emotional states. As another example, Gaddis, Connelly, and Mumford (2004) had leaders display either positive or negative affect after a failure experience. Leaders who displayed negative affect were judged by followers as less effective and responded with poorer quality performance compared to leaders who displayed more positive emotions.

It is perhaps easier to think of behavior as an outcome of other processes, including internal states and motivations, than as mediator or moderator. For example, an empathetic focus on a victim may lead one to a behavioral outcome that expresses helping (e.g., donating hours of babysitting, contributing money; Batson, 1998). Oftentimes, however, our research ends prior to the actual behavioral expression of these processes. For example, we may ask people to indicate on a questionnaire how many hours they would be willing to babysit to help out a person in an unfortunate position, but the actual behavioral expression of this intention is not assessed, and as mentioned previously, decades of research have addressed how the realities of a situation may reduce the likelihood that an expressed behavior will result from an intention (Fishbein & Ajzen, 1975).

It may also currently be difficult for social and personality researchers to generate interesting and meaningful research questions that center around behavior as a mediator, a moderator, or even as an outcome given the field's current focus on internal states such as attitudes and emotions. Part of the reason for this may be illustrated in the examples provided above. Using behavior as a moderator often involves the use of confederates, which can be a resource-consuming approach to research. And of course, assessing behavior as an outcome involves the time- and resource-consuming strategy of behavioral assessment. However, given the importance of behavior in validating other forms of assessment, more research questions need to be generated that include the assessment of behavior as a final outcome measure.

Selecting or Developing the Behavioral Observation System

Researchers who are knowledgeable about behavioral observation make the recommendation that, when possible, new researchers should try to borrow from observational systems that have already been created (Bakeman, 2000; Furr & Funder, 2007). Systems exist to code a wide variety of social behaviors, including emotional displays (FACS coding; Ekman, Friesen, & Hager 2002), aggressive behavior (Fagot & Hagen, 1985), personality (Riverside Behavioral Q-sort [RBQ]; Funder, Furr, & Colvin, 2000), and group interaction (SYMLOG; Bales & Cohen, 1979). The ability to utilize an existing system, with an already established track record of producing usable and valid data that can be reliably collected, can put a researcher far ahead in the game of behavior assessment.

If a researcher chooses to develop a novel coding system, the researcher needs to keep two primary factors in mind when selecting what sorts of behaviors to include in the system: (1) the level of analysis at which the behavior is to be observed and measured (molecular or molar), and (2) whether the system is intended to generalize across situations or apply specifically to a single situation (Furr & Funder, 2007). The answers to these questions are often dictated by the researcher's theoretical orientation and specific research question.

LEVEL OF ANALYSIS

Behaviors can be observed and measured at many different levels of analysis. For example, traditional behaviorists measured behavior at a very molecular level, such as number of bar presses. Some social psychologists who are interested in the expression of emotion also tend to observe and measure behavior at a molecular level. For example, FACS coding (Ekman, Friesen, & Hager, 2002) involves the coding of micromovements of facial muscles. Observers of nonverbal behavior are often interested in eyebrow flashes, body orientation, and the use of discrete gestures, all of which would be considered molecular level behaviors. For example, Hall and Friedman (1999) had observers record frequency counts of head nods, smiles, and hand gestures, as well as touch, forward lean, and interruptions in order to understand the interplay of status and gender in a structured interaction. What is important to keep in mind is that these very specific behaviors are consistent with the level of analysis of the researcher's theoretical approach and specific research question. An advantage of measuring behavior at this very molecular level is that the assessments involved require very little inference on the part of the observer about the social meaning of the behavior. Often the judgment is simply whether the behavior has occurred or not, and if the behavior is easily discerned from background noise, such a judgment should be relatively straightforward.

Behavior can also be measured at extremely molar levels. For example, Bernieri, Reznick, and Rosenthal (1988), in a study of interaction synchrony, had observers make global judgments of how smoothly the behavior of mother-infant pairs was coordinated in genuine interactions versus artificially generated pseudointeractions. Similarly, the Leadership Trait Questionnaires (LTQ; Northouse, 2007) asks both leaders and subordinates to rate the leader on ten behaviorally based traits, such as being articulate, perceptive, and self-confident. Note that these more molar, behaviorally based judgments involve a good deal more inference on the part of the observer than do specific discrete behaviors such as "gestures." In fact, a trait such as "self-confident" involves the observation of a number of more specific behaviors, such as participation rates or interruptions, from which position on the trait in question is inferred. And the greater the amount of inference involved, the greater might be the potential problems of interrater agreement (Funder et al., 2000). Consequently, it becomes important for the researcher to carefully specify what behaviors he or she thinks are indicative of the underlying (and nonobserved) trait, as a great deal of slippage can occur between the identification of a trait and its operational definition. However, again, the effort that might be involved in achieving sufficient levels of interrater reliability would be worth it if this level of analysis is appropriate for the researcher's conceptual network and specific research question.

A classic example of a more molar system is the Bales Interaction Process Analysis (IPA) system (Bales, 1950). The IPA was originally developed to systematically categorize small-group discussions in a manner that reflected Bales' theoretical ideas concerning group problem-solving. In that earlier work, Bales proposed that a group moves through a particular sequence of task phases as it moves from the beginning to the completion of a task: (1) orientation (gathering information and clarifying the task); (2) evaluation (assessing that information); and (3) control (deciding what to do). Twelve categories of discussion acts were developed to capture movement through those phases. For example, the categories of "gives orientation" and "asks for orientation" reflect activity in the orientation phase. The categories of "gives opinion" and "asks for opinion" reflect activity in the evaluation phase. Note then that the categories are meant to code the process meaning of verbal (and nonverbal) statement, and not their literal content. The implication of this is that the degree of inference needed on the part of the coder is quite high and intercoder reliability can be difficult to achieve without extensive training efforts.

The RBQ is an excellent example of a midlevel observation system (Funder, Furr, & Colvin, 2000). The RBQ asks observers to make behavioral judgments such as "appears relaxed and comfortable," "seems to enjoy the interaction," or "exhibits a high degree of intelligence." Similarly, the Leadership Behavior Description Questionnaire (LBDQ; Ohio State Leadership Studies, 1964) asks followers to make behavioral judgments of a leader such as "acts as spokesperson for the group," "makes accurate decisions," and "keeps the work moving at a rapid pace." Although a variety of molecular behaviors may go into the assessment of these midlevel categories (e.g., "seems to enjoy the interaction" might be indicated by a participant smiling frequently and actively engaging in discussion with their interaction partner), the level of inference needed in order to make judgments of midlevel categories is much less than for the types of molar judgments described above. A corresponding decrease in the amount of training required in order to achieve an appropriate level of reliability is also a benefit to assessments made at this level.

GENERALIZABILITY OF THE SYSTEM

The researcher also needs to decide whether the system will be useful across a variety of situations, or whether the system is appropriate only for use in a single type of situation. For example, the RBQ (Funder, Furr, & Colvin, 2000) was specifically developed to be useful across a wide variety of situations involving interpersonal interactions. Observers who use this system are able to sample a variety of potential behaviors that may underlie a particular RBQ rating. For example, "dominates the interaction" may be indicated by extensive talking in one setting and prominent body language in another, making the system flexible across a variety of situations. Indeed, the RBQ has been implemented in a variety of interpersonal situations (Funder, Furr, & Colvin, 2000). The Bales IPA (1950) or SYMLOG systems (Bales & Cohen, 1979) are also flexible systems that can be used across a variety of situations. The flexibility of the Bales IPA is due to the fact that utterances are coded for their process meaning, rather than coded for literal content.

In contrast, a wide variety of systems have been developed that focus on the coding of behaviors that are specific to a particular situation. For example, Foushee and colleagues (Foushee, 1984; Foushee, Lauber, Baetge, & Acomb, 1986) developed a system for observing the behavior of a flight crew within the cockpit of an airplane. Although this system was highly appropriate for the situation for which it was developed, and although the observations provided by the system were highly predictive of flight crew performance, the system has little use in other settings because many of the behaviors observed are not relevant to or are not performed in settings other than airplane cockpits (e.g., uses preflight checklist).

Kelly (2000), in a discussion of observation systems that have been used for the observation of group processes, made a distinction between process-focused systems and setting-focused systems. Process-focused systems, such as the Bales IPA, code the process meaning, rather than the literal content, of verbal utterances. Setting-focused systems may utilize either process or content coding, but are distinguished by having an application to only a specific group-task-situation. The avoidance of literal content makes process-focused systems flexible over many types of groups and many types of tasks, except where such group or task features vary too greatly from the theoretical categories proposed by the system. However, it is sometimes difficult to use these systems to test hypotheses that differ from the theoretical underpinnings of the system. In contrast, setting-focused systems are valuable for analyzing interaction in specific groups in specific situations, but cannot be used with any other kind of groups or even with the same group in any other performance context since categories are often idiosyncratically defined. The usefulness of these systems for theory-building is also limited.

Kelly (2000) also describes activity-focused systems that concentrate on the single dimension of vocalization/silence. These systems do not take into account the literal content of a vocalization, but merely record content-free features of the vocalizations such as tone of voice, turn-taking, interruptions, and so forth (e.g., Chapple, 1970; Dabbs & Ruback, 1987; Jaffee & Feldstein, 1970). The obvious benefits of such systems are the ease and reliability with which such observations can be made and the flexibility of the system in terms of applicability to many group-task-setting situations. An obvious drawback is the lack of conceptual clarity of the meaning of sound/silence patterns.

Choosing the Task and Setting

Once the behaviors of interest have been identified, the researcher must decide on the best setting in which to observe those behaviors. Direct observation of behavior can occur in both natural and contrived (e.g., laboratory) settings. The choice of setting must naturally depend on the research question of interest. But it also depends on the particular behaviors of interest as well.

It is not uncommon to equate behavioral observation with qualitative assessment of behavior as it occurs in natural settings, and although the equation is not accurate, the use of natural settings is certainly one choice that researchers might make. There are a wide range of overt, public social behaviors that are available for observation and that can be meaningfully fit into an appropriate theoretical framework. For example, a broad range of research examining children's levels of aggression has drawn heavily on behavioral observation of children in schools (Fagot & Hagan, 1985; Ostrov & Keating, 2004; Pelligrini, 2001). The various systems that have been implemented make use of both specific, discrete actions (e.g., hitting), as well as verbal utterances indicative of relational aggression (e.g., Crick, 1996).

Naturally occurring behaviors or classes of behaviors can vary in terms of frequency. Higher frequency behaviors have a higher likelihood of being captured in a natural setting. The assessment of lower frequency or novel behaviors may be aided by the creation of a behavior-eliciting task in the lab to ensure that those behaviors occur. For example, in order to examine aggressive behavior, which for most people is a low frequency behavior, participants were required to engage in a task with a confederate that involved provocation on the part of the confederate, with the participant later being given the chance to retaliate with some sort of aggressive behavior (Buss, 1961). In this way, a low frequency behavior can be reliably elicited in an experimental context.

Training Coders and Establishing Reliability

Proper training of observers or coders is essential to the behavioral assessment process. However, this training process can be one of the most time-consuming and costly aspects of proper behavior assessment. Some simple instances of behavioral observation, such as a mere frequency count of a discrete behavior like smiling, require little observer training, and in fact some behaviors can be easily assessed with mechanical counters such as a pedometer. Similarly, a popular behavior measure used by intergroup researchers involves assessing seating

distance between participants when the participants are allowed to position their own chair (e.g., Goff, Steele, & Davies, 2008). Other assessments require extensive training. For example, FACS training requires hundreds of hours of training for each coder (Ekman, Friesen, & Hager, 2002). Similarly, a moderately complex observation system developed for coding group interaction was estimated to require approximately 60 hours of training per coder in order for them to achieve appropriate levels of interrater reliability (Weingart, Hyder, & Prietula, 1996).

The degree of training involved depends on a number of factors, including the unitization of the activities being observed and the degree of inference involved in selecting an appropriate coding category. For example, in FACS coding, coders are instructed to distinguish and code extremely minute differences in facial muscle contractions, and correspondingly, training is a fairly laborious process. In contrast, coders using the RBQ (Furr, Funder, & Colvin, 2000) are asked to make midlevel judgments (e.g., expresses criticism, exhibits social skill) of a focal interactant in an interaction sequence. Funder and colleagues estimate that RBQ training requires approximately 2 hours per coder.

When developing a novel observation system, training coders and developing the observation system is often a recursive process. Issues of definition of the behavior, including issues of threshold, interdependence, or discernability often lead to a redefinition of how a behavior is operationalized in the observation system. When differences exist for how a particular behavior is characterized and coded, the resolution of those differences can lead to a clearer understanding of the parameters of the behavior in question.

Good behavioral assessment should also involve some sort of indication of the reliability of the system. That is, two or more observers should observe the same event and code the same behavior in the same way. Different indices of reliability exist for different types of data (e.g., categorical vs. interval). A thorough explanation of all these indices along with their statistical applications is beyond the scope of this chapter. However, LeBreton and Senter (2008) and von Eye and Mun (2005) provide comprehensive coverage of these topics.

Most behavioral data is ordinal or categorical in nature. That is, most systems involve categorizing a discrete behavior into one or more unordered categories. To assess reliability for these data, most indices involve some derivation of percent agreement.

Simple percent agreement (total number of agreements in categorizing the behavior divided by the total number of observations) is easy to calculate and is easily understood by most readers. However, total percent agreement can overestimate reliability especially when only a few categories are used for the categorization. Cohen's Kappa (1960) is recommended for assessing reliability for categorical behavior systems where errors can be made in the placement of the observed behavior into a specific category. Cohen's Kappa takes into account not only total agreement, but also corrects for chance agreement in situations where such chance error is likely to occur (e.g., few categories). Cohen's Kappa does, however, tend to provide a lower than expected reliability estimate when there is an unequal frequency of codes across categories. In this case, a weighted Kappa may be the more appropriate index of reliability.

For interval data (e.g., a frequency count of smiling), most researchers use some variation of a correlation coefficient. However, a Pearson correlation assesses only the relative pattern of responses between coders, and does not take into account absolute agreement. Intraclass correlations (McGraw & Wong, 1996), on the other hand, take into account both the relative pattern of responses and absolute agreement as well. Intraclass produces a coefficient that can be interpreted similarly to a correlation coefficient.

Strengths and Weakness of Behavior Observation

We have previously mentioned some of the strengths and weaknesses of behavioral observation, but some aspects of these qualities merit further reflection. One of the primary strengths of behavioral observation relative to self-reports of behavior is that it tends to be less subject to some sources of bias, such as lack of an accurate memory for events, biasing reports so as to appear in a positive and socially desirable light, and various response sets that may occur when reporting on behavior. Memory biases not only include the degradation of a memory trace, but the fact that much of our behavior is simply not noted at a conscious enough level to be stored in memory. For example, behavior that is routinized or habitual is likely not to be consciously noted or recorded in memory. (Just think of the times when we end up in our regular parking space at work with no real memory of the trip that brought us to that location.) And some researchers have suggested that such habitual behavior may make up as much as

40% of our daily activities (Verplanken, 2010). Furthermore, memories can be reexamined and reinterpreted in order to fit more easily into schemas that we hold for ourselves or others (Loftus & Cahill, 2007).

These points all relate to the most important strength of behavioral observation. Given that we have no direct access to a person's internal cognitions and emotions, our best objective indicator of those thoughts and emotions is what a person says and what a person does. Therefore, the systematic recording of those behaviors gives us particularly useful information about the internal psychological workings of individuals.

But behavioral assessment is not without weaknesses as well. As we have noted, observation systems vary quite widely on factors such as the size of the behavioral unit being observed and the degree of inference needed in order to categorize a particular behavior. In terms of implementation of a system, we have already noted that the amount of training necessary to achieve appropriate levels of interrater reliability varies with factors such as size of the behavioral unit and degree of inference. And although we have referred to behavioral assessment as being "objective," observers can also have expectations or biases that color their coding or interpretation of behavior (Rosenthal & Rubin, 1978). Consider, for example, an observer who is recording specific aggressive behavioral acts enacted by young children. Suppose further that this observer believes that boys are more aggressive than girls. The same specific behavior—a pointed finger, perhaps— might be interpreted as an aggressive behavior when exhibited by a boy and not when exhibited by a girl. That is, the observer's expectations or stereotypes may bias how a specific act is interpreted or fit within a behavioral recording system.

As with any research approach, replication is one of the best tools that we have in our arsenal to overcome weaknesses in research methods. Given the potential strengths of behavioral assessment, and given the increasing availability of tools for collecting these data, research using behavior may reach a critical enough mass for replications to occur. We end this section on behavior assessment by mentioning some of these emerging tools and technologies that might aid us in this endeavor.

New Technologies in Behavior Assessment

Behavior assessments are often made online or live as the focal person is behaving. This is especially true when the behaviors of interest are relatively straightforward and easily distinguished from other behaviors, such as large gestures, laughter, or talking. However, it is also a common procedure to record an ongoing interaction for later coding. Here, the accuracy of behavioral assessment is only as good as the instrument used, and instruments are subject to failure. Videotaped recordings of behavior may be of poor quality, making coding, especially of verbal behavior, quite difficult. Electronic instruments, such as video-recorders, are also subject to instrument decay or deterioration over time.

Despite the potential problems with using mechanical recordings of behavior, recent years have witnessed the introduction of new technologies that may prove to be particularly useful for behavioral assessment. We review several of these technologies here. Note, however, that some of these technologies do not have extensive research applications to date. They are, thus, presented as potential aids to behavioral research.

THE ELECTRONICALLY ACTIVATED RECORDER (EAR)

The Electronically Activated Recorder (EAR; Mehl, 2009) is a developing behavioral sampling technology and technique that is proving useful in sampling behavior as it occurs in a natural context. The EAR is a pocket sized audio-recorder that periodically records small audio samples of the ambient sounds from a person's environment. The EAR can be unobtrusively carried in the participant's pocket and audio samples can be collected with minimal amounts of reactivity as the person goes through his or her natural daily activities. Behavioral information is then coded from the sampled audio data. EAR has been used to assess a number of common social behaviors, such as talking (Mehl, Vazire, Ramirez-Esparza, Slatcher, & Pennebaker, 2007), swearing (Mehl, Gosling, & Pennebaker, 2006), and class attendance (Mehl et al., 2006). Many personality researchers consider experience sampling to be the best proxy for direct behavioral observation (Spain, Eaton, & Funder, 2000). However, EAR allows for the sampling of behavioral data independent of the participants' self-reports, and thus provides a behaviorally grounded criteria against which to assess other personality measures (Mehl, 2009).

VIRTUAL REALITY

Behavioral assessments can and have been applied within the context of immersive virtual environment technologies (IVET). Earlier we mentioned that it may be difficult for social and personality psychologists to conceptualize research where behavior serves as a moderator. IVETs, however, provide a vehicle for delivering behavioral manipulations. For example, IVETs can be used to manipulate subtle nonverbal cues or other behavioral characteristics of avatars in order to better understand their function in social interaction. A variety of behavioral dependent measures can also be conceptualized, including social interaction behaviors such as social distance between a participant and an avatar, vocal utterances, nonverbal cues such as body orientation or gaze directed toward the avatar, and so forth.

For example, Bailenson et al. (2008) manipulated physical proximity between a teacher and a student in order to examine its effects on student learning outcomes. They did so to simulate typical classroom environments in which only a subset of students can be at desks in closest proximity to the teacher. They found that student performance was improved when the student sat in a seat that was closer versus farther from the teacher. In another experiment, Bailenson and colleagues (2008) manipulated the presence of a model costudent or distracting costudent to assess the effect of the presence of such costudents on learning outcomes. They found that the behavior of virtual colearners influenced learning patterns of participants. Of particular interest, they found that eliminating the presence of costudents altogether had the most beneficial effect on learning.

In earlier work, Bailenson, Blascovich, Beall, and Loomis (2003) used IVET to study the interpersonal distance maintained between participants and virtual humans. They found that distance maintained was influenced by direction of avatar approach (front versus back), avatar gaze behavior (mutual vs. nonmutual with the participant), and violations of personal space. Manipulating environmental conditions via IVET provides a particularly powerful means for examining both behavioral influences and consequences.

WEBCAMS, SURVEILLANCE MONITORS, AND THE INTERNET

Recordings of public behavior are ubiquitous with the advent of webcams and surveillance recording machines. Security cameras record the behavior of passersby, live webcams broadcast the behavior of selected exhibits on the Internet. In fact, cell phones can also easily record the behavior of others in practically any location. For the most part, the behaviors recorded are public behaviors and thus can ethically be used as a medium for behavior assessment. The Internet itself can provide a wealth of information on behavior (Wallace, 2001). On YouTube, for example, people post videos involving many sort of social situations or behavior, and in fact, viewers can post comments or feedback about the posted videotape. The Internet can itself be used to assess behavior. With webcams, the behavior of people in distributed locations can be observed and coded.

Online participant observation is also an emerging method for behavioral assessment (Utz, 2010). Online participant observation is especially useful for studying sensitive topics (e.g., discrimination), difficult-to-access groups (e.g., viewers of online pornography, criminals), and interpersonal interaction (e.g., online dating sites). Advantages of participant observation include a fairly naturalistic record of behavior if the observer's identity is unknown. Beyond possible ethical issues involved in covert participant observation, researchers are limited in their ability to interpret some text due to lack of information concerning motivation and emotions. Generalizability to other groups or even to similar groups that meet offline can also be limited. Utz also provides a scheme for the types of behavioral data that can be collected including text messages, avatars, group size, and so forth.

Social networking Web sites, such as Facebook, are also now being used increasingly by personality and social psychological researchers to study various questions relevant to behavior. Self-reported behavioral information is a hallmark of such sites, but there are also opportunities for researchers to assess actual behaviors enacted by users with respect to interactions with other users or in obtaining information about other users. For example, Waggoner, Smith, and Collins (2009) used Facebook to assess differences in impression formation for passive versus active perceivers. Passive perceivers (defined as those Facebook users who were provided with preselected information about target individuals and whose searching behavior was, thus, constrained) were contrasted with active perceivers (those users who were free to choose the type and amount of information they received about a target person). Results indicated that active perceivers, whose behavior was not constrained, liked targets less but were less confident regarding their judgments of target personality than were passive perceivers. Manipulating the behavior of social network Website users provides a fascinating new approach

to the study of an increasing ubiquitous human behavior: Web use.

The challenge for using these technologies is in developing appropriate research questions that could be addressed using available recordings. That is, the researcher must limit his or her questions to those where the recordings would provide meaningful data. The potential of the resource, however, is exciting.

CODER COMPUTER SUPPORT SYSTEMS
Coding from digital recordings of behavior has been made easier with the advent of various computer observational support systems, such as the Observer Video-Pro (Lucas et al., 2000), the NVivo (http://www.qsrinternational.com), or the MAXQDA (http://www.maxqda.com). These systems aid the task of observation by offering direct data entry of data into a computer, often in conjunction with an automatic time stamping of the ongoing interaction. The interface eliminates errors due to transcription and the time stamping increases the researcher's ability to assess coding reliability. Generally, these systems allow you to import observations from analog/digital videotapes or digital media files. Observation streams can be reviewed and edited on the computer. In conjunction with this, software allows you to define a number of behaviors and assign a key code to each behavior. These keys are pressed to record the occurrence of an event during an observation session.

Observation of Personal Living Spaces (PLSs)
An intriguing new technique for discerning personality traits through observation has been initiated by Gosling and his colleagues (Carney et al., 2008; Gosling et al., 2002). Rather than directly observing behavior, however, Gosling and colleagues observe the remnants or traces that behavior has left behind by observing personal living spaces (PLSs) such as dorm rooms or offices. The Personal Living Space Cue Inventory (PLSCI; Gosling et al., 2005) is an observation tool that allows the user to comprehensively document aspects of individual's personal living spaces (PLSs), such as whether the space is generally tidy or colorful, whether the clocks are set on time, or whether the space was light or stuffy. These descriptors have also been linked to various personality traits. For example, the Big Five personality trait of Openness to Experience has been linked to PLSs that are distinctive and colorful, whereas the traits of Conscientiousness has been linked to

PLSs that are tidy and decorated in a conventional manner (Carney et al., 2008; Gosling et al., 2002).

Integrating Behavior Into Social And Personality Psychology Theory

We have argued, as have others, that behavioral assessment is essential for researchers who study personality and social behavior because behavior often provides an objective look into the hearts and minds of research participants. Since we do not have direct access to internal states that are the precursors of behavior, such as attitudes and predispositions, other than as they are processed through other mechanisms subject to potential bias (e.g., self-reports), overt behavior provides the most direct access to these sorts of psychological states. While it is true that we may also be interested in cognitions and emotions for their own sake, knowledge of how internal states impact behavioral outcomes is an essential part of understanding the human condition.

However, merely assessing and quantifying behavior is not enough to provide meaningful insight into human psychology. Those behaviors needs to be translated into psychologically meaningful constructs—that is, constructs that are theoretically useful for making sense of people's psychological states. And further, that behavior needs to be integrated into our social and personality psychology theories.

Interpretation of Behavior as Psychologically Meaningful Constructs

A problem with some aspects of behavioral observation is that the psychological meaning of a specific behavior is often unclear. For example, a single cooperative choice in a Prisoner's Dilemma Game may be reflective of a person's underlying cooperativeness. However, it may also reflect a more complex strategy for gaining future resources. For example, a tit-for-tat strategy, where one responds on a subsequent move with what one's partner has responded on for the previous move, is an effective strategy for establishing a pattern of cooperation. But it is also an effective strategy for reliably gaining resources. The behavior itself is ambiguous with respect to the motive that underlies its enactment. As another example, striking out at another person, an overt behavior that should be fairly easy to reliably notice and record, could be motivated by fear, and thus reflect a self-protective response, or by anger, and thus reflect an exertion of frustration, power, or dominance over the other.

Other examples of psychologically ambiguous behaviors include those often produced by activity-focused systems. As described previously, activity-focused systems are those that focus on the presence or absence of an activity such as talking. Although this single dimension of behavior has been used to generate complex descriptions of personality (Chapple, 1970), the precise psychological motivation behind a specific pattern of behavior is difficult to discern. For example, does rapid and uninterruptable speech indicate that the speaker is extraverted, nervous, or dominant? Are long "turns" of speech also possible indicators of those same psychological states?

In some instances, we put the burden of this translation on the observers by asking them to make at least some degree of inference in assessing the behaviors. Coding systems that operate at the more molecular level, for example, often explicitly ask observers to develop trait or character inferences based on their observation of sometimes long, but sometimes very short (thin slices; Ambady & Rosenthal, 1993), sequences of behavior. In general, the ambiguity of a behavior increases as the coding level decreases.

Although we argue that behavior is a key indicator of people's internal cognitive and emotional states, specifying exactly what those behaviors indicate remains a challenge for behavioral researchers.

Using Behavior in Our Social and Personality Psychology Theories

We suggested earlier that it may be difficult for social and personality researchers to generate interesting and meaningful research questions that center around behavior. Part of this is due to the field's current focus on internal states—cognition, emotions, and motivations. Part of this is due to the increasing emphasis on multistudy papers in our top journals. Given the often time-consuming task of behavioral observation, it would be difficult to accrue the number of publications needed for academic success when packing those publications with multiple studies that include behavioral observation. And finally, the further away from behavior we've gone as a field, the more difficult it has become to conceptualize our variables in behavioral terms.

Many of the currently popular theories in social and personality psychology reflect this internal focus. For example, in terror management theory (Solomon, Greenberg, & Pyszczynski, 1991), the mortality salience hypothesis states that reminders of one's mortality will increase the needs of individuals to value their own cultural worldview and self-esteem. This may result in behavioral changes, but more typically, these motivational changes are indexed by outcomes such as increased stereotypical thinking and biased intergroup evaluation. And it is those internal changes that are assessed and reported in research publications.

The currently popular theory of persuasion in attitudes research, the elaboration likelihood model (Petty & Wegener, 1999), similarly focuses on the cognitive variable of elaborative thought processing as the mediator between source messages and attitude change. The impact of attitude change on actual behavior is not addressed, although theoretically much is known regarding when attitudes predict behavior.

Again, this is not to say that these inner states are not important. It is certainly important to predict and understand another person's emotional or cognitive reactions to stimuli. We are only saying that this is not the whole picture when trying to understand people. Sometimes we are interested in internal processes in and of themselves. But at other times, these internal processes are meant as precursors to action, and it is important that the action itself be included in the assessment picture as well.

There has been a recent rise in theories and research programs that emphasize behavior. For example, Gollwitzer's work on implementation intentions (Gollwitzer, 1999; 2010) includes both the assessment of internal cognitions—a specific cognitive plan for carrying out an activity—as well as an assessment of the activity itself. With a focus on behavior as the outcome, Gollwitzer and colleagues have shown how different forms of intentions affect the occurrence of an actual behavior (e.g., Gawrilow & Gollwitzer, 2008; Gollwitzer & Sheeran, 2006). Chartrand and Bargh's (1999; Bargh & Morsella, 2010) work on behavioral mimicry also has a strong behavioral component and offers interesting evidence that the environment can automatically determine behavior. And research on interaction synchrony and rapport (Tickle-Degnen, 2006) demonstrates that behavioral coordination can have a profound impact on relational outcomes.

It is also worth noting that social psychological and personality research featuring actual behaviors are more likely to have impact on real-world problems as well as on policymakers (including those who fund our less behavior-oriented research) (see Omoto, chapter 32, this volume). For example, research on stereotype threat has helped to identify what interventions can be undertaken to reduce academic performance deficits in those students who are the target of negative group-based stereotypes. Actual behavioral differences ("performance deficits") between students are tangible and more easily identified as problematic by educators and policymakers alike. Put another way, behavior attracts attention.

It is not that we want to strip the assessment of internal processes from our research, but rather we want to complement those assessments with assessments of external behavioral processes. We believe it would be a mistake to ignore the complexities of the actual enactment of behavior when building a comprehensive understanding of human interaction.

Concluding Thoughts

In this chapter, we have attempted to reintroduce behavior and behavior assessment to personality and social psychology. Although early research in our fields was characterized by studies that included observations of behavior—and sometimes quite dramatic behavior—this cannot be said to be true for research conducted at least for the past 25 years. Social and personality psychology attempts to understand how the thoughts, feelings, *and behaviors* of individuals are influenced by individual characteristics and by other people. It is time to more completely embrace this definition by grounding our assessments whenever appropriate in behavioral observation.

References

Ambady, N., & Rosenthal, R. (1993). Half a minute: Predicting teacher evaluations from thin slices of nonverbal behavior and physical attractiveness. *Journal of Personality and Social Psychology, 64,* 431–441.

Achenbach, T. M. (1991). *Manual for the Child Behavior Checklist/4–18 and 1991 profile*. University of Vermont, Department of Psychiatry, Burlington, VT.

Agnew, C. R. (1999). Power over interdependent behavior within the dyad: Who decides what a couple does? In L. J. Severy & W. B. Miller (Eds.), *Advances in population: Psychosocial perspectives* (vol. 3, pp. 163–188). London: Kingsley.

Agnew, C. R., Carlston, D. E., Graziano, W. G., & Kelly, J. R. (Eds.). (2010). *Then a miracle occurs: Focusing on behavior in social psychological theory and research*. New York: Oxford University Press.

Agnew, C. R., Carlston, D. E., Graziano, W. G., & Kelly, J. R. (2010). Behavior and miracles. In C. R. Agnew, D. E. Carlston, W. G. Graziano, & J. R. Kelly (Eds.), *Then a miracle occurs: Focusing on behavior in social psychological theory and research* (pp. 3–11). New York: Oxford University Press.

Agnew, C. R., & Kelly, J. R. (2010). Behavior between people: Emphasizing the "act" in interaction. In C. R. Agnew, D. E. Carlston, W. G. Graziano, & J. R. Kelly (Eds.), *Then a miracle occurs: Focusing on behavior in social psychological theory and research* (pp. 275–282). New York: Oxford University Press.

Ajzen, I. (1991). The theory of planned behavior. *Organizational Behavior and Human Decision Processes, 50*, 179–211.

Ajzen, I., & Fishbein, M. (1977). Attitude-behavior relations: A theoretical analysis and review of empirical research. *Psychological Bulletin, 84*, 888–918.

Aron, A. (2010). Behavior, the brain, and the social psychology of close relationships. In C. R. Agnew, D. E. Carlston, W. G. Graziano, & J. R. Kelly (Eds.), *Then a miracle occurs: Focusing on behavior in social psychological theory and research* (pp. 283–298). New York: Oxford University Press.

Bailenson, J. N. Blascovich, J., Beall, A. C., & Loomis, J. M. (2003). Interpersonal distance in immersive virtual environments. *Personality and Social Psychology Bulletin, 29*, 819–833.

Bailenson, J. N., Yee, N., Blascovich, J., Beall, A. C., Lundblad, N., & Jin, M. (2008). The use of virtual reality in the learning sciences: Digital transformations of teachers, students, and social context. *Journal of the Learning Sciences, 17*, 102–141.

Bakeman, R. (2000). Behavioral observation and coding. In H. T. Reis & C. K. Judd (Eds.), *Handbook of research methods in social psychology* (pp. 138–159). New York: Cambridge University Press.

Bales, R. F. (1950). *Interaction process analysis: A method for the study of small groups*. Oxford, UK: Addison-Wesley.

Bales, R. F., & Cohen, S. P. (1979). *SYMLOG: A System for the Multiple Level Observation of Groups*. New York: Macmillan.

Bargh, J. A., & Morsella, E. (2010). Unconscious behavioral guidance systems. In C. R. Agnew, D. E. Carlston, W. G. Graziano, & J. R. Kelly (Eds.), *Then a miracle occurs: Focusing on behavior in social psychological theory and research* (pp. 89–118). New York: Oxford University Press.

Batson, C. D. (1998). Altruism and prosocial behavior. In D. T. Gilbert, S. T. Fiske, & G. Lindzey, (Eds.), *The handbook of social psychology* (pp. 282-316). New York: McGraw Hill.

Baumeister, R. F., Vohs, K. D., & Funder, D. C. (2007). Psychology as the science of self-reports and finger movements: Whatever happened to actual behavior? *Perspectives on Psychological Science, 2*, 396–403.

Bem, D. J. (1972). Self-perception theory. In L. Berkowitz (Ed.), *Advances in experimental social psychology* (Vol. 6, pp. 1-62). New York: Academic.

Bernieri, F. J., Reznick, J. S., Rosenthal, R. (1988). Synchrony, pseudosynchrony, and dissynchrony: Measuring the entrainment process in mother-infant interactions. *Journal of Personality and Social Psychology, 54*, 243–253.

Bolger, N., Stadler, G., Paprocki, C., & DeLongis, A. (2010). Grounding social psychology in behavior in daily life: The case of conflict and distress in couples. In Agnew, C. R., Carlston, D. E., Graziano, W. G., & Kelly, J. R. (Eds.), *Then a miracle occurs: Focusing on behavior in social psychological theory and research* (pp. 368–390). New York: Oxford University Press.

Buss, A. (1961). The *psychology of aggression, New* York: Wiley.

Carney, D. R., Jost, J. T., Gosling, S. D., & Potter, J. (2008). The secret lives of liberals and conservatives: Personality Profiles, interaction styles, and the things they leave behind. *Political Psychology, 29*, 807–840.

Chapple, E. D. (1970). *Culture and biological man: Explorations in behavioral anthropology*. New York: Holt, Rinehart, and Winston.

Chartrand, T. L., & Bargh, J. A. (1999). The chameleon effect: The perception-behavior link and social interaction. *Journal of Personality and Social Psychology, 76*, 893–910.

Cialdini, R. B., Reno, R. R., & Kallgren, C. A. (1990). A focus theory of normative conduct: Recycling the concept of norms to reduce littering in public places. *Journal of Personality and Social Psychology, 58*, 1015–1026.

Cohen, J. A. (1960). Coefficient of agreement for nominal scales. *Educational and Psychological Measurement, 20*, 37–46.

Crick, N. R. (1996). The role of overt aggression, relational aggression, and prosocial behavior in the prediction of children's future social adjustment. *Child Development, 67*, 2317–2327.

Dabbs, J. M., & Ruback, R. B. (1987). Dimensions of group process: Amount and structure of vocal interaction. In L. Berkowitz (Ed.), *Advances in experimental social psychology* (pp. 123–169). New York: Academic.

Darley, J. M., & Latanè, B. (1968). Bystander intervention in emergencies: Diffusion of responsibility. *Journal of Personality and Social Psychology, 28*, 377–383.

Ekman, P., Friesen, W. V., & Hager, J. C. (2002). *The facial action coding system* (2nd ed.). Salt Lake City, UT: Research Nexus eBook.

Fagot, B. T. & Hagan, R. (1985). Aggression in toddlers: Responses to the assertive acts of boys and girls. *Sex Roles, 12*, 341–351.

Fishbein, M., & Ajzen, I. (1975). *Belief, attitude, intention, and behavior: An introduction to theory and research*. Reading, MA: Addison-Wesley.

Foushee, H. C. (1984). Dyads and triads at 35,000 feet. *American Psychologist, 39*, 885–893.

Foushee, H. C., Lauber, J. K., Baetge, M. M., & Acomb, D. B. (1986). *Crew factors in flight operations: III. The operational significance of exposure to short-haul air transport operations*. Moffet Field, CA: NASA Ames Research Center (NASA Technical Memorandum 88322).

Funder, D. C. (2006). Toward a resolution of the personality triad: Persons, situations, and behaviors. *Journal of Research in Personality, 40*, 21–34.

Funder, D. C., Furr, R. M., & Colvin, C. R. (2000). The Riverside Behavioral Q-Sort: A tool for the description of social behavior. *Journal of Personality, 68*, 451–489.

Furr, R. M., & Funder, D. C. (2007). Behavioral observation. In R. W. Robins, R. C. Fraley, & R. F. Krueger (Eds.). (2007). *Handbook of research methods in personality psychology* (pp. 273–291). New York: Guilford.

Furr, R. M., Wagerman, S. A., & Funder, D. C. (2010). Personality as manifest in behavior: Direct behavioral observation using the Revised Riverside Behavioral Q-Sort (RBQ-3.0). In C. R. Agnew, D. E. Carlston, W. G. Graziano, & J. R. Kelly. (Eds.), *Then a miracle occurs: Focusing on behavior in social psychological theory and research* (pp. 186–204). New York: Oxford University Press.

Gaddis, B, Connelly, S., & Mumford, M. D. (2004). Failure feedback as an affective event: Influences of leader affect on subordinate attitudes and performance. *Leadership Quarterly, 15*, 663–686.

Gawrilow, C., & Gollwitzer, P. M. (2008). Implementation intentions facilitate response inhibition in children with ADHD. *Cognitive Therapy and Research, 32*, 261–280.

Gladwell, M. (2000). *The tipping point: How little things can make a big difference*. New York: Little, Brown and Company.

Gladwell, M. (2005). *Blink: The power of thinking without thinking*. New York: Little, Brown and Company.

Gladwell, M. (2008). *Outliers: The story of success*. New York: Little, Brown and Company.

Goff, P. A., Steele, C. M., & Davies, P. G. (2008). The space between us: Stereotype threat and distance in interracial contexts. *Journal of Personality and Social Psychology, 94,* 91–107.

Gollwitzer, P. M. (1999). Implementation intentions: Strong effects of simple plans. *American Psychologist, 54,* 493–503.

Gollwitzer, P. M., & Sheeran, P. (2006). Implementation intentions and goal achievement: A meta-analysis of effects and processes. *Advances in Experimental Social Psychology, 38,* 69–119.

Gollwitzer, P. M., Wieber, F., Myers, A. L., & McCrea, S. M. (2010). How to maximize implementation intention effects. In C. R. Agnew, D. E. Carlston, W. G. Graziano, & J. R. Kelly (Eds.), *Then a miracle occurs: Focusing on behavior in social psychological theory and research* (pp. 275–282). New York: Oxford University Press.

Gosling, S. D., Craik, K. H., Martin, N. R., & Pryor, M. R. (2005). The Personal Living Space Cue Inventory: An analysis and evaluation. *Environment and Behavior, 37,* 683–705.

Gosling, S. D., Ko, S. J., Mannarelli, T., & Morris, M. E. (2002). A room with a cue: Judgments of personality based on offices and bedrooms. *Journal of Personality and Social Psychology, 82,* 379–398.

Hall. J. A., & Friedman, G. B. (1999). Status, gender, and nonverbal behavior: A study of structured interactions between employees of a company. *Personality and Social Psychology Bulletin, 25,* 1082-1091.

Hartshorne, H., & May, M. A. (1928). *Studies in the nature of character.* New York: Macmillan.

Holmes, J. G., & Cavallo, J. V. (2010) The atlas of interpersonal situations: A theory-driven approach to behavioral signatures. In C. R. Agnew, D. E. Carlston, W. G. Graziano, & J. R. Kelly (Eds.), *Then a miracle occurs: Focusing on behavior in social psychological theory and research* (pp. 321–341). New York: Oxford University Press.

Jaffe, J., & Feldstein, S. (1970). *Rhythms of dialogue.* New York: Academic.

Kelly, J. R. (2000). Interaction process analysis in task performing groups. In A. P. Beck & C. M. Lewis (Eds.), *Process in therapeutic groups: A handbook of systems of analysis* (pp. 49-65). Washington, DC: American Psychological Association.

LaPiere, R. T. (1934). Attitudes vs. actions. *Social Forces, 13,* 230–237.

LeBreton, J. M., & Senter, J. L. (2008). Answers to twenty questions about interrater reliability and interrater agreement. *Organizational Research Methods, 11,* 815–852.

Loftus, E. F., & Cahill, L. (2007). Memory distortion: From misinformation to rich false memory. In J. S. Nairne (Ed.), *The foundations of remembering: Essays in honor of Henry L. Roediger, III* (pp. 413–425). New York: Psychology Press.

Lucas, P. J. J., Noldus, R. J. H., Trienes, A. H. M., Hendriksen, H. J., & Roland G. J. (2000). The Observer Video-Pro: New software for the collection, management, and presentation of time-structured data from videotapes and digital media files. *Behavior Research Methods, Instruments, and Computers, 32,* 197–206.

McGraw, K. O., & Wong, S. P. (1996). Forming inferences about some intraclass correlation coefficients. *Psychological Methods, 1,* 30–46.

Mehl, M. R. (2009). Naturalistic observations of daily behavior in personality psychology. *European Journal of Personality, 23,* 414–416.

Mehl, M. R., Gosling, S. D., & Pennebaker, J. W. (2006). Personality in its natural habitat: Manifestations and implicit folk theories of personality in daily life. *Journal of Personality and Social Psychology, 90,* 862–877.

Mehl, M. R., Vazie, S., Ramirez-Esparza, N., Slatcher, R. B., & Pennebaker, J. W. (2007). Are women really more talkative than men? *Science, 317,* 82.

Milgram, S. (1975). *Obedience to authority.* New York: Harper & Row.

Mischel, W. (1968). *Personality and assessment.* New York: Wiley.

Moreland, R. L., Fetterman, J. D., Flagg, J. J., & Swanenburg, K. L. (2010). Behavioral assessment practices among social psychologists who study small groups. In C. R. Agnew, D. E. Carlston, W. G. Graziano, & J. R. Kelly (Eds.), *Then a miracle occurs: Focusing on behavior in social psychological theory and research* (pp. 28–56). New York: Oxford University Press.

Newtson, D., & Engquist, G. (1976). The perceptual organization of ongoing behavior. *Journal of Experimental Social Psychology, 2,* 436–450.

Nisbett, R., & Wilson, T. (1977). Telling more than we can know: Verbal reports on mental processes. *Psychological Review, 84,* 231–259.

Northouse, P. G. (2007). *Leadership theory and practice* (4th ed.). London: Sage.

Ohio State Leadership Studies. (1964). *Leader behavior description questionnaire* (LBDQ). Retrieved from *http://fisher.osu.edu/offices/fiscal/lbdq.*

Ostrov, J. M., & Keating, C. F. (2004). Gender differences in preschool aggression during free play and structured interactions: An observational study. *Social Development, 13,* 255–277.

Paulhus, D. L. (1991). Measurement and control of response bias. In J. P. Robinson, P. R. Shaver, & L. S. Wrightsman (Eds.), *Measures of personality and social psychological attitudes* (pp. 17–60). San Diego: Academic.

Paulhus, D. L., & Holden, R. R. (2010). Measuring self-enhancement: From self-report to concrete behavior. In C. R. Agnew, D. E. Carlston, W. G. Graziano, & J. R. Kelly (Eds.), *Then a miracle occurs: Focusing on behavior in social psychological theory and research* (pp. 227–246). New York: Oxford University Press.

Pellegrini, A. D. (2001). Practitioner review: The role of direct observation in the assessment of young children. *Journal of Child Psychology and Psychiatry and Allied Disciplines, 42,* 861–869.

Petty, R. E., & Wegener, D. T. (1999). The elaboration likelihood model: Current status and controversies. In S. Chaiken & Y. Trope (Eds.), *Dual process theories in social psychology* (pp. 41–72). New York: Guilford.

Rosenthal, R., & Rubin, D. B. (1978). Interpersonal expectancy effects: The first 345 studies. *Behavioral and Brain Sciences, 3,* 377–386.

Sande, G. N., Goethals, G. R., & Radloff, C. E. (1988). Perceiving one's own traits and others': The multifaceted self. *Journal of Personality and Social Psychology, 54,* 13-20.

Sherif, M., Harvey, O. J., White, B. J., Hood, W. R., & Sherif, C. W. (1961): *Intergroup conflict and cooperation: The Robbers Cave experiment.* Norman: University of Oklahoma Book Exchange.

Snyder, M. (1984). When belief creates reality. In L. Berkowitz (Ed.), *Advances in experimental social psychology* (Vol. 18, pp. 248-305). New York: Academic.

Solomon, S., Greenberg, J., & Pyszczynski, T. (1991). Terror management theory of self-esteem. In C. R. Snyder & D. R. Forsyth (Eds.), *Handbook of social and clinical psychology: The health perspective* (pp. 21–40). Elmsford, NY: Pergamon.

Spain, J. S., Eaton, L. G., & Funder, D. C. (2000). Perspectives on personality: The relative accuracy of self vs. others for the prediction of behavior and emotion. *Journal of Personality, 68,* 837–867.

Tickle-Degnen, L. (2006). Nonverbal behavior and its functions in the ecosystem of rapport. In M. L. Patterson & V. Manusov (Eds.), *Handbook of nonverbal communication (pp. 381-420).* Thousand Oaks, CA: Sage.

Utz, S. (2010). Using automated "field notes" to observe the behavior of online subjects. In S. D. Gosling & J. A. Johnson (Eds.), *Advanced methods for conducting online behavioral research* (pp. 91–108). Washington, DC: American Psychological Association.

Waggoner, A. S., Smith, E. R., & Collins, E. C. (2009). Person perception by active versus passive perceivers. *Journal of Experimental Social Psychology, 45,* 1028–1031.

Wallace, P. (2001). *The psychology of the Internet.* New York: Cambridge University Press.

Webb, E. J., Campbell, D. T., Schwartz, R. D., Sechrest, L, & Grove J. B. (1981). *Nonreactive measures in the social sciences.* Boston: Houghton Mifflin.

Weingart, L. R. (1997). How did they do that: The ways and means of studying group processes. *Research in Organizational Behavior, 19,* 189–239.

Weingart, L. R., Hyder, E. B., & Prietula, M. J. (1996). Knowledge matters: The effect of tactical descriptions on negotiation behavior and outcome. *Journal of Personality and Social Psychology, 70,* 1205–1217.

Wicker, A. W. (1969). Attitudes vs. actions: The relationship of verbal and overt behavioral responses to attitude objects. *Journal of Social Issues, 25,* 41–78.

Williams, K. D., & Sommer, K. L. (1997). Social ostracism by coworkers: Does rejection lead to loafing or compensation? *Personality and Social Psychology Bulletin, 23,* 693–706.

Verplanken, B. (2010). Habit: From overt action to mental events. In C. R. Agnew, D. E. Carlston, W. G. Graziano, & J. R. Kelly (Eds.), *Then a miracle occurs: Focusing on behavior in social psychological theory and research* (pp. 89–118). New York: Oxford University Press.

von Eye, A., & Mun, E. Y. (2005). *Analyzing rater agreement: Manifest variable methods.* Mahwah, NJ: Erlbaum.

Neuroscience Approaches in Social and Personality Psychology

David M. Amodio *and* Eddie Harmon-Jones

Abstract

Social neuroscience is an interdisciplinary approach to studying the mind and behavior, noted for its appreciation for the dynamic interactions of situational and dispositional processes as they relate to neural and biological mechanisms. In this chapter, we describe the methodological approach of social neuroscience and review research that has applied this approach to address the interplay of the person and situation in the domains of social cognition, attitudes, emotion and motivation, intergroup relations, and personality. We provide critical discussion of how neuroscience may contribute to classic questions in personality and social psychology, and we describe how the social neuroscience approach promotes the integration of dispositional and situational accounts of the mind and behavior.

Keywords: social neuroscience, emotion, attitudes, intergroup, review, psychophysiology, cognitive neuroscience, personality and neuroscience

Neuroscience Approaches to Social and Personality Psychology

The recent interest in neural and biological components of social and personality processes may seem new, but is actually a return to form for the field of social and personality psychology. Founding psychologists such as James and Wundt were trained in physiology, and they approached issues of thought, emotion, memory, and perception with a firm belief that mental processes were rooted in the brain. To these psychologists, the mind and the brain were symbiotic, and a consideration of neural processes, along with dispositional and interpersonal processes, provided a natural and comprehensive approach to understanding the mind and behavior. Early psychological research on social processes, such as bluffing to other players during a poker game (Riddle, 1925) or responding to socially taboo words and phrases (Darrow, 1929), incorporated psychophysiological measures to complement behavioral observations. Indeed, early research on intergroup interactions and prejudice used physiological measures to

examine anxiety during an interracial encounter (Rankin & Campbell, 1955). Hence, physiological measures have long served as an important component of an integrated approach to social-personality psychology.

As the field of psychology developed, a shift toward behaviorism effectively vanquished the role of the mind and brain from the study of behavior, and the field of neuroscience branched away from psychology. Although research on neural function continued at lower levels of analysis (e.g., cellular and molecular), it no longer made contact with the higher-level processes of social and personality psychology. When a focus on mental function reemerged during the cognitive revolution, it was generally held separate from neural and biological function (with some notable exceptions, e.g., Cacioppo & Petty, 1983; Frith, Morton, & Leslie, 1991; Gazzaniga, 1985; Shapiro & Crider, 1969). However, with recent advances in brain imaging technology, research on cognitive neuroscience has surged over the past decade, making increasing contact with questions of social cognition (Ochsner & Lieberman, 2001). In this way, social and personality psychologists have begun to reintegrate neural and biological approaches into the range of methods used to understand the social mind and behavior.

In this chapter, we review the contemporary social neuroscience approach to social-personality psychology. This general approach began to appear with increasing frequency in the laboratories of social psychologists, cognitive neuroscientists, and neurologists during the late 1990s. The term "social neuroscience" was coined in print by Cacioppo and Berntson (1992; see also Carlston, 1994) and tends to describe the broad enterprise of examining the interplay of social and physiological levels of analysis. More recent formulations by Ochsner and Lieberman (2001) and Klein and Kihlstrom (1998) incorporated ideas from cognitive neuroscience and neuropsychological patient literatures, respectively, prompting new aspects of social neuroscience referred to as "social cognitive neuroscience" and "social neuropsychology." Over the past decade, social neuroscience has been the subject of several dedicated research conferences, culminating in the formation of the Social and Affective Neuroscience Society in 2008 and the Society for Social Neuroscience in 2010. Whereas social neuroscience was seen as a novelty at social-personality meetings merely a decade ago, it is now fully integrated into the social/personality psychologist's methodological repertoire.

The present volume highlights the interplay of social and personality factors in studies of the mind and behavior. The social neuroscience approach fits this theme well. Integrative at its core, social neuroscience encompasses the study of personality and individual differences as well as situational and environmental effects, as they interface with cognitive processes and neural mechanisms. In this chapter, we use the term "social neuroscience" to refer to this general integrative approach, although it might just as easily be called "social-personality neuroscience."

In what follows, we begin with an overview of the methodological approaches used in social neuroscience. We then describe social neuroscience research across major areas of social and personality psychology, with a focus on how neuroscience and physiological approaches pertain to social-personality theory.

The Social Neuroscience Approach

Broadly speaking, social neuroscience refers to an integrative approach that can be applied to any scientific question concerning social processes and the brain. However, the types of questions that are addressed with this approach vary considerably across disciplines. To the social psychologist, *social neuroscience* refers to an interdisciplinary research approach that integrates theories and methods of neuroscience (and other biological fields) to address social psychological questions. To a cognitive neuroscientist, it often refers to research that addresses questions about the neural substrates of social processes, with a focus on understanding neural function. To an animal behaviorist, social neuroscience research may address questions about the neural and hormonal mechanisms associated with low-level social behaviors, such as dominance and affiliation. Thus, many "social neuroscience" studies examine questions outside the typical purview of social-personality psychology, and therefore it is helpful for consumers of this literature to carefully consider the question asked by a particular study. In this section, we describe the two main types of questions asked in human social neuroscience and their corresponding methodological approaches. We also describe the critical role of reverse inference in drawing conclusions from neuroscience findings.

Brain Mapping Approach

Brain-mapping studies ask "Where in the brain is _____?" For example, Where in the brain is fear? Where is episodic memory? Where is love? Where is the self? Human brain mapping is a cornerstone of modern cognitive neuroscience. It concerns the mapping of basic psychological processes to particular regions of the brain.

Early forms of brain mapping involved the probing of exposed brain tissue by a neurosurgeon while a patient reported his or her experience. Today, relatively noninvasive neuroimaging measures, such as functional magnetic resonance imaging (fMRI), are often used for a similar purpose. In cognitive neuroscience, this approach is used to map relatively low-level psychological processes such as basic forms of sensation, perception, and specific aspects of learning and memory. As a general rule, lower-level cognitive processes can be mapped more directly onto specific physiological responses than more complex high-level processes.

In social psychology, researchers have attempted to map very high-level psychological processes, such as social emotions, the self-concept, trait impressions, and political attitudes, onto the brain as well. This is where things get trickier. For example, to study the neural basis of romantic love, researchers have scanned participants' brains while they viewed pictures of strangers versus their significant others

(Aron, Fisher, Mashek, Strong, Li, & Brown, 2005). Similarly, to study the neural basis of the self, researchers have scanned the brain while subjects judged whether trait adjectives described them versus another person (Kelley et al., 2002; Mitchell, Banaji, & Macrae, 2005). Such studies apply the same logic to identifying the neural substrates of very high-level processes as neuroscientists have applied in the neural mapping of very low-level processes, such as edge detection in vision. Although high-level psychological ascriptions of brain activity may have heuristic value, they may risk obscuring the important low-level mechanisms that the observed brain activations likely represent.

A defining feature of the brain mapping approach is that it seeks to create a valid mapping of psychological processes onto a pattern of neurophysiological responses. Pure brain-mapping studies are undertaken with few prior assumptions about the psychological function of a brain region—indeed, the point of such studies is to establish ideas about function through the process of induction across multiple studies using a variety of conceptually similar tasks and manipulations. This approach is potentially useful for generating new ideas about commonalities in the cognitive processes that may underlie two otherwise distinct psychological functions. For example, some researchers have observed that social exclusion and physical pain activate a common region of the anterior cingulate cortex (figure 6.1; among many other nonoverlapping areas) and concluded that social and physical pain share some common psychological features (Eisenberger, Lieberman, & Williams, 2003; but see Sommerville, Heatherton, & Kelley, 2006). Although this approach does not tell us exactly how or why social and physical forms of pain might be related, simply because the true function of the neural activity is difficult to discern, it nevertheless provokes new ideas about potential relationships between psychological processes. But because brain activations alone are usually ambiguous with regard to their specific psychological functions, they do not always provide a reliable index of a psychological variable. Thus, the brain-mapping approach is not appropriate for testing hypotheses about the relationship between two psychological variables or the effects of an experimental manipulation on a psychological variable.

Hypothesis Testing Approach

The hypothesis testing approach in social neuroscience is used to test relationships between psychological variables. This approach begins with the assumption

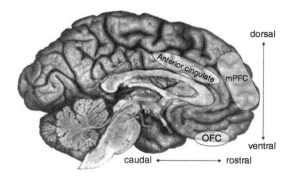

Fig. 6.1 Medial aspect of the left hemisphere of the brain. mPFC = medial prefrontal cortex, OFC = orbital frontal cortex.

that a particular brain region reflects a specific psychological process. In this regard, it does not concern brain mapping, but instead relies on past research to have already established the validity of neural indicators. For example, a social psychologist who studies intergroup prejudice might hypothesize that implicit racial bias is rooted in mechanisms of classical fear conditioning (Amodio, Harmon-Jones, & Devine, 2003). To test this hypothesis, one might measure brain activity in the amygdala (figure 6.2)—a structure implicated in fear conditioning in many previous studies—while a participant completes a behavioral task designed to elicit implicit racial bias. In this case, the construct validity of the neural measure of fear conditioning (amygdala activity) is already reasonably established (but see Amodio & Ratner, 2011a), and the question concerns not the meaning of brain activations, but experimental effects among psychological variables. It is the hypothesis testing approach of social neuroscience that is of primary interest to social-personality psychologists.

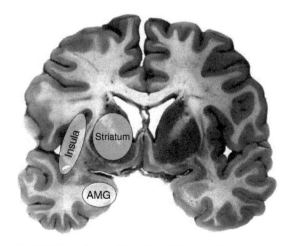

Fig. 6.2 View of coronal slice through brain, with structures on the left side labeled. AMG = amygdala.

Whereas brain-mapping studies may inform our understanding of the brain, hypothesis-testing studies attempt to inform psychological theories of the mind.

Critically, brain mapping and psychological hypothesis testing approaches should not be combined within a single experiment; major inferential problems occur as a result (Amodio, 2010a). This is because a test of a psychological hypothesis assumes that the mapping of a psychological variable to a neural structure is already established (e.g., that the neural measure has construct validity). The brain mapping approach is used to establish the mapping between a psychological variable and neural structure (i.e., to establish construct validity of the neural measure). When these approaches are combined, there is a risk of defining the neural operationalization of a psychological construct on the basis of whether it supports one's theoretical hypothesis—an example of tautological inference.

To illustrate, imagine that a researcher wants to test the hypothesis that empathy involves self-reflection. Given previous research linking self-judgments to activity in the medial frontal cortex (mPFC, figure 6.1), he decides to use a measure of mPFC during an empathy task (e.g., viewing pictures of people in pain) to index the engagement in self-reflection. However, the region of mPFC that has been linked to the self is rather large and idiographic across individuals and, this area has been associated with several other psychological responses, including mentalizing, evaluation, and self-regulation. Therefore, it is difficult to know whether observed mPFC activity on a given task represents self-reflection or some other process. This ambiguity undermines the construct validity of mPFC activity as a measure of the "self".

To deal with this problem, the researcher might simply examine a correlation between mPFC activity and scores on an empathy questionnaire to see which, if any, portions of the task-related mPFC ativity might relate to empathy. But this can compound the problem. Given his hypothesis that empathy involves self-reflection, the researcher might simultaneously infer that any mPFC region correlated with the questionnaire must be the "self" region (establishing the construct) and that "self" activity is indeed associated with greater empathy (testing the psychological hypothesis). This blurs the important steps of establishing construct validity (brain mapping) and internal validity (hypothesis testing). Because the construct is validated on the basis of the hypothesis-testing correlation analysis,

the logic of the test is circular (Amodio, 2010a; Barrett, 2009). This analytical approach is fairly common in social neuroscience research, primarily because the social psychological processes of interest are complex and difficult to localize. Nevertheless, this approach is problematic, and consumers of social/personality neuroscience should be aware of such practices and cautious of their use.

Reverse Inference

When considering the two general approaches described above, the issue of *reverse inference* is often a concern. Reverse inference refers to a form of reasoning used heavily in social and cognitive neuroscience to infer the psychological meaning of a brain activation based on previous findings (Poldrack, 2006). In some studies (e.g., simple brain-mapping studies), a psychological process is manipulated and the resulting pattern of brain activity is observed. The inference that the psychological manipulation produced the brain activity may be described as a forward inference, in that the brain activity clearly follows from the manipulation. The inference is based on the known validity of the manipulation. By contrast, the inference of a psychological process from an observed pattern of brain activity is a *reverse inference*. In this case, the precise meaning of the brain activation is ambiguous and inferred from other studies that have used a particular manipulation to activate the same area. The practice of reverse inference becomes increasingly problematic to the extent that the source of inference—in this case, a brain activation—could reflect different psychological processes (Cacioppo et al., 2003; Poldrack, 2006). In studies of low-level vision, reverse inference is a comparatively lesser problem (but still a serious issue). For example, retinotopic mapping of stimuli onto primary visual cortex provides a relatively constrained index of basic visual processing. But as psychological variables become more complex, as they do with social and personality processes, the mapping between a particular brain region and a psychological process becomes less certain. In these cases, reverse inference can be a serious problem.

All cognitive and social neuroscience studies rely on reverse inference. That is, to the extent that a neural activation is interpreted as reflecting a psychological process, the use of reverse inference is unavoidable. However, researchers can take steps to bolster the strength of a reverse psychological inference by enhancing the construct validity of a neural indicator and the strength of their experimental designs, such as through the careful use of theory, converging evidence from other studies (including animal research), and the use of behavioral tasks that provide valid manipulations of a construct and interpretable behavioral data.

What Types of Social and Personality Questions Are Amenable to a Neuroscience Analysis?

First and foremost, the brain is a *mechanism*, and an extremely complex one at that. Hence, neuroscience models and methods are especially useful for the study of psychological mechanisms, such as those involved in action control, perception, and attention. Psychological phenomena that are not mechanisms, but correspond more closely to appraisals (e.g., attitudes and beliefs), subjective psychological states, abstract psychological structures (e.g., the self), and high-level representation, may be less amenable to a neuroscience level of analysis. For a social/personality psychologist who is considering the potential benefit of a neuroscience approach, the most critical issue is whether one's question concerns basic psychological mechanisms. Can the components of one's mechanistic model be described in terms of low-level functions, such as perception, sensation, low-level cognition, and low-level motivation? If so, then neuroscience models may be particularly useful. If the psychological phenomena of interest cannot be conceptualized at a low level of analysis, but rather are most meaningful at a high level of construal (e.g., the self), then it may be more difficult to make valid inferential connections between psychological theory and the brain.

Methods of Social and Personality Neuroscience

Contemporary social neuroscience makes use of a wide range of methods that are often used in combination with the more traditional tools of personality and social psychology. In addition to new technologies for measurement, social neuroscience methodology relies on the use of experimental designs, valid manipulations of psychological states and processes, and careful inference and interpretation. Here, we describe the most prominent methods currently used in the field and briefly discuss their relative advantages as they relate to experimental designs, issues of construct validity, and psychological inference. A more detailed description of methods in neuroscience approaches to social and personality psychology is provided by

Harmon-Jones and Beer (2009), and recent discussions of inference and validity in social neuroscience can be found in Amodio (2010a), Barrett (2009), and Cacioppo et al. (2003).

Early studies taking a social neuroscience approach primarily used peripheral physiological measures, such as electrocardiogram (e.g., heart rate), galvanic skin response (i.e., skin conductance, a measure of sympathetic activation vis-à-vis palm sweating), and electromyography (e.g., measures of facial muscle activity related to emotional expressions). More recently, neuroimaging measures have become popular. The two most common neuroimaging techniques include functional magnetic resonance imaging (fMRI), which measures the flow of oxygenated blood in the brain, and electroencephalography (EEG), which measures electrical activity produced from the firing of neuron populations. EEG is used to examine event-related potentials (ERPs), which represent a burst of EEG activity in response to a discrete event, such as a stimulus presentation or subject response (Amodio & Bartholow, 2011). fMRI yields high spatial resolution and thus is optimal for determining the location of activity within the brain. But because it assesses slow-moving blood flow, its temporal resolution is relatively poor. By contrast, EEG/ERP yields high temporal resolution and is thus optimal for assessing the timing of a neural process, but its spatial resolution is comparatively poor. Given their relative strengths, researchers may select fMRI or EEG methods to suit their particular question, or use both approaches in complementary studies within a program of research. Neuroimaging and psychophysiological approaches may also be combined with measures of hormones, immune factors, and DNA, for example, to provide convergent evidence for a physiological process of interest. However, as with traditional methods in social-personality psychology, the utility of these measures depends on the quality of the question, the experimental paradigm, and careful interpretation.

Major Content Areas of Social Neuroscience

In this section, we provide a broad review of the social neuroscience literature in the areas of social cognition and the self, attitudes, emotion and motivation, intergroup relations, and individual differences. Although our review distinguishes these five areas of research for convenience, their content overlaps substantially. In each area, we will integrate methods and levels of analysis, and we will discuss how research in each area has contributed to social-personality psychology theories.

Social Cognition and the Self

The earliest studies conducted at the intersection of social psychology and neuroscience examined basic processes of automaticity and control, as well as the processing involved in perceiving the self and other people. Together, these areas of research have laid the foundation for social neuroscience studies of more complex social-personality processes.

AUTOMATIC AND CONTROLLED PROCESSING

Theories of automatic and controlled processes represent a cornerstone of modern social cognition (Wegner & Bargh, 1998). Mechanisms of automaticity and control also constitute a central topic in cognitive psychology, and thus a large body of cognitive neuroscience research has been devoted to their elucidation. These processes have been studied primarily in two different broad research literatures on memory and cognitive control.

Automaticity

Research on systems of learning and memory is particularly relevant to social-personality theories of automaticity and implicit processes. Traditional models of learning and memory often distinguish between neural correlates of explicit (declarative) and implicit (nondeclarative) memory processes, and neuroscience research suggests these forms of memory reflect distinct neural substrates (Squire & Zola, 1996). Although implicit and automatic refer to different properties of a process (i.e., degree of awareness vs. degree of intentionality), implicit forms of memory, such as classical fear conditioning and procedural memory (i.e., skill or habit learning), have important automatic characteristics and thus are relevant to the present discussion. Studies of nonhuman animals have identified the amygdala as a critical structure in the learning and expression of fear conditioning (LeDoux, Iwata, Cicchetti, & Reis, 1988; Fendt & Fanselow, 1999), a role that has been corroborated in fMRI studies of fear conditioning in humans (LaBar, Gatenby, Gore, LeDoux, & Phelps, 1998). The neuroscience research suggests that automatic fear-related responses function somewhat independently from other types of automatic responses.

Other research on procedural memory has focused on the basal ganglia, a set of interconnected structures that include the striatum (figure 6.2; caudate, putamen, and nucleus accumbens), globus pallidus, and their dopaminergic inputs from the midbrain (substantia nigra and ventral tegmentum). Research has identified regions of basal ganglia as

being critical for implicit skill learning, such as when subjects learn response associations that are embedded implicitly in a task procedure (Foerde, Knowlton, & Poldrack, 2006; Squire & Zola, 1996). These forms of learning and memory more closely resemble the type of automatic processes studied in the social and personality psychology literature, in that they drive actions that may be activated and implemented without conscious awareness or intention. It is notable that, in recent years, studies of economic decisions and reward learning have also focused on the role of basal ganglia, but as a substrate for error prediction or the computation of "value" (e.g., Hare, O'Doherty, Camerer, Schultz, & Rangel, 2008). Research has yet to resolve these different interpretations. However, given the strong anatomical connectivity between the basal ganglia and both motor cortices and PFC regions linked to goal representations, the interpretation that the basal ganglia are centrally involved in goal driven behaviors (including automatic responses) remains plausible.

In the social cognition literature, automaticity is often demonstrated in sequential priming tasks, when a prime word is shown to facilitate the categorization of an associated target word (Gaertner & McLaughlin, 1983; Dovidio, Evans, & Tyler, 1986). This idea was originally adapted from cognitive psychology research on semantic associations between words, such as "bread-butter" or "doctor-nurse" (Meyer & Schaneveldt, 1971, 1976). In fMRI studies, semantic priming has been associated with activity in left posterior PFC (figure 6.3; e.g., Blaxton et al., 1996; Demb et al., 1995; Raichle et al., 1994; Wagner, Gabrieli, & Verfaellie, 1997) and temporal cortex (Rissman, Eliassen, & Blumstein, 2003; Schacter & Buckner, 1998; Squire, 1992), as well as

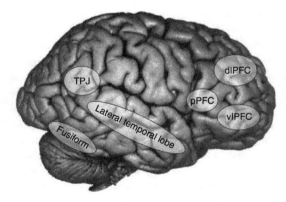

Fig. 6.3 Lateral aspect of the right hemisphere of the brain. dlPFC = dorsolateral prefrontal cortex, vlPFC = ventrolateral prefrontal cortex, pPFC = posterior prefrontal cortex, TPJ = temporo-parietal junction.

reduced activity in regions linked to attention (e.g., in the parietal cortex, figure 6.3; Gabrieli, 1998). Given other research implicating the left PFC in approach-related motivation and action tendencies (Harmon-Jones, 2003a), this pattern of neural correlates suggests a link between automatic semantic processes and goal-driven behavior (Amodio, 2008), consistent with the idea that "thinking is for doing" (Fiske, 1992).

Together, the neuroscience research on fear-conditioning, procedural memory and reward, and semantic associations has helped to distinguish different types of automatic processes. In doing so, these studies clarify the functions of automaticity and shed new light on how automatic processes operate and change. These advances have already begun to inspire new theories of implicit social cognition (e.g., Amodio & Ratner, 2011b).

Control
Cognitive neuroscience research on mechanisms of control has examined subjects' brain activity while they completed classic cognitive control tasks, such as the Stroop color naming task, the Eriksen Flankers Task, or the Go/No-Go task. Tasks such as these typically include two main types of trials, which require either a high or low degree of control. In one set of trials, subjects make responses that are facilitated by existing semantic associations (e.g., the color-naming Stroop task), perceptual cues (e.g., the Eriksen Flankers task), or expectancy (e.g., the Go/No-Go). Responses on these trials are thought to benefit from automatic processing. On other trials, the participant must override the automatic influence in order to deliver the correct, but countervailing task response. Control-related behavior on these tasks has been consistently associated with activity in the anterior cingulate cortex (ACC) and PFC regions of the brain.

In particular, the ACC responds to instances when a prepotent, or automatic, response is inconsistent with the task goal, such as when the text of a color word interferes with one's goal to name the ink color (Carter et al., 1998; MacDonald, Cohen, Stenger, & Carter, 2000). Botvinick, Braver, Barch, Carter, and Cohen (2001) proposed that the ACC serves a *conflict monitoring* function, such that it is involved in detecting conflict between alternative response tendencies and, when conflict arises, it signals regions of the PFC involved in implementing one's intended response over other tendencies. Consistent with the conflict monitoring hypothesis, anatomical research on monkeys has revealed that the ACC is strongly interconnected with motor structures as well as PFC regions associated with high-level representations of goals and actions (Miller & Cohen, 2001). Some researchers have extended this theorizing to suggest that ACC activity on control tasks may simply reflect a distress signal or social pain (Eisenberger et al., 2003; Inzlicht, McGregor, Hirsh, & Nash, 2009). However, most cognitive control tasks that elicit ACC activity do not involve distress or pain, complicating this interpretation. Finally, several studies have shown that conflict-related ACC activity occurs in the absence of awareness (Berns, Cohen, & Mintun, 1997; Nieuwenhuis, Ridderinkhof, Blom, Band, & Kok, 2001), suggesting that it represents a preconscious component of control that initiates the engagement of more deliberative components. The findings of cognitive neuroscience research on conflict monitoring and control have been applied to questions regarding self-regulation in social-personality contexts such as stereotyping and prejudice (Amodio, Shah, Sigelman, Brazy, & Harmon-Jones, 2004; Amodio, Kubota, Harmon-Jones, & Devine, 2006; Amodio, Devine, & Harmon-Jones, 2008; Bartholow, Dickter, & Sestir, 2006), individual differences related to anxiety and neuroticism (Amodio, Master, Yee, & Taylor, 2008; Robinson, Ode, Wilkowski, & Amodio, 2007), political orientation (Amodio, Jost, Master, & Yee, 2007), religiosity (Inzlicht et al., 2009), and social exclusion (Eisenberger et al., 2003).

Although several regions of the PFC are activated during attempts at response control, a general pattern has been observed in the literature whereby left-sided PFC regions are associated with the implementation of intended actions, whereas right-sided PFC activity has been associated with the intentional inhibition of action (Aron, 2007). It is notable that EEG and fMRI research is almost always conducted on right-handed participants, and observed hemispheric asymmetries in patterns of control are likely related to the lateral specialization of hand (and foot) dominance (Harmon-Jones, 2006).

In sum, cognitive neuroscience research on control has highlighted different subcomponents of controlled processing. Although aspects of these subcomponents have been considered in previous social and personality psychology theories (e.g., Wegner, 1994; Wegener & Petty, 1997), the neuroscience literature has provided important clarifications of these components, as well as methods for assessing aspects of control that function rapidly and without conscious awareness.

PERCEPTION OF THE SELF AND OTHERS

The Self

The self is one of social-personality psychology's earliest and most enduring constructs (see Crocker & Canevello, chapter 11, this volume) and, not surprisingly, it was among the first constructs to be examined in neuroscientific studies of social psychological processes (e.g., Craik et al., 1999; Klein, Loftus, & Kihlstrom, 1996). Most of this research has examined brain activity associated with self-reflection and judgments about the self in comparison to judgments of others (see also Uleman & Saribay, chapter 14, this volume). Using positron emission tomorgraphy (PET) to measure cerebral blood flow, Craik et al. (1999) found that judgments of trait words as relating to the self versus others were associated with large activations in the mPFC. In a similar study that used fMRI, Kelley et al. (2002) found that reflections on one's own traits activated a region of ventral mPFC to a greater extent than did reflecting on the traits of another person (in this study, George W. Bush). The finding of ventral mPFC activity in response to self-related judgments has been replicated in several studies (e.g., Gutchess, Kensinger, & Schacter, 2007; Heatherton et al., 2006; Kircher et al., 2002; Pfeifer, Lieberman, Dapretto, 2007; Saxe, Moran, Scholz, & Gabrieli, 2006; Schmitz, Kawahara-Baccus, & Johnson, 2004; Turner, Simons, Gilbert, Frith, & Burgess, 2008; Zhang, Lawson, Guo, & Jiang, 2006; Zhu, Zhang, Fan, & Han, 2007). Studies of other aspects of the self, such as agency and self-discrepancies, have observed regions of the brain typically involved in more general aspects of visual perception, conflict monitoring, and cognitive control (Blakemore, Oakley, & Frith, 2003; Farrer et al., 2008). Thus, brain activations during self-related judgments likely pertain to the process of self-reflection, but not to other aspects of self-related processing.

Although neuroimaging research on the self is a popular topic in social cognitive neuroscience, the findings of this area of research must be considered in light of some important interpretational concerns. For example, in Kelley et al. (2002), the activity level of the mPFC during judgments of the self and other was lower than activity during a baseline condition, in which participants viewed a fixation cross on the computer display. That is, self-related processing is often associated with a deactivation in mPFC activity relative to baseline. This below-baseline effect is observed in most studies of the self, and it represents a major interpretational problem.

If mPFC activity reflects "self" processing, why would this region be more activated when subjects stare at a fixation point than when they are explicitly reflecting on the self? This observation has led some researchers to suggest that research participants spontaneously focus on the self when at rest (to a greater extent than when instructed to think about the self), and this observation has prompted theories about a baseline "default" network of brain activity that supports thoughts about the self and other people (e.g., Gusnard, Akbudak, Shulman, & Raichle, 2001; Gusnard & Raichle, 2001). Although the idea that humans reflect on the self and others by default is interesting, it is inconsistent with daily diary research showing that, when probed at random points during the day and asked to report on what one was doing at the moment, participants rarely (8% of 4,700 responses) reported that they were engaged in some form of self-reflection (Csikszentmihalyi & Figurski, 1982). Ultimately, a construct like "the self" is a very broad and complex construct that may not be easily localized to a circumscribed set of neural structures.

Perceiving Faces

Information about conspecifics and social relationships is eminent in perception and cognition, and the initial stage of social processing often begins with face perception (see Uleman & Saribay, chapter 14, this volume). Research on visual perception suggests that some components of the visual system are specialized for seeing faces, and these face-specialized processes have beem localized in the fusiform gyrus in fMRI studies (figure 6.1; Kanwisher, McDermot, & Chun, 1997). Although the idea of a specialized face area has been debated, with some arguing that fusiform responses to faces reflect expertise rather than a "face module" (Haxby, Hoffman, & Gobbini, 2000), the finding that this region responds to faces more than to other objects is consistent.

Faces are also known to elicit a characteristic ERP component that peaks 170 ms after the presentation of a face. This "N170" component is consistently larger to faces than to nonface stimuli that are matched on other visual dimensions (Bentin, Allison, Puce, Perez, & McCarthy, 1996; Carmel & Bentin, 2002), making it a valuable neural marker of the engagement of low-level face-specific perception processes marking the encoding of facial features (e.g., Eimer, 2000). The N170 is believed to reflect activity in multiple temporal-occipital structures linked to face processing (Deffke et al., 2007), including the fusiform (figure 6.1; e.g., Haxby,

Hoffman, & Gobbini, 2000; Puce, Allison, Gore, & McCarthy, 1995) and other temporal regions (e.g., Desimone, 1991; Perrett, Rolls, & Caan, 1982). Together, fMRI and ERP studies of face perception have shown that faces are perceived very quickly and at relatively low levels in the hierarchy of visual processing. These studies also establish a way to measure online face perception processes without requiring behavioral or self-reported responses.

Mentalizing and Theory of Mind
Once an object is perceived as a face, a perceiver rapidly begins to evaluate and infer information about the individual (Todorov, Said, Engell, & Oosterhof, 2008). The process of inferring another person's unique motives and perspectives is referred to as *mentalizing*, which is the process underlying one's *theory of mind* (Frith & Frith, 1999). Early studies of mentalizing in the brain used PET to measure activity involved in inferences about the thoughts of other people or characters. These studies were motivated in part by an effort to understand autism and its links to deficits in theory of mind (Frith, 1989; Baron-Cohen, Tager-Flusberg, & Cohen, 1993). In this line of research, theory of mind is best characterized by tasks involving false belief or deceptive intent—tasks on which successful performance depends on one's ability to take another person's perspective. In an early study on this topic, Fletcher et al. (1995) examined brain activity while normal subjects read a set of short stories. Mentalizing stories involved jokes or lies as a literary device—that is, they made sense to the extent that the reader understood that a character was the victim of a lie or joke. Hence, the stories required an understanding of a character's false belief. Control stories did not rely on such devices, but rather involved straightforward physical descriptions. Although several brain regions were activated by both types of stories, only the mPFC was uniquely more active during the mentalizing stories. A similar set of mentalizing activations were observed in another study when subjects viewed movies of people showing deceptive intent (Grezes, Frith, & Passingham, 2004).

Castelli, Happe, Frith, and Frith (2000) connected their findings on mentalizing with the attribution literature in social psychology. They measured brain activity while participants viewed a set of videos inspired by the famous Heider and Simmel (1944) animations, in which three shapes moved in an anthropomorphic fashion that implied human interaction. The authors found that the viewing of this type of animation also elicited mPFC activity, compared with control videos in which the movement of the shapes was not interpreted anthropomorphically. More recent work has linked the process of dispositional attribution to activity in the mPFC (Harris, Todorov, & Fiske, 2005; cf. Heider, 1958). Since these initial studies, a large body of research has associated activity of the mPFC with a range of tasks involving mentalizing and complex aspects of person perception (Amodio & Frith, 2006; Frith & Frith, 1999; Saxe, Carey, & Kanwisher, 2004). These tasks also typically elicit activity in regions of the superior temporal lobe (or temporal-parietal junction) and the temporal poles—regions associated with the perception of biological motion and to conceptual representations of social information, respectively (Frith & Frith, 1999). Converging findings from the developmental literature corroborate the idea that mPFC development underlies the emergence of theory of mind abilities in children (Bunge, Dudukovic, Thomason, Valdya, & Gabrieli, 2002).

Since the initial finding that mentalizing activated regions of mPFC, researchers have asked whether other forms of person perception might involve the same brain regions. A series of studies by Mitchell, Macrae, and colleagues proposed that social-cognitive aspects of person perception, such as the ascription of trait attributes to a person, might also activate areas of mPFC (even if they do not necessarily require mentalizing). For example, when subjects judged noun-adjective word pairs that described a person, compared with those describing an inanimate object, activity was found in regions of interest within the mPFC, as well as areas of the temporal cortex and the temporal-parietal junction (figure 6.3; Mitchell, Heatherton, & Macrae, 2002). This pattern of activity has been seen across several studies using similar tasks (e.g., Mitchell et al., 2005; Mitchell, Macrae, & Banaji, 2006). Other researchers have observed activity in similar regions when simply viewing faces in an easy memory task (Gobbini, Leibenluft, Santiago, & Haxby, 2004), demonstrating that activity in this region in response to faces does not necessarily imply the inference of traits. Some research has found that viewing and making trait judgments of unfamiliar faces or dissimilar people is associated with activity in more dorsal regions of the mPFC, whereas more familiar and/or similar faces are associated with activity in more ventral regions, near areas activated by self-reflection (Gobbini et al., 2004; Mitchell et al., 2006).

It is notable, however, that the mPFC is a large region of cortex, and the specific locus of person-related activity varies considerably across studies (Gilbert et al., 2006).

As with neuroimaging studies of the self, activity associated with forming impressions of both people and inanimate objects is typically lower than baseline mPFC activity (e.g., Mitchell, Macrae, & Banaji, 2004). If the process of person perception is truly located in the mPFC, then the data imply that subjects engage more strongly in person perception during baseline periods (i.e., viewing a fixation cross) than when they are explicitly engaged in the person perception process. This explanation assumes that people naturally reflect on others when at rest (presumably while also thinking about the self; but see Csikszentmihalyi & Figurski, 1982). As with interpretations of the mPFC as reflecting activation of the self, this issue complicates the idea that the mPFC is the neural substrate of person perception. Other researchers have proposed that this region serves a domain-general process of coordinating one's responses with complex (e.g., externally guided) plans (Amodio & Frith, 2006; Amodio et al., 2006), such as when a research subject prepares for an upcoming trial during intertrial intervals (when mPFC activity is usually highest). This interpretation of mPFC function helps to account for the broad range of findings involving this region.

Although the potential contribution of brain-mapping abstract constructs like "the self" and "social cognition" to theories of social-personality psychology has yet to be established, fMRI research on mentalizing, person perception, and the self has inspired interesting debates about the processes through which a person judges another's thoughts or intentions. For example, "simulation" theory posits that people consider how they would respond in the other person's situation and then respond to that person accordingly. "Theory" theory posits that people have an implicit theory of how a person would respond in a particular situation and, rather than reflecting on the self, form their perceptions based on this theory. As evidence for "theory" theory, some researchers have noted that brain activity associated with self and other judgments is related to different regions of the mPFC, implying that people do not activate representations of the self when considering the responses of others (Saxe, 2005). Other researchers have argued in favor of simulation theory, based on the observation that judgments of similar or familiar others activate a region close to areas activated by self-reflection, (Mitchell, 2005). Although a lively debate, these interpretations are tentative because they have relied primarily on reverse inferences about the function of brain areas (cf. Poldrack, 2006), assuming that these regions of the mPFC truly represent the "self" and "social cognition". Indeed, the strongest evidence in such debates comes from behavioral studies, which provide more clearly interpretable data (Saxe, 2005).

Empathy

Empathy is broadly defined as concern for another's welfare (Batson, 1991). By some definitions, empathy involves experiencing another's perspective and affective response (Lamm, Batson, & Decety, 2007; see also Castano, chapter 17, this volume). As with mentalizing and theory of mind, empathy is complex and involves a broad set of neural and psychological processes associated with affect, perception, social cognition, self-regulation, mimicry, and action (Decety, 2010). Building on neuroscience studies of mentalizing, research on the neural substrates of empathy have focused primarily on the role of the mPFC (Decety, 2010; Rameson & Lieberman, 2009). Many studies have examined empathy by measuring brain activity while a subject views another person experiencing pain. For example, Singer et al. (2004) used fMRI to measure brain activity while participants experienced a painful stimulus or viewed a loved one receiving the same stimulus. A set of structures, including the rostral ACC and anterior insula, were active in both conditions, relative to baseline. Rostral ACC activity was greater in response to observing a loved one's pain among subjects with higher scores on a trait empathy scale. Other research has found similar brain regions to be more strongly activated when participants observed racial ingroups (as opposed to racial outgroups) experiencing pain (Xu, Zuo, Wang, & Han, 2009). There are also suggestive findings from lesion patient studies, in which damage to the ventromedial PFC and ACC are associated with impaired empathy (Shamay-Tsoory, Tomer, Berger, & Aharon-Peretz, 2003). Given that the ACC is involved in a wide range of processes involving expectancy violation, these findings may reflect some aspect of expectancy violation or concern when either the self or another person is subjected to pain, rather than suggesting that empathy is related to the experience of pain per se. Overall, this body of research has focused primarily on the brain mapping of empathic processes.

Related to work on empathy, a "mirror neuron" system has been proposed as a brain network devoted to understanding other people through their actions (Iacoboni & Dapretto, 2006). The mirror neuron idea originated from single-unit recording in the macaque premotor cortex, in which the same neuron fired when the monkey moved its hand toward a food reward and when it watched an experimenter move his hand toward the reward (Gallese, Fadiga, Fogassi, & Rizzolatti, 1996). "Mirror neuron" is not a literal term, in the sense that no single neuron can be described as providing a mirroring function. Rather, "mirror neurons" refer loosely to areas of the brain that are activated both when an individual observes the behavior of another person, and when one performs the same behavior. Brain regions implicated in the "mirror neuron" network include premotor cortex, inferior frontal cortex, superior temporal sulcus, anterior insula, and the amygdala (Iacoboni & Dapretto, 2006; Rizzolatti & Sinigaglia, 2010), although the patterns and locations of activity in these regions vary considerably from study to study. Although the notion that we relate to other people by representing their actions and mental states in the same way we represent our own has intuitive appeal, more recent theoretical analyses have questioned the plausibility of mirror neurons as mechanisms of action understanding (Decety, 2010; Hickock, 2009; Saxe, 2005; Vivona, 2009). Aside from questions about the neural substrates, the fact that so many social interactions often require complementary responses (e.g., conversing or dancing), rather than mimicry, calls into question the idea that human social behavior is rooted in a mirroring system. Hence, more research will be needed to assess the utility of the mirror neuron idea.

Humanization

Humanization refers to the process of seeing another person as possessing the characteristics unique to the human species, including the human rights associated with being a member of society. Hence, dehumanization refers to the process of denying a person these qualities (Haslam, 2006). High status groups and members of one's ingroup are typically perceived as possessing these qualities; low-status individuals and members of the outgroup are often seen as lacking these qualities (Leyens et al., 2001; Leyens et al., 2003). The process of "humanization" is also associated with empathy and mentalizing, but whereas humanization processes typically apply only to people, empathy and mentalizing may also

relate to nonhumans and inanimate objects, as a form of anthropomorphism (Epley, Waytz, & Cacioppo, 2007). Research on dehumanization has connected the neuroscience work on mentalizing and the mPFC to the topic of intergroup relations (Harris & Fiske, 2009). For example, a study by Harris and Fiske (2006) demonstrated that mPFC activity was greater when participants viewed pictures of valued others (e.g., members of the ingroup, people of high social status) compared with "dehumanized" individuals, such as drug abusers and homeless people.

Why the mPFC?

What is the significance of the mPFC as it relates to the self, person perception, and mentalizing? Mitchell argued (2009) that the fact that these "social" processes all activate the same general brain region indicates that social psychology is a "natural kind," meaning that social psychological processes have a unique and privileged place in neural activity. Taking a different approach to this issue, Amodio and Frith (2006) considered the neuroanatomical properties of the mPFC in its relation to social cognition. They noted that the mPFC is a highly interconnected region of brain uniquely situated to integrate information about internal processes (e.g., motor responses, visceral states) and higher-level representations of goals, reward contingencies, and complex expectancies. In their analysis, the mPFC is thought to be involved in any process that involves a complex interplay of internal states and the tracking of abstract external contingencies for one's response—a type of process exemplified by social cognition. According to this view, the mPFC is not the neural instantiation of the self or social cognition, and "social psychology" is not a natural kind in the brain. Rather, thinking about the self and others is most likely to involve the neural and cognitive processes supported by this region. More research is needed to understand the significance of the mPFC for social cognition.

Summary

To date, social neuroscience research on social-cognitive processes has primarily focused on brain mapping. In this way, it has been primarily exploratory and used to elucidate the understanding of neural function. How has this research informed social-personality psychology? Neuroscience studies of cognitive control have informed social psychological theories by delineating different components of the self-regulatory process. Similarly, neuroscience research on learning and memory systems has provided a useful framework for understanding automatic and implicit forms of social cognition (Amodio, 2008; Amodio & Ratner, 2011b). By contrast, the contribution of extant brain-mapping studies of the self and person perception for theories of social-personality psychology remains less clear.

Attitudes

The attitude is a foundational construct in the field of social psychology (Thurstone, 1928; see also Ajzen, chapter 15 this volume), and attitudes were the subject of the earliest psychophysiological studies of social psychological processes. Rankin and Campbell (1955) measured changes in skin conductance levels (i.e., galvanic skin response) while White participants in their study interacted with White and Black experimenters. Skin conductance responses, which reflect activity of the sympathetic nervous system, were interpreted as instances of heightened anxiety. Although participants in their study reported similar liking for the two experimenters, they exhibited larger skin conductance responses to Black than White experimenters on average. The authors interpreted the results as evidence for negative attitudes toward African Americans—the first evidence of implicit racial bias.

The attitude construct is complex, and although it is often defined simply as liking/disliking, the psychological and physiological processes that give rise to an attitude are very complicated. The classic tripartite model of attitudes includes cognitive, affective, and behavioral components. However, at the physiological level of analysis, an attitude likely corresponds to several other processes, such as motivational tendencies, action representations, changes in attention, and basic motor tendencies, among others. For this reason, it is very difficult—and perhaps inadvisable—to map the high-level construct of an attitude onto specific physiological systems. Indeed, there are ongoing debates on whether an "attitude" is properly conceptualized as an abstract appraisal or a psychological mechanism (Fazio, 2007; Harmon-Jones, Harmon-Jones, Amodio, & Gable, in press; Schwarz, 2007). To the extent that an attitude is not defined as a mechanism, a neuroscience analysis of attitudes may not be useful. If a researcher is simply interested in assessing a subject's affective response to an object, peripheral physiological responses may provide more useful indicators.

The use of physiological methods to examine attitudes was developed significantly by the research of Cacioppo and his colleagues. These methods allowed researchers to assess changes in a participants' response unobtrusively and often unconsciously, using a range of physiological indicators including skin conductance (Cacioppo & Sandman, 1978), heart rate (Cacioppo, Sandman, & Walker, 1978), facial EMG (Cacioppo & Petty, 1979), EEG spectral power (Cacioppo, Petty, & Snyder, 1979), and ERPs, among others. This early social psychophysiology research on attitudes focused on the psychological processes involved in persuasion, which leads to attitude change. Of special interest was the role of information processing. For example, Cacioppo and colleagues focused on asymmetries in parietal cortical activity associated with semantic versus nonsemantic processing of a stimulus (e.g., Cacioppo, Petty, & Quintanar, 1982). This focus contrasts with other researchers' focus on hemispheric asymmetries in frontal cortical brain regions that were associated with emotion and motivation (Davidson & Fox, 1982). Other research examined subtle and implicit affective responses to pro- versus counterattitudinal messages by measuring subtle changes in facial expressions during message processing (Cacioppo & Petty, 1979). Cacioppo and Petty's early use of psychophysiological methods to study attitudes and persuasion blazed the trail for future neuroscience approaches in social and personality psychology.

Peripheral physiological measures have been especially useful for assessing the affective component of attitudes, by way of assessing arousal (e.g., Rankin & Campbell, 1955). However, skin conductance measures are limited because they cannot distinguish between positive versus negative responses. In order to draw stronger inferences about the valence of a physiological response, facial EMG may be used to measure activity in muscle groups associated with different facial expressions linked to emotion (Dimberg, 1982; Cacioppo & Petty, 1979). Activity of the corrugator supercilii muscle, located just above and running parallel to the brow, is commonly described as brow-furrowing, and it is associated with many forms of negative affect, including anger and disgust. Activity of the zygomaticus major muscle, which runs across the cheek from the corners of the mouth to the cheekbones, is related to smiling, and it is associated with many forms of positive affect. Thus, EMG provides information about an emotional expression, from which researchers may infer valence, approach/withdrawal orientation, or any other psychological process linked to a facial expression.

Although emotional expressions can usually be observed directly, EMG allows researchers to quantify their activity with precision, providing continuous online assessments of affective response without requiring an overt response from the participant. Facial EMG has also been shown to be sensitive to microexpressions—changes in facial muscle activity that are imperceptible to the naked eye (Cacioppo, Bush, & Tassinary, 1992). Other research has used EMG to measure subtle emotional responses to subliminally presented stimuli. Dimberg, Thunberg, and Elmehed (2000) demonstrated changes in EMG measures of the zygomaticus and corrugator responses to subliminally presented pictures depicting facial expressions of happiness versus anger. Harmon-Jones and Allen (2001) also used facial EMG to demonstrate that repeated presentations of a neutral stimulus caused an increase in zygomatic activity, as well as more positive attitudes, as a way to examine the role of affect in the mere exposure effect.

NEURAL ASSESSMENTS OF ATTITUDES

The first brain-based assessments of attitudes used measures of frontal cortical activity to assess affective responses to different stimuli and situations. This earlier research showed that responses to positive stimuli were associated with greater left-sided PFC activity, whereas responses to aversive stimuli were associated with greater right-sided PFC activity (Davidson, Ekman, Saron, Senulis, & Friesen, 1990; Davidson & Fox, 1982). Subsequent research by Harmon-Jones and his colleagues (Harmon-Jones, 2003; Harmon-Jones & Allen, 1998) clarified that, at the physiological level of analysis, responses to positive and negative stimuli were organized according to approach-withdrawal processes rather than to positive-negative valence. This research raises questions about whether the concept of "valence" is meaningfully represented at the neural or physiological level of analysis.

ERP methods have also been used to examine attitudes. Early psychophysiology research observed that unexpected stimuli, such as a loud tone among a series of soft tones in an oddball task, reliably elicit a positive-going ERP response approximately 300–500 ms after the deviant stimulus, maximal over parietal scalp sites (Squires, Donchin, Herning, & McCarthy, 1977; Sutton, Braren, Zubin, & John, 1965). This ERP component was named the P300, for its positive polarity and its approximate peak at 300 ms. However, given that the latency of its peak varies considerably across tasks, it is often referred to as the P3 (because it is the third positive-going peak following the stimulus) or *late positive potential* (LPP). The P3 was interpreted as reflecting the engagement of attention, associated with a surprise response, and the updating of one's mental set (Donchin, 1981). More recent research has linked the LPP to activity of norepinephrine systems in response to an unexpected event (Nieuwenhuis, Aston-Jones, & Cohen, 2005), suggesting the LPP reflects a complex set of processes associated with attention and arousal.

Cacioppo, Crites, Berntson, and Coles (1993) noted that the LPP component, in conjunction with the oddball task, could be used to assess individuals' evaluations of attitude objects. For example, the authors found that a negative "oddball" stimulus that appeared within a series of positive objects elicited an LPP response, much like a high-pitched tone amongst a series of low-pitched tones. Other research showed that the magnitude of the evaluative oddball effect varied as a function of its evaluative extremity, such that extremely negative trait words elicited larger LPP amplitudes than moderately negative trait words, when they were embedded within a series of positive words (Cacioppo, Crites, Gardner, & Berntson, 1994; Crites & Cacioppo, 1996; Ito, Larsen, Smith, & Cacioppo, 1998). These LPP effects were also found to be sensitive to individual differences in attitudes, such that they were responsive to subjects' ideographically liked versus disliked objects (Crites & Cacioppo, 1996). The LPP/oddball method of attitude assessment has even been shown to reveal people's true attitudes when they attempted to misreport the attitude (Crites, Cacioppo, Gardner, & Berntson, 1995) or when implicit evaluations differed from explicit task instructions (Ito & Cacioppo, 2000). This technique of examining attitudes by measuring the LPP during the oddball task has since been used to assess a variety of attitudes, including intergroup attitudes (as described below).

Hemispheric asymmetries in ERP responses have also been related to attitudes. In one study, Cunningham, Espinet, DeYoung, and Zelazo (2005) measured the LPP while participants made evaluative (good vs. bad) and nonevaluative (abstract vs. concrete) judgments about socially relevant concepts. The concepts were then rated for goodness and badness. Concepts rated as "bad" caused greater LPPs over the right frontal hemisphere, while concepts rated "good" caused greater LPPs over the left frontal hemisphere. Similarly, van de Laar, Licht,

Franken, and Hendriks (2004) found that cocaine-addicted individuals, but not nonaddicted individuals, showed larger positive slow wave responses over the left (but not right) frontal cortex to cocaine-related photographs as compared to neutral photographs. Along similar lines, Gable and Harmon-Jones (2010) observed greater left than right frontal LPPs to pictures of desserts, and Ohgami et al. (2006) found ERP evidence that reward cues caused greater left frontal cortical activity.

With the introduction of functional neuroimaging tools with good spatial resolution, such as fMRI, researchers have begun to explore the specific neural systems that underlie attitude processes. Whereas peripheral physiology measures provide indicators of preference, studies of brain activity linked to attitudes often seek to address questions about mechanism. This raises the question of whether an attitude represents a mechanism, per se, or an appraisal of an object. As noted above, a neuroscience analysis of the attitude construct is informative to the extent that it reflects mechanism. Initial fMRI studies of attitudes focused on brain mapping. For example, Cunningham, Johnson, Gatenby, Gore, and Banaji (2003) measured brain activity while subjects viewed and evaluated pleasant versus unpleasant words. They observed greater amygdala activity to negative than positive words. However, later findings suggested this effect was driven by the arousal associated with particular words and not the valence, per se (cf. Whalen, 1998), whereas the valence of the words was associated with activity in the insula, among other regions (Cunningham, Raye, & Johnson, 2004). Although these findings do not address psychological questions about attitudes, they begin to map out the neural correlates of evaluation.

Research in neuroeconomics has examined how people evaluate goods and money and how they process potential rewards (Fehr & Camerer, 2007; Glimcher, Camerer, Fehr, & Poldrack, 2009). By engaging subjects in economic games, often with real cash rewards, these studies of attitudes provide a higher degree of ecological validity than measures of word judgments. Much of this research has found greater activation in regions of the basal ganglia, such as the ventral striatum and nucleus accumbens, when participants viewed high-value stimuli. Similar brain activations have been observed during the evaluation of people (Delgado, Frank, & Phelps, 2005). Although some researchers have interpreted these activations as reflecting the neural computation of value, the broader literature on basal ganglia function suggests that these neural activations reflect the learning and coordination of motor plans linked to reward-driven actions (Alexander, DeLong, & Strick, 1986). This line of research on evaluations is useful because it links evaluation processes more directly to goals and behavior, whereas contemporary social psychology research on attitudes focuses on the representation of attitudes in cognition, with less emphasis on links to behavior.

Emotion and Motivation

Affect and emotion range from relatively low-level aspects of reward and punishment; to discrete basic emotions, such as joy, anger, and fear; to highly complex emotion processes such as guilt, jealousy, compassion, and schadenfreude (see Clore & Robinson, chapter 13, this volume), and they are almost always intertwined with motivation. Although some research has attempted to study brain activations unique to complex emotional responses (e.g., Moll, Zahn, Oliveira-Souza, Krueger, & Grafman, 2005), interpretation of such findings is difficult (Barrett & Wager, 2006). Indeed, a meta-analysis of brain activations in response to manipulations of different emotional states failed to reveal clear patterns of activity for specific emotional states (Phan, Wager, Taylor, & Liberzon, 2002). Although one could interpret this finding as evidence against mechanistic distinctions among different emotions, this pattern of null results likely reflects the limitations of trying to assess fine-grained processes using comparatively coarse measures (e.g., fMRI) and methods (e.g., meta-analysis). Like attitudes, emotion constructs correspond to a complex set of more basic processes at the neurophysiological level of analysis and, therefore, common distinctions in the subjective experience of emotions should not cleanly map onto the organization of the brain and physiology. For this reason, most progress has been made in studying the neural activity associated with lower-level emotion processes, such as motivational, attentional, and autonomic processes, and basic mechanisms underlying fear and reward responses.

At the physiological level of analysis, emotional processes overlap substantially with motivational processes. In the affective neuroscience literature, it is generally assumed that approach motivation and responses to rewards involve a positive affective system, whereas avoidance motivation and responses to punishments involve a negative affective system. Indeed, motivational dispositions toward approach and withdrawal are often associated with emotions. However, an emotion is not a single "thing," but rather a multicomponent process made up of basic processes such as feelings of pleasure or displeasure, facial/body expressions, particular appraisals, and particular action plans and activation states (Frijda, 1993). Moreover, these components are not perfectly correlated with one another (Lang, 1995).

Approach and withdrawal motivational processes likely involve neural *systems* rather than specific brain structures. However, a systems-level analysis of approach-withdrawal motivation has yet to be thoroughly investigated due to the empirical difficulties of mapping the precise timecourse of these microprocesses. In addition, much of the research on the neuroscience of emotion and motivation has proceeded under a "brain mapping" approach rather than a "hypothesis testing" approach, as defined earlier. Consequently, this review will focus on brain regions that have received the most research attention. These are the amygdala, nucleus accumbens/ventral striatum, the orbitofrontal cortex, and the prefrontal cortex. While considering the reviewed research, it is important to keep in mind the difficulty of making one-to-one associations between psychological and physiological processes. For example, if fMRI data indicate amygdala activity in response to viewing a face, it is almost impossible to claim that this activation reflects a certain psychological variable like fear, given that different subnuclei of the amygdala support a wide range of psychological variables, including uncertainty (Whalen, 1998), positive affect (Anderson et al., 2003), and motivational relevance (Cunningham, Van Bavel, & Johnsen, 2008; Whalen, 1998).

Perception of Motivational Relevance

Many of the stimuli that arouse motivation are perceived via the visual or auditory system. Novel and significant events attract our attention and engage the orienting response, and they are typically associated with approach and avoidance behavior (Thorndike, 1911) or the emotion evoked by an event (Bradley, 2009; Maltzman, 1979). The processes of orienting and attending have been posited to "stem from the activation of defensive and appetitive motivational systems that evolved to protect and sustain the life of the individual" (Bradley, 2009, p. 1). In this way, attention, emotion, and motivation are inextricably linked. Emotion is often theoretically defined, fundamentally, as a disposition to act, or to behave effectively to events that threaten or promote life (Frijda, 1986; Lang, 1985). The associated motivational tendencies are realized in general systems of approach and avoidance, with approach processes often acting to promote survival and avoidance processes often acting to prevent threats to well-being. Some theorists suggest that judgments of positivity reflect approach motivation, judgments of negativity reflect avoidance motivation, and judgments of arousal index the intensity of activation or motivation (Bradley, 2009). Although this may often be the case, the relationship between emotional valence and motivational direction (i.e., approach motivation is positive) is not always so direct. For instance, anger, a negatively valenced emotion, is often associated with approach motivation (Carver & Harmon-Jones, 2009). We return to this point later.

Fear Processing

As noted above, human neuroimaging research has converged with the animal research to reveal that the amygdala is important for processing fear. For instance, the amygdala region is more activated by a neutral stimulus paired with an aversive event (conditioned stimulus) compared to another neutral stimulus that does not predict an aversive event (LaBar et al., 1998). Moreover, amygdala activation correlates with the degee of skin conductance response (an indication of arousal) to the conditioned stimulus (LaBar et al., 1998). Going beyond these correlations, research has revealed that patients with lesions of the right, left, or bilateral amygdala do not demonstrate a conditioned response as measured by skin conductance, even though they respond normally to the unconditioned (aversive) stimulus (Bechara et al., 1995). These results fit well with the animal research demonstrating that the amygdala—specifically, the central nucleus—plays a critical role in fear conditioning.

Interestingly, although the amygdala is important for the acquisition of fear, as measured implicitly by skin conductance to fear-conditioned stimuli, it does not appear to be important for the acquisition of fear learning measured explicitly. Individuals who suffer bilateral amygdala damage acquire explicit knowledge about the relationship between the conditioned stimulus and the aversive unconditioned stimulus (Gazzaniga, Irvy, & Mangun, 2002). This type of explicit knowledge is associated with the hippocampus (Squire & Zola-Morgan, 1991). Individuals with a damaged hippocampus but intact amygdala show normal skin conductance responses to conditioned stimuli but no explicit knowledge of the relationship between the conditioned stimulus and unconditioned stimulus (Bechara et al., 1995).

More recent human neuroimaging research has revealed that the amygdala becomes activated in response to a variety of emotive stimuli in addition to fear-provoking ones (Whalen, 1998). For instance, experiments have revealed that positive stimuli also evoke greater amygdala activity than neutral stimuli (Breiter et al., 1996). Other studies have independently manipulated valence and intensity and found that amygdala activity is more associated with processing affective intensity than with processing any specific valence (Anderson et al., 2003). Consistent with results obtained from these studies, Whalen (1998) observed that the amygdala is generally associated with vigilance to motivationally relevant stimuli (see also Anderson & Phelps, 2001; Cunningham et al., 2008). Although these findings appear to contradict the fear conditioning literature, they likely reflect the role of a different part of the amygdala—the basal nucleus—which supports the initiation of appetitive and goal-driven responses to stimuli, such as rewards (Holland & Gallagher, 1999; LeDoux, 2000). Contemporary fMRI methods lack the resolution to sufficiently discern the subnuclei in the amygdala, and this sometimes leads to confusion over interpretations of the amygdala as relating to motivational and emotional responses such as fear (e.g., freezing), withdrawal, and approach.

Along these lines, research has revealed that extraversion is correlated directly with amygdala activation to positive (relative to negative) emotional pictures and that neuroticism is correlated directly with amygdala activation to negative (relative to positive) emotional pictures (Canli et al., 2001). Extraversion has also been found to correlate directly with amygdala activation to happy (relative to fearful) faces (Canli, Sivers, Whitfield, Gotlib, & Gabrieli, 2002). Similarly, individual differences in promotion focus (sensitivity to gains) is associated with amygdala activation to positive (relative to negative) word stimuli, whereas individual differences in prevention focus (sensitivity to losses) is associated with amygdala activation to negative (relative to positive) word stimuli (Cunningham, Raye, & Johnson, 2005). These findings demonstrate that the amygdala is responsive to both appetitive and aversive stimuli, although this pattern likely reflects the roles of different subnuclei of the amygdala.

Reward Processing

In humans, fMRI research has linked the anticipation of rewards to activity in regions of the basal ganglia, such as the nucleus accumbens. For instance, Knutson, Wimmer, Kuhnen, and Winkielman (2008) found that anticipation of viewing rewarding stimuli (e.g., erotic female nudes, viewed by heterosexual men) increased nucleus accumbens activity and financial risk taking. Nucleus accumbens activity also increased in anticipation of making a risky decision, that is, a relatively high-risk ($1.00) as compared to a low-risk ($0.10) financial gamble. Moreover, the risk taking was partially mediated by increases in nucleus accumbens activation.

Research on dopamine and the nucleus accumbens has revealed differential mechanisms associated with the "wanting" and "liking" of a reward. Specific subregions of the nucleus accumbens, in combination with specific neurotransmitters, are involved in "liking" or postgoal positive affect. For instance, microinjection of morphine, which activates opioid receptors, into posterior and medial regions of the accumbens shell increases positive affective reactions to sweet tastes (Peciña & Berridge, 2000). Other research has revealed that the nucleus accumbens is critical in regulating effort-related functions, such that lever pressing schedules that require minimal work are unaffected by accumbens dopamine depletions, whereas lever-pressing schedules that require greater work are impaired by accumbens dopamine depletions (Salamone, 2007).

The orbital frontal cortex (figure 6.1; OFC) is another brain region that is widely implicated in studies of reward contingencies, such as in reversal learning (Schoenbaum, Setlow, & Ramus, 2003), and in the self-monitoring of emotional responses. In reversal learning, an animal is taught that responding to one cue produces reward, whereas acting similarly to another cue produces nonreward or punishment. After the animal learns to respond correctly, the experimenter switches the cue-outcome associations, and the animal must learn to change its behavior. During cue-outcome learning across reversals, the OFC is activated (O'Doherty, Critchley, Deichmann, & Dolan, 2003).

The reversal-learning function of the OFC relates to the process of self-monitoring in humans. Self-monitoring is defined as the ability to evaluate one's behavior in the moment in reference to higher-order goals or the reactions of other people (Prigatano, 1991; Stuss, 1991; Stuss & Benson, 1984). This is the process "by which individuals evaluate their behavior in the moment to make sure that the behavior is consistent with how they want to behave and how other people expect them to behave" (Beer, John, Scabini, & Knight, 2006, p. 872). Individuals with OFC damage have an impaired ability to prioritize solutions to interpersonal problems (Saver & Damasio, 1991), a tendency to greet strangers in an overly familiar manner (Rolls, Hornak, Wade, & McGrath, 1994), and to behave with disruptive manners in hospital settings (Blair & Cipolotti, 2000). They also tease strangers inappropriately and are more likely to disclose unnecessary or inappropriate personal information when answering questions (Beer, Heerey, Keltner, Scabini, & Knight, 2003; Kaczmarek, 1984). This self-monitoring perspective on OFC is consistent with the previously reviewed research on the emotional functions of this region.

PFC Asymmetries Associated with Emotion and Motivation

The asymmetric involvement of prefrontal cortical regions in positive affect (or approach motivation) and negative affect (or withdrawal motivation) was suggested over 70 years ago by observations of persons who had suffered damage to the right or left anterior cortex (Goldstein, 1939). Later research supported these observations using the Wada test, which involves injecting amytal, a barbiturate derivative, into one of the internal carotid arteries, suppressing the activity of one hemisphere. Amytal injections in the left side were found to produce depressed affect, whereas injections in the right side produced euphoria (Alema, Rosadini, & Rossi, 1961; Perria, Rosadini, & Rossi, 1961; Rossi & Rosadini, 1967; Terzian & Cecotto, 1959). These effects were interpreted as reflecting the release of one hemisphere from contralateral inhibitory influences. According to this view, activation in the right hemisphere, when not inhibited by the left hemisphere, caused depression; and disinhibited left hemisphere caused euphoria.

Subsequent studies appeared to confirm these results, finding that persons who had suffered left hemisphere damage or lesions tended to show depressive symptoms (Black, 1975; Gasparrini, Satz, Heilman, & Coolidge, 1978; Gainotti, 1972; Robinson & Price, 1982), whereas persons who had suffered right hemisphere lesions tended to show manic symptoms (Gainotti, 1972; Robinson & Price, 1982; Sackeim et al., 1982). Other research has revealed asymmetries underlying appetitive and avoidant behaviors in nonhuman animals, in species ranging from great apes and reptiles (Deckel, Lillaney, Ronan, & Summers, 1998; Hopkins, Bennett, Bales, Lee, & Ward, 1993) to chicks (Güntürkün et al., 2000), amphibians (Rogers, 2002), and spiders (Ades & Ramires, 2002).

More recent research suggests that in humans these affect-related asymmetric activations are often specific to the frontal cortex. This research often uses asymmetric activation in right versus left frontal cortical areas as a dependent variable, usually assessed by EEG recordings. Frontal cortical asymmetry is assessed by comparing activation levels between homologous areas on the left and right sides. Difference scores are widely used in this research, and their use is consistent with the amytal and lesion research described above that suggests that asymmetry may be the key variable, with one hemisphere inhibiting the other hemisphere.

Much of this evidence has been obtained with EEG measures of brain activity, or more specifically, power (square of the voltage amplitude) of activity within the alpha frequency band (8-13 Hz) of the EEG. Research has revealed that alpha power is inversely related to regional brain activity using hemodynamic measures (Cook, O'Hara, Uijtdehaage, Mandelkern, & Leuchter, 1998) and behavioral tasks (Davidson, Chapman, Chapman, & Henriques, 1990). Source localization of EEG signals (Pizzagalli, Sherwood, Henriques, & Davidson, 2005) and fMRI results (Berkman & Lieberman, 2010) obtained in emotion-frontal asymmetry studies converge in suggesting that the dorsolateral PFC (figure 6.3) is responsible for these alpha asymmetry effects. These findings are further corroborated by evidence from studies of transcranial magnetic stimulation, discussed later (Schutter, 2009; Schutter, van Honk, d'Alfonso, Postma, & de Haan, 2001).

Trait Affective Styles and Resting Frontal Cortical Asymmetry

Depression has been found to relate to resting frontal asymmetric activity, with depressed individuals showing relatively less left than right frontal brain activity (Jacobs & Snyder, 1996; Schaffer, Davidson, & Saron, 1983), even when in remission status (Henriques & Davidson, 1990). Other research has revealed that trait positive affect in healthy subjects is associated with greater left than right frontal cortical activity, whereas trait negative affect is associated with greater right than left frontal activity (Tomarken, Davidson, Wheeler, & Doss, 1992).

Subsequent studies observed that trait behavioral activation, construed as approach motivation (Carver & White, 1994), was related to greater left than right frontal activity at resting baseline (Amodio, Master, et al., 2008; Harmon-Jones &

Allen, 1997; Sutton & Davidson, 1997). These studies suggest that asymmetric frontal cortical activity could be associated with motivational direction instead of affective valence. However, avoidance and approach motivation are mostly associated with negative and positive affect, respectively (Carver & White, 1994), and consequently, the interpretation is clouded. Similarly, the finding that promotion (versus prevention) forms of regulatory focus are associated with greater relative left (versus right) frontal activation at baseline (Amodio et al., 2004) could be interpreted from either the motivational direction or affective valence view. That is, the distinction between emotional valence and motivational direction has been somewhat ambiguous given the methods used in past research, and researchers have tended to interpret relatively greater left than right frontal cortical activity as reflecting greater approach motivation and positive affect, and relatively greater right than left frontal cortical activity as reflecting greater withdrawal motivation and negative affect. Although these claims fit well into dominant emotion theories that associate positive affect with approach motivation and negative affect with withdrawal motivation (Lang, 1995; Watson, 2000), they do not comport well with known physiological structure and function, as discussed below.

State Affect and Asymmetric Frontal Activity

Research has also demonstrated that asymmetric frontal brain activity is associated with state emotional responses. For instance, Davidson and Fox (1982) found that 10-month-old infants exhibited increased left frontal activation in response to a film clip of an actress generating a happy facial expression as compared to a sad facial expression. Frontal brain activity has been found to relate to facial expressions of positive and negative emotions, as well. For example, Ekman and Davidson (1993) found increased left frontal activation during voluntary facial expressions of smiles of enjoyment. Coan, Allen, and Harmon-Jones (2001) found that voluntary facial expressions of fear produced relatively less left frontal activity.

Some positive affects are lower in approach motivation, whereas others are higher in approach motivation. An important question remains regarding the findings relating affective valence to asymmetric frontal cortical activity: Do positive affects of any approach motivational intensity cause increases in relative left frontal activation? An experiment by Harmon-Jones, Harmon-Jones, Fearn, Sigelman,

and Johnson (2008) addressed this issue by manipulating positive affect and approach motivation independently while measuring frontal EEG. Participants who wrote about positive/high-approach and positive/low-approach events both reported elevated positive affect, but only the positive/high-approach manipulation produced an increase in left-frontal activity. These results support the hypothesis that it is the approach motivational component of positive affective experiences, and not the positive valence per se, that causes greater relative left frontal cortical activation (as measured by EEG).

Anger and Asymmetric Frontal Cortical Activity

The experiment by Harmon-Jones et al. (2008), described above, suggests that approach motivation and positive affect are not perfectly associated with each other. More convincing evidence for the dissociation of affective valence and motivational direction (e.g., positive affect = approach motivation) comes from research on anger. Anger is a negatively valenced emotion that evokes behavioral tendencies of approach (e.g., Darwin, 1872; Ekman & Friesen, 1975; Plutchik, 1980; Young, 1943). Anger is associated with attack, particularly offensive aggression (e.g., Berkowitz, 1993; Blanchard & Blanchard, 1984; Lagerspetz, 1969). Offensive aggression can be distinguished from defensive aggression, which is associated with fear. Other research also suggested that anger was associated with approach motivation (e.g., Izard, 1991; Lewis, Alessandri, & Sullivan, 1990; Lewis, Sullivan, Ramsay, & Alessandri, 1992). More recent studies examined whether trait behavioral approach (or behavioral activation) sensitivity (BAS) related to anger-related responses. Several studies have found that trait BAS, as assessed by Carver and White's (1994) scale, is positively related to state and trait anger (Carver, 2004; Harmon-Jones, 2003b; Smits & Kuppens, 2005). Therefore, the emotion of anger provides a critical test case to disentangle interpretations of frontal cortical asymmetry as relating to valence or motivational direction.

In an initial test of this hypothesis, Harmon-Jones and Allen (1998) assessed trait anger using the Buss and Perry (1992) questionnaire and assessed asymmetric frontal activity by examining baseline, resting EEG activity. In this study of adolescents, trait anger related to higher left frontal activity and lower right frontal activity at baseline. Asymmetric activity in other brain regions did not relate to anger, a finding that has been observed in all subsequent observations of this effect. Replications have revealed that these results were not due to anger being evaluated as a positive feeling (Harmon-Jones, 2004), and this general effect has been replicated in other laboratories (e.g., Hewig, Hagemann, Seifert, Naumann, & Bartussek, 2004; Rybak, Crayton, Young, Herba, & Konopka, 2006). Other research has manipulated asymmetrical frontal cortical activity using transcranial magnetic stimulation and found that the disruption of right PFC increased approach responses to angry faces compared with disruption of the left PFC (d'Alfonso, van Honk, Hermans, Postma, & de Haan, 2000; van Honk & Schutter, 2006).

Researchers have also tested the motivational direction model of frontal cortical asymmetry by manipulating state anger. Harmon-Jones and Sigelman (2001) found that individuals who were insulted evidenced greater relative left frontal activity than individuals who were not insulted. Additional analyses revealed that within the insult condition, reported anger and aggression were positively correlated with relative left frontal activity. Neither of these correlations was significant in the no-insult condition. Harmon-Jones, Peterson, and Harris (2009) conceptually replicated the above research and extended it by showing that anger and jealousy in responses to social rejection caused increased relative left frontal activity. This pattern of state anger and approach motivation has been conceptually replicated in other laboratories as well (e.g., Jensen-Campbell, Knack, Waldrip, & Campbell, 2007; Verona, Sadeh, & Curtin, 2009).

Considered as a whole, EEG asymmetry studies of emotion and motivation have provided a critical test of how emotions are organized in the brain. Although the subjective appraisal of emotion is usually described in terms of valence (e.g., pleasant vs. unpleasant), this large body of research demonstrates that with regard to asymmetric frontal activity, emotional responses are organized in terms of their approach versus withdrawal motivational orientation (Harmon-Jones et al., in press).

Emotion Regulation

The idea that people often seek to regulate their emotional response dates back to classic theories of Freud and Descartes, who suggested that reason is needed to overcome passion (in Freud's terms, the ego must adjudicate the sway of the id). Contemporary views on emotion regulation have similarly focused on the role of cognitive control in modulating lower-level emotional processes

(Davidson, Jackson, & Kalin, 2000). In social cognitive neuroscience, researchers have focused on regions of the PFC as the neural substrate of control and on regions of the subcortex, such as the amygdala, as the substrate of emotion, particularly negative emotion (Ochsner & Gross, 2005). For example, in many emotion regulation studies, subjects view aversive (vs. neutral) images during an fMRI scan. On some trials, subjects are instructed to simply view the image. On other trials, subjects may be instructed to decrease their affective response to the image. In one study using this method, Ochsner, Bunge, Gross, and Gabrieli (2002) found that the simple viewing of aversive images was associated with increased activity in the amygdala. When subjects attempted to reduce their affective response, activations in lateral prefrontal cortex (PFC, figure 6.3) were observed and interpreted as reflecting the engagement of control, whereas amygdala activity on such trials did not differ from baseline (Ochsner et al., 2002). Several other studies have observed similar effects (e.g., Banks, Eddy, Angstadt, Nathan, & Phan, 2007; Cunningham et al., 2004; Ochsner et al., 2002; Lieberman, Hariri, Jarcho, Eisenberger, & Bookheimer, 2005; Lieberman et al., 2007; Phan et al., 2005; Urry et al., 2006).

As more direct evidence for the down-regulation hypothesis, researchers have observed a negative correlation between activity in the lateral PFC during emotion regulation trials and amygdala activity during baseline (no-regulation) trials (e.g., Hariri, Mattay, Tessitore, Fera, & Weinberger, 2003; Ochsner et al., 2002). This negative correlation is typically interpreted as demonstrating the direct "down-regulation" of emotion, in the direction of the PFC acting on the amygdala. There are problems with this interpretation, however. Despite observed correlations between regions of lateral PFC and the amygdala, these regions share very few anatomical connections, and of these, most run from the amygdala to the PFC (Ghashghaei & Barbas, 2002). Thus, the idea that the PFC "down-regulates" emotion may be incorrect, or at least inconsistent with neuroanatomy.

If the PFC does not directly down-regulate emotion, how might it otherwise play a role? One recent study suggests that PFC activity interpreted as controlling emotion may actually reflect the control of eye gaze (van Reekum et al., 2007). The authors found that, when instructed to reduce one's affective response to aversive images, subjects' gaze avoided the most aversive parts of the image, as measured by eye-tracking sensors. Interestingly, increases in PFC activity (and decreases in amygdala activity) associated with the voluntary reduction of negative affect were statistically explained by these changes in eye gaze. This important finding suggests that PFC activations previously interpreted as reflecting the direct down-regulation of affect may actually reflect an indirect mechanism, whereby the control of attention away from the aversive stimulus lessens the emotional impact. The notion of an indirect pathway for emotion regulation is consistent with previous physiological studies (Gross & Levenson, 1993, 1997).

Neuroscience research on emotion regulation highlights the idea that psychological conceptions of emotion do not map cleanly onto specific underlying neural structures (Amodio, 2008; Cacioppo et al., 2003). Rather, psychological constructs of emotions (e.g., subjective feelings) more likely reflect a summary appraisal of several interacting physiological mechanisms that function in concert to promote adaptive responses to an emotion-eliciting situation. If so, then questions about the neural correlates of emotion and emotion regulation may need to be reconsidered and perhaps replaced by questions about more basic processes of motivation, attention, arousal, and action that support the adaptive functions associated with subjective experiences of emotion.

Intergroup Processes

One of the most active areas in the field of social neuroscience examines prejudice, stereotyping, and intergroup relations (for a review, see Amodio, 2008). The area has provided fertile ground for social neuroscience research because it concerns the confluence of multiple psychological processes across multiple levels of analysis. That is, researchers can simultaneously examine issues of automaticity and control, emotion and cognition, motivation, attitudes, and a range of individual differences, all within the context of social cognition and social behavior, and with broad societal implications (see also Tropp & Molina, chapter 22, this volume).

Seeing Groups

How early is a person's social category perceived in the person perception process? Several studies have examined this question by testing whether faces of ingroup and outgroup members are perceived differently in basic visual processes. A study by Golby, Eberhardt, Chiao, and Gabrieli (2001) observed greater activity in the fusiform gyrus in response to

ingroup than outgroup faces, and this difference predicted later recognition of the faces. Several studies have also examined this question using the N170 component of the ERP while participants viewed faces of Black and White people in the context of various tasks. However, the findings have been mixed, with some studies observing no differences (Caldara, Rossion, Bovet, & Hauert, 2004; Caldara et al., 2003; Wiese, Stahl, & Schweinberger, 2009), some finding larger effects of visual processing for the ingroup (Ito & Urland, 2005) and others for the outgroup (Walker, Silvert, Hewstone, & Nobre, 2008). These inconsistent findings are likely due to task differences. Also, few extant studies have controlled for important low-level visual factors (e.g., luminance and contrast) in their stimuli, and therefore more research is needed to understand what aspects of group membership might contribute to N170 effects.

In an effort to address these methodological issues, Ofan, Rubin, and Amodio (2011) presented White participants with "two-tone" faces of Black and White people. These two-tone faces were created by transforming grayscale images into images consisting only of pure white or black pixels. Images of White and Black faces were then equated for luminance and contrast by equating the proportion of black and white pixels in each face. In addition, the authors proposed that differences in face processing might relate to participants' degree of implicit racial bias. Participants with stronger pro-White bias, as assessed using a sequential evaluative priming task, may perceive Black outgroup faces as less normative compared with White ingroup faces. Given past work showing that N170 amplitudes are larger in response to non-normative faces (e.g., Halit, de Haan, & Johnson, 2000), the authors predicted that participants with stronger pro-White implicit bias would exhibit larger N170s to Black faces than to White faces. Indeed, this pattern was found (Ofan et al., in press). These results suggest that social group differences are indeed registered at the earliest stages of visual face processing, but that the effect of group differences on these processes varies as a function of the context and the perceiver's goals and attitudes.

Brain Mapping of Racial Bias

Physiological research on responses to race provided the first evidence that implicit forms of racial bias may differ from explicit self-reports (Rankin & Campbell, 1955; Vanman, Paul, Ito, & Miller, 1997). The earliest neuroscience studies of intergroup bias attempted to map this implicit response to the brain. At the time of these early neuroimaging studies, new findings were emerging from the study of fear conditioning in nonhuman animals that identified the amygdala as a key neural structure involved in the fear response (Davis & Whalen, 2001; LeDoux, 2000). Given other research suggesting that fear-related responses might underlie observations of implicit racial bias (Fazio, Jackson, Dunton, & Williams, 1995; Greenwald, McGhee, & Schwartz, 1998), the amygdala seemed to be a logical candidate for the neural substrate of prejudice.

A pair of initial studies by Hart et al. (2000) and Phelps et al. (2000) used fMRI to measure participants' brain activity while viewing faces of ingroup and outgroup members. Both studies used blocked designs, such that participants would view a series of White faces in one block and a series of Black faces in a different block. Hart et al. (2000) included both White and African American participants, whereas Phelps et al. (2000) included only White participants. In both studies, the authors focused on the amygdala as the proposed substrate of racial prejudice. Each face was viewed for several seconds, and measures of brain activity were averaged across the entire block, as a function of race. Although these studies did not allow for inferences about the "implicitness" of a response to race, given that the blocked task design allowed for slow and potentially deliberative responses, it was assumed that the amygdala only operates in an implicit manner, and thus any differences in amygdala activity to ingroup versus outgroup faces would indicate a neural form of implicit bias.

Interestingly, neither study found a significant effect for ingroup versus outgroup race in amygdala responses. Rather, the effects were more complex. Hart el al. (2000) observed that although passive viewing of both ingroup and outgroup faces elicited a similar degree of amygdala activity, amygdala responses to ingroup faces habituated more quickly than activity to outgroup faces. In Phelps et al. (2000), subjects viewed faces and indicated whether each face was the same or different from the previous trial. Although the authors did not observe an effect for race in amygdala activity, individual differences in amygdala response to Black versus White faces from the fMRI measure were correlated with subjects' scores on a Black-White IAT and also their degree of startle-eyeblink modulation to Black versus White faces. None of these measures were associated with explicit self-report measures of racial

attitudes. These patterns of results were consistent with the idea that the amygdala may be involved in implicit responses to race. By suggesting a neural correlate of implicit bias, these studies provided a foothold for future research to consider how mechanisms of learning and memory associated with the amygdala might be involved in implicit intergroup processes.

Social-Personality Research on Intergroup Bias and the Brain

From a social psychological perspective, identifying a neural substrate of implicit racial bias was interesting because it could offer new clues as to how implicit racial biases are learned, activated, expressed in behavior, and potentially altered or extinguished. Furthermore, such research could help to clarify important individual differences in people's abilities to respond without prejudice. For example, it could help us understand whether egalitarians respond without prejudice because they are very effective in regulating their responses or because they do not have biased responses in the first place. To address these questions, Amodio et al. (2003) conducted a study in which they used the startle-eyeblink method to examine fear-related amygdala responses to race.

Amodio et al.'s (2003) study was designed to address multiple goals. First, the authors sought to identify a uniquely affective form of implicit racial bias. Previous theories assumed that implicit bias reflected associations between a target group and related attributes within a semantic network (Fazio et al., 1995; Greenwald & Banaji, 1995). This type of theory explained observations of priming between target groups and judgments of stereotypic and evaluative words. Interestingly, priming effects for evaluative word associations were frequently interpreted as an affective form of bias. However, it is difficult to make this claim based on a measure of semantically based word associations. Amodio et al. (2003) noted that although the amygdala is associated with fear-related affective responses, it is not able to process semantic information (see also Amodio & Devine, 2006). Therefore evidence for differences in amygdala activity to Black versus White faces using the startle-eyeblink measure would provide strong evidence for an affective basis of implicit bias. By using a startle-eyeblink index of amygdala activity, the authors could also assess rapid changes in amygdala activity in response to an ingroup versus outgroup face, which would strengthen the interpretation that the amygdala response reflects "automatic" processing. Furthermore, the startle eyeblink method assesses activity of the amygdala's central nucleus—the region specifically involved in the learned fear response. By contrast, fMRI measures of amygdala activity cannot distinguish activity in the central nucleus from other regions that are not associated with fear. Thus, the startle eyeblink measure provided the best method for linking implicit racial bias to fear and threat-related affect.

Amodio et al.'s (2003) second goal was to understand why some people with sincere low-prejudice attitudes nevertheless show anti-Black bias on implicit measures, whereas other low-prejudice people do not. Previous research had shown that among people with strong internal motivations to respond without prejudice, those who were also very worried about appearing prejudiced in front of others exhibited high levels of implicit racial bias (e.g., on the IAT), whereas those who were not worried about social pressures exhibited low levels of implicit bias (Devine, Plant, Amodio, Harmon-Jones, Vance, 2002). Thus, Amodio et al. (2003) asked whether the subset of low-prejudice people who did not show implicit affective bias in behavior either (1) did not have a bias in the first place or (2) were biased but were very effective in regulating their bias.

To address these questions, participants viewed pictures of White, Black, and Asian faces. Some trials included a startle probe at 400 ms following picture onset, which assessed amygdala responses prior to the opportunity for controlled processing, and other trials included a startle probe at 4000 ms, assessing amygdala activity after an opportunity for controlled processing. At 400 ms, startle-eyeblink responses revealed greater amygdala activity to Black than White faces, but only among people with low internal motivation to respond without prejudice (i.e., high-prejudice subjects). At 4000 ms, there was greater amygdala activity to Black versus White faces for people with low internal motivations, as well as those with high internal motivation who were also very concerned about external social pressures. Subjects with strong internal motivations who did not worry about external social pressures—the ones who showed low implicit bias in other research—did not show a different startle response to Black versus White faces. These data suggested that indeed, some low-prejudice people did not show any signs of implicit affective bias to begin with, which might explain why they often do not show bias on

behavioral measures such as the IAT (Devine et al., 2002). Although other low-prejudice people, who worry about external pressures, do show signs of bias in their amygdala activity, a second study found that they are effective at controlling their expression of bias in more deliberative behaviors (Amodio et al., 2003, Study 2). Thus, this research was the first to show significant differences in amygdala activity to Black versus White faces, and this effect was moderated by individual differences. This research also provided evidence for a uniquely affective form of implicit bias, and it suggested that some low-prejudice people possess implicit negative affective association with racial outgroups, whereas other low-prejudice people do not.

By linking the amygdala to implicit affective racial associations in several studies, this body of research suggested that affective racial bias may reflect a form of fear conditioning. Therefore, knowledge about how fear responses are learned, expressed, and potentially unlearned could be applied to the topic of implicit affective intergroup bias. For example, fear-conditioned responses are learned rapidly, often after a single experience, and they are expressed primarily in autonomic responses and nonverbal behaviors (such as freezing and avoidance). Such associations are also very difficult and perhaps impossible to extinguish (Bouton, 1994; cf. Schiller, et al., 2010); instead of being unlearned, new learning is needed to override the effects of older fear-conditioned associations. Interestingly, most theories of implicit social cognition suggest that implicit associations are learned slowly, only after repeated exposure (e.g., Smith & DeCoster, 2000)—an idea that is inconsistent with fear conditioning. Nevertheless, behavioral studies have shown that measures of implicit evaluative bias predict nonverbals associated with freezing and avoidance (Amodio & Devine, 2006; Dovidio, Kawakami, Johnson, Johnson, & Howard, 1997; Fazio et al., 1995), consistent with the models of amygdala-based learning. Finally, the fact that evaluative biases are so difficult to extinguish is also consistent with research suggesting that fear-conditioned associations are relatively permanent.

Since these initial studies, several event-related fMRI studies have observed that amygdala activity is greater to outgroup than ingroup faces under some conditions but not others, and that these effects are typically subtle (Cunningham et al., 2004; Lieberman et al., 2005; Wheeler & Fiske, 2005; Ronquillo et al., 2007). That is, differences in amygdala activity to Black versus White faces tend to emerge only in a minimally demanding task. As tasks become more demanding, such as when searching for a "dot" on the image, when imagining whether the target likes a particular vegetable, or when attempting to match the face to written group labels, amygdala activations tend not to be found (Liberman et al., 2005; Wheeler & Fiske, 2005). Other research suggests that amygdala effects are lessened when the outgroup face is not looking directly at the subject (i.e., has averted gaze; Richeson, Todd, Trawalter, & Baird, 2008).

It is also notable that amygdala activity to Black compared with White faces may reflect participants' concern about appearing prejudiced in such studies. That is, participants are usually aware that a task concerns reactions to race after a few trials of viewing Black and White faces. To the extent that a participant is worried about showing prejudice toward Black faces, each Black face serves as a threat stimulus—that is, a trial on which the subject may reveal bias, either to others or to the self. Thus, it is possible that amygdala responses to race are due to this anxiety, rather than to previously learned affective associations. Other research has shown that the amygdala responds to motivationally relevant stimuli, such as to rewarding stimuli (Holland & Gallagher, 1999) or to one's ingroup members (e.g., in the context of an implied competition; Van Bavel, Packer, & Cunningham, 2008), although these responses may reflect the basal nucleus rather than the central nucleus of the amygdala. These findings suggest some alternative explanations for observations of amygdala activity associated with responses to race, highlighting the complexity of these processes and the need for careful interpretations and additional research.

Stereotyping

Whereas much research has examined the neural correlates of race-related affect and evaluation, very little has investigated social stereotypes. Stereotypes are cognitive structures stored in memory that represent a set of attributes associated with a social group (Devine, 1989). Amodio and Devine (2006; see also Amodio, 2008; Amodio & Mendoza, 2010) noted that stereotypes are rooted in mechanisms of semantic memory and selection, which are associated with neural activity in the temporal lobes and lateral posterior PFC (e.g., Brodmann areas 45 and 47). Behavioral and neuroscience research on semantic learning systems has uncovered the dynamics of

how such associations are learned and expressed in behavior, and by accessing this literature, researchers can apply findings from the memory literature to understand stereotyping processes (Amodio, 2008; Amodio & Ratner, 2011b). For example, whereas affective associations are learned quickly and are relatively indelible, semantic associations may be learned and unlearned through a process of repeated pairings and nonpairings. Semantic learning systems are more likely to be expressed in trait impressions, goal representations, and goal-driven behaviors, and thus they are more likely to emerge in verbal responses (Amodio & Devine, 2006).

Some fMRI studies have examined neural activity associated with the completion of stereotyping tasks (Knutson, Mah, Manly, & Grafman, 2007; Mitchell, Ames, Jenkins, & Banaji, 2009; Quadflieg et al., 2009), but these studies have not explored the mechanisms of stereotypes per se. Rather, these studies have focused on brain activity associated with more general aspects of task completion, such as response conflict and inhibition, or face perception. In a brain lesion study, patients with mPFC damage did not show bias on a male versus female IAT (Milne & Grafman, 2001). However, it is likely that this mPFC damage interfered with the general process of response conflict that drives the IAT effect, rather than representions of stereotype knowledge (a function typically ascribed to the lateral PFC and temporal lobes). Thus, the neural mechanisms of stereotyping remain largely unstudied, although researchers have already applied findings from the broader cognitive neuroscience literature on semantic selection and representation to help understanding the representation and functions of stereotypes (Amodio, 2008; Amodio & Ratner, 2011b).

Control and the Regulation of Intergroup Bias

Given that racial stereotypes and implicit evaluations may be automatically activated, regulatory processes are needed to reduce their expression in behavior. Social-personality psychologists have begun to apply findings from neuroscience studies of cognitive control to understand how expressions of intergroup bias may be regulated (Amodio, Devine, & Harmon-Jones, 2007; Amodio & Devine, 2010). Amodio et al. (2003; see also Richeson et al., 2003) proposed that PFC regions were likely involved in the control of behavioral responses to race, but that control operated on behavior rather than the putative source of bias in the amygdala. Indeed, Amodio et al. (2003) found that participants who were highly motivated to respond without prejudice were generally unable to control the activation of affective responses to race directly, but rather were highly effective at controlled behavioral expression of bias. This finding suggests that the mechanisms of control are complex, and that research was needed to understand the different ways in which control functions to guide intergroup behavior.

Detecting the Need for Control
Despite holding nonprejudiced beliefs, many self-avowed egalitarians still often express stereotypes and affective biases in their behavior. In light of recent neuroscience models positing that control involves two major components, conflict monitoring and regulative control (Botvinick et al., 2001), Amodio et al. (2004) wondered whether such "slips" might reflect a failure to detect the need for control by the conflict monitoring system, or rather a failure to implement control once its need has been detected. The authors measured EEG in low-prejudice participants while they completed the weapons identification task—a sequential priming task that requires enhanced control on some trials to override the influence of automatic stereotypes. The use of a behavioral "control" task was critical because it (1) clearly manipulated the engagement of controlled processing and (2) provided behavioral indicators of both automatic bias and the degree of successful control—both of which are needed to interpret associated brain activity as being involved in control.

Amodio et al. (2004) focused on two ERP measures of ACC activity—the error-related negativity component and the N2 component associated with successful control—and found that both were more strongly activated on trials where control over stereotypes was needed (see also Bartholow et al., 2006; Correll, Urland, & Ito, 2006). Importantly, heightened ACC activity was observed both when control succeeded and when it failed. In the case of failure, the finding suggested that when low-prejudice people respond with unwanted stereotypes, it is the result of failing to implement a controlled response rather than a failure to detect that control is needed. A conceptually related ERP study by Bartholow et al. (2006) found that alcohol administration selectively impaired the regulative component of control without affecting the conflict monitoring component in the process of stereotyping inhibition,

providing further support for the distinction between these two components of control in the regulation of intergroup bias.

Amodio, Devine, et al., (2008) conducted a follow-up study to address why some low-prejudice people—those who have strong internal motivation to respond without prejudice but are also very concerned about external social pressures—are especially prone to unintended expressions of bias. The authors asked whether these individuals were less sensitive to conflicts between activated stereotypes and egalitarian response goals. Consistent with this hypothesis, these high-internal/high-external motivation subjects showed lower levels of ACC activity on task trials that required control over automatic stereotypes, similar to subjects reporting high-prejudice beliefs. By contrast, participants who were highly internally motivated and unconcerned about external pressures showed strong ACC responses when stereotype control was needed. A second study showed that these groups did not differ in domain-general forms of control and that the observed differences were specific to racial stereotypes (as expected, given that groups were determined by their motivations to respond without prejudice). Other research suggests that mechanisms for engaging control in response to external cues (e.g., cues from other people) involve more rostral regions of the ACC and mPFC, in contrast to ACC-related mechanisms involved in control based on internal cues (Amodio et al., 2006). This finding suggests that when controlling responses according to external social cues, people rely on mentalizing and social cognition processes associated with the mPFC in other research (Amodio & Frith, 2006; Mitchell et al., 2006).

Implementing Control
Many theories in social and cognitive psychology posit that, once the need for control is detected, other mechanisms are engaged to implement a controlled response (Devine, 1989; Shiffrin & Schneider, 1977). Neuroscience research has implicated the PFC in this function (Botvinick et al., 2001; Kerns et al., 2004; Badre & Wagner, 2007). However, the specific target of control is not always clear—it could be the emotional response, the stereotype itself, the expressed behavior, the way a person is perceived, or some other process. Neuroscience can help clarify this issue, as an analysis of the neuronal circuitry of the PFC provides clues about the targets of control. In particular, this circuitry suggests that the PFC

modulates goal-directed action processes as well as the modulation of sensory input and perceptual processing (Miller & Cohen, 2001). By contrast, the PFC has few connections to the amygdala, and to the extent that the amygdala is the source of implicit affective bias, it is unlikely to be a direct target of control.

Several studies have observed patterns of PFC activity associated with responses to race, but their role in response control has not been clear. In the earliest example, Richeson et al. (2003) found that subjects who showed greater PFC activity when viewing Black versus White faces in one experimental session were more likely, in a subsequent experimental session, to perform more poorly on a cognitive control task following a stressful interracial interaction. The authors reasoned that subjects who spontaneously engaged control when viewing faces were also more likely to engage control during an interracial interaction, which in turn interfered with their performance on the Stroop task. A study by Cunningham et al. (2004) measured brain activity to faces of Black and White people using fMRI. Participants simply indicated whether faces appeared on the right or left side of the visual field. Like Richeson et al. (2003), Cunningham et al. (2004) assumed that people spontaneously engage some form of control during passive face viewing. Indeed, the ACC and several regions of the PFC were more active to Black faces than White faces, although some PFC regions were more active to White faces than Black faces. Similarly, a study by Lieberman et al. (2005) found a reduction in amygdala activity and an increase in some PFC regions (e.g., the right ventrolateral PFC, figure 6.3) when participants viewed Black versus White faces and were instructed to match the faces to written labels.

Taken together, these studies are provocative, suggesting a possible role of the PFC in the control of racial bias. However, without the manipulation of response control or a behavioral measure of control, interpretations of these studies are unclear. That is, the PFC is involved in a wide range of functions, and therefore one cannot necessarily infer the engagement of "control" from the observation of PFC activity alone, as this would be a poorly supported reverse inference. A second issue is that researchers often assume that the target of control is the amygdala (i.e., the putative source of implicit bias). Indeed, Cunningham et al. (2004) and Lieberman et al. (2005) each found a region of lateral PFC (a different region in each paper) that was inversely correlated with an index of amygdala activity to Black versus White faces. These authors interpreted this correlation as evidence for a neural mechanism of prejudice control. However, these regions of lateral PFC are known to have few, if any, anatomical connections to the amygdala (Ghashghaei & Barbas, 2002), and therefore the interpretation of this "down-regulatory" effect is likely to be incorrect. For example, it is possible that observed PFC activations were associated with task demands and changes in attention that were indirectly associated with a reduction in amygdala responses (as in Wheeler & Fiske, 2005).

Other research has examined the role of the PFC in modulating behavioral intentions and the perceptual processing of race in a way that is more consistent with PFC anatomy. Previous work by Amodio et al. (2003) observed that controlled processes operated on behavior, but not directly on amygdala activity. In a later study, Amodio et al. (2007) demonstrated that increased left PFC activity was associated with the behavioral intention to engage in prejudice-reducing behaviors. More recently, Amodio (2010b) proposed that mechanisms of control promote intentional behavior by modulating attention to and perception of cues that control is needed. For example, Monteith's (1993) self-regulation model posits that, once the goal to control intergroup responses is formed, an individual becomes vigilant to cues that control is needed, such as the presence of an outgroup member (see also Richeson & Trawalter, 2008). Amodio (2010b) predicted that control-related PFC activity would serve to allocate greater attentional resources to the perception of outgroup faces, which in turn would facilitate better response control (i.e., more accurate responding despite any biasing effects of racial stereotypes). Indeed, while White participants in the study by Amodio (2010b) completed the weapons identification task, greater left PFC activity throughout the task predicted larger attentional ERP responses to Black versus White face primes just 180 ms after a face appeared, as well as greater response control. Furthermore, the effect of PFC activity on response control was mediated by attentional ERP responses to Black faces, among low-prejudice participants. These findings are consistent with anatomical models of the PFC, as well as behavioral research showing that people are effective at controlling their actions and perceptual attention, but ineffective at directly controlling their thoughts or emotions (Gross & Levenson, 1993; Wegner, Schneider, Carter, & White, 1987).

Intergroup Emotion and the Brain

Research on intergroup emotion examines responses such as love, hate, threat, disgust, and guilt in an intergroup context, and their implications for social interactions and discrimination (Mackie & Smith, 1998; Fiske, Cuddy, Glick, & Xu, 2002; Devine, Monteith, Zuwerink, & Elliot, 1991). Other research has focused on the role of intergroup anxiety in interracial interactions (Stephan & Stephan, 1985). Several social neuroscience studies have been conducted to probe these processes further. However, as noted above, the study of emotion (and affect) at the neural level of analysis is challenging because emotions and affect typically describe psychological states rather than mechanisms. When one begins to describe mechanisms associated with an emotion, a lower level of analysis that involves motivational, attentional, and/or autonomic functions is often necessary. Thus, social neuroscience research on intergroup emotion often focuses on these lower-level mechanisms.

Several studies have examined the physiological correlates of intergroup emotional responses within a social interaction. Early physiological studies showed that despite reports of liking for outgroup members, White participants revealed heightened skin conductance levels and facial EMG patterns indicating negative emotion in response to outgroup members (Rankin & Cambell, 1955; Vanman et al., 1997; Vrana & Rollock, 1998). As noted above, initial cognitive neuroscience studies of intergroup emotion focused on the amygdala as a key substrate, on the basis of animal research linking the amygdala to the learning and expression of fear (e.g., Amodio et al., 2003; Hart et al., 2000; Phelps et al., 2000). However, a simple mapping of implicit bias to the amygdala is not informative about the emotional quality of implicit bias per se. Rather, it links the construct of implicit bias to a set of mechanisms involved in the response to a learned threat, such as the activation of the autonomic nervous system, heightened attention and perceptual vigilance, behavioral inhibition and the preparation for "fight or flight" behaviors (Amodio, 2008). This research suggests a mechanism underlying implicit bias, which in turn suggests new ideas for how implicit bias might relate to behavior, learning, and other low-level psychological functions. In general, though, relatively few studies have examined the role of the brain in intergroup emotional processes. Here we note a few examples.

Role of Self-Directed Negative Affect

Guilt is an important intergroup emotion experienced among egalitarians after responding unintentionally with prejudice, and it is associated with new goals to regulate one's prejudices in future situations (Monteith, 1993; Monteith, Ashburn-Nardo, Voils, & Czopp, 2002). Amodio et al. (2007) showed that guilt resulting from the unintentional expression of prejudice is associated with a decrease in left PFC activity, relative to baseline, and a reduction in approach motivation. Other negative emotions, such as shame, sadness, and anxiety, were not associated with changes in PFC activity in this situation. Importantly, when an opportunity to reduce future prejudice arose, subjects' degree of guilt predicted a shift toward greater left PFC activity, which was associated with stronger approach motivation toward behaviors designed to reduce prejudice. Thus, this research used EEG measures of brain activity to show that guilt is a complex intergroup emotion that coordinates shifts from inhibition to approach-motivated responses to promote prosocial behavior.

Intergroup Anxiety

In actual intergroup situations, anxiety is often a factor. Using cardiovascular assessments of threat versus challenge appraisals, Mendes, Blascovich, Lickel, and Hunter (2002) observed stronger threat responses during interactions with outgroup members on the basis of race or socioeconomic status, compared with ingroup members. Based on earlier research suggesting that anxiety can interfere with performance and controlled processing (e.g., Easterbrook, 1959; Baumeister & Showers, 1986), prejudice researchers have proposed that intergroup anxiety might undermine attempts to control implicit racial bias, leading to greater expressions of prejudice (Lambert et al., 2003; Richeson & Trawalter, 2005). However, the mechanism through which anxiety might interfere with control has been unclear, particularly because self-report assessments of anxiety are typically uncorrelated with changes in behavioral control.

Taking a neuroscience perspective on this issue, Amodio (2009) proposed that anxiety might affect the control of intergroup responses through a neural pathway that operates independently of subjective emotional responses. That is, he noted that social threats are typically associated with the release of norepinephrine within the brain, which has been shown to modulate ACC activity and conflict monitoring processes (Aston-Jones & Cohen, 2005). According to this model, high norepinephrine signaling to the ACC sensitizes the conflict monitoring processes, such that vigilance to conflict is very high, but the ability to implement an intended response becomes impaired. Through this pathway, high anxiety should impair the control of automatic stereotyping effects on behavior. Although one cannot measure brain norepinephrine during an interracial interaction, one of its downstream effects is the release of the hormone *cortisol* in the bloodstream, which can be measured in saliva. Thus, Amodio (2009) measured salivary cortisol changes in response to an interracial versus same-race interaction. As part of the interaction, participants completed a stereotype inhibition task that assessed response control. Interaction-related increases in cortisol predicted worse control during the interracial interaction. This effect was not observed during the same-race interaction. Also, although participants reported greater subjective anxiety in the interracial interaction condition, self-reported anxiety was unrelated to cortisol levels or behavior. Thus, this research applied a neuroscience model to propose a specific mechanism through which intergroup anxiety might enhance some aspects of control (e.g., vigilance) but impair other aspects (e.g., response implementation) during an intergroup interaction.

Personality and Individual Differences

Personality is the study of enduring psychological dispositions and their influence on thought, emotion, and behavior (see Fleeson, chapter 3, this volume). For researchers interested in personality processes, physiological processes that operate on a longer timecourse, such as genes and hormones, are of special interest. Some research in this area has examined direct correlations between personality traits, such as those described by the "Big Five." Increasingly, however, researchers have used neural and physiological models of continuity and change to help understand the complexities of personality processes and individual differences. In this section, we describe just few examples of this growing area of research.

Affective Style

Research by Davidson and colleagues suggested that enduring affective styles, associated broadly with depression and anxiety, relate to different patterns of neural function (Davidson & Irwin, 1999). Specifically, these styles relate to differences in frontal cortical asymmetries, as described in previous sections, which are also associated with differential approach versus withdrawal tendencies (Davidson, 1998; see also Heller, Nitschke, & Miller, 1998). Although much research has examined state changes in frontal EEG asymmetry to study emotion and motivation, more stable, trait-like components of the asymmetry (e.g., at rest or baseline) have been taken to reflect a substrate of affective personality style. These trait-like patterns have been observed in adults, children, and nonhuman primates using a range of measures, and individual differences in these styles have been linked to various assessments of mental and biological health (Kern et al., 2008; Rosenkranz et al., 2003). More recently, trait-like patterns of activity in other brain regions, including the amygdala and regions of the basal ganglia, have been included in an expanded framework of affective style (e.g., Fox, Shelton, Oakes, Davidson, & Kalin, 2008).

Role of Genes in Personality and Social Psychology

Psychologists have long suspected that many personality traits are substantially heritable, with longitudinal studies showing strong continuity in temperament from childhood to adulthood (Caspi, 2003; Cramer & Block, 1998). Over the past several decades, research on heritability using twin designs has supported this view (Caspi, Roberts, & Shiner, 2005; Plomin, DeFries, McClearn, & Rutter, 1997). Across the "Big Five" personality dimensions, a review of heritability estimates suggests that these traits are approximately 50% due to genetic similarities (Bouchard & Loehlin, 2001). The traits neuroticism and extraversion tend to show the largest heritability estimates, consistent with theory and research suggesting that these factors are dominant over other traits (Eaves, Eysenck, Martin, 1989; Tellegen et al., 1988). Significant heritability has also been observed for attitudes, such as toward social policy (e.g., the death penalty, immigration), racial beliefs, and hobbies (e.g., doing crossword puzzles) (Olson, Vernon, Harris, & Lang, 2001).

More recently, researchers have used a molecular genetics approach to explore the relationships between particular gene polymorphisms found in DNA and personality traits (Plomin & Caspi, 1999). The most well known example of this candidate-gene approach is the effort to associate differences in emotional processing with variations in the serotonin transporter gene—a gene that codes for proteins involved in the reuptake of serotonin from the synapse (Hariri & Holmes, 2006; Canli & Lesch, 2007). Lesch et al. (1996) found that trait neuroticism was associated with individual differences (i.e., polymorphisms) in this gene. Other research has observed suggestive associations between gene polymorphisms related to dopamine function and traits of extraversion and sensation seeking (Smillie, Cooper, Proitsi, Powell, & Pickering, 2010), although a meta-analysis suggests that evidence for these relationships is mixed across studies (Munafò, Yalcin, Willis-Owen, Flint, 2008). Another method for garnering convergent insight into the genetic and neurotransmitter systems involved in social processes is the experimental administration of various drug challenges. These studies provide insight into the molecular involvement in aspects of personality and various behaviors, such as extraversion and economic decision-making (Depue, Luciana, Arbisi, Collins, & Leon, 1994; Crockett, Clark, Tabibnia, Lieberman, & Robbins, 2008)

A growing body of evidence suggests that environmental experiences can directly and indirectly modulate the expression of DNA (Caspi et al., 2003; Champagne & Curley, 2005; Way & Gurbaxani, 2008), consistent with psychological theories that highlight the importance of both personal and environmental factors. Although this approach has generated much excitement, it is notable that effects in this literature have been difficult to replicate (Caspi et al., 2005; Munafò et al. 2003). It is likely that the extreme complexity involved in traversing such distal levels of analysis—from DNA to complex behaviors, traits, and mental states—remains beyond the grasp of extant theoretical models. Therefore, much of the current work in this area continues to explore gene-behavior associations in an effort to incrementally constrain our understanding of their causal relationship, slowly progressing toward a coherent genetic account of personality and behavior.

Hormones and Psychological Dispositions

Although genes provide a close analog to the concept of personality as an enduring trait, the role of hormones in individual differences and social behavior has received much more attention. Hormones are characterized as providing a broader "organizational" function, in that they help to orchestrate the coordinated response of multiple physiological and brain mechanisms. By comparison, specific neural activations are typically interpreted as reflecting very specific, low-level aspects of a psychological response. Furthermore, whereas neural processes typically relate to specific state-related responses, the effects of hormones on behavior are slower, ranging from a few seconds, in the case of hormonal responses to specific events, to the course of a lifetime, in the case of baseline hormonal function. Hormonal influences in early development can set the stage for enduring dispositions in biological and mental processes. For example, prenatal exposure to sex hormones has been shown to have long-term implications for gender development and adult sexual behavior (Singh, Vidaurri, Zambarano, & Dabbs, 1999).

As with gene effects, hormone effects can vary substantially as a function of the situation. For example, testosterone levels may vary with changes in power and social status (Josephs, Sellers, Newman, & Mehta, 2006; Mazur & Booth, 1998), and individual differences in the testosterone response following a competition predict who chooses to seek a rematch (Mehta & Josephs, 2006). Experimental administration of testosterone can also increase attention to potential social threats, such as angry faces (van Honk et al., 1999). More recent research suggests that testosterone plays a larger role in orchestrating social behavior, such that it may promote greater cooperation in reciprocal social exchanges (Eisenegger et al., 2010).

Another steroidal hormone, cortisol, is widely studied as a physiological response to stress (Dickerson & Kemeny, 2004). Cortisol is produced by the adrenal glands following activation along the hypothalamic-pituitary-adrenal axis, and it functions broadly to regulate metabolism and arousal in dispositional (i.e., baseline) diurnal processes and also in response to specific arousing events. Cortisol secreted into the blood can be detected in saliva, and thus salivary cortisol concentrations may be measured non-invasively and with relatively low cost in the typical psychological laboratory (Schultheiss & Stanton, 2009).

Cortisol reactivity in response to a stressor coordinates an adaptive response (e.g., fight or flight), but after chronic exposure, heightened levels of cortisol become maladaptive (McEwen, 1998; Sapolsky, Romero, & Munck, 2000). For example, higher baseline cortisol levels have been associated with unhealthy profiles, including perceived stress, anxiety, depression, and cardiovascular stress (Cohen et al., 2006; Gallagher, Reid, & Ferrier, 2009). Although cortisol reactivity in response to a stressful event has been examined in different contexts, a meta-analysis by Dickerson and Kemeny (2004) suggests that it is especially sensitive to socioevaluative stressors, such as when a subject must give an extemporaneous speech to a panel of disapproving peer judges. Thus, cortisol research has highlighted the primacy of social interactions in human motivation and stress responses. As an outcome measure, cortisol provides a useful assessment of the stress response that does not rely on self-report. Furthermore, the connection between psychological distress and biological responses highlights connections between the mind and body, and it underlines the important effects that social and dispositional factors have on physical health. Research on immune variables, such as proinflammatory cytokines, provides a similar link that pertains even more directly to healing and illness processes (Maier & Watkins, 1998; Segerstrom & Miller, 2004).

It is notable that the greatest power of the social neuroscience approach lies in its ability to probe mechanism, and researchers have recently begun to conceptualize hormones and immune variables as mechanism variables. For example, Amodio (2009) measured salivary cortisol as a downstream correlate of within-brain norepinephrine activity to test a mechanism through which intergroup anxiety affects the control of racial stereotypes. Maier and Watkins (1998) provided a detailed analysis of how changes in cytokines and other associated immune and endocrine variables can act as mechanisms to alter cognition, emotion, and behavior, and to promote an organism's health. These examples suggest that endocrine and immune approaches will increasingly be used to understand psychobiological mechanisms associated with social and personality processes in future research.

The Future of Social Neuroscience in Social-Personality Psychology

Over the past decade, physiological approaches have reemerged as an important facet of social-personality research, now augmented by advances in neural, pharmacological, endocrinological, immunological, and genetic approaches. This time, we think neuroscience is here to stay. Recently a novelty in social-personality circles, the neuroscience perspective is now woven into the natural discourse of social-personality inquiry. Neuroscience data are increasingly integrated into the literature reviews of mainstream social-personality manuscripts, and psychophysiological methods complement the traditional tools of behavioral psychology, now without the fanfare of a novelty act. Social neuroscience is also becoming more prevalent in the training of new social-personality psychologists. These are healthy developments for the field.

The purpose of this volume is to highlight the interplay of personality and social psychological approaches. It is interesting to consider this aim from the perspective of social neuroscience, a field in which traditional boundaries between the person and the situation are reinterpreted as complex, dynamic, and inherently multilevel interactions. For example, neuroscientific models reveal how our perception of a situation is influenced by dispositional factors, such as personality, goals, and mental sets (following ideas from the New Look movement). At the same time, research on genetics shows that even our DNA may be influenced by situational factors at the time of conception, and that gene expression—often held to be the purest expression of personality—is strongly influenced by the situation. Thus, from the social neuroscience perspective, a dynamic interplay of personal and situational influences operates at every level of analysis.

In this regard, the social neuroscience approach is helping to build connections between the fields of social and personality psychology in two ways. The first way is through its influence on theory and research. As noted above, social neuroscience research reveals the dynamic symbiosis between situational and personal factors that exists across levels of analysis, in line with the interactionist view that the effects of personality and the situation can only genuinely be studied in the context of each other. The second way is by bringing together researchers from different disciplines to lend their respective expertise to integrative research questions, and by promoting education and training in interdisciplinary approaches used in social neuroscience research.

Conclusion

Although neuroscience has reemerged on the social-personality scene, it still needs to establish itself as a substantive contributor to social and personality psychology theory. Success in this endeavor will depend on researchers' ability to ground their social neuroscience research in rigorous methodology and to relate it to central questions and theories of social and personality psychology. Researchers in the field are clearly rising to this challenge. As we described in this chapter, neuroscience theories and methods have begun to shed new light on the mechanisms of person perception, emotion, stereotyping and prejudice, and some aspects of personality processes. Once the functions of specific neural structures, and their associated networks, are better understood, the contributions of linking social-personality processes to the brain will be increasingly realized. We look forward to new contributions from the social neuroscience approach in years to come.

Acknowledgments

Work on this article was supported by grants from the National Science Foundation to David Amodio (BCS 0847350) and Eddie Harmon-Jones (BCS 0643348, BCS 0921565).

References

Ades, C., & Ramires, E. N. (2002). Asymmetry of leg use during prey handling in the spider Scytodes globula (scytodidae). *Journal of Insect Behavior, 15*, 563–570.

Alema, G., Rosadini, G., & Rossi, G. F. 1961. Psychic reactions associated with intracarotid amytal injection and relation to brain damage. *Excerpta Medica, 37*, 154–155.

Alexander, G.E., DeLong, M.R., & Strick, P.L. (1986). Parallel organization of functionally segregated circuits linking basal ganglia and cortex. *Annual Review of Neuroscience, 9*, 357–381.

Amodio, D. M. (2008). The social neuroscience of intergroup relations. *European Review of Social Psychology, 19*, 1–54.

Amodio, D. M. (2009). Intergroup anxiety effects on the control of racial stereotypes: A psychoneuroendocrine analysis. *Journal of Experimental Social Psychology, 45*, 60–67.

Amodio, D. M. (2010a). Can neuroscience advance social psychological theory? Social neuroscience for the behavioral social psychologist. *Social Cognition, 28*, 695–716.

Amodio, D. M. (2010b). Coordinated roles of motivation and perception in the regulation of intergroup responses: Frontal cortical asymmetry effects on the P2 event-related potential and behavior. *Journal of Cognitive Neuroscience, 22*, 2609–2617.

Amodio, D. M., & Bartholow, B. D. (2011). Event-related potential methods in social cognition. In C. Klauer, A. Voss, & C. Stahl (Eds.), *Cognitive methods in social psychology.* (pp. 303–339) New York: Guilford.

Amodio, D. M. & Devine, P. G. (2006). Stereotyping and evaluation in implicit race bias: Evidence for independent constructs and unique effects on behavior. *Journal of Personality and Social Psychology, 91*, 652–661.

Amodio, D. M., & Devine, P. G. (2010). Regulating behavior in the social world: Control in the context of intergroup bias. In R. R. Hassin, K. N. Ochsner, & Y. Trope (Eds.). *Self control in society, mind, and brain* (pp. 49–75). New York: Oxford University Press.

Amodio, D. M., Devine, P. G., & Harmon-Jones, E. (2007). A dynamic model of guilt: Implications for motivation and self-regulation in the context of prejudice. *Psychological Science, 18*, 524–530.

Amodio, D. M., Devine, P. G., & Harmon-Jones, E. (2008). Individual differences in the regulation of intergroup bias: The role of conflict monitoring and neural signals for control. *Journal of Personality and Social Psychology, 94*, 60–74.

Amodio, D. M., & Frith, C. D. (2006). Meeting of minds: The medial frontal cortex and social cognition. *Nature Reviews Neuroscience, 7*, 268–277.

Amodio, D. M., Harmon-Jones, E., & Devine, P. G. (2003). Individual differences in the activation and control of affective race bias as assessed by startle eyeblink responses and self-report. *Journal of Personality and Social Psychology, 84*, 738–753.

Amodio, D. M., Jost, J. T., Master, S. L., & Yee, C. M. (2007). Neurocognitive correlates of liberalism and conservatism. *Nature Neuroscience, 10*, 1246–1247.

Amodio, D. M., Kubota, J. T., Harmon-Jones, E., & Devine, P. G. (2006). Alternative mechanisms for regulating racial responses according to internal vs. external cues. *Social Cognitive and Affective Neuroscience, 1*, 26–36.

Amodio, D. M., Master, S. L., Yee, C. M., & Taylor, S. E. (2008). Neurocognitive components of behavioral inhibition and activation systems: Implications for theories of self-regulation. *Psychophysiology, 45*, 11–19.

Amodio, D. M., & Mendoza, S. A. (2010). Implicit intergroup bias: Cognitive, affective, and motivational underpinnings. In B. Gawronski & B. K. Payne (Eds.) *Handbook of implicit social cognition* (pp. 353–374). New York: Guilford.

Amodio, D. M., & Ratner, K. G. (2011a). A social neuroscience analysis of the regulation of intergroup responses. In J. Decety & J. T. Cacioppo (Eds.), *Handbook of social neuroscience.* Oxford, UK: Oxford University Press.

Amodio, D. M., & Ratner, K. G. (2011b). A memory systems model of implicit social cognition. *Current Directions in Psychological Science, 20*, 143-148.

Amodio, D. M., Shah, J. Y., Sigelman, J., Brazy, P. C., & Harmon-Jones, E. (2004). Implicit regulatory focus associated with resting frontal cortical asymmetry. *Journal of Experimental Social Psychology, 40*, 225–232.

Anderson, A. K., Christoff, K., Stappen, I., Panitz, D., Ghahremani, D. G., Glover, G., et al. (2003). Dissociated neural representations of intensity and valence in human olfaction. *Nature Neuroscience, 411*, 196–202.

Anderson, A. K., & Phelps, E. A. (2001). Lesions of the human amygdala impair enhanced perception of emotionally salient events. *Nature, 411*, 305–309.

Aron, A. R. (2007). The neural basis of inhibition in cognitive control. *Neuroscientist, 13*, 214–228.

Aron, A., Fisher, F., Mashek, D. A., Strong, G., Li, H., & Brown, L. L. (2005). Reward, motivation, and emotion systems associated with early-stage romantic love. *Journal of Neurophysiology, 94*, 327–337.

Aston-Jones, G., & Cohen, J. D. (2005). An integrative theory of locus coeruleus-norepinephrine function: Adaptive gain and optimal performance. *Annual Review of Neuroscience, 28*, 403–450.

Badre D., & Wagner, A. D. (2007). Left ventrolateral prefrontal cortex and the control of memory. *Neuropsychologia, 45*, 2883–2901.

Banks, S. J., Eddy, K. T., Angstadt, M., Nathan, P. J., & Luan Phan, K. (2007). Amygdala-frontal connectivity during emotion regulation. *Social Cognitive and Affective Neuroscience, 2*, 303–312.

Baron-Cohen, S., Tager-Flusberg, H., & Cohen, D. J. (Eds.). (1993). *Understanding other minds: Perspectives from autism.* Oxford, UK: Oxford University Press.

Barrett, L. F. (2009). Understanding the mind by measuring the brain: Lessons from measuring behavior (Commentary on Vul et al., 2009). *Perspectives on Psychological Science, 4*, 314–318.

Barrett, L. F., & Wager, T. D. (2006). The structure of emotion: Evidence from neuroimaging studies. *Current Directions in Psychological Science, 15*, 79–83.

Bartholow, B. D., Dickter, C. L., & Sestir, M. A. (2006). Stereotype activation and control of race bias: Cognitive control of inhibition and its impairment by alcohol. *Journal of Personality and Social Psychology, 90,* 272–287.

Batson, C. D. (1991). *The altruism question: Toward a social-psychological answer.* Hillsdale, NJ: Erlbaum.

Baumeister, R. F., & Showers, C. J. (1986). A review of paradoxical performance effects: Choking under pressure in sports and mental tests. *European Journal of Social Psychology, 16,* 361–383.

Bechara, A., Damasio, H., Tranel, D., & Damasio, A. R. (1997). Deciding advantageously before knowing the advantageous strategy. *Science, 275,* 1293–1294.

Bechara, A., Tranel, D., Damasio, H., Adolphs, R., Rockland, C., & Damasio, A. R. (1995). Double dissociation of conditioning and declarative knowledge relative to the amygdala and hippocampus in humans. *Science, 269,* 1115–1118.

Beer, J. S., Heerey, E. H., Keltner, D., Scabini, D., & Knight, R. T. (2003). The regulatory function of self-conscious emotion: Insights from patients with orbitofrontal damage. *Journal of Personality and Social Psychology, 85,* 594–604.

Beer, J. S., John, O. P., Scabini, D., & Knight, R. T. (2006). Orbitofrontal cortex and social behavior: Integrating self-monitoring and emotion-cognition interactions. *Journal of Cognitive Neuroscience, 18,* 871–879.

Bentin, S., Allison, T., Puce, A., Perez, E., & McCarthy, G. (1996). Electrophysiological studies of face perception in humans. *Journal of Cognitive Neuroscience, 8,* 551–565.

Berkman, E. T., & Lieberman, M. D. (2010). Approaching the bad and avoiding the good: Lateral prefrontal cortical asymmetry distinguishes between action and valence. *Journal of Cognitive Neuroscience, 22,* 1970–1979.

Berkowitz, L. (1993). *Aggression: Its causes, consequences, and control.* New York: McGraw-Hill.

Berns, G. S., Cohen, J. D., & Mintun, M. A. (1997). Brain regions responsive to novelty in the absence of awareness. *Science. 276,* 1272–1275.

Black, W. (1975). Unilateral brain lesions and MMPI performance: A preliminary study. *Perceptual and Motor Skills, 40,* 87–93.

Blair, R. J. R., & Cipolotti, L. (2000). Impaired social response reversal: A case of "acquired sociopathy." *Brain, 123,* 1122–1141.

Blakemore, S.-J., Oakley, D. A., & Frith, C. D. (2003). Delusions of alien control in the normal brain. *Neuropsychologia, 41,* 1058–1067.

Blanchard R. J., & Blanchard D. C. (1984). Affect and aggression: An animal model applied to human behavior. In: R. J. Blanchard, & D. C. Blanchard (Eds.), *Advances in the study of aggression* (pp. 1–62). Orlando, FL: Academic.

Blaxton, T. A., Bookheimer, S. Y., Zeffiro, T. A., Figlozzi, C. M., William, D. D., & Theodore. W. H. (1996). Functional mapping of human memory using PET: Comparisons of conceptual and perceptual tasks. *Canadian Journal of Experimental Psychology, 50,* 42–56.

Botvinick, M. M., Braver, T. S., Barch, D. M., Carter, C. S., & Cohen, J. D. (2001). Conflict monitoring and cognitive control. *Psychological Review, 108,* 624–652.

Bouchard, T. J., Jr., & Loehlin, J. C. (2001). Genes, evolution, and personality. *Behavioral Genetics, 31,* 243–273.

Bouton, M. E. (1994). Conditioning, remembering, and forgetting. *Journal of Experimental Psychology: Animal Behavior Processes, 20,* 219–231.

Bradley, M. M. (2009). Natural selective attention: Orienting and emotion. *Psychophysiology, 46,* 1–11.

Breiter, H. C., Etcoff, N. L., Whalen, P. J., Kennedy, W. A., Rauch, S. L., R. L. Buckner, et al. (1996). Response and habituation of the human amygdala during visual processing of facial expression. *Neuron, 17,* 875–887.

Bunge, S. A., Dudukovic, N. M., Thomason, M. E., Valdya, C. J., & Gabrieli, J. D. E. (2002). Immature frontal lobe contributions to cognitive control in children: Evidence from fMRI. *Neuron, 33,* 301–311.

Buss, A. H., & Perry, M. (1992). The aggression questionnaire. *Journal of Personality and Social Psychology, 63,* 452–459.

Cacioppo, J. T. (1994). Social neuroscience: Autonomic, neuroendocrine, and immune responses to stress. *Psychophysiology, 31,* 113–128.

Cacioppo, J. T., & Berntson, G. G. (1992). Social psychological contributions to the decade of the brain: Doctrine of multilevel analysis. *American Psychologist, 47,* 1019–1028.

Cacioppo, J. T., Berntson, G. G., Lorig, T. S., Norris, C. J., Rickett, E., & Nusbaum, H. (2003). Just because you're imaging the brain doesn't mean you can stop using your head: A primer and set of first principles. *Journal of Personality and Social Psychology, 85,* 650–661.

Cacioppo, J. T., Bush, L. K., & Tassinary, L. G. (1992). Microexpressive facial actions as a function of affective stimuli: Replication and extension. *Personality and Social Psychology Bulletin, 18,* 515–526.

Cacioppo, J. T., Crites, S. L., Jr., Berntson, G. G., & Coles, M. G. H. (1993). If attitudes affect how stimuli are processed, should they not affect the event-related brain potential? *Psychological Science, 4,* 108–112.

Cacioppo, J. T., Crites, S. L., Jr., Gardner, W. L., & Berntson, G. G. (1994). Bioelectrical echoes from evaluative categorization: I. A late positive brain potential that varies as a function of trait negativity and extremity. *Journal of Personality and Social Psychology, 67,* 115–125.

Cacioppo, J. T., & Petty, R. E. (1979). Attitudes and cognitive response: An electrophysiological approach. *Journal of Personality and Social Psychology, 37,* 2181–2199.

Cacioppo, J. T., & Petty, R. E. (1983). Foundations of social psychophysiology. In J. T. Cacioppo & R. E. Petty (Eds.), *Social psychophysiology: A sourcebook* (pp. 3–36). New York: Guilford.

Cacioppo, J. T., Petty, R. E., & Quintanar, L. R. (1982). Individual differences in relative hemispheric alpha abundance and cognitive responses to persuasive communications. *Journal of Personality and Social Psychology, 43,* 623–636.

Cacioppo, J. T., Petty, R. E., & Snyder, C. W. (1979). Cognitive and affective response as a function of relative hemispheric involvement. *International Journal of Neuroscience, 9,* 81–89.

Cacioppo, J. T., & Sandman, C. A. (1978). Physiological differentiation of sensory and cognitive tasks as a function of warning, processing demands, and reported unpleasantness. *Biological Psychology, 6,* 181–192.

Cacioppo, J. T., Sandman, C. A., & Walker, B. B. (1978). The effects of operant heart-rate conditioning on cognitive elaboration and attitude change. *Psychophysiology, 15,* 330–338.

Caldara, R., Rossion, B., Bovet, P., & Hauert, C. (2004). Event-related potentials and time course of the "other-race" face classification advantage. *NeuroReport, 15,* 905.

Caldara, R., Thut, G., Servoir, P., Michel, C., Bovet, P., & Renault, B. (2003). Face versus non-face object perception and the "other-race" effect: A spatio-temporal event-related potential study. *Clinical Neurophysiology, 114,* 515–528.

Canli, T., & Lesch, K. P. (2007). Long story short: The serotonin transporter in emotion regulation and social cognition. *Nature Neuroscience, 10,* 1103–1109.

Canli, T., Omura, K., Haas, B. W., Fallgatter, A., Constable, R. T., & Lesch, K. P. (2005). Beyond affect: A role for genetic variation of the serotonin transporter in neural activation during a cognitive attention task. *Proceedings of the National Academy of Sciences, USA, 102,* 12224–12229.

Canli, T., Sivers, H., Gotlib, I. H., & Gabrieli, J. D. E. (2002). Amygdala activation to happy faces as a function of extraversion. *Science, 296,* 2191.

Canli, T., Zhao, Z., Desmond, J. E., Kang, E., Gross, J., & Gabrieli, J. D. E. (2001). An fMRI study of personality influences on brain reactivity to emotional stimuli. *Behavioral Neuroscience, 115,* 33–42.

Carlston, D. E. (1994). Associated systems theory: A systematic approach to the cognitive representation of persons and events. In R. S. Wyer (Ed.), *Associated systems theory: Advances in social cognition* (Vol. 7, pp. 1–78). Hillsdale, NJ: Erlbaum.

Carmel, D., & Bentin, S. (2002). Domain specificity versus expertise: factors influencing distinct processing of faces. *Cognition, 83,* 1–29.

Carter, C. S., Braver, T. S., Barch, D. M., Botvinick, M. M., Noll, D., & Cohen, J. D. (1998). Anterior cingulate cortex, error detection, and the online monitoring of performance. *Science, 280,* 747–749.

Carver, C. S. (2004). Negative affects deriving from the behavioral approach system. *Emotion, 4,* 3–22.

Carver, C. S., & Harmon-Jones, E. (2009). Anger is an approach-related affect: Evidence and implications. *Psychological Bulletin, 135,* 183–204.

Carver, C. S., & White, T. L. (1994). Behavioral inhibition, behavioral activation, and affective responses to impending reward and punishment: The BIS/BAS scales. *Journal of Personality and Social Psychology, 67,* 319–333.

Caspi, A. (2008). The child is father of the man: Personality continuities from childhood to adulthood. *Journal of Personality and Social Psychology, 78,* 158–172.

Caspi, A., & Moffitt, T. E. (2006). Gene-environment interaction research, joining forces with neuroscience. *Nature Reviews Neuroscience, 7,* 583–590.

Caspi, A., Roberts, B. W., & Shiner, R. L. (2005). Personality development: Stability and change. *Annual Review of Psychology, 56,* 453–484.

Caspi, A., Sugden, K., Moffitt, T. E., Taylor, A., Craig, I. W., Harrington, H., et al. (2003). Influence of life stress on depression: Moderation by a polymorphism in the 5-HTT gene. *Science, 301,* 386–389.

Castelli, F., Happe, F., Frith, U., & Frith, C. (2000). Movement and mind: A functional imaging study of perception and interpretation of complex intentional movement patterns. *NeuroImage, 12,* 314–325.

Champagne, F. A., & Curley, J. P. (2005). How social experiences influence the brain. *Current Opinion in Neurobiology, 15,* 704–709.

Coan, J. A., Allen, J. J. B., & Harmon-Jones, E. (2001). Voluntary facial expression and hemispheric asymmetry over the frontal cortex. *Psychophysiology, 38,* 912–925.

Cohen, S., Schwartz, J. E., Epel, E., Kirschbaum, C., Sidney, S., & Seeman, T. (2006). Socioeconomic status, race, and diurnal cortisol decline in the Coronary Artery Risk Development in Young Adults (CARDIA) study. *Psychosomatic Medicine, 68,* 41–50.

Cook, I. A., O'Hara, R., Uijtdehaage, S. H. J., Mandelkern, M., & Leuchter, A. F. (1998). Assessing the accuracy of topographic EEG mapping for determining local brain function. *Electroencephalography and Clinical Neurophysiology, 107,* 408–414.

Correll, J., Urland, G. R., & Ito, T. A. (2006). Event-related potentials and the decision to shoot: The role of threat perception and cognitive control. *Journal of Experimental Social Psychology, 42,* 120–128.

Craik, F. I. M., Moroz, T. M., Moscovitch, M., Stuss, D. T., Winocur, G., Tulving, E., et al. (1999). In search of the self: A positron emission tomography study. *Psychological Science, 10,* 26–34.

Cramer, P., & Block, J. (1998). Preschool antecedents of defense mechanism use in young adults: A longitudinal study. *Journal of Personality and Social Psychology, 74,* 159–169.

Crites, S. L., & Cacioppo, J. T. (1996). Electrocortical differentiation of evaluative and nonevaluative categorizations. *Psychological Science, 7,* 318–321.

Crites, S. L., Cacioppo, J. T., Gardner, W. L., & Berntson, G. G. (1995). Bioelectrical echoes from evaluative categorization: II. A late positive brain potential that varies as a function of attitude registration rather than attitude report. *Journal of Personality and Social Psychology, 68,* 997–1013.

Crockett M. J., Clark, L., Tabibnia, G., Lieberman, M. D., & Robbins, T. W. (2008). Serotonin modulates behavioral reactions to unfairness. *Science, 320,* 1739.

Csikszentmihalyi, M., & Figurski, T. J. (1982). Self-awareness and aversive experience in everyday life. *Journal of Personality, 50,* 15–28.

Cunningham, W. A., Espinet, S. D., DeYoung, C. G., & Zelazo, P. D. (2005). Attitudes to the right and left: Frontal ERP asymmetries associated with stimulus valence and processing goals. *NeuroImage, 28,* 827–834.

Cunningham, W. A., Johnson, M. K., Gatenby, J. C., Gore, J. C., & Banaji, M. R. (2003). Neural components of social evaluation. *Journal of Personality and Social Psychology, 85,* 639–649.

Cunningham, W. A., Raye, C. L., & Johnson, M. K. (2004). Implicit and explicit evaluation: fMRI correlates of valence, emotional intensity, and control in the processing of attitudes. *Journal of Cognitive Neuroscience, 16,* 1717–1729.

Cunningham, W. A., Raye, C. L., & Johnson, M. K. (2005). Neural correlates of evaluation associated with promotion and prevention regulatory focus. *Cognitive, Affective, and Behavioral Neuroscience, 5,* 202–211.

Cunningham, W. A., Van Bavel, J. J., & Johnsen, I. R. (2008). Affective flexibility: Evaluative processing goals shape amygdala activity. *Psychological Science, 19,* 152–160.

d'Alfonso, A., van Honk, J., Hermans, E. J., Postma, A., & de Haan, E. (2000). Laterality effects in selective attention to threat after repetitive transcranial magnetic stimulation at the prefrontal cortex in female subjects. *Neuroscience Letters, 280,* 195–198.

Damasio, A. R. (1994). *Descartes' error: Emotion, rationality, and the human brain.* New York: Putnam.

Darrow, C. W. (1929). Differences in the physiological reactions to sensory and ideational stimuli. *Psychological Bulletin, 26,* 185–201.

Darwin, C. (1872/1965). The expressions of the emotions in man and animals. New York: Oxford University Press.

Davidson, R. J. (1998). Affective style and affective disorders: Perspectives from affective neuroscience. *Cognition and Emotion, 12,* 307–320.

Davidson, R. J., Chapman, J. P., Chapman, L. J., & Henriques, J. B. (1990). Asymmetric brain electrical-activity discriminates between psychometrically-matched verbal and spatial cognitive tasks. *Psychophysiology, 27,* 528–543.

Davidson, R. J., Ekman, P., Saron, C. D., Senulis, J. A., & Friesen, W. V. (1990). Approach-withdrawal and cerebral asymmetry: Emotional expression and brain physiology: I. *Journal of Personality and Social Psychology, 58,* 330–341.

Davidson, R. J., & Fox, N. A. (1982). Asymmetrical brain activity discriminates between positive and negative affective stimuli in human infants. *Science, 218,* 1235–1237.

Davidson, R. J., & Irwin, W. (1999). The functional neuroanatomy of emotion and affective style. *Trends in Cognitive Science, 3,* 11–21.

Davidson, R. J., Jackson, D. C., & Kalin, N. H. (2000). Emotion, plasticity, context, and regulation: Perspectives from affective neuroscience. *Psychological Bulletin, 126,* 890–909.

Davis, M. (2006). Neural systems involved in fear and anxiety measured with fear-potentiated startle. *American Psychologist, 61,* 741–756.

Davis, M. & Whalen, P. J. (2001). The amygdala: Vigilance and emotion. *Molecular Psychiatry, 6,* 13–34.

Decety, J. (2010). To what extent is the experience of empathy mediated by shared neural circuits? *Emotion Review, 2,* 204–207.

Deckel, A. W., Lillaney, R., Ronan, P. J., & Summers, C. H. (1998). Lateralized effects of ethanol on aggression and serotonergic systems in *Anolis carolinensis. Brain Research, 807,* 38–46.

Deffke, I., Sander, T., Heidenreich, J., Sommer, W., Curio, G., Trahms, L., et al. (2007). MEG/EEG sources of the 170-ms response to faces are co-localized in the fusiform gyrus. *NeuroImage, 35,* 1495–1501.

Delgado, M. R., Frank, R. H., & Phelps, E. A. (2005). Perceptions of moral character modulate the neural systems of reward during the trust game. *Nature Neuroscience, 8,* 1611–1618.

Demb, J. B., Desmond, J. E., Wagner, A. D., Vaidya, Chandan J., Glover, G. H., et al. (1995). Semantic encoding and retrieval in the left inferior prefrontal cortex: A functional MRI study of task difficulty and process specificity. *Journal of Neuroscience, 15,* 5870–5878.

Depue, R. A., Luciana, M., Arbisi, P., Collins, P. F., & Leon, A. (1994). Dopamine and the structure of personality: Relation of agonist-induced dopamine activity to personality. *Journal of Personality and Social Psychology, 67,* 485–498.

Desimone, R. (1991). Face-selective cells in the temporal cortex of monkeys. *Journal of Cognitive Neuroscience, 3,* 1–8.

Devine, P. G. (1989). Stereotypes and prejudice: Their automatic and controlled components. *Journal of Personality and Social Psychology, 56,* 5–18.

Devine, P. G., Monteith, M. J., Zuwerink, J. R., & Elliot, A. J. (1991). Prejudice with and without compunction. *Journal of Personality and Social Psychology, 60,* 817–830.

Devine, P. G., Plant, E. A., Amodio, D. M., Harmon-Jones, E., Vance, S. L. (2002). The regulation of explicit and implicit race bias: The role of motivations to respond without prejudice. *Journal of Personality and Social Psychology, 82,* 835–848.

Dickerson, S. S., & Kemeny, M. E. (2004). Acute stressors and cortisol responses: A theoretical integration and synthesis of laboratory research. *Psychological Bulletin, 130,* 355–391.

Dimberg, U. (1982). Facial reactions to facial expressions. *Psychophysiology, 19,* 643–647.

Dimberg, U., Thunberg, M., & Elmehed, K. (2000). Unconscious facial reactions to emotional facial expressions. *Psychological Science, 11,* 86–89.

Donchin, E. (1981). Surprise! . . . Surprise? *Psychophysiology, 18,* 493–513.

Dovidio, J. F., Evans, N., & Tyler, R. B. (1986). Racial stereotypes: The contents of their cognitive representations. *Journal of Experimental Social Psychology, 22,* 22–37.

Dovidio, J. F., Kawakami, K., Johnson, C., Johnson, B., & Howard, A. (1997). On the nature of prejudice: Automatic and controlled processes. *Journal of Experimental Social Psychology, 33,* 510–540.

Easterbrook, J. A. (1959). The effect of emotion on cue utilization and the organization of behavior. *Psychological Review, 66,* 183–201.

Eaves, L. J., Eysenck, H. J., & Martin, N. G. (1989). Genes, culture, and personality: An empirical approach. San Diego, CA: Academic.

Eimer, M. (2000). Event-related brain potentials distinguish processing stages involved in face perception and recognition. *Clinical Neurophysiology, 111,* 694–705.

Eisenberger, N. I., Lieberman, M. D., & Williams, K. D. (2003). Does rejection hurt? An fMRI study of social exclusion. *Science, 302,* 290–292.

Eisenegger, C., Naef, M., Snozzi, R., Heinrichs, M., & Fehr, E. (2010). Prejudice and the truth about the effect of testosterone on human bargaining behavior. *Nature, 463,* 356–361.

Ekman, P., & Davidson, R. J. (1993). Voluntary smiling changes regional brain activity. *Psychological Science, 4,* 342–345.

Ekman, P., & Friesen, W. V. (1975). *Unmasking the face: A guide to recognizing emotions from facial clues.* Englewood Cliffs, NJ: Prentice-Hall.

Epley, N. Waytz, A., & Cacioppo, J. T. (2007). On seeing human: A three-factor theory of anthropomorphism. *Psychological Review, 114,* 864–886.

Farrer, C., Frey, S. H., Van Horn, J. D., Tunik, E., Turk, D., Inati, S., et al. (2008). The angular gyrus computes action awareness representations. *Cerebral Cortex, 18,* 254–261.

Fazio, R. H. (2007). Attitudes as object-evaluation associations of varying strength. *Social Cognition, 25,* 603–637.

Fazio, R. H., Jackson, J. R., Dunton, B. C., & Williams, C. J. (1995). Variability in automatic activation as an unobtrusive measure of racial attitudes: A bona fide pipeline? *Journal for Personality and Social Psychology, 69,* 1013–1027.

Fehr, E., & Camerer, C. F. (2007). Social neuroeconomics: The neural circuitry of social preferences. *Trends in Cognitive Sciences, 11,* 419–427.

Fendt, M., & Fanselow, M. S. (1999). The neuroanatomical and neurochemical basis of conditioned fear. *Neuroscience and Biobehavioral Review, 23,* 743–760.

Fiske, S. T. (1992). Thinking is for doing: Portraits of social cognition from daguerreotype to laserphoto. *Journal of Personality and Social Psychology, 63,* 877–889.

Fiske, S. T., Cuddy, A. J. C., Glick, P., & Xu, J. (2002). A model of (often mixed) stereotype content: Competence and warmth respectively follow from perceived status and competition. *Journal of Personality and Social Psychology, 82,* 878–902.

Fletcher, P. C., Happe, F., Frith, U., Baker, S. C., Dolan, R. J., Frackowiak, R. S., et al. (1995). Other minds in the brain: A functional imaging study of "theory of mind" in story comprehension. *Cognition, 57,* 109–128.

Foerde, K., Knowlton, B. J., & Poldrack, R. A. (2006). Modulation of competing memory systems by distraction. *Proceedings of the National Academy of Sciences, USA, 103,* 11778–11783.

Fox, A. S., Shelton, S. E., Oakes, T. R., Davidson, R. J., & Kalin, N. H. (2008). Trait-like brain activity during adolescence predicts anxious temperament in primates. *PLoS ONE, 3,* e2570.

Frijda, N. H. (1986). *The emotions.* New York: Cambridge University Press.

Frijda, N. H. (Ed.). (1993). Appraisal and beyond [Special issue]. *Cognition and Emotion.* Hillsdale, NJ: Erlbaum.

Frith, U. (1989). *Autism: Explaining the enigma.* Oxford: Blackwell.

Frith, C. D., & Frith, U. (1999). Interacting minds—A biological basis. *Science, 286,* 1692–1695.

Frith, U., Morton, J., & Leslie, A. M. (1991). The cognitive basis of a biological disorder: Autism. *Trends in Neurosciences, 14,* 433–438.

Gable, P. A., & Harmon-Jones, E. (2010). Late positive potential to appetitive stimuli and local attentional bias. *Emotion, 10,* 441–446.

Gabrieli, J. D. (1998). Cognitive neuroscience of human memory. *Annual Review of Psychology, 49,* 87–115.

Gaertner, S. L., & McLaughlin, J. P. (1983). Racial stereotypes: Associations and ascriptions of positive and negative characteristics. *Social Psychology Quarterly, 46,* 23–30.

Gainotti, G. (1972). Emotional behavior and hemispheric side of the lesion. *Cortex, 8,* 41–55.

Gallagher, P., Reid, K., & Ferrier, I. N. (2009). Neuropsychological functioning in health and mood disorder: Modulation by glucocorticoids and their receptors. *Psychoneuroendocrinology, 34,* S196–S207.

Gallese, V., Fadiga, L., Fogassi, L., & Rizzolatti, G. (1996). Action recognition in the premotor cortex. *Brain, 119,* 593–609.

Gasparrini, W. G., Satz, P., Heilman, K., & Coolidge, F. L. (1978). Hemispheric asymmetries of affective processing as determined by the Minnesota Multiphasic Personality Inventory. *Journal of Neurology, Neurosurgery, and Psychiatry, 41,* 470–473.

Gazzaniga, M. S. (1985). *The social brain.* New York: Basic Books.

Gazzaniga, MS., Irvy, R.B, & Mangun, G. R. (2002). *Cognitive neuroscience.* 2nd ed. New York: Norton.

Ghashghaei, H. T., & Barbas, H. (2002). Pathways for emotions: Interactions of prefrontal and anterior temporal pathways in the amygdala of the rhesus monkey. *Neuroscience, 115,* 1261–1279.

Gilbert, S. J., Spengler, S., Simons, J. S., Steele, J. D., Lawrie, S. M., Frith, C. D., et al. (2006). Functional specialization within rostral prefrontal cortex (Area 10): A meta-analysis. *Journal of Cognitive Neuroscience, 18,* 932–948.

Glimcher, P. W., Camerer, C. F., Fehr, E., & Poldrack, R. A. (Eds.). (2009). *Neuroeconomics: Decision making and the brain.* New York: Academic.

Gobbini, M. I., Leibenluft, E., Santiago, N., & Haxby, J. V. (2004). Social and emotional attachment in the neural representation of faces. *NeuroImage, 22,* 1628–1635.

Golby, A. J., Eberhardt, J. L., Chiao, J. Y., & Gabrieli, J. D. E. (2001). Fusiform response to same and other race faces. *Nature Neuroscience, 4,* 845–850.

Goldstein, K. (1939). *The organism: An holistic approach to biology, derived from pathological data in man.* New York: American Book.

Greenwald, A. G., & Banaji, M. R. (1995). Implicit social cognition: Attitudes, self-esteem, and stereotypes. *Psychological Review, 102,* 4–27.

Greenwald, A. G., McGhee, D. E., & Schwartz, J. K. L. (1998). Measuring individual differences in implicit cognition: The Implicit Association Test. *Journal of Personality and Social Psychology, 74,* 1464–1480.

Grezes, J., Frith, C., & Passingham, R. F. (2004). Brain mechanisms for inferring deceit in the actions of others. *Journal of Neuroscience, 24,* 5500–5505.

Gross, J. J., & Levenson, R. W. (1993). Emotional suppression: Physiology, self-report, and expressive behavior. *Journal of Personality and Social Psychology, 64,* 970–986.

Gross, J. J., & Levenson, R. W. (1997). Hiding feelings: The acute effects of inhibiting negative and positive emotion. *Journal of Abnormal Psychology, 106,* 95–103.

Güntürkün, O., Diekamp, B., Manns, M., Nottelmann, F., Prior, H., Schwarz, A., et al. (2000). Asymmetry pays: Visual lateralization improves discrimination success in pigeons. *Current Biology, 10,* 1079–1081.

Gusnard, D. A., Akbudak, E., Shulman, G. L., & Raichle, M. E. (2001). Medial prefrontal cortex and self-referential mental activity: Relation to a default mode of brain function. *Proceedings of the National Academy of Sciences, USA, 98,* 4259–4264.

Gusnard, D. A., & Raichle, M. E. (2001). Searching for a baseline: Functional imaging and the resting human brain. *Nature Reviews Neuroscience, 2,* 685–694.

Gutchess, A. H., Kensinger, E. A., & Schacter, D. L. (2007). Aging, self-referencing, and medial prefrontal cortex. *Social Neuroscience, 2,* 117–133.

Halit, H., de Haan, M., & Johnson, M. (2000). Modulation of event-related potentials by prototypical and atypical faces. *NeuroReport, 9,* 1871–1875.

Hare, T., O'Doherty, J., Camerer, C., Schultz, W., & Rangel, A. (2008). Dissociating the role of the orbitofrontal cortex and the striatum in the computation of goal values and prediction errors. *Journal of Neuroscience, 28,* 5623–5630.

Hariri, A. R., & Holmes, A. (2006). Genetics of emotional regulation: The role of the serotonin transporter in neural function. *Trends in Cognitive Sciences, 10,* 182–191.

Hariri, A. R., Mattay, V. S., Tessitore, A., Fera, F., & Weinberger, D. R. (2003). Neocortical modulation of the amygdala response to fearful stimuli. *Biological Psychiatry, 53,* 494–501.

Hariri, A. R., Mattay, V. S., Tessitore, A., Kolachana, B. S., Fera, F., Goldman, D., et al. (2002). Serotonin transporter genetic variation and the response of the human amygdala. *Science, 297,* 400–403.

Harmon-Jones, E. (2003). Anger and the behavioural approach system. *Personality and Individual Differences, 35,* 995–1005.

Harmon-Jones, E. (2003). Clarifying the emotive function of asymmetrical frontal cortical activity. *Psychophysiology, 40,* 838–848.

Harmon-Jones, E. (2004). On the relationship of anterior brain activity and anger: Examining the role of attitude toward anger. *Cognition and Emotion, 18,* 337–361.

Harmon-Jones, E. (2006). Unilateral right-hand contractions cause contralateral alpha power suppression and approach motivational affective experience. *Psychophysiology, 43,* 598–603.

Harmon-Jones, E. & Amodio, D. M. (in press). Electroencephalographic methods in psychology. In H. Cooper, P. Camic, R. Gonzalez, D. Long, A. Panter, & K. Sher (Eds.), *APA Handbook of Research Methods in Psychology.* Washington, DC: American Psychological Association.

Harmon-Jones, E., & Allen, J. J. B. (1997). Behavioral activation sensitivity and resting frontal EEG asymmetry: Covariation of putative indicators related to risk for mood disorders. *Journal of Abnormal Psychology, 106,* 159–163.

Harmon-Jones, E., & Allen, J. J. B. (1998). Anger and prefrontal brain activity: EEG asymmetry consistent with approach motivation despite negative affective valence. *Journal of Personality and Social Psychology, 74,* 1310–1316.

Harmon-Jones, E., & Allen, J. J. B. (2001). The role of affect in the mere exposure effect: Evidence from psychophysiological and individual differences approaches. *Personality and Social Psychology Bulletin, 27,* 889–898.

Harmon-Jones, E., & Beer, J. S. (Eds., 2009). *Methods in social neuroscience.* New York: Guilford.

Harmon-Jones, E., Harmon-Jones, C., Amodio, D. M., & Gable, P. A. (in press). Attitudes toward emotions. *Journal of Personality and Social Psychology.*

Harmon-Jones, E., Harmon-Jones, C., Fearn, M., Sigelman, J. D., & Johnson, P. (2008). Action orientation, relative left frontal cortical activation, and spreading of alternatives: A test of the action-based model of dissonance. *Journal of Personality and Social Psychology, 94,* 1–15.

Harmon-Jones, E., Peterson, C. K., & Harris, C. R. (2009). Jealousy: Novel methods and neural correlates. *Emotion, 9,* 113–117.

Harmon-Jones, E., & Sigelman, J. D. (2001). State anger and prefrontal brain activity: Evidence that insult-related relative left-prefrontal activation is associated with experienced anger and aggression. *Journal of Personality and Social Psychology, 80,* 797–803.

Harris, L. T., & Fiske, S. T. (2006). Dehumanizing the lowest of the low: Neuro-imaging responses to extreme outgroups. *Psychological Science, 17,* 847–853.

Harris, L. T., & Fiske, S. T. (2009). Social neuroscience evidence for dehumanised perception. *European Review of Social Psychology, 20,* 192–231.

Harris, L. T., Todorov, A., & Fiske, S. T. (2005). Attributions on the brain: Neuro-imaging dispositional inferences, beyond theory of mind. *NeuroImage, 28,* 763–769.

Hart, A. J., Whalen, P. J., Shin, L. M., McInerney, S. C., Fischer, H, & Rauch, S. L. (2000). Differential response in the human amygdala to racial outgroup vs. ingroup face stimuli. *NeuroReport, 11,* 2351–2355.

Haslam, N. (2006). Dehumanization: An integrative review. *Personality and Social Psychology Review, 10,* 252–264.

Haxby, J., Hoffman, E., & Gobbini, M. (2000). The distributed human neural system for face perception. *Trends in Cognitive Sciences, 4,* 223–232.

Heatherton, T. F., Wyland, C. L., Macrae, C. N., Demos, K. E., Denny, B. T., & Kelley, W. M. (2006). Medial prefrontal activity differentiates self from close others. *Social Cognitive and Affective Neuroscience, 1,* 18–25.

Heeger, D. J. & Ress, D. (2002). What does fMRI tell us about neuronal activity? *Nature Reviews Neuroscience, 3,* 142–151.

Heider, F., & Simmel, M. (1944). An experimental study of apparent behavior. *American Journal of Psychology, 57,* 243–259.

Heller, W., Nitschke, J. B., & Miller, G. A. (1998). Lateralization in emotion and emotional disorders. *Current Directions in Psychological Science, 7,* 26–32.

Henriques, J. B. & Davidson, R. J. (1990). Regional brain electrical asymmetries discriminate between previously depressed and healthy control subjects. *Journal of Abnormal Psychology, 99,* 22–31.

Hewig, J., Hagemann, D., Seifert, J., Naumann, E., & Bartussek, D. (2004). On the selective relation of frontal cortical activity and anger-out versus anger-control. *Journal of Personality and Social Psychology, 87,* 926–939.

Hickok, G. (2009). Eight problems for the mirror neuron theory of action understanding in monkeys and humans. *Journal of Cognitive Neuroscience, 21,* 1229–1243.

Holland, P. C., & Gallagher, M. (1999). Amygdala circuitry in attentional and representational processes. *Trends in Cognitive Sciences, 3,* 65–73.

Hopkins, W. D., Bennett, A. J., Bales, S. L., Lee, J., & Ward, J. P. (1993). Behavioral laterality in captive bonobos (*Pan paniscus*). *Journal of Comparative Psychology, 107,* 403–410.

Huettel, S. A., Song, A. W., & McCarthy, G. (2009). *Functional magnetic resonance imaging* (2nd ed.). Sunderland, MA: Sinauer Associates.

Iacoboni, M., & Dapretto, M. (2006). The mirror neuron system and the consequences of its dysfunction. *Nature Reviews Neuroscience, 7,* 942–951.

Inzlicht, M., McGregor, I., Hirsh, J. B., & Nash, K. A. (2009). Neural markers of religious conviction. *Psychological Science, 20,* 385–392.

Ito, T. A., & Cacioppo, J. T. (2000). Electrophysiological evidence of implicit and explicit categorization processes. *Journal of Experimental Social Psychology, 35,* 660–676.

Ito, T. A., Larsen, J. T., Smith, N. K., & Cacioppo (1998). Negative information weighs more heavily on the brain: The negativity bias in evaluative categorizations. *Journal of Personality and Social Psychology, 75,* 887–900.

Ito, T., & Urland, G. (2005). The influence of processing objectives on the perception of faces: An ERP study of race and gender perception. *Cognitive, Affective, and Behavioral Neuroscience, 5,* 21–36.

Izard, C. E. (1991). *The psychology of emotions.* New York: Plenum.

Jacobs, G. D., & Snyder, D. (1996). Frontal brain asymmetry predicts affective style in men. *Behavioral Neuroscience, 110,* 3–6.

Jensen-Campbell, L. A., Knack, J. M., Waldrip, A. M., & Campbell, S. D. (2007). Do Big Five personality traits associated with self-control influence the regulation of anger and aggression? *Journal of Research in Personality, 41,* 403–424.

Josephs, R. A., Sellers, J. G., Newman, M. L., & Mehta, P. H. (2006). The mismatch effect: When testosterone and status are at odds. *Journal of Personality and Social Psychology, 90,* 999–1013.

Kaczmarek, B. L. J. (1984). Neurolinguistic analysis of verbal utterances in patients with focal lesions of frontal lobes. *Brain and Language, 21,* 52–58.

Kanwisher, N. G., McDermott, J., & Chun, M. M. (1997). The fusiform face area: A module in human extrastriate cortex specialized for face perception. *Journal of Neuroscience, 17,* 4302–4311.

Kelley, W. M., Macrae, C. N., Wyland, C. L., Caglar, S., Inati, S., & Heatherton, T. F. (2002). Finding the self? An event-related fMRI study. *Journal of Cognitive Neuroscience, 14,* 785–794.

Kern, S., Oakes, T. R., Stone, C. K., McAuliff, E. M., Kirschbaum, C., & Davidson, R. J. (2008). Glucose metabolic changes in the prefrontal cortex are associated with HPA axis response to a psychosocial stressor. *Psychoneuroendocrinology, 33,* 517–529.

Kerns, J. G., Cohen, J. D., MacDonald, A. W., Cho, R. Y., Stenger, V. A., & Carter, C. S. (2004). Anterior cingulate conflict monitoring and adjustments in control. *Science, 303,* 1023–1026.

Kircher, T. T. J., Brammer, M., Bullmore, E., Simmons, A., Bartels, M., & David, A. S. (2002). The neural correlates of intentional and incidental self processing. *Neuropsychologia, 40,* 683–692.

Klein, S. B., & Kihlstrom, J. F. (1998). On bridging the gap between social-personality psychology and neuropsychology. *Personality and Social Psychology Review, 2,* 228–242.

Klein, S. B., Loftus, J., & Kihlstrom, J. F. (1996). Self-knowledge of an amnesic patient: Toward a neuropsychology of personality and social psychology. *Journal of Experimental Psychology: General, 125,* 250–260.

Knutson, K. M., Mah, L., Manly, C. F., & Grafman, J. (2007). Neural correlates of automatic beliefs about gender and race. *Human Brain Mapping, 28,* 915–930.

Knutson, B., Wimmer, G. E., Kuhnen, C. M., & Winkielman, P. (2008). Nucleus accumbens activation mediates the influence of reward cues on financial risk taking. *NeuroReport, 19,* 509–513.

LaBar, K. S., Gatenby, J. C., Gore, J. C., LeDoux, J. E., & Phelps, E. A. (1998). Human amygdala activation during conditioned fear acquisition and extinction: A mixed-trial fMRI study. *Neuron, 20,* 937–945.

Lagerspetz, K. M. J. (1969). Aggression and aggressiveness in laboratory mice. In S. Garattini & E. B. Sigg (Eds.), *Aggressive behavior.* (pp. 77–85). New York: Wiley.

Lambert, A. J., Payne, B. K., Jacoby, L. L., Shaffer, L. M., Chasteen, A. L., & Khan, S. R. (2003). Stereotypes as dominant responses: On the "social facilitation" of prejudice in anticipated public contexts. *Journal of Personality and Social Psychology, 84,* 277–295.

Lamm, C., Batson, C. D., & Decety, J. (2007). The neural substrate of human empathy: Effects of perspective-taking and cognitive appraisal. *Journal of Cognitive Neuroscience, 19,* 42–58.

Lang, P. J. (1985). The cognitive psychophysiology of emotion: Fear and anxiety. In A. H. Tuma & J. D. Maser (Eds.), *Anxiety and the anxiety disorders* (pp. 131–170). Hillsdale, NJ: Erlbaum.

Lang, P. J. (1995). The emotion probe. *American Psychologist, 50,* 372–385.

Lang, P. J., Bradley, M. M., & Cuthbert, B. N. (1997). International affective picture system (IAPS): Technical manual and affective ratings (Tech. Rep. No. A-4). Gainesville: The Center for Research in Psychophysiology, University of Florida.

LeDoux, J. E. (2000). Emotion circuits in the brain. *Annual Review of Neuroscience, 23,* 155–184.

LeDoux, J. E., Iwata, J., Cicchetti, P. & Reis, D. J. (1988). Different projections of the central amygdaloid nucleus mediate autonomic and behavioral correlates of conditioned fear. *Journal of Neuroscience, 8,* 2517–2529.

Lesch, K. P., Bengel, D., Heils, A., Sabol, S. Z., Greenberg, B. D., Petri, S., et al. (1996). Association of anxiety-related traits with a polymorphism in the serotonin transporter gene regulatory region. *Science, 274,* 1527–1531.

Lewis, M., Alessandri, S. M., & Sullivan, M. W. (1990). Violation of expectancy, loss of control, and anger expressions in young infants. *Developmental Psychology, 26,* 745–751.

Lewis, M., Sullivan, M. W., Ramsey, D. S., & Alessandri, S. M. (1992). Individual differences in anger and sad expressions during extinction: Antecedents and consequences. *Infant Behavior and Development, 15,* 443–452.

Leyens, J. P., Cortes, B. P., Demoulin, S., Dovidio, J., Fiske, S. T., Gaunt, R., et al. (2003). Emotional prejudice, essentialism, and nationalism. *European Journal of Social Psychology, 33,* 703–718.

Leyens, J. P., Rodriguez-Perez, A., Rodriguez-Torres, R., Gaunt, R., Paladino, M. P., Vaes, J., et al. (2001). Psychological essentialism and the differential attribution of uniquely human emotions to ingroups and outgroups. *European Journal of Social Psychology, 31,* 395–411.

Lieberman, M. D., Eisenberger, N. I., Crockett, M. J., Tom, S. M., Pfeifer, J. H., & Way, B. M. (2007). Putting feelings into words: Affect labeling disrupts amygdala activity to affective stimuli. *Psychological Science, 18,* 421–428.

Lieberman, M. D., Hariri, A., Jarcho, J. M., Eisenberger, N. I., & Bookheimer, S. Y. (2005). An fMRI investigation of race-related amygdala activity in African-American and Caucasian-American individuals. *Nature Neuroscience, 8,* 720–722.

Lykken, D. T., & Venables, P. H. (1971). Direct measurement of skin conductance: A proposal for standardization. *Psychophysiology, 8,* 656–672.

MacDonald, A. W., III, Cohen, J. D., Stenger, V. A., & Carter, C. S. (2000). Dissociating the role of the dorsolateral prefrontal cortex and anterior cingulate cortex in cognitive control. *Science, 288,* 1835–1838.

Mackie, D. M., & Smith, E. R. (1998). Intergroup relations: Insights from a theoretically integrative approach. *Psychological Review, 105,* 499–529.

Maier, S. F. & Watkins, L. R. (1998). Cytokines for psychologists: Implications of bi-directional immune-to-brain communication for understanding behavior, mood, and cognition. *Psychological Review, 105,* 83–107.

Maltzman, I. (1979). Orienting reflexes and significance: A reply to O'Gorman. *Psychophysiology, 16,* 274–282.

Mazur, A., & Booth, A. (1998). Testosterone and dominance in men. *Behavioral Brain Science, 21,* 353–397.

McEwen, B. (1998). Protective and damaging effects of stress mediators. *New England Journal of Medicine, 338,* 171–179.

Mehta, P. H., & Josephs, R. A. (2006). Testosterone change after losing predicts the decision to compete again. *Hormones and Behavior, 50,* 684–692.

Mendes, W. B., Blascovich, J., Lickel, B., & Hunter, S. (2002). Cardiovascular reactivity during social interactions with white and black men. *Personality and Social Psychology Bulletin, 28,* 939–952.

Meyer, D. E., & Schvaneveldt, R. W. (1971). Facilitation in recognizing pairs of words: Evidence of a dependence between retrieval operations. *Journal of Experimental Psychology, 90,* 227–234.

Meyer, D. E., & Schvaneveldt, R. W. (1976). Meaning, memory, structure, and mental processes. *Science, 192,* 27–33.

Miller, E. K., & Cohen, J. D. (2001). An integrative theory of prefrontal cortex function. *Annual Review of Neuroscience, 24,* 167–202.

Milne, E., & Grafman, J. (2001). Ventromedial prefrontal cortex lesions in humans eliminate implicit gender stereotyping. *Journal of Neuroscience, 21,* 1–6.

Mitchell, J. P. (2009). Social psychology as a natural kind. *Trends in Cognitive Sciences, 13,* 246–251.

Mitchell, J. P., Ames, D. L., Jenkins, A. C., & Banaji, M. R. (2009). Neural correlates of stereotype application. *Journal of Cognitive Neuroscience, 21,* 594–604.

Mitchell, J. P., Banaji, M. R., & Macrae, C. N. (2005). General and specific contributions of the medial prefrontal cortex to knowledge about mental states. *NeuroImage, 28,* 757–762.

Mitchell, J. P., Heatherton, T. F., & Macrae, C. N. (2002). Distinct neural systems subserve person and object knowledge. *Proceedings of the National Academy of Sciences, USA, 99,* 15238–15243.

Mitchell, J. P., Macrae, C. N., & Banaji, M. R. (2004). Encoding-specific effects of social cognition on the neural correlates of subsequent memory. *Journal of Cognitive Neuroscience, 24,* 4912–4917.

Mitchell, J. P., Macrae, C. N., & Banaji, M. R. (2006). Dissociable medial prefrontal contributions to judgments of similar and dissimilar others. *Neuron, 50,* 655–663.

Moll, J., Zahn, R., de Oliveira-Souza, R., Krueger, F., & Grafman, J. (2005). The neural basis of human moral cognition. *Nature Reviews Neuroscience, 6,* 799–809.

Monteith, M. J. (1993). Self-regulation of prejudiced responses: Implications for progress in prejudice-reduction efforts. *Journal of Personality and Social Psychology, 65,* 469–485.

Monteith, M. J., Ashburn-Nardo, L., Voils, C. I. & Czopp, A. M. (2002). Putting the brakes on prejudice: On the development and operation of cues for control. *Journal of Personality and Social Psychology, 83,* 1029–1050.

Munafo, M. R., Clark, T. G., Moore, L. R., Payne, E., Walton, R., Flint, J. (2003). Genetic polymorphisms and personality in healthy adults: A systematic review and meta-analysis. *Molecular Psychiatry, 8,* 471–484.

Munafo, M. R., Yalcin, B., Willis-Owen, S. A., Flint, J. (2008). Association of the dopamine D4 receptor (DRD4) gene and approach-related personality traits: Meta-analysis and new data. *Biological Psychiatry, 63,* 197–206.

Nieuwenhuis, S., Aston-Jones, G. & Cohen, J. D. (2005). Decision making, the P3, and the locus coeruleus-norepinephrine system. *Psychological Bulletin, 131,* 510–532.

Nieuwenhuis, S., Ridderinkhof, K. R., Blom, J., Band, G. P. H., & Kok, A. (2001). Error-related brain potentials are differently related to awareness of response errors: Evidence from an antisaccade task. *Psychophysiology, 38,* 752–760.

Ochsner, K. N., Bunge, S. A., Gross, J. J., & Gabrieli, J. D. E. (2002). Rethinking feelings: An fMRI study of the cognitive regulation of emotion. *Journal of Cognitive Neuroscience, 14,* 1215–1929.

Ochsner, K. N. & Gross, J. J. (2005). The cognitive control of emotion. *Trends in Cognitive Sciences, 9,* 242–249.

Ochsner, K. N., & Lieberman, M. D. (2001). The emergence of social cognitive neuroscience. *American Psychologist, 56,* 717–734.

O'Doherty, J., Critchley, H., Deichmann, R., & Dolan, R. J. (2003). Dissociating valence of outcome from behavioral control in human orbital and ventral prefrontal cortices. *Journal of Neuroscience, 23,* 7931–7939.

Ofan, R. H., Rubin, N., Amodio, D. M. (in press). Seeing race: N170 responses to race and their relation to automatic racial attitudes and controlled processing. *Journal of Cognitive Neuroscience.*

Ohgami, Y., Kotani, Y., Tsukamoto, T., Omura, K., Inoue, Y., Aihara, Y., et al. (2006). Effects of monetary reward and punishment on stimulus-preceding negativity. *Psychophysiology, 43,* 227–236.

Olson, J. M., Vernon, P. A., Harris, J. A., & Jang, K. L. (2001). The heritability of attitudes: A study of twins. *Journal of Personality and Social Psychology, 80,* 845–860.

Peciña, S., & Berridge, K. C. (2000). Opioid site in nucleus accumbens shell mediates food intake and hedonic "liking": Map based on microinjection fos plumes. *Brain Research, 863,* 71–86.

Perrett, D., Rolls, E., & Caan, W. (1982). Visual neurons responsive to faces in the monkey temporal cortex. *Experimental Brain Research, 47,* 329–342.

Perria, P., Rosadini, G., & Rossi, G. F. (1961). Determination of side of cerebral dominance with amobarbital. *Archives of Neurology, 4,* 175–181.

Pfeifer, J. H., Lieberman, M. D., & Dapretto, M. (2007). "I know you are but what am I?!": Neural Bases of self- and social knowledge in children and adults. *Journal of Cognitive Neuroscience, 19,* 1323–1337.

Phan, K. L., Wager, T. D., Taylor, S. F., & Liberzon, I. (2002). Functional neuroanatomy of emotion: A meta-analysis of emotion activation studies in PET and fMRI. *NeuroImage, 16,* 331–348.

Phan, K. L., Fitzgerald, D. A., Nathan, P. J., Moore, G. J., Uhde, T. W., & Tancer, M. E. (2005). Neural substrates for voluntary suppression of negative affect: A functional magnetic resonance study. *Biological Psychiatry, 57,* 210–219.

Phelps, E. A., O'Connor, K. J., Cunningham, W. A., Funayama, E. S., Gatenby, J. C., Gore, J. C., et al. (2000). Performance on indirect measures of race evaluation predicts amygdala activation. *Journal of Cognitive Neuroscience, 12,* 729–738.

Pizzagalli, D. A., Sherwood, R. J., Henriques, J. B., & Davidson, R. J. (2005). Frontal brain asymmetry and reward responsiveness: A source-localization study. *Psychological Science, 16,* 805–813.

Plomin, R., & Caspi, A. (1999). Behavioral genetics and personality. In L. A. Pervin (Ed.), *Handbook of personality theory and research* (pp. 251–276). New York: Guilford.

Plomin, R., DeFries, J. C., McClearn, G. E. & Rutter, M. (1997). *Behavioral genetics* (3rd ed.) New York: Freeman.

Plutchik, R. (1980). *Emotion: A psychoevolutionary synthesis.* New York: Harpercollins College Division.

Poldrack, R. A. (2006). Can cognitive processes be inferred from neuroimaging data? *Trends in Cognitive Sciences, 10,* 59–63.

Prigatano, G. P. (1991). Disturbances of self-awareness of deficit after traumatic brain injury. In G. P. Prigatano & D. L. Schacter (Eds.), *Awareness of deficit after brain injury: Clinical and theoretical issues* (pp. 111–126). New York: Springer.

Puce, A., Allison, T., Gore, J., & McCarthy, G. (1995). Face-sensitive regions in human extrastriate cortex studied by functional MRI. *Journal of Neurophysiology, 74,* 1192–1199.

Quadflieg, S., Turk, D. J., Waiter, G. D., Mitchell, J. P., Jenkins, A. C., & Macrae, C. N. (2009). Exploring the neural correlates of social stereotyping. *Journal of Cognitive Neuroscience, 21,* 1560–1570.

Raichle, M. E., Fiez, J. A., Videen, T. O., MacLeod, A. K., Pardo, J. V., P. T. Fox, et al. (1994). Practice-related changes in human brain functional anatomy during nonmotor learning. *Cerebral Cortex, 4,* 8–26.

Rameson, L. T., & Lieberman, M. D. (2009). Empathy: A social cognitive neuroscience approach. *Social and Personality Psychology Compass, 3,* 94–110.

Rankin, R. E., & Campbell, D. T. (1955). Galvanic skin response to negro and white experimenters. *Journal of Abnormal and Social Psychology, 51,* 30–33.

Richeson, J. A., Baird, A. A., Gordon, H. L., Heatherton, T. F., Wyland, C. L., Trawalter, S., et al. (2003). An fMRI investigation of the impact of interracial contact on executive function. *Nature Neuroscience, 6,* 1323–1328.

Richeson, J. A., Todd, A. R., Trawalter, S., & Baird, A. A. (2008). Eye-gaze direction modulates race-related amygdala activity. *Group Processes and Intergroup Relations, 11,* 233–246.

Richeson, J. A., & Trawalter, S. (2005). Why do interracial interactions impair executive function? A resource depletion account. *Journal of Personality and Social Psychology, 88,* 934–947.

Richeson, J. A., & Trawalter, S. (2008). The threat of appearing prejudiced and race-based attentional biases. *Psychological Science, 19,* 98–102.

Riddle, E. M. (1925). Aggressive behavior in a small social group. *Archives of Psychology, 78.*

Rissman, J., Eliassen, J. C., & Blumstein, S. E. (2003). An event-related fMRI investigation of implicit semantic priming. *Journal of Cognitive Neuroscience, 15,* 1160–1175.

Rizzolatti, G., & Sinigaglia, C. (2010). The functional role of the parieto-frontal mirror circuit: interpretations and misinterpretations. *Nature Reviews Neuroscience, 11,* 264–274.

Robinson, M. D., Ode, S., Wilkowski, B. M., & Amodio, D. M. (2007). Neurotic contentment: A self-regulation view of neuroticism-linked distress. *Emotion, 7,* 579–591.

Robinson, R. G., & Price, T. R. (1982). Post-stroke depressive disorders: A follow-up study of 103 patients. *Stroke, 13,* 635–641.

Rogers, L. J. (2002). Lateralised brain function in anurans: Comparison to lateralisation in other vertebrates. *Laterality: Asymmetries of Body, Brain and Cognition, 7,* 219–239.

Rolls, E. T., Hornak, J., Wade, D., & McGrath, J. (1994). Emotion-related learning in patients with social and emotional changes associated with frontal lobe damage. *Journal of Neurology, Neurosurgery, and Psychiatry, 57,* 1518–1524.

Ronquillo, J., Denson, T. F., Lickel, B., Lu, Z., Nandy, A, & Maddox, K. B. (2007). The effects of skin tone on race-related amygdala activity: An fMRI investigation. *Social Cognitive and Affective Neuroscience, 2,* 39–44.

Rosenkranz, M. A., Jackson, D. C., Dalton, K. M., Dolski, I., Ryff, C. D., Singer, B. H., et al. (2003). Affective style and in vivo immune response: Neurobehavioral mechanisms. *Proceedings of the National Academy of Sciences, 100,* 11148–11152.

Rossi, G. F., & Rosadini, G. R. (1967). Experimental analyses of cerebral dominance in man. In D. H. Millikan, & F. L. Darley (Eds.), *Brain mechanisms underlying speech and language.* (pp. 167–184) New York: Grune & Stratton.

Rybak, M., Crayton, J. W., Young, I. J., Herba, E., & Konopka, L. M., (2006). Frontal alpha power asymmetry in aggressive children and adolescents with mood and disruptive behavior disorders. *Clinical EEG and Neuroscience, 37,* 16–24.

Sackeim, H., Greenberg, M. S., Weimen, A. L., Gur, R. C., Hungerbuhler, J. P., & Geschwind, N. (1982). Hemispheric asymmetry in the expression of positive and negative emotions: Neurologic evidence. *Archives of Neurology, 39,* 210–218.

Salamone, J. D. (2007). Functions of mesolimbic dopamine: Changing concepts and shifting paradigms. *Psychopharmacology, 191,* 389.

Sapolsky, R. M., Romero, L. M., & Munck, A. U. (2000). How do glucocorticoids influence stress responses? Integrating permissive, suppressive, stimulatory, and preparative actions. *Endocrine Reviews, 21,* 55–89.

Saver, J. L., & Damasio, A. R. (1991). Preserved access and processing of social knowledge in a patient with acquired sociopathy due to ventromedial frontal damage. *Neuropsychologia, 29,* 1241–1249.

Saxe, R. (2005). Against simulation: The argument from error. *Trends in Cognitive Sciences, 9,* 174–179.

Saxe, R., Carey, S., & Kanwisher, N. (2004). Understanding other minds: Linking developmental psychology and functional neuroimaging. *Annual Review of Psychology, 55,* 87–124.

Saxe, R., Moran, J. M., Scholz, J., & Gabrieli, J. (2006). Overlapping and non-overlapping brain regions for theory of mind and self reflection in individual subjects. *Social Cognitive and Affective Neuroscience, 1,* 229–234.

Schacter, D. L., & Buckner, R. L. (1998). Priming and the brain. *Neuron, 20,* 185–195.

Schaffer, C. E., Davidson, R. J., & Saron, C. (1983). Frontal and parietal electroencephalogram asymmetry in depressed and nondepressed subjects. *Biological Psychiatry, 18,* 753–762.

Schiller, D., Monfils, M. H., Raio, C. M., Johnson, D. C., Ledoux, J. E., & Phelps, E. A. (2010). Preventing the return of fear in humans using reconsolidation update mechanisms. *Nature, 463,* 49–53.

Schmitz, T. W., Kawahara-Baccus, T. N., & Johnson, S. C. (2004). Metacognitive evaluation, self-relevance, and the right prefrontal cortex. *NeuroImage, 22,* 941–947.

Schoenbaum, G., Setlow, B., & Ramus, S. J. (2003). A systems approach to orbitofrontal cortex function: Recordings in rat orbitofrontal cortex reveal interactions with different learning systems. *Behavioural Brain Research, 146,* 19–29.

Schultheiss, O. C., & Stanton, S. J. (2009). Assessment of salivary hormones. In E. Harmon-Jones & J. S. Beer (Eds.), *Methods in social neuroscience* (pp. 17–44). New York: Guilford.

Schutter, D. J. L. G. (2009). Transcranial magnetic stimulation. In E. Harmon-Jones & J. S. Beer (Eds.), *Methods in social neuroscience.*(pp. 233–258) New York: Guilford.

Schutter, D. J. L. G., van Honk, J., d'Alfonso, A. A. L., Postma, A., & de Haan, E. H. F. (2001). Effects of slow rTMS at the right dorsolateral prefrontal cortex on EEG asymmetry and mood. *NeuroReport, 12,* 445–447.

Schwarz, N. (2007). Attitude construction: Evaluation in context. *Social Cognition, 25,* 638–656.

Segerstrom, S. C., & Miller, G. E. (2004). Stress and the human immune system: A meta-analytic review of 30 years of inquiry. *Psychological Bulletin, 130,* 601–630.

Shamay-Tsoory, S. G., Tomer, R., Berger, B. D., & Aharon-Peretz, J. (2003). Characterization of empathy deficits following prefrontal brain damage: The role of the right ventromedial prefrontal cortex. *Journal of Cognitive Neuroscience, 15,* 324–337.

Shapiro, D., & Crider A. (1969). Psychophysiological approaches in social psychology. In G. Lindzey & E. Aronson (Eds.), *Handbook of social psychology* (2nd. ed., Vol. 3, pp. 1–49). Reading, MA: Addison-Wesley.

Shiffrin, R., & Schneider, W. (1977). Controlled and automatic human information processing: II. Perceptual learning, automatic attending, and a general theory. *Psychological Review, 84,* 127–190.

Singer, T., Seymour, B., O'Doherty, J., Kaube, H., Dolan, R. J., & Frith, C. D. (2004). Empathy for pain involves the affective but not sensory components of pain. *Science, 303,* 1157–1162.

Singh, D., Vidaurri, M., Zambarano, R. J., Dabbs, J. M., Jr. (1999). Lesbian erotic role identification: Behavioral, morphological, and hormonal correlates. *Journal of Personality and Social Psychology, 76,* 1035–1049.

Smillie, L. D., Cooper, A. J., Proitsi, P., Powell, J. F., & Pickering, A. D. (2010). Variation in DRD2 dopamine gene predicts extraverted personality. *Neuroscience Letters, 468,* 234–237.

Smith, E. R., & DeCoster, J. (2000). Dual process models in social and cognitive psychology: Conceptual integration and links to underlying memory systems. *Personality and Social Psychology Review, 4,* 108–131.

Smits, D. J. M., & Kuppens, P. (2005). The relations between anger, coping with anger and aggression, and the BIS/BAS system. *Personality and Individual Differences, 39,* 783–793.

Somerville, L. H., Heatherton, T. F., & Kelley, W. M. (2006). Anterior cingulate cortex responds differentially to expectancy violation and social rejection. *Nature Neuroscience, 9,* 1007–1008.

Squire, L. R. (1992). Memory and the hippocampus: A synthesis from findings with rats, monkeys, and humans. *Psychological Review, 99,* 195–231.

Squire, L. R., & Zola, S. M. (1996). Structure and function of declarative and nondeclarative memory systems. *Proceedings of the National Academy of Sciences, 93,* 13515–13522.

Squire, L. R., Zola-Morgan, S. (1991). The medial temporal lobe memory system. *Science, 253,* 1380–1386.

Squires, K. C., Donchin, E., Herning, R. I., & McCarthy, G. (1977). On the influence of task relevance and stimulus probability on event-related potential components. *Electroencephalography and Clinical Neurophysiology, 42,* 1–14.

Stephan, W. G., & Stephan, C. W. (1985). Intergroup anxiety. *Journal of Social Issues, 41,* 157–175.

Stuss, D. T. (1991). Self, awareness, and the frontal lobes: A neuropsychological perspective. In J. Strauss & G. R. Goethals (Eds.), *The self: Interdisciplinary approaches.* (pp. 255–278) New York: Springer.

Stuss, D. T., & Benson, D. F. (1984). Neuropsychological studies of the frontal lobes. *Psychological Bulletin, 95,* 3–28.

Sutton, S. K. & Davidson, R. J. (1997). Prefrontal brain asymmetry: A biological substrate of the behavioral approach and inhibition systems. *Psychological Science, 8,* 204–210.

Sutton, S., Braren, M., Zubin, J., & John, E. R. (1965). Evoked-potential correlates of stimulus uncertainty. *Science, 150,* 1187–1188.

Taylor, S. E., Klein, L. C., Lewis, B. P., Gruenewald, T. L., Gurung, R. A. R., & Updegraff, J. A. (2000). Biobehavioral responses to stress in females: Tend-and-befriend, not fight-or-flight. *Psychological Review, 107,* 411–429.

Taylor, S. E., Way, B. M., Welch, W. T., Hilmert, C. J., Lehman, B. J., & Eisenberger, N. I. (2006). Early family environment, current adversity, the serotonin transporter polymorphism, and depressive symptomatology. *Biological Psychiatry, 60,* 671–676.

Tellegen, A., Lykken, D. X, Bouchard, T. J., Wilcox, K., Segal, N., & Rich, S. (1988). Personality similarity in twins reared apart and together. *Journal of Personality and Social Psychology, 54,* 1031–1039.

Terzian, H., & Cecotto, C. (1959). Determination and study of hemisphere dominance by means of intracarotid sodium amytal injection in man: II. Electroencephalographic effects. *Bolletino della Societa Ztaliana Sperimentale, 35,* 1626–1630.

Thorndike, E. L. (1911). *Animal intelligence: Experimental studies.* New York: Macmillan.

Thurstone, L. L. (1928). Attitudes can be measured. *American Journal of Sociology, 33,* 529–554.

Todorov, A., Said, C. P., Engell, A. D., & Oosterhof, N. N. (2008). Understanding evaluation of faces on social dimensions. *Trends in Cognitive Sciences, 12,* 455–460.

Tomarken, A. J., Davidson, R. J., Wheeler, R. E., & Doss, R. C. (1992). Individual differences in anterior brain asymmetry and fundamental dimensions of emotion. *Journal of Personality and Social Psychology, 62,* 676–687.

Turner, M. S., Simons, J. S., Gilbert, S. J., Frith, C. D., & Burgess, P. W. (2008). Distinct roles for lateral and medial rostral prefrontal cortex in source monitoring of perceived and imagined events. *Neuropsychologia, 46,* 1442–1453.

Urry, H. L., van Reekum, C. M., Johnstone, T., Kalin, N. H., Thurow, M. E., Schaefer, H. S., et al. (2006). Amygdala and ventromedial prefrontal cortex are inversely coupled during regulation of negative affect and predict the diurnal pattern of cortisol secretion among older adults. *Journal of Neuroscience, 26,* 4415–4425.

Van Bavel, J. J., Packer, D. J., & Cunningham, W. A. (2008). The neural substrates of in-group bias: A functional magnetic resonance imaging investigation. *Psychological Science, 11,* 1131–1139.

van de Laar, M. C., Licht, R., Franken, I. H. A., & Hendriks, V. M. (2004). Event-related potentials indicate motivational relevance of cocaine cues in abstinent cocaine addicts. *Psychopharmacology, 177,* 121–129.

van Honk, J., & Schutter, D. J. L. G. (2006). From affective valence to motivational direction. *Psychological Science, 17,* 963–965.

van Honk, J., Tuiten, A., Verbaten, R., Van den Hout, M., Koppeschaar, H., Thijssen, J., et al. (1999). Correlations among salivary testosterone, mood, and selective attention to threat in humans. *Hormones and Behavior, 36,* 17–24.

van Reekum, C. M., Johnstone, T., Urry, H. L., Thurow, M. E., Schaefer, H. S., Alexander, A. L., et al. (2007). Gaze fixations predict brain activation during the voluntary regulation of picture-induced negative affect. *NeuroImage, 36,* 1041–1055.

Vanman, E. J., Paul, B. Y., Ito, T. A., & Miller, N. (1997). The modern face of prejudice and structural features that moderate the effect of cooperation on affect. *Journal of Personality and Social Psychology, 73,* 941–959.

Verona, E., Sadeh, N., & Curtin, J. J. (2009). Stress-induced asymmetric frontal brain activity and aggression risk. *Journal of Abnormal Psychology, 118,* 131–145.

Vivona, J. M. (2009). Leaping from brain to mind: A critique of mirror neuron explanations of countertransference. *Journal of the American Psychoanalytic Association, 57,* 525–550.

Vrana, S. R., & Rollock. D. (1998). Physiological response to a minimal social encounter: Effects of gender, ethnicity, and social context. *Psychophysiology, 35,* 462–469.

Vul, E., Harris, C., Winkielman, P., & Pashler, H. (2009). Puzzlingly high correlations in fMRI studies of emotion, personality, and social cognition. *Perspectives on Psychological Science, 4,* 274–290.

Wagner, A. D., Gabrieli, J. D. E., & Verfaellie, M. (1997). Dissociations between familiarity processes in explicit recognition and implicit perceptual memory. *Journal of Experimental Psychology: Learning, Memory, and Cognition, 23,* 305–323.

Walker, P., Silvert, L., Hewstone, M., & Nobre, A. (2008). Social contact and other-race face processing in the human brain. *Social Cognitive and Affective Neuroscience, 3,* 16.

Watson, D. (2000). *Mood and temperament.* New York: Guilford.

Way, B. M., & Gurbaxani, B. M. (2008). A genetics primer for social health research. *Social and Personality Psychology Compass, 2,* 785–816.

Wegner, D. M. & Bargh, J. A. (1998). Control and automaticity in social life. In D. T. Gilbert & S. T. Fiske, & G. Lindzey (Eds.), *The handbook of social psychology, Vols. 1 and 2 (4th ed.).* (pp. 446–496). New York, NY: McGraw-Hill.

Wegner, D. M., Schneider, D. J., Carter, S., & White, T. (1987). Paradoxical effects of thought suppression. *Journal of Personality and Social Psychology, 53,* 5–13.

Whalen, P. J. (1998). Fear, vigilance, and ambiguity: Initial neuroimaging studies of the human amygdala. *Current Directions in Psychological Science, 7,* 177–188.

Wheeler, M. E., & Fiske, S. T. (2005). Controlling racial prejudice and stereotyping: Social cognitive goals affect amygdala and stereotype activation. *Psychological Science, 16,* 56–63.

Wiese, H., Stahl, J., & Schweinberger, S. R. (2009). Configural processing of other-race faces is delayed but not decreased. *Biological Psychology, 81,* 103–109.

Xu, X., Zuo, X., Wang, X., & Han, S. (2009). Do you feel my pain? Racial group membership modulates empathic neural responses. *Journal of Neuroscience, 29,* 8525–8529.

Young, P. T. (1943). *Emotion in man and animal: Its nature and relation to attitude and motive.* New York: Wiley.

Zhang, Q., Lawson, A., Guo, C., & Jiang, Y. (2006). Electrophysiological correlates of visual affective priming. *Brain Research Bulletin, 71,* 316–323.

Zhu, Y., Zhang, L., Fan, L., & Han, S. (2007). Neural basis of cultural influence on self-representation. *NeuroImage, 34,* 1310–1316.

CHAPTER 7

Evolutionary Perspectives

Steven W. Gangestad

Abstract

Evolutionary perspectives on human behavior are almost as old as the science of psychology itself. Functionalists such as James, Dewey, and Angell, however, lacked explicit evolutionary theories and methodologies to inspire generative research programs, and their movement dissipated. Today, a new brand of functionalism has emerged, one that draws its inspiration from massive developments in evolutionary biology in the past half-century. This chapter has several aims. First, it offers an overview of evolutionary biology as applied to human psychology. Second, it discusses the concept of an ecological niche, and addresses the critical issue of the nature of the niche that humans entered and defined. This niche has the unusual feature that individuals' fitness was highly dependent on their ability to attract, form, and maintain cooperative coalitions with others and, hence, to harness the competencies of others to their own competencies. Third, it describes several broad, evolution-inspired proposals about human social behavior, which illustrate how evolutionary perspectives offer integrative understandings of psychological phenomena and generate new research programs. Fourth, it addresses individual differences from an evolutionary perspective. Rather than representing alternatives to social or cultural perspectives, evolutionary perspectives offer means by which to construct a personality and social psychology that is foundationally integrative.

Keywords: evolutionary psychology; adaptationism; human niche; social selection; developmental systems

Evolutionary Perspectives

Evolutionary perspectives on personality and social psychology are almost as old as the science of psychology itself. In the late 1800s, scholars such as William James and John Dewey were inspired by Darwin's notion of evolved adaptation. Their interpretations of the self, social emotions, social learning, and other phenomena reflected a Darwinian outlook (e.g., James, 1890, 1904; Dewey, 1896). The school of functionalism became defined, its goals outlined in James Rowland Angell's 1906 Presidential Address to the American Psychological Association:

> The psychologist of this stripe is wont to take his cue from the basal conception of the evolutionary movement, i.e., that for the most part organic

structures and functions possess their present characteristics by virtue of the efficiency with which they fit into the extant conditions of life broadly designated the environment. With this conception in mind he then proceeds to attempt some understanding of the manner in which the psychical contributes to the furtherance of the sum total of organic activities, not alone the psychical in its entirety, but especially the psychical in its particularities—mind as judging, mind as feeling, etc. . . . This is the point of view which instantly brings the psychologist cheek by jowl with the general biologist. (Angell, 1907, p. 69)

As Angell (1907) also noted, "Functional psychology is at the present moment little more than a point of view, a program, an ambition" (p. 61).

It never became much more. As an evolution-inspired movement, it diffused within a decade after Angell's address. It did influence subsequent developments (e.g., Clark Hull, 1937, 1943, viewed Darwin as an inspiration for his theories of adaptive learning). And specific notions developed by functionalists have had long-standing influence on psychology (e.g., symbolic interactionism, theories of the self). But no well-defined approach that has drawn its inspiration from explicit evolutionary biological theory can trace continuous intellectual activity within it from the present back to the 1800s.

Perhaps the primary reason for this fact lay more with the state of evolutionary biology than psychology. Darwin's notion of evolved adaptation was abstractly inspirational, but specific evolutionary approaches, theories, and methodologies that could be used to derive and test explicit theoretical propositions about psychological (or, for that matter, physiological) outcomes of adaptation had not yet been developed. Indeed, evolutionary approaches that could inspire specific research programs would not blossom for another half-century (see discussions of adaptationism and cost-benefit models below).

In the past quarter-century, a new functionalism has emerged. This functionalism does draw very explicitly on theories within evolutionary biology. Its practitioners do see themselves "cheek by jowl" with general biologists. Evolutionary psychology has emerged as an important perspective within personality and social psychology (see, e.g., Buss & Kenrick, 1998).

This chapter has several primary aims. First, I provide an overview of evolutionary biology, as applied to studies of human psychology. Second, I describe the concept of an ecological niche and address the critical question of what niche humans entered and defined. Third, on this basis, I discuss several broad, evolution-inspired proposals about human social behavior, which illustrate how evolutionary perspectives offer integrative understandings of psychological phenomena and generate new research programs. Fourth, I discuss individual differences from an evolutionary perspective. I end with several reflections.

In particular, evolution-mindedness inspires the following broad proposals: (1) Human sociality can be understood in the context of a broader niche or way of living humans evolved to be adapted to; this framework serves to both integrate and generate empirical findings and specific theoretical

conjectures in social and personality psychology; (2) Perhaps most central to this understanding is that humans are highly unusual organisms not merely in the *extent* of their sociality, but also in its kinds: Given the importance of cooperative activity in the human niche, the fitness of individual humans has long depended critically on their abilities to harness the competencies of other individuals, through formation of and participation within coalitions; (3) Many social psychological phenomena are reflective of adaptations that evolved to promote individual fitness and success by enhancing social capital, attracting valued social partners, and effectively harnessing cooperative activities; (4) Many individual differences, as well as cultural differences, may reflect variations in strategy to attract and harness coalitional partners, adaptively contingent on individual circumstances that affect what strategies are successful.

Evolutionary Approaches: An Overview
In their most general sense, evolutionary approaches to understanding behavior include any that invokes evolution-minded thinking. Specific approaches (e.g., adaptationism) utilize particular sets of working assumptions and methodologies in evolutionary biology.

Charles Darwin and the Theory of Evolution by Natural Selection
DARWIN'S THEORY: FIVE FACTS AND THREE INFERENCES
Naturally, Charles Darwin (1859) is credited with deriving the theory of evolution by natural selection. (In fact, Darwin and Alfred Russell Wallace introduced the theory in an 1858 collaborative paper.) Ernst Mayr (1982) famously distilled the fundamental claims of Darwin's theory into 5 facts and 3 inferences.

Fact 1. All species have such great potential fertility that their population size would increase exponentially if all individuals that are born would reproduce successfully.

Fact 2. Except for minor annual fluctuations and occasional major fluctuations, populations normally display stability.

Fact 3. Natural resources are limited and, in a stable environment, are fairly constant.

Inference 1. Because more individuals are produced than can be supported by the available resources but population size remains stable, there must be a fierce struggle for existence among the individuals of the population resulting in the survival (or successful reproduction) of only a part, often a very small part, of the progeny of each generation.

Fact 4. No two individuals are exactly the same; every population displays variability.

Fact 5. Much of this variation is heritable. That is, it is transmitted from parents to offspring, such that parental and offspring features positively covary.

Inference 2. Survival in this struggle is not random but depends in part on the hereditary constitution of the surviving individuals, which constitutes a process of *natural selection.*

Inference 3. Over generations, this process of natural selection leads to a continuing gradual change of populations, that is, to *evolution* and to the production of new species.

What was foundationally novel in Darwin's thinking? As Mayr (1982) notes, Darwin did not invent the notion of evolution or introduce the idea that evolution involves adaptation to the environment; he was not the first to recognize any of the five facts, or first to claim a role for heredity in evolution. (Lamarck's theory, albeit quite different from Darwin's, did much of this; Malthus recognized several of the facts.) The key novelty in Darwin's theory was a perspective shift from *essentialist thinking* about species to *population thinking.* In essentialist thinking, each species has an essential core. Individual differences are variations around this core, but they and their causes are irrelevant to the concept of the species. Individuals deviating from the mean do not lack the core essence. In *population thinking,* there is no core essence to a species. Individual differences reflect, in part, differences in the make-ups of individuals. Universal features reflect the fact that individuals share common make-ups (though that commonality does not imply an "essence"). Mean values on features that vary across individuals represent abstractions of features of individuals within a population, not a "real" essence that individuals share.

This frame shift permitted Darwin to see the possibility for change or evolution in a novel way. Evolution does not consist of change in the essence of species. Rather, it consists of changes in the distribution of make-ups of individuals in populations. Put otherwise, evolution consists of *changes, over time, in the distribution of whatever is heritable within a population.*

THE MODERN SYNTHESIS

A crucial component of Darwin's theory is the idea that something that affects individuals' features can differentiate individuals and be heritable—transmittable from parents to offspring. Indeed, evolution consists of changes in the distribution of these heritable "factors." Of course, these factors would ultimately be identified as genes (a shortening of "pangens," adopted from Darwin), themselves consisting of nucleotide sequences known as DNA.

The modern synthetic theory of evolution, established in the first half of the last century, combined a Darwinian view of evolution with Mendelian gene theory. Inheritance consists of passing down of heritable units, genes. Variation in genes ultimately derives from mutations, alterations induced by errors of DNA copying. Evolution consists of changes in gene frequencies (i.e., distributions of genetic variants) in a population. To the extent that genes affect observable features of individuals and how individuals interact with their environments (i.e., phenotypes), evolution results in changes in the distribution of phenotypic features. And because some features are better adapted to individuals' environments than others, selection—differential reproduction as a function of phenotypic features—can result in changes in gene frequencies or evolution. (See, e.g., Mayr, 1982, 1991.)

The early geneticists often assumed a 1:1 correspondence between genetic loci and phenotypic features (e.g., a gene site and smooth vs. rough peas). But these links are rare. Complex features of organisms are the function of many genes. Human stature, for instance, is associated with genetic variation at thousands of loci, the most important 20 of which still account for just 3% of the variance (Perola et al., 2007). Fisher (1918) demonstrated how "effects" of genes at multiple individual loci and their interactions on phenotypes translate into associations between trait values of individuals of varying relatedness (e.g., parents and offspring), and thereby showed that genetics is compatible with gradual evolution. A marriage between Darwinism and Mendelian gene theory in sight, a number of scholars—notably, Fisher (1958), Wright (1968), and Haldane (1932)—asked fundamental questions about how selection operates to affect gene frequencies by applying mathematical techniques: e.g., What is the power of selection? What role does population size play? How does selection affect the nature and quantity of genetic variation? Insights achieved through mathematical modeling led to both development and acceptance of the modern synthesis.

Adaptationism

By 1960, many problems in evolutionary quantitative genetics had been worked out fairly well. The framework of the modern synthesis was nearly complete. But ignorance of many processes underlying the evolutionary process remained vast, partly because quantitative geneticists did not have to assume anything about phenotypes or the processes that link genes to phenotypes to address the basic questions they asked. In the 1960s, evolutionary theory increasingly turned to fill in these gaps. What phenotypes are favored by selection? In particular, how does thinking about specific selection pressures inform our understanding of organisms' features? These issues are core to the approach within evolutionary biology referred to as adaptationism, the modal approach adopted by evolutionary psychologists.

ADAPTATION, FUNCTION, ADAPTIVENESS, AND EXAPTATION

Darwinian theory argues that species evolve through natural selection—differential reproduction of individuals with different phenotypes and genotypes—but that is not to say that all features evolve because they were directly favored by selection. Williams (1966) drew a distinction between two different kinds of evolved features, *adaptations* and *byproducts*. Within this context, the evolutionary concept of *function* takes on special meaning, and the notion of adaptation must be distinguished from adaptiveness.

Adaptation

In evolutionary biology, *adaptation* refers to two related phenomena: first, a *process* whereby organisms are shaped through natural selection to be adapted to their environments; second, a *feature* that evolved through selection because it enhanced the fitness of its carriers. The process of adaptation occurs through the evolution of adaptations.

Function

Evolutionary biologists use the term *function* in a special way, one tied to the concept of adaptation. Through an organism's interactions with the world, a trait has effects. One or more of the trait's effects may lead its beholder to have greater fitness than others lacking the trait. A beneficial effect that led selection to favor the trait is a trait's *function*.

Simple examples illustrate. Simply put, bird wings are adaptations *for* the function of flight. Eyes are adaptations *for* the function of seeing. Release of gonadotropins by human fetuses into the bloodstream of their mothers appears to be an adaptation *for* the function of increasing the likelihood fetuses will be retained by the mother (Haig, 1993).

Evolutionary biology's special concept of function is distinct from a more general concept used by physiologists and psychologists. Causal role functional analysis (Godfrey-Smith, 1993) examines processes through which an organism performs an activity. Some psychologists, for instance, address the question of how people read by examining the roles of various psychological capacities, and thereby perform causal role functional analysis. But that analysis does not reveal *evolutionary* functions. The evolutionary concept of function explicitly refers to historical selection. Though psychological processes function in reading in a causal role sense, their *evolutionary functions* do not directly pertain to reading (see also Millikan, 1989).

Adaptiveness

The concept of adaptiveness is distinct from adaptation. A trait is adaptive if it offers its beholders fitness benefits in a current context. Because adaptation is defined with reference to *historical*, not contemporary, events, current adaptiveness is neither a necessary nor sufficient feature of an adaptation. It is not necessary because features that evolved due to past adaptiveness need not remain adaptive. The human appendix likely evolved in distant ancestors for the function of breaking down cellulose. Humans no longer benefit from the function. The human appendix is an adaptation (albeit in vestigial form)—it exists because it was selected for benefits—but not currently adaptive (see Sterelny & Griffiths, 1999.)

Exaptation

Current adaptiveness is not sufficient to define a trait as an adaptation because a trait's adaptiveness may not have the historical depth to have affected trait evolution. Gould and Vrba (1982) introduced the concept of *exaptation* to highlight the difference between adaptiveness that, historically, did play a role in the evolution of a trait, and adaptiveness that did not. A trait is an exaptation to a particular beneficial effect if the trait gives rise to that beneficial effect, but the beneficial effect had no impact on the shaping of the trait historically. When foraging for fish, the black heron may raise its wing to reduce glare of the sunlight off the water and increase visibility of prey under the water's surface. The wing itself evolved through selection for flight. There is no evidence that the wing was modified by selection for water shading.

The wing is therefore an adaptation for flight, and exapted to water shading (Gould & Vrba, 1982). Or consider reading. We can read (and reading might even yield fitness benefits) but not because selection favored traits for their effects on reading. Reading is possible because traits evolved for reasons unrelated to the benefits of reading can be used to read.

Secondary Adaptation

Often, a trait that acquires a new benefit undergoes subsequent modification that improves its proficiency in delivering the benefit. Gould and Vrba (1982) refer to this process as secondary adaptation. Adaptation (vs. exaptation) is the proper term, they claim, because selection for the benefit led to change. From a historical standpoint, a trait that evolved for one function but is later adapted for a different benefit underwent primary adaptation for the first function, was exapted to a new benefit, and then was secondarily adapted for the new benefit. Apes evolved fully extendable elbows, arguably for swinging through branches. Humans no longer benefit from ability to swing through branches. But fully extendable elbows may have exapted to, and then secondarily modified for, accurately throwing of objects.

By-Products

When selection occurs due to the beneficial effect of a particular trait, it inevitably modifies the phenotype in many ways. A trait that has a selected beneficial effect is an adaptation. Other traits also modified but with no beneficial effects themselves are *by-products* of selection (also *incidental effects* or *spandrels*; Gould & Lewontin, 1979). Vertebrate bones are composed of calcium phosphate. Bones are adaptations that enable effective movement. Calcium phosphate is white and, hence, so too are bones. The whiteness of bones has no beneficial effect itself, however; it's a by-product of selection.

Selection for a single adaptation may potentially lead to a multitude of by-products. The precise distance between the eyes in humans may be partly due to selection for effective binocular vision. But it also affects the precise distance between each eye and any other morphological structure (e.g., the right and left kneecaps, the appendix, and so on). In all likelihood, virtually all of these distances are mere by-products of selection.

HOW EVOLUTIONARY BIOLOGISTS IDENTIFY ADAPTATION

Evolutionary biologists are interested in understanding the selective forces that shaped an organism.

Adaptationism is a methodology for "carving" the organism into those phenotypic features that evolved due to net fitness benefits historically and nonfunctional by-products (e.g., Thornhill, 1997; see Sterelny & Griffiths, 1999, for other types of adaptationism). It furthermore yields inferences about the *specific nature* of selective forces that shaped the organism. That is, it not only identifies adaptations, but also biological function, what those adaptations are *for*.

How does one identify a feature as an adaptation? As already noted, demonstrating that the feature is beneficial is not sufficient. Williams (1966) argued that adaptations must meet stringent standards of evidence, ones captured by the concept of *functional* or *special design*. A trait or constellation of traits exhibits special design for a particular function if it performs that function effectively and, furthermore, it is difficult to imagine another scenario that would have led to the evolution of the trait or constellation of traits. The classic example is the vertebrate eye (see, e.g., Williams, 1992). Its detailed features are effective for seeing, and it is difficult to imagine an evolutionary scenario through which they would have evolved other than one in which its details were selected for their optical properties and thereby the function of sight.

Naturally, not all special design arguments are as compelling as this one, but a variety of human psychological capacities arguably demonstrate evidence of special design. Consider two examples. First, people experience incest aversion to the extent that they coresided, as a child, with a sibling of the other sex, or experienced an association between their mother and the sibling. Lieberman, Tooby, and Cosmides (2007) inferred that people were selected to use these two cues to infer relatedness and hence avoidance of sexual attraction to (likely) siblings. Second, when heterosexual women are fertile in their menstrual cycles, they are particularly sexually attracted to a variety of male features (masculine features, features associated with developmental robustness). These changes have been claimed to reflect adaptation for the function of favoring (ancestrally) fit sires of offspring (see Thornhill & Gangestad, 2008). A host of psychological features important to human functioning in social groups may similarly possess special design for particular function: for example, impression management strategies, bases for selection of coalition partners, discrimination of trustworthiness of others, particular emotional expressions, features underlying the formation and maintenance of close friendships and other "communal relationships," social comparison processes, envy, romantic love, regulation of reproductive hormones such as testosterone as a function of mating and paternal status, discrimination of kin based on cues in scent, and many others. (For a treatment of the related modularity argument of evolutionary psychology, see Barrett & Kurzban, 2006. See also Confers et al., 2010.)

Evolutionary psychologists have also argued, based on *lack* of special design, that other features are by-products. Men find the scent of fertile women more attractive than the scent of women in their infertile luteal phase. Although men's varying attraction to female scents probably reflects adaptation (e.g., to attend to fertile women preferentially), there is no compelling evidence that women possess *adaptation* to smell better when fertile. They likely smell differently as a *by-product* of changing hormone levels, which males have been selected to detect and differentially evaluate (see Thornhill & Gangestad, 2008). As already noted, then, adaptationism does *not* argue that all features are indeed adaptations. Most are *not*. Rather, adaptationism specifies evidentiary bases for deciding which features are adaptations and which are not. For further reading, see Williams (1966), Thornhill (1990, 1997), Tooby & Cosmides (1992), Andrews, Gangestad, and Matthews (2002), and Gangestad (2008).

EVOLUTIONARY ECONOMICS: COST-BENEFIT MODELING

Adaptationism is partly concerned with identifying adaptations, traits evolved because they enhanced fitness ancestrally. In the 1960s (to a limited extent, even before), evolutionary biologists developed evolutionary economic approaches to shed light on what features would in fact enhance fitness. In this approach, "utility" is fitness. A phenotypic feature may provide a level of fitness benefits. But every phenotypic feature has costs as well (even if only due to opportunity costs—those incurred because resources allocated to one trait could have been applied to another). Selection favors the trait level that maximizes net benefits—benefits minus costs. This approach tries to model costs and benefits to then decide (typically via mathematical derivation) what level of trait would have maximized net benefits.

By now, this approach has been used to address a very large number of questions concerning what selection favors: for example, What is the right size to grow to? What affects the optimal number of

sperm to inseminate? What affects optimal family size? How much should a parent invest in an offspring? Under what circumstances should individuals mate with siblings? How choosy should individuals with particular value on the mating market be? Modeling of this sort has transformed theoretical biology (e.g., Parker & Maynard Smith, 1990; Parker, 2006).

Three observations are warranted. First, cost-benefit models can address what behavioral outcomes selection favors. They do not address the precise nature of the adaptations that produce those behavioral outcomes. For instance, modeling makes fairly clear that humans would have been selected to avoid sexual relations with siblings (for one model of incest avoidance, see Kokko & Ots, 2006). But how do humans identify close relatives, and what psychological processes lead us to then avoid incest? The selection models do not, by themselves, address those questions. Adaptationist analyses are needed. Selection-based arguments and adaptationist analyses are complementary, not identical.

Second, formal cost-benefit models are desirable but not always specifiable. Evolutionary biologists and psychologists sometimes engage in informal thought experiments—imagined scenarios about what selection might favor. (See for instance, the later section on friendship.) Informal selection-based thinking can be important to hypothesis-generation (even if, ultimately, one would like to see the informal model formalized; see, e.g., Kokko, Jennions, & Brooks, 2006).

Third, selection operates on individuals but, ultimately, genes replicate. Individuals can pass on their genes (or help kin pass on genes they carry), but cannot be represented in future generations. The gene-centered approach in evolutionary biology emphasizes that, ultimately, changes in phenotypic features—for example, the evolution of phenotypic features—depend on the success of genes promoting their carriers' ability to help them be represented in future generations. The value of a cost-benefit analysis is not that it can tell us how selection affects the gene-propagating effects of individuals' traits, which affect the distribution of genes and hence phenotypes, in future generations.

THEORY IN ADAPTATIONIST PSYCHOLOGY: TWO LEVELS

Two different levels of theory in evolutionary psychology must be discriminated, theory of *proximate* causation and theory of *ultimate* causation. Ultimate causes are those that brought about evolution per se.

Cost-benefit theory and other forms of reasoning about what selection would have favored (whether directly, as in the case of adaptations, or indirectly, as in the case of by-products) address ultimate causation. Proximate causes are those operating to affect behavior in the present. Theory explaining how they operate does not appeal to evolutionary causes. Consider, for instance, an example discussed earlier: avoidance of incest. Lieberman et al. (2007) found that people who had, during childhood, coresided longer with an opposite sex sibling, as well as witnessed the sibling with their mothers, had relatively strong aversion to incest. The ultimate causes of these phenomena were the selection pressures that favored particular adaptations leading individuals to be averse to sex with others inferred to be siblings based on specific cues (e.g., childhood coresidence). They are in the purview of evolutionary biology. The proximate causes of the phenomena are the psychological processes leading individuals to respond to particular features (e.g., childhood coresidence) with an aversion to incest. They are the purview of psychology.

One might ask what evolutionary theorizing adds to the proximate explanation of behavior (in this case, incest aversion). The answer is nothing. The proximate causes of the behavior are psychological in nature, not evolutionary. Those psychological processes are what they are, no matter what evolutionary process shaped them or their developmental underpinnings. What, then, is the value of evolutionary theorizing in psychology? It does not lie in it offering a new language for understanding psychological process. Rather, *it has value in the context of theory development and discovery of psychological process*. In absence of explicit evolutionary theory (e.g., concerning selection against mating with close relatives), it is very unlikely that anyone would have thought to examine whether childhood coresidence and maternal perinatal association as psychological causes of sexual aversion to specific individuals. The same is true of many psychological phenomena discovered through explicit evolutionary theorizing (see, e.g., Confers et al., 2010).

Developmental Systems Theory and Evolutionary Biology

IS DARWINISM GENETIC DETERMINISM?

It is perhaps easy to imagine that a Darwinian view of life is one of genetic determinism. Genes affect phenotypes, such as behavioral tendencies. Selection operates on phenotypes, resulting in changes in gene frequencies. Temporal changes in gene frequencies result in alterations in phenotypes. Current behavioral phenotypes, then, are to be understood as the result of the precise distribution of genes in a population, itself the result of a history of selection. Genes determine behavior, and selection determines genes.

As others have emphasized, this scenario caricatures a Darwinian view of life (see, e.g., Confers et al. 2010). Phenotypic outcomes themselves can result in environmental sensitivity. Prolonged exposure to intense sunlight results in deposition of melanin into skin tissues ("tanning"), an adaptive response to exposure to intense, harmful ultraviolet (UV) rays. The response itself has been selected and, presumably, through changes in gene frequencies. But tanning itself *is* a response to an environmental feature—prolonged exposure to sunlight. Similarly, specific abilities to learn result from selection and changes in gene frequencies, but obviously learning itself occurs through an individual's specific interactions with environments.

One might argue that, despite recognition of these environmental influences, explanation of behavior in this way still invokes a more restricted but nonetheless powerful form of genetic determinism. Adaptive behavior might be contingent on environmental features, but the nature of the contingencies may be thought of as a function of genes and hence genetically preprogrammed. That is, while behavior itself may not be genetically determined, one might say that behavioral *strategies* are (see, e.g., Eagly & Wood, 2006).

It is hence important to recognize other roles for environmental features in evolutionary biology: roles in development. Genetic changes may lead to evolutionary change in phenotypes via their effects on phenotypes, but the processes through which genes affect phenotypes do not involve *nothing but* genes. Genes affect phenotypes in the context of a broader matrix of elements—at cellular levels, cytoplasmic elements, and at broader levels, the environment in which the organism is embedded.

DEVELOPMENTAL SYSTEMS PERSPECTIVES

Some developmental systems theorists have argued that, while recognizing roles for experiences, some evolutionists still implicitly endorse a kind of genetic determinism through concept of a *genetic program*: the idea that genes play an active, *orchestrating* role in development, whereas other elements (environments, experience) play passive roles, ones *orchestrated by* genes. The genes, in such accounts, have a privileged causal status and, in that sense, the genes ultimately "determine" the developmental outcome (see, e.g., Lickliter & Honeycutt, 2003; see also Ploeger, van der Maas, & Raijmakers, 2008).

These concerns can be couched in terms of centuries-old debates between preformationist and epigenetic views of development. Preformationism states that the features of the adult (or developed) form are embodied in the features of the embryo (or undeveloped) form. Development consists of the fuller expression of these already-present features. Epigenesis is the view that developed features do not reside in any form in the undeveloped organism. Elements that do reside within (and around) the undeveloped form interact to give rise to *emergent* developed features. No serious biologist today is a literal preformationist (e.g., believes that tiny homunculi reside in embryos and grow into adults). But developmental systems theorists argue that the idea of a genetic program implies a kind of preformationism. It implies that the developmental outcome is "prespecified" or determined by the genetic program.

An implication concerns the durability of selected phenotypes. In the traditional view, again, evolution consists of changes in distributions of genes, which affect phenotypes. Selection favors some phenotypes over others, leading to changes in gene frequencies. Ultimately, then, selection causally affects phenotypes: It causes distributions of genes, which causes distributions of phenotypes. (See Oyama, 1985, and West-Eberhard, 2003, on implications of developmental systems for a broadening of this conceptualization of evolution.) But genes are only part of the developmental system leading to phenotypes. In principle, introduction of nongenetic novelties (e.g., new environments) into the developmental system could yield completely different phenotypes. Nothing about past selection on genes necessitates that, in novel environments, phenotypes selected *in the past* will develop in novel environments. (Imagine, for instance, a new environment in which a system that regulated production of testosterone is completely altered.) If so, how will selection-based and adaptationist analyses shed light on human psychological processes? (For a similar argument, see Buller, 2005.)

Evolutionary psychologists have responded to this argument in at least two ways. The first is a *theoretic-empirical response*. Developmental systems that selection favors *should* robustly lead to adaptive design (e.g., Tooby et al., 2003). A system whose adaptive outcomes were highly sensitive to perturbations *wouldn't* be adaptive (see, e.g., Waddington, 1957, on canalization). Empirically, Tooby et al. (2003) argue, evidence for robust development is widespread. Virtually everyone develops two arms, legs, and eyes, and a functional heart, liver, and stomach. Why, they claim, should one not expect the same of psychological adaptations?

The *pragmatic response* does not deny that adaptations may not develop robustly, but says the possibility is *merely* a possibility. Suppose we adopt a *working assumption* that development of selected design *is* robust. If true, selection may well have yielded adaptations that we can observe today, even in novel environments, and selection-based thinking will help identify them. If not, selection-based thinking won't be useful—*but that's an outcome that we can assess.* The proof of the recipe is in the eating: Does adaptationism generate productive research programs, or not (e.g., Buss & Reeve, 2003)?

How has the adaptationist recipe worked thus far? By some accounts, very well (e.g., Confers et al., 2010); evolutionary approaches have generated many research findings. At the same time, vast regions of the landscape of human social behavior have hardly been explored via this approach. Much work in the kitchen must yet be done; dining room deliveries await.

Phylogenetic Analysis

When many laypersons think about human evolution, they associate it with the idea that humans evolved from ancestral primates. Adaptationism, the analysis of adaptations and by-products *within a species*, seems not to address this particular aspect of evolution. Phylogenetics does. Specifically, it concerns how species evolved from common ancestors.

A *phylogeny* (from Greek roots for "class" and "origin"—the origin of a biological class) describes an organism's lineage, typically represented within a *phylogenetic tree*. The "tree of life" reflects the history of all organisms. In theory, all have a common ancestor in deep-time history. This organism is the base of the tree. At some point, this species diverged into two, each of which diverged into two, and so on. The tree "grew" and separated into major branches, each one a grouping of organisms, all with a common ancestor. Each separation of a branch into two is a speciation event, and has a "distance" from the present. Hundreds of thousands of "tips" of the tree's twigs represent living species or species that became extinct. As time passes, the tree grows, but only at the tips (as history cannot be changed): Some divide (i.e., more speciation events occur); others end (i.e., some living species will become extinct).

The lineage of a living species is the "route" in the tree (from base to tip) leading to the species—though often lineages are traced "backward" in time, from tip to base. A variety of forms of evidence—most recently, comparisons of genetic make-ups—can be used to infer lineages. Humans (representing the *hominin* family), one "tip" of a branch, had a common ancestor with modern chimpanzees and bonobos (and earlier, extinct hominin species, e.g., Neanderthals) ~5–7 million years ago (mya). Within ~15 mya, we had common ancestors with modern gorillas and orangutans. Tracing the lineage to ~25 mya, humans share ancestors with all apes (hominoids), modern and extinct. At ~50 mya, we share an ancestor with all primates, and at ~200 mya, all mammals, and so on.

Phylogenies have major implications for understanding human features. Each trait humans possess, adaptation or by-product, has a point of origin on the tree. At some time, the trait emerged, and was maintained through an evolutionary force (often, selection) to the present. Inferences about when a trait arose in a lineage appeal to phylogenetics. For instance, all extant chordates (vertebrates plus lampreys) possess a functional estrogen receptor. The common ancestor of these species existed ~450 mya. Estrogen, then, probably became a functional hormone in the lineage leading to humans ~450 mya (Thornton et al., 2003). Theories of the function of estrogens in humans should be sensitive to this fact. A theory that estrogens evolved in a uniquely *human* environment is wrong. Estrogens could have acquired a *new* benefit in the hominin lineage. But they surely had functions in the lineage even in very distant ancestors. (They appear to importantly regulate fertility in all or nearly all female vertebrates).

Some features *are* uniquely human in the primate lineage. These may inform our understanding of what selection pressures led humans to differ from close relatives. They can only be identified, however, through phylogenetic analysis. To know what features evolved in hominins, we must know whether primate species with close ancestors possess them.

Evolutionary psychologists have not attended much to phylogenetic analyses to date. A number of scholars have recently called for greater attention to them. See Fraley et al. (2005); Gosling and Graybeal (2007); Thornhill (2007); Thornhill and Gangestad (2008); Eastwick (2009).

The Human Niche
The Concept of an Ecological Niche
THE TRADITIONAL CONCEPT
Adaptation occurs through selection, and results in a population of organisms being better adapted to their environments. The concept of an *ecological niche* has been used to conceptualize the environment to which organisms adapt (e.g., Elton, 1927). To be adapted to an environment, an organism must "make a living." It must extract energy from the environment, convert it into fitness-enhancing activities (ultimately, reproduction), and survive threats from other organisms extracting energy from it or its kind (through predation or parasitism). The concept of a niche (derived from the French word for "nest") presumes that, within a community of organisms, there are different ways of successfully making a living. In this way, a niche is similar to a person's career or profession (making a living through being a carpenter, an accountant, or a professional athlete). To say that a population has evolved to be better adapted to its environment is to say that its members have evolved features that permit them to more successfully make their living. Just as specific skill sets promote success in particular professions, specific aptitudes best promote success in particular niches. Hence, selection favors different features in different niches. In some niches, for instance, being highly intelligent promotes success, whereas in others, it foolishly squanders energy on a skill set (building a large, complexly organized brain) that does little to promote success.

THE TRADITIONAL CONCEPT CRITIQUED
Traditionally, niches have been thought to be definable by environmental features external to the organism, without reference to any specific organism under consideration. The environment, in this view, poses "problems" for the organism to solve. The organism's evolved solutions to these problems constitute adaptation. Solutions fit prespecified problems in the way that keys fit locks. "Adaptations" are features "adapted" to features of the environment. (See, for instance, Elton, 1927; Hutchinson, 1965; also Sterelny & Griffiths, 1999.)

Richard Lewontin (1982, 1983, 1985) has been a strident critic of this conception of a niche and, by implication, adaptation. Organisms, he argues, do not merely *find themselves* in niches; they *create* them, in at least two ways. First, they choose their environments, to which they are already somewhat adapted. Migratory birds, for instance, travel to find biotic environments (e.g., insect populations) to which they are already suited. Second, they construct features of their environments. Beavers don't adapt to ponds they find; their dams make them. Organisms, then, don't merely "fill" niches. Niches exist when organisms create them.

Once again, an analogy with human careers can be drawn. Traditionally, niches are like careers that one could find cataloged. Lewontin's conception, by contrast, sees niches as creations of their inhabitants. Some service professions (such as waiters), for instance, were originally created because individuals saw a way to create demand for service. (For parallel ideas about persons in relation to their situations and social worlds, see Snyder, 1983.)

Lewontin's critique has implications for the concept of adaptation. "Adaptation" implies that an organism has adapted to, or solved a problem posed by, its environment. But to the extent that organisms create their environments, this term is potentially misleading. I noted earlier that exaptation refers to a trait that happens to be adapted for a use, without it having evolved for that use. If organisms find and create environments, exaptation may be common. It makes sense that organisms would find or create niches to which they already have adaptive traits—that is, ones in which their traits could be exapted to new uses. (Birds were able to move into an aerial niche because of incipient "wings" evolved for other reasons and feathers for insulation. At that stage, those "wings" were exapted to flight.) If many, perhaps most, adaptive features preexisted the niche to which they are adapted, what role does the niche play in adaptation? Are organisms shaped to fit their environments, as keys are to locks? Or do they choose and create environments to which they are fit, as though keys that *find* suitable locks?

Though Lewontin's critique correctly accuses the unqualified traditional conception to be overly naive, more nuanced views of niches that do partly explain adaptation are possible (Sterelny & Griffiths, 1999). Organisms may create niches, but they also adapt *to* them. And lineages of organisms tend to specialize in niches (e.g., horses graze on grasses; Eldridge, 1995); not *every* species creates its own. Only occasionally do organisms "break out of" a niche space within which close ancestors lived, and thereby construct a new niche.

The Niche Humans Entered and Defined
PRIMATE NICHES AND THE EVOLUTION OF MIOCENE APES

What can we say about the hominin niche or way of "making a living"? And what does it tell us about ancestral human *social* adaptations?

Humans, of course, are primates. Most primates are arboreal omnivores. Typically, their diets heavily consist of readily collected items. Features that distinguish monkeys from most mammals, such as opposable thumbs and abilities to grasp with hands and feet, are features well suited to foraging leaves and fruits by moving on all fours along tree branches (while also consuming small amounts of insects and occasional hunted meats).

In the Old World, apes and monkeys diverged from a common ancestor approximately 25 mya (see Begun, 2003). Apes typically possess anatomical features that distinguish them from most monkeys. They lack tails, possess adaptations for greater flexibility of limb movement, long arms, powerful hands, and broad chests, all of which appear adapted for suspension under branches as well as a mode of travel under the forest canopy, swinging from branch to branch, as do others. Most apes likely became fruit-eating specialists: particularly well adapted to gathered fruits and nuts from the understories of lush subtropical forests. Because optimizing the ripeness of fruit to consume is a cognitively more complex task than gathering leaves, even monkeys with relatively more fruit in their diets have larger brains (relative to body size) than ones foraging mostly leaves (e.g., Kaplan et al., 2007; Walker et al., 2006). Apes too, then, evolved large brains. Because fruit ripeness can be discriminated as a product of color, apes increasingly came to heavily rely on vision (less on olfaction) for sensory information.

About 16 mya, a land bridge formed between Africa and Eurasia, leading to a mass exodus of mammals out of Africa. At that time, subtropical forests covered much of Eurasia, and apes flourished there. Perhaps 100 or more ape species existed shortly thereafter, many in Europe (e.g., Begun, 2003). In the late Miocene epoch (ending 5.5 mya), major mountain ranges (e.g., Alps, Himalayas) were built, causing European climates to became temperate and the Middle East dry. Apes did not adapt to these changes and, in just a few million years, virtually all vanished. Natural populations of modern apes, aside from humans, are found only in subtropical Africa (chimpanzees, bonobos, gorillas) and Southeast Asia (orangutans, siamangs, gibbons). The lineages surviving today may have migrated from Europe back into the African continent within the last 10 million years (Begun, 2003).

THE HOMININ NICHE CONTRASTED WITH THE TYPICAL APE NICHE

Humans are apes, but hardly typical ones. Not surprisingly, we do owe some morphological features to a uniquely ape heritage: Hands suited for grasping; fully extendable elbows; flexible hips; heavy reliance on vision. But unlike other apes, our legs are longer than our arms. Our hands are not powerful. We aren't well suited to swing from branch to branch. More generally, we are not well adapted for the typical ape niche: foraging of fruits from the understory of tropical forests. Humans are one of those rare instances of a species that moved into a niche distinct in rather fundamental ways from that of its ancestors or close relatives.

Human forager diets contrast sharply with the diets of our closest living relative, the chimpanzee. Chimpanzees derive 95% of their diets from collected foods, largely fruit. Hunting produces just 2% of their calories. By contrast, human foragers derive 30–70% of their calories from hunted game. Much of the rest of their diet replies on other extracted foods, such as roots, only 8% requiring no extraction. The niche in which humans evolved has hence been characterized in terms of our abilities to forage a variety of *high caloric-density but difficult-to-extract foods* (through hunting and root extraction; Kaplan et al., 2000). Hominins may have created this niche because ancestors were forced out of dense arboreal settings and onto savannas. Some ancestral ape features were exapted and then secondarily modified for new uses (e.g., the extendable elbow permitted throwing; flexible hips set the stage for the evolution of bipedalism, walking, and running). Some (e.g., long arms) were selected out. Possibly, the already relatively advanced cognitive abilities of ancestral hominins may have been the "incipient wings" that fundamentally allowed them to create a new niche.

THE HUMAN ADAPTIVE COMPLEX

In evolving to fill or define their niche, humans were selected to possess a variety of core features, distinct from those of ancestors, that permitted humans to "make a living" in the niche particularly well. I draw on discussion of Kaplan et al.'s (2000) description of the human adaptive complex, but augmented and modified in the context of Sterelny's (2007) model.

Embodied Cognitive Capital

Humans take a long time to become good at foraging. Hunters, for instance, don't hit their peak productivity until they are in their mid-40s. Through learning and innovation, humans learn to forage effectively. The way in which humans "make a living," then, is at least partly through acquisition of skills and information over time—an accumulation of "embodied cognitive capital" that pays off over time (see Kaplan et al., 2003).

A Long Lifespan and a Conservative Approach to Mortality Risks

The longer and more costly the acquisition of a form of embodied capital that increases production, the longer the period of production postacquisition must be to "pay for" the acquisition. (E.g., one can recoup the costs of an expensive college education if living a long time earning a high salary, but not if death immediately follows college.) Humans' commitment to making a living through expensively acquired embodied capital is only possible if they have a prolonged postacquisition period of productive living. We hence have evolved to live long and to age relatively slowly.

A Long Period of Juvenile Dependence

When acquiring skill sets, individuals may not be able to sustain themselves energetically. Whereas chimpanzees are dependent on mothers for caloric subsidies until they are 2–3 years old, human forager offspring don't begin paying their own way until nearly 20. The human commitment to making a living through foraging difficult-to-extract resources hence required a way of directing production surpluses to juveniles.

Biparental Care

In chimpanzees and most mammals, mothers subsidize the diets of young offspring. Adult males rarely do so. In human foraging societies, by contrast, adult males typically forage large subsidies. On average in foraging societies, males produce about 65% of all calories, women about 35% (e.g., Marlowe, 2001). (In a meaningful proportion of societies, however, women produce more calories than men; see Schlegel & Barry, 1986.) Kaplan et al. (2000) argue that biparental care was essential to pay for prolonged juvenile dependence, which a single parent could not do alone while also engaging in direct care for small children and infants. (This argument has been challenged [see, e.g., Hawkes, 2004], and challenges have been countered [Marlowe, 2003; Gurven & Hill, 2009]; debate will likely continue.)

Extensive Cooperation

Human foragers live in multifamily groups. Group-living affords advantages, such as protection from predation and efficiencies of mate-search. In humans, it also facilitated foraging high-density, relatively large but difficult-to-extract packages of nutrients. First, human hunting and fishing may have been more efficient when performed by multiperson parties compared to single individuals. Groups of hunters can surround and trap large game, which single hunters cannot do. Second, many game are too large for single individuals or families to wholly consume. By sharing meat, individuals can increase their own rates of consumption: sharing when they generate surpluses, and receiving when others do. Adaptive sharing may rely on sophisticated social adaptations (e.g., ones tracking costs and benefits of sharing and receiving, histories of who has given and received; Trivers, 1971; see also Gurven, 2004). Third, early humans could benefit from learning from others. Success in hunting and other forms of foraging could be enhanced through technological and strategic innovation (e.g., advances in weaponry, mass fishing techniques, means of water travel, strategies in hunting, techniques of designing or producing technologies), which could spread through social learning (e.g., Ramsey et al., 2007). Humans tend to be strongly predisposed to reciprocate and cooperate, tendencies reinforced by individuals' willingness to punish, at a cost to themselves, noncooperative behavior (e.g., Gintis, 2000; Lehmann & Keller, 2006).

Reliance on Coalitional Success
In many species, individuals live in groups (presumably because of the benefits that group-living affords), but individuals' successes are nonetheless largely their own creations. The skill sets of other group members largely matter as features of *competitors*; inclusion of highly fit group members hurt one's success, all else equal. In some species, individual success relies on assistance from kin (e.g., Silk et al., 2009), and those with fit kin may succeed better than those with weak kin, all else equal.

In human foraging groups, other group members also matter as competitors, and kin too are important. But given reliance on cooperation to make a living, nonkin matter in additional ways: *Individuals' success and fitness depended not only on their own skills and those of kin, but also on the skill sets of others with whom they cooperated.* Individual success depended partly on *coalitional strengths.* Human coalitional action may have arisen in the context of foraging (where, again, groups could be more successful than individuals, and meat-sharing yielded benefits), but it spread to many activities: sharing information, building shelters, defending territories, exerting political influence, tending to others sick or injured. The ramifications for human social adaptations run very deep. In human societies, *others embody potential fitness-enhancing resources*

to be tapped. Humans hence possess adaptations for garnering those fitness-enhancing resources. They assess who has attributes they can tap through coalitions, and compete to be chosen as coalition partners themselves (see Nesse, 2009). The next section of this chapter discusses some of the adaptations.

No other close relative has extensive adaptations similar in kind, de Waal (1989) argued, though chimpanzees form alliances that benefit each member's standing in the group dominance hierarchy as well as defend group territories against males from neighboring groups (de Waal, 1989; Wrangham & Peterson, 1996), cooperation is deeply embedded in human means of subsistence, and not obviously pertinent to chimpanzee subsistence.

Big Brains
Humans possess large brains, relative to body size. Kaplan et al. (2000) argue that they evolved to facilitate foraging of difficult-to-extract foods (by enhancing hunting ability or technological innovation). Others argue that complex forms of human sociality led to the evolution of big brains (e.g., Flinn et al., 2005). (Group size, a marker of social complexity, covaries with brain size across primate species, and human forager group size is relatively large; Dunbar, 1998; Walker et al., 2006.) These theories are not mutually exclusive (see below). In any event, humans clearly have unusual cognitive capacities for both innovation and social functioning. (Displays of intelligence may signal mate quality as well; Miller, 2000.)

Additional features emerged. Importantly, human societies embody multiple forms of culture. One form consists of information and technology generated and commonly represented in the society. A second form consists of norms concerning appropriate behavior and sanctions regulating them (e.g., Hill, 2007). (See also Schaller et al., 2009.)

COMPONENTS OF THE HUMAN ADAPTIVE COMPLEX COEVOLVED

One might wonder what features within the human adaptive complex evolved first, and which ones followed. In fact, the components of the human adaptive complex probably incrementally coevolved, and necessarily so (Kaplan et al., 2000). Each component entails costs, which must be offset by benefits. But benefits of each component cannot be fully realized in absence of other components. The effects of the components on benefits are synergistic.

Kaplan et al. (2000) ask us to consider, for instance, how a prolonged period of skill acquisition and hence juvenile dependence could have evolved. The cost is very large in energetic terms; forager children run tremendous deficits in energy production in their first 18 years of life. The only way that it could pay is if it were followed by a long period of production of surpluses, partly directed toward juveniles—which would require other components of the complex: for example, a long lifetime during which deficits can be made up, and prolonged childcare. To illustrate, Kaplan et al. imposed a chimpanzee mortality schedule on the production curve of humans. If humans lived only as long as typical chimpanzees, adults would never make up the calorie deficit accrued during childhood, an outcome that could not possibly evolve. At the same time, the costs of growing and maintaining a large brain and allocating substantial amounts of energy to mortality reduction (immune defense, somatic repair) can only be offset by benefits made possible through a prolonged juvenile period. Single components could not have evolved, in full, by themselves. The components must have evolved incrementally in concert. The special adaptations for social life in the distinctively human adaptive complex (for biparental care, pair-bonding, extensive cooperation, and harnessing the capabilities of others to promote one's own success through coalitions) likely coevolved with other components too.

ALTERNATIVE VIEWS OF THE HUMAN NICHE

I've sketched out one view of the human niche. But there are alternative views, and debate continues. In broad terms, most models are of two sorts: *ecological* and *social*. Kaplan et al.'s (2000) is an ecological model. It emphasizes that the primary selection pressures giving rise to derived human features (e.g., a large brain) fundamentally pertained to what ancestors foraged (specifically, difficult-to-extract foods), and how they did it. By contrast, a noteworthy social model is the ecological dominance model (Flinn et al., 2005). It claims that humans evolved to a point at which they were so good at extracting resources from their environments they no longer needed to worry about obtaining sufficient nutrients. As a result, the primary "forces of nature" humans faced were each other, not predators or food sources. Humans evolved an array of psychological features that led us to take advantage of other people, as well as prevent others from doing so to us. We also evolved coalitional psychologies as a means of competing with each other in groups. A metaphor for the arena of selection in this model is "social chess" (Humphrey, 1976): We evolved to

anticipate what others' perspectives are—and their perspectives of our perspectives, their perspectives of our perspectives of their perspectives, and so on—leading to runaway selection of elaborate social strategies at this "game" (see also Dunbar, 1998, Dunbar & Schultz, 2007).

Sterelny (2007) registers two primary complaints about the ecological dominance model. First, it invokes a flaw in reasoning. It presumes that humans became good enough at producing nutritious foods, so that threats came from elsewhere, notably, other humans. But selection does not favor what is "good enough"; it favors what is best. And if producing even more nutrients could increase fitness (e.g., through ability to rear even more offspring), selection would favor doing so. Second, though levels of strategic reasoning and defense against being cheated have evolved, the theory exaggerates the importance of "social chess." Human foragers would have been favored to cooperate, but with discretion about whom to cooperate with. The primary task increasing the benefits gained from cooperation, then, would be to *find suitable others* with whom to cooperate productively. Social features do play a fundamental role in the human niche, but in a way that contrasts with traditional social hypotheses. Because humans sustained themselves through cooperative activities, coalition formation and maintenance is embedded within virtually all aspects of life. If, within the human niche, the means of production itself became increasingly cooperation-based, a correct model does not pit social and ecological selection pressures against each other. As noted earlier, the analysis I present draws heavily on Kaplan et al.'s model, but placed in the broader social-ecological framework proposed by Sterelny (2007) (also elaborated by Kaplan et al., 2007).

One additional model deserves mention. Gintis (2000) and Bowles and Gintis (2004) argue that widespread, virtually indiscriminate cooperation permitted entire human groups to succeed, grow, and repopulate new others at the expense of other groups. Others argue that no design evidence to date requires group-level selection to explain (e.g., Kurzban & Aktipsis, 2007). Swayed by the latter arguments, I emphasize here within-group selection on ability to garner profitable coalition partners rather than between-group selection.

Social Adaptations Special to the Human Niche: Illustrations Pertaining to Coalitional Behavior

I now consider specific implications of the niche in which humans evolved for an understanding of key components of human social and personality psychology. Not surprisingly, social psychologists have already studied much of what the human adaptive complex leads us to expect in the way of human social psychology. One need not possess a theory of the human niche to observe that people possess big brains and long lifespans—or behave with each other in particular ways. At the same time, evolutionary perspectives on the human niche can contribute to an understanding of human social life in at least two important ways. First, they may offer broad, integrative theoretical conceptualizations of many discrete facts. Second, they can generate novel insights and programs of research about human sociality. In discussing specific implications, I emphasize both *integrative* and *generative* contributions.

The next two sections concern human social adaptations. In the current section, I deliberately focus on implications of a core component of sociality evolved in the human niche: Individuals' success and fitness depended on not only their own skills, but also on the skill sets of others with whom they cooperated. I do so not because this component is more important than any other (though it might be); rather, I use it to illustrate how evolution-inspired views can lead to coherent, integrative, systematic exploration of human adaptations. Other realms (e.g., mating, biparental care) could have been used as well. The following section briefly discusses a variety of additional components of human sociality from an evolutionary perspective.

REPUTATIONS MATTER: PEOPLE EVALUATE OTHERS AS COALITION PARTNERS

Again, humans have long engaged in extensive coalitional behavior to achieve a variety of ends, and success of individuals' coalitions affected their fitness ancestrally: coalitions to forage, build shelters, defend territories, gain social or political influence, and, in modern environments, all manner of aims (e.g., do psychological research, write papers). Strength of their coalitions, then, was important to individual success. Coalitional strength, in turn, was affected by (1) individuals' abilities to assess others' abilities to contribute to coalitional success, and (2) individuals' abilities to be attractive coalition partners to others (in particular, other good coalition partners). Selection hence likely enhanced these abilities in humans.

Naturally, large literatures in social psychology address ways in which these abilities affect human social interaction. Theories of person perception, for instance, concern how individuals ascribe enduring personal dispositions (e.g., abilities, motivations, altruism, selfishness) to an individual's acts-in-context or sequences of such acts (e.g., Heider, 1958; Funder, 1999). Impression management theory concerns how individuals strategically communicate information about themselves and their personal qualities, in light of how others draw inferences from their acts and displays (e.g., Goffman, 1959; Schlenker, 1980). Evolutionary perspectives, however, offer novel insights on these phenomena.

What features do valuable coalition members possess? I highlight three kinds (see also Newcomb, 1990; Fiske et al., 2007; Vigil, 2009): *capacity*, *trustworthiness*, and *compatibility*.

Capacity

Capacity reflects features that promote effective task performance. Task-relevant competencies are highly important: If the task is to build a shelter, knowledge of how to build one; if it is to physically dominate another group, physical prowess; if one seeks a coalition to increase one's own social status, status (and status-enhancing attributes, e.g., physical attractiveness). Stamina to perform hard work also affects capacity. (See Vigil, 2009.)

Trustworthiness

Cooperative activities leave individuals open to cheating. A coalition member may reap the benefits of cooperative activity but not fully share in its costs (e.g., through loafing, hoarding of products yielded), and thereby "steal," literally or figuratively, the efforts of others. Trustworthiness reflects a propensity to engage cooperatively in a way others perceive as fair (see Simpson, 2007). Whereas capacity tends to be embodied in persons, trust is often generated through repeated interactions with others (e.g., Kurzban, Rigdon, & Wilson, 2008; Zak et al., 2005), and hence relationship-specific. Distrust need not imply suspicion of motives to cheat. A person perceived to be impulsive or emotionally unstable may also be distrusted.

Compatibility

Compatibility, related to but partly distinct from trustworthiness, reflects the ability of an individual to work effectively in coordinated ways with others. Once again, it is often relationship-specific (e.g., effective coordination can require compatibility of goals and work styles). At the same time, individuals differ in their ability to work effectively with others in general, as partly reflected in the personality trait of agreeableness.

If these three attribute-sets importantly reflect on one's ability to be a good coalition member, they should be three kinds of attributes that people are motivated to display to others, as well as attributes that people strive to judge in others. Much evidence indicates that they are (for a recent review, see Vigil, 2009; see also Miller, 2009; Fiske et al., 2007).

Do Emotions Signal these Abilities and Appraisals?
A long tradition, dating to Darwin (1872), examines the communicative functions of emotional expressions. These expressions appear to have been shaped to part of signaling systems, which require specialized features evolved to communicate one's state or quality to other organisms, and specialized features in perceiver organisms to act on the signals (see Gangestad & Thornhill, 2007). Though much work characterizes the stereotypic muscle movements that characterize expressions (e.g., Ekman, 1980), much less has been done to understand the functional significance of signaling. To evolve, signaling systems must have offered net benefits to signalers and to receivers. What were these benefits? One general model focuses on how emotional expressions play roles in implicit negotiation of social problems (Morris & Keltner, 2000). In this view, relational problems (e.g., caused by a minor transgression) evoke emotional reactions from actors (e.g., embarrassment or shame), leading perceivers to expressing emotions that resolve the matter in one way (e.g., acceptance) or another (e.g., disgust) (see also Wubben et al., 2009). In this way, emotional expressions importantly regulate social interaction.

Recently, Vigil (2009) proposed that emotional expressions in general communicate capacity (e.g., joy, courage, confidence, hope anger), trustworthiness (e.g., acceptance, interest), one's own appraisal of another's capacity (e.g., admiration, fear), or trustworthiness (e.g., compassion, sympathy), or a mixture of these qualities (e.g., appraisal of someone as low trust and low capacity may be displayed by disgust). Relatedly, Fiske et al. (2002) propose that perceptions of particular combinations of features of capacity and trust (in their terms, competence and warmth) elicit specific emotions (pity, envy, admiration, and contempt).

The comprehensiveness of this explanation of emotional expression has yet to be fully evaluated. (Sell et al., 2009, for instance, propose a related but alternative evolutionary perspective on one emotion, anger.) In addition, from an evolutionary perspective, evolved signals should be honest; were they not fundamentally honest, perceivers should not have evolved to attend to them. It will thus also be important to establish, from an evolutionary standpoint, how emotional expressions of capacity and trustworthiness have evolved to be honest ones, not susceptible to cheating. (On honest signals of intent, see Andrews, 2001.)

COALITIONAL PSYCHOLOGY
If humans are disposed to engage cooperatively in coalitions, they should be disposed to elicit cooperative behavior from coalition members. Individuals do favor ingroup over outgroup members, even when membership is decided on arbitrary bases (e.g., Mullen et al., 1992). Consistent with it being driven by perceived benefits of coalitional cooperation, the bias appears to be largely due to favoritism toward ingroup members, not dislike of outgroup members (Brewer, 1999, 2007; Yamagishi & Mifune, 2009; but see Levin & Sidanius, 1999, for evidence that certain forms of ingroup bias, e.g., associated with social dominance orientation, relate to outgroup derogation). Relatedly, people may not automatically encode the race of others. People encode coalitional affiliation, with which race may often be perceived to be related. When race fails to predict coalitional alliance, individuals may cease to encode it (Kurzban, Tooby, & Cosmides, 2001). (Though lab manipulations disassociating coalitional association with race may erase immediate encoding of race, they do not necessarily erase engrained implicit associations of race with negative traits developed over sustained histories; e.g., Dovidio et al., 1997.)

TWO FORMS OF STATUS: DOMINANCE AND PRESTIGE
In social groups of many species, individuals differ in status. One's status rank is a function of access to fitness-enhancing benefits afforded through preferential treatment by group members. In most primate societies, status is a function of *dominance*, one's ability to gain access to valued resources through physical prowess. Because physical altercations with dominant individuals are costly, others often forego competing for valued resources in the presence of dominant others. Dominant individuals may also be preferred as coalition partners. These forms of preferential treatment render dominance a form of social status.

In human groups, status rank has distinct forms. In addition to gaining status through dominance, individuals may gain *prestige* (Henrich & Gil-White,

2001), preferential treatment bestowed on individuals who possess certain abilities or capacities that others value, such specific forms of knowledge, the ability to innovate, and skill at coordinating the activities of others in effective cooperative behavior (e.g., leadership). The emergence of prestige-based status can be understood in the context of the human niche. Humans' way of living came to rely on knowledge and innovation. Because individual success was importantly affected by a person's social coalitions, others' skills, competencies, and abilities to engage in effective coalitional behavior became resources for others. As emphasized, the success of individuals depended partly on their ability to harness the competencies of others through coalitional behavior. Individuals who possess valued competencies that others can harness are preferred social partners. The preferential treatment of individuals with these competencies constitutes status. Other primate social groups are not characterized by prestige rank because the competencies of individuals (aside from physical prowess) do not importantly function as a resource for others to harness. (An exception occurs in the context of mating. Males' fitness is enhanced to the extent that they mate with females that competently rear offspring. For instance, chimpanzee males prefer to mate with females over 40 years old, who most successfully rear offspring [Muller et al., 2006].)

Prestige can be earned through a variety of different competencies. Because individuals will be particularly preferred as social partners when they are better than others at some task, individuals may benefit from specialization: Becoming very good at one particular form of competence. The evolution of prestige as a form of social rank, then, may also favor diversification of skill within a group (see also Baumeister et al., 2006). Tooby and Cosmides (1996) note an additional advantage to specialization: Individuals are particularly sought after as social partners when the benefits that they can provide due to their competencies are both valued and *difficult to replicate or replace*. Hence, having an unusual talent, skill, or knowledge-set useful to many others is highly valuable. Social motivation to acquire such attributes may have been just as important to human innovation as our highly evolved intellectual capacities.

SOCIAL COMPARISONS AND SPECIALIZATION
To best benefit from coalitions, individuals should cooperate with others who specialize in skills and knowledge that they themselves lack and, in return,

offer coalition partners with valued skills. People should hence possess means of identifying and protecting their own strengths, as well as finding others who possess complementary skills. Beach and Tesser (2000) offer an evolution-inspired social comparison theory that specifies ways people do so.

Social comparisons lead to evaluation of oneself relative to specific target persons on some dimension of competence. Relative rather than absolute performance is typically key. Being best at a task may more favorably affect one's social prospects than being, in absolute terms, better, but in relative terms only second best, at another task (e.g., Frank, 1985). Several elements influence the importance of particular comparisons and their implications for self-assessment (e.g., Beach & Tesser, 2000): performance, closeness, and self-relevance.

Performance reflects the direction of a social comparison with a specific other, positive (when one outperforms the other) or negative (when the other out-performs oneself). *Closeness* reflects the extent to which individuals are likely and important potential coalition partners as well as potential competitors. Comparisons with these individuals, who affect one's own fitness, are more relevant to adaptive self-assessment than are comparisons to others largely irrelevant to one's own fitness (e.g., members of distant groups). *Self-relevance* reflects the importance of a particular domain or specialization to oneself. As one commits more effort to establish oneself as valued by others in a domain, the domain becomes increasingly self-relevant. Self-relevance hence reflects, to a large degree, the extent to which their success in attracting valuable social coalitions depends on their relative performance in the domain.

Self-relevance modulates the impact of self-assessment on evaluations of self. When a domain is self-relevant, positive performance assessments bolster commitment to the specialization. Negative performance assessments motivate actions to defend and maintain one's standing in a domain. By contrast, when a domain is not self-relevant, negative self-assessments have a different effect: They lead individuals to value people whose performance is superior, those who possess skills that can complement one's own as coalition partners.

As affected by these three elements, then, social comparisons lead people to be attracted to specializations in which they perform well relative to others who are important to them, and respond positively toward important others whose specializations are complementary, with whom they can reap benefits of cooperation.

I have emphasized that peoples' competencies represent resources that others can harness through coalitions. Ancestrally, some people were better than others at doing so, partly due to their psychological features, and selection led these features—adaptations—to evolve. In many instances, the competition selection operated on was of the sort spelling bees are: Contestants show off their talents, and the best is picked. In others, however, selection may have favored tendencies to engage in conflict. Envy is evoked by self-assessment of relative inferiority to pertinent competitors in self-relevant domains (Hill & Buss, 2006), particularly when individuals cannot readily remove a threat by improving or changing specialization. Envious individuals are motivated to diminish the perceived social value of their competitors (e.g., through gossip or direct aggression; see review by Smith & Kim, 2007; for a model of how evaluations of competence and competition affect stereotype content, see Fiske et al., 2002).

SOCIAL SPHERES: A CONCEPTUALIZATION OF INDIVIDUALS' SOCIAL CAPITAL

Social worlds comprise the networks of individuals with whom individuals interact. Evolution-minded scholars have recently conceptualized social worlds to reflect the fact that, in human groups, others partly represent resources for individuals (Geary et al., 2003; Vigil, 2007, 2009). The concept of a *social sphere* represents the aggregation of all possible social interactions available to an individual at a given point in time, and hence the sociorelational risks and opportunities (Geary et al., 2003; Vigil, 2007, 2009; see also Newcomb & Chou, 1989). Others embody fitness-enhancing resources one can harness (via cooperation and coalitional behavior), as well as represent potential threats (via competition). The notion of a social sphere represents others in terms of these potential benefits and costs.

Social spheres differ across individuals (and, within individuals, across time) in various ways. At a broad level, they vary in the *overall net benefits* afforded, one's *social capital*. A high-prestige individual has social partnerships that offer opportunities more valuable than the opportunities afforded by the social partnerships of a low-prestige individual. They also differ on more specific dimensions: *size* (total number of potential interactants), *mean or net capacity* of the interactants, and *mean or net relational proximity* (perceived trustworthiness or reliability of the relationships). A person's net benefits approach a maximum when they have many potential social partners who offer resources to draw

on, each with high capacity and close relational proximity. Of course, most people's social spheres do not possess all of these features.

The value of capacity and trustworthiness in social partners operates somewhat differently. One can enjoy the benefits of having a highly competent partner even in a short-term, one-shot collaboration. By contrast, people typically garner benefits from trustworthy partners over repeated interactions over which trust deepens. The benefits of a high capacity and trustworthy partner may also be nonadditive. For instance, the value of coalition partners' trustworthiness may be minimal in settings in which lack key relevant competencies.

Social sphere size and mean relational proximity trade off against one another. Maintaining trust in relationships requires time, effort, and other resources (e.g., to share), and hence the more one invests in trust in relationships the smaller one's social sphere. By contrast, one can potentially acquire many relationship partners, but only at a cost of mean relational proximity (Vigil, 2009; see also Tooby & Cosmides, 1996). Individuals might be expected to invest in social sphere size and relational proximity in ways that maximize net social capital. Two different individuals might do so in different ways, one investing more in size, the other in relational proximity, a topic I discuss when I turn to individual differences.

This model of social spheres is explicitly evolution-inspired, based on the premise that other people's capacities and other qualities are resources others can harness for their own ends through coalitional behavior. This premise, in turn, follows from a particular view of the human niche. The social sphere concept captures the idea that, in human evolution, social relationships were important vehicles for individual fitness-enhancement.

AFFORDANCES IN THE SOCIAL WORLD

I noted above that the concept of a social sphere assumes that individuals perceive opportunities and risks in their social world. Perception of opportunities and risks may be conceptualized in terms of Gibson's (1979) idea of *affordances*. Affordances are perceived ways one may interact with an object or entity that benefit or cost individuals. According to Gibson, the way we fundamentally perceive objects is in terms of the opportunities they present and their risks. For humans, tables afford placing objects on them, stairs afford climbing, and cups afford pouring liquid into them. Similarly, other individuals represent opportunities and risks—for example, possibilities of coalitions of particular types, in light of their specific competencies, as well as risks incurred through coalitional interaction or direct competition (e.g., due to lack of trust or incompatible interaction styles). Our interactions with others are shaped by these affordances (see also McArthur & Baron, 1983). One hence might say that a social sphere embodies the affordances of a person's total aggregation of social relationships.

Gibson (1979) emphasized that affordances are not readily classified as either subjective or objective aspects of perception. They are subjectively perceived in the sense that they characterize perceptions of the perceiving individual and no other. (E.g., an individual's precise set of friends is unique.) They are objective, however, in the sense that they may accurately reflect the opportunities available to *that* individual. (E.g., the benefits a person sees in his or her friendships may be accurately perceived.) Relatedly, affordances are neither exclusively person- or situation-referenced. They are person-referenced because, once again, individuals perceive opportunities offered by their social worlds in ways that no one else does. They are situation-referenced in that perceptions fundamentally define situations (e.g., Ross & Nisbett, 1991); for any two individuals with a common friend, their interactions with that friend constitute different situations, as each perceives different affordances in the friend. Affordances furthermore do not reflect person-situation *interactions*; an interaction assumes that each component can be defined independently of the other and, as just noted, situations are defined partly by affordances specific to persons. (This point, I note, parallels one made earlier about ecological niches: Lewontin claims that, because organisms create their niches, niches cannot be defined independently of the organism inhabiting it.) Rather, affordances are a function of person-in-context: a particular person placed in a context perceives affordances in that context (see also Reis & Holmes, chapter 4, this volume).

Because an individual may perceive opportunities and risks differently depending on context, the affordances of one's social sphere need not be constant. For instance, one's social sphere may offer opportunities suitable for some pursuits but not others. (See Buss, 2009a, on a related view on how adaptive problems define situations.) Programs of research have impressively demonstrated how manipulations of the salience of goals can influence the opportunities and risks offered by people, and how selective attention is accordingly affected (e.g., Maner et al., 2003, 2005; Griskevicius et al., 2009).

FRIENDSHIP

Not all coalitions are of the same sort. Much coalitional activity can be understood in terms of a simple model of cooperation, *mutualism*. Mutualism exists when two or more individuals can only obtain a benefit through collective action (see, for instance, West et al., 2006). If hunting returns per person increase when a party of hunters works together, relative to them working alone, hunters benefit from collective action. If individuals can build a set of shelters together more effectively than each building one, they benefit from working together. (Of course, the individual whose shelter is built first must help build the remaining ones. Again, in some cooperative activities, individuals can "steal" the efforts of others. But if individuals benefit from future cooperation with the same set of individuals or observers, they likely are best off establishing trust.) Some political alliances too represent mutualism; individuals with common interests may work together to further them. Cooperation arising from mutualism is not difficult to explain: Each person, once again, obtains benefits through collective action. Many important human relationships with nonkin, however, seem to be a different kind: friendships.

In relationships that people subjectively consider their closest friendships, individuals do not exchange benefits in a tit-for-tat way, and they do not form a coalition to collectively achieve a specific goal (e.g., hunt game, build shelters). Close friends often benefit each other in absence of expectation that they will receive benefits in return, either now or in the future. They are steadfastly "there" for each other, and respond to each other based on need. (Clark & Mills, 1993, refer to these relationships as "communal," in contrast to "exchange" relationships.) People think of their close friends as among the most important figures in their lives. And they become attached to their friends. They share in their friends' joys and pains, and suffer distress when friendships are lost. The psychological features that underlie the formation and maintenance of friendships demand a special evolutionary analysis. How were the adaptations leading to friendship formation and maintenance selected? That is, how did individuals' fitness come to depend on features leading to the formation and maintenance of friendships?

Tooby and Cosmides (1996) propose that the evolution of friendships can be explained in a series of steps. First, they imagine a scenario in which individuals act in self-interested ways and simultaneously benefit others as side effects (positive externalities; e.g., one person knows the way back to camp and allows the other to follow). If the recipient of such a benefit were to provide a low-cost benefit to the other in response, both individuals could benefit at low cost, encouraging the other to provide another low-cost benefit in the future. The pair becomes more likely to interact repeatedly, exchanging low-cost benefits. For these benefits to be gained, however, each individual must be able to discriminate the consequences of their actions for others. One individual, for instance, must understand, at some level, that she received a benefit in response to *the act of benefiting the other*, an act that must be discriminable.

The evolution of this psychological capacity may be no trivial matter (e.g., it would seem to require the ability to take another's perspective and perceptions of benefits and costs; Tooby & Cosmides, 1996). Once it has evolved, however, the stage is set for individuals to select each other as frequent interaction partners, each mutually benefiting the other at low cost. For any given individual, however, not all such partners are equally beneficial. If one is to interact frequently with a particular individual, at a cost of being able to interact with others, it is best if that individual (1) has particular strengths that are especially beneficial to oneself (e.g., ones that complement one's own, and offer benefits to oneself at low cost to the other); (2) has goals and interests that are compatible with one's own; (3) understands oneself well (due to similarities in circumstance, personal history, or values) so that mutually beneficial activities are efficiently coordinated, (4) values and can benefit from one's own strengths, even at low cost to oneself, so that the other also values continued interaction. The upshot is that, given opportunity to select frequent-interaction partners, individuals benefit from choosing partners unusually valuable to oneself. As a result of frequent interaction, compatibility grows (e.g., due to others' deepened knowledge of oneself) and their value as partners deepens.

The stage is now set for the distinctive qualities of friendships to emerge. Each partner serves as a highly important resource to the other: Each individual's ability to engage in fitness-enhancing activities depends on the relationship with the other. Moreover, because (1) the other person was selected to be particularly valuable to one's self in the first place, and (2) that value has been enhanced through repeated interaction, each person becomes exceptionally difficult for the other to replace. If the other dies, for instance, one cannot immediately find a replacement who promotes one's own fitness-relevant well-being to a similar extent. As the other's well-being is critically important to one's own, *each individual benefits by investing in the other's well-being*. If the other is sick, one aids the other. If the other has other immediate needs, one offers help. Each individual protects the other against harm as though the threat were to oneself because, effectively, it is. The relationship has the features of a close friendship.

As Tooby and Cosmides (1996) emphasize, the properties of friendship have self-reinforcing qualities. If one friend has a very large stake in the well-being of the other friend, then the first will be willing to go to great lengths to aid the other. That in turn means that the second has a great stake in the well-being of the first. Though, once again, friends often select each other because they have qualities valuable to each other, even friendships that begin with weak initial compatibilities can, over time, develop, through this self-reinforcement process, into friendships characterized by "deep engagement" (Tooby & Cosmides, 1996).

Naturally, individuals' option sets of friends are constrained by who values them as a friend. Competition for coalition partners, then, is partly competition for friends. Features that enable individuals to attract highly valuable friends should have been favored by selection in human history. (See DeScioli & Kurzban, 2009b, for additional perspectives on friendships.)

Evolutionary Perspectives on Additional Domains of Social Behavior

In the last section, I deliberately focused on implications of one core component of sociality evolved in the human niche to illustrate how evolution-inspired views can lead to coherent, integrative, systematic exploration of human adaptations. But evolution-inspired frameworks have generated productive research programs investigating other domains of human sociality. Space does not permit detailed description of these programs. I touch on some approaches in four broad areas—mating, kinship, norms and morality, and cultural variation.

Mating and Pair-Bonding

In any sexually reproducing species, gene-propagation into future generations crucially depends on successfully attracting mates and conceiving offspring. In human history, formation of pair-bonds has likely also been important to reproductive success. Mate selection, sexual attraction, and romantic relationships (e.g., attachment, fidelity, conflict) have been fruitfully investigated by evolution-inspired research more than any other single topic (e.g., Buss, 2008). I have repeatedly noted that, in human ancestry, individuals competed to gain favor as potential coalition partners. In most places, I perhaps should have added "and potential mates." That human mateships are important forms of coalitions, with unique qualities shaped by their special fitness implications, is an understatement. For overviews of evolutionary views of mate selection, sexual attraction, and mating in humans, see Buss (2003), Thornhill and Gangestad (2008), and chapters in Buss (2005), Crawford and Krebs (2008), and Dunbar and Barrett (2007).

Kinship

As Hamilton (1964) famously showed, genes that lead individuals to benefit kin at expense to oneself are, under specifiable conditions, favored by selection. From this perspective, it is not surprising that kin relations are very important in both traditional and modern societies (e.g., Brown, 1991) and that people are willing to make costly sacrifices for close kin (e.g., sibs), even more than close friends (Burnstein et al., 1994). In light of their special qualities, kin relations have received remarkably little attention in traditional social psychology.

As I noted earlier, a key evolution-inspired question is how individuals detect kin relatedness. Naturally, in modern societies individuals know their siblings, uncles, aunts, and so on by being told. But these labels are susceptible to manipulation and, furthermore, kin detection systems almost surely evolved prior to the evolution of language. Lieberman et al. (2007), once again, have done seminal work on evolved kin detection systems.

The significance of kin relations from an evolutionary perspective cannot be distilled simply into relatedness translates into altruism. Kin play other special roles. Because they share many mutations that are especially harmful when "doubled-up" (i.e., when both parents pass on the same mutation to an offspring) close kin are poor mates. Incest is not only frowned on culturally; people are especially disgusted by the thought of sex with close kin if exposed to putative evolved cues of kinship (Lieberman et al., 2007). Kin also have conflicts of interest, on which evolutionary theory sheds light (see Salmon & Shackelford, 2007; Buunk et al., 2008).

Norms and Morality

Universally, human cultural groups specify norms for proper behavior and sanctions against norm violations (Brown, 1991). Indeed, norms constitute an important form of human culture (and one quite distinct from the accumulation of knowledge and technologies specific to particular human groups; Hill, 2007). Norms may serve at least two social functions. Many conventions may be viewed as means of solving coordination problems: Though often arbitrary, they yield interaction efficient for all individuals, without biasing outcomes to favor some people over others. Agreement to drive on one side of the road reduces conflicts, and so too do many other social conventions. Norm formation of this sort solves coordination problems that cooperation entails. In cooperative activity, an individual's behavior must be coordinated with others' for outcomes to be achieved efficiently (e.g., Sterelny, 2007). Conventions can hence increase the net benefits of cooperative activity. Other norms, of course, yield benefits to some group members but not others, as in socially stratified societies. Once capacities to form norms to solve coordination problems arose, individuals could influence the formation of norms and thereby potentially create ones that enhanced their own success (e.g., Kaplan et al., 2005).

Moral rules, which imply right and wrong, form a special category. Wrongness is linked with the idea that transgressors "deserve" punishment. In lab experiments, people often punish wrongdoers, even at a cost to themselves (see Bowles & Gintis, 2004). As cooperation yields the possibility that an individual "steals" the fruits of others' efforts, moral condemnation may have evolved as a defense against cheating partners. Willingness to punish transgressors (even as a third party) may be desired in a coalition partner; hence, its costs could be recouped in future cooperative opportunities. As DeScioli and Kurzban (2009a) emphasize, however, any theory of the functions of moral judgment and punishment must account for their "special design": how the details of how individuals judge wrongness and the conditions under which they will pay costs to punish wrongdoers point to specific function. This topic will no doubt continue to receive much attention from evolution-inspired scholars.

Cultural Variation

Cultures obviously vary. They vary with respect to accumulated knowledge widespread among members, and with respect to the precise norms that regulate behavior (see Adams, chapter 8, this volume). These facets of cultural variation can readily be explained by an evolutionary framework that assumes, first, humans have evolved to solve many problems through innovation and technology and, second, humans have evolved capacities for regulation of efficient interaction through partly arbitrary norms (see, e.g., Richerson & Boyd, 2005). Some cultural psychologists have emphasized, however, that cultural groups differ at more fundamental levels—that the psychological processes that characterize individuals vary across human groups (e.g., Heine & Buchtel, 2009; Henrich, Heine, & Norenzayan, 2010). For instance, individuals in some Asian cultures lack the processes that bolster positive views of the self so well documented in Western cultures and, more generally, possess a concept of self markedly different from the sense of self in Western cultures (e.g., Markus & Kitayama, 1991). And East Asians may think differently in more general ways (e.g., with respect to focus on analysis of individual objects) than Westerners (e.g., Nisbett et al., 2001; Nisbett & Masuda, 2003). How do evolutionary perspectives explain these variations?

One approach explains them as outcomes of "evoked culture." As noted earlier, humans generally possess adaptive capacities to mobilize and store concentrations of melanin in skin cells in response to exposure to sunlight—to "tan." If we were to measure concentrations of melanin in skin cells across individuals, some variation would be a function of recent exposure to sunlight. The capacity to tan is evolved. Actual levels of tanning are evoked. One cannot fully understand the process whereby tanning is evoked in absence of an appreciation of the specialized evolved capacity involving transport of melanin. In a similar way, humans may possess evolved capacities for expressing particular psychological features under ecological and socioecological conditions in which, ancestrally, they were adaptive. Variation in "evoking" features ecological across human groups may, as a result, give rise to variation in psychological features (e.g., Tooby & Cosmides, 1992; Gangestad et al., 2006; Nettle, 2009).

One ecological feature that evolution-inspired work has explored is pathogen prevalence. Parasites represent threats to long-lived organisms; more than half of all species parasitize the other half (Windsor, 1998). Long-lived organisms possess immune systems that function to defend against pathogens. The human immune system is energetically very expensive. For instance, neutrophils, our most common leukocytes, live minutes to days (e.g., Lichtman et al., 2006) and, hence, turnover costs are extraordinary. Indeed, the neutrophils a person produces in one year weigh more than his or her full body weight. These costs are paid precisely because of the net benefits of defense against pathogens.

Humans also possess psychological immune systems (e.g., that producing disgust responses) that lead us to navigate the world in ways that reduce risks of infection (Tybur et al., 2009). These too are costly because, in reducing risks, we also miss opportunities. Moreover, they may activate costly physiological responses. (Mere exposure to pictures of infected faces leads to physiological increases in inflammatory immune reactions; Schaller et al., 2010.) Hence, selection may have favored both physiological and psychological immune systems to be sensitive to the risks of parasitic infection, such as pathogen prevalence. Worldwide, a variety of psychological features vary as a function of parasite prevalence (contemporary or historical). Regions characterized by greater risk of parasitic infection, compared to ones with little parasitic risk, tend to be more collectivistic and ethnocentric in nature (e.g., Fincher et al., 2008), tendencies that may function to avoid exposure to outgroup members' pathogens to which ingroup members are not adapted (see also Nettle, 2009, and references therein). (For an alternative view of ecocultural influences on collectivism and associated thought patterns also consistent with the evoked culture framework, see Uskal et al., 2008.)

Individual Differences in Evolutionary Perspective

An integrative personality and social psychology must address variation across individuals' behavioral responses to apparently similar circumstances. Optimally, it does so using the same principles used to explain general tendencies in individuals' behavior, rather invoking special theories or forces to explain individual differences. (For an early statement of this perspective, see Lewin, 1931.) Evolutionary perspectives do so, using both selection-based thinking about social strategies and evolutionary genetics.

Most individual differences arise from one of several possibilities (see also Buss, 2009b). First, individual differences are adaptive but vary due to variation in individuals' circumstances. If individuals pursue a strategy for maximizing net fitness returns, and best strategy depends on circumstances, selection may lead individuals' behavioral tendencies to vary by circumstances. Second, individual differences are adaptive because selection favors certain nontypical behavioral strategies when they are rare, but disfavors them when they become common. Selection has therefore maintained a mix of behavioral tendencies in the population. Third, some variants are maladaptive. A number of distinct evolutionary processes lead to and maintain variation in fitness. Fourth, a special case mixes the first and third possibilities. Some variants in the population may be disposed to be less successful than others. But individuals who are disadvantaged respond in ways that optimize their outcomes, given their condition.

Adaptive Contingent Variation

AN ILLUSTRATION: VARIATIONS ACROSS INDIVIDUALS IN HOW THEY BUILD SOCIAL SPHERES

Social spheres, once again, reflect opportunities and risks represented by individuals' potential social interactants, and vary on multiple dimensions, for example, size and mean reciprocity potential of partners. Social sphere size and reciprocity potential trade off; expanding number of partners and building trust with specific partners both require time and energy, which are limited. Different individuals may maximize their net social capital by making this trade-off differently.

Consider, for instance, a high capacity person who gains much by participating in opportunistic coalitions with other high capacity individuals. This person may maximize social capital by expanding social networks at the expense of trustworthiness of their partnerships. A low capacity individual with few opportunities to reap benefits through opportunistic coalitions may, by contrast, maximize social capital by investing in relationships' trustworthiness and durability (Vigil, 2009). Two individuals with the same choices, then, are best off making different choices, given their individual circumstances and social affordances. This example illustrates adaptive variation in behavioral tendencies (see also Krebs & Davies, 1993; Buss & Greiling, 1999).

VARIATIONS IN SELF-MONITORING: ADAPTIVE VARIATIONS IN STRATEGIES FOR BUILDING SOCIAL SPHERES?

Self-monitoring refers to efforts to control expressive behavior in response to situational demands, a form of impression management (Snyder, 1974). Individuals high in self-monitoring (Snyder, 1974; Snyder & Gangestad, 1986) are able and willing to control their expressive behavior and may hence appear to possess different attitudes, interests, and views across social settings. Individuals low in self-monitoring are either unable or unwilling to do so, and tend to appear to "be the same person" across social settings (for a review, see Snyder, 1987).

The social worlds of individuals of high and low self-monitoring differ. The consummate high self-monitoring individual appears to pursue a large social sphere offering many coalitional opportunities, at the expense of investing heavily in a few relationships (e.g., Snyder et al., 1983). The consummate low self-monitoring individual invests in a few durable relationships, at the expense of a large social sphere (Snyder et al., 1983; Snyder & Simpson, 1984; Omoyat et al., 2010). Variations in social spheres, then, appear to be linked with variations in impression management strategies. The latter may well be adaptive components to social strategies. Ability to opportunistically enter coalitions of many kinds requires being able to express the interests and aims of a wide variety of potential coalition partners. By contrast, trust-building demands consistency, predictability, and, being who one appears to be.

Self-monitoring relates to social motivations as well. High self-monitoring individuals care about status and "getting ahead" (Gangestad & Snyder, 2000), and partly through associations with high status individuals. Low self-monitoring individuals care about trust and reliability in social partners. These social motivations too are consistent with high and low self-monitoring embodying different strategies to build social capital. A critical question is why: How do the circumstances of high and low self-monitoring individuals differ, leading them to adaptively pursue different social strategies? Future research may address whether it has to do with differences in overall competencies (a scenario described earlier) or differences in the kinds of competencies that high and low self-monitors possess, leading to differences in social strategies, or some other possibility. (For other possible illustrations of adaptive variations, see Figueredo et al., 2001; Ellis et al., 2009; Watve & Yajnik, 2007.)

Negative Frequency-Dependent Selection

Frequency-dependent selection occurs when the success of a genetic variant depends on its frequency in the population (e.g., Crow, 1986). Genes in the major histocompatibility complex (MHC) are examples. They code for cell-surface markers that the immune system uses to recognize self-cells and, hence, foreign entities such as pathogens. Because foreign pathogens may be adapted to genetic variants they frequently encounter, genetic variants are favored when rare, all else equal. Partly as a result, scores of possible genetic variants exist at human MHC loci, most rare (Hedrick, 1998). Equilibrium exists when each genetic variant exists at a frequency at which it selected to be neither more or less common.

Frequency-dependent selection may operate on social strategies. Mealey (1995) proposed that rare psychopathy can be maintained in the population. When psychopaths are common, others are on the lookout for them. When they are absent, others never suspect them. Selection could hence maintain genetic variants predisposing psychopathy at low levels. Nettle (2006) argued that, more generally, genetic variation in Big Five personality traits are partly maintained by frequency-dependent selection (see also Penke et al., 2007). Genes that predispose particular specialized skills could, in theory, similarly be subject to frequency-dependent selection. A small number of individuals in a group with, say, highly developed spatial skills (perhaps at the expense of other abilities) could be valued (Wilson, 1994, 1998).

Variations in Fitness

Why, in natural populations of animals, are some individuals better fit to their circumstances than others? If selection favors those who are fit, why does any variation in fitness persist? A number of processes can lead to variations in fitness.

First, even two genetically identical individuals exposed to different environments may vary in fitness: Variations in nutritional status of the mother during gestation, nutritional status during development, exposure to toxins pre- and postnatally, history of infection during development, differences in social support available, and so on can affect fitness.

Second, deleterious mutation is common. On average, individuals probably possess hundreds of slightly deleterious mutations—rare genetic variants that ultimately will be selected out of the population. Most all of these were inherited from parents. When only slightly deleterious, mutations can persist for many generations before being eliminated. (Individuals have only a few new mutations, on average; Keightley & Charlesworth, 2005). At equilibrium, mutational effects on fitness enter the population at the same rate as they are removed by selection, a state of "mutation-selection balance." At this equilibrium level, individuals do not possess the same number of mutations; a substantial amount of variation in fitness due to differences in levels of mutations is maintained. Mutation is probably the single biggest reason for genetic variation in fitness (Lynch et al., 1999).

Third, selection may vary spatially across the range of the population. Trait levels favored at one end of the range may differ from those favored at the other end. Through migration and mating, however, genetic variants selected at one end occasionally make their way from one end to the other end. Though favored where they were selected, these variants are disfavored elsewhere. As a result, individuals vary in fitness due to genetic factors.

Fourth, variation can similarly be maintained when selection varies temporally. Genetic variants favored at one time remain in the population for some time after selection no longer favors them. As a result, at any given time individuals vary in fitness.

Fifth, genetic variants may be favored in combination with certain other genes, but disfavored in combination with other genes. These effects are referred to as epistatic effects on fitness (or, when gene combinations occur at a single locus, dominance effects). One form is sexually antagonistic selection. On certain dimensions, trait levels favored in males and females differ. (Examples might be circulating levels of testosterone and estrogen, which may have masculinizing and feminizing effects on physical features, respectively.) A gene affecting these levels could, in theory, be favored when in males but disfavored when in females, or vice versa. Net selection could be very weak, and genetic variants of this sort could accumulate. If so, males will, on average, be less than optimally masculine and females less than optimally feminine. Moreover, individuals within each sex will vary on these qualities and, hence, fitness.

What Accounts for Genetic Variation in Personality?

As reviewed in Bouchard and Loehlin (2001), about 50% of the variance in personality traits, on average, is associated with genetic variations. Which evolutionary process likely explains this genetic variation in personality? Cases have been made for each. Penke et al. (2007) and Nettle (2006) argued for mixtures of temporally varying, spatially varying, and frequency-dependent selection. Nettle (2006), for instance, noted that many personality variations reflect trade-offs in ways of doing tasks. The bold, impulsive person risks getting into fitness-compromising situations (e.g., being face-to-face with a predator), whereas the cautious individual risks missing out on opportunities. The precise balance favored may depend on particular environmental features (e.g., density of predators), which may vary spatially and temporally. At any given point in time and space, then, personality variations may be found. Selection for specialization may furthermore select for variation in personality.

Cross-national surveys do reveal some differences in Big Five personality traits. In one study (Schmitt et al., 2009), East Asians (Hong Kong, Japan, Korea, Taiwan) had the lowest levels of agreeableness, conscientiousness, openness, and extraversion, and the highest levels of neuroticism. Nonetheless, regional differences were small, with mean percentage of variance accounted just 3%. Small island and mainland Italian populations differ in Big Five traits—but differences explain, on average, less than 1% of the variance (Camperio Ciani et al., 2007). The vast majority of personality variation is within-culture, not between-culture (which is not to deny important variations in psychological features across groups; e.g., Heine & Buchtel, 2009).

Penke et al. (2007) argue that signatures of the genetic effects on personality point to temporally varying, spatially varying, and frequency-dependent selection, as opposed to effects of mutations. Large effects of fairly common genetic variants, for instance, aren't likely due to a build-up of deleterious mutations. In fact, however, evidence for these signatures is scant. For instance, using a genome-wide scan, Shifman et al. (2007) failed to find any loci accounting for >1% of the variance in neuroticism, and concluded, "the heritability of neuroticism probably arises from loci each explaining much less than 1%" (p. 302). (See also Gangestad, 2011.)

That slightly deleterious mutations explain much variation in personality, then, cannot be ruled out. If so, it seems likely that personality has been subject to stabilizing selection, which occurs when a trait value close to the mean is favored, and extreme values are disfavored. Mutations affecting the trait exist at mutation-selection balance, which means that some individuals at extremes on the trait are (in ancestral conditions) less fit (see, for instance, Bouchard & Loehlin, 2001; McDonald, 1995). Clearly, however, more research is needed before the processes that maintain variation in personality are fully identified (Buss, 2009b).

Making the Best of a Bad Job

As noted earlier, one model of individual differences reflects a combination of models. Suppose individuals differ in certain features affecting their competitive abilities due to variation in environmental events (e.g., conditions affecting early development)

or genetic factors (e.g., mutations). For instance, individuals differ in their physical prowess, intellectual abilities, or physical attractiveness due to these processes (e.g., Gangestad et al., 2010). The social worlds of individuals with disfavored traits have fewer social opportunities than those advantaged. As a result, their optimal choices differ from the optimal choices of those who are advantaged. In the terms of behavioral ecologists, they "make the best of a bad job" (e.g., Krebs & Davies, 1993).

Suppose, for instance, variation in individuals' size and strength leads to variation in ability to physically dominate others. It doesn't pay weaker individuals to challenge stronger ones. Various submissive displays function to communicate to dominant individuals that the signaler poses no threat (de Waal, 1989). Submissiveness, in this scenario, reflects an adaptive strategy for someone disadvantaged. The submissive individual makes the best of a bad job.

Some personality variations may be of this sort. Consider once again variations in individuals' approach to their social worlds I discussed earlier. Individuals of high capacity (or able to attract high capacity coalition partners) may be best off building large social networks, whereas individuals less able to attract high capacity partners may be best off investing in trust in a smaller sphere of social partners. But what leads to variation in ability to attract high capacity partners in the first place? In theory, individuals investing in small spheres of social partners could be making the best of a bad job. This is merely a hypothesis, but one leading to testable predictions. For instance, it suggests that individuals able to attract diverse social networks are prone to be healthier, age more slowly, and live longer in general. In fact, research supports these links, though their causes remains unknown (e.g., Cohen & Janicki-Deverts, 2009). Alternative evolution-minded hypotheses are possible and testable.

Why the Big Five?

A well-known finding in personality psychology is that variance on most any self- or peer-reported measure shares at least moderate variance with one or more of five dimensions, the Big Five: surgency, agreeableness, conscientiousness, openness, and emotional stability (see Fleeson, chapter 3, this volume). From an evolutionary perspective, why these dimensions?

As Buss (1991) noted, one reason lies with *perceivers*: people have been selected to discriminate other people on these dimensions. Once again,

I harken back to the idea that humans harness other individuals' competencies in fitness-enhancing ways. Selection should have favored displays of features valued in coalition partners, but also dispositions to evaluate others' propensities to be good coalition partners. Surgency and openness to experience (which some refer to as intellect; e.g., Digman, 1997) may affect capacity. Emotional stability and conscientiousness may affect trustworthiness. Agreeableness reflects individuals' desire to be compatible coalition partners. In fact, small to moderate correlations between the five mean that an even bigger two can be distilled: one dimension defined by surgency and openness and hence reflective of engagement, the other dimension defined by conscientousness, agreeableness, and emotional stability and reflective of restraint (e.g., Digman, 1997; DeYoung, 2006; Hirsch et al., 2009.) As Digman (1998) notes, these higher-order factors define two-factor personality systems, for example, power and intimacy, status and peer-popularity, agency and communion—or, in terms discussed earlier, capacity and trustworthiness/compatibility.

This reason, however, can only partly explain the Big Five and its reduction to an even bigger two. Why are there five dimensions? Why not more, or fewer? In theory, for instance, it would be possible that individuals who are most surgent would also be the most emotionally stable, such that these two dimensions would not be largely independent. The fact that they *are* two distinct dimensions must say something about the distribution of qualities found in people *in the world*, and not merely a function of *perceiver* qualities. And why do the five dimensions covary weakly to moderately in the way they do?

The distribution of qualities found in the world must have something to do with the nature of psychological processes that generate behavior in actors. I consider two nonmutually exclusive possibilities. First, it may be a function of the physiological structures regulating behavior that could be altered to produce variability. A car's brake system has nothing to do with the engine and, hence, variation in brake performance is largely independent of engine performance. Similarly, personality researchers have argued that neural systems responsible for positive affect (pertaining to surgency) are different from those responsible for negative affect (pertaining to emotional stability). As these systems evolved or develop through distinct processes (e.g., different genes regulate their development and performance), variation in the "performance" of these systems is largely independent, leading the two personality

dimensions to be largely independent (e.g. Watson et al., 1999; also DeYoung, 2006; Hirsch et al., 2009).

Second, the distribution of qualities found in the world may be a function of the adaptive social strategies available to people. Certain sets of traits make for adaptive constellations of traits. Others don't. This point was illustrated with self-monitoring: Clusters of high self-monitoring and low self-monitoring tendencies work together. The distribution of individuals found in the five-factor space (and the weak to moderate correlations between these factors) may partly reflect the space of adaptive options available to people. For instance, one reason emotional stability positively covaries with conscientious may be that both promote trustworthiness. Strategically, if one invests in one, it may also pay to invest in the other.

Reflections

In this final section, I offer reflections: Thoughts about how evolutionary perspectives can contribute to the integrative personality and social psychology that lies in the future.

An evolutionary perspective intrinsically emphasizes integration. It steadfastly attempts to understand human behavior in light of principles and theories that not only explain social and personality psychology within a common framework, but also offers explanation of other aspects of the biological world (e.g., the behavior of nonhuman animals, nonpsychological phenomena such as life histories, energetic trade-offs, and so on). As noted in discussion of individual differences, evolutionary perspectives do not invoke new theories and principles to explain them; their explanation must appeal to explanations with the same grounding as explanations of social behavior more generally. More generally, evolutionary perspectives seek to understand through appeal to general principles social psychological phenomena that are often explained by highly local theories. Hence, for instance, evolutionary psychology does not explain behavior within "communal" relationships or friendships in terms of special rules that apply to them; rather, they explain it within a broader framework that specifies how patterns of behavior specific to friendships can arise out of more general evolved features. At the same time, evolutionary perspectives demand recognition that some kinds of relationships are fundamentally different in character, in light of special features that can *only* be appreciated through evolutionary principles (e.g., mateship, kinship).

This feature of evolutionary perspectives offers both opportunities and challenges. As observed at the outset, today's evolutionary psychology does not represent the first broad approach in psychology inspired by Darwinian theory. An ambitious program of evolution-inspired functionalism arose in the late 1800s—and diffused within two decades. It did so because evolutionary biology had not yet offered specific, well-formulated, well-established, highly integrative metatheories, theories, and methodologies. Darwin's theory inspired scientific passion, but in abstract ways that did not translate into concrete, critically derived theory. Evolutionary biology now does offer highly developed theories and methodologies. If today's evolutionary psychology is to avoid the fate of last century's functionalism, however, it must remain inspired by this theory. Much of the broadly integrative, generative features of evolution-inspired theories of human sociality derive from their being informed by specific theories in evolutionary biology (e.g., fitness cost-benefit analysis, life history theory, signaling theory, evolutionary genetics). Evolutionary psychologists should be "cheek by jowl" with biologists not only in spirit, but also in their sophisticated appreciation of evolutionary biological theory. This presents challenges to a new breed of functionalists: They must be familiar with broad landscapes of evolutionary theory as well as social and personality psychology.

Evolutionary perspectives demand an appreciation of anthropological theory too. I emphasized the need to understand unique components of human behavior in the context of the ecological niche that ancestral humans created and evolved within. Organisms must "make a living" in a context in which other organisms are selected to do so as well. How they are selected to do so in better ways importantly informs our understanding of adaptation. Humans, it appears, have constructed a niche quite different from that of ancestors shared with our closest living ancestors. While the theory I discuss may not fully identify that niche, future efforts should attend to it. Relatedly, human sociality must be understood in a broader context of evolution-informed human functioning, both in psychological and nonpsychological domains (e.g., life history, physical growth, endocrinology, immunology, energy utilization). Functional analysis of these domains can inform functional analyses of behavior.

Perhaps the most fundamental implication of an evolutionary perspective on human sociality and personality is a frame shift. Traditional approaches to personality and social psychology sometimes contrast social and cultural influences with biological influences on behavior. From an evolutionary perspective, it makes no sense to do so. "Biological" simply means, "pertaining to life forms," no more and no less. As nothing on Earth has "social" features aside from life forms, social features are *inherently* biological. Physiology, endocrinology, immunology, and neurology are too but, by definition, no more and no less than sociality. From an evolutionary perspective, then, the sociality of an organism is to be understood in the context of its more general functioning in the biological world, no differently from how this approach would ultimately attempt to understand an organism's physiological features. Once appreciated, this viewpoint leads one to see the theoretical and methodological tools that evolutionary biology has to offer not as alternatives to constructing "social" or "cultural" understandings of human behavior. Rather, evolutionary perspectives offer means by which to construct a personality and social psychology that, at its foundations, is integrative.

As already noted, however, evolutionary biology fundamentally addresses causal processes—those involved in evolution or ultimate causes—that operate at a level different from than those addressed by psychology, proximate causes of behavior. The value of evolutionary theorizing to psychology, then, does not lie in it offering an array of new causal processes involved in psychological processes per se. Rather, as emphasized repeatedly in this chapter, evolutionary theorizing has value to psychology in the context of theory development and discovery of psychological process. Evolution-minded thinking can lead researchers to identify phenomena one would never think to investigate in the absence of explicit evolutionary theory. Though evolution-minded approaches have offered valuable insights to date, vast domains of human social behavior remain unexplored through this approach. For this reason too, then, evolutionary approaches offer opportunities and challenges to an integrative personality and social psychology.

Acknowledgment

Rachael Falcon provided extensive commentary and offered a number of very helpful insights and suggestions.

References

Andrews, P. W. (2001). The psychology of social chess and the evolution of attribution mechanisms: Explaining the fundamental attribution error. *Evolution and Human Behavior, 22,* 11–29.

Andrews, P. A., Gangestad, S. W., & Matthews, D. (2002). Adaptationism—How to carry out an exaptationist program. *Behavioral and Brain Sciences, 25,* 489–504.

Angell, J. R. (1907). The province of functional psychology. *Psychological Review, 14,* 61–91.

Barrett, H. C., & Kurzban, R. (2006). Modularity in cognition: Framing the debate. *Psychological Review, 113,* 628–647.

Baumeister, R. F., Maner, J. K., & DeWall, C. N. (2006). Evoked culture and evoked nature: Coevolution and the emergence of cultural animals. *Psychological Inquiry, 17,* 128–130.

Beach, S. R., & Tesser, A. (2000). Self-evaluation maintenance and evolution: Some speculative notes. In J. M. Suls & L. Wheeler (Eds.), *Handbook of social comparison: Theory and research* (pp. 123–140). New York: Plenum.

Begun, D. R. (2003). Planet of the apes. *Scientific American, 289,* 74–83.

Bowles, S., & Gintis, H. (2004). The evolution of strong reciprocity: Cooperation in heterogeneous populations. *Theoretical Population Biology, 65,* 17–28.

Bouchard, T. J., Jr., & Loehlin, J. C. (2001). Genes, evolution, and personality. *Behavior Genetics, 31,* 243–273.

Brewer, M. B. (1999). The psychology of prejudice: In-group love or out-group hate? *Journal of Social Issues, 55,* 429–444.

Brewer, M. B. (2007). The importance of being "We": Human nature and intergroup relations. *American Psychologist, 62,* 728–738.

Brown, D. E. (1991). *Human universals.* New York: McGraw-Hill.

Buller D. J. (2005). *Adapting minds: Evolutionary psychology and the persistent quest for human nature.* Cambridge, MA: MIT Press.

Burnstein, E., Crandall, C., & Kitayama, S. (1994). Some neo-Darwinian decision rules for altruism: Weighting cues for inclusive fitness as a function of the biological importance of the decision. *Journal of Personality and Social Psychology, 67,* 773–789.

Buss, D. M. (1991). Evolutionary personality psychology. *Annual Review of Psychology, 42,* 459–491.

Buss, D. M. (2003). *The evolution of desire* (Rev. ed.). New York: Basic Books.

Buss, D. M. (2005). *The handbook of evolutionary psychology.* Hoboken, NJ: Wiley.

Buss, D. M. (2008). *Evolutionary psychology: The new science of the mind* (3rd ed.). Boston: Allyn & Bacon.

Buss, D. M. (2009a). Adaptive problems define situations: An evolutionary approach to person-situation interactions. *Journal of Research in Personality, 43,* 241–242.

Buss, D. M. (2009b). How can evolutionary psychology successfully explain personality and individual differences? *Perspectives in Psychological Science, 4,* 359–366.

Buss, D. M. & Greiling, H. (1999). Adaptive personality differences. *Journal of Personality, 67,* 209–243.

Buss, D. M., & Kenrick, D. T. (1998). Evolutionary social psychology. In D. T. Gilbert, S. T. Fiske, & G. Lindzey (Eds.), *Handbook of social psychology* (4th ed., pp. 982–1026). New York: McGraw-Hill.

Buss, D. M., & Reeve, H. K. (2003). Evolutionary psychology and developmental dynamics: Comment on Lickliter and Honeycutt (2003). *Psychological Bulletin, 129,* 848–853.

Buunk, A. P., Park, J. H., & Dubbs, S. L. (2008). Parent-offspring conflict in mate preferences. *Review of General Psychology, 12,* 47–62.

Camperio Ciani, A. S., Capiluppi, C., Veronese, A., & Sartori, G. (2007). The adaptive value of personality differences revealed by small island population dynamics. *European Journal of Personality, 21,* 3–22.

Clark, M. S., & Mills, J. (1993). The difference between communal and exchange relationships: What it is and is not. *Personality and Social Psychology Bulletin, 19,* 684–691.

Cohen, S., & Janicki-Deverts, D. (2009). Can we improve our physical health by altering our social networks? *Perspectives on Psychological Science, 4,* 375–378.

Confers, J. C., Easton, J. A., Fleishman, D. S., Goetz, C. D., Lewis, D. M. G., Perilloux, C., et al. (2010). Evolutionary psychology: Controversies, questions, prospects, and limitations. *American Psychologist, 65,* 110–126.

Crawford, C. & Krebs, D (Eds.). (2008). *Foundations of evolutionary psychology.* Hillsdale, NJ: Erlbaum.

Crow, J. F. (1986). *Basic concepts in population, quantitative, and evolutionary genetics.* New York: Freeman.

Darwin, C. (1859). *On the origin of species.* London: John Murray.

Darwin, C. (1872). *The expression of emotion in man and animals.* London: John Murray.

de Waal, F. (1989). *Peacemaking among primates.* Cambridge, MA: Harvard University Press.

DeYoung, C. G. (2006). Higher-order factors of the Big Five in a multi-informant sample. *Journal of Personality and Social Psychology, 91,* 1138–1151.

Dewey, J. (1896). The reflex arc concept in psychology. *Psychological Review, 3,* 357–370.

DeScioli, P., & Kurzban, R. (2009a). Mysteries of morality. *Cognition, 112,* 281–299.

DeScioli, P., & Kurzban, R. (2009b). The alliance hypothesis for human friendship. *PLoS ONE, 4,* e5802.

Digman, J. M. (1997). Higher-order factors of the Big Five. *Journal of Personality and Social Psychology, 73,* 1246–1256.

Dovidio, J. F., Kawakami, K., Johnson, C., Johnson, B., & Howard, A. (1997). On the nature of prejudice: Automatic and controlled processes. *Journal of Experimental Social Psychology, 33,* 510–540.

Dunbar, R. I. M. (1998). The social brain hypothesis. *Evolutionary Anthropology, 6,* 178–190.

Dunbar, R. I. M., & Barrett, L. (Eds.). (2007). *Oxford handbook of evolutionary psychology.* Oxford, UK: Oxford University Press.

Dunbar, R. I. M., & Shultz, S. (2007). Evolution in the social brain. *Science, 317,* 1344–1347.

Eagly, A. H., & Wood, W. (2006). Three ways that data can misinform: Inappropriate partialling, small samples, and anyway, they're not playing our song. *Psychological Inquiry, 17,* 131–137.

Eastwick, P. W. (2009). Beyond the Pleistocene: Using phylogeny and constraint to inform the evolutionary psychology of human mating. *Psychological Bulletin, 135,* 794–821.

Ekman, P. (1980). *Face of man.* New York: Garland STPM.

Eldridge, N. (1995). *Reinventing Darwin.* New York: Wiley.

Ellis, B. J., Figueredo, A. J., Brunbach, B. H., & Schlomer, G. L. (2009). Fundamental dimensions of environmental risk. *Human Nature, 20,* 204–268.

Elton, C. S. (1927). *Animal ecology.* London: Sidgwick and Jackson.

Figueredo, A. J., Corral-Verdugo, V., Frias-Armenta, M., Bachar, K. J., White, J., McNeill, P. L., et al. (2001). Blood, solidarity, status, and honor: The sexual balance of power and spousal abuse in Sonora, Mexico. *Evolution and Human Behavior, 22,* 295–328.

Fincher, C. L., Thornhill, R., Murray, D. R., & Schaller, M. (2008). Pathogen prevalence predicts human cross-cultural variability in individualism/collectivism. *Proceedings of the Royal Society B, 275,* 1279–1285.

Fisher, R. A. (1918). The correlation between relatives based on the supposition of Mendelian inheritance. *Transactions of the Royal Society of Edinburgh, 52,* 399–433.

Fisher, R. A. (1958). *The genetical theory of natural selection.* New York: Oxford University Press.

Fiske, S. T., Cuddy, A. J. C., & Glick, P. (2007). Universal dimensions of social cognition: Warmth and competence. *Trends in Cognitive Science, 11,* 77–83.

Fiske, S. T., Cuddy, A. J. C., Glick, P., & Xu, J. (2002). A model of (often mixed) stereotype content: Competence and warmth follow respectively from perceived status and competition. *Journal of Personality and Social Psychology, 82,* 878–902.

Flinn, M. V., Geary, D. C., & Ward, C. V. (2005). Ecological dominance, social competition, and coalitionary arms races: Why humans evolved extraordinary intelligence. *Evolution and Human Behavior, 26,* 10–46.

Fraley, R. C., Brumbaugh, C. C., & Marks, M. J. (2005). The evolution and function of adult attachment: A comparative and phylogenetic analysis. *Journal of Personality and Social Psychology, 89,* 731–746.

Frank, R. (1985). *Choosing the right pond: Human behavior and the quest for status.* New York: Oxford University Press.

Funder, D. C. (Ed.). (1999). *Personality judgment: A realistic approach to person perception.* New York: Academic.

Gangestad, S. W. (2008). Biological adaptation and human behavior. In C. Crawford & D. Krebs (Eds.), *Foundations of evolutionary psychology.* (pp. 153–173) Hillsdale, NJ: Erlbaum.

Gangestad, S. W. (2011). Evolutionary processes explaining the genetic variance in personality: An exploration of scenarios. In D. M. Buss & P. Hawley (Eds.), *The evolution of personality and individual differences.* (pp. 376–399) New York: Oxford University Press.

Gangestad, S. W., & Buss, D. M. (1993). Pathogen prevalence and human mate preferences. *Ethology and Sociobiology, 14,* 89–96.

Gangestad, S. W., Haselton, M. G., & Buss, D. M. (2006). Evolutionary foundations of cultural variation: Evoked culture and mate preferences. *Psychological Inquiry, 17,* 75–95.

Gangestad, S. W., Merriman, L., & Emery Thompson, M. (2010). Men's oxidative stress, developmental instability, and physical attractiveness. Manuscript submitted for publication.

Gangestad, S. W., & Snyder, M. (2000). Self-monitoring: Appraisal and reappraisal. *Psychological Bulletin, 126,* 530–555.

Gangestad, S. W., & Thornhill, R. (2007). The evolution of social inference processes: The importance of signaling theory. In J. P. Forgas, M. G. Haselton, & W. von Hippel (Eds.), *Evolutionary psychology and social cognition.* (pp. 33–48) New York: Psychology Press.

Geary, D. C., Byrd-Craven, J., Hoard, M. K., Vigil, J., & Numtee, C. (2003). Evolution and development of boys' social behavior. *Developmental Review, 23,* 444–470.

Gibson, J. J. (1979). *The ecological approach to visual perception.* Boston: Houghton Mifflin.

Gintis, H. (2000). Strong reciprocity and human sociality. *Journal of Theoretical Biology, 206,* 169–179.

Godfrey-Smith, P. (1993). Functions: Consensus without unity. *Pacific Philosophical Quarterly, 74,* 196–208.

Goffman, E. (1959). *The presentation of self in everyday life.* New York: Anchor.

Gosling, S. D., & Graybeal, A. (2007). Tree thinking: A new paradigm for integrating comparative data in psychology. *Journal of General Psychology, 134,* 259–277.

Gould, S. J., & Lewontin, R. C. (1979). The spandrels of San Marco and the panglossian paradigm: A critique of the adaptationist programme. *Proceedings of the Royal Society: Series B, 205,* 581–598.

Gould, S. J., & Vrba, E. S. (1982) Exaptation: A missing term in the science of form. *Paleobiology, 8,* 4–15.

Griskevicius, V., Tybur, J. M., Gangestad, S. W., Perea, E. F., Shapiro, J. R., & Kenrick, D. T. (2009). Aggress to impress: Hostility as an evolved context-dependent strategy. *Journal of Personality and Social Psychology, 96,* 980–994.

Gurven, M. (2004). To give or not to give: The behavioral ecology of human food transfers. *Behavioral and Brain Sciences, 27,* 543–583.

Gurven, M., & Hill, K. (2009). Why do men hunt? A reevaluation of "man the hunter" and the sexual division of labor. *Current Anthropology, 50,* 51–74.

Haig, D. (1993). Genetic conflicts in human pregnancy. *Quarterly Review of Biology, 68,* 495–532.

Haldane, J. B. S. (1932). *The causes of evolution.* New York: Harper.

Hamilton, W. D. (1964). The genetical evolution of social behaviour: I, II. *Journal of Theoretical Biology, 7,* 1–52.

Hawkes, K. (2004). Mating, parenting, and the evolution of human pairbonds. In B. Chapais & C. M. Berman (Eds.), *Kinship and behavior in primates* (pp. 443–473). Oxford, UK: Oxford University Press.

Hedrick, P. W. (1998). Balancing selection and the MHC. *Genetica, 104,* 207–214.

Heider, F. (1958). *The psychology of interpersonal relations.* New York: Wiley.

Heine, S. J., & Buchtel, E. E. (2009). Personality: The universal ad the culturally specific. *Annual Review of Personality, 60,* 369–394.

Henrich, J., & Gil-White, F. (2001). The evolution of prestige: Freely conferred deference as a mechanism for enhancing the benefits of cultural transmission. *Evolution and Human Behavior, 22,* 165–196.

Henrich, J., Heine, S. J., & Norenzayan, A. (2010). The weirdest people in the world? *Behavioral and Brain Sciences, 33,* 61–83.

Hill, K. (2007). Evolutionary biology, cognitive adaptations, and human culture. In S. W. Gangestad & J. A. Simpson (Eds.), *The evolution of mind: Fundamental questions and controversies* (pp. 348–356). New York: Guilford.

Hill, S. E., & Buss, D. M. (2006). Envy and positional bias in the evolutionary psychology of management. *Managerial and Decision Economics, 27,* 131–143.

Hirsch, J. B., DeYoung, C. G., & Peterson, J. B. (2009). Metatraits of the Big Five differentially predict engagement and restraint of behavior. *Journal of Personality, 77,* 1085–1102.

Hull, C. L. (1937). Mind, mechanism, and adaptive behavior. *Psychological Review, 44,* 1–32.

Hull, C. L. (1943). *Principles of behavior.* New York: Appleton-Century-Crofts.

Humphrey, N. K. (1976). The social function of intellect. In P. P. G. Bateson & R. A. Hinde (Eds.), *Growing points in ethology* (pp. 303–317). Cambridge, UK: Cambridge University Press.

Hutchinson, G. E. (1965). *The ecological theater and the evolutionary play*. New Haven, CT: Yale University Press.

James, W. (1890). *Principles of psychology*. New York: Holt.

James, W. (1904). The Chicago school. *Psychological Bulletin, 1,* 1–5.

Kaplan, H. S., Gangestad, S. W., Gurven, M., Lancaster, J., Mueller, T., & Robson, A. (2007). The evolution of diet, brain, and life history among primates and humans. In W. Roebroeks (Ed.), *Brains, guts, food, and the social life of early hominins* (pp. 47–90). Leiden, Netherlands: Leiden University Press.

Kaplan, H., Gurven, M., Hill, K. & Hurtado, A. M. (2005). The natural history of human food sharing and cooperation: A review and a new multi-individual approach to the negotiation of norms. In S. Bowles, R. Boyd, E. Fehr & H. Gintis (Eds.)., *The moral sentiments and material interests: The foundations of cooperation in economic life.* (pp. 75–113) Cambridge, MA: MIT Press.

Kaplan, H. S., Gurven, M., & Lancaster, J. B. (2007). Brain evolution and the human adaptive complex. In S. W. Gangestad & J. A. Simpson (Eds.), *The evolution of mind: Fundamental questions and controversies* (pp. 259–269). New York: Guilford.

Kaplan, H., Hill, K., Lancaster, J., & Hurtado, A. M. (2000). A theory of human life history evolution: Diet, intelligence, and longevity. *Evolutionary Anthropology, 9,* 156–185.

Kaplan, H., Lancaster, J., & Robson, A. J. (2003). Embodied capital and the evolutionary economics of the human life span. *Population and Development Review, 29,* 152–182.

Keightley, P. D., & Charlesworth, B. (2005). Genetic instability of *C. elegans* comes naturally. *Trends in Genetics, 21,* 67–70.

Kokko, H., Jennions, M. D., & Brooks, R. (2006). Unifying and testing models of sexual selection. *Annual Review of Ecology, Evolution and Systematics, 37,* 43–66.

Kokko, H. & Ots, I. (2006). When not to avoid inbreeding. *Evolution, 60,* 467–475.

Krebs, J. R., & Davies, N. B. (1993). *An introduction of behavioural ecology* (3rd ed.). Oxford, UK: Blackwell.

Kurzban, R., & Aktipis, C. A. (2007). On detecting the footprints of multilevel selection in humans. In S. W. Gangestad & J. A. Simpson (Eds.), *The evolution of mind: Fundamental questions and controversies* (pp. 226–232). New York: Guilford.

Kurzban, R., Rigdon, M. L., & Wilson, B. J. (2008). Incremental approaches to establishing trust. *Experimental Economics, 11,* 370–389.

Kurzban, R., Tooby, J., & Cosmides, L. (2001). Can race be erased? Coalitional computation and social categorization. *Proceedings of the National Academy of Sciences, USA, 98,* 15387–15392.

Lehmann, L., & Keller, L. (2006). The evolution of cooperation and altruism: A general framework and a classification of models. *Journal of Evolutionary Biology, 19,* 1365–1376.

Levin, S., & Sidanius, J. (1999). Social dominance and social identity in the United States and Israel: Ingroup favoritism or outgroup derogation? *Political Psychology, 20,* 99–126.

Lewin, K. (1931). The conflict between the Aristotelian and Galileian modes of thought in contemporary psychology. *Journal of General Psychology, 5,* 141–177.

Lewontin, R. C. (1982). Organism and environment. In H. C. Plotkin (Ed.), *Learning, development, and culture* (pp. 151–170). New York: Wiley.

Lewontin, R. C. (1983) Gene, organism and environment. In D. S. Bendall (Ed.), *Evolution from molecules to men.* (pp. 273–285) Cambridge, UK: Cambridge University Press.

Lewontin, R. C. (1985). Adaptation. In R. Levin & R. C. Lewontin (Eds.), *The dialectical biologist* (pp. 65–84). Cambridge, MA: Harvard University Press.

Lichtman, M., Beutler, E., Kaushansky, K., Kipps, T., Seligsohn, U, & Prchal, J. (2006). *Williams hematology* (7th ed.). New York: McGraw-Hill.

Lickliter, R., & Honeycutt, H. (2003). Developmental dynamics: Toward a biologically plausible evolutionary psychology. *Psychological Bulletin, 129,* 819–835.

Lieberman, D., Tooby, J., & Cosmides, L. (2007). The architecture of human kin detection. *Nature, 445,* 727–731.

Lynch, M., Blanchard, J., Houle, D., Kibota, T., Schultz, S., Vassilieva, L., et al. (1999). Perspective: Spontaneous deleterious mutation. *Evolution, 53,* 645–663.

Maner, J. K., Kenrick, D. T., Becker, D. V., Delton, A. W., Hofer, B., Wilbur, C. J., et al. (2003). Sexually selective cognition: Beauty captures the mind of the beholder. *Journal of Personality and Social Psychology, 85,* 1107–1120.

Maner, J. K., Kenrick, D. T., Becker, D. V., Robertson, T. E., Hofer, B., Neuberg, S. L., et al. (2005). Functional projection: How fundamental social motives can bias interpersonal perception. *Journal of Personality and Social Psychology, 88,* 63–78.

Markus, H. R., & Kitayama, S. (1991). Culture and the self: Implications for cognition, emotion, and motivation. *Psychological Review, 98,* 224–253.

Marlowe, F. (2001). Male contribution to diet and female reproductive success among foragers. *Current Anthropology, 42,* 755–760.

Marlowe, F. W. (2003). A critical period for provisioning by Hadza men: Implications for pair bonding. *Evolution and Human Behavior, 24,* 217–229.

Mayr, E. (1982). *The growth of biological thought: Diversity, evolution, and inheritance.* Cambridge, MA: Harvard University Press.

Mayr, E. (1991). *One long argument: Charles Darwin and the genesis of modern evolutionary thought.* Cambridge, MA: Harvard University Press.

McArthur, L. Z., & Baron, R. M. (1983). Toward an ecological theory of social perception. *Psychological Review, 90,* 215–238.

McDonald, K. (1995). Evolution, the 5-factor model, and levels of personality. *Journal of Personality, 63,* 525–567.

Mealey, L. (1995). The sociobiology of sociopathy: An integrated evolutionary model. *Behavioral and Brain Sciences, 18,* 523–541.

Miller, G. F. (2000). *The mating mind: How sexual choice shaped the evolution of human nature.* New York: Anchor Books.

Miller, G. F. (2009). Spent: Sex, evolution, and consumer behavior. New York: Viking.

Millikan, R. (1989). In defense of proper functions. *Philosophy of Science, 56,* 288–302.

Morris, M. W., & Keltner, D. (2000). How emotions work: The social functions of emotional expression in negotiation. *Research in Organizational Behavior, 22,* 1–50.

Mullen, B., Brown, R., & Smith, C. (1992). Ingroup bias as a function of salience, relevance, and status: An integration. *European Journal of Social Psychology, 22,* 103–122.

Muller, M. N., Emery Thompson, M., & Wrangham, R. W. (2006). Male chimpanzees prefer mating with old females. *Current Biology, 16,* 2234–2238.

Nesse, R. (2009). Social selection and the origins of culture. In M. Schaller, A. Norenzayan, S. J. Heine, T. Yamagishi, & T. Kameda (Eds.), *Evolution, culture, and the human mind* (pp. 137–150). New York: Psychology Press.

Nettle, D. (2006). The evolution of personality variation in humans and other animals. *American Psychologist, 61,* 622–631.

Nettle, D. (2009). Ecological influences on human behavioural diversity: A review of recent findings. *Trends in Ecology and Evolution, 24,* 618–624.

Newcomb, M. D. (1990). Social support and personal characteristics: A developmental and interactional perspective. *Journal of Social and Clinical Psychology, 9,* 54–68.

Newcomb, M. D. & Chou, C. (1989). Social support among young adults: Latent variable models of quantity and satisfaction within six life areas. *Multivariate Behavioral Research, 24,* 233–256.

Nisbett, R. E., & Masuda, T. (2003). Culture and point of view. *Proceedings of the National Academy of Sciences, USA, 100,* 11163–11170.

Nisbett, R. E., Peng, K. P., Choi, I, & Norenzayan, A. (2001). Culture and systems of thought: Holistic versus analytic cognition. *Psychological Review, 108,* 291–310.

Oyama, S. (1985). *The ontogeny of information.* Cambridge, UK: Cambridge University Press.

Omoyat, C. M., Jr., Fuglestad, P. T., & Snyder, M. (2010). Balance of power and influence in relationships: The role of self-monitoring. *Journal of Social and Personal Relationships, 27,* 23–46.

Parker, G. A. (2006). Behavioural ecology: Natural history as science. In J. R. Lucas & L. W. Simmons (Eds.), *Essays in animal behaviour: Celebrating 50 years of animal behaviour* (pp. 23–56) Amsterdam, Netherlands: Elsevier.

Parker, G. A., & Maynard Smith, J. (1990). Optimality theory in evolutionary biology. *Nature, 348,* 27–33.

Penke, L., Denissen, J. J. A., & Miller, G. F. (2007). The evolutionary genetics of personality. *European Journal of Personality, 21,* 549–587.

Perola, M., Sammalisto, S., Hiekkalinna, T., Martin, N. G., Visscher, P. M., Montgomery, G. W., et al. (2007). Combined genome scans for body stature in 6,602 European twins: Evidence for common Caucasian loci. *PLoS Genetics, 3,* e97. doi:10.1371/journal.pgen.0030097

Ploeger, A., van der Maas, H. L. J., & Raijmakers, M. E. J. (2008). Is evolutionary psychology a metatheory for psychology? A discussion of four major issues in psychology from an evolutionary developmental perspective. *Psychological Inquiry, 19,* 1–18.

Ramsey, G., Bastien, M. L., & van Schaik, C. (2007). Animal innovation defined and operationalized. *Behavioral and Brain Sciences, 30,* 393–407.

Richerson, P. J., & Boyd, R. (2005). *Not by genes alone: How culture transformed human evolution.* Chicago: University of Chicago Press.

Ross, L., & Nisbett, R. E. (1991). *The person and the situation.* New York: McGraw-Hill.

Salmon, C. A., & Shackelford, T. K. (Eds.). (2007). *Family relationships: An evolutionary perspective.* New York: Oxford University Press.

Schaller, M., Norenzayan, A., Heine, S. J., Yamagishi, T., & Kameda, T. (Eds.). (2009). *Evolution, culture, and the human mind.* New York: Psychology Press.

Schaller, M., Miller, G. E., Gervais, W. M., Yager, S., & Chen, E. (2010). Mere visual perception of others' disease symptoms facilitates a more aggressive immune response. *Psychological Science, 21,* 649–652.

Schlegel, A., & Barry, H., III. (1986). The cultural consequences of female contribution to subsistence. *American Anthropologist, 88,* 142–150.

Schlenker, B. R. (1980). *Impression management: The self-concept, social identity, and interpersonal relations.* Monterey, CA: Brooks-Cole.

Schmitt, D. M. Allik, J., McCrae, R. R. & Benet-Martínez, V. (2009). The geographic distribution of Big Five personality traits: Patterns and profiles of human self-description across 56 nations. *Journal of Cross-Cultural Psychology, 38,* 173–212.

Sell, A., Tooby, J., & Cosmides, L. (2009). Formidability and the logic of human anger. *Proceedings of the National Academy of Sciences, USA, 106,* 15073–15078.

Shifman, S., Bhomra, A., Smiley, S., Wray, N. R., James, M. R., Martin, N. G., et al. (2007). A whole genome association of neuroticism using DNA pooling. *Molecular Psychiatry, 13,* 302–312.

Silk, J. B., Beehner, J. C., Bergman, T. J., Crockford, C., Engh, A. L., Moscovice, L. R., et al. (2009). The benefits of social capital: Close social binds among female baboons enhance offspring survival. *Proceedings of the Royal Society: B, 276,* 3099–3104.

Simpson, J. A. (2007). Foundations of interpersonal trust. In A. W. Kruglanski & E. T. Higgins (Eds.), *Social psychology: Handbook of basic principles* (2nd ed., pp. 587–607). New York: Guilford.

Smith, R. H., & Kim, S. H. (2007). Comprehending envy. *Psychological Bulletin, 133,* 46–64.

Snyder, M. (1974). Self-monitoring of expressive behavior. *Journal of Personality and Social Psychology, 30,* 526–537.

Snyder, M. (1983). The influence of individuals on situations: Implications for understanding the links between personality and social behavior. *Journal of Personality, 51,* 497–516.

Snyder, M. (1987). *Public appearances/private realities: The psychology of self-monitoring.* New York: Freeman.

Snyder, M., Gangestad, S., & Simpson, J. A. (1983). Choosing friends as activity partners: The role of self-monitoring. *Journal of Personality and Social Psychology, 45,* 1061–1072.

Snyder, M., & Gangestad, S. (1986). On the nature of self-monitoring: Matters of assessment, matters of validity. *Journal of Personality and Social Psychology, 51,* 125-139.

Snyder, M., & Simpson, J. A. (1984). Self-monitoring and dating relationships. *Journal of Personality and Social Psychology, 47,* 1281–1291.

Sterelny, K. (2007). Social intelligence, human intelligence, and niche construction. *Philosophical Transactions of the Royal Society: B, 362,* 719–730.

Sterelny, K., & Griffiths, P. E. (1999). *Sex and death: An introduction to the philosophy of biology.* Chicago: University of Chicago Press.

Thornhill, R. (1990). The study of adaptation. In M. Bekoff & D. Jamieson (Eds.), *Interpretation and explanation in the study of behavior* (Vol. 2, pp. 31–62). Boulder, CO: Westview.

Thornhill, R. (1997). The concept of an evolved adaptation. In G. Bock (Ed.), *Characterizing human psychological adaptations* (pp. 4–13). London: Wiley.

Thornhill, R. (2007). The importance of developmental biology to evolutionary biology and vice versa. In S. W. Gangestad & J. A. Simpson (Eds.), *The evolution of mind: Fundamental questions and controversies* (pp. 203–209). New York: Guilford.

Thornhill, R., & Gangestad, S. W. (2008). *The evolutionary biology of human female sexuality*. New York: Oxford University Press.

Thornton, J. W., Need, E., & Crews, D. (2003). Resurrecting the ancestral steroid receptor: Ancient origin of estrogen signaling. *Science* 301: 1714–1717.

Tooby, J., & Cosmides, L. (1992). Psychological foundations of culture. In J, Barkow, L. Cosmides, & J. Tooby (Eds.), *The adapted mind* (pp. 19–136). New York: Oxford University Press.

Tooby, J., & Cosmides, L. (1996). Friendship and the banker's paradox: Other pathways to the evolution of adaptations for altruism. *Proceedings of the British Academy, 88,* 119–143.

Tooby, J., Cosmides, L., & Barrett, H. C. (2003). The second law of thermodynamics is the first law of psychology: Evolutionary developmental psychology and the theory of tandem, coordinated inheritances: Comment on Lickliter and Honeycutt (2003). *Psychological Bulletin, 129,* 858–865.

Trivers, R. L. (1971). The evolution of reciprocal altruism. *Quarterly Review of Biology, 45,* 35–57.

Tybur, J. M., Lieberman, D., & Griskevicius, V. (2009). Microbes, mating, and morality: Individual differences in three functional domains of disgust. *Journal of Personality and Social Psychology, 97,* 103–122.

Uskal, A. K., Kitayama, S., & Nisbett, R. E. (2008). Ecocultural bases of cognition: Farmers and fisherman are more holistic than herders. *Proceedings of the National Academy of Sciences, USA, 105,* 8552–8556.

Vigil, J. M. (2007). Asymmetries in the friendship preferences and social styles of men and women. *Human Nature, 18,* 143–161.

Vigil, J. M. (2009). A socio-relational framework of sex differences in the expression of emotion. *Behavioral and Brain Sciences, 32,* 375–428.

Waddington, C. H. (1957). *Strategy of the genes*. London, UK: Allen & Unwin.

Walker, R., Burger, O., Wagner, J. & Von Rueden, C. R. (2006). Evolution of brain size and juvenile periods in primates. *Journal of Human Evolution, 51,* 480–489.

Watson. D., Wiese, D., Vaidya, J., & Tellegen, A. (1999). The two general activation systems of affect: Structural findings, evolutionary considerations, and psychobiological evidence. *Journal of Personality and Social Psychology, 76,* 820–838.

Watve, M. G., & Yajnik, C. S. (2007). Evolutionary origins of insulin resistance: A behavioral switch hypothesis. *BMC Evolutionary Biology, 7,* 61; doi:10.1186/1471-2148-7-61.

West, S. A., Griffin, A. S., & Gardner, A. (2006). Social semantics: Altruism, cooperation, mutualism, strong reciprocity, and group selection. *Journal of Evolutionary Biology, 20,* 415–432.

West-Eberhard, M. J. (2003). *Developmental plasticity and evolution*. New York: Oxford University Press.

Williams, G. C. (1966). *Adaptation and natural selection: A critique of some current evolutionary thought*. Princeton, NJ: Princeton University Press.

Williams, G. C. (1992). *Natural selection: Domains, levels, and challenges*. New York: Oxford University Press.

Wilson, D. S. (1994). Adaptive genetic variation and human evolutionary psychology. *Ethology and Sociobiology, 15,* 219–235.

Wilson, D. S. (1998). Adaptive individual differences within single populations. *Philosophical Transactions of the Royal Society: B, 353,* 199–205.

Windsor, D. A. (1998). Most of the species on Earth are parasites. *International Journal of Parasitology, 28,* 1939–1941.

Wrangham, R. & Peterson, D. (1996). *Demonic males: Apes and the origins of human violence*. Boston, MA: Houghton Mifflin.

Wright, S. (1968). *Evolution and genetics of populations*. Chicago: Chicago University Press.

Wubben, M. J. J., De Cremer, D., & Van Dijk, E. (2009). How emotion communication guides reciprocity: Establishing cooperation through disappointment and anger. *Journal of Experimental Social Psychology, 45,* 987–990.

Yamagishi, T., & Mifune, N. (2009). Social exchange and solidarity: In-group love or out-group hate? *Evolution and Human Behavior, 30,* 229–237.

Zak, P. J., Kurzban, R., & Matzner, W. T. (2005). Oxytocin is associated with human trustworthiness. *Hormones and Behavior, 48,* 522–527.

CHAPTER

8

Context in Person, Person in Context
A Cultural Psychology Approach to Social-Personality Psychology

Glenn Adams

Abstract

This chapter applies a cultural psychology framework to provide a macrosocial account of social-personality psychology. Extending the standard social-psychological emphasis on the importance of context, the first section considers the *cultural constitution of personal experience*. A history of engagement with particular cultural affordances shapes a person with an associated set of residual tendencies such that what appear to be "personal" dispositions are instead a form of *context in person*: embodied traces of a person's engagement with ecological structures of mind that continually reconstitute the person's habitual ways of being. Extending an emphasis on importance of subjective construal, the second section considers the *psychological constitution of cultural worlds*. As people act on subjective interpretations, their behavior leaves traces on objective realities to create a form of *person in context*: everyday constructions of reality that bear the influence of personal activity. In this way, a cultural psychology analysis balances the traditional social psychological emphasis on "the power of the situation" with a restored emphasis on the power of the culturally grounded person as (re)constructor of intentional worlds.

Keywords: action, cultural affordance, ecological, habitus, identity, intentional world, mutual constitution, selfways

In this chapter, I approach the guiding theme of this *Handbook*—the integration of social and personality psychology—from a perspective of cultural psychology. Contrary to common understandings, the point of a cultural psychology analysis is not merely to examine how psychological phenomena vary across cultural settings; instead, a cultural psychology analysis highlights how "psyche and culture . . . make each other up" (Shweder, 1990; p. 1). That is, a cultural psychology analysis emphasizes the extent to which person-based structures of experience that are the focus of most psychological research exist in a dynamic relationship of *mutual constitution* with socially constructed *affordances* (i.e., qualities of an object or environment that allow performance of an action; see Gibson, 1977) embedded in the structure of everyday worlds. One can apply a cultural psychology framework not just to make sense of

"cross-cultural" variation, but more generally to provide a macrosocial account of social-personality psychology: one that balances the traditional social psychological emphasis on "the power of the situation" with a restored emphasis on the power of the person as creator of intentional worlds (see Gjerde, 2004).

With its defining focus on the mutual constitution of cultural worlds and psychological experience, a cultural psychology analysis extends an earlier discussion of the relationship between social and personality psychology by Lee Ross and Richard Nisbett (1991), who proposed that the field of social psychology rests on a small set of basic principles.[1] The first principle, the "power of the situation," refers to the typically underappreciated extent to which subtle contextual features moderate the course of psychological experience. In contrast to the general thrust of psychological science and its emphasis on personal dispositions, this principle emphasizes environmental regulation of action and experience. The second principle, "the importance of subjective construal," refers to the role of human imagination in the creation of meaning from inherently ambiguous stimuli. In contrast to the layperson's sense of direct access to an objective reality (i.e., *naive realism*), this social-psychological principle emphasizes the dynamic construction of experience from typically underspecified, environmental inputs.[2]

A cultural psychology analysis elaborates these social-psychological principles by adding considerations of history and materiality. Extending "the power of the situation," one direction of the mutual constitution relationship refers to the *cultural constitution of psychological experience*. Psychological development is not simply the natural outgrowth of inborn programming or unfolding of genetic potential; instead, it reflects the incorporation and embodiment—literally, "taking into the body"—of blueprints for psychological experience deposited over historical time in the structure of everyday cultural worlds. The idea here is not a weak form of contextualism that emphasizes the "power of the situation" to regulate personal experience, but rather a strong form of contextualism in which cultural realities are *constitutive* of psychological experience. In terms of species-typical tendencies, this means that what we have come to regard as normal human development would not be possible without the tools or scaffolding that socially constructed, historically evolved, cultural affordances provide. In terms of individual personalities, this means that a history of engagement with particular sets of cultural affordances shapes a person with an associated set of residual tendencies such that what appear to be "personal" dispositions are instead a form of *context in person*: embodied traces of a person's engagement with ecological structures of mind that continually reconstitute the person's habitual ways of being.

Extending the idea of subjective construal, the other side of this mutual constitution relationship refers to the *psychological constitution of cultural worlds*. Cultural worlds do not exist apart from human action; instead, people continually reproduce environmental extensions of the person into which they inscribe, objectify, and *realize* (literally, "make real"; see Berger & Luckmann, 1966; Moscovici, 1984) their beliefs and desires. Again, the idea here is not a relatively weak form of constructivism that emphasizes the dynamic role of human imagination in the interpretation of reality, but rather a strong form of constructivism in which human subjectivity is *constitutive* of everyday realities. As people act on subjective interpretations, their behavior leaves traces on objective realities to create a form of *person in context*: everyday constructions of reality that bear the influence of personal activity.

In the sections that follow, I consider the intersection of social and personality psychology in terms of both directions of the mutual constitution process. Reflecting the emphasis of existing work, the first and largest section of the paper considers the cultural constitution of personal experience: the extent to which the structure of persons bears the embodied influence of contextual scaffolding. In the second section, I consider the equally important, but typically less well articulated, psychological constitution of cultural worlds: the extent to which the cultural-ecological context bears the accumulated influence of personal activity. In both sections, the goal is not to provide a comprehensive catalog of relevant research; indeed, the discussion draws disproportionately on theory and research from African settings that are unrepresentative of work in both mainstream and cultural psychology. Instead, the goal is to provide a heuristic framework for reimagining social-personality psychology in a "macrosocial" direction.

Context in Person: Sociocultural Constitution of Psychological Experience

One of the most significant developments in social-personality psychology during the past two decades has been unprecedented attention to the cultural constitution of psychological experience. A key insight of this work is the suggestion that psychological tendencies observed in the typical experiment are not "just so," but instead reflect the particular cultural-psychological ecologies of the worlds in which the science developed. One of the most important statements of this idea is a review of cultural variation in constructions of self by Hazel Markus and Shinobu Kitayama (1991).

Independent Constructions of Self

Markus and Kitayama (1991) proposed that theory and research in psychological science had primarily considered (and had treated as normative or "just natural") historically particular patterns of experience associated with what they referred to as *independent self-construal*: an atomistic understanding of self as a bounded entity, inherently separate from social and physical context, composed of defining or essential attributes abstracted from particular situational performances. The key feature of independent self-construal is not devaluation of relational connection, but instead an experience of such connection—for better or worse—as the secondary, manufactured product of inherently separate selves. Subsequent research has linked these constructions of self to a variety of implications for cognition, motivation, and emotion.

With respect to perception and cognition, research has linked independent constructions of self with *analytic* tendencies to focus attention on properties of people and objects as the primary unit of reality (Nisbett, Peng, Choi, & Norenzayan, 2001; see also Kühnen, Hannover, & Schubert, 2001; Kühnen & Oyserman, 2002). The experience of self as a bounded entity abstracted from context reflects and promotes perceptual tendencies to a focus on discrete objects and their defining attributes independent of their background fields (Masuda & Nisbett, 2001; Nisbett et al., 2001). In turn, the tendency to focus on defining attributes of objects reflects and promotes tendencies to understand or explain everyday events with disproportionate emphasis on actors' personal traits or dispositions (i.e., the "fundamental attribution error," Ross, 1977; see Cousins, 1989; Lee, Hallahan, & Herzog, 1996; Miller, 1984; Shweder & Bourne, 1984; Suh, 2002). Similarly, the focus on defining properties of bounded objects reflects and promotes analytic tendencies of taxonomic categorization, whereby people categorize objects on the basis of common attributes (e.g., rather than functional relationship; see Nisbett et al., 2001). Finally, perceptual or cognitive tendencies to abstract objects from context are associated with analytic reasoning styles whereby people view the world as operating according to universal abstract rules and laws (Norenzayan, Smith, Kim, & Nisbett, 2002).

With respect to motivation, research has linked independent constructions of self with *promotion-focused* tendencies (Higgins, 1996; see also Lee, Aaker, & Gardner, 2000) to express authentic dispositions and take advantage of opportunities for self-enhancement (Heine, Lehman, Markus, & Kitayama, 1999; Kitayama, Markus, Matsumoto, & Norasakkunkit, 1997). Independent constructions of self as a bundle of defining attributes foster motivations to express these attributes (e.g., beliefs and preferences) via acts of disclosure and personal choice (Kim & Sherman, 2007; Savani, Markus, & Conner, 2008). Similarly, research has associated independent constructions of self with motivations to highlight one's uniqueness (Kim & Markus, 1999) and influence one's surroundings to fit one's preferences, goals, or wishes (Morling, Kitayama, & Miyamoto, 2002). Likewise, the focus on defining attributes of independent selves reflects and promotes an emphasis on cultivation of self-esteem (e.g., Singelis, Bond, Lai, & Sharkey, 1999) and a tendency to maintain positively biased self-views (Heine & Hamamura, 2007) via "self-serving" patterns of memory and attribution (Endo & Meijer, 2004). This motivation to seek self-enhancement (at the expense of self-improvement) is especially evident in tendencies to persist at a task longer after success feedback than failure feedback (Heine et al., 2001).

With respect to affect and emotion, research has linked independent constructions of self to tendencies of experience and expression that highlight positive personal attributes and affirm the self as an independent entity (Kitayama, Markus, & Kurokawa, 2010). For example, research has associated independent constructions of self with an emphasis on the personal meaning of emotional experience (rather than normative or consensual understandings; Mesquita, 2001; Oishi, Diener, Scollon, & Biswas-Diener, 2004) and positive evaluation of self-conscious emotions (e.g., pride) that signal personal accomplishment (Eid & Diener, 2001). Likewise, research has associated independent constructions with a self-indulgent preference for high-arousal positive affective states (Tsai, 2007).

Research has also linked independent constructions of self to a set of implications for relational and collective belonging. Contrary to stereotypes about solitary, relationship-disdaining individualists, a cultural psychology perspective suggests that the relevant feature of independent constructions is a "promotion-focused" experience of relational belonging as a somewhat voluntary, effortful choice of atomistic "free agents" who strive to create connection in contexts of inherent separation. Independent constructions of self afford open, uninhibited pursuit of pleasurable companionship and a sense of freedom both to choose attractive partners and to avoid onerous obligations (e.g., to relatives). They resonate strongly with *market pricing* models of relationality (Fiske, 1991) that emphasize a free market of relationship in which people are at liberty to choose whether to initiate, maintain, or dissolve connections. They also resonate strongly with *equality matching* models of relationality (Fiske, 1991) and conceptions of a highly disordered "state of nature" in which "all [people] are created equal . . . with unalienable rights [that] include . . . liberty and the pursuit of happiness" in mutually rewarding, companionate relationship. These conceptions find expression in tendencies for people to report a relatively large number of friends (Adams & Plaut, 2003); to report a sense of freedom from enemies (Adams, 2005); and to emphasize verbally oriented, emotional intimacy as the essence of social support (Kim, Sherman, & Taylor, 2008). The foundation of psychological science in these models is evident both in (1) the valorization of romantic or mating relationship as the prototypical case of love and intimacy (see Adams, Anderson, & Adonu, 2004) and (2) the abundance of research on such topics as attraction and commitment to explain relationship initiation and persistence in the face of competing alternatives (e.g., Rusbult, 1980).

Similarly independent constructions of self afford a voluntaristic experience of collective belonging as a product of personal choice that grants people liberty (and requires them) to create their own group memberships (Triandis, Bontempo, Villareal, Asai, & Lucca, 1988). The high degree of social mobility associated with voluntaristic, independent models is associated with a relatively limited experience of obligation and high conditionality of group identification (Oishi, Ishii, & Lun, 2009), meaning that people feel free to invest in group memberships, or not, to the extent that doing so serves their current personal projects. In general, independent constructions of self afford a sense of freedom to create a relatively large number of thin connections dependent on the extent to which they satisfy personal goals.

As another manifestation of this relatively thin construction of sociality, Yuki (2003) has proposed that independent constructions promote a "common identity" experience of belonging (Prentice, Miller, & Lightdale, 1994)—as assimilation to a representation of an identity category—that resonates strongly with self-categorization theoretical perspectives (e.g., Turner, Hogg, Oakes, Reicher, & Wetherell, 1987). From this perspective, the glue that holds collective identity together is not actual connection among people, but instead a sense of *imagined community* (Anderson, 1983) with abstract or hypothetical others in the same category. As I note in a later section, this sense of imagined community typically rests on cultural artifacts (e.g., monuments, national media, standardized national languages; see Anderson, 1983; Billig, 1995; Reicher & Hopkins, 2001) that afford particular constructions of the collective self and convey knowledge about prototypical members.

INTERDEPENDENT CONSTRUCTIONS OF SELF

In contrast to the independent constructions of self that inform scientific imagination and conceptions of normative, Markus & Kitayama (1991) suggested that the more typical patterns of subjectivity in human communities across time and space have been more relational understandings of self-in-context that they referred to as interdependent self-construal. The key feature of interdependent self-construal is not greater value of relationship, but instead an experience—again, for better or worse—of embeddedness in community (in both its senses of "place" and "network of social relations").

One of many statements of this idea in African contexts is the Kuranko (Sierra Leone) saying that "One's birth is like the bird-scaring rope" (Jackson, 1982, p. 17). The bird-scaring rope is an agricultural tool that consists of a network of rope with bits of metal tied to stakes and stretched back and forth across a field. By tugging from a central point, a farmer sets in motion the whole network of rope and produces a cacophony of clanking metal that scares marauding birds away from the maturing rice crop. This tool serves as an apt metaphor for personal experience in many West African settings. People emphasize that they do not exist in isolation; rather, their actions reflect the influence of others in the community. When one person is agitated, the whole network shakes. Likewise, people emphasize that their actions trigger consequences for others that reverberate across networks of social relations like a tug of the bird-scaring rope.

Again, research has linked interdependent constructions of self to a variety of implications for cognition, motivation, and emotion. With respect to perception and cognition, research has linked interdependent constructions of self with *holistic* tendencies to focus attention on contextual forces or relationships as the primary unit of reality (Nisbett et al., 2001). The experience of self as a relational node embedded in context reflects and promotes "field-dependent" perceptual tendencies to focus on relations among objects in their surrounding context or background field (Masuda & Nisbett, 2001; Nisbett et al., 2001). In turn, research has associated this holistic perceptual focus with the tendency to make sense of situations by considering relationships among objects or events and to make *situational attributions* when understanding the sources of action (Lee et al., 1996; Shweder & Bourne, 1984). Similarly, the holistic focus on relationships between objects and attention to background context reflects and promotes tendencies to categorize objects according to functional relationship rather than defining attributes (Nisbett et al., 2001). Finally, perceptual or cognitive tendencies that emphasize background context promote dialectic reasoning styles and tolerance for logical contradiction (Peng & Nisbett, 1999).

With respect to motivation, research has linked interdependent constructions of self with *prevention-focused* tendencies (Higgins, 1996; see also Lee et al., 2000) to meet obligations, live up to normative expectations, and attend to domains that require self-improvement (e.g., Kitayama et al., 1997). Interdependent constructions of self as a node in a network of interpersonal connection are associated with a deemphasis on expression of personal attributes (Savani et al., 2008), motivations to act in ways that fit in with others (Kim & Markus, 1999), and an emphasis on adjusting or accommodating oneself to one's surroundings (Morling et al., 2002). Likewise, research has associated interdependent constructions of self with motivations to maintain relatively unbiased self-views (Heine & Hamamura, 2007) via attention to information that indicates shortcomings or failure to meet normative standards and obligations (Kitayama et al., 1997). This motivation to prevent shortcomings (rather than promote self-enhancement) is especially evident in tendencies to persist at a task longer after failure feedback than success feedback (Heine et al., 2001).

With respect to affect and emotion, research has linked interdependent constructions of self to tendencies of experience and expression that emphasize adjustment of self to interpersonal context (Kitayama et al., 2010). For example, research has associated interdependent constructions of self with emphases on external, "objective," or *consensual meaning of emotional experience* (Mesquita, 2001; Oishi et al., 2004) and positive evaluation of emotions that signal one's shortcomings (e.g., guilt; see Eid & Diener, 2001). Likewise, research has associated interdependent constructions with preference for low-arousal positive affective states (e.g., contentment) and deemphasis on expression of elated happiness due to its potentially disruptive effects on interpersonal relationships (Tsai, 2007).

Research has also linked interdependent constructions of self to implications for relational and collective belonging. A cultural psychology perspective suggests that the relevant feature of interdependent constructions is an experience of relationality as environmentally afforded connection. This sense of inherent connection affords a "prevention-focused" orientation to relationship that emphasizes

painstaking management of obligations for material support—what Coe (in press) has referred to as "the materiality of care" (see also Adams & Plaut, 2003; Kim et al., 2008)—and an acute awareness of the potential hazards of embeddedness in thickly overlapping networks of enduring interpersonal connection (Adams, 2005). Interdependent constructions resonate strongly with *authority ranking* models of relationality (Fiske, 1991) that promote a sense of vertical positioning characterized by reciprocal obligations of deferent obedience and benevolent supervision. They also resonate with *communal sharing* models of relationality (Fiske, 1991) that emphasize fundamental connectedness, for better or worse, in prefabricated webs of interpersonal connection. In many West African settings, these conceptions find expression in tendencies for people to report a relatively small number of friends (Adams & Plaut, 2003), to be vigilant for attacks from envious personal enemies (including family and other intimate spaces; Adams, 2005; Geschiere, 1997), and to emphasize silence and concealment rather than self-disclosure and revelation (e.g., Ferme, 2001; Shaw, 2000). Rather than valorize "manufactured" romantic or mating relationships, interdependent constructions resonate with an experience of kinship as the prototype of human relationality.

Similarly, interdependent constructions of self afford a relationally embedded experience of collective belonging associated with a "common-bond" experience of group membership as a network of actual connections (Prentice et al., 1994; Yuki, 2003). Although this relationally embedded notion of collective belonging may provide a strong sense of tangible bonds, it also places constraints on the number of bonds that people can claim (in part because of the corresponding experience of substantial obligation; see Triandis et al., 1988). In contrast to assumptions that "group-oriented" collectivists will show stronger patterns of group-relevant phenomena, Yuki (2003) proposes that the more relational experience of collective belonging associated with interdependent constructions will promote relatively weak patterns of the phenomena detailed by the social identity tradition. This includes ingroup favoritism, (Karp, Jin, Yamagishi, & Shinotsuka, 1993; Yamagishi, Jin, & Kiyonari, 1999), especially in the case of minimal groups or other artificially imposed categories. Likewise, in direct contrast to stereotypes about the self-effacing character of the collectivist self (see Shaw, 2000, for a critique), this perspective associates interdependent constructions with less of the depersonalized assimilation of self to category that social identity and social categorization theoretical traditions emphasize.

To further elaborate this idea, consider an example from African settings. As a challenge to stereotypes about the importance of collective belonging (manifest in alleged proclivities for ethnic violence), historians have emphasized the extent to which ethnicity in African settings has typically been a colonial invention and postcolonial reproduction. Beyond obviously artificial, national identities (e.g., Ghanaian or Nigerian), researchers have noted the extent to which even apparently "primordial" or timeless group categories such as Dagaare (Lentz, 2006), Tutsi (Mamdani, 2001), or Yoruba (Peel, 2001) are likewise sociopolitical constructions that arose in the context of the colonial encounter. (For a common example, colonial authorities sometimes encouraged the imagination of ethnic communities and associated "state societies" to facilitate indirect rule via installation of local rulers rather than relatively expensive colonial administrators.) At a more fundamental level, researchers suggest that the phenomenon of ethnicity itself—that is, the experience of collective belonging to an imagined community of people who may share language, appearance, and customs but are otherwise distant strangers—was also in many cases a product of the colonial encounter. Resonating with Yuki's (2003) account, researchers propose that people in many African societies have experienced collective belonging not in terms of imagined community in an abstract category, but rather as deeply embedded connection in locally rooted networks characterized by a long history of tangible interactions (see Hawkins, 2002; and Lentz, 2006, for examples from what is now Northern Ghana). One implication of this perspective is that the "standard" patterns of belonging meticulously documented in such mainstream traditions as social identity theory and self-categorization theory are partly the product of human invention—that is, cultural innovations for imagination of community—rather than a natural law of human psychology (for discussions of cultural affordances that scaffold imagination of national community, see Anderson, 1983; Reicher & Hopkins, 2001; Winichakul, 1994).

Beyond Self-Construal: Cultural-Ecological Scaffolding of Self

Especially as appropriated in mainstream social-personality psychology, the notions of independent and interdependent self-construal are somewhat limiting to the extent that they entail problematic reifications of both culture and self. With respect to *culture*, the association of independent self-construal with North American or "Western" settings and interdependent self-construal with Asian or "Eastern" settings can promote notions of bounded, monolithic entities with timeless, traditional essences that lead to the reproduction of stereotypes and exotification (Adams & Markus, 2004; Lewis & Wigan, 1997; Okazaki, David, & Abelmann, 2007; Said, 1978). With respect to *self*, the focus on "self-construal" reflects and reproduces the tendency in psychology to locate the source of action and experience in internal essences that crystallize during early childhood, persist throughout the lifespan, and direct experience as a trait-like structure that one can measure with an individual difference variable.

A formulation that resonates more clearly with a cultural psychology analysis is one that Markus and Kitayama (along with Patricia Mullally) later referred to as *selfways*: scaffolding or affordances for psychological functioning embedded in the structure of everyday cultural ecologies (Markus, Mullally, & Kitayama, 1997). The notion of selfways makes explicit the idea that the influence of culture on self is not a matter of reified cultural traditions shaping, once-and-for-all, an essentially independent or interdependent self. Instead, the notion of selfways affords more fluid understandings of culture and self. With respect to *culture*, the notion of selfways suggests fluid forms of cultural influence infused in diffuse institutions, practices, and artifacts rather than calcified traditions associated with rigidly bounded groups (Adams & Markus, 2004). This more fluid notion of cultural influence focuses on the ecological scaffolding that promotes psychological tendencies rather than labeling tendencies as the product of some reified cultural tradition. With respect to *self*, the notion of selfways makes explicit that the foundations of psychological experience are not limited to internal architecture, but also reside in the structure of everyday cultural worlds. Rather than trait-like construals that solidify during early childhood and persist via inertia throughout the life course, the notion of selfways treats the cultural construction of self as the repeated reconstitution of relatively fluid, habitual tendencies that are the product of ongoing engagement with ecologically inscribed, psychological resources.

INDEPENDENT SELFWAYS

Theory and research has associated independent selfways with a variety of ecological realities. With respect to distal ecological forces, independent selfways often feature a high degree of market integration and organizational scale that allow for depersonalized economic transactions between anonymous strangers (Henrich et al., 2005). Independent selfways often feature voluntary settlement patterns (Kitayama, Ishii, Imada, Takemura, & Ramaswamy, 2006) and relatively high levels of spatial and social mobility (Oishi & Kisling, 2009) that both reflect and promote a sense of independence from any particular social or geographical context (Giddens, 1991). Similarly, independent selfways often include collective realities of relative affluence (amid pockets of individual scarcity) that afford high degrees of mobility (e.g., via roads, mass transit, and other transportation infrastructure), convenient access to resources (e.g., fuel, electricity, and water), and a sense of financial independence: the ability to enact one's preferences and pursue life projects with relative freedom from material constraint (Markus, Ryff, Curhan, & Palmersheim, 2004). In turn, high levels of mobility and affluence are associated with "neolocal" residence (i.e., the practice of leaving a parental home to occupy a separate residence upon reaching adulthood), self-contained housing (i.e., with its own kitchen, bath, and toilet rather than communal or public amenities), and a small ratio of persons to rooms—all of which afford an experience of privacy and interpersonal insulation.

With respect to proximal forces, independent selfways often involve sociocultural organization of bodily functions in ways that reflect and afford a sense of privacy and interpersonal separation. These include bedtime rituals of parent-child separation to foster an experience of independent subjectivity (e.g., Shweder, Jensen, & Goldstein, 1995). These also include food rituals—such as individual place settings, individually wrapped meals from drive-through windows of fast food restaurants, "modern" conveniences that allow one to prepare and consume food quickly with a minimum of labor, and a high frequency of eating alone—that reflect and afford a socially disembedded experience of the biological activity of eating (see e.g., Rozin, 2007). Other proximal realities of independent selfways include low-context communication practices that assume relatively little common ground between speakers and rely on direct or explicit reference (Hall, 1976), linguistic features (e.g., pronoun use; Kashima & Kashima, 1998) that reflect and promote a sense of bounded actors abstracted from relational or physical context, and a host of "promotion-focused"

childcare practices (Higgins, 1996)—including visually and verbally oriented interaction with infants as more or less equal partners (Keller, Schölmerich, & Eibl-Eibesfeldt, 1988; LeVine et al., 1994; see Greenfield, Keller, Fuligni, & Maynard, 2003)—that emphasize exploration (Rothbaum, Weisz, Pott, Miyake, & Morelli, 2000), bolstering (Higgins, 1996); nurturance (Higgins, 1997); and the emotional value of children (Kağıtçıbaşı & Ataca, 2005).

A relatively recent focus of cultural psychological research has been the inscription of different selfways in material artifacts (see Morling & Lamoreaux, 2008). To cite only a few examples, researchers have associated independent selfways with magazine advertisements that emphasize originality, freedom, and rejection of traditional roles (Kim & Markus, 1999); media interviews with Olympic athletes and other forms of reportage that locate the source of performance in individual ability or effort (Markus, Uchida, Omorogie, Townsend, & Kitayama, 2006); popular music that valorizes self-expression and independence (Snibbe & Markus, 2005); and pictures in children's books that valorize excitedly happy affective states (Tsai, Louie, Chen, & Uchida, 2007). As a result of these artifacts and practices, people in worlds informed by independent selfways inhabit objective realities that—regardless of personal endorsement—reflect and promote intersubjective understandings of individuality and self-expression as normal and normative ways of being (Chiu, Gelfand, Yamagishi, Shteynberg, & Wan, 2010).

INTERDEPENDENT SELFWAYS

The preceding section describes a set of realities that mainstream psychology tends to portray as "just natural" (and then bases a science of human experience on interactions with this "natural" environment). Accordingly, it is useful to recall the extent to which these realities are highly unusual in the context of human history (Arnett, 2008; Henrich, Heine, & Norenzayan, 2010).

To get some sense for this particularity, consider ecological realities associated with the relatively interdependent selfways common across a variety of West African worlds. These realities include such distal ecological forces as limited spatial and social mobility (e.g., due to difficulty of transportation) that both reflect and promote a sense of rootedness in community and place; Giddens, 1991; Tengan, 1991). These realities often (but not always) involve labor-intensive, subsistence activities; difficult access to basic amenities (e.g., fuel, electricity, and water);

and a collective reality of scarcity (with nearly half of the population living on less than $1.25 per day; United Nations Development Program, 2010) that demand extensive coordination within and between domestic units and reciprocal obligations of support to ensure viable existence. Similarly, these realities often include residence in communal or compound houses with multiple generations of relatives who are typically linked by patrilineal descent (occasionally by matrilineal descent; Oppong, 1974) and often include relationships (e.g., cowife and siblings of the same father by different mothers) that arise from the widespread practice of polygynous marriage (up to 25% of all conjugal unions; see Dodoo, 1998). These residential realities require people to share space and amenities (e.g., bedrooms, kitchen, bath, and toilet) in ways that—regardless of personal endorsement—constitute an experience of embedded interdependence.

With respect to proximal forces, the interdependent selfways common in many West African settings include sociocultural organization of bodily functions—for example, eating from a common bowl, drinking from a common cup, and sleeping together in a common bed (Morelli, Rogoff, Oppenheim, & Goldsmith, 1992 Keller, 2003)—in ways that afford an experience of embeddedness in community (see Fiske, 1991). They include "prevention-focused" childcare practices (Higgins, 1996)—including bodily contact, parental control, and familial obligation (LeVine et al., 1994; Keller, 2003)—that emphasize prudence (cf. Higgins, 1996), security, and contribution of children to the family's economic survival (LeVine et al., 1994; Kağıtçıbaşı, 1996; Keller, 2003). They include practices of ritualized avoidance and deferential respect that constitute the experience of authority-ranked relationality (Radcliffe-Brown, 1940; see Fiske, 1991), rituals of memory (e.g., libation and offerings; Cole, 2001; Fiske, 1991) that promote a sense of ongoing relationship with departed ancestors, and socially distributed forms of childcare (e.g., fosterage; Bledsoe, 1990; Goody, 1982) that promote experience of broad connection rather than intense dyadic attachment (Weisner, 2005). Together with an abundance of material artifacts—including bumper stickers (Adams, 2005), lorry slogans (van der Geest, 2009), wall posters (Adams & Dzokoto, 2003), movies (Meyer, 1998), and news reports of penis-shrinking sorcerers (Adams & Dzokoto, 2007), to name only a few—these everyday realities reflect and promote intersubjective understandings of relationality as normal and normative ways of being.

It is important to note that mainstream science regards many features of interdependent selfways and associated psychological tendencies in West African settings as either suboptimal ways of being—for example, reminiscent of insecure attachment (Ainsworth, 1967) and authoritarian parenting (Baumrind, 1968)—or provisionally adaptive responses to undesirable circumstances (e.g., poverty and other life-threatening situations; see Main, 1990, on the topic of "avoidant attachment"). In response, a cultural psychology perspective emphasizes two strategies (Adams & Salter, 2007). The first strategy is to provide "normalizing" accounts of apparently harmful ways of being. Without denying the possibility that habitual ways of being can reflect adaptation to undesirable circumstances, a cultural psychology perspective emphasizes the extent to which those ways of being can also be part of larger, historically evolved systems that constitute viable paths to human welfare. The second, arguably more important, strategy is to denaturalize understandings of "normal" functioning. A cultural psychology perspective emphasizes that patterns portrayed as normal in mainstream science are not "just natural" expressions of optimal human development, but instead are the product of particular realities, with their own harmful side-effects, that mainstream scientific work typically obscures.

To these strategies I add a third point that resonates with an emphasis on the psychological constitution of cultural reality and a corresponding understanding of everyday ecologies as human products. Again, this point does not deny that many ways of being associated with interdependent selfways might reflect adaptation to undesirable cultural ecologies. However, it simultaneously emphasizes the historical processes that produced these cultural ecologies. Perspectives in postcolonial studies (Appiah, 1992, Mbembe, 1992; Mudimbe, 1988) propose that the poverty, instability, and other undesirable features associated with life in many West African spaces are an ongoing product of the same colonial domination and resource extraction (e.g., of capital and slave labor) that made possible the abundance and security that people in the scientific center enjoy (see Ferguson, 2006; Shaw, 2000). From this perspective, any potentially problematic features of the interdependent selfways that I have described in this section do not develop and persist in isolation; instead, they are a byproduct of the independent selfways that psychological science trumpets as normative human standards.

SUMMARY: SELFWAYS AS HABITUS

From this cultural psychology perspective, contextual variation in self and experience is less the product of conscious indoctrination into different value systems than it is something that arises in bottom-up fashion as people repeatedly engage everyday realities that elicit or shape psychological habits. A useful concept in this regard is *habitus* (see Bourdieu, 1977), which refers to direct inscription of ecological affordances on a person's habitual modes of affect, cognition, motivation, and being in the world. This notion provides a useful alternative to prevailing understandings of sociocultural influences on self. Perhaps reflecting their origins in the discipline of psychology, typical formulations have tended to locate sociocultural influence in individual endorsement of cultural values (see Oyserman, Coon, & Kemmelmeier, 2002) or individual construal of self as independent or interdependent (Matsumoto, 1999). More recently, theorists and researchers have proposed a conceptual move away from individual endorsement toward intersubjective knowledge of modal community tendencies as carriers of sociocultural influence (Chiu et al, 2010). The notion of habitus extends this conceptual move beyond relatively conscious, intersubjective knowledge to emphasize relatively nonconscious processes of environmental regulation via implicit ecological blueprints embedded in the structure of everyday cultural world. From this perspective, tendencies that psychologists have associated with different varieties of self-construal are not essential features of an independent or interdependent self, but instead reflect routine engagement with ecologically inscribed selfways that continually reconstitute those tendencies.

Beyond Cultural Variation: Sociocultural Bases of Psychological Experience

The preceding discussion conforms to most people's understanding of a cultural psychology approach as a means for investigating diversity in psychological functioning along "cultural-group" dimensions. However, a cultural psychology approach is a broader understanding—the extent to which the foundation for psychological experience is present in the structures of everyday cultural worlds—that applies beyond questions of cultural diversity to topics across the spectrum of psychological science (see Cole, 1996).

SOCIOCULTURAL BASES OF SPECIES-TYPICAL TENDENCIES

With respect to general tendencies, a cultural psychology analysis considers the extent to which apparently natural psychological capacities are particular technologies of mind made possible by common cultural ecologies. From this perspective, human beings share a set of species-typical tendencies that are the product of near-universal engagement with widely distributed cultural tools.

For example, researchers have noted how many apparently "natural" cognitive or perceptual abilities are associated with cultural ecologies in which language and literacy practices are standard features. Tomasello (1999) argues that many forms of higher cognition characteristic of species-typical humans are not themselves innate, but instead depend on cultural tools that have developed via processes of cumulative cultural evolution. Similarly, research suggests that many near-universal and species-typical cognitive and perceptual abilities—including the use of graphic conventions to represent and perceive depth in two-dimensional drawings, memory for disconnected lists of information, spontaneous use of strategies for organizing memory, use of taxonomic versus functional categories to organize test objects, and willingness to go beyond personal experience in answering logical problems—are not innate properties of the human organism, but instead reflect near-universal engagement with widespread institutions of literacy and formal school-based education (Rogoff, 1990; see also Scribner & Cole, 1981).

Likewise, the near-universal penetration of market economic activity carries with it cultural affordances that systematically evoke certain forms of experience and are becoming increasingly common across a variety of "traditional" settings (Greenfield, Maynard, & Marti, 2009). For example, researchers have noted that apparently "standard" tendencies to diverge from unrestrained self-interest and make relatively egalitarian offers in one-shot economic games are not "just natural" features of human's genetic inheritance, but instead are associated with integration into market economies that require abstract forms of impersonal cooperation (Henrich et al., 2005). Similarly, researchers who observed a Zinacanatec Mayan setting over time documented increasing integration into market economic activity that was, in turn, associated with increased reliance on technology, individuation and opportunities for expression of individual choice, and specialization for economic tasks (Greenfield et al, 2009). The researchers also noted associated changes due to increased urban residence, including increased contact with strangers, contact with people of different ethnicities, and increases in the range of economic and social possibilities for women (Greenfield et al., 2009).

Finally, technological advances have contributed to a global cultural space that has a similar impact on identity-development processes of youth from a variety of national settings, despite differences in local traditions of identity construction. Youth around the world encounter manifestations of global popular culture that include film, music, and fashion distributed via such widely (although unevenly; see Ferguson, 2006) available mechanisms as satellite television, cell phones, and Internet cafes. As a result, they often develop a form of bicultural identity reflecting the influence of engagement with local communities of origin and an "imagined" global community (Arnett, 2002). This bicultural identity increases the range of options for construction of personal identity and therefore grants some measure of increased authorship over one's life story. However, this bicultural identity also creates challenges for identity integration and increases potential for intergenerational conflict (Arnett, 2002).

In all of these cases, the emphasis of a cultural psychology analysis is not cultural diversity, but rather cultural-ecological structures—whether unique to a particular community or shared across human societies—that continually reconstitute apparently "natural" features of human psychological functioning. One noteworthy implication of these ideas is that failure to observe a difference in comparisons of samples from two communities does not mean lack of a cultural difference. Rather than "natural" features of the human organism, the observed similarity can be the product of universal engagement with the same cultural-ecological affordances. Likewise, a study with university students from different national settings does not necessarily constitute a cross-cultural comparison. Although the students may differ in national cultures, they share engagement with ecological affordances associated with university cultural spaces.

PERSONAL IDENTITY

With respect to personal dispositions, one application of a cultural psychology analysis might be to investigate variation in personality across "cultural" settings (see McCrae & Allik, 2002). Instead, I consider a more general issue: the extent to which personal dispositions reflect the particular sociocultural ecologies that a person inhabits. Just as a cultural psychology perspective does not deny the existence of genetically inherited, species-typical capacities, it likewise does not deny the existence of genetically inherited temperaments or predispositions—what one might refer to as "traits"—that vary across individuals. However, just as genetically inherited capacities require complementary input from cultural-ecological affordances to produce species-typical skills of recognizable human beings, so too do genetically linked predispositions require complementary input from cultural-ecological affordances to produce normally functioning, recognizably human persons.

Content of Identity Stories

Among the most important ecological affordances in this regard are resources for the life stories that constitute personal identity (McAdams, 2001). One contribution of cultural ecologies to the construction of personal identity concerns content. What matters for inclusion in one's identity story—category identities such as gender, nationality, ethnicity, lineage, class, and ageset; or role identities such as sibling, parent, child, patron, client, and foster parent—depends on the cultural world that one inhabits. Cultural ecologies vary not only in the availability and content of these identities, but also the extent to which they function as *master identities*: structures that organize self-experience across a broad range of situations. For example, the influence of gender on experience of personal identity varies greatly across settings, determining many aspects of a person's life story (e.g., occupation) in some worlds, but exerting more limited influence in others. Likewise, the influence of different roles varies across settings. In many African spaces, the roles of sibling or parent exert strong influence on one's evolving life story and matter more than the "manufactured" role of spouse. In other worlds informed by the notion of a "sacred couple" (Shweder et al., 1995), the role of spouse is a master identity that looms large in the life story, and the search for a (soul)mate is one of the defining themes of a person's life.

Cultural ecologies also vary in conceptions of the life course in ways that impact personal identity stories. Some cultural ecologies emphasize initiation ceremonies, parenthood, and "becoming an ancestor" upon one's death as defining scenes in life stories (e.g., Cole, 2001; Oppong, 1973). Other cultural ecologies emphasize school graduations, marriage, professional employment, home ownership, retirement, and "going to heaven" as defining scenes.

One of the most important variations in life course imagination concerns "leaving home." In many cultural ecologies that inform mainstream psychology, the expectation is that a person will leave the family home to start an independent life in a new location soon after reaching adulthood. Many identity tasks that mainstream psychology portrays as "just natural" features of a healthy life course—establishing a "secure" attachment bond between parents and children or resolving Eriksonian identity crises (1968)—may reflect adjustment to this culturally variable, life-course mandate of separation (Bellah, Madsen, Sullivan, Swindler, & Tipton, 1985). One can contrast this with the situation in many West African communities, in which the expectation is one of enduring connection—often a lifetime spent in or near the same residence—that persists even after one's death through practices such as libation, offerings of food, and divination (e.g., Fiske, 1991, pp. 281–283). In these worlds, problems of adjustment concern embeddedness as an ecological fact of life and successful management of developmental tasks associated with "being a relative" (Reisman, 1992).

Organization of Identity Stories

Beyond content, different cultural ecologies also impact the process and organization of identity stories. One of the most important functions of identity stories is to integrate or abstract an experience of sameness or unitary essence from an individual's different performances or presentations of self across time and audiences (Goffman, 1959; McAdams, 2001). In turn, one of the most important features of different cultural ecologies is the degree to which they afford or promote such integration and abstraction. A typical pattern across human history has been one in which everyday realities afford an experience of identity tied to situated performances (e.g., occupational role, family position). In contrast, a history of engagement with "modern" spaces promotes a relatively integrated experience of being as a bundle of essential features, abstracted from situated performances, that define a person's authentic self-identity (Baumeister, 1987; Giddens, 1991).

From this perspective, the experience of personal identity is not the unfolding and expression of some core, authentic essence, but instead is a sociocultural construction: the product of cultural affordances that permit abstraction and integration of identity across situations. Indeed, research suggests that cultural ecologies vary in the extent to which they both afford such abstraction and require it for social approval and well-being. For example, Suh (2002) used a measure of transituational consistency to assess identity integration among students in Korea and the United States. Results indicated not only that identity consistency was greater among American students than Korean students, but also that relationships of identity consistency scores with both self-reports of participant life-satisfaction and third-party ratings of participant likability ratings were significantly stronger (and more positive) among American students than Korean students. Suh (2002) interpreted this pattern as an indication of the extent to which the independent selfways prominent in American settings both afford and require (for social approval and life satisfaction) abstraction of a consistent identity to a greater extent than do the relatively interdependent selfways of Korean settings. In summary, a cultural psychology analysis emphasizes the extent to which identity stories reflect not only the collective identities, role identities, and conceptions of life course that are prominent in different cultural ecologies (Erikson, 1968; Reisman, 1992), but also local affordances for abstracted or situated experience of identity associated with different selfways (Suh, 2002).

ATTITUDES AND DISPOSITIONS

Although few psychologists would deny that the construction and experience of personal identity reflects considerable sociocultural influence, prevailing approaches in mainstream psychology regard other person factors—for example, attitudes, preferences, traits, and habitual self-construals—as deeply embodied, essential features of individual organisms. Perhaps reflecting the tendency to see context-abstracted persons as the source of agency and experience, prevailing understandings hold that, whether conceived as genetically inherited traits or habitual dispositions acquired during early socialization, it is these internal structures that guide behavior and experience. From this mainstream perspective, the primary task of an integrated social-personality psychology is to determine the properties of situations that moderate the operation of these guiding dispositions. This prevailing model does not necessarily deny the possibility of change in guiding dispositions (as the enormous body of research on such topics as attitude change suggests). However, the implicit conceptions at work in this model portray such change as a case of rewriting a person's operating code with a new set of internal guides to replace earlier ones. As a productive contrast to this prevailing view of personal dispositions, a cultural psychology analysis emphasizes two points.

Cultural-Ecological Variation

The first concerns the issue of cultural-ecological variation in the extent to which local realities permit (or require) individual exercise of personal dispositions. Cultural ecologies associated with independent selfways typically promote *disjoint* constructions of action as the self-directed product of internal dispositions, and these ecologies afford the opportunity to exercise these personal dispositions. In contrast, cultural ecologies associated with interdependent selfways typically promote *conjoint* constructions of action as a collaborative production of personal dispositions in concert with environmental affordances (e.g., Markus & Kitayama, 2004). Accordingly, even if/when people across settings are similarly shaped to have dispositional stances, these dispositional stances typically have a greater impact on action and experience in worlds informed by independent selfways than worlds informed by interdependent selfways. For example, research suggests that subjective emotional experience informs life satisfaction judgments to a greater extent in "individualist" settings than "collectivist" settings (where normative standards are equally strong predictors of life satisfaction judgments; Suh, Diener, Oishi, & Triandis, 1998). Similarly, research suggests that personal preferences serve as a guide for product choice to a greater extent in middle-class American settings than similarly situated, middle-class Indian settings, for whom product choices also reference preferences of important relatives (Savani et al., 2008).

Another example comes from research on the importance of attraction in everyday life. Rather than a "just natural" law of human psychology, a cultural psychology analysis suggests that the importance of attraction for everyday life (see Langlois et al., 2000) is a feature of the promotion-focused relationality associated with independent selfways. These cultural ecologies promote a "free market" experience of relationship in which choice, preference (as a determinant of choice), and attraction (as a determinant of preference) loom large as determinants of relational and other life outcomes. People who possess attractive qualities receive greater attention from others, have a greater range of social opportunities, and therefore experience more satisfying social and other life outcomes than people who do not possess attractive qualities. This theoretical framework suggests the hypothesis that attraction will be less important for life outcomes in worlds informed by interdependent selfways, where everyday ecologies render choice and personal preferences less relevant for relationship creation. In support of this hypothesis, researchers observed that (1) discrimination in judgments of expected life outcomes as a function of target attractiveness and (2) the relationship between personal attractiveness and life satisfaction was greater among participants in North American settings, urban areas, and other situations where independent selfways inform relationship experience than in West African settings, rural areas, and other situations where interdependent selfways inform relationship experience (Anderson, Adams, & Plaut, 2008; Plaut, Adams, & Anderson, 2009).

In short, worlds informed by independent selfways both afford and require recruitment and enactment of personal dispositions—whether attitudes (Ybarra & Trafimow, 1998), assessments of individual happiness (Suh et al., 1998), product preferences (Savani et al., 2008), or interpersonal attractions (Anderson et al., 2008)—to an extent that worlds informed by interdependent selfways do not. Indeed, the association of independent selfways with the "fundamental attribution error" (Ross, 1977)— the tendency to overweight personal dispositions and underweight ecological affordances in assessing the causes of behavior—may be a reflection of this variability in affordances for exercise of personal dispositions. In other words, dispositional attributions may be less "erroneous" in settings informed by disjoint rather than conjoint models of agency.

Sociocultural Sources

Beyond the issue of cultural variation, the defining feature of a cultural psychology analysis is to bridge the conceptual divide between embodied personal dispositions and the cultural-ecological structures that continually tune those dispositions. From this perspective, ecological structures do not merely moderate the direction of preexisting dispositions; instead, a history of engagement with particular ecological structures continually reconstitutes configurations of affect, motivation, and cognition. Rather than deeply embodied, essential characteristics, a cultural psychology perspective highlights the extent to which personal dispositions are lightly embodied traces of "context in person": an acquired environmental charge resulting from a history of engagement with ecological affordances for psychological experience embedded in the structure of local worlds (Mischel, 1968).

There are a number of noteworthy resonances between this notion of context in person and other theoretical perspectives. One is the "environmental associations" interpretation of implicit attitudes, which highlights the extent to which a person's "automatic" affective stances toward objects reflect histories of engagement with ecological representations that portray the object with positive or negative connotations (e.g., Karpinski & Hilton, 2001). Related to this is recent work on the "social tuning" of attitudes (and the perspective of shared reality theory more generally; see Sinclair, Lowery, Hardin, & Colangelo, 2005; Hardin & Higgins, 1996), which emphasizes the extent to which people collaboratively construct situated attitudes and other personal stances in the course of creating common ground with particular audiences. Another point of resonance is with discourse analytic perspectives, which emphasize how people's reports of attitudes and other personal stances are not the expression of some essential internal attribute, but instead reflect embodied representation of culturally inscribed rituals and discursive repertoires that people reproduce in situated performances of persuasion and justification (Durrheim & Dixon, 2004). Yet another point of resonance is with the concept of *habitus* and practice theory more generally (see Bourdieu, 1977). As I noted earlier, and in contrast to the prevailing emphasis on individual endorsement of value ideology or intersubjective knowledge of modal community tendencies (Chiu et al., 2010) as carriers of sociocultural influence, the concept of *habitus* emphasizes relatively nonconscious processes of environmental regulation via implicit cultural affordances embedded in the structure of everyday worlds.

PROPENSITIES FOR PREJUDICE

To illustrate further with a specific example, consider one of the most enduring topics of research on personal dispositions in social-personality psychology: research on individual tendencies of prejudice and stereotyping. An emphasis on structures of persons as source of prejudicial action is evident in the diverse forms of racist and sexist dispositions that psychologists have proposed (e.g., ambivalent, aversive, paternalistic, modern, old-fashioned, and symbolic); the substantial research effort that investigators have devoted to measurement of these dispositions (e.g., Ambivalent Sexism Inventory, Glick & Fiske, 1996; "Bogus Pipeline" method, Jones & Sigall, 1971; "Bona Fide Pipeline" method, Fazio, Jackson, Dunton, & Williams, 1995; Implicit Associations Test, Greenwald, McGhee, & Schwartz, 1998; Modern Racism Scale, McConahay, 1986;

Social Dominance Orientation, Pratto, Sidanius, Stallworth, & Malle, 1994; and Symbolic Racism Scale, Henry & Sears, 2002); and the overriding emphasis on—indeed, approaching a faith in—changing these dispositions as the goal of antiracism interventions (e.g., research on the contact hypothesis; Allport, 1954; see Pettigrew & Tropp, 2006; see also Tropp & Molina, chapter 22, this volume). This work continues to generate important insights about superficially benevolent or subtle expressions of bias (Devine, 1989; Glick & Fiske, 1996), the myriad ways in which apparently principled action implicates such bias (e.g., Knowles, Lowery, Hogan, & Chow, 2009) and the extent to which such bias does not require that perpetrators act with intention or awareness (Krieger & Fiske, 2006). However, the relatively exclusive focus on personal dispositions of stereotyping and prejudice (a.k.a., "the prejudice problematic"; Wetherell & Potter, 1992) produces an atomistic account of racism that focuses on changing hearts and minds while neglecting the cultural-ecological structures that afford racist subjectivity and reproduce racist inequality (see Wright & Lubensky, 2008).

In contrast, the defining feature of a cultural psychology analysis is again to bridge the conceptual divide between embodied personal dispositions and the cultural-ecological structures that continually tune those dispositions (Adams, Biernat, Branscombe, Crandall, & Wrightsman, 2008). From this perspective, a more fruitful conception of the prejudice, stereotypes, and other tendencies of personal bias featured in mainstream research is as the embodied traces of cultural-ecological tools for domination. These tools include *cultural practices*, such as games that reproduce genocidal oppression as children's play; *cultural artifacts*, such as the portrait of Andrew Jackson on the U.S. $20 note, that accord high honor to notorious perpetrators of slavery, genocide, and ethnic cleansing; and *official holidays*, such as Thanksgiving Day, that celebrate the dispossession of indigenous societies (Kurtiş, Adams, & Yellow Bird, 2010; Yellow Bird, 2004). They include ecological representations of identity categories that associate *African American* with *crime* or animality (Eberhardt, Goff, Purdie, & Davies, 2004; Goff, Williams, Eberhardt, & Jackson, 2008); that model hostile treatment toward African Americans (e.g., Weisbuch, Pauker, & Ambady, 2009); and that fail to associate women and people from devalued ethnic minority groups with prestigious professions (Fryberg & Townsend, 2008; Dasgupta & Asgari, 2004). They include discursive repertoires that justify racism or dismiss the role of historical oppression in creating and maintaining present inequality (e.g., Augoustinos & LeCouteur, 2004; Riggs & Augoustinos, 2005). A recognition of the cultural psychological foundations of racism and sexism suggests a shift in emphasis of intervention efforts from changing personal dispositions to transforming the ecologically embedded structures that continually reconstitute those dispositions (Dasgupta & Asgari, 2004).

Likewise, regarding the consequences of being the target of systemic bias, accounts in social-personality psychology have often focused on personal dispositions that carry the wounds of past domination to the present and can reproduce future domination in situations from which oppression might otherwise be absent. For example, a history of experience with worlds of domination might promote dispositions of stigma consciousness (Pinel, 1999) or rejection sensitivity (Mendoza-Denton, Downey, Davis, Purdie, & Pietrzak, 2002) that lead people to avoid certain domains or to interact in "hyper"-vigilant ways that elicit negative treatment from otherwise "unbiased" others. Similarly, a history of engagement with worlds of domination can promote forms of internalized oppression associated with such concepts as *colonial mentality* (e.g., David & Okazaki, 2006; Fanon, 1965). Such accounts strike a delicate balance between acknowledging the subtle ways in which systems of oppression can cause harm without portraying targets in somewhat pathological terms that border on "blaming victims" for their ongoing oppression.

Without denying that a history of engagement with systems of domination can shape habitual tendencies of vigilance or similar responses to collective trauma, a focus on cultural constitution of psychological experience proposes a normalizing account of those tendencies (Adams & Salter, 2007). Rather than personal dispositions that reproduce oppression, this focus highlights how apparently pathological, personal propensities are intimately linked with—and represent continual tuning to—broader systems of domination. From this perspective, an exclusive focus on vigilance-oriented dispositions as a proximal source of ongoing suffering, without a corresponding emphasis on the cultural ecologies that reproduce and require that vigilance, can also be a cultural-psychological tool or discursive repertoire that serves to reproduce domination.

Despite potential problems, an emphasis on personal dispositions tuned to worlds of domination is critically important to catalog the ways in which

worlds of domination cause harm. Contributing to this effort, a cultural psychology analysis emphasizes that ecological structures of domination can be sufficient to elicit discrimination-like outcomes regardless of the personal dispositions of oppressed-group targets and even in the absence of discriminatory differential treatment. Perhaps the best-known example of this idea is the phenomenon of stereotype threat (Steele, 1997), whereby standard constructions of testing situations (e.g., portraying tests as diagnostic measures of ability; Steele & Aronson, 1995; see also Croizet, 2008) can be sufficient to elicit underperformance among people from negatively stereotyped groups. One need not resort to deeply embodied, personal dispositions to explain these patterns; instead, a cultural psychology analysis locates their roots in an ongoing history of engagement with—and self-protective tuning of responses to—material bases of racist oppression embedded in the structure of everyday worlds.

Summary

Rather than a comprehensive discussion of prejudice from a cultural psychology perspective (see Adams et al., 2008), the purpose of this section has been to use the case of prejudice-relevant dispositions to illustrate the idea of "context in person." A cultural psychology perspective emphasizes the extent to which much of psychological experience—not only the psychological correlates of independent and interdependent selfways that have been the focus of most work in cultural psychology, but also habits and dispositions that are the topic of mainstream psychology more generally—is not the "just natural" expression of internal essence. Instead, it reflects the sociocultural constitution of the person: the continual tuning of subjectivity to historically evolved structures for mind embedded in the stuff of everyday worlds. This idea has been an enduring theme in the interdisciplinary exercise of social psychology (e.g., Mead, 1934). A cultural psychology perspective is one of several theoretical bases from which to recapture this theme.

Person in Context: Psychological Constitution of Cultural Worlds

The preceding focus on the cultural constitution of psychological experience resonates with the objectivism and environmentalist roots of social psychology evident in discussions of automaticity (Bargh & Chartrand, 1999; Devine, 1989) and ecological affordances (Gibson, 1977; McArthur & Baron, 1983). However, an exclusive emphasis on contextual determinants neglects what may be the defining element of psychological science (as opposed to behavioral science or neuroscience): namely, a subjectivist appreciation for the role of dynamic construction processes—and related concepts of activity (versus behavior; Bruner, 1990), agency, meaning, construal and imagination—in the perception, interpretation, and (re-)production of everyday reality (Griffin & Ross, 1991). One can theorize the impact of dynamic construction processes in two ways.

UPSTREAM IMPACTS ON ACTION

The typical way in which psychologists have considered dynamic construction processes is with respect to the upstream side of action. For example, psychologists have considered the necessarily "subjective" perception of "objective" physical stimuli. Whether the topic is visual perception (e.g., Segall, Campbell, & Herskovitz, 1963), auditory perception (Bregman, 1990), memory (Bartlett, 1932), or identity (Mead, 1934), people do not have direct access to objective reality; instead, they build an emergent experience of reality from underspecified inputs. Likewise, social psychologists have emphasized the phenomenon of subjective construal, whereby people agentically interpret situations that are inherently ambiguous (e.g., whether a remark about a person's appearance is a put-down, come-on, ingratiation, or relatively innocent compliment; Ross & Nisbett, 1991; Griffin & Ross, 1991).

In similar fashion, cultural psychologists emphasize that the intersection of cultural-ecological niches does not wholly determine a person's experience; instead, people exercise some agency over selection and meaning of cultural resources that they appropriate. An important implication for a cultural psychology analysis is that each act of interpretation constitutes a form of selection pressure on the evolution of cultural realities (Heath, Bell, & Sternberg, 2001; Lau, Chiu, & Lee, 2001; McIntyre, Lyons, Clark, & Kashima, 2004; Norenzayan & Atran, 2004; Schaller, Conway, & Tanchuk, 2002). As people preferentially attend to and act on interpretations of some features of a situation, they not only ensure the continued relevance or reproduction of those features (in slightly altered form), but also produce continued irrelevance of or silence about other possible features (Trouilliot, 1995).

As an illustration, consider a classic study of sleeping arrangements among people in Chicago, Illinois, United States, and Bubaneswar, Orissa, India (Shweder et al., 1995). Noting that people in the former city tend to sleep with fewer people to

a space than do people in the latter city, researchers considered whether this pattern reflected differences in desired ways of being or was merely a function of material resources impinging on a universal desire for privacy. When the researchers asked participants to allocate sleeping space to a 7-member family under different conditions of resource availability, participants tended to reproduce locally typical sleeping patterns regardless of material affordances. That is, Chicagoans tended to preserve the privacy of the "sacred" conjugal couple even in conditions of resource scarcity, and Bubaneswaris tended to preserve the local patterns of cosleeping (e.g., to protect vulnerable members and guarantee female chastity) under conditions of resource abundance. This study suggests that, even when cultural ecologies appear to be static and unchanging across generations, this appearance of inertia often reflects the dynamic exercise of human agency and preferential selection to maintain desired cultural ecologies in the face of structural forces (e.g., acquisition of resources) that might enable other ways of being.

DOWNSTREAM CONSEQUENCES OF ACTION

The second way in which one can theorize dynamic construction processes is with respect to the downstream side of action. As people act on their interpretations or construals of events, they inscribe observable traces of their subjectivity on intersubjective space and material realities. These materialized traces of psychological experience influence the subsequent flow of interpretation and activity not only for producers and their immediate interaction partners, but also for present and future third-party observers who come in contact with those behavioral products. For example, a person who expresses greater or less interest in a phone conversation as a function of perceived attractiveness of the conversation partner elicits behavior from the partner that observers find more or less interesting (Snyder, Tanke, & Berschied, 1977). A man who responds with aggression (versus laughter) when another person calls him "Asshole!" reconstructs normative understandings of the event as a personal attack or insult that demands retaliation (rather than a ridiculous loss of self-control that one should ignore), and suggests to observers that any man's personal honor requires that he do the same (Cohen, Nisbett, Bowdle, & Schwarz, 1996; see Vandello & Cohen, 2004). A person who responds with liking or approval of someone who maintains high identity consistency across diverse situations reproduces normative understandings of this consistency as authenticity (versus insensitivity or failure to accommodate self to situations) and increases the likelihood of others will strive for such consistency (Suh, 2002). A mother who routinely asks her child about subjective emotional experience of daily events (rather than normative understandings of those events) directs her child's emerging autobiography in ways that habitually reference subjective emotional experience (versus normative understandings) as a guide to interpretation of events (Wang & Brockmeier, 2002; see also Pasupathi, 2001, for a discussion of ways in which conversation partners shape emerging autobiography and personal identity). A man who responds to somatic manifestations of anxiety by raising the alarm that a passerby has stolen his penis not only produces a construction of that interaction as an incident of magical theft, but also reproduces the associated realities (e.g., charged atmosphere of anxiety, belief in a world populated by magical penis thieves) that reconstitute fertile ground for others to report similar experience (Adams & Dzokoto, 2007). By drawing attention to such downstream consequences of action, a cultural psychology perspective extends the idea of subjective construal in historical and material directions. When people act on subjective construals they produce material realities that bear the traces of their subjectivity and thereby inscribe personal psychology into ecological context.

To illustrate this idea of "person in context," consider a classic study among students at Kyoto University (Japan) and the University of Oregon (United States; Kitayama et al., 1997). Researchers asked students in these universities to provide situations from their own lives in which they experienced success and failure. The researchers then exposed different samples of students from these universities to a random sample of 100 success situations and 100 failure situations from each university, and they asked them to consider whether (and how much) their self-esteem would rise or fall if they experienced those situations. Besides an effect of participant background, such that European American students at Oregon (who reported net self-esteem gain) tended to report higher self-esteem in response to situations than did Japanese students at Kyoto (who reported net self-esteem loss), results also revealed an effect of situation source. Regardless of participant background, Oregon-produced situations tended to elicit self-enhancing responses and Kyoto-produced settings tended to elicit less self-enhancing (or more self-critical) responses. This study suggests that the patterns of promotion-focused self-enhancement and prevention-focused self-criticism observed in American and Japanese settings (e.g., Heine et al., 1999) reside not only in the psychological habits of persons, but also in the enhancement-affording or criticism-affording situations that people in these settings create. These situations bear the self-evaluation tendencies of their producers, and exert influence on the self-evaluation of subsequent actors who encounter them.

Dynamic Construction of Personal Identity

To further illustrate dynamic construction processes, consider again the phenomenon of identity. Integration and stability in personal identity are not the mere reflection of some authentic, internal core. Instead, the apparent stability of personal identity requires continual acts of (re-)creation as a person collaborates with a relatively stable set of audiences (Hammack, 2008; Pasupathi, 2001) and draws on relatively stable configurations of ecological affordances—including selfways, subject positions (Hermans, 2001), and collective identity stereotypes—to keep the story going.

> [Identity] stories are based on biographical facts, but go considerably beyond the facts as people selectively appropriate aspects of their experience and imaginatively construe both past and future to construct stories that make sense to them and to their audiences, that vivify and integrate life and make it more or less meaningful. (McAdams, 2001, p. 101)

In terms of upstream influences, a person can exercise agency and direction over the identity process by "selectively appropriating" elements of past autobiography or local affordances and "imaginatively construing" them in ways that make sense for the person's particular identity story. For example, research suggests that people do not recall autobiographical events in neutral or "objective" fashion, but instead do so in ways that serve identity needs of the present (e.g., emphasizing success over failure to preserve a sense of moral adequacy, personal efficacy, or self-esteem; Wilson & Ross, 2003). In terms of downstream influences, the identity stories that people tell themselves and others have important consequences for self-knowledge and motivation (e.g., Pasupathi, 2001; Wilson & Ross, 2003); in particular, psychologists have noted the extent to which identity stories provide a person with a sense of meaning, direction, and purpose. For example, I manage the self-direction to drag myself away from a warm bed at 5:00 AM to work on this chapter because it is the logical next scene in an identity story that necessarily draws on local affordances, but requires my active participation.

An important consideration here is the extent to which such self-direction occurs via the psychological constitution of everyday worlds that provide the proximal ecological support for desired action. In terms of the example, part of the self-direction necessary to get out of bed requires that I imaginatively anticipate my attempts to subvert this exercise of purpose by placing the alarm clock across the room to prevent repeated use of the "snooze" button. That is, I recognize the limitations of my self-directive capacity (i.e., "willpower") in the moment of temptation, and preemptively arrange worlds that reflect my "higher" intentions and will afford behavior consistent with those intentions. Similar examples include putting a mirror on the refrigerator to remind oneself to eat more healthily, forgoing a parking pass to force oneself to use more environmentally responsible forms of transportation, joining a support group to help continually reconstitute one's identity as survivor of serious illness or recovering addict, or seeking out new social networks to help reconstitute nonracist subjectivity. In all of these examples, people exercise a distal or "culturally mediated" form of self-regulation whereby they actively construct the ecological affordances that will provide proximal regulation (via the cultural-ecological constitution of psychological experience) in some future moment.

More generally, a cultural psychology perspective suggests the extent to which integration and stability in identities occur via the psychological constitution of everyday realities that provide the ecological foundation for those identities. An interesting program of research in this regard concerns the "behavioral residue" of personality: for example, the extent to which the content and arrangement of artifacts in a room represent material expressions of personal traits (e.g., Gosling, Ko, Mannarelli, & Morris, 2002). Similar work comes from research on place-making: the process by which people transform natural space, often through use of tangible objects, by individually or jointly infusing it with meaning. For example, people constitute relationships in part through the collaborative production of a jointly constructed, material reality; that is, they buy jointly owned objects, decorate and furnish homes, create gardens, and otherwise inscribe their relationality on the structure of everyday worlds (Lohmann, Arriaga, & Goodfriend, 2003). Likewise, research has examined the extent to which people express collective identities by displaying national flags (Skitka, 2005), wearing clothing with university symbols, and otherwise "basking in reflected glory" (Cialdini et al., 1976). All of these cases illustrate the psychological constitution of cultural-ecological realities, by which actors deposit traces of their psychological experience in the material stuff of everyday worlds. However, rather than see such behavioral residue as the end-product of experience, a cultural psychology analysis emphasizes the extent to which the associated artifacts—unmade beds, joint purchases, national flags—provide scaffolding that continually reconstitutes the associated personal, relational, and collective experience (see Mischel, 1968; Ross & Nisbett, 1991).

One important implication of this discussion is to propose greater space for the exercise of human agency. Researchers who emphasize the "automaticity of everyday life" have provocatively asserted that perhaps 95% of psychological experience occurs via environmental regulation of habitual responses, allowing people to apply the remaining 5% of psychological experience that is open to self-reflection or personal control toward meaningful, self-defining pursuits (Bargh, 1997; Bargh & Chartrand, 1999). Without necessarily disputing this assessment, a cultural psychology analysis proposes the psychological constitution of cultural realities as an additional, typically underappreciated process by which people exercise agency. People exercise reflection and intention not only to direct current activity, but also to construct worlds into which they deposit their subjectivity and thereby permit a form of "automatic" intentional influence during future moments in other settings when their action and experience are under environmental regulation. Accordingly, some discussions of ecological regulation may understate the impact of human agency because they fail to appreciate the extent to which the ecology of human experience is not a "just natural" environment. Instead it is a cultural product that mediates the imagination and motivation of the intentional activity that created it. Environments, ecologies. and situations are "not natural," but instead come with imaginative possibilities and constraints, motivational directions, and other psychological traces built into them.

Intentional Worlds

A cultural psychology concept that highlights the psychological constitution of cultural realities is the notion of "intentional worlds": constructions of everyday reality that bear the psychological traces of previous actors and evolve over generations of activity to serve collectively desired ends. The "intention" in intentional worlds does not necessarily refer to the mental states of people who produce, appropriate, or fall under the influence of these cultural products. People may appropriate cultural tools without self-conscious reflection, they may engage them with little intention or awareness about their (often "unintended") consequences, and they may reproduce them with little intention or awareness about the extent to which they inscribe their own beliefs and desires. Rather, the adjective "intentional" refers to the directive force of the resulting cultural worlds, which systematically orient action toward particular ends.[3]

SELFWAYS AS INTENTIONAL WORLDS

Reflecting conventional understandings of a cultural psychology perspective, one can use the concept of intentional worlds to rethink the ecologically inscribed selfways that afford psychological experience in different communities. From this perspective, local selfways are not the fading remnant of age-old traditions, but instead are constantly evolving technologies that reflect the inventive imagination of the culturally grounded persons who select, reproduce, and extend features of local realities into the next historical moment.

In some cases—especially related to childhood socialization—the selective reproduction of ecological affordances proceeds with a fair measure of intention and awareness about the consequences of those affordances. For example, research suggests that adult caregivers talk to young children in ways designed to scaffold locally normative forms of self-understanding. In one study, American moms used elaborative conversational style that focused on the child's personal opinions, roles, and feelings. In contrast, Chinese moms rarely elaborated; instead, they repeated factual questions and showed concern for moral rules and behavioral standards (Kulkofsky, Wang, & Koh, 2009). In both cases, caregivers actively participated in the psychological constitution of different selfways. That is, they intervened in conversation to impose their own beliefs and desires on the cultural-ecological affordances that scaffold their children's emerging autobiography.

In other cases—especially related to production of marketable cultural goods—the selective reproduction of ecological affordances may proceed with considerable awareness and intention about the role of preferences in the selection process, but with little awareness or concern about consequences for local selfways. For example, an analysis of children's books

suggested that authors in Taiwanese settings produce characters who model relatively low-arousal positive affect, but authors in American settings produce characters who model relatively high-arousal positive affect (Tsai et al., 2007). Likewise, content analysis of televised interviews with Olympic medalists suggests that Japanese interviews featured a balance of positive and negative evaluations and emphasized the background or social context of performance, but American interviews emphasized positive personal characteristics of the performers (Markus et al., 2006). Presumably, the primary motivation of the producers of these artifacts is to tell stories that resonate with consumers' sensibilities and preferences, thereby increasing the demand for their product. Even so, regardless of whether producers intend to design local selfways, their products constitute intentional worlds that shape consumers' subjectivity (see Morling & Lamoreaux, 2008).

BEYOND CULTURAL VARIATION: INTENTIONAL WORLDS OF DOMINATION

Although one can apply the notion of intentional worlds to understand the psychological constitution of cultural variation, it (and a cultural psychology perspective in general) has implications for topics across the spectrum of social-personality psychology. For example, this notion resonates strongly with Bakhtinian perspectives on the dialogical nature of personhood or self (Bakhtin, 1981; Hermans, 2001), which emphasize how other people's beliefs and desires constitute multiple ecological affordances (i.e., subject positions from which a person authors an experience of self-identity).

Likewise, the cultural psychology notion of intentional worlds resonates strongly with research on behavioral confirmation processes. This research examines how people deposit their beliefs and expectations—regarding classroom performance (Rosenthal & Jacobsen, 1968), attractiveness (Snyder et al., 1977), rejection (Downey, Freitas, Michaelis, & Khouri, 1998), hostility (Dodge & Crick, 1990), or competition (Kelley & Stahelski, 1970)—into local ecologies via immediacy behaviors and other observable manifestations. For example, research suggests that people often act on anxious expectations about interracial interaction by increasing interpersonal distance as measured by physical arrangement in space (e.g., chair distance; see Goff, Steele, & Davies, 2008; Word, Zanna, & Cooper, 1973). These inscriptions of person in context bear the social influence of their producers and can elicit belief-confirming behavior (e.g., emotional distance or racialized affect) from the often unwitting targets of the expectancy.

A particularly promising way in which the notion of intentional worlds can inform social-personality psychology concerns the phenomenon of privilege. Consider again the topic of stereotype threat. Conventional discussions of this topic have emphasized how particular constructions of the test situation—specifically, as a diagnostic measure of one's essential intelligence or intellectual merit (Croizet, 2008; Steele, 1997)—cause underperformance among people from negatively stereotyped groups relative to their "true" ability in the absence of those harmful constructions. However, an exclusive emphasis on the harmful consequences of stereotype threat for people from disadvantaged groups obscures a key point about the psychology of oppression. Specifically, the same constructions of the test that artificially undermine oppressed group performance via stereotype threat also serve to artificially inflate dominant group performance via the phenomenon of stereotype lift (Walton & Cohen, 2003; Croizet, 2010). This often obscured point has two important implications for the present topic.

The first concerns understandings of *performance* and *ability*. If mainstream constructions of the test situation provide a platform for people from dominant groups that leads them to overperform relative to their "true ability" (such that they score higher than they otherwise would in the absence of the performance-enhancing construction of the test), then how is one to understand their personal ability? Is it most evident in their inflated performance under "standard" constructions of the test situation or their "corrected" performance under "more neutral" constructions of the test situation? Without denying the possibility of performance-relevant dispositions (whether acquired skills or essential abilities; Dweck, Hong, & Chiu, 1993), a cultural psychology analysis of "mind in society" (Vygotsky, 1978) emphasizes that any performance is a joint product of such dispositions and the particular, culturally evolved technologies present in an activity setting (see various perspectives in activity theory). This casts doubt on the possibility of observing raw talent from any particular measure.

The second implication concerns understandings of the test gap. The phenomenon of stereotype lift makes clear that the test gap is not merely the result of barriers that impede performance of people from oppressed groups, but also results from affordances that benefit the performance of people from dominant groups. Some readers may find it strange to refer to standard constructions of the test situation as oppressive or to propose (as I do in the preceding paragraph) that one might replace them with "more neutral" constructions. After all, the tendency in mainstream psychological science is to regard the test situation as a paragon of neutrality. In contrast, the phenomenon of stereotype lift suggests that the test situation is *not* a neutral setting in which to observe raw ability, but instead arises and persists precisely because it does important societal work. In particular, standard constructions of the test situation launder inequality. They reproduce the same differential outcomes as the raw exercise of power, but do so in a way that legitimizes the resulting inequality as the result of differences in intellectual merit (see Jackman, 1994). Indeed, the very notion of raw, internal ability—especially as an inherited entity that indicates merit—may itself produce racist inequality (see Croizet, 2010 on the "racism of intelligence"). When this notion is in play, it not only constitutes an unfair pressure that depresses performance of people with devalued identities, but also serves as a performance-enhancing ideology that unfairly inflates the performance of people with overvalued identities. Accordingly, one can speak of mainstream constructions of the test situation as "intentional worlds" of domination: apparently "neutral" constructions of reality that (1) are infused with dominant group beliefs and desires (e.g., about merit as the source of test scores) and (2) systematically reproduce differential outcomes and racial advantage.

As another example of intentional worlds of domination, consider the work that my colleagues and I have conducted on representations of history and identity as tools of oppression and liberation (Kurtiş et al., 2010; Salter & Adams, 2010). Numerous observers have noted a bidirectional relationship between memory and identity that one can observe not only at the personal level (e.g., Wilson & Ross, 2003), but also at the collective level (e.g., Sahdra & Ross, 2007). Our work considers how commemorative holidays, museums, official monuments, textbooks, and other representations of history serve as cultural technologies for memory that both reflect creators' identity concerns and direct users' actions in identity-consistent ways (Kurtiş et al., 2010; see also Loewen, 1995; Rowe, Wertsch, & Kosyaeva, 2002; Wertsch, 2002).

In one direction, corresponding to the sociocultural constitution of psychological experience, people build a sense of identity using ecologically inscribed tools (e.g., representations of history) that tend to glorify collective triumphs and deny or silence acts of collective wrongdoing (e.g., Baumeister & Hastings, 1997; Loewen, 1995; Wertsch, 2002). In the other direction, corresponding to this section's focus on the psychological constitution of cultural reality, people do not recall the past in neutral or disinterested fashion; instead, they selectively re-member and re-produce representations of the past in ways that address present identity concerns (Sahdra & Ross, 2007; Wohl, Branscombe, & Klar, 2006). For example, white American students prefer relatively mainstream commemorations of the American Thanksgiving holiday that glorify European colonization of the North American continent: celebrating it as an opportunity to express gratitude for fulfillment of divinely ordained destiny, but remaining silent about the violent destruction of indigenous societies as a result of European colonization (Kurtiş et al., 2010). Likewise, white American students prefer relatively mainstream representations of Black History Month (BHM) that emphasize peaceful coexistence in ethnically diverse communities and individual achievements of African American heroes, but remain silent about the systems of racial domination that required heroic resistance (Salter & Adams, 2010). These preferences inform subsequent actions—failure to mention racial violence in one's own Thanksgiving celebrations or BHM assignment—that reconstitute the culturally inscribed silences that in turn promote national identification and identity-defensive activity (e.g., denial about racism in American society and opposition to antiracist policy; Kurtiş et al., 2010; Nelson, Adams, Branscombe, & Schmitt, 2010; Salter & Adams, 2010). From this perspective, the proliferation of nation-glorifying, racism-denying representations in American society is not an accident or coincidence but occurs instead through incremental acts of everyday reproduction by ordinary people acting on personal understandings and preferences.

This section's emphasis on the psychological constitution of cultural reality focuses on a question about which canonical approaches to cultural psychology remain relatively silent: How or why do prevailing constructions of reality arise and persist? The conception of cultural realities as intentional worlds proposes an answer to this question. Particular constructions of reality arise and persist because people selectively reproduce bits of everyday realities that resonate with their beliefs and

desires, which include a (barely conscious) sense of group position or collective interest (Blumer, 1958; Bobo, 1999). Although privilege and domination sometimes occur through deliberate acts of direct discrimination or conscious exercise of racial power, their more typical form may be preferential reproduction of apparently "neutral" cultural tools that nevertheless have "disparate impact" and reproduce dominant-group advantage. For example, relatively innocuous constructions of behavior as choice not only resonate with middle-class understandings of action and desires for perceived control, but also "just happen" to reproduce racial inequality when people withhold aid or justice from victims because they made bad "choices" (e.g., for "choosing" to live in ethnic enclaves or to stay in New Orleans during Hurricane Katrina; see Stephens, Hamedani, Markus, Bergsieker, & Eloul, 2009). Similarly, models of ideal affect that emphasize high arousal positive states not only resonate with white American understandings and desires (Tsai, 2007), but also delegitimize the experience of dissatisfaction that often accompanies motivation for social change (Ahmed, 2008; Becker & Maracek, 2008). From this perspective, understandings of choice or ideal affect that prevail in North American settings (and mainstream psychological science) are not essentially neutral constructions that have unfortunate side-effects; instead, they are dynamically reproduced cultural tools that may evolve and persist precisely because they serve interests of domination.

Extending the Social (and Personal) in Social-personality Psychology

To conclude this chapter, consider a teacher who commemorates Black History Month with mass-marketed, mainstream artifacts that—by emphasizing cultural diversity rather than social justice and focusing on individual achievements of black heroes without mentioning the racism that required heroic resistance—reflect and promote racism denial. Even if the teacher displays these artifacts without ego-defensive motivations to deny the extent of racism in U.S. society, the products she chooses to deposit in the world nevertheless bear identity-defensive beliefs and desires of the people who produced them. Similarly, even if the teacher personally intends to promote awareness of racism and support for reparative policy, her actions nevertheless reconstitute ecologies filled with cultural tools that promote denial of racism and opposition to reparative policy. In other words, the motivations and intentions associated with the teacher's action are not reducible to her personal motivation to deny racism or personal intention to oppose antiracist policy; instead, the relevant motivations and intentions reside in the cultural tools for memory and identity on which the teacher draws.

This example illustrates well a primary goal of the chapter: to extend the "social" of social-personality psychology in ways that escape the prevailing individualism of mainstream psychological science. In keeping with the reductionist roots of psychological science, social-personality psychologists have typically retreated to atomistic philosophical positions that portray phenomena as the aggregate of separate individual experience. In contrast, a cultural psychology analysis illuminates a more *collective* understanding of mind, not in the intellectually discredited sense of a collective entity having its own motivations or intentions (Allport, 1924); nor merely in the sense of individual motivations and intentions when collective identity is salient (as in self-categorization theory; Turner et al. 1987); but instead in the sense of intentional worlds: motivation and intention deposited as psychological traces into the structure of everyday cultural ecologies. The key to this extension is an emphasis on the history and materiality of persons and situations.

Regarding the former, a cultural psychology analysis emphasizes the extent to which species-general, community-specific, or individual patterns reflect the sociocultural constitution of personal experience: the inscription of context in person over the course of development as one engages and acquires the psychological charge of ecologically embedded, cultural tools. From this perspective, even the sense of abstracted independence that informs mainstream psychological science is not "just natural," but instead is a social product that reflects the historical evolution of cultural technologies (i.e., independent selfways) that promote and maintain it.

Regarding the latter, a cultural psychology analysis emphasizes the extent to which situations and everyday ecologies reflect the psychological constitution of cultural realities: that is, the inscription of person in context as people imaginatively re-make material realities into which they deposit their beliefs and desires. Humans do not exist in a natural environment, but instead inhabit cultural ecologies that bear the accumulated, material sediment from a social history of human activity. Besides avoiding pitfalls of an exclusive emphasis on environmental determinants of action (see Reicher & Haslam, 2006; Wrong, 1961), this emphasis on the psychological constitution of cultural realities extends the "personal" in social-personality psychology beyond the narrow concern with embodied dispositions to emphasize more enduring manifestations of personal agency embedded in everyday intentional worlds (Gjerde, 2004). From this perspective, one should locate the power of the person not only in proximal self-direction of momentary experience, but also (and more profoundly) in the imagi-native capacity to construct situations (i.e., ecological manifestations of person in context) that provide distal or "culturally mediated" forms of self-regulation, even in the absence of proximal self-direction.

Acknowledgments

I thank Tuğçe Kurtiş for her considerable input into this chapter, especially at the final stages of production. I also thank the Culture and Psychology Research Group at the University of Kansas and Hazel Rose Markus for valuable suggestions on an earlier draft. This work has benefitted from countless conversations with colleagues during a fellowship at the Center for Advanced Study in the Behavioral Sciences at Stanford University—particularly the *Agency and Objects*, *Culture and Race*, and *Identities* discussion groups—and I am grateful to CASBS for support. Finally, I gratefully acknowledge the unmistakable influence of work by Lee Ross, who (along with Mark Lepper) taught me social psychology.

Address correspondence concerning this article to Glenn Adams, Department of Psychology, University of Kansas, 1415 Jayhawk Blvd., Lawrence, KS 66045–7556. Email: *adamsg@ku.edu*.

Notes

[1] Indeed, in Shweder's (1990) defining statement of a cultural psychology analysis, he appreciatively cites the work of Ross and Nisbett as one of the multidisciplinary sites where ideas compatible with a cultural psychology analysis flourish.

[2] Ross and Nisbett also noted a third principle of "tension systems" but, unlike the other two themes, did not devote a separate chapter to it. Although they undoubtedly meant it in more senses, this third principle is evident in the mutual constitution framework as a dynamic-tension relationship between the other two principles.

[3] It is noteworthy in this regard that, in addition to his famous definition of cultural psychology as the study of mutual constitution, Shweder (1990) less famously defined cultural psychology as the study of intentional worlds. Although the idea of mutual constitution has been central to a cultural psychology perspective in social-personality psychology (e.g., Fiske, Kitayama, Markus, & Nisbett, 1998; Kashima, 2000) social psychologists have typically ignored the idea of intentional worlds.

References

Adams, G. (2005). The cultural grounding of personal relationship: Enemyship in North American and West African worlds. *Journal of Personality and Social Psychology, 88,* 948–968.

Adams, G., Anderson, S. L., & Adonu, J. K. (2004). The cultural grounding of closeness and intimacy. In D. Mashek & A. Aron (Eds.), *The handbook of closeness and intimacy* (pp. 321–339). Mahwah, NJ: Erlbaum.

Adams, G., Biernat, M., Branscombe, N. R., Crandall, C. S., & Wrightsman, L. S. (2008). Beyond prejudice: Toward a sociocultural psychology of racism and oppression. In G. Adams, M. Biernat, N. R. Branscombe, C. S. Crandall, & L. S. Wrightsman (Eds.), *Commemorating* Brown*: The social psychology of racism and discrimination* (pp. 215–246). Washington, DC: American Psychological Association.

Adams, G., & Dzokoto, V. A. (2007). Genital-shrinking panic in Ghana: A cultural-psychological analysis. *Culture and Psychology, 13,* 83–104

Adams, G., & Dzokoto, V. A. (2003). Self and identity in African studies. *Self and Identity, 2,* 345–359.

Adams, G., & Markus, H. R. (2004). Toward a conception of culture suitable for a social psychology of culture. In M. Schaller & C. S. Crandall (Eds.), *Psychological foundations of culture* (pp. 335–360). Hillsdale, NJ: Erlbaum.

Adams, G., & Plaut, V. C. (2003). The cultural grounding of personal relationship: Friendship in North American and West African worlds. *Personal Relationships, 10,* 333–348.

Adams, G., & Salter, P. S. (2007). Health psychology in African settings: A cultural psychological analysis. *Journal of Health Psychology, 12,* 539–551.

Ahmed, S. (2008). Multiculturalism and the promise of happiness. *New Formations, 63,* 121–137.

Ainsworth, M. D. (1967). *Infancy in Uganda.* Baltimore: Johns Hopkins.

Allport, F. H. (1924). The group fallacy in relation to social science. *Journal of Abnormal and Psychology and Social Psychology, 19,* 60–73.

Allport, G. W. (1954). *The nature of prejudice* (8th ed.). Oxford, UK: Addison-Wesley.

Anderson, B. (1983). *Imagined communities: Reflections on the origin and spread of nationalism.* London: Verso.

Anderson, S. L., Adams, G., & Plaut, V. C. (2008). The cultural grounding of personal relationship: The importance of attractiveness in everyday life. *Journal of Personality and Social Psychology, 95,* 352–368.

Appiah, K. A. (1992). *In my father's house: Africa in the philosophy of culture.* New York: Oxford University Press.

Arnett, J. J. (2002). The psychology of globalization. *American Psychologist, 57,* 774–783.

Arnett, J. J. (2008). The neglected 95%: Why American psychology needs to become less American. *American Psychologist, 63,* 602–614.

Augoustinos, M., & LeCouteur, A. (2004). On whether to apologize to indigenous Australians: The denial of White guilt. In N. R. Branscombe & B. Doosje (Eds.), *Collective guilt: International perspectives* (pp. 2336–2261). New York: Cambridge University Press.

Bakhtin, M. (1981). *The dialogic imagination: Four essays by M. M. Bakhtin* (M. E. Holquist, Ed., C. Emerson & M. Holquist, Trans.). Austin: University of Texas Press.

Bargh, J. A. (1997). The automaticity of everyday life. In R. S. Wyer Jr. (Ed.), *Advances in social cognition* (Vol. 10, pp. 1–61). Mahwah, NJ: Erlbaum.

Bargh, J. A., & Chartrand, T. L. (1999). The unbearable automaticity of being. *American Psychologist, 54,* 462–479.

Bartlett, F. C. (1932). *Remembering: A study in experimental and social psychology.* Cambridge, UK: Cambridge University Press.

Baumeister, R. F. (1987). How the self became a problem: A psychological review of historical research. *Journal of Personality and Social Psychology, 52,* 163–176.

Baumeister, R. F., & Hastings, S. (1997). Distortions of collective memory: How groups flatter and deceive themselves. In J. W. Pennebaker, D. Paez, & B. Rime (Eds.), *Collective memory of political events: Social psychological perspectives* (pp. 277–293). Mahwah, NJ: Erlbaum.

Baumrind, D. (1968). Authoritarian vs. authoritative parental control. *Adolescence, 3,* 255–272.

Becker, D., & Maracek, J. (2008). Dreaming the American dream: Individualism and positive psychology. *Social and Personality Psychology Compass, 2,* 1767–1780. DOI: 10.1111/j.1751-9004.2008.00139.x

Bellah, R., Madsen, R., Sullivan, W., Swindler, A., & Tipton, S. (1985). *Habits of the heart: Individualism and commitment in American life.* New York: Harper & Row.

Berger, P. L., & Luckmann, T. (1966), *The social construction of reality: A treatise in the sociology of knowledge,* Garden City, NY: Anchor Books.

Billig, M. (1995). *Banal nationalism.* London: Sage.

Bledsoe, C. (1990). No success without struggle: Social mobility and hardship for foster children in Sierra Leone. *Man, 25,* 70–88.

Blumer, H. (1958). Race prejudice as a sense of group position. *Pacific Sociological Review, 1,* 3–7.

Bobo, L. D. (1999). Prejudice as group position: Microfoundations of a sociological approach to racism and race relations. *Journal of Social Issues, 55,* 445–472.

Bourdieu, P. (1977). *Outline of a theory of practice.* Cambridge: Cambridge University Press.

Bregman, A. S. (1990). *Auditory scene analysis: The perceptual organization of sound.* Cambridge, MA: MIT Press.

Bruner, J. (1990). *Acts of meaning.* Cambridge, MA: Harvard University Press.

Chiu, C. Y., Gelfand, M., Yamagishi, T., Shteynberg, G., & Wan, C. (2010). Intersubjective culture: The role of intersubjective perceptions in cross-cultural research. *Perspectives on Psychological Science, 5,* 482–493.

Cialdini, R. B., Borden, R. J., Thorne, A., Walker, M., Freeman, S., & Sloan, L. (1976). Basking in reflected glory: Three (football) field studies. *Journal of Personality and Social Psychology, 34,* 366–375.

Coe, C. (in press). What is love? The materiality of care in Ghanaian transnational families. *International Migration.*

Cohen, D., Nisbett, R. E., Bowdle, B. F., & Schwarz, N. (1996). Insult, aggression, and the Southern culture of honor: An "experimental ethnography." *Journal of Personality and Social Psychology, 70,* 945–960.

Cole, J. (2001). *Forget colonialism? Sacrifice and the art of memory in Madagascar.* Berkeley: University of California Press.

Cole, M. (1996). *Cultural psychology: A once and future discipline.* Cambridge, MA: Harvard University Press.

Cousins, S. D. (1989). Culture and selfhood in Japan and the U.S. *Journal of Personality and Social Psychology, 56,* 124–131.

Croizet, J.-C. (2008). The pernicious relationship between merit assessment and discrimination in education. In G. Adams,

M. Biernat, N. R. Branscombe, C. S. Crandall, & L. S. Wrightman (Eds.), *Commemorating* Brown: *The social psychology of racism and discrimination* (pp. 153–172). Washington, DC: American Psychological Association.

Croizet, J. C. (2011). The racism of intelligence: How mental testing practices have constituted an institutionalized form of group domination. In H. L. Gates (Ed.), *Handbook of African American citizenship*. Oxford: Oxford University Press.

Dasgupta, N., & Asgari, S. (2004). Seeing is believing: Exposure to counterstereotypic women leaders and its effect on the malleability of automatic gender stereotyping. *Journal of Experimental Social Psychology, 40,* 642–658.

David, E. J. R., & Okazaki, S. (2006). Colonial mentality: A review and recommendation for Filipino American psychology. *Cultural Diversity and Ethnic Minority Psychology, 12,* 1–16.

Devine, P. G. (1989). Stereotypes and prejudice: Their automatic and controlled components. *Journal of Personality and Social Psychology, 56,* 5–18.

Dodge, K. A., & Crick, N. R. (1990). Social information-processing bases of aggressive behavior in children. *Personality and Social Psychology Bulletin, 16,* 8–22.

Dodoo, F. N.-A. (1998). Marriage type and reproductive decisions: A comparative study in sub-Saharan Africa. *Journal of Marriage and the Family, 60,* 232–242.

Downey, G., Freitas, A. L., Michaelis, B., & Khouri, H. (1998). The self-fulfilling prophecy in close relationships: Rejection sensitivity and rejection by romantic partners. *Journal of Personality and Social Psychology, 75,* 545–560.

Durrheim, K., & Dixon, J. (2004). Attitudes in the fiber of everyday life: The discourse of racial evaluation and the lived experience of desegregation. *American Psychologist, 59,* 626–636.

Dweck, C. S., Hong, Y., & Chiu, C. Y. (1993). Implicit theories: Individual differences in the likelihood and meaning of dispositional inference. *Personality and Social Psychology Bulletin, 19,* 644–656.

Eberhardt, J. L., Goff, P. A., Purdie, V. J., & Davies, P. G. (2004). Seeing Black: Race, crime, and visual processing. *Journal of Personality and Social Psychology, 87,* 876–893.

Eid, M., & Diener, E. (2001). Norms for experiencing emotions in different cultures: Inter- and intranational differences. *Journal of Personality and Social Psychology, 81,* 869–885.

Endo, Y., & Meijer, Z. (2004). Autobiographical memory of success and failure experiences. In Y. Kashima, Y. Endo, E. S. Kashima, C. Leung, & J. McClure (Eds.), *Progress in Asian social psychology* (Vol. 4, pp.67–84). Seoul, Korea: Kyoyook-Kwahak-Sa Publishing Company.

Erikson, E. H. (1968). *Identity: Youth and crisis.* New York: Norton.

Fanon, F. (1965). *The wretched of the earth.* New York: Grove.

Fazio, R. H., Jackson, J. R., Dunton, B. C., & Williams, C. J. (1995). Variability in automatic activation as an unobtrusive measure of racial attitudes. *Journal of Personality and Social Psychology, 96,* 1013–1027.

Ferme, M. C. (2001). *The underneath of things: Violence, history, and the everyday in Sierra Leone.* Berkeley: University of California Press.

Ferguson, J. (2006). *Global shadows: Africa in the neoliberal world order.* Durham, NC: Duke University Press.

Fiske, A. P. (1991). *Structures of social life: The four elementary forms of social relations: Communal sharing, authority ranking, equality matching, and market pricing.* New York: Free Press.

Fiske, A., Kitayama, S., Markus, H. R., & Nisbett, R. E. (1998). The cultural matrix of social psychology. In D. Gilbert & S. Fiske & G. Lindzey (Eds.), *The handbook of social psychology* (4th ed., pp. 915–981). San Francisco: McGraw-Hill.

Fryberg, S. A., & Townsend, S. S. M. (2008). The psychology of invisibility. In G. Adams, M. Biernat, N. R. Branscombe, C. S. Crandall, & L. S. Wrightsman (Eds.), *Commemorating* Brown: *The social psychology of racism and discrimination* (pp. 173–193). Washington, DC: American Psychological Association.

Geschiere, P. (1997). *The modernity of witchcraft: Politics and the occult in postcolonial Africa.* Charlottesville: University of Virginia Press.

Gibson, J. J. (1977). The theory of affordances. In R. Shaw & J. Bransford (Eds.), *Perceiving, acting, and knowing: Toward an ecological psychology* (pp. 67–82). Hillsdale, NJ: Erlbaum.

Giddens, A. (1991). *Modernity and self-identity: Self and society in the late modern age.* Cambridge, UK: Polity.

Gjerde, P. F. (2004). Culture, power, and experience: Toward a person-centered cultural psychology. *Human Development, 47,* 138–157.

Glick, P., & Fiske, S. T. (1996). The ambivalent sexism inventory: Differentiating hostile and benevolent sexism. *Journal of Personality and Social Psychology, 70,* 491–512.

Goff, P. A., Steele, C. M., & Davies, P. G. (2008). The space between us: Stereotype threat and distance in interracial contexts. *Journal of Personality and Social Psychology, 94,* 91–107.

Goff, P. A., Williams, M. J., Eberhardt, J. L., & Jackson, M. C. (2008). Not yet human: Implicit knowledge, historical dehumanization, and contemporary consequences. *Journal of Personality and Social Psychology, 94,* 292–306.

Goffman, E. (1959). *The presentation of self in everyday life.* New York: Anchor Books.

Goody, E. (1982). *Parenthood and social reproduction: Fostering and occupational roles in West Africa.* Cambridge, UK: Cambridge University Press.

Gosling, S. D., Ko, S., J., Mannarelli, T., & Morris, M. E. (2002). A room with a cue: Personality judgments based on offices and bedrooms. *Journal of Personality and Social Psychology, 82,* 379–398.

Greenfield, P. M., Keller, H., Fuligni, A., & Maynard, A. (2003). Cultural pathways through universal development. *Annual Review of Psychology, 54,* 461–490.

Greenfield, P. M., Maynard, A. E., & Martí, F. A. (2009). Implications of commerce and urbanization for the learning environments of everyday life: A Zinacantec Maya family across time and space. *Journal of Cross-Cultural Psychology, 40,* 935–952.

Greenwald, A. G., McGhee, D. E., & Schwartz, J. K. L. (1998). Measuring individual differences in implicit cognition: The Implicit Associations Test. *Journal of Personality and Social Psychology, 64,* 1464–1480.

Griffin, D., & Ross, L. (1991). Subjective construal, social inference, and human misunderstanding. In M. P. Zanna (Ed.), *Advances in experimental social psychology* (Vol. 24, pp. 319–359). San Diego, CA: Academic.

Hammack, P. L. (2008). Narrative and the cultural psychology of identity. *Personality and Social Psychology Review, 12,* 222–247.

Hardin, C. D., & Higgins, E. T. (1996). Shared reality: How social verification makes the subjective objective. In R. Sorrentino & E. T. Higgins (Eds.), *Handbook of motivation and cognition* (Vol. 3, pp. 28–84). New York: Guilford.

Hawkins, S. (2002). *Writing and colonialism in Northern Ghana: The encounter between the LoDagaa and "The world on paper," 1892–1991.* Toronto: University of Toronto Press.

Heath C., Bell C., & Sternberg E. (2001). Emotional selection in memes: The case of urban legends. *Journal of Personality and Social Psychology, 81,* 1028–1041.

Heine, S. J., & Hamamura, T. (2007). In search of East Asian self-enhancement. *Personality and Social Psychology Review, 11,* 1–24.

Heine, S. J., Kitayama, S., Lehman, D. R., Takata, T., Ide, E., Leung, C., et al. (2001). Divergent consequences of success and failure in Japan and North America: An investigation of self-improving motivations and malleable selves. *Journal of Personality and Social Psychology, 81,* 599–615.

Heine, S. J., Lehman, D. R., Markus, H. R., & Kitayama, S. (1999). Is there a universal need for positive self-regard? *Psychological Review, 106,* 766–794.

Henrich, J., Boyd, R., Bowles, S., Camerer, C., Fehr, E., & Gintis, H., et al. (2005). "Economic man" in cross-cultural perspective: Behavioral experiments in 15 small-scale societies. *Behavioral and Brain Sciences, 28,* 795–855.

Henrich, J., Heine, S. J., & Norenzayan, A. (2010). The weirdest people in the world? *Behavioral and Brain Sciences, 33,* 61–83.

Henry, P. J., & Sears, D. O. (2002). The symbolic racism 2000 scale. *Political Psychology, 23,* 253–283.

Hermans, H. J. M. (2001). The dialogical self: Toward a theory of personal and cultural positioning. *Culture and Psychology, 7,* 243–281.

Higgins, E. T. (1996). The "self digest": Self-knowledge serving self-regulatory functions. *Journal of Personality and Social Psychology, 71,* 1062–1083.

Higgins, E. T. (1997). Beyond pleasure and pain. *American Psychologist, 52,* 1280–1300.

Jackman, M. R. (1994). *The velvet glove: Paternalism and conflict in gender, class, and race relations.* Berkeley: University of California Press.

Jackson, M. S. (1982). *Allegories of the wilderness: Ethics and ambiguity in Kuranko narratives.* Bloomington: Indiana University Press.

Jones, E. E., & Sigall, H. (1971). The bogus pipeline: A new paradigm for measuring affect and attitude. *Psychological Bulletin, 76,* 349–364.

Kağıtçıbaşı, Ç. (1996). *Family and human development across cultures: A view from the other side.* Mahwah, NJ: Erlbaum.

Kağıtçıbaşı, Ç., & Ataca, B. (2005). Value of children and family change: A three-decade portrait from Turkey. *Applied Psychology, 54,* 317–337.

Karp, D. R., Jin, N., Yamagishi, T., & Shinotsuka, H. (1993). Raising the minimum in the minimal group paradigm. *Japanese Journal of Experimental Social Psychology, 32,* 231–240.

Karpinski, A., & Hilton, J. L. (2001). Attitudes and the implicit association test. *Journal of Personality and Social Psychology, 81,* 774–788.

Kashima, Y. (2000). Conceptions of culture and person for psychology. *Journal of Cross-Cultural Psychology, 31,* 14–32.

Kashima, E. S., & Kashima, Y. (1998). Culture and language: The case of cultural dimensions and personal pronoun use. *Journal of Cross-Cultural Psychology, 29,* 461–486.

Keller, H. (2003). Socialization for competence: Cultural models of infancy. *Human Development, 46,* 288–311.

Keller, H., Schölmerich, A., & Eibl-Eibesfeldt, I. (1988). Communication patterns in adult-infant interactions in Western and non-Western cultures. *Journal of Cross-Cultural Psychology, 19,* 427–445.

Kelley, H. H., & Stahelski, A. J. (1970). Social interaction basis of cooperators' and competitors' beliefs about others. *Journal of Personality and Social Psychology, 16,* 66–91.

Kim, Y. H., Chiu, C. Y., Peng, S., Cai, H., & Tov, W. (2010). Explaining East-West differences in the likelihood of making favorable self-evaluations: The role of evaluation apprehension and directness of expression. *Journal of Cross-Cultural Psychology, 4,* 62–75.

Kim, H., & Markus, H. R. (1999). Deviance or uniqueness, harmony or conformity? A cultural analysis. *Journal of Personality and Social Psychology, 77,* 785–800.

Kim, H. S., & Sherman, D. K. (2007). "Express yourself": Culture and the effect of self-expression on choice. *Journal of Personality and Social Psychology, 92,* 1–11.

Kim, H. S., Sherman, D. K., & Taylor, S. E. (2008). Culture and social support. *American Psychologist, 63,* 518–526.

Kitayama, S., Ishii, K., Imada, T., Takemura, K., & Ramaswamy, J. (2006). Voluntary settlement and the spirit of independence: Evidence from Japan's "Northern frontier." *Journal of Personality and Social Psychology, 91,* 369–384.

Kitayama, S., Markus, H. R., & Kurokawa, M. (2010). Culture, emotion, and well-being: Good feelings in Japan and the United States. *Cognition and Emotion, 14,* 93–124.

Kitayama, S., Markus, H. R., Matsumoto, H., & Norasakkunkit, V. (1997). Individual and collective processes in the construction of the self: Self-enhancement in the United States and self-criticism in Japan. *Journal of Personality and Social Psychology, 72,* 1245–1267.

Knowles, E. D., Lowery, B. S., Hogan, C. M., & Chow, R. M. (2009). On the malleability of ideology: Motivated construals of color blindness. *Journal of Personality and Social Psychology, 96,* 857–869.

Krieger, L. H., & Fiske, S. T. (2006). Behavioral realism in employment discrimination law: Implicit bias and disparate treatment. *California Law Review, 94,* 997–1062.

Kühnen, U., Hannover, B., & Schubert, B. (2001). The semantic-procedural interface model of the self: The role of self-knowledge for context-dependent versus context-independent modes of thinking. *Journal of Personality and Social Psychology, 80,* 397–409.

Kühnen, U., & Oyserman, D. (2002). Thinking about the self influences thinking in general: Cognitive influences of salient self-concept. *Journal of Experimental Social Psychology, 38,* 492–499.

Kulkofsky, S., Wang, Q., & Koh, J. B. K. (2009). Functions of memory sharing and mother-child reminiscing behaviors: Individual and cultural variations. *Journal of Cognition and Development, 10,* 92–114.

Kurtiş, T., Adams, G., & Yellow Bird, M. (2010). Generosity or genocide? Identity implications of silence in American Thanksgiving commemorations. *Memory, 18,* 208–224.

Langlois, J. H., Kalakanis, L., Rubenstein, A. J., Larson, A., Hallam, M., & Smoot, M. (2000). Maxims or myths of beauty? A meta-analytic and theoretical review. *Psychological Bulletin, 126,* 390–423.

Lau, I. Y. M., Chiu, C. Y., & Lee, S.-I. (2001). Communication and shared reality: Implications for the psychological foundations of culture. *Social Cognition, 19,* 350–371.

Lee, A. Y., Aaker, J. L., & Gardner, W. L. (2000). The pleasures and pains of distinct self-construals: The role of interdependence in regulatory focus. *Journal of Personality and Social Psychology, 78,* 1122–1134.

Lee, F., Hallahan, M., & Herzog, T. (1996). Explaining real life events: How culture and domain shape attributions. *Personality and Social Psychology Bulletin, 22,* 732–741.

Lentz, C. (2006). *Ethnicity and the making of history in Northern Ghana.* Edinburgh: Edinburgh University Press.

LeVine, R. A., Dixon, S., LeVine, S., Richman, A., Leiderman, P. H., Keefer, C. H., et al. (1994). *Child care and culture: Lessons from Africa.* New York: Cambridge University Press.

Lewis, M. W., & Wigen, K. E. (1997). *The myth of continents: A critique of metageography.* Berkeley: University of California Press.

Loewen, J. (1995). *Lies my teacher told me: Everything your American history textbook got wrong.* New York: Touchstone.

Lohmann, A., Arriaga, X. B., Goodfriend, W. (2003). Close relationships and placemaking: Do objects in a couple's home reflect couplehood? *Personal Relationships, 10,* 437–449.

Main, M. (1990). Cross-cultural studies of attachment organization: Recent studies, changing methodologies, and the concept of conditional strategies. *Human Development, 33,* 48–61.

Mamdani, M. (2001). *When victims become killers: Colonialism, nativism, and the genocide in Rwanda.* Princeton, NJ: Princeton University Press.

Markus, H. R., & Kitayama, S. (1991). Culture and self: Implications for cognition, emotion, and motivation. *Psychological Review, 98,* 224–253.

Markus, H. R., & Kitayama, S. (2004). Models of agency: Sociocultural diversity in the construction of action. In V. Murphy-Berman & J. J. Berman (Eds.), *Nebraska symposium on motivation: Vol. 49. Cross-cultural differences in perspectives on self* (pp. 1–57). Lincoln: University of Nebraska Press.

Markus, H. R., Mullally, P. R., & Kitayama, S. (1997). Selfways: Diversity in modes of cultural perception. In U. Neisser & D. A. Jopling (Eds.), *The conceptual self in context: Culture, experience, self-understanding. The Emory symposia in cognition.* (pp. 13–61). New York: Cambridge University Press.

Markus, H. R., Ryff, C. D., Curhan, K. B., & Palmersheim, K. A. (2004). In their own words: Well-being at midlife among high school educated and college-educated adults. In O. G. Brim, C. D. Ryff, & R. C. Kessler (Eds.), *How healthy are we? A national study of well-being at midlife* (pp. 273–319). Chicago: University of Chicago Press.

Markus, H. R., Uchida, Y., Omoregie, H., Townsend, S. S. M., & Kitayama, S. (2006). Going for the gold: Models of agency in Japanese and American contexts. *Psychological Science, 17,* 103–112.

Masuda, T., & Nisbett, R. E. (2001). Attending holistically vs. analytically: Comparing the context sensitivity of Japanese and Americans. *Journal of Personality and Social Psychology, 81,* 922–934.

Matsumoto, D. (1999). Culture and self: An empirical assessment of Markus and Kitayama's theory of independent and interdependent self-construal. *Asian Journal of Social Psychology, 2,* 289–310.

Mbembe, A. (1992). Provisional notes on the postcolony. *Africa, 62,* 3–37.

McAdams, D. P. (2001). The psychology of life stories. *Review of General Psychology, 5,* 100–122.

McArthur, L. Z., & Baron, R. M. (1983). Toward an ecological theory of social perception. *Psychological Review, 90,* 215–238.

McConahay, J. B. (1986). Modern racism, ambivalence, and the Modern Racism Scale. In J. F. Dovidio & S. L. Gaertner (Eds.), *Prejudice, discrimination, and racism* (pp.91–125). Orlando, FL: Academic.

McCrae, R. R., & Allik, J. (Eds.).(2002). *The five-factor model of personality across cultures.* New York: Kluwer.

McIntyre, A., Lyons, A., Clark, A. E., & Kashima, Y. (2004). The microgenesis of culture: Serial reproduction as an experimental simulation of cultural dynamics. In M. Schaller, & C. S. Crandall (Eds.), *The psychological foundations of culture* (pp. 227–258). Mahwah, NJ: Erlbaum.

Mead, G. H. (1934). *Mind, self, and society* (Charles W. Morris, Ed.) Chicago: University of Chicago Press.

Mendoza-Denton, R., Downey, G., Davis, A., Purdie, V., & Pietrzak, J. (2002). Sensitivity to status-based rejection: Implications for African American students' college experience. *Journal of Personality and Social Psychology, 83,* 896–918.

Mesquita, B. (2001). Emotions in collectivist and individualist contexts. *Journal of Personality and Social Psychology, 80,* 68–74.

Meyer, B. (1998). The power of money: Politics, sorcery, and Pentecostalism in Ghana. *African Studies Review, 41,* 15–38.

Miller, J. G. (1984). Culture and the development of everyday social explanation. *Journal of Personality and Social Psychology, 46,* 961–978.

Mischel, W. (1968). *Personality and assessment.* New York: Wiley.

Morling, B., Kitayama, S., & Miyamoto, Y. (2002). Cultural practices emphasize influence in the United States and adjustment in Japan. *Personality and Social Psychology Bulletin, 28,* 311–323.

Morling, B., & Lamoreaux, M. (2008). Measuring culture outside the head: A meta-analysis of cultural products. *Personality and Social Psychology Review, 12,* 199–221.

Morelli, G. A., Rogoff, B., Oppenheim, D., & Goldsmith, D. (1992). Cultural variation in infants' sleeping arrangements: Questions of independence. *Developmental Psychology, 28,* 604–613.

Moscovici, S. (1984). The phenomena of social representations. In R. M. Farr & S. Moscovici (Eds.), *Social representations* (pp. 3–69). Cambridge, UK: Cambridge University Press

Mudimbe, V. Y. (1988). *The invention of Africa: The geography of a discourse.* Bloomington: Indiana University Press.

Nelson, J. C., Adams, G., Branscombe, N. R., & Schmitt, M. T. (2010). The role of historical knowledge in perception of race-based conspiracies. *Race and Social Problems, 2,* 69–80.

Nisbett, R. E., Peng, K., Choi, I., & Norenzayan, A. (2001). Culture and systems of thought: Holistic vs. analytic cognition. *Psychological Review, 108,* 291–310.

Norenzayan, A., & Atran, S. (2004). Cognitive and emotional processes in the cultural transmission of natural and non-natural beliefs. In M. Schaller & C. Crandall (Eds.), *The psychological foundations of culture* (pp 149–169). Mahwah, NJ: Erlbaum.

Norenzayan, A., Smith, E. E., Kim, B. J., & Nisbett, R. E. (2002). Cultural preferences for formal versus intuitive reasoning. *Cognitive Science, 26,* 653–684.

Oishi, S., Diener, E., Scollon, C. N., & Biswas-Diener, R. (2004). Cross-cultural consistency of affective experiences across cultures. *Journal of Personality and Social Psychology, 86,* 460–472.

Oishi, S., Ishii, K., & Lun, J. (2009). Residential mobility and conditionality of group identification. *Journal of Experimental Social Psychology, 45,* 913–919.

Oishi, S., & Kisling, J. (2009). The mutual constitution of residential mobility and individualism. In R. S. Wyer Jr., C-Y. Chiu, Y. Y. Hong, & S. Shavitt (Eds.), *Understanding culture: Theory, research, and application* (pp. 223–238). New York: Psychology Press.

Okazaki, S., David, E. J. R., & Abelmann, N. (2007). Colonialism and psychology of culture. *Social and Personality Psychology Compass, 2,* 90–106. DOI: 10.1111/j.1751–9004.2007.00046.x

Oppong, C. (1973). *Growing up in Dagbon.* Tema, Ghana: Ghana Publishing Corporation.

Oppong, C. (1974). *Marriage among a matrilineal elite: A family study of Ghanaian senior civil servants.* Cambridge, UK: Cambridge University Press.

Oyserman, D., Coon, H. M., & Kemmelmeier, M. (2002). Rethinking individualism and collectivism: Evaluation of theoretical assumptions and meta-analyses. *Psychological Bulletin, 128,* 3–72.

Pasupathi, M. (2001). The social construction of the personal past and its implications for adult development. *Psychological Bulletin, 127,* 651–672.

Peel, J. D. Y. (2001). *Religious encounter and the making of the Yoruba.* Indianapolis; Bloomington: Indiana University Press.

Peng, K., & Nisbett, R. E. (1999). Culture, dialectics, and reasoning about contradiction. *American Psychologist, 54,* 741–754.

Pettigrew, T. F., & Tropp, L. R. (2006). A meta-analytic test of intergroup contact theory. *Journal of Personality and Social Psychology, 90,* 751–783.

Pinel, E. C. (1999). Stigma consciousness: The social legacy of stereotypes. *Journal of Personality and Social Psychology, 76,* 114–128.

Plaut, V. C., Adams, G., & Anderson, S. (2009). Does attractiveness buy happiness? "It depends where you're from." *Personal Relationships, 16,* 619–630.

Pratto, F., Sidanius, J., Stallworth, L. M., & Malle, B. F. (1994). Social dominance orientation: A personality variable predicting social and political attitudes. *Journal of Personality and Social Psychology, 67,* 741–763.

Prentice, D. A., Miller, D. T., & Lightdale, J. R. (1994). Asymmetries in attachments to groups and to their members: Distinguishing between common-identity and common-bond groups. *Personality and Social Psychology Bulletin, 20,* 484–493.

Radcliffe-Brown, A. (1940). On joking relationships. *Africa, 13,* 195–210.

Reicher, S., & Haslam, A. S. (2006). On the agency of individuals and groups: Lessons from the BBC prison study. In T. Postmes & J. Jetten (Eds.), *Individuality and the group: Advances in social identity* (pp. 237–257). Thousand Oaks, CA: Sage.

Reicher, S., & Hopkins, N. (2001). *Self and nation.* London: Sage.

Reisman, P. (1992). *First find your child a good mother.* New Brunswick, NJ: Rutledge University Press.

Riggs, D. W., & Augoustinos, M. (2005). The psychic life of colonial power: Racialised subjectivities, bodies, and methods. *Journal of Community and Applied Social Psychology, 15,* 461–477.

Rogoff, B. (1990). *Apprenticeship in thinking: Cognitive development in social context.* New York: Oxford University Press.

Rosenthal, R., & Jacobson, L. (1968). *Pygmalion in the classroom.* New York: Holt, Rinehart, and Winston.

Ross, L. (1977). The intuitive psychologist and his shortcomings. In L. Berkowitz (Ed.), *Advances in experimental social psychology* (Vol. 10, pp.173–220). New York: Academic.

Ross, L. D., & Nisbett, R. E. (1991). *The person and the situation: Perspectives of social psychology.* New York: McGraw-Hill.

Rothbaum, F., Weisz, J., Pott, M., Miyake, K., & Morelli, G. (2000). Attachment and culture: Security in the United States and Japan. *American Psychologist, 55,* 1093–1104.

Rowe, S., Wertsch, J., & Kosyaeva, T. (2002). Linking little narratives to big ones: Narrative and public memory in history museums. *Culture and Psychology, 8,* 96–112.

Rozin, P. (2007). Food and eating. In S. Kitayama & D. Cohen (Eds.). *Handbook of cultural psychology* (pp. 391–416). New York: Guilford.

Rusbult, C. E. (1980). Commitment and satisfaction in romantic associations: A test of the investment model. *Journal of Experimental Social Psychology, 16,* 172–186.

Sahdra, B., & Ross, M. (2007). Group identification and historical memory. *Personality and Social Psychology Bulletin, 33,* 384–395.

Said, E. W. (1978). *Orientalism.* New York: Vintage.

Salter, P. S., & Adams, G. (2010). *Representations of black history as instruments of liberation and oppression.* Unpublished manuscript. University of Kansas. Lawrence, KS.

Savani, K., Markus, H. R., & Conner, A. L. (2008). Let your preference be your guide? Preferences and choices are more tightly linked for North Americans than for Indians. *Journal of Personality and Social Psychology, 95,* 861–876.

Schaller, M., Conway, L. G., & Tanchuk, T. L. (2002). Selective pressures on the once and future contents of ethnic stereotypes: Effects of the communicability of traits. *Journal of Personality and Social Psychology, 82,* 861–877.

Scribner, S., & Cole, M. (1981). *The psychology of literacy.* London: Harvard University Press.

Segall, M. H., Campbell, D. T., & Herskovits, M. J. (1963). Cultural differences in the perception of geometric illusions. *Science, 139,* 769–771.

Shaw, R. (2000). "Tok af, lef af": A political economy of Temne techniques of secrecy and self. In I. Karp & D. A. Masolo (Eds.), *African philosophy as cultural inquiry* (pp. 25–49). Bloomington: Indiana University Press.

Shweder, R. A. (1990). Cultural psychology: What is it? In J. Stigler, R. Shweder, & G. Herdt (Eds.), *Cultural psychology: Essays on comparative human development* (pp. 1–46). Cambridge, UK: Cambridge University Press.

Shweder, R. A., & Bourne, E. J. (1984). Does the concept of the person vary cross-culturally? In A. J. Marsella & G. M. White (Eds.), *Cultural conceptions of mental health and therapy* (pp. 97–137). New York: Kluwer.

Shweder, R. A., Jensen, L. A., & Goldstein, W. M. (1995). Who sleeps by whom revisited: A method for extracting the moral goods implicit in practice. In J. J. Goodnow, P. J. Miller, & F. Kessel (Eds.), *Cultural practices as contexts for development: New directions for child development* (pp. 21–39). San Francisco: Jossey-Bass.

Sinclair, S., Lowery, B. S., Hardin, C. D., & Colangelo, A. (2005). Social tuning of automatic racial attitudes: The role of affiliative motivation. *Journal of Personality and Social Psychology, 89,* 583–592.

Singelis, T. M., Bond, M. H., Lai, S. Y., & Sharkey, W. F. (1999). Unpacking culture's influence on self-esteem and embarrassability: The role of self-construals. *Journal of Cross-Cultural Psychology, 30,* 215–331.

Skitka, L. J. (2005). Patriotism or nationalism? Understanding post–September 11, 2001 flag-display behavior. *Journal of Applied Social Psychology, 35*, 1995–2011.

Snibbe, A. C., & Markus, H. R. (2005). You can't always get what you want: Educational attainment, agency, and choice. *Journal of Personality and Social Psychology, 88*, 703–720.

Snyder, M., Tanke, E. D., Berschied, E. (1977). Social perception and interpersonal behavior: On the self-fulfilling nature of social stereotypes. *Journal of Personality and Social Psychology, 35*, 656–666.

Steele, C. M. (1997). A threat in the air: How stereotypes shape intellectual identity and performance. *American Psychologist, 52*, 613–629.

Steele, C. M., & Aronson, J. (1995). Stereotype threat and the test performance of African Americans. *Journal of Personality and Social Psychology, 69*, 797–811.

Stephens, N. M., Hamedani, M. G., Markus, H. R., Bergsieker, H. B., & Eloul, L. (2009). Why did they "choose" to stay? Perspectives of Hurricane Katrina observers and survivors. *Psychological Science, 20*, 878–886.

Suh, E. M. (2002). Culture, identity consistency, and subjective well-being. *Journal of Personality and Social Psychology, 83*, 1378–1391.

Suh, E. M., Diener, E., Oishi, S., & Triandis, H. C. (1998). The shifting basis of life satisfaction judgments across cultures: Emotions versus norms. *Journal of Personality and Social Psychology, 74*, 482–493.

Tengan, E. (1991). *The land as being and cosmos: The institution of the Earth Cult among the Sisaala of northern Ghana*. Frankfurt, Germany: Peter Lang.

Tomasello, M. (1999). A puzzle and a hypothesis. In *The cultural origins of human cognition* (pp. 1–12). Cambridge, MA: Harvard University Press.

Triandis, H. C., Bontempo, R., Villareal, M. J., Asai, M., & Lucca, N. (1988). Individualism and collectivism: Cross-cultural perspectives on self-ingroup relationships. *Journal of Personality and Social Psychology, 54*, 323–338.

Trouillot, M. R. (1995). *Silencing the past: Power and the production of history*. Boston: Beacon Press.

Tsai, J. L., (2007). Ideal affect: Cultural causes and behavioral consequences. *Perspectives on Psychological Science, 2*, 242–259.

Tsai, J. L., Louie, J. Y., Chen, E. E., Uchida, Y. (2007). Learning what feelings to desire: Socialization of ideal affect through children's storybooks. *Personality and Social Psychology Bulletin, 33*, 17–30.

Turner, J. C., Hogg, M. A., Oakes, P. J., Reicher, S. D., & Wetherell, M. S. (1987). *Rediscovering the social group: A self-categorization theory*. Oxford: Blackwell.

United Nations Development Program (2010). *The real wealth of nations: Pathways to human development (Human Development Report 2010)*. New York: Palgrave Macmillan.

van der Geest, S. (2009). Anyway! Lorry inscriptions in Ghana. In J.-B. Gewald, S. Luning, & K. van Walraven (Eds.), *The speed of change: Motor vehicles and people in Africa, 1890–2000* (pp. 253–293). Leiden, Netherlands: Brill.

Vandello, J. A., & Cohen, D. (2004). When believing is seeing: Sustaining norms of violence in cultures of honor. In M. Schaller & C. Crandall (Eds.), *The psychological foundations of culture* (pp. 281–304). Mahwah, NJ: Erlbaum.

Vygotsky, L. S. (1978). *Mind in society: The development of higher psychological processes*. Cambridge, MA: Harvard University Press.

Wang, Q., & Brockmeier, J. (2002). Autobiographical remembering as cultural practice: Understanding the interplay between memory, self, and culture. *Culture and Psychology, 8*, 45–64.

Walton, G. M., & Cohen, G. L. (2003). Stereotype lift. *Journal of Experimental Social Psychology, 39*, 456–467.

Weisbuch, M., Pauker, K., & Ambady, N. (2009). The subtle transmission of race bias via televised nonverbal behavior. *Science, 326*, 1711–1714.

Weisner, T. S. (2005). Commentary: Attachment as a cultural and ecological problem with pluralistic cultural and ecological solutions. *Human Development, 48*, 89–94.

Wertsch, J. V. (2002). *Voices of collective remembering*. Cambridge, UK: Cambridge University Press.

Wetherell, M., & Potter, J. (1992). *Mapping the language of racism*. New York: Cambridge University Press.

Wilson, A. E., & Ross, M. (2003). The identity function of autobiographical memory: Time is on our side. *Memory, 11*, 137–149.

Winichakul, T. (1994). *Siam mapped: A history of the geo-body of a nation*. Honolulu: University of Hawaii Press.

Wohl, M. J. A., Branscombe, N. R., & Klar, Y. (2006). Collective guilt: Emotional reactions when one's group has done wrong or been wronged. *European Review of Social Psychology, 17*, 1–37.

Word, C. O., Zanna, M. P., & Cooper, J. (1973). The nonverbal mediation of self-fulfilling prophecies in interracial interaction. *Journal of Experimental Social Psychology, 10*, 109–120.

Wright, S. C., & Lubensky, M. (2008). The struggle for social equality: Collective action vs. prejudice reduction. In S. Demoulin, J. P. Leyens & J. F. Dovidio (Eds.), *Intergroup misunderstandings: Impact of divergent social realities.* (pp. 291–310). New York: Psychology Press.

Wrong, D. H. (1961). The oversocialized conception of man in modern sociology. *American Sociological Review, 26*, 183–193.

Yamagishi, T., Jin, N., & Kiyonari, T. (1999). Bounded generalized reciprocity: In-group favoritism and in-group boasting. *Advances in Group Processes, 16*, 161–197.

Ybarra, O., & Trafimow, D. (1998). How priming the private self or collective self affects the relative weights of attitudes or subjective norms. *Personality and Social Psychology Bulletin, 24*, 362–370.

Yellow Bird, M. (2004). Cowboys and Indians: Toys of genocide, icons of colonialism. *WicazoSa Review, 18*, 33–48.

Yuki, M. (2003). Intergroup comparison versus intragroup relationships: A cross-cultural examination of social identity theory in North American and East Asian cultural contexts. *Social Psychology Quarterly, 66*, 166–183.

Conceptual and Methodological Issues in the Analysis of Data from Dyads and Groups

Deborah A. Kashy *and* M. Brent Donnellan

Abstract

This chapter provides a detailed introduction to the analysis of nonindependent data from dyads and groups. We begin the chapter by examining current practices regarding dyadic and group research in social and personality psychology. We then present a set of basic definitions, as well as a brief introduction to multilevel modeling (MLM). Throughout the chapter we present SPSS syntax that can be used to specify the models we describe using variants of MLM. The remainder of the chapter is broken into two sections—the first focuses on dyadic contexts, and the second focuses on group contexts. For dyads we discuss both cross-sectional and longitudinal designs, and we provide a detailed discussion of the actor-partner interdependence model (APIM), dyadic growth models, and lagged models. For groups we limit our presentation to methods for cross-sectional research; we describe the APIM for groups, the one-with-many design, and we provide a brief introduction to the social relations model. Examples of how these methods have been used to advance social and personality psychological science are given throughout.

Keywords: actor-partner interdependence model, dyadic data analysis, groups, nonindependent data, one-with-many design, quantitative methods, research methods, social relations model

Relationships and interpersonal processes are central to the science of both social and personality psychology. Social psychology is predicated on the notion that features of situations contribute to behavior, and it is widely argued that the most important situations in life are interpersonal (Kelley & Thibaut, 1978; Reis, Collins, & Berscheid, 2000). Likewise, major individual differences manifest themselves in interpersonal behavior (e.g., aggressiveness, shyness) and recently proposed transactional perspectives suggest that personality development is shaped, in part, by social relationships and social experiences (e.g., Roberts, Wood, & Smith, 2005). Given the importance of interpersonal phenomena to social and personality psychology, the goal of this chapter is to outline the methodological issues that are most relevant when analyzing data that result from empirical studies of groups and dyads.

A Brief Overview of Current Practices

Prior to describing issues related to data analysis, we decided to first obtain a clearer understanding of current methodological practices involving dyads and groups. To this end, we conducted a brief survey of 12 issues of the *Journal of Personality and Social Psychology* (*JPSP*) from 2008 and 2009 (Vol. 95, issue 3, through Vol. 97, issue 2), focusing on the Interpersonal Relations and Group Processes (IRGP) and Personality Processes and Individual Differences (PPID) sections. We expected that these sections would be the mostly likely place to find studies that were based on studies of dyads and groups. Our search yielded 124 research articles (78 from IRGP, 46 from PPID) describing a total of 410 studies (284 from IRGP, 126 from PPID).

We classified each study as a function of whether it was a study of (1) individuals working alone with no actual or implied partner or partners (e.g., individuals completing a personality questionnaire), (2) individuals working with one partner (i.e., a dyadic context), or (3) individuals working with multiple partners (i.e., a group context). It was a little surprising and even a bit disconcerting to find that 79% of all studies published in these two sections of the flagship journal in social and personality psychology were based on the study of individuals in isolation (76% in IRGP and 85% in PPID).

Nevertheless, dyad and group research is clearly an important component of both personality and social psychology, as reflected in the fact that 24% of the studies in IRGP and 15% of the studies in PPID were dyadic or group-based studies. We then refined our coding categories to delineate whether the interaction partner or partners were themselves participants, or whether the partners' behavior was constrained in some way (e.g., because they were confederates of the experimenter, or because these partners were actually preprogrammed responses by a computer). Of the 59 dyadic studies, 27 involved what we termed "fictitious" dyads for which most fell into three broad categories: 12 studies used confederates, 5 studies used computer-mediated interactions in which the "partner's" responses were preprogrammed, and 10 studies involved an initial exchange of information with a fictitious partner, with the unfulfilled expectation of an interaction to follow. Thus, across the 410 studies published in the IRGP and PPID sections from 12 months of JPSP, only 31 studies (7.6 percent; 20 studies in IRGP and 11 studies in PPID) involved dyads comprised of two "unconstrained" participants.

Similar results emerged for group research in that we found that of the 28 group studies, 13 involved fictitious group interaction in which the only interaction was between the participant and a computer (i.e., a set of preprogrammed "partners"). One additional group study involved interactions between the participant and a set of confederates. Thus, of the 410 studies we surveyed, only 14 studies (3.4 percent; 10 studies in IRGP and 4 studies in PPID) included groups comprised of three or more unconstrained participants.

In addition to gaining a more precise understanding of the kinds of studies that social and personality psychologists were conducting for papers published in the premier journal in the field, we also wanted to gain a sense of how researchers using dyadic and group methods analyzed their data. Specifically we were interested in whether researchers tested for and/or modeled nonindependence in their analyses. Of the 31 dyadic studies, 14 studies

clearly used analyses that treated dyad as the unit of analysis. Four other studies evaluated the degree of nonindependence by estimating and testing an intraclass correlation, and because they found little evidence of nonindependence, these studies then used individual as the unit of analysis. Of the remaining five studies, three clearly used individual as the unit, ignoring (or at least not acknowledging) dyadic effects, and two did not provide sufficient information to evaluate this question (e.g., no mention in the text, no degrees of freedom for tests). Likewise, of the 14 group studies, 12 modeled the nonindependence within groups, and two did not.

These findings suggest that the majority of researchers investigating interpersonal processes using dyadic or group research paradigms are familiar with issues of nonindependence, and they typically analyze their data in ways that take the interdependent nature of such data into account. Multilevel modeling (MLM) was the most commonly occurring data analytic approach used in these studies, as it was applied in 12 of the dyadic studies and 7 of the group studies (see also Christ, Sibley, & Wagner, chapter 10, this volume). The remaining studies used a range of approaches including traditional methods (e.g., ANOVA, multiple regression, structural equation modeling) and specialized models (e.g., the social relations model, or behavioral genetic analyses). Our survey also indicated that 11 of the 31 dyadic studies (35%) included an over-time component. Seven of these studies were daily diary or experience sampling studies that occurred over the course of a few weeks, and the other studies varied in length (e.g., 6 months to 8 years) and frequency of observation (e.g., monthly or yearly). Thus, longitudinal approaches are a small but nonetheless significant part of dyadic research.

All in all, it seems that researchers who study groups and dyads are using more or less appropriate data analytic techniques. However, the broader issue is that relatively few studies using dyads and groups are being conducted by social and personality psychologists. That is, the overwhelming prevalence of individual-focused research and the frequent use of fictitious dyads or groups in JPSP suggest that a chapter describing methods that model interdependence in a clear and accessible manner may be useful in expanding the methodological repertoire of social and personality researchers. Accordingly, the central goal of this chapter is to demonstrate some of the unique insights that can emerge from a series of dyadic and group data analytic models.

The first section introduces key definitions that play important roles in determining the appropriate data analytic approach. For simplicity, in this part of the discussion we use the term "group" to refer to both dyads (i.e., n = 2) and larger groups (i.e., n > 2). We then briefly describe some basics of multilevel modeling because that approach is used to estimate many of the models we detail. In the remainder of the chapter we provide a conceptual overview of each model, as well as a pragmatic discussion of estimation methods. We will not describe methods for analyzing dyadic and group data that simply correct significance testing for bias due to violations of independence because an extensive presentation of that material can be found in Kashy and Kenny (2000) and in Kenny, Kashy, and Bolger (1998).

Basic Definitions Associated with the Analysis of Data from Groups and Dyads
Between, Within, and Mixed Variables

An important factor in determining the appropriate data analytic approach for group-based data is the nature of the variables under investigation. A *between* variable varies from group to group, but does not vary across individuals within the same group. In other words, all members of a group have the same score on this type of variable. Examples of between variables include relationship length in dating research, gender in research on same-sex friends, and overall group productivity scores.

A *within* variable varies within the group (i.e., it varies across members of the same group), but when averaged across the group members, each group has an identical average score. Gender in heterosexual married couples is a prototypical within variable, since every couple is comprised of both a man and a woman. Likewise, family role (e.g., mother, father, child) in a study of three-person families would also be a within group variable. An example of a continuous within variable is percent time talking in a group with *n* individuals; this variable can vary from person to person, but those percentages average to 1/*n* for each group.

The third type of variable in dyadic and group research is a *mixed* variable, in which variation exists within groups and between groups. Many variables in group research are mixed in nature such that the group members' scores differ from person to person in the group, and some groups have higher average scores than others. Attachment anxiety is an example of a mixed variable from relationship research, because the two partners may differ from one another in anxiety, and some couples are higher in

anxiety, on average, than other couples. Identification with the group is also an example of a mixed variable, as some individuals may strongly identify with their group whereas other individuals do not, and average levels of identification may differ across groups as well. Most outcome variables we discuss in this chapter are mixed variables such that each individual within the group provides an outcome score, and those scores vary both within and between groups.

Nonindependence

The issue of nonindependence is crucial for analyses involving data from groups. When we say that an outcome score is nonindependent (i.e., dependent) within groups, what we mean is that the scores for people within the same group are related to one another (e.g., there is a nonzero correlation between the scores from individuals in the same group). Most often nonindependence results in a positive correlation between group members' scores (e.g., relationship satisfaction in couples). This occurs when an outcome is structured such that if one group member has a high score, other group members also have relatively high scores. However, it is also possible for there to be a negative correlation between group members' scores. This occurs when an outcome is structured such that if one group member has a high score, other group members have relatively low scores. The percent of points scored in a basketball game is one example of this: If the team has a star player who scores a large percentage of the points, by necessity the other players will have lower percentages.

Nonindependence has two primary roles in statistical models of dyadic and group data. First, its presence violates the independence of observations assumption that is the basis of traditional statistical methods such as ANOVA or regression, and it biases standard errors. Therefore, inferential tests need to be modified to account for the dependence of the scores. The second issue is perhaps the more interesting one—nonindependence presents an opportunity for personality and social psychologists to understand how and why individuals are connected to one another. It is this component of nonindependence that is the focus of the models and methods discussed below.

Distinguishability

Distinguishability is a key factor in both dyadic and group research paradigms. Members of a group are said to be conceptually *distinguishable* if there is a meaningful variable that can be used to identify or differentiate the individuals. For example, researchers who study adult heterosexual romantic relationships typically treat gender as the key distinguishing variable (e.g., husbands versus wives). Likewise, family researchers distinguish family members by family role (e.g., mother, father, and daughter). Distinguishability is an important factor in models of dyads and groups because it suggests that there may be population-level differences in both processes and outcomes for individuals who fall into the different roles. As a result, replications occur across—but not within—groups.

In contrast, when members of groups are *indistinguishable*, there is no systematic (or nonarbitrary) way to order the scores. Examples of indistinguishable dyads include same-sex friends, homosexual couples, or identical twins. Examples of indistinguishable groups could include friendship groups, roommates, and psychotherapy group members. In essence, indistinguishability implies that the individuals within the dyad or group are sampled from the same population. Accordingly, indistinguishable group members can be treated as replications within their groups as well as across groups.

Ultimately, distinguishability is both a theoretical and empirical issue. If the scores do not actually differ across the proposed distinguishing variable, then treating the data as indistinguishable typically increases the precision of estimates as well as the power of statistical tests. Thus, simply assuming distinguishability may lead to distortions in the empirical literature. This is an especially relevant issue with respect to the role of gender in heterosexual relationships. For example, researchers sometimes treat data from husbands and wives as distinguishable when they might be empirically indistinguishable. Kenny, Kashy, and Cook (2006) refer to this practice as the "first sin of dyadic data analysis" and admonish researchers to evaluate the evidence for distinguishability on a routine basis. After introducing MLM, we describe a way of testing distinguishability for the standard dyadic design using this method.

A Brief Introduction to MLM for Dyadic and Group Data

Multilevel modeling (MLM; also known as hierarchical linear modeling) is an important tool for dyadic and group researchers because it is specifically designed to handle hierarchically nested data that are nonindependent. In other words, this approach is specifically intended to handle clustered

observations. For example, in studies of marital satisfaction, the two individuals are nested within couple, and so their satisfaction scores are likely to be (strongly) related. MLM can also be used for repeated measures data, with each individual providing a series of outcome scores over time. Again, because multiple observations are obtained from each individual, observations are nested within individuals and are therefore likely to be nonindependent. In each of these examples, there are upper-level sampling units (couples and individuals respectively) and lower-level sampling units (individuals and time respectively). In MLM, outcome scores must be measured for each lower-level unit, and predictors can be measured at either the upper or lower levels. In our brief introduction we first describe a typical multilevel analysis for group data, and then we note how this analysis must be modified to accommodate dyadic data. Until otherwise specified, our discussion of MLM presumes that group or dyad members are indistinguishable.

MLM for Group Data

As an example, consider a study of task complexity, neuroticism, and perceptions of group cohesion in small, newly acquainted groups. Participants first complete individual assessments of neuroticism and then they are assigned to five-person groups. Each of these groups is then randomly assigned to work on either a series of simple tasks or a series of complex tasks. After the groups finish the tasks, each participant completes a measure of perceived group cohesiveness. Researchers might have hypotheses about the impact of neuroticism on cohesion and perhaps about main effects of task complexity for cohesion. It is even quite likely that researchers might hypothesize an interaction between task complexity and neuroticism for statistically predicting cohesion.

In this example individuals are nested within groups, and so in MLM terms, individual is the lower-level unit whereas group is the upper-level unit, and the outcome (cohesiveness) is collected for each lower-level unit. There are two predictor variables in this study: neuroticism and task complexity. Neuroticism is lower-level variable that is mixed, and task complexity is an upper-level variable that varies between groups. Note that for purposes of this example (and as a general recommendation) the continuous predictor variable, neuroticism, has been grand-mean centered (i.e., scores have been deviated from the average score across all participants), and the categorical predictor, task complexity, has been effects-coded such that groups who complete the simple task have task scores equal to minus one (−1.0), and groups that complete the complex task have task scores equal to one (1.0).

A subset of the data that could be generated by this study is presented in table 9.1. MLM analyses typically require that the data is structured such that there is a separate record for each lower-level unit (i.e., person). Thus, a five-person group generates five data records, and the total number of rows or records for the entire study equals the total number of participants involved in the research (as opposed to the total number of groups). Each record then includes the person's outcome score (e.g., **cohesive**), any lower-level predictor variables (e.g., **neuro**), and any upper-level predictor variables (e.g., **taskC**). Note that in the table the values of upper-level predictor variables are repeated for each individual within the same group, illustrating that upper-level variables are what we have described as between variables. Finally, a key component of the data set is a variable that denotes group membership (e.g., **groupID**). Researchers not familiar with MLM software may have the initial impulse to construct a dataset in which each group represents a row in the data file. Such a data structure, which is commonly used for structural equation modeling, would typically denote each individual's score with separate variable names (e.g., **cohesive1–cohesive5**; **neuro1–neuro5**). This structure would not work well with most MLM analysis packages. Although SPSS has restructuring capabilities, we recommend the researchers give considerable thought to how data will be recorded in light of the analytic techniques that will be used.

MLM is often described as a multistep process in which a "lower-level" regression is first computed separately for each "upper-level" unit. In the current example, this can be understood in conceptual terms to mean that a separate regression is computed for each group, and in each of these regressions the individuals' perception of group cohesiveness (Y) is predicted as a function of that individual's neuroticism score (X). More formally, the lower level model for person i in group j would be:

$$Y_{ij} = b_{0j} + b_{1j}X_{ij} + e_{ij}, \qquad (1)$$

where b_{0j} represents the predicted cohesiveness score for group j for a person who is average in neuroticism (recall that neuroticism is grand-mean centered), and b_{1j} represents the change in cohesiveness rating as neuroticism increases by one unit for group j. The next step of the analysis involves treating the slopes and intercepts from the first-step analyses as outcome variables in two "upper-level" regressions. For these level-two analyses, the regression coefficients from the first step are assumed to be a function of our group-level predictor, task complexity, or Z. These two equations would be:

$$b_{0j} = a_0 + a_1 Z_j + d_j \qquad (2)$$

$$b_{1j} = c_0 + c_1 Z_j + f_j \qquad (3)$$

Equation 2 predicts the intercepts from equation 1 as a function of the upper level variable, Z. For the example, a_0 is the grand mean of the cohesiveness ratings for all group members, regardless of task complexity, and a_1 estimates whether individuals in groups who were assigned to more complex tasks perceived their groups as more or less cohesive, on average, compared to those assigned to simple tasks. Likewise, equation 3 treats the first-step regression coefficients as a function of Z. Here c_0 estimates whether individuals higher in neuroticism perceive more cohesiveness, and c_1 estimates the degree to

Table 9.1 Data from three groups in the study of group cohesiveness, neuroticism, and task complexity example

GroupID	PersonID	Cohesive	Neuro	TaskC
1	1	8	2.18	1
1	2	7	.18	1
1	3	5	−2.82	1
1	4	6	−1.82	1
1	5	7	−.82	1
2	1	10	.18	−1
2	2	13	1.18	−1
2	3	9	−.82	−1
2	4	7	1.18	−1
2	5	8	.18	−1
3	1	7	−2.82	1
3	2	4	−.82	1
3	3	5	1.18	1
3	4	7	−.82	1
3	5	5	−1.18	1

Note. Neuroticism scores have been grand-mean centered. Task complexity is coded as complex tasks = 1, simple tasks = −1.

which the relationship between perceived cohesiveness and neuroticism differs as a function of task complexity.

There are three random effects represented in these three equations. First, there is the error component, e_{ij}, in the lower-level equation (i.e., equation 1). This represents variation in responses across the lower-level units, after controlling for the effects of the lower-level predictor variable; its variance can be represented as σ_e^2. In the example, this component represents variation in cohesiveness ratings from individual to individual within a group, controlling for the effects of neuroticism. There are also random effects in each of the two second-step regression equations. The random effect d_j in the first of the second-step regressions represents variation in the intercepts that is not explained by Z. For the example, d_j represents variation in the group mean cohesiveness scores that is not explained by task complexity.

The variance in d_j is a combination of σ_d^2, which can be referred to as group variance, and σ_e^2. The intraclass correlation that measures the degree of nonindependence in cohesiveness ratings within groups is then defined as:

$$\rho = \frac{\sigma_d^2}{\sigma_d^2 + \sigma_e^2} \tag{4}$$

The random effect in the second of the second-step equations is f_j and represents the degree to which the size of the neuroticism-cohesiveness relationship varies from group to group after controlling for Z (task complexity). The variance in f_j is a combination of σ_f^2 and σ_e^2, where σ_f^2 can be referred to as the neuroticism-by-group variance or the variance in the neuroticism-cohesiveness slopes. Finally, although not specifically depicted in the models, in the most general MLM case, the random effects for the intercept and slope are allowed to covary (e.g., if a group is relatively high in cohesiveness, is the link between neuroticism and cohesiveness weaker for that group?), adding a fourth random component to the model.

The multistep conceptualization is handy when explaining MLM but it is does not accurately reflect the way that MLM programs typically estimate the model we have described. Instead, the two sets of equations are combined into a single equation:

$$Y_{ij} = (a_0 + d_j) + a_1 Z_j + (c_0 + f_j) X_{ij} \\ + c_1 Z_j X_{ij} + e_{ij} \tag{5}$$

The intercept in this equation involves two components: a_0 is the fixed effect piece that estimates the grand mean of cohesiveness, and d_j is the random effects piece that indicates that the intercept also varies from group to group. The main effect (also termed the first-order effect) of Z, is comprised of only a fixed effect represented by a_1: It is the mean difference in cohesiveness for complex versus simple tasks. However, like the intercept, the main effect of X has both a fixed effect component, c_0, which measures the average neuroticism-cohesiveness relationship across groups, and a random effect component, f_j, which estimates the degree to which the effect of neuroticism varies from group to group. The coefficient for the interaction, c_1, is the last fixed effect and it estimates the degree to which the neuroticism-cohesiveness relationship is moderated by task complexity, or XZ. The final term in the model is the random error component: e_{ij}.

Given our three variables **cohesive**, **neuro**, and **taskC**, and the group identification number, **groupID**, that specifies which group each individual was in, the SPSS syntax that can be used to estimate this basic multilevel model would be:

MIXED
cohesive WITH **neuro taskC**
/FIXED = neuro **taskC neuro*taskC**
/PRINT = SOLUTION TESTCOV
/RANDOM INTERCEPT **neuro** |
SUBJECT(**groupID**) COVTYPE(UNR).

The FIXED statement specifies that the outcome, **cohesive**, is a function of the person's X, **neuro**, the person's value on Z, **taskC**, and the XZ interaction. The PRINT statement requests that the program print out both the fixed effect estimates (SOLUTION) and the tests of the random effects (TESTCOV). Finally, the RANDOM statement is used to model the random effects, including a random intercept and a random slope for the lower-level predictor, **neuro**. In this statement, the SUBJECT(**groupID**) option specifies that individuals at the same level of **groupID** are members of the same group. Finally, the COVTYPE(UNR) option requests separate estimates of the intercept variance, the slope variance, and the intercept-slope correlation.

MLM with Dyadic Data

What changes are required to adapt these models to the dyadic case? This question is sometimes a source of confusion because each upper-level unit has only two observations in the case of a dyad (as opposed to five in the previous example), and so there isn't sufficient information to truly estimate a separate regression for each dyad. Perhaps surprisingly, this constraint is not reflected in the lower-level MLM equation, as this equation is identical to the model presented for groups (i.e., equation 1). The only change relative to the five-person group case comes in the upper-level model of the slopes, denoted as equation 3 earlier. This equation changes for dyadic data in that the random component for the slopes, f_j, is fixed to zero, and so equation 3 is modified to be:

$$b_{1j} = c_0 + c_1 Z_j \qquad (6)$$

Viewing MLM from the perspective of a single combined equation can be especially useful for dyadic data. This combined model is:

$$Y_{ij} = (a_0 + d_j) + a_1 Z_j + c_0 X_{ij} + c_1 Z_j X_{ij} + e_{ij} \qquad (7)$$

Thus, the modified version of the single MLM equation for dyads looks much like a standard moderated regression equation (imagine a_0, a_1, c_0, and c_1 as b_0, b_1, b_2, and b_3 respectively) with the only major difference being the presence of a random effect for the intercepts. As is the case for group data, the presence of this random effect in the intercepts models the nonindependence of scores for the two dyad members. Similarly, the intraclass correlation can be estimated as the proportion of variance in these intercepts, or $\sigma_d^2 (\sigma_d^2 + \sigma_e^2)$.

If we amend our example into a study of perceived cohesiveness, neuroticism, and task complexity in dyads (i.e., each individual works with only one other person), the only *required* change in the syntax is in the RANDOM statement:

/RANDOM INTERCEPT | SUBJECT(**dyadID**)
COVTYPE(VC).

where **dyadID** is a variable that denotes dyad membership. This change drops **neuro** from the list of random effects and changes the covariance type to VC or "variance components," which simply requests that the program estimate the variance of the intercepts.

One additional modification of the standard MLM formulation is useful in dyadic data analysis. As we have noted, in the standard MLM formulation, nonindependence is modeled as a variance, but an alternative is to treat the scores from the two dyad members as repeated measures of the same construct such that each dyad member would have

an error. These terms reflect the part of the outcome score that is not explained by the lower-level predictor, and would be correlated across dyad members. Such a formulation models the nonindependence between dyad members as a covariance rather than a variance. This is particularly important when the outcome measure is structured such that when one dyad member has a higher score, the other person's score tends to be lower (e.g., variables involving compensation, competition, or division of a limited resource). Nonindependence in dyadic data can be negative in these cases (i.e., the correlation between dyad members' scores is negative rather than positive) and negative nonindependence can be captured by a covariance, but not by a variance (recall that it is impossible for a variance to be negative!). Thus, the standard MLM formulation can be problematic, and we strongly urge researchers to use the repeated measures formulation rather than the random intercept approach when analyzing dyadic data. Finally, if the nonindependence is positive, then this covariance in the residuals equals the variance of the intercepts (σ_d^2) described earlier. To make this change, the RANDOM statement would be replaced by the following REPEATED statement:

/REPEATED = **personID** | SUBJECT(**dyadID**)
COVTYPE(CS).

The **personID** variable in the last syntax statement arbitrarily denotes the two dyad members as a "1" and "2." The COVTYPE here requests a residual structure known as compound symmetry, which constrains the residual variances to be equal across the dyad members and specifies that there is a covariance between the residuals as well. The equal variance constraint is particularly important because the dyad members are indistinguishable, and so the model specifies that the residuals are sampled from the same underlying population.

Finally, as was the case for groups, the data for MLM analyses with dyads should be structured such that each member of the dyad has a separate line or record in the file. Thus, the total number of records would be the number of participants in the project (i.e., 2 times the number of dyads, assuming no missing data). A complete treatment of MLM is beyond the scope of this chapter, and so we refer readers to one or more of several accessible texts such as Hox (2002), Kreft and de Leeuw (2004), and Snijders and Bosker (1999) in addition to the chapter by Christ et al. in this volume (chapter 10). Kenny et al. (2006) provide an expanded treatment for dyadic analyses with particular reference to MLM.

As a final point, we note that many of the models we discuss can also be estimated in a structural equation modeling framework, and interested readers can consult Kashy and Donnellan (2008); Kashy, Donnellan, Burt, and McGue (2008); and Ackerman, Donnellan, and Kashy (2011) for examples.

Testing Distinguishability in the Standard Dyadic Design with MLM

As we have noted, there is a distinction between *conceptual distinguishability* and *empirical distinguishability* (Kenny et al., 2006). Conceptual distinguishability refers to whether there is a within-dyad categorical variable that can be used to systematically identify members in principle. Empirical distinguishability refers to whether such a conceptual distinction actually matters in terms of observed differences in means, variances, and covariances for dyad members. This distinction between conceptual and empirical distinguishability is well illustrated in studies of heterosexual dyads. Although researchers can (and generally do) distinguish couple members by gender, there is no guarantee that this classification has any empirical basis or consequence for the particular analysis. As noted elsewhere (e.g., Ackerman et al., 2011; Kenny et al., 2006), we recommend that researchers evaluate distinguishability by gender empirically rather than simply assuming that gender matters for a particular analysis.

For purposes of this discussion, say that our study of cohesiveness, neuroticism, and task complexity was run using dyads comprised of one man and one woman, and we want to know whether gender empirically distinguishes the data from the two dyad members. Another way to phrase this question is whether gender moderates the fixed and random effects. For example, is the within-person link between neuroticism and cohesiveness stronger for women than for men? To conduct this test using MLM, two models must be estimated, and both of these models should use maximum likelihood estimation (ML) rather than the typical program default of restricted maximum likelihood (REML). The ML option should be used because the distinguishable model generally differs from the indistinguishable model in its fixed effects as well as its random effects. Maximum likelihood estimation is requested by adding the statement

/METHOD = ML

to the syntax.

In the first model, dyad members are treated as distinguishable both in terms of their fixed and random effects. For the fixed effects part of the model, this involves including gender as a main effect (to estimate differences in the intercepts or average values of cohesiveness) and as a factor that interacts with the other predictors in the model. For the random effects part of the model, gender is treated as a random effect by specifying that the covariance type is heterogeneous compound symmetry (i.e., CSH) rather than compound symmetry (i.e., CS). Assuming that gender is coded one for men and minus one for women, the full syntax for the distinguishable model would be:

```
MIXED
cohesive WITH neuro taskC gender
/FIXED = gender neuro taskC gender*neuro
         gender*taskC neuro*taskC
         gender*neuro*taskC
/PRINT = SOLUTION TESTCOV
/METHOD = ML
/REPEATED = gender | SUBJECT(dyadID)
         COVTYPE(CSH).
```

In the second model, dyad members are treated as indistinguishable. Note that gender is included in the variable list in this syntax to ensure that the exact same data set is used for the two analyses. If it were not included, but there were missing data for the gender variable, the data sets actually used in the two analyses would differ, potentially invalidating the subsequent tests and conclusions.

```
MIXED
cohesive WITH neuro taskC gender
/FIXED = neuro taskC neuro*taskC
/PRINT = SOLUTION TESTCOV
/METHOD = ML
/REPEATED = gender | SUBJECT(dyadID)
         COVTYPE(CS).
```

A chi-square difference test can then be computed by subtracting the deviances (i.e., the −2*log likelihood values) for the two models. For this example, the distinguishable model has four more fixed effects than the indistinguishable model (i.e., **gender, gender*neuro, gender*taskC,** and **gender*neuro*taskC**). There is also one additional random effect in the distinguishable model because heterogeneous compound symmetry allows the residual variances for men and women to differ but homogeneous compound symmetry does not. If the χ^2 difference with 5 degrees of freedom were not statistically significant, the data would be assumed to be consistent with the null hypothesis that the dyad members are indistinguishable. If, however, the χ^2 were statistically significant, then there would be support for the alternative hypothesis that dyad members are empirically distinguishable by gender. In other words, a statistically significant test statistic indicates that the model that takes account of gender fits the data better than a model that ignores gender.

Testing for distinguishability with a few variables is also fairly simple using SEM packages, and these procedures are well described in Kenny et al. (2006, pp. 129–131; see also Ackerman et al., 2011). The SEM approach is more cumbersome with multiple variables, and thus we expect that researchers testing fairly complicated multivariate models will want to develop facility with the MLM approach.

Models for Dyadic Research
The Actor-Partner Interdependence Model (APIM)

The APIM is one of the most commonly used models for analyzing data from dyads (e.g., Brock & Lawrence, 2009; Butler, Egloff, Wilhelm, Smith, Erickson, & Gross, 2003; Dailey, 2008; Badr & Carmack Taylor, 2008; Lakey & Canary, 2002; Luo, Chen, Yue, Zhang, Zhaoyang, & Xu, 2008; McIsaac, Connolly, McKenney, Pepler, & Craig, 2008; Proulx, Buehler, & Helms, 2009; Tran & Simpson, 2009). The APIM is a particularly elegant and useful model for examining how individual differences are associated with relationship outcomes, or for examining whether individual characteristics

have interpersonal consequences. For instance, Cuperman and Ickes (2009) used this model to examine how two previously unacquainted individuals' personalities, as measured by the Big Five domains, predicted their own and their partner's behavior in unstructured dyadic social interactions. Results from this study highlighted the importance of agreeableness for both actual interpersonal behavior (e.g., number of speaking turns) and perceptions of behavior (e.g., perceptions of rapport with partner). Extensive details on this model can be found in Ackerman et al. (2011) and Kenny et al. (2006).

The basic specification of the APIM is that outcomes are affected by the characteristics of the individual as well as characteristics of the individual's partner (see figure 9.1). In the terminology associated with the APIM, the effect of the person's own predictor variable on the person's own outcome variable is called an *actor effect*, whereas the effect of the partner's predictor variable on the person's outcome is called a *partner effect*. Cuperman and Ickes (2009) found evidence of both actor and partner effects for agreeableness predicting number of speaking turns, such that individuals higher in agreeableness spoke more (an actor effect), and individuals who had partners who were higher in agreeableness spoke more as well (a partner effect). Separate actor and partner effects can be estimated only for predictors that vary both within and between dyads (i.e., mixed variables). However, as discussed in Kenny et al. (2006), the model allows for moderation of

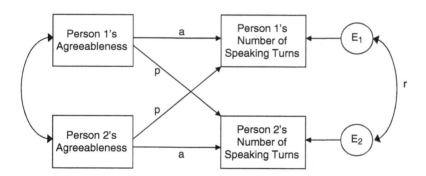

a = actor effect estimate pooled across and within dyads. Does a person's agreeableness predict his or her number of speaking turns, controlling for the partner's agreeableness?

p = partner effect estimate pooled across and within dyads. Does the partner's agreeableness predict the person's number of speaking turns, controlling for the person's agreeableness?

r = partial intraclass correlation for number of speaking turns, controlling for agreeableness

Fig. 9.1 APIM for indistinguishable dyads based on the variables assessed in Cuperman and Ickes (2009).

actor and partner effects by both between- and within-dyads predictors.

The APIM can be applied to distinguishable or indistinguishable dyads. For instance, beyond its frequent use in marital and dating studies, the APIM for distinguishable dyads has been used in studies of parent-child relationships, (e.g., Dailey, 2008) and patient-doctor relationships (e.g., LeBlanc, Kenny, O'Connor, & Légaré, 2009). When the model is used with distinguishable dyads, the actor and partner effects are typically allowed to vary across the distinguishing variable. For example, Proulx et al. (2009) estimated separate actor and partner effects for husbands and wives in their examination of the degree to which spouses' hostility predicted their own and their partner's depressive symptoms three years later. The model has also been applied to the indistinguishable case, as in studies of friendships (Cillessen, Jiang, West, & Laszkowski, 2005), unacquainted dyads (Cuperman & Ickes, 2009), and same-sex roommates (Ackerman et al., 2011). With indistinguishable dyads only a single actor and a single partner effect are estimated, as the estimates are pooled within dyads as well as between dyads.

To estimate the APIM for dyads using MLM, the data must be structured as a *pairwise* data set. table 9.2 uses fictitious data from five dyads to illustrate the pairwise data structure using variables from Cuperman and Ickes (2009). As we discussed earlier in our introduction to MLM with dyads, in this structure there is a data record for each individual, so with 100 dyads there would be 200 records

of data. A variable representing dyad membership (e.g., **dyadID**), as well as a variable that differentiates the two individuals (e.g., **personID**), should be included. Each record would also include the individual's outcome (e.g., **speak**), and that individual's predictor score (e.g., **act_agree**). The unique component of the pairwise data set is that each person's data record also includes his or her partner's predictor score (e.g., **part_agree**). Thus, each person's predictor score is included in the data set twice—one time it is associated with the person's own outcome for speaking turns, and the other time it is associated with the person's partner's outcome. In table 9.2 the cross-over pattern for actor and partner predictor variables is illustrated for the first dyad. For person 1, the person's own agreeableness score (i.e., the actor score) is 3.8, and the person's partner's agreeableness score (i.e., the partner score) is 2.7. In contrast, for person 2, the actor score is 2.7 and the partner score is 3.8.

THE APIM FOR INDISTINGUISHABLE DYADS

The two-step conceptualization of the APIM using MLM includes a lower-level regression equation in which each person's outcome, Y_{ij} for person i in dyad j, is predicted to be a function of that person's predictor, XA_{ij}, and the partner's predictor, XP_{ij}. The lower-level model that depicts both actor and partner effects is:

$$Y_{ij} = b_{0j} + b_{1j}XA_{ij} + b_{2j}XP_{ij} + e_{ij} \qquad (8)$$

In this equation, b_{1j} estimates the actor effect for dyad j, and b_{2j} estimates the partner effect for dyad j. The upper-level models, assuming that there are no upper-level predictor variables, would be:

$$b_{0j} = a_0 + d_j \quad b_{1j} = c_0 \quad b_{2j} = h_0 \qquad (9)$$

Thus, like the MLM example for a simple dyadic model, only the intercepts are allowed to vary across dyads. Assuming that the actor and partner variables have been grand-mean centered, the actor effect, c_0, would estimate the effect of the person's own agreeableness on his or her own number of speaking turns, and the partner effect, h_0, would estimate the effect of the partner's agreeableness on the person's number of speaking turns. The SPSS syntax for a basic actor-partner model that does not include a dyad-level (i.e., level 2) predictor would be:

MIXED
speak WITH **act_agree part_agree**
/FIXED = **act_agree part_agree**

Table 9.2 Data depicting the pairwise data structure for an APIM analysis with indistinguishable dyads

DyadID	PersonID	Speak	Act_agree	Part_agree
1	1	83	3.8	2.7
1	2	72	2.7	3.8
2	1	55	4.1	3.7
2	2	68	3.7	4.1
3	1	108	4.3	4.0
3	2	130	4.0	4.3
4	1	89	2.9	3.4
4	2	76	3.4	2.9
5	1	46	2.3	2.8
5	2	52	2.8	2.3

One additional feature of the actor-partner model is that actor and partner effects can interact to create a new upper-level variable. We can form the interaction in the usual way by computing a product term; in the Cuperman and Ickes (2009) example this interaction might capture a synergistic phenomenon such that two individuals who are both high in agreeableness combine to make an especially animated interaction in which both individuals have many speaking turns. Alternatively, it may be more appropriate to form the interaction by computing the absolute difference between the person's X and the partner's X scores to create a measure of dissimilarity. Such an "interaction" or dyad-level variable might capture the phenomenon that discrepancies in agreeableness matter for the flow of the interaction. These kinds of effects are referred to as dyadic indexes in the literature (see chapter 12 in Kenny et al., 2006). The important thing to note here is that the lower-level actor and partner effects should also be included in models involving these couple-level variables. This is the case regardless of how an interaction between actor and partner effects is defined and operationalized (Griffin, Murray, & Gonzalez, 1999). We refer the reader to chapters 7 and 12 of Kenny et al. (2006) for a more thorough discussion of the issues involving dyadic indexes.

THE APIM FOR DISTINGUISHABLE DYADS

The APIM can also be adapted to handle distinguishable dyads. The key difference in the distinguishable case is that the actor and partner effects may differ as a function of the distinguishing variable. We use the Proulx et al. (2009) study that examined whether actor and partner effects for married partners' hostility predicted depressive symptoms three years later as an example (see figure 9.2). In this case the actor effect for women estimates whether the wife's hostility predicts her own subsequent depression, and the husband's actor effect estimates whether his hostility predicts his own subsequent depression. The partner effect for the wife to the husband estimates whether the wife's hostility predicts her husband's subsequent depression, and the partner effect for the husband to the wife estimates whether his hostility predicts her later depression. To estimate this model in MLM, the data set should include a measure of **gender** (or G, coded as husbands = 1 and wives = -1), which is a

within-dyads variable that systematically distinguishes between the two spouses. Each record in the data set will also include an actor hostility score (**act_hostile**) and a partner hostility score (**part_hostile**), as well as a depression score for the actor (**depress**). We outline two strategies for handling distinguishable dyads.

The first strategy is identical to the one presented above for handling indistinguishable dyads, but now the effects-coded gender variable is added to the model to represent the distinguishing variable. This variable is included as a main effect to capture differences in average responses for husbands and wives. It is also included in interactions with the actor and partner effects. These interactions estimate the degree to which actor and partner effects differ for husbands and wives. Tests of the gender interactions serve the important purpose of determining whether the dyad members are truly distinguishable in their actor and partner effects.

The distinguishable APIM level-one model is:

$$Y_{ij} = b_{0j} + b_{1j}XA_{ij} + b_{2j}XP_{ij} + b_{3j}G_{ij} \\ + b_{4j}XA_{ij}G_{ij} + b_{5j}XP_{ij}G_{ij} + e_{ij} \tag{10}$$

And the level-two equations are:

$$b_{0j} = a_0 + d_j \quad b_{1j} = c_0 \quad b_{2j} = h_0 \\ b_{3j} = k_0 \quad b_{4j} = m_0 \quad b_{5j} = p_0 \tag{11}$$

In these models, k_0 estimates the average gender difference on Y or depressive symptoms, m_0 estimates the degree to which actor effects differ as a function of the person's gender, and likewise, p_0 estimates the degree to which partner effects differ by gender. If m_0 is not statistically significant, the implication is that a_W and a_H in figure 9.2 do not differ, and could be substituted with a general actor effect, a, as in the indistinguishable model. The same is true for the partner effects p_{WH} and p_{HW} and the test of the partner by gender interaction, p_0.

As we noted in our introduction to MLM, in the distinguishable case we would probably want to allow for heterogeneity of variance across levels of the distinguishing variable. This is consistent with the idea that dyad members are sampled from different populations, and therefore may have different population means and standard deviations. In the example, including heterogeneous compound symmetry would allow the residual variances in depressive symptoms to differ for husbands and wives. The syntax below specifies a model that includes actor and partner effects for the mixed predictor (i.e.,

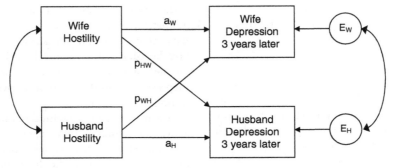

Fig. 9.2 APIM for distinguishable dyads.

act_hostile and **part_hostile**) and a distinguishing variable, **gender**. By including interactions between the distinguishing variable and the actor and partner effects, the model allows the actor and partner effects to differ as a function of the distinguishing variable. Moreover, by changing the COVTYPE to CSH (heterogeneous compound symmetry) this syntax also allows for heterogeneous variances as a function of the distinguishing variable:

> MIXED
> **depress** WITH **gender act_hostile part_hostile**
> /FIXED = **gender act_hostile part_hostile**
>   **gender*act_hostile gender*part_hostile**
> /PRINT = SOLUTION TESTCOV
> /REPEATED = **gender** | SUBJECT(**dyadID**)
>   COVTYPE(CSH).

A second strategy for the analysis of distinguishable dyads is the two-intercept model, which was originally suggested by Raudenbush, Brennan, and Barnett (1995). To estimate this model we create two redundant dummy variables, W = 1 if the outcome score is from the wife, and W = 0 otherwise; and H = 1 if the outcome score is from the husband, and H = 0 otherwise. (These variables are designated as **wife** and **husband** in the computer syntax below.) We then use these two dummy codes in the lower level model for member i of dyad j:

$$Y_{ij} = b_{1j}W_{ij} + b_{2j}H_{ij} \qquad (12)$$

In this model there is no intercept, at least not in the usual sense, but rather there are two intercepts, b_1 and b_2. The intercept for wives is estimated as b_1 and the intercept for husbands is estimated as b_2. In addition, there is no error term in the model, making this a very unusual model. Importantly, in this model both b_1 and b_2 are random effects, and so the model has a variance-covariance matrix of b_1

and b_2 with three elements: the variance of b_1 or s_1^2 (the error variance for wives), the variance of b_2 or s_2^2 (the error variance for husbands), and the covariance between the two or s_{12} (the degree of nonindependence).

To specify the distinguishable APIM using the two-intercept approach, the actor and partner variables need to be multiplied by each of the two dummy variables (i.e., W and H).

The full lower-level model is:

$$Y_{ij} = b_{1j}W_{ij} + b_{2j}H_{ij} + b_{3j}W_{ij}XA_{ij} + b_{4j}H_{ij}XA_{ij} \\ + b_{5j}W_{ij}XP_{ij} + b_{6j}H_{ij}XP_{ij} \qquad (13)$$

Thus, the actor effects for wives are given by the b_{3j}'s, and the actor effects for husbands are given by the b_{4j}'s, and likewise for the partner effects: b_{5j} and b_{6j}.

The syntax below estimates the two-intercept model that also includes separate actor and partner effects for husbands and wives:

> MIXED
> **depress** WITH **wife husband act_hostile**
>   **part_hostile**
> /FIXED = **wife husband wife *act_hostile husband**
>   ***act_hostile**
>   **wife *part_hostile husband*part_hostile**
> | NOINT
> /PRINT = SOLUTION TESTCOV
> /REPEATED = **gender** | SUBJECT(**dyadID**)
>   COVTYPE(CSH).

Including the NOINT option, which suppresses the traditional intercept from the model, is key to specifying the two-intercept approach. By suppressing the intercept and including the dummy coded values for the distinguishing variable, we force the program to compute two intercepts, one for husbands and one for wives. Similarly, we obtain estimates of separate actor and partner effects by including interactions between these dummy codes and the actor and partner variables.

Finally, it is often useful to use both of the methods for specifying the APIM with distinguishable dyads when conducting a comprehensive analysis. The first approach we described provides estimates and tests of the interactions between actor and partner effects and the distinguishing factor (e.g., the test of whether the effect of the person's own hostility on his/her depressive symptoms differs for husbands and wives). If such interactions emerge, then estimating and testing the simple slopes separately for each level of the distinguishing variable (e.g., what is the effect of own hostility for wives? what is the effect of own hostility for husbands?) is a natural way to break down the interaction.

Over-Time Dyadic Models

Longitudinal studies of dyads are becoming relatively common, a factor we attribute in part to the increasing familiarity with and use of MLM, as well as greater appreciation for the importance of stability and change in close relationships (e.g., Conger, Lorenz, & Wickrama, 2004; Karney & Bradbury, 1997). Indeed, our survey of studies in *JPSP* found that 11 of the 31 dyadic studies (35%) included a longitudinal component. Seven of these studies were daily diary or experience sampling studies that occurred over the course of a few weeks, whereas the other studies varied in length (e.g., 6 months to 8 years) and frequency of observation (e.g., monthly or yearly).

In this section we consider dyadic designs in which each member of the dyad is measured at multiple times. By multiple times, we mean more than once and we strongly suggest that researchers attempt to collect as many waves as possible. There is a truism in longitudinal research that "two waves of data are better than one, but maybe not much better" (Rogosa, Brandt, & Zimowski, 1982, p. 744). Increasing the number of time points in a longitudinal study allows researchers to test more complicated models and generally increases statistical power (e.g., Hertzog, Lindenberger, Ghisletta, & von Oertzen, 2006). For example, the precision of parameter estimates in growth models and the reliability of the estimate of the rate of change increases with additional waves of data collection (Willett, Singer, & Martin, 1998). This is especially true when researchers collect only a few waves of data (see figure 4 in Willett et al., 1998).

In over-time data from dyads there are three factors that define the structure of the data: time,

person, and dyad. Researchers sometimes conceptualize these kinds of data to be a three-level nested model in which time points are nested within persons and persons are nested within dyads (e.g., Theiss & Knobloch, 2009; see the top panel of figure 9.3). As pointed out by Laurenceau and Bolger (2005), however, the problem is that time and person are usually crossed rather than nested. That is, for a given dyad, the time point is usually the same for the two persons as depicted in the bottom panel of figure 9.3 (i.e., both partners are usually assessed at the *same* time). As a result, there may be an additional dyadic covariance that should be included in the model: a covariance between the two dyad members' residuals at a specific point in time.

In the sections below we describe three data analytic models that can be applied to longitudinal dyadic data: the over-time standard APIM, the cross-lagged model, and the dyadic growth-curve model. With each model we focus on the analysis of data from distinguishable dyads, and then we briefly discuss how the model would change if dyad members were indistinguishable. Prior to describing these models, however, we provide some general

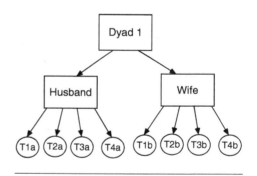

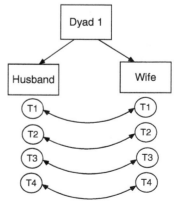

Fig. 9.3 Three-level nested versus crossed depiction of over-time dyadic data.

comments about issues of design and measurement in longitudinal studies.

DESIGN ISSUES TO BE CONSIDERED WHEN STUDYING DYADS OVER TIME

Social and personality psychologists study phenomena longitudinally because they are interested in how people and relationships change over time and because they would like to use temporal precedence to constrain inferences about causality from correlational data. In light of these general objectives, there are several general methodological issues that researchers need to consider as they design their studies to maximize the chances that the time and effort required to collect such data will yield interpretable results. Donnellan and Conger (2007) provide an overview of general considerations for longitudinal studies and provide an introduction to the key issues. Much of this section draws from their discussion.

One of the most important considerations for longitudinal studies is whether it is reasonable to expect that the variable(s) of interest will change over the data collection period. Therefore researchers interested in describing and statistically predicting change need to identify and target those time periods in which change is most likely to occur (e.g., changes in global relationship satisfaction across the transition to parenthood; changes in child behavior as infants develop into toddlers). This means that researchers might need to pay considerable attention to sample selection considerations. The use of haphazard strategies to select dyads can produce a sample in which couples are at different points in their relationship with some exhibiting considerably more stability than others. Such a mixture of couple types may make it difficult to detect a systematic trajectory of change.

In addition, researchers need to pay attention to the constructs of interest and to the measures of those constructs. Variables such as marital quality are often quite stable over time especially in terms of the rank-order stability of the measures (see e.g., Johnson, Amoloza, & Booth, 1992). In other words, couples who are relatively happy and satisfied at time t-1 tend to be relatively happy and satisfied at time t. In light of these issues, longitudinal studies of satisfaction can result in rather disappointing data given that researchers may not find particularly strong predictors of change. Indeed, the degree of stability of measures has severe implications for researchers who envision using prospective models or lagged models in their work. Consider that a researcher might want to use neuroticism at time t-1 to predict dyadic coping at time t controlling for dyadic coping at time t-1. This kind of finding would bear on theoretical models linking personality attributes to processes of adaptation (e.g., Karney & Bradbury, 1995). However, if dyadic coping is a highly stable characteristic, then this type of lagged model may not produce interesting or interpretable results.

As an illustration, imagine that dyadic coping scores are very similar over time such that the correlation between a person's coping score at time t-1 and at time t is very large. Statistically, this will mean that coping at time t-1 will account for the lion's share of the variance in coping at time t and it will be quite difficult to find additional predictors of coping at time t. Moreover, this problem is exacerbated further when the predictor is strongly correlated across partners as well. In these cases, researchers may find themselves estimating what we consider to be the least interesting over-time dyadic model (the over-time standard APIM) when they had intended to estimate a prospective or lagged model, simply because the over-time stability is too high to draw meaningful inferences about longitudinal processes. This means that researchers will not be in a particularly strong position to constrain their causal inferences from a given analysis in meaningful and interesting ways.

Researchers also need to keep in mind that all over-time models assume a degree of measurement invariance across the study period (e.g., Pitts, West, & Tein, 1996; Vandenberg & Lance, 2000). Longitudinal measurement equivalence is required to draw valid inferences about continuity or change across time (e.g., Horn & McArdle, 1992). The core issue is that longitudinal models assume that the measures assess the same underlying construct in the same way at each time point. It might seem like this issue is most relevant and perhaps most problematic in long-term longitudinal studies; however, repeatedly asking the same question over short periods of time can also change the nature of the assessment instrument (e.g., asking participants if they are happy and satisfied with their relationship every day for two weeks). The evaluation of measurement invariance is a relatively technical issue which is infrequently addressed in the substantive literature. Indeed, this issue was not discussed in any of the 11 over-time studies in our review. Nonetheless, issues of measurement invariance can be evaluated using confirmatory factor analytic techniques (see Brown, 2006 for an accessible treatment).

As an example, consider that growth curve models are based on fairly strong assumptions about measurement properties. In essence the basic model requires that measures "weigh" people in the same way at each wave. A score of 3.5 on the focal measure must have the same meaning at all occasions. Otherwise, observed differences across waves may amount to the act of "comparing apples and spark plugs" (Vandenberg & Lance, 2000, p. 9). This stricter form of measurement invariance can be satisfied when indictors of the measure (e.g., items) have the same factor loadings over time and when the same indicator at different time points has the same intercept for the same level of the latent variable (see Brown, 2006, p. 257). Less restrictive forms of measurement invariance are required for lagged models and the standard APIM, given that variable means are not actually part of the model. Here it is important that the indicators have the same factor loadings at each wave (e.g., Brown, 2006, p. 257) so that researchers can be confident that their measures produce the same rank-ordering at each wave. In essence, the measure needs to "rank" people in the same way at each wave. It is often easier to satisfy this requirement of consistently "ranking" objects over time. We refer interested readers to accessible discussions of measurement invariance by Schmitt and Kuljanin (2008).

A few additional methodological issues warrant discussion. First, researchers need to coordinate the study length and measurement intervals with the phenomena of interest. All too often the length of longitudinal studies is determined by the beginning and end of the academic calendar or some other arbitrary designation, rather than the period during which change is expected to occur. We suspect that this strategy will generally produce frustrating null results for researchers who wish to test the plausibility of causal hypotheses or to test mediational models (e.g., Cole & Maxwell, 2003). Our reasoning is deceptively simple: causes produce effects that play out over time and the strength of these causal effects varies over time (Gollob & Reichardt, 1987). Relationship dissatisfaction may not immediately lead to relationship dissolution and the impact of life stress on relationships is likely to be moderated by time. Researchers need to match the frequency and intensity of measurement to the anticipated underlying causal processes.

Accordingly, we suggest that researchers pay careful attention to the frequency of assessments as well as the intervals between assessments.

These design decisions should derive from theoretical concerns and preexisting knowledge about the processes under investigation. In the absence of strong conceptual guidance, or in the common situation in which a given longitudinal study has multiple research goals, we suggest that researchers collect as many waves of data as possible using the shortest intervals. For some variables, daily measures may be appropriate, but for others change occurs slowly, and so measurement intervals on the order of months may be needed. Regardless of the interval length, it is helpful to emphasize the importance of sampling enough time-points to model change. Thus, the total number of observations is an important consideration, as is the frequency of observation. All in all, researchers who apply longitudinal techniques successfully will give considerable attention to design basics related to the selection of measures, the timing and frequency of assessment occasions, and the selection of the sample.

THE OVER-TIME STANDARD APIM

The first over-time model we describe is what Kenny et al. (2006) refer to as the over-time standard APIM. This is the least interesting longitudinal model, as temporal ordering is not a consideration. In this model both the predictor and outcome are measured at each time-point (i.e., both are time-varying), and the model specifies that the predictor measured at time t has actor and partner effects on the outcome, which is also measured at time t. The primary role of time in this model is that it allows for replications of the cross-sectional relationships between the predictor(s) and outcome. Thus, the repeated observations in the over-time APIM are used essentially to increase the precision of the estimates of the actor and partner effects, drawing on the virtues of aggregation (e.g., Rushton, Brainerd, & Pressley, 1983). Accordingly, it is important that the model assumes that the relations between variables are stationary. In other words, there should be no systematic differences in the strength of the actor and partner effects at time t as opposed to time $t-1$ or time $t+1$, and so any variation should be attributable to sampling error.

An example of the over-time standard APIM model is provided by Davila and Kashy (2009), who used a 14-day diary study of heterosexual dating couples to examine the degree to which a person's standing on daily attachment security predicted adaptive daily support processes for that same person and for that person's partner. The lower-level equation for this model using the Davila and Kashy example with distinguishable dyad members would be:

$$Y_{ijt} = b_{0j} + b_{1j} XA_{ijt} + b_{2j} XP_{ijt} + b_3 G_{ij} + b_{4j} XA_{ijt} G_{ij} + b_{5j} XP_{ijt} G_{ij} + e_{ijt}, \quad (14)$$

where G represents gender (i.e., the distinguishing variable), XA represents the person's own attachment security (**Act_secure**) on day t, XP represents the partner's attachment security (**Part_secure**) on day t, and Y represents the measure of daily social support (**support**) on day t. Note that this model is almost identical to equation 10 for the distinguishable APIM. The key difference is that t is an additional subscript for the measures (e.g., Y_{ijt}, XA_{ijt}), which represents the fact that the variables are measured for each person i in dyad j at t points in time.

Table 9.3 provides an example of the data structure for this model, which Kenny et al. (2006) refer to as a pairwise person-period data set. In this data set, each person would have fourteen records representing day 1 through day 14, and so each dyad would have 28 records. For each day, the person's outcome is associated with that person's daily attachment, and the person's partner's daily attachment. For instance, on day 1 person 1's support score is 17, that person's attachment security on that day is 6.3, and his partner's daily attachment is 5.6. In addition, the data in table 9.3 also includes redundant dummy codes for **man** and **woman** to assist in specifying the random effects for the model.

Using Davila and Kashy's (2009) variables as an example, the syntax to estimate this model would be:

MIXED
support WITH **man woman Act_secure Part_secure gender**
/FIXED = **gender Act_secure Part_secure Act_secure*gender Part_secure*gender**
/PRINT = SOLUTION TESTCOV
/RANDOM = **man woman man*Act_secure woman*Act_secure man*Part_secure woman*Part_secure** | SUBJECT(**dyadID**) COVTYPE(UN)
/REPEATED = **day*gender** | SUBJECT(**dyadID**) COVTYPE(AR1).

Note that the RANDOM statement in the above syntax includes separate intercepts, actor effects, and partner effects for men and women, and the covariance type is UN or unspecified. This means that we are allowing for different variances in intercepts, actor effects, and partner effects across gender. More importantly, perhaps, is that all of the covariances between the six effects are estimated. It may be the case that some of these covariances are very close to zero, and so a more restricted random effects model might be needed. One reasonable simplification is to include all the variances, but limit the covariances to the covariance between the two intercepts, the covariance between the two actor effects, and the covariance between the two partner effects. This would be accomplished by replacing

Table 9.3 Data illustrating the person-period data structure using the example variables measured in Davila and Kashy (2009).

DyadID	Person	Day	Support	Act_secure	Part_secure	Gender	Man	Woman
1	1	1	17	**6.3**	**5.6**	1	1	0
1	1	2	18	7.1	5.0	1	1	0
1	1	3	18	6.5	5.4	1	1	0
1	1	⋮	⋮	⋮	⋮	⋮	⋮	⋮
1	1	14	16	7.4	6.1	1	1	0
1	2	1	14	**5.6**	**6.3**	−1	0	1
1	2	2	12	5.0	7.1	−1	0	1
1	2	3	16	5.4	6.5	−1	0	1
1	2	⋮	⋮	⋮	⋮	⋮	⋮	⋮
1	2	14	13	6.1	7.4	−1	0	1

Note. Gender is coded 1 for men and −1 for women.

the RANDOM statement with the following three RANDOM statements:

/RANDOM = **man woman** | SUBJECT(**dyadID**)
      COVTYPE(UN)

/RANDOM = **man*Act_secure woman*Act_secure**
      | SUBJECT(**dyadID**)
      COVTYPE(UN)

/RANDOM = **man*Part_secure woman*Part_secure**
      | SUBJECT(**dyadID**)
      COVTYPE(UN)

Finally, an important issue with the over-time standard APIM is the necessity of modeling the non-independence that arises because variables are measured over time, which is commonly called *autocorrelation* (see e.g., Hillmer, 2001). Autocorrelation occurs when observations that are closer in time are more similar to one another. Because time does not play an explicit role in the analysis, non-independence of observations over time due to autocorrelation is represented in the syntax via the REPEATED statement. In fact, the only statement in the syntax that includes the time variable (**day**) is this REPEATED statement, which specifies an autoregressive-lag 1 autocorrelation structure using the AR1 covariance type. This structure dictates that the residuals at any time t, are related only to residuals at time t-1.

LAGGED MODELS FOR DYADS
Like the over-time APIM, lagged dyadic models treat time as replications of a basic process model.

However, in this type of model the focus is on the degree to which both dyad members' past behavior predicts their current behavior. Thus, this model introduces controls for prior levels and it is therefore more useful for constraining causal inferences than the previous model. Here, time matters in terms of what came before and what came after.

In the most basic dyadic lagged model, actor and partner scores on a variable assessed at time t-1 are used to predict the person's score on that same variable at time t (see figure 9.4) Lags other than t-1 are possible, but these are not widely used in practice and they are usually not strongly anticipated by theoretical or conceptual considerations (they also naturally require more waves of data to estimate reliably). For example, in a moment-by-moment study of marital communication we might have scores measuring the level of negativity for each spouse's speaking turn. We would then predict a person's current negativity to be a function of his or her own past negativity and his or her partner's past negativity. The lower-level model for an indistinguishable lagged dyadic model would be:

$$Y_{ijt} = b_{0j} + b_{1j}YA_{ij,t-1} + b_{2j}YP_{ij,t-1} + e_{ijt} \qquad (15)$$

In this equation, Y_{ijt} is the negativity score for person i in dyad j at time t, $YA_{ij,t-1}$ is that same person's negativity in his or her previous speaking turn, and $YP_{ij,t-1}$ is person i's partner's negativity during his or her previous speaking turn. In an example of this type, actor effects are typically viewed as estimates of behavioral stability, and partner effects can

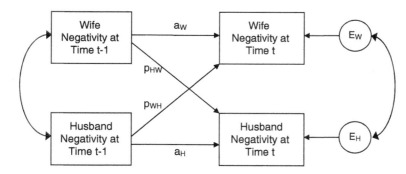

a_W and a_H are estimates of *stability* in negativity, or the degree to which a person's negativity in his or her previous speaking turn predicts that person's negativity in the current speaking turn.

p_{WH} and p_{HW} are estimates of *reciprocity* of negativity, or the degree to which a person's partner's negativity in his or her previous speaking turn predicts the person's subsequent negativity in the current speaking turn.

Fig. 9.4 Lagged APIM model.

be viewed as estimates of partner influence or reciprocity. Thus, the actor effect in the example measures the degree to which a person's negative communication is stable from one speaking turn to the next, and the partner effect measures whether the partner's past negativity is reciprocated.

This type of model seems particularly compelling when observations are made from moment to moment, or perhaps day to day. Moreover, it seems prudent to estimate this model when the study includes many repeated observations to increase the precision of the estimates. To estimate a distinguishable model, we can expand equation 15 to include interactions with the distinguishing variable (e.g., gender or G). This would result in:

$$Y_{ijt} = b_{0j} + b_{1j}YA_{ij,t-1} + b_{2j}YP_{ij,t-1} + b_{3j}G_{ij} \\ + b_{4j}YA_{ij,t-1}G_{ij} + b_{5j}YP_{ij,t-1}G_{ij} + e_{ijt} \quad (16)$$

To estimate a lagged model in SPSS, researchers first need to create a pairwise person-period data set in which each record includes both the person's outcome at time t (e.g., act_neg) and the partner's outcome at time t (e.g., part_neg; see table 9.4). Each record should also include identification variables

for dyad (dyadID), individual (personID), and time (timeID). We suggest that researchers first create centered actor and partner variables by subtracting the grand-mean from the original scores. These centered actor and partner variables are then used to create the lagged scores. SPSS includes a Lag(X) function that can be used to create the actor and partner scores at time t-1. It is critical to note that use of the Lag(X) function when a data set has missing data can be problematic. Our best advice for researchers is to include blank records for missing observations so that each individual and each dyad have the same number of records in the data set. The SPSS syntax to create the lagged variables would be:

IF (timeID ne 0) act_negPast=LAG(act_negC).
IF (timeID ne 0) part_negPast=LAG(part_negC).

As this syntax makes explicit and as depicted in table 9.4, there is no lagged actor or partner score for the first observed time point (timeID = 0). Indeed this raises an important point with lagged models: If the study includes n repeated observations for each person, estimates from these models are based on n - 1 data points. Thus, lagged analyses

Table 9.4 Data illustrating a lagged data set in the pairwise person-period data structure

DyadID	PersonID	TimeID	Act_Neg	Part_Neg	Act_NegC	Part_NegC	Act_NegPast	Part_NegPast
1	1	0	4	5	−2.34	−1.34		
1	1	1	5	6	−1.34	−.34	−2.34	−1.34
1	1	2	4	7	−2.34	.66	−1.34	−.34
1	1	3	3	8	−3.34	1.66	−2.34	.66
1	2	0	5	4	−1.34	−2.34		
1	2	1	6	5	−.34	−1.34	−1.34	−2.34
1	2	2	7	4	.66	−2.34	−.34	−1.34
1	2	3	8	3	1.66	−3.34	.66	−2.34
2	1	0	5	5	−1.34	−1.34		
2	1	1	8	7	1.66	.66	−1.34	−1.34
2	1	2	7	6	.66	−.34	1.66	.66
2	1	3	8	3	1.66	−3.34	.66	−.34
2	2	0	5	5	−1.34	−1.34		
2	2	1	7	8	.66	1.66	−1.34	−1.34
2	2	2	6	7	−.34	.66	.66	1.66
2	2	3	3	8	−3.34	1.66	−.34	.66

case is somewhat more complex in that each person has multiple "partners." Thus, in the APIM for groups, the partner effect is defined as *the effect of the average of the other group members' inputs on the person's outcomes*. As an example, consider a study of group identification and productivity. The actor effect would measure whether individuals who identify with the group more are more productive, and the partner effect would measure whether individuals whose other group members identify with the group more are more productive. Researchers who focus on groups typically examine actor effects but often ignore partner effects. Nonetheless, partner effects capture the interdependence between individuals that exists in multiperson groups, and so partner effects in this context address key questions concerning how group members affect one another.

In contrast to the APIM for dyads, the APIM for groups has been used in only a handful of studies. Bonito (2000) used the APIM in a study examining the correspondence between perceived and actual group participation in three-person groups, and Bonito, DeCamp, Coffman, and Fleming (2006) examined how participation in small-group discussions is affected by the distribution of information within the group. Reid and Ng (2006) also used actor-partner analyses to study group participation, but in this study, the focus was on perceived status in an intergroup setting.

We illustrate implementation of the APIM for groups using MLM with our hypothetical study of identification and productivity. To use MLM as the data analytic approach for this design, data must be formatted such that each individual has a data record that includes a group identification variable (e.g., **groupID**) and a person identification variable (e.g., **personID**). Each record then includes the individual's outcome score (e.g., **product**), and the individual's score on the predictor (e.g., **Act_identity**; see table 9.6). We then calculate the average of the other group members' scores on the predictor (e.g., **Part_identity**). The required syntax to compute the partner variable, allowing for unequally sized groups is:

```
SORT CASES BY groupID.
AGGREGATE
/OUTFILE = * MODE = ADDVARIABLES
/PRESORTED
/BREAK = groupID
/ID_mean = MEAN(Act_identity)
/N_BREAK = N.
COMPUTE Part_identity = (Id_mean*N_BREAK
    – Act_Identity)/(N_BREAK – 1).
EXECUTE.
```

Once the data set is prepared, the APIM for groups with indistinguishable members is relatively straightforward to estimate using MLM. The SPSS syntax for the example is:

Table 9.6 Data depicting actor and partner effects for the APIM with groups

GroupID	Person	Product	Act_Identity	ID_mean	N_Break	Part_Identity
1	1	6	7	6.80	5	6.75
1	2	7	9	6.80	5	6.25
1	3	5	6	6.80	5	7.00
1	4	7	7	6.80	5	6.75
1	5	6	5	6.80	5	7.25
2	1	4	5	5.86	7	6.00
2	2	5	4	5.86	7	6.17
2	3	3	6	5.86	7	5.83
2	4	4	6	5.86	7	5.83
2	5	3	7	5.86	7	5.67
2	6	4	6	5.86	7	5.83
2	7	3	7	5.86	7	5.67

Note. ID_mean is the average identity score across members of the same group, N_Break is the number of members in the group, and Part_Identity is the average of the other group member's identity scores (excluding the actor).

```
MIXED
product WITH Act_identity Part_identity
/FIXED = Act_identity Part_identity
/PRINT = SOLUTION TESTCOV
/REPEATED = personID | SUBJECT(groupID)
        COVTYPE(CSR).
```

In this syntax we have used the REPEATED statement to estimate nonindependence within groups. As in the case of dyads, this specification allows for the possibility that scores from members of the same group are negatively correlated. Given that the lower limit of the intraclass correlation is $-1/(n-1)$, negative values are less likely to occur as group size increases. Kenny, Mannetti, Pietro, Livi, and Kashy (2002) provide a detailed discussion of the APIM analysis for small groups using multilevel modeling.

The One-with-Many Design (OWM)

The OWM design is a family of designs in which there is a focal individual (i.e., the "one") who is linked to or paired with a set of partners (i.e., the "many"). In some ways, this is a well-established design in that researchers often study how individuals perceive and/or interact with multiple others (e.g., strangers, friends, family members). For example this design is often used when each participant (the one) is asked to rate a set of targets' personalities (the many; e.g., Friedman, Oltmanns, &

Turkheimer, 2007) or other attributes such as physical attractiveness (Wood & Brumbaugh, 2009). Kenny and Winquist (2001) refer to these designs as *one-perceiver, many-targets* designs (1PMT) because the data are generated by "one" rater who makes multiple ratings. In contrast, in the *many-perceivers, one-target* design (MP1T) the ratings come from the "many." For instance, studies that use multiple informant reports typically have this MP1T data structure, as in Donnellan, Conger, and Burzette (2007), in which mothers and fathers separately reported on their adolescent child's personality.

Somewhat less common is the *reciprocal* design, in which both the one and the many provide data (see figure 9.5). Kenny et al. (2010) describe a study of doctor-patient communication using a reciprocal design in which multiple patients with the same doctor rated the doctor's communication skills, and the doctors also rated their communication skills with each patient. Marcus, Kashy, and Baldwin (2009) describe a similar study in which therapists reported their alliance with each of their clients (i.e., the therapist's report that his or her relationship with a patient is collaborative, mutually trusting, and promotes clinical improvement) and the clients also each rated their alliance with their therapist.

The focus of the reciprocal OWM design described here is on questions of consensus, coordination, and

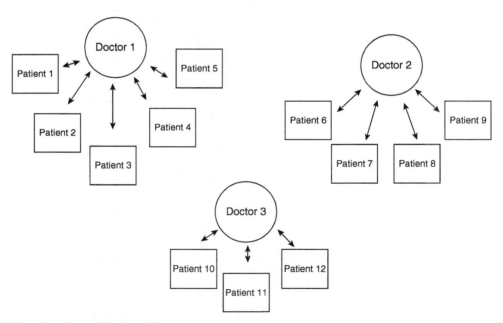

Fig. 9.5 The reciprocal one-with-many design.

agreement at two levels: the dyad and the focal person. Variation in the ratings or behavioral data generated by the focal persons is decomposed into a focal-person component and a residual component. The focal-person component measures similarity in the focal person's behaviors or ratings across the partners. For instance, in the Kenny et al. (2010) example, this is the degree to which some doctors think they communicate clearly with all of their patients whereas other doctors think that they are not very clear with any of their patients. The residual component measures whether doctors think that they communicate clearly with some patients but not with others. The data from the partners (e.g., patients) are also decomposed into focal-person and residual components, but in this case the focal-person component measures consensus or similarity of behavior by "the many" with the focal person. In the communication example, the focal-person component measures whether the patients of some doctors all tend to report that their doctor communicates clearly, but the patients of other doctors all report that their doctors are not clear. The residual component measures whether there is variation in scores from "the many" who are associated with the same focal person: Do some patients who see the same doctor report that the doctor communicates clearly whereas others report that the same doctor is not clear?

A key question in the OWM reciprocal design concerns covariation in these effects. Specifically, the two focal-person effects can be correlated, and for the Kenny et al. (2010) example this correlation addresses whether doctors who generally see themselves as communicating clearly with their patients are generally perceived by their patients as communicating clearly. Thus, this parameter addresses issues of the *generalized accuracy* of self-perceptions on the part of the focal person. The two dyad effects can also be correlated, and this correlation assesses *dyadic accuracy*, or whether a doctor who reports uniquely clear communication with a particular patient is seen in return by that client as communicating clearly.

MLM is the natural data analytic approach for the OWM design; however the focus of the analysis we describe here is on the random effects (i.e., variance and covariance) rather than the fixed effects. The focal person is the upper-level unit and the "many" are the lower-level units. The MLM equations for this design are based on the two-intercept approach described earlier (Raudenbush et al., 1995), in which two dummy variables are created to

denote which person provided the outcome score. Thus, we would have a doctor dummy variable, D (**doctor** in the syntax below), which is coded 1 if the data are provided by the doctor and 0 if the data came from the patient, and we would have a patient dummy variable, P (**patient**), which is coded 0 if the data are provided by the doctor and the 1 if the data are provided by the patient. Using these two dummy variables allows us to specify a model with separate intercepts for doctors' and patients' ratings, as well as separate residuals for doctors' and patients' ratings. The lower-level MLM equation is:

$$Y_{ijk} = b_{01j}D + b_{02j}P + De_{1ij} + Pe_{2ij} \qquad (18)$$

Where i refers to the patient, j refers to the doctor, and k denotes whether the data were provided by the doctor (i.e., $k = 1$) or the patient (i.e., $k = 2$). In this equation, b_{01j} estimates the average of the communication skills ratings made by doctor j, averaging across j's patients. In contrast, b_{02j} estimates the average of the communication skills ratings made by doctor j's clients. The error component, e_{1ij}, reflects the unique part of doctor j's rating of patient i after removing doctor j's average effect, and the second error component e_{2ij}, reflects the unique part of patient i's rating of doctor j after removing doctor j's average effect.

The basic level-two model aggregates results across doctors and has both a fixed and a random effect. These equations are:

$$b_{01j} = a_{01} + d_{1j} \qquad b_{02j} = a_{02} + d_{2j} \qquad (19)$$

In these models, a_{01} is the grand mean for doctor ratings and a_{02} is the grand mean for patient ratings. More importantly, d_{1j} and d_{2j} represent the random component of the ratings associated with the doctor. Thus, the doctor variance from the doctors' ratings is based on the variance in d_{1j}, and the doctor variance from the patients' ratings is based on the variance in d_{2j}. The correlation between these is a function of the covariance between these two random effects. Finally, the dyadic correlation is based on the covariance between the two error terms from the lower-level model (i.e., De_{1ij} and Pe_{2ij}).

To estimate the OWM with this example, the SPSS syntax would be:

```
MIXED
commskill WITH doctor patient
/FIXED = doctor patient | NOINT
/PRINT = SOLUTION TESTCOV
```

/RANDOM **doctor patient** | SUBJECT(**doctorID**)
   COVTYPE(UNR)
/REPEATED = **role** | SUBJECT
        (**doctorID*patientID**)
        COVTYPE(UNR).

In this syntax, **commskill** is the measure of perceived communication skill, and **role** is a variable that designates whether the doctor or the patient made the rating. The RANDOM statement is used to obtain the focal person variance for the doctor's ratings and patient's ratings, and the specification of UNR requests the correlation between these two focal person effects (i.e., generalized reciprocity). The REPEATED statement specifies the dyadic or residual variances as well as the dyadic correlation. Marcus et al. (2009) present a more detailed discussion of the OWM that also includes how additional predictors or covariates can be included in the analysis.

The Social Relations Model (SRM)

The SRM (Kenny, 1994; Kenny & La Voie, 1984; Warner, Kenny, & Stoto, 1979) is a model of social behavior and interpersonal perception that can be applied in research contexts in which each person participates in more than one dyad within their group. In recent years this model has been used to examine topics ranging from perceptions of leadership (Kenny & Livi, 2009) to the anthropomorphism of dogs (Kwan, Gosling, & John, 2008). It has also been used to examine individual differences in negotiation (Elfenbein, Curhan, Eisenkraft, Shirako, & Baccaro, 2008), dating preferences based on speed dating procedures (Finkel & Eastwick,

2008), and friendship development (Back, Schmukle, & Egloff, 2008). (David Kenny maintains a very useful Web site that provides links to a bibliography of all SRM studies, as well as data analysis programs specifically designed for SRM analyses, at http:// davidakenny.net/srm/srm.htm.)

Like the OWM design, the SRM is a variance decomposition model. In formal terms, according to the SRM each dyadic score is comprised of four components. Consider as an example a study of interpersonal perception between well-acquainted roommates. In the example, members of four-person suites are asked to rate one another's agreeableness. Figure 9.6 presents the breakdown of two suitemates' ratings: Anne's rating of Beth's agreeableness and Beth's rating of Anne's agreeableness. The SRM suggests that dyadic scores are comprised of group-level, individual-level, and dyad-level effects. Specifically, Anne's rating of Beth includes a *group mean*, which reflects the average level of the perceived agreeableness for the suite (i.e., some groups of suitemates are more agreeable on average than others). Next, at the individual level Anne may tend to think that everyone is agreeable, and so Anne's rating of Beth may reflect her general tendency to view everyone in a positive light. The tendency for a person to exhibit a consistent level of response across all partners is called a *perceiver effect*. The *target effect* is also an individual-level effect, and it measures the tendency for others to agree in their perceptions of an individual. Thus, for Anne's rating of Beth, the target effect measures the tendency for Beth to be seen as agreeable by all of her suitemates. The *relationship effect* measures the unique component of the dyadic score. For Anne's rating of Beth, the relationship

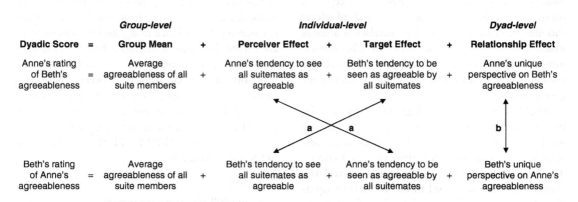

a = generalized reciprocity, **b** = dyadic reciprocity

Figure 9.6 The SRM decomposition.

effect measures the degree to which Anne considers Beth to be especially agreeable, more agreeable than Anne tends to see others, and more agreeable than others tend to see Beth. Thus, the relationship effect reflects the unique combination of two individuals after removing their individual-level tendencies.

In the SRM, the focus is not on the absolute size of perceiver, target, or relationship effects for any particular person or dyad. Instead, the focus is on the extent to which the variation in dyadic behavior reflects variation in group effects, individual effects (i.e., perceiver and target effects), and unique dyadic or relationship effects. Thus, the *perceiver variance* measures the degree to which some individuals rate all partners high on a specific outcome variable and other individuals rate all partners low on the outcome variable. In the example, perceiver variance occurs if some individuals think that all of their suitemates are agreeable, but others think that all of their suitemates are disagreeable. Note that the perceiver variance in the SRM is analogous to the focal-person variance in the OWM design when the ratings are from the focal person. That is, both capture the degree to which a person's perceptions or behavior is consistent across partners.

Target variance measures the degree to which some individuals are rated high on a particular outcome variable by all partners and other individuals are rated low on the outcome variable by all partners. For instance, some individuals may be seen as agreeable by everyone in the group, and others may be uniformly seen as disagreeable. The target variance in the SRM is analogous to the focal-person variance in the OWM design when the ratings are from the partners, and in both models this variance is a measure of consensus: The degree to which individuals agree in their ratings of a common target.

Relationship variance measures the degree to which ratings vary depending on the specific individuals in the dyad after removing variance due to those individuals' perceiver and target effects. For the agreeableness data, the relationship variance would measure the degree to which perceptions of agreeableness are unique to the particular dyadic combinations. The SRM provides a more accurate estimate of unique dyadic variance because it removes *both* the perceiver and target effects from each rating. In contrast, the residual from the OWM when scores come from the focal person includes both target effects and relationships effects, since each target (e.g., patient) is rated by only one perceiver (e.g., the doctor) and therefore these two factors cannot be disentangled. Likewise, the residual

from the OWM when scores come from the partners includes variance due to perceiver effects and relationship effects, as each perceiver (e.g., the patients) rates only a single target (e.g., the doctor).

The SRM can be used to measure two types of reciprocity: generalized reciprocity and dyadic reciprocity. Recall that in the OWM, generalized reciprocity was specific to the focal person.

In contrast, in the SRM generalized reciprocity refers to all group members and so it is based on the correlation between each group member's perceiver and target effects (see path *a* in figure 9.6). For instance, in the agreeableness example, generalized reciprocity measures whether individuals who generally see others as agreeable are also seen by others as agreeable.

Dyadic reciprocity is measured by correlating the two group members' relationship effects (see path *b* in figure 9.6). Thus dyadic reciprocity would emerge if two group members perceive one another in a uniquely similar way. Thus, if Anne sees Beth as uniquely high in agreeableness, does Beth see Anne in this way as well? In the SRM, dyadic reciprocity is a property of every dyad within the group whereas in the OWM, dyadic reciprocity was specific to dyads comprised of the focal person and each of his or her partners.

A complete discussion of all of the ways the SRM has been used in social and personality psychology is beyond the scope of this chapter. Indeed, we have limited our introduction to an example of a single interpersonal perception variable. Nonetheless, the SRM has also been used to study metaperception (i.e., the way we think we are viewed by others) and accuracy in metaperception (e.g., Levesque, 1997; Malloy, Albright, & Scarpatti, 2007; Santuzzi, 2007), as well as interpersonal behavior and accuracy in behavioral predictions (e.g., Levesque & Kenny, 1993; Malloy, Barcelos, Arruda, DeRosa, & Fonseca, 2005) among other things. In addition, a variety of sources discussing the SRM and its implementation are available (e.g., Kenny, 1994; Kenny et al., 2006; Kenny & Kashy, 2010). On his Web site Kenny provides stand-alone data analysis programs that can be used to estimate the SRM effects, and Kenny and Kashy (2010) present a brief discussion of how this model can be estimated using multilevel modeling with a particular emphasis on the SAS package.

Summary and Conclusion

We began this chapter with a brief discussion of current methodological practices in social and personality psychology, and we observed that current research in this field is strongly tied to an individual-as-unit perspective given the kinds of studies published in *JPSP* during the late 2000s. However, social and personality psychologists have clear interests in understanding *interpersonal* behavior, and thus, the focus on individuals may represent a limitation in current research. Accordingly, we have tried to provide an accessible introduction to the methodological issues relevant for studies involving dyads and groups. We also presented several statistical models that are specifically designed to examine interpersonal behavior in studies involving more than one person.

In particular, the actor-partner interdependence model for both dyads and groups is a useful tool for understanding how interdependent individuals affect one another's thoughts, feelings, and behavior. The over-time models for dyadic data are perhaps particularly important given the increasing use of longitudinal designs in the field. We noted several design considerations that are relevant for conducting these kinds of studies, and provided examples of dyadic growth models and lagged models. Finally, we briefly described the one-with-many design and social relations model for use with dyadic group data. In each of these discussions we have tried to refer readers to additional readings and resources, as this chapter can only serve as an introduction to some relatively complex methods.

In closing, we hope that social and personality psychologists will broaden their empirical research to more consistently incorporate actual interpersonal contexts into their substantive areas. It is difficult to identify all of the potential applications of the methods we describe, but we suspect that researchers who specialize in topical areas will be in a good position to apply these methods once they have been introduced to them. As Reis et al. (2000) note, "Most human behavior takes place in the context of the individual's relationships with others." Although many questions require an individual focus for the purposes of methodological control and experimental rigor, there is much to be learned by incorporating relationships into our research. In line with this goal, the models and methods we described should serve as important tools for advancing personality and social psychology.

References

Ackerman, R. A., Donnellan, M. B., & Kashy, D. A. (2011). Working with dyadic data in studies of emerging adulthood: Specific recommendations, general advice, and practical tips. In F. Fincham & M. Cui (Eds.), *Romantic relationships in emerging adulthood.* (pp. 67–97). New York: Cambridge University Press.

Back, M. D., Schmukle, S. C., & Egloff, B. (2008). Becoming friends by chance. *Psychological Science, 19,* 439–440.

Badr, H., & Carmack Taylor, C.L. (2008). Effects of relationship maintenance on psychological distress and dyadic adjustment among couples coping with lung cancer. *Health Psychology, 27,* 616–627.

Biesanz, J., Deeb-Sossa, N., Papadakis, A., Bollen, K. A., & Curran, P. (2004). The role of coding time in estimating and interpreting growth curve models. *Psychological Methods, 9,* 30–52.

Bonito, J. A. (2000). The effect of contributing substantively on assessments of participation. *Small Group Research, 31,* 528–553.

Bonito, J. A., DeCamp, M. H., Coffman, M., & Fleming, S. (2006.) Participation, information, and control in small groups: An actor-partner interdependence model. *Group Dynamics: Theory, Research, and Practice, 10,* 16–28.

Brock, R. L., & Lawrence, E. (2009). Too much of a good thing: Underprovision versus overprovision of partner support. *Journal of Family Psychology, 23,* 181–192.

Brown, T. A. (2006). *Confirmatory factor analysis for applied research.* New York: Guilford.

Butler, E. A., Egloff, B., Wilhelm, F. H., Smith, N. C., Erickson, E. A., & Gross, J. J. (2003). The social consequences of expressive suppression. *Emotion, 3,* 48–67.

Cillessen, A. H. N., Jiang, S. L., West, T. V., & Laszkowski, D. K. (2005). Predictors of dyadic friendship quality in adolescence. *International Journal of Behavioral Development, 29,* 165–172.

Cole, D. A., & Maxwell, S. E. (2003). Testing mediational models with longitudinal data: Questions and tips in the use of structural equation modeling. *Journal of Abnormal Psychology, 112,* 558-577.

Conger, R. D., Lorenz, F. O., & Wickrama, K. A. S. (Eds.). (2004). *Continuity and change in family relations.* Mahwah, NJ: Erlbaum.

Cuperman, R., & Ickes, W. (2009). Big Five predictors of behavior and perceptions in initial dyadic interaction: Personality similarity helps extraverts and introverts, but hurts "disagreeable." *Journal of Personality and Social Psychology, 97,* 667–684.

Dailey, R. M. (2008). Assessing the contribution of nonverbal behaviors in displays of confirmation during parent-adolescent interactions: An actor-partner interdependence model. *Journal of Family Communication, 8,* 62–91.

Davila, J., & Kashy, D. A. (2009). Secure base processes in couples: Daily associations between support experiences and attachment security. *Journal of Family Psychology, 23,* 76–88.

Donnellan, M. B., & Conger, R. D. (2007). Designing and implementing longitudinal studies. In R. W. Robins, R. C. Fraley, & R. Krueger (Eds.), *The handbook of research methods in personality psychology.* (pp. 21–36). Guilford.

Donnellan, M. B., Conger, R. D, & Burzette, R. G. (2007). Personality development from late adolescence to young adulthood: Differential stability, normative maturity, and evidence for the maturity-stability hypothesis. *Journal of Personality, 75,* 237–264.

Elfenbein, H. A., Curhan, J. R., Eisenkraft, N., Shirako, A., & Baccaro, L. (2008). Are some negotiators are better than others? Individual differences in bargaining outcomes. *Journal of Research in Personality, 42,* 1463–1475.

Finkel, E. J., & Eastwick, P. W. (2008). Speed-dating. *Current Directions in Psychological Science, 17,* 193–197.

Friedman, J.N.W., Oltmanns, T.F., & Turkheimer, E. (2007). Interpersonal perception and personality disorders: Utilization of a thin slice approach. *Journal of Research in Personality, 41,* 667-688.

Gollob, H. F., & Reichardt, C. S. (1987). Taking account of time lags in causal models. *Child Development, 58,* 80-92.

Griffin, D., Murray, S., & Gonzalez, R. (1999). Difference score correlations in relationship research: A conceptual primer. *Personal Relationships, 6,* 505–518.

Hertzog, C., Lindenberger, U., Ghisletta, P., & von Oertzen, T. (2006). On the power of latent growth curve models to detect correlated change. *Psychological Methods, 11,* 244–252.

Hillmer, S. (2001). Time series regressions. In D. S. Moskowitz & S. L. Hershberger (Eds.), *Modeling intraindividual variability with repeated measures data: Methods and applications.* (pp. 203-233). Mahwah, NJ: Erlbaum.

Horn, J. L., & McArdle, J. J. (1992). A practical and theoretical guide to measurement invariance in aging research. *Experimental Aging Research, 18,* 117–144.

Hox, J. (2002). *Multilevel analyses: Techniques and applications.* Mahwah, NJ: Erlbaum.

Johnson, D. R., Amoloza, T., & Booth, A. (1992). Stability and developmental change in marital quality: A three wave panel analysis. *Journal of Marriage and the Family, 54,* 582–594.

Karney, B., & Bradbury, T. N. (1995). The longitudinal course of marital quality and stability: A review of theory, methods, and research. *Psychological Bulletin, 118,* 3–34.

Karney, B. R., & Bradbury, T. N. (1997). Neuroticism, marital interaction, and the trajectory of marital satisfaction. *Journal of Personality and Social Psychology, 72,* 1075–1092.

Kashy, D. A., & Donnellan, M. B. (2008). Comparing MLM and SEM approaches to analyzing developmental dyadic data: Growth curve models of hostility in families. In N. A. Card & T. D. Little (Eds.), *Analysis of interdependent developmental data.* (pp. 165-190). Mahwah, NJ: Erlbaum.

Kashy, D. A., Donnellan, M. B., Burt, S. A., & McGue, M. (2008). Growth curve models for indistinguishable dyads using multilevel modeling and structural equation modeling: The case of adolescent twin's conflict with their mothers. *Developmental Psychology, 44,* 316–329.

Kashy, D. A., & Kenny, D. A. (2000). The analysis of data from dyads and groups. In H. T. Reis & C. M. Judd (Eds.), *Handbook of research methods in social psychology* (pp. 451-477). Cambridge, UK: Cambridge University Press.

Kelley, H. H., & Thibaut, J. W. (1978). *Interpersonal relations: A theory of interdependence.* New York: Wiley.

Kenny, D. A. (1994). *Interpersonal perception: A social relations analysis.* New York: Guilford.

Kenny, D. A., & Kashy, D. A. (2010). Dyadic data analysis using multilevel modeling. In J. Hox & J. K. Roberts (Eds.), *The handbook of advanced multilevel analysis.* (pp. 335-370). London: Taylor & Francis.

Kenny, D. A., Kashy, D. A., & Bolger, N. (1998). Data analysis in social psychology. In D. Gilbert, S. Fiske, & G. Lindzey (Eds.), *The handbook of social psychology* (4th ed., Vol. 1, pp. 233–265). New York: McGraw-Hill.

Kenny, D. A., Kashy, D. A., & Cook, W. L. (2006). *Dyadic data analysis.* New York: Guilford.

Kenny, D. A., & La Voie, L. (1984). The social relations model. In L. Berkowitz (Ed.), *Advances in experimental social psychology* (Vol. 18, pp. 142–182). Orlando: Academic.

Kenny, D. A., & Livi, S. (2009). A componential analysis of leadership using the Social Relations Model. In F. J. Yammarino & F. Dansereau (Eds.), *Multi-Level Issues in Organizational Behavior and Leadership (Vol. 8 of Research in Multi-level Issues;* pp. 147-191). Bingley, UK: Emerald.

Kenny, D. A., Mannetti, L., Pietro, A., Livi, S., & Kashy, D. A. (2002). The statistical analysis of data from small groups. *Journal of Personality and Social Psychology, 83,* 126–137.

Kenny, D. A., Veldhuijzen, W., van der Weijden, T., LeBlanc, A., Lockyer, J., Légaré, F., et al. (2010). Interpersonal perception in the context of doctor-patient relationships: A dyadic analysis of doctor-patient communication. *Social Science and Medicine, 70,* 763–768.

Kenny, D. A., & Winquist, L. A. (2001). The measurement of interpersonal sensitivity: Consideration of design, components, and unit of analysis. In J. A. Hall & F. J. Bernieri (Eds.), *Interpersonal sensitivity: Theory and measurement* (pp. 265–302). Mahwah, NJ: Erlbaum.

Kreft, I., & de Leeuw, J. (2004). *Introducing multilevel modeling.* Thousand Oaks, CA: Sage.

Kwan, V. S. Y., Gosling, S. D., & John, O. P. (2008). Anthropomorphism as a special case of social perception: A cross-species social relations model analysis of humans and dogs. *Social Cognition, 26,* 129–142.

Lakey, S. G., & Canary, D. J. (2002). Actor goal achievement and sensitivity to partner as critical factors in understanding interpersonal communication competence and conflict strategies. *Communication Monographs, 69,* 217–235.

Langer, A., Lawrence, E., & Barry, R. A. (2008). Using a vulnerability-stress-adaptation framework to predict physical aggression trajectories in newlywed marriage. *Journal of Consulting and Clinical Psychology, 76,* 756–768.

Laurenceau, J-P., & Bolger, N. (2005). Using diary methods to study marital and family processes. *Journal of Family Psychology, 19,* 86–97.

LeBlanc, A., Kenny, D. A., O'Connor, A. M., & Légaré, F. (2009). Decisional conflict in patients and their physicians: A dyadic approach to shared decision making. *Medical Decision Making, 29,* 61–68.

Levesque, M. J. (1997). Meta-accuracy among acquainted individuals: A social relations analysis of interpersonal perception and metaperception. *Journal of Personality and Social Psychology, 72,* 66–74.

Levesque, M. J., & Kenny, D. A. (1993). Accuracy of behavioral predictions at zero acquaintance. *Journal of Personality and Social Psychology, 65,* 1178–1187.

Luo, S., Chen, H., Yue, G., Zhang, G., Zhaoyang, R., & Xu, D. (2008). Predicting marital satisfaction from self, partner, and couple characteristics: Is it me, you, or us? *Journal of Personality, 76,* 1231–1265.

Malloy, T. E., Albright, L., & Scarpati, S. (2007). Awareness of peers' judgments of oneself: Accuracy and process of metaperception. *International Journal of Behavior Development, 31,* 603–610.

Malloy, T. E., Barcelos, S., Arruda, E., DeRosa, M., & Fonseca, C. (2005). Individual differences and cross-situational consistency of dyadic social behavior. *Journal of Personality and Social Psychology, 89,* 643–654.

Marcus, D., Kashy, D., & Baldwin, S. (2009). Studying psychotherapy using the one-with-many design: The therapeutic alliance as an exemplar. *Journal of Counseling Psychology, 56*(4), 537–548.

McIsaac, C., Connolly, J., McKenney, K. S., Pepler, D., & Craig, W. (2008). Conflict negotiation and autonomy processes in adolescent romantic relationships: An observational study of interdependency in boyfriend and girlfriend effects. *Journal of Adolescence, 31,* 691–707.

Pitts, S. C., West, S. G., & Tein, J. Y. (1996). Longitudinal measurement models in evaluation research: Examining stability and change. *Evaluation and Program Planning, 19,* 333–350.

Proulx, C. M., Buehler, C., & Helms, H. (2009). Moderators of the link between marital hostility and change in spouses' depressive symptoms. *Journal of Family Psychology, 23,* 540–550.

Raudenbush, S. W., Brennan, R. T., & Barnett, R. C. (1995). A multivariate hierarchical model for studying psychological change within married couples. *Journal of Family Psychology, 9,* 167–174.

Reid, S. A., & Ng, S. H. (2006). The dynamics of intragroup differentiation in an intergroup social context. *Human Communication Research, 32,* 504–525.

Reis, H. T., Collins, W., & Berscheid, E. (2000). The relationship context of human behavior and development. *Psychological Bulletin, 126,* 844–872.

Roberts, B. W., Wood, D., & Smith, J. L. (2005). Evaluating the five factor theory and social investment perspective on personality trait development. *Journal of Research in Personality, 39,* 166–184.

Rogosa, D., Brandt, D., & Zimowski, M. (1982). A growth curve approach to the measurement of change. *Psychological Bulletin, 92,* 726–748.

Rushton, J. P., Brainerd, C. J., & Pressley, M. (1983). Behavioral development and construct validity: The principle of aggregation. *Psychological Bulletin, 94,* 18–38.

Schwarzer, R., & Knoll, N. (2007). Functional roles of social support within the stress and coping process: A theoretical and empirical overview. *International Journal of Psychology, 42,* 243–252.

Santuzzi, A. M. (2007). Perceptions and metaperceptions of negative evaluation: Group composition and interpersonal accuracy in a social relations model. *Group Processes and Intergroup Relations, 10,* 383–398.

Schmitt, N., & Kuljanin, G. (2008). Measurement invariance: Review of practice and implications. *Human Resource Management Review, 18,* 210–222.

Selfhout, M., Denissen, J., Branje, S., & Meeus, W. (2009). In the eye of the beholder: Perceived, actual, and peer-rated similarity in personality, communication, and friendship intensity during the acquaintanceship process. *Journal of Personality and Social Psychology, 96,* 1152–1165.

Singer, J. D., & Willett, J. B. (2003). *Applied longitudinal data analysis: Modeling change and event occurrence.* New York: Oxford University Press.

Snijders, T., & Bosker, R. (1999). *Multilevel analysis: An introduction to basic and advanced multilevel modeling.* Thousand Oaks, CA: Sage.

Theiss, J. A., & Knobloch, L. K. (2009). An actor-partner interdependence model of irritations in romantic relationships. *Communication Research, 36,* 510–537.

Trail, T. E., Shelton, J. N., & West, T.V. (2009). Interracial roommate relationships: Negotiating daily interactions. *Personality and Social Psychology Bulletin, 35,* 671–684.

Tran, S., & Simpson, J.A. (2009). Prorelationship maintenance behaviors: The joint roles of attachment and commitment. *Journal of Personality and Social Psychology, 97,* 685–698.

Vandenberg, R. J., & Lance, C. E. (2000). A review and synthesis of the measurement invariance literature: Suggestions, practices, and recommendations for organizational research. *Organizational Research Methods, 3,* 4–69.

Warner, R. M., Kenny, D. A., & Stoto, M. (1979). A new round robin analysis of variance for social interaction data. *Journal of Personality and Social Psychology, 37,* 1742–1757.

Willett, J. B., Singer, J. D., & Martin, N. C. (1998). The design and analysis of longitudinal studies of development and psychopathology in context: Statistical models and methodological recommendations. *Development and Psychopathology, 10,* 395–426.

Wood, D., & Brumbaugh, C. C. (2009) Using revealed mate preferences to evaluate market force and differential preference explanations for mate selection. *Journal of Personality and Social Psychology, 96,* 1226–1244.

Multilevel Modeling in Personality and Social Psychology

Oliver Christ, Chris G. Sibley, *and* Ulrich Wagner

Abstract

An integrated personality and social psychology needs to take into account different levels of analysis by definition. In both disciplines, it is widely accepted that personality and the social context affects social behavior and that social behavior, in turn, also informs us about personality. The challenge for an integrated personality and social psychology is to simultaneously analyze the complex relations between the different levels of analysis for both theoretical as well as statistical reasons. Innovations in statistical analysis in the last three decades have made it possible to simultaneously take into account different levels of analysis. Our purpose in this chapter is to review the basics of as well as recent advances in multilevel modeling, to develop a framework of multilevel analyses for an integrated personality and social psychology, and to illustrate the importance of multilevel modeling for theory development and testing using examples from research on personality and social behavior. It is our hope that this chapter will help to increase the application of multilevel modeling in personality and social psychology and to further advance the development of an integrated personality and social psychology.

Keywords: integrated personality and social psychology, multilevel modeling, multilevel random coefficient model, multilevel framework, multilevel theory

Personality and social psychology both target human behavior: "Social psychologists examine how external, situational causes operate, personality psychologists study how people's inner traits and processes operate" (Baumeister, 1999, p. 367). In both disciplines, it is widely accepted that personality affects social behavior and that social behavior, in turn, also informs us about personality (e.g., Funder & Fast, 2010; Rhodewalt, 2008; Snyder & Cantor, 1998). Both fields systematically study thoughts, emotions, and behaviors of the person, and both acknowledge that people operate in social context (Baumeister, 1999; Rhodewelt, 2008; Snyder & Ickes, 1985). "Personality and social psychology therefore links the biology and development of the individual with the systems of interpersonal relationships, social structure, and culture within which the person is formed and functions" (Brewer, Kenny, & Norem, 2000, p. 2).

In both disciplines, the importance of different levels of analysis is emphasized. For instance, the social psychologist Thomas F. Pettigrew (1996, 1997; see also Doise, 1980) presented an elegant model distinguishing between three levels of analysis (see Figure 10.1). The broadest, or macrolevel, encompasses expansive entities such as societies, nations, cultures, economic and political systems, institutions and organizations. The mesolevel of analysis involves face-to-face interactions. At the lowest level of analysis, the microlevel, human beings are considered one at a time. Moreover, Pettigrew outlined six possible causal routes between the levels, whereby the micro-meso link (route B) and vice versa (route E) are at the center of an integrated personality and social psychology (Pettigrew, 1997). Studies located here are concerned with the interaction between characteristics of individuals and features of the situation or groups individuals are members of.

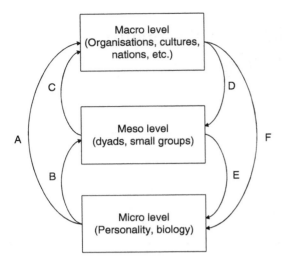

Fig. 10.1 Levels of analysis adapted from Pettigrew (1996).

Many of the examples presented later in this chapter stand exemplarily for either the micro-meso link (e.g., Reis, Sheldon, Gable, Roscoe, & Ryan 2000) or the meso-micro link (e.g., DeHart & Pelham, 2007; Poteat, Espelage, & Green, 2007) or combinations of the two (e.g., Weingart, Brett, Olekalns, & Smith, 2007). Routes C (meso-macro link) and D (macro-meso link) are of importance especially for social psychologists who analyze social interactions in relation to their societal context, like differences in interaction patterns between cultures (Heine, 2010; see also Pettigrew, 1997; Oishi, Kesebir, & Snyder, 2009). Routes A (micro-macro link) and F (macro-micro link) are also of central interest for the field, especially for personality psychology. A classic example for route A forms research by McClelland (1961; for a critical reexamination see Gilleard, 1989) who attempted to show that cross-national variation in personality structure (i.e., need for achievement; microlevel) directly influences national economic development (macrolevel). Research by Doty, Peterson, and Winter (1991) provides exemplary research assessing Pettigrew's route F. Based on archival data, Doty et al. compared periods of high-threat and low-threat (macrolevel) on different indicators of authoritarianism (microlevel). Supporting the theoretical link between threat and authoritarianism, societal measures of authoritarianism decreased between the high-threat and the low-threat periods.

Proponents of personality science also explicitly point to the importance of including different levels of analysis. For instance, Diener and Napa Scollon (2002; see also Revelle, 1995; Sheldon, 2008) argued that future research in personality psychology should pursue multilevel analyses of phenomena in contexts where individual differences are viewed in light of cultures and situations. They identified as one challenge for the future of personality psychology the identification of models that can explain the mechanism through which distal traits operate on behaviors, or the genesis of traits (microlevel), or how they interact with situations (mesolevel). Moreover, they point to the importance of connecting culture and society (macrolevel) to personality dispositions. Thus, to fully understand personality and social behavior, different levels of analysis have to be taken into account.

A multilevel approach has consequences for data collection and statistical analysis. We confine our review to multilevel models in which lower-level data (e.g., data from a sample of people) are nested within higher-level units (e.g., people sampled from different nations). There are a variety of different types of data that conform to this type of hierarchical structure in the fields of personality and social psychology, including studies of people nested within groups, and also multiple behavioral observations or self-reports nested within people. Traditional methods used in personality and social psychology do not account for the hierarchical nature of observations. Rather, they tend to focus on a given level and, as a result, may distort the analysis and interpretation of research findings in personality and social psychology (e.g., Kenny & Judd, 1986; Kenny & La Voie, 1985).

Innovations in statistical analysis in the last three decades have made it possible to account for the hierarchical nature of observations. The purpose of this chapter is to introduce the basics of multilevel analysis concentrating on multilevel random coefficient modeling (MRCM; see Kreft & de Leeuw, 1998; Raudenbush & Bryk, 2002; Snijders & Bosker, 1999). Multilevel analysis is the appropriate statistical method to handle hierarchical data. Multilevel analysis is therefore of basic importance for an integrated personality and social psychology, for both theory development and testing. We will illustrate the importance of multilevel analysis for theorizing and testing using examples from research on personality and social behavior. Before doing so however, we first outline important consequences of multiple levels of analysis. We then present one type of multilevel analysis, namely MRCM.

When and Why We Need Multilevel Analyses: Some Examples

Whenever data is collected at multiple levels of analysis, a hierarchical data structure results. The defining characteristic of hierarchical data structure is that observations at one level of analysis are nested within observations at another level. In personality and social psychology, multiple levels of analysis result from different research designs.

Diary or event sampling methods are a common port of call for researchers interested in studying integrated trait and situational processes (Bolger & Romero-Canyas, 2007). In such studies, multiple individuals each provide data in multiple situations or at different time intervals (Reis & Gable, 2000). This provides a sample of social interactions or events experienced by people, from a sample of people. Repeated observations within people constitute the level 1 unit of analysis and the individual characteristics of people constitute the level 2 unit. Importantly, the two levels of analysis are hierarchically related. Repeated observations (level 1) are nested within people (level 2). The convention in multilevel research is that larger numbers indicate levels higher in the hierarchy.

A good example of this kind of hierarchical data structure is provided by DeHart and Pelham (2007). These authors were interested in changes in state implicit self-esteem after negative events. They hypothesized that people with low explicit trait self-esteem or low self-concept clarity would report lower state implicit self-esteem on days where they experienced more (versus fewer) negative events. In contrast, for people with high explicit trait self-esteem or high self-concept clarity, no relation between state implicit self-esteem and the number of negative events experienced on a given day was expected. In order to test these hypotheses, the authors collected repeated assessments of negative daily events and state implicit self-esteem. Moreover, participants provided information on trait explicit self-esteem as well as self-concept clarity. Thus, this research design resulted in a hierarchical nature of the data since the repeated measures of negative daily events and state implicit self-esteem (level 1) were nested within participants (level 2).

DeHart and Pelham (2007) used multilevel modeling to estimate within-person (i.e., variance in negative daily events and state implicit self-esteem between the repeated assessments) and between-person effects (i.e., variance in negative daily events, state implicit self-esteem, trait explicit self-esteem, and self-concept clarity between participants) independently. Their multilevel analysis revealed that trait explicit self-esteem and self-concept clarity moderated the within-person association between daily negative events and state implicit self-esteem.

As expected, people with low trait explicit self-esteem or low self-concept clarity experienced decreases in state implicit self-esteem when they experienced negative life events. In contrast, for people with high trait explicit self-esteem or high self-concept clarity, state implicit self-esteem remained stable after negative events.

Research by Reis et al. (2000) provides another example of a study using multilevel modeling to examine processes within people. Using data recorded on multiple days by each person, Reis et al. (2000) examined whether daily variation in emotional well-being was predicted by the fulfillment of basic needs on a daily level (state versions of needs) and also by person-level needs (trait versions of needs). Participants provided daily reports on well-being and need satisfaction (autonomy, competence, and relatedness). In addition, trait measures of self-determination, effectance, and connectedness were collected prior to the daily recording. Again, the daily reports of the individuals constituted the level 1 unit of analysis, and differences between individuals constituted the level 2 unit of analysis.

Reis et al. (2000) were interested in whether within-person variability in emotional well-being may be understood in terms of the degree to which three basic needs—autonomy, competence, and relatedness—are satisfied in daily activity. They therefore analyzed the within-person effects of the fulfillment of basic needs on well-being. The focus here was on level 1 (within-person variability in well-being and basic needs). The authors were also interested in the relationship between trait level predictors (i.e., self-determination, effectance, and connectedness) and person-level variance in emotional well-being. Here, the appropriate level of analysis would be at level 2; that is between-person variability in well-being and basic needs, or *differences across persons*. Finally, Reis et al. examined the interaction between state and trait versions of the same general needs to determine whether some individuals were dispositionally more responsive to daily variation than were others. Their multilevel analysis indicated that at level 1 (within persons), all three needs were significantly associated with well-being. In addition, at level 2 (between persons), all three trait measures related positively to mean levels of well-being. Moreover, state and trait versions of needs significantly interacted in the prediction of well-being: Persons with higher scores on the trait variable showed greater increases in daily well-being as a function of each unit of increment in that need.

As mentioned above, researchers may also be interested in questions that involve sampling multiple people from multiple different groups or dyads (see Kenny, Mannetti, Pierro, Livi, & Kashy, 2002; see also Kashy & Donnellan, chapter 9, in this volume). In this case, persons constitute the level 1 unit of analysis, and dyads or groups constitute the level 2 unit of analysis. People are thus nested within the dyad or group to which they belong. Weingart et al. (2007), for example, were interested in the effects of group members' social motives and the social-cognitive composition of the group on group members' strategic negotiation behavior. Within the negotiation literature, two primary negotiation strategies are distinguished: An integrative strategy, consisting of behaviors that maximize the amount of resources available, and a distributive strategy, consisting of behaviors that divide resources among the parties. Moreover, different social motives can be distinguished (cooperative vs. individualistic) that drive the strategic behavior of people.

Weingart et al. (2007) were interested in the impact of the social-motive context of the group on strategic behavior of group members as well as the interaction between the social-motive context and individuals' social motives. Specifically, the authors hypothesized that group composition influences group members' use of negotiation strategy such that the more cooperators there are in the group, the more integrative behaviors will be exhibited by group members. In contrast, the more individualists there are in the group, the more distributive behavior will be exhibited. Moreover, an interaction of group composition with the social motives of the individual group members was expected. The authors expected that as the number of cooperators in the group increased (relative to the number of individualists), cooperators will increase their use of integrative strategies to a greater extent than will individualists. In contrast, as the number of individualists in the group increases (relative to the number of cooperators), cooperators will increase their use of distributive strategies to a greater extent than will individualists.

In order to test these hypotheses, Weingart et al. (2007) conducted an experiment in which management students were randomly assigned to 4-person groups forming five experimental conditions: 2 homogeneous conditions (all cooperators and all individualists) and 3 heterogeneous groups (3 cooperators and 1 individualist, 2 cooperators and 2 individualists, 1 cooperator and 3 individualists). This research design resulted in a hierarchical data structure:

The 144 participants (level 1) were nested into 36 groups (level 2). Results of the multilevel analyses showed that cooperative negotiators adjusted their use of integrative and distributive strategies in response to the social-motive composition of the group, but individualistic negotiators did not.

This same type of multilevel analysis, where people are nested within groups, also readily applies to naturalistic or quasi-experimental contexts, in which group membership cannot be manipulated. Poteat et al. (2007), for example, tested the contextual effects of adolescent peer groups on individuals' homophobic and social dominance attitudes. These authors assumed that the social climate of the peer group, as characterized along the hierarchy-enhancing continuum, would explain differences in attitudes toward gay men and lesbians between peer groups. Accordingly, the authors gathered data from 213 high school students from the 7th to 11th grade. Based on friendship nomination data, N = 115 students were matched to 18 peer groups (16 cliques composed of 3 or more members and 2 dyads). Thus, the hierarchical structure of the data was that students (level 1) were nested in peer groups (level 2). To test for the contextual effect of the peer group in predicting individuals' homophobic attitudes, multilevel modeling was used. The analyses showed that differences in homophobic attitudes across the peer groups can be partly explained on the basis of the hierarchy-enhancing or -attenuating climate of the group.

Cross-cultural research, in which multiple people are sampled from multiple cultures or nations, provides another case where multilevel modeling offers a viable way to analyze data appropriately (van de Vijver & Leung, 2001). In samples of people drawn from multiple different nations, people are the level 1 unit of analysis and nations or cultures constitute the level 2 unit of analysis. Pehrson, Vignoles, and Brown (2009), for example, examined the relationship between national identification and anti-immigrant prejudice. The authors hypothesized that this relationship depends on how national groups are defined by their members. A common distinction within the nationalism literature is made between ethnic and civic nationalism. Ethnic nationalism defines national group membership in a way that excludes immigrants (i.e., nation is defined in terms of some supposed shared ancestral, linguistic, and/or cultural homogeneity), whereas civic nationalism defines national group membership in a more inclusive way (i.e., nation is defined in more voluntaristic terms, using criteria such as citizenship and participation that this entails).

Pehrson et al. (2009) expected to find an association between national identification and anti-immigrant prejudice in nations where ethnic definition of nationality is widely endorsed, whereas they expected to find no correlation in nations where the civic definition is dominant. To test these hypotheses, the authors used data from the International Social Survey Program (ISSP) 2003 module on national identity. This dataset included 37,030 respondents from 31 nations. Thus, the hierarchical structure of the dataset was that respondents (level 1) were nested in nations (level 2). Multilevel analysis revealed the expected variation in the strength of the within-person relation between national identification and anti-immigrant prejudice. This variance was explained by differences in the overall endorsement of ethnic versus civic definition of nationality between the nations. The relationship between national identification and prejudice was stronger in countries where people on average defined the nation in ethnic terms.

Research by Kuppens, Realo, and Diener (2008) provides another excellent example of the use of multilevel modeling to analyze nested data. Kuppens and colleagues examined the relationship between the frequency of positive and negative emotions that people experienced and their level of life satisfaction across nations. They reasoned that the relations between positive and negative emotions and life satisfaction depended on how national culture differentially emphasizes and values such experiences, causing positive and negative emotions to be differentially weighted in their relation with life satisfaction. They hypothesized that the cultural value dimensions of survival/self-expression and individualism/collectivism would moderate the relations between positive and negative emotions, respectively. To test these hypotheses, the authors analyzed data on the self-reported frequency of emotional experiences and life satisfaction judgment taken from the International College Survey 2001. The dataset included 8,557 respondents from 46 countries. Multilevel analyses showed that across nations, the experience of positive emotions was more strongly related to life satisfaction than the absence of negative emotions. Yet, the cultural dimensions of individualism and survival/self-expression moderated these relationships. Negative emotional experiences were more negatively related to life satisfaction in individualistic than in collectivistic nations, and positive emotional experiences had a larger positive relationship with life satisfaction in nations that stress self-expression than in nations that value survival.

These examples show that a hierarchical data structure is common, not only, but particularly in an integrated personality and social psychology. Kreft and de Leeuw (1998, p. 1) nicely point to this fact in their book on multilevel modeling: "Once you know that hierarchies exist, you see them everywhere."

A hierarchical data structure has two important consequences (for a detailed discussion, see Nezlek, 2001). First, in many cases, level 1 observations are not independent. Second, single-level analyses, which ignore the hierarchical data structure, often yield misleading results, particularly when results are generalized from one level of analysis to another. This relates to the fact that in many research designs commonly used in social psychology the assumption of independent observations is violated. For instance, the repeated measures of one individual from a diary study have in common the characteristics of that individual. Similarly, individuals from the same dyad or group will tend to be more similar to one another than are individuals who are members of different dyads or groups. As a result, the mean correlation of variables measured for persons of one group is higher than the average correlation between variables measured in individuals from different groups. Single-level analyses like Ordinary Least Squares multiple regression are founded on the assumption of independent observations. Ignoring the hierarchical data structure and thus the nonindependence of observations often results in estimates of standard errors that are too small. This may in turn result in the false or spurious detection of significant results (Hox, 2010).

In the case of hierarchical data, phenomena are simultaneously examined at different levels of analysis. Relationships between variables of interest at different levels of analysis are independent. For instance, a relationship between two variables at level 1 can be positive, whereas at level 2 the relationship between the same aggregated variables may be negative. This is only one example; any type of relationship at one level can coexist with any type of relationship at another level. Using a single-level analysis, either performed on the lower or higher level, can provide misleading results and inferences. In the past, aggregation and disaggregation were used in order to use single-level analysis procedures for data analysis (Hox, 2010; Snijders & Bosker, 1999). Both strategies have been used to move variables to one single level of analysis, in the case of aggregation to the higher-level, in the case of disaggregation to the lower-level. Aggregation means that lower-level data is used to construct a structural variable (e.g., using the mean of a lower-level variable for each higher-level unit), disaggregation means that higher-level variables are disaggregated to a lower-level unit.

Aggregation and disaggregation carry the risk of fallacies, namely analyzing the data at one level, and formulating conclusions at another level (Pettigrew, 1996). Using aggregation, the ecological fallacy is often made. The ecological fallacy occurs when relations between variables from a higher-level of analysis are interpreted at a lower-level of analysis. Using disaggregation, the compositional or atomistic fallacy is often made. Here, the relations between variables at a lower-level are interpreted at a higher-level of analysis. Just to give an example: Social psychologists have found that dependent on the level of analysis, different relations between percentage of minorities and intergroup attitudes can be observed (e.g., Wagner, Christ, Pettigrew, Stellmacher, & Wolf, 2006). Within smaller units (i.e., comparing districts within a nation), a higher percentage of minorities is related to more positive intergroup attitudes. In contrast, using larger units (i.e., comparing nations), the percentage of minorities is related to more negative intergroup attitudes.

In multilevel modeling, variables from different levels of analysis are analyzed simultaneously, using a statistical model that accounts for dependency of observations. Thus, multilevel modeling yields unbiased standard errors. Moreover, relations between variables from different levels are analyzed at their appropriate level, thereby avoiding ecological and atomistic fallacies.

What is Multilevel Modeling?
A Brief Introduction

We will introduce as one type of multilevel analysis the so called multilevel random coefficient model (MRCM), which provides a highly reliable analysis suited for hierarchical data structures. In this chapter, we will only outline the very basics of MRCM. There exist a number of excellent and detailed introductions to multilevel analysis (e.g., Hox, 2010; Kreft & de Leeuw, 1998; Raudenbush & Bryk, 2002; Snijders & Bosker, 1999). Moreover, there are several articles describing the application of multilevel analysis to certain kinds of data like event- and interval-contingent data (Nezlek, 2001) as well as diary data (Nezlek, 2003) or to personality and social psychology more generally (Nezlek, 2007a, 2008; West, Ryu, Kwok, & Cham, 2011).

Central to MRCM is that coefficients describing phenomena on one level are analyzed at another level. For instance, a regression model may first be estimated at level 1. The coefficients of this lower-level analysis

are then modeled as dependent variables at a higher level of analysis. Thus, for each coefficient, two parameters are estimated. The first parameter, the so called fixed-effect, is the central tendency of this parameter or, put another way, the mean or average size of the effect. The second parameter, the so called random-effect, reflects random error or variation across level 2 units in the effect. The random error indicates that coefficients from the lower-level analysis (intercept and slopes) vary between higher-levels of analysis. A critical strength of multilevel modeling is that it allows such variation to be modeled using higher-level predictors to explain the variation. This is hugely important in personality and social psychological research as so many of our theories are about the effects of factors at one level of analysis (e.g., social norms) on outcomes or associations at another level of analysis (e.g., individual behavior).

In the following, we will concentrate our presentation of MRCM at two levels. In multilevel analysis, however, more than two levels can be used (see Raudenbush & Bryk, 2002). It is a straightforward expansion of the basic two-level multilevel model we will describe. We base our nomenclature on Raudenbush and Bryk (2002). Here, level 1 coefficients are referred as βs (subscripted 0 for the intercept, 1 for the first coefficient, 2 for the second, etc.). The basic level 1 model is:

$$Y_{ij} = \beta_{0j} + r_{ij} \qquad (1)$$

In this model, there are i observations for j level 2 units of a continuous variable Y, which are modeled as a function of the intercept of each level 2 unit and error (r_{ij}). In MRCM, it is assumed that each level 1 error, r_{ij}, is normally distributed with a mean of zero and a constant level 1 variance, σ^2. In this case, it is an unconditional model at level 1, since Y is not modeled as a function of another variable at level 1.

The level 1 coefficients are then modeled at level 2. Level 2 coefficients are typically referred to as γ. For each level 1 coefficient, there are separate level 2 equations. The basic level 2 model is:

$$\beta_{0j} = \gamma_{00} + u_{0j} \qquad (2)$$

In this model, the mean of Y for each of j units of analysis (β_{0j}) is modeled as a function of only the grand mean (γ_{00}) and error (u_{0j}). The error u_{0j} is assumed to have a mean of zero and a level 2 variance τ_{00}. Such models are described as unconditional at level 2 since β_{0j} is not modeled as a function of another variable at level 2.

Raudenbush and Bryk (2002, pp. 23–24) discuss how this simple model is equivalent to a one-way ANOVA with random effects. Thought of in this way, each person or level 2 unit would represent a different group and γ_{00} would represent the grand-average across all groups (persons). In this case, u_0 would represent between-group variability, and r_{ij} would represent all remaining variability that occurred within groups.

Normally, each multilevel analysis starts with such an unconditional model before more complex models are analyzed. Only the intercept is entered in this model. With such models, one is able to estimate the proportion of variance in Y that occurs at each level. The total variance of Y is the sum of the variances at each level. In the most basic model with only two levels, the total variance is $r_{ij} + u_{0j}$. The model including only the intercept, which is often referred to as the fully unconditional or intercept-only model, enables estimation of the so called intraclass correlation, which is an estimate for the extent of nonindependence of observations. This coefficient is given by:

$$\rho = \frac{\tau_{00}}{\tau_{00} + \sigma^2} \qquad (3)$$

ρ in this equation reflects the proportion of variance in multiple ratings that can be explained by the grouping structure of the data relative to the total variation (for example multiple attitude ratings nested within persons). As Hox (2010, p. 15) commented, the intraclass correlation coefficient "can also be interpreted as the expected correlation between two randomly drawn units that are in the same group." In the context of personality research, for example, where multiple observations are nested within persons, this therefore reflects the expected correlation between two randomly chosen observations, such as two different observations of the same participant. This can be thought of as the average level of nonindependence in the data.

Combining equations 1 and 2, the combined (or mixed) model is given as:

$$Y_{ij} = \gamma_{00} + u_{0j} + r_{ij}. \qquad (4)$$

Identifying significant, systematic variation in multiple observations or ratings made within the individual (such as regularities in working models of attachment, behavior across different situations, or prejudice toward different groups) also begs the question: Are there measurable or observable characteristics of the individual that might predict this systematic between-persons variation? This question

is actually a fairly simple extension of the random intercept model with no predictors described in equations 1 and 2 above. All we do is to make the analysis conditional, that is, add a level 2 predictor to the model.

It is worth emphasizing at this point that Fournier, Moskowitz, and Zuroff (2008), and others have applied models of this type to distinguish between dispositions and signatures in personality theory. As Fournier et al. (2008, p. 532) eloquently argued when discussing the concept of variance proportions in personality science, "The larger the between-subject variation in behavior, the more we need elevation (i.e., dispositions) in order to account for the behavior of individuals. In contrast, the larger the within-subject variation in behavior the more we need shape (i.e., signatures) in order to account for the behavior of individuals." This distinction is important because it emphasizes that within-person variability can itself be considered an individual difference, to the extent that such variation conforms to a measurable signature or pattern *within the individual* (see also Fleeson, 2001, 2007b; Mischel & Shoda, 1995).

The former fully unconditional model can be easily extended to include level 1 and level 2 predictor variables. For instance, at level 1, the level 1 predictor X can be added. Hereby, variance in the intercept can be explained at level 1. The extended model is:

$$Y_{ij} = \beta_{0j} + \beta_1 X_{ij} + r_{ij} \qquad (5)$$

In this case, the effect of X on Y is constrained to be the same fixed value for each level 2 unit. Thus, it is assumed that there is no variability in the relation between X and Y (note that this is indicated by the absence of a subscript j for β_1). This model (as it is the case for the fully unconditional model) is a random-intercept model. However, this model can be further extended by estimating the variability of the regression coefficients (both intercept and slopes) across level 2 units (by adding random u components). Thus, both the level 1 intercept and one or more level 1 slopes are allowed to vary randomly over the population of level 2 units. The level 1 model is identical to the equation just shown. At level 2, however, we now model the variance in both the intercept and the slopes. In the case of one level 1 predictor variable, the level 2 model is:

$$\beta_{0j} = \gamma_{00} + u_{0j}, \qquad (6)$$

$$\beta_{1j} = \gamma_{10} + u_{1j}, \qquad (7)$$

where γ_{00} is the average intercept across the level 2 units, γ_{10} is the average regression slope across the level 2 units, u_{0j} is the unique increment to the intercept associated with the level 2 unit j, and u_{1j} is the unique increment to the slope associated with the level 2 unit j. The dispersion of the level 2 random effects are τ_{00}, which is the unconditional variance in the level 1 intercept; τ_{11}, which is the unconditional variance in the level 1 slopes; and τ_{01}, which is the unconditional covariance between the level 1 intercepts and slopes. This random-coefficient regression model allows us to estimate the variability in the regression coefficients across the level 2 units. In the next step, level 2 predictor variables can be included in the model to explain this variability in the coefficients at level 2.

Having included a randomly varying slope and including a level 2 predictor variable results in the full model called an intercepts- and slopes-as-outcome model. This results in the following model:

$$\beta_{0j} = \gamma_{00} + \gamma_{01}W_j + u_{0j}, \qquad (8)$$

$$\beta_{1j} = \gamma_{10} + \gamma_{11}W_j + u_{1j}, \qquad (9)$$

The level 1 coefficients are modeled as a function of W. Equation 8 models the intercept of Y by W, equation 9 states that the relation between Y and X is dependent on the value of W. In this case, W is a level 2 moderator and if W has a significant effect on β_{1j} then this is called a cross-level interaction (relationship at one level varies as a function of variables at another level).

Centering

One important issue in multilevel modeling is how one centers predictor variables. Centering helps interpretation of the model parameters. It is relatively straightforward at level 2, but more complicated at level 1. Here, level 1 covariates can be centered at the grand mean or they can be deviated around the mean of cluster j to which case i belongs (group mean centering). Both centering options produce parameter estimates that differ in value and also meaning. Which centering option should be used depends on the substantive research question. Enders and Tofighi (2007; see also Raudenbush & Bryk, 2002; Kreft & de Leeuw, 1998; Kreft, de Leeuw, & Aiken, 1995) have summarized which centering options should be used for different prototypical research questions. For instance, if a level 1 predictor is of substantive interest the predictor variable should be centered at the group mean. By centering at the

group mean, one gets a pure pooled within-cluster regression coefficient since centering at the group mean removes all between-cluster (level 2) variation in the predictor variable. In addition, the estimate of the variance of the slope is more accurate. If a level 2 predictor is of main interest and one would like to control for level 1 predictor variables, then the level 1 predictor variables should be centered at the grand mean. Hereby, it is guaranteed that the effect of the level 2 predictor is controlled for level 1 covariates. If group mean centering would be used, then one would not, even when including the level 1 predictor in the multilevel model, control for this covariate. Group mean centering deletes all level 2 variance in the level 1 predictor. In contrast, grand mean centering only leads to a linear transformation of the scale of the predictor, all level 2 variance is retained in the grand-mean-centered predictor.

When the influence of a predictor at both levels of analysis is of interest, then both centering options can be used. In this case, one is interested in whether the influence of the predictor variable is the same at both levels of analysis. The predictor variable has to be decomposed into its within- (level 1) and between-level (level 2) components. This is done by using the group mean as a level 2 predictor (between-level component). Including in the multilevel model the grand-mean-centered or group-mean-centered predictor variables, the same estimates will result (see Kreft et al., 1995).

In many cases a cross-level interaction is of interest. That is, the relation of a level 1 predictor with the outcome is dependent on a level 2 covariate. In this case, group mean centering is again the method of choice. Only in this case it is guaranteed that it really is a cross-level interaction. Using grand mean centering, it is not possible to differentiate between a cross-level interaction and a between-group interaction (see Hofmann & Garvin, 1998). A group-level interaction would suggest that the level 2 component of the level 1 predictor variable interacts with the level 2 covariate.

Centering is important for a number of more complex multilevel analyses, especially in longitudinal multilevel models and using event- and interval-contingent data. Using longitudinal multilevel models or event- and interval-contingent data, time can be included as a level 1 predictor. Depending on the way time is centered, different research questions can be answered. For an overview, see Singer and Willett (2003) and Hox (2010) for longitudinal multilevel models, for event- and interval-contingent data, a detailed overview is provided by Nezlek (2001).

Nonlinearity and Categorical Outcomes

In most applications of MRCM, only simple linear relations are estimated. However, nonlinear effects can also be estimated by including quadratic effects or polynoms of a higher order. In a recent paper, Bauer and Cai (2009; see also Snijders & Berkhof, 2008) demonstrated that failing to model nonlinear relations between a level 1 predictor and outcome leads to possible spurious effects of the variance of the random slope and the cross-level interaction. Thus, it is important to test whether the relation between a level 1 predictor and outcome is nonlinear.

Multilevel modeling is not restricted to continuous outcomes. It is also possible to examine categorical outcomes. Although the estimation procedure is different compared to continuous outcomes, the logic of multilevel modeling is the same. Snijders and Bosker (1999) give a good overview of multilevel modeling with dichotomous outcomes. A more general overview on multilevel modeling with discrete outcomes is given by Agresti, Booth, Hobert, and Caffo (2000).

Important Extensions of the Basic MRCM
Multilevel Mediation

For an integrated personality and social psychology, it is of central importance to test not only moderation, but also mediational hypotheses (Baron & Kenny, 1986; Shrout & Bolger, 2002). In the case of multiple levels of analysis, two different kinds of mediation can be separated: upper-level and lower-level mediation (Kenny, Kashy, & Bolger, 1998; Krull & MacKinnon, 2001). In upper-level mediation, the effect of a level 2 or upper-level variable is mediated by level 1 processes. In lower-level mediation, the effect of a level 1 or lower-level variable is mediated by level 2 processes.

Both types of mediation or indirect effect can be easily tested using the standard single-level procedures to establish mediational effects (Krull & MacKinnon, 2001; see Zhang, Zyphur, & Preacher, 2009, for an overview on problems and solutions in testing multilevel mediational models). These standard procedures are, however, only appropriate for lower-level mediation as long as fixed-effect models are estimated. As Kenny, Korchmaros, and Bolger (2003) emphasize, lower-level mediational analysis becomes more complicated when effects are considered to be random. In lower-level mediation, all mediational links, from the independent variable on the mediator and from the mediator on the dependent variable, can vary randomly across the level 2

or upper-level units. If the mediational links varies across the level 2 units, the random effects for the independent variable-mediator link and for the mediator-dependent variable link can be correlated. The problem for lower-level mediation models is, however, that the random effects cannot be estimated in one step and therefore the covariance between random effects cannot be directly estimated. As shown by Kenny et al. (2003) the formulae for the indirect effect and its standard error have to be modified to include the covariance between the random effects.

Bauer, Preacher, and Gil (2006) recently presented direct procedures to test random indirect effects in lower-level mediation models. The procedures proposed by Bauer et al. (2006) are not yet in widespread use in social or personality psychology (but see Overall and Sibley, 2009, for a recent example of their application in event sampling research). Moreover, multilevel structural equation modeling has the potential to directly test lower-level mediation models with random effects (Mehta & Neale, 2005; Preacher, Zhang, & Zyphur, 2011).

Multilevel Structural Equation Modeling

One important recent extension of multilevel analysis is the combination with structural equation modeling. The advantage of multilevel structural equation modeling (ML-SEM) is that it combines the best of both worlds (Mehta & Neale, 2005). It allows one to develop full SEMs at different levels of analysis (so far, this is restricted to two levels of analysis except in formulating growth models). Thus, it is possible to model complex relationships between variables of interest. Moreover, measurement error can be taken into account by using multiple indicators for latent variables overcoming the assumption in regular multilevel modeling that variables are measured without error. Therefore, more accurate estimates are provided in ML-SEM.

Wagner et al. (2006), for example, used ML-SEM to test the relation between the proportion of ethnic minorities in a given social area (districts; a district is an administrative unit of about 50,000 inhabitants in Germany) and negative intergroup attitudes toward minorities in Germany. Moreover, Wagner and colleagues assumed, based on intergroup contact theory, that the proportion of ethnic minorities was negatively related to prejudice. They tested whether the mean quantity of intergroup contact within a given region mediated the effects of proportion of ethnic minorities on negative intergroup attitudes. Both quantity of intergroup contact as well as negative intergroup attitudes were measured at the individual level (level 1), whereas the proportion of ethnic minorities was an official statistic (percentage of ethnic minorities within districts; level 2) matched to the individual data. For both quantity of intergroup contact and negative intergroup attitudes, multiple indicators were available, allowing estimation of latent variables in the mediational model.

An additional feature of ML-SEM is that a measurement model can be tested at different levels of analysis simultaneously (multilevel confirmatory factor analysis). This enables researchers to assess the invariance of the measurement model across levels. This is important since factor structure may be, but is not necessarily, the same at different levels of analysis (van de Vijver & Leung, 2001). For instance, multilevel CFA enables researchers to compare the structure of a construct at individual and cultural levels (e.g., Fuzhong, Duncan, Harmer, Acock, & Stoolmiller, 1998; Selig, Card, & Little, 2008; Zyphur, Kaplan, & Christian, 2008). Wu (2009), for instance, used multilevel CFA to determine whether the general self-efficacy scale has the same unidimensional structure within and between 25 countries. Model fit of the multilevel CFA with a single latent factor both on the within level (within nations based on individual data) and between level (between nations) was acceptable and showed that on both levels of analysis, a single-factor structure was adequate.

ML-SEM is still a new area of methodological research (e.g., Bauer, 2003; Curran; 2003; du Toit & du Toit, 2003; Muthén, 1991, 1994; Rovine & Molenaar, 2000). In recent years, SEM software advances have made it easier to apply ML-SEM to the analysis of hierarchical data. For an excellent introduction in ML-SEM presenting examples of ML-SEM using the software package *Mplus* (Muthén & Muthén, 1998–2007), the reader is referred to the book of Heck and Thomas (2008; see also Hox, 2010; Muthén & Asparouhov, 2011).

Level 2 Variables as Outcome

The multilevel models described so far are restricted to the case where the dependent variable is measured at level 1, such as individual attitudes or behavior. Although in many situations level 1 dependent variables are of main concern, there are situations where level 2 outcomes are of interest. Snijders and Bosker (1999) differentiated between macro-micro situations (routes D, E, and F in Figure 10.1) and micro-macro situations (routes A, B, C in Figure 10.1). In

macro-micro situations, the dependent variable is measured at level 1, and predictor variables are measured at level 1 and/or level 2. In micro-macro situations, the dependent variable is measured at level 2, and predictor variables are again be measured either at level 1 or level 2. Croon and van Veldhoven (2007) pointed out that the study of multilevel models has mainly focused on macro-micro situations; micro-macro situations were almost neglected. The same statement can be made for multilevel applications in personality and social psychology. All of the examples we have presented or will present in this chapter have dependent variables in focus measured at level 1. In many cases, however, level 2 outcomes are of interest. For instance, within an integrated trait and process approach to personality, based on diary studies, the repeated observations of one person constitute the level 1 unit of analysis and individual characteristics of the person constitute the level 2 unit. In this case, individual characteristics of people are typically used as predictor variables in multilevel models. But it is also important from a theoretical point of view to analyze the impact of the repeated observations (in different situations) on individual characteristics of the persons. Likewise, when people from different dyads or groups are examined, typically the dependent variables are measured at the person level (level 1), although level 2 outcomes at the level of the dyad or the group are equally important, such as dyad or group interaction pattern, norm, or productivity. Thus, one of the promising developments will be micro-macro analyses.

Most textbooks on multilevel modeling are restricted to models that are appropriate to the macro-micro situation. Moreover, most software packages for multilevel modeling (e.g., MLwiN, HLM) are mainly designed for the macro-micro situation.

Croon and van Veldhoven (2007) proposed a latent variable model for analyzing data from micro-macro situations. Their model applies to situations in which some or all predictor variables are measured at level 1. The authors showed that simply aggregating the lower-level predictor variables, as often done in research that aggregates data to a higher-level, leads to biased estimates when using Ordinary Least Square regression analysis. They proposed a two-stage latent variable approach in which the unobserved group mean for each higher-level unit is estimated using weights obtained by applying basic ANOVA formulae. The adjusted group means are then used to run ordinary least square regressions at the higher level to predict the higher-level outcome. The authors showed analytically and in a simulation study that the results based on the adjusted group means are unbiased (for an application, see van Woerkom & Croon, 2009).

More recently, Lüdtke et al. (2008) showed that using a multilevel latent covariate approach (e.g., Muthén & Asparouhov, 2011; see also above) to estimate the unobserved group mean of level 1 predictor variables outperforms under certain circumstances the two-stage approach of Croon and van Veldhoven. Thus, the multilevel latent covariate approach as implemented in *Mplus* (Muthén & Muthén, 1998–2007) can be easily used to estimate multilevel models capturing micro-macro situations.

A Framework for Multilevel Modeling Within an Integrated Personality and Social Psychology

In the previous section, we presented the basics of MRCM and important extensions of multilevel modeling. In the following we will outline a conceptual and analytic framework of multilevel analyses for an integrated personality and social psychology. We have argued that an integrated personality and social psychology needs to take into account different levels of analysis by definition. We will build on a previous framework by Nezlek (2007b) for understanding relationships among traits, states, situations, and behaviors outlined. We extend this framework to incorporate relational data at the mesolevel of analysis (small groups or dyadic data; see Kenny et al., 2002) as well as connections between personality and the macrolevel of analysis (cultures, nations; see Pettigrew, 1996, 1997).

A modified version of the model developed by Pettigrew (1996) is presented in Figure 10.1. As can be seen, we adopt the simple division between the micro-, meso- and macrolevel of analysis, but indicate more precisely at which level different kinds of research questions can be analyzed using MRCM. Since we have focused in the presentation of the basic MRCM on two levels of analysis, we will restrict the presentation of our framework on two levels of analysis. More complex models, involving all levels of analysis, are, however, possible.

To summarize thus far, there are three common types of multilevel analysis in an integrated personality and social psychology: (1) multiple observations of people's behavior or attitudes across different times and different contexts nested within different people; (2) multiple observations of different people nested within different dyads or small groups; and (3) multiple observations of different people nested within different nations or cultures. In the following, we will summarize possible kinds of analysis that can be done using MRCM.

Multiple Situations or Contexts Nested in Persons

In many cases, personality and social psychologists approach social behavior by tracking persons over different situations or in different contexts. Here, the main concern is the person-situation relation (Higgins, 1991). Central to this person-situation approach is that persons are observed over multiple situations or contexts. Independent of the theoretical approach researchers have, this data structure enables researchers to simultaneously examine within-person *and* between-person variability. Although this approach focuses on the link between the microlevel and the mesolevel of analysis, the structure of the data is counterintuitive in the sense that different situations or contexts are nested within persons. Thus, situations or contexts constitute level 1 and persons level 2 in the multilevel model.

John B. Nezlek (2007b; see also Bolger & Romero-Canyas, 2007; Fleeson, 2007a) proposed a multilevel framework aiming to conceptualize research questions in terms of between-person variability (traits), within person-variability (states), situations, and behaviors. Nezlek (2007b) recommended an integrated strategy that guides the analyses needed to answer such questions about the interaction between persons and situations and consequences for social behavior. The framework addresses four primary questions: (1) The relationship between trait- and state-level measures per se, and relationships between traits and individual differences in the situations people encounter or choose; (2) State-level relationships between or among state-level measures such as relationships between states, relationships between states and situations, and relationships between situations and behaviors; (3) The variation of state-level relationships as a function of trait-level measures; and (4) Changes of relationships as outlined in questions 1, 2, and 3 over time.

All of these four primary questions can be answered using multilevel analysis. For instance, the relationship between traits and state-level measures (question 1) can be estimated at level 2. The dependent variable in this case is a random coefficient for the state-level measure (β_{0j}) representing the mean of the state-level measure for person j. At level 2, a trait-level measure can be included in the multilevel model to estimate the relation between the trait-level measure and the state-level measure. Relationships among state-level measures, situations, and behaviors (question 2) can be estimated at level 1. To test for variation in state-level relationships as a function of trait-level measures (question 3), cross-level interactions have to be included in the multilevel model. To model change and stability of trait-level measures or the relationship between state-level measures and trait-level measures over time (question 4), time can be included in the multilevel analysis either by including dummy variables that represent when measures were collected or by adding a further level of analysis representing when measures have been collected. There are many possible questions that can be answered using multilevel analysis. For instance, differences between situations and within-level interactions can be estimated. For a more detailed description of this multilevel model, see Nezlek (2007b).

A similar data structure occurs when event- and interval-contingent data is collected (see for overviews Nezlek, 2001, 2003; Mroczek, 2007). In most cases, diaries are used, and respondents are asked to describe the social interactions they have (in most cases event-contingent data) or their reactions to daily events like stressors (in most cases interval-contingent data). Later in this chapter, we will introduce exemplary studies that have used these types of designs.

Persons Nested in Dyads or Small Groups

An integrated person-situation approach must focus on the analysis of the behavior of individuals *dependent* on situations and contexts (Mischel & Shoda, 1995). Such situations and contexts are most often operationalized as dyadic or group-level factors, meaning that people interact and influence each other within groups (see chapter 9, on analysis of dyads and groups, in the current volume). Analyses within an integrated personality and social psychology framework often focus on social interactions within dyads (Malloy & Kenny, 1986) or groups (Moritz & Watson, 1998). In such cases, persons are typically not followed up over multiple situations, but are observed while interacting with a partner or within a group. Again, both conceptually as well as statistically, the hierarchical nature of the data has to be taken into account. There are two different types of approaches one can adopt in this case, the traditional multilevel analysis (Hoyle, Georgesen, & Webster, 2001) or a revised multilevel strategy (Kenny et al., 2002).

In the traditional multilevel analysis, the within variability (between persons from one dyad or group; level 1) and the between variability (between dyads or groups; level 2) are modeled. At level 1, within-group predictors can be used to explain within group variability in the dependent variable. At level 2, between-group predictors, either group means of level 1 predictor variables or variables measured at level 2, and thus having variance only at that level, can be used to explain between-group variance in the dependent variable.

Kenny et al. (2002) proposed an alternative multilevel strategy based on the actor-partner interdependence model (APIM; Kashy & Kenny, 2000; Kenny, 1996). The main difference between the APIM and the traditional multilevel approach is how the group effect is conceptualized. In the traditional multilevel approach, the group mean is used. In the APIM, the group effect is defined only as the effect due to other members of the group, thus excluding the individual. So the group effect only refers to the others in the group, not the entire group as in the traditional approach. Central to the APIM is the assumption that a person's independent variable score affects his or her score on the dependent or outcome variable (an actor effect), but also his or her partner's dependent variable score (a partner effect).

Moreover, the traditional multilevel approach does not allow for negative nonindependence. However, in some circumstance, negative correlations between group members are possible: The higher one member scores, the lower the others score. It is possible to incorporate negative nonindependence in traditional multilevel computer programs (Snijders & Kenny, 1999; for an easy-to-follow introduction, see Campbell & Kashy, 2002).

Again, we will present later in the chapter typical examples of this approach.

Persons Nested in Cultures or Nations

Gordon Allport (1968, p. 9) posed the fundamental question, "how [. . .] the individual [can] be both a cause and a consequence of society," many years ago. The relationship between personality and a broader social context, here culture, still remains a central focus for cultural psychology looking at personality in a specific cultural context and examining and comparing personality across cultures many decades later (van de Vijver & Leung, 2001).

Again, in its simplest design, persons are nested in the broader context (different nations, cultures, etc.) yielding a hierarchical data structure as outlined before. Level 1 is constituted by persons, level 2 by different nations or cultures. Using multilevel analysis (for an overview of typical applications, see the edited book by van de Vijver, van Hermert, & Poortinga, 2007), it can be examined whether certain personality characteristics have the same correlates in different cultures, whether personality and social behavior relate in the same way in different cultures, and so on. It can be tested whether personality is influenced by culture or whether personality influences culture (e.g., Hofstede & McCrae, 2004).

Applications of Multilevel Analysis in Personality and Social Psychology

MRCM has immense potential for the study of personality and social behavior. The diverse array of applications provided by this analytic method stem, in part, from the flexibility of MRCM to test research questions framed at different levels of analysis, that is, within-person, between-person, between-group or culture, or any combination thereof.

In this section we summarize some of the different types of research questions that MRCM has been used for.

Examples of MRCM to examine personality or within person processes

ANALYSIS OF VARIANCE COMPONENTS:
TRACKING CONSISTENCIES WITHIN
THE INDIVIDUAL

MRCM has proven extremely useful for researchers interested in individual differences in many areas, including early research on individual differences in working models of attachment and also the study of individual differences in prejudice. For example, a key premise of attachment theory is that people develop multiple working models of their different attachment partners (including romantic partners, parents, siblings, and close friends) (Bowlby, 1969/1982; see also Mikulincer & Shaver, chapter 19, this volume). These multiple different working models are theorized to exist in a hierarchical structure in which they are nested under a more global or abstracted working model that predicts how people will respond to others more generally (Collins & Read, 1994). Attachment theory therefore implies that there should be a high degree of consistency (or a high intraclass correlation) between the multiple working models referring to specific others (e.g., mother, father, romantic partner, close friend) held by a given individual. If, in contrast, between-persons variation in working models (u_0) were

nonsignificant, then this would suggest that there would be no reliable consistencies between a given individual's ratings of one attachment figure and their ratings of other attachment figures.

In an early study, La Guardia, Ryan, Couchman, and Deci (2000) tested exactly this idea by measuring individuals' attachment ratings toward multiple people (for an overview on attachment theory, see Mikulincer & Shaver, chapter 19, in this book). In this analysis each participant represented a level 2 unit, and the multiple attachment ratings toward different relationship partners made by each individual represented the level 1 units. La Guardia et al. reasoned that cognitive representations of specific others should be coherently organized and therefore possibly explained by individual differences in more global and abstracted constructs (indexed by the percentage of between-person variance) versus the degree to which models of one's relationships with specific others are the product of experiences and beliefs unique to that particular relationship (indexed by the within-person variance). The authors found support for both perspectives, with intraclass correlations of $\rho = 0.36$ for working model of self and $\rho = 0.28$ for working models of others. These findings suggest that a reasonable portion (roughly a quarter to a third) of the variance in relationship-specific attachment ratings is systematic across a variety of relationships with specific others. This systematic variation indicates regularities in attachment orientations across peoples' relationships—regularities that are potentially attributable to more global individual differences such as domain-specific attachment and/or personality.

More recently, Fournier et al. (2008) used this application of MRCM to examine the extent to which people's self-reported behavior was consistent across different situations. Behavioral characteristics were recorded by asking participants to rate items such as "I expressed affection with words or gestures" (which measured agreeableness) toward multiple different groups they interacted with using a social interaction diary. Situations were classified into four types, which reflected the nature of relations with different interaction partners (e.g., whether the relationship was one defined by agreeableness versus dominance or agreeableness versus submissiveness). This yielded a data structure in which ratings of different types of behaviors in four different situations were nested within persons.

Analyses indicated a fairly even split between the between-person component of variation with behaviors indicative of dominance, agreeableness, submissiveness, and quarrelsomeness all displaying intraclass correlations of around $\rho = 0.50$. As Fournier et al. (2008, p. 541) concluded on the basis of these and other results, "Although there is irrefutable evidence of traits in behavior, there is also more to the organization of behavior than traits." By indexing the proportion of between-persons variation relative to within-persons variation (which it should be noted contains unidentified error), MRCM allows researchers to estimate the extent to which multiple observations of behavior reflect individual differences in dispositions, versus the extent to which behavior is possibly attributable to idiosyncratic effects of the situation. Not surprisingly, both of these factors seem to matter, and to affect behavior fairly equally.

Researchers have also begun to use MRCM to examining the consistency of individual differences in prejudice expressed toward multiple different groups and social categories. In a well-known and oft-cited quote, Allport (1954/1979, p. 68) argued that "One of the facts of which we are most certain is that people who reject one out-group will tend to reject other out-groups. If a person is anti-Jewish, he is likely to be anti-Catholic, anti-Negro, anti any out-group." This early observation is often cited as evidence for an individual-difference genesis of prejudice.

Duckitt and Sibley (2007) recently used MRCM to examine the extent to which variation in affect thermometer ratings of 24 different groups and social categories that tend to be targets of negative attitudes (e.g., unattractive people, drug users, prostitutes, Africans, and feminists) occurred at the between-persons versus within-persons level. Following Allport (1954/1979) they reasoned that if there is a dispositional component to prejudice; then there should be a significant and reasonably between-persons variance component (and thus a reasonably intraclass correlation) in ratings of these multiple different social groups. This was indeed the case, with $\rho = 0.17$. This suggests that there are regularities in prejudice toward a diverse range of groups that is attributable to global individual differences in dispositions (rather than, for example, that attitudes toward different groups are entirely unrelated to one another within individuals, as would have been indicated by an intraclass correlation coefficient that approached $\rho = 0.00$). As this example indicates, analysis of the intraclass correlation in multilevel modeling provides an important additional method for examining the extent to which behavior and attitudes are consistent or trait-like within persons.

EFFECTS OF INDIVIDUAL DIFFERENCES ON MULTIPLE OBSERVATIONS NESTED WITHIN INDIVIDUALS

In this section we concern ourselves with the simple application of MRCM to predict the component of variation indicative of dispositions, that is, the between-persons component, where multiple observations are nested within persons.

Sibley and Overall (2008), for instance, used MRCM to examine the extent to which individual differences in sociotropic and autonomous personality predicted sociability in interactions with romantic partners, friends, family, and acquaintances. Sociability ratings were collected by asking participants to complete a social interaction diary recording their experiences in the interactions they had each day (and were therefore nested within persons). Results indicated that measures of sociotropic and autonomous personality consistently predicted variation in sociability across social interactions with a range of different partners. This is exactly what one would expect to observe if measures of sociotropy and autonomy do indeed index global tendencies to consistently respond with respective approach versus avoidance strategies across all situations and types of social relationship; if they do, in other words, reflect dispositions.

Similarly, Tong et al. (2006) examined whether the Big Five dimensions of personality predicted variation in the self-reported emotions (e.g., anger, fear, sadness, and happiness) experienced by Singaporean police officers at multiple random times during a typical work day. Multiple observations of emotional experience were nested within persons (emotions therefore represented the level 1 unit). People represented the level 2 unit, and individuals' scores on the Big Five were entered as level 2 predictors of level 1 emotions. Results indicated that neuroticism and conscientiousness reliably predicted individual differences in the experience of a range of different emotions, with police officers higher in neuroticism, for example, generally experiencing more anger, sadness, and fear during their work day, and less happiness. One important thing to note regarding this study is that each Big Five dimension of personality was entered into separate analyses. Tong et al.'s (2006) analyses therefore did not control for covariance between the different Big Five dimensions. As with a classical regression, this can easily be achieved, if desired, by simply entering all level 2 predictors simultaneously.

Examples of MRCM to Examine Personality X Situation or Person X Situation Processes

A further application of MRCM we will discuss here is useful when one is interested to know whether an individual difference factor, such as gender or extraversion, affects the extent to which one within-person measure (such as differences across types of situation) predicts another within-person measure (such as specific behaviors or the experience of specific emotions). This is one example of a cross-level interaction because it tests whether level 2 and level 1 variables interact to predict a separate level 1 outcome. This is a fairly common application of MRCM. It has been used extensively in research on personality and related areas to examine the extent to which hypothesized global dispositions or traits systematically predict contingencies in behavior in certain situations or contexts but not others. In the personality literature, this is related to a central premise of Mischel and Shoda's (1995) cognitive-affective systems theory of personality (CAPS), which states that personality signatures can be expressed as *if . . . then . . .* contingencies. This model therefore implies that people with a high level of a trait should generally respond consistently when the *if . . .* condition is satisfied (see also Mendoza-Denton & Ayduk, chapter 18, and Simpson & Winterheld, chapter 20, in this volume.)

Research on dependency and accommodation processes in interpersonal relationships provides a good example of one specific application of this general *if . . . then . . .* principle. Models of the risk regulation system and accommodation in close relationships imply that people should have dispositional tendencies to deal with feelings of interpersonal dependence (low personal control in intimate relationships) in different ways (Murray, Holmes, & Collins, 2006; Rusbult, Verette, Whitney, Slovik, & Lipkus, 1991). These tendencies should come into play in situations of conflict. In such situations some people should respond by directly approaching and discussing problems with their partners, whereas others will be more likely to withdraw. Accommodative tendencies should reflect specific patterns of contingent behavior, in which case they should therefore be most predictive of relevant outcomes in social interactions of high conflict or dependency.

Overall and Sibley (2008) tested this idea using MRCM. Overall and Sibley first measured general self-reported tendencies to respond with accommodation versus withdrawal in situations of conflict (e.g., "When my partner is upset and says something mean, I try to patch things up and solve the problem"). Participants then completed a social interaction diary and reported their feelings of value/acceptance and felt interpersonal control in all social interactions with their romantic partner for two weeks. Social interactions and corresponding ratings of value/acceptance and control within each interaction therefore constituted level 1 variables nested within persons (level 2 units). The single accommodation score calculated for each person, in contrast, represented a dispositional or trait-like measure that occurred at level 2.

Overall and Sibley (2008) found good support for a contingency model of accommodation and dependency, and reported that while high-dependency (low control) situations predicted decreased feelings of value and acceptance, this effect was buffered by dispositional differences in accommodation. People who scored high in accommodation (and therefore tended to approach conflict and dependency by openly discussing problems) retained more positive feelings toward their partner in situations of high dependency. In other words, the cross-level interaction between level 1 dependency and level 2 accommodation (y_{11}) was significant. This provides a good example of a specific *if . . . then . . .* contingency that mixes dispositional and situational factors occurring at different levels of analysis and therefore requires MRCM to test appropriately.

MRCM has also proven extremely useful for the assessment of social-cognitive models of depression. Generally speaking, such models suggest that there are reliable individual differences in the ways in which people tend to make attributions or generate explanations for negative events, and this individual difference is critical for understanding why similar events might have dramatic differences in the extent to which they adversely affect some people but not others (e.g., Abramson, Metalsky, & Alloy, 1989). Hankin, Fraley, and Abela (2005) tested this idea using a daily diary study. Each day for 35 days, participants completed a measure of their daily depressive symptoms and a measure assessing their negative-event specific inferences about the most negative event to occur each day. Diary ratings were therefore nested within participants. Each participant also completed a measure of general individual differences in depressogenic cognitive style.

The MRCM analyses conducted by Hankin et al. (2005) indicated that on days where people made more negative-event specific inferences they also experienced heightened depressive symptoms.

However, individual differences in general depressogenic cognitive style moderated the extent to which this effect occurred. Specifically, when people made negative-event-specific inferences they experienced similarly high daily depressive symptoms regardless of individual differences in depressogenic cognitive style. However, depressogenic cognitive style predicted reliable differences in daily depressive symptoms when negative daily inferences were low. When people's days were fairly good, people high in depressogenic cognitive style still experienced more daily depression, whereas those low in this type of cognitive style were far lower in daily depression. This study provides a good example of where innovations provided by MRCM allow researchers to conduct appropriate tests of important person x situation interactions that have long been theorized on in models of depression.

Examples of MRCM in Cross-Cultural Research

MRCM also lends itself to cross-cultural analysis of data collected in multiple nations or cultures. In such cases, participants are generally treated as level 1 units that are nested within different nations (or level 2 units). Research by Napier and Jost (2008) provides an excellent example of the creative application of MRCM to test predictions using existing (and we might add publicly available) large-scale multilevel datasets (in their case analyses of data from the World Values Survey and General Social Survey).

The World Values Survey provides data on various measures collected in a wide range of different nations. Participants in this case can be viewed as level 1 units that are nested with nations (which form the level 2 units). Napier and Jost (2008) were concerned with a central question: Why are conservatives happier than liberals? Using data from ten nations contained in the World Values Survey, Napier and Jost (2008, study 2) calculated the average slope between individuals' self-rated left- versus right-wing orientation and self-reported life satisfaction. They reported that the average slope across nations was significant, suggesting that people that were more right-wing in orientation tended to report increased life satisfaction. Napier and Jost (2008, study 2) also explored the possibility that variation across nations in the magnitude of this slope might be explained by national-level differences in quality of life. To examine this possibility they matched United Nations data on the Human Development Index (HDI, an overall quality-of-life

indicator) in each nation, and then tested whether HDI scores moderated the extent to which right-wing orientation predicted individuals' life satisfaction (a cross-level interaction). The interaction was marginally significant, suggesting that while right-wingers tend be more satisfied with their lives across nations; this effect is magnified in nations where the quality of life is fairly low.

In another innovative analysis of publicly available data, Napier and Jost (2008, study 3) analyzed data from different years of the General Social Survey collected in the United States. This data is collected on a yearly basis, and Napier and Jost were interested in the association of political orientation and happiness in cross-sectional U.S. samples from 1974 to 2004. They therefore conducted analyses of these data where participants (again, the level 1 units) were nested within years (level 2 units). They key thing to keep in mind in this case, and what is creative about their analysis of this data, was that they structured the dataset by treating the years of data collection as independent level 2 units, and the independent cross-sectional samples of U.S. participants surveyed each year were level 1 units. In each year of data collection participants reported their self-rated political orientation as liberal versus conservative and also their level of happiness. At level 2, Napier and Jost matched the data collected each year with the yearly Gini Index (a measure of income inequality) from the U.S. Census Bureau.

Consistent with their cross-cultural analyses, Napier and Jost (2008, study 3) reported that there was a significant slope for political orientation and happiness. Put another way, the average slope for this effect across years of data collection was significant. Variation in this slope across years, however, was explained by relative (yearly) variation in income inequality. This cross-level interaction, in which the Gini Index moderated the relation between political orientation and individual happiness, occurred because conservatives tended to be reasonably happy in a given year regardless of levels of systemic inequality. For liberals, in contrast, increased systemic income inequality predicted decreased personal happiness in that time period. The use of MRCM in this context allowed Napier and Jost to combine data from different publicly available datasets to test novel predictions derived from system justification theory (Jost & Banaji, 1994) regarding the interplay between individual-level attitudes, and national-level or year-level indicators of inequality in society. In Napier and Jost's (2008, p. 571) words, their findings suggest that "viewing the status quo (with its attendant degree of inequality) as fair and legitimate serves a palliative function." Conservatives, these data suggest, are not bothered by inequality to the same extent that liberals are, at least in terms of its effect on individual levels of happiness and life satisfaction.

Recent research by Liu and colleagues (in press) provides another example of the use of MRCM for the analysis of large-scale cross-cultural data. Liu et al (in press) were interested in the effects that historical perceptions might have on willingness to fight to defend one's country in any subsequent conflict. They collected data from more than 6,000 individuals in 30 different nations. Participants (level 1) were treated as being nested within nations (level 2 units). They conducted a MRCM analysis examining the effect of the perceived importance individuals placed on historical calamities (e.g., World War I, World War II) on their self-reported willingness to fight. This analysis therefore took the form of a level 1 predictor (historical calamities) predicting a level 1 outcome (willingness to fight) adjusted for the nested structure of the data. Thus, the authors used MRCM to estimate the average slope for this relation across the 30 nations contained in their sample, adjusted for differences in the reliability of this slope across different nations. Averaged across nations, people that perceived historical calamities as more important were more willing to fight for their country. This finding suggests that history matters: the importance that is placed on historical events, and how those events may be mobilized within society, may translate into important outcomes relating to intergroup conflict and peace.

Recent research by Liu and Sibley (2010) provides another good an example of the use of MRCM to examine the possible interaction of individual-level factors (such as attitudes) and more general economic or societal conditions. Liu and Sibley (2010) examined individual and societal factors that predict intentions of making personal sacrifices to one's living standard in order to help protect the natural environment. Unsurprisingly, across the 30 nations included in the analysis, people that perceived global warming as a more important problem were more likely to express a willingness to make personal sacrifices for the health of the planet (e.g., drive less, accept higher prices, and conserve energy). The average slope for this relationship was significant when averaged across the 30 nations included in the analysis.

However, Liu and Sibley (2010) were also interested in whether cross-national differences in economic conditions might explain differences in the extent to which perceptions of the importance of global warming predicted intentions. They included a random component in their model, which indicated, as expected, that there was significant variation across nations in the slope of the relation between global warming attitudes and behavioral intentions. Moreover, variation in this slope was explained by cross-national differences in the United Nations Human Development Index (HDI). These results indicated that there was a cross-level interaction in which viewing global warming as important predicted self-reported intentions to make personal sacrifices *more so in nations that had a high HDI*. That is; attitudes were more strongly predictive of behavioral intentions regarding this issue in those nations that already had an extremely high standard of living, where the costs of minor sacrifices to one's standard of living would, presumably, have less of an impact on the individuals' overall quality of life. People care, it seems, and more importantly are willing to do something about the environment, when they can afford to.

The aforementioned studies focused primarily on the effects of individual-level variables on other individual variables averaged across nations, and also examined how such associations can be moderated by cultural- or nation-level variables such as systemic inequality or national standard of living. MRCM has also been used, however, to focus more specifically on the effects that nation-level variables, such as differences in the effect that government policy has on individuals living within the nation. Torney-Purta, Wilkenfeld, and Barber (2008) focused on this latter type of issue in a complex multilevel analysis of the human rights attitudes of 88,000 14-years-olds from 27 different nations. For each nation, Torney-Purta et al. (2008) created an indicator representing the extent of government focus on human rights. This index was based on information from the United Nations and the frequency with which human rights was mentioned by each nation in specific international documents. They also matched data from each nation with Freedom House Ratings, an indicator of the extent to which a nation promotes civil liberty and political rights in education.

The authors then conducted a three-level MRCM (with students nested within schools nested within nations) to examine the extent to which nation-level indicators of human rights education and promotion predicted students' scores on specific items assessing knowledge test of human rights, and also attitudes toward human rights. Torney-Purta et al.

(2008) reported that nation-level differences in governmental focus on human rights and freedom predicted an increased level of knowledge in students regarding the purpose of the United Nations and the purpose of the Convention on the Rights of the Child controlling for levels of general knowledge unrelated to human rights issues. These knowledge items were dichotomous (students scored either correctly or incorrectly when answering). Torney-Purta et al. (2008) therefore employed a form of multilevel logistic regression (or a binominal hierarchical generalized linear model) to test this model.

The results of the study conducted by Torney-Purta et al. (2008) are particularly promising because they indicate that governmental policy can directly predict student learning in this important domain, a finding that MRCM allowed the authors to reliably detect. Moreover, in a second set of analyses, Torney-Purta et al. (2008) also reported that students' knowledge of human rights–related issues predicted positive attitudes toward immigrants' rights, although national-level predictors were nonsignificant in this analysis. This raises the interesting possibility of a mediational model in which nation-level indictors that are determined by governments affect student knowledge, which might in turn translate into more supportive attitudes toward human rights–related issues—something that could be examined in greater detail using recent advances in analyses of random indirect effects using the procedures recently developed by Bauer et al. (2006).

Multilevel Analysis as an Important Statistical Tool for an Integrated Personality and Social Psychology

An integrated personality and social psychology needs to take into account different levels of analysis by definition, since "personality and social psychology. . . links the biology and development of the individual with the systems of interpersonal relationships, social structure, and culture within which the person is formed and functions" (Brewer et al., 2000, p. 2). The challenge for an integrated personality and social psychology is to simultaneously analyze the complex relations between the different levels of analysis for both theoretical as well as statistical reasons.

It is a challenge for theoreticians to clearly specify levels of theory (i.e., person, group, situation) and their interrelation (see e.g., Klein, Tosi, & Canella, 1999 for a discussion of multilevel theories in organizational research; see also Rousseau, 1985).

Moreover, the simultaneous consideration of different levels of analysis is also a challenge for statistical reasons. In the present chapter, we have presented the MRCM (e.g., Kreft & de Leeuw 1998; Raudenbush & Bryk, 2002; Snijders & Bosker, 1999) as a statistical method that allows the simultaneous consideration of different levels of analysis. MRCM is a flexible statistical tool to test different kinds of research questions in personality and social psychology. We have proposed a multilevel framework for multilevel modeling within an integrated personality and social psychology that differentiates between three types of multilevel analysis in an integrated personality and social psychology: (1) observing persons over multiple situations or contexts; (2) observing persons in dyads or small groups; and (3) observing persons between different cultures or nations. We have outlined a range of possible research questions that can be answered using MRCM. We have also summarized sample studies that we hope may help researchers to apply MRCM to own research questions.

In the last two decades, many new developments in multilevel modeling have emerged. This has led to important extensions of the MRCM. Among these are tests for multilevel mediation, the combination of multilevel modeling and structural equation modeling (ML-SEM), and models for level 2 variables as outcomes. MRCM is now implemented in many standard statistical software packages like SPSS, SAS, and R, beside specialized packages like HLM and MlWin. These new developments together with the basics of MRCM will help to further develop the field of an integrated personality and social psychology.

The study of social psychology and personality is inherently one of different levels of analysis. Every person is unique, and every person also exists in social context. MRCM allows theoretical processes occurring at both the person and social or group level to be modeled simultaneously. We hope that this chapter may aid in the development of more detailed and explicit multilevel theories to fully make use of the different multilevel modeling techniques provided by MRCM. For many concepts and phenomena within personality and social psychology, only single-level theories exist. A good starting point is to review the research literature from a multilevel perspective and to look for similarities and differences across levels. Exemplary for this approach is a recent review by Penner, Dovidio, Piliavin, and Schroeder (2005) on prosocial behavior. Kozlowski and Klein (2000) have summarized issues that are central to the development of multilevel theories and that provide conceptual guidance for the development of specific multilevel models. Moreover, they provide principles to guide researchers through the problem of the specification of multilevel models. Likewise, Markovsky (1996) formulated criteria for multilevel theory construction. It is our strong believe that multilevel modeling techniques will help to move personality and social psychology toward an integrated personality and social psychology.

Our purpose in this chapter has been to review the basics and recent advances of multilevel modeling, to develop a framework of multilevel analyses for an integrated personality and social psychology, and to illustrate the importance of multilevel modeling for theorizing and testing using examples from research on personality and social behavior. Our goal is to convince readers that multilevel modeling is of key importance for the development of an integrated personality and social psychology. We hope that this chapter will, in a small way, push researchers to use multilevel modeling and to start to research phenomena within the fields of personality and social psychology from different levels of analysis.

References

Abramson, L. Y., Metalsky, G. I., & Alloy, L. B. (1989). Hopelessness depression: A theory-based subtype of depression. *Psychological Review, 96,* 358–372.

Agresti, A., Booth, J. G., Hobert, J. P., & Caffo, B. (2000). Random-effects modeling of categorical response data. *Sociological Methodology, 30,* 27–80.

Allport, G. W. (1954/1979). *The nature of prejudice.* Reading, MA: Addison-Wesley.

Allport, G. W. (1968). The historical background of modern social psychology. In G. Lindzey & E. Aronson (Eds.), *The handbook of social psychology* (2nd ed., pp. 1–80). Reading, MA: Addison-Wesley.

Baron, R. M., & Kenny, D. A. (1986). The moderator-mediator variable distinction in social psychological research: Conceptual, strategic, and statistical considerations. *Journal of Personality and Social Psychology, 51,* 1173–1182.

Bauer, D. J. (2003). Estimating multilevel linear models as structural models. *Journal of Educational and Behavioral Statistics, 28,* 135–167.

Bauer, D. J., & Cai, L. (2009). Consequences of unmodeled nonlinear effects in multilevel models. *Journal of Educational and Behavioral Statistics, 34,* 97–114.

Bauer, D. J., Preacher, K. J., & Gil, K. M. (2006). Conceptualizing and testing random indirect effects and moderated mediation in multilevel models: New procedures and recommendations. *Psychological Methods, 11,* 142–163.

Baumeister, R. F. (1999). On the interface between personality and social psychology. In L. Pervin & O. John (Eds.), *Handbook of personality: Theory and research* (pp. 367–377). New York: Guilford.

Bolger, N., & Romero-Canyas, R. (2007). Integrating personality traits and processes. In Y. Shoda, D. Cervone, &

G. Downey (Eds.), *Persons in context: Building a science of the individual* (pp. 201–210). New York: Guilford.

Bowlby, J. (1969/1982). *Attachment and loss: Vol. 1. Attachment* (2nd ed.). New York: Basic Books.

Brewer, M. B., Kenny, D. A., & Norem, J. K. (2000). Personality and social psychology at the interface: New directions for interdisciplinary research. *Personality and Social Psychology Review, 4,* 2.

Campbell, L., & Kashy, D. A. (2002). Estimating actor, partner, and interaction effects for dyadic data using PROC MIXED and HLM: A user-friendly guide. *Personal Relationships, 9,* 327–342.

Collins, N. L., & Read, S. J. (1994). Cognitive representations of attachment: The structure and function of working models. In K. Bartholomew & D. Perlman (Eds.), *Advances in personal relationships: Vol. 5. Attachment processes in adulthood* (pp. 53–90). London: Kingsley.

Croon, M. A., & van Veldhoven, J. P. M. (2007). Predicting group-level outcome variables from variables measured at the individual level: A latent variable multilevel model. *Psychological Methods, 12,* 45–57.

Curran, P. J. (2003). Have multilevel models been structural equation models all along? *Multivariate Behavioral Research, 38,* 529–569.

DeHart, T., & Pelham, B. W. (2007). Fluctuations in state implicit self-esteem in response to daily negative events. *Journal of Experimental Social Psychology, 43,* 157–165.

Diener, E., & Napa Scollon, C. (2002). Our desired future for personality psychology. *Journal of Research in Personality, 36,* 629–637.

Doise, W. (1980). Levels of explanation in the European Journal of Social Psychology. *European Journal of Social Psychology, 10,* 213–231.

Doty, R. M., Peterson, B. E., & Winter, D. G. (1991). Threat and authoritarianism in the United States, 1978–1987. *Journal of Personality and Social Psychology, 61,* 629–640.

Duckitt, J., & Sibley, C. G. (2007). Right-wing authoritarianism, social dominance orientation, and the dimensions of generalized prejudice. *European Journal of Personality, 21,* 113–130.

du Toit, S., & du Toit, M. (2003). Multilevel structural equation modeling. In J. De Leeuw & I. G. G. Kreft (eds.), *Handbook of quantitative multilevel analysis* (pp. 273–321). Boston: Kluwer.

Enders, C. K., & Tofighi, D. (2007). Centering predictor variables in cross-sectional multilevel models: A new look at an old issue. *Psychological Methods, 12,* 121–138.

Fleeson, W. (2001). Toward a structure- and process-integrated view of personality: Traits as density distributions of states. *Journal of Personality and Social Psychology, 80,* 1011–1027.

Fleeson, W. (2007a). Studying personality process: Explaining change in between-persons longitudinal and within-person multilevel models. In R. C. Robins, R. C. Fraley, & R. Krueger (Eds.), *Handbook of research methods in personality psychology* (pp. 523–542). New York: Guilford.

Fleeson, W. (2007b). Situation-based contingencies underlying trait-consistent manifestation in behavior. *Journal of Personality, 75,* 825–861.

Fournier, M. A., Moskowitz, D. S., & Zuroff, D. C. (2008). Integrating dispositions, signatures, and the interpersonal domain. *Journal of Personality and Social Psychology, 94,* 531–545.

Funder, D. C., & Fast, L. A. (2010). Personality in social psychology. In S. T. Fiske, D. T. Gilbert, & G. Lindzey, (eds.),

The handbook of social psychology (5th ed., Vol. 1, pp. 668–697). Hoboken, NJ: Wiley.

Fuzhong, L., Duncan, T. E., Harmer, P., Acock, A., & Stoolmiller, M. (1998). Analyzing measurement models of latent variables through multilevel confirmatory factor analysis and hierarchical linear modeling approaches. *Structural Equation Modeling, 5,* 294–306.

Gilleard, C. J. (1989). The achieving society revisited: A further analysis of the relation between national economic growth and need achievement. *Journal of Economic Psychology, 10,* 21–34.

Hankin, B. L., Fraley, R. C., & Abela, J. R. Z. (2005). Daily depression and cognitions about stress: Evidence for a trait-like depressogenic cognitive style and the prediction of depressive symptoms in a prospective daily diary study. *Journal of Personality and Social Psychology, 88,* 673–685.

Heck, R. H., & Thomas, S. L. (2008). *An introduction to multilevel modeling techniques* (2nd ed.). New York: Routledge.

Heine, S. J. (2010). Cultural psychology. In S. T. Fiske, D. T. Gilbert, & G. Lindzey (Eds.), *The handbook of social psychology* (5th ed., Vol. 2, pp. 1423–1464). Hoboken, NJ: Wiley.

Higgins, E. T. (1991). Personality, social psychology, and person-situation relations: Standards and knowledge activation as a common language. In L. A. Pervin (Ed.), *Handbook of personality: Theory and research* (pp. 301–338). New York: Guilford.

Hofmann, D. A., & Garvin, M. B. (1998). Centering decisions in hierarchical linear models: Implications for research in organizations. *Journal of Management, 24,* 623–641.

Hofstede, G., & McCrae, R. R. (2004). Personality and culture revisited: Linking traits and dimensions of culture. *Cross-Cultural Research, 38,* 52–88.

Hox, J. (2010). *Multilevel analysis: Techniques and applications* (2nd ed.). New York: Routledge.

Hoyle, R. H., Georgesen, J. C., & Webster, J. M. (2001). Analyzing data from individuals in groups: The past, the present, and the future. *Group Dynamics: Theory, Research, and Practice, 5,* 41–47.

Jost, J. T., & Banaji, M. R. (1994). The role of stereotyping in system-justification and the production of false consciousness. *British Journal of Social Psychology, 33,* 1–27.

Kashy, D. A., & Kenny, D. A. (2000). The analysis of data from dyads and groups. In H. Reis & C. M. Judd (Eds.), *Handbook of research methods in social psychology* (pp. 451–477). New York: Cambridge University Press.

Kenny, D. A. (1996). Models of nonindependence in dyadic research. *Journal of Social and Personal Relationships, 13,* 279–294.

Kenny, D. A., & Judd, C. M. (1986). Consequences of violating the independence assumption in analysis of variance. *Psychological Bulletin, 99,* 422–431.

Kenny, D. A., & La Voie, L. (1985). Separating individual and group effects. *Journal of Personality and Social Psychology, 48,* 339–348.

Kenny, D. A., Kashy, D. A., & Bolger, N. (1998). Data analysis in social psychology. In D. Gilbert, S. T. Fiske, & G. Lindzey (Eds.), *The handbook of social psychology* (4th ed., Vol. 1, pp. 223–265). New York: McGraw-Hill.

Kenny, D. A., Korchmaros, J. D., & Bolger, N. (2003). Lower-level mediation in multilevel models. *Psychological Methods, 8,* 115–128.

Kenny, D. A. Mannetti, L., Pierro, A., Livi, S., & Kashy, D. (2002). The statistical analysis of data from small groups. *Journal of Personality and Social Psychology, 83,* 126–137.

Klein, K. J., Tosi, H., & Cannella, A. A., Jr. (1999). Multilevel theory building: Benefits, barriers, and new developments. *Academy of Management Review, 24,* 243–248.

Kozlowski, S. W. J., & Klein, K. J. (2000). A multilevel approach to theory and research in organizations: Contextual, temporal, and emergent processes. In K. J. Klein & S. W. J. Kozlowski, (Eds.), *Multilevel theory, research, and methods in organizations: Foundations, extensions, and new directions* (pp. 3–90). San Francisco: Jossey-Bass.

Kreft, I. G. G., & de Leeuw, J. (1998). *Introducing multilevel modeling.* Newbury Park, CA: Sage.

Kreft, I. G. G., De Leeuw, J., & Aiken, L. (1995). The effects of different forms of centering on hierarchical linear models. *Multivariate Behavioral Research, 30,* 1–22.

Krull, J. L., & MacKinnon, D. P. (2001). Multilevel modeling of individual and group level mediated effects. *Multivariate Behavioral Research, 36,* 249–277.

Kuppens, P., Realo, A., & Diener, E. (2008). The role of positive and negative emotions in life satisfaction judgement across nations. *Journal of Personality and Social Psychology, 95,* 66–75.

La Guardia, J. G., Ryan, R. M., Couchman, C. E., & Deci, E. L. (2000). Within-person variation in security of attachment: A self-determination theory perspective on attachment, need fulfillment, and well-being. *Journal of Personality and Social Psychology, 79,* 367–384.

Liu, J. H., & Sibley, C. G. (2010). Towards a global political psychology of mitigating greenhouse gas emissions among young citizens of the world: There is hope for the future. Manuscript submitted for publication.

Liu, J. H., Paez, D., Hanke, K., Rosa, A., Hilton, D. J., Sibley, C.G., et al. (in press). Cross-cultural dimensions of meaning in the evaluation of events in world history? Perceptions of historical calamities and progress in cross-cultural data from 30 societies. *Journal of Cross-Cultural Psychology.*

Lüdtke, O., Marsh, H. W., Robitzsch, A., Trautwein, U., Asparouhov, T., & Muthén, B. (2008). The multilevel latent covariate model: A new, more reliable approach to group-level effects in contextual studies. *Psychological Methods, 13,* 203–229.

Malloy, T. E., & Kenny, D. A. (1986). A social relations model: An integrative method for personality research. *Journal of Personality, 54,* 199–225.

Markovsky, B. (1996). Theory, science, and "micro-macro" bridges in structural social psychology. *Current Research in Social Psychology, 1,* 30–42.

McClelland, D. C. (1961). *The achieving society.* Princeton, NJ: Van Nostrand.

Mehta, P. D., & Neale, M. C. (2005). People are variables too: Multilevel structural equation modeling. *Psychological Methods, 10,* 259–284.

Mischel, W., & Shoda, Y. (1995). A cognitive-affective system theory of personality: Reconceptualizing situations, dispositions, dynamics, and invariance in personality structure. *Psychological Review, 102,* 246–268.

Moritz, S. E., & Watson, C. B. (1998). Levels of analysis issues in group psychology: Using efficacy as an example of a multilevel model. *Group Dynamics: Theory, Research, and Practice, 2,* 285–298.

Mroczek, D. K. (2007). The analysis of longitudinal data in personality research. In R. C. Robins, R. C. Fraley, & R. Krueger (Eds.), *Handbook of research methods in personality psychology* (pp. 543–572). New York: Guilford.

Murray, S. L., Holmes, J. G., & Collins, N. L. (2006). Optimizing assurance: The risk regulation system in relationships. *Psychological Bulletin, 132,* 641–666.

Muthén, B. O. (1991). Multilevel factor analysis of class and student achievement components. *Journal of Educational Measurement, 28,* 338–354.

Muthén, B. O. (1994). Multilevel covariance structure analysis. *Sociological Methods and Research, 22,* 376–398.

Muthén, B. O., & Asparouhov, T. (2011). Beyond multilevel regression modeling: Multilevel analysis in a general latent variable framework. In J. Hox & J. K. Roberts (Eds.), *The handbook of advanced multilevel analysis* (pp. 15–40). New York: Taylor & Francis.

Muthén, L. K., & Muthén, B. O. (1998–2007). *Mplus user's guide* (5th ed.). Los Angeles, CA: Muthén & Muthén.

Napier, J. L., & Jost, J. T. (2008). Why are conservatives happier than liberals? *Psychological Science, 19,* 565–572.

Nezlek, J. B. (2001). Multilevel random coefficient analyses of event- and interval-contingent data in social and personality psychology. *Personality and Social Psychology Bulletin, 27,* 771–785.

Nezlek, J. B. (2003). Using multilevel random coefficient modeling to analyze social interaction diary data. *Journal of Social and Personal Relationships, 20,* 437–469.

Nezlek, J. B. (2007a). Multilevel modeling in research on personality. In R. C. Robins, R. C. Fraley, & R. Krueger (Eds.), *Handbook of research methods in personality psychology* (pp. 502–523). New York: Guilford.

Nezlek, J. B. (2007b). A multilevel framework for understanding relationships among traits, states, situations, and behaviors. *European Journal of Personality, 21,* 789–810.

Nezlek, J. B. (2008). An introduction to multilevel modeling for social and personality psychology. *Social and Personality Psychology Compass, 2,* 842–860.

Oishi, S., Kesebir, S., & Snyder, B. H. (2009). Sociology: A lost connection in social psychology. *Personality and Social Psychology Review, 13,* 334–353.

Overall, N. C., & Sibley, C. G. (2008). When accommodation matters: Situational dependency within daily interactions with romantic partners. *Journal of Experimental Social Psychology, 44,* 238–249.

Overall, N. C., & Sibley, C. G. (2009). When rejection-sensitivity matters: Regulating dependence within daily interactions with family and friends. *Personality and Social Psychology Bulletin, 35,* 1057–1070.

Pehrson, S., Vignoles, V. L., & Brown, R. (2009). National identification and anti-immigrant prejudice: Individual and contextual effects of national definitions. *Social Psychology Quarterly, 72,* 24–38.

Penner, L. A., Dovidio, J. F., Schroeder, D. A., & Piliavin, J. A. (2005) Prosocial behavior: Multilevel perspectives. *Annual Review of Psychology, 56,* 365–392.

Pettigrew, T. F. (1996). *How to think like a social scientist.* New York: HarperCollins.

Pettigrew, T. F. (1997). Personality and social structure: Social psychological contributions. In Hogan, R., Johnson, J., & Briggs, S. (Eds.), *Handbook of personality psychology* (pp. 417–438). San Diego, CA: Academic.

Poteat, V. P., Espelage, D. L., & Green, H. D. (2007). The socialization of dominance: Peer group contextual effects on homophobic and dominance attitudes. *Journal of Personality and Social Psychology, 92,* 1040–1050.

Preacher, K. J., Zhang, Z., & Zyphur, M. J. (2011). Alternative methods for assessing mediation in multilevel data: The advantages of multilevel SEM. *Structural Equation Modeling, 18,* 161–182.

Raudenbush, S. W., & Bryk, A. S. (2002). *Hierarchical linear models* (2nd ed.). Newbury Park, CA: Sage.

Reis, H. T., & Gable, S. L. (2000). Event-sampling and other methods for study everyday experience. In H. T. Reis & C. M. Judd (eds.), *Handbook of research methods in social and personality psychology* (pp. 190–222). New York: Cambridge University Press.

Reis, H. T., Sheldon, K. M., Gable, S. L., Roscoe, J., & Ryan, R. M. (2000). Daily well-being: The role of autonomy, competence, and relatedness. *Personality and Social Psychology Bulletin, 26,* 419–435.

Revelle, W. (1995). Personality processes. *Annual Review of Psychology, 46,* 295–328.

Rhodewalt, F. (2008). Personality and social behavior: An overview. In F. Rhodewalt (Ed.). *Personality and Social Behavior* (pp. 1–8). New York: Psychology Press.

Rousseau, D. (1985). Issues of level in organizational research: Multilevel and cross-level perspectives. In L. L. Cummings & B. M. Staw (Eds.), *Research in organizational behavior* (Vol. 7, pp. 1–37). Greenwich, CT: JAI Press.

Rovine, M. J., & Molenaar, P. C. (2000). A structural equation modeling approach to multilevel random coefficients model. *Multivariate Behavioral Research, 35,* 51–88.

Rusbult, C. E., Verette, J., Whitney, G. A., Slovik, L. F., & Lipkus, I. (1991). Accommodation processes in close relationships: Theory and preliminary empirical evidence. *Journal of Personality and Social Psychology, 60,* 53–78.

Selig, J. P., Card, N. A., & Little, T. D. (2008). Latent variable structural equation modeling in cross-cultural research: Multigroup and multilevel approaches. In F. J. R. van de Vijver, D. A. van Hermert, & Y. H. Poortinga (Eds.), *Multilevel analysis of individuals and cultures* (pp. 93–119). New York: Erlbaum.

Sheldon, K. M. (2008). The interface of motivational science and personology: Self-concordance, quality motivation, and multi-level personality integration. In J. Shah & W. Gardner (Eds.), *Handbook of motivational science* (pp. 465–476). New York: Guilford.

Shrout, P. E., & Bolger, N. (2002). Mediation in experimental and nonexperimental studies: New procedures and recommendations. *Psychological Methods, 7,* 422–445.

Sibley, C. G., & Overall, N. C. (2008). The boundaries between attachment and personality: Localized versus generalized effects in daily social interaction. *Journal of Research in Personality, 42,* 1394–1407.

Singer, J. D., & Willett, J. B. (2003). *Applied longitudinal data analysis: Modeling change and event occurrence.* New York: Oxford University Press.

Snijders, T., & Berkhof, J. (2008). Diagnostic checks for multilevel models. In J. de Leeuw & E. Meijer (Eds.), *Handbook of multilevel analysis* (pp. 141–175). Berlin: Springer.

Snijders, T., & Bosker, R. (1999). *Multilevel analysis.* London: Sage.

Snijders, T., & Kenny, D. A. (1999). The social relations model for family data. A multilevel approach. *Personal Relationships, 6,* 471–486.

Snyder, M., & Cantor, N. (1998). Understanding personality and social behavior: A functionalist strategy. In D. T. Gilbert, S. T. Fiske, & G. Lindzey (Eds.), *The handbook of social psychology* (4th ed., Vol. 1, pp. 635–679). Boston: McGraw-Hill.

Snyder, M., & Ickes, W. (1985). Personality and social behavior. In G. Lindzey & E. Aronson (Eds.), *Handbook of social psychology* (3rd ed., Vol. 2, pp. 883–948). New York: Random House.

Tong, E. M. W., Bishop, G. D., Enkelmann, H. C., Why, Y. P., Diong, S. M., Ang, J., et al. (2006). The role of the Big Five in appraisals. *Personality and Individual Differences, 41,* 513–523.

Torney-Purta, J., Wilkenfeld, B., & Barber, C. (2008). How adolescents in 27 countries understand, support, and practice human rights. *Journal of Social Issues, 64,* 857–880.

Wagner, U., Christ, O., Pettigrew, T. F., Stellmacher, J., & Wolf, C. (2006). Prejudice and minority proportion: Contact instead of threat effects. *Social Psychology Quarterly, 69,* 380–390.

Weingart, L. R., Brett, J. M., Olekalns, M., & Smith, P. L. (2007). Conflicting social motives in negotiating groups. *Journal of Personality and Social Psychology, 93,* 994–1010.

West, S. G., Ryu, E., Kwok, O.-M., & Cham, H. (2011). Multilevel modeling: Current and future applications in personality research. *Journal of Personality, 79,* 2–50.

Wu, C.-H. (2009). Factor analysis of the general self-efficacy scale and its relationship with individualism/collectivism among twenty-five countries: Application of multilevel confirmatory factor analysis. *Personality and Individual Differences, 46,* 699–703.

Van de Vijver, F. J. R., & Leung, K. (2001). Personality in cultural context: Methodological issues. *Journal of Personality, 69,* 1007–1031.

Van de Vijver, F. J. R., van Hermert, D. A., & Poortinga, Y. H. (2007). *Multilevel analysis of individuals and cultures.* New York: Erlbaum.

Van Woerkom, M., & Croon, M. (2009). The relationships between team learning activities and team performance. *Personnel Review, 38,* 560–577.

Zhang, Z., Zyphur, M. J., & Preacher, K. J. (2009). Testing multilevel mediation using hierarchical linear models: Problems and solutions. *Organizational Research Methods, 12,* 695–719.

Zyphur, M. J., Kaplan, S. A., & Christian, M. S. (2008). Assumptions of cross-level measurement and structural invariance in the analysis of multilevel data: Problems and solutions. *Group Dynamics: Theory, Research, and Practice, 12,* 127–140.

Substantive Areas Approached from Personality and Social Psychology Perspectives

Self and Identity
Dynamics of Persons and Their Situations

Jennifer Crocker *and* Amy Canevello

Abstract

In this chapter, we examine how the self both creates and results from experience—both its high points and low points. At a metatheoretical level, we consider how social and personality psychologists typically conceive of and study the self, drawing on the topic of self-esteem to illustrate typical views of the self as dispositional characteristics of persons, the product of situations, or the interaction between them. This Person × Situation framework has stimulated a great deal of research and had considerable heuristic value for social and personality psychologists who study the self and identity. However, because it views both the person and the situation as static rather than the result of dynamic processes, it fails to account for how people and situations mutually create each other in a process that unfolds over time. Through dynamic processes of reciprocal influence between persons and situations, self and identity can change surprisingly rapidly—change sustained by the situations people create for themselves over time. We consider methodological approaches in personality and social psychology to test these dynamic models of self and identity.

Keywords: self-esteem, relationships, goals, motives, contingencies, self-transcendence, compassion

Introduction

The capacity to conceive of the self distinguishes humans from other animals, and plays a key role in many of our most human abilities and foibles. Without selves, people could not introspect, articulate goals, evaluate their abilities and progress, plan for the future, exert self-control, empathize, take the perspective of others, or feel humble or proud. And without selves, people would never be self-centered, self-serving, self-promoting, self-critical, self-affirming, or self-denigrating. They would not have self-images, or feel self-conscious, ashamed, guilty, or embarrassed. They would never lack self-confidence—or have it, for that matter. Self-esteem would never be an issue, nor would garnering the approval or disapproval of others. The self is both a gift and a curse, contributing to some of the best and some of the worst moments in human experience (Leary, 2004).

In this chapter, we examine how the self both creates and results from experience—both its high points and low points. At a metatheoretical level, we consider how social and personality psychologists typically conceive of and study the self, drawing on the topic of self-esteem to illustrate typical views of the self as dispositional characteristics of persons, the product of situations, or the interaction between them. This Person X Situation framework has stimulated a great deal of research and had considerable heuristic value for social and personality psychologists who study the self and identity. However, because it views both the person and the situation as static rather than the result of dynamic processes, it fails to account for how people and situations mutually create each other in a process that unfolds over time. We propose a dynamic metatheoretical perspective on persons and situations and how they shape the self, and consider changes in the traditional methodological approaches of personality and social psychology required to test it.

At a more substantive level, we consider progress, remaining issues, and limitations in the standard person, situation, and Person X Situation approaches to the self, using self-esteem as an example. We consider not only level of self-esteem, but also stability, contingencies, and motivations relevant to self-esteem, and self-transcendence as an alternative to self-esteem. We illustrate a dynamic approach by examining how people can create what they experience through their self- and other-relevant interpersonal goals, and how that experience, in turn, shapes self-esteem and self-construals. In a process of reciprocal influence, self-esteem and self-construals shape interpersonal goals over time, creating the potential for upward and downward spirals in the experience of self. This process, we suggest, explains how the self, which affords many uniquely human abilities, also contributes to human suffering.

Defining the Self

What is the self? Trying to answer this apparently simple question reveals the vexing complexities of the self. Baumeister (1998) suggested that the self comprises three types of experience—reflexive consciousness (or self-awareness), interpersonal relationships, and the executive, or self as doer. Baumeister (1998) declined to define the self, suggesting that people understand the colloquial meaning of the word "self," which conveys the same meaning as the self in psychological terminology. But relying on colloquial understanding leaves us in the position of the proverbial man looking for his lost keys under the lamppost, because that is where the light is. Colloquial definitions illuminate only familiar conceptions of self.

The *American Heritage Dictionary* defines the self as: "1) the total, essential, or particular being of a person; the individual. 2) The essential qualities distinguishing one person from another; individuality. 3) An individual's consciousness of his own being or identity; ego. 4) One's own interests, welfare, or advantage." As this definition suggests, most people experience themselves as stable, coherent, continuous over time, unique, and separate from other selves. The idea that each human has an essential self that is distinct from other selves makes intuitive sense. In part, it reflects the physical boundaries of the human body; our physical selves are separated at the skin. It also reflects the need for social animals to distinguish one from another for social relationships

and transactions. Knowing the reputation of individuals—who is trustworthy or untrustworthy, who can be counted on to help in times of need, who is brave, who might violate norms, and so on—requires people to distinguish one person from another, and to learn the essential character of individuals. Humans also understand that they have reputations; others draw conclusions about whether the self is trustworthy or not, reliable, brave, and so on. This view of the self as stable and continuous underlies contemporary research on the self; how could self-esteem, self-verification, self-criticism, self-protection, self-presentation, self-consciousness, self-regulation, or any of the myriad other self-relevant phenomena exist without some essential, coherent, stable, continuous, and separate self?

Yet, looking for the definition of self away from the ground already illuminated by the lamplight, we encounter a different view of the self. For thousands of years, Buddhist teaching has argued that the existence of the self is an illusion. That is, although we experience the self as stable, continuous, and separate from other people, animals, and things, the self may consist of no more or less than an impermanent, fluid, ever-shifting stream of momentary thoughts and feelings that come and go in our minds, resulting from electrical activity in particular neurons in the brain; the idea that we are separate from other selves or even other species and things, is an illusion. The self is an idea, a construct, not a reality; in Buddhist thought, this idea causes human suffering. Indeed, awareness that a separate, permanent self is an illusion constitutes enlightenment in Buddhist philosophy:

> When the Buddha confronted the question of identity on the night of his enlightenment, he came to the radical discovery that we do not exist as separate beings. He saw into the human tendency to identify with a limited sense of existence and discovered that this belief in an individual small self is a root illusion that causes suffering and removes us from the freedom and mystery of life. He described this as interdependent arising, the cyclical process of consciousness creating identity by entering form, responding to contact of the senses, then attaching to certain forms, feelings, desires, images, and actions to create a sense of self. In teaching, the Buddha never spoke of humans as persons existing in some fixed or static way. Instead, he described us as a collection of five changing processes: the processes of the physical body, of feelings, of perceptions, of responses, and of the flow of consciousness that experiences them all.

Our sense of self arises whenever we grasp at or identify with these patterns. The process of identification, of selecting patterns to call "I," "me," "myself," is subtle and usually hidden from our awareness.(Jack Kornfield, *A Path with Heart*, p. 199)

Traditional Personality and Social Psychological Conceptions of Self

These two views of the self—as stable, coherent, and separate versus impermanent, interconnected, and fluid, an ever-shifting stream of momentary thoughts and feelings that come with electrical activity in the brain—roughly correspond to traditional personality and social psychological conceptions of the self. Personality psychologists tend to focus on individual differences, and view self and identity as stable features of the person. To be sure, experience, including culture, early experiences, and developmental processes, mold self and identity. By adulthood, however, these processes result in stable individual differences in self and identity. People who are relatively high in self-esteem, for example, in one situation will be relatively high in other situations, even if the situation tends to raise or lower self-esteem for most people (Endler & Magnusson, 1976). These individual differences have consequences for self-relevant thoughts, emotions, motivations, and behaviors. The self, in the personality psychology view, represents an independent variable, or input that shapes experience.

Social psychologists, on the other hand, tend to focus on situational influences on self and identity, and view the self as malleable, shifting, and shaped by immediate circumstances, accessible information, and concepts. To some degree, social psychologists' view of the self resembles the Buddhist view that a permanent, stable self is an illusion. The self, in the social psychology view, represents a dependent variable, an output that is shaped by situations and experience.

Of course, these characterizations of personality and social psychological approaches to the self are oversimplified. Although personality researchers focus on stability in the self over time, they recognize that situations matter, even if relative differences between people may remain relatively stable (Endler & Magnusson, 1976). Most social and personality psychologists assume that personality and situations interact to produce behavior and experiences; stable characteristics of people shape behavior more in some situations than others. Mischel and Shoda (1995) called these interactions "*if . . . then . . .* contingencies" of behavior, in which

personality is reflected in "signature" patterns of behaviors that emerge predictably under particular circumstances. And social psychologists generally recognize that situations affect some people more than others. Typically, persons and situations are assumed to be independent of one another; that is, anyone can find themselves in a wide variety of situations. Consequently, a great deal of research examines Person X Situation interactions as predictors of behavior.

Even this view of persons and situations as independent, interacting factors that shape behavior may be oversimplified. Persons are shaped by their situations, and situations are shaped by persons (Bowers, 1973; Snyder & Ickes, 1985). For example, people are not randomly distributed across situations; people choose many of their situations or circumstances, including accessible information, locations, and relationships, and personality characteristics such as self-esteem may shape the situations and relationships people choose, and how they understand and experience those situations (Reis, 2009; Snyder & Ickes, 1985; see also Reis & Holmes, chapter 4, this volume). Characteristics of people shape how people treat interaction partners, so people sometimes end up creating the reality they experience. For example, people with negative self-views often seek relationship partners who share those negative views (Swann, Rentfrow, & Guinn, 2003), and highly rejection sensitive people, who anxiously expect rejection, overreact to perceived slights in their relationships, eventually driving their relationship partners away and creating the very reality they feared (Downey, Freitas, Michaelis, & Khouri, 1998).

The self can easily be studied through the lens of the person, situation, and Person X Situation frameworks. Many self-relevant constructs function as both traits and states; individual differences in self-relevant variables are often stable over time, yet within a person, levels of these variables fluctuate meaningfully. Personality psychologists tend to focus more on understanding the stability of between-person differences, whereas social psychologists focus more on identifying the causes or predictors of within-person fluctuations.

Viewing Self-Esteem Through the Person, Situation, and Person X Situation Lenses

Self-esteem is a judgment about the worth or value of the self—the whole self (i.e., global self-esteem: Rosenberg, 1965); specific aspects of the self such as appearance, intelligence, or athletic prowess (domain-specific self-esteem: Rosenberg, Schooler, Schoenbach, & Rosenberg, 1995; Woike & Baumgardner, 1993); or one's groups and identities (collective self-esteem: Crocker & Luhtanen, 1990). In this chapter, we focus on global self-esteem because it is both the most frequently studied form of self-esteem, and the most emotionally potent. Self-esteem is both a personality trait and a psychological state; people have average or typical levels of self-esteem that remain relatively stable over weeks, months, and even years (Rosenberg, 1965), and they experience fluctuations in self-esteem around that average or typical level (Crocker & Wolfe, 2001; Kernis, Cornell, Sun, Berry, & Harlow, 1993; Rosenberg, 1979).

Whether assessed as trait or a state, self-esteem feels good; people with high self-esteem experience more pleasant feelings such as happiness and life satisfaction and fewer unpleasant feelings such as depression and anxiety than people with low self-esteem (Brockner et al., 1983; Crocker, Sommers, & Luhtanen, 2002; Diener, 1984; Pelham & Swann, 1989; Tennen & Herzberger, 1987).

Individual Differences in Self-Esteem: Level, Stability, Contingencies, and Motives

Personality approaches treat self-esteem as a trait—a stable individual difference in the chronic tendency to feel that one has worth or value as a person. The vast majority of studies of self-esteem focus on individual differences in *level* of self-esteem—whether it is high or low—but researchers have also investigated individual differences in other aspects of self-esteem, such as stability, contingencies, and motives.

LEVEL OF SELF-ESTEEM

Researchers usually measure global self-esteem with self-report questionnaires such as the Rosenberg Self-Esteem Inventory (RSEI; Rosenberg, 1965), a well-validated measure of global self-esteem (Blascovich & Tomaka, 1991). Participants indicate their agreement or disagreement with items such as, "I feel I am a person of worth, at least on an equal basis with others," and "At times, I feel I am no good at all." Most people in the United States, Canada, and Northern Europe have high self-esteem, as indicated by their responses to questionnaires. For example, on average, people score well above the neutral midpoint on the RSEI (Baumeister, Campbell, Krueger, & Vohs, 2003; Baumeister, Tice, & Hutton, 1989).

Low self-esteem people have moderately positive views of themselves, but their self-views are uncertain

and unclear; they have self-doubts (Campbell, 1990; Campbell et al., 1996). People with high self-esteem think they have a host of desirable attributes; self-esteem correlates strongly with positive self-judgments of popularity, attractiveness, relationships, abilities, and morality (Baumeister et al., 2003; J. D. Brown, 1986; Campbell, 1986; Diener, Wolsic, & Fujita, 1995; Gabriel, Critelli, & Ee, 1994; Harter, 1993; Wylie, 1979). They hold these positive self-views with certainty and clarity (Campbell, 1990; Campbell et al., 1996). These positive self-views do not jibe closely with reality; when measured objectively, characteristics of high and low self-esteem people differ only slightly, if at all (Baumeister et al., 2003), leading some to describe the positive self-views of high self-esteem people as illusory (Taylor & Brown, 1988). For example, although high self-esteem people rate themselves much higher in attractiveness than do low self-esteem people, observer ratings of attractiveness show small and inconsistent differences in the attractiveness of high and low self-esteem people, and these differences virtually disappear when appearance is not enhanced by hair styles, clothing, jewelry, makeup, and so on (Diener et al., 1995; Gabriel et al., 1994).

High self-esteem people have unrealistically positive views of their personal qualities for several reasons. For example, they take more credit for their successes and make more excuses for failure than do low self-esteem people (Bradley, 1978; Miller & Ross, 1975). High self-esteem people respond to self-threat in ways that maintain and protect their self-esteem, such as derogating others and comparing themselves with others who are worse off (Blaine & Crocker, 1993), and they define traits to emphasize their positive and deemphasize their negative qualities (Beauregard & Dunning, 2001). For example, high self-esteem students might define intelligence in ways that reflect their own particular skills, such as analytical reasoning ability, speed of judgment, or originality, and not the skills they lack.

Although North Americans and Western Europeans tend to have high self-esteem, regional and cultural variations in self-esteem suggest limits on the tendency to think highly of the self. For example, average self-esteem in Japan is much closer to the neutral midpoint of the scale than in the United States and Canada, and the longer Japanese students live in North America, the higher their self-esteem (Heine, Lehman, Markus, & Kitayama, 1999). Cultural psychologists suggest that lower mean levels of self-esteem in Japan reflect construals of self that emphasize fitting in rather than standing out, and norms that support self-criticism rather than self-enhancement (e.g., Heine et al., 1999; Markus & Kitayama, 1991). Other researchers cite evidence that despite cultural variation in the magnitude of the effect, average levels of self-esteem are universally above the neutral midpoint of self-esteem scales, that people in Eastern cultures self-enhance on domains that are important to them (Constantine Sedikides & Gregg, 2008), and that implicit measures of self-esteem, such as positive ratings of the letters in one's own name, suggest equally high self-esteem in Japan, China, and the United States (Yamaguchi et al., 2007). At the same time, explicit self-esteem remains lower in Japan.

Interest in individual differences in level of self-esteem partly reflects the assumption that self-esteem causes behavior, success at achieving goals, or psychological disorders. Researchers and policy-makers often assume that high self-esteem causes desirable behavior such as school achievement, whereas low self-esteem causes undesirable outcomes such as prejudice, delinquency, drug use, or aggression (Mecca, Smelser, & Vasconcellos, 1989). High self-esteem correlates positively with outcomes such as school achievement, popularity, and mental health (Trzesniewski et al., 2006; Wylie, 1979), but these correlations are typically small, with global self-esteem accounting for only about 4% of the variance in school achievement, for example, and less than that in many other variables (Baumeister et al., 2003; Smelser, 1989; Wylie, 1979).

In a major review of the literature on the benefits of self-esteem, Baumeister and his colleagues concluded that, "Overall, the benefits of high self-esteem fall into two categories: enhanced initiative and pleasant feelings. We have not found evidence that boosting self-esteem (by therapeutic interventions or school programs) causes benefits. Our findings do not support continued widespread efforts to boost self-esteem in the hope that it will by itself foster improved outcomes" (Baumeister et al., 2003, p. 1). Of course, pleasant feelings and enhanced initiative are significant in themselves. But the assumption that global feelings of self-worth or self-esteem cause most good things in life, whereas low self-esteem causes most social problems, often does not stand up to scrutiny.

The controversial conclusion that global self-esteem has little benefit aside from pleasant feelings and persistence has been challenged. For example, a recently published longitudinal study of 1,037

adolescents in Dunedin, New Zealand, showed that those who scored low on a widely used measure of global self-esteem predicted objective measures of poorer mental and physical health, worse economic prospects, and higher criminal behavior in adulthood (Trzesniewski et al., 2006). Finding that adolescent self-esteem predicts a wide range of problems in adulthood is provocative, but despite many positive features of this study, it does not show that adolescent self-esteem predicts *change* in these outcomes, consistent with a causal effect of self-esteem, nor does it rule out the possibility that the association between adolescent self-esteem and adult problems is due to the association between adolescent self-esteem and adult self-esteem. In other words, because self-esteem tends to be stable, the association between adolescent self-esteem and adult problems could simply be due to the correlation between adult self-esteem and adult problems, which provides no information about the causal direction of the association. Another study on the same sample showed that global self-esteem at age 11 predicted decreased aggression and other externalizing problems at age 13 (Donnellan, Trzesniewski, Robins, Moffitt, & Caspi, 2005). Although this cannot demonstrate a causal effect of self-esteem on externalizing problems, it provides stronger evidence than studies that do not test whether self-esteem predicts future outcomes. As with other studies of consequences of self-esteem, however, the effect was small.

Typical personality studies on correlates and consequences of trait self-esteem suffer from some major limitations. First, as noted, self-esteem is typically measured with self-report questionnaires with high face validity; research participants can easily guess that a study concerns self-esteem from items such as, "I feel like a person of worth, at least on an equal basis with others." To address this issue, researchers have developed measures of implicit self-esteem, such as liking for letters that are the initials of one's name (Koole et al., 2003), or reaction times to associate positive words with the self (Farnham, Greenwald, & Banaji, 1999). These measures do not correlate strongly with one another (Bosson, Swann, & Pennebaker, 2000), and their validity as measure of personality is not well-established (Schimmack & Diener, 2003), although accumulating research points to the potential usefulness of these implicit measures (e.g., Jordan, Spencer, & Zanna, 2005; Rudman, Dohn, & Fairchild, 2007).

Second, because self-esteem correlates with a host of individual differences, from positive affect to social anxiety, researchers cannot rule out all plausible alternative explanations for the effects of self-esteem. For example, recent research indicates that positive emotions benefit physical health, including predicting decreased morbidity and mortality and improved immune response (Pressman & Cohen, 2005; Robles, Brooks, & Pressman, 2009). Together with the strong association between high self-esteem and positive emotions, these findings suggest that health benefits of high self-esteem may be due to positive affect rather than self-esteem per se. To be sure, this difficulty of possible third variables that could explain effects of self-esteem also applies to other individual differences, but it may be particularly problematic with self-esteem because of the wide range of things with which it correlates, and the lack of an objective behavioral indicator of self-esteem.

Third, many people with low self-esteem do not experience the negative outcomes hypothesized to result from low self-esteem (e.g., Trzesniewski et al., 2006), suggesting that even if low self-esteem contributes to problems such as poor mental and physical health or aggression, it is but one factor of many contributing factors. Factors such as social support or psychological resilience may buffer low self-esteem people from negative outcomes. Similarly, associations between low self-esteem and problematic outcomes may emerge only under certain conditions, such as stress or self-threat. These possibilities require that researchers shift from a strictly individual difference perspective to examine Person X Situation interactions as predictors of outcomes.

These considerations suggest a related limitation of personality-oriented research on individual differences in self-esteem: the paucity of theoretical accounts of how and why trait self-esteem might affect outcomes such as substance abuse, aggression, physical health, or popularity. The idea that low trait self-esteem causes problems such as aggression has such intuitive appeal that it hardly seems to need a theoretical rationale. Where such rationales are offered, researchers rarely test them directly in process models that examine change over time. In light of the thousands of studies examining correlates and consequences of self-esteem over the past half century, development and testing of such process models is long overdue.

Although level of global self-esteem—whether it is high or low—does not seem to have much causal influence on behavior, other aspects of self-esteem might. One aspect that seems promising is fragility of self-esteem, reflected in self-esteem that rises and falls over time, or is contingent on success, approval of others, or other accomplishments.

STABILITY OF SELF-ESTEEM

Unstable self-esteem reflects a fragile sense of self-worth, buffeted by events such as success and failure, or acceptance and rejection by others (Kernis, 2003; Kernis & Waschull, 1995). In theory, stability of self-esteem is independent of its level; both high and low self-esteem can be stable or unstable over time. In reality, people with low self-esteem also tend to have more unstable self-esteem, although these two aspects are sufficiently distinct that their unique effects can be examined (Crocker et al., 2002; Kernis et al., 1993; Kernis & Waschull, 1995). Although low self-esteem might be inherently more fragile, high self-esteem might appear to be more stable because the skewed distribution of self-esteem scores means that people with high self-esteem cannot increase much.

Instability of self-esteem can be measured in several ways, including self-reports (Rosenberg, 1979), computing the within-person standard deviation of self-esteem across repeated measurements (Kernis, Grannemann, & Barclay, 1989), or fluctuations of self-esteem in response to specific events such as acceptances and rejections (Crocker et al., 2002). Self-reports of self-esteem stability do not correlate with the standard deviation of self-esteem in repeated measurements, but do correlate strongly with level of self-esteem, suggesting that self-reports do not provide a valid indicator of self-esteem stability (Kernis et al., 1989).

Within-person standard deviations of self-esteem assessed in multiple reports provides a face-valid indicator of self-esteem stability, and has strong predictive power (Kernis & Waschull, 1995), but has its own limitations. Within-person standard deviations provide no information about the direction of changes in self-esteem: self-esteem could be steadily increasing or decreasing, or it could fluctuate around the person's mean level of self-esteem, without changing systematically over time. When self-esteem fluctuates around a mean level, those fluctuations could be random (i.e., unrelated to internal or external events), or they could reflect events such as success or failure, or rejection or acceptance (Crocker, Karpinski, Quinn, & Chase, 2003; Crocker et al., 2002). Personality-oriented researchers tend to use standard deviations of self-esteem to index (in) stability, assuming that fluctuations reflect a characteristic of the person rather than his or her experiences.

Individual differences in stability (i.e., standard deviation) of self-esteem predict several outcomes even when the effects of level of trait self-esteem are controlled (Kernis & Waschull, 1995). For example, people with high and stable self-esteem are less defensive and aggressive than people with high but unstable self-esteem (Kernis et al., 1989). Unstable self-esteem is associated with less intrinsic motivation (Waschull & Kernis, 1996), less clarity about the self-concept, and more tension or pressure (Kernis, Brown, & Brody, 2000). People with unstable self-esteem are particularly vulnerable to depression, especially if they have low and unstable self-esteem (Franck & De Raedt, 2007; Roberts & Monroe, 1994).

Why do some people have more unstable self-esteem? Kernis proposed that self-esteem fluctuates when people are ego-involved in events (Greenier et al., 1999). They tend to view successes and failures as reflections of their worth and value as human beings, so when things go well they feel valuable and worthy, but when things go badly, they feel worthless. People with unstable self-esteem tend to base their self-esteem what others think of them, or their accomplishments (Kernis, 2003). Presumably, their self-esteem goes up when they succeed or others accept them, and goes down when they fail or others reject them. However, when instability of self-esteem is measured with the within-person standard deviation of self-esteem, we cannot know whether change in self-esteem due to these events accounts for self-esteem instability.

CONTINGENCIES OF SELF-ESTEEM
Related to the self-esteem stability, researchers have investigated individual differences in contingent self-esteem, or the degree to which self-esteem follows "*if . . . then . . .*" contingency rules. For example, people who feel worthless when they fail or others disapprove of them are said to have contingent self-esteem. Many researchers have suggested that some people have contingent self-esteem, whereas others have noncontingent or secure self-esteem (e.g., Deci & Ryan, 1995; Kernis, 2003); this view mirrors the idea that some people have unstable self-esteem, whereas others have stable self-esteem. Others have suggested that nearly everyone stakes their self-esteem more on success in some areas than others; the difference lies not in whether or not self-esteem is contingent, but what it is contingent on (Coopersmith, 1967; Crocker & Wolfe, 2001; James, 1910; Kernis, 2003; Kuiper & Olinger, 1986). For example, over a century ago, William

James observed that his self-esteem was staked on his skill and reputation as a psychologist, but did not depend on his skill as a linguist (James, 1910). James proposed a formula in which self-esteem = success/pretensions. In other words, the more people succeed in the domains in which their self-esteem is staked, the higher their global self-esteem.

Measures of contingent self-esteem reflect these differing points of view. For example, Paradise and Kernis (1999) constructed a measure of contingent self-esteem as a whole, whereas Crocker and her colleagues constructed a measure of seven common contingencies of self-esteem in college students (Crocker, Luhtanen, Cooper, & Bouvrette, 2003). Contingencies of self-worth are stable over time, although not as stable as many personality traits (Crocker, Luhtanen, et al., 2003).

James's formulation of self-esteem served as the basis for Crocker and Wolfe's (2001) theory of contingencies of self-worth. They suggested that positive and negative events in domains of contingent self-worth raise or lower momentary self-esteem around a person's typical or trait level of self-esteem (Crocker, Karpinski, et al., 2003; Crocker, Luhtanen, et al., 2003; Crocker & Wolfe, 2001). Although trait levels of self-esteem might be stable and independent of success or failure, fluctuations in state self-esteem around that trait level occur when people succeed or fail in areas on which their self-esteem is staked. For example, among a sample of college seniors applying to graduate school, the more self-esteem was staked on academic success, the more acceptances by graduate programs increased self-esteem and rejections decreased self-esteem (Crocker et al., 2002). Unfortunately, the "high" associated with success in domains of contingency does not last; within a day or two, self-esteem tends to revert to its typical, or trait level. The good news is that the "low" associated with failure in domains of contingency also doesn't last; self-esteem rebounds within a day or two.

Crocker and Wolfe (2001) proposed that individual differences in contingencies of self-worth may be more important predictors of behavior than level of self-esteem. Increases in self-esteem feel good, whereas decreases in self-esteem feel bad (Crocker et al., 2002); accordingly, people are highly motivated to succeed and avoid failure in domains of contingent self-worth. Ups and downs of state self-esteem may motivate people more than individual differences in trait levels of self-esteem, which change little and therefore have little power to reinforce behavior. To obtain the good feeling, or high associated with a boost in self-esteem, people may work hard to succeed or at least avoid failure. For example, students who base their self-esteem on academics report studying more hours than students whose self-esteem is not contingent on academics (Crocker, Luhtanen, et al., 2003).

Despite the motivation that contingencies of self-worth generate, Crocker and Park (Crocker & Park, 2004) argued that pursuing self-esteem by trying to succeed and avoid failure in domains of contingency has costs for learning, self-regulation, relationships, and mental health. When self-esteem is at stake, people focus on proving themselves by demonstrating their ability rather than identifying where they need to grow or evolve as a person (Niiya & Crocker, 2009). Although the boost to self-esteem that follows success in contingent domains creates a pleasurable "high," self-esteem quickly returns to normal even following significant successes such as admission to graduate school. Consequently, people pursuing self-esteem may become addicted, seeking more and more success to obtain the same self-esteem "high" (Baumeister & Vohs, 2001). As if running on a treadmill, people who pursue self-esteem may never achieve their goal of definitively establishing their worth and value (Crocker & Nuer, 2003). And although people may work hard to avoid failure in domains of contingency, they also protect self-esteem by self-handicapping, or creating justifications for failure that can actually undermine their performance (Niiya, Brook, & Crocker, 2010; Tice, 1991).

Preoccupation with one's own worth and value that accompanies contingencies of self-worth can make people poor relationship partners (Park & Crocker, 2005). And some contingencies of self-worth—those that place self-esteem at the mercy of other people or events—predict increased depression (Sargent & Crocker, 2006). Some contingencies of self-worth are nearly impossible to satisfy, with negative consequences for mental health. The dysfunctional attitudes scale (DAS: Weissman & Beck, 1978), which includes items such as, "If I fail at my work, than I am a failure as a person," and "I am nothing if a person I love doesn't love me," predicts both anxiety and depression (G. P. Brown, Hammen, Craske, & Wickens, 1995; Kuiper & Olinger, 1986).

In sum, research suggests that contingencies of self-worth represent another important aspect of self-esteem. The increases and decreases in self-esteem that accompany success and failure in these domains serve as both a carrot and a stick, driving people to succeed. However, the carrot of permanent increases in self-esteem is always just out of reach, and to avoid the stick of drops in self-esteem, people sometimes engage in counterproductive strategies such as self-handicapping.

Like level of self-esteem, research on contingencies of self-worth as a personality characteristic suffers from shortcomings. Contingencies tend to correlate with other personality characteristics, and it is virtually impossible to rule out every potentially correlated variable as alternative explanations (c.f., Crocker & Luhtanen, 2003). One strength of research on contingencies of self-worth is the more elaborated process models of how contingencies shape behavior and outcomes (Crocker & Park, 2004; Crocker & Wolfe, 2001; Deci & Ryan, 1995; Kernis, 2003).

SELF-ESTEEM MOTIVES

As the preceding discussion suggests, people can be highly motivated by self-esteem; they want to feel valuable and worthy, and don't want to feel valueless or unworthy. Of course, self-esteem motives such as validation-seeking and self-image goals are not the only self-relevant motivations people can have; people may also seek verification of their self-views (i.e., confirmation that others see their negative as well as their positive qualities), and they may seek accurate information about the self (Swann et al., 2003; Trope, 1986). But self-esteem motives may be stronger than self-verification and accuracy motives (Sedikides, 1993). Psychologists have long recognized the motivational power of self-esteem. For example, Maslow included self-esteem in his hierarchy of needs (Maslow, 1968). Although self-esteem motives are often considered universal, people differ in motives related to self-esteem. As noted previously, people who are high in global self-esteem show more self-serving biases and positive illusions about the self. However, it is unclear whether these biases result from a greater motivation to enhance self-esteem among high self-esteem people, self-verification strivings, or generalization from high global self-esteem to other beliefs and conclusions about the self.

Researchers have developed a few measures intended to directly assess individual differences in motivations to maintain, enhance, and protect self-esteem. For example, Dykman (1998) developed a measure of individual differences in validation seeking, which assesses chronic striving to prove one's basic self-worth through external symbols of achievement and acceptance by others (Dykman, 1998).

The scale has high test-retest reliability over 10 weeks ($r = 0.76$), consistent with the proposition that it measures a stable disposition. People high in validation-seeking tend to be anxious, depressed, and low in trait self-esteem, and report that their self-esteem is unstable, suggesting that people seek to validate their self-worth when they feel insecure or negative about themselves. They report using more self-blame and disengagement coping strategies in stressful situations, and they increase in depressive symptoms when experiencing high stress. The validation-seeking scale provides a useful measure of self-esteem motivation. However, the items tend to assume low self-esteem, and assess the desire to avoid feeling worthless (e.g., "It seems like I'm constantly trying to prove that I'm 'okay' as a person."). Consequently, they may not capture the validation-seeking of high self-esteem people, who want to prove not simply that they are good enough, but that they are great.

Several personality questionnaires assess the more public side of self-esteem motivation—trying to control how others view the self—rather than the more private side of validation-seeking. These measures capture the motivation to construct desired images and avoid constructing negative images of the self in daily life (i.e., impression motivation), including public self-consciousness, fear of negative evaluation, social anxiety, and embarrassability (Nezlek & Leary, 2002). However, they assess specific aspects of impression motivation (e.g., fear of negative evaluation) or constructs that correlate with impression motivation (e.g., public self-consciousness, social anxiety) but do not directly assess the motivation to construct desired impressions and avoid negative impressions.

We created a measure of self-image goals—trying to get others to see the self in positive ways and not in negative ways (Canevello & Crocker, 2010; Crocker & Canevello, 2008). The measure has moderate test-retest reliability ($r = 0.49$, Canevello & Crocker, 2010), suggesting that it is less stable than many personality traits. People with chronically high self-image goals (averaged over multiple reports) also score high on validation-seeking, but the correlation between these constructs is small enough ($r = 0.34$) to suggest that they capture distinct aspects of self-esteem motivation (Crocker, unpublished data). People high in self-image goals view the relationship between the self and others as competitive and zero-sum, so that one person's success detracts from others, and they believe people should take care of themselves even at the expense

of others (Crocker & Canevello, 2008). Students high in self-image goals increase in symptoms of anxiety and depression over the first semester of college (Crocker, Canevello, Breines, & Flynn, 2010; Nezlek & Leary, 2002). These findings suggest that people have self-image goals when they lose trust that their needs can be met collaboratively with others; consequently, they attempt to control how others view them as a means to getting their needs met.

In sum, although high self-esteem people tend to self-enhance more than do low self-esteem people, research suggests that self-esteem motivation is more characteristic of low than high self-esteem people. These findings suggest either that high self-esteem is not associated with motivation to maintain, enhance, or boost self-esteem (perhaps because high self-esteem people do not need more self-esteem), or that existing measures do not capture the nature of self-esteem motivation in high self-esteem people. Alternatively, high self-esteem people may be motivated to maintain, protect, and enhance self-esteem only when their self-esteem is threatened, a Person X Situation possibility we consider later. The process by which validation-seeking leads to symptoms of depression and anxiety is not yet clear. Process models for the effects of self-image goals have been proposed; we defer discussion of those models for a later section.

SELF-TRANSCENDENCE

Whereas self-esteem motivation reflects preoccupation with one's self-worth, self-transcendence refers to the ability to rise above concerns about self-worth. Leary and his colleagues called this a hypoegoic state, characterized by low self-awareness, focus on the present, and concrete thoughts about the self (Leary, Adams, & Tate, 2006). In contrast to the tens of thousands of studies of self-esteem and related constructs, only a small number of studies have investigated individual differences in the capacity to transcend concerns about self-worth.

Mindfulness refers to a state of dispassionate and nonjudgmental awareness of the present (e.g., Kirk Warren Brown, Ryan, & Creswell, 2007; Kirk W. Brown, Ryan, Creswell, & Niemiec, 2008). Mindful awareness practices such as meditation foster awareness of self as fluid, connected, and impermanent, as described in the Buddhist tradition. The detached, rather than overidentified, sense of self arising from mindfulness represents a type of self-transcendence. Brown and Ryan (2003) developed a measure of dispositional mindfulness, assessing individual differences in the chronic tendency toward mindful awareness. If mindfulness fosters self-transcendence, then people high in dispositional mindfulness should be less defensive in response to self-threats. Studies of romantic relationship conflict support this hypothesis (Barnes, Brown, Krusemark, Campbell, & Rogge, 2007). For example, in one study couples discussed a conflict that currently challenged their relationship. Dispositional mindfulness predicted less hostility and anxiety both before and during the discussion.

Self-compassion, in Buddhist thought, refers to kindness toward the self, recognition that failures and flaws reflect one's humanity, and a mindful perspective regarding negative aspects of the self (Neff, Rude, & Kirkpatrick, 2007; Neff, Wayment, & Bauer, 2008). Neff proposed that self-compassion is a healthier way to relate to the self than self-esteem, which involves self-judgment rather than self-kindness (Neff, 2009; Neff et al., 2008). Consistent with this idea, self-compassion correlates positively with life satisfaction, emotional intelligence, social connectedness, and mastery goals, and correlates negatively with self-criticism, depression, anxiety, rumination, thought suppression, perfectionism, performance goals, and disordered eating behaviors (C. E. Adams & Leary, 2007; Neff, 2003; Neff, Hsieh, & Dejitterat, 2005; Neff et al., 2007). People high in self-compassion show increased reflective and affective wisdom, personal initiative, curiosity and exploration, happiness, optimism, and positive affect.

Although self-compassion and self-esteem correlate strongly, self-compassion predicts many aspects of psychological health beyond their associations with self-esteem (Neff & Vonk, 2009). Controlling for self-esteem, self-compassion negatively relates to instability of self-esteem (within-person standard deviation of self-esteem); global self-esteem contingency; basing self-esteem on others' approval, performance, or physical appearance; social comparison tendency; public self-consciousness; rumination about the self; anger; and need for cognitive closure (Neff & Vonk, 2009). As Neff and Vonk (2009, p. 39) note:

> Individuals who are harshly self-critical should tend to have lower self-esteem than those who treat themselves kindly. When the shared variance between the two constructs is partialled out, however, the different foundations of these two forms of positive self-affect become visible. What is left of self-esteem after accounting for self-compassion levels is likely to be the mere positivity of self-representations, which may not help much when these self-representations are threatened. What is left of self-compassion after accounting for self-esteem, on the other hand, are the warm feelings associated with an inclusive, open-hearted acceptance of oneself without judgment or evaluation.

Researchers have only recently begun to study self-compassion as a personality trait, and much remains to be done. Longitudinal research demonstrating that self-compassion predicts improved psychological functioning and well-being over time would strengthen the case for a causal link between self-compassion and psychological health. Nonetheless, initial studies support the idea that dispositional self-compassion provides an alternative to self-esteem as a route to psychological health. It seems unlikely that the pursuit of self-compassion would have the same negative consequences as the pursuit of self-esteem.

An alternative route to self-transcendence involves caring about the well-being of others. Of course, people can care for others with the hope that others will view the self positively (Helgeson, 1994); this ego-involved type of concern for others is not self-transcendent. Compassionate goals focus on supporting others, not to obtain something for the self, but out of concern for others' well-being (Crocker & Canevello, 2008). When people have compassionate goals, they want to be a constructive force in their interactions with others, and avoid harming them.

We developed a measure of compassionate goals to compare their effects with the effects of self-image goals (Crocker & Canevello, 2008). Like our measure of self-image goals, test-retest reliability over 10 weeks ($r = 0.21$) suggested that compassionate goals are not a stable personality trait (Canevello & Crocker, 2010). Correlations of compassionate goals with other constructs suggests that they involve self-transcendence; compassionate goals correlate positively with spiritual transcendence (a sense of connectedness with other people and living things) and self-compassion, and negatively with zero-sum beliefs that success for one person must be at the expense of others, and psychological entitlement (Crocker & Canevello, 2008).

Individual differences in chronic compassionate goals (averaged across multiple reports from the same person over time) predict increases in perceived available support from others, interpersonal trust, and feelings of closeness, and decreased loneliness, anxiety, and depression over the first semester of college (Crocker & Canevello, 2008; Crocker et al., 2010). Studies of roommate pairs in the first semester of college show that one roommate's compassionate goals predict increases in the other roommate's reports of support received from and responsiveness of the first roommate, and increases in relationship quality over time for both roommates (Canevello & Crocker, 2010; Crocker & Canevello, 2008). We discuss process models of how compassionate goals lead to improvements in mental health, relationship quality, and self-esteem in a later section.

In sum, research on self-transcendence as a personality trait is in its infancy, yet the research to date suggests that self-transcendence, including self-compassion and compassionate goals toward others provides a healthy alternative to self-esteem or the pursuit of self-esteem.

CONCLUSIONS AND FUTURE DIRECTIONS

Most research on self-esteem from a personality perspective focuses on level of trait self-esteem, and what it correlates with or predicts. Much less research has focused on fragility of self-esteem, as revealed by instability of self-esteem over time and contingencies of self-worth, and self-esteem motives. Even less has focused on the possibility of transcending concerns about the worth and value of the self, either through self-compassion or compassionate goals toward others. These relatively new directions for personality-oriented research on self-esteem present many exciting opportunities for research, including longitudinal research examining whether these aspects of self-esteem predict changes in mental health, interpersonal relationships, self-regulation, and behaviors over time. As with other personality research, one challenge is demonstrating that these aspects of self-esteem contribute something new, that is, that their effects cannot be explained by other personality variables.

One limitation of research on individual differences in various aspects of self-esteem is the assumption that they are unchanging, and perhaps unchangeable. Can self-esteem dispositions change? If so, what changes them, and how? These questions cannot be answered by studying aspects of self-esteem only as inputs, or independent variables.

One potentially important direction for research on individual differences in self-esteem and its aspects involves development of process models that explain how and why self-esteem predicts (or doesn't

predict) outcomes and behavior. Process-oriented personality research not only provides a much deeper understanding of personality; it also provides an essential step toward understanding how personality can change, and how one might intervene to produce that change.

Situational Variability in Self-Esteem Level, Stability, Contingencies, Motives, and Self-Transcendence

Whereas personality psychologists typically focus on individual differences in self-esteem and its aspects, social psychologists focus on situational determinants of self-esteem and its aspects. As with personality approaches, most research has focused on level of self-esteem, but some research has examined situational variability in self-esteem contingencies, motives, and self-transcendence. Social psychological approaches that treat aspects of self-esteem as outputs, or dependent variables, can reveal just how malleable these aspects of self-esteem are. Most studies examining situational variability in aspects of self-esteem take place in the laboratory, where situations can be precisely controlled and manipulated. These studies have the advantage of enabling researchers to know the exact parameters of the situation, and through manipulating those parameters, researchers can draw conclusions about the causal effects of situations.

LEVEL OF SELF-ESTEEM

Situation-induced changes in level of self-esteem are hard to detect using measures of trait self-esteem; trait measures ask about general tendencies over time, and one experience in the laboratory is unlikely to change how people answer these questions. Consequently, researchers have developed measures of state self-esteem. Sometimes researchers create ad hoc measures of self-esteem for a particular study. For example, McFarland and Ross (1982) examined the effects of attributions for success and failure on state self-esteem by having participants rate how much they experienced feelings such as proud, good, superior, and valuable; Leary used a similar approach to examine the effects of social inclusion and exclusion on state self-esteem (Leary, Tambor, Terdal, & Downs, 1995). These scales have face validity as measures of how people feel about themselves at the moment, but they blur the distinction between emotional states and self-esteem, and lack rigorous assessment of their validity. Heatherton and Polivy (1991) developed a measure of state self-esteem assessing momentary performance, social, and appearance self-esteem. These three factors together correlate strongly with the RSEI, which assesses global trait self-esteem (Rosenberg, 1965). Other researchers (e.g., Crocker, Voelkl, Testa, & Major, 1991; Niiya, Crocker, & Bartmess, 2004) have modified the RSEI to reflect momentary or daily self-esteem by rephrasing items to focus on self-esteem right now, or today.

Regardless of how it is measured, research clearly demonstrates situational influences on state self-esteem. In theory, any situation or information that reflects on the worth or value of the self in that context could affect self-esteem. In a classic study, job applicants completed questionnaires, including a measure of self-esteem, in the presence of another applicant, who was actually a confederate of the researchers (Morse & Gergen, 1970). The competitor was either well-dressed, well-groomed, and self-confident (dubbed "Mr. Clean") or dressed in a smelly sweatshirt, ripped trousers, and apparently confused (dubbed "Mr. Dirty"). Applicants who thought they were competing with Mr. Clean for the job dropped in self-esteem; those who thought they were competing with Mr. Dirty increased in self-esteem. Apparently, people's judgments of their own worth and value in a particular context depends on how they compare to others in that context.

Other studies show that self-esteem increases when people succeed, receive positive feedback, or are socially accepted and included, and decreases when people fail, receive negative feedback, or are socially rejected and excluded (e.g., Leary et al., 1995; McFarland & Ross, 1982; Niiya et al., 2004). These findings are not restricted to highly controlled laboratory experiments. Diary studies show that real-life experiences such as receiving good or bad grades, interpersonal stress, and changes in perceived relationship quality predict change in self-esteem over time; grades on exams or papers also predict change in self-esteem over time (Crocker, Karpinski, et al., 2003; Stinson et al., 2008).

How much self-esteem drops when people receive negative feedback, are rejected or excluded, or compare unfavorably to those around them depends on the meaning people give to these situations; it is not the situation itself, but the significance people give it, that influences self-esteem. For example, the effect of success and failure depend on the attributions people make for their performance; failure leads to drops in self-esteem when it is attributed to internal, stable, and global causes (e.g., I'm an idiot) but not when it is attributed to unstable,

external, or specific causes (e.g., I was upset about something) (McFarland & Ross, 1982). Comparing unfavorably with in-group members leads to lower self-esteem than comparing unfavorably to out-group members (Major, Sciacchitano, & Crocker, 1993), because in-group members provide a more relevant comparison standard.

The importance of interpretations is illustrated by research on stigma (Crocker, Major, & Steele, 1998; Crocker & Major, 1989; Major & O'Brien, 2005; Major, Quinton, & McCoy, 2002). Stigmatized identities provide a clear instance of situational devaluation, and social scientists usually assume that the experience of stigma lowers self-esteem (Crocker et al., 1998). Yet, targets of prejudice and discrimination do not always have low self-esteem, because they sometimes interpret the meaning of negative events in ways that are self-protective (Crocker & Major, 1989; Major, McCoy, & Quinton, 2002). For example, attributing negative events to prejudice or discrimination can protect self-esteem, but attributing positive events to one's stigmatized identity can hurt self-esteem (Crocker, Cornwell, & Major, 1993; Crocker et al., 1991). Reading about discrimination against one's in-group lowers self-esteem, but only for people who endorse a meritocracy ideology that success is a function of talent and hard work (Major, Kaiser, O'Brien, & McCoy, 2007).

In sum, research demonstrates that self-esteem is not only a fixed trait; state self-esteem fluctuates in situations of success and failure, acceptance and rejection, and valuation and devaluation of identities. The effects of these situations on self-esteem depends, however, on the meaning people make of them; some beliefs, attributions, and comparisons magnify these effects of situations on self-esteem, whereas others attenuate them.

STABILITY OF SELF-ESTEEM

Do contexts influence stability of self-esteem? To our knowledge, no research has addressed this question, perhaps because situational influences on stability of self-esteem are difficult to study in the laboratory; stability is typically operationalized as variability in self-esteem over time, usually at least several days. Personality approaches assume that instability measured over time reflects a dispositional characteristic of the person, but it could as easily reflect aspects of the situations, with some people in situations that promote self-esteem stability, and others in situations that promote self-esteem instability. Some situations may raise more doubts about the worth and value of the self, creating vulnerability, and consequent fluctuations, in self-esteem. For example, self-esteem may be more unstable in unfamiliar situations, where people are uncertain of their worth and value. Self-esteem may be more unstable in situations where people feel more stigmatized, or perceive more threats to their social identities. Other situations may involve more occasions of success and failure or acceptance and rejection, leading to greater instability of self-esteem in those contexts. Experience sampling studies or daily report studies could examine whether self-esteem is more unstable in some situations than others. Situational influences on stability of self-esteem could be a fruitful area for research, particularly in light of the negative effects of unstable self-esteem reviewed earlier.

CONTINGENCIES OF SELF-ESTEEM

Do situations influence contingencies of self-esteem? It seems plausible that different qualities are valued in different contexts, so context could activate or create different contingencies of self-esteem. For example, on the football field, physical strength is valued, so athletic ability may become a more important contingency of self-esteem in sports contexts. On a date, appearance and charm may be valued, so appearance may become a more important contingency in that context.

Although this question has rarely been studied directly, research supports the idea that situations can activate contingencies of self-esteem. In one line of research, Baldwin and his colleagues hypothesized that some significant others are more contingently accepting than others; reminders of these significant others may activate contingencies of self-worth (Baldwin, 1992). In support of this hypothesis, several studies show that priming conditionally accepting relationship partners leads to more negative self-evaluations, and strengthens cognitive associations between success and acceptance, and failure and rejection (Baldwin, 1994; Baldwin & Sinclair, 1996) For example, graduate students who were subliminally exposed to pictures of the scowling, disapproving face of their department chair rated their research ideas more negatively than those who were exposed to the smiling, approving face of another person (Baldwin, Carrell, & Lopez, 1990).

Building on the idea that reminders of conditionally accepting relationship partners activate contingencies of self-esteem, Arndt, Schimel, and their colleagues showed that priming participants with a conditionally accepting other (relative to

a nonconditionally accepting other), or being liked for accomplishments rather than intrinsic aspects of the self increases defense of self-esteem (Arndt, Schimel, Greenberg, & Pyszczynski, 2002; Schimel, Arndt, Pyszczynski, & Greenberg, 2001). Again, these studies provide indirect support for the idea that conditional acceptance, or reminders of conditionally accepting significant others, activates contingencies of self-worth.

To our knowledge, only one study has directly examined whether situations influence contingencies of self-esteem (Garcia & Crocker, 2007). In that study, undergraduate women from underrepresented racial and ethnic groups completed multiple brief reports of their momentary contingencies of self-esteem several times per day, in both academic and nonacademic contexts. More than 2/3 of the variance in contingencies of self-esteem occurred within participants, suggesting that contingencies may be more state-like than trait-like. Furthermore, participants' self-esteem was more contingent when they were in academic contexts (classrooms, the library) than other contexts. Garcia and Crocker (2007) hypothesized that their participants felt devalued or that their ability was suspect in academic contexts, leading to increased academic contingency. However, their study did not include a control sample of majority students, so this remains speculation.

In sum, the idea that situations influence contingencies of self-esteem seems plausible, but very little research has directly examined this issue. Situational influences on contingencies of self-worth would be a fruitful area for future research.

SELF-ESTEEM MOTIVES

In contrast to research on stability and contingencies of self-esteem, a great deal of research has examined situational influences on self-esteem motives. In generally, this research finds that anticipated, actual, and perceived self-threats of various sorts predict defense of self-esteem and self-images, which researchers interpret as evidence that self-esteem motives have been activated (e.g., Leary, Terry, Allen, & Tate, 2009; Pyszczynski, Greenberg, Solomon, Arndt, & Schimel, 2004; Tesser, 1988, 2000). Studies have variously threatened people's private images of themselves (i.e., self-esteem threats), other people's images of them (i.e., public image threats), and control over negative events (Leary et al., 2009).

Leary and his colleagues recently criticized much of this research for confounding these three types of self-threats, and argued that these three types of threats have distinct antecedents and consequences. Although this may be true, all three types of threats likely threaten self-esteem, as Leary et al. (2009) acknowledge; in our view (and data), private self-esteem concerns strongly implicate public image concerns (Crocker, Luhtanen, Blaine, & Broadnax, 1994) and loss of control, and vice versa (see Tetlock & Manstead, 1985, for a review). Public and private self-images are like conjoined twins; forcing a separation may do them both in. In fact, self-esteem threats, public image threats, and control threats all likely activate the self-preservation, or fight or flight physiological system (Dickerson & Kemeny, 2004; Henry & Wang, 1998). Different antecedents may reflect different means of threatening the self, and different consequences of these types of self-threat may reflect distinct strategies to restore self-esteem afforded by different situations, rather than implicate fundamentally different psychological processes. At the least, however, researchers should follow Leary et al.'s (2009) advice to be as precise as possible about the conceptual variable they intend to manipulate, the match of their operationalization to this conceptual variable, and potential confounds.

In most research on self-threats, self-esteem motives are not measured directly, but inferred from defensive responses to self-esteem threats, leaving open the possibility that some nonmotivational process accounts for the effects. For example, people tend to take credit for success and avoid responsibility for failure, which as noted previously can enhance and protect state self-esteem. But researchers have debated whether this findings stem from a motive to enhance and protect self-esteem, or from nonmotivated cognitive inferences; if people generally think they have value and worth and rate their abilities highly, it may be logical to conclude that failures result from external or unstable causes such as lack of effort, whereas successes result from internal and stable causes such as high ability (Bradley, 1978; Miller & Ross, 1975). Of course, this is not an either/or question; both nonmotivated inferential processes and motivations to maintain self-esteem and avoid negative affect may lead people to take credit for success and avoid blame for failure.

Accumulated research, too voluminous to review thoroughly here, provides compelling evidence that self-threats arouse self-esteem motives. Tesser's self-evaluation maintenance model posits that self-esteem is threatened when people are outperformed by a close other in a domain that is relevant to their sense of self (Tesser, 1988). For example, tennis champion Serena Williams might not feel threatened when outperformed at Scrabble by her sister Venus, and she might not feel threatened when outperformed at tennis by the winner of the men's singles championship, but according to the self-evaluation maintenance model, her self-esteem would be threatened if defeated by her sister at tennis. People can maintain self-esteem in this situation by either distancing from the close other, diminishing the relevance of the domain to the self, or altering their own or the other's performance so the social comparison favors the self (Tesser, 1988). For example, one study showed that people actually give more difficult clues to a friend than to a stranger, to hamper the friend's performance on a self-relevant task (Tesser & Smith, 1980).

Sociometer theory proposes that threats to relational value, (i.e., one's potential includibility in relationships and social groups) threaten self-esteem, and that self-esteem functions to monitor relational value, as a sort of early warning system that one is in danger of exclusion or rejection (Leary & Baumeister, 2000). According to sociometer theory, self-esteem motives and the motive to be included and accepted are indistinguishable. As noted, experiences of rejection and inclusion affect state self-esteem; they also can have powerful and widespread effects on cognition, self-regulation, prosocial behavior, and antisocial behavior (Baumeister, DeWall, Ciarocco, & Twenge, 2005; Baumeister, Twenge, & Nuss, 2002; Twenge, Baumeister, DeWall, Ciarocco, & Bartels, 2007; Twenge, Baumeister, Tice, & Stucke, 2001; Twenge, Catanese, & Baumeister, 2003). We find it difficult to interpret these effects as reflecting self-esteem or social inclusion motivation; becoming less intelligent, less able to self-regulate, more aggressive, and less helpful, would not seem to indicate the desire to restore self-esteem or increase one's includibility.

Terror management theory proposes that reminders of one's mortality activate the desire to defend self-esteem and one's worldview (Greenberg, Pyszczynski, & Solomon, 1986; Pyszczynski et al., 2004). According to terror management theory, without self-esteem people would be overwhelmed with terror resulting from awareness of the inevitability and unpredictability of their own death. Self-esteem depends on belief in a cultural worldview that specifies standards for what makes a person valuable, and satisfying those standards. Research based on terror management theory supports the view that reminders of one's mortality (i.e., mortality salience) increase self-esteem motivation, as indicated by bolstering self-esteem and one's world-view (see Pyszczynski et al., 2004, for a review). For example, mortality salience increases self-serving biases, such as viewing bogus positive feedback from astrological charts or personality questionnaires as especially valid (Dechesne, Janssen, & van Knippenberg, 2000).

In sum, considerable research is consistent with the view that self-threats of various sorts activate self-esteem motives, although many manipulations confound self-esteem threats, public image threats, and control threats, and motives are inferred, rather than directly measured, leaving some room for alternative interpretations. Despite alternative interpretations for some studies, when considered as a whole the evidence for situational influences on self-esteem motives seems compelling.

SELF-TRANSCENDENCE

Research also suggests situational influences on self-transcendence, or the capacity to rise above concerns about self-image or self-esteem. The most widely studied situational influence on self-transcendence is self-affirmation (Sherman & Cohen, 2006; Steele, 1988). Steele proposed that the purpose of the self-system is to maintain self-integrity, "a phenomenal experience of the self—self-conceptions and self-images—as adaptively and morally adequate, that is, as competent, good, coherent, unitary, stable, capable of free choice, capable 1 of controlling important outcomes, and so on" (Sherman & Cohen, 2006; Steele, 1988). When self-integrity—including self-esteem—is threatened, affirming the self even in an unrelated area enables people to transcend concerns about self-esteem.

Self-affirmation has been manipulated in a variety of ways, but the most common manipulation involves having people rank order or write about their most important values (see McQueen & Klein, 2006, for a review). In a typical self-affirmation study, people rank-order a list of values (e.g., politics, business, art, religion, social relationships) from most important to least important, and either write a paragraph about their most important value and why it is important to them (experimental condition), or their least important value and why it might be important to others (control condition). Self-affirmation manipulations such as this reduce or eliminate a wide range of responses to self-threats, including self-evaluation maintenance processes (Tesser, 2000), cognitive dissonance reduction (Steele & Liu, 1983), defensive responses to self-threatening

health information (Sherman, Nelson, & Steele, 2000), rumination about a frustrated goal (Koole, Smeets, van Knippenberg, & Dijksterhuis, 1999), perceptions of racism among Latinos (G. Adams, Tormala, & O'Brien, 2006), and even ideological close-mindedness and inflexibility during negotiation (Cohen et al., 2007; see Sherman & Cohen, 2006, for a recent review). Self-affirmation manipulations also have cognitive effects, such as increasing attention to threatening words (Klein & Harris, 2009), and physiological effects, such as decreasing physiological stress responses (Creswell et al., 2005; Sherman, Bunyan, Creswell, & Jaremka, 2009).

Although evidence that self-affirmation reduces defensiveness is strong, why it does so is less clear (Crocker, Niiya, & Mischkowski, 2008; Sherman & Cohen, 2006). Nonetheless, we interpret evidence of reduced defensiveness as indicating that self-affirmation enables people to transcend concerns about self-esteem, at least temporarily.

Little research has examined situational influences on self-compassion. In one study, participants recalled a negative event that made them feel bad about themselves (Leary, Tate, Adams, Batts Allen, & Hancock, 2007). The researchers induced a self-compassionate perspective by asking participants to list ways other people also experience similar events (common humanity), express kindness toward themselves (self-kindness), and describe their feelings in an objective and nonemotional fashion (mindfulness). Relative to three other conditions (boosting self-esteem, expressive writing, and a control condition), the self-compassion induction reduced negative feelings about the event, while increasing the personal responsibility participants accepted for the event.

In sum, research from a social psychological perspective clearly demonstrates situational influences on level of self-esteem, self-esteem motives, and self-transcendence; little research has examined situational influences on self-esteem stability or contingencies of self-esteem. Consistent with a Buddhist conception of self, this research suggests that self-esteem is fluid and impermanent, reflecting the momentary activation of self-relevant goals, thoughts, and judgments.

One strength of research that manipulates situational variables and measures their effects on self-esteem and its aspects is the ability to draw inferences about the causal effects of situations on the self. Apart from issues concerning operationalization of variables, this research suffers from an important limitation; people do not all respond in the same way to situational influences on self-esteem and related aspects. Studies that examine only the effect of situations treat individual differences in response to situational influences as error, or unexplained variance. Yet, a large body of research indicates that people differ in their response to situational influences on the self. This research marries the personality and social psychological approaches by examining Person X Situation interactions.

Person X Situation Interactions

Person X Situation interactions in self-esteem research asks two questions: Does dispositional self-esteem or aspects of self-esteem moderate the effects of events, and do person, or dispositional variables moderate effects of events on self-esteem and its aspects. Research has examined both of these questions, and the answer is a clear "yes."

SELF-ESTEEM AS A MODERATOR OF EFFECTS OF SITUATIONS OR EVENTS

By far the largest number of studies has examined whether level of trait self-esteem moderates how people respond to events, especially self-threats. Both high and low self-esteem people attempt to maintain, protect, and enhance the self, but they often use different strategies. Because high self-esteem people hold positive self-views with certainty and clarity, they do not expect to experience failure or rejection (Campbell, 1990). Consequently, they eagerly approach situations, anticipating positive outcomes (Heimpel, Elliot, & Wood, 2006; Leonardelli, Lakin, & Arkin, 2007). High self-esteem people do not feel the need to protect self-esteem from the possibility of future failures, they take credit for success, and respond favorably to it (Baumeister & Tice, 1985; Baumeister et al., 1989; Blaine & Crocker, 1993; Tice & Baumeister, 1990; Wood, Heimpel, Newby-Clark, & Ross, 2005). After failure or setbacks, however, high self-esteem people are defensive (Blaine & Crocker, 1993); for example, they blame failure on external or unstable causes (Bradley, 1978), and derogate others (Crocker & Luhtanen, 1990; Fein & Spencer, 1997).

Because low self-esteem people hold less positive, certain, and clear self-views (Campbell, 1990), they anticipate the possibility of failure or rejection and prepare for it in advance more than high self-esteem people (Baumeister & Tice, 1985; Baumeister et al., 1989; Blaine & Crocker, 1993; Tice & Baumeister, 1990; Wood et al., 2005). In public, low self-esteem people are more modest about themselves (Baumeister et al., 1989), and when failure is possible they

self-handicap to protect self-esteem from the possibility of failure (Tice & Baumeister, 1990, 1993). When they succeed, low self-esteem people feel anxious, do not think any more positively about themselves, and focus on the negative aspects of success (Wood et al., 2005).

PERSON X SITUATION EFFECTS ON STATE SELF-ESTEEM

Dispositional variables moderate the effects of situations and events on state self-esteem. People with more fragile or vulnerable self-esteem are, not surprisingly, more likely to drop in self-esteem following failure or setbacks. For example, people with contingent self-esteem experience larger drops in self-esteem when they fail, but mastery goals or incremental theories of intelligence can buffer the self-esteem of highly contingent people from failure (Dweck, Chiu, & Hong, 1995; Grant & Dweck, 2003; Niiya & Crocker, 2003, 2007). When they exert high effort, however, the self-esteem of highly contingent people drops even if they are learning oriented (Niiya et al., 2010). Diary studies show that these findings extend beyond the laboratory. For example, the more students base their self-esteem on academics, the more their self-esteem goes up when they get good grades and goes down when they get bad grades (Crocker, Karpinski, et al., 2003). In a sample of college seniors applying to graduate school, basing self-esteem on academics predicted how much self-esteem went up on days students received an acceptance, and went down on days they received a rejection (Crocker et al., 2002).

Instability of self-esteem and self-compassion also moderate reactions to events, although few studies have examined these issues. People with unstable self-esteem feel worse following negative events and better following positive events (Greenier et al., 1999). Self-compassion also moderates reactions to success and failure; students higher in self-compassion who perceived a recent midterm grade as a failure reported using more emotion-focused coping strategies and fewer avoidance-focused coping strategies (Neff et al., 2005).

In sum, most personality and social psychologists think in terms of Person X Situation interactions; few personality psychologists believe that situations do not affect the expression of personality, and few social psychologists believe that individual differences do not affect how people respond to situations (e.g., Holmes & Wood, 2009; Reis, 2009). In the domain of the self and self-esteem, most studies have examined how trait self-esteem moderates reactions to events such as success and failure, and how preexisting vulnerabilities, such as self-esteem contingencies moderate how self-esteem fluctuates in response to positive or negative events. Few studies have examined how instability of self-esteem or indicators of self-transcendence (i.e., self-compassion) moderate responses to situations or events such as success and failure. To date, research on instability of self-esteem and self-compassion has seldom examined how these individuals moderate responses to specific events either manipulated in the laboratory or assessed repeatedly in diary studies; studies such as this are needed to disentangle causal associations.

Limitations of the Person, Situation, and Person X Situation Approaches to the Self

Although the Person X Situation framework has stimulated a great deal of research and had considerable heuristic value for social and personality psychologists, in our view it limits understanding of the self because it treats both the person and the situation as static. In laboratory experiments, individual differences are usually measured only once, but nonetheless are assumed to reflect enduring dispositions. Most aspects of the situation are held constant, varying only in ways fixed by the experimenter across experimental conditions. For example, in Crocker's laboratory research on contingencies of self-worth, contingencies are typically measured once, and success or failure manipulated as an independent variable (e.g., Niiya et al., 2010; Niiya et al., 2004). Of course, the same construct, such as self-esteem, may be an individual difference person variable in the Person X Situation interaction in one study, and an outcome, or dependent variable, in a second study; for example, contingencies of self-worth could be consequences of success and failure. Still, these studies cannot reveal how persons and situations mutually influence each other in a process that unfolds over time.

Self and identity are not static, fixed traits or individual differences, nor are they solely responses to situations. Furthermore, people and situations are not orthogonal or independent of one another, as Person X Situation approaches assume. In reality, people and situations (especially social situations) are both dynamic, changing over time. People shape the situations they experience and those situations, in turn, change people in a constantly evolving process of mutual influence (Bowers, 1973; Endler & Magnusson, 1976; Snyder & Ickes, 1985).

For social psychologists, many or most situations of interest are social or interpersonal in nature (Reis, 2009), and interpersonal relationships may constitute some of the most important influences on self and identity (e.g., Leary, 2007). People can create their interpersonal situations in their own minds, independent of "objective" reality, through their interpretations of others' behavior (Andersen & Chen, 2002; Baldwin, 1992; Snyder, 1984; Swann, De La Ronde, & Hixon, 1994; Swann, Hixon, & De La Ronde, 1992). Alternatively, people can create their objective interpersonal situations when their self-relevant goals and interpretations of others' behavior shape the relationship partners they seek and how they interact with others, which affects others' interpersonal situation or context (Swann et al., 1994; Swann et al., 1992). Others may then respond to this altered situation in ways that change the interpersonal situation for the self.

For example, research on rejection sensitivity demonstrates a self-fulfilling prophecy in which people who anxiously expect rejection overinterpret the behavior of relationship partners as rejecting, and overreact to the perceived rejection, which undermines their relationships and drives relationship partners away, confirming and reinforcing their initial anxious expectation of rejection (Downey et al., 1998) with implications for each persons' experience and self. Analyses of persons (i.e., stable dispositions), fixed situations, and their interaction do not capture this dynamic, evolving, mutually constituting dance between the person and the situation.

Interpersonal and Intrapersonal Dynamics of the Self

Research on the self, and self-esteem in particular, has begun to adopt this dynamic view of the mutual influences of persons and situations over time. Swann and his colleagues' research on self-verification theory examines how people seek out and create social environments that confirm their self-views (even negative self-views), and selectively attend to, encode, recall, and interpret information in ways that confirm their self-views (see Swann et al., 2003, for a review). Swann and his colleagues' research on self-verification theory nicely illustrates the interdependence of persons and their social situations, challenging the view that persons and situations are independent variables that can be understood by measuring persons and manipulating the situation.

When people shape their situations, do those situations then shape the self? Research on self-verification theory is not well-suited to answer this question, because it assumes that people create situations consistent with their self-views; self-verification strivings should lead to stability rather than change in the self. Other research, however, suggests that the self can shape situations, which in turn change the self.

DYNAMICS OF RISK REGULATION IN RELATIONSHIPS

Murray and her colleagues' risk-regulation model of relationships also takes a dynamic perspective on the self (Murray, Holmes, & Collins, 2006). According to the risk-regulation model, self-esteem shapes people's perceptions of partners' caring and esteem for them, which then determines whether or not they risk rejection by becoming dependent on and connected to partners. When people with low self-esteem believe that partners don't care and have low regard for them, they react in self-protective ways that alienate partners and undermine relationship quality. For example, when low self-esteem people felt rejected by partners one day, they reported being more cold, critical, and negative toward partners the following day (Murray, Bellavia, Rose, & Griffin, 2003), which alienates their partners; partners of low self-esteem people report long-term decreases in love and relationship satisfaction (Murray, Griffin, Rose, & Bellavia, 2003). When people with high self-esteem believe that partners don't care and have low regard for them, they react in ways that draw their partners closer, leading to better relationship outcomes. Over time, people may "recalibrate," their relationship behaviors as a function of more or less adaptive reactions to potential risk. Furthermore, relationship partners' regard for the self predicts change in self-perceptions over time, so people who idealize their relationship partners actually create the partners they want (Murray, Holmes, & Griffin, 1996).

DYNAMICS OF SELF-ESTEEM AND SOCIAL BONDS

Stinson and colleagues (Stinson et al., 2008) also demonstrated a reciprocal and dynamic association between self-esteem and social bonds over time. As Murray and Holmes' research shows, people with low trait self-esteem are overly sensitive to cues about others' regard for them and adopt self-protective interaction styles that limit their connections to others, whereas people with high trait self-esteem adopt relationship-promoting interaction styles that foster social bonds (Murray, 2005; Murray, Griffin, et al., 2003; Murray et al., 2006). The reduced

quality of social bonds should then predict lowered self-esteem, which in turn promotes interaction styles emphasizing self-protection or relationship-promotion. Data collected across 10 weeks supports this reciprocal, dynamic process: Week 0 self-esteem predicted higher quality social bonds at Weeks 2 and 4, which predicted increased self-esteem from Weeks 0 to 6, which then predicted increased social bonds at Weeks 8 and10 (Stinson et al., 2008).

The Stinson et al. study examined individuals, not their relationship partners, so it is unclear whether this dynamic, self-reinforcing cycle of low self-esteem and poor quality social relationships operated only in the minds of the research participants, or if they interacted in ways that caused others to withdraw or reject them. In addition, Stinson et al. did not examine the process by which low self-esteem impairs social bonds, and social bonds in turn impair self-esteem. Nonetheless, this study exemplifies research on the dynamics of self-esteem, in which self-esteem and relationships (or perceptions of relationships) mutually influence each other over time.

Taken together, the studies by Stinson et al. (2008) and Murray and her colleagues illustrate the dynamic process by which the self shapes social situations, which in turn shape the self. The dynamic models of Stinson et al. (2008) and Murray and her colleagues focus on self-esteem, but dynamic models could also be developed for contingencies of self-esteem, self-esteem motives, and self-transcendence. How do these aspects of the self shape the interpersonal situations people experience, and how do those situations, in turn, shape these aspects of the self?

DYNAMICS OF INTERPERSONAL GOALS, SELF-ESTEEM, AND OTHERS' REGARD

Canevello and Crocker (2010) showed that self-image goals predict decreased responsiveness to the needs of college roommates, who are less responsive in return. Canevello and Crocker (2011) examined reciprocal influences between people's chronic interpersonal goals, their self-esteem, their partners' esteem for them, and their partners' self-esteem. In a longitudinal study, they found that interpersonal goals can have paradoxical effects; when people try to get others to view them in a positive light (i.e., when they have self-image goals), their responsiveness to relationship partners decreases and their partners' responsiveness also decreases. As a result of these processes, their partners' regard for them decreases, their own self-esteem decreases, and their partners' self-esteem decreases. In contrast, when people chronically have compassionate goals, their responsiveness increases, and their partner's responsiveness also increases. As a result, their partners' regard for them increases, their own self-esteem increases, and their partners' self-esteem increases.

Canevello and Crocker (2011) also examined reciprocal effects of self-esteem on interpersonal goals. The lower people's self-esteem, the more their self-image goals increased and their compassionate goals decreased over the course of the study. Thus, interpersonal goals shape relationship processes that predict change in self-esteem, and self-esteem predicts change in interpersonal goals, creating the potential for upward and downward spirals of self-esteem and relationship processes. Truly interpersonal dynamic models could extend research on the self to examine how one person's self shapes another person's self over time. When effects are reciprocal, upward and downward spirals could lead to rapid improvement or deterioration in relationships, which in turn lead to relatively rapid change in the self.

Conclusions

Theoretical accounts of the dynamic processes by which the self and social situations mutually influence each other may better capture the reality of the self than Person X Situation analyses that assume that persons and situations are static and independent of one another. Furthermore, dynamic models can illuminate when and how the self changes, and the process by which people shape their situations and situations shape persons, providing a deeper understanding of the self for both personality and social psychologists.

Studying dynamic processes of the self will require some social and personality psychologists to expand their methodological repertoire beyond laboratory experiments and cross-sectional correlational designs. Dynamic processes can only be detected in studies that involve multiple assessments over time, such as experience sampling and daily or weekly diary studies, or laboratory studies with multiple measurements. Short-term longitudinal studies can illuminate associations and processes that might be missed in experimental or simple correlational designs, and in long-term longitudinal studies that assess participants yearly, or even less often. Furthermore, to study the mutual influence of persons and their social situations researchers must include other people, such as friends, roommates, romantic partners, or coworkers, in their studies. Studies of the self, including studies of the social self, rarely include other people. When they

do, others are usually in the role of confederates of the experimenter, who are trained to keep their behavior constant, so their behavior will not be influenced by characteristics of the research participant. Yet, in our view such a research strategy intentionally removes the very dynamic processes that self and identity researchers should be studying (e.g., Sadler & Woody, 2003).

We suspect that some researchers resist using longitudinal designs to study self and identity and do not include relationship partners in their studies because these methods sacrifice the power of laboratory experiments to test causal associations. However, longitudinal designs in which participants and their relationship partners are repeatedly assessed can provide information pointing to plausible causal pathways, and can rule out causal associations between variables. For example, lagged analyses that test residual change from one time point to the next permit conclusions concerning the plausibility of causal associations. Quasi-experimental designs, although not ideal, can also provide information about the plausibility of causal associations (e.g., Shadish, Cook, & Campbell, 2002; West, 2009).

Finally, we note that experiments do not always provide the basis for strong causal inferences about process. Manipulating independent variables can provide evidence of causal associations, but the gap between the conceptual independent variable and the operationalization of that variable in a particular study can lead to erroneous conclusions about causal processes. In the study of the self, for example, researchers have studied "self-affirmation" by having participants write about important values; these manipulations reduce defensiveness, as we noted previously. However, whether this manipulation actually affirms the self has not been established (Sherman & Cohen, 2006); it may, instead, enable people to transcend the self (Crocker et al., 2008). Thus, although they are often held up as the gold standard of research designs in social and personality psychology, laboratory experiments are not without their weaknesses.

Although we propose that social and personality psychology could benefit from a more dynamic, reciprocal, and interpersonal approach to the study of persons and situations, there may also be limits to dynamic processes. For example, dynamic processes may not operate in all situations. Dynamic effects may emerge in some social situations, whereas other situations may in fact be static. We suspect that dynamic processes of the self in social situations occur most often during times of change. Consequently, they may emerge during transitions (e.g., adolescence and early adulthood, the transition to college, or the transition to retirement) but not in times of relative stability. Further, some types of situations and particular types of dispositions may be most likely to be constructed in this dynamic way. For example, people higher in openness to experience may be more likely to experience dynamic processes. Although we are far from having all of the answers to these questions, it is clear that raising them will stimulate further research and clarify our understanding of self and identity.

References

Adams, C. E., & Leary, M. R. (2007). Promoting self-compassion-ate attitudes toward eating among restrictive and guilty eaters. *Journal of Social and Clinical Psychology, 26,* 1120–1144.

Adams, G., Tormala, T. T., & O'Brien, L. T. (2006). The effect of self-affirmation on perception of racism. *Journal of Experimental Social Psychology, 42,* 616–626.

Andersen, S. M., & Chen, S. (2002). The relational self: An interpersonal social-cognitive theory. *Psychological Review, 109,* 619–645.

Arndt, J., Schimel, J., Greenberg, J., & Pyszczynski, T. (2002). The intrinsic self and defensiveness: Evidence that activating the intrinsic self reduces self-handicapping and conformity. *Personality and Social Psychology Bulletin, 28,* 671–683.

Baldwin, M. W. (1992). Relational schemas and the processing of social information. *Psychological Bulletin, 112,* 461–484.

Baldwin, M. W. (1994). Primed relational schemas as a source of self-evaluative reactions. *Journal of Social and Clinical Psychology, 13,* 380–403.

Baldwin, M. W., Carrell, S. E., & Lopez, D. F. (1990). Priming relationship schemas: My advisor and the Pope are watching me from the back of my mind. *Journal of Experimental Social Psychology, 26,* 435–454.

Baldwin, M. W., & Sinclair, L. (1996). Self-esteem and "if then" contingencies of interpersonal acceptance. *Journal of Personality and Social Psychology, 71,* 1130–1141.

Barnes, S., Brown, K. W., Krusemark, E., Campbell, W. K., & Rogge, R. D. (2007). The role of mindfulness in romantic relationship satisfaction and responses to relationship stress. *Journal of Marital and Family Therapy, 33,* 482–500.

Baumeister, R. F. (1998). The self. In D. T. Gilbert, S. T. Fiske & G. Lindzey (Eds.), *The handbook of social psychology* (4 ed., Vol. 2, pp. 680-740). New York: McGraw-Hill.

Baumeister, R. F., Campbell, J. D., Krueger, J. I., & Vohs, K. D. (2003). Does high self-esteem cause better performance, interpersonal success, happiness, or healthier lifestyles? *Psychological Science in the Public Interest, 4,* 1–44.

Baumeister, R. F., DeWall, C. N., Ciarocco, N. J., & Twenge, J. M. (2005). Social exclusion impairs self-regulation. *Journal of Personality and Social Psychology, 88,* 589–604.

Baumeister, R. F., & Tice, D. M. (1985). Self-esteem and responses to success and failure: Subsequent performance and intrinsic motivation. *Journal of Personality, 53,* 450–467.

Baumeister, R. F., Tice, D. M., & Hutton, D. G. (1989). Self-presentational motivations and personality differences in self-esteem. *Journal of Personality, 57,* 547–579.

Baumeister, R. F., Twenge, J. M., & Nuss, C. K. (2002). Effects of social exclusion on cognitive processes: Anticipated alone-ness reduces intelligent thought. *Journal of Personality and Social Psychology, 83,* 817–827.

Baumeister, R. F., & Vohs, K. D. (2001). Narcissism as addiction to esteem. *Psychological Inquiry, 12,* 206–210.

Beauregard, K. S., & Dunning, D. (2001). Defining self-worth: Trait self-esteem moderates the use of self-serving trait definitions in social judgment. *Motivation and Emotion, 25,* 135–161.

Blaine, B., & Crocker, J. (1993). Self-esteem and self-serving biases in reactions to positive and negative events: An integrative review. In R. F. Baumeister (Ed.), *Self-esteem: The puzzle of low self-regard* (pp. 55–85). Hillsdale, NJ: Erlbaum.

Blascovich, J., & Tomaka, J. (1991). Measures of self-esteem. In J. P. Robinson, P. R. Shaver, & L. S. Wrightsman (Eds.), *Measures of personality and social psychological attitudes* (pp. 115–160). San Diego, CA: Academic.

Bosson, J. K., Swann, W. B., Jr., & Pennebaker, J. W. (2000). Stalking the perfect measure of implicit self-esteem: The blind men and the elephant revisited? *Journal of Personality and Social Psychology, 79,* 631–643.

Bowers, K. S. (1973). Situationism in psychology: An analysis and a critique. *Psychological Review, 80,* 307–336.

Bradley, G. W. (1978). Self-serving biases in the attribution process: A reexamination of the fact or fiction question. *Journal of Personality and Social Psychology, 36,* 56–71.

Brockner, J., Gardner, M., Bierman, J., Mahan, T., Thomas, B., Weiss, W., et al. (1983). The roles of self-esteem and self-consciousness in the Wortman-Brehm model of reactance and learned helplessness. *Journal of Personality and Social Psychology, 45,* 199–209.

Brown, G. P., Hammen, C. L., Craske, M. G., & Wickens, T. D. (1995). Dimensions of dysfunctional attitudes as vulnerabilities to depressive symptoms. *Journal of Abnormal Psychology, 104,* 431–435.

Brown, J. D. (1986). Evaluations of self and others: Self-enhancement biases in social judgments. *Social Cognition, 4,* 353–376.

Brown, K. W., & Ryan, R. M. (2003). The benefits of being present: Mindfulness and its role in psychological well-being. *Journal of Personality and Social Psychology, 84,* 822–848.

Brown, K. W., Ryan, R. M., & Creswell, J. D. (2007). Mindfulness: Theoretical foundations and evidence for its salutary effects. *Psychological Inquiry, 18,* 211–237.

Brown, K. W., Ryan, R. M., Creswell, J. D., & Niemiec, C. P. (2008). Beyond me: Mindful responses to social threat. In H. Wayment & J. Brauer (Eds.), *Transcending self-interest: Psychological explorations of the quiet ego.* Washington, DC: American Psychological Association.

Campbell, J. D. (1986). Similarity and uniqueness: The effects of attribute type, relevance, and individual differences in self-esteem and depression. *Journal of Personality and Social Psychology, 50,* 281–294.

Campbell, J. D. (1990). Self-esteem and clarity of the self-concept. *Journal of Personality and Social Psychology, 59,* 538–549.

Campbell, J. D., Trapnell, P. D., Heine, S. J., Katz, I. M., Lavallee, L. F., & Lehman, D. R. (1996). Self-concept clarity: Measurement, personality correlates, and cultural boundaries. *Journal of Personality and Social Psychology, 70,* 141–156.

Canevello, A., & Crocker, J. (2010). Creating good relationships: Responsiveness, relationship quality, and interpersonal goals. *Journal of Personality and Social Psychology, 99,* 78–106.

Canevello, A., & Crocker, J. (2011). Interpersonal goals, others' regard for the self, and self-esteem: The paradoxical consequences of self-image and compassionate goals. *European Journal of Social Psychology, 41,* 422-434.

Cohen, G. L., Sherman, D. K., Bastardi, A., Hsu, L., McGoey, M., & Ross, L. (2007). Bridging the partisan divide: Self-affirmation reduces ideological closed-mindedness and inflexibility in negotiation. *Journal of Personality and Social Psychology, 93,* 415–430.

Coopersmith, S. (1967). *The antecedents of self-esteem.* San Francisco: Freeman.

Coyne, J. C., Pepper, C. M., & Flynn, H. (1999). Significance of prior episodes of depression in two patient populations. *Journal of Consulting and Clinical Psychology, 67,* 76–81.

Creswell, J. D., Welch, W. T., Taylor, S. E., Sherman, D. K., Gruenewald, T. L., & Mann, T. (2005). Affirmation of personal values buffers neuroendocrine and psychological stress responses. *Psychological Science, 16,* 846–851.

Crocker, J., & Canevello, A. (2008). Creating and undermining social support in communal relationships: The role of compassionate and self-image goals. *Journal of Personality and Social Psychology, 95,* 555–575.

Crocker, J., Canevello, A., Breines, J. G., & Flynn, H. (2010). Interpersonal goals and change in anxiety and dysphoria in first-semester college students. *Journal of Personality and Social Psychology, 98,* 1009–1024.

Crocker, J., Cornwell, B., & Major, B. M. (1993). The stigma of overweight: Affective consequences of attributional ambiguity. *Journal of Personality and Social Psychology, 64,* 60–70.

Crocker, J., Karpinski, A., Quinn, D. M., & Chase, S. (2003). When grades determine self-worth: Consequences of contingent self-worth for male and female engineering and psychology majors. *Journal of Personality and Social Psychology, 85,* 507–516.

Crocker, J., & Luhtanen, R. K. (1990). Collective self-esteem and ingroup bias. *Journal of Personality and Social Psychology, 58,* 60–67.

Crocker, J., & Luhtanen, R. K. (2003). Level of self-esteem and contingencies of self-worth: Unique effects on academic, social, and financial problems in college students. *Personality and Social Psychology Bulletin, 29,* 701–712.

Crocker, J., Luhtanen, R., Blaine, B., & Broadnax, S. (1994). Collective self-esteem and psychological well-being among white, black, and Asian college students. *Personality and Social Psychology Bulletin, 20,* 502–513.

Crocker, J., Luhtanen, R., Cooper, M. L., & Bouvrette, S. A. (2003). Contingencies of self-worth in college students: Measurement and theory. *Journal of Personality and Social Psychology, 85,* 894–908.

Crocker, J., & Major, B. M. (1989). Social stigma and self-esteem: The self-protective properties of stigma. *Psychological Review, 96,* 608–630.

Crocker, J., Major, B., & Steele, C. M. (1998). Social stigma. In D. Gilbert, S. T. Fiske, & G. Lindzey (Eds.), *Handbook of social psychology* (4th ed., Vol. 2, pp. 504–553). New York: McGraw-Hill.

Crocker, J., Niiya, Y., & Mischkowski, D. (2008). Why does writing about important values reduce defensiveness? The role of positive, other-directed feelings. *Psychological Science, 19,* 740–747.

Crocker, J., & Nuer, N. (2003). The relentless quest for self-esteem. *Psychological Inquiry, 14,* 31–34.

Crocker, J., & Park, L. E. (2004). The costly pursuit of self-esteem. *Psychological Bulletin, 130,* 392–414.

Crocker, J., Sommers, S. R., & Luhtanen, R. K. (2002). Hopes dashed and dreams fulfilled: Contingencies of self-worth and admissions to graduate school. *Personality and Social Psychology Bulletin, 28,* 1275–1286.

Crocker, J., Voelkl, K., Testa, M., & Major, B. M. (1991). Social stigma: Affective consequences of attributional ambiguity. *Journal of Personality and Social Psychology, 60,* 218–228.

Crocker, J., & Wolfe, C. T. (2001). Contingencies of self-worth. *Psychological Review, 108,* 593–623.

Dechesne, M., Janssen, J., & van Knippenberg, A. (2000). Derogation and distancing as terror management strategies: The moderating role of need for closure and permeability of group boundaries. *Journal of Personality and Social Psychology, 79,* 923–932.

Deci, E. L., & Ryan, R. M. (1995). Human autonomy: The basis for true self-esteem. In M. H. Kernis (Ed.), *Efficacy, agency, and self-esteem* (pp. 31–49). New York: Plenum.

Dickerson, S. S., & Kemeny, M. E. (2004). Acute stressors and cortisol responses: A theoretical integration and synthesis of laboratory research. *Psychological Bulletin, 130,* 355–391.

Diener, E. (1984). Subjective well-being. *Psychological Bulletin, 95,* 542–575.

Diener, E., Wolsic, B., & Fujita, F. (1995). Physical attractiveness and subjective well-being. *Journal of Personality and Social Psychology, 69,* 120–129.

Donnellan, M. B., Trzesniewski, K. H., Robins, R. W., Moffitt, T. E., & Caspi, A. (2005). Low self-esteem is related to aggression, antisocial behavior, and delinquency. *Psychological Science, 16,* 328–335.

Downey, G., Freitas, A. L., Michaelis, B., & Khouri, H. (1998). The self-fulfilling prophecy in close relationships: Rejection sensitivity and rejection by romantic partners. *Journal of Personality and Social Psychology, 75,* 545–560.

Dweck, C. S., Chiu, C., & Hong, Y. (1995). Implicit theories and their role in judgments and reactions: A world from two perspectives. *Psychological Inquiry, 6,* 267–285.

Dykman, B. M. (1998). Integrating cognitive and motivational factors in depression: Initial tests of a goal orientation approach. *Journal of Personality and Social Psychology, 74,* 139–158.

Endler, N. S., & Magnusson, D. (1976). Toward an interactional psychology of personality. *Psychological Bulletin, 83,* 956–974.

Farnham, S. D., Greenwald, A. G., & Banaji, M. R. (1999). Implicit self-esteem. In D. Abrams & M. A. Hogg (Eds.), *Social identity and social cognition* (pp. 230–248). Malden, MA: Blackwell.

Fein, S., & Spencer, S. J. (1997). Prejudice as self-image maintenance: Affirming the self through derogating others. *Journal of Personality and Social Psychology, 73,* 31–44.

Franck, E., & De Raedt, R. (2007). Self-esteem reconsidered: Unstable self-esteem outperforms level of self-esteem as vulnerability marker for depression. *Behaviour Research and Therapy, 45,* 1531–1541.

Gabriel, M. T., Critelli, J. W., & Ee, J. S. (1994). Narcissistic illusions in self-evaluations of intelligence and attractiveness. *Journal of Personality, 62,* 143–155.

Garcia, J. A., & Crocker, J. (2007). Women of color in the academy: Effects of context and identity on contingent self-worth. In A. J. Fuligni (Ed.), *Contesting stereotypes and creating identities: Social categories, social identities, and educational participation* (pp. 160–179). New York: Russell Sage.

Grant, H., & Dweck, C. S. (2003). Clarifying achievement goals and their impact. *Journal of Personality and Social Psychology, 85,* 541–553.

Greenberg, J., Pyszczynski, T., & Solomon, S. (1986). The causes and consequences of the need for self-esteem: A terror management theory. In R. F. Baumeister (Ed.), *Public self and private self* (pp. 189–207). New York: Springer-Verlag.

Greenier, K. D., Kernis, M. H., McNamara, C. W., Waschull, S. B., Berry, A. J., Herlocker, C. E., et al. (1999). Individual differences in reactivity to daily events: Examining the roles of stability and level of self-esteem. *Journal of Personality, 67,* 185–208.

Harter, S. (1993). Causes and consequences of low self-esteem in children and adolescents. In R. G. Baumeister (Ed.), *Self-esteem: The puzzle of low self-regard* (pp. 87–116). New York: Plenum.

Heatherton, T. F., & Polivy, J. (1991). Development and validation of a scale for measuring state self-esteem. *Journal of Personality and Social Psychology, 60,* 895–910.

Heimpel, S. A., Elliot, A. J., & Wood, J. V. (2006). Basic personality dispositions, self-esteem, and personal goals: An approach-avoidance analysis. *Journal of Personality, 74,* 1293–1319.

Heine, S. J., Lehman, D. R., Markus, H. R., & Kitayama, S. (1999). Is there a universal need for positive self-regard? *Psychological Review, 106,* 766–795.

Helgeson, V. S. (1994). Relation of agency and communion to well-being: Evidence and potential explanations. *Psychological Bulletin, 116,* 412–428.

Henry, J. P., & Wang, S. (1998). Effects of early stress on adult affiliative behavior. *Psychoneuroendocrinology, 23,* 863–875.

Holmes, J. G., & Wood, J. V. (2009). Interpersonal situations as affordances: The example of self-esteem. *Journal of Research in Personality, 43,* 250–250.

James, W. (1910). The self. In W. James (Ed.), *Psychology: The briefer course* (pp. 41–49). New York: Holt.

Jordan, C. H., Spencer, S. J., & Zanna, M. P. (2005). Types of high self-esteem and prejudice: How implicit self-esteem relates to ethnic discrimination among high explicit self-esteem individuals. *Personality and Social Psychology Bulletin, 31,* 693–702.

Kernis, M. H. (2003). Toward a conceptualization of optimal self-esteem. *Psychological Inquiry, 14,* 1–26.

Kernis, M. H., Brown, A. C., & Brody, G. H. (2000). Fragile self-esteem in children and its associations with perceived patterns of parent-child communication. *Journal of Personality, 68,* 225–252.

Kernis, M. H., Cornell, D. P., Sun, C.-R., Berry, A., & Harlow, T. (1993). There's more to self-esteem than whether it is high or low: The importance of stability of self-esteem. *Journal of Personality and Social Psychology, 65,* 1190–1204.

Kernis, M. H., Grannemann, B. D., & Barclay, L. C. (1989). Stability and level of self-esteem as predictors of anger arousal and hostility. *Journal of Personality and Social Psychology, 56,* 1013–1023.

Kernis, M. H., & Waschull, S. B. (1995). The interactive roles of stability and level of self-esteem: Research and theory. In M. P. Zanna (Ed.), *Advances in experimental social psychology* (Vol. 27, pp. 93–141). San Diego, CA: Academic.

Klein, W. M. P., & Harris, P. R. (2009). Self-affirmation enhances attentional bias toward threatening components of a persuasive message. *Psychological Science, 20,* 1463–1467.

Koole, S. L., Pelham, B. W., Spencer, S. J., Fein, S., Zanna, M. P., & Olson, J. M. (2003). On the nature of implicit self-esteem: The case of the name letter effect. In *Motivated social perception: The Ontario symposium* (Vol. 9, pp. 93–116). Mahwah, NJ: Erlbaum.

Kornfield, J. (1993). A path with heart. New York: Bantam.

Koole, S. L., Smeets, K., van Knippenberg, A., & Dijksterhuis, A. (1999). The cessation of rumination through self-affirmation. *Journal of Personality and Social Psychology, 77,* 111–125.

Kuiper, N. A., & Olinger, L. J. (1986). Dysfunctional attitudes and a self-worth contingency model of depression. In P. C. Kendall (Ed.), *Advances in cognitive-behavioral research and therapy* (pp. 115–142). Orlando, FL: Academic.

Leary, M. R. (2004). *The curse of the self: Self-awareness, egotism, and the quality of human life.* New York: Oxford University Press.

Leary, M. R. (2007). Motivational and emotional aspects of the self. *Annual Review of Psychology, 58,* 317–344.

Leary, M. R., Adams, C. E., & Tate, E. B. (2006). Hypo-egoic self-regulation: Exercising self-control by diminishing the influence of the self. *Journal of Personality, 74,* 1803–1831.

Leary, M. R., & Baumeister, R. F. (2000). The nature and function of self-esteem: Sociometer theory. In M. Zanna (Ed.), *Advances in experimental social psychology* (Vol. 32, pp. 1–62). San Diego, CA: Academic.

Leary, M. R., Tambor, E. S., Terdal, S. K., & Downs, D. L. (1995). Self-esteem as an interpersonal monitor: The sociometer hypothesis. *Journal of Personality and Social Psychology, 68,* 518–530.

Leary, M. R., Tate, E. B., Adams, C. E., Batts Allen, A., & Hancock, J. (2007). Self-compassion and reactions to unpleasant self-relevant events: The implications of treating oneself kindly. *Journal of Personality and Social Psychology, 92,* 887–904.

Leary, M. R., Terry, M. L., Allen, A. B., & Tate, E. B. (2009). The concept of ego threat in social and personality psychology: Is ego threat a viable scientific construct? *Personality and Social Psychology Review, 13,* 151–164.

Leonardelli, G. J., Lakin, J. L., & Arkin, R. M. (2007). A regulatory focus model of self-evaluation. *Journal of Experimental Social Psychology, 43,* 1002–1009.

Major, B., Kaiser, C. R., O'Brien, L. T., & McCoy, S. K. (2007). Perceived discrimination as worldview threat or worldview confirmation: Implications for self-esteem. *Journal of Personality and Social Psychology, 92,* 1068–1086.

Major, B., McCoy, S. K., & Quinton, W. (2002). Antecedents and consequences of attributions to discrimination: Theoretical and empirical advances. In M. P. Zanna (Ed.), *Advances in experimental social psychology* (Vol. 34, pp. 251–349). San Diego, CA: Academic.

Major, B., & O'Brien, L. T. (2005). The social psychology of stigma. *Annual Review of Psychology, 56,* 393–421.

Major, B., Quinton, W. J., & McCoy, S. K. (2002). Antecedents and consequences of attributions to discrimination: Theoretical and empirical advances. In M. P. Zanna (Ed.), *Advances in experimental social psychology* (Vol. 34, pp. 251–330). San Diego: Academic Press.

Major, B., Sciacchitano, A. M., & Crocker, J. (1993). In-group versus out-group comparisons and self-esteem. *Personality and Social Psychology Bulletin, 19,* 711–721.

Markus, H. R., & Kitayama, S. (1991). Culture and the self : Implications for cognition, emotion, and motivation. *Psychological Review, 98,* 224–253.

Maslow, A. H. (1968). *Motivation and personality.* New York: Harper & Row.

McFarland, C., & Ross, M. (1982). Impact of causal attributions on affective reactions to success and failure. *Journal of Personality and Social Psychology, 43,* 937–946.

McQueen, A., & Klein, W. M. P. (2006). Experimental manipulations of self-affirmation: A systematic review. *Self and Identity, 5,* 289–354.

Mecca, A. M., Smelser, N. J., & Vasconcellos, J. (1989). *The social importance of self-esteem.* Berkeley: University of California Press.

Miller, D. T., & Ross, M. (1975). Self-serving biases in attribution of causality: Fact or fiction? *Psychological Bulletin, 82,* 213–225.

Mischel, W., & Shoda, Y. (1995). A cognitive-affective system theory of personality: Reconceptualizing situations, dispositions, dynamics, and invariance in personality structure. *Psychological Review, 102,* 246–268.

Morse, S., & Gergen, K. J. (1970). Social comparison, self-consistency, and the concept of self. *Journal of Personality and Social Psychology, 16,* 148–156.

Murray, S. L. (2005). Regulating the risks of closeness: A relationship-specific sense of felt security. *Current Directions in Psychological Science, 14,* 74–78.

Murray, S. L., Bellavia, G. M., Rose, P., & Griffin, D. W. (2003). Once hurt, twice hurtful: How perceived regard regulates daily marital interactions. *Journal of Personality and Social Psychology, 84,* 126–147.

Murray, S. L., Griffin, D. W., Rose, P., & Bellavia, G. M. (2003). Calibrating the sociometer: The relational contingencies of self-esteem. *Journal of Personality and Social Psychology, 85,* 63–84.

Murray, S. L., Holmes, J. G., & Collins, N. L. (2006). Optimizing assurance: The risk regulation system in relationships. *Psychological Bulletin, 132,* 641–666.

Murray, S. L., Holmes, J. G., & Griffin, D. W. (1996). The self-fulfilling nature of positive illusions in romantic relationships: Love is not blind, but prescient. *Journal of Personality and Social Psychology, 71,* 1155–1180.

Neff, K. D. (2003). The development and validation of a scale to measure self-compassion. *Self and Identity, 2,* 223–250.

Neff, K. D. (2009). The role of self-compassion in development: A healthier way to relate to oneself. *Human Development, 52,* 211–214.

Neff, K. D., Hsieh, Y.-P., & Dejitterat, K. (2005). Self-compassion, achievement goals, and coping with academic failure. *Self and Identity, 4,* 263–287.

Neff, K. D., Rude, S. S., & Kirkpatrick, K. L. (2007). An examination of self-compassion in relation to positive psychological functioning and personality traits. *Journal of Research in Personality, 41,* 908–916.

Neff, K. D., & Vonk, R. (2009). Self-compassion versus global self-esteem: Two different ways of relating to oneself. *Journal of Personality, 77,* 23–50.

Neff, K. D. (2008). Self-compassion: Moving beyond the pitfalls of a separate self-concept. In H. A. Wayment & J. J. Bauer (Eds.), *Transcending self-interest: Psychological explorations of the quiet ego.* (pp. 95–105). Washington, DC US: American Psychological Association.

Nezlek, J. B., & Leary, M. R. (2002). Individual differences in self-presentational motives in daily social interaction. *Personality and Social Psychology Bulletin, 28,* 211–223.

Niiya, Y., Brook, A. T., & Crocker, J. (2010). Contingent self-worth and self-handicapping: Do contingent incremental theorists protect self-esteem? *Self and Identity, 9,* 276–297.

Niiya, Y., & Crocker, J. (2003). *Mastery goals buffer contingent self-esteem from failure.* Unpublished manuscript, University of Michigan.

Niiya, Y., & Crocker, J. (2007). Gakushu shikosei ha shippai ga jisonshin ni ataeru kyoui wo kansho suruka [Do mastery goals buffer self-esteem from failure threat?]. *Shinrigaku Kenkyu [Japanese Journal of Psychology], 78,* 504–511.

Niiya, Y., & Crocker, J. (2009). Mastery goals and contingent self-worth: A field study. *International Review of Social Psychology, 21,* 135–155.

Niiya, Y., Crocker, J., & Bartmess, E. (2004). From vulnerability to resilience: Learning orientations buffer contingent self-esteem from failure. *Psychological Science, 15,* 801–805.

Paradise, A. W., & Kernis, M. H. (1999). *Development of the contingent self-esteem scale.* Unpublished manuscript, University of Georgia.

Park, L. E., & Crocker, J. (2005). Interpersonal consequences of seeking self-esteem. *Personality and Social Psychology Bulletin, 31,* 1587–1598.

Pelham, B. W., & Swann, W. B., Jr. (1989). From self-conceptions to self-worth: On the sources and structure of global self-esteem. *Journal of Personality and Social Psychology, 57,* 672–680.

Pressman, S. D., & Cohen, S. (2005). Does positive affect influence health? *Psychological Bulletin, 131,* 925–971.

Pyszczynski, T., Greenberg, J., Solomon, S., Arndt, J., & Schimel, J. (2004). Why do people need self-esteem? A theoretical and empirical review. *Psychological Bulletin, 130,* 435–468.

Reis, H. T. (2009). Relationships are situations, and situations involve relationships. *Journal of Research in Personality, 43,* 266–266.

Roberts, J. E., & Monroe, S. M. (1994). A multidimensional model of self-esteem in depression. *Clinical Psychology Review, 14,* 161–181.

Robles, T. F., Brooks, K. P., & Pressman, S. D. (2009). Trait positive affect buffers the effects of acute stress on skin barrier recovery. *Health Psychology, 28,* 373–378.

Rosenberg, M. (1965). *Society and the adolescent self-image.* Princeton, NJ: Princeton University Press.

Rosenberg, M. (1979). *Conceiving the self.* New York: Basic Books.

Rosenberg, M., Schooler, C., Schoenbach, C., & Rosenberg, F. (1995). Global self-esteem and specific self-esteem: Different concepts, different outcomes. *American Sociological Review, 60,* 141–156.

Rudman, L. A., Dohn, M. C., & Fairchild, K. (2007). Implicit self-esteem compensation: Automatic threat defense. *Journal of Personality and Social Psychology, 93,* 798–813.

Sadler, P., & Woody, E. (2003). Is who you are who you're talking to? Interpersonal style and complementarity in mixed-sex interactions. *Journal of Personality and Social Psychology, 84,* 80–95.

Sargent, J., & Crocker, J. (2006). Contingencies of self-worth and symptoms of depression in college students. *Journal of Social and Clinical Psychology, 25,* 628–646.

Schimel, J., Arndt, J., Pyszczynski, T., & Greenberg, J. (2001). Being accepted for who we are: Evidence that social validation of the intrinsic self reduces general defensiveness. *Journal of Personality and Social Psychology, 80,* 35–52.

Schimmack, U., & Diener, E. (2003). Predictive validity of explicit and implicit self-esteem for subjective well-being. *Journal of Research in Personality, 37,* 100–106.

Sedikides, C. (1993). Assessment, enhancement, and verification determinants of the self-evaluation process. *Journal of Personality and Social Psychology, 65,* 317–338.

Sedikides, C., & Gregg, A. P. (2008). Self-enhancement: Food for thought. *Perspectives on Psychological Science, 3,* 102–116.

Shadish, W. R., Cook, T. D., & Campbell, D. T. (2002). *Experimental and quasi-experimental designs for generalized causal inference*. Boston, MA: Houghton, Mifflin.

Sherman, D. K., Bunyan, D. P., Creswell, J. D., & Jaremka, L. M. (2009). Psychological vulnerability and stress: The effects of self-affirmation on sympathetic nervous system responses to naturalistic stressors. *Health Psychology, 28*, 554–562.

Sherman, D. K., & Cohen, G. L. (2006). The psychology of self-defense: Self-affirmation theory. In M. P. Zanna (Ed.), *Advances in experimental social psychology* (Vol. 38, pp. 183–242). San Diego, CA: Academic.

Sherman, D. K., Nelson, L. D., & Steele, C. M. (2000). Do messages about health risks threaten the self? Increasing the acceptance of threatening health messages via self-affirmation. *Personality and Social Psychology Bulletin, 26*, 1046–1058.

Smelser, N. (1989). Self-esteem and social problems: An introduction. In A. M. Mecca, N. J. Smelser, & J. Vasconcellos (Eds.), *The social importance of self-esteem* (pp. 1–23). Berkeley: University of California Press.

Snyder, M. (1984). When belief creates reality. In L. Berkowitz (Ed.), *Advances in experimental social psychology* (Vol. 18, pp. 238–305). Orlando, FL: Academic.

Snyder, M., & Ickes, W. (1985). Personality and social behavior. In G. Lindzey & E. Aronson (Eds.), *Handbook of social psychology* (3rd ed., Vol. 2, pp. 883–947). New York: Random House.

Steele, C. M. (1988). The psychology of self-affirmation: Sustaining the integrity of the self. In L. Berkowitz (Ed.), *Advances in experimental social psychology* (Vol. 21, pp. 261–302). New York: Academic.

Steele, C. M., & Liu, T. J. (1983). Dissonance processes as self-affirmation. *Journal of Personality and Social Psychology, 45*, 5–19.

Stinson, D. A., Logel, C., Zanna, M. P., Holmes, J. G., Cameron, J. J., Wood, J. V., et al. (2008). The cost of lower self-esteem: Testing a self- and social-bonds model of health. *Journal of Personality and Social Psychology, 94*, 412–428.

Swann, W. B., Jr., De La Ronde, C., & Hixon, J. G. (1994). Authenticity and positivity strivings in marriage and courtship. *Journal of Personality and Social Psychology, 66*, 857–869.

Swann, W. B., Jr., Hixon, J. G., & De La Ronde, C. (1992). Embracing the bitter "truth": Negative self-concepts and marital commitment. *Psychological Science, 3*, 118–121.

Swann, W. B., Jr., Rentfrow, P. J., & Guinn, J. S. (2003). Self-verification: The search for coherence. In M. R. Leary & J. P. Tangney (Eds.), *Handbook of self and identity* (pp. 367–383). New York: Guilford.

Taylor, S. E., & Brown, J. D. (1988). Illusion and well-being: A social-psychological perspective on mental health. *Psychological Bulletin, 103*, 193–210.

Tennen, H., & Herzberger, S. (1987). Depression, self-esteem, and the absence of self-protective attributional biases. *Journal of Personality and Social Psychology, 52*, 72–80.

Tesser, A. (1988). Toward a self-evaluation maintenance model of social behavior. In L. Berkowitz (Ed.), *Advances in experimental social psychology* (Vol. 21, pp. 181–227). San Diego, CA: Academic.

Tesser, A. (2000). On the confluence of self-esteem maintenance mechanisms. *Personality and Social Psychology Review, 4*, 290–299.

Tesser, A., & Smith, J. (1980). Some effects of friendship and task relevance on helping: You don't always help the one you like. *Journal of Experimental Social Psychology, 16*, 582–590.

Tetlock, P. E., & Manstead, A. S. R. (1985). Impression management versus intrapsychic explanations in social psychology: A useful dichotomy? *Psychological Review, 92*, 59–77.

Tice, D. M. (1991). Esteem protection or enhancement? Self-handicapping motives and attributions differ by trait self-esteem. *Journal of Personality and Social Psychology, 60*, 711–725.

Tice, D. M., & Baumeister, R. F. (1990). Self-esteem, self-handicapping, and self-presentation: The strategy of inadequate practice. *Journal of Personality, 58*, 443–464.

Tice, D. M., & Baumeister, R. F. (1993). The social motivations of people with low self-esteem. In R. F. Baumeister (Ed.), *Self-esteem: The puzzle of low self-regard* (pp. 37–53). New York: Plenum.

Trope, Y. (1986). Self-enhancement and self-assessment in achievement behavior. In R. M. Sorrentino & E. T. Higgins (Eds.), *Handbook of motivation and cognition: Foundations of social behavior* (pp. 350–378). New York: Guilford.

Trzesniewski, K. H., Donnellan, M. B., Moffitt, T. E., Robins, R. W., Poulton, R., & Caspi, A. (2006). Low self-esteem during adolescence predicts poor health, criminal behavior, and limited economic prospects during adulthood. *Developmental Psychology, 42*, 381–390.

Twenge, J. M., Baumeister, R. F., DeWall, C. N., Ciarocco, N. J., & Bartels, J. M. (2007). Social exclusion decreases prosocial behavior. *Journal of Personality and Social Psychology, 92*, 56–66.

Twenge, J. M., Baumeister, R. F., Tice, D. M., & Stucke, T. S. (2001). If you can't join them, beat them: Effects of social exclusion on aggressive behavior. *Journal of Personality and Social Psychology, 81*, 1058–1069.

Twenge, J. M., Catanese, K. R., & Baumeister, R. F. (2003). Social exclusion and the deconstructed state: Time perception, meaninglessness, lethargy, lack of emotion, and self-awareness. *Journal of Personality and Social Psychology, 85*, 409–423.

Waschull, S. B., & Kernis, M. H. (1996). Level and stability of self-esteem as predictors of children's intrinsic motivation and reasons for anger. *Personality and Social Psychology Bulletin, 22*, 4–13.

Weissman, A. N., & Beck, A. T. (1978). *Development and validation of the Dysfunctional Attitude Scale: A preliminary investigation*. Paper presented at the annual meeting of the American Psychological Association, Toronto, Canada.

West, S. G. (2009). Alternatives to randomized experiments. *Current Directions in Psychological Science, 18*, 299–304.

Woike, B. A., & Baumgardner, A. H. (1993). Global-specific incongruencies in self-worth and the search for self-knowledge. *Personality and Social Psychology Bulletin, 19*, 290–295.

Wood, J. V., Heimpel, S. A., Newby-Clark, I. R., & Ross, M. (2005). Snatching defeat from the jaws of victory: Self-esteem differences in the experience and anticipation of success. *Journal of Personality and Social Psychology, 89*, 764–780.

Wylie, R. (1979). *The self-concept: Theory and research on selected topics* (2nd ed., Vol. 2). Lincoln: University of Nebraska Press.

Yamaguchi, S., Greenwald, A. G., Banaji, M. R., Murakami, F., Chen, D., Shiomura, K., et al. (2007). Apparent universality of positive implicit self-esteem. *Psychological Science, 18*, 498–500.

Motivation and Goal Pursuit
Integration Across the Social/Personality Divide

Julie K. Norem

Abstract

This chapter reviews motivation research that integrates person and situation perspectives. Personality and social psychologists pursue approaches to the study of human motivation that tend to be complementary and integrated, because they have had similar reactions to historical influences. Research tends to focus either on general motives, or on specific goals and goal pursuit processes. Within each focus, one can distinguish between implicit and explicit motives and goals, and approach and avoidance versions of motives and goal constructs. The chapter reviews implicit motive theory, self-determination theory, and research on goal structure, content, appraisal and pursuit. Implicit theories, life tasks, and self-regulation strategies (e.g., defensive pessimism) exemplify perspectives on motivation that integrate personal and situational factors using a functional approach. The chapter calls for further research on the relationship between implicit and explicit motivational variables, on congruence versus conflict in motivational systems, and on the integration of self-concept and motivational systems.

Keywords: motivation, goals, implicit motives, self-determination theory, self-regulation, life tasks, approach, avoidance, defensive pessimism, functional approach

Human activity is outrageously varied and complex, within and across situations, cultural contexts, daily and epic time periods, and individuals. Personality and social psychologists work to organize understanding of that variety and complexity, in part by accounting for the psychological forces that initiate, focus, and fuel it: that is, by studying motivation. As in all scientific endeavors, we avoid the seduction of explaining a single, specific activity in favor of looking for a finite system of structures (e.g., needs, interests, motives, goals) and related processes (e.g., priming, activation, approach and avoidance, self-regulation strategies) that explain reliable patterns and predictable deviations from those patterns, in thoughts, feelings, and behavior.

The study of motivation dates from the beginning of psychology as a discipline, and motivational questions—often at different levels of analysis—are fundamental to virtually every subfield of psychology.

Researchers interested in particular phenomena will often pursue questions that include motivation, even if motivation research is not their main focus: for example, the literature on stereotyping includes research on the motivation to stereotype and the motivation not to stereotype (Amodio, Devine, & Harmon-Jones, 2007). Attempts to stay within the historical or prototypical boundaries of personality and social psychology are doomed either to distort those boundaries beyond recognition, or to ignore significant and arguably relevant material.

With that caveat, one can identify, with broad strokes, general patterns that distinguish areas within the study of motivation. Personality psychologists, congruent with their focus on individual differences and person variables, have typically started by thinking about ways in which relatively broad and stable needs and motives are organized within individuals and vary across individuals. They then examine the ways in which differences in motives influence goal-setting, goal pursuit, and patterns of behaviors.

Social psychologists may assume that there are motives and needs that influence human beings generally, and then begin their empirical pursuits by looking at goals—often as they are situationally elicited, influenced, or defined. Consistent with historical emphasis, then, personality psychologists are more likely to look at systematic patterns of behavior associated with individual differences, while social psychologists are more likely to look at differences in behavior as a function of situational manipulations or variations in conditions relevant to elicitation and strength of the motive.

Yet, despite the historical rifts between personality and social psychology, (most notoriously those evident in the debate and subsequent cold war about the relative influence on behavior of dispositions and situations; see Kenrick & Funder, 1988), there is little active antagonism along those lines among researchers interested in motivation. There are, of course, disagreements among researchers (or, more frequently, isolation of foci); however those disagreements do not fall into the categories that have sometimes distinguished personality and social psychology. Within theoretical frameworks, many motivation researchers use both correlational and experimental methodologies, cite diverse theoretical sources, and assume the mutual influence of situations and persons (e.g., Deci & Ryan, 1985a; Elliot, 2008; Gollwitzer, 1999; Kuhl, 2001; Mayer, Faber, & Xu, 2007; Schultheiss, 2008; Snyder & Cantor, 1998). Indeed, motivation research provides an especially strong demonstration of the potential for integration of personality and social psychological perspectives, and the benefits that accrue from such attempts.

While particular research programs may be more strongly identified with either social psychology or personality psychology—often as a function of the self-identification and training of the researchers involved—that boundary becomes increasingly porous as research accumulates. There are several alternative frameworks that have more heuristic value for understanding motivation research than the personality/social distinction.

This chapter will use two very general distinctions to organize review of motivation research. The first is between a focus on broad, general human motives on the one hand, and a focus on relatively more specific goals one the other. The second distinction is between a focus on explicit (readily

consciously accessible) motivations and implicit (inaccessible, nonconscious or largely automatic) motivations. These two distinctions can be combined to create a 2 x 2 framework that provides a useful starting heuristic, although that heuristic breaks down fairly quickly under the weight of potentially relevant literature. Content area (e.g., achievement-related motivation) provides a plausible alternative organizational principle, as does a distinction between motivational content and motivational processes. Subsets of research will be differentiated by those rubrics, although they also crumble if applied too rigidly or stretched too broadly. Finally, approach-avoidance is a frequent cross-cutting distinction that adds precision and explanatory power within and across virtually all of these distinctions.

Selection of particular research or areas for discussion is driven by criteria that vary across examples. Emphasis is given to approaches that attempt to integrate across traditional personality/social boundaries, either by inclusion of both person and situation variables, or by more complex examination of the ways in which individuals navigate across the many situations of their lives over time. Extensive consideration is given to implicit motive theory and self-determination theory, for example, because each of these perspectives has generated an uncommon depth and breadth of research, more or less continuously, over several decades. Each perspective includes not only person and situation variables but also a variety of levels and kinds of each sort of variable. While neither tidily integrates every disparate finding, they are both notably fecund grand perspectives. Each represents an impressive attempt to integrate social and personality perspectives and acknowledge the complexity of human motivation. In contrast, different schemes for categorizing motivations are reviewed because they help to illustrate the breadth of research and theorizing that fall under the heading of motivation, and provide a survey of the terrain for personality and social psychologists looking for starting points and potential connections across literatures.

Goal research tends to be more scattered and less driven by grand theories of human nature, personality, or motivation than work on broad motives. It tends to focus on particular kinds of goals, particular domains of goals, particular kinds of situations or life contexts, or particular processes of goal-setting, goal activation, and goal pursuit. The specific research reviewed in the goals section of this chapter was selected to illustrate the variety of goal concepts in the literature, influential past or contemporary foci, and general trends and findings within those foci. Much of the work on goals and goal pursuit has been strongly influenced by cognitive perspectives; relatively little can be neatly divided along social/personality lines. That does not mean, however, that this work is necessarily well integrated, either within a particular focus, or with other key perspectives in personality and social psychology. Instead, the diverse literature represented by goal research seems ripe for attempts at more comprehensive integration by personality and social psychologists, and identifying some key questions that might move us toward that process occupies the final section of the chapter.

Historical Influences

One reason there is no simple, comprehensive framework in motivational research is that much of the research was developed in the context of reactions to overly simplistic or extreme theoretical traditions. Moreover, including ideas embraced and those rejected, many influences from historical approaches to motivation are common to both personality and social psychologists, which mitigates some of the obstacles to integrating perspectives across that boundary. Both groups reacted against strict behaviorist approaches (e.g., Bandura, 1974; Deci, 1975; Tolman, 1932; Lewin, 1936). Both reacted against orthodox psychoanalytic approaches and simple drive-reduction theories (e.g., G. Allport, 1937; Eysenck, 1967; Hull, 1951; Kelly, 1955; Kihlstrom, 2009; Mischel, 1968) and both have been influenced by the "New Look" premise that perception is influenced by motivation (Atkinson, 1957; Bruner & Postman, 1949; Kunda, 1990; Norem, 2009).

Neo-Freudian and ego-psychology's emphasis on competence/mastery (or "effectance") motivation, ego-development, and self-protection (e.g., Adler, 1930; Horney, 1968; White, 1959) is echoed in a wide range of social and personality psychology, from work on the motivation to understand and control (e.g., Kruglanski, Orehek, Dechesne, & Pierro, 2010; Rotter, 1966) to work on self-enhancement, self-validation, and self-protection (e.g., Bosson, Brown, Zeigler-Hill, & Swann, 2003; Hepper, Gramzow, & Sedikides, 2010; Kurt & Paulhus, 2008). The humanists' insistence that people are more than the sum of their learned contingencies, and are motivated by factors beyond simple hedonism (Maslow, 1971; Rogers, 1951) is also evident in motivation work (e.g., Deci & Ryan, 1985).

Specific responses to common influences show considerable variation, of course. Some researchers focus on identifying basic or fundamental motivations hypothesized to influence behavior across a wide variety of situations and circumstances. The "fundamental" status of these motives, depending on specific theoretical perspective, derives from the ubiquity of their influence on human behavior, their evolutionary significance, or their ability to capture something crucial about human nature.

Motives
Perspectives on Basic or Fundamental Motives
APPROACH AND AVOIDANCE

Approach and avoidance describe both general (e.g., avoiding novel situations whenever possible) and specific (e.g., leaning toward attractive stimuli) tendencies that characterize our reactions to the world. Elliot and Covington (2001) argue that approach and avoidance are fundamental, overarching categories of motivation that encompass individual differences in response tendencies, appraisals, and situations. Approach/avoidance distinctions appear in early accounts of motivation as diverse as Bentham (1779/1948), Freud (1915/1963), Eysenck (1967), Lewin (1935), and Maslow (1955). Approach and avoidance tendencies can also be seen across a variety of animate species, from humans to amoeba, because those tendencies relate to fundamental evolutionary problems—how to approach necessary resources and avoid potential threat—that every species must face (Tooby & Cosmides, 1992).

Approach-avoidance reactions are immediate, automatic, and often reflexive, suggesting that they are deeply implicated in our neural, cognitive, and hormonal architectures, and related to our automatic evaluation of stimuli as good or bad (Bargh, 1997; Chen & Bargh, 1999). Multiple levels of approach and avoidance reaction operate, such that initial automatic responses may be overridden by other goals and self-regulatory strategies at other levels of analysis (Cacioppo & Berntson, 1999); approach and avoidance also can characterize motivation and responses at several levels of a motivational hierarchy (Elliot & Church, 1997).

There are several theoretical models that posit plausible neurophysiological structures that may correspond (more or less roughly) to separate approach and avoidance systems (e.g., Cloninger, 1987; Gray, 1990; LeDoux, 1996; Zuckerman, 1994). Davidson has shown a stable, early-developing pattern of hemispheric asymmetry in activation associated with approach-based positive affect versus avoidance-based negative affect (Davidson, 1995; cf. Ito & Cacioppo, 1999). Relative left frontal EEG activity, correlated with approach, is related to risk-taking, positive mood, and anger (Harmon-Jones & Allen, 1997; Harmon-Jones, Peterson, Gable, & Harmon-Jones, 2008; for reviews, see Coan & Allen, 2003, and Elliot, 2008). (See also Amodio & Harmon-Jones, chapter 6, this volume).

Behavioral Inhibition and Behavioral Approach

Gray (1990) describes two neural systems that represent general motivational tendencies to approach or avoid classes of stimuli. The behavioral activation system (BAS) orients an organism toward reward, nonpunishment, and escape from punishment and regulates positive affect (happiness) and movement toward stimuli. The behavioral inhibition system (BIS) orients toward punishment, nonreward, and novelty, and regulates anxiety. Self-report BIS/BAS tendencies predict greater anxiety in anticipation of a punishment and greater happiness in anticipation of a reward, respectively (Carver & White, 1994). Further research suggests that individual differences in BIS/BAS systems influence autonomic, immune, and behavioral responses to reward-relevant stimuli (e.g., Balconi, Falbo, & Brambilla, 2009).

Regulatory Focus Theory

Research on regulatory focus theory (RFT) is related to the categorization of motivation as approach-avoidance (Higgins, 1998; for a recent review, see Molden, Lee, & Higgins, 2008). RFT posits two self-regulatory systems represented by differences in attentional focus that are similar to those encompassed by BIS/BAS. A promotion focus directs goal-relevant action when the need or desire to achieve ideals (or self-realization) and victories is salient; a prevention focus takes over when safety and security needs are primary.

Regulatory focus can become a personality characteristic, but it can also be manipulated by situational variables, or be a feature of institutional or societal structures (Higgins & Silberman, 1998). RFT thus represents greater integration of personality and social perspectives than previously mentioned work. Each focus promotes different corresponding strategies for goal pursuit, with prevention-focus resulting in vigilant strategies and promotion-focus resulting in eager strategies (Higgins, 2000). For example, promotion focus (whether an individual difference or situationally induced) leads to greater speed but less accuracy on tasks where

both contribute to performance, while prevention focus leads to greater accuracy, but slower responding (Forster, Higgins, & Bianco, 2003).

When decisions or actions are made in generally neutral or positive contexts, promotion focus will tend to lead to greater openness to novelty (Liberman, Idson, Camacho, & Higgins, 1999) and choice of riskier options in the pursuit of gain or avoidance of nongain (Galinsky, Leonardelli, Okhuysen, & Mussweiler, 2005; Zhou, Pham, Mick, Iacobucci, & Huber, 2004). Individuals can be sensitive to situations, however, and change their strategies in ways that fit with their regulatory focus and with the constraints and affordances of situations (e.g., Scholer, Stroessner, & Higgins, 2008). Thus, prevention focus could lead to riskier decisions and behavior when more moderate approaches seem unlikely to succeed in avoiding losses, as when negative potential events loom large because of their probability or magnitude (hence, possibly, discussions of using nuclear devices to stop the British Petroleum oil pipe leak in the Gulf of Mexico).

According to RFT, failure and success should be related to different affect under prevention versus promotion focus. Under conditions of success and failure, respectively, promotion focus is related to cheerfulness and dejection, while prevention is related to calmness and agitation (Roney, Higgins, & Shah, 1995; Shah & Higgins, 2001). Correspondingly, people should also work harder after failure under a prevention focus, but persist less under a promotion focus. In contrast, success should lead to less vigilance, relative quiescence, and consequently less effort after success under prevention focus, while success should energize and motivate increased effort under promotion focus (e.g., Werth & Forster, 2007).

The relevance of approach-avoidance dimensions across individuals, situations, specific motives, specific versions of goals, and even different species demonstrates its power as a motivational construct. There are, however, alternative proposals for categorizing fundamental motivational tendencies that focus on differences across motives in content or domain. These approaches often include approach and avoidance versions of specific goals as induced by situational manipulations or as a consequence of factors within persons.

CATEGORIZATION OF MOTIVES

Social psychologists have long been interested in a variety of general motivations for human behavior. Not surprisingly, they have typically been less interested than personality psychologists in individual differences in those motivations, and more interested in the specific processes (especially cognitive processes) by which these motivations influence specific goals and related behavior, the situational factors that elicit or inhibit particular motivations, and the interpersonal dynamics with which they are associated. Nevertheless, for every general motivation, individual difference work has informed understanding of category boundaries, goal-setting, and motivation strength.

Motive Classes Derived From Basic Questions

Fiske (2004) summarizes five general motives on which social psychology has focused over the years: belonging, understanding, controlling, protecting/enhancing self, and trusting. She relates each general motive to different traditions that have emphasized different questions or problems: for example, therapeutic traditions ranging from Freud (1914/1953) to Maslow (1957) influence models of the ego/self that need enhancement and protection. Those who emphasize consciousness and functional processes—for example, William James, as well as the humanist tradition and work by Erikson (1950)—influenced research on basic trust. A focus on goal pursuit under the influence of drives, habits, and incentives ties together traditional learning theories, Lewin's notion of life space, achievement motivation theories, social comparison, and cognitive dissonance (Festinger, 1954), effectance theory (White, 1959), and interdependence theory (Thibaut & Kelley, 1959), because a major component of human goal pursuit is the process of trying to assert control.

How people try to understand the self, other, and the social world is the focus of models of information processing, impression formation research, and Kelly's (1955) personal construct theory, as well as Gestalt approaches (Boring, 1950), and work by Heider (1958) and Asch (1946). Finally, from early work on social influence (F. Allport, 1924) and social facilitation (Zajonc, 1965), through attachment theory (e.g., Bowlby, 1969) and sociological theories of roles and norms (Bales, 1950; Goffman, 1956), one sees an emphasis on the human need to belong to social groups.

One can quibble, as Fiske recognizes, with particular assignments of theorists or traditions (many more than described here) to one motive as opposed to another (e.g., it seems reasonable to include attachment theory as highly relevant to work on trusting as a social model, and its focus on internal

working models would appear to make it a candidate for a significant role in the cast of those contributing to the study of understanding self and others). Whatever specific disagreements or agreements one might have with her heuristic historical synthesis, however, glancing at the references makes clear the extent to which ideas from both personality and social psychology have guided its formulation and the work that exemplifies each category.

Evolutionarily Based Fundamental Motive Theories

Fiske's rationale for her description of five general motive classes is its heuristic value in both tracing historical influences in psychology and in providing an organizational framework for considering contemporary research. In contrast, Kenrick, Neuberg, Griskevicius, Becker, and Schaller (2010) argue explicitly that there are classes of motives that are fundamental because of their implications for evolutionary fitness. This perspective assumes that the paramount evolutionary goal is to produce viable offspring who themselves survive to reproductive age; in the service of that goal, people are motivated to accomplish more specific goals: disease-avoidance, affiliation, self-protection, status, mate-acquisition, mate-retention, and child-rearing. Kenrick, Li, and Butner (2003) argue that these goals are managed by distinct motivational systems. Within these systems, a given stimulus will have different implications and elicit different motivated responses (see also Gangestad, chapter 7, this volume).

In support of their framework, Kenrick and his colleagues cite several studies showing motive-specific effects. For example, the specific content of automatically activated stereotypes varies with the motives operating during activation. When "darkness" is primed (via a darkened room), self-protective concerns are also activated; as a result, when viewing a black man in a darkened room, white individuals were more likely to think of threatening aspects of black stereotypes than other stereotypic and equally negative aspects (Schaller, Park, & Faulkner, 2003). Similar specific effects were found for attention, memory (Ackerman et al., 2006), and encoding (Maner et al., 2005). There were no sex differences in these effects. Self-protection motives also increase conformity among both men and women.

In contrast, when mating motives are activated, there are significant differences in average responses between males and females (Griskevicius, Cialdini, & Kenrick, 2006). While both men and women initially attend preferentially to the faces of attractive members of the opposite sex, corresponding to hypotheses about sex-differentiated patterns in mate selection, men show enhanced memory for faces of beautiful women, but women show no such effect for faces of attractive men (Becker, Kenrick, Guerin, & Maner, 2005). When researchers activate mating motives, women tend to become more agreeable and conforming, while men conform less (in what is interpreted as a dominance display; Griskevicius, Goldstein, Mortensen, Cialdini, & Kenrick, 2006).

Bargh, Gollwitzer, and Oettingen (2010) also argue that there are categories of goals that have particular evolutionary relevance, and that those goals are especially likely to have nonconscious representations and to be vulnerable to activation and operation outside of conscious awareness. Their list includes self-protection, mating, the need to understand one's environment, the need to belong to social groups and the need to have supportive relationships.

There is enough work on motivation to provide impressive empirical justification for each of the systems offered. There is also room for vigorous debate about the comprehensiveness, historical interpretations, and internal integrity of specific categorical boundaries. As Fiske (2004) aptly notes, the goals and interests (to name two motivational constructs) of individual researchers will be important determinants of the how useful different categorizations of motivation will be. Their potential will also be tested by whether they are able to move us toward better understanding of individual differences and systems of motives (rather than single motives operating in isolation) as they influence ongoing behavior and self-regulation attempts.

IMPLICIT MOTIVE THEORY

Other researchers have built their theories by researching in depth a finite number of general motivations that they consider basic and fundamental. One of the best-known examples of a "basic motive" approach is work on implicit motives.

Contemporary work on implicit motives has roots in Henry Murray's (1938) work, which was itself seeded by influences from Freud and Jung (Murray, 1940), as well as Morton Prince and the neo-associationism tradition (Kihlstrom, 2009). According to Murray, a need is "a construct which stands for a force in the brain region . . . which organizes perception, apperception, intellection, conation, and action in such way as to transform in a certain direction an existing unsatisfying situation" (Murray, 1938, pp. 123–124). Murray began with

the assumption that motives are at least partly "hidden" from the individual: that is, that they operate outside of conscious awareness and are difficult to access via introspection or standard self-report methods (albeit not because, as Freud maintained, they were actively repressed). Murray also emphasized the importance of the "press" of the situation. Thus, from the beginning, this research tradition has integrated personality and social perspectives by considering individual differences and person variables and the influence of both specific situations and broader social and cultural contexts.

Murray devoted considerable effort to compiling a list of what he believed to be universal psychological needs (which are traditionally denoted by a short-hand label as indicated in parentheses): for example, need for achievement (n ach), need for power (n power), and need for affiliation (n aff). Historical attempts to compile comprehensive lists of motives have largely been abandoned, in part because of a lack of consensus, and in part because such lists become potentially endless as motives are increasingly subdivided to account for specific behaviors. The majority of research has been devoted to n ach, n power, n aff, and need for intimacy (n intimacy). N ach is the motivation to accomplish something or to "do better" (than oneself or than others) relative to some standard, or to overcome an obstacle. N power, in Murray's framework, is the motivation to have an impact on other people; it includes typical conceptions of dominance, but extends more broadly to other forms of impact, including influence. High n power individuals want be influential and to feel more effective than other people (Murray, 1938).

N aff was initially defined as the desire to create and maintain emotionally positive relationships with others, while n intimacy is the motivation to have warm and close interactions with others (Atkinson, Heyns, & Veroff, 1954; McAdams, 1980; Shipley & Veroff, 1952). Perhaps not surprisingly, these motives tend to correlate with each other, and they may be thought of as different aspects of a core motivation such as belongingness or dependence (Boyatzis, 1973). Mehrabian argued that there were two social motives: n aff and fear of rejection (e.g., Mehrabian & Ksionzky, 1974). Similarly, Weinberger and colleagues argue that n aff represents a "dark side" to the need to be with others because it stems from a fear of rejection or loneliness, while need for intimacy represents the "bright side" of our desires for mutually satisfying relationships (Weinberger, Cotler, & Fishman, 2010).

The idea that motives have different "faces" has historically been an important part of the implicit motive perspective, and it corresponds to the approach/avoidance distinction discussed previously. Rather than assuming superordinate approach and avoidance motivational systems, this perspective argues that there are approach and avoidance versions of each major motive. Thus, n ach is composed of both hope for success and fear of failure; n power includes both hope of power and fear of weakness; n aff or n intimacy combines hope for closeness and fear of rejection or loneliness (Atkinson & Birch, 1970). At times these forms of motivation can facilitate one another, as when hope for success and fear of failure both drive persistence on a task. Sometimes, however, they can create conflict or impasses, as when hope for success impels risk-taking, while fear of failure inhibits it (Atkinson, 1957).

Implicit motives can take a third form, reflected in fear of the fundamental incentive class at the core of each motive. In this situation, the motive involves neither active pursuit nor active avoidance; rather, it operates more like an "antimotive" that encourages passive avoidance (Schultheiss, 2008). Matina Horner (1972) argued that some individuals fear success, which can result in self-sabotage, motivational paralysis, or conflicted emotions in achievement situations. There is also evidence that some individuals fear (or dislike) power (Schultheiss et al., 2005; Winter, 1973). Accounts of self-handicapping tendencies fit well with the idea that these motives can take potentially conflicting forms, and have potentially conflicting influences (Baumeister & Scher, 1988; Berglas & Jones, 1978).

Implicit motive constructs are similar to traditional trait conceptions in that there is stable and systematic variation in chronic motive strength across individuals. Unlike most conceptions of traits, however, implicit motives are also hypothesized to be dynamic, sensitive to situations, and relatively specific in their influences on categories of variables and over time. From the beginning, then, implicit motive theory bridged personality and social psychology. Implicit motives are dispositional, that is, at least somewhat stable units of individual difference. Nevertheless, both subtle and bold features of situations can arouse these universal tendencies. Indeed, McClelland argued that societies vary in the extent to which they inculcate achievement motivation in their members (McClelland, 1976). The impact of situations, in turn, should vary as a function of the strength of motives within individuals, which makes implicit motive theory compatible with interactionist perspectives (Furr & Funder, 2004).

Like physiological needs, implicit psychological motives are dynamic: within a given time frame, it is possible to satisfy a particular need, and immediately after satisfaction, there should be a drop in the strength of that motivation, and thus, its influence on other variables. Hunger can be satisfied such that after a meal, food is not very appealing and we are not motivated to seek or consume it; instead, other motivations will come to the fore (like the need for a nap!). Similarly, n ach or n power can be temporarily satisfied, after which other motivations will exert more noticeable influences until previous satisfaction of achievement or power motivation begins to give way to resurging need. Motives are also dynamic in that they can be elicited by situational cues: for example, n ach should be elicited by situational cues concerning the importance of performing relative to a standard ("see how high you can score"), while n power should be elicited by opportunities to influence other people or otherwise have an impact ("who will win this contest?"). Focus on the dynamic nature of motivation, from this perspective, has the potential to provide us with ways to consider the ongoing interaction among motives, not just fluctuations in motive strength within a motive.

Efforts to develop reliable and valid measures of implicit motives focused on coding of stories written in response to pictures from the Thematic Apperception Test (TAT; Atkinson, 1957; McClelland, Atkinson, Clark, & Lowell, 1953; Morgan & Murray, 1935; Murray, 1943). Use of the TAT was based on the assumption that implicit motives will influence interpretation of each picture, and thus the themes, structures, and emotions expressed in the stories individuals write. Theoretically, the projected effects of implicit motives should be apparent in the stories regardless of the conscious intentions of the writer. Currently, the most commonly used measure of implicit motives is the Picture-Story Exercise (PSE), for which there are a standardized set of pictures and standardized scoring systems for n ach, n power, and n aff (McClelland, Koestner, & Weinberger, 1992; Pang & Schultheiss, 2005; Winter, 1993; see Mayer, Faber, & Xu, 2007, for a review of motivation measures).

Profiles of Implicit Motives
Rich profiles of those high in each motive have emerged from accumulation of research results.

Early research showed that those high in n ach tend to choose moderately difficult tasks and individualized feedback. Research also shows that high n ach individuals are successful in performance-oriented groups and organizations, but only up to a point; they have somewhat weak people skills, and (perhaps as a consequence), typically do not make good leaders (Atkinson & Raynor, 1978; Feather, 1961; Heckhausen, 1977; Winter & Carlson, 1988). There are a variety of intriguing physiological correlates of some implicit motives, but a relative lack of research reporting those correlates for n ach. There is some evidence that, among men who are high in n ach, there are lower levels of urine excretion in achievement-arousing conditions, and those conditions also produce better recall (Schultheiss, 2008). Schultheiss hypothesizes that n ach might be associated with a release of arginine-vasopressin (AVP), which promotes water retention and is correlated with episodic memory processes.

Individuals who are high in n aff are often less popular, but are perceived as more self-confident and higher in approval-seeking. They function well in "flat" organizational structures (Litwin & Siebrecht, 1967), and tend to avoid those who are different from themselves (Atkinson & O'Connor, 1966; Byrne, 1961; McClelland, 1987). N aff tends to be associated with parasympathetic nervous system activity, better immune functioning under stress, and better immunocompetence in general (Jemmott, 1987; McClelland, 1989). These relationships may relate to positive affect arousal, in that there are greater IgA increases among high n aff individuals under positive affect conditions. There also appears to be a bidirectional relationship between progesterone and n aff. Women taking progesterone via birth control pills are higher in n aff than both women who do not take the pill and than men. Within individuals, women are also higher in n aff during luteal phase, higher-progesterone-producing days of their menstrual cycles. Arousal of n aff (using film-clips with relevant content) leads to faster progesterone production, which may further be related to oxytocin increases that have anxiolytic effects in the brain, down-regulating "fight-flight" responses and up-regulating "tend-befriend" responses (Schultheiss, Wirth, & Stanton, 2004; Wirth & Schultheiss, 2006).

High n power individuals tend to be aggressive and irresponsible (Winter, 1988), but also strategic (McClelland, 1975). High n power is generally correlated with interpersonal intelligence and success in organizations, but also with the tendency to be autocratic, attention-seeking, and open to flattery (McClelland & Boyatzis, 1982). Arousal of n power is associated with increases in sympathetic nervous system arousal, especially among dispositionally high n power individuals. Among men, high n power shows small correlations with basal testosterone levels, but n power also interacts with both anticipation of and outcomes of dominance exchanges to predict changes in testosterone (Schultheiss, 2007, 2008). Among women, both "winners" and "losers" who are high in n power show increases in testosterone after a contest (Schultheiss, Brunstein, Elliot, & Dweck, 2005); however, estradiol changes in high n power women are similar to testosterone changes in men as a function of the outcome of a dominance exchange. High n power women showed increases in estradiol after winning, and decreases after losing (Stanton & Schultheiss, 2007). For both women and men who are high in n power, defeat (or "stressed n power") is associated with increased cortisol levels and compromised immune function.

The nuanced relations between implicit motives and hormones provide support for arguments that these motives are fundamental in the sense that they have ongoing, interactive connections to physiological systems—particularly hormonal systems, which themselves are often considered essential to understanding drive and other motivational constructs at a physiological level of analysis.

Relationships Between Implicit and Explicit Motives
Implicit and explicit measures of the same motive typically do not correlate: indeed, meta-analysis shows that the average correlation is close to zero, and the average overlap in variance is about 1%. In this case, though, the lack of correlation does not seem to indicate a troubling lack of convergent validity, because there are lucid and consistently different patterns of correlates for implicit versus explicit measures of motivation. McClelland (1980) argued that the conscious self-report of n ach corresponded more to an individual's values or desired self-concept than to implicit motives. Biernat (1989) found that implicit n ach predicts task performance, but not whether people will volunteer for leadership positions, while explicit n ach predicts volunteering for those positions, but not actual task performance. The hormonal changes associated with implicit n power are not related to explicit measures of n power (Schultheiss, 2008). Brunstein and Maier (2005) found similar results looking across motives: broadly speaking, implicit motives predicted performance, while explicit motives were

better predictors of self-reported commitments and judgments. Spangler (1992) found that implicit and explicit motives respond to different kinds of cues, with verbal cues more likely to elicit explicit motives, and nonverbal cues (especially emotional cues) eliciting implicit motives. Congruent with those findings, implicit motives relate to the accessibility of specific emotional experiences, while explicit motives appear to be linked to the accessibility of self-concept-related memories (Woike, McLeod, & Goggin, 2003).

To the extent that implicit and explicit motivations are distinct, there is a potential for their relationship within individuals to vary from close congruence to conflict. To the extent that there are stable differences from individual to individual in the extent of this congruence, it represents a potentially new individual difference variable for investigation—one that may be particularly powerful in explaining why some individuals are more or less vulnerable to situational influences. Schultheiss (2008) has suggested that there may be chronic individual differences in what he terms "regulatory competence," where competence refers to one's ability bring implicit and explicit motivations into alignment.

SELF-DETERMINATION THEORY

Self-determination theory (SDT), developed by Edward Deci and Richard Ryan, presents a perspective on motivation that begins with the assumption that there are three basic and universal human needs: autonomy, competence, and relatedness. In contrast to the conception of implicit motives developed by Murray, McClelland, Atkinson, and their collaborators, Deci and Ryan (2000) define needs in terms of "nutriments," which are necessary for psychological health, development, and well-being. All other motives are hypothesized to derive from the ways in which the three fundamental needs are satisfied or thwarted. Although there are individual difference variables within the "minitheories" of which SDT is comprised, the basic needs are not conceived of as varying in strength from individual to individual; instead, what varies are the degree and means of satisfaction, and the relationship of need satisfaction efforts and consequences to aspects of the self and other psychological states.

Basic psychological needs theory of SDT explains the general assumptions guiding the larger framework and the other three subsidiary theories. Basic psychological needs theory specifies that psychological needs define what is necessary for wellness and optimal functioning, and that basic psychological needs are universal and active throughout the life span. It further specifies that all motivations and goals have an impact on wellness through their relationships to the satisfaction of basic needs, and that basic needs contribute (both individually and interactively) to within and between person differences in wellness (Ryan & Deci, 2002). Though some of these assumptions, at least in nascent form, guided earlier development of pieces of SDT, they are most explicitly and comprehensively stated in basic psychological needs theory.

Intrinsic Versus Extrinsic Motivation

The SDT framework itself began with the distinction between intrinsic and extrinsic motivation. Motivation is intrinsic when an activity is pursued for its own sake, for example, because it is pleasurable, fun, or interesting. In contrast, the motivation for an activity is extrinsic when that activity is pursued for reasons extrinsic to the experience or activity itself, for example, for money or other rewards, or under threat of punishment. Cognitive evaluation theory was developed to explain findings from research on these sources of motivation that did not fit traditional incentive-based or expectancy x value accounts of motivation. These findings suggested that, rather than intrinsic and extrinsic incentives adding together to a "sum" or total amount of motivation, under some circumstances, extrinsic incentives tended to decrease intrinsic motivation (e.g., Calder & Staw, 1975; Deci, Koestner, & Ryan, 1999; cf. Eisenberger, Pierce, & Cameron, 1999). Cognitive evaluation theory posits that individuals evaluate the functional significance of incentives in terms of the extent to which we experience them as controlling and as providing information about competence. If an incentive is extrinsic, but provides information about competence, it tends not to subtract from intrinsic motivation. If, however, an incentive is experienced as controlling, it will decrease intrinsic motivation.

Extensive research across a variety of situations and contexts, experiments and field studies, and variously aged samples, supports the SDT proposition that increases in autonomy and competence help to maintain and increase intrinsic motivation (Ryan & Deci, 2000). When people's feelings are acknowledged (Koestner, Ryan, Bernieri, & Holt, 1984), or when they feel they have choice in their activities (Zuckerman, Porac, Lathin, Smith, & Deci, 1978), they tend to feel more intrinsically motivated. In contrast, deadlines (Amabile,

DeJong, & Lepper, 1976), and feeling watched (Lepper & Greene, 1975) tend to decrease intrinsic motivation.

Internalization, Autonomy, and Self-Regulation

Although intrinsic incentives and motivation tend to coincide with satisfaction of autonomy needs, extrinsic incentives can become autonomous through the process of internalization. In other words, our reasons for and experience while engaging in activities can change over time; indeed, we can self-regulate, to varying extents, our interest (Sansone & Thoman, 2006). According to organismic integration theory, individuals internalize attitudes, rules, expectations, values, and behavior patterns from their social environment and from other people who are important to them (Deci & Ryan, 1985a; Ryan & Deci, 2008). A child, for example, may initially make her bed only because her parents tell her to do so. Over time, however, if she feels that she does the task well, if her parents do not supervise her while she does it, and if she is able to choose when she does it, she may come to value the activity and its results herself. Importantly, it is at that point that we would expect her to continue to make her bed even when she could get away with not doing it.

Development of this sort of self-regulated, autonomous behavior—that is, being able to motivate oneself to do tedious or frustrating things, even when no one is "making you"—is one hallmark of psychological maturity. Indeed, autonomous self-regulation is related to psychological health and actual performance (Reis, Sheldon, Gable, Roscoe, & Ryan, 2000; Ryan & Deci, 2000; Sheldon, Ryan, Deci, & Kasser, 2004). More autonomous motivation relates to better adherence to prescription medication protocols (G. Williams, Rodin, Ryan, Grolnick, & Deci, 1998), more weight loss and better weight loss maintenance (G. Williams, Grow, Freedman, Ryan, & Deci, 1996), and greater engagement and well-being in both school and work contexts (Baard, Deci, & Ryan, 2004; Chirkov & Ryan, 2001). Recent research suggests that autonomy support plays a role in the development of intimate romantic relationships (Lynch, La Guardia, & Ryan, 2007) and close friendships (Deci, La Guardia, Moller, Scheiner, & Ryan, 2006).

Individual Differences in Causality Orientations

Context variables (including cultural "ambience," specific reinforcements, and the other people present) influence the extent to which individuals feel more autonomously motivated or more controlled (G. Williams, Freedman, & Deci, 1998). SDT also includes, however, constructs describing relatively stable individual differences in the tendency to interpret situations, other people, and contexts as supportive of autonomy. Causality orientation theory describes three "orientations" that represent different general tendencies to interpret the environment in ways that increase or decrease autonomous motivation (Deci & Ryan, 1985b). These orientations are assessed using the General Causality Orientations Scale (Deci & Ryan, 1985b; Ryan & Connell, 1989). Each orientation is hypothesized to be the result of developmental influences (i.e., not innate), and each corresponds to a characteristic pattern of interpretations and outcomes.

People with a strong autonomy orientation tend to interpret their social environments (including the attitudes of other people) as generally supportive, and as providing useful competence information (M. Gagné & Deci, 2005; Hodgins & Knee, 2002). These individuals are typically high in self-esteem, and aware of their own needs, interests, and values, which they use to guide their choices and behavior (see, e.g., Koestner, Bernieri, & Zuckerman, 1992; Loevinger et al., 1985).

In contrast, those with a more controlled orientation look for cues in the social environment, cues from other people, or to their own "introjected" guidelines, as opposed to internalized values and desires, to guide their behavior (Neighbors & Knee, 2003). They are more conforming and higher in public self-consciousness (J. Williams, Mathews, & MacLeod, 1996) and self-monitoring (Zuckerman, Gioioso, & Tellini, 1988) and they demonstrate less consistency among their attitudes, traits, and behaviors (e.g., Koestner et al., 1992).

Those with an impersonal orientation tend to feel generally unmotivated and to perceive that they have little control over themselves or their environment. They are more likely to be depressed, to have an external locus of control, and to experience social anxiety (Deci & Ryan, 1985b).

Assumption of Universality

SDT focuses on autonomy and competence as hypothesized basic and universal psychological needs. (Relatedness has received relatively less and more recent emphasis.) SDT posits that autonomy is invariant across development and culture and necessary for psychological health and well-being (Ryan, Deci, Grolnick, & La Guardia, 2006). The construct of autonomy fundamentally implicates the self as the desired instigator and regulator of behavior. This perspective has been criticized for being culture-bound, or even culturally insensitive or biased, based on work suggesting that independence and the bounded individual self are more highly valued in more individualistic Western cultural contexts (such as the United States) than in more collectivistic Eastern cultural contexts (such as Japan) (see, e.g., Iyengar & DeVoe, 2003; Jordan, 1991; Markus & Kitayama, 1991).

Theoretically, SDT views autonomy as reflecting "the self-endorsement and valuing of one's own practices" (Ryan & Deci, 2008, p. 667). This conception of autonomy does not reject the influence of cultural context on particular practices or structure of the self-concept. Instead, it considers autonomy in terms of evaluation processes that reflect the extent to which any given practice is internalized so that it feels self-directed. In the case where, for example, there may be a cultural press toward contributions to group outcomes rather than individual outcomes, SDT would not see individuals who work hard for the group outcome (perhaps even sacrificing other personal outcomes) as people who were necessarily controlled rather than autonomous. Rather, to the extent that they had internalized valuing collective outcomes, their motivation would be considered autonomous, and it would be predicted to correlate positively with indicators of well-being.

There are several studies that support the SDT-based argument about the importance of autonomous motivation across varied cultural contexts. For example, Chirkov, Ryan, Kim, and Kaplan (2003) found that, in samples from Russia, the United States, Turkey, and South Korea, autonomous reasons for performing both collectivistic and individualistic practices were associated with greater well-being, independent of culture (see also: Sheldon et al., 2004). In Japan (Yamauchi & Tanaka, 1998) and South Korea (Kim, 2004), autonomy in schoolchildren was associated with more interest in schoolwork and learning and greater well-being. Relationship satisfaction is also related to autonomy support in China, the United States, and Russia (Lynch, La Guardia, & Ryan, 2009).

Work on the numerous constructs associated with SDT illustrates the power of an approach that integrates individual differences in person-centered structures and processes with an attempt to look systematically at forces outside the individual, at both the level of specific situations and broader cultural contexts. Internalization processes within this perspective provide one of the few nonpsychodynamic explanations of the ways that cultural and social prescriptions can become part of an individual, rather than simply acting on individuals from the "outside." Accounts of that process move well beyond approaches that consider person variables separately from situational variables, and beyond more mechanical person x situation approaches. They allow us to consider the ways that situational influences develop over time in conjunction with both automatic and more active interpretations by the individuals in those situations. They also provide a model for trying to understand when person variables are likely to exert more influence and when situation variables are likely to be strongest—something hard to find in most literatures.

Goals

Goals are typically defined as representations of endpoints that people try to reach or avoid, although there is variation in the specific definitions used in the literature (Elliot & Fryer, 2008; Elliot & Niesta, 2009). Goals are more proximal influences on behavior than more distal motive concepts, and can be viewed as instantiations of general motives. As units of analysis, goals are flexible, in that they are person variables—a goal only has motivational power and significance if individuals are engaged (consciously or nonconsciously) in pursuing it—but they can be represented and manipulated by situational parameters. Level of aspiration, for example, is a facet of goal pursuit that chronically varies between people, but can also be manipulated in the laboratory. Not surprisingly, then, personality and social psychologists have often studied similar aspects of goals, with relatively more focus on variation between individuals or variations in situations respectively.

Research on goals can be organized by goal content, goal structure, and processes associated with goal pursuit, including goal-setting and self-regulation. More recently, there has also been rapid growth of research on automatic processes associated with goal pursuit. The relative specificity of many goal concepts means that they often predict quite specific behaviors that vary across situations in ways that broad motive-based approaches cannot distinguish. Moreover, goal-based accounts often address processes that are missing or less well elaborated by those focusing primarily on broad motives or primarily on situational factors. These approaches provide the pieces that, when integrated, allow us to understand how motives are translated into goals by people reacting to their own perceptions, experience, choice, and creation of situations or context.

Goals: Appraisal, Structure, and Content

Researchers focusing on particular types of goals or dimensions of appraisals often integrate results from both person-centered and situation-centered research, yielding deep and detailed understanding within their particular focus. Understanding different types of goals and how people vary in their appraisal of them facilitates consideration of the strategies they develop to pursue those goals.

Presaging the "Cognitive Revolution" that overtook psychology in the late 1900s (Simon, 1985), expectancy x value approaches to motivation established that the individual's understanding of incentives and probabilities of success are fundamental contributors to their motivation (Atkinson, 1964; Eccles & Wigfield, 2002; Rotter, 1966). This influence led to a large literature on goal-setting and goal-striving (Lewin, 1951). The Gestalt view of perception as an active process (Sheerer, 1954) also sent tendrils into goals research, encouraging a move from exclusive focus on "objective" characteristics of situations and contingencies toward study of the ways in which those representations are influenced by individuals constructing their perceptions of the world through different lenses, which include motivation and affect (Brunswik, 1956; Kelly, 1955).

GOAL APPRAISAL

The specific goals individuals set for themselves are influenced by the perceived likelihood of attaining a goal and its desirability (Ajzen & Fishbein, 1980). Desirability is influenced by personality factors (Roberts, Wood, & Caspi, 2008), anticipated affect (Baumeister, Vohs, DeWall, & Zhang, 2007), counterfactual thinking (e.g., Epstude & Roese, 2008), and by the relative nearness of the goal, with desirability being more salient for distant goals. In contrast, feasibility is more salient for psychologically closer goals (Liberman & Trope, 1998). Likelihood estimations are influenced both by outcome expectancies and self-efficacy beliefs (Bandura, 1977).

The goals that individuals pursue include those assigned or imposed by others. The latter may be transformed into more personal goals, depending on factors such as the relationship between assigned goals and personal values, legitimacy of the assignment source, and individual skills (Locke & Latham, 2006). Goals that individuals see as congruent with their core values, interests, and desires are considered

intrinsic, while those adopted because of internalized "shoulds" or external forces are considered extrinsic (Sheldon & Elliot, 1999). Social context may influence goal selection and goal-setting, as when individuals are confronted with tasks that are normative for a given life transition. A normative task may be translated into an intrinsic or an extrinsic goal: for example, a religious confirmation may represent a personal, spiritual destination, or a ritual one endures to receive presents or avoid parental condemnation.

Broad traits are also associated with patterns of appraisals for goals. Conscientiousness, extraversion, and agreeableness positively correlate with importance ratings for personal projects, while conscientiousness and extraversion correlate with visibility ratings for interpersonal projects. Openness and low neuroticism correlate positively with enjoyment ratings (Little, Lecci, & Watkinson, 1992; see also, Stimson, Grant, Choquet, & Garrison, 2007).

Ozer and his colleagues are developing a taxonomy of appraisal dimensions that could be used to characterize both individuals and situations (Kaiser & Ozer, 1997; Stauner, Stimson, & Ozer, 2009). Such a taxonomy would facilitate examination of the interactions between individual differences and situational parameters, in ways that might help us go beyond finding correlations between traits and appraisals.

GOAL STRUCTURE AND CONTENT

Goals vary in terms of how concrete (specific) or abstract they are (Locke & Latham, 1990; Wegner, Vallacher, Macomber, Wood, & Arps, 1984). Individuals differ in their preferences for more abstract or more specific goal identification, as well as the level of abstraction at which they identify their actions (Vallacher & Wegner, 1989). More concrete or specific goals are typically necessary when pursuing difficult goals and when encountering obstacles (Vallacher & Wegner, 1987).

Goals vary in regulatory focus, for example, whether they are prevention goals or promotion goals or, more broadly, whether they are approach or avoidance goals. Importantly, in each of these cases, a specific endpoint or outcome can often be defined differently along these dimensions, by individuals or by external framing. The influence of approach and avoidance on the framing of goals is at least partially independent. Broad approach-avoidance goal content dimensions can be used to consider other content categories: for example, self-protection goals versus self-enhancement goals; or belongingness goals framed either as "make new friends so I'm not lonely" or "make new friends so life is more interesting."

Gable has found that social avoidance and social approach goals are associated with negative and positive social outcomes, respectively (Gable, 2006). The relationship between social avoidance goals and outcomes is mediated by a reactivity process characterized by stronger reactions to negative outcomes and an emphasis on potential threat in social situations. In contrast, the relationship between social approach goals and social outcomes is mediated by an exposure process, whereby people with stronger appetitive motivation and approach goals are more likely to seek out, create, and take advantage of potentially positive social opportunities (Gable, 2006; Strachman & Gable, 2006).

Facets of the self can operate as goals, with particular content related to specific affective consequences. Possible selves (Markus & Nurius, 1986) are mental representations of ways that individuals would like to be (ideal selves), feel they ought to be (ought selves), fear becoming (feared selves), or wish to avoid (undesired selves; Ogilvie, 1987). Discrepancies between one's ideal self and actual self are related to dejection emotions, while discrepancies between one's ought self and actual self are related to agitation emotions (Higgins, Klein, & Strauman, 1985). Discrepancy between actual and feared or undesired selves moderates these relationships (Carver, Lawrence, & Scheier, 1999; Heppen & Ogilvie, 2003).

The approaches above are particularly useful in that they consider individuals' understanding and appraisal of their goals in ways that include structural aspects of personality (e.g., self-systems and traits) and factors outside the individual (e.g., external imposition of goals, normative demands), as well as the agency of the individual. In doing so, they also begin to bring vital affective factors—initially missing from early social cognition work—into goal research.

Goal Pursuit and Self-Regulation
GOAL SELECTION AND COMMITMENT

The process of selecting and committing to a goal and then pursuing it can be complex, and requires consideration of situational opportunities and limitations, as well as individual factors (Bandura, 1990; Gollwitzer, 1999; Kruglanski et al., 2002). Several researchers have analyzed these processes and their varying implications for affect and outcome.

Mind-Set Theory of Action Phases

The mind-set theory of action phases describes how people select among goals through a series of four phases, each with a corresponding facilitative mind-set (Gollwitzer, 1999; Heckhausen & Gollwitzer, 1987). The predecisional phase involves evaluating the desirability and feasibility of the goals, a process facilitated by an open, deliberative mind-set that is relatively objective, realistic, and open to information (Bayer & Gollwitzer, 2005; Fujita, Gollwitzer, & Oettingen, 2007; F. Gagné & Lydon, 2001). The end of the predecisional phase is a decision to act: namely, setting a goal.

Once individuals have committed themselves to a goal, they begin to plan, which induces an implemental mind-set (Gollwitzer & Bayer, 1999). In this closed mind-set, information irrelevant to their goal is disregarded, and people generate implementation intentions: that is, they select particular means to move toward their goal. This increases commitment and facilitates action by encouraging generation of if-then contingencies and increasing accessibility of goal-relevant information (Gollwitzer, 1999; Gollwitzer & Sheeran, 2006). An implemental mind-set creates a narrow focus on positive information: perceptions of vulnerability decrease, and illusory optimism increases (Gollwitzer & Kinney, 1989; Taylor & Gollwitzer, 1995). This, in turn, enhances perceptions of the desirability and feasibility of the goal, which then strengthens commitment.

Personality Systems Interaction Theory

In his personality systems interaction theory, Kuhl (2001) describes two volitional dispositions related to mind-set. State-orientation individual tends to excel at the cognitive representation of their goals, but have difficulty enacting their intentions: they get stuck in thought, particularly under difficult or stressful task demands. Action-oriented individuals, in contrast, process information more automatically and efficiently, and tend to be able to carry out their intentions more quickly and effectively (Goschke & Kuhl, 1996). Action-oriented individuals reap the motivational benefits of positive affect derived from an implemental mind-set, which energizes their efforts and decreases perceptions of potential difficulties (Kazén, Kaschel, & Kuhl, 2008). Action orientation also facilitates shielding goals, for example, protecting them from competing demands by controlling attention, emotion, and one's environment (Kuhl & Beckmann, 1994).

Fantasy Realization Theory

Oettingen's (2000) theory of fantasy realization describes the process of goal selection and goal pursuit in terms of three mental strategies that mediate the effects of expectations on goal commitment, effort, and subsequent outcomes: mental contrasting, dwelling, and indulging. Mental contrasting is when current conditions are compared to a positive imagined future. Dwelling involves thinking only about a present negative reality, while indulging involves thinking only about a positive future reality.

Mental contrasting and high expectations are associated with feeling energized, making specific plans, and exerting effort, while mental contrasting and low expectations are associated with less commitment and effort. Dwelling and indulging lead to moderate commitment, independent of expectations for success (Oettingen, Pak, & Schnetter, 2001). Mental contrasting increases planning and energization, and thus goal commitment (Oettingen & Stephens, 2009). Indulging in positive fantasies, however, leads to weaker commitment and less success (Oettingen & Mayer, 2002).

Each of these process-based approaches includes situational factors as defined by individuals' understandings of their own goals and contexts. Variation in situations should influence that understanding, though not independently of individual dispositions. Presumably, other personality structures should also interact to influence goal selection and commitment, but that largely remains to be explored in further research.

SELF-REGULATION

Selecting goals and committing to them is only part of the process (Heckhausen, Wrosch, & Schulz, 2010). Regulating behavior so as to realize one's goals is also essential. Individuals pursuing goals need to exert control over attention, perception, and behavior: they need to self-regulate for successful goal pursuit (Carver & Scheier, 1981).

Self-Regulatory Strength

Muraven, Baumeister, and Tice (1999) propose that self-regulatory strength is analogous to muscle strength: it can be exhausted after exertion, leading to self-regulatory depletion, but can be strengthened through regular exercise (for a review, see DeWall, Baumeister, Schurtz, & Gailliot, 2010). For example, prior thought suppression leads to less success in refraining from alcohol consumption (Muraven, Collins, & Neinhaus, 2002), and coping with stressful work days leads to less exercise (Sonnentag & Jelden, 2005), while self-regulatory exercises increase performance on self-regulatory tasks (Gailliot, Plant, Butz, & Baumeister, 2007).

Affect and Self-Regulation

Positive affect can facilitate goal pursuit, and negative affect can derail it; however, the relationship between affect and goal pursuit is a function of both the nature of the goal pursued and the self-regulation strategies of the individual. Kazen and Kuhl (2005) found that positive affect was correlated with successful behavioral intentions. Positive affect is also associated with selective attention toward reward stimuli (Tamir & Robinson, 2007) and a more narrow focus on specific action tendencies and the goal at hand (Gable & Harmon-Jones, 2008). Tice, Bratslavsky, and Baumeister (2001) found that feeling distraught was associated with difficulty in delay of gratification and increased procrastination because people felt that inaction would alleviate their negative affect.

Individual differences, goal content, and goal structure, however, qualify the generality of these results. For example, positive affect facilitates shielding of goals, but only when goal attainment is relatively distant. When goal attainment is proximate, positive affect tends to lower shields around a goal, while negative affect increases them (Fishbach & Dhar, 2005). The calm experienced when prevention-focused individuals succeed can lead to subsequent decreases in effort, while the anxiety they feel when they perceive negative feedback or encounter obstacles can increase effort (Werth & Forster, 2007). Higgins's (2006) discussion of regulatory fit between promotion-focus and eager strategies and prevention-focus and vigilant strategies highlights the importance of considering self-regulation strategies in the context of individual goals and particular contexts (Renkema & Van Yperen, 2008).

Positive affect can hinder motivation and performance on complex and ill-defined tasks (Markman, Lindberg, Kray, & Galinsky, 2007; Oettingen & Mayer, 2002; Tamir, 2009). The same focus on reward stimuli that may increase motivation may blind individuals to negative cues that signal the need for further preparation or effort, lead them to overly optimistic estimations of chances for success, or to overly superficial or heuristic processing. Positive affect prior to or during contemplation of goal pursuit may even provide enough satisfaction to forestall further effort (Brunstein & Gollwitzer, 1996; Oettingen et al., 2001)

Integrating Influences on Goal Appraisal and Goal Pursuit

Much of the integration of personality and social approaches to motivation is relatively implicit: that is, researchers use multiple perspectives to study goals and goals pursuit, without much regard for whether a perspective is primarily social or personality oriented in pedigree. Some researchers, however, more explicitly attempt to integrate perspectives, particularly with respect to understanding how individuals confront external situations: sometimes seeing ostensibly similar circumstances in very different ways; sometimes see ostensibly different circumstances similarly.

ACHIEVEMENT SITUATIONS: MOTIVES, BELIEFS, AND GOALS

From a social-cognitive perspective, beliefs about oneself and about the nature of competence and ability should influence what people are trying to do in their lives, and the characteristic ways they go about doing it. Dweck and her colleagues have shown that naive theories about ability and performance influence approaches to achievement situations. Entity theorists (who believe ability and intelligence are fixed) tend to focus on setting performance goals: that is, goals that represent specific desired or feared outcomes. Incremental theorists (who believe ability and performance can be incrementally increased with effort) focus on learning goals: that is, goals concerning improving skills and understanding (Dweck, 1999; Dweck & Leggett, 1988; Hong, Chiu, Dweck, Lin, & Wan, 1999). Incremental theorists exert more effort after mistakes or failure, and attribute good performances to effort. Entity theorists attribute outcomes to ability. Mistakes indicate a lack of ability, are feared, and generate defensive strategies and helplessness (Blackwell, Trzesniewski, & Dweck, 2007; Robins & Pals, 2002).

Elliot and his colleagues crossed mastery/performance goals with approach/avoidance motivation to describe four kinds of achievement goals: mastery-approach, mastery-avoidance, performance-approach, and performance-avoidance. Individuals who set mastery-approach goals work to develop competence by mastering increasingly difficult tasks. Those who set mastery-avoidance goals work to avoid doing worse than they have done previously. Performance-approach goals focus on demonstrating normative competence: that is, doing well relative to others; while performance-avoidance goals focus on avoiding demonstration of incompetence (Elliot & Church, 1997; Elliot & Harackiewicz, 1996).

Achievement goals are proximal predictors of both intrinsic motivation and performance. Approach goals are associated with better performance overall, with mastery-approach associated with better outcomes than performance-approach. Performance approach goals, however, do not undermine interest, whereas performance avoidance goals do (Rawsthorne & Elliot, 1999). Performance-avoidance is associated with better outcomes than mastery-avoidance (Cury, Elliot, Da Fonseca, & Moller, 2006).

Focusing on the way that general orientations and beliefs lead to specific achievement goals illuminates several aspects of goal pursuits and motivation, including interest, effort expenditure, and outcomes. This approach can be applied to a variety of achievement situations, and readily suggests connection to individual differences in self-regulatory strategies (e.g., Elliot & Church, 2003).

PERSONAL GOALS AS PERSONALITY

A number of researchers have approached the study of goals by considering them as middle-level units of personality that are influenced by general motivations; specific situational constraints, affordances, and demands; and the active, problem-solving efforts of individuals. Little (1989; Palys & Little, 1983) has extensively studied individuals' "personal projects," which he describes as personally engrossing sets of actions. Klinger (e.g., Klinger & Cox, 2004) studies a related concept he calls "personal concerns." Emmons and his colleagues have looked at "personal strivings" as general motivational categories that organize individual efforts (Emmons, 1989; Emmons & King, 1988). These approaches share the assumption that, although there may be species-general motivations that all humans share, there is wide latitude for investment of personal meaning as those motivations are translated into specific goals.

Cantor and her colleagues have studied how individuals navigate life transitions by looking at the age-graded life tasks salient in those transitions, and the variations in the ways that individuals construe those tasks and individualize them (Cantor, 1990; Cantor, Norem, Niedenthal, Langston, & Brower, 1987). Individual goals interact with group structures to influence engagement with the group and personal identity negotiation (Cantor, Kemmelmeier, Basten, & Prentice, 2002). Life tasks guide the ways that individuals organize their efforts

(Cantor, Norem, Langston, & Zirkel, 1991; Harlow & Cantor, 1995; Zirkel & Cantor, 1990), and the relevance and affective implications of situations and activities are a function of the extent to which they represent avenues for life task pursuit (Fleeson & Cantor, 1995; Sanderson & Cantor, 1999).

SELF-REGULATION STRATEGIES, PERSONALITY, AND GOALS: DEFENSIVE PESSIMISM

Many of the aspects of goal content and appraisal discussed earlier are influenced by both individual and situational factors. Whether preparing for an upcoming exam is difficult, ill-defined, or complex may be a function the number of problems on the exam and how many competing goals an individual may be pursuing, such as finding time to study for the exam without missing hours at one's job.

For those who are anxious, for example, performance situations are importantly different situations than they are for nonanxious individuals. Anxiety complicates their goal pursuit—and is inseparable from that pursuit—because it presents a potential source of performance disruption and is fundamental to their framing of specific goals in specific situations. Thus, they need a strategy for goal pursuit that, ideally, addresses both achieving their goals and managing their anxiety so that it does not interfere with their performance.

Self-handicapping is a relatively ineffective (albeit common) strategy used by anxious individuals; it helps to down-regulate anxiety, but often impedes effort expenditure and commitment, and consequently, performance; self-handicappers' performance is especially likely to deteriorate over time. Defensive pessimism, in contrast, attempts to address anxiety management, while moving people toward their goals. Defensive pessimism as a strategy involves first setting low expectations (i.e., being pessimistic), and then thinking through all the negative things that might happen (in concrete and vivid detail) when anticipating a performance or goal-relevant situation (Norem & Illingworth, 1993). Focusing on concrete negative possibilities aids specific action planning and switches focus from anxiety to the task at hand. In Gollwitzer's terms, defensive pessimism facilitates implementation intentions, and moves individuals from the immobilization of state orientation to an action orientation. This approach does little to alleviate their negative affect (and may even exacerbate it initially). It does, however, lead to better outcomes, in that defensive pessimists typically perform as well as nonanxious individuals who focus on maintaining

positive affect (Sanna, 1998), and better than anxious individuals who do not use defensive pessimism (see Norem, 2008, for a review). Defensive pessimists perform more poorly and are less satisfied under positive affect conditions than negative affect conditions, and for them, negative affect is positively correlated with performance (Norem & Illingworth, 2004; Sanna, 1998).

Even when external circumstances or objective characteristics of a goal seem similar for everyone, internal characteristics and understandings may contribute to very different goal contexts (Norem & Andreas Burdzovic, 2007). For those who might be vulnerable to stereotype-threat (Steele, 1988), for example, defensive pessimism may be a particularly apt strategy. Among African American students at predominantly white institutions, Brower and Ketterhagen (2004) found that those who used defensive pessimism performed better and had higher retention rates than those who did not. Perry and Skitka (2009) showed that African American women who used defensive pessimism actually performed better on a math test under experimentally induced conditions of stereotype threat.

These approaches promote the study of motivation as it is embedded in the rich contexts of people's understanding of their lives. They describe what people are trying to do across a variety of specific situations—a focus on "action agendas," that characterizes a functionalist approach to the study of motivation (Cantor, 1990; Omoto, Snyder, & Martino, 2000; Snyder & Cantor, 1998).

AUTOMATIC PROCESSES AND IMPLICIT GOALS

Much of the previously discussed goal research implicates an agentic self and assumes that the processes involved in goal-setting and subsequent goal pursuit are primarily conscious. Some aspects of goal activation, and the influence of goals on cognition, affect, and behavior during goal pursuit, however, result from processes outside of conscious awareness (Bargh, 1997). Building on dual-process models that contrasted automatic with controlled processes (e.g., Chaiken & Trope, 1999; Posner & Snyder, 1975; Shiffrin & Schneider, 1977), studies of priming and of cognitive structures outside of conscious awareness point to many parallels between implicit and explicit processes (for a review, see Bargh & Huang, 2009). As with conscious goals, implicit goals direct attention toward goal-relevant stimuli (e.g., Maner et al., 2005; McCulloch, Ferguson, Kawada, & Bargh, 2008). For example, under an implicit achievement motivation prime, working on easier tasks (and thus succeeding) increased motivation for subsequent tasks, while working on a more difficult task (and failing) subsequently led to decreased effort (Chartrand & Bargh, 2002). The mood effects associated with success versus failure in this study parallel those in studies where achievement goals are explicit (e.g., Carver & Scheier, 1982), and presumably influence subsequent evaluation of the desirability of related tasks. Congruent with that assumption, work by Aarts and colleagues shows that implicit conditioning of positive or negative affect associated with a goal increases effort or disengagement, respectively (e.g., Aarts, Custers, & Holland, 2007; Aarts, Custers, & Marien, 2008).

Researchers have demonstrated the nonconscious priming of interpersonal and impression formation goals (Chartrand & Bargh, 1996; Fitzsimons & Bargh, 2003). Jost, Pietrzak, Liviaton, Mandisodza, and Napier (2008) demonstrated how priming an implicit system justification motive can account for people's conscious advocacy of systems that operate against their own self-interests, or interfere with social desirability motivations that might otherwise determine conscious responses.

Among many psychologists, skepticism about nonconscious processing has given way to enthusiasm (e.g., Bargh et al., 2010). The idea that implicit motivation could be activated by subtle situational cues, and influence behavior in ways that run parallel to or even oppose conscious intentions is congruent with earlier theory and research on implicit motives. Newer research, however, extends the range of motivations and potential primes beyond those systematically studied previously, and provides a more elaborated and specific model of both nonconscious and conscious cognitive structures and processes.

Future Directions

Looking across the several paradigms of motivation research in this chapter reveals some fascinating convergence: research programs starting with different assumptions, questions, and measures point both to further compelling questions and to intriguing suggestions of constructs that might provide answers. Three of those interrelated questions are discussed here.

Conscious Versus Nonconscious Goal Pursuit

At the level of general motivations and specific goals, it is clear that both conscious and nonconscious goal-setting and goal pursuit processes

influence affect, perception, cognition, and behavior. Currently, however, we know relatively little about the interaction of conscious and nonconscious (implicit) motivation. Specifically, we know very little about "who (or what) is in charge" when both implicit and explicit motives and goals are activated. Do conscious self-regulation efforts and controlled processing trump the effects of an activated implicit goal and consequent automatic processes? Or, are our conscious, agentic selves at the mercy of whatever situational cues happen to prime nonconscious goals?

Research suggesting that people often are unaware of influences on their behavior would seem to support the argument that nonconscious influences are generally more powerful than we think (Wegner, 2002; Wilson, 2002); and that they exert influence over which we have little control, even if we try to believe otherwise (Bargh, 1997). Evidence of a goal turnoff effect, where behavior that fulfills a goal activated outside of awareness seems to satisfy that goal and "turn it off" so that it does not affect behavior subsequently, suggests that we may run into obstacles created by goals processes we are not consciously monitoring (Meece & Miller, 2001; Zhong & Liljenquist, 2006). There are also extreme cases, where nonconscious goals seem to override self-interest and, possibly, conscious intentions, as in the case of environmental dependency syndrome, where lesions in prefrontal cortex lead people to lack awareness of their own goals and to respond only to external cues (L'hermitte, 1986); or where "lower" automatic systems operate against conscious efforts (Morsella, 2005).

There are also, however, studies that suggest that conscious intentions can override automatic processes by shifting attention, influencing perceptions, increasing vigilance, or encouraging increased effort and more effective strategies directed toward conscious goals. Warnings or information about stereotyping or responding prejudicially can lead people to be more vigilant about cues that might elicit prejudice and they can tune their perceptions and increase their self-regulation efforts so as to facilitate egalitarian goals (Mendoza, Gollwitzer, & Amodio, 2010; Monteith, 1993).

Mindfulness—the conscious effort to be aware of one's thoughts, feelings, and impressions in the moment—lowers prejudiced responding in response to automatic activation of stereotypes (Legault, Green-Demers, Grant, & Chung, 2007). Niemiec, Brown, and Ryan (2007) found that highly mindful participants did not show automatic defensive reactions to mortality salience manipulations, and Moller et al. (2006) showed that, when people are allowed "true choice," they do not show automatic ego depletion effects. Jamieson and Harkins (2007, 2009, 2010) found that the automatic effects of stereotype threat can be understood as potentiating prepotent responses, which can lead to poor performance when the prepotent response is not a good fit for the task. They also showed, however, that very simple instructions allowed participants to override their prepotent responses, which eliminated performance deficits under threat conditions.

Overall, at this point, we have relatively few studies that directly pit nonconscious and conscious goals against one another in ways that allow direct comparison of their influence (Kihlstrom, 2008). Many of the effects related to automatic processes have been found in otherwise relatively sterile motivational contexts: that is, in laboratory studies where there is reason to suspect that participants' personal, conscious goals are not being actively pursued. As a result, they may be more vulnerable to automatic processes outside of their awareness, precisely because they are not engaged in conscious shielding or self-regulation efforts, and have little investment in the outcomes measured (Fishbach, Friedman, & Kruglanski, 2003). Fuller understanding of the consequences and implications of automaticity for goal pursuit also awaits further exploration of the extent to which nonconscious goals and related processes are ultimately inaccessible (Kihlstrom, 2009).

There would seem to be considerable potential for exploring the interactions between implicit and explicit motivational processes—and in the process, to illuminate the conditions under which situational influences on motivation vary. Implicit motive theory suggests that those high in a particular implicit motive might be especially "primable" by cues relevant to that motive, but somewhat immune to competing primes. This could be tested by either a between-subjects or within-subjects design (or both), given the dynamic nature of implicit motive levels. Findings suggesting that implicit and explicit motivations influence different kinds of behaviors and outcomes raise the question of whether there are categories of behavior that are relatively unaffected by priming: for example, performance might be more strongly affected by achievement-relevant primes than self-presentation is. Schultheiss's concept of regulatory competence is a reasonable candidate in the search for moderators of these effects: Those who are able to bring their explicit and implicit motivations in line may be less vulnerable

to automatic processes that might otherwise interfere with conscious self-regulation attempts.

Congruence and Conflict in Motive/Goal Systems

Of course conscious and nonconscious goals and processes need not operate in conflict: they can potentially be congruent or facilitative (Monteith, Ashburn-Nardo, Voils, & Czopp, 2002; Moskowitz, 2001). Indeed, a number of studies have shown that congruence across goal levels is related to more successful goal pursuits and greater well-being and satisfaction (Brunstein, Schultheiss, & Grässmann, 1998). Incongruence between implicit motives and conscious goals correlates with lower satisfaction (Hofer & Chasiotis, 2003) and increased psychosomatic complaints (Baumann, Kaschel, & Kuhl, 2005).

In general, conflict between motivations or goals, whether across levels or within, is underresearched relative to its seeming relevance to daily life and emotional experience (Emmons & King, 1988; Emmons, King, & Sheldon, 1993). Conflict among goals, or confusion about standards is related to poorer self-regulation (Baumeister, Heatherton, & Tice, 1994) and even the presence of multiple motivations (without active conflict) is related to negative outcomes (Kiviniemi, Snyder, & Omoto, 2002). Thus the question of dynamic relations among motives and goals within individuals begs for further research and integration across perspectives.

We need more research to define the important aspects of congruence and conflict themselves: Is congruence the absence of conflict, or does it involve more active integration or facilitation among goals, greater tolerance for conflict, or better regulation of attention? Is it achieved by dropping conflicting versions of goals, by creative synthesis, or by superordinate appraisal (e.g., "all my goals are autonomous")?

Prior research has generated a number of appraisal dimensions that are influential in goal pursuit. Further research on those dimensions, compared across goals and contexts, within individuals, might enrich our understanding of congruence and conflict among explicit goals and motivations. Congruence or conflict at an implicit level could be explored by presenting competing cues that have already been shown to elicit different motivations, to see how they influence behavior when presented simultaneously under different conditions.

There are tantalizing hints about individual differences and self-regulation efforts that can increase congruence, and they point to exciting avenues for future research.

Individuals' awareness of their own feelings, including affect and bodily sensations, seems key to promoting congruence, especially between automatic and hedonically driven implicit processes on the one hand and effortful, analytic processes on the other (Job & Brandstatter, 2009; Schultheiss, Jones, Davis, & Kley, 2008). Self-determined individuals are more congruent (Elliot & Thrash, 2002), as are those higher in private body awareness. State-oriented individuals are less congruent (especially under stress), possibly because they inhibit awareness of affect. Researchers could examine situational factors (in field studies) or manipulations (in the laboratory) that promote or inhibit affective or bodily awareness or internalization of goals to see whether they reduce or increase congruence in goals or motives across levels, and whether changes in congruence are associated with subsequent outcomes.

Self and Self-Regulation

Congruence not just among goals and motives, but between goals and self is also related to well-being (e.g., Sheldon et al., 2004) and relatively underresearched, especially with respect to how individuals manage or fail to pursue goals that feel appropriately aligned with other aspects of their self-concepts. The self is directly implicated in self-protection and self-enhancement, but also in need to belong, competence, control, and autonomy motivations. Self-relevance amplifies virtually every process and consequence of goal pursuit (Alicke & Sedikides, 2009), as exemplified in the extreme case of fused identities that lead to extreme motivations and actions (Swann, Gomez, Seyle, Morales, & Huici, 2009).

There are hints concerning influences on self/goal congruence: for example, stress increases "self-infiltration," whereby people misremember imposed goals as self-selected (Quirin, Koole, Baumann, Kazen, & Kuhl, 2009). Self-infiltration could increase incongruence both among goals and between goals and self, because external demands are internalized but not integrated (Ryan & Deci, 2006). We may need further descriptive research that compares self-appraisal dimensions with goal appraisal dimensions to further our understanding of self/goal congruence.

The concept of self-regulatory resources has potential here, in that it provides a way to consider multiple competing demands on individuals, and to look at allocation of motivational resources across different contexts. Those who feel they have more choice about their distribution of self-regulatory resources, for example, may feel more self/goal congruence, even under competing demands or stress.

Self/goal congruence may also involve more than the relationship between any particular goal and self: It may be, at least partially, a function of the relationship between one's self-system and one's system of motives and goals. What happens if, for example, the relative prominence or influence of one or more major implicit motives is incongruent with one's self-concept: If one is high in n aff, but a salient part of one's identity is being a high-achiever, does that create a disruptive sense that motivations do not align with self?

Summary

Motivation is a part of almost every key question and major research area in personality and social psychology because, in our attempts to understand human behavior, we want to know why people initiate, try, pursue, or disengage in whatever it is that we are studying—and those are motivational questions. The limits of purely situational or purely dispositional accounts of motivation have been clear to both personality and social psychologists since strict behaviorism and dogmatic psychoanalysis gave way to other approaches in psychology.

While there are differences in emphasis and approach between personality and social psychologists who study motivation, there is also considerable agreement about major motivations, approach and avoidance distinctions, the importance of exploring both implicit and explicit motivations, the significance of goals as organizers of coherent action, their impact on affective experience, and the consequential role of self-regulation. The majority of motivational constructs and theories that have been central to personality and social psychologists exist in versions that reflect the relative differences in emphasis between those groups in complementary ways. Approach and avoidance, for example, are instantiated in general behavioral tendencies, the different faces of implicit motives, and specific versions of goals and regulatory focus, but can be manipulated or induced by situational factors such as framing, and have different consequences depending on the situation. Similarly, implicit motives vary in chronic strength across individuals, but can be activated by situational primes. Goal appraisals have been studied as a function of external constraints and as expressions of personality, and goal pursuit can be viewed as an general set of stages, the relative difficulty of which varies as a function of general personality orientations.

Neither the focus of past research, nor the crucial questions for future research break down along a clear line dividing personality and social psychology. Instead, we have converging results across multiple research programs that point toward the next big questions, and those questions require even more integration across approaches. The idea, for example, that we need to find out more about the relationship between implicit and explicit motives and goals comes not from a personality perspective or a social perspective, but from research that crosses those boundaries to reveal that both externally primed automatic processes and internal implicit motives influence different behaviors than, and can interfere with, their explicit counterparts.

Motivation research offers an ideal arena in which to see the advantages of integration across traditional divisions between social and personality psychology. Indeed, personality and social psychologists are motivated to answer many of the same motivational questions, use many of the same motivational constructs, and face many of the same complexities. We have much in common in our endeavors to understand human motivation, and little to gain from distinctions between sides of the same coin.

References

Aarts, H., Custers, R., & Holland, R. W. (2007). The nonconscious cessation of goal pursuit: When goals and negative affect are coactivated. *Journal of Personality and Social Psychology, 92*, 165–178.

Aarts, H., Custers, R., & Marien, H. (2008). Preparing and motivating behavior outside of awareness. *Science, 319,* 1639.

Ackerman, J. M., Shapiro, J. R., Neuberg, S. L., Kenrick, D. T., Becker, D. V., Griskevicius, V., et al. (2006). They all look the same to me (unless they're angry): From out-group homogeneity to out-group heterogeneity. *Psychological Science, 17*(10), 836–840.

Adler, A. (1930). *Problems of neurosis.* Oxford, UK: Cosmopolitan.

Ajzen, I., & Fishbein, M. (1980). *Understanding attitudes and predicting social behavior.* Englewood Cliffs, NJ: Prentice-Hall.

Alicke, M. D., & Sedikides, C. (2009). Self-enhancement and self-protection: What they are and what they do. *European Review of Social Psychology, 20*(1), 1–48.

Allport, F. H. (1924). *Social psychology.* Boston: Houghton Mifflin.

Allport, G. W. (1937) The functional autonomy of motives. *American Journal of Psychology, 50,* 141–156.

Amabile, T. M., DeJong, W., & Lepper, M. (1976). Effects of externally imposed deadlines on subsequent intrinsic motivation. *Journal of Personality and Social Psychology Bulletin, 34,* 92–98.

Amodio, D. M., Devine, P. G., & Harmon-Jones, E. (2007). A dynamic model of guilt: Implications for motivation and self-regulation in the context of prejudice. *Psychological Science, 18*(6), 524–530.

Amodio, D. M., & Harmon-Jones, E. (2011). Neuroscience Approaches in Social and Personality Psychology. In K. Deaux & M. Snyder (Eds.), *Handbook of personality and social psychology* (pp. xxx–xxx). New York: Oxford University Press.

Asch, S. E. (1946). Forming impressions of personality. *Journal of Abnormal and Social Psychology, 41,* 258–290.

Atkinson, J. W. (1957). Motivational determinants of risk-taking behavior. *Psychological Review, 64,* 359–372.

Atkinson, J. W. (1964). *An introduction to motivation.* Oxford, UK: Van Nostrand.

Atkinson, J. W., & Birch, D. (1970). The dynamics of action. Oxford, UK: Wiley.

Atkinson, J. W., Heyns, R. W., & Veroff, J. (1954). The effect of experimental arousal of the affiliation motive on thematic apperception. *Journal of Abnormal and Social Psychology, 49,* 405–410.

Atkinson, J. W., & O'Connor, P. (1966). Neglected factors in studies of achievement-oriented performance: Social approval as an incentive and performance decrement. In J. W. Atkinson & N. T. Feather (Eds.), *A theory of achievement motivation* (pp. 299–326). New York: Wiley.

Atkinson, J. W., & Raynor, J. O. (1978). *Personality, motivation, and achievement.* Oxford, UK: Hemisphere.

Baard, P. P., Deci, E. L., & Ryan, R. M. (2004). Intrinsic need satisfaction: A motivational basis of performance and well-being in two work settings. *Journal of Applied Social Psychology, 34,* 2045–2068.

Balconi, M., Falbo, L., & Brambilla, E. (2009). BIS/BAS responses to emotional cues: Self report, autonomic measure and alpha band modulation. *Personality and Individual Differences, 47,* 858–863.

Bales, R. F. (1950). Interaction process analysis: A method for the study of small groups. Oxford, UK: Addison-Wesley.

Bandura, A. (1974). Behavior theory and the models of man. *American Psychologist, 29*(12), 859–869.

Bandura, A. (1977). Self-efficacy: Toward a unifying theory of behavioral change. *Psychological Review, 84,* 191–215.

Bandura, A. (1990). Perceived self-efficacy in the exercise of personal agency. *Journal of Applied Sport Psychology, 2*(2), 128–163.

Bargh, J. A. (1997). The automaticity of everyday life. In R. S. Wyer Jr. (Ed.), *The automaticity of everyday life: Advances in social cognition* (Vol. 10, pp. 1–61). Mahwah, NJ: Erlbaum.

Bargh, J. A., Gollwitzer, P. M., & Oettingen, G. (2010). Motivation. In S. T. Fiske, D. T. Gilbert, & G. Lindzey (Eds.), *Handbook of social psychology* (5th ed., pp. 268–316.). New York: Wiley.

Bargh, J. A., & Huang, J. Y. (2009). The selfish goal. In G. Moskowitz & H. Grant (Eds.), *The psychology of goals* (pp. 127–150). New York: Guilford.

Baumann, N., Kaschel, R., & Kuhl, J. (2005). Striving for unwanted goals: Stress-dependent discrepancies between explicit and implicit achievement motives reduce subjective well-being and increase psychosomatic symptoms. *Journal of Personality and Social Psychology, 89,* 781–799.

Baumeister, R. F., Heatherton, T. F., & Tice, D. M. (1994). *Losing control: How and why people fail at self-regulation.* San Diego, CA: Academic.

Baumeister, R. F., & Scher, S. J. (1988). Self-defeating behavior patterns among normal individuals: Review and analysis of common self-destructive tendencies. *Psychological Bulletin, 104,* 3–22.

Baumeister, R. F., Vohs, K. D., DeWall, C. N., & Zhang, L. (2007). How emotion shapes behavior: Feedback, anticipation, and reflection, rather than direct causation. *Personality and Social Psychology Review, 11,* 167–203.

Bayer, U. C., & Gollwitzer, P. M. (2005). Mindset effects on information search in self-evaluation. *European Journal of Social Psychology, 35,* 313–327.

Becker, D. V., Kenrick, D. T., Guerin, S., & Maner, J. K. (2005). Concentrating on beauty: Sexual selection and sociospatial memory. *Personality and Social Psychology Bulletin, 31*(12), 1643–1652.

Bentham, J. (1779/1948). *An introduction to the principles of morals and legislation.* Oxford: Blackwell.

Berglas, S., & Jones, E. E. (1978). Drug choice as a self-handicapping strategy in response to noncontingent success. *Journal of Personality an Social Psychology, 36,* 405–417.

Biernat, M. (1989). Motives and values to achieve: Different constructs with different effects. *Journal of Personality, 57,* 69–95.

Blackwell, L. S., Trzesniewski, K. H., & Dweck, C. S. (2007). Implicit theories of intelligence predict achievement across an adolescent transition: A longitudinal study and an intervention. *Child Development, 78,* 246–263.

Boring, E. G. (1950). *A history of experimental psychology.* Englewood Cliffs, NJ: Prentice Hall.

Bosson, J. K., Brown, R. P., Zeigler-Hill, V., & Swann, W. B., Jr. (2003). Self-enhancement tendencies among people with high explicit self-esteem: The moderating role of implicit self-esteem. *Self and Identity, 2,* 169–187.

Bowlby, J. (1969). Disruption of affectional bonds and its effects on behavior. *Canada's Mental Health Supplement, 59.*

Boyatzis, R. E. (1973). Affiliation motivation. In D. C. McClelland & R. S. Steele (Eds.), *Human motivation: A book of readings* (pp. 252–276). Morristown, NJ: General Learning.

Brower, A. M., & Ketterhagen, A. (2004). Is there an inherent mismatch between how black and white students expect to succeed in college and what their colleges expect from them? *Journal of Social Issues, 60*(1), 95–116.

Bruner, J. S., & Postman, L. (1949). Perception, cognition, and behavior. *Journal of Personality, 18,* 14–31.

Brunstein, J. C., & Gollwitzer, P. M. (1996). Effects of failure on subsequent performance: The importance of self-defining goals. *Journal of Personality and Social Psychology, 70,* 395–407.

Brunstein, J. C., & Maier, G. W. (2005). Implicit and self-attributed motives to achieve: Two separate but interacting needs. *Journal of Personality and Social Psychology, 89*(2), 205–222.

Brunstein, J. C., Schultheiss, O. C., & Grässmann, R. (1998). Personal goals and emotional well-being: The moderating role of motive dispositions. *Journal of Personality and Social Psychology, 75*(2), 494–508.

Brunswik, E. (1956). *Perception and the representative design of psychological experiments* (2nd ed.). Berkeley: University of California Press.

Byrne, D. (1961). Interpersonal attraction as a function of affiliation need and attitude similarity. *Human Relations, 14,* 283–289.

Cacioppo, J. T., & Berntson, G. G. (1999). The affect system: Architecture and operating characteristics. *Current Directions in Psychological Science, 8*(5), 133–137.

Calder, B. J., & Staw, B. M. (1975). The interaction of intrinsic and extrinsic motivation: Some methodological notes. *Journal of Personality and Social Psychology, 31,* 76–80.

Cantor, N. (1990). From thought to behavior: "Having" and "doing" in the study of personality and cognition. *American Psychologist, 45,* 735–750.

Cantor, N., Kemmelmeier, M., Basten, J., & Prentice, D. A. (2002). Life-task pursuit in social groups: Balancing self-exploration and social integration. *Self and Identity, 1*(2), 177–184.

Cantor, N., Norem, J., Langston, C., & Zirkel, S. (1991). Life tasks and daily life experience. *Journal of Personality, 59*(3), 425–451.

Cantor, N., Norem, J. K., Niedenthal, P. M., Langston, C. A., & Brower, A. M. (1987). Life tasks, self-concept ideals, and cognitive strategies in a life transition. *Journal of Personality and Social Psychology, 53,* 1178–1191.

Carver, C. S., Lawrence, J. W., & Scheier, M. F. (1999). Self-discrepancies and affect: Incorporating the role of feared selves. *Personality and Social Psychology Bulletin, 25,* 783–792.

Carver, C. S., & Scheier, M. F. (1981). *Attention and self-regulation: A control-theory approach to human behavior.* New York: Springer.

Carver, C. S., & Scheier, M. F. (1982). Outcome expectancy, locus of attribution for expectancy, and self-directed attention as determinants of evaluations and performance. *Journal of Experimental Social Psychology, 18*(2), 184–200.

Carver, C. S., & White, T. L. (1994). Behavioral inhibition, behavioral activation, and affective responses to impending reward and punishment: The BIS/BAS scales. *Journal of Personality and Social Psychology, 67,* 319–333.

Chaiken, S., & Trope, Y. (1999). *Dual process theories in social psychology.* New York: Guilford.

Chartrand, T. L., & Bargh, J. A. (1996). Automatic activation of social information processing goals: Unconscious priming reproduces effects of explicit conscious instructions. *Journal of Personality and Social Psychology, 71,* 464–478.

Chartrand, T. L., & Bargh, J. A. (2002). Unconscious motivations: Their activation, operation, and consequences. In A. Tesser, D. Stapel, & J. Wood (Eds.), *Self and motivation: Emerging psychological perspective* (pp. 13–41). Washington, DC: American Psychological Review.

Chen, M., & Bargh, J. A. (1999). Consequences of automatic evaluation: Immediate behavioral predispositions to approach or avoid the stimulus. *Personality and Social Psychology Bulletin, 25,* 215–224.

Chirkov, V. I., & Ryan, R. M. (2001). Parent and teacher autonomy-support in Russian and U.S. adolescents: Common effects on well-being and academic motivation. *Journal of Cross-Cultural Psychology, 32,* 618–635.

Chirkov, V. I., Ryan, R. M., Kim, Y., & Kaplan, U. (2003). Differentiating autonomy from individualism and independence: A self-determination theory perspective on internalization of cultural orientations and well-being. *Journal of Personality and Social Psychology, 84,* 97–110.

Cloninger, C. R. (1987). A systematic method for clinical description and classification of personality variants: A proposal. *Archives of General Psychiatry, 44,* 573–588.

Coan, J. A., & Allen, J. J. B. (2003). Frontal EEG asymmetry and the behavioral activation and inhibition systems. *Psychophysiology, 40*(1), 106–114.

Cury, F., Elliot, A. J., Da Fonseca, D., & Moller, A. C. (2006). The social-cognitive model of achievement motivation and the 2 x 2 achievement goal framework. *Journal of Personality and Social Psychology, 90*(4), 666–679.

Davidson, R. J. (1995). Brain asymmetry, emotion, and affective style. In R. J. Davidson & K. Hugdahl (Eds.), *Brain asymmetry* (pp. 361–387). Cambridge, MA: MIT Press.

Decharms, R. (1958). Affiliation motivation and productivity in small groups. *Journal of Abnormal and Social Psychology, 55,* 222–226.

Deci, E. L. (1975). *Intrinsic motivation.* New York: Plenum.

Deci, E. L., Koestner, R., & Ryan, R. M. (1999). A meta-analytic review of experiments examining the effects of extrinsic rewards on intrinsic motivation. *Psychological Bulletin, 125,* 627–668.

Deci, E. L., La Guardia, J. G., Moller, A. C., Scheiner, M. J., & Ryan, R. M. (2006). On the benefits of giving as well as receiving autonomy support: Mutuality in close friendships. *Personality and Social Psychology Bulletin, 32,* 313–327.

Deci, E. L., & Ryan, R. M. (1985a). *Intrinsic motivation and self-determination in human behavior.* New York: Plenum.

Deci, E. L., & Ryan, R. M. (1985b). The General Causality Orientations Scale: Self-determination in personality. *Journal of Research in Personality, 19,* 109–134.

Deci, E. L., & Ryan, R. M. (2000). The "what" and "why" of goal pursuits: Human needs and the self-determination of behavior. *Psychological Inquiry, 11,* 227–268.

DeWall, C. N., Baumeister, R. F., Schurtz, D. R., & Gailliot, M. T. (2010). Acting on limited resources: The interactive effects of self-regulatory depletion and individual differences. In R. H. Hoyle (Ed.), *Handbook of personality and self-regulation* (pp. 243–262). Malden, MA: Wiley-Blackwell.

Dweck, C. S. (1999). Self-theories: Their role in motivation, personality, and development. New York: Psychology Press.

Dweck, C. S., & Leggett, E. L. (1988). A social-cognitive approach to motivation and personality. *Psychological Review, 95,* 256–273.

Eccles, J. S., & Wigfield, A. (2002). Motivational beliefs, values, and goals. *Annual Review of Psychology, 53,* 109–132.

Eisenberger, R., Pierce, W. D., & Cameron, J. (1999). Effects of reward on intrinsic motivation—negative, neutral, and positive: Comment on Deci, Koestner, and Ryan. *Psychological Bulletin, 125,* 677–691.

Elliot, A. J. (2008). *Handbook of approach and avoidance motivation.* Mahwah, NJ: Erlbaum.

Elliot, A. J., & Church, M. A. (1997). A hierarchical model of approach and avoidance achievement motivation. *Journal of Personality and Social Psychology, 72,* 218–232.

Elliot, A. J., & Church, M. A. (2003). A motivational analysis of defensive pessimism and self-handicapping. *Journal of Personality, 71,* 369–396.

Elliot, A. J., & Covington, M. V. (2001). Approach and avoidance motivation. *Educational Psychology Review, 13*(2), 73–92.

Elliot, A. J., & Fryer, J. W. (2008). The goal construct in psychology. In Shah, J. Y., & Garner, W. L. (Eds.), *Handbook of motivation science* (pp. 235–250). New York: Guilford.

Elliot, A. J., & Harackiewicz, J. M. (1996). Approach and avoidance achievement goals and intrinsic motivation: A mediational analysis. *Journal of Personality and Social Psychology, 70*(3), 461–475.

Elliot, A. J., & Niesta, D. (2009). Goals in the context of the hierarchical model of approach-avoidance motivation. In G. B. Moskowitz & H. Grant (Eds.), *The psychology of goals* (pp. 56–76). New York: Guilford.

Elliot, A. J., & Thrash, T. M. (2002). Approach-avoidance motivation in personality: Approach and avoidance temperaments and goals. *Journal of Personality and Social Psychology, 82*(5), 804–818.

Emmons, R. A. (1989). The personal striving approach to personality. In L. A. Pervin (Ed.), *Goal concepts in personality and social psychology.* Hillsdale, NJ: Erlbaum.

Emmons, R. A., & King, L. (1988). Conflict among personal strivings: Immediate and long-term implications for psychological and physical well-being. *Journal of Personality and Social Psychology, 54*(6), 1040–1048.

Emmons, R. A., King, L. A., & Sheldon, K. (1993). Goal conflict and the self-regulation of action. In Wegner, D. M., & J. W. Pennebaker (Eds.), *Handbook of mental control* (pp. 528–551). Englewood Cliffs, NJ: Prentice-Hall.

Epstude, K., & Roese, N. J. (2008). The functional theory of counterfactual thinking. *Personality and Social Psychology Review, 12,* 168–192.

Erikson, E. H. (1950). *Childhood and society.* New York: Norton.

Eysenck, H. (1967). *The biological basis of personality.* Springfield, IL: Charles Thomas.

Feather, N. T. (1961). The relationship of persistence at a task to expectation of success and achievement related motives. *Journal of Abnormal and Social Psychology, 63,* 552–561.

Festinger, L. (1954). Motivations leading to social behavior. In M. R. Jones (Ed.), *Nebraska symposium on motivation, 1954.* (pp. 191–219). Lincoln: University of Nebraska Press.

Fishbach, A., & Dhar, R. (2005). Goals as excuses or guides: The liberating effect of perceived goal progress on choice. *Journal of Consumer Research, 32,* 370–377.

Fishbach, A., Friedman, R. S., & Kruglanski, A. W. (2003). Leading us not unto temptation: Momentary allurements elicit overriding goal temptation. *Journal of Personality and Social Psychology, 84,* 296–309.

Fiske, S. T. (2004). *Social beings: A core motives approach to social psychology.* New York: Wiley.

Fitzsimons, G. M., & Bargh, J. A. (2003). Thinking of you: Unconscious pursuit of interpersonal goals associated with relationship partners. *Journal of Personality and Social Psychology, 84,* 148–164.

Fleeson, W., & Cantor, N. (1995). Goal relevance and the affective experience of daily life: Ruling out situational explanations. *Motivation and Emotion, 19,* 25–57.

Forster, J., Higgins, E. T., & Bianco, A. T. (2003). Speed/accuracy decisions in task performance: Built-in trade-off or separate strategic concerns? *Organizational Behavior and Human Decision Processes, 90*(1), 148–164.

Freud, S. (1914/1953). On narcissism: An introduction. In J. Strachey (Ed.), *The standard edition of the complete psychological works of Sigmund Freud* (Vol. 14, pp. 67–102). London: Hogarth.

Freud, S. (1915/1963). Instincts and their vicissitudes. (C. M. Baines, Trans.). In P. Reiff (Ed.), *General psychological theory: Papers on metapsychology.* New York: Macmillan.

Fujita, K., Gollwitzer, P. M., & Oettingen, G. (2007). Mindsets and preconscious open-mindedness to incidental information. *Journal of Experimental Psychology, 43,* 48–61.

Furr, R. M., & Funder, D. C. (2004). Situational similarity and behavioral consistency: Subjective, objective, variable-centered, and person-centered approaches. *Journal of Research in Personality, 38*(5), 421–447.

Gable, P. A. (2006). Approach and avoidance social motives and goals. *Journal of Personality, 74,* 175–222.

Gable, P. A., & Harmon-Jones, E. (2008). Approach-motivated positive affect reduces breadth of attention. *Psychological Science, 19,* 476–482.

Gagné, F. M., & Lydon, J. E. (2001). Mindset and relationship illusions: The moderating effects of domain specificity and relationship commitment. *Personality and Social Psychology Bulletin, 27,* 1144–1155.

Gagné, M., & Deci, E. L. (2005). Self-determination theory and work motivation. *Journal of Organizational Behavior, 26,* 331–362.

Gailliot, M. T., Plant, E. A., Butz, D. A., & Baumeister, R. F. (2007). Increasing self-regulatory strength can reduce the depleting effect of suppressing stereotypes. *Personality and Social Psychology Bulletin, 33,* 281–294.

Galinsky, A. D., Leonardelli, G. J., Okhuysen, G. A, & Mussweiler, T. (2005). Regulatory focus at the bargaining table: Promoting distributive and integrative success. *Personality and Social Psychology Bulletin, 31,* 1087–1098.

Gangestad, S. (2011). Evolutionary perspectives. In K. Deaux & M. Snyder (Eds.), *The handbook of personality and social psychology* (pp. xxx–xxx). New York: Oxford University Press.

Goffman, E. (1956). Embarrassment and social organization. *American Journal of Sociology, 62,* 264–271.

Gollwitzer, P. M. (1999). Implementation intentions: Strong effects of simple plans. *American Psychologist, 54,* 493–503.

Gollwitzer, P. M., & Bayer, U. C. (1999). Deliberative versus implemental mindsets in the control of action. In S. Chaiken & Y. Trope (Eds.), *Dual-process theories in social psychology* (, pp. 403–422): New York: Guilford.

Gollwitzer, P. M., & Kinney, R. F. (1989). Effects of deliberative and implemental mind-sets on illusion of control. *Journal of Personality and Social Psychology, 56,* 531–542.

Gollwitzer, P. M., & Sheeran, P. (2006). Implementation intentions and goal achievement: A meta-analysis of effects and processes. *Advances in Experimental Social Psychology, 38,* 69–119.

Goschke, T., & Kuhl, J. (1996). Remembering what to do: Explicit and implicit memory for intentions. In M. Brandimonte, G. O. Einstein, & M. A. McDaniel (Eds.), *Prospective memory: Theory and applications.* (pp. 53–91). Mahwah, NJ: Erlbaum.

Gray, J. A. (1990). Brain systems that mediate both emotion and cognition. *Cognition and Emotion, 4,* 269–288.

Griskevicius, V., Cialdini, R. B., & Kenrick, D. T. (2006). Peacocks, Picasso, and parental investment: The effects of romantic motives on creativity. *Journal of Personality and Social Psychology, 91*(1), 63–76.

Griskevicius, V., Goldstein, N. J., Mortensen, C. R., Cialdini, R. B., & Kenrick, D. T. (2006). Going along versus going alone: When fundamental motives facilitate strategic (non)conformity. *Journal of Personality and Social Psychology, 91*(2), 281–294.

Harlow, R. E., & Cantor, N. (1995). To whom do people turn when things go poorly? Task orientation and functional social contacts. *Journal of Personality and Social Psychology, 69,* 329–340.

Harmon-Jones, E., & Allen, J. J. B. (1997). Behavioral activation sensitivity and resting frontal EEG asymmetry: Covariation of putative indicators related to risk for mood disorders. *Journal of Abnormal Psychology, 106,* 159–163.

Harmon-Jones, E., Peterson, C., Gable, P. A., & Harmon-Jones, C. (2008). Anger and approach-avoidance motivation. In A. J. Elliot (Eds.), *Handbook of approach and avoidance motivation* (pp. 399–413). New York: Psychology Press.

Heckhausen, H. (1977). Achievement motivation and its constructs: A cognitive model. *Motivation and Emotion, 1,* 283–329.

Heckhausen, H., & Gollwitzer, P. M. (1987). Thought contents and cognitive functioning in motivational versus volitional states of mind. *Motivation and Emotion, 11,* 101–120.

Heckhausen, J., Wrosch, C., & Schulz, R. (2010). A motivational theory of life-span development. *Psychological Review, 117*(1), 32–60.

Heider, F. (1958). *The psychology of interpersonal relations.* New York: Wiley.

Heppen, J. B., & Ogilvie, D. M. (2003). Predicting affect from global self-discrepancies: The dual role of the undesired self. *Journal of Social and Clinical Psychology, 22,* 347–368.

Hepper, E. G., Gramzow, R. H., & Sedikides, C. (2010). Individual differences in self-enhancement and self-protection strategies: An integrative analysis. *Journal of Personality, 78,* 781–814.

Higgins, E. T. (1998). From expectancies to worldviews: Regulatory focus in socialization and cognition. In J. M. Darley & J. Cooper (Eds.), *Attribution and social interaction: The legacy of Edward E. Jones.* (pp. 243–309). Washington, DC: American Psychological Association.

Higgins, E. T. (2000). Making a good decision: Value from fit. *American Psychologist, 55,* 1217–1230.

Higgins, E. T. (2006). Value from hedonic experience and engagement. *Psychological Review, 113,* 439–460.

Higgins, E. T., Klein, R., & Strauman, T. (1985). Self-concept discrepancy theory: A psychological model for distinguishing among different aspects of depression and anxiety. *Social Cognition, 3*(1), 51–76.

Higgins, E. T., & Silberman, I. (1998). Development of regulatory focus: Promotion and prevention as ways of living. In J. Heckhausen & C. S. Dweck (Eds.), *Motivation and self-regulation across the life span.* (pp. 78–113). New York: Cambridge University Press.

Hodgins, H. S., & Knee, C. R. (2002). The integrating self and conscious experience. In E. L. Deci & R. M. Ryan (Eds.), *Handbook of self-determination research* (pp. 87–100). Rochester, NY: University of Rochester Press.

Hofer, J., & Chasiotis, A. (2003). Congruence of life goals and implicit motives as predictors of life satisfaction: Cross-cultural implications of a study of Zambian male adolescents. *Motivation and Emotion, 27*(3), 251–272.

Hong, Y., Chiu, C., Dweck, C. S., Lin, D. M. S., & Wan, W. (1999). Implicit theories, attributions, and coping: A meaning system approach. *Journal of Personality and Social Psychology, 77*(3), 588–599.

Horner, M. S. (1972). Toward an understanding of achievement-related conflicts in women. *Journal of Social Issues, 28,* 157–175.

Horney, K. (1968). The technique of psychoanalytic therapy. *American Journal of Psychoanalysis, 28,* 3–12.

Hull, C. L. (1951). *Essentials of behavior.* New Haven, CT: Yale University Press.

Ito, T. A., & Cacioppo, J. T. (1999). The psychophysiology of utility appraisals. In D. Kahneman, E. Diener, & N. Schwarz (Eds.), *The foundations of hedonic psychology* (pp. 470–488). New York: Russell Sage.

Iyengar, S. S., & DeVoe, S. E. (2003). Rethinking the value of choice: Considering cultural mediators of intrinsic motivation. In V. Murphy-Berman & J. J. Berman (Eds.), *Nebraska Symposium on Motivation: Cross-cultural differences in perspectives on self* (Vol. 49, pp. 129–174). Lincoln: University of Nebraska Press.

Jamieson, J. P., & Harkins, S. G. (2007). Mere effort and stereotype threat performance effects. *Journal of Personality and Social Psychology, 93*, 544–564.

Jamieson, J. P., & Harkins, S. G. (2009). The effect of stereotype threat on the solving of quantitative GRE problems: A mere effort interpretation. *Personality and Social Psychology Bulletin, 35*, 1301–1314.

Jamieson, J. P., & Harkins, S. G. (2010). Evaluation is necessary to produce stereotype threat performance effects. *Social Influence, 5*, 75–86.

Jemmott, J. B. (1987). Social motives and susceptibility to disease: Stalking individual differences in health risks. *Journal of Personality, 55*, 267–298.

Job, V., & Brandstatter, V. (2009). Get a taste of your goals: Promoting motive goal congruence through affect-focus goal fantasy. *Journal of Personality, 77*, 1527–1559.

Jordan, J. V. (1991). The relational self: A new perspective for understanding women's development. In J. Strauss & G. Goethals (Eds.), *The self: Interdisciplinary approaches* (pp. 136–149). Cambridge, MA: Harvard University Press.

Jost, J. T., Pietrzak, J., Liviaton, I., Mandisodza, A. N., & Napier, J. L. (2008). System justification as conscious and unconscious goal pursuit. In J. Y. Shah & W. L. Gardner (Eds.), *Handbook of motivation science* (pp. 591–605). New York: Guilford.

Kaiser, R. T., & Ozer, D. J. (1997). Emotional stability and goal-related stress. *Personality and Individual Differences, 22*(3), 371–379.

Kazen, M., Kaschel, R., & Kuhl, J. (2008). Individual differences in intention initiation under demanding conditions: Interactive effects of state vs. action oriented and enactment difficulty. *Journal of Research in Personality, 42*(3), 693–715.

Kazen, M., & Kuhl, J. (2005). Intention memory and achievement motivation: Volitional facilitation and inhibition as a function of affective contents of need-related stimuli. *Journal of Personality and Social Psychology, 89*(3), 426–448.

Kelly, G. (1955). *The psychology of personal constructs.* New York: Norton.

Kenrick, D. T., & Funder, D. C. (1988). Profiting from controversy: Lessons from the person-situation debate. *American Psychologist, 43*(1), 23–34.

Kenrick, D. T., Li, N. P., & Butner, J. (2003). Dynamical evolutionary psychology: Individual decision rules and emergent social norms. *Psychological Review, 110*(1), 3–28.

Kenrick, D. T., Neuberg, S. L., Griskevicius, V., Becker, D. V., & Schaller, M. (2010). Goal-driven cognition and functional behavior: The fundamental-motives framework. *Current Directions in Psychological Science, 19*, 63–67.

Kihlstrom, J. F. (2008). The psychological unconscious. In O. P. John, R. W. Robins, & L. A. Pervin (Eds.), *Handbook of personality: Theory and research* (3rd ed., pp. 583–602). New York: Guilford.

Kihlstrom, J. F. (2009). Commentary: "So that we might have roses in December": The functions of autobiographical memory. *Applied Cognitive Psychology, 23*(8), 1179–1192.

Kim, A. (2004). *Investigating self-regulation in Korean students.* Paper presented at the Second International Conference on Self-Determination Theory. Ottowa, Canada.

Kiviniemi, M. T., Snyder, M., & Omoto, A. M. (2002). Too many of a good thing? The effects of multiple motivations on stress, cost, fulfillment, and satisfaction. *Personality and Social Psychology Bulletin, 28*(6), 732–743.

Klinger, E., & Cox, W. M. (2004). Motivation and the theory of current concerns. In W. M. Cox & E. Klinger (Eds.), *Handbook of motivational counseling: Concepts, approaches, and assessment.* (pp. 3–27). New York: Wiley.

Koestner, R., Bernieri, F., & Zuckerman, M. (1992). Self-determination and consistency between attitudes, traits, and behaviors. *Personality and Social Psychology Bulletin, 18*, 52–59.

Koestner, R., Ryan, R. M., Bernieri, F., & Holt, K. (1984). Setting limits on children's behavior: The differential effects of controlling versus informational styles on intrinsic motivation and creativity. *Journal of Personality, 52*, 233–248.

Kruglanski, A. W., Orehek, E., Dechesne, M., & Pierro, A. (2010). Lay epistemic theory: The motivational, cognitive, and social aspects of knowledge formation. *Social and Personality Psychology Compass, 4*, 939–950.

Kruglanski, A. W., Shah, J. Y., Fishbach, A., Friedman, R., Chun, W. Y., & Sleeth-Keppler, D. (2002). A theory of goal systems. In M. P. Zanna (Ed.), *Advances in Experimental Social Psychology* (Vol. 34, pp. 331–378). San Diego: Academic.

Kuhl, J. (2001). A functional approach to motivation: The role of goal-enactment and self-regulation in current research on approach and avoidance. In A. Efklides, J. Kuhl, & R. M. Sorrentino (Eds.), *Trends and prospects in motivation research.* (pp. 239–268). Dordrecht Netherlands: Kluwer Academic.

Kuhl, J., & Beckmann, J. (1994). *Volition and personality.* Göttingen, Germany: Hoegrefe.

Kunda, Z. (1990). The case for motivated reasoning. *Psychological Bulletin, 108*, 480–498.

Kurt, A., & Paulhus, D. L. (2008). Moderators of the adaptiveness of self-enhancement: Operationalization, motivational domain, adjustment facet, and evaluator. *Journal of Research in Personality, 42*, 839–853.

LeDoux, J. E. (1996). *The emotional brain: The mysterious underpinnings of emotional life.* New York: Simon & Schuster.

Legault, L., Green-Demers, I., Grant, P., & Chung, J. (2007). On the self-regulation of implicit and explicit prejudice: A self-determination theory perspective. *Personality and Social Psychology Bulletin, 33*, 732–749.

Lepper, M. R., & Greene, D. (1975). Turning play into work: Effects of adult surveillance and extrinsic rewards on children's intrinsic motivation. *Journal of Personality and Social Psychology, 31*, 479–486.

Lewin, K. (1935). *A dynamic theory of personality.* New York: McGraw-Hill.

Lewin, K. (1951). *Field theory in social science.* New York: Harper.

L'hermitte, F. (1986). Human anatomy and the frontal lobes: Part II. Patient behavior in complex and social situations: The "environmental dependency syndrome." *Annals of Neurology, 19*, 335–343.

Liberman, N., Idson, L. C., Camacho, C. J., & Higgins, E. T. (1999). Promotion and prevention choices between stability and change. *Journal of Personality and Social Psychology, 77*(6), 1135–1145.

Liberman, N., & Trope, Y. (1998). The role of feasibility and desirability considerations in near and distant future decisions: A test of temporal construal theory. *Journal of Personality and Social Psychology, 75*, 5–18.

Little, B. R. (1989). Personal projects analysis: Trivial pursuits, magnificent obsessions, and the search for coherence. In D. M. Buss & N. Cantor (Eds.), *Personality psychology: Recent trends and emerging issues* (pp. 15–41). New York: Springer-Verlag.

Little, B. R., Lecci, L., & Watkinson, B. (1992). Personality and personal projects: Linking Big Five and PAC units of analysis. *Journal of Personality, 60*(2), 501–525.

Litwin, G. H., & Siebrecht, A. (1967). Integrators and entrepreneurs: Their motivation and effect on management. *Hospital Progress, 48*(9), 67–71.

Locke, E. A., & Latham, G. P. (2006). New directions in goal-setting theory. *Current Directions in Psychological Science, 15,* 265–268.

Loevinger, J., Cohn, L. D., Bonneville, L. P., Redmore, C. D., Streich, D. D., & Sargent, M. (1985). Ego development in college. *Journal of Personality and Social Psychology, 48*(4), 947–962.

Lynch, M. F., La Guardia, J. G., & Ryan, R. M. (2007). On being yourself: Ideal, actual, and relationship-specific trait self-concept and the support of autonomy. Unpublished manuscript submitted for publication.

Lynch, M. F., La Guardia, J. G., & Ryan, R. M. (2009). On being yourself in different cultures: Ideal and actual self-concept, autonomy support, and well-being in China, Russia, and the United States. *Journal of Positive Psychology, 4,* 290–304.

Maner, J. K., Kenrick, D. T., Becker, D. V., Robertson, T. E., Hofer, B., Neuberg, S. L., et al. (2005). Functional projection: How fundamental social motives can bias interpersonal perception. *Journal of Personality and Social Psychology, 88,* 63–78.

Markman, K. D., Lindberg, M. J., Kray, L. J., & Galinsky, A. D. (2007). Implications of counterfactual structure for creativity and analytical problem solving. *Personality and Social Psychology Bulletin, 33,* 312–324.

Markus, H., & Nurius, P. (1986). Possible selves. *American Psychologist, 41,* 954–969.

Markus, H. R., & Kitayama, S. (1991). Culture and the self: Implications for cognition, emotion, and motivation. *Psychological Review, 92,* 224–253.

Maslow, A. (1955). Deficiency motivation and growth motivation. In M. R. Jones (Ed.), *Nebraska Symposium on Motivation: 1955* (pp. 1–30). Lincoln: University of Nebraska Press.

Maslow, A. (1957). Philosophy of psychology. In J. E. Fairchild (Ed.), *Personal problems and psychological frontiers.* Oxford: Sheridan House.

Maslow, A. (1971). *The farther reaches of human nature.* Oxford, UK: Viking.

Mayer, J., Faber, M., & Xu, X. (2007). Seventy-five years of motivation measures (1930–2005): A descriptive analysis. *Motivation and Emotion, 31*(2), 83–103.

McAdams, D. P. (1980). A thematic coding system for the intimacy motive. *Journal of Research in Personality, 14,* 413–432.

McClelland, D. C. (1975). *Power: The inner experience.* New York: Irvington.

McClelland, D. C. (1976). *The achieving society* (2nd ed.). Oxford: Irvington.

McClelland, D. C. (1980). Motive dispositions: The merits of operant and respondent measures. In L. Wheeler (Ed.), *Review of personality and social psychology* (Vol. 1, pp. 10–41). Beverly Hills, CA: Sage.

McClelland, D. C. (1987). *Human motivation.* New York: Cambridge University Press.

McClelland, D. C. (1989). Motivational factors in health and disease. *American Psychologist, 44,* 675–683.

McClelland, D. C., Atkinson, J. W., Clark, R. A., & Lowell, E. L. (1953). *The achievement motive.* Norwalk, CT: Appleton-Century-Crofts.

McClelland, D. C., & Boyatzis, R. E. (1982). Leadership motive pattern and long-term success in management. *Journal of Applied Psychology, 67,* 737–743.

McClelland, D. C., Koestner, R., & Weinberger, J. (1992). How do self-attributed and implicit motives differ? In C. P. Smith, J. W. Atkinson, D. C. McClelland, & J. Veroff (Eds.), *Motivation and personality: Handbook of thematic content analysis* (pp. 49–72). Cambridge, UK: Cambridge University Press.

McCulloch, K. D., Ferguson, M. J., Kawada, C., & Bargh, J. A. (2008). Taking a closer look: On the operation of unconscious impression formation. *Journal of Experimental Social Psychology, 44,* 614–623.

Meece, J. L., & Miller, S. D. (2001). A longitudinal analysis of elementary school students' achievement goals in literacy activities. *Contemporary Educational Psychology, 26,* 454–480.

Mehrabian, A., & Ksionzky, S. (1974). *A theory of affiliation.* Lexington, MA: Heath.

Mendoza, S. A., Gollwitzer, P. M., & Amodio, D. M. (2010). Reducing the expression of implicit stereotypes: Reflexive control through implementation intentions. *Personality and Social Psychology Bulletin, 36,* 512–523.

Mischel, W. (1968). *Personality and assessment.* Hoboken, NJ: Wiley.

Molden, D. C., Lee, A. Y., & Higgins, E. T. (2008). Motivations for promotion and prevention. In J. Y. Shah & W. L. Gardner (Eds.), *Handbook of motivation science.* (pp. 169–187). New York: Guilford.

Moller, A. C., Deci, E. L., & Ryan, R. M. (2006). Choice and ego-depletion: The moderating role of autonomy. *Personality and Social Psychology Bulletin, 32,* 1024–1036.

Monteith, M. J. (1993). Self-regulation of prejudiced responses: Implications for progress in prejudice-reduction efforts. *Journal of Personality and Social Psychology, 65,* 469–485.

Monteith, M. J., Ashburn-Nardo, L., Voils, C., & Czopp, A. M. (2002). Putting the brakes on prejudice: On the development and operation of cues for control. *Journal of Personality and Social Psychology, 83,* 1029–1050.

Morgan, C. D., & Murray, H. H. (1935). A method for investigating fantasies: The Thematic Apperception Test. *Archives of Neurology and Psychiatry, 34,* 289–305.

Morsella, E. (2005). The function of phenomenal states: Supramodular interaction theory. *Psychological Review, 112,* 1000–1021.

Moskowitz, G. B. (2001). Preconscious control and compensatory cognition. In G. B. Moskowitz (Ed.), *Cognitive social psychology: The Princeton Symposium on the Legacy and Future of Social Cognition* (pp. 333–358). Mahwah, NJ: Erlbaum.

Muraven, M., Baumeister, R. F., & Tice, D. M. (1999). Longitudinal improvement of self-regulation through practice: Building self-control strength through repeated exercise. *Journal of Social Psychology, 139*(4), 446–457.

Muraven, M., Collins, R. L., & Neinhaus, K. (2002). Self-control and alcohol restraint: An initial application of the Self-Control Strength Model. *Psychology of Addictive Behaviors, 16*(2), 113–120.

Murray, H. A. (1938). *Explorations in personality*. New York: Oxford University Press.

Murray, H. A. (1940). What should psychologists do about psychoanalysis? *Journal of Abnormal and Social Psychology, 35*(2), 150–175.

Murray, H. A. (1943). *Thematic Apperception Test*. Cambridge, MA: Harvard University Press.

Neighbors, C., & Knee, C. R. (2003). Self-determination and the impact of social comparison information. *Journal of Research in Personality, 37*(6), 529–546.

Niemiec, C. P., Brown, K. W., & Ryan, R. M. (2007). Being present when facing death: The role of mindfulness in terror management processes. Unpublished manuscript submitted for publication.

Norem, J. K. (2008). Defensive pessimism, anxiety, and the complexity of self-regulation. *Social and Personality Compass, 2*(1), 121–134.

Norem, J. K. (2009). Psychological defensiveness: Repression, blunting, and defensive pessimism. In M. R. Leary & R. H. Hoyle (Eds.), *Handbook of individual differences in social behavior* (pp. 480–492). New York: Guilford.

Norem, J. K., & Andreas Burdzovic, J. A. (2007). Understanding journeys: Latent individual growth analysis as a tool for studying individual differences in change over time. In A. D. Ong & M. V. Dulmen (Eds.), *The Oxford handbook of methods in positive psychology* (pp. 477–486). Oxford, UK: Oxford University Press.

Norem, J. K., & Illingworth, K. S. S. (1993). Strategy dependent effects of reflecting on self and tasks: Some implications of optimism and defensive pessimism. *Journal of Personality and Social Psychology, 65*, 822–835.

Norem, J. K., & Illingworth, K. S. S. (2004). Mood and performance among strategic optimists and defensive pessimists. *Journal of Research in Personality, 38*, 351–366.

Oettingen, G. (2000). Expectancy effects on behavior depend on self-regulatory thought. *Social Cognition, 18*, 101–129.

Oettingen, G., & Mayer, D. (2002). The motivating function of thinking about the future: Expectations versus fantasies. *Journal of Personality and Social Psychology, 83*, 1198–1212.

Oettingen, G., Pak, H., & Schnetter, K. (2001). Self-regulation of goal-setting: Turning free fantasies about the future into binding goals. *Journal of Personality and Social Psychology, 80*, 736–753.

Oettingen, G., & Stephens, E. J. (2009). Fantasies and motivationally intelligent goal setting. In G. B. Moskowitz & H. Grant (Eds.), *The psychology of goals* (pp. 153–178). New York: Guilford.

Ogilvie, D. M. (1987). The undesired self: A neglected variable in personality research. *Journal of Personality and Social Psychology, 52*(2), 379–385.

Omoto, A. M., Snyder, M., & Martino, S. C. (2000). Volunteerism and the life course: Investigating age-related agendas for action. *Basic and Applied Social Psychology, 22*, 181–197.

Palys, T. D., & Little, B. R. (1983). Perceived life satisfaction and the organization of personal project systems. *Journal of Personality and Social Psychology, 44*, 1221–1230.

Pang, J. S., & Schultheiss, O. C. (2005). Assessing implicit motives in U. S. college students: Effects of picture type and position, gender and ethnicity, and cross-cultural comparisons. *Journal of Personality Assessment, 85*, 280–294.

Perry, S.P., & Skitka, L. J. (2009). Making lemonade? Defensive coping style moderates the effect of stereotype threat on women's math testperformance. *Journal of Research in Personality, 43*, 918–920.

Posner, M. I., & Snyder, C. R. R. (1975). Attention and cognitive control. In R. L. Solso (Ed.), *Information processing and cognition: The Loyola Symposium* (pp. 55–85). New York: Wiley.

Quirin, M., Koole, S. L., Baumann, N., Kazen, M., & Kuhl, J. (2009) You can't always remember what you want: The role of cortisol in self-ascription of assigned goals. *Journal of Research in Personality, 43*, 1026–1043.

Rawsthorne, L. J., & Elliot, A. J. (1999). Achievement goals and intrinsic motivation: A meta-analytic review. *Personality and Social Psychology Review, 3*(4), 326–344.

Reis, H. T., Collins, W. A., & Berscheid, E. (2000). The relationship context of human behavior and development. *Psychological Bulletin, 126*(6), 844–872.

Reis, H. T., Sheldon, K. M., Gable, S. L., Roscoe, J., & Ryan, R. M. (2000). Daily well-being: The role of autonomy, competence, and relatedness. *Personality and Social Psychology Bulletin, 26*, 419–435.

Renkema, L. J., & Van Yperen, N. W. (2008). On goals and strategies: Distinguishing performance goals and regulatory strategy. *International Review of Social Psychology, 21*, 97–108.

Roberts, B. W., Wood, D., & Caspi, A. (2008). The development of personality traits in adulthood. In O. P. John, R. W. Robins, & L. A. Pervin (Eds.), *Handbook of personality*. New York: Guilford.

Robins, R. W., & Pals, J. L. (2002). Implicit self-theories in the academic domain: Implications for goal orientation, attributions, affect, and self-esteem change. *Self and Identity, 1*, 313–336.

Rogers, C. R. (1951). Perceptual reorganization in client-centered therapy. In R. R. Blak & G. V. Ramsey (Eds.), *Perception: An approach to personality* (pp. 307–327). New York: Ronald Press.

Roney, C. J. R., Higgins, E. T., & Shah, J. (1995). Goals and framing: How outcome focus influences motivation and emotion. *Personality and Social Psychology Bulletin, 21*, 1151–1160.

Rotter, J. B. (1966). Generalized expectancies for internal versus external control of reinforcement. *Psychological Monographs: General and Applied, 80*, 1–28.

Ryan, R. M., & Connell, J. P. (1989). Perceived locus of causality and internalization: Examining reasons for acting in two domains. *Journal of Personality and Social Psychology, 57*, 749–761.

Ryan, R. M., & Deci, E. L. (2000). Self-determination theory and the facilitation of intrinsic motivation, social development, and well-being. *American Psychologist, 55*, 68–78.

Ryan, R. M., & Deci, E. L. (2002). An overview of self-determination theory: An organismic–dialectical perspective. In E. L. Deci & R. M. Ryan (Eds.), *Handbook of self-determination research* (pp. 3–33). Rochester, NY: University of Rochester Press.

Ryan, R. M., & Deci, E. L. (2006). Self-regulation and the problem of human autonomy: Does psychology need choice, self-determination, and will? *Journal of Personality, 74*, 1557–1585.

Ryan, R. M., & Deci, E. L. (2008). Self-determination theory and the role of basic psychological needs in personality and the organization of behavior. In O. P. John, R. W. Robins, & L. A. Pervin (Eds.), *Handbook of personality: Theory and research* (3rd ed., pp. 654–678). New York: Guilford.

Ryan, R. M., Deci, E. L., Grolnick, W. S., & La Guardia, J. G. (2006). The significance of autonomy and autonomy support in psychological development and psychopathology. In D. Cicchetti & D. J. Cohen (Eds.), *Developmental psychopathology* (pp. 795–849). Hoboken, NJ: Wiley.

Sanderson, C. A., & Cantor, N. (1999). A life task perspective on personality coherence: Stability versus change in tasks, goals, strategies, and outcomes. In D. Cervone and Y. Shoda (Eds.), *The coherence of personality: Social-cognitive bases of consistency, variability, and organization* (pp. 372–292). New York: Guilford.

Sanna, L. J. (1998). Defensive pessimism and optimism: The bitter-sweet influence of mood on performance and prefactual and counterfactual thinking. *Cognition and Emotion, 12*(5), 635–665.

Sansone, C., & Thoman, D. B. (2006). Maintaining activity engagement: Individual differences in the process of self-regulating motivation. *Journal of Research in Personality, 74,* 1697–1720.

Schaller, M., Park, J. H., & Faulkner, J. (2003). Prehistoric dangers and contemporary prejudices. *European Review of Social Psychology, 14,* 105–137.

Scholer, A. A., Stroessner, S. J., & Higgins, E. T. (2008). Responding to negativity: How a risky tactic can serve a vigilant function. *Journal of Experimental Social Psychology, 44,* 767–774.

Schultheiss, O. C. (2007). A biobehavioral model of implicit power motivation arousal, reward, and frustration. In E. Harmon-Jones & P. Winkielman (Eds.), *Social neuroscience: Integrating biological and psychological explanations of social behavior* (pp. 176–196). New York: Guilford.

Schultheiss, O. C. (2008). Implicit motives. In O. P. John, R. W. Robins, & L. A. Pervin (Eds.), *Handbook of personality: Theory and research* (3rd ed.). New York: Guilford.

Schultheiss, O. C., Brunstein, J. C., Elliot, A. J., & Dweck, C. S. (2005). An implicit motive perspective on competence. In *Handbook of competence and motivation.* (pp. 31–51). New York: Guilford.

Schultheiss, O. C., Jones, N. M., Davis, A. Q., & Kley, C. (2008). The role of implicit motivation in hot and cold goal pursuit: Effects on goal progress, goal rumination, and emotional well-being. *Journal of Research in Personality, 42,* 971–987.

Schultheiss, O. C., Wirth, M. M., & Stanton, J. (2004). Effects of affiliation and power motivation arousal on salivary progesterone and testosterone. *Hormones and Behavior, 46,* 592–599.

Schultheiss, O. C., Wirth, M. M., Torges, C. M., Pang, J. S., Villacorta, M. A., & Welsh, K. M. (2005). Effects of implicit power motivation on men's and women's implicit learning and testosterone changes after social victory or defeat. *Journal of Personality and Social Psychology, 88*(1), 174–188.

Shah, J., & Higgins, E. T. (2001). Regulatory concerns and appraisal efficiency: The general impact of promotion and prevention. *Journal of Personality and Social Psychology, 80,* 693–705.

Sheerer, M. (1954). Cognitive theory. In G. Lindsey (Ed.), *Handbook of social psychology* (Vol. 1, pp. 91–142). Reading, MA: Addison-Wesley.

Sheldon, K. M., & Elliot, A. J. (1999). Goal striving, need satisfaction, and longitudinal well-being: The self-concordance model. *Journal of Personality and Social Psychology, 76,* 482–497.

Sheldon, K. M., Ryan, R. M., Deci, E. L, & Kasser, T. (2004). The independent effects of goal contents and motives on well-being: It's both what you pursue and why you pursue it. *Personality and Social Psychology Bulletin, 30,* 475–486.

Shiffrin, R. M., & Schneider, W. (1977). Controlled and automatic human information processing: Part II. Perceptual learning, automatic attending, and a general theory. *Psychological Review, 84,* 127–190.

Shipley, T. E., Jr., & Veroff, J. (1952). A projective measure of need for affiliation. *Journal of Experimental Psychology, 43,* 349–356.

Simon, H. A. (1985). *Artificial intelligence: Current status and future potential.* Washington, DC: Academy Press.

Snyder, M., & Cantor, N. (1998). Understanding personality and social behavior: A functionalist strategy. In D. T. Gilbert & S. T Fiske, (Eds.), *The handbook of social psychology* (4th ed., pp. 635–679). New York: McGraw-Hill.

Sonnentag, S., & Jelden, S. (2005). *The recovery paradox: Why we don't exercise after stressful days.* Paper presented at the Annual Conference of the Society for Industrial and Organizational Psychology.

Spangler, W. D. (1992). Validity of questionnaire and TAT measures of need for achievement: Two meta-analyses. *Psychological Bulletin, 112,* 140–154.

Stanton, S. J., & Schultheiss, O. C. (2007). Basal and dynamic relationships between implicit power motivation and estradiol in women. *Hormones and Behavior, 52*(5), 571–580.

Stauner, N., Stimson, T. S., & Ozer, D. J. (2009). The factor structure of personal goals in an undergraduate population. Poster presented at the Annual Meeting of the Society for Personality and Social Psychology, Tampa, FL.

Strachman, A., & Gable, S. L. (2006). What you want (and do not want) affects what you see (and do not see): Avoidance goals and social events. *Personality and Social Psychology Bulletin, 32,* 1446–1458.

Steele, C. M. (1988). The psychology of self-affirmation: Sustaining the integrity of the self. In L. Berkowitz (Ed.), *Advances in experimental social psychology: Vol. 21. Social psychological studies of the self: Perspectives and programs* (pp. 261–302). San Diego, CA: Academic.

Stimson, G., Grant, M., Choquet, M., & Garrison, P. (2007). *Drinking in context: Patterns, interventions, and partnerships.* New York: Routledge/Taylor & Francis.

Swann, W. B., Jr., Gomez, A., Seyle, D. C., Morales, J. F., & Huici, C. (2009). Identity fusion: The interplay of personal and social identities in extreme group behavior. *Journal of Personality and Social Psychology, 96*(5), 995–1011.

Tamir, M. (2009). What do people want to feel and why? Pleasure and utility in emotion regulation. *Current Directions in Psychological Science, 18,* 101–105.

Tamir, M., & Robinson, M. D. (2007). The happy spotlight: Positive mood and selective attention to rewarding information. *Personality and Social Psychology Bulletin, 33,* 1124–1136.

Taylor, S. E., & Gollwitzer, P. M. (1995). The effects of mindsets on positive illusions. *Journal of Personality and Social Psychology, 69,* 213–226.

Thibaut, J. W., & Kelley, H. H. (1959). *The social psychology of groups.* Oxford, UK: Wiley.

Tice, D. M., Bratslavsky, E., & Baumeister, R. F. (2001). Emotional distress regulation takes precedence over impulse control: If you feel bad, do it! *Journal of Personality and Social Psychology, 80,* 53–67.

Tolman, E. C. (1932). *Purposive behavior in animals and men.* New York: Appleton-Century.

Tooby, J., & Cosmides, L. (1992). The psychological foundations of culture. In J. H. Barkow, L. Cosmides & J. Tooby (Eds.), *The adapted mind: Evolutionary psychology and the generation of culture* (pp. 19–136). New York: Oxford University Press.

Vallacher, R. R., & Wegner, D. M. (1987). What do people think they're doing? Action identification and human behavior. *Psychological Review, 94,* 215–228.

Vallacher, R. R., & Wegner, D. M. (1989). Levels of personal agency: Individual variation in action identification. *Journal of Personality and Social Psychology, 57,* 660–671.

Wegner, D. M. (2002). *The illusion of conscious will.* Cambridge, MA: MIT Press.

Wegner, D. M., Vallacher, R.R., Macomber, G., Wood, R., & Arps, K. (1984). The emergence of action. *Journal of Personality and Social Psychology, 46,* 269–279.

Weinberger, J., Cotler, T., & Fishman, D. (2010). The duality of affiliative motivation. In O. C. Schultheiss & J. C. Brunstein (Eds.), *Implicit motivation* (pp. 31–71). Oxford, UK: Oxford University Press.

Werth, L., & Forster, J. (2007). The effects of regulatory focus on braking speed. *Journal of Applied Social Psychology, 37*(12), 2764–2787.

White, R. W. (1959). Motivation reconsidered: The concept of competence. *Psychological Review, 66,* 297–333.

Williams, G. C., Freedman, Z., & Deci, E. L. (1998). Supporting autonomy to motivate patients with diabetes for glucose control. *Diabetes Care, 21,* 1644–1651.

Williams, G. C., Grow, V. M., Freedman, Z., Ryan, R. M., & Deci, E. L. (1996). Motivational predictors of weight loss and weight-loss maintenance. *Journal of Personality and Social Psychology, 70,* 115–126.

Williams, G. C., Rodin, G. C., Ryan, R. M., Grolnick, W. S., & Deci, E. L. (1998). Autonomous regulation and long-term medication adherence in adult outpatients. *Health Psychology, 17,* 269–276.

Williams, J. M. G., Mathews, A., & MacLeod, C. (1996). The emotional Stroop task and psychopathology. *Psychological Bulletin, 120,* 3–24.

Wilson, T. D. (2002). *Strangers to ourselves: Discovering the adaptive unconscious.* Cambridge, MA: Belknap Press of Harvard University Press.

Winter, D. G. (1973). *The power motive.* New York: Free Press.

Winter, D. G. (1988). The power motive in women—and men. *Journal of Personality and Social Psychology, 54,* 510–519.

Winter, D. G. (1993). Power, affiliation, and war: Three tests of a motivational model. *Journal of Personality and Social Psychology, 65,* 532–545.

Winter, D. G., & Carlson, L. A. (1988). Using motive scores in the psychobiographical study of an individual: The case of Richard Nixon. In D. P. McAdams & R. L. Ochberg (Eds.), *Psychobiography and life narratives* (pp. 75–103). Durham, NC: Duke University Press.

Wirth, M. M., & Schultheiss, O. C. (2006). Effects of affiliation arousal (hope of closeness) and affiliation stress (fear of rejection) on progesterone and cortisol. *Hormones and Behavior, 50,* 786–795.

Woike, B. A., McLeod, S., & Goggin, M. (2003). Implicit and explicit motives influence accessibility to different autobiographical knowledge. *Personality and Social Psychology Bulletin, 29*(8), 1046–1055.

Yamauchi, H., & Tanaka, K. (1998). Relations of autonomy, self-referenced beliefs, and self-regulated learning among Japanese children. *Psychological Reports, 82,* 803–816.

Zajonc, R. B. (1965). Social facilitation. *Science, 149,* 269–274.

Zhong, C., & Liljenquist, K. (2006). Washing away your sins: Threatened morality and physical cleansing. *Science, 313,* 1451–1452.

Zhou, R., Pham, M. T., Mick, D. G., Iacobucci, D., & Huber, J. (2004). Promotion and prevention across mental accounts: When financial products dictate consumers' investment goals. *Journal of Consumer Research, 31,* 125–135.

Zirkel, S., & Cantor, N. (1990). Personal construal of life tasks: Those who struggle for independence. *Journal of Personality and Social Psychology, 58,* 172–185.

Zuckerman, M. (1994). Impulsive unsocialized sensation-seeking: The biological foundations of a basic dimension of personality. In J. E. Bates & T. D. Wachs (Eds.), *Temperament: Individual differences at the interface of biology and behavior* (pp. 219–255). Washington, DC: American Psychological Association.

Zuckerman, M., Gioioso, C., & Tellini, S. (1988). Control orientation, self-monitoring, and preference for image versus quality approach to advertising. *Journal of Research in Personality, 22*(1), 89–100.

Zuckerman, M., Porac, J., Lathin, D., Smith, R., & Deci, E. L. (1978). On the importance of self-determination for intrinsically motivated behavior. *Personality and Social Psychology Bulletin, 4,* 443–446.

Five New Ideas About Emotion and Their Implications for Social-Personality Psychology

Gerald L. Clore *and* Michael D. Robinson

Abstract

Emotions are important to personality and social psychology and to the relationship between them. In this chapter, we contrast traditional views of emotion with more recent social-personality views and then contrast these with emerging new perspectives. We consider five questions and conclude that: (1) the components of emotion are not sufficiently correlated to implicate underlying affective programs for specific emotions in the brain; (2) an iterative processing view of emotion elicitation can accommodate both subcortical, unconscious affect and cognitively rich, conscious emotion; (3) emotions influence perceptions in a manner consistent with a resource-based view of both; (4) rather than triggering behavior directly, emotional experience appears to serve a self-teaching function; (5) positive and negative emotions affect thinking styles by promoting or inhibiting the cognitive orientations that are dominant in particular situations. The chapter is thus both historical and modern, emphasizing new developments and their implications for social and personality psychology.

Keywords: emotion, cognition, experience, components, perception, behavior, decision-making

The Early History of Emotion (1884–1980)

William James (1884) was the first psychologist to seek a scientific understanding of emotions. It is well known that he emphasized peripheral bodily inputs to the experience of emotion (Ellsworth, 1994). Less well known is his suggestion that emotional experiences and reactions are as diverse as rocks found in a typical New Hampshire field. The diversity of "things" called emotion, then, would seem to require some organizing principles. In their absence, only a chaotic understanding of emotion could occur.

Subsequent to James's (1884) initial statement, empirical progress was made. Many of these developments were reviewed by Woodworth and Schlosberg in their comprehensive text *Experimental Psychology* (1954). Their review of the emotion literature at that time suggested that: (1) different measures of emotion often do not, though sometimes do, converge; (2) emotional arousal has an uncertain physiological basis; (3) no general statements can be made in relation to Darwin's (1998/1872) hypothesis that individuals are biologically prepared to recognize emotional displays; and (4) the organization of subjective emotional experiences can best be characterized in terms of a two-dimensional space defined by the valence (displeasure-pleasure) and arousal (deactivated-activated) of such experiences.

The emotion-relevant chapters of Woodworth and Schlosberg (1954) are both informative and somewhat depressing. What is informative is that their conclusions have held up remarkably well over time. Different measures of emotion do not strongly converge (Lang, 1994), subjective emotional arousal still has an uncertain physiological basis (Russell & Barrett, 1999), debates continue as to how well individuals can read the emotional displays of others (Ekman, 1993; Fridlund, 1994), and the two-dimensional space advocated by Schlosberg (1952) continues to do well in characterizing subjective experiences of emotion, but continues to be debated as well (Mauss & Robinson, 2009).

What is somewhat depressing is how little apparent progress in understanding emotion has occurred since the review of Woodworth and Schlosberg (1954). Part of the problem, we suggest, is a bias in the emotion literature to emphasize physiological processes relative to the social-personality determinants of emotion. The physiological determinants of emotion are important, but appear limited in their explanatory value (Lazarus, 1991). For example, it has been shown that the physiological reactions often linked to emotion—among them increases in heart rate, blood pressure, respiration frequency, and so on—serve too many masters to be *particularly* explanatory in an emotion-related context (Obrist & Light, 1988; Wright & Kirby, 2003; Zillmann & Zillmann, 1996).

Social-personality perspectives on emotion, we suggest, have considerable potential merit for helping us to understand emotion-related processes and outcomes. Such perspectives—whether in relation to traits, appraisals, or emotion-regulation processes—converge on what should be the common currency of emotional reactions, irrespective of which particular inputs are involved. Specifically, emotional reactions concern *meaning* and *interpretation* (Clore, Schwarz, & Conway, 1994; Lazarus, 1991; Ortony, Clore, & Collins, 1988). Social-personality psychological perspectives should thus be in a unique position to answer important questions concerning emotion that have vexed and stymied emotion researchers not adopting such social-personality perspectives. This point is generally made in the body of our review.

Emotion in the Modern Personality and Social Psychology Era (1980-Present)

The 1980s in both personality and social psychology tended to neglect emotional and motivational factors (Dunning, 1999; Kunda & Sinclair, 1999). Personality psychologists focused on such descriptive considerations as which traits belong together (Pervin, 1994), and social psychologists were focused on the cues used in social judgments, using highly artificial paradigms (Funder, 1995). For different reasons, but perhaps reflecting the zeitgeist of the 1980's, research in personality and social psychology during that decade tended to sidestep the "hot" factor: emotional arousal.

The 1990s and beyond were very different. Emotion became a central interest to both personality and social psychologists. Personality psychologists recognized that all "Big Five" traits (John & Srivastava, 1999) could be understood in affective terms (Paulhus & John, 1998), and that they all had implications for emotional experiences (McCrae & Costa, 1991). Various investigators (e.g., Clark & Watson, 1999; Depue & Collins, 1999; Larsen & Ketelaar, 1991; Zelenski & Larsen, 1999), converged on the idea that many personality variables reflected emotional reactivity and emotion regulation (Block, 2002; Rothbart, Ahadi, & Evans, 2000). Much of this work emphasized temperamental (genetic, inborn, early-appearing) bases of individual differences in emotional experience (Clark & Watson, 1999).

Social psychologists, too, began to focus on affect and emotion to explain social phenomena. Murphy and Zajonc (1993) showed that subliminal exposure to positive versus negative facial expressions biased subsequent liking for Chinese ideographs. Bechara, Damasio, Tranel, and Damasio (1997) demonstrated that damage to emotional areas of the brain (e.g., the ventromedial prefrontal cortex) impaired decision-making. And an extensive literature developed concerning emotional influences on judgment and decision-making (Loewenstein, Weber, Hsee, & Welch, 2001; Slovic, Finucane, Peters, & MacGregor, 2002). Studies also found that mood manipulations could affect judgments and social behavior (Forgas, 2002; Schwarz & Clore, 2007). In addition, Berkowitz (1993) advanced a model of aggression in which any negative experience (e.g., exposure to pain, hot temperatures, negative emotional inductions) might render the person more interpersonally aggressive (also see Anderson & Bushman, 2002).

A variety of findings made it clear that emotion belongs to both personality and social psychology (Watson, 2000). For example, data show that the personality trait of neuroticism predicts higher levels of negative emotion (Meyer & Shack, 1989), and extraversion predicts higher levels of positive emotion (Lucas & Fujita, 2000). There are also robust social-situational influences on positive and negative emotional states. Positive emotional states are higher on days with more frequent social interactions and vigorous activities (e.g., exercise), whereas negative emotional states are higher on days with greater levels of stress or health-related problems (for relevant results, see Clark & Watson, 1988; Watson, 2000). Emotion, then, is both a personality variable and a variable influenced by momentary situational factors and cannot be understood exclusively from *either* a personality or a social perspective.

Emotion as an Interactive Personality-Social Entity

Mischel's (1968) critique of personality psychology was not meant in the way many interpreted it (Mischel, 2009). He did not claim that situations are more important predictors than persons, as some social psychologists have assumed (Ross & Nisbett, 1991). Rather, his point was that personality traits would be limited in their predictive power to the extent that situational influences on behavior and emotion were neglected. Greater predictive power would presumably be obtained to the extent that personality dispositions are defined in terms of *reactions* to particular types of situations (Mischel, 2004). This is broadly an interactive, person by situation framework (Mischel, 2009; see also Mendoza-Denton & Ayduk, chapter 18, this volume). Thus, for example, individual differences in test anxiety should appear primarily in response to taking tests (Endler, 2002), individual differences in rejection sensitivity should appear following cues to rejection (Romero-Canyas, Downey, Berenson, Ayduk, & Kang, 2010), and individual difference in forgiveness should appear after the transgressions of others (Hoyt, Fincham, McCullough, Maio, & Davila, 2005).

The naive view of personality traits critiqued by Mischel (1968) no longer has much currency in the emotion literature. Personality traits are often viewed in terms of emotional reactivity to particular types of situations. For example, positive emotional inductions result in greater increases in positive emotion among extraverts relative to introverts (Gross, Sutton, & Ketelaar, 1998; Larsen & Ketelaar, 1991), and negative emotional inductions result in greater increases in negative emotion among neurotic relative to stable individuals (Gross et al., 1998; Zelenski & Larsen, 1999). Results of this interactive type are typically confirmed in experience-sampling studies of daily experiences (for a review, see Bolger, Davis, & Rafaeli, 2003). Also consider the striking meta-analytic results of Deffenbacher (1992). Trait anger is a poor predictor of state anger in most situations ($r \sim 0.2$), but quite a robust predictor of state anger in response to provocation ($r \sim 0.6$). Thus, trait anger individuals are not angry generally, but only in response to provocation (also see the meta-analysis of Bettencourt, Talley, Benjamin, & Valentine, 2006). Such results make it clear that situational determinants of emotion are moderated by personality factors.

In summary, personality and social psychologists have increasingly considered emotion as central to their respective literatures. And, emotional reactions cannot be understood from exclusively person- or situation-centric frameworks. Rather, emotional reactions are best approached from a combined personality-social perspective. The domain of emotion, then, is one in which major advances in linking personality and social processes are possible and have been realized to some extent. With this context in mind, we focus on five key questions concerning emotion.

Question 1: What is an Emotion?
Traditional Perspective
William James (1884) sought to answer the question "What is an emotion?" and ended up concluding that it was synonymous with the perception of bodily changes. Exactly what these bodily changes are and how they are perceived was left underspecified. Additionally, work on the bodily changes associated with emotion has not resulted in a coherent body of findings, at least not one that would be of general service to investigators interested in emotion rather than physiology (Mauss & Robinson, 2009). Nor is it clear that individuals can perceive their bodily changes, as they are often clueless about them (Pennebaker, 1982).

Additionally confusing has been the idea that emotions involve "innate affect programs," an idea that can be traced to Darwin initially (1998/1872). The idea here is that emotional life is the product of a small number of evolved, tightly organized basic emotions that are, to some extent, homologous across species. But emotions do not appear to operate in this manner as the multiple manifestations of such a purported affect program are generally poorly correlated (Ellsworth, 1994; Lang, 1994). In the face of such dissociations, one could advance an account of the biological components of emotion while ignoring its subjective experiential component. LeDoux (1996) initially proposed such an account, but later (LeDoux, 2002) admitted that any theory failing to account for the subjective experience of emotion cannot capture the ways in which emotion participates in human social life.

Further, the traditional biological view of emotion proposes that innate affect programs are discrete, with separate brain modules for each discrete emotion—e.g., sadness, disgust, fear, anger, surprise, and happiness. While some data of this type can be marshaled, they are ultimately not convincing. For example, LeDoux (1996) suggested a link between amygdala activation and fear, but the amygdala also responds to anger, positive emotions, and even nonemotional inductions (Baxter & Murray, 2002). In their review of imaging data, Duncan and Barrett (2007) concluded that emotion specificity does not seem to characterize the manner in which the brain reacts to emotional stimuli (see also Amodio & Harmon-Jones, chapter 6, this volume).

The View from Personality and Social Psychology

Cannon's (1929) research was an early precursor to modern social-cognitive perspectives on emotion. On the basis of his research, Cannon concluded that the biological changes associated with emotional arousal were too slow to serve as inputs to the experience of emotion, as James (1884) had suggested. Equally important, physiological arousal patterns were too undifferentiated to account for the diversity of emotional experiences, even with respect to the fundamental distinction between positive and negative emotions (Lang, 1994). Biological indicators of emotion, then, lack the sort of specificity posited by the "affect programs" idea (for similar considerations in the hormonal and cardiovascular realms, see McEwen, 2002).

Building on Cannon's (1929) analysis to a considerable extent, Schachter and Singer (1962) reasoned that physiological arousal is a nonspecific input to emotional experience that must be interpreted in a social psychological manner. In their classic test of this idea, they manipulated physiological arousal by injecting adrenaline or an inert substance. Participants then waited with another person (posing as a fellow participant, but actually a confederate) who engaged in either happy, playful behaviors or expressed anger concerning the experiment. In the absence of an explanation for their experience of arousal, adrenaline-injected participants tended to react like the confederate and to rate their own emotional reactions accordingly.

Schachter and Singer (1962) viewed physiological arousal as a noncognitive contribution to emotional experience. However, cognitive appraisals are clearly a primary determinant of measurable levels of physiological arousal (Gross, 1998; Mauss & Robinson, 2009; Stemmler, 1992). Thus, subsequent social-personality perspectives on emotion essentially invert James's (1884) theory of emotion

in that interpretative activity precedes rather than follows its physiological manifestations (Lazarus & Alfert, 1964; Ochsner & Gross, 2008; Smith, Glazer, Ruiz, & Gallo, 2004). Further advances in understanding the physiological determinants of emotion are reviewed next.

A New View

We suggest that the time has come to reject the idea of emotions as innate affective programs, at least among human beings. Despite nearly a century of efforts to provide support for this idea, research has shown, over and over again, that the various components of emotion—physiological, expressive, behavioral, and subjective—are loosely coupled at best and uncorrelated at worst (Ellsworth, 1994; Lang, 1994). Fresh thinking on this important problem is needed. In place of this discrete biological view of emotion, a new view holds that emotions are reliably distinguished by interpretations of concurrent situations rather than by facial expressions, physiology, neural processing, or indeed feeling states (Barrett, 2006).

NATURAL KINDS

On the basis of a timely review of available data, Barrett (2006) proposed that emotions are not "natural kinds." Meteorologists distinguish among kinds of clouds, but most would agree that those categories are constructed rather than discovered. Chemical elements like gold or iron are better candidates for natural kinds, as they are discrete in nature. The distinctions among emotions are probably more like the distinctions among clouds than chemical elements. The fact is that physiological patterns and brain activation patterns do not support a discrete perspective of emotion (e.g., Barrett, 2006; Lindquist, et al, in press). In addition, emotional behavior varies too widely, and emotional experiences are not sufficiently discrete, for the "affect program" idea to be viable (Russell, 2003; Russell & Barrett, 1999).

AFFECT

Psychometric work establishes that emotional reactions are well captured by two dimensions of "core (subjective) affect"—valence and arousal (Russell, 2003). Valence is an embodied representation of value, and arousal is an embodied representation of the urgency of a situation (Clore & Schnall, 2005). These affective reactions inform other systems within the individual about the goodness-badness and urgency of events.

EMOTIONS

From this view, emotions are situated affective reactions, reactions that are made specific by the situation in which they occur. Thus, "sadness" involves negative affect to personal loss, "anger" involves negative affect to blameworthy action, "fear" involves negative affect to potential, rather than actual, threatening outcomes, and so on. Each kind of situation has implications for thought and action (and for the neural and physiological processes that support them), all of which are further shaped by particular details of the situation. Emotions, then, can be best thought of as situationally constrained affective reactions (Clore & Ortony, 2008). In this sense, emotions are situated constructions rather than purely biological entities. Support for this idea has been found in recent studies showing that contextual details drive our perceptions of facial expressions of emotion (Barrett & Kensinger, 2010), as well as emotional tones of voice (Bliss-Moreau, Barrett, & Owren, 2010), much more than hitherto thought.

From this perspective, specific emotions do not show tightly organized sets of responses at the biological level because they are not organized at that level. Instead, the joints of our emotional nature lie in our social ecology (a theme further developed in understanding emotional influences on perception). Emotions are constructed from and dedicated to coping with the concurrent social realities that we face. Humans share the emotions of lower animals, but also display a greater variety of emotions, reflecting the greater variety of situations that humans find psychologically significant.

CULTURE

In this new view, Barrett (2006) argues that the notion of discrete emotions is a cultural concept rather than a natural consequence of our biological systems. In place of the traditional "affect program" view, Barrett proposes a "conceptual act model," in which emotions are elaborations of core affect that are configured by cultural ideas about emotion as well as by more immediate situational demands. The cultural concepts of discrete emotions then help us assimilate the reactions we observe in ourselves and others into useful, stereotypic emotion categories, which are useful for representational and communication purposes (Barrett, Mesquita, Ochsner, & Gross, 2007).

Further Implications of the New View

Coan (2010) observes that, traditionally, emotion has been seen as a latent entity that causes a variety of coordinated responses. This is the model that most of us have always assumed, and it is intuitively appealing. But Coan presents an emergent variable model that has some distinct advantages. Rather than emotions causing responses, emotions are inferences concerning such responses (for a fuller discussion, see Buck, 2010, and the corresponding special issue of *Emotion Review*). In a related way, sociologists have suggested that socioeconomic status (SES) is not a latent entity, but rather an abstract way of conceptualizing diverse indicators of SES that are often not highly correlated (Galobardes, Shaw, Lawlor, Smith, & Lynch, 2006).

Consider James's (1884) classic example of encountering a bear in the woods. The emergent variable view of emotion does not assume a fear circuit, but rather emphasizes the situational context and the multiple manners in which the brain solves several problems in parallel. In Coan's (2010, p. 279) terms:

> First, . . . the bear must be avoided, and avoidance-based behavioral action plans are formed. Second, the body must become physiologically prepared for quick and vigorous action, and ANS arousal meets that need. Third, elements of the experience must, by virtue of their life-threatening intensity, be tagged as highly salient in memory, resulting in amygdala activity. Finally, the ensemble of activity is experienced in consciousness (possibly at a later time) as a state of fear.

These changes are organized by the situation, not by an innate fear program. Should the situation change, the response pattern would change as well. Thus, if a bear were encountered in the zoo, the amygdala may well respond, as it is relatively insensitive to context, at least initially (Storbeck, Robinson, & McCourt, 2006). However, the sight of the bear in this very different context, would not trigger ANS arousal or avoidance behavior because the situation does not call for those problems to be solved. The configuration of bodily or subjective changes thus reflects the configuration of the situation. In sum, a situated view of emotion may solve many of the problems with traditional "affect program" views of emotion.

Question 2: How do Emotions Arise?
Traditional Perspective

From the early Greeks onward, attempts to understand human nature have made a sharp distinction between passion and reason. Plato pictured the soul as a charioteer trying to direct two horses, Descartes advocated a philosophical dualism between the bodily passions and the soul, and Kant believed that passion threatens our capacity to act from the motive of rational duty. Freud drew on a related set of distinctions, envisioning a ceaseless contest between id, ego, and superego. Similar metaviews have led modern social psychologists to propose dual-process theories of mental function (Chaiken & Trope, 1999).

The closest modern psychology gets to the passion-reason distinction is that between emotion and cognition. Emotion is thought to reflect our animal nature, whereas cognition is thought to reflect our uniquely human nature. As an example of such a framework, Maclean's (1952) influential triune brain theory linked emotions to the biologically prepared functions of the limbic system, which we share with rats, rabbits, and weasels. Similarly, Schneirla (1959) noted that apparently emotional behaviors were evident in flatworms, army ants, and even paramecia, species that have very limited reasoning capacities if any. In more modern thinking, Lang (1995) suggested that the functions of the amygdala are fundamentally similar in rats and humans, and Gray's (1990) theory of personality was similarly based on assumed parallels between the emotional circuitry of rats and humans. Multiple theorists, then, regard emotions as especially primitive biological entities.

Multiple Views from Personality and Social Psychology

Bargh (1997), Zajonc (1998), and others (e.g., Winkielman, Knutson, Paulus, & Trujillo, 2007) have argued that human emotions are elicited by circuits shared with lower mammalian species (LeDoux, 1996; Maclean, 1952; Panksepp, 1998). On the other hand, other social-personality psychologists have contended that the unique cognitive capacities of human beings change the manner in which emotions are elicited, such that they are much more dependent on cognitive interpretations of emotion-eliciting situations (Clore & Ortony, 2000; Lazarus, 1991; Schachter & Singer, 1962). In his APA Gold Medal Award address of 1980, Bob Zajonc championed the former view of emotion elicitation, in effect arguing for the independence of affect elicitation and cognition. He made this case with characteristic charm and passion and cited this bit of poetry from E. E. Cummings:

since feeling is first
who pays any attention

to the syntax of things
will never wholly kiss you

A primary source of data was and still is the *mere exposure* effect—repeated exposure to neutral stimuli results in higher liking for such stimuli subsequently (Zajonc, 1998). Much of this research has involved Chinese ideographs. Because such ideographs are not meaningful to non-Chinese individuals, liking for them would seem to bypass considerations of meaning or interpretation. Further, mere exposure effects of this type tend to be more pronounced with unconscious exposures, further making a case for the unconscious mediation of such effects (Bornstein, 1989). Even so, much of cognition—if not the vast majority of it—operates unconsciously (Deheane, 2001; Kihlstrom, 1987). Accordingly, it may be hazardous to interpret lack of awareness as evidence that a process is noncognitive.

Indeed, prominent modern theories of the mere exposure effect view it in at least quasi-cognitive terms. According to Bornstein and D'Agostino (1994), this phenomenon occurs because people misattribute stimulus familiarity, caused by repeated presentation, with liking. More recently, Winkielman and Cacioppo (2001) showed that repeated stimuli resulted in greater zygomatic or smile muscle activity, an affective rather than a cognitive reaction to fluency. Even so, fluency depends on implicit memory processes (Schacter, 1987). For this reason, we have viewed fluency accounts of the mere exposure effect as cognitive rather than noncognitive (Storbeck et al., 2006).

Although we have often argued for cognitive perspectives of affect and emotion elicitation (e.g., Clore & Ortony, 2000; Robinson, 1998), we offer a more integrated view in the present chapter. After all, an emphasis on single perspectives stymied the otherwise informative Lazarus-Zajonc debate (van Reekum & Scherer, 1997) and perhaps also the more recent exchange between Berkowitz and Harmon-Jones (2004) and Clore and Centerbar (2004) on anger. Here, we contend that substantial progress concerning affect and emotion elicitation can be made by viewing affect and emotion in terms of recursive processes (e.g., Rolls, 1999).

A New View

An iterative processing model of attitudes proposed by Cunningham and Zelazo (2007) holds promise, we believe, for understanding emotion elicitation in humans. This model proposes that exposure to an emotionally significant object initiates an iterative sequence of processes, which the authors refer to as an "evaluative cycle." Evaluative reactions are thought to begin with minimal, subcortical reactions to a novel stimulus, which is then evaluated repeatedly, augmented each time with more and more contextual information. Evaluations based on a few iterations of this recursive cycle are automatic and occur without awareness, but subsequent iterations are likely to involve additional processes that allow the system to become reflective or conscious. This neurologically informed view of evaluative activity helps explain several phenomena, as reviewed next.

ATTITUDES

An advantage of the iterative processing model (Cunningham & Zelazo, 2007) is that it helps refine our notion of the processing basis of the assessments that generate implicit and explicit attitudes. Social psychologists often assume that implicit attitudes are the same as conscious, explicit attitudes except that we are unaware of them. Is this a viable idea? We suggest that it is not.

Consider the finding that white research participants often respond to pictures of unknown black faces with amygdala activation and negative associations on the Implicit Association Test (IAT). Are such sources of data evidence of unconscious attitudes that are the same as explicit attitudes except that they are hidden from view? No. Cunningham et al. (2010) suggest that such implicit reactions are diffuse and relatively gross, but will become iteratively reprocessed many times before becoming an explicit attitude. Such considerations are consistent with Devine's (1989) model of prejudice, which contends that truly egalitarian individuals nevertheless exhibit stereotyping at the implicit level of processing. They are also consistent with the fact that implicit and explicit attitudes are often not highly correlated (Hofmann, Gawronski, Gschwendner, Le, & Schmitt, 2005) and, in some domains, are not correlated at all (Nosek, 2007).

EMOTION

Can emotions be unconscious? There has been a great deal of recent interest in this possibility (Barrett, Niedenthal, & Winkielman, 2005), although the answer depends on how one defines emotion. If emotions are identified with affective processing in sub-cortical brain regions, then emotions can be nonconscious by definition. Consistent with that approach, Morris, Öhman, and Dolan (1998) showed that subliminal threat primes were capable of activating the amygdala. Similar dynamics can also occur with degraded appetitive stimuli such as the injection of a solution with very low (and not consciously detectable) concentrations of morphine (Berridge, 1999).

On the other hand, if emotions are states that involve subjective experience, then such demonstrations concern early affective processes rather than emotions as such (Clore, Storbeck, Robinson, & Centerbar, 2005). Indeed, equating emotion with early affective processes is problematic. For example, the amygdala and the insula, both purported to respond to emotional information, actually respond to many sources of stimulation, some of which are not emotional or even affective (Duncan & Barrett, 2007). But equally, how to go from subjective experience back to brain processing is also unclear, or at least very much a work in progress (Barrett et al., 2007). The Cunningham and Zelazo (2007) model, however, although it views full blown emotions as conscious states, accommodates both early and late processes in one and the same account.

EMOTION REGULATION

The iterative evaluation model of Cunningham and Zelazo (2007) also provides insights concerning emotion regulation. In their model, emotion regulation can be understood as top-down processes that alter bottom-up affective influences. Thus, for example, the same amygdala activation to threatening stimuli should be less problematic for individuals capable of regulating such bottom-up processes. There is neural support for this idea. A review of the evidence (Davidson, Putnam, & Larson, 2000) indicates that violent individuals have frontal lobes less capable of top-down control and other reviews (Blair, Mitchell, & Blair, 2005) indicate that psychopathic individuals and individuals suffering from major depression exhibit similar control deficits (DeRubeis, Siegle, & Hollon, 2008). Other evidence comes from studies asking individuals to down-regulate their negative reactions to stimuli. Such instructions activate regions of the frontal lobes and can reduce amygdala activation to otherwise distressing stimuli (Ochsner & Gross, 2008).

Such emotion regulation processes also vary within the normal range of personality, as illustrated in research on anger and aggression. Dominant social cognitive models of aggression have tended to emphasize bottom-up affective processes (e.g., Berkowitz, 1993). Thus, the activation of hostile thoughts (whether by violent media exposure or other means) is often assumed to cause individuals to behave more aggressively (Anderson & Bushman, 2002). However, the second author and his research team have suggested that a bottom-up approach to aggression is incomplete. The impact of stimuli that prime anger and aggression is not automatic, but depends on skills for coping with such situations. For individuals high on agreeableness, for example, accessible hostile thoughts are much less predictive of anger and aggression (Meier & Robinson, 2004). In addition, agreeable individuals are able to disengage from hostile primes in an attention paradigm and tend to recruit more prosocial thoughts following the activation of hostile thoughts (Wilkowski, Robinson, &Meier (2006). Indeed, training individuals to recruit such prosocial thoughts following hostile primes has been found to lower levels of subsequent laboratory aggression (Meier, Wilkowski, & Robinson, 2008). Thus, emotion regulation can involve multiple kinds of top-down modulations of bottom-up influences. More generally, consistent with Cunningham and Zelazo's (2007) iterative reprocessing model, the process of emotion regulation involves more than viewing cognition as a lid on a boiling pot of emotion. Rather, top-down processes also regulate emotion by altering and shaping the inputs on which the automatic bottom-up processes operate.

Question 3: Do Emotions Influence Perception and If So How So?
Traditional Perspective
Investigators have taken a variety of different approaches to visual perception, but a common assumption is that understanding visual perception is primarily a matter of understanding the optics of the eye, sensory receptors, and their transduction. Perception of the world is believed to occur in a passive manner through a set of modular processes that are insulated from ascriptions of meaning (Pylyshyn, 2003). In this view, motivational and emotional factors should be irrelevant to the actual process of perception.

The View from Personality and Social Psychology
In sharp contrast to such bottom-up views of perception, Bruner (1957) proposed that motivational and emotional factors routinely influence perception, either by leading individuals to see what they want to see, are motivated to see, or expect to see. Simply stated, Bruner contended that motivational and emotional states should sensitize individuals to

relevant stimulus inputs. He also assumed that understanding such processes would require the expertise of personality and social psychological researchers.

This position was known as the "New Look" in perception. After a period of popularity, it fell out of favor, in part because it proposed "perceptual defense" processes, an idea derived from Freudian theory, which was subsequently shown to be problematic (Ericksen, 1960). But New Look ideas should not rise and fall by this particular phenomenon (Bruner, 1992; 1994). Increasingly, some of the insights of the original New Look movement have been resurrected by motivationally inclined social-personality psychologists (e.g., Balcetis & Lassiter, 2010; Brendl, Markman, & Messner, 2003; Veltkamp, Aarts, & Custers, 2008).

A New View
One of the problems with the New Look movement was that it had no central theory; rather, its data were primarily demonstrations (Bruner, 1994). A recent theoretical perspective, centrally emphasizing resources, has been shown to be predictive of many nonoptical influences on visual perception (Proffitt, 2006). We first review components of the theory before reviewing research extending it to emotional experiences, approach motivation, and the beneficial effects of social support.

ECONOMY OF ACTION
A cardinal principle from the field of behavioral ecology is that survival requires an "economy of action," whereby the energy spent by an animal, over time, cannot exceed the energy consumed (Krebs, Davies, & Parr, 1993). For example, predators cannot expend more energy in catching their prey than they acquire from eating them (Proffitt, 2006). Decisions about action must therefore be balanced to maximize energy gain and minimize energy loss. Of course animals are incapable of computing that balance explicitly and humans would find it impractical to do so. But since people trust their senses, a natural way of regulating behavior to match resources would be to adjust visual perceptions (e.g., of distances and inclines) by taking into account one's current resources or energetic state (Proffitt, 2006).

EFFORT
Imagine competing in a marathon that involved running up a long hill with a five degree incline. Would that incline look the same after running

25 miles as it did earlier in the race? Research that addresses this question finds that hills look steeper and distances look further when viewed in a state of physical exhaustion (Proffitt, 2006). Such effects are not limited to self-reports of perception, as they are also found when they are assessed through an angle-matching procedure using a kind of adjustable protractor (Bhalla & Proffitt, 1999; Proffitt, Bhalla, Gossweiler, & Midgett, 1995; Proffitt, Stefanucci, Banton, & Epstein, 2003; Witt, Proffitt, & Epstein, 2004). These results make sense if one assumes that "perception is for action" (Gibson, 2009): To the extent that actions are more effortful, perceptions should mirror that state. With respect to our primary interest in emotions, perceptions thus constitute an implicit probe of anticipated effort, an important component of several appraisal theories of emotion (e.g., Scherer, 1984; Smith & Ellsworth, 1985).

ENERGY

To this ecological perspective, Proffitt (2006) has added a *bioenergetic* view. In this view, perceptions of distances, slopes, and heights should reflect not only perceived levels of effort, but also one's current energy level. Support for this idea comes from findings that hills are perceived as especially steep by individuals who are physically exhausted, elderly, or who are wearing a heavy backpack, all conditions that would seem to implicate energy depletion (for a review, see Zadra & Clore, 2011). The energy hypothesis has received further, and perhaps more direct sources of support, by Schnall, Zadra, and Proffitt (2011). After a demanding Stroop task (Gailliot et al., 2007), some participants were given a glucose-rich fruit drink, while others got a diet version of the same drink. Afterward, they all estimated the incline of a steep hill while wearing a heavy backpack. The results were as hypothesized. The provision of a glucose-rich energy drink (relative to a nonnutritive diet drink) made the hill look flatter. Such results directly support the bioenergetic predictions of Proffitt's (2006) model.

SADNESS

Recent evidence indicates that emotions, too, bias such visual perceptions. Reasoning that the emotion of sadness is associated with low energy as a result of a loss of resources (Roseman, 1984), Reiner, Stefanucci, Proffitt, and Clore (2011) induced states of sadness or happiness with a standard autobiographical recall task. Subsequently, participants were asked to estimate the slant of a hill while standing at the bottom of it. Those who had written about a sad event were sadder than those who had written about a happy event, and participants in the sad condition viewed the same hill as steeper (23 degrees) than did those in the happy condition (16 degrees). Comparisons to a neutral induction condition revealed that the action was due to the induction of sadness rather than happiness, in that perceived slants were equal in the happy and neutral induction conditions. The results suggest that negative emotional states may be experienced as a burden, not unlike wearing a heavy backpack.

FEAR

Fear is not a low energy state, but rather one associated with a greater perception of threat (Watson, 2000). Accordingly, the perceptual biases induced by sadness and fear should be different. To model fear-related biases in perceptual terms, investigators in a recent study (Stefanucci, Proffitt, Clore, & Parekh, 2008) asked participants to estimate the steepness of a downhill slope. As predicted, verbal and visual estimates of slant were biased in a fearful condition, relative to a control condition, such that downhill slopes were perceived as steeper after the induction of fear. In related research, fearful individuals also overestimated the distance from a multistory balcony to the ground, relative to nonfearful individuals (Stefanucci, 2007). Additional results of this type were reported by Stefanucci and Storbeck (2009) and Teachman, Stefanucci, Clerkin, Cody, and Proffitt (2008). In the latter case, individuals with a greater fear of heights exhibited stronger biases, perceiving the distance to the ground as greater than did others.

APPROACH MOTIVATION

Pleasant stimuli (e.g., food, friends, love) are those to be approached, as they generally confer energy and resources (Watson, 2000). In a series of four studies, Ode, Winters, and Robinson (in press) presented pleasant, neutral, and unpleasant words and then asked for perceptual estimates concerning the words. In Study 1, it was found that pleasant stimuli were perceived to be larger than they were, relative to neutral and unpleasant stimuli. In Study 4, it was found that pleasant stimuli were perceived to have been presented for a longer period of time than they actually were, a bias not observed in response to neutral and unpleasant stimuli. Similar results were found in the other studies. Thus, consistent with a resource-based model of perception (Proffitt, 2006), appetitive motivational states appear to bias perceptions in a manner signaling their attainability.

SOCIAL RESOURCES

We are a social species and social support is important to our day-to-day resource acquisition. In a relevant set of studies, Schnall, Harber, Stefanucci, and Proffitt (2008) found that being with a friend can make hills appear significantly less steep, and that the magnitude of this effect is predicted by the duration of the friendship. In addition, they found that merely thinking of a friend was sufficient to make inclines look flatter and hence easier to ascend. In other research, Schnall (in press) asked students at the University of Virginia how far it would be to walk from the psychology department to Monticello, the historic home of Thomas Jefferson, a few miles away. She found that estimates were significantly shorter when she asked how far it would be to walk with a friend to Monticello. Thus, perceived availability of social support significantly reduces the perceived distance of a trek to be made.

Broader Implications

We have reviewed research showing that inclines look steeper and distances look greater when resources for coping with them are low, effects that can be reversed by adding physical resources (glucose) or social resources (friends). Additionally, it appears that the negative emotions of sadness and fear have predictable influences on perceptions of physical layout as well. These results imply that resource considerations may be important in understanding emotion and social psychological phenomena more broadly considered (Zadra & Clore, 2011).

EMOTION

In line with the affect-as-information hypothesis (Schwarz & Clore, 1983), Zadra and Clore (2011) propose that emotion provides information that is useful for estimating resource availability. Sadness, for example, may act like a gas gauge, signaling that resources have been lost, and fear carries information about threats to resources. Both make obstacles seem bigger, which should lead to more conservative decisions about action. But such considerations raise an important question. If energy levels influence perceptions directly, why would emotional states also influence them? An answer is that whereas feeling energetic or exhausted necessarily concerns only the present, emotions can concern past, future, or even imagined actions. Hence they can inform resource management decisions well beyond the present.

Indeed, emotions might be viewed as situated concerns about resources. If so, do the emotions that have sometimes been classified as "basic" implicate a concern with resources in a particularly direct and obvious way? Perhaps so, because all species must cope with danger, attack, opportunity, toxins, and novelty. It is not surprising, from a resource perspective, then, that the emotions deemed "basic"—including fear, anger, joy, disgust, and surprise—are those that seem to most directly implicate the potential gain or loss of resources.

SOCIAL RESOURCES

The common social emotions can also be interpreted from a resource perspective, but one emphasizing social rather than purely intrapsychic resources. Thus, love is attachment to a social resource, jealousy concerns a threat to social resources from someone else, and envy involves perceptions of undesirable or unfair distributions of resources. Grief is distress over the loss of an especially close social resource, and homesickness can be viewed similarly. Anger consists of being upset at a loss of resources from someone else's blameworthy action, whereas gratitude involves being pleased at a gain in resources from someone else's praiseworthy action.

Guilt is a curious emotion, however, because it seems to be associated with penalizing the self perhaps unduly so. Yet, guilt too should be a useful emotion for maintaining social resources. The behavioral economist Robert Frank (1988) provides useful insights along such lines. Consider, for example, a situation in which one is tempted to obtain some benefit at the expense of a friend. The situation may be tempting because immediate benefits are generally more compelling than delayed costs (Herrnstein, 1990). But Frank (1988) notes that by being felt immediately, guilt can counter such immediate rewards, providing a subjectively compelling reason for not taking advantage of one's friend. Guilt thus brings the otherwise delayed pain of being discovered as a false friend into the present, where it can compete on even terms with whatever immediate benefits the transgression might produce.

Indeed, social emotions appear to provide the glue that ensures that individuals do their part to fulfill interpersonal obligations. Emotions of love and gratitude, for example, motivate the mutuality required for relationships to work. When people are faced with the cost of doing their part, they can easily get distracted, but gratitude can motivate them to reciprocate, even when doing so is costly (Bartlett & DeSteno, 2006). And reciprocation, in turn, should breed trust and intensify interpersonal bonds. The genius of social emotions is that they make one want to act in ways that maintain one's social resources in the long-term, despite the fact that few of such considerations would be conscious.

Question 4: How Do Emotions Affect Behavior?
Traditional Perspective

It is widely assumed that emotions have strong, direct effects on behavior, thus explaining their functional basis. As Russell (2003, p. 161) states: "Everyone knows that fear brings flight and anger brings fight." From this commonsense, traditional perspective, it is not surprising that many prominent theories of emotion emphasize its behavioral effects. Frijda (1986) suggested that emotions are basically felt action tendencies. Lang, Bradley, and Cuthbert (1997), following Schneirla (1959), similarly define emotions in terms of action tendencies first and foremost, though such motivated action tendencies might be inhibited in particular contexts. Emotions have been characterized in terms of stereotyped, survival-relevant action inclinations, including flight in the case of fear, avoidance in the case of disgust, withdrawal in the case of sadness, vengeful approach in the case of anger, and so forth.

Problems with the Traditional Perspective

Anyone who has experienced a near collision when driving knows that the feeling of fear generally arrives only after the collision has been averted. The brake pedal is depressed instantaneously without waiting for the experience of fear to encourage it. Such considerations suggest that conscious emotional experiences are often too delayed to trigger immediate adaptive responding (Cannon, 1929).

More generally, the social psychological literature is not very encouraging to the idea that emotions activate specific action tendencies (e.g., Barrett, 2006). Additionally, Fredrickson (1998) notes that evolutionary accounts of emotion that emphasize effects on immediate action do not seem relevant to understanding positive emotions like happiness and contentment. When one feels contented or calm, there would seem nothing urgent to do. The fact that most of our emotions are of this pleasant hedonic type (Diener, Suh, Lucas, & Smith, 1999) thus poses problems for behavioral theories of emotion. Further, most instances of human emotion do not occur in situations in which the immediate survival of the self is at issue (Parkinson, Fischer, & Manstead, 2005).

Such problems for the traditional action-oriented perspective on emotion are usually handled by insisting that emotions may not show up in behavior because action tendencies are sometimes suppressed by the frontal cortex (Lang et al., 1997). This suppression-related view of the frontal cortex, however, is not correct. The frontal cortex plays a more fundamental role in redefining the emotional situation, thereby keeping such action tendencies from being activated in the first place (Luu, Tucker, & Derryberry, 1998; Storbeck et al., 2006). In short, there are a number of problems for traditional theories of emotion that emphasize action tendencies.

A New View

Baumeister, Vohs, DeWall, and Zhang (2007) reviewed a number of social and personality literatures and concluded that emotion often affects behavior indirectly rather than directly. We expand on their analysis in the section that follows, beginning with their distinction between affect and emotion.

DISTINGUISHING AFFECT AND EMOTION

Affect refers to quick, automatic, valenced reactions of positivity or negativity that do not require physiological arousal and most typically are stimulus-based rather than felt. Flashes of automatic affect may be triggered simply by exposure to affectively relevant stimuli. Such affective reactions are likely to provide important information concerning whether such stimuli should be approached or avoided and do in fact seem to guide behavior in such an automatic fashion (Chen & Bargh, 1999; Robinson, 1998).

In contrast to often unconscious affective reactions, full blown, conscious emotional states involve emotional arousal, are triggered relatively slowly, and are experienced in terms of implications for the self (Lazarus, 1991). Both the slowness of such reactions and their link to self-representations make conscious emotions quite different feedback signals. Rather than facilitating immediate action patterns, emotions are likely to provide a wider perspective on one's actions. For example, Schwarz and Clore (2007) suggest that emotions provide information concerning the adequacy of the self's functioning and Carver and Scheier (1998) consider emotions as second-order feedback signals that inform the self concerning the adequacy of goal progress rather than altering action tendencies.

THE FUNCTION OF (CONSCIOUS) EMOTIONAL EXPERIENCES

In related terms, Baumeister et al. (2007) suggest that emotions facilitate learning rather than providing an impetus to immediate action. Consistent with this view, emotions are often experienced as disruptions (Carver & Scheier, 1998) that disengage the individual from immediate responding (Mandler, 2003). However, they also inform the individual that a significant concern is at stake (Lazarus, 1991), commandeer attention (Robinson, 1998), and make salient key elements to be remembered when similar situations arise in the future (LeDoux, 1996).

As an example, consider the emotion of regret. Clearly, this emotion cannot undo the behaviors that led to it, which have already passed (Gilovich & Medvec, 1995). However, the emotion of regret stimulates counterfactual thinking—that is, imagining having taken a different course of action. Such counterfactuals are remembered and can be recalled prior to acting or not acting in similar future circumstances (Roese, 1997). Consider also the emotion of guilt. Again, feeling guilty cannot undo past transgressions, but it may provide a learning experience that leads the individual to avoid engaging in similar actions next time (Baumeister, Stillwell, & Heatherton, 1995).

EMOTION AS A TRIGGER OF THOUGHT

Much of social behavior is relatively thoughtless according to influential social psychological (Bargh & Chartrand, 1999; Dijksterhuis & Aarts, 2010) and personality (McCrae & Costa, 1994; Mischel & Shoda, 1995) theories. The arousal of emotion is important in part because it stops such mindless processing and, in doing so, calls for a reorganization of the self's efforts (Carver & Scheier, 1998; Lazarus, 1991). Indeed, if it were not for emotions, people would not bother to think as much as they do (Baumeister et al., 2007).

Of course, merely stimulating thought might not be sufficient to make emotions adaptive. For example, rumination on sadness often exacerbates rather than alleviates depression over the long term (Lyubomirsky & Nolen-Hoeksema, 1993). Yet, this example, too, is consistent with our central claims. Rumination, whether adaptive or not, represents an attempt to solve long-term problems of the self, regardless of whether such efforts are successful or not (Wells, 2006). A similar case can be made for worries (Borkovec, Ray, & Stöber, 1998), obsessions (Mallinger, 2009), and intrusive thoughts (Clark &

Rhyno, 2005). Fortunately for most of us, such emotion-induced cognitive tendencies toward problem-solving are likely to be adaptive (Klinger, 1999).

EMOTION AND DECISION-MAKING

An implication of the preceding analysis is that people will often make decisions on the basis of previous emotional experiences or at least simulations of such experiences. Baumeister et al. (2007) referred to this idea as the "how *will* I feel about it?" heuristic and suggested that past experiences, and their memorial traces, should provide some guidance in making similar decisions in the future. This is certainly the case. A large body of work has shown that much of human decision-making is guided by affective forecasts—that is, simulations of whether a chosen course of action will likely result in beneficial or problematic outcomes, in part based on previous experiences with similar situations in the past (Wilson & Gilbert, 2005).

Interestingly, the affective forecasting literature generally emphasizes the error-prone nature of such decision-making processes (Wilson & Gilbert, 2005). Essentially, people have beliefs about the emotional consequences of choices that are exaggerated (Robinson & Clore, 2002). They may quite accurately expect that benefits will be pleasing and costs will be distressing, but they tend to believe that these emotions will be more intense and last longer than they do.

Baumeister et al. (2007) suggest that such exaggerations of affective forecasting may actually be beneficial. If one imagined only a temporary discomfort over losing one's job, for example, one might not be sufficiently motivated to work hard. On the other hand, it is also adaptive for actual emotional reactions to emotional events to be manageable and short-lived so that one can move on (Gilbert, Pinel, Wilson, Blumberg, & Wheatley, 1998). In short, although anticipated emotions are often exaggerated, that very fact may allow previous emotional experience to serve as an effective guide to decision-making.

Question 5: How Do Emotions Regulate Thought?
Traditional Perspective

The history of Western philosophy from Aristotle and before treats emotion and thinking as separate entities. For example, Descartes (2009) viewed emotions as mechanical and animal-like in nature (bestial, in fact), whereas thoughts were the product of a disembodied soul. Biologically inclined theories of emotion, too, maintain that distinct and purportedly independent brain circuits mediate emotion on the one hand and thinking on the other (LeDoux, 1996; Panksepp, 1998). And when the relation between cognition and emotion is considered, emotions are often assumed to undermine rational thought (Drevets & Raichle, 1998; McClure, Botvinick, Yeung, Greene, & Cohen, 2007). Such a view is essentially a continuation of the Cartesian tradition, which Damasio (1994) criticized in his popular book titled, *Descartes' Error.*

The View from Personality and Social Psychology

The social psychology literature has, for some 30 years now, emphasized interactions between emotion and cognition, many of which cannot be viewed from a traditional Cartesian perspective (e.g., Bower, 1981). Thus, positive and negative emotional states clearly influence cognitive processing. For example, the induction of positive states facilitates the use of social cognitive scripts (Bless, Clore, Schwarz, Golisano, Rabe, & Wolk, 1996), the occurrence of semantic and affective priming (Storbeck & Clore, 2008), and the operation of associative memory processes (Kuhl, 1994). The induction of negative emotional states, facilitates careful attention to argument quality in persuasive messages (Schwarz, Bless, & Bohner, 1991), directs attention to local details in attention tasks (Gasper & Clore, 2002), and lowers susceptibility to false memories (Storbeck & Clore, 2005).

A number of possible explanations have been proposed for such emotional effects on cognition. These include proposals that positive affect broadens attention (Derryberry & Tucker, 1994), creates a broaden and build orientation (Fredrickson, 1998), promotes heuristic processing (Schwarz & Clore, 2007), leads to the use of general knowledge structures (Bless, 2001), activates positive memories (Bower, 1981), depletes cognitive resources (Worth & Mackie, 1987), activates substantive processing (Forgas, 2001), elicits stimulus assimilation (Fiedler, 2001), or encourages relational processing (Storbeck & Clore, 2005). Despite their variety, all of these explanations have one assumption in common. All assume that positive and negative affect activate particular styles of cognitive processing. As an alternative to this assumption that positive affect triggers one kinds of processing and negative affect another, a new model (e.g., Clore & Huntsinger, 2009) assumes greater flexibility in the emotional effects on cognition, and we review relevant evidence.

A New View

A new approach to affective influences on cognition assumes that the affective components of moods and emotions confer value on whatever is in mind at the time. Positive affect confers positive value, and negative affect confers negative value. In this account positive and negative states and reactions often serve as "go" and "stop" signs for accessible cognitions and inclinations (a similar emphasis can be found in Briñol & Petty, 2008; Clore, et al., 2001; Martin, Ward, Achee, & Wyer, 1993; Wyer, Clore, & Isbell, 1999).

This approach relies on two basic principles. The *accessibility principle* is that positive affect should facilitate the processing tendency that is dominant or accessible in particular situations (Clore et al., 2001). For example, if stereotypes are accessible, positive affect should facilitate stereotyping to a greater extent than negative affect. On the other hand, if the dominant response in a situation favors individuation, then positive affect should result in reduced stereotyping. Positive affect should thus facilitate dominant processing tendencies in a task-specific manner.

The *accessibility principle* is complemented by an *attribution principle*. It is not always the case that affective reactions are seen as relevant to the judgment or task at hand. To the extent that they are not, they may have very different cognitive consequences. In this respect, a well-cited study found that positive moods, due to irrelevant, temporary factors (e.g., sunny rather than rainy weather), nonetheless led individuals to report that their lives as a whole were more satisfying (Schwarz & Clore, 1983). Such effects were not observed when individuals were asked about the weather beforehand because, in that condition, the affective reactions would be more properly attributed to transient factors and would therefore not be included in the life satisfaction judgments.

An important question is whether the attribution principle acts to control affective influences not only on evaluative judgments but on cognitive processes more generally. If so, and putting the two principles together, positive affective states should facilitate and negative states should inhibit the use of accessible cognitions, inclinations and styles of thought to the extent that the relevant affect is viewed as a reaction to the task at hand. We review multiple sources of evidence. In the experiments reviewed, participants were randomly assigned to a condition designed to induce a mildly positive or negative affective state (e.g., writing about a positive versus negative event from the past, a well-validated method of inducing moods and emotions in the laboratory).

ATTRIBUTION EFFECTS

In two sets of studies, induced states of positive affect led to greater global than local perceptual tendencies (Gasper, 2004) and to higher levels of being persuaded by presented arguments (Sinclair, Mark, & Clore, 1994). Important to the attribution principle, however, both sets of studies also showed that such emotion-cognition effects were attenuated or eliminated under conditions in which individuals were led to attribute their affective reactions to task-irrelevant influences. The attribution principle has thus been supported in several lines of investigation in which processing tendencies rather than judgments constituted the dependent measure.

THE FLEXIBLE EFFECTS OF
EMOTIONAL STATES

An implication of the affect-as-information hypothesis and particularly of the attribution principle is that the effects of affective reactions, moods, and emotions on cognition and behavior should be flexible. That is, it should be possible to change the effects of emotion with relatively minor changes in a situation to the extent that such changes alter the apparent object of the affect (Clore & Huntsinger, 2009).

Martin et al. (1993) were the first to show such effects by varying the implicit questions to which positive and negative affect seemed relevant. Thus, when instructions emphasized doing well, positive affect indicated that participants had done well, so they tended to stop working sooner on the task than those in negative states. But when instructions emphasized continuing for as long as the task was enjoyable, positive affect indicated that participants were enjoying the task, so they persisted longer than those in negative states. Similar contextual effects have been found by Briñol and Petty (2008) and Fishbach and Trope (2008). Such results are consistent with the view that affective influences on thought and behavior depend on the cognitions and inclinations that are most accessible in the situations in which the affect is experienced.

In this section, we refer to affect without regard to whether it reflects moods, emotions, or other affective reactions. In should be noted that the particularities of specific emotions can alter and limit these general affective influences in important ways, although that is not part of the current focus.

STEREOTYPING

In social situations, a variety of stereotypes may become accessible as people encounter others differing in age, gender, ethnicity, or other characteristics. It is therefore not surprising that positive moods are generally associated with greater stereotyping (Isbell, 2004). On the other hand, some studies have shown that for egalitarian individuals, counter-stereotypic information is more accessible in such situations (Moskowitz, Gollwitzer, Wasel, & Schaal, 1999). If so, and in view of the accessibility principle mentioned above, the induction of positive (versus negative) emotional states should lead to *greater* stereotyping only among nonegalitarian individuals (for whom stereotypes are highly accessible) but should lead to *less* stereotyping among egalitarian individuals (for whom stereotypes are less accessible). Just such a pattern was reported in a study of gender stereotyping (Huntsinger, Sinclair, Dunn, & Clore, 2011). The results illustrate the accessibility principle and suggest an important role for individual differences in understanding the cognitive consequences of emotional states.

GLOBAL-LOCAL FOCUS

Recall that Gasper (2004; Gasper & Clore, 2002) found that the induction of positive (versus negative) emotional states resulted in an increased global (rather than local) perceptual focus. Such results are understandable because a global focus of attention is normative in attention paradigms of this type (Navon, 1977). However, work by Trope and colleagues (Trope & Liberman, 2010) has shown that priming can change people's focus to produce either a more global focus (i.e., seeing the forest rather than the trees) or a more local focus (i.e., seeing the trees rather than the forest). According to the accessibility-attribution model, the induction of happy emotional states should enhance whatever focus of attention a situation makes most accessible. Thus, happy states should enhance a local focus of attention when a local focus is most accessible. Two experiments found precisely this pattern: Happy emotional states led to an increased global focus after global responding had been primed, but to an increased local focus after local responding had been primed (Huntsinger, Clore, &Bar-Anan, 2011). Rather than viewing emotion-cognition relations as invariant, therefore, these results reinforce the central premise of the model. Whereas it is often descriptively accurate to say that positive and negative affect lead to adoption of a global and a local focus, respectively, this generalization appears to hold simply because a global focus is often the dominant orientation. Positive affect then promotes and negative affect inhibits that dominant orientation.

CULTURE AS ACCESSIBILITY

Culture is thought to operate, in part, by making particular patterns of thinking more accessible (Cohen, 2009; see also Adams, chapter 8, this volume). According to the accessibility principle, such cultural differences in cognition should be particularly pronounced in the context of induced positive emotional states. Recent investigations have tested the hypothesis in relation to holistic vs. analytic reasoning (Koo, Clore, Kim, & Choi, in press). Holistic reasoning has been found to be especially prevalent among East Asian participants (Nisbett, Peng, Choi, & Norenzayan, 2001). The experimenters manipulated positive versus negative emotional states among both Americans and Koreans as they responded to the same reasoning task examined by Nisbett et al. (2001). As hypothesized, American/Korean differences in holistic thinking were particularly pronounced in positive emotional states and absent in negative emotional states. That is, positive affect promoted the tendency for Koreans to reason holistically and for Americans to reason analytically. These results nicely illustrate predictions of the new view of emotional influences on cognition.

Implications for Personality and Social Psychology

The five new ideas challenge traditional thinking about emotion. We have suggested that the notion of biological "affect programs" is problematic, that emotions arise interactively from bottom-up (affective) and top-down (cognitive and contextual) factors, that a resource-based model appears to have potential for helping us understand emotion, that emotional experience influences behavior not so much directly, but indirectly by dramatizing important lessons, and that rather than being dedicated to particular styles of thought, positive and negative affect confer value on whatever cognitions and inclinations are most accessible at the time. We also contrasted our "new view" perspectives with traditional social-personality perspectives concerning the same questions. For example, we presented a more integrated framework for understanding the role of

affective evaluation in emotion and suggested that new theoretical frameworks can be used to generate predictions concerning emotional effects on perception and cognition. In addition, we linked our new view perspective to some central social-personality variables such as attitudes, emotion regulation, social support, and culture.

Aside from such considerations, do the five new ideas about emotion have implications for the study of personality and social psychology? We believe they do and accordingly widen our discussion along such lines.

Emotional Reactions: State, Trait, or Both?

We are accustomed to think that our emotional reactions reflect the situation we are in just as we are accustomed to think of our behaviors in such situational terms (Ross & Nisbett, 1991). However, developmental and personality psychologists have demonstrated that such views of emotions are myopic as they neglect the fact that there are pronounced individual differences in typical emotional experiences (Watson, 2000) and reactions to emotional stimuli (Zelenski & Larsen, 1999); and it is also true that individuals appear genetically programmed to experience certain emotional states more frequently and intensely than others (Tellegen et al., 1988). It is accordingly incorrect to suggest that emotional reactions are based on situational factors exclusively. This is most definitely not true (Headey & Wearing, 1989; McCrae & Costa, 1994).

Although our review primarily focused on inductions of emotion, relative to personality factors, this was less true for our analysis of perceptual biases. In this section, we reported (among other findings) that dispositionally anxious individuals estimated that the distance from a balcony to the ground was further (e.g., Stefanucci, 2007). Additionally, anxious individuals exhibit a number of other perceptual, cognitive, and judgment biases (Eysenck, Derakshan, Santos, & Calvo, 2007; Gasper & Clore, 1998; Mathews & MacLeod, 2005; Robinson, 1998). The upshot of such considerations is that trait emotionality factors are likely to be important in moderating many of the effects we reported, but that further work of a personality-related type is necessary to demonstrate this point.

Personality and Top-Down Factors in Affective Processing

Biological theories of emotion and personality predominate. For example, Gray's influential theory of personality (reviewed in Corr, 2008) contended that the subcortical circuits responsible for vigilance to threats and reward-pursuit provide a more or less adequate explanation of individual differences in neuroticism (anxiety in Gray's original framework) and extraversion (impulsivity in Gray's original framework). Depue and Collins (1999) presented additional arguments for the idea that extraversion can be understood in terms of variations in the subcortical brain regions responsible for dopamine release. However, Matthews (2008; Matthews & Gilliland, 1999) argued that such subcortical views of extraversion and neuroticism have little direct support and neglect top-down cognitive factors in understanding these traits.

In our review, we challenged the idea that subcortical evaluative processes provide a sufficient understanding of emotion. It is also true that such subcortical views appear insufficient in understanding variations in human personality. Canli et al. (2001) conducted a well-cited study in which they exposed individuals to affective stimuli while imaging the brain's responses to them. Extraversion predicted greater brain activation to positive affective stimuli, and neuroticism predicted greater brain activation to negative affective stimuli. However, the brain regions implicated were decidedly more frontal (top-down) than subcortical (bottom-up). Moreover, there are numerous sources of fMRI data suggesting that many clinical disorders (e.g., depression) are associated with insufficient top-down control of bottom-up emotional arousal in structures such as the amygdala (Davidson, 1999; Davidson et al., 2000; DeRubeis et al., 2008).

Additionally, Wilkowski and Robinson (2008a) argued and provided results (Wilkowski & Robinson, 2007; 2008b) to support the point that trait variations in anger can be understood in terms of the insufficient control of hostile thoughts, once activated. Further, individuals exhibiting higher levels of top-down control following activated hostile thoughts are: (1) less aggressive in the laboratory, (2) more capable of forgiving provocations in daily life, and (3) more capable of translating forgiveness into lower levels of subsequent anger (Wilkowski, Robinson, & Troop-Gordon, 2010). In general terms, then, people are not passive victims of automatic affect, and consideration of top-down processes afford significant insights into personality functioning. Clearly, such work is of a personality by situation type, consistent with interactive frameworks for emotion (Endler, 2002; Zelenski & Larsen, 1999) and personality (Deffenbacher, 1992; Snyder & Ickes, 1985).

Emotion from a Broader Social-Personality Perspective

In this section, we adopt a broader perspective on emotion in social-personality psychology. In doing so, we are mindful that there was a time during which social and personality perspectives on behavior, and to some extent emotion, were seen as mutually competing. The present *Handbook* should correct this problematic conception. However, it is still true that more can be said concerning emotion in relation to the goals of the *Handbook*. We raise a set of questions and answer them in support of such a broader conception.

WHY SHOULD SOCIAL AND PERSONALITY PSYCHOLOGISTS CONCERN THEMSELVES WITH EMOTION?

If an individual exhibits an emotional reaction, we can be relatively confident that the situation or outcome is hedonically important to the individual (Lazarus, 1991). Social and personality psychologists should focus on emotional outcomes, then, to the extent that they are interested in such hedonically important outcomes and processes. It might be that investigators are not interested in such hedonic outcomes, but we suggest that nonhedonic depictions of social and personality processes are likely to be sterile and descriptive (Pervin, 1994). The fact is that individuals care about their emotions and thus social and personality investigations of an emotional type get to the core of individuals' goals, strategies, and concerns (Klinger, 1977).

IS EMOTION A PERSONALITY OR SOCIAL OUTCOME?

As should be clear, emotion belongs to the interface of social and personality psychology. Some events—such as a relationship breakup or an excellent test score—may be hedonically important to any individual. However, even in relation to such outcomes, individuals differ in their emotional reactivity (Goldstein & Strube, 1994; Romero-Canyas et al., 2010). In turn, personality variables moderate emotional reactions to affective stimuli. For example, Meier and Robinson (2004) showed that accessible hostile thoughts, whether assessed or manipulated, led to greater blame, greater anger, and greater aggression at low levels of the Big Five trait of agreeableness. Although most of the findings covered in the present review were of a social cognitive type, we emphasized the need for personality-oriented investigations to complement our largely social cognitive focus.

WHAT ARE THE IMPLICATIONS FOR UNDERSTANDING PERSONALITY BY SITUATION INTERACTIONS?

We view emotional reactions as an excellent realm for understanding personality by situation interactions. In this respect, it is apparent that extraverts are more reactive to positive events (Zelenski & Larsen, 1999) or priming conditions (Robinson, Moeller, & Ode, 2010), neurotics are more reactive to negative events (Suls & Martin, 2005) or priming conditions (Robinson, Ode, Moeller, & Goetz, 2007), and agreeable individuals appear to self-regulate their hostile thoughts in a top-down manner (Robinson, 2007). Such interactions are important in ruling out exclusively situational or personality perspectives concerning affective processing tendencies or emotional reactions (Larsen & Ketelaar, 1991; Robinson & Compton, 2008). The fact is that emotional reactions are better modeled in terms of person by situation effects than in terms of either source of variance considered alone (see Moeller, Robinson, & Bresin, 2010).

Acknowledgments

The authors acknowledge support from NIH (Clore: MH 50074) and NSF (Robinson: BCS 0843982).

References

Anderson, C. A., & Bushman, B. J. (2002). Human aggression. *Annual Review of Psychology, 53,* 27–51.

Balcetis, E., & Lassiter, G. D. (2010). *The social psychology of visual perception.* New York: Psychology Press.

Bargh, J. (1997). The automaticity of everyday life: A manifesto. In: R. S. Wyer (Ed.), *Advances in social cognition* (pp. 1–61). Mahwah, NJ: Erlbaum.

Bargh, J. A., & Chartrand, T. L. (1999). The unbearable automaticity of being. *American Psychologist, 54,* 462–479.

Barrett, L. F. (2006). Are emotions natural kinds? *Perspectives in Psychological Science, 1,* 28–58.

Barrett, L. F., & Kensinger, L. A. (2010). Context is routinely encoded during emotion perception. *Psychological Science, 21,* 595–599.

Barrett, L. F., Mesquita, B., Ochsner, K. N., & Gross, J. J. (2007). The experience of emotion. *Annual Review of Psychology, 58,* 373–403.

Barrett, L. F., Niedenthal, P. M., & Winkielman, P. (2005). *Emotion and consciousness.* New York: Guilford.

Bartlett, M. Y., & DeSteno, D. (2006). Gratitude and prosocial behavior: Helping when it costs you. *Psychological Science, 17,* 319–325.

Baumeister, R. F., Stillwell, A. M., & Heatherton, T. F. (1995). Personal narratives about guilt: Role in action control and interpersonal relationships. *Basic and Applied Social Psychology, 17,* 173–198.

Baumeister, R. F., Vohs, K. D., DeWall, N., & Zhang, L. (2007). How emotion shapes behavior: Feedback, anticipation, and reflection, rather than direct causation. *Personality and Social Psychology Review, 11,* 167–203.

Baxter, M. G., & Murray, E. A. (2002). The amygdala and reward. *Nature Reviews Neuroscience, 3,* 563–573.

Bechara, A., Damasio, H., Tranel, D., & Damasio, A. R. (1997). Deciding advantageously before knowing the advantageous strategy. *Science, 275,* 1293–1294.

Berkowitz, L. (1993). *Aggression: Its causes, consequences, and control.* New York: McGraw-Hill.

Berkowitz, L., & Harmon-Jones, E. (2004). Toward an understanding of the determinants of anger. *Emotion, 4,* 107–130.

Berridge, K. C. (1999). Pleasure, pain, desire, and dread: Hidden core processes of emotion. In D. Kahneman, E. Diener, & N. Schwarz (Eds.), *Well-being: The foundations of hedonic psychology* (pp. 525–557). New York: Russell Sage.

Bettencourt, B. A., Talley, A., Benjamin, A. J., & Valentine, J. (2006). Personality and aggressive behavior under provoking and neutral conditions: A meta-analytic review. *Psychological Bulletin, 132,* 751–777.

Bhalla, M., & Proffitt, D. R. (1999). Visual-motor recalibration in geographical slant perception. *Journal of Experimental Psychology: Human Perception and Performance, 25,* 1076–1096.

Blair, J., Mitchell, D., & Blair, K. (2005). *The psychopath: Emotion and the brain.* Malden, MA: Blackwell.

Bless, H. (2001). The relation between mood and the use of general knowledge structures. In L. L. Martin & G. L. Clore (Eds.), *Mood and social cognition: A user's guidebook* (pp. 9–29). Mahwah, NJ: Lawrence.

Bless, H., Clore, G., Schwarz, N., Golisano, V., Rabe, C., & Wolk, M. (1996). Mood and the use of scripts: Does happy mood really lead to mindlessness? *Journal of Personality and Social Psychology, 71,* 665–679.

Bliss-Moreau, E., Barrett, L. F. & Owren, M. (2010). I like the sound of your voice: Affective learning about the human voice. *Journal of Experimental Social Psychology, 46,* 557-563.

Block, J. (2002). *Personality as an affect-processing system: Toward and integrative theory.* Mahwah, NJ: Erlbaum.

Bolger, N., Davis, A., & Rafaeli, E. (2003). Diary methods: Capturing life as it is lived. *Annual Review of Psychology, 54,* 579–616.

Borkovec, T. D., Ray, W. J., & Stöber, J. (1998). Worry: A cognitive phenomenon intimately linked to affective, physiological, and interpersonal behavioral processes. *Cognitive Therapy and Research, 22,* 561–576.

Bornstein, R. F. (1989) Exposure and affect: Overview and meta-analysis of research, 1968–1987. *Psychological Bulletin, 106,* 265–289.

Bornstein, R. F., & D'Agostino, P. R. (1994). The attribution and discounting of perceptual fluency: Preliminary tests of a perceptual fluency/attributional model of the mere exposure effect. *Social Cognition, 12,* 103–128.

Bower, G. H. (1981). Mood and memory. *American Psychologist, 36,* 129–148.

Brendl, C. M., Markman, A. B., & Messner, C. (2003). The devaluation effect: Activating a need devalues unrelated objects. *Journal of Consumer Research, 29,* 463–473.

Briñol, P., & Petty, R. E. (2008). Embodied persuasion: Fundamental processes by which bodily responses can impact attitudes. In G. R. Semin & E. R. Smith (Eds.), *Embodiment grounding: Social, cognitive, affective, and neuroscientific approaches* (pp. 184–207). Cambridge, UK: Cambridge University Press.

Bruner, J. (1957). On perceptual readiness. *Psychological Review, 64,* 123–152.

Bruner, J. (1992). Another look at New Look 1. *American Psychologist, 47*, 780–783.

Bruner, J. (1994). The view from the heart's eye: A commentary. In P. M. Niedenthal & S. Kitayama (Eds.), *The heart's eye: Emotional influences in perception and attention* (pp. 269–286). New York: Academic.

Buck, R. (2010). Emotion is an entity at both biological and ecological levels: The ghost in the machine is language. *Emotion Review, 2*, 286–287.

Canli, T., Zhao, Z., Desmond, J. E., Kang, E., Gross, J., & Gabrieli, J. D. E. (2001). An fMRI study of personality influences on brain reactivity to emotional stimuli. *Behavioral Neuroscience, 115*, 33–42.

Cannon, W. B. (1929). *Bodily changes in pain, hunger, fear and rage*. Oxford, UK: Appleton.

Carver, C. S., & Scheier, M. F. (1998). *On the self-regulation of behavior*. New York: Cambridge University Press.

Chaiken, S., & Trope, Y. (1999). *Dual-process theories in social psychology*. New York: Guilford.

Chen, M., & Bargh, J. A. (1999). Consequences of automatic evaluation: Immediate behavioral predispositions to approach or avoid the stimulus. *Personality and Social Psychology Bulletin, 25*, 215–224.

Clark, D. A., & Rhyno, S. (2005). Unwanted intrusive thoughts in nonclinical individuals: Implications for clinical disorders. In D. A. Clark (Ed.), *Intrusive thoughts in clinical disorders: Theory, research, and treatment* (pp. 1–29). New York: Guilford.

Clark, L. A., & Watson, D. (1988). Mood and the mundane: Relations between daily life events and self-reported mood. *Journal of Personality and Social Psychology, 54*, 296–308.

Clark, L. A., & Watson, D. (1999). Temperament: A new paradigm for trait psychology. In L. A. Pervin & O. P. John (Eds.), *Handbook of personality: Theory and research* (2nd ed., pp. 399–423). New York: Guilford.

Clore, G. L., & Centerbar, D. B. (2004). Analyzing anger: How to make people mad. *Emotion, 4*, 139–144.

Clore, G. L. & Huntsinger, J. R. (2009). How the object of affect guides its impact. *Emotion Review, 1*, 39–54.

Clore, G. L., & Ortony, A. (2000). Cognition in emotion: Never, sometimes, or always? In R. D. Lane & L. Nadel (Eds.), *The cognitive neuroscience of emotion* (pp. 24–61). New York: Oxford University Press.

Clore, G. L., & Ortony, A. (2008). Appraisal theories: How cognition shapes affect into emotion. In M. Lewis, J. M. Haviland-Jones, & L. F. Barrett (Eds.), *Handbook of emotions* (3rd ed., pp. 628–642). New York: Guilford.

Clore, G. L., & Schnall, S. (2005). The influence of affect on attitudes. In D. Albarracin, B. T. Johnson, & M. P. Zanna (Eds.), *The handbook of attitudes* (pp. 437–489). Mahwah, NJ: Erlbaum.

Clore, G. L., Schwarz, N., & Conway, M. (1994). Affective causes and consequences of social information processing. In R. S. Wyer & T. K. Srull (Eds.), *Handbook of social cognition* (pp. 323–417). Hillsdale, NJ: Erlbaum.

Clore, G. L., Storbeck, J., Robinson, M. D., & Centerbar, D. B. (2005). Seven sins in the study of unconscious affect. In L. F. Barrett, P. M. Niedenthal, & P. Winkielman (Eds.), *Emotion and consciousness* (pp. 384–408). New York: Guilford.

Clore, G. L., Wyer, R. S., Dienes, B., Gasper, K., Gohm, C., & Isbell, L. (2001). Affective feelings as feedback: Some cognitive consequences. In L. L. Martin & G. L. Clore (Eds.), *Theories of mood and cognition: A user's handbook* (pp. 27–62). Mahwah, NJ: Erlbaum.

Coan, J. A. (2010). Emergent ghosts of the emotion machine. *Emotion Review, 2*, 274–285.

Cohen, A. B. (2009). Many forms of culture. *American Psychologist, 64*, 194–204.

Corr, P. J. (2008). *The reinforcement sensitivity theory of personality*. New York: Cambridge University Press.

Cunningham, W. A., & Zelazo, P. D. (2007). Attitudes and evaluations: A social cognitive neuroscience perspective. *Trends in Cognitive Sciences, 11*, 97–104.

Cunningham, W. A., Johnson, M. K., Raye, C. L., Gatenby, J. C., Gore, J. C., & Banaji, M. R. (2010). Separable neural components in the processing of black and white faces. *Psychological Science, 15*, 806–813.

Damasio, A. (1994). *Descartes' error: Emotion, reason, and the human brain*. New York: Avon Books.

Darwin, C. (1998/1872). *The expression of the emotions in man and animals* (3rd ed.). New York: Oxford University Press.

Davidson, R. J. (1999). Neuropsychological perspectives on affective styles and their cognitive consequences. In T. Dalgleish & M. J. Power (Eds.), *Handbook of cognition and emotion* (pp. 103–123). New York: Wiley.

Davidson, R. J., Putnam, K. M., & Larson, C. L. (2000). Dysfunction in the neural circuitry of emotion regulation—a possible prelude to violence. *Science, 289*, 591–594.

Deffenbacher, J. L. (1992). Trait anger: Theory, findings, and implications. In C. D. Spielberger & J. N. Butcher (Eds.), *Advances in personality assessment* (Vol. 9, pp. 177–201). Hillsdale, NJ: Erlbaum.

Dehaene, S. (2001). *The cognitive neuroscience of consciousness*. London: MIT Press.

Depue, R. A., & Collins, P. F. (1999). Neurobiology of the structure of personality: Dopamine, facilitation of incentive motivation, and extraversion. *Behavioral and Brain Sciences, 22*, 491–569.

Derryberry, D., & Tucker, D. M. (1994). Motivating the focus of attention. In P. M. Niedenthal & S. Kitayama (Eds.), *The heart's eye: Emotional influences in perception and attention* (pp. 167–196). San Diego, CA: Academic.

DeRubeis, R. J., Siegle, G. J., & Hollon, S. D. (2008). Cognitive therapy versus medication for depressions: Treatment outcomes and neural mechanisms. *Nature Reviews Neuroscience, 9*, 788–796.

Descartes, R. (2009). Selections from meditations on first philosophy. In J. P. Lizza (Ed.), *Defining the beginning and ending of life: Readings on personal identity and bioethics* (pp. 30–41). Baltimore: Johns Hopkins University Press.

Devine, P. G. (1989). Stereotypes and prejudice: Their automatic and controlled components. *Journal of Personality and Social Psychology, 56*, 5–18.

Diener, E., Suh, E. M., Lucas, R. E., & Smith, H. E. (1999). Subjective well-being: Three decades of progress. *Psychological Bulletin, 125*, 276–302.

Dijkerhuis, A., & Aarts, H. (2010). Goals, attention, and (un)consciousness. *Annual Review of Psychology, 61*, 467–490.

Drevets, W. C., & Raichle, M. E. (1998). Reciprocal suppression of regional blood flow during emotional versus higher cognitive processes: Implications for interactions between emotion and cognition. *Cognition and Emotion, 12*, 353–385.

Duncan, S., & Barrett, L. F. (2007). Affect is a form of cognition: A neurobiological analysis. *Cognition and Emotion, 21*, 1184–1211.

Dunning, D. (1999). A newer look: Motivated social cognition and the schematic representation of social concepts. *Psychological Inquiry, 10*, 1–11.

Ellsworth, P. C. (1994). William James and emotion: Is a century of fame worth a century of misunderstanding? *Psychological Review, 101,* 222–229.

Ekman, P. (1993). Facial expression and emotion. *American Psychologist 48,* 384–392.

Endler, N. S. (2002). Multidimensional interactionism: Stress, anxiety, and coping. In L. Bäckman & C. von Hofsten (Eds.), *Psychology at the turn of the millennium: Vol. 1. Cognitive, biological, and health perspectives* (pp. 281–305). Hove, England: Psychology Press.

Eriksen, C. W. (1960). Discrimination and learning without awareness: A methodological survey and evaluation. *Psychological Review, 67,* 279–300.

Eysenck, M. W., Derakshan, N., Santos, R., & Calvo, M. G. (2007). Anxiety and cognitive performance: Attentional control theory. *Emotion, 7,* 336–353.

Fiedler, K. (2001). Affective states trigger processes of assimilation and accommodation. In L. L. Martin & G. L. Clore (Eds.), *Theories of mood and cognition: A user's guidebook* (pp. 85–98). Mahwah, NJ: Erlbaum.

Fishbach, A., & Trope, Y. (2008). Implicit and explicit counteractive self-control. In J. Y. Shah & W. L. Gardner (Eds.), *Handbook of motivational science* (pp. 281–294). New York: Guilford.

Forgas, J. P. (2001). The affect infusion model (AIM): An integrative theory of mood effects on cognition and judgments. In L. L. Martin & G. L. Clore (Eds.), *Theories of mood and cognition: A user's guidebook* (pp. 99–134). Mahwah, NJ: Erlbaum.

Forgas, J. P. (2002). Feeling and doing: Affective influences on interpersonal behavior. *Psychological Inquiry, 13,* 1–28.

Frank, R. H. (1988). *Passions within reason: The strategic role of the emotions.* New York: Norton.

Fredrickson, B. L. (1998). What good are positive emotions? *Review of General Psychology, 2,* 300–319.

Fridlund, A. (1994). *Human facial expression: An evolutionary view.* San Diego, CA: Academic.

Frijda, N. H. (1986). *The emotions.* New York: Cambridge University Press.

Funder, D. C. (1995). On the accuracy of personality judgment: A realistic approach. *Psychological Review, 102,* 652–670.

Gailliot, M. T., Baumeister, R. F., DeWall, N., Maner, J. K., Plant, E. A., Tice, D. M., et al. (2007). Self-control relies on glucose as a limited energy source: Willpower is more than a metaphor. *Journal of Personality and Social Psychology, 92,* 325–336.

Galobgardes, B., Shaw, M., Lawlor, D. A., Smith, G. D., & Lynch, J. (2006). Indicators of socioeconomic position. In J. M. Oakes & J. S. Kaufman (Eds.), *Methods in social epidemiology* (pp. 47–85). San Francisco, CA: Jossey-Bass.

Gasper, K. (2004). Do you see what I see? Affect and visual information processing. *Cognition and Emotion, 18,* 405–421.

Gasper, K., & Clore, G. L. (1998). The persistent use of negative affect by anxious individuals to estimate risk. *Journal of Personality and Social Psychology, 74,* 1350–1363.

Gasper, K., & Clore, G. L. (2002). Attending to the big picture: Mood and global vs. local processing of visual information. *Psychological Science, 13,* 34–40.

Gibson, J. J. (2009). The perception of the visual world (1950). In B. F. Gentile & B. O. Miller (Eds.), *Foundations of psychological thought: A history of psychology* (pp. 161–179). Thousand Oaks, CA: Sage.

Gilbert, D. T., Pinel, E. C., Wilson, T. D., Blumberg, S. J., & Wheatley, T. P. (1998). Immune neglect: A source of durability bias in affective forecasting. *Journal of Personality and Social Psychology, 75,* 617–638.

Gilovich, T., & Medvec, V. H. (1995). The experience of regret: What, when, and why. *Psychological Review, 102,* 379–395.

Goldstein, M. D., & Strube, M. J. (1994). Independence revisited: The relation between positive and negative affect in a naturalistic setting. *Personality and Social Psychology Bulletin, 20,* 57–64.

Gray, J. A. (1990). Brain systems that mediate both emotion and cognition. *Cognition and Emotion, 4,* 269–288.

Gross, J. J. (1998). The emerging field of emotion regulation: An integrative review. *Review of General Psychology, 2,* 271–299.

Gross, J. J., Sutton, S. K., & Ketellar, T. (1998). Relations between affect and personality: Support for the affect-level and affective reactivity views. *Personality and Social Psychology Bulletin, 24,* 279–288.

Headey, B., & Wearing, A. (1989). Personality, life events, and subjective well-being: Toward a dynamic equilibrium model. *Journal of Personality and Social Psychology, 57,* 731–739.

Herrnstein, R. J. (1990). Rational choice theory: Necessary but not sufficient. *American Psychologist, 45,* 356–367.

Hofmann, W., Gawronski, B., Gschwendner, T., Le, H., & Schmitt, M. (2005). A meta-analysis on the correlation between the Implicit Association Test and explicit self-report measures. *Personality and Social Psychology Bulletin, 31,* 1369–1385.

Hoyt, W. T., Fincham, F. D., McCullough, M. E., Maio, G., & Davila, J. (2005). Responses to interpersonal transgressions in families: Forgiveness, forgivability, and relationship-specific events. *Journal of Personality and Social Psychology, 89,* 375–394.

Huntsinger, J. R., Clore, G. L. & Bar-Anan, Y. (2011). Mood and global-local focus: Priming a local focus reverses the link between mood and global-local processing. *Emotion, 10,* 722–726.

Huntsinger, J. R., Sinclair, S., Dunn, E., & Clore, G. L. (2011). Affective regulation of stereotype activation: It's the (accessible) thought that counts. *Personality and Social Psychology Bulletin, 36,* 564–577.

Isbell, L. (2004). Not all happy people are lazy or stupid: Evidence of systematic processing in happy moods. *Journal of Experimental Social Psychology, 40,* 341–349.

James, W. (1884). What is an emotion? *Mind, 9,* 188–205.

John, O. P., & Srivastava, S. (1999). The Big Five trait taxonomy: History, measurement, and theoretical perspectives. In L. A. Pervin & O. P. John (Eds.), *Handbook of personality: Theory and Research* (2nd ed., pp. 102–138). New York: Guilford.

Kihlstrom, J. F. (1987). The cognitive unconscious. *Science, 237,* 1445–1452.

Klinger, E. (1977). *Meaning and void: Inner experience and the incentives in people's lives.* Oxford, UK: University of Minnesota Press.

Klinger, E. (1999). Thought flow: Properties and mechanisms underlying shifts in content. In J. A. Singer & P. Salovey (Eds.), *At play in the fields of consciousness: Essays in honor of Jerome L. Singer* (pp. 29–50). Mahwah, NJ: Erlbaum.

Koo, M., Clore, G. L., Kim, J., & Choi, I. (in press). Affective facilitation and inhibition of cultural influences on reasoning. *Cognition and Emotion.*

Krebs, J. R., Davies, N. B., & Parr, J. (1993). *An introduction to behavioural ecology* (3rd ed.). Cambridge, MA: Blackwell.

Kuhl, J. (1994). Motivation and volition. In G. d'Ydevalle, P. Bertelson, & P. Eelen (Eds.), *Current advances in psychological science: An international perspective* (pp. 311–340). Hillsdale, NJ: Erlbaum.

Kunda, Z., & Sinclair, L. (1999). Motivated reasoning with stereotypes: Activation, application, and inhibition. *Psychological Inquiry, 10,* 12–22.

Lang, P. J. (1994). The varieties of emotional experience: A meditation on James-Lange theory. *Psychological Review, 101,* 211–221.

Lang, P. J. (1995). The emotion probe: Studies of motivation and attention. *American Psychologist, 50,* 372–385.

Lang, P. J., Bradley, M. M., & Cuthbert, B. N. (1997). Motivated attention: Affect, activation, and action. In P. J. Lang, R. F. Simons, & M. T. Balaban (Eds.), *Attention and orienting: Sensory and motivational processes* (pp. 97–135). Mahwah, NJ: Erlbaum.

Larsen, R. J., & Ketelaar, T. (1991). Personality and susceptibility to positive and negative emotional states. *Journal of Personality and Social Psychology, 61,* 132–140.

Lazarus, R. S. (1991). *Emotion and adaptation.* New York: Oxford University Press.

Lazarus, R. S., & Alfert, E. (1964). Short-circuiting of threat by experimentally altering cognitive appraisal. *Journal of Abnormal and Social Psychology, 69,* 195–205.

LeDoux, J. (1996). *The emotional brain: The mysterious underpinnings of emotional life.* New York: Simon & Schuster.

LeDoux, J. (2002). *Synaptic self: How our brains become who we are.* New York: Viking.

Lindquist, K.A., Wager, T.D., Kober, H., Bliss-Moreau, E., & Barrett, L.F. (in press). The brain basis of emotion. A meta-analytic review. *Behavioral and Brain Sciences, 35.*

Loewenstein, G. F., Weber, E. U., Hsee, C. K., & Welch, N. (2001). Risk as feelings. *Psychological Bulletin, 127,* 267–286.

Lucas, R. E., & Fujita, F. (2000). Factors influencing the relation between extraversion and pleasant affect. *Journal of Personality and Social Psychology, 79,* 1039–1056.

Luu, P., Tucker, D. M., & Derryberry, D. (1998). Anxiety and the motivational basis of working memory. *Cognitive Therapy and Research, 22,* 577–594.

Lyubomirsky, S., & Nolen-Hoeksema, S. (1993). Self-perpetuating properties of dysphoric rumination. *Journal of Personality and Social Psychology, 65,* 339–349.

Maclean, P. D. (1952). Some psychiatric implications of physiological studies on frontotemporal portion of limbic system (visceral brain). *Electroencephalography and Clinical Neurophysiology 4,* 407–418.

Mallinger, A. (2009). The myth of perfectionism: Perfectionism in the obsessive personality. *American Journal of Psychotherapy, 63,* 103–131.

Mandler, G. (2003). Emotion. In D. K. Freedheim (Ed.), *Handbook of psychology: History of psychology* (Vol. 1, pp. 157–175). Hoboken, NJ: Wiley.

Martin, L. L., Ward, D. W., Achee, J. W., & Wyer, R. S. (1993). Mood as input: People have to interpret the motivational implications of their moods. *Journal of Personality and Social Psychology, 64,* 317–326.

Mathews, A., & MacLeod, C. (2005). Cognitive vulnerability to emotional disorders. *Annual Review of Clinical Psychology, 1,* 167–195.

Matthews, G. (2008). Reinforcement sensitivity theory: A critique from cognitive science. In P. J. Corr (Ed.), *The reinforcement sensitivity theory of personality* (pp. 482–507). New York: Cambridge University Press.

Matthews, G., & Gilliland, K. (1999). The personality theories of H. J. Eysenck and J. A. Gray: A comparative review. *Personality and Individual Differences, 26,* 583–626.

Mauss, I. B., & Robinson, M. D. (2009). Measures of emotion: A review. *Cognition and Emotion, 23,* 209–237.

McClure, S. M., Botvinick, M. M., Yeung, N., Greene, J. D., & Cohen, J. D. (2007). Conflict monitoring in cognition-emotion competition. In J. J. Gross (Ed.), *Handbook of emotion regulation* (pp. 204–226). New York: Guilford.

McCrae, R. R., & Costa, P. T. (1991). Adding Leibe and Arbeit: The full five-factor model and well-being. *Personality and Social Psychology Bulletin, 17,* 227–232.

McCrae, R. R., & Costa, P. T. (1994). The stability of personality: Observation and evaluations. *Current Directions in Psychological Science, 3,* 173–175.

McEwen, B. (2002). *The end of stress as we know it.* Washington, DC: Joseph Henry Press/Dana Press.

Meier, B. P., & Robinson, M. D. (2004). Does quick to blame mean quick to anger? The role of agreeableness in dissociating blame and anger. *Personality and Social Psychology Bulletin, 30,* 856–867.

Meier, B. P., Robinson, M. D., & Wilkowski, B. M. (2006). Turning the other cheek: Agreeableness and the regulation of aggression-related primes. *Psychological Science, 17,* 136–142.

Meier, B. P., Wilkowski, B. M., & Robinson, M. D. (2008). Bringing out the agreeableness in everyone: Using a cognitive self-regulation model to reduce aggression. *Journal of Experimental Social Psychology, 44,* 1383–1387.

Meyer, G. J., & Shack, J. R. (1989). Structural convergence of mood and personality: Evidence for old and new directions. *Journal of Personality and Social Psychology, 57,* 691–706.

Mischel, W. (1968). *Personality and assessment.* New York: Wiley.

Mischel, W. (2004). Toward an integrative science of the person. *Annual Review of Psychology, 55,* 1–22.

Mischel, W. (2009). From personality and assessment (1968) to personality science (2009). *Journal of Research in Personality, 43,* 282–290.

Mischel, W., & Shoda, Y. (1995). A cognitive-affective system theory of personality: Reconceptualizing situations, dispositions, dynamics, and invariance in personality structure. *Psychological Review, 102,* 246–268.

Moeller, S. K., Robinson, M. D., & Bresin, K. (2010). Integrating trait and social-cognitive views of personality: Neuroticism, implicit stress priming, and neuroticism-outcome relationships. *Personality and Social Psychology Bulletin, 36,* 677–689.

Morris, J. S., Öhman, A., & Dolan, R. J. (1998). Conscious and unconscious emotional learning in the human amygdala. *Nature, 393,* 467–470.

Moskowitz, G. B., Gollwitzer, P. M., Wasel, W., & Schaal, B. (1999). Preconscious control of stereotype activation through chronic egalitarian goals. *Journal of Personality and Social Psychology, 77,* 167–184.

Murphy, S. T., & Zajonc, R. B. (1993). Affect, cognition, and awareness: Affective priming with optimal and suboptimal stimulus exposures. *Journal of Personality and Social Psychology, 64,* 723–739.

Navon, D. (1977). Forest before trees: The precedence of global features in visual perception. *Cognitive Psychology, 9,* 353–383.

Nisbett, R. E., Peng, K., Choi, I., & Norenzayan, A. (2001). Culture and systems of thought: Holistic versus analytic cognition. *Psychological Review, 108,* 291–310.

Initial Impressions of Others

James S. Uleman *and* S. Adil Saribay

Abstract

"Initial impressions" bring together personality and social psychology like no other field of study—"personality" because (1) impressions are about personalities, and (2) perceivers' personalities affect these impressions; and "social" because (3) social cognitive processes of impression formation, and (4) sociocultural contexts have major effects on impressions. To make these points, we first review how people explicitly describe others: the terms we use, how these descriptions reveal our theories about others, the important roles of traits and types (including stereotypes) in these descriptions, and other prominent frameworks (e.g., narratives and social roles). Then we highlight recent research on the social cognitive processes underlying these descriptions: automatic and controlled attention, the many effects of primes (semantic and affective) and their dependence on contexts, the acquisition of valence, spontaneous inferences about others, and the interplay of automatic and control processes. Third, we examine how accurate initial impressions are, and what accuracy means, as well as deception and motivated biases and distortions. Fourth, we review recent research on effects of target features, perceiver features, and relations between targets and perceivers. Finally, we look at frameworks for understanding explanations, as distinct from descriptions: attribution theory, theory of mind, and simulation theory.

Keywords: traits, stereotypes, social cognition, attention, priming, spontaneous inferences, automaticity, accuracy, deception, attribution, theory of mind, simulation

Who are you? How should we describe you? A colleague once asked me (JSU) if I knew what it was like to be a bat, referring to Nagel's (1974) famous essay on consciousness and the mind-body problem. I said that I didn't even know what it was like to be me. Where should I begin? What should I leave out, so the account takes less than a lifetime, and is responsive to his question? What about the influences and processes I'm oblivious to or have forgotten? How accurate are my impressions, and against what standards of accuracy? Is there one truth or many? These are the kinds of questions this chapter addresses (but does not answer), by noting how social and personality psychologists approach them, in theory and in research. We hope to give you an overview of the terrain in this area.

In some ways, the impressions studied by social and by personality psychologists could not be more different. The initial impressions studied by social psychologists are fleeting and dissipate in the face of extended interactions; exist only in the minds of perceivers; can be manipulated or managed; and are presumed to be flawed guides to future behavior. The initial impressions studied by personality psychologists are stable and coherent over time and place; exist apart from particular perceivers; and should provide true guides to future acts.

However, our view is that they are inseparable, two sides of the same coin. Both are social constructions (like the economy or the legal system). Both concern the nature of persons: what their characteristics are; what causes them to behave in particular ways in specific situations, as well as more generally; what they think and feel; and so on. And both arise from the same initial evidence: other people's behaviors in particular situations. Social psychologists focus on perceivers and what they make of this evidence; personality psychologists focus on targets and what produces this evidence. But perceivers have personalities too; and targets act in the actual or imagined presence of perceivers. Individual differences are part of the picture throughout. So these two emphases are not only two sides of the same coin, they are two intertwined aspects of a conceptual Gordian knot. Cutting through this knot to divide it into social and personality halves does violence to all these interrelations. So this apparent division is largely a matter of (real) professional territoriality, that is, different scientific traditions and academic audiences. Because this chapter focuses on *initial* impressions, we draw more heavily from social psychologists' work. But the complementary concerns of personality psychologists, with their long-term perspectives, make important contributions too.

How we form impressions of others has long been a fundamental question in both social and personality psychology, because our interactions depend in fundamental ways on our impressions of others. (Of course we might start with questions about impressions of social situations or relationships. But Western, and especially U.S. psychology has been individualistic for a long time, for cultural (Lehman, Chiu, & Schaller, 2004) and ideological (Ichheiser, 1949) reasons. We begin with *the terms we explicitly use to describe* other people. What are these terms, and when do we use them? How are they related to each other, and what do their relations reveal about our theories about other people?

We also form *implicit (unspoken and unconscious) impressions*, and our explicit descriptions are based on processes of which we are largely unaware. What are some of these processes? What captures our attention, unbidden? What produces positive or negative evaluations? How do we unconsciously infer inner qualities (e.g., traits) from outer observables (e.g., behaviors)? The second section of this chapter reviews some of these processes. Distinctions between explicit and implicit impressions, and automatic and controlled processes are central.

Research on *accuracy* has been oddly independent of research on processes, in part because Cronbach's (1955) devastating critique of accuracy research intimidated other researchers for decades, and Mischel's (1968) critique of personality research raised questions about whether there is anything to

be accurate about. But now there are more sophisticated approaches to these questions, and this is a lively area of research. We review conceptions of accuracy in trait judgments and sample current results. We also describe recent research on deception (lying), and some motivated biases and distortions in forming initial impressions.

The fourth section surveys some of the *features of targets, of perceivers, and of their relations with each other* that affect initial impressions. Faces and other visual information form most of the work on targets. We also note recent work on impressions in cyberspace, and reputation. Relations include power and psychological distance.

Finally we note recent work on *explanations of others' behaviors*, focusing on three frameworks: (1) attribution theory, (2) theory of mind, and (3) simulation theory and self-reference. Explanations are more than descriptions. They are more motivated and judgmental, and carry clearer implications for responsibility, credit, and blame. They depend on large and often implicit theories, such as Tetlock's (2002) politician, theologian, and prosecutor frameworks.

Lay Descriptions of Others

How do people describe one another? Park (1986) had members of her seminar at Northwestern University describe each other every week for 7 weeks. She content-analyzed the results into five categories: traits and habits; behaviors; attitudes, feelings, and beliefs; demographics; and physical and biological characteristics. Traits dominated the descriptions (65%), followed by behaviors (23%). Traits were used more and behaviors were used less as targets became better known. So traits are central in describing others.

People differ in how they describe others, even at "zero acquaintance" (Kenny & West, 2008). In their classic demonstration, Dornbush, Hastorf, Richardson, Muzzy, and Vreeland (1965) asked summer campers to describe their tent mates. On average, when one perceiver described two different targets, the categories overlapped 57%, but when two perceivers described the same target, categories overlapped only 45%. Perceivers affected category choice more than targets did. People differ in which categories are chronically accessible (come easily to mind; Higgins, 1996), and this produces different descriptions, and memories. Thus an important determinant of individual (i.e., personality) differences in describing and remembering targets is differences in the chronic accessibility of perceivers' concepts.

Looking beyond initial impressions (as we occasionally do), familiarity with the target affects category use. Idson and Mischel (2001) found that traits usually outnumbered mental states. But relatively fewer traits were used the longer perceivers had liked (but not disliked) targets, and the more situations they had seen them in. Fewer traits were used for important (vs. unimportant) targets. Familiarity also affects how targets are categorized automatically. Unfamiliar faces get categorized by salient stereotyped categories, whereas familiar faces do not (Quinn, Mason, & Macrae, 2009.) Thus descriptions of unfamiliar targets contain more traits, fewer mental states, and are less conditional on situations than familiar others.

Communicating descriptions to an audience changes the descriptions. Zajonc's (1960) classic study showed that descriptions are more "differentiated, complex, unified, and organized" (p. 166) when perceivers expect to communicate. Lassiter, Geers, and Apple (2002) found that this organization produced fewer units of behavior, fewer remembered behaviors, and less positive affect. When people know something about their audience, communications are "tuned" to the audience. Todorov (2002) showed not only that these tuned descriptions affect memory for and attitudes toward targets, but also these descriptions mediate tuning's effects. Wyer and Gruenfeld (1995) provided a thoughtful review of related literature.

Perceivers' cultures also affect descriptions. Westerners use more trait terms and fewer relational and contextually qualified terms than Asians. For example, Shweder and Bourne (1984) asked residents of Chicago and Orissa, India, to describe close acquaintances. Americans use more context-free descriptions (71.7%), including unqualified traits, than did Oriyas (50.4%), and more abstractions than Oriyas (74.6% vs. 35.2%). Self-descriptions show similar cultural differences (Rhee, Uleman, Lee, & Roman, 1995). Although this difference is often explained by individualist versus collectivist conceptions of individuals, Kashima, Kashima, Kim, and Gelfand (2006) suggest that it reflects cultural differences in linguistic practices. Westerners, more than Asians, objectify and decontextualize descriptions not only of individuals, but also of relationships and even groups (also see Adams, chapter 8, this volume).

Traits' Relations to Each Other

Implicit theories of traits' relations to each other, that is, implicit personality theories (IPT), have been studied primarily through factor analyses of trait ratings (Schneider, 1973). The same Big Five factors of personality—openness to experience, conscientiousness, extraversion, agreeableness, and neuroticism—emerge from ratings of traits' semantic similarity, co-occurrence likelihoods, and the prototypicality of acts, as well as from ratings of complete strangers, well-known others, and the self (John, 1990). A long-standing controversy concerns whether IPT reflects actual relations among traits or merely semantic relations, which distort judgments of actual relations. Borkenau (1992) found that distortion happens occasionally, but cannot fully account for IPT.

Poon and Koehler (2008) looked for individual differences in inferring traits and behaviors from other traits and behaviors, with particular attention to Dweck's (Dweck, Chiu, & Hong, 1995) entity theorists (who believe traits are fixed) and incremental theorists (who believe traits are malleable). For semantically similar (vs. unrelated) traits and behaviors, inferences were more extreme for entity than incremental theorists. Thus, moderately reliable theories (0.57 over 8 weeks) about the reliability of trait and behavioral information affect inferences among them. Poon and Koehler (2006) found that priming entity knowledge made participants more confident about trait inferences.

How universal is this Big Five structure? With some important caveats, Heine and Buchtel (2009) concluded that "there is good evidence that the Big Five reflect the universal structure of personality" (p. 378), when scales are based on translated English rating scales. But studies based on indigenous Chinese, Filipino, Spanish, or Greek traits uncovered six or seven factors, only some of which correspond to the Big Five. Saucier (2003a) reports evidence that the seven factors from studies of Filipino and Hebrew traits may be more universal than the Big Five. Heine and Buchtel (2009) describe some interesting functional evolutionary ideas about possible origins of the Big Five factor structure. (See also Fleeson, chapter 3, this volume.)

Rosenberg, Nelson, and Vivekananthan (1968) suggested that most IPTs are dominated by two correlated but distinct evaluative dimensions: social warmth and competence. Recently Judd, James-Hawkins, Yzerbyt, and Kashima (2005) have termed these "the fundamental dimensions of social judgment," and examined their relations in judging groups. Although usually related positively in judging individuals, they are negatively related in judging groups. They are sometimes called the "Big Two" dimensions, in homage to the Big Five.

How well do the Big Five describe individual targets? All the analyses above are based on data aggregated over many targets, but individual targets show idiosyncratic trait structures, and individual perceivers organize traits in idiosyncratic ways. Exploratory factor analyses of ratings of single targets, rated repeatedly over many days, do not yield the familiar Big Five for most targets. Nesselroade and Molenaar (1999) report that fewer than a third of their targets showed the Big Five pattern, and Borkenau and Ostendorf (1998) put this figure at 10%. Thus multiple ratings of single individuals over time rarely yield the Big Five.

Finally, most traits are hierarchically organized, for example, being charitable is a way of being generous, which is a way of being kind, which is a way of being good. Targets' familiarity and likability affect the preferred level of description, and there is a basic (default) level for most hierarchies (John, Hampson, & Goldberg, 1991). Each factor has several hierarchical subcomponents; for example, extraversion includes sociability, lack of restraint, assertiveness, and adventurousness.

Conceptions of Traits

Traits terms are used in many ways (Uleman, 2005). Most personality researchers (e.g., McCrae & Costa, 2003) think of traits as relatively stable internal causes of behavior, with predictive utility across many situations. On the other hand, Wright and Mischel (1987) showed that traits' meanings are implicitly (and sometimes explicitly; Wright & Mischel, 1988) conditional on the situation in which they are used. Thus two youthful targets may be described as *aggressive* even though one aggresses only toward peers and the other only toward adult authorities. More generally, most of us seem to have theories about the kinds of personality differences that are revealed in different situations. Higgins and Scholer (2008) note that behaviors in "high-demand [stressful] situations" best reveal coping abilities, whereas behaviors in "low-demand situations" best reveal preferences, values, and tastes. All these approaches treat traits as causal rather than merely descriptive (of people and/or behaviors). Kressel and Uleman (2010) showed that isolated trait terms have the properties of causes (of behavior), even when lacking explanatory and descriptive functions. This suggests that traits are theory-based concepts (Murphy & Medin, 1985) with inherently causal meanings, even though they are also the most abstract level at which behaviors are described (Semin & Fiedler, 1991). They can both describe and explain behavior.

Traits are part of the "(folk) theory of mind" (section "Explanations," below), a set of concepts that people use to understand others (and themselves). Malle (2004) presents the most articulated version available for American adults, developed to account for their explanations of behaviors. Malle's fundamental distinction is between *intentional* behaviors (i.e., *actions*, which have *reasons*) and *unintentional* behaviors (which have *causes*). Causes of unintended behaviors ("She failed organic chemistry.") can be in the situation or the person, and include traits (e.g., *stupid*). Actions have three kinds of explanations: (1) *enabling factors*, which include traits such as abilities; (2) *reasons*, based on targets' *values*, *beliefs*, and *desires*; and (3) *causal histories of reasons*, that is, the background or origin of the targets' reasons (including traits, e.g., *ambitious*) without the reasons themselves. Thus traits play several different roles and have different meanings in folk theories of mind.

Understanding others also involves narratives (e.g., Schank & Abelson, 1995). Read (1987) argued that explaining an extended sequence of behavior—and (we would add) even describing it—requires a scenario, including targets' plans and goals. He conceives of most traits as goal-based categories. Read, Jones, and Miller (1990) showed that ratings of how effective behaviors are at attaining trait-related goals predicts ratings of behaviors' typicality (in the graded structure of trait categories) as well as confidence in making trait inferences from behaviors. (See also Read & Miller, 2005.)

Working with a prototype conception of personality trait and state categories, Chaplin, John, and Goldberg (1988) found that trait and state category "prototypes are not defined by averages . . . but by ideal (or extreme) attribute values. Like other ideal-based categories, traits and states serve particular goals. Trait concepts permit people to predict the present from the past; state concepts identify those behaviors that can be controlled by manipulating the situation" (p. 541).

Dweck and her colleagues have produced the most extensive research on individual differences in person concepts, with their entity and incremental theorists (e.g., Levy, Plaks, & Dweck, 1999). Different judgments and explanations of individual, as well as group characteristics (Levy, Plaks, Hong, Chiu, & Dweck, 2001), follow from these two orientations. Entity theorists emphasize traits, trait-consistent information, and evaluations in their descriptions. Hong, Chiu, Dweck, and Sacks (1997) found that entity theorists make more implicit evaluative inferences (assessed via evaluative priming). McConnell (2001) showed that incremental theorists make memory-based judgments and entity theorists make on-line judgments. Plaks, Stroessner, Dweck, and Sherman (2001) showed that entity theorists attended more to stereotype-consistent information, whereas incremental theorists attended more to stereotype-inconsistent information. Plaks, Grant, and Dweck (2005) showed that attention is also differentially affected by how consistent new information is with perceivers' theories of change.

Church et al. (2003) examined lay theories of behavior in two cultures, with their questionnaire about beliefs about traits and situations. The five trait beliefs concern traits' stability, cross-situational consistency, predictive validity, ease of inference from a few behaviors, and accuracy for describing and understanding others. The five situational beliefs are roughly parallel. These two belief sets formed two factors that are essentially orthogonal. Dweck's measures are only moderately related to them. Thus, beliefs about the trait- and context-driven nature of human behavior (Church et al. 2003), as well as dispositionist, situationist, and interactionist thinking (Baumann & Skitka 2006; Norenzayan, Choi, & Nisbett, 2002) are not mutually exclusive, and vary by individual as well as culture.

Types

Traits are not the only terms we use to describe others. One of the most important alternatives is types, including stereotypes. Andersen and Klatzky (1987) showed that social types (e.g., *clown, bully*) are more distinctive, and visually and associatively richer than related traits. People can also answer behavioral questions about others more quickly when they are described in terms of types rather than traits, suggesting more efficient information processing (Andersen, Klatzky, & John, 1990). Saucier (2003b) reported 2- and 8-factor structures of 372 common English types. The two factors were contemptibleness (including *moron, rat, monster*), implying social rejection and derogation; and admirableness (*hero, star*). The 8-factor solution included some factors that resemble the Big Five, but more that suggest types have unique functions and are often highly evaluative. Ethnophaulisms (racial and ethnic slurs) constitute one class of evaluative types that has received particular attention from Mullen (e.g., Leader, Mullen, & Rice, 2009).

As some ethnophaulisms suggest, we may see others as not fully human. Haslam and colleagues distinguish uniquely human attributes from human nature. The former "implicate culture, social learning, and higher cognition, whereas human nature implicates what is natural, innate, and affective" (Haslam, Loughnan, Kashima, & Bain, 2008, p. 58). Human nature is universal, essential, and the concept emerges early in individual development, whereas uniquely human qualities are infrequent and emerge in maturity (e.g., Haslam, Bain, Douge, Lee, & Bastian, 2005). The denial of uniquely human qualities is the basis for *animalistic dehumanization*, wherein people (especially outgroups) are likened to animals. The denial of human nature is the basis for *mechanistic dehumanization*, wherein people are likened to machines (Haslam et al., 2008). These are empirically distinct across a number of cultures (e.g., Australia, China, and Italy; Haslam, Kashima, Loughnan, Shi, & Suitner, 2008).

Leyens and colleagues (Leyens et al., 2000) studied variations in descriptions of the emotions of essentialized social group members. They differentiate primary emotions (simpler, physiological, externally caused) from secondary emotions or *sentiments* (*French*; complex, cognitively oriented, and internally caused). The latter are more "uniquely human" versus animal (Demoulin et al., 2004). Ingroups are accorded more *sentiments* than are outgroups; and there is a reluctance to attribute *sentiments* to outgroups (Cortes, Demoulin, Rodriguez-Torres, Rodriguez-Perez, & Leyens, 2005).

Essentialism—the belief that types are based on intrinsic, inherited qualities—plays an important role in stereotyping others, especially when the stereotypes have a plausible biological basis such as with gender, race, and sexual orientation (see Yzerbyt, Judd, & Corneille, 2004). Carnaghi et al. (2008) found that the use of nouns rather than adjectives to describe others is associated with more essentialistic beliefs about them. Gelman (2003) argued that preschoolers naturally employ essentialistic concepts in developing their folk psychologies.

Stereotypes

Stereotyping is a huge topic, so we touch on only a few highlights. Schneider notes that at a minimum, "stereotypes are qualities perceived to be associated with particular groups or categories of people" (2004, p. 24). Some but not all theorists hold that stereotypes are also negative, inaccurate, and/or consensual. In practice, the categories most often studied as "stereotypes" have been those most socially, politically, and legally fraught, for example, race, ethnicity, gender, and age. *Prejudice* is the affective or attitudinal/evaluative component of stereotypes, and *discrimination* is the behavioral consequence. So all the theoretical and empirical complexities associated with attitudes and their relations to behavior apply to prejudice, including the distinction between implicit and explicit processes and measures. In addition, much of the research on social identity, self-categorization, and intergroup perceptions involves stereotypes.

Notwithstanding race, gender, and so forth, many social features can be used to categorize others. Weeks and Vincent (2007) showed that people spontaneously use religion, even when another salient category (race) is available. Lieberman, Oum, and Kurzban (2008) showed that kinship is as important a category as sex or age. Kinzler, Shutts, DeJesus, and Spelke (2009) showed that when 5-year-old children were asked to "choose friends" from among novel others, who did or did not share their own language or race, same-language trumped same-race. Paladino and Castelli (2008) showed that simply categorizing others as ingroup versus outgroup members (based on ethnicity, nationality, age, political views, or even a minimal group paradigm) has immediate motoric approach-avoidance consequences. The last three papers present evolutionary arguments.

The stereotype content model (SCM; Fiske, Cuddy, Glick, & Xu, 2002), and its successor, the BIAS map (Behaviors from Intergroup Affect and Stereotypes; Cuddy, Fiske, & Glick, 2007), describe relations among social structure, stereotype contents, and the emotions and behaviors associated with them. Perceptions of group members vary along two dimensions: competence (confident, independent, competitive, intelligent), which is predicted by their social status; and warmth (tolerant, warm, good-natured, sincere), predicted by their low social competitiveness with perceivers. In the resulting two-dimensional space, groups with negative stereotypes (low competence and low warmth, e.g., the poor, and homeless) cluster together, and are opposite groups with positive stereotypes (high competence and high warmth, e.g., professionals, ingroup members). The model naturally accommodates ambivalent stereotypes: low competence and high warmth (e.g., the elderly), and high competence but low warmth (e.g., the wealthy). Each quadrant or cluster elicits characteristic emotions: contempt and resentment (low-low), pride and admiration (high-high), pity and sympathy (low-high), and envy and jealousy (high-low) respectively.

The BIAS map includes behaviors by distinguishing active from passive, and harm from facilitation. Active facilitation includes helping, and active harm includes attacking. Passive facilitation ("acting with") includes associating with or using, and passive harm ("acting without") includes excluding. Using a combination of surveys and experiments, Cuddy et al. (2007) showed that the effects of stereotypes on behaviors are mediated by particular emotions. Furthermore, a meta-analysis by Talaska, Fiske, and Chaiken (2008) showed that emotional reactions to social groups predict discriminatory behavior twice as well as stereotypes do.

This framework has generated two other interesting findings. First, when perceivers think about their emotional responses to groups, those in the low competence, low warmth (contempt) quadrant do not activate brain regions that are typically activated by observing people (the medial prefrontal cortex). This suggests perceivers dehumanize such group members (Harris & Fiske, 2006). However, when perceivers have a more individuating goal (judging targets' food preferences), this effect disappears (Harris & Fiske, 2007).

Second, these two dimensions of warmth and competence (the Big Two) have a compensatory relationship in comparative judgments of groups. Yzerbyt, Provost, and Corneille (2005) found that when a group was higher on one dimension, it was seen as lower on the other. Kervyn, Yzerbyt, Judd, and Nunes (2009) showed how this compensatory relationship plays out through confirmatory biases in impression formation. They define the compensation effect as "the tendency to differentiate two social targets in a comparative context on the two fundamental dimensions by contrasting them in a compensatory direction" (p. 829). This compensatory relationship is unique to these two dimensions, and contrary to the well-known halo effect (Yzerbyt, Kervyn, & Judd, 2008).

Given that many stereotypes are ambivalent, why do evaluations of stereotyped group members seem so univalent? Quinn, Hugenberg, and Bodenhausen (2004) showed that, consistent with research on retrieval-induced forgetting, cued-recall rehearsal of some targets' traits (e.g., Susan—independent) inhibits free recall of nonrehearsed traits (e.g., liberal, opinionated), regardless of their valence. However, activating an applicable stereotype (e.g., feminist) changes this effect, facilitating free recall of nonrehearsed traits that are evaluatively consistent with rehearsed traits, and inhibiting recall of evaluatively inconsistent traits. This effect may underlie "the momentary experience of evaluative consistency in person perception" (p. 519). Gawronski, Peters, Brochu, and Strack (2008) presented a general theory and supportive evidence on how and when cognitive consistency operates to reconcile conflicting evaluations and beliefs in prejudiced behavior.

People belong to many social groups. For example, Weeks and Lupfer (2004) found that "lower-class Black targets were primarily categorized by race, whereas middle-class Black targets were primarily categorized by social class," spontaneously (p. 972). Multiple categories facilitate subtyping, in which targets who disconfirm a stereotype are put into a subcategory that preserves the stereotype itself, or subgrouping, in which stereotypes are differentiated (Richards & Hewstone, 2001). More generally, goals and situational factors can determine which categories or subcategories are activated, often automatically (e.g., Gilbert & Hixon, 1991). Crisp and Hewstone (2007) reviewed research on multiple social categorization, and its implications for reducing and preserving stereotyping.

Finally, important individual differences in stereotyping and prejudice are tapped by both explicit and implicit prejudice measures; see the section on unconscious processes, below. Sibley and Duckitt (2008) performed a meta-analysis of 71 studies looking at relations between the Big Five, prejudice, right wing authoritarianism (RWA), and social dominance orientation (SDO). SDO and RWA mediated most effects, consistent with "a dual-process motivational model of ideology and prejudice" (p. 248).

Other Frameworks for Describing Others

People are often described through stories or narratives. Being complex, such impressions almost always combine descriptions, judgments, and explanations. Narratives can arise to simply convey information, to form impressions (Wyer, Adaval, & Colcombe, 2002), or to judge guilt (e.g., Pennington & Hastie, 1992).

Park has long contended (1986) that people form complex multidimensional *person models* of others, organized around central concepts and used to generate attributions, explanations, and predictions through simulation. In a methodological tour de force, Park, DeKay, and Kraus (1994) presented participants with brief self-descriptions of how several targets behaved in five different settings: work, home, social, chore, and leisure (Study 1). Kenny's (1994) social relations model (which decomposes

ratings into components due to targets, to perceivers or judges, and to their statistical interaction) showed that perceivers organized the behavioral information with some consistency across situations, producing a large target effect. A large judge x target effect showed that different perceivers (judges) developed different person models, even though all perceivers had the same information. Perceivers also wrote brief descriptions of the targets, and there seemed to be only a few different central concepts for each target, based more on how behaviors were combined (i.e., the person models) than on how each behavior was interpreted.

In Study 2, participants read the five self-descriptive statements for each of four targets from Study 1, and then wrote free descriptions and five descriptive traits for each. Then they rated each target on many traits, completed a recognition memory test for the original statements, and chose which of three possible person models (adapted from Study 1) best captured their impressions. Even though participants all read the same descriptions, they developed different models (as seen in their free descriptions and model choices), and these predicted differences in trait ratings and recognition memory, including false recognition of conceptually related foils. There was no relation between model choices and perceivers' self-descriptions. The authors suggest that person models are spontaneously constructed during impression formation, and are flexible combinations of traits, narratives, and other elements organized around central concepts. Many of these effects were replicated and extended by Mohr and Kenny (2006), who also saw them as explaining the robust finding that there is typically low consensus among perceivers of the same targets.

A completely different approach can be found in Carlston's (1994) associated systems theory. It describes relations among four systems: sensory (esp. visual appearance), verbal (esp. traits), affective (esp. responses to others), and action (esp. behavioral responses). While the theory has not received extensive testing (cf. Claypool & Carlston, 2002), it organizes several literatures and underscores the complexity of our representations of others.

Finally, social roles describe others, including role stereotypes. Social roles are also common in self-descriptions. For example, Rhee et al. (1995) coded self-descriptions from 353 American and Korean college students, using "probably the most elaborate and sophisticated coding scheme to date" (Kashima et al., 2006, p. 390). Traits were the most common description (30%), but 22% were social identities. Most of these were social roles. Social roles can be classified into ascribed versus attained, voluntary versus involuntary, and hierarchical categories. Such distinctions play little part in impression formation research, even though many languages (e.g., Japanese) make elaborate role distinctions in forms of address. Rather, research often treats roles as situational or contextual explanations for behavior, contrasting them with dispositional explanations, perhaps because Westerners think of people as "occupying" or "playing" roles, whereas they "have" dispositions.

One exception to the neglect of roles is Alan Fiske's (1992) proposal that there are four basic types of social relationships: (1) communal sharing, as among close kin; (2) authority ranking, among superiors and subordinates; (3) equality matching, or egalitarian relationships; and (4) market pricing, based on equitable exchanges. Fiske, Haslam, and Fiske (1991) predicted that when one makes errors that substitute one person for another—by misnaming them, misremembering who did what to whom, or acting toward one person as though they were another—these confusions are more likely between others with whom one has the same kind of basic relationship. Across seven studies, they found that these relationship types "and gender predict the pattern of errors as well as or better than the age or race of the people confused" (p. 673). This suggests that people implicitly categorize others in terms of these four types of relationships, and that even when these types do not appear in descriptions, they affect memories of and actions toward others.

Processes of Impression Formation

Where do our descriptions of others come from? As noted above, they are shaped and constrained by our concepts, theories, and culture. And as elaborated below ("Features of Targets, Perceivers, and Relations"), they depend on the stimuli that others emit: appearance, behavior, and so forth. But how can we understand the pathways from receiving stimuli to producing descriptions or explanations of others? This is the purview of "social cognition," which investigates the cognitive and motivational processes that construct our phenomenological social world. Our treatment here must be brief, but see Carlston (forthcoming) and Uleman, Saribay, and Gonzalez (2008) for more detail.

Dual-process theories dominate this area, and many dichotomies feature the distinction between *automatic* and *controlled* cognitive processes.

Thoroughly automatic processes take place outside of awareness, without intentions, without conscious control, and quickly and efficiently (free from interference by concurrent cognitive operations). Controlled processes have the opposite features (Bargh, 1994). But these features do not always co-occur, so it is important to specify how a process is or is not automatic (Moors & De Houwer, 2007).

Closely related to this (oversimplified) dichotomy is the one between implicit and explicit measures. In promoting this distinction, Greenwald and Banaji (1995, p. 4) focused on awareness. "The signature of implicit cognition is that traces of past experience affect some performance [e.g., a measure], even though the influential earlier experience is not remembered in the usual sense—that is, it is unavailable to self-report or introspection." But implicit measures are often treated as though they are thoroughly automatic. So De Houwer, Teige-Mocigemba, Spruyt, and Moors (2009) redefined implicit measures as "outcomes of measurement procedures that are caused in an automatic manner" (p. 347), even though Nosek and Greenwald (2009) demur. De Houwer et al. (2009) provide a useful conceptual analysis of how automaticity's features apply to two prominent implicit measures (the Implicit Association Test, or IAT, and affective priming).

A study that illustrates many of these concepts (Rydell, McConnell, Mackie, & Strain, 2006) independently manipulated and measured explicit and implicit attitudes toward a target person, Bob. In the first block of 100 trials, participants formed an impression by reading brief descriptions of positive behaviors performed by Bob. Each behavior was preceded by a subliminal negative word. Participants' explicit evaluations of Bob at the end of this series were positive, but an IAT showed negative implicit associations with him. Then they read 100 additional behavioral descriptions of Bob, which were now negative, each preceded by a subliminal positive word. After this second block of trials, explicit attitudes had become negative but implicit associations with Bob were positive. Participants were not aware of the subliminal stimuli, their implicit attitudes, or the connection between the two. Implicit attitudes were thus formed without intentions, and were completely at odds with explicit attitudes. (This study did not examine efficiency or controllability.)

Automatic processes are important in many ways including directing attention, activating concepts (including traits and stereotypes), in evaluative conditioning and priming, in forming inferences, and in interactions with controlled processes.

Attention

Several theories, including evolution, suggest that some stimuli should automatically capture our attention. Subliminally presented threatening faces attract more attention than neutral faces, but only when presented in the left visual field (Mogg & Bradley, 1999). Concurrent tasks that reduce working memory can eliminate the ability of angry faces to capture attention (Van Dillen & Koole, 2009). In deliberate searches of multiface arrays, there is conflicting evidence for an "angry face" effect. Juth, Lundqvist, Karlsson, and Öhman (2005) found that happy (vs. angry or fearful) faces were detected faster and more accurately among neutral distracters, but socially anxious participants showed the angry face effect, suggesting important personality differences. Implicating more functional and motivational moderators, Öhman and Juth (2010, p. 59) report that the angry face effect is restricted to "male targets in the context of familiar [vs. novel] faces—a common situation for interpersonal violence." Thus these automatic effects are not invariant, and are moderated by several variables.

Goals are among the most important moderators. For example, participants with experimentally created egalitarian goals are less successful at ignoring words related to egalitarianism (Moskowitz, 2002). Maner, Gailliot, and Miller (2009) found that participants exposed to mating primes and not in a committed relationship showed automatic attention to physically attractive opposite-sex others. Maner, Gailliot, Rouby, and Miller (2007) showed automatic "attentional adhesion" to potential rivals by participants primed with mate-guarding, but only if they were insecure in their own relationships.

Attention operates at several levels, from automatic attention capture to deliberate information search. At the automatic level, negative information is more likely to capture attention (Pratto & John, 1991), although this can be moderated by affective context (Smith et al., 2006). The encoding flexibility model (Sherman, Lee, Bessenoff, & Frost, 1998) describes how attention is flexibly deployed between consistent and inconsistent information about a stereotyped target; when cognitive resources are scarce, inconsistent information attracts more attention. Unprejudiced perceivers seek stereotype-inconsistent information (Wyer, 2005). De Bruin and Van Lange (2000) found that people search first for, and are more influenced by information relevant to

morality than competence. And differentially attending to those we like, including ingroup members, unintentionally biases stimulus sampling in the social environment, with interesting consequences for impression formation (Denrell, 2005).

Other people's attention is often signaled by their gaze direction, and this in turn captures perceivers' attention, often without awareness. Indeed, gaze following is one of the foundations of competent social interaction from infancy onward (Frischen, Bayliss, & Tipper, 2007).

Priming

Brief, even subliminal exposures to stimuli can activate concepts that then influence impressions. The classic study by Higgins, Rholes, and Jones (1977) exposed participants to traits (e.g., *adventurous* or *reckless*) which influenced their impressions of a target who behaved in ways that could be interpreted either way. Besides such assimilation effects, priming can produce contrast effects. Förster, Liberman, and Kuschel's (2008) "global/local processing style model" (GLOMO) describes some of the variables that determine whether assimilation or contrast occurs. See also Bless and Schwarz (2010) for important alternative accounts of assimilation and contrast effects.

There are several types of priming (Förster, Liberman & Friedman, 2008). Repetition priming (when the same stimulus is repeated) typically increases perceptual fluency and reduces response times. Semantic priming can activate semantically related concepts (which then disambiguate stimuli, or bias subsequent judgments), goals (which direct behavior and ensure persistence by deactivating competing goals), or behaviors themselves. Procedural priming makes particular cognitive operations more likely. Affective or evaluative priming influences evaluations outside of awareness. Even cultural orientations, including individualism and collectivism, can be primed (Oyserman & Lee, 2008).

Semantic primes' effects depend on many variables (Weisbuch, Unkelbach, & Fiedler, 2008). For example, Petty, DeMarree, Briñol, Horcajo, and Strathman (2008) showed that subtle primes work best for people high in the need for cognition, whereas blatant primes work best for those who are low in the need for cognition.

Stereotypes are primed by many stimuli including simply faces (e.g., Rule, Macrae, & Ambady, 2009). Stereotyping is supported by differential attention and attribution processes (Sherman, Stroessner, Conrey, & Azam, 2005); is reinforced through nonconscious mimicry by those who agree with stereotyped statements (Castelli, Pavan, Ferrari, & Kashima, 2009); and is supported by perceivers' nonconscious positive moods (Huntsinger, Sinclair, & Clore, 2009). Goal activation and goal satisfaction influence the application of stereotypes and the mere presence of other ingroup members can prompt egalitarian goals and affect implicit attitudes (Castelli & Tomelleri, 2008). Activated stereotypes and implicit evaluations predict different behaviors (Amodio & Devine, 2006). Kunda and Spencer's (2003) widely cited framework describes which goals operate in social interactions with stereotyped group members, and how they affect both stereotype activation and application. See Schneider (2004) for more.

Affective or evaluative priming occurs when the first stimulus of a pair (e.g., *sunshine*) speeds up the evaluation of a second stimulus (e.g., *puppy*) when their valences match. This occurs with stimulus onset asynchronies as brief as 300 ms, even when perceivers are unaware of the priming stimulus (Fazio, Sanbonmatsu, Powell, & Kardes, 1986), and does not depend on explicit evaluations (Bargh, Chaiken, Raymond, & Hymes, 1996). Evaluative priming is widely used as an implicit measure of attitudes toward the first stimuli (Fazio & Olson, 2003). But it can also affect explicit evaluative judgments of the second stimulus (Ferguson, Bargh, & Nayak, 2005).

Valence Acquisition
Stimuli, including other people, acquire positive or negative valence in many ways. Some of the most interesting recent research is in the attitudes literature. Duckworth, Bargh, Garcia, and Chaiken (2002) showed that completely novel stimuli are automatically evaluated within milliseconds. The bases of these automatic evaluations are unknown, but this work suggests that many novel stimuli are inherently valenced (Zajonc, 1980).

Single events can confer valence on otherwise neutral people. Balance theory (Heider, 1958) and research show that we like the friends of our friends, as well as the enemies of our enemies (Tashakkori & Insko, 1981). Strangers may also be (dis)liked because they resemble significant others who are (dis)liked, even when that resemblance is not recognized (Andersen, Reznik, & Glassman, 2005). Such *social cognitive transference* is largely automatic. Evaluations based on explicit information (e.g., target's membership in a valenced group) can persist well after the information itself is forgotten (Castelli,

Zogmaister, Smith, & Arcuri, 2004). And perceivers' current emotions can also confer valence. DeSteno, Dasgupta, Bartlett, and Cajdric (2004) found that induced anger (vs. sadness or neutrality) created implicit negative attitudes toward minimal outgroups.

Over many trials, repeated *mere exposure* to stimuli (including other people) can make them more positively valued, through greater familiarity and processing fluency, even if that exposure is subliminal (Bornstein, 1989). Thus rapid supraliminal or subliminal exposure to outgroup members' faces increases liking for new faces from those outgroups (Zebrowitz, White, & Wieneke, 2008), and exposure to white faces can increase whites' prejudice (Smith, Dijksterhuis, & Chaiken, 2008). People's liking for average over distinctive faces seems to be based on mere exposure, even though attractiveness ratings are not (Rhodes, Halberstadt, Jeffery, & Palermo, 2005).

Explicit evaluations of others, based on the same behaviors, can be quite ideosyncratic. Schiller, Freeman, Mitchell, Uleman, and Phelps (2009) detected large individual differences during impression formation in fMRI activation of the amygdala and posterior cingulate cortex by particular behaviors, and these predicted subsequent evaluations of the actors. "Subjects regarded different segments of person-descriptive information as being relevant or irrelevant for their subsequent evaluations. The idiosyncratic basis for this . . . shapes how subjects weigh different types of information and which information is selected for additional processing" (p. 511).

Evaluative conditioning (EC), through repeated pairings with valenced objects, can impart positive or negative valence to previously neutral people. Walther, Nagengast, and Trasselli (2005) suggest that EC does not depend on awareness or on highly invariant contingencies, unlike classical or signal conditioning; resists extinction; is subject to counterconditioning; produces evaluations that spread to other stimuli that were already associated with the target; and is based on association mechanisms. So it likely plays an important role in many familiar social phenomena. See also Ferguson (2007).

Attitudinal ambivalence occurs when evaluations of others are simultaneously positive and negative. Van Harreveld, van der Pligt, and de Liver (2009) describe this conscious phenomenon and its consequences for decision-making, in their model of ambivalence-induced discomfort (MAID). A different sort of ambivalence arises when implicit (inaccessible) and explicit (accessible) attitudes differ (Rydell et al., 2006). Son Hing, Chung-Yan, Hamilton, and Zanna (2008) describe several interesting implications of such a two-dimensional (positive-negative and implicit-explicit) model for prejudice. And Rydell and McConnell (2006) provide a convincing dual "systems of reasoning" approach to how differing implicit and explicit attitudes toward the same object (e.g., person) can themselves change and also affect behavior.

Spontaneous Inferences from Behaviors

Early models of impression formation assumed that "behaviors will typically not be spontaneously encoded in terms of trait (attribute) concepts unless a specific processing objective requires it" (Wyer & Srull, 1986, p. 328). Research on "spontaneous trait inferences" (STIs), using more than a half-dozen paradigms, challenged this assumption. Reading descriptions of targets' trait-diagnostic behaviors with the intent to memorize or familiarize oneself with them produces trait inferences, with little or no effort or awareness, and these inferences affect subsequent judgments (Uleman, Newman, & Moskowitz, 1996). Implied traits are activated (lexical decision and probe recognition paradigms) and bound to representations of the target (false recognition and savings-in-relearning paradigms; Carlston & Skowronski, 2005; Todorov & Uleman, 2004). STIs are more likely in individualistic (Anglo) than collectivist (Hispanic) cultures (Zárate, Uleman, & Voils, 2001), and more likely by those high on idiocentrism (Duff & Newman, 1997) and the personal need for structure (Moskowitz, 1993). Once STIs are formed about one member of a social group that is high (but not low) in entitativity, they generalize to other group members (Crawford, Sherman, & Hamilton, 2002).

Besides traits, people spontaneously infer goals (Hassin, Aarts, & Ferguson, 2005), justice concepts (Ham & Van den Bos, 2008), counterfactual behaviors (Roese, Sanna, & Galinsky, 2005), and nonsocial causes (Hassin, Bargh, & Uleman, 2002). Both traits and situational causes may be activated simultaneously (Ham & Vonk, 2003). Target valences are inferred spontaneously, especially by extraverts, and persist for days (Bliss-Moreau, Barrett, & Wright, 2008). Moreover, some affect prompted by targets' behaviors (e.g., disgust) is spontaneously retrieved on subsequent encounters with their faces (Todorov, Gobini, Evans, & Haxby, 2007), as detected by fMRI. There are other neuroscience STI studies. Mitchell, Cloutier, Banaji, and Macrae (2006)

located a region of dorsal medial prefrontal cortex that is spontaneously activated (fMRI) by trait-diagnostic, but not by nondiagnostic behaviors. Van Overwalle, Van den Eede, Baetens, and Vandekerckhove (2009) report differential ERP evidence for spontaneous and intentional trait versus goal inferences.

Spontaneous trait transference (STT) refers to communicators becoming associated with the trait implications of behaviors they ascribe to others (Skowronski, Carlston, Mae, & Crawford, 1998). Several interesting differences between STIs and STTs implicate different cognitive processes (e.g., Carlston & Skowronski, 2005). Participants with the task of judging the veracity of trait-implying statements show no evidence of STIs, but STTs persist (Crawford, Skowronski, Stiff, & Scherer, 2007). STTs do not occur when representations (photos) of both communicator and target are present at encoding (Goren & Todorov, 2009).Gawronski and Walther (2008) present evidence for their transfer of attitudes recursively (TAR) model, in which communicators become associated with the *evaluative* (not trait) implications of behaviors ascribed to others. They provide a lucid discussion of differences (in predictions and mechanisms) among STT, balance theory, EC, and TAR, including evidence that TAR is inferential rather than associative.

Control and Automatic Processes

The old dichotomy between controlled and automatic processes is too simple. Not only do (1) the several criteria for automaticity not always co-occur, but also (2) virtually all processes of interest to social psychologists involve both control and automatic processes, and (3) there are many kinds of mental control (e.g., Wegner & Pennebaker, 1993). One fruitful approach to this complexity is provided by Jacoby's (1991) process dissociation procedure (PDP), which defines control in terms of the difference in performance on the same basic task under two conditions: one in which automatic and controlled processes work together to facilitate performance, and the other in which they oppose each other. Often the former condition involves simply performing the task as intended, and the latter condition involves eliminating or *controlling* effects of prior information on performance, by excluding it. Hence the definition of control is straightforward and natural. Control exists to the extent that performance differs between the two conditions. Once control (C) is estimated, a pair of equations provides estimates of A, automatic processes. See

Ferreira, Garcia-Marques, Sherman, and Sherman (2006) for multiple illustrations.

Most PDP research on person perception involves stereotyping, because of the strong interest in controlling its undesirable effects. For example, in Payne's (2001) weapons identification task, participants must identify a stimulus as a tool or a gun as quickly as possible, while trying to avoid the influence of preceding photos of a black or white man on each trial. On black-gun trials, automatic processes (stereotypic associations of black men with violence) and controlled processes (detecting a gun rather than a tool) both contribute to rapid accurate performance. But on black-tool trials, they oppose each other. Typical results show both C and A making significant contributions, so the interesting questions concern variables that influence their magnitude. Payne (2008) provides an excellent overview of research using this approach, including its use in conjunction with social neuroscience conceptions of control (Amodio, Devine, & Harmon-Jones, 2008).

More complex multinomial models of control and automatic processes' joint operation are possible. A particularly well developed one, the quad model (Sherman et al., 2008) includes two parameters that usually represent automatic processes (AC, activation; and G, guessing) and two for control processes (D, detection; and OB, overcoming bias). AC is the probability that a particular construct, evaluation, or behavioral impulse is activated by the stimulus, as in priming. D is the probability of detecting the correct response, strategically. OB is the probability that a correction occurred, given that AC could produce a response different from what D suggested. And G is the probability of guessing a correct response, given that neither AC nor D suggested a response. The model has shown adequate fit to data from semantic and evaluative priming tasks, weapons identification, the IAT, and the Go/No-Go Associations Test (GNAT). Sherman et al. (2008) describe several cases in which reanalyses with the quad model modify previous conclusions. For example, context effects on "automatic associations" may result from changes in control processes as well. Training to reduce biased stereotypic associations can both decrease AC and increase D. Implicit biases that increase with alcohol consumption were shown to result simply from decreases in OB. And individual differences in controlling race bias (Amodio et al., 2008) were traced to differences in AC and D, but not OB.

Virtually all applications of the quad model to date have used reaction times, but it is not restricted to these. Burke and Uleman (2006) described a study of the effects of spontaneous trait inferences on subsequent trait ratings of targets. They showed heightened AC of implied traits to targets; minimal G; and significant individual differences—for participants run in the first part of the semester. Participants run at the end of the semester showed less AC and greater G, supporting informal observations that these Ps unconsciously learned less and guessed more.

The quad model will change our view of automatic and controlled processes, from the idea that each is tapped by particular tasks, or that if they co-occur they always compete with each other, to the view that there are several kinds of each, and that they complement and compete with each other, depending on task demands and conditions. The prospect of correlating quad parameters with behaviors and social neuroscience markers is particularly exciting.

Accuracy of Initial Impressions

Gauging perceivers' accuracy depends on having criteria against which to compare their perceptions. When objective criteria for accuracy exist (e.g., height, income), there are few problems. But subjective criteria or ratings (e.g., how tall or successful?) present special problems, including how perceivers interpret the question (Uleman, 2005) and frame the comparisons they are making. Thus a woman may be judged as the same height as a man, but relatively "tall" because she is implicitly compared with other women (Biernat, 2003). Many of the criteria of interest to personality and social psychologists are subjective (e.g., traits) with shifting comparison frames.

If subjective ratings of a target are used as criteria, are a target's self-ratings, or a composite of others' ratings more valid? There seems to be no general answer. Vazire and Mehl (2008) present evidence that each has substantial predictive validity for a range of everyday behaviors' frequencies, and each often has unique validity. Behaviors are probably the least controversial criteria for accuracy (Kenny & West, 2008), especially (and perhaps only) when the behaviors are unambiguous.

The accuracy of stereotypes has been a research topic in its own right. Jussim (2005) has been particularly vigorous in documenting the accuracy (as well as the errors) of stereotypes, often with behavioral evidence in natural settings such as schools. He provides an excellent discussion of how to distinguish between accuracy and self-fulfilling prophecies, the importance of differentiating levels of analysis in analyzing stereotypes, and how accuracy can sometimes lead to discrimination.

Accuracy in Trait Judgments

There are at least four major conceptions of accuracy in trait judgments. Kruglanski (1989) viewed traits as useful social constructs based on consensus, with their reality moot. Gill and Swann described "pragmatic accuracy" as "accuracy that facilitates the achievement of relationship-specific interaction goals" (Gill & Swann, 2004, p. 405). They found that both group members and romantic partners had more functional, pragmatically accurate perceptions of others in task- and relationship-relevant domains than otherwise. Gagné and Lydon (2004) found that in relationships, bias and accuracy coexist in different areas. Perceivers are "more accurate in epistemic-related relationship judgments while being more positively biased in esteem-related relationship judgments" (p. 322).

Funder's realistic accuracy model (RAM; 1995) assumes traits are "real," and advocates multifaceted criteria to assess them. So Letzring, Wells, and Funder (2006) used self-ratings, ratings by knowledgeable peers, and clinical interviews to establish criteria for accuracy, in a study of perceptions of triads of strangers. Reminiscent of Brunswik's (1956) lens model, RAM holds that accuracy depends on (1) the relevance of behavioral cues to a trait, (2) how available these cues are for observation, (3) the ease with which they can be detected, and (4) how they are used. In an interesting extension, Letzring (2008) found that the accuracy of *observers* of triadic interactions was positively related to the number of "good judges" (good social skills, agreeable, well adjusted) within the triads. This suggests that good judges are not only better at detecting and using relevant cues, but that they also elicit them in ways other observers can use.

Ickes (2009) focuses on empathy in social interactions; has developed innovative methods for defining and measuring accuracy in knowing what interaction partners were thinking and feeling; and has generated a wealth of interesting results.

The most quantitatively sophisticated views of accuracy emerge from Kenny's social relations model (SRM; Kenny, 1994) and PERSON model (Kenny, 2004). This work isolates several sources of accuracy, in both targets and perceivers. The SRM decomposes ratings of many targets, by many perceivers, into independent components attributable to targets, to perceivers, and to their unique

interactions ("relationship effects"). The PERSON model decomposes the variance in such ratings into components that are more psychologically meaningful (namely Personality, Error, Residual, Stereotype, Opinion, and Norm; but note that Kenny's quantitative definitions of these mnemonic terms are not always obvious). PERSON generates predictions and explanations of several interesting phenomena, once appropriate parameters from past research are employed. For example, the surprising degree of consensus among perceivers at "zero acquaintance" and from "thin slices" of behavior is attributable largely to Stereotypes ("shared assumptions based on physical appearance"; Kenny, 2004, p. 268). With increasing acquaintance, asymptoting at about 100 acts after a few hours of interaction, consensus hardly increases, but is based entirely on Personality (perceivers' consistent shared interpretation of the target's acts). Yet consensus only accounts for about 30% of the variance in impressions. The remainder is based on Opinion (the consistent, private, and "unique view that the perceiver has of the target," Kenny, 2004, p. 268).

PERSON accounts for other important results. First, consensus partly depends on how much perceivers observe the *same* target behaviors. Yet this effect only makes a large difference for extraversion (among the Big Five, usually employed in these studies), probably because perceivers typically observe the same behaviors in groups, and group settings are uniquely appropriate for extraverted behaviors. Second, O is the dominant contributor to accuracy under standard conditions. Kenny (2004, p. 272) notes that Swann has called this "circumscribed accuracy" and claimed it reflects behaviors that are uniquely available to the perceiver. But most research suggests that it represents unique *interpretations* of target's behaviors by the perceiver, not unique *behaviors*. There is much more to PERSON, and to Kenny's general approach, than can be described here (e.g., Kenny & West, 2008). It simultaneously takes into account accuracy and bias of various sorts (e.g., Kenny & Acitelli, 2001); accounts for changes in perceptions over time; and models many of the findings from natural and experimental settings. As the field becomes more sophisticated and software becomes friendlier, it will become increasingly influential.

Deception

Bond and DePaulo (2008) analyzed how well perceivers can detect strangers' deception, across 247 experimental studies, and found that their ability is negligible. Perceivers differ from each other in suspiciousness, but not in accuracy. Overall, they judge others as truthful. Some targets are more credible (believable) than others, based partly on physical appearance. Credibility differences among targets are larger than differences in trust/suspicion among perceivers, but these are also unrelated to detecting deception. Results are essentially the same when testing lies by acquaintances, and high-stakes lies. These studies, however, exclude important factors that lead to detecting deception in real-world settings. Park, Levine, McCornack, Morrison, and Ferrara (2002) asked over 200 undergraduates to describe incidents of detecting deception in their own lives. People usually relied on information from third parties, and physical evidence. Becoming suspicious in the first place was critically important; and that the process often took days to months or longer. All of this suggests that cues from liars' behavior alone are not only few and far between, they are also relatively unimportant in detecting deception. (See also Kassin & Kovera, chapter 30, this volume.)

Motivated Biases and Distortions

Motivated biases and distortions occur in many ways. When the self-concept is threatened (e.g., via failure feedback), stereotypes are more likely activated and applied, and this restores self-esteem (Fein & Spencer, 1997). Furthermore, self-concept threat selectively activates the relevant (vs. irrelevant) content in a stereotype, which is then selectively applied to stereotyped (vs. nonstereotyped) targets (Govorun, Fuegen, & Payne, 2006).

In general, perceivers are motivated to draw inferences about others that are harmonious with their current self-concepts, if not also self-affirming (see Dunning, 2003, for a review). In defining positive traits, perceivers (particularly those with high self-esteem) emphasize self-descriptive manifestations of these traits, and evaluate others who fit these definitions more positively (e.g., Beauregard & Dunning, 2001). When a target is known to be competent in a given domain, perceivers infer that s/he possesses self-descriptive attributes (McElwee, Dunning, Tan, & Hollmann, 2001). Thus a violinist who learns that a well-liked target is musical assumes she plays the violin.

Repressors show less evidence of STIs from negative (vs. positive) behaviors, but this bias disappears when they must respond quickly. This suggests that they attend to threat cues early in processing and engage in avoidance at later stages (Caldwell & Newman 2005).

Defensive projection involves perceiving in others qualities that are unacceptable in oneself. Newman, Duff, and Baumeister (1997) argued that defensive projection is not directly motivational, but is a by-product of cognitively suppressing thoughts of self-relevant but undesirable qualities. This suppression then makes these thoughts hyperaccessible, so they affect perceptions of others. Perceivers led to believe they have an undesirable trait that they are asked to suppress perceive this trait in another group, and the success of suppression predicts the strength of projection (Newman, Caldwell, Chamberlin, & Griffin, 2005). Others argue that perceiving negative qualities in others may function to deny their relevance to oneself: Perceivers who received feedback that they were high on an undesirable trait (anger or dishonesty), and then had a chance to project the trait onto a target, showed less accessibility and self-attribution of the trait (Schimel, Greenberg, & Martens, 2003).

Functional projection occurs when people perceive qualities in targets that are functionally related to their own mental states (Maner et al., 2005). For instance, following the activation of self-protection goals, white U.S. participants perceive more anger (but not other, functionally irrelevant emotions) only in faces of outgroups implicitly associated with threat (e.g., black males and Arabs, but not black females or whites). Similarly, white U.S. males perceive more sexual arousal in white female faces after a mating goal is primed. Chronic self-protection and mating goals show similar effects.

Mortality salience (MS, i.e., thoughts of one's own death) motivates people to increase the search and preference for stimuli that validate their cultural worldview. Those high in MS prefer stereotype-consistent outgroup targets (Schimel et al., 1999) and targets who praise or endorse their worldview (Greenberg et al., 1990). MS also increases seeking and preferring order and stability in the social world. So MS increases primacy effects in impression formation and the preference for Heiderian interpersonal balance (Landau et al., 2004), especially for perceivers high in the personal need for structure.

Ideological beliefs affect person perception in motivational ways. Rich targets are seen as more competent (e.g., intelligent), and poor targets as warmer, consistent with the SCM (Fiske et al., 2002). The source of affluence (inheritance or hard work) and perceivers' belief in the Protestant work ethic influences these impressions (Christopher et al., 2005). Conversely, exposure to targets who

from attributions of causality, accompanied by attributions of intention, foreseeability, capacity, and so forth. Only then was blame attributed. Haidt (2001) turned this formulation on its head and posited that intuitions (often emotionally based) come first, followed by rationalizations and reasoning. And most of the reasoning happens socially, between people, rather than through inner speech. Thus, "moral intuitions and emotions drive moral reasoning" (p. 830). Not all moral reasoning depends on others' opinions (Haidt & Kesebir, 2010), but much of it does. Haidt's formulation has precedents. Alicke (2000) showed clearly that people's evaluation of causality in culpable events is affected by outcomes over which the target had little or no control.

Theory of Mind

"Theory of mind" attempts to delineate how people (and other mammals) infer the mental events that occur in others' minds. Malle (2004) developed an adult folk theory that organizes people's explanations for others' behaviors in natural settings, in the spirit of Heider (1958), and provides an alternative to classical attribution theory. Explanations are communications, not simply private thoughts. So they follow conversational (Gricean) rules, and carry implications of praise and/or blame in addition to mere causality. The central distinction is between accidental behaviors (e.g., stumbling) and intentional acts, not between situational and dispositional causes. Intentionality judgments depend on multiple cues, and the ability to make them emerges early in life. Sensitivity to the various features of animacy occurs during infancy (Rakison & Poulin-Dubois, 2001). By 16 months, infants distinguish intentional acts from accidental behaviors, and are less likely to repeat an adult's action that is followed by "Whoops" (and hence accidental) than by "There!" (Carpenter, Akhtar, & Tomasello, 1998). Even 6- to10-month-old infants form impressions, and prefer puppets who intentionally help rather than hinder other puppets (Hamlin, Wynn, & Bloom, 2007).

In Malle's (2004) framework, only *behaviors* (accidental) are explained by *causes,* whereas *acts* are explained by *reasons.* Causes can be situational or personal (including traits), whereas reasons depend on the target's values, beliefs, and desires. If such immediate mental states are unknown, a *causal history of reasons* explanation is offered, in personal (e.g., "he is lazy") and/or situational terms. Finally, acts may be explained in terms of situational and/or

personal enabling factors, again including traits. This framework has considerable support and leads to novel predictions. For example, Malle et al. (2007) found good evidence for three kinds of actor-observer asymmetries (although not the traditional one).

Reeder's multiple inference model (Reeder, Vonk, Ronk, Ham, & Lawrence, 2004) is consistent with Malle's framework. It contends that people explain others' intentional acts in terms of motives (i.e., reasons, based on values, beliefs, and desires); that multiple motives are considered; that these motives have specific content; and that these are reconciled with situational pressures to produce trait inferences (or not). Specific motives mediate specific trait inferences. Reeder, Monroe, and Pryor (2008) showed that the nature of situational constraints affect the motives and traits inferred about the "teacher" in Milgram's obedience situation. Reeder (2009) discusses the model more generally, contrasting it with traditional attribution theory.

The theory of mind or "mindreading" perspective is also consistent with Idson and Mischel's (2001) findings noted above, and with Royzman, Cassidy, and Baron's (2003) "epistemic egocentrism," which shows that adults retain much of the failure in perspective-taking seen in young children's failure at the false-beliefs task.

Simulation Theory and the Self-Referential Perceptions of Others

Simulation theory (e.g., Perner & Kühberger, 2005) is less an explicit deductive theory than the other two, involving not so much inferring the other's mental state or situation from general principles as imagining oneself in the other's situation, and reading off from that simulation an explanation of why the other acted as that way, and what the other might feel and do. Much research on understanding others emphasizes the self as a starting point (Alicke, Dunning, & Krueger, 2005). People seem to use self-knowledge automatically to make inferences about others, and assume self-other similarity by default (Epley, Keysar, Van Boven, & Gilovich, 2004; Krueger, 2003; Mussweiler, 2003), particularly for ingroup members (Robbins & Krueger, 2005). Others' emotions are understood by feeling them in ourselves (Niedenthal, Barsalou, Ric, & Krauth-Gruber, 2005), as are other aspects of people's behavior (Chartrand, Maddux, & Lakin, 2005). People spontaneously project both their chronic and primed goals onto others (Kawada, Oettingen, Gollwitzer, & Bargh, 2004). They also assimilate impressions of romantic partners to themselves, an adaptive process in high-functioning relationships (Murray, Holmes, Bellavia, Griffin, & Dolderman, 2002).

Children require practice in correcting these automatic egocentric inferences (Epley, Morewedge, & Keysar, 2004). This correction seems to fit an "anchoring-and-adjustment" model. Egocentric biases increase under time pressure, decrease with accuracy motivation, are adjusted serially and insufficiently, and stop at satisfactory but not necessarily accurate points (Epley, Keysar, et al., 2004). Although the self is a reasonable basis for inference about others, and even an adaptive strategy in the absence of information about others, adults make egocentric inferences even when they have ready access to concrete knowledge of others' beliefs (Keysar, Lin, & Barr, 2003; Royzman et al., 2003).

Van Boven and Loewenstein (2003) proposed a dual-judgment model, in which people first imagine being in the other's situation. An "empathy gap" occurs in self-predictions (i.e., predictions of one's own future acts are colored by current mental states), and this gap also appears in predicting others. Thus thirsty perceivers projected more thirst than warranted for others in a different situation, and this was mediated by self-predictions.

Judging others (vs. self) can use different information (folk theories vs. introspection, respectively), producing divergent inferences about intrapersonal and interpersonal insight (Pronin, Kruger, Savitsky, & Ross, 2001). Others may also be seen as different from self in having less essential humanness (Haslam et al., 2005), being more driven by ulterior motives or self-interest (Reeder, Pryor, Wohl, & Griswell, 2005), and more susceptible to influence and bias (Ehrlinger, Gilovich, & Ross, 2005; Van Boven, White, Kamada, & Gilovich, 2003). See Pronin, Gilovich, and Ross (2004) for a review. People project more when targets are similar to self, but rely on stereotypes more for dissimilar targets (Ames, 2004). As noted earlier, motivated biases link self with other perception in many ways. In general, people are motivated to see others in ways that support current self-views, or better yet, self-enhance (Balcetis & Dunning, 2005; Dunning, 2003).

To summarize, people are beset by egocentric biases and knowledge when perceiving others for cognitive (e.g., high accessibility of the self) and motivational (e.g., self-enhancement) reasons. Mental state inferences are no longer a "haphazard enterprise" (Davis, 2005, p. 53) but are systematically studied tools of perceivers. And there is a lively debate between simulation theory versus theory-of-mind accounts of mindreading (Perner & Kühberger; 2005; Saxe, 2005).

Conclusion

More than most other areas of research, impression formation lies at the very heart of social and personality psychology. Other's personalities are the object of study; perceivers' personalities affect their perceptions; and both of these classes of "personality" variables interact with each other and a variety of situational or "social" variables. Finally, the very metaconcept of personality is based on impressions of others. Initial impressions are the beginning of these stories.

So who are you, at least to strangers like us? It should be clear that there is no simple or complete answer. The answer depends on what you do and how we interpret it; on the social categories to which you belong, and what we are interested in or attuned to; on how you look, and what that means to us; and on who is asking, and when, and why, as well as what we all want to believe. Rather than a single answer, there is a Rashomon of realities (Kurosawa, 1950), each with its own truths and biases. Impressions are conjoint social constructions by targets and perceivers, their personalities and cultures. Understanding them requires analyses at multiple levels (cultural, personal, social, neuronal) in multiple time frames (lifetimes, years, immediate situations, and milliseconds) and degrees of awareness (explicit and implicit), and from multiple points of view (self, perceiver, consensus, and some future eye-of-God scientific framework that integrates all of these). There is no sword to cut this Gordian knot. It must be unraveled and assembled one thread at a time. But we hope you find, as we do, that the skeins and fabrics that have emerged so far are fascinating.

References

Alicke, M. D. (2000). Culpable control and the psychology of blame. *Psychological Bulletin, 126*, 556–574.

Alicke, M. D., Dunning, D. A., & Krueger, J. I. (Eds.). (2005). *The self in social judgment*. New York: Psychology Press.

Ambady, N., Bernieri, F. J., & Richeson, J. A. (2000). Toward a histology of social behavior: Judgmental accuracy from thin slices of the behavioral stream. In M. P. Zanna (Ed.), *Advances in experimental social psychology* (Vol. 32, pp. 201–272). San Diego, CA: Academic.

Ames, D. R. (2004). Inside the mind reader's tool kit: Projection and stereotyping in mental state inference. *Journal of Personality and Social Psychology, 87*, 340–353.

Amodio, D. M., & Devine, P. G. (2006). Stereotyping and evaluation in implicit race bias: Evidence for independent constructs and unique effects on behavior. *Journal of Personality and Social Psychology, 91,* 652–661.

Amodio, D. M., Devine, P. G., & Harmon-Jones, E. (2008). Individual differences in the regulation of intergroup bias: The role of conflict monitoring and neural signals for control. *Journal of Personality and Social Psychology, 94,* 60–74.

Andersen, S. M., & Klatzky, R. L. (1987). Traits and social stereotypes: Levels of categorization in person perception. *Journal of Personality and Social Psychology, 53,* 235–246.

Andersen, S. M., Klatzky, R. L., & John, M. (1990). Traits and social stereotypes: Efficiency differences in social information processing. *Journal of Personality and Social Psychology, 59,* 192–201.

Andersen, S. M., Reznik, I., & Glassman, N. S. (2005). The unconscious relational self. In R. R. Hassin, J. S. Uleman, & J. A. Bargh (Eds.), *The new unconscious* (pp. 421–481). New York: Oxford University Press.

Anderson, C., & Shirako, A. (2008). Are individuals' reputations related to their history of behavior? *Journal of Personality and Social Psychology, 94,* 320–333.

Balcetis, E., & Dunning, D. A. (2005). Judging for two: Some connectionist proposals for how the self informs and constrains social judgment. In M. D. Alicke, D. A. Dunning, & J. I. Krueger (Eds.), *The self in social judgment: Studies in self and identity.* (pp. 181–211). New York: Psychology Press.

Bargh, J. A. (1994). The four horsemen of automaticity: Awareness, intention, efficiency, and control in social cognition. In R. S. Wyer, Jr., & T. K. Srull (Eds.), *Handbook of social cognition: Vol. 1. Basic processes* (2nd ed., pp. 1–40). Hillsdale, NJ: Erlbaum.

Bargh, J. A., Chaiken, S., Raymond, P., & Hymes, C. (1996). The automatic evaluation effect: Unconditional automatic attitude activation with a pronunciation task. *Journal of Experimental Social Psychology, 32,* 104–128.

Barrett, L. F., Tugade, M. M., & Engle, R. W. (2004). Individual differences in working memory capacity and dual-process theories of the mind. *Psychological Bulletin, 130,* 553–573.

Bartholow, B. D., Pearson, M. A., Gratton, G., & Fabiani, M. (2003). Effects of alcohol on person perception: a social cognitive neuroscience approach. *Journal of Personality and Social Psychology, 85,* 627–638.

Bauman, C. W., & Skitka, L. J. (2006). Ethnic group differences in lay philosophies of behavior in the United States. *Journal of Cross-Cultural Psychology, 37,* 438–445.

Beauregard, K. S., & Dunning, D. (2001). Defining self-worth: Trait self-esteem moderates the use of self-serving trait definitions in social judgment. *Motivation and Emotion, 25,* 135–161.

Biernat, M. (2003). Toward a broader view of social stereotyping. *American Psychologist, 58,* 1019–1027.

Blair, I. V., Judd, & C. M., Chapleau, K. M. (2004). The influence of Afrocentric facial features in criminal sentencing. *Psychological Science, 15,* 674–679.

Blanchard-Fields, F. (1994). Age differences in causal attributions from an adult developmental perspective. *Journal of Gerontology: Series B. Psychological Sciences and Social Sciences, 49,* 43–51.

Blanchard-Fields, F., Chen, Y., Horhota, M., & Wang, M. (2007). Cultural differences in the relationship between aging and the correspondence bias. *Journal of Gerontology: Series B. Psychological Sciences and Social Sciences, 62,* 362–365.

Bless, H., & Schwarz, N. (2010). Mental construal and the emergence of assimilation and contrast effects: The inclusion/exclusion model. In M. P. Zanna (Ed.), *Advances in experimental social psychology* (Vol. 42, pp. 319–373). New York: Academic.

Bliss-Moreau, E., Barrett, L. F., & Wright, C. I. (2008). Individual differences in learning the affective value of others under minimal conditions. *Emotion, 8,* 479–493.

Bond, C. F., Jr., & DePaulo, B. M. (2008). Individual differences in judging deception: Accuracy and bias. *Psychological Bulletin, 134,* 477–492.

Borkenau, P. (1992). Implicit personality theory and the five-factor model. *Journal of Personality, 60,* 295–327.

Borkenau, P., & Ostendorf, F. (1998). The Big Five as states: How useful is the five-factor model to describe intraindividual variations over time? *Journal of Research in Personality, 32,* 202–221.

Bornstein, R. F. (1989). Exposure and affect: Overview and meta-analysis of research, 1968–1987. *Psychological Bulletin, 106,* 265–289.

Boothroyd, L. G., Jones, B. C., Burt, D. M., DeBruine, L. M., & Perrett, D. I. (2008). Facial correlates of sociosexuality. *Evolution and Human Behavior, 29,* 211–218.

Brinsmead-Stockham, K., Johnston, L., Miles, L., & Macrae, C. (2008). Female sexual orientation and menstrual influences on person perception. *Journal of Experimental Social Psychology, 44,* 729–734.

Brunswik, E. (1956). *Perception and the representative design of psychological experiments* (2nd ed.). Berkeley: University of California Press.

Burke, C., & Uleman, J. S. (2006, January). *Mental control over the effects of implicit impressions.* Paper presented in the symposium (Unintentional) Social Inference at the annual meeting of the Society for Personality and Social Psychology, Palm Springs, CA.

Caldwell, T. L., & Newman, L. S. (2005). The timeline of threat processing in repressors: More evidence for early vigilance and late avoidance. *Personality and Individual Differences, 38,* 1957–1967.

Campanella, S., & Belin, P. (2007). Integrating face and voice in person perception. *Trends in Cognitive Sciences, 11,* 635–643.

Carlston, D. E. (Ed.). (forthcoming). *The Oxford handbook of social cognition.* New York: Oxford University Press.

Carlston, D. E. (1994). Associated systems theory: A systematic approach to cognitive representations of persons. In R. S. Wyer, Jr. (Ed.), *Advances in social cognition* (Vol. 7, pp. 1–78). Hillsdale, NJ: Erlbaum.

Carlston, D. E., & Skowronski, J. J. (2005). Linking versus thinking: Evidence for the different associative and attributional bases of spontaneous trait transference and spontaneous trait inference. *Journal of Personality and Social Psychology, 89,* 884–898.

Carnaghi, A., Maass, A., Gresta, S., Bianchi, M., Cadinu, M., & Arcuri, L. (2008). *Nomina sunt omina*: On the inductive potential of nouns and adjectives in person perception. *Journal of Personality and Social Psychology, 94,* 839–859.

Carpenter, M., Akhtar, N., & Tomasello, M. (1998). Fourteen-through 18-month-old infants differentially imitate intentional and accidental actions. *Infant Behavior and Development, 21,* 315–330.

Castelli, L., Pavan, G., Ferrari, E., & Kashima, Y. (2009). The stereotyper and the chameleon: The effects of stereotype use on perceivers' mimicry, *Journal of Experimental Social Psychology, 45,* 835–839.

Castelli, L., & Tomelleri, S. (2008). Contextual effects on prejudiced attitudes: When the presence of others leads to more egalitarian responses. *Journal of Experimental Social Psychology, 44,* 679–686.

Castelli, L., Zogmaister, C., Smith, E. R., & Arcuri, L. (2004). On the automatic evaluation of social exemplars. *Journal of Personality and Social Psychology, 86,* 373–387.

Chaplin, W. F., John, O. P., & Goldberg, L. R. (1988). Conceptions of states and traits: Dimensional attributes with ideals as prototypes. *Journal of Personality and Social Psychology, 54,* 541–557.

Chartrand, T. L., Maddux, W. W., & Lakin, J. L. (2005). Beyond the perception-behavior link: The ubiquitous utility and motivational moderators of nonconscious mimicry. In Hassin, R. R., Uleman, J. S., & Bargh, J. A. (Eds.), *The new unconscious* (pp. 334–361). New York: Oxford University Press.

Chen, Y., & Blanchard-Fields, F. (1997). Age differences in stages of attributional processing. *Psychology and Aging, 12,* 694–703.

Choi, Y. W., Gray, H. M., & Ambady, N. (2005). The glimpsed world: Unintended communication and unintended perception. In R. R. Hassin, J. S. Uleman, & J. A. Bargh (Eds.), *The new unconscious* (pp. 309–333). New York: Oxford University Press.

Christopher, A. N., Morgan, R. D., Marek, P., Troisi, J. D., Jones, J. R., & Reinhart, D. F. (2005). Affluence cues and first impressions: Does it matter how the affluence was acquired? *Journal of Economic Psychology, 26,* 187–200.

Church, A. T., Ortiz, F. A., Katigbak, M. S., Avdeyeva, T. V., Emerson, A. M., Vargas Flores, J. deJ., et al. (2003). Measuring individual and cultural differences in implicit trait theories. *Journal of Personality and Social Psychology, 85,* 332–347.

Claypool, H. M., & Carlston, D. E. (2002). The effects of verbal and visual interference on impressions: An associated-systems approach. *Journal of Experimental Social Psychology, 38,* 425–433

Chiao, J. Y., Adams, R. B., Jr., Tse, P. U., Lowenthal, W. T., Richeson, J. A., & Ambady, N. (2008). Knowing who's boss: fMRI and ERP investigations of social dominance perception. *Group Processes and Intergroup Relations, 11,* 201–214.

Conway, M. (2000). Individual differences in attentional resources and social cognition: Elaboration and complexity in representations of others and self. In U. von Hecker, S. Dutke, & G. Sedek (Eds.), *Generative mental processes and cognitive resources: Integrative research on adaptation and control* (pp. 5–38). Dordrecht, The Netherlands: Kluwer.

Cortes R. P., Demoulin, S., Rodriguez-Torres, R., Rodriguez-Perez, A., & Leyens J-P. (2005). Infrahumanization or familiarity? Attribution of uniquely human emotions to the self, the ingroup, and the outgroup. *Personality and Social Psychology Bulletin, 31,* 245–253.

Crawford, M. T., Sherman, S. J., & Hamilton, D. L., (2002). Perceived entitativity, stereotype formation, and the interchangeability of group members. *Journal of Personality and Social Psychology, 83,* 1076–1094.

Crawford, M. T., Skowronski, J. J., Stiff, C., & Scherer, C. R., (2007). Interfering with inferential, but not associative, processes underlying spontaneous trait inference. *Personality and Social Psychology Bulletin, 33,* 677–690.

Crisp, R. J., & Hewstone, M. (2007). Multiple social categorization. In M. P. Zanna (Ed.), *Advances in experimental social psychology* (Vol. 39, pp. 163–254). San Diego: Elsevier Academic.

Cronbach, L. (1955). Processes affecting scores on "understanding of others" and "assumed similarity." *Psychological Bulletin, 52,* 177–193.

Cuddy, A. J. C., Fiske, S. T., & Glick, P. (2007). The BIAS map: Behaviors from intergroup affect and stereotypes. *Journal of Personality and Social Psychology, 92,* 631–648.

Davis, M. H. (2005). A "constituent" approach to the study of perspective taking: what are its fundamental elements? In B. F. Malle & S. D. Hodges (Eds.), *Other minds: How humans bridge the divide between self and others* (pp. 44–55). New York: Guilford.

De Bruin, E. N. M., & Van Lange, P. A. M. (2000). What people look for in others: Influences of the perceiver and the perceived on information selection. *Personality and Social Psychology Bulletin, 26,* 206–219.

De Houwer, J., Teige-Mocigemba, S., Spruyt, A., & Moors, A. (2009). Implicit measures: A normative analysis and review. *Psychological Bulletin, 135,* 347–368.

Demattè, M. L., Österbauer, R., & Spence, C. (2007). Olfactory cues modulate facial attractiveness. *Chemical Senses, 32,* 603–610.

Demoulin, S., Leyens, J-P, Paladino, M. P., Rodriguez-Torres, R., Rodriguez-Perez, A., & Dovidio, J. F. (2004). Dimensions of "uniquely" and "non-uniquely" human emotions. *Cognition and Emotion, 18,* 71–96.

Denrell, J. (2005). Why most people disapprove of me: Experience sampling in impression formation. *Psychological Review. 112,* 951–978.

DeSteno, D., Dasgupta, N., Bartlett, M., & Cajdric, A. (2004). Prejudice from thin air: The effect of emotion on automatic intergroup attitudes. *Psychological Science, 15,* 319–324.

Dornbush, S. M., Hastorf, A. H., Richardson, S. A., Muzzy, R. E., & Vreeland, R. S. (1965). The perceiver and perceived: Their relative influence on categories of interpersonal perception. *Journal of Personality and Social Psychology, 1,* 434–440.

Duckworth, K. L., Bargh, J. A., Garcia, M., & Chaiken, S. (2002). The automatic evaluation of novel stimuli. *Psychological Science, 13,* 513–519.

Duff, K. J., & Newman, L. S. (1997). Individual differences in the spontaneous construal of behavior: Idiocentrism and the automatization of the trait inference process. *Social Cognition, 15,* 217–241.

Dunning, D. (2003). The zealous self-affirmer: How and why the self lurks so pervasively behind social judgment. In S. J. Spencer, S. Fein, M. P. Zanna, & J. M. Olson (Eds.), *Motivated SOCIAL perception: The Ontario symposium* (Vol. 9, pp. 45–72). Mahwah, NJ: Erlbaum.

Dweck, C. S., Chiu, C., & Hong, Y. (1995). Implicit theories and their role in judgment and reactions: A world from two perspectives. *Psychological Inquiry, 6,* 267–285.

Eberhardt, J. L., Dasgupta, N., & Banaszynski, T. L. (2003). Believing is seeing: The effects of racial labels and implicit beliefs on face perception. *Personality and Social Psychology Bulletin, 29,* 360–370.

Epley, N., Keysar, B., Van Boven, L., & Gilovich, T. (2004). Perspective taking as egocentric anchoring and adjustment. *Journal of Personality and Social Psychology, 87,* 327–339.

Epley, N., Morewedge, C. K., & Keysar, B. (2004). Perspective taking in children and adults: equivalent egocentrism but differential correction. *Journal of Experimental Social Psychology, 40,* 760–768

Ehrlinger, J., Gilovich, T., & Ross, L. (2005). Peering into the bias blind spot: People's assessments of bias in themselves

Oyserman, D., & Lee, S. W. S. (2008). Does culture influence what and how we think? Effects of priming individualism and collectivism. *Psychological Bulletin, 134,* 311–342.

Paladino, M.-P., & Castelli, L. (2008). On the immediate consequences of intergroup categorization: Activation of approach and avoidance motor behavior toward ingroup and outgroup members. *Personality and Social Psychology Bulletin, 34,* 755–768.

Park, B. (1986). A method for studying the development of impressions of real people. *Journal of Personality and Social Psychology, 51,* 907–917.

Park, B., DeKay, M. L., & Kraus, S. (1994). Aggregating social information into person models: Perceiver-induced consistency. *Journal of Personality and Social Psychology, 66,* 437–459.

Park, H. S., Levine, T. R., McCornack, S. A., Morrison, K., & Ferrara, M. (2002). How people really detect lies. *Communications Monographs, 69,* 144–157.

Payne, B. K. (2001). Prejudice and perception: The role of automatic and controlled processes in misperceiving a weapon. *Journal of Personality and Social Psychology, 81,* 181–192.

Payne, B. K. (2008). What mistakes disclose: A process dissociation approach to automatic and controlled processes in social psychology. *Social and Personality Psychology Compass, 2,* 1073–1092.

Pennington, N., & Hastie, R. (1992). Explaining the evidence: Tests of the story model for juror decision making. *Journal of Personality and Social Psychology, 62,* 189–206.

Penton-Voak, I. S., Perrett, D., Castles, D., Kobayashi, T., Burt, M., Murray, L. K., et al. (1999). Menstrual cycle alters face preference. *Nature, 399,* 741–742.

Penton-Voak, I. S., Pound, N., Little, A. C., & Perrett, D. I. (2006). Personality judgments from natural and composite facial images: More evidence for a "kernel of truth" in social perception. *Social Cognition, 24,* 607–640.

Perner, J., & Kühberger, A. (2005). Mental simulation: Royal road to other minds? In B. F. Malle & S. D. Hodges (Eds.), *Other minds: How humans bridge the divide between self and others* (pp. 174–189). New York: Guilford.

Peters, E., Hess, T. M., Västfjäll, D., & Auman, C. (2007). Adult age differences in dual information processes. *Perspectives on Psychological Science, 2,* 1–23.

Petty, R. E., DeMarree, K. G., Briñol, P., Horcajo, J., & Strathman, A. J. (2008). Need for cognition can magnify or attenuate priming effects in social judgment. *Personality and Social Psychology Bulletin, 34,* 900–912.

Phelps, E. A., O'Connor, K. J., Cunningham, W. A., Gatenby, J. C., Funayama, E. S., Gore, J. C., et al. (2000). Amygdala activation predicts performance on indirect tests of racial bias. *Journal of Cognitive Neuroscience, 12,* 729–738.

Phillips, L. H., MacLean, R. D. J., & Allen, R. (2002). Aging and the perception and understanding of emotions. *Journal of Gerontology: Series B. Psychological Sciences and Social Sciences, 57,* 526–530.

Plaks, J. E., Grant, H., & Dweck, C. S. (2005). Violations of implicit theories and the sense of prediction and control: Implications for motivated person perception. *Journal of Personality and Social Psychology, 88,* 245–262.

Plaks, J. E., Stroessner, S. J., Dweck, C. S., & Sherman, J. W. (2001). Person theories and attention allocation: Preferences for sterotypic versus counterstereotypic information. *Journal of Personality and Social Psychology, 80,* 876–893.

Poon, C. S. K., & Koehler, D. J. (2008). Person theories: Their temporal stability and relation to intertrait inferences. *Personality and Social Psychology Bulletin, 34,* 965–977.

Poon, C. S. K., & Koehler, D. J. (2006). Lay personality knowledge and dispositionist thinking: A knowledge-activation framework. *Journal of Experimental Social Psychology, 42,* 177–191.

Pratto, F., & John, O. P. (1991). Automatic vigilance: The attention-grabbing power of negative social information. *Journal of Personality and Social Psychology, 61,* 380–391.

Pronin, E., Gilovich, T., & Ross, L. (2004). Objectivity in the eye of the beholder: Divergent perceptions of bias in self versus others. *Psychological Review, 111,* 781–799.

Pronin, E., Kruger, J., Savitsky, K., & Ross, L. (2001). You don't know me, but I know you: The illusion of asymmetric insight. *Journal of Personality and Social Psychology, 81,* 639–656.

Quinn, K. A., Hugenberg, K., & Bodenhausen, G. V. (2004). Functional modularity in stereotype representation. *Journal of Experimental Social Psychology, 40,* 519–527.

Quinn, K. A., Mason, M. F., & Macrae, N. (2009). Familiarity and person construal: Individuating knowledge moderates the automaticity of category activation. *European Journal of Social Psychology, 39,* 852–861.

Rakison, D. H., & Poulin-Dubois, D. (2001). Developmental origin of the animate-inanimate distinction. *Psychological Bulletin, 127,* 209–228.

Read, S. J. (1987). Constructing causal scenarios: A knowledge structure approach to causal reasoning. *Journal of Personality and Social Psychology, 52,* 288–302.

Read, S. J., Jones, D. K., & Miller, L. C. (1990). Traits as goal-based categories: The importance of goals in the coherence of dispositional categories. *Journal of Personality and Social Psychology, 58,* 1048–1061.

Read, S. J., & Miller, L. C. (2005). Explanatory coherence and goal-based knowledge structures in making dispositional inferences. In B. F. Malle & S. D. Hodges (Eds.), *Other minds: How humans bridge the divide between self and others* (pp. 124–139). New York: Guilford.

Reeder, G. D. (2009). Mindreading: Judgments about intentionality and motives in dispositional inference. *Psychological Inquiry, 20,* 1–18 and 73–83.

Reeder, G. D., Monroe, A. E., & Pryor, J. B (2008). Impressions of Milgram's obedient teachers: Situational cues inform inferences about motives and traits. *Journal of Personality and Social Psychology, 95,* 1–17.

Reeder, G. D., Pryor, J. B., Wohl, M. J. A., & Griswell, M. L. (2005). On attributing negative motives to others who disagree with our opinions. *Personality and Social Psychology Bulletin, 31,* 1498–1510.

Reeder, G. D., Vonk, R., Ronk, M. J., Ham, J., & Lawrence, M. (2004). Dispositional attribution: Multiple inferences about motive-related traits. *Journal of Personality and Social Psychology, 86,* 530–544.

Rentfrow, P. J., & Gosling, S. D. (2006). Message in a ballad: The role of music preferences in interpersonal perception. *Psychological Science, 17,* 236–242.

Rhee, E., Uleman, J. S., Lee, H. K, & Roman, R. J. (1995). Spontaneous self-descriptions and ethnic identities in individualistic and collectivistic cultures. *Journal of Personality and Social Psychology, 69,* 142–152.

Rhodes, G., Halberstadt, J., Jeffery, L., & Palermo, R. (2005). The attractiveness of average faces is not a generalized mere exposure effect. *Social Cognition, 23,* 205–217.

Richards, X., & Hewstone, M. (2001). Subtyping and subgrouping: Processes for the prevention and promotion of stereotype change. *Personality and Social Psychology Review, 5,* 52–73.

Richeson, J. A., Todd, A. R., Trawalter, S., & Baird, A. A. (2008). Eye-gaze direction modulates race-related amygdala activity. *Group Processes and Intergroup Relations, 11,* 233–246.

Richeson, J. A., & Trawalter, S. (2005). On the categorization of admired and disliked exemplars of admired and disliked racial groups. *Journal of Personality and Social Psychology, 89,* 517–530.

Rim, S., Uleman, J. S., & Trope, Y. (2009). Spontaneous trait inference and construal level theory: Psychological distance increases nonconscious trait thinking. *Journal of Experimental Social Psychology, 45,* 1088–1097.

Robbins, J. M., & Krueger, J. I. (2005). Social projection to ingroups and outgroups: A review and meta-analysis. *Personality and Social Psychology Review, 9,* 32–47.

Robins, R. W., Mendelsohn, G. A., Connell, J. B., & Kwan, V. S. Y. (2004). Do people agree about the causes of behavior? A social relations analysis of behavior ratings and causal attributions. *Journal of Personality and Social Psychology, 86,* 334–344.

Roese, N. J., Sanna, L.J., & Galinsky, A. D. (2005). The mechanics of imagination: Automaticity and control in counterfactual thinking. In R. R. Hassin, J. S. Uleman, & J. A. Bargh (Eds.), *The new unconscious* (pp. 138–170). New York: Oxford University Press.

Rosenberg, S., Nelson, C., & Vivekananthan, P. S. (1968). A multidimensional approach to the structure of personality impressions. *Journal of Personality and Social Psychology, 9,* 283–294.

Royzman, E. B., Cassidy, K. W., & Baron, J. (2003). "I know, you know": Epistemic egocentrism in children and adults. *Review of General Psychology, 7,* 38–65.

Rule, N. O., Ambady, N., & Hallett, K. C. (2009). Female sexual orientation is perceived accurately, rapidly, and automatically from the face and its features. *Journal of Experimental Social Psychology, 45,* 1245–1251.

Rule, N. O., Macrae, C. N., & Ambady, N. (2009). Ambiguous group membership is extracted automatically from faces. *Psychological Science, 20,* 441–443.

Rydell, R. J., & McConnell, A. R. (2006). Understanding implicit and explicit attitude change: A systems of reasoning analysis. *Journal of Personality and Social Psychology, 91,* 995–1008.

Rydell, R. J., McConnell, A. R., Mackie, D. M., & Strain, L. M. (2006). Of two minds: Forming and changing valence-inconsistent implicit and explicit attitudes. *Psychological Science, 17,* 954–958.

Saucier, G. (2003a). An alternative multi-language structure for personality attributes. *European Journal of Personality, 17,* 179–205.

Saucier, G. (2003b). Factor structure of English-language personality type-nouns. *Journal of Personality and Social Psychology, 85,* 695–708.

Saxe, R. (2005). Against simulation: The argument from error. *Trends in Cognitive Science, 9,* 174–179.

Schaller, M. (2007). Evolutionary bases of first impressions. In N. Ambady & J. J. Skowronski (Eds.), *First impressions* (pp. 15–34). New York: Guilford.

Schank, R. C., & Abelson, R. P. (1995). Knowledge and memory: The real story. In R. S. Wyer (Ed.), *Advances in social cognition* (Vol. 8, pp. 1–85). Hillsdale, NJ: Erlbaum.

Schiller, D., Freeman, J. B., Mitchell, J. P., Uleman, J. S., & Phelps, E. A. (2009) A neural mechanism for first impressions. *Nature Neuroscience, 12,* 508–514.

Schimel, J., Greenberg, J., & Martens, A. (2003). Evidence that projection of a feared trait can serve a defensive function. *Personality and Social Psychology Bulletin, 29,* 969–979.

Schimel, J., Simon, L., Greenberg, J., Pyszczynski, T., Solomon, S., Waxmonsky, J., et al. (1999). Stereotypes and terror management: Evidence that mortality salience enhances stereotypic thinking and preferences. *Journal of Personality and Social Psychology, 77,* 905–926.

Schneider, D. J. (1973). Implicit personality theory: A review. *Psychological Bulletin, 79,* 294–309.

Schneider, D. J. (2004). *The psychology of stereotyping.* New York: Guilford.

Semin, G. R., & Fiedler, K. (1991). The linguistic category model, its bases, applications, and range. *European Review of Social Psychology, 2,* 1–30.

Shaver, K. G. (1985). *The attribution of blame: Causality, responsibility, and blameworthiness.* New York: Springer-Verlag.

Sherman, J. W., Gawronski, B., Gonsalkorale, K., Hugenberg, K., Allen, T., & Groom, C. J. (2008). The self-regulation of automatic associations and behavioral impulses. *Psychological Review, 115,* 314–335.

Sherman, J. W., Lee, A. Y., Bessenoff, G. R., & Frost, L. A. (1998). Stereotype efficiency reconsidered: Encoding flexibility under cognitive load. *Journal of Personality and Social Psychology, 75,* 589–606.

Sherman, J. W., Stroessner, S. J., Conrey, F. R., & Azam, O. A. (2005). Prejudice and stereotype maintenance processes: Attention, attribution, and individuation. *Journal of Personality and Social Psychology, 89,* 607–622.

Shweder, R. A., & Bourne, E. J. (1984). Does the concept of the person vary cross-culturally? In R. A. Shweder & R. A. LeVine (Eds.), *Culture theory* (pp. 158–199). Cambridge, UK: Cambridge University Press.

Sibley, Chris G.(1); Duckitt, J. (2008). Personality and prejudice: A meta-analysis and theoretical review. *Personality and Social Psychology Review, 12,* 248–279.

Skowronski, J. J., Carlston, D. E., Mae, L., & Crawford, M. T. (1998). Spontaneous trait transference: Communicators take on the qualities they describe in others. *Journal of Personality and Social Psychology, 74,* 837–848.

Slessor, G., Phillips, L. H., & Bull, R. (2008). Age-related declines in basic social perception: evidence from tasks assessing eye-gaze processing. *Psychology and Aging, 23,* 812–822.

Smith, E. R., & Collins, E. C. (2009). Contextualizing person perception: Distributed social cognition. *Psychological Review, 116,* 343–364.

Smith, N. K., Larsen, J. T., Chartrand, T. L., Cacioppo, J. T., Katafiasz, H. A. & Moran, K. E. (2006). Being bad isn't always good: Affective context moderates the attention bias toward negative information. *Journal of Personality and Social Psychology, 90,* 210–220.

Smith, P. K., Djiksterhuis, A., & Chaiken, S. (2008). Subliminal exposure to faces and racial attitudes: Exposure to whites makes whites like blacks less. *Journal of Experimental Social Psychology, 44,* 50–64.

Son Hing, L. S., Chung-Yan, G. A., Hamilton, L. K., & Zanna, M. P. (2008). A two-dimensional model that employs explicit and implicit attitudes to characterize prejudice. *Journal of Personality and Social Psychology, 94,* 971–987.

Sullivan, S., & Ruffman, T. (2004). Social understanding: How does it fare with advancing years? *British Journal of Psychology, 95*, 1–18.

Talaska, C. A., Fiske, S. T., & Chaiken, S. (2008). Legitimating racial discrimination: Emotions, not beliefs, best predict discrimination in a meta-analysis. *Social Justice Research, 21*, 263–296.

Tashakkori, A., & Insko, C. A. (1981). Interpersonal attraction and person perception: Two tests of three balance models. *Journal of Experimental Social Psychology, 17*, 266–285

Tetlock, P. E. (2002). Social functionalist frameworks for judgment and choice: Intuitive politicians, theologians, and prosecutors. *Psychological Review, 109*, 451–471.

Todorov, A. (2002). Communication effects on memory and judgment. *European Journal of Social Psychology, 32*, 531–546.

Todorov, A., Gobbini, M. I., Evans, K. K, & Haxby, J. V. (2007). Spontaneous retrieval of affective person knowledge in face perception. *Neuropsychologia, 45*, 163–173.

Todorov, A., Mandisodza, A. N., Goren, A., & Hall, C. C. (2005). Inferences of competence from faces predict election outcomes. *Science, 308*, 1623–1626.

Todorov, A., Pakrashi, M., & Oosterhof, N. N. (2009). Evaluating faces on trustworthiness after minimal time exposure. *Social Cognition, 27*, 813–833.

Todorov, A., & Uleman, J. S. (2004). The person reference process in spontaneous trait inferences. *Journal of Personality and Social Psychology. 87*, 482–493.

Trope, Y., & Liberman, N. (2000). Temporal construal and time-dependent changes in preference. *Journal of Personality and Social Psychology, 79*, 876–889.

Uleman, J. S. (2005). On the inherent ambiguity of traits and other mental concepts. In B. F. Malle & S. D. Hodges (Eds.), *Other minds: How humans bridge the divide between self and others* (pp. 253–266). New York: Guilford.

Uleman, J. S., Newman, L. S., & Moskowitz, G. B. (1996). People as flexible interpreters: Evidence and issues from spontaneous trait inference. In M. P. Zanna (Ed.), *Advances in experimental social psychology* (Vol. 28, pp. 211–279). San Diego, CA: Academic.

Uleman, J. S., Saribay, S. A., & Gonzalez, C. (2008). Spontaneous inferences, implicit impressions, and implicit theories. *Annual Review of Psychology, 59*, 329–360.

Van Boven, L., & Loewenstein, G. (2003). Social projection of transient drive states. *Personality and Social Psychology Bulletin, 29*, 1159–1168.

Van Boven, L., White, K., Kamada, A., & Gilovich, T. (2003). Intuitions about situational correction in self and others. *Journal of Personality and Social Psychology, 85*, 249–258.

Van Dillen, L. F., & Koole, S. L. (2009). How automatic is "automatic vigilance"? The role of working memory in attentional interference of negative information. *Cognition and Emotion, 23*, 1106–1117.

Van Harreveld, F., van der Pligt, J., & de Liver, Y. N. (2009). The agony of ambivalence and ways to resolve it: Introducing the MAID model. *Personality and Social Psychology Review, 13*, 45–61.

Van Overwalle, F., Van den Eede, S., Baetens, K., & Vandekerckhove, M. (2009). Trait inferences in goal-directed behavior: ERP timing and localization under spontaneous and intentional processing. *Social Cognitive and Affective Neuroscience, 4*, 177–190.

Vazire, S. & Gosling, S. D. (2004). E-perceptions: Personality impressions based on personal websites. *Journal of Personality and Social Psychology, 87*, 123–132.

Vazire, S., & Mehl, M. R. (2008). Knowing me, knowing you: The accuracy and unique predictive validity of self-ratings and other-ratings of daily behavior. *Journal of Personality and Social Psychology, 95*, 1202–1216.

Vescio, T. K., Snyder, M., & Butz, D. A. (2003). Power in stereotypically masculine domains: A social influence strategy × stereotype match model. *Journal of Personality and Social Psychology, 85*, 1062–1078.

von Hippel, W. (2007). Aging, executive functioning, and social control. *Current Directions in Psychological Science, 16*, 240–244.

Walther, E., Nagengast, B., & Trasselli, C. (2005). Evaluative conditioning in social psychology: Facts and speculations. *Cognition and Emotion, 19*, 175–196.

Weeks, M., & Lupfer, M. B. (2004). Complicating race: The relationship between prejudice, race, and social class categorizations. *Personality and Social Psychology Bulletin, 30*, 972–984.

Weeks, M., & Vincent, M. A. (2007). Using religious affiliation to spontaneously categorize others. *International Journal for the Psychology of Religion, 17*, 317–331.

Wegner, D. M., & Pennebaker, J. W. (Eds.), (1993). *Handbook of mental control*. Englewood-Cliffs, NJ: Prentice-Hall.

Weisbuch, M., Unkelbach, C., & Fiedler, K. (2008). Remnants of the recent past: Influences of priming on first impressions. In N. Ambady & J. J. Skowronski (Eds.), *First impressions* (pp. 289–312). New York: Guilford.

Wright, J. C., & Mischel, W. (1987). A conditional analysis of dispositional constructs: The local predictability of social behavior. *Journal of Personality and Social Psychology, 53*, 1159–1177.

Wright, J. C., & Mischel, W. (1988). Conditional hedges and the intuitive psychology of traits. *Journal of Personality and Social Psychology, 55*, 454–469.

Wyer, N. A. (2005). Not all stereotypic biases are created equal: Evidence for a stereotype-disconfirming bias. *Personality and Social Psychology Bulletin, 30*, 706–720.

Wyer, R. S., Jr., Adaval, R., & Colcombe, S. J. (2002). Narrative-based representations of social knowledge: Their construction and use in comprehension, memory, and judgment. In M. P. Zanna (Ed.), *Advances in experimental social psychology* (Vol. 34, pp. 131–197). San Diego, CA: Academic.

Wyer, R. S., Jr., & Gruenfeld, D. H. (1995). Information processing in social contexts: Implications for social memory and judgment. In M. P. Zanna (Ed.), *Advances in experimental social psychology* (Vol. 27, pp. 49–91). San Diego: Academic.

Wyer, R. S., Jr., & Srull, T. K. (1986). Human cognition in its social context. *Psychological Review, 93*, 322–359.

Ybarra, O. & Park, D. C. (2002). Disconfirmation of person expectations by older and younger adults: Implications for social vigilance. *Journal of Gerontology: Series B. Psychological Sciences and Social Sciences, 57*, 435–443.

Yzerbyt, V., Judd, C. M., & Corneille, O. (Eds.). (2004). *The psychology of group perception: Perceived variability, entitativity, and essentialism*. New York: Psychology Press.

Yzerbyt, V. Y., Kervyn, N., & Judd, C. M. (2008). Compensation versus halo: The unique relations between the fundamental dimensions of social judgment. *Personality and Social Psychology Bulletin, 34*, 1110–1123.

Yzerbyt, V. Y., Provost, V., & Corneille, O. (2005). Not so competent but warm . . . Really? Compensatory stereotypes in the French-speaking world. *Group Processes and Intergroup Relations, 8,* 219–308.

Zajonc, R. B. (1960). The process of cognitive tuning in communication. *Journal of Abnormal and Social Psychology, 61,* 159–167.

Zajonc, R. B. (1980). Feeling and thinking: Preferences need no inferences. *American Psychologist, 35,* 151–175.

Zárate, M. A., Uleman, J. S., & Voils, C. I. (2001). Effects of culture and processing goals on the activation and binding of trait concepts. *Social Cognition, 19,* 295–323.

Zebrowitz, L. A. (2006). Finally, faces find favor. *Social Cognition, 24,* 657–701.

Zebrowitz, L. A., Fellous, J., Mignault, A., & Andreoletti, C. (2003). Trait impressions as overgeneralized responses to adaptively significant facial qualities: Evidence from connectionist modeling. *Personality and Social Psychology Review, 7,* 194–215.

Zebrowitz, L. A., White, B., & Wieneke, K. (2008). Mere exposure and racial prejudice: Exposure to other-race faces increases liking for strangers of that race. *Social Cognition, 26,* 259–275.

In sum, the work described above provides indirect evidence for the importance of trait accessibility when it comes to the prediction of behavior. Arguably, personality dispositions are more readily accessible for individuals who are low rather than high in self-monitoring tendency and for individuals who are high rather than low in private self-consciousness. The research by Eichstaedt and Silvia (2003) and by Markus (1977) is consistent with this interpretation. As mentioned earlier, these investigators showed that individuals with high standing on a trait dimension, or individuals for whom a given trait is particularly important, respond faster to trait-relevant information, suggesting that for these individuals the trait in question is highly accessible.

Accessibility of Attitudes

More direct evidence for the importance of a disposition's accessibility can be found in research on attitude strength and its role as a moderator of the attitude-behavior relation. People have positive or negative reactions to virtually any concrete object or event, and to any abstract construct or other discriminable aspect of their world. Indeed, evaluations are the most important aspect of a construct's connotative meaning (Osgood, Suci, & Tannenbaum, 1957). There is good evidence to show that these favorable or unfavorable attitudes are automatically activated when people are exposed to actual or symbolic representations of an object or construct (Bargh, Chaiken, Govender, & Pratto, 1992; Bargh, Chaiken, Raymond, & Hymes, 1996). Nevertheless, even though attitudes are automatically activated, they can differ in strength. Generally speaking, strong attitudes involve issues of personal relevance and are held with great conviction or certainty. However, there is considerable disagreement regarding the definition and measurement of attitude strength (Raden, 1985). Its definition often refers, among other things, to attitudinal extremity, confidence in one's attitude, low attitudinal ambivalence, involvement with the attitude object, direct experience with it, its centrality or importance, and its temporal stability (see Krosnick, Boninger, Chuang, Berent, & Carnot, 1993). These different indicators of attitude strength tend to correlate with each other, even though the correlations can be relatively low (Krosnick & Petty, 1995; Raden, 1985).

Recent theorizing has relied on the notion of attitude accessibility as an anchor and unifying framework for the multifaceted construct of attitude strength. Fazio (1990a) defined attitude as the link, in memory, between the attitude object and a favorable or unfavorable evaluation. The stronger this link, the stronger the attitude and the more accessible it should be. An attitude's accessibility in memory is assessed most directly by means of reaction times. The faster a person can provide an evaluation of a given object or construct, the more accessible and hence stronger the person's attitude (Fazio, 1990b). Some proposed aspects of attitude strength can be viewed as antecedents of the attitude's accessibility or strength while others are likely consequences. Thus, an object's or issue's importance or personal relevance, direct experience with the attitude object, and attitudinal extremity will tend to result in strong and highly accessible attitudes, whereas ambivalence regarding an issue will tend to slow down evaluative responses, an indication of lower accessibility. In partial support of this suggestion, attitudes formed after direct experience with the attitude object are found to be more readily accessible, as indicated by response latencies, than are attitudes based on second-hand information (Berger & Mitchell, 1989; Fazio, Chen, McDonel, & Sherman, 1982). On the other side of the equation, strong, highly accessible attitudes are likely to produce relative stable attitudes that are resistant to change and hence are good predictors of later behavior.

Strong attitudes are chronically accessible, but attitudes, like other cognitive schemas, can also be primed to make them temporarily more accessible (Bargh, 2006; Higgins, Rholes, & Jones, 1977). Thus, for example, repeated expressions of an attitude have been shown to produce faster responses to attitudinal questions on subsequent occasions (Powell & Fazio, 1984; Roese & Olson, 1994).

Attitudes and Behavior

Because attitudes are internal dispositions that reflect approach-avoidance tendencies, they are expected to induce corresponding behavior toward the attitude object. Many theorists have distinguished between two modes of information processing, a controlled mode and a spontaneous mode (see Chaiken & Trope, 1999). The labels used to identify these two modes of operation include systematic versus heuristic (Chaiken, 1980), rational versus experiential (Epstein, 1990), deliberative versus spontaneous (Fazio, 1990a), associative versus propositional (Gawronski & Bodenhausen, 2006), System I versus System II (Kahneman & Frederick, 2005), central versus peripheral (Petty & Cacioppo, 1986), associative versus rule-based (Sloman, 1996;

Smith & DeCoster, 2000) and reflective versus impulsive (Strack & Deutsch, 2004). When applied to the attitude construct, this distinction implies that attitudes can be formed and produced spontaneously, without much cognitive effort, or in a more controlled fashion, after some degree of cognitive effort or scrutiny.

Perhaps the most comprehensive conceptual framework to draw out the implications of this distinction for the attitude-behavior relation is Fazio's (1986; 1990a) MODE model. Consistent with the logic of other dual-process theories, the MODE model posits that attitudes can influence behavior in two ways: in a deliberative and in a spontaneous fashion. The acronym MODE stands for "*motivation* and *opportunity* act as *de*terminants of spontaneous versus deliberative attitude-to-behavior processes" (Fazio, 1995, p. 257). When people are sufficiently motivated and have the cognitive capacity to do so, they can retrieve or construct their attitudes in an effortful manner. When motivation or cognitive capacity is low, attitudes become available only if they are strong enough to be readily accessible in memory. Building on past work concerning the effects of attitudes on perceptions and judgments (see Eagly, 1998; Higgins, 1996 for reviews), the model assumes that attitudes can influence or bias perception and judgments of information relevant to the attitude object, a bias that is congruent with the valence of the attitude. The more accessible or stronger the attitude, the greater this bias and therefore the attitude's impact on behavior.

Controlled/Explicit Attitudinal Responses

Research findings regarding the relation between explicit verbal attitudes and actual behavior in many ways parallel the results of research on the relation between personality traits and behavior. General attitudes tend to predict aggregated patterns of behavior directed at the attitude object, but they generally fail to predict any particular action (see Ajzen, 2005).

PATTERNS OF BEHAVIOR

Focusing on religiosity, Fishbein and Ajzen (1974) were the first to demonstrate that general attitudes can predict broad patterns of behavior. College students expressed their attitudes toward religion and the church on five standard attitude scales and then indicated which of 100 behaviors in the domain of religion they had performed. Among the behaviors were praying before or after meals, taking a religious course for credit, reading the Bible in one's free

time, donating money to a religious institution, and dating a person against parents' wishes. The number of behaviors on the list participants reported to have performed served as an aggregate measure of their religious behavior. This broad measure of behavior could be predicted very well from the general attitudes toward religion; the mean correlation across the different attitude scales was .63.

Werner (1978) reported very similar results in relation to the abortion controversy. Male and female college students expressed their attitudes toward abortion on demand and also reported the extent to which they had performed each of 83 activities related to abortion. Among these activities were trying to convince a friend or acquaintance that abortion should be greatly restricted or prohibited, encouraging a woman with an unwanted pregnancy to have an abortion, and circulating an antiabortion petition. Attitude toward abortion was found to be a highly accurate predictor of a multiple-act index based on all 83 activities. For the total sample of respondents, the attitude-behavior correlation was .78.

An apparent weakness of investigations of this kind is their reliance on self-reports of behavior (Schuman & Johnson, 1976). However, Weigel and Newman (1976) reported the same results for observed behavior in the domain of environmental protection. Using a community sample of participants, the investigators measured attitudes toward environmental quality and, 3 to 8 months later, observed 14 behaviors related to the environment. The behaviors involved signing and circulating three different petitions concerning environmental issues, participating in a litter pick-up program, and participating in a recycling program on eight separate occasions. The results revealed a correlation of .62 between general attitudes toward environmental quality and an overall index based on all 14 behavioral observations.

In a similar fashion, Bandura, Blanchard, and Ritter (1969) reported a strong association between general attitudes toward snakes and an aggregate of observed behaviors in relation to a snake. The investigators assessed attitudes toward snakes by means of two standard attitude scales and then recorded the behavior of undergraduates in a graded series of interactions with a live snake that ranged from approaching the snake in an enclosed glass cage to passively permitting the snake to crawl in one's lap. The two attitude measures were found to correlate strongly ($r = .73$ and $r = .56$) with the aggregated behavioral criterion.

INDIVIDUAL BEHAVIORS

The strong relations between general attitudes and behavioral patterns contrast sharply with the results obtained when general attitudes are used to predict individual behaviors. As was true of personality traits, general attitudes are found to have very low predictive validity in relation to specific behaviors (see Ajzen, 2005). Consider, for example, the Fishbein and Ajzen (1974) study on religious attitudes and behavior. Whereas the general attitudes toward religiosity were found to be good predictors of a person's overall pattern of religious behavior, the mean correlations of the five attitude measures with the 100 individual behaviors was only about .14. Similar results emerged in the Weigel and Newman (1976) study, where attitudes toward environmental quality correlated, on average, 0.29 with the 14 individual behaviors related to the environment.

Many earlier investigations had foreshadowed these weak attitude-behavior relations (see Wicker, 1969 for a review). In their analysis of the literature, Ajzen and Fishbein (1977) concluded that most studies conducted in the 1950s and 1960s had examined the relation between very general attitudes and quite specific behaviors. Thus, investigators attempted to predict job performance, absenteeism, and turnover from job satisfaction attitudes (e.g., Bernberg, 1952; Vroom, 1964); conformity with the judgments made by a black person (Himelstein & Moore, 1963) or willingness to have one's picture taken with a black individual (De Fleur & Westie, 1958; Linn, 1965) from attitudes toward blacks; attendance at labor union meetings from attitudes toward labor unions (Dean, 1958); participation in psychological research from attitudes toward psychological research (Wicker & Pomazal, 1971); and so forth. The majority of these studies reported very low and often nonsignificant correlations. More recent meta-analytic syntheses (Kraus, 1995; Schütz & Six, 1996; Talaska, Fiske, & Chaiken, 2008) reveal similarly low correlations between general attitudes and specific actions.

These kinds of findings led Wicker (1969) to doubt the ability of verbal attitudes to predict actual behavior and, indeed, to question the utility of the attitude construct itself. Wicker's far-reaching conclusion is, however, belied by the results of research on behavioral aggregates reviewed in the previous section. This research has demonstrated that even though general attitudes often fail to predict individual behaviors, they have good predictive validity in relation to overall patterns of behavior. Moreover, in the following section we will see that the ability

of general attitudes to predict specific actions is at least in part a function of the attitude's strength.

Attitude Strength and Prediction of Behavior

Unless individuals operate under time pressure or under cognitive load, explicit measures of attitude are likely to be produced in a controlled fashion. When individuals complete an attitude questionnaire, they typically have enough time and opportunity to carefully consider their responses. Virtually all early failures to find strong attitude-behavior correspondence relied on such explicit measures of attitude. We now consider the extent to which attitude accessibility moderates the relation between broad explicit attitudes and specific behaviors. As a general rule, controlled attitudinal responses should predict individual behaviors better when attitudes are strong rather than weak. Several lines of research support this expectation.

Sample and Warland (1973) were perhaps the first to show that strongly held attitudes are better predictors of behavior than weakly held attitudes. These investigators assessed college students' attitudes toward student government as well as their certainty with respect to their responses. Based on these certainty scores, participants were divided into low and high attitude strength groups. The correlation between attitudes toward student government and participation in undergraduate student elections was only .10 for respondents with low certainty in their attitudes, but .47 for respondents with high certainty. Using alternative indicators of attitude strength, other investigators have obtained similar results (e.g., Sivacek & Crano, 1982).

Further support is provided by research on the role of direct experience in attitude formation (Fazio & Zanna, 1978; Regan & Fazio, 1977). Compared to attitudes based on second-hand information, attitudes based on direct experience are known to be held with greater confidence (Fazio & Zanna, 1981) and, as noted earlier, to be more readily accessible in memory (Berger & Mitchell, 1989; Fazio et al., 1982). As would therefore be expected, attitudes based on direct experience tend to be better predictors of behavior. To illustrate, in the direct experience condition of their experiment, Regan and Fazio (1977) gave participants an opportunity to try each of five different types of intellectual puzzles, whereas in the second-hand information condition they gave participants a description of each puzzle type and showed them previously solved examples of the puzzles. Expressed interest in each puzzle type served as a measure of attitude while behavior (order and proportion of each puzzle type attempted) was observed during a 15-minute free-play period. Correlations between attitudes and the two measures of behavior were .51 and .54 under direct experience conditions and .22 and .20 when participants had been given only second-hand information about the puzzles.

Spontaneous/Implicit Attitudinal Responses

As noted earlier, exposure to any meaningful construct automatically activates the person's attitude toward the construct in question (Bargh et al., 1992; Bargh et al., 1996). Investigators have taken advantage of this phenomenon to develop implicit measures of attitude that avoid reliance on explicit evaluations of the attitude object. Generally speaking, implicit measures are based on the assumption that activation of a positive attitude (favorable evaluation) speeds up responses to other positive stimuli and slows down responses to negative stimuli. Conversely, activation of a negative attitude is assumed to facilitate responses to negative stimuli and to interfere with responses to positive stimuli (see Petty, Fazio, & Briñol, 2009). Two approaches to implicit attitude measurement are in common use, evaluative priming (Fazio, Jackson, Dunton, & Williams, 1995) and the Implicit Association Test (IAT; Greenwald, McGhee, & Schwartz, 1998). Although these methods can be used to assess many different kinds of attitudes, they have been applied most frequently to the assessment of implicit prejudice with respect to various outgroups. For instance, to assess racial prejudice with the evaluative priming method, participants may be shown pictures of black and white persons on a computer screen, each picture followed by a positive word (e.g., *attractive*) or by a negative word (e.g., *disgusting*). The participant's task is to respond as quickly as possible to the second stimulus, for example by rating it as good or bad, or by reading it out loud. Prejudicial attitudes toward blacks are inferred when negative words elicit faster responses after a photo of a black than a white person, and when positive words produce faster responses when they follow a photo of a white rather than a black person.

When the IAT is used to measure implicit attitudes toward blacks, participants are seated in front of a computer screen and may be shown, one at a time, pictures of black or white individuals and positive or negative words. They are asked to respond as quickly as possible by pressing one computer key if they see either the picture of a black person or a positive word and another key if they see a white person or a negative word. Later the task is reversed such that one key is used for black person or negative word and another key for white person or positive word. By comparing response latencies (the speed with which the keys are pressed) in the two situations it is possible to infer the preference for white over black stimulus persons. Such a preference is indicated if participants respond faster to the white/positive and black/negative combinations than to the white/negative and black/positive combinations.

IMPLICIT ATTITUDES AND BEHAVIOR

Because implicit attitude measures are assumed to be less subject to social desirability biases than explicit measures, and to be capable of reflecting subtle attitudes of which people may not be fully aware (Petty et al., 2009), there was an expectation that they would have better predictive validity in relation to actual behavior. Empirical research, however, has not borne out this expectation. In a recent comprehensive meta-analysis of 184 independent data sets that compared the predictive validities of explicit and implicit attitude measures (Greenwald, Poehlman, Uhlmann, & Banaji, 2009), the correlation between implicit measures and behavior was found to be .27, compared to a correlation of .36 for explicit measures.

When implicit attitude measures are obtained, individuals are instructed to respond as quickly as possible and their response latencies are used to derive an attitude score. Nevertheless, because implicit attitude measures rely on differences in reaction times between a critical stimulus (e.g., blacks) and a comparison stimulus (e.g., whites), the absolute latency is not taken into account. Systematic overall differences in response latencies could be taken as an indication of attitude strength that may moderate the extent to which implicit attitudes predict behavior. Unfortunately, it appears that investigators have, thus far, not examined this possibility. They have, however, considered another factor that may influence the predictive validity of implicit attitudes. Like expressions of attitude, overt behaviors can differ in the extent to which they are produced in a spontaneous or controlled manner; implicit attitudes would be expected to predict the former but not necessarily the latter (see Gawronski & Bodenhausen, 2006).

A number of studies have directly tested this hypothesis, mostly in the context of racial attitudes and discrimination. Consistent with expectations, implicit measures of prejudice are often found to be superior to explicit measures for the prediction of various nonverbal (spontaneously produced) behaviors such as blinking and eye contact, smiling, and spatial distance (e.g., Dovidio, Kawakami, Johnson, Johnson, & Howard, 1997; Fazio, 1995; T. D. Wilson, Lindsey, & Schooler, 2000) as well as judging the suitability of a candidate with ambiguous qualifications (Olson & Fazio, 2007). (For reviews, see Fazio & Olson, 2003 and Olson & Fazio, 2009). However, even the implicit attitude measures in these studies usually have relatively low predictive validity, with correlations rarely exceeding the .30 level observed in research with explicit measures.

RECAPITULATION

The results of research on the relation between dispositions and behavior can be summarized as follows. General personality traits and attitudes toward objects, issues, or events have good predictive validity in relation to broad, aggregated patterns of behavior in the domain of interest, but these general dispositions tend to be relatively poor predictors of individual behaviors. The low predictive validity of attitudes in relation to individual behaviors is found irrespective of whether the attitude is assessed by means of explicit or implicit methods. However, general personality traits and explicit attitudes are found to predict individual behaviors better when they are relatively strong, that is, when they are readily accessible in memory, than when they are weak. This finding demonstrates that general dispositions can influence not only broad patterns of behavior but, when they are sufficiently strong, can also have an impact on individual behaviors. Yet, this conclusion is problematic. When we demonstrate the moderating effect of dispositional strength, we not only identify a subset of individuals for whom the dispositions are relatively good predictors of behavior, we also identify a subset of individuals for whom the dispositions are relatively poor predictors of behavior (Zedeck, 1971). Consideration of a disposition's strength therefore does not provide a general solution to the prediction of individual behaviors from general dispositions (see Ajzen, 2005). In the following section I discuss an alternative approach based on the concept of compatibility between measures of dispositions and measures of behavior.

Compatibility

Any behavior can be defined in terms of four elements: the action involved, the target at which the action is directed, the context in which it occurs, and the time or time frame of its occurrence (Ajzen, 2005; Ajzen & Fishbein, 1980). A disposition is said to be compatible with a behavior if both are measured at the same level of generality or specificity; that is, if the measure of the disposition involves the same action, target, context, and time elements as the measure of behavior. Further, consistency between dispositions and behavior is a function of the degree to which measures of these variables are compatible with each other. The more similar the target, action, context, and time elements of the dispositional measure are to the corresponding elements of the behavioral measure, the stronger should be the relation between them.

The finding that general personality and attitudinal dispositions tend to be good predictors of broad, aggregated patterns of behavior is quite consistent with the compatibility principle. When we aggregate multiple behaviors, we essentially generalize across different actions, performed in different contexts and at various points in time. The only element that remains constant is the target of the different actions. For instance, a multiple-act indicator of altruistic behavior would aggregate across such actions as donating blood, giving money to charities, volunteering time to help the elderly, serving as a big brother or sister to a child, and so forth, actions that are performed in different contexts and at different times. Because it generalizes across the action, context, and time elements, a behavioral aggregate of this kind is compatible with a measure of altruism, a disposition that could be assessed by means of a questionnaire.

Good correspondence between broad dispositions and general patterns of behavior is, however, only one implication of the compatibility principle. The principle also implies that individual behaviors can be predicted from compatible dispositions that refer to the particular behaviors in question. As was shown in Table 15.1, it is possible to conceive of dispositions at a high level of generality, as in the case of general attitudes and personality traits, or at a much lower level of generality. Outcome expectancies, attitudes toward a behavior, intentions, and habits are dispositions at a relatively low level of generality that refer to a particular behavior. Thus, outcome expectancies are beliefs about the likely outcomes of performing a given behavior (Bandura, 1997), attitudes toward a behavior are favorable or unfavorable evaluations of performing the behavior, intentions refer to readiness to perform the behavior, and habits involve a tendency to perform a well-practiced behavior. According to the principle of compatibility, these kinds of dispositions should correlate well with actual performance of the particular behavior in question.

The Theory of Planned Behavior

The principle of compatibility is a central feature of the theory of planned behavior (TPB; Ajzen, 1991, 2005), an extension of the theory of reasoned action (Ajzen & Fishbein, 1980). This popular theory assumes that performance of a particular behavior is determined, in an immediate sense, by the intention to perform the behavior in question, and it also deals with the dispositional antecedents of intentions, dispositions that are closely tied to the behavior under consideration. According to the TPB, intentions are determined by three dispositional factors: attitude toward the behavior, subjective norm, and perceived behavioral control.

ATTITUDE TOWARD A BEHAVIOR

As noted earlier, attitudes are evaluative reactions to any discriminable aspect of a person's environment or the self. Consistent with this conception, attitude toward a behavior is defined as the person's degree of favorable or unfavorable evaluation of a particular behavior. In the TPB, this attitude is assumed to be based on the person's readily accessible *behavioral beliefs* with respect to the behavior. Each behavioral belief links the behavior to an outcome, and each outcome has a certain subjective value. It is assumed that these behavioral beliefs and outcome evaluations combine to produce an overall positive or negative attitude toward the behavior. Specifically, the subjective value or evaluation of each accessible outcome contributes to the attitude in direct proportion to the person's subjective probability that performing the behavior will produce the outcome in question. In this *expectancy-value model* of attitude (Fishbein, 1963; Peak, 1955), the subjective probability of each outcome is multiplied by the evaluation of the outcome, and the resulting products are summed across all accessible outcomes.

To illustrate, in a pilot study on alcohol and drug use among college students, Armitage, Conner, Loach, and Willetts (1999) identified the following accessible beliefs about using alcohol and marijuana: "Makes me more sociable," "Leads to me having poorer physical health," "Will result in my becoming dependent on it," "Will result in me getting into trouble with authority," and "Makes me feel good." In the main study, they assessed, on 7-point scales, the perceived likelihood that drinking alcohol and

that using marijuana would produce each of these outcomes as well as the evaluation of each outcome. In addition, they measured attitudes toward the two behaviors directly by asking participants to evaluate each behavior on four bipolar adjective scales (*bad-good, unfavorable-favorable, negative-positive, unsatisfying-satisfying*). With respect to drinking alcohol, this attitude measure correlated .58 with the summed likelihood x evaluation products; the corresponding correlation for using marijuana was .78.

Several meta-analyses provide general evidence in support of the expectancy-value model as applied to attitudes toward a behavior. Two of these analyses (Armitage & Conner, 2001; van den Putte, 1993) examined prediction across a broad range of behaviors and reported mean correlations of .53 and .50 between the expectancy-value index of beliefs and a direct attitude measure. In a more limited meta-analysis of research on condom use (Albarracín, Johnson, Fishbein, & Muellerleile, 2001) the mean correlation was .56.

There is also empirical support for the idea that attitudes are a function of beliefs that are readily accessible. In a pilot study, Ajzen, Nochols, and Driver (1995) asked participants to list outcomes of different leisure activities and then selected frequently mentioned outcomes for further investigation. In the main study, participants were asked to evaluate each outcome and to rate its probability. The results showed that responses to the most frequently mentioned outcomes had lower latencies than responses to outcomes that were emitted less frequently. More important, highly accessible behavioral beliefs have been shown to correlate more strongly with an independent measure of attitude than do less accessible beliefs (Petkova, Ajzen, & Driver, 1995; van den Putte, 1993; van der Pligt & Eiser, 1984).

SUBJECTIVE NORM

In addition to holding beliefs about the likely outcomes of a behavior, people also consider the wishes of important social referents. These perceived expectations are termed *normative beliefs* and, according to the TPB, the normative beliefs regarding different social referents (e.g., spouse, close friends, coworkers, physician) combine to produce an overall perceived social pressure to perform the behavior of interest, or subjective norm. Drawing an analogy to the expectancy-value model of attitude toward a behavior, it is assumed that the prevailing subjective norm is determined by the total set of readily accessible normative beliefs concerning the expectations of important referents. Each normative belief is multiplied by the person's motivation to comply with the referent, and the resulting products are summed across all accessible referents.

Similar to tests of the expectancy-value model of attitudes, tests of the subjective norm model usually involve correlating the summed products of normative belief strength times motivation to comply with a direct measure of subjective norm. Empirical evidence is supportive of a correlation between normative beliefs on one hand and perceived social pressure or subjective norm on the other. The strength of this correlation is conveyed in the above-cited meta-analysis of research with the theory of planned behavior by Armitage and Conner (2001). Across 34 sets of data dealing with diverse kinds of behavior, the mean correlation between normative beliefs and subjective norms was .50.

PERCEIVED BEHAVIORAL CONTROL

Many factors, internal and external, can impair (or facilitate) performance of a given behavior. People should be able to act on their intentions to the extent that they have the information, intelligence, skills, abilities, and other internal factors required to perform the behavior and to the extent that they can overcome any external obstacles that may interfere with behavioral performance (see Ajzen, 1985). Perhaps less self-evident than the importance of actual control, but more interesting from a psychological perspective, is the role of *perceived* behavioral control—the extent to which people believe that they can perform a given behavior if they are inclined to do so. The conceptualization of perceived behavioral control in the TPB owes much to Albert Bandura's work on self-efficacy (Bandura, 1977, 1997). In Bandura's social cognitive theory, people's beliefs about their capabilities to exercise control over events that affect their lives function as proximal determinants of human motivation and action. A considerable body of research attests to the powerful effects of self-efficacy beliefs on motivation and performance. The strongest evidence comes from studies in which level of self-efficacy was experimentally manipulated and the effects of this manipulation on perseverance at a task and/or on task performance was observed. Much of this research has been conducted in situations where intentions to perform the behavior of interest can be taken for granted. Under these conditions, perseverance and task performance are found to increase with perceived self-efficacy (e.g., Bandura

& Adams, 1977; Cervone & Peake, 1986; Litt, 1988; Weinberg, Gould, Yukelson, & Jackson, 1981; see Bandura & Locke, 2003, for a review).

However, in the theory of planned behavior, the role of perceived behavioral control goes beyond its effect on perseverance in at least two ways. First, the TPB is a general model designed to be applicable to any behavior, not only behaviors that individuals are motivated to perform. Thus, the more confident people are that they are capable of performing the behavior, the stronger should be their behavioral intentions. Conversely, people who do not believe that they are capable of performing the behavior under investigation will be unlikely to form an intention to do so. Perceived behavioral control can thus influence behavioral performance indirectly by its effects on intentions to engage in the behavior and more directly by its effects on perseverance in the face of difficulties encountered during execution. In addition, perceived behavioral control can potentially serve as a proxy for actual control. In most TPB applications, measures of actual control are unavailable. Indeed, with respect to many behaviors, it would be difficult to identify, let alone measure, the various internal and external factors that may facilitate or inhibit behavioral performance. To the extent that perceptions of control are veridical, they can serve as a proxy for actual control and contribute to the prediction of behavior.

Like attitudes and subjective norms, perceptions of behavioral control are assumed to follow consistently from readily accessible beliefs, in this case beliefs about resources and obstacles that can facilitate or interfere with performance of a behavior. Analogous to the expectancy-value model of attitudes, the power of each control factor to facilitate or inhibit behavioral performance is expected to contribute to perceived behavioral control in direct proportion to the person's subjective probability that the control factor is present. Perceived power and subjective probability are multiplied, and the resulting products are summed across all accessible control factors. In support of this model, empirical evidence shows strong correlations between direct measures of perceived behavioral control and the composite of control beliefs. For example, in an analysis of 16 of their own studies in the health domain, Gagné and Godin (2000) found a median correlation of .57 between control belief composites and direct measures of perceived behavioral control, and in a meta-analysis of 18 studies on a variety of different behaviors, Armitage and Conner (2001) reported a mean correlation of .52.

Predicting Intentions

A large body of research attests to the ability of theory of planned behavior to predict intentions from attitudes toward the behavior, subjective norms, and perceived behavioral control (see Armitage & Conner, 2001; Fishbein & Ajzen, 2010, for reviews). In two meta-analytic syntheses of research on condom use, the mean multiple correlations for the prediction of intentions were found to be .71 (Albarracín et al., 2001) and .65 (Sheeran & Taylor, 1999), and in two meta-analyses of research on physical activity, the mean multiple correlations were .55 (Downs & Hausenblas, 2005) and .67 (Hagger, Chatzisarantis, & Biddle, 2002). Meta-analyses covering a variety of different behaviors (Armitage & Conner, 2001; Notani, 1998; Rivis & Sheeran, 2003; Schulze & Wittmann, 2003) have revealed mean multiple correlations ranging from .59 to .66.

Intentions and Behavior

In the theory of planned behavior, intentions are assumed to be the immediate antecedents of corresponding behavior. The expectation that intentions predict behavior is supported by several systematic reviews of the empirical literature. Some investigators have examined research in delimited behavioral domains, such as condom use and exercise. Meta-analyses of studies in these domains have revealed mean intention-behavior correlations ranging from .44 to .56 (Albarracín et al., 2001; Godin & Kok, 1996; Hagger et al., 2002; Hausenblas, Carron, & Mack, 1997; Sheeran & Orbell, 1998). Meta-analyses spanning research in different behavioral domains—from physical activity, health screening, and illicit drug use to playing video games, donating blood, and smoking cigarettes—have reported mean intention-behavior correlations ranging from .44 to .62 (e.g., Armitage & Conner, 2001; Notani, 1998; Randall & Wolff, 1994; Sheppard, Hartwick, & Warshaw, 1988). In a meta-analysis of such meta-analyses, Sheeran (2002) reported an overall mean correlation of .53 between intention and behavior. Note that these meta-analyses did not consider the degree of intention-behavior compatibility even though compatibility undoubtedly varied across studies. Despite this failure to take compatibility into account, the results show that intentions are quite accurate predictors of corresponding behaviors.

We noted that, according to the TPB, only readily accessible behavioral, normative, and control beliefs provide the cognitive foundation for attitudes, subjective norms, and perceived control,

respectively. When we identify people's readily accessible beliefs we obtain a snapshot of the kinds of considerations that influence their attitudes, subjective norms, and perceptions of control and that therefore guide their intentions and actions at a given point in time. What may be less obvious is that the beliefs that are readily accessible in memory can change over time. The fact that different beliefs may be accessible on different occasions can help explain some of the discrepancies between measured intentions and actual behavior (Ajzen, Brown, & Carvajal, 2004; Sheeran, 2002). Intentions assessed at time 1 will be influenced by the beliefs that are accessible at that time. Behavior, however, is performed at a later point in time, and at that time different beliefs may have become accessible, producing different intentions. In short, intentions measured at time 1 can be expected to predict behavior at time 2 only to the extent that the same beliefs (or beliefs of equivalent valence) are readily accessible at the two time points (Ajzen & Sexton, 1999).

CAUSAL EFFECT OF INTENTIONS ON BEHAVIOR

The empirical research reviewed above shows that intentions can indeed be used to predict behavior, but because most of the research is correlational in nature, these findings are not definitive proof that intentions have a causal impact on behavior. There is growing evidence, however, for a causal relation between intentions and actions coming mainly from intervention studies. In a meta-analysis of 47 studies in which an intervention was shown to have had a significant effect on intentions, this effect was also shown to promote a change in actual behavior (Webb & Sheeran, 2003). On average, the interventions reviewed produced medium to large changes in intentions (mean $d = 0.66$), followed by small to medium changes in behavior (mean $d = 0.36$).

Specific Personality Dispositions: Habits and Behavior

The theory of planned behavior focuses on dispositions of an attitudinal nature, that is, on beliefs and attitudes as precursors of intentions and actions. More closely related to the personality construct is research on the relation between habits and behavior. Whereas general personality dispositions like conscientiousness refer to a tendency to perform a broad range of behaviors in a given domain, habit refers to the tendency to perform a specific behavior. A measure of the tendency to perform a specific behavior should, of course, be a good predictor of the actual performance of this behavior.

Strong empirical tests of this proposition are awaiting the development of valid and reliable measures of habit strength that are independent of the behavior to be predicted (Verplanken, 2006; Verplanken & Orbell, 2003). In the absence of such measures, most research on the relation between habit strength and behavior has relied on the frequency with which the behavior was performed in the past as a measure of habit strength. With repeated performance, behavior is said to habituate, to come under the direct control of stimulus cues, and thus to automatically activate the habitual action (e.g., Aarts & Dijksterhuis, 2000; Aarts, Verplanken, & van Knippenberg, 1998; Ouellette & Wood, 1998). Consistent with this proposition is the general observation that past behavior is a good predictor of future behavior. Indeed, reviews of the relevant literature have revealed strong correlations in various domains between past and later behavior (see Ouellette & Wood, 1998; Sandberg & Conner, 2008). Thus, although the assumption that the frequency of past behavior is a good proxy for habit strength has been challenged (e.g., Ajzen, 2002), to the extent that frequency of past behavioral performance indeed reflects habit strength, these findings suggest that personality dispositions can be defined at the level of an individual behavior, and that such specific dispositions are good predictors of the corresponding action.

Recapitulation

To summarize briefly, personality and social psychologists have learned a great deal about the relations between internal dispositions and overt behavior. Broad personality traits and general attitudes can bias perceptions and judgments and thereby influence performance of behaviors relevant to the personality trait or attitude under consideration. Thus, individuals who score high on a personality measure of conscientiousness will tend to exhibit a general pattern of conscientious behavior, and scores on a measure of attitude toward religion will tend to correlate well with the general pattern of religious behavior. However, as a general rule, broad personality traits are poor predictors of individual behaviors, and the same is true for general attitudes, whether they are produced in a controlled fashion (explicit attitude measure) or spontaneous fashion (implicit attitude measure). The predictive validity of broad personality traits and attitudes tends to improve only for individuals with relatively strong and readily accessible dispositions.

We can obtain better prediction of individual behaviors by relying on internal dispositions that are compatible with the behavior in terms of its action, target, context, and time elements. Habits may be viewed as personality dispositions reduced to the level of particular behaviors, and there is evidence to suggest that such specific trait dispositions do indeed predict performance of corresponding behaviors. A widely used conceptual framework in the attitude domain is provided by the theory of planned behavior. According to the TPB, human social behavior is guided by three kinds of considerations: beliefs about the likely outcomes of the behavior and the evaluations of these outcomes (behavioral beliefs), beliefs about the normative expectations of important others and motivation to comply with these expectations (normative beliefs), and beliefs about the presence of factors that may facilitate or impede performance of the behavior and the perceived power of these factors (control beliefs). In their respective aggregates, behavioral beliefs produce a favorable or unfavorable attitude toward the behavior; normative beliefs result in perceived social pressure or subjective norm; and control beliefs give rise to perceived behavioral control or self-efficacy. In combination, attitude toward the behavior, subjective norm, and perception of behavioral control lead to the formation of a behavioral intention and, given a sufficient degree of actual control over the behavior, people carry out their intentions when the opportunity arises. It can be seen that the TPB incorporates the three types of low generality internal dispositions shown in Table 15.1: cognitive (behavioral, normative, and control beliefs), evaluative (attitude toward the behavior), and behavioral (intention).

Persuasion: Changing Attitudes and Behavior

Current research on persuasion is guided in large measure by the distinction between spontaneous and controlled processes discussed earlier. In the most influential conceptual frameworks—the elaboration likelihood model (Petty & Cacioppo, 1981) and the heuristic-systematic model (Chaiken, 1980)—these processing modes are endpoints on a continuum that ranges from relatively shallow to deep. Most approaches in contemporary cognitive and social psychology, however, postulate two qualitatively distinct information processing systems, one relatively automatic that operates largely below awareness and a more conscious controlled system (e.g., Epstein, 1991; Kahneman & Frederick, 2005;

Sloman, 1996; Strack & Deutsch, 2004). It is usually assumed that the spontaneous system is anchored in parts of the brain that developed relatively early from an evolutionary perspective, whereas the controlled system is a more recent addition. The dual-system conception harkens back to earlier conceptualizations, such as Freud's (1900) distinction between primary and secondary mental processes, but Epstein (1980, 1991) provided the first and most detailed comparison of the two systems in contemporary theorizing. In his cognitive-experiential self-theory, the experiential (spontaneous) system is an automatic learning system that routinely influences not only motor behavior but also conscious thought. It is characterized by associative information processing that is relatively fast and effortless, guided by affective (pleasure-pain) principle, and broad generalizations. The categories and associations in this system, once established, change only slowly as a result of repetitive or intense experiences. The rational (controlled) system is distinguished by effortful analytic information processing that relies on logical connections and symbolic (linguistic, numerical) representations. Processing in this system is relatively slow, but change—which relies on logic and evidence—can occur more rapidly than in the experiential system.

The distinction between explicit and implicit attitudes discussed in a previous section parallels the distinction between controlled and spontaneous information processing systems. Indeed, some theorists (e.g., DeCoster, Banner, Smith, & Semin, 2006; Rydell, McConnell, Mackie, & Strain, 2006; T. D. Wilson et al., 2000) have argued that individuals can hold both explicit and implicit attitudes toward the same objects, attitudes that differ from each other and are perhaps stored in different brain regions. In this view, explicit attitudes are formed in an effortful manner as a result of reflection and logical connections that are forged between the attitude object and other constructs. Change in explicit attitudes can occur rapidly as new information becomes available and is assimilated by the individual. In contrast, implicit attitudes are acquired in a slow process whereby associations are formed between the attitude object and various attributes on the basis of similarity and contiguity. As is characteristic of the spontaneous system, such implicit attitudes are assumed to change only gradually by the same kinds of associative automatic processes. In light of these considerations, it seems reasonable to suggest that changes in explicit attitudes are best brought about by engaging individuals in a logical process of reasoning, whereas implicit attitudes can be changed gradually by creating new automatic associations to the attitude object (see Gawronski & Bodenhausen, 2006).

Explicit Attitudes and Persuasion

Persuasive communication involves the use of verbal messages to influence attitudes and behavior. Through a process of reasoning, communicators attempt to exert influence by force of the arguments contained in their messages. Scientific work on persuasive communication began in earnest during World War II in an attempt to determine the effects of wartime propaganda (Hovland, Lumsdaine, & Sheffield, 1949). This was followed by a period of intensive experimental research at Yale University in the 1950s under the direction of Carl Hovland (Hovland, Janis, & Kelley, 1953; Sherif & Hovland, 1961). Although it was extremely prolific and highly influential, the program of research initiated by the Hovland group produced very few generalizable conclusions. By the late 1960s, disappointment with this approach had become widespread (see Eagly & Himmerlfarb, 1974; Fishbein & Ajzen, 1975). As is usually the case, realizing where this approach went wrong is much easier in retrospect than it was at the time. Consistent with the dominant theoretical orientation at the time, Hovland and his associates adopted a learning theory framework. Perhaps without meaning to, they therefore cast the receiver in a rather passive role whose task was to learn the information and recommended position presented in a message. Attention and comprehension would assure that the information was absorbed, and persuasion would thus follow.

This view of the receiver flies in the face of much that is now known about controlled information processing (see Petty, Ostrom, & Brock, 1981). People are far from passive receivers of information (Bruner, 1973; Neisser, 1976). Research on impression formation, for example, has shown that people draw far-ranging inferences about the attributes of another person on the basis of very limited information (Asch, 1946; Wiggins, 1973). Similarly, it is possible to produce changes in beliefs by merely making people aware of inconsistencies among their beliefs or values (McGuire, 1960b; Rokeach, 1971) in a process McGuire termed the *Socratic effect*: After reviewing their beliefs, people tend to change some of them in the direction of increased logical consistency. Also, early lines of research demonstrated the potential importance of active information processing in the context of persuasive communication.

Thus it was shown that a persuasive communication designed to produce a change in one belief will lead to changes in other, related, beliefs (McGuire, 1960a; Wyer & Goldberg, 1970).

In short, there is every reason to expect that receivers of a persuasive communication can engage in an active process of deliberation that involves reviewing the information presented, accepting some arguments, rejecting others, and drawing inferences about issues addressed that go beyond the arguments in the original message. The image of the passive learner fostered in the Hovland tradition is thus highly misleading and misses the most important aspect of persuasive communication: the receiver's capacity for reasoning and for being swayed by the merits of a cogent argument.

Central Processing

Of course, for receivers to exert the effort involved in scrutinizing and evaluating the merits of arguments contained in a message they must be sufficiently motivated and have the cognitive capacity to do so. This is a central tenet of both Chaiken's heuristic-systematic model (Chaiken, 1980) and Petty and Cacioppo's elaboration likelihood model (ELM; Petty & Cacioppo, 1986). When receivers are motivated and able to process information, they are said to be operating in the systematic or central processing mode. According to the ELM, during exposure to a persuasive communication, receivers generate arguments of their own, either in support of the advocated position (pro arguments) or opposed to it (con arguments). These cognitive responses determine the direction and degree of change in attitudes. To the extent that the number of thoughts generated on the pro side exceeds the number of thoughts on the con side, the receiver will change in the advocated direction. When elaboration leads to the production of more unfavorable than favorable thoughts, however, either no change or a boomerang effect (change in the opposite direction) may occur. When receivers are operating in the central mode, therefore, an effective message must contain strong arguments, arguments that are likely to engender many supportive thoughts and few counterarguments. The change in attitudes produced in the central mode is expected to be lasting and resistant to counterpropaganda (see Petty & Cacioppo, 1986).

In an extensive program of research, Petty, Cacioppo, and their associates have provided strong evidence for the predictions derived from the ELM (see Petty & Wegener, 1999). For example, in an early investigation, Petty and Cacioppo (1979,

Experiment 2) demonstrated the effect of motivation to process message arguments on cognitive responses and attitude change. They exposed college students to one of two persuasive communications that advocated instituting a comprehensive exam as a prerequisite for graduation. One message contained strong, cogent arguments in support of the proposed policy, whereas the second message contained weak arguments. Furthermore, some of the participants were led to believe that the new policy would apply to them (high personal relevance) while others were told that the comprehensive exam was to be instituted at a remote university and would thus not apply to them (low personal relevance). High relevance was intended to generate motivation to elaborate on the message arguments. After listening to the message, participants were asked to list the thoughts they had while they were listening and to indicate their degree of agreement with the advocated policy. As expected, the strong message produced more favorable thoughts and fewer unfavorable thoughts than did the weak message, especially under conditions of high personal relevance. Moreover, consistent with this pattern of cognitive responses, the quality of the message (strong vs. weak) had a much greater effect on attitudes under high than under low relevance conditions. When personal relevance was high, the strong message resulted in more agreement with the advocated position than did the weak message; the effect of message strength had a much smaller effect when personal relevance was low.

Research in the context of the ELM has also provided evidence that central attitude change depends not only on motivation to process a persuasive communication but also on the recipients' cognitive capacity to do so. When ability to process information is reduced by means of distraction, strong messages tend to lose their effectiveness whereas weak messages can actually become more effective due to the receivers' reduced ability to elaborate on the (weak) message arguments (e.g., Petty, Wells, & Brock, 1976). Conversely, repeated exposure to the same message, which enables receivers to continue central processing of its arguments, tends to increase the effectiveness of a strong message while reducing the effectiveness of a weak message (Cacioppo & Petty, 1980).

Individual Differences
NEED FOR COGNITION
Personality or individual difference variables have played a relatively minor role in this research program.

According to the ELM, any personality trait that would predispose individuals to process a message more or less centrally could moderate the effect of the message. Thus, Cacioppo and Petty (1982) proposed that high need for cognition could serve to motivate receivers to engage in central message processing, and they developed a scale to assess this trait. Consistent with expectations, compared to individuals low in need for cognition, individuals who score high on this trait are found to engage in more issue-relevant thinking (Cacioppo, Petty, Kao, & Rodriguez, 1986), and their newly formed attitudes are more resistant to a countermessage (Haugtvedt & Petty, 1992) and more predictive of later behavior (Cacioppo, Petty, Kao, & Rodriguez, 1986).

ATTITUDE FUNCTIONS

The functional approach to attitude formation and change provides another perspective on the role of individual differences in persuasion. The functional approach is based on the assumption that attitudes fulfill certain psychological needs or serve certain motives (Herek, 1987; Katz, 1960; Maio & Olson, 2000; Smith, Bruner, & White, 1956). Among other needs, attitudes are said to have a *knowledge function* (explaining events and making sense of the world), a *utilitarian function* (helping the individual obtain rewards and avoid punishments), a *social adjustive function* (maintaining satisfactory relationships), a *value-expressive function* (expressing core values and important beliefs), and an *ego-defensive function* (protecting one's self-esteem). Importantly, the same attitude can serve different functions for different individuals, that is, different individuals may hold a given attitude for different reasons. It follows that a persuasive communication will be most effective if it is tailored to deal with the most important underlying function or functions served by the attitude.

The functional matching hypothesis has received considerable empirical support (e.g., Murray, Haddock, & Zanna, 1996; Shavitt, 1990; Snyder & DeBono, 1985; see Watt, Maio, Haddock, & Johnson, 2008 for a review). For instance, Clary, Snyder, Ridge, Miene, and Haugen (1994) first asked participants to rate the importance of a series of reasons for volunteering, corresponding to the social-adjustive function (building social relationships), knowledge function (learning useful skills), the utilitarian function (gaining prestige), the value-expressive function (value of helping others), and the ego-defensive function (being a good person). They then selected each participant's most and least

important function of volunteering and asked them to watch a videotaped appeal to engage in volunteering activities. In the functionally matched condition of the experiment, the message targeted the participant's most important function whereas in the mismatched condition, it targeted the least important function. Consistent with expectations, participants judged the functionally matched appeal to be more persuasive and emotionally appealing than the functionally mismatched appeal. Moreover, their intentions to volunteer were significantly higher following exposure to the matched as opposed to the mismatched appeal.

Relying on the elaboration likelihood model of persuasion, Petty and Wegener (1998) proposed that functionally matched messages may be more effective than mismatched messages because they motivate individuals to process the communication centrally. As such, receivers should be sensitive to both the strengths and to the weaknesses of a functionally matched communication. In one of their experiments, participants were indeed shown to be more sensitive to message strength in functionally matched as opposed to mismatched messages, suggesting that they processed the former more carefully than the latter. In a second experiment, the investigators found that this effect was more pronounced for participants low as opposed to high in need for cognition. In other words, the functionally matched communication apparently served to motivate central processing among low need-for-cognition individuals who are normally unlikely to engage in such processing. While demonstrating that matched messages can be more effective when they contain strong arguments (especially for recipients low in need for cognition), these studies also showed that a functionally matched message will tend to be less effective than a mismatched message if the message contains weak arguments. However, there is also evidence to suggest that functionally matched messages are perceived to contain better arguments and thus to enhance the overall effectiveness of the message (Lavine & Snyder, 1996).

Shallow/Heuristic Processing

Central or systematic processing is not the only way in which receivers can approach a persuasive communication. When they are either not sufficiently motivated to carefully scrutinize the contents of the message, or when they don't have the cognitive capacity to do so, they can rely instead on simple cognitive shortcuts or heuristics (Tversky & Kahneman, 1974). Thus, receivers can base acceptance of the

However, most attempts to change volitional behavior have relied on deliberative rather than automatic processes. When comparing automatic to deliberative processes, the elaboration likelihood model has important implications for behavior change. It suggests that modifications of attitude or behavior brought about by exposure to peripheral cues or by temporary priming of cognitive schemas will tend to dissipate quickly because these methods fail to bring about fundamental changes in cognitive structure. Peripheral or automatic influence processes are therefore unlikely to have a lasting effect on future behavior. In contrast, central processing is expected to produce a strong new attitude that persists over time and is thus available to influence later behavior (Petty & Cacioppo, 1986). Furthermore, research with the ELM has shown that central attitude change can be expected to occur only when the message contains strong arguments and receivers have the motivation and ability to systematically process these arguments.

However, in light of research on the attitude-behavior relation discussed in previous sections, we can expect that changing broad attitudes, such as attitudes toward African Americans, the handicapped, or the elderly, may well influence general patterns of behavior with respect to members of these groups, but not necessarily any particular behavior we might be interested in, such as employing an African American, a handicapped person, or an elderly individual. To effect changes in particular behaviors, investigators have found it useful to rely on theoretical frameworks that focus on the antecedents of individual behaviors, most notably the health-belief model (Rosenstock, 1966; Rosenstock, Strecher, & Becker, 1994), social cognitive theory (Bandura, 1977, 1997), the transtheoretical stage model of change (Prochaska & DiClemente, 1983), and the theory of planned behavior (Ajzen, 1991). Although they differ in specifics, there is much in common to these approaches in that they all adopt a reasoned action perspective. According to the health-belief model, people's decisions regarding the performance of particular health-protective behaviors take into account their perceived susceptibility or risk of contracting a given illness, perceptions of the severity of the illness, beliefs about the costs and benefits of performing the recommended health behavior, and perceived self-efficacy in relation to the behavior. Some of the same factors are invoked in protection-motivation theory (Rogers, 1975), the information-motivation-behavioral skills model (Fisher & Fisher, 1992), and the AIDS risk reduction model (Catania, Kegeles, & Coates, 1990).

Although social cognitive theory includes a consideration of outcome expectancies (see Bandura, 1997), its main focus is the concept of self-efficacy. As we saw earlier, there is good evidence to show that experimental manipulations of perceived self-efficacy can have strong and lasting effects on later behavior (see Bandura & Locke, 2003).

According to Prochaska and DiClementi's (1983; Prochaska & Norcross, 2002) transtheoretical model, behavior change involves five stages: *precontemplation, contemplation, preparation, action,* and *maintenance.* Prior to having formed any intention to change their behavior in the foreseeable future people are said to be in the precontemplation stage. Once they have formed an intention to do so but have not yet acted on their intention they are in the contemplation stage. When they reach the preparation stage, people begin to perform the behavior but they don't do so consistently. They move into the action stage when they start to engage in the behavior consistently. Finally, after performing the behavior consistently for several months, they are considered to be in the maintenance stage. Different processes are assumed to be involved in the transition from one stage to the next, with the implication that different intervention strategies are required at different stages. Among the critical factors that move people from stage to stage are decisional balance (the pros and cons of changing one's behavior) and self-efficacy (confidence in one's ability to change). However, empirical evidence has failed to support the hypothesis that a given process (e.g., development of high self-efficacy) is important only at a certain transition point. Although some processes seem to be more important at certain stages than at others, research suggests that all processes can influence behavior change to some degree throughout the sequential stages of change (Armitage & Arden, 2002; Armitage, Povey, & Arden, 2003; Courneya, 1995; de Vries & Backbier, 1994; see Fishbein & Ajzen, 2010 for a discussion).

Changing Intentions

Many of the variables and processes captured in the above models are also part of the theory of planned behavior (Ajzen, 1991) described earlier. In this theory, an important distinction is made between individuals who do not currently intend to perform a desired behavior and individuals who do intend to perform it but don't act on their intentions (see also Gollwitzer's [Gollwitzer & Bayer, 1999] distinction between deliberative versus implementational mindsets). In other words, Prochaska and DiClementi's (1983) five stages of change are reduced to two critical stages: Forming an intention to engage in a behavior and implementing the intention. Behavior change interventions can therefore be focused on producing intentions to engage in a desired behavior, or on implementing an existing intention to perform the behavior. Intention-focused interventions must produce changes in the behavioral, normative, and control beliefs that guide performance of the behavior. To accomplish this goal, interventions based on the TPB have used a variety of methods. Investigators have attempted to change intentions (and consequent behavior) by enrolling individuals in an intensive two-week workshop designed to change job-search strategies (Van Ryn & Vinokur, 1992), by introducing a prepaid bus ticket to encourage bus use (Bamberg, Ajzen, & Schmidt, 2003), by means of a short lecture delivered by a dental health educator to persuade mothers to limit their babies' sugar intake (Beale & Manstead, 1991), by placing a poster in student dormitories to encourage testicular self-examination (Brubaker & Wickersham, 1990), and by a variety of other intervention methods (see Hardeman et al., 2002 for a review).

To give just one example, Brubaker and Fowler (1990) conducted an intervention to encourage men to perform testicular self-examinations (TSE) for early detection of testicular cancer. In addition to testing the effectiveness of the intervention in terms of behavior change, the investigators collected information about changes in the theoretical determinants of this behavior. Male college students were exposed to a tape-recorded message based on the TPB that was designed to challenge unfavorable beliefs about performing TSE. Participants in a second condition of the experiment were exposed to a message of equal length that provided general information about testicular cancer, and participants in a control condition were encouraged to perform TSE but were not exposed to a persuasive communication. All participants then completed a questionnaire that assessed the TPB constructs: beliefs about TSE, attitudes toward performing TSE, subjective norms, perceptions of behavioral control, and intentions to perform TSE. Four weeks later, the participants reported whether they had performed TSE in the interim.

The results of the study demonstrated the effectiveness of the theory-based intervention. In the no-message control group, about 19 percent of the participants reported having performed TSE at the end of the four-week period. This compares with about 44 percent in the general information group and fully 71 percent in the theory-based message condition. A structural equation analysis confirmed the hypothesis that participants in the theory-based message condition were most likely to change their beliefs about performing TSE; that these changes in beliefs affected attitudes toward the behavior, subjective norms, and perceptions of behavioral control; and that changes in these three factors raised intentions to perform TSE which, in turn, led to the observed increase in reported testicular self-examination.

Implementation Intentions

Individuals fail to carry out existing intentions for any number of reasons (see Ajzen, 2002). Thus, they may procrastinate until it is too late or they may change their minds because of unanticipated difficulties or consequences. Also, when asked to explain why they failed to act on their intentions, people often mention that they simply forgot or that it slipped their minds (Orbell, Hodgkins, & Sheeran, 1997; Sheeran & Orbell, 1999). In those instances, a very effective means for closing the intention-behavior gap is to prompt people to formulate an implementation intention (Gollwitzer, 1999). Simply asking them when, where, and how they will carry out their intentions greatly increases the likelihood that they will do so. The beneficial effects of implementation intentions have been found with respect to such normal, everyday activities as completing a project during Christmas vacation (Gollwitzer & Brandstätter, 1997), taking a daily vitamin C pill (Sheeran & Orbell, 1999), and eating healthy food (Verplanken & Faes, 1999); as well as for disagreeable tasks, such as performing a breast self-examination (Orbell, Hodgkins, & Sheeran, 1997) and resuming functional activities following surgery (Orbell & Sheeran, 2000).

Summary and Conclusions

In this chapter I reviewed theory and research on internal dispositions and their effects on behavior. Internal dispositions can vary in generality from very broad personality traits and attitudes to dispositions defined narrowly in terms of a particular behavior, such as outcome expectancies, attitude toward the behavior, intentions, and habits. Broad dispositions can influence general patterns of behavior, but their influence on any individual behavior tends to be modest. However, internal dispositions are known to differ in terms of their accessibility or, more generally, in terms of their strength. The predictive validity of broad personality traits and general attitudes tends to increase with the strength of these dispositions.

of subjective perceptions of message quality. *Journal of Experimental Social Psychology, 32,* 580–604.

Linn, L. S. (1965). Verbal attitudes and overt behavior: A study of racial discrimination. *Social Forces, 43,* 353–364.

Litt, M. D. (1988). Self-efficacy and perceived control: Cognitive mediators of pain tolerance. *Journal of Personality and Social Psychology, 54,* 149–160.

Maio, G. R. E., & Olson, J. M. E. (Eds.). (2000). *Why we evaluate: Functions of attitudes.* Mahwah, NJ: Erlbaum.

Markey, P. M., Markey, C. N., & Tinsley, B. J. (2004). Children's behavioral manifestations of the five-factor model of personality. *Personality and Social Psychology Bulletin, 30,* 423–432.

Markus, H. (1977). Self-schemata and processing information about the self. *Journal of Personality and Social Psychology, 35,* 63–78.

McCrae, R. R., & John, O. P. (1992). An introduction to the five-factor model and its applications. *Journal of Personality, 60,* 175–215.

McGowan, J., & Gormly, J. (1976). Validation of personality traits: A multicriteria approach. *Journal of Personality and Social Psychology, 34,* 791–795.

McGuire, W. J. (1960a). Cognitive consistency and attitude change. *Journal of Abnormal and Social Psychology, 60,* 345–353.

McGuire, W. J. (1960b). A syllogistic analysis of cognitive relationships. In M. J. Rosenberg, C. I. Hovland, W. J. McGuire, R. P. Abelson, & J. W. Brehm (Eds.), *Attitude organization and change: An analysis of consistency among attitude components* (pp. 65–111). New Haven, CT: Yale University Press.

Milgram, S. (1963). Behavioral study of obedience. *Journal of Abnormal and Social Psychology, 67,* 371–378.

Mischel, W. (1968). *Personality and assessment.* New York: Wiley.

Mischel, W., & Peake, P. K. (1982). Beyond deja vu in the search for cross-situational consistency. *Psychological Review, 89,* 730–755.

Moreland, R. L., & Zajonc, R. B. (1977). Is stimulus recognition a necessary condition for the occurrence of exposure effects? *Journal of Personality and Social Psychology, 35,* 191–199.

Murray, S. L., Haddock, G., & Zanna, M. P. (1996). On creating value-expressive attitudes: An experimental approach. In C. Seligman, J. M. Olson, M. P. Zanna, C. E. Seligman, J. M. E. Olson, & M. P. E. Zanna (Eds.), *The psychology of values: The Ontario symposium* (Vol. 8, pp. 107–133). Hillsdale, NJ: Erlbaum.

Neisser, U. (1976). *Cognition and reality: Principles and implications of cognitive psychology.* San Francisco: Freeman.

Notani, A. S. (1998). Moderators of perceived behavioral control's predictiveness in the theory of planned behavior: A meta-analysis. *Journal of Consumer Psychology, 7,* 247–271.

Olson, M. A., & Fazio, R. H. (2001). Implicit attitude formation through classical conditioning. *Psychological Science, 12,* 413–417.

Olson, M. A., & Fazio, R. H. (2007). Discordant evaluations of blacks affect nonverbal behavior. *Personality and Social Psychology Bulletin, 33,* 1214–1224.

Olson, M. A., & Fazio, R. H. (2009). Implicit and explicit measures of attitude: The perspective of the MODE model. In R. E. Petty, R. H. Fazio, & P. Briñol (Eds.), *Attitudes: Insights for the new implicit measures* (pp. 19–63). New York: Psychology Press.

Orbell, S., Hodgkins, S., & Sheeran, P. (1997). Implementation intentions and the theory of planned behavior. *Personality and Social Psychology Bulletin, 23,* 945–954.

Orbell, S., & Sheeran, P. (2000). Motivational and volitional processes in action initiation: A field study of the role of implementation intentions. *Journal of Applied Social Psychology, 30,* 780–797.

Osgood, C. E., Suci, G. J., & Tannenbaum, P. H. (1957). *The measurement of meaning.* Urbana: University of Illinois Press.

Ouellette, J. A., & Wood, W. (1998). Habit and intention in everyday life: The multiple processes by which past behavior predicts future behavior. *Psychological Bulletin, 124,* 54–74.

Page, M. M. (1969). Social psychology of a classical conditioning of attitudes experiment. *Journal of Personality and Social Psychology, 11,* 177–186.

Paunonen, S. V. (2003). Big Five factors of personality and replicated predictions of behavior. *Journal of Personality and Social Psychology, 84,* 411–422.

Peak, H. (1955). Attitude and motivation. In M. R. Jones (Ed.), *Nebraska symposium on motivation* (Vol. 3, pp. 149–189). Lincoln: University of Nebraska Press.

Petkova, K. G., Ajzen, I., & Driver, B. L. (1995). Salience of anti-abortion beliefs and commitment to an attitudinal position: On the strength, structure, and predictive validity of anti-abortion attitudes. *Journal of Applied Social Psychology, 25,* 463–483.

Petty, R. E., & Cacioppo, J. T. (1979). Issue involvement can increase or decrease persuasion by enhancing message-relevant cognitive responses. *Journal of Personality and Social Psychology, 37,* 1915–1926.

Petty, R. E., & Cacioppo, J. T. (1981). *Attitudes and persuasion: Classic and contemporary approaches.* Dubuque, IA: Brown.

Petty, R. E., & Cacioppo, J. T. (1986). *Communication and persuasion: Central and peripheral routes to attitude change.* New York: Springer Verlag.

Petty, R. E., Cacioppo, J. T., & Goldman, R. (1981). Personal involvement as a determinant of argument-based persuasion. *Journal of Personality and Social Psychology, 41,* 847–855.

Petty, R. E., Fazio, R. H., & Briñol, P. (2009). The new implicit measures. In R. E. Petty, R. H. Fazio, & P. Briñol (Eds.), *Attitudes: Insights from the new implicit measures* (pp. 3–18). New York: Psychology Press.

Petty, R. E., Ostrom, T. M., & Brock, T. C. (Eds.). (1981). *Cognitive responses in persuasion.* Hillsdale, NJ: Erlbaum.

Petty, R. E., & Wegener, D. T. (1998). Matching versus mismatching attitude functions: Implications for scrutiny of persuasive messages. *Personality and Social Psychology Bulletin, 24,* 227–240.

Petty, R. E., & Wegener, D. T. (1999). The elaboration likelihood model: Current status and controversies. In S. Chaiken & Y. Trope (Eds.), *Dual-process theories in social psychology.* (pp. 41–72). New York: Guilford.

Petty, R. E., Wells, G. L., & Brock, T. C. (1976). Distraction can enhance or reduce yielding to propaganda: Thought disruption versus effort justification. *Journal of Personality and Social Psychology, 34,* 874–884.

Pleyers, G., Corneille, O., Luminet, O., & Yzerbyt, V. (2007). Aware and (dis)liking: Item-based analyses reveal that valence acquisition via evaluative conditioning emerges only when there is contingency awareness. *Journal of Experimental Psychology: Learning, Memory, and Cognition, 33,* 130–144.

Powell, M. C., & Fazio, R. H. (1984). Attitude accessibility as a function of repeated attitudinal expression. *Personality and Social Psychology Bulletin, 10,* 139–148.

Prochaska, J. O., & DiClemente, C. C. (1983). Stages and processes of self-change of smoking: Toward an integrative model of change. *Journal of Consulting and Clinical Psychology, 51*, 390–395.

Prochaska, J. O., & Norcross, J. C. (2002). Stages of change. In J. C. Norcross (Ed.), *Psychotherapy relationships that work: Therapist contributions and responsiveness to patients* (pp. 303–313). New York: Oxford University Press.

Raden, D. (1985). Strength-related attitude dimensions. *Social Psychology Quarterly, 48*, 312–330.

Randall, D. M., & Wolff, J. A. (1994). The time interval in the intention-behaviour relationship: Meta-analysis. *British Journal of Social Psychology, 33*, 405–418.

Regan, D. T., & Fazio, R. H. (1977). On the consistency between attitudes and behavior: Look to the method of attitude formation. *Journal of Experimental Social Psychology, 13*, 28–45.

Richeson, J. A., & Ambady, N. (2003). Effects of situational power on automatic racial prejudice. *Journal of Experimental Social Psychology, 39*, 177–183.

Rivis, A., & Sheeran, P. (2003). Social influences and the theory of planned behaviour: Evidence for a direct relationship between prototypes and young people's exercise behaviour. *Psychology and Health, 18*, 567–583.

Roese, N. J., & Olson, J. M. (1994). Attitude importance as a function of repeated attitude expression. *Journal of Experimental Social Psychology, 30*, 39–51.

Rokeach, M. (1971). Long-range experimental modification of values, attitudes, and behavior. *American Psychologist, 26*, 453–459.

Rogers, R. W. (1975). A protection motivation theory of fear appeals and attitude change. *Journal of Psychology, 91*, 93–114.

Rosenstock, I. (1966). Why people use health services. *Milbank Memorial Fund Quarterly, 44*, 94–124.

Rosenstock, I. M., Strecher, V. J., & Becker, M. H. (1994). The health belief model and HIV risk behavior change. In R. J. DiClemente & J. L. Peterson (Eds.), *Preventing AIDS: Theories and methods of behavioral interventions. AIDS prevention and mental health* (pp. 5–24). New York: Plenum.

Rydell, R. J., McConnell, A. R., Mackie, D. M., & Strain, L. M. (2006). Of two minds: Forming and changing valence-inconsistent implicit and explicit attitudes. *Psychological Science, 17*, 954–958.

Sandberg, T., & Conner, M. (2008). Anticipated regret as an additional predictor in the theory of planned behavior: A meta-analysis. *British Journal of Social Psychology, 47*, 589–606.

Sample, J., & Warland, R. (1973). Attitude and prediction of behavior. *Social Forces, 51*, 292–304.

Scheier, M. F., Buss, A. H., & Buss, D. M. (1978). Self-consciousness, self-report of aggressiveness, and aggression. *Journal of Research in Personality, 12*, 133–140.

Schulze, R., & Wittmann, W. W. (2003). A meta-analysis of the theory of reasoned action and the theory of planned behavior: The principle of compatibility and multidimensionality of beliefs as moderators. In R. Schulze, H. Holling, & D. Böhning (Eds.), *Meta-analysis: New developments and applications in medical and social sciences.* (pp. 219–250). Cambridge, MA: Hogrefe & Huber Publishers.

Schuman, H., & Johnson, M. P. (1976). Attitudes and behavior. *Annual Review of Sociology, 2*, 161–207.

Schütz, H., & Six, B. (1996). How strong is the relationship between prejudice and discrimination? A meta-analytic answer. *International Journal of Intercultural Relations, 20*, 441–462.

Shavitt, S. (1990). The role of attitude objects in attitude functions. *Journal of Experimental Social Psychology, 26*, 124–148.

Sheeran, P. (2002). Intention-behavior relations: A conceptual and empirical review. In W. Stroebe & M. Hewstone (Eds.), *European review of social psychology* (Vol. 12, pp. 1–36). Chichester, UK: Wiley.

Sheeran, P., & Orbell, S. (1998). Do intentions predict condom use? Meta-analysis and examination of six moderator variables. *British Journal of Social Psychology, 37*, 231–250.

Sheeran, P., & Orbell, S. (1999). Implementation intentions and repeated behaviour: Augmenting the predictive validity of the theory of planned behaviour. *European Journal of Social Psychology, 29*, 349–369.

Sheeran, P., & Taylor, S. (1999). Predicting intentions to use condoms: A meta-analysis and comparison of the theories of reasoned action and planned behavior. *Journal of Applied Social Psychology, 29*, 1624–1675.

Sheppard, B. H., Hartwick, J., & Warshaw, P. R. (1988). The theory of reasoned action: A meta-analysis of past research with recommendations for modifications and future research. *Journal of Consumer Research, 15*, 325–342.

Sherif, M., & Hovland, C. I. (1961). *Social judgment: Assimilation and contrast effects in communication and attitude change.* New Haven, CT: Yale University Press.

Sivacek, J., & Crano, W. D. (1982). Vested interest as a moderator of attitude-behavior consistency. *Journal of Personality and Social Psychology, 43*, 210–221.

Sloman, S. A. (1996). The empirical case for two systems of reasoning. *Psychological Bulletin, 119*, 3–22.

Smith, E. R., & DeCoster, J. (2000). Dual-process models in social and cognitive psychology: Conceptual integration and links to underlying memory systems. *Personality and Social Psychology Review, 4*, 108–131.

Smith, M. B., Bruner, J., & White, R. (1956). *Opinions and personality.* New York: Wiley.

Snyder, M. (1974). Self-monitoring of expressive behavior. *Journal of Personality and Social Psychology, 30*, 526–537.

Snyder, M., & DeBono, K. G. (1985). Appeals to image and claims about quality: Understanding the psychology of advertising. *Journal of Personality and Social Psychology, 49*, 586–597.

Staats, A. W., & Staats, C. K. (1958). Attitudes established by classical conditioning. *Journal of Abnormal and Social Psychology, 57*, 37–40.

Strack, F., & Deutsch, R. (2004). Reflective and impulsive determinants of social behavior. *Personality and Social Psychology Review, 8*, 220–247.

Talaska, C. A., Fiske, S. T., & Chaiken, S. (2008). Legitimating racial discrimination: Emotions, not beliefs, best predict discrimination in a meta-analysis. *Social Justice Research, 21*, 263–296.

Tversky, A., & Kahneman, D. (1974). Judgment under uncertainty: Heuristics and biases. *Science, 185*, 1124–1131.

van den Putte, B. (1993). *On the theory of reasoned action.* Unpublished dissertation, University of Amsterdam, The Netherlands.

van der Pligt, J., & Eiser, J. R. (1984). Dimensional salience, judgment, and attitudes. In J. R. Eiser (Ed.), *Attitudinal judgment* (pp. 43–63). New York: Springer-Verlag.

Van Ryn, M., & Vinokur, A. D. (1992). How did it work? An examination of the mechanisms through which an intervention for the unemployed promoted job-search behavior. *American Journal of Community Psychology, 20*, 577–597.

Verplanken, B. (2006). Beyond frequency: Habit as mental construct. *British Journal of Social Psychology, 45,* 639–656.

Verplanken, B., & Orbell, S. (2003). Reflections on past behavior: A self-report index of habit strength. *Journal of Applied Social Psychology, 33,* 1313–1330.

Verplanken, B., & Faes, S. (1999). Good intentions, bad habits, and effects of forming implementation intentions on healthy eating. *European Journal of Social Psychology, 29,* 591–604.

Vroom, V. H. (1964). *Work and motivation.* New York: Wiley.

Watt, S. E., Maio, G. R., Haddock, G., & Johnson, B. T. (2008). Attitude functions in persuasion: Matching, involvement, self-affirmation, and hierarchy. In W. D. Crano & R. Prislin (Eds.), *Attitudes and attitude change* (pp. 189–211). New York: Psychology Press.

Webb, T. L., & Sheeran, P. (2003). Can implementation intentions help to overcome ego-depletion? *Journal of Experimental Social Psychology, 39,* 279–286.

Weigel, R. H., & Newman, L. S. (1976). Increasing attitude-behavior correspondence by broadening the scope of the behavioral measure. *Journal of Personality and Social Psychology, 33,* 793–802.

Weinberg, R. S., Gould, D., Yukelson, D., & Jackson, A. (1981). The effect of preexisting and manipulated self-efficacy on a competitive muscular endurance task. *Journal of Sport Psychology, 3,* 345–354.

Werner, P. D. (1978). Personality and attitude-activism correspondence. *Journal of Personality and Social Psychology, 36,* 1375–1390.

Wicker, A. W. (1969). Attitudes versus actions: The relationship of verbal and overt behavioral responses to attitude objects. *Journal of Social Issues, 25,* 41–78.

Wicker, A. W., & Pomazal, R. J. (1971). The relationship between attitudes and behavior as a function of specificity of attitude object and presence of a significant person during assessment conditions. *Representative Research in Social Psychology, 2,* 26–31.

Wiggins, J. S. (1973). *Personality and prediction: Principles of personality assessment.* Reading, MA: Addison-Wesley.

Wilson, T. D., Lindsey, S., & Schooler, T. Y. (2000). A model of dual attitudes. *Psychological Review, 107,* 101–126.

Wilson, W. R. (1979). Feeling more than we can know: Exposure effects without learning. *Journal of Personality and Social Psychology, 37,* 811–821.

Wyer, R. S. J., & Goldberg, L. (1970). A probabilistic analysis of the relationships among belief and attitudes. *Psychological Review, 77,* 100–120.

Zajonc, R. B. (1968). Attitudinal effects of mere exposure. *Journal of Personality and Social Psychology, 9,* 1–27.

Zedeck, S. (1971). Problems with the use of "moderator" variables. *Psychological Bulletin, 76,* 295–310.

From Help-Giving to Helping Relations
Belongingness and Independence in Social Interaction

Arie Nadler

Abstract

This chapter surveys social psychological research on help-giving and helping relations from the 1950s until today. The first section reviews research on help-giving and considers the conditions under which people are likely to help others: The personality dispositions that characterize helpful individuals and the motivational and attributional antecedents of helpfulness. The second section reviews research on helping relations, which transcends the help-giving perspective by looking at the long-term consequences of help on helpers and receivers and by examining help in the context of enduring and emotionally significant relationships, such as in families, communities, and organizations. Research on helping relations has shown that because independence is key to positive personal and collective identity, people are often reluctant to seek or receive needed help, and that in the long term, help can increase psychological and physical well-being for helpers but can discourage self-reliance for recipients. The third section analyzes helping from an intra- and intergroup perspective, considering how the provision of help can advance helpers' reputations within a group or promote positive social identity of ingroups relative to outgroups. Help is conceptualized as a negotiation between the fundamental psychological needs for belongingness and independence. Conceptual and applied implications are discussed.

Keywords: help-giving, helping relations, help-seeking, reactions to help, belongingness, independence, interpersonal relations, intergroup relations, coping, interactive effects of personality and situation variables on behavior

Past Themes and Present Emphases

Helping others is a universal social phenomenon across time and cultures (Hunt, 1990). In spite (or maybe because) of this it has embodied an enigma for generations of scholars trying to reconcile helping with the basic motivations for self-preservation and self-reward (Cronin, 1991). Thinkers like Rousseau and Maslow suggested that people help because they are *innately* good; Hobbes and Freud held that people help in spite of their egotistic nature because *society* compels them to do so; and Locke and Skinner held the morally neutral position that people *learn* to be selfish or generous to others (de Waal, 2009).

The history of empirical research on the social psychology of helping, which is the focus of the present chapter, is more recent, beginning in the 1960s with Darley and Latané's work on bystander intervention (1968, 1970). It has since grown to encompass an independent field of social psychological research, pursued under three different terms: prosocial behavior, altruism, and helping. Research on *prosocial behavior* attends to positive social interaction in the broadest sense, including such behaviors as cooperation, emergency intervention, and philanthropy (e.g., Dovidio, Piliavin, Schroeder, & Penner, 2006). *Altruism* research centers on self-sacrificial acts to save others in extreme situations (Oliner & Oliner, 1988), or to any acts carried out with the intention of benefiting another (Aronson, Wilson, & Akert, 2004; Batson, 1991). *Helping* research examines the provision of aid in situations that may or may not be life-threatening, through acts that may or may not be motivated by the intention to benefit another (McGuire, 1994). "Helping" does not imply self-sacrifice or totality in the correspondence of behavior with emotion and motivation. Because the present chapter emphasizes the multicausal nature of helping and the different levels at which helping relations play out, the term *helping* rather than *prosocial behavior* or *altruism* is used.

Reviews of social psychological research on helping have been guided by diverse approaches. Batson (1998) surveyed help-giving research according to the different theoretical lenses through which helping propensities can be understood, for example, social learning or attributional theory. Penner, Dovidio, Piliavin, and Schroeder (2005) organized their review of helping according to scales of research and analysis: micro (individual variation in prosocial tendencies), meso (helping at the interpersonal level), and macro (helping within groups and large organizations). Piliavin (2009) considered the field via the central questions that have guided research on help-giving, such as the origins of altruism and whether altruism can be learned. These and other reviews principally cast helping as *agential behavior*, asking why and when some people offer help to others in need. The present chapter extends this perspective to consider questions of *helping relations*: How helping constitutes relationships between help-givers and help-receivers and how both sides are changed by the helping interaction.

Helping relations departs from the help-giving perspective with respect to the *aims, scale,* and *context* of helping research. Help-giving studies aim to explain and predict people's willingness to help others, whereas the helping relations perspective seeks to examine both the psychological processes leading up to a helping exchange (e.g., willingness to seek help; Nadler, 1991), and posthelp consequences for both the help-giver (e.g., well-being; Brown et al., 2009) and recipient (e.g., dependence; Nadler & Fisher, 1986). While help-giving research centers on helping at the *interpersonal* level, helping relations also attends to helping between *groups* with different relational characteristics (e.g., advantaged vs. disadvantaged groups; Nadler, 2002). Finally, for the most part, research on help-giving examines helping in the context of relatively short-lived social interactions between strangers. Research on helping relations has added the considerations of seeking, giving, and receiving help in relatively *enduring* (e.g., organizational), and *emotionally significant* (e.g., familial) social contexts.

The duality of help-giving and helping relations brings the insight that helping relations bear on two fundamental, and often conflicting, psychological needs: the need for belongingness (Baumeister & Leary, 1995) and the need for independence (Jordan, 1997). Belongingness constitutes the psychological glue that connects people in meaningful interpersonal relations and is the basis of the social solidarity that makes group life possible (Reicher & Haslam, 2009). At the same time, psychology views independence as a basic human motivation and as a marker of successful development (Rogoff, 2003). Further, independent achievements warrant elevated status in groups, while dependence elicits negative appraisals by self and others (Van Vugt & van Lange, 2006; Flynn, 2003). Helping contexts draw a tension between these two fundamental needs. While the motivation for belongingness drives helpfulness and reliance, the motivation for independence inhibits willingness to seek and receive help. These two needs and the tension that binds them is the psychological arena of the present chapter.

The situationist approach to social behavior dominated social psychology in the 1960s and 1970s, when the field of helping research began to take shape. Empirical disappointment with personality dispositions as predictors of social behavior generally (Mischel, 1968) and of help-giving in particular (e.g., Gergen, Gergen, & Meter, 1972) brought researchers, for the most part, to dismiss the explanatory value of personal characteristics. In more recent years the negative appraisal of personality variables in explaining social behavior has been revisited (Mischel, 2004), including with regard to helping (Graziano & Eisenberg, 1997). It is now commonly accepted that social behavior is best explained as the combined product of personality and situational variables rather than the deterministic outcome of one or the other (Penner, 2002).

Consistent with this change, which is reflected in the overall theme of the present volume, we emphasize the interaction between personal characteristics and situational variables in explaining and predicting help-giving and helping relations. These include situational fluctuations in the experience of belongingness and hence concern for others (e.g., when the person in need is viewed as similar), and personal variation in the inclination to feel and act accordingly (e.g., dispositional empathy). Similarly, certain conditions can inhibit or intensify the desire for self-reliance, thus affecting receptiveness to help (e.g., when help reflects on an ego-central dimension), particular with respect to variability in the desire for independence (e.g., individual differences in self-esteem).

The first part of the present chapter focuses on help-giving. At the center of this research are three questions: When do people help? Who helps? and Why do people help? (see also Dovidio et al., 2006). Research on the question of *when* people help has sought to identify the situational and normative factors that predict when people will help others; research on the question of *who* helps has centered on portraiture of the "altruistic personality" and its antecedents; and research on the question of *why* people help has examined the attributional processes implicated in helping and whether the motivation to help is characteristically empathic as opposed to egoistic.

The second part of this review considers research on help-seeking, and the consequences of helping for both helper and recipient in interpersonal and intergroup relations. It concludes with an overview of helping relations in enduring and emotionally significant social contexts. The final section considers applied and conceptual implications of this review and focuses on how tension between the needs for belongingness and independence can be weaved to create socially meaningful and individually empowering helping relations.

Help-Giving Research
When Do People Help? Situations and Norms
SITUATIONAL DETERMINANTS
Almost all textbooks in social psychology attribute the initiation of helping research to the fatal stabbing of Kitty Genovese in Queens, New York, in 1964, while 38 bystanders watched behind their windows. The Genovese case encapsulated horror over apathy to human suffering at a time when cultural values of conformity and social order were being reevaluated, and it implied that the invisible strings of social connection were fraying in the modern world. The Genovese murder was a lens through which social psychologists of the time tried to glimpse a sharper understanding of social behavior, and by which to demonstrate the relevance of social psychology to bettering society.

In their classic work on bystander intervention Darley & Latané (1968) proposed that intervention

was an outcome of a sequential decision-making process in which the bystander must (1) notice the event, (2) interpret it as an emergency, (3) assume responsibility to intervene, (4) decide how to do so, and (5) act. Failure to notice, interpret, or assume responsibility was said to produce failure to intervene. Consistent with this model, subsequent researchers found that people witnessing an emergency intervened less frequently when their attention was distracted by extraneous stimuli (Mathews & Cannon, 1975) or by a pressing assignment (Darley & Batson, 1973). Milgram (1970) suggested that the hyperstimulation of urban life reduced urbanites' willingness to help each other compared to residents of smaller towns and rural areas, an interpretation supported in a comparison of helping behavior in small, medium, and large American cities by Levine, Martinez, Brase, and Sorenson (1994), and of low- versus high-density living arrangements in Israeli dorms (Nadler, Bar-Tal, & Drukman, 1982; cf. Steblay, 1987, for a review of rural vs. urban differences in helping).

Once an event has been noticed, the manner in which others respond can ambiguate or disambiguate its *interpretation* as an emergency. For example, all bystanders intervened when a confederate said in response to a sound of crash, "This sounds serious," as opposed to only 25% of bystanders in a control condition (Staub, 1974). Spontaneous communication, and hence intervention, in an emergency is higher when participants sit facing each other (Darley, Lewis, & Teger, 1973) and when they are prior friends rather than strangers (Rutkowski, Gruder, & Romer, 1983).

Once a situation has been correctly identified as an emergency, bystanders will intervene if they *assume responsibility* to act. If other bystanders are present responsibility may be diffused, reducing the probability of intervention by any one participant singly. However, if there is a physical reason why other bystanders cannot intervene, such as blindness, responsibility is not diffused and intervention is more likely (Ross & Braband, 1973). Imagining oneself to be among an anonymous group is sufficient to reduce one's personal responsibility and subsequent willingness to help. In an experiment by Garcia, Weaver, Moskowitz, and Darley (2002), participants who were asked to imagine themselves in a social situation with a friend were more likely to display generosity in an unrelated subsequent context (volunteering their time to help another experimenter) than those who had been asked to imagine themselves in the equivalent social situation while in the midst of a large crowd.

Another early model of helping conceives the likelihood of direct versus indirect intervention according to the relative costs of helping or not helping (Piliavin, Dovidio, Gaertner, & Clark, 1981). Intervention involves personal risk and investing resources, whereas nonintervention entails an emotional cost such as guilt. If costs for not helping are high (e.g., a person's life is threatened with a knife) and the costs for helping are low (e.g., the bystander has a gun) direct intervention is likely. If the costs for helping are also high (e.g., the bystander is unarmed) indirect intervention is more likely (e.g., calling the police).

Research on bystander intervention, like research on conformity and obedience, faults groups for their capacity to unhinge individual bonds of solidarity and care (Zimbardo, 1969). Yet, neither empirical research (e.g., Rutkowski et al., 1983; Schwartz & Gottlieb, 1976) nor a reanalysis of the Kitty Genovese case (Manning, Levine, & Collins, 2007) warrants such a whole-hog conclusion. It depends on the nature of the group. The presence of others can be deleterious when bystanders don't know each other or when interaction between them is inhibited. When group members feel belongingness through shared social identity, the presence of other group members facilitates intervention. For example, Levine, Cassidy, Brazier, and Reicher (2002) found that observers were more likely to stop a violent fight when ingroup members suggested taking such a course of action, or intervened themselves (Levine & Crowther, 2008).

NORMATIVE INFLUENCES

Social norms outline what people should or should not do in social situations (Higgins & Spiegel, 2004), and can be *situation-specific*, *general*, or *personal*. A *situation-specific* norm, such as an instruction, addresses social expectations in a particular scenario, and may either promote or inhibit helping; for example, children who have been told that they may leave the room to obtain pencils are twice as likely to intervene in an emergency occurring outside of their room than those who have not been so told (Staub, 1971). A *general norm* guides behavior across a wide range of social situations. Here, two such norms are relevant for help-giving. The norm of *reciprocity* dictates that people should help those who help them in like proportion (Gouldner, 1960). In spite of its cross-cultural applicability (Gergen, Ellsworth, Maslach, & Seipel, 1975), the norm of reciprocity applies differently to exchange relations (e.g., relations at work) than to communal relations (e.g., relations between family members or close friends; Clark & Mills, 1993). In communal relations people tend to help according to need, regardless of whether they have received help from the beneficiary in the past. In exchange relations people tend to give in like proportion to what they get. These norms are not interchangeable. For example, monetary payment defines exchange relationships and is thus an unacceptable reward for help exchanged between close neighbors (Webley & Lea, 1993).

A second general norm that is relevant to help-giving is that of *social responsibility*, by which people are expected to help those who depend on them (Berkowitz, 1972). Evidence for the predictive power of this norm is mixed, possibly because it is both general and specific at the same time (Batson, 1998) and thus varies across situations (Latané & Darley, 1970); for example, parents are generally expected to help their own children, but the extent they will do so depends on the child's assumed mastery of the task at hand.

Whereas general norms such as reciprocity encompass broad expectations about the behavior appropriate to a variety of social situations, *personal norms* guide the behavior of a specific individual in a given situation. Personal norms reflect one's values and moral standards (Schwartz & Howard, 1984). As such, personal norms bridge between the general social norm that applies to all people (e.g., all individuals should help those who helped them) and the personal norm-based tendency to act in a particular way in a unique instance. For example, people who are morally committed to the environment are more willing to recycle but not necessarily more willing to donate blood (Hopper, 1991; Schwartz & Howard, 1982). Conceptually relevant personality dispositions determine the degree to which personal norms will have an effect on helping. The predictive power of personal norms on helping is higher for people who have a dispositional tendency to act in line with their beliefs (Schwartz & Howard, 1982).

Who Helps? Developmental Antecedents and Personal Dispositions

While early research on help-giving dismissed the predictive value of personality characteristics, more recent studies indicate that this exclusion has been premature (Graziano & Eisenberg, 1997). For example, a longitudinal study by Eisenberg et al.

(2002) reported that indices of preschool sharing were positively related to prosocial tendencies in young adults, indicating the stability of individual differences in the inclination to help others. Research on individual variation in willingness to help has centered on the *developmental, demographic,* and *personality* antecedents of helping.

DEVELOPMENTAL ANTECEDENTS

Developmental research indicates that helpfulness has biological and social antecedents. On hearing the audiotaped crying of a newborn, one-day-old babies respond by crying in what appears to be "empathic" distress (Martin & Clark, 1982); this suggests that empathic reaction to others' pain is, at least in part, biologically determined. Twin studies indicate that 25–50% of the variance in helpfulness is genetically determined (Robinson, Zahn-Waxler, & Emde, 2001; Rushton, Fulker, Neale, Nias, & Eysenck, 1986). Physiological studies have linked empathy to increased activity in the middle insula and the medial and lateral premotor areas of the brain (Lamm, Batson, & Decety, 2007), and to heightened levels of the hormone oxytocin (Zak, Stanton, & Ahmadi, 2007).

Parental socialization and the modeling of social behavior seem to foster helpfulness in childhood. Europeans who sheltered Jews under the Nazi regime (London, 1970; Oliner & Oliner, 1988) and whites who made personal sacrifices to advance the U.S. civil rights movement (Rosenhan, 1970) remember their parents as being emotionally warm people who emphasized commitment to moral values. Parents to helpful children use inductive, rather than punitive, socialization techniques— explaining why a certain behavior is wrong and emphasizing its effects on others. These socialization practices engage the child in moral reasoning and perspective-taking, both of which are well established in promoting helping (Bar-Tal & Raviv, 1982; Eisenberg & Fabes, 1991).

Social modeling also encourages helpfulness (Bandura, 1977). Children who observed someone demonstrate generosity donated more than those who observed a nongenerous model (Rushton, 1975), and adults who saw someone help a stranded motorist were more helpful than those who did not (e.g., Bryan & Test, 1967). Exposure to virtual helping via films and electronic media also affects responsiveness to the needs of others. For example, six-year-old children who watched a rescue scene from the movie *Lassie* were more likely to stop playing a game in order to comfort a distressed animal

than children in control groups (Sprafkin, Liebert, & Poulous, 1975). On the other hand, exposure to violent behavior reduces willingness to help others (Anderson & Bushman, 2001) and desensitizes people to others' need for help (Bushman & Anderson, 2009). For example, individuals who had been exposed to videotaped violence were later less likely to report that they had heard a fight in an adjoining room or to view the fight as serious, and were less likely to help a person using crutches, than those who had not been similarly exposed (Bushman & Anderson, 2009). The question of how repeated exposures to violence influence helpfulness as an enduring propensity remains open. Posing it directs attention to the personal characteristics that are related to helpfulness.

INDIVIDUAL CHARACTERISTICS: GENDER AND PERSONALITY

Gender

In general, men are more likely than women to intervene in emergencies that pose physical danger, and women are more likely than men to help in situations that require long-term care and emotional support (Becker & Eagley, 2004), a variation that has been interpreted on physiological, social, and evolutionary grounds. The *physiological* explanation attributes men's greater willingness to intervene in dangerous situations to the greater physical strength of the average man (Piliavin & Unger, 1985). The *social* explanation attributes these differences to gendered expectations that women express nurturance and that men exhibit courage and risk-taking (Eagly & Crowley, 1986); the *evolutionary* view posits that reproductive success is promoted by aggressive behavior by men and nurturant behavior by women (Buss, 1995).

The "Altruistic Personality"

Penner and Finkelstein (1998) define the prosocial personality as reflecting a stable and enduring tendency to "*think. . . feel. . .* and *act* in a way that benefits" others (emphases added; p. 526). This suggests that dispositional helpfulness represents a cluster of affective, behavioral, and cognitive characteristics. Recent research supports this *tripartite view* of the helpful personality. Other-oriented dispositional empathy is a key affective characteristic of the helpful person (Davis, 1983). This quality predicts heroic helping in extreme situations (Midlarsky, Jones, & Corley, 2005; Oliner & Oliner, 1988), and sustained volunteering (Penner & Finkelstein, 1998). Agreeableness, a dimension of the five-factor model of personality (Costa & McCrae, 1985), is associated with "altruism, nurturance, and emotional support" (Digman, 1990, p. 422) and is highly correlated with dispositional empathy (Graziano, Habashi, Sheese, & Tobin, 2007). It also predicts help-giving in laboratory studies (Graziano et al., 2007) and willingness to volunteer (Carlo, Okun, Knight, & de Guzman, 2005) and donate blood (Ferguson, 2004).

In the behavioral dimension, helpful individuals score higher not only on agreeableness but also on conscientiousness (Graziano & Tobin, 2002; King, George, & Hebl, 2005), a dispositional tendency for efficient, planned, and goal-organized behavior (McCrae & John, 1992). On a 56-item helping inventory developed by Penner, Fritzsche, Craiger, and Freifeld (1995), higher scorers loaded on an affective factor of other-oriented empathy, as well as on a behavioral factor of acting in a helpful way (i.e., "helpfulness"). With respect to the cognitive dimension, helpful individuals evidence high commitment to general moral values. For example, Europeans who saved Jews under the Nazi regime believed that their responsibility for the fate of the less fortunate extended beyond the boundaries of the ingroup (i.e., "extensivity"; Oliner & Oliner, 1988).

The predictive utility of personality dispositions depends on the helping situation. In life-threatening emergencies, especially when the person in need is a family member or a close friend, most people will help regardless of their scores on one or another personality scale. In support of this Graziano et al. (2007) found that scores on agreeableness had no predictive value in a situation that was life-threatening to one's good friend or sibling, but were predictive when helping involved doing a simple favor. This may explain why bystander research, which studies relatively extreme social situations, has not found effects for personality dispositions.

Why Help? Motivational and Attributional Processes

The question of *why* people help brings to light the intrapsychological processes that underlie help-giving. This research has pivoted on two themes: The relation of help to empathy, and the role of causal attributions in responding to the need for help.

MOTIVATION: ALTRUISM OR DISGUISED EGOISM?

The most common explanation for why people help is the empathy-altruism hypothesis (Batson,

1991)—that need evokes empathic arousal, which then motivates the potential helper to "benefit the person for whom the empathy is felt" (Batson, 1998, p. 300). Although much research has substantiated the link between empathy and help-giving (e.g., Batson, Duncan, Ackerman, Buckley, & Birch, 1981; Batson et al., 1991; see also Castano, chapter 17, this volume), the altruistic interpretation has been challenged. The alternative positions hold that all giving is selfishly motivated: "Scratch an altruist and watch a hypocrite bleed" (Ghiselin, 1974, p. 247).

An egoistic alternative, the "aversive-arousal reduction" hypothesis, is that help is a learned behavior that ameliorates the dysphoria occasioned by others' distress (Cialdini, Darby, & Vincent, 1973; Schaller & Cialdini, 1988; Yinon & Landau, 1987). To pit the empathy-altruism hypothesis against the aversive-arousal reduction hypothesis, Batson et al. (1981) created the "physical escape" experimental paradigm, which gave participants the option of responding to another's distress by helping or leaving the scene. This series of experiments found that research participants who had been empathically aroused chose to help an individual in distress even when they could have ameliorated their own dysphoria by leaving, whereas participants who had not been empathically aroused simply left. Findings were consistent whether empathy was induced using experimental instructions, assessed on a dispositional empathy scale, or manipulated through an induction of perceived similarity with the victim (Batson, 1991). Likewise, Stocks, Lishner, and Decker (2009) found that inducing empathy increased helpfulness regardless of whether participants anticipated they would remember or soon forget about the distressed individual.

Other egoistic alternatives to the empathy-altruism hypothesis include the possibility, which has not been supported, that empathically aroused individuals are more likely to help because of their apprehension about others' evaluations of them (Fultz, Schaller, & Cialdini, 1988), and the suggestion, which has been partially supported, that empathically aroused people are motivated to share vicariously in the joy of the recipient being helped (Smith, Keating, & Stotland, 1989). Still another egoistic alternative is that since high empathy results in feelings of "oneness" with the victim, helping cannot be validly conceptualized as an altruistic behavior directed at increasing the *other's* welfare (Cialdini, Brown, Lewis, Luce, & Neuberg, 1997). This possibility is supported by the finding that perceived oneness with the victim mediates the link between empathic arousal and helping (Maner et al., 2002).

Does "true" altruism exist? Although Maner et al. (2002) express the skeptical position that "evidence for true altruism remains elusive" (p. 1601), the overall empirical picture warrants a more affirmative conclusion. According to Batson (1998, p. 302), "the empathy-altruism hypothesis should *tentatively* be accepted as true" (italics in the original) under certain conditions and for certain individuals. These conditions (e.g., social proximity between helper and recipient) and individuals (i.e., those high in dispositional empathy) are characterized by mutual feelings of belongingness and, resultantly, concern for others' welfare.

This view is consistent with Graziano and Habashi's (2010) conceptualization of help-giving as a two-stage process. On encountering a person in need people first experience personal distress, triggering a "fight or flight" motivation to leave the scene. In the second stage, this urge may be suppressed and supplanted by empathic concern, such as when the victim of misfortune is an emotionally close other—a family member or close friend—with whom we have relations of interdependence (Brown & Brown, 2006). Further, the suppression of the flight reaction and its replacement by a caring reaction is more likely for individuals who are dispositionally empathic, such as those high on agreeableness (Graziano et al., 2007).

ATTRIBUTION: DID THEY DESERVE IT?
In an early study of bystander intervention a confederate was made to collapse in a New York subway car (Piliavin, Rodin, & Piliavin, 1969). In half of the cases he was visibly drunk and in the other half visibly ill. Fellow train travelers intervened on behalf of the ill person more than they did on behalf of the one who was drunk. The researchers' explanation was that when we witness another person in need we immediately ask ourselves: Do they deserve our help? Based on the answer to this question we may decide to help them—or not.

Weiner's (1993) attributional analysis of help-giving proposes that if potential helpers attribute the person's predicament to *controllable causes*, such as lack of effort or callous behavior, they will judge that person as *responsible* for their plight, feel *anger*, and *abstain* from helping him or her. If, however, the predicament is attributed to *causes beyond the person's control*, such as lack of ability or situational constraints, observers *exonerate* the person from

responsibility, feel *sympathy* toward him or her (or pity, if the person belongs to a stigmatized group), and decide to *help*. This view fashions potential helpers as judges, adjudicating the primary charge of responsibility (Weiner, 1993).

Consistent with this, people assign less responsibility to sufferers of ostensibly intractable medical problems (e.g., Alzheimer's or heart disease), feel greater sympathy toward them, and are more willing to help them than they do to sufferers of problems that are seen to have a controllable or behavioral cause (e.g., drug addiction or obesity; Weiner, Perry, & Magnusson, 1988). A meta-analysis of 39 studies on the link between help and perceived causes of need supports the model of attribution-affect-behavior (Rudolph, Roesch, Greitemeyer, & Weiner, 2004), a model that Weiner puts forward as a general theory of social motivation applying to the prediction and explanation of aggression as well as to helping (Weiner, 2006).

The link between attributions of responsibility and help-giving has important implications for help-giving at the societal level. Personal and situational characteristics affect judgments of deservedness, which determine willingness for social solidarity with outgroups in need. Regarding personal characteristics, empirical findings show that politically conservative, but not liberal, respondents endorsed assistance to communities that had been hit by flooding in the United States only if those communities had taken preventive measures before the floods (i.e., by building a dam; Skitka, 1999). Regarding situational characteristics, people respond more positively to those described as "poor" than to those described as "welfare recipients" (Henry, Reyna, & Weiner, 2004), since the latter term evokes an image of nonworking individuals who are to blame for their own hardship. In summary, people are inclined to distance themselves from those they see as responsible for their own plight and to show solidarity with those they view as blameless. Thus, "universal belongingness" and the care that it affords is conditional on judgments of blame and responsibility.

In a related theoretical framework Brickman et al. (1982) suggested that helping decisions are also affected by whether or not potential recipients are seen as capable agents of their problem's solution. If recipients are viewed as lacking the ability to take part in their own problem-solving, they will likely receive dependency-oriented help, which consists of full solutions and which implies that recipients are weak and chronically dependent. When, however, recipients are viewed as potential agents of change they will likely receive autonomy-oriented help, which consists of tools for resolving difficulties and which implies that recipients' dependency is transient (Nadler, 1997, 1998, 2002).

The distinction between autonomy- and dependency-oriented help calls for a reexamination of the "empathic arousal-altruism" hypothesis (Batson, 1998). Research guided by this hypothesis has assessed whether increased empathy leads to helping aimed at alleviating recipients' immediate distress. Faced with a choice between a goal of future independence versus immediate respite, what kind of help will empathic observers provide? Paradoxically, it may be possible that empathic helpers favoring the goal of autonomy will provide less, rather than more, assistance to help-needy others (e.g., will offer instructions and hints rather than answers and solutions). Whether, under what conditions, and for which individuals empathy will take an "independence-oriented" form remains an open question.

Helping Relations
Help-Seeking and the Consequences of Help for the Recipient, the Helper, and Their Relationship

To receive help is a mixed blessing (Nadler & Fisher, 1986). Help can be experienced as an expression of meaningful belongingness between oneself and the helper, eliciting positive feelings, favorable self-perceptions, and gratitude (Fisher, Nadler, & Whitcher-Alagna, 1982). But it can also feel like a barricade to independence, drawing a sense of indebtedness (Greenberg, 1980) and loss of freedom, and inducing an aversive psychological state of "reactance" (Brehm, 1966). One method people use to restore their sense of freedom is to reciprocate help less than expected (El-Alayli & Messe', 2004). This and other aversive consequences of dependency (e.g., feelings of inequity or unworthiness) have been conceptualized as *threats to recipients' self-esteem*. When help threatens sense of self, relations between helper and recipient are likely to suffer; oftentimes, people will prefer to bear through hardships alone rather than accept assistance to ease them (Nadler & Fisher, 1986).

POSITIVE CONSEQUENCES OF RECEIVING HELP: GRATITUDE

Much of the positive consequences of receiving help have been subsumed under the emotion of *gratitude* (Mikulincer & Shaver, 2009). This feeling has been conceptualized as both a "dispositional" tendency and as a "state." Dispositional gratitude is the enduring tendency to feel grateful for the role of others' benevolence in the positive things in one's life (Emmons & McCullough, 2004; McCullough, Emmons, & Tsange, 2002; McCullough, Tsang, & Emmons, 2004). This personal disposition is said to result from the "upward" conduction of day-to-day gratitude to create a more pervasive grateful mood (the "conductance hypothesis"; McCullough et al., 2004). A grateful disposition is associated with higher ratings of life satisfaction, happiness, and hope (McCullough et al., 2002). State gratitude is defined as a "positive emotional reaction to the receipt of benefit that is perceived as having resulted from the good intentions of another" (p. 139, Tsang, 2006). Consistent with this definition, benefits provided under role-based obligations (Graham, 1988; Lane & Anderson, 1976) do not produce gratitude. Gratitude is felt only when the helpful act is perceived by the recipient as representing the helper's autonomous decision (Weinstein, De Haan & Ryan, 2010). Nor does assistance bring gratitude when helpers are adversarial or competitive toward recipients; rather, such help is often viewed suspiciously (Nadler, Fisher, & St3reufert, 1974) and is rejected (Worchel, Wong, & Scheltema, 1989). Finally, feeling of gratitude and its expression contribute to the maintenance of helpfulness. Expressions of gratitude decrease the helper's uncertainty as to whether or not their help is positively received and increases their willingness to provide more help to the grateful recipient (Grant & Gino, 2010).

Feeling grateful and feeling indebted are not the same. Gratitude is a positive emotion associated with a desire for social closeness with the helper (Mayer, Salovey, Gomberg-Kaufman, & Blainey, 1991), while indebtedness is associated with uneasiness toward the benefactor (Greenberg, 1980). Supporting this distinction, research shows that feeling grateful is a function of the perceived benevolence of the helper while feeling indebted is not (Tsang, 2006). Further, feelings of gratitude are better predictors of subsequent giving to the helper than feelings of indebtedness (Tsang, 2007). Thus, gratitude is an emotional reaction associated with the perception that the helper truly cares. Reciprocal and recurring feelings of gratitude within a dyad or group are evidenced in relations marked by mutual belongingness and genuine solidarity.

NEGATIVE CONSEQUENCES OF RECEIVING HELP: SELF-THREAT AND SELF-SUPPORT

Much of the research on the negative consequences of receiving help has been conducted within the framework of the threat to self-esteem model, which addresses the *positive, negative,* and *short-* and *long-term* consequences of receiving help (Fisher, Nadler, & Whitcher-Alagna, 1982; Nadler & Fisher, 1986; Shell & Eisenberg, 1992). This model posits that help can be a supportive or threatening experience for the recipient, depending on whether the salient quality of help is care and concern or a sense of relative unworthiness. Accordingly, short- and long-term responses to help may range from feelings of gratitude, mutual belongingness, and solidarity to help-aversion, diminished affect, and negative perceptions of the self, the helper, and the helping act (Nadler & Fisher, 1986). Dispositional characteristics also play a role in the long-term consequences of self-threatening help, spawning greatest efforts toward independence among recipients who enjoy feeling self-efficacious and in control (Fisher & Nadler, 1976). For recipients who lack those feelings, self-threatening help grows into enduring perceptions of worthlessness and chronic dependency on others (Nadler, 2009; Nadler & Fisher, 1986).

The self-threat or support incumbent in aid is produced by interaction of the *personal* and *situational characteristics* of the recipient, the helper, and the helping act (Fisher et al., 1982; Nadler & Fisher, 1986).

Characteristics of the Helper
Requiring help from someone who is amply blessed with needed resources is more threatening when helpers are similar others (Nadler & Fisher, 1986). Dependency on similar others generates "comparison stress," which causes people to avoid seeking the help they need (Nadler, 1991) and to respond negatively on its receipt (Nadler & Fisher, 1986). These effects were observed when levels of donor-recipient similarity were experimentally induced (Nadler, Fisher, & Streufert, 1976) and when the helper was an acquaintance as opposed to a stranger (Nadler, Fisher, & Ben-Itzhak, 1983). Further, these effects are more likely to arise in exchange relations, in which interactants monitor each other's relative performance, than in communal relations, which are based on expectations of mutual care in times of need. Consistent with this, field research shows that people will turn to close friends and family members as preferred sources of help in hard times (Wills, 1991).

Characteristics of Help
Dependency is more self-threatening when help implies inadequacy on ego-relevant dimensions (e.g., intelligence). Under such circumstances people are less likely to seek help (Nadler, 1987) and will respond more negatively to its receipt (Nadler et al., 1976). For example, women suffering from osteoarthritis were found to respond negatively to spousal help only when functional independence was important to their self-image (Matire, Stephens, Druley, & Wojno, 2002).

Help is also more threatening when it is offered in a manner that makes the recipient's dependency *explicit* rather than *implicit.* Dependency is explicit when (1) the recipient is identifiable, and when help is (2) imposed, (3) conspicuous, and (4) dependency-oriented. Receiving help is more self-threatening when recipients need to identify themselves before seeking help than when they are allowed to remain anonymous (Nadler & Porat, 1978). Assumptive help, which is imposed on the recipient rather than requested (Schneider, Major, Luhtanen, & Crocker, 1996), is more self-threatening and reduces competence-based self-esteem (Deelstra et al., 2003). Participants who *conspicuously* received helpful information, in the form of spoken instructions from an experimenter, were more adversely affected than those who received help subtly, by overhearing the same information in an answer the experimenter gave to a fellow research participant (Bolger & Amarel, 2007); thus, "masking" help as nonhelp dilutes the implication of inadequacy. In a similar manner, autonomy-oriented assistance is more implicit than dependency-oriented help; the meaning conveyed to recipients is that help satisfies a temporary rather than a chronic deficit.

Characteristics of the Recipient
Age, culture, gender, and personality all affect the degree of self-threat in receiving help. Young children do not devaluate themselves for being dependent on help, since relative dependence is expected by both themselves and others (Shell & Eisenberg, 1992). At the other extreme of the age continuum, older people whose independence is threatened by frailty of body or mind are particularly concerned about their need for assistance from others (Langer & Rodin, 1976). Regarding cultural background, Israelis raised in a collectivist culture—a kibbutz—were more willing to seek help than those raised in a more competitive, urban environment, especially when the assignment was a group task (Nadler, 1986).

One of the most robust findings on recipient characteristics is that given the same level of difficulty, men seek less help than women, whether the challenge is material or psychological (Galdas, Cheater, & Marshall, 2005; Veroff, 1981). These findings seem to reflect a traditional ideal of self-reliance as a "masculine" rather the "feminine" quality (Addis & Mahalik, 2003); for example, Nadler, Fisher, and Ben-Itzhak (1983) found that women who were motivated to present themselves positively, interacting with an attractive man, displayed dependency, while men in a similar situation, interacting with an attractive woman, displayed independence. Indeed, it is the adherence of men and women to respective gender roles, rather than the biological fact of being a man or a woman, that predicts willingness to express dependence (Nadler, Maler, & Friedman, 1984).

Some personality dispositions are related to the need for independence and affect receptivity to help (Nadler, 1991, 1997, 1998). People who score high on need for achievement scales are less willing to seek help than those who score low, since achievers are apt to desire independent credit for their accomplishments (e.g., Tessler & Schwartz, 1972; Nadler, 1986). People who are characterized as having a "dependent personality"—i.e., for whom dependency is consistent with self-image—find it easier to rely on help than those who are not so characterized (Bornstein, 1992). In experiments, people characterized as having high self-esteem are less receptive to help than those characterized with low self-esteem (Nadler, 1986, 1991, 1998; Wills & DePaulo, 1991), whether self-esteem is experimentally induced (Nadler, Altman, & Fisher, 1979) or measured on standard scales (Nadler, 1987; Nadler et al., 1976; Nadler, Mayseless, Chemerinski, & Peri, 1985; Nadler, 1986; Tessler & Schwartz, 1972). People with high self-esteem may be reluctant to seek help because they perceive dependence as inconsistent with their positive self-image. Consistent with this, sufferers of domestic violence who have high self-esteem are less likely to seek counseling than those who have low self-esteem (Frieze, 1979), probably because help-seeking is inconsistent with self-image for those who would otherwise view themselves as competent and independent. Finally, shy individuals, who worry more than nonshy people about the negative evaluations of others (Jones, Cheek, & Briggs, 1986), take longer than others to seek help (DePaulo, Dull, Greenberg, & Swaim, 1989; Wills & DePaulo, 1991).

It should be emphasized that personal characteristics almost always interact with situational variables in predicting responses to help, and that no personality disposition can account for the range of effects on help receptivity on its own. High self-esteem individuals are less willing to seek and receive help when the task is ego-relevant, but not when irrelevant (Nadler, 1986); people with more dependent personalities are readier to rely on others on the condition that the helper has higher status than themselves (Bornstein, 1992); and in the main, members of collective cultures are more willing to seek help when the task is collective rather than individualistic (Nadler, 1986).

CONSEQUENCES OF HELP FOR RECIPIENT COPING

Viewing helpfulness as a component of enduring relationships rather than as one-off events raises questions about the links between seeking and receiving help and long-term coping and performance. In the long run, does help work as intended? How much help is too much? Or too little? Overwhelmingly, studies show that both over- and underutilization of help are detrimental to long-term coping (Nadler, 1998). Habitual reliance on help diminishes recipients' prospects for future independence, while habitual aversion to help results in lower task performance. Weiss and Knight (1980) reported that individuals with high self-esteem were more hesitant to seek help from team members and hence performed worse on tasks that required frequent consultation than those with low self-esteem. In a study at a large chemical plant, Nadler, Ellis, and Bar (2003) found that employees who characteristically sought moderate levels of help had better job performance, rated independently by supervisors, than employees who consistently sought high or low amounts of help. With regard to educational settings, Ryan, Patrick, and Shim (2005) had teachers rate their students as underutilizers, overutilizers, or adequate utilizers of help, finding that profiles of both over- and underutilization were associated with poorer academic performance than a profile of moderate, situationally appropriate help-seeking. Research shows that children who receive too much help from an emotionally close adult internalize an implied message of helplessness and thence make less effort to cope autonomously (Leone, 2009).

CONSEQUENCES OF HELP-GIVING FOR THE HELPER

Helping, especially sustained, benefits helpers. Positive self-regard is cited as a major reason why people decide to volunteer (Omoto & Snyder, 1995) and continue to do so over time (Midlarsky

& Kahana, 1994). Empirically, sustained helping benefits helpers' physical and psychological health (also see Oishi, chapter 24, this volume). Over a 5-year period people who had provided emotional support to another person, such as their spouse, evidenced reduced mortality independent of other variables (e.g., prior physical and mental health; Brown, Nesee, Vinokur, & Smith, 2003; Brown, Bulanda, & Lee, 2005). Among widowers, helping others in the 6 months following the spouse's death was associated with less depression at the end of the year following the loss (Brown, House, Brown, & Smith, 2008). In addition to general enhancement of psychological well-being (Brown et al., 2009), volunteering makes people feel useful at times when they are most vulnerable to feeling useless, such as old age (Omoto, Snyder, & Martino, 2000).

One explanation for the return on helping is that the positive emotional state it induces speeds recovery from stressful life events (Fredrickson, Manusco, Branigan, & Tugade, 2000). Another explanation centers on the self-transcendence of helping. Sustained helping, such as volunteering, contributes to a feeling of self-actualization and a "sense of mattering" to others (Piliavin, 2009; Taylor & Turner, 2001). Compared to the temporary positive affect of a helping encounter, sustained helping nourishes eudaimonic, as opposed to hedonic, well-being: A sense of self-realization and meaning in life (Ryan & Deci, 2001). In a cyclical way, people who feel psychologically connected to a relevant community are more likely to volunteer in that community, which in turn feeds into the volunteer's sense of connectedness (Omoto & Snyder, 2009). These observations are consistent with Viktor Frankl's (1984) insight, based on his experiences as a prisoner in a Nazi concentration camp, that by finding existential meaning in the midst of the darkest of circumstances people increase their chances of coping.

The concepts "sense of mattering," "community feeling," and "finding existential meaning through helping" are all different expressions of the fulfillment of the fundamental human need for belongingness. They reflect a transformation from knowing that "I am part of a group" to an identity-relevant feeling and knowledge that "I belong to a group."

CONSEQUENCES FOR HELPER-RECIPIENT RELATIONS: IMPLICATIONS FOR STATUS

Beyond its positive effects on helpers' well-being, sustained helping has positive consequences on the way others view the helper. Helping signals to observers that the actor has enough resources to take care of his or her needs *and also* those of others. This heightens status (Boone, 1998). "Costly signaling" theory (Zahavi & Zahavi, 1997), which comes from ethology, states that animals willingly incur the short-term costs of giving—for example, feeding nestlings that are not their own—in exchange for the long-term benefits of attractiveness to others as a potential mate or ally. Seeming "waste" may actually make a good evolutionary investment. Consistent with this logic, and as is true for any successful advertising campaign, such behavior is more frequent once an audience of other birds had assembled near the nest (Doutreland & Covas, 2007).

While evolutionary theorists view the distal purpose of all social behavior as the increase of mating opportunities, the benefits of costly signaling in humans are more proximally associated with the social and material advantages of high status (Blau, 1963; Flynn, 2003; Hardy & Van Vugt, 2006), conceptualized as the "competitive altruism" hypothesis (Van Vugt & van Lange, 2006). People give more help to group members when helping is visible and public. Further, those who seek help more often than they receive it undermine their status in the group (Lee, 1997), and people characterized as high self-monitors—that is, those who are more status conscious—build a reputation of generosity by providing more help than they ask for (Flynn, Reagans, Amanatullah, & Ames, 2006).

Intergroup Helping Relations

The shift in social psychology from studying the "physical group," a set of copresent individuals, to the study of the "psychological group," the experience of shared identity with others, has also influenced the study of helping. This theoretical development alerted researchers that when interactants' social identity is salient, interpersonal helping encounters between members of separate groups should be analyzed as intergroup helping interactions (Stürmer & Snyder, 2009). Another reason for the growing research interest in helping across group boundaries is the increasing research on volunteerism with stigmatized outgroups (e.g., mentally ill patients). We address three research directions on intergroup helping: (1) the role of social identity and self-categorization, (2) intergroup helping relations as status relations, and (3) helping between blacks and whites in the United States.

SELF-CATEGORIZATION AND CROSS-GROUP HELPING RELATIONS

The social identity perspective on intergroup relations holds that people are more likely to benefit ingroup than outgroup members (Van Vugt & Park 2009). As a direct example, Levine, Prosser, Evans, and Reicher (2005) found that bystanders who encountered an injured student intervened more often when the target's t-shirt identified him as a fan of the same as opposed to a rival soccer club. The common ingroup identity model (Gaertner & Dovidio, 2000) states that ingroup favoritism can be ameliorated by extending group boundaries so that members view the ingroup and outgroup as belonging to the same overarching category (Dovidio et al., 1997). Consistent with this, when Levine et al. induced a common group identity by emphasizing that both helpers and targets were "soccer fans," no difference was found in rates of help (2005).

A real-world illustration of the effects of common group identity on helping is provided by Reicher et al.'s (2006) analysis of the saving of Bulgarian Jews from Nazi deportation in 1941. Based on historical documents assembled by Todorov (2001) Reicher et al. concluded that a key reason for the rescue was the emphasis by the Bulgarian leadership of the common identity of Bulgarian Jews with other Bulgarians. An example of this inclusive message is contained in a speech by Todor Polakov (a Communist parliamentarian of the time) who declared to the National Assembly: "Bulgarian Jews . . . speak Bulgarian. . . . They sing Bulgarian songs and tell Bulgarian stories" (Reicher et al., 2006, p. 58).

The motivations for helping ingroup members differ from those of helping outgroup members. Ingroup members feel similar, and similarity is an antecedent of empathy, which in turn drives up help. In contrast, help to outgroup members is more often based on cost-reward considerations, such that helpers are more likely to help if they like the recipients and view a relationship with them as potentially rewarding (Stürmer & Snyder, 2009). Consistent with this, Penner and Finkelstein found that dispositional empathy predicted AIDS volunteerism among homosexual men but not heterosexual women (1998). On the other hand, attractiveness of the target is a stronger predictor of helping directed toward an outgroup than an ingroup member (Stürmer, Snyder, & Omoto, 2005). Empathy also predicts intentions to help a culturally similar other (e.g., both helper and recipient are ethnic Germans)

but not a dissimilar other (e.g., the helper is ethnically German and the recipient a German Muslim citizen; Stürmer, Snyder, Kropp, & Siem, 2006).

INTERGROUP HELPING RELATIONS BETWEEN DIFFERENTIALLY ADVANTAGED GROUPS

Another line of research on intergroup helping has focused on helping interactions between more and less advantaged groups. This research is grounded in the intergroup helping as status relations model (IHSR; Nadler, 2002), which integrates findings on helping relations with the central tenets of the social identity perspective (Turner & Reynolds, 2001). The IHSR model posits that helping between groups is a function of status relations and goals. When status differences are secure (i.e., are perceived as legitimate and stable) high-status groups tend to provide dependency-oriented help to lower status groups as needed, for which lower status groups are usually grateful. However, when status relations are insecure (i.e., perceived as illegitimate and unstable), high-status groups tend to exaggerate offers of dependency-oriented help (Nadler, Harpaz-Gorodeisky, & Ben-David, 2009, Experiments 2 and 3) and to do so irrespective of need. This scenario is labeled *defensive helping* (Nadler et al., 2009).

Real-world illustrations of defensive helping are numerous. Researchers in Canada (Jackson & Essess, 2000) and Australia (Cunningham & Platow, 2007) found that citizens of those countries would not recommend autonomy-oriented help to new immigrants when they regarded them as a source of economic competition. Such findings are mediated by dispositional characteristics. In both Canadian (Jackson & Essess, 2000) and Israeli (Halabi, Dovidio, & Nadler, 2008) samples, defensive helping is more characteristic of members of high-status groups who score high on social dominance orientation (SDO; Sidanius & Pratto, 1999), a dispositional tendency to view group inequality as justified.

The induction of common group identity between high- and low-status groups reduces the motivation to engage in defensive helping. When members of a high-status group perceived a common identity with a low-status group that threatened their advantage, the high-status group provided *autonomy-oriented help* (Nadler et al., 2009, Experiment 3). This suggests that the induction of common group identity transforms a defensive motivation for helping into an altruistic motivation; helpers may become more sensitive to recipients' long-term needs and provide them with the kind of help that promotes future independence and equality. These findings support the interpretation that the provision of help by a high-status group, especially when its social advantage is threatened, reflects a motivation to maintain the social inequality from which it benefits, but also that the defensive motivation can be altruistically transformed by redrawing the boundaries between the groups.

Lower status groups resent dependency-oriented help from the higher status group when status relations are perceived as insecure because of its inconsistency with their motivation for equality under these conditions. They respond negatively to receiving such help (Halabi, Dovidio, & Nadler, 2008; Halabi, Nadler, & Dovidio, in press) and refrain from seeking it (Nadler & Halabi, 2006). Under these conditions low status groups remain receptive to autonomy-oriented help (Nadler & Halabi, 2006, Experiment 4). Status insecurity augurs the possibility of social change, and help plays into the contrary motivations of high- and low-status groups to gird or unfix patterns of dependence.

A concept that is closely related to defensive helping is *strategic helping* (van Leeuwen & Tauber, 2009), which is the management of ingroup reputation through help given to a third party. For example, in a study by Hopkins et al. (2007), Scottish participants who learned that English participants considered them cruel were more generous toward Welsh participants than to members of their own group. In other words, the maligned Scottish group displayed uncommon generosity—giving more to the outgroup than the ingroup—in order to remedy its injured reputation. In another experimental demonstration, van Leeuwen (2007) informed half of her Dutch participants that the Netherlands' merger into the EU endangered its independent status. On a subsequent measure participants who had heard this threatening message voiced greater support for Dutch assistance to victims of the 2004 Asian tsunami—especially regarding water management, an area central to Dutch national identity—than those who had not.

HELPING RELATIONS ACROSS
RACIAL BOUNDARIES

Intergroup helping between European- and African-Americans have attracted relatively much research attention. One reason is that this context encapsulates a more general concern that prejudicial attitudes inhibit help. Findings on cross-racial helping center on the idea of aversive racism (Dovidio &

Gaertner, 2004)—that discrimination is latent when social costs are high, but becomes perceptible when social costs are low. Blatant discrimination in helping is counternormative and rare, but when norms for helping are ambiguous or when not helping can be rationalized, whites are more likely to discriminate against blacks by retracting help. For example, the decision not to intervene can be rationalized by interpreting an event as a nonemergency (Dovidio, Piliavin, Gaertner, Schroeder, & Clark, 1991), as in a recent study by Kunstman and Plant (2008) in which white helpers who were slower to help a black victim than a white victim in a crisis reported the emergency as being less serious.

An early study of aversive racism found that white bystanders gave the same amount of help to black and white victims when the bystander was alone (94% and 81%, respectively), but gave less help to black victims when other bystanders were present (38% and 75%, respectively; Gaertner & Dovidio, 1977). It seems that when responsibility can be diffused, white helpers can avoid helping black victims without appearing prejudiced. Reviewing the then-available literature Crosby, Bromley, and Saxe (1980) determined that whites help black and white victims equally in face-to-face interactions when the costs of discrimination are high. Twenty-five years later, a meta-analysis of 31 studies of interracial helping concludes, similar to the conclusions of Crosby et al., that when the costs of *helping* are high, and the costs of discriminatory nonhelping low, whites help white victims more than they help black victims (Saucier, Miller, & Doucet, 2005).

How can discriminatory nonhelping be ameliorated? Research on the beneficial consequences of common group identity suggests that extending group boundaries beyond the racial dividing line will decrease aversive racism in helping. Supporting this, a recent study found that the induction of common group identity increased willingness to help across racial boundaries and that this increase was mediated by an empathic concern for members of the outgroup (Dovidio et al., 2009). Another way to ameliorate racial discrimination in helping is to give members of the advantaged group information that important ingroup members regard the stigmatized outgroup favorably (Sechrist & Milford, 2007).

On the other side of the helping paradigm, dependency on the help of the advantaged majority can threaten the disadvantaged group's feelings of self-worth. African Americans who received help from a white helper had lower ratings of competence-based self-esteem than whites who received the same help (Schneider et al., 1996). Similarly, Arab Israeli students working on a scholastic task were found less willing to seek and receive help from a member of the advantaged Jewish Israeli majority group than the reverse (Halabi et al., 2008; Nadler & Halabi, 2006). Members of stigmatized groups seem to feel the same. Paraplegics (Nadler, Sheinberg, & Jaffe, 1981) and parents of mentally retarded children (Nadler, Lewinstein, & Rahav, 1991) are unwilling to seek needed help when they suspect this might reinforce their, or their children's, stigmatized condition.

Helping in Close and Enduring Relationships

Overall, research has looked less often where helping occurs most frequently: In close and significant relationships. This neglect may be attributed, partly at least, to the wish to formulate general and context-free principles of social behavior. Social psychological research that addressed helping in close and enduring relations has traced helping via themes of kinship, attachment, and volunteerism, and more recently, social exclusion and trauma.

HELPING KIN VS. NON-KIN

Questions of kinship and helping have their origins in evolutionary analyses of altruistic behavior (see Gangestad, chapter 7, this volume). In animal species self-sacrificial altruism is more common on behalf of kin than non-kin. For example, ground nesting birds, such as the killdeer, defend their nestlings from predators by displaying a "broken wing" behavior that puts them at risk. At the sight of the predator the mother bird moves away slowly from the nest as if her wing were broken, thereby attracting the predator's attention from her nestlings to herself (Goldsmith, 1991). Helping kin brings genetic benefits for the altruist, since it protects genes for passage to the next generation. Thus, the "inclusive fitness" hypothesis (Hamilton, 1964) states that the greater the genetic relatedness between helper and beneficiary, the higher the likelihood of self-sacrificial altruism. In humans, people are more willing to help those in life or death situations who are genetically related to them, and are more apt to help those who have higher reproductive potential (healthy rather than sick, and premenopausal women rather than postmenopausal women; Burnstein, Crandall, & Kitayama, 1994). Further, young adults, who typically feel closer to their intimate friends than to their siblings (Kruger, 2003),

are nevertheless more willing to provide costly, sacrificial help (e.g., donating a kidney) to siblings than to close friends (Stewart-Williams, 2007).

Korchmoros and Kenny challenged the evolutionary explanation of the kinship-helping link (Korchmoros & Kenny, 2001, 2006), asserting that we help those to whom we feel obligated and emotionally close, and that since social life is built around kinship units there is an inherent propinquity between biological relation and emotional closeness. They supported this explanation empirically by showing that the relationship between kinship and helping is mediated by emotional closeness and operates on psychological rather than evolutionary mechanisms. While both approaches may be valid, the determinism of evolutionary theory can obscure important relational insights. For example, in recent decades the structure of kinship units has shifted so that genetic relatedness is more often partial or absent in families, yet there is no evidence that this diminishes emotional attachment between parents and children. Golombok, Cook, Bish, and Murray (1995) report that the quality of parenting in families where the child is genetically related only to the mother (via assisted reproduction through donor insemination) or unrelated to either parent (as with adopted children) is higher than in families where children were conceived naturally, and that genetic relatedness has no link to children's emotional relationships with their parents. The higher quality of parenting in adoptive and reproduction-assisted families implies that psychological commitment carries greater weight than genetic relatedness in determining the quality of family ties. The kinship/helping relationship can therefore be more parsimoniously phrased as indicating that we experience greater care and give more help to those with whom we share a feeling of belongingness. In many, but not all, cases these individuals are genetically related.

HELPING RELATIONS AND ATTACHMENT

Attachment theory asserts that interactions with significant care-takers in early childhood fosters life-long positions about the availability of others in times of stress (also see Mikulincer & Shaver, chapter 19, this volume). These assumptions result in three different strategies of coping, based on people's standing on two orthogonal dimensions: Attachment anxiety and avoidance (Mikulincer & Shaver, 2007). Stress activates the care-giving system in interpersonal relationships (Bowlby, 1982) via two related but distinct support mechanisms: The "secure base" and "safe haven" (Collins, Ford, Guichard, Kane, & Feeney, 2009). Secure-base support refers to the ongoing sustenance and encouragement that people provide to emotionally close others, while safe-haven support addresses help provided in acute situations when one of the partners experiences distress that can be alleviated by the other. Because of the present emphasis on helping in times of need our concern is with safe-haven support.

People who have an *anxious* attachment style are uncertain and worried about the availability of significant others. Responses to their own and to others' distress is harder to moderate, exhibited as neediness and overreliance when seeking support, and domineeringness and vigilance for signs of gratitude when providing it (Shaver, Mikulincer, & Shemesh-Iron, 2009). People whose attachment style is *avoidant* are skeptical and withdrawn in their relationships, seeking to minimize interdependence. Avoidant people report less responsiveness to the needs of close others (Kunce & Shaver, 1994) as well as strangers (e.g., cancer patients; Westmaas & Silver, 2001), and are likewise less likely to seek out such responsiveness. For example, among women who waited to participate in an anxiety-provoking experiment, those who were securely attached sought more support from their partners as their anxiety increased, while avoidant women sought less support as their anxiety increased (Simpson, Rholes, & Nelligan, 1992). *Securely attached* people score low on both the dimensions of anxiety and avoidance, and tend to be more responsive to the needs of loved ones (Simpson et al., 1992). The higher willingness of securely attached individuals to seek help from others when in need does not necessarily mean they are less concerned about their independence, but that they are more certain of others' availability, and more willing to make themselves available to others in return (Mikulincer & Shaver, 2007).

The links between attachment security and caring has been observed outside of the context of close interpersonal bonds in the responses of secure and insecure individuals to the suffering of strangers. In field studies, avoidant individuals were less responsive to cancer patients (Westmaas & Silver, 2001), and attachment insecurity was positively correlated with egoistic motivations for volunteering (Gillath et al. 2005). Links between attachment and care-giving can also be experimentally induced. Recent research indicates that inducing attachment security, by subliminally priming participants with secure attachment figures, led participants to exhibit

more compassion toward a suffering stranger and greater willingness to help that person (Mikulnicer, Shaver, Gillath, & Nitzberg, 2005). This emphasizes that attachment has conceptually consistent effects on helping outside close relationships, and suggests that the attachment system operates preconsciously.

SOCIAL EXCLUSION AND HELPING

At the other extreme of belongingness is the experience of rejection and exclusion. Since relational bonds are fertile ground for care and helping toward others, active exclusion from those bonds can lower sensitivity to others' needs (DeWall & Baumeister, 2006) and reduce willingness to help. Recent research on the effects of social exclusion on helping supports this proposition. For example, children who suffer peer rejection are less helpful than those who do not (e.g., Asher & Coie, 1990; Gest, Graham-Bermann, & Hartup, 2001). Twenge, Baumeister, DeWall, Ciarocco, and Bartels (2007) measured the effects of exclusion—induced by telling participants that they would be alone later in life, or that they had been rejected by others—on a variety of helping responses ranging from donating money to helping pick up dropped pencils. Findings show that exclusion reduces helpfulness, and that this effect is mediated by reduced empathy. Other findings indicate that emotional disengagement following social exclusion is strategic and situational, not ingrained. In a mixed-motive game, participants who had suffered an experience of social exclusion behaved cooperatively up until the other player made a single noncooperative move (Twenge et al., 2007). Once burned, participants turned highly competitive. Thus, given a safe opportunity, excluded people may try to build bridges to others, while remaining vigilant lest their goodwill be taken advantage of.

SUSTAINED HELPING: VOLUNTEERING

Data collected in the United States, UK, Ireland, and Germany indicates that between 25% and 50% of adults above the age of 18 are involved in some form of sustained volunteer activity (Dovidio et al., 2006). Social psychological research on volunteerism has addressed three questions: The determinants of the *initiative to volunteer*, factors that contribute to *sustained volunteering*, and the *consequences of volunteering* for volunteers themselves. Initiating volunteership is more common among those with higher levels of education and income (Penner et al., 2005), possibly because educated and wealthier people have greater control over their time. Women and people higher in dispositional empathy also initiate volunteering more often (Atkins, Hart, & Donnely, 2005; Penner, 2002).

In their functional analysis of volunteering, Snyder, Clary, and Stukas (2000) proposed that the decision to volunteer fulfills at least one of six psychological functions: expressing personal values of humanitarian concern, acquiring new learning and understanding, gaining material rewards such as career-related benefits, strengthening social relationships, serving as a protective mechanism against bad feelings or personal problems, and providing psychological growth. According to the *volunteer process model* the persistence of volunteering can be predicted by matching precipitating motivations to volunteer with the consequences of the actual experience (Omoto & Snyder, 2002). Another approach suggests that volunteering will be sustained when significant others view it positively, and when it becomes an important part of the volunteer's identity (Piliavin, 2003).

A shared experience of trauma can generate willingness to assist fellow victims in greater need. Frequent responses in the days and weeks following the September 11th attacks were to help others by donating blood, contributing money, or volunteering to aid victims (Schuster et al., 2001). Lebanese children who had been traumatized by war-related violence in Lebanon reported being involved in helping others more than those had not (Macksoud & Aber, 1996), and Israeli survivors of terrorist attacks reported that helping other victims of violence facilitated their coping with the trauma they had suffered (Kleinman, 1989). Experiencing trauma vicariously is sufficient to enhance volunteerism: People distressed by 9/11 through written and televised stories exhibited survivor guilt and grief, which brought on a greater willingness to volunteer on behalf of direct victims (Wayment, 2004). This *altruism born of suffering* (Staub & Vollhardt, 2008; Vollhardt, 2009) may arise from the greater empathy that exists among sufferers of a similar or shared trauma, or from the sense of the traumatized person that by helping one regains control and efficacy—often the first casualties of a traumatic experience.

The link between trauma and helping is an emerging area of study that relays new questions: Why and when do some trauma sufferers prefer to isolate themselves while others become more responsive to others? Can altruism born of suffering extend to help outside the traumatized ingroup—victims and even perpetrators in the adversarial party?

Summary, Conclusions, and Implications

Giving and receiving help pivot on two central needs in human relationships: Belongingness and independence. The interplay of these needs illuminates the diverse goals, temporal spans, beliefs about, and consequences of helping. Belongingness is expressed in the expectation that people who share the same relational bond will help each other when the need arises. From this perspective the goal of helping is to alleviate the victim's difficulties as fast and fully as one can. Yet, because dependency is inconsistent with the fundamental psychological need for self-reliance, needing help does not mean being receptive to help in any form; from the recipient's perspective, help should pave the way to future independence. Social psychologists have sought to identify the situational and personality determinants of actions intended to ameliorate another's immediate distress, without placing an equivalent emphasis on receptivity to help and the consequences of receiving it for the recipient's long-term independence. The present emphasis on the role of belongingness and independence in help-giving and helping relations corrects this oversight and offers a more balanced account of helping.

Help-Giving and Belongingness

Early research on help-giving indicates that people help relative strangers in situations ranging from the quotidian to the extreme. Readiness to help arises as an interaction between the helping context and the helper's personal disposition; the helper's act may express empathic concern with the other's predicament, compliance with social norms, or self-serving motivations. From an evolutionary perspective helping strangers of the same species may favor natural selection as long as help is reciprocated at some future time (i.e., *reciprocal altruism*; Trivers, 1985). More recent research shows that while helping strangers is common, people give more empathy-based assistance to those with whom they share a sense of belongingness. This is true in helping family members (Brown & Brown, 2006), ingroup members (Levine et al., 2002), and when outgroup members share a common social category with the helper (Levine et al., 2005).

Recent analysis suggests that belongingness is the primary foundation for people's willingness to make costly sacrifices for each other. Consistent with this, soldiers who exhibited heroic altruism in battle cited the intense social bonds they shared with fellow combatants as the reason for their self-sacrificial heroism (Stouffer et al., 1949). The link between interdependence, social bonds, and helping is said to have an evolutionary advantage in that "social bonds evolved primarily to motivate costly long term investment" (Brown & Brown, 2006; p. 1) in the welfare of close others.

Importantly, the research reviewed in the previous sections shows that the link between belongingness and help-giving is not a one-way street. Not only are people willing to invest in helping those with whom they share a sense of belongingness, but sustained helping, such as volunteering, in turn nourishes feelings of communality (Omoto & Snyder, 2009). In fact, most of the positive physical and psychological benefit of sustained volunteering is attributed to enhanced feelings of belongingness.

Independence and the Recipient of Help
In interpersonal and intergroup helping contexts dependency can threaten recipients' self-esteem or social identity, respectively, and people in need may prefer continued hardship to self-threatening dependency. The finding that most adults with mental health disorders do not seek professional help to ease their difficulties (Montjabi, Olfson, & Mechanic, 2002) is one expression of this. The corollary to this link is that having others depend on one's help is a source of high status and positive reputation for the helper.

The view of a helping encounter as an arena where the two fundamental needs for belongingness and independence play out allows for a more complex articulation of the question of helping than has been commonly expressed. Overemphasis on the help-giving side of the helping equation may arise from the positioning of much helping research under the banner of "altruism" rather than looking to where help matters most: In transforming need into agency. Yet, as the present review emphasizes, such a monolithic view of helping obscures the important interactional dynamics that such social encounters entail. The beliefs, feelings, and actions of the helper and the recipient all determine the quality of the helping interaction and its long-term consequences. Importantly, the present emphasis on the different kinds of help and their implications transcends the common dichotomization of giving versus not giving help.

For recipients who view themselves as independent and only temporarily in need, receiving a full solution to a problem (i.e., dependency-oriented help) is inconsistent with self-perception. In this scenario some kinds of help can be detrimental for both sides. In one study Nadler et al. (1983) found

that the receipt of assumptive and dependency-oriented help was experienced by the recipient as self-threatening, interpreted as an expression of the helper's motivation to display their superiority and resulted in negative expectations about the quality of future relations with them. Intergroup relations may be similarly adversely affected by such helping interactions. Halabi, Nadler, and Dovidio (2009) have recently found that members of disadvantaged group within the Israeli society, Israeli-Arabs, motivated to gain intergroup equality, viewed dependency-oriented help from a member of the advantaged group, Israeli-Jews, as motivated by ulterior motivations, while the helpers saw the same assistance as an expression of their good will and benevolence. As recently noted by Nadler, Halabi, and Harapaz-Gorodeisky (2009) such helping interactions lead to interpersonal and intergroup misunderstandings that result in exacerbated social tensions between the interactants. Under these conditions autonomy-oriented help, which involves recipients in the alleviation of their difficulties, is more likely to be accepted gratefully, to advance future independent coping and to foster equality between the two parties.

Paradoxically, the danger of excessive or dependency-oriented help is more common when the helper and recipient share a significant relational bond, since empathy can propel the desire to fully and immediately ameliorate the recipient's hardship. An important area for future research is to determine the personal and situational conditions under which empathy will translate into concern for the recipient's future independence and not only into the alleviation of the recipient's present distress.

When the need for help is extreme or the person experiencing it feels helpless, dependency-oriented help is situationally appropriate. To paraphrase a well-known metaphor, only cooked fish will allay impending starvation. Teaching the hungry how to use a fishing rod will come later. By the same token, people who are resigned to chronic helplessness do not welcome autonomy-oriented assistance because it threatens such individuals' self-perceptions. The implication of this analysis is that, depending on the particular state of need, a "truly helpful" act is an outcome of (1) the recipient's characteristics, (2) the helper's awareness and motivation to increase the recipient's short- and long-term well-being, and (3) the administration of an appropriate form of help to increase both. This view departs from the implicit assumption that has governed much of past research, which is that help is uniformly good and more help is even better.

Personality and Situational Determinants of Interpersonal and Intergroup Helping

Since its inception, research on helping has shifted from dismissing the importance of personality dispositions to accepting that a range of personal variables influence help (Graziano & Habashi, 2010). The present review documents this change. In the main, dispositional variables affect help-giving to the degree that they reflect people's sense of belonging with others. For example, *agreeableness*, which indexes personal variations in the wish to maintain positive relations with others (Graziano et al., 2007), and *dispositional empathy*, which indexes the degree to which people are affectively tuned to the way others feel (Davis), are determinants of help-giving (Graziano & Eisenberg, 1997; Penner & Orom, 2009). Dispositional variables that reflect the subjective importance of independence and individual achievement affect recipients' receptivity to help and its consequences. Levels of achievement motivation, self-esteem, and enduring beliefs about self-control (Nadler, 1997, 1998) are examples of such variables. These dispositional differences interact with conceptually relevant situational characteristics. Thus for example, agreeableness does not predict help-giving when an emotionally close other, such as a family member, faces immediate danger (Graziano et al., 2007). In these circumstances everyone intervenes. Similarly, self-esteem does not predict receptivity to help on tasks in which independence is not ego-relevant (e.g., when performance is related to luck; Nadler, 1991).

Both dispositional and situational variables affect interpersonal and intergroup helping. Although the relevant variables at each of these levels of analysis are not the same, the underlying psychological processes that they reflect are similar. Intergroup helping is predicted by such situational and dispositional factors as status security, ingroup commitment, and SDO, while interpersonal helping is predicted by such factors as similarity and self-esteem. Yet, at both of these levels power relations and empathic concern are explanatory concepts used to account for the dynamics of helping.

Concluding Comments and Applied Implications

Since its beginnings in the mid-20th century, the social psychology of helping has changed in its interests and foci. Yet, help research has remained a thriving area of social psychological inquiry. Help-giving and helping relations are rich, diverse phenomena that express the most basic motivations of social life: the need to belong to others and the need to be independent. Furthermore, the findings and concepts of helping research have never tracked far from real-world contexts (Nadler, 2009). In its beginnings, research on help-giving was stimulated by concern about social apathy, and its findings remain relevant to generating a more caring society. Evidence for the psychological and physical benefits of sustained helping is important to the understanding of well-being. The interplay of help-giving, help-getting, and self-reliance are immediately relevant to shaping learning and work environments that are both challenging and supportive, and may be especially significant to institutionalized helping programs between differentially advantaged groups, such as affirmative action (Pratkanis & Turner, 1996), postconflict peace building projects (Nadler & Saguy, 2004), and international aid (Fisher, Nadler, Little, & Saguy, 2008).

The shift from the emphasis on help-giving to the study of helping relations reflects changes within and outside of social psychology. The study of help-giving began in the postwar period when urbanization and social change made certain needs for help more salient, such as apathy and increasing feelings of social alienation. This was paralleled by behaviorist and situationist emphases in social psychology, which directed the field's attention to specifying the situational determinants of help-giving. Since then, social psychological research has given increased attention to the role of personality and to the cognitive and affective processes at work in interpersonal and intergroup relations.

At the center of research on helping relations are issues of empowerment, well-being, and equality between helper and recipient. This research highlights people's strengths. Help is seen as a vehicle for personal or social change rather than a temporary palliative to distress. This perspective on helping is consistent with current emphases in positive psychology, which go beyond successful coping with adversity to identifying psychological processes and variables that culminate in a more fulfilling social and personal life (Lopez & Snyder, 2009).

We end with a variation on the question with which we began: What kind of help is good help? The common answer—that which relieves another's misfortune—is articulated from the helper's perspective. The task of determining what constitutes good help is more complex for recipients, for whom immediate benefits can be less important than long-term independence. From this perspective, the best help is the action, or set of actions, that promotes independence and leads to greater equality in helper-recipient relationships. These qualities emphasize the concerns of belongingness and independence. They need not be mutually exclusive. Helping relations can both express the genuine care that comes with feelings of belongingness as well as reflect recipients' strengths and their potential to be become self-reliant and enjoy equality and mutual respect. The dual attention to belongingness and independence is at the heart of this view.

Acknowledgments

Preparation of this manuscript was supported by the Argentina Chair for Research on the Social Psychology of Conflict and Cooperation, Tel Aviv University. I thank and Talia Fried and Lily Tchemerinski-Chai for their assistance in preparation of this chapter and Gal Harpaz-Gorodeisky, Samer Halabi, and Svetlana Kommisaruk for their comments on earlier versions.

References

Addis, M. E., & Mahalik, J. R. (2003). Men, masculinity, and the contexts of help-seeking. *American Psychologist, 58,* 5–14.

Anderson, C. A., & Bushman, B. J. (2001). Effects of violent games on aggressive behavior, aggressive cognition, aggressive affect, physiological arousal, and prosocial behavior: A meta-analytic review of the scientific literature. *Psychological Science, 12,* 353–359.

Aronson, E., Wilson, T. D., & Akert, R. M. (2004). *Social psychology.* Upper Saddle River, NJ: Pearson Prentice Hall.

Asher, S. R., & Coie, J. D. (Eds.). (1990). *Peer rejection in childhood.* New York: Cambridge University Press.

Atkins, R., Hart, D., & Donnelly, T. M. (2005). The association of childhood personality type with volunteering during adolescence. *Merrill-Palmer Quarterly, 51,* 145–162.

Bandura, A. (1977). *Social learning theory.* Englewood Cliffs, NJ: Prentice Hall.

Bar-Tal, D., & Raviv, A. (1982). *A cognitive-learning model of helping behavior development: Possible implications and applications.* In N. Eisenberg (Ed.), *The development of prosocial behavior* (pp. 199–218). New York: Academic.

Batson, C. D. (1991). *The altruism question: Toward a social-psychological answer.* Hillsdale, NJ: Erlbaum.

Batson, C. D. (1998). *Altruism and prosocial behavior.* In D. T. Gilbert, S. T. Fiske, & G. Lindzey (Eds.), *The handbook of social psychology* (4th ed., Vol. 2, pp. 282–315). New York: McGraw-Hill.

Batson, C. D., Batson, J. G., Slingsby, J. K., Harrell, K. L., Peekna, H. M., & Todd, R. M. (1991). Empathic joy and the empathy-altruism hypothesis. *Journal of Personality and Social Psychology, 61,* 413–426.

Batson, C. D., Duncan, B., Ackerman, P., Buckley, X., & Birch, K. (1981). Is empathic emotion a source of altruistic motivation? *Journal of Personality and Social Psychology, 40,* 290–302.

Baumeister, R. F., & Leary, M. R. (1995). The need to belong: Desire for interpersonal attachment as a fundamental human motivation, *Psychological Bulletin, 117,* 497–529.

Becker, S., & Eagly, A. H. (2004). The heroism of women and men. *American Psychologist, 59,* 163–178.

Berkowitz, L. (1972). Social norms, feelings, and other factors affecting helping behavior and altruism. In L. Berkowitz (Ed.), *Advances in experimental and social psychology* (Vol. 5, pp. 63–102). New York: Academic.

Blau, P. M. (1963). *The dynamics of bureaucracy: A study of interpersonal exchange in two government agencies.* Chicago: University of Chicago Press.

Bolger, N., & Amarel, D. (2007). Effects of social support visibility on adjustment to stress: Experimental evidence. *Journal of Personality and Social Psychology, 92,* 458–475.

Boone, J. L. (1998). The evolution of magnanimity: When is it better to give than to receive? *Human Nature, 9,* 1–21.

Bornstein, R. F. (1992). The dependent personality: Developmental, social, and clinical perspectives. *Psychological Bulletin, 112,* 3–23.

Bowlby, J. (1982). *Attachment and loss: Vol. 1. Attachment* (2nd ed.). New York: Basic. (Original work published 1969)

Brehm, J. W. (1966). *A theory of psychological reactance.* New York: Academic.

Brickman, P., Rabinovitz, V. C., Karuza, J., Coates. D., Cohn. D., & Kidder, L. (1982). Models of helping and coping. *American Psychologist, 37*(4), 368–384.

Brown, S. L., & Brown, R. M. (2006). Selective investment theory: Recasting the functional significance of close relationships. *Psychological Inquiry, 17,* 1–29.

Brown, S. L., Bulanda, J. R., & Lee, G. L. (2005). The significance of cohabitation: Marital status and mental health benefits among middle-aged and older adults. *Journal of Gerontology: Social Sciences, 60,* 21–29.

Brown, S. L., House, J. S., Brown, R. M., & Smith, D. M. (2008). Coping with spousal loss: The buffering effects of helping behavior. *Personality and Social Psychology Bulletin, 34,* 849–861.

Brown, S. L., Nesee, R. M., Vinokur, A. D., & Smith, D. M. (2003). Providing social support may be more beneficial than receiving it. *Psychological Science, 14,* 320–327.

Brown, S. L., Smith, D. M., Schulz, R., Kabeto, M. U., Ubel, P. A., Poulin, M., et al. (2009). Caregiving behavior is associated with decreased mortality risk. *Psychological Science, 20*(4), 488–494.

Bryan, J. H., & Test, M. A. (1967). Models and helping. *Journal of Personality and Social Psychology, 6,* 400–407.

Burnstein, E., Crandall, C., & Kitayama, S. (1994). Some neo-Darwinian decision rules for altruism: Weighing cues for inclusive fitness as a function of the biological importance of the decision. *Journal of Personality and Social Psychology, 67,* 773–789.

Bushman, B. J., & Anderson, C. A. (2009). Comfortably numb: Desensitizing effects of violent media on helping others. *Psychology Science, 20,* 273–277.

Buss, D. M. (1995). Psychological sex differences: Origins through sexual selection. *American Psychologist, 50,* 164–168.

Carlo, G., Okun, M. A., Knight, G. P., & de Guzman, M. R. T. (2005). The interplay of traits and motives on volunteering: Agreeableness, extraversion, and prosocial value motivation. *Personality and Individual Differences, 38,* 1293–1305.

Cialdini, R. B., Brown, S. L., Lewis, B. P., Luce, C., & Neuberg, S. L. (1997). Reinterpreting the empathy-altruism relationship: When one into one equals oneness. *Journal of Personality and Social Psychology, 73,* 481–494.

Cialdini, R. B., Darby, B. K., & Vincent, J. E. (1973). Transgression and altruism: A case for hedonism. *Journal of Experimental Social Psychology, 9,* 502–516.

Clark, M. S., & Mills, J. R. (1993). The difference between communal and exchange relationships: What it is and is not. *Personality and Social Psychology Bulletin, 19,* 684–691.

Collins, N. L., Ford, M. B., Guichard, A. C., Kane, H. S., & Feeney, B. C. (2009). Responding to need in intimate relationships: Social support and caregiving processes in couples. In M. Mikulincer & P. Shaver (Eds.), *Prosocial emotions, motives and behavior* (pp. 367-389). Washington, DC: Psychology Press.

Costa, P. T, Jr., & McCrae, R. R. (1985). *The NEO personality inventory.* Odessa, FL: Psychological Assessment Resources.

Cronin, H. (1991). *The ant and the peacock.* New York: Cambridge University Press.

Crosby, F., Bromley, S., & Saxe, L. (1980). Recent unobtrusive studies of black and white discrimination and prejudice: A literature review. *Psychological Bulletin, 87,* 546–563.

Cunningham, E., & Platow, M. J. (2007). On helping lower status out-groups: The nature of the help and the stability of the intergroup status hierarchy. *Asian Journal of Social Psychology, 10*(4), 258–264.

Darley, J. M., & Batson, C. D. (1973). From Jerusalem to Jericho: A study of situational and dispositional variables in helping behavior. *Journal of Personality and Social Psychology, 27,* 100–108.

Darley, J. M., & Latané, B. (1968). Bystander intervention in emergencies: Diffusion of responsibility. *Journal of Personality and Social Psychology, 8,* 377–383.

Darley, J. M., Latané, B. (1970). Norms and normative behavior: Field studies of social interdependence. In J. Macauley & L. Berkowitz (Eds.), *Altruism and helping behavior* (pp. 83–101). New York: Academic.

Darley, J. M., Lewis, L. D., & Teger, A. (1973). Do groups always inhibit individuals' response to potential emergencies? *Journal of Personality and Social Psychology, 26,* 395–400.

Davis, M. H. (1983). Measuring individual differences in empathy: Evidence for a multidimensional approach. *Journal of Personality and Social Psychology, 44*(1), 113–126.

de Waal, F. (2009). *Primates and philosophers: How morality evolved.* Princeton, NJ: Princeton University Press.

Deelstra, J. T., Peeters, M. C. W., Schaufeli, W. B., Stroebe, W., van Doornen, L. O., & Zijlstra, F. R. H. (2003). Receiving instrumental support at work: When help is not welcome. *Journal of Applied Psychology, 88,* 324–331.

DePaulo, B. M., Dull, W. R., Greenberg, J. M., & Swaim, G. W. (1989). Are shy people reluctant to ask for help? *Journal of Personality and Social Psychology, 56,* 834–844.

DeWall, C. N., & Baumeister, R. F. (2006). Alone but feeling no pain: Effects of social exclusion on physical pain tolerance and pain threshold, affective forecasting, and interpersonal empathy. *Journal of Personality and Social Psychology, 91,* 1–15.

Digman, J. M. (1990). Personality structure: Emergence of the five-factor model. *Annual Review of Psychology, 41,* 417–440.

Doutreland, C., & Covas, R. (2007). Helping has signaling characteristics in a cooperatively breeding bird. *Animal Behavior, 74,* 734–747.

Dovidio, J. F., & Gaertner, S. L. (2004). Aversive racism. In M. P. Zanna (Ed.), *Advances in experimental social psychology* (Vol. 36, pp. 1–51). San Diego, CA: Academic.

Dovidio, J. F., Gaertner, S. L., Validzic, A., Matoka A., Johnson, B., & Frazier, S. (1997). Extending the benefits of recategorization: Evaluations, self-disclosure, and helping. *Journal of Experimental Social Psychology, 33,* 401–420.

Dovidio, J. F., Johnson, J. D., Gaertner, S. L., Pearson, A. R., Saguy, T., & Nardo, L. A. (2009). Empathy and intergroup relations. In M. Mikulincer & P. Shaver (Eds.), *Prosocial emotions motives and behavior* (pp. 393-408). Washington, DC: Psychology Press

Dovidio, J. F., Piliavin, J.A., Gaertner, S. L., Schroeder, D. A., & Clark, R. D., III (1991). The arousal:cost-reward model and the process of intervention: A review of the evidence. In M. S. Clark (Ed.), *Review of personality and social psychology: Vol. 12. Prosocial behavior* (pp. 86–118). Newbury Park, CA: Sage.

Dovidio, J. F., Piliavin, J. A., Schroeder, D. A., & Penner, L. A. (2006). *The social psychology of prosocial behavior.* Mahwah, NJ: Erlbaum.

Eagly, A. H., & Crowley, M. (1986). Gender and helping behavior: A meta-analytic review of the social psychological literature. *Psychology Bulletin, 100,* 283–308.

Eisenberg, N., & Fabes, R. A. (1991). Prosocial behavior and empathy: A multimethod developmental perspective. In M. S. Clark (Ed.), *Review of personality and social psychology: Vol. 12. Prosocial behavior* (pp. 34–61). Newbury Park, CA: Sage.

Eisenberg, N., Guthrie, I. K., Cumberland, A., Murphy, B. C., Shepard, S. A., Zhou, Q., et al. (2002). Prosocial development in early adulthood: A longitudinal study. *Journal of Personality and Social Psychology, 82,* 993–1006.

El-Alayli, A. L., & Messe', L. A. (2004). Reactions toward an unexpected or counternormative favor given: Does it matter if we think we can reciprocate? *Journal of Experimental Social Psychology, 40,* 633–641.

Emmons, R. A., & McCullough, M. E. (2004). *The psychology of gratitude.* New York: Oxford University Press.

Ferguson, E. (2004). Conscientiousness, emotional stability, perceived control, and the frequency, recency, rate, and years of blood donor behavior. *British Journal of Health Psychology, 9,* 293–314.

Fisher, J. D., & Nadler, A. (1976). Getting help from the rich and the poor: The effects of donor's level of resources on the recipient's self perceptions and subsequent self help behavior. *Journal of Experimental Social Psychology, 12,* 139–150.

Fisher, J. D., Nadler, A., Little, J. S., & Saguy, T. (2008). Help as a vehicle to reconciliation, with particular reference to help for extreme health needs. In A. Nadler, T. E. Malloy, & J. D. Fisher (Eds.), *Social psychology of inter-group reconciliation* (pp. 447–468). New York: Oxford University Press.

Fisher, J. D., Nadler, A., Whitcher-Alagna, S., (1982). Recipient reactions to aid: A conceptual review. *Psychological Bulletin, 91,* 27–54.

Flynn, F. J. (2003). How much should I give and how often? *Academy of Management Journal, 46,* 539–553.

Flynn, F. J., Reagans, R., Amanatullah, E. T., & Ames, D. R. (2006). Helping one's way to the top: Self-monitors achieve status by helping others and knowing who helps whom. *Journal of Personality and Social Psychology, 91,* 1123–1137.

Frankl, V. E. (1984). *Man's search for meaning.* New York: Washington Square Press.

Fredrickson, B. L., Mancuso, R. A., Branigan, C., & Tugade, M. M. (2000). The undoing effect of positive emotions. *Motivation and Emotion, 24,* 237–258.

Frieze, I. (1979). Perceptions of battered wives. In I. Frieze, D. Bar-Tal, & J. S. Carroll (Eds.), *New approaches to social problems* (pp. 79-108). San Francisco: Jossey-Bass.

Fultz, J., Schaller, M., & Cialdini, R. B. (1988). Empathy, sadness, and distress: Three related but distinct vicarious affective responses to another's suffering. *Personality and Social Psychology Bulletin, 14,* 312–325.

Gaertner, S. L., & Dovidio, J. F. (1977). The subtlety of white racism, arousal, and helping behavior. *Journal of Personality and Social Psychology, 35,* 691–707.

Gaertner, S. L., & Dovidio, J. F. (2000). *Reducing intergroup bias: The common ingroup identity model.* Philadelphia: Psychology Press.

Galdas, P. M., Cheater, F., & Marshall, P. (2005). Men and health seeking behavior: Literature review. *Journal of Advanced Nursing, 49*(6), 616–631.

Garcia, S. M., Weaver, K., Moskowitz, G. B., & Darley, J. M. (2002). Crowded minds: The implicit bystander effect. *Journal of Personality and Social Psychology, 83,* 843–853.

Gergen, K. J., Ellsworth, P., Maslach, C., & Seipel, M. (1975). Obligation, donor resources, and reactions to aid in three cultures. *Journal of Personality and Social Psychology, 31,* 390–400.

Gergen, K. J., Gergen, M. M., & Meter, K. (1972). Individual orientations to prosocial behavior. *Journal of Social Issues, 28,* 105–129.

Gest, S. D., Graham-Bermann, S. A., & Hartup, W. W. (2001). Peer experience: Common and unique features of number of friendships, social network centrality, and sociometric status. *Social Development, 10*(1), 23–40.

Ghiselin, M. (1974). *The economy of nature and the evolution of sex.* Berkley: University of California Press.

Gillath, O., Shaver, P. R., Mikulincer, M., Nitzberg, R. E., Erez, A., & van Ijzendoorn, M. H. (2005). Attachment, caregiving, and volunteering: Placing volunteerism in an attachment-theoretical framework. *Personal Relationships, 12,* 425–446.

Goldsmith, T. H. (1991). *The biological roots of human nature: Forging links between evolution and behavior.* New York: Oxford University Press.

Golombok, S., Cook, R., Bish, A., & Murray, C. (1995). Families created by the new reproductive technologies: Quality of parenting and social and emotional development of the children. *Child Development, 66,* 285–298.

Gouldner, A. W. (1960). The norm of reciprocity: A preliminary statement. *American Sociological Review, 25*(2), 161–178.

Graham, S. (1988). Children's developing understanding of the motivational role of affect: An attributional analysis. *Cognitive Development, 3,* 71–88.

Grant, A.M., & Gino, F., (2010). A little thanks goes a long way: Explaining why gratitude expression motivates prosocial behavior. *Journal of Personality and Social Psychology, 98,* 946-955.

Graziano, W. G., & Eisenberg, N. (1997). Agreeableness and altruism. In S. Briggs, R. Hogan, & W. Jones (Eds.), *Handbook of personality* (pp. 725–895). New York: Academic.

Graziano, W. G., & Habashi, M. M. (2010). Motivational processes underlying both prejudice and helping. *Personality and Social Psychology Review, 14,* 314–331.

Graziano, W. G., Habashi, M. M., Sheese, B. E., & Tobin, R. M. (2007). Agreeableness, empathy, and helping: A person × situation perspective. *Journal of Personality and Social Psychology, 93,* 583–599.

Graziano, W. G., & Tobin, R. M. (2002). Agreeableness: Dimension of personality or social desirability artifact? *Journal of Personality, 70,* 695–727.

Greenberg, J. (1980). Attentional focus and locus of performance causality as determinants of equity behavior. *Journal of Personality and Social Psychology, 38,* 579–585.

Halabi, S., Dovidio, J. F., & Nadler, A. (2008). When and how high status groups offer help: Effects of social dominance orientation and status threat. *Political Psychology, 29,* 841–858.

Hamilton, W. D. (1964). The genetic evolution of social behavior. *Journal of Theoretical Biology, 7,* 1–52.

Hardy, C., & Van Vugt, M. (2006). Nice guys finish first: The competitive altruism hypothesis. *Personality and Social Psychology Bulletin, 32,* 1402–1413.

Henry, P. J., Reyna, C., & Weiner, B. (2004). Hate welfare but help the poor: How the attributional content of stereotypes explains the paradox of reactions to the destitute in America. *Journal of Applied Social Psychology, 34*(1), 34–58.

Higgins, E. T., & Spiegel, S. (2004). Promotion and prevention strategies for self-regulation: A motivated cognition perspective. In R. F. Baumeister & K. D. Vohs (Eds.), *Handbook of self-regulation: Research, theory and applications* (pp. 171–187). New York: Guilford.

Hopkins, N., Reicher, S., Harrison, K., Cassidy, C., Bull, R., & Levine, M. (2007). Helping to improve the group stereotype: On the strategic dimension of prosocial behavior. *Personality and Social Psychology Bulletin, 33,* 776–788.

Hopper, J. R. (1991). Recycling as altruistic behavior: Normative and behavioral strategies to expand participation in a community recycling program. *Environment and Behavior, 23,* 195–220.

Hunt, M. (1990). *The compassionate beast: What science is discovering about the humane side of humankind.* New York: Morrow.

Jackson, L. M., & Esses, V. M. (2000). Effects of perceived economic competition on people's willingness to help empower immigrants. *Group Processes and Intergroup Relations, 3,* 419–435.

Jones, W. H., Cheek, J. M., & Briggs, S. R. (Eds.). (1986). *Shyness: Perspectives on research and treatment.* New York: Plenum.

Jordan, J. V. (1997). Do you believe that the concepts of self and autonomy are useful in understanding women? In J. V. Jordan(Ed.), *Women's growth in diversity: More writings from the Stone Center*(pp. 29-32). New York: Guilford.

King, E. B., George, J. M., & Hebl, M. R. (2005). Linking personality to helping behaviors at work: An interactional perspective. *Journal of Personality, 73,* 585–608.

Kleinman, S. B. (1989). A terrorist hijacking: Victims' experiences initially and 9 years later. *Journal of Traumatic Stress, 2,* 49–58.

Korchmoros, J. D., & Kenny, D. A. (2001). Emotional closeness as a mediator of the effect of genetic relatedness on altruism. *Psychological Science, 12,* 262–265.

Korchmaros, J. D., & Kenny, D. A. (2006). An evolutionary and close-relationship model of helping. *Journal of Social and Personal Relationships, 23,* 21–43.

Kruger, D. J. (2003). Evolution and altruism: Combining psychological mediators with naturally selected tendencies. *Evolution and Human Behavior, 24,* 118–125.

Kunce, L. J., & Shaver, P. R. (1994). An attachment-theoretical approach to caregiving in romantic relationships. In K. Bartholomew & D. Perlman (Eds.), *Advances in personal relationships* (Vol. 5, pp. 205–237). London: Kingsley.

Kunstman, J. W., & Plant, E. A. (2008). Racing to help: Racial bias in high emergency helping situations. *Journal of Personality and Social Psychology, 65*(6), 1499–1510.

Lamm, C. C., Batson, D. & Decety, J. (2007). The neural substrate of human empathy: Effects of perspective taking and cognitive appraisal. *Journal of Cognitive Neuroscience, 19*, 42–58.

Lane, J., & Anderson, N. H. (1976). Integration of intention and outcome in moral judgment. *Memory and Cognition, 4*, 1–5.

Langer, E. J., & Rodin, J. (1976). The effects of choice and enhanced personal responsibility for the aged: A field experiment in an institutional setting. *Journal of Personality and Social Psychology, 34*, 191–198.

Latané, B., & Darley, J .M. (1970). *The unresponsive bystander: Why doesn't he help?* New York: Appleton-Century-Crofts.

Lee, F. (1997). When the going gets tough, do the tough ask for help? Help seeking and power motivation in organizations. *Organizational Behavior and Human Decision Processes, 72*, 336–363.

Leone, G. (2009). *Le ambivalenze dell'aiuto* [The ambivalence of helping]. Rome: Carocci.

Levine, M., & Crowther, S. (2008). The responsive bystander: How social group membership and group size can encourage as well as inhibit bystander intervention. *Journal of Personality and Social Psychology, 95*(6), 1429–1439

Levine, M., Cassidy, C., Brazier, G., & Reicher, S. D. (2002). Self-categorization and bystander non-intervention: Two experimental studies. *Journal of Applied Social Psychology, 32*, 1452–1463.

Levine, M., Prosser, A., Evans, D., & Reicher, S. (2005). Identity and emergency intervention: How social group membership and inclusiveness of group boundaries shape helping behavior. *Personality and Social Psychology Bulletin, 31*, 443–453.

Levine, R. V., Martinez, T. S., Brase, G., & Sorenson, K. (1994). Helping in 36 U. S. cities. *Journal of Personality and Social Psychology, 67*, 69–82.

London, P. (1970). The rescuers: Motivational hypothesis about Christians who saved Jews from the Nazis. In J. Macaulay & L. Berkowitz (Eds.), *Altruism and helping behavior* (pp. 241–250). New York: Academic.

Lopez, S. J., & Snyder, C. R. (2009). *Oxford handbook of positive psychology* (2nd ed.). New York: Oxford University Press.

Macaulay, J. & Berkowitz, L. (Eds.). (1970). *Altruism and helping behavior: Social psychological studies of some antecedents and consequences.* New York: Academic.

Macksoud, M., & Aber, L. J. (1996). The war experiences and psychosocial development of children in Lebanon. *Child Development, 67*, 70–88.

Maner, J. K., Luce, C. L., Neuberg, S. L., Cialdini, R. B., Brown, S., & Sagarin, B. J. (2002). The effects of perspective taking on motivations for helping: Still no evidence for altruism. *Personality and Social Psychology Bulletin, 28*, 1601–1610.

Manning, R., Levine, M., & Collins, A. (2007). The Kitty Genovese murder and the social psychology of helping: The parable of the 38 witnesses. *American Psychologist, 62*, 555–562.

Martin, G. B., & Clark, R. D., III (1982). Distress crying in infants: Species and peer specificity. *Developmental Psychology, 18*, 3–9.

Mathews, K. E., & Cannon, L. K. (1975). Environmental noise level as a determinant of helping behavior. *Journal of Personality and Social Psychology, 32*, 571–577.

Matire, L. M., Stephens, M. A. P., Druley, J. A., & Wojno, W. C. (2002). Negative reactions to received spousal care: Predictors and consequences of miscarried support. *Health Psychology, 21*, 167–176.

Mayer, J. D., Salovey, E., Gomberg-Kaufman, S., & Blainey, K. (1991). A broader conception of mood experience. *Journal of Personality and Social Psychology, 60*, 100–111.

McCrae, R. R., & John, O. P. (1992). An introduction to the five-factor model and its applications. *Journal of Personality, 60*, 175–215.

McCullough, M. E., Emmons, R. A., & Tsang, J. (2002). The grateful disposition: A conceptual and empirical topography. *Journal of Personality and Social Psychology, 82*, 112–127.

McCullough, M. E., Tsang, J., & Emmons, R. A. (2004). Gratitude in intermediate affective terrain: Links of grateful moods to individual differences and daily emotional experience. *Journal of Personality and Social Psychology, 86*, 295–309.

McGuire, A. M. (1994). Helping behaviors in the natural environment: Dimensions and correlates of helping. *Personality and Social Psychology Bulletin, 20*(1), 45–56.

Midlarsky, E., & Kahana, E. (1994). *Altruism in later life.* Thousand Oaks, CA: Sage.

Midlarsky, E., Jones, S., & Corley, R. (2005). Personality correlates of heroic rescue during the holocaust. *Journal of Personality, 73*, 907–934.

Mikulincer, M., & Shaver, P. R. (2007). Contributions of attachment theory and research to motivation science. In J. Shah & W. Gardner (Eds.), *Handbook of motivation science* (pp. 201–216). New York: Guilford.

Mikulincer, M., & Shaver, P. (2009). Does gratitude promote prosocial behavior? The moderating role of attachment security. In M. Mikulincer & P. Shaver (Eds.), *Prosocial emotions motives and behavior* pp. 267-283). Washington, DC: Psychology Press.

Mikulincer, M., Shaver, P. R., Gillath, O., & Nitzberg, R. E. (2005). Attachment, caregiving, and altruism: Boosting attachment security increases compassion and helping. *Journal of Personality and Social Psychology, 89*, 817–839.

Milgram, S. (1970). The experience of living in cities. *Science, 167*, 1461–1468.

Mischel, W. (1968). *Personality and assessment.* New York: Wiley.

Mischel, W. (2004). Toward an integrative science of the person. *Annual Review of Psychology, 55*, 1–22

Montjabi, R., Olfson, M., & Mechanic, D. (2002). Perceived need and help-seeking in adults with mood, anxiety, or substance use disorders. *Archives of General Psychiatry, 59*, 77–84.

Nadler, A. (1986). Self esteem and help seeking and receiving: Empirical and theoretical perspectives. In B. A. Maher (Ed.), *Progress in experimental personality research* (Vol. 14, pp. 115–165). New York: Academic.

Nadler, A. (1987). Determinants of help seeking behavior: The effects of helper's similarity, task centrality, and recipient's self esteem. *European Journal of Social Psychology, 17*, 57–67.

Nadler, A. (1991). Help seeking behavior: Psychological costs and instrumental benefits. In M. S. Clark (Ed.), *Review of personality and social psychology* (Vol. 12, pp. 290–312). New York: Sage.

Nadler, A. (1997). Autonomous and dependent help seeking: Personality characteristics and the seeking of help. In B. Sarason, I. Sarason, & R. G. Pierce (Eds.), *Handbook of personality and social support* (pp. 258–302). New York: Plenum.

Nadler, A. (1998). Esteem, relationships, and achievement explanations of help seeking behavior. In S. A. Karabenick (Ed.), *Strategic help seeking: Implications for learning and teaching* (pp. 61–96). Hillsdale, NJ: Erlbaum.

Nadler, A. (2002). Inter-group helping relations as power relations: Helping relations as affirming or challenging intergroup hierarchy. *Journal of Social Issues, 58,* 487–503.

Nadler, A. (2009). Interpersonal and intergroup helping relations as power relations: Implications for real world helping. In S. Stürmer & M. Snyder (Eds.), *The psychology of prosocial behavior: Group processes, intergroup relations, and helping* (pp. 269-289). Oxford, UK: Wiley-Blackwell.

Nadler, A., Altman, A., & Fisher, J. D. (1979). Effects of positive and negative information about the self on recipient's reactions to aid. *Journal of Personality, 47,* 616–629.

Nadler, A., Bar-Tal, D., & Drukman, O. (1982). Density does not help: Help giving, help seeking, and help reciprocating of students living in high rise and lower dormitories. *Population and Environment: Behavioral and Social Issues, 5,* 26–42.

Nadler, A., Ellis, S., & Bar, I. (2003). To seek or not to seek: The relationship between help seeking and job performance evaluations as moderated by task-relevant expertise. *Journal of Applied Social Psychology, 33*(1), 91–109.

Nadler, A., & Fisher, J. D. (1986). The role of threat to self esteem and perceived control in recipient reactions to aid: Theory development and empirical validation. In L. Berkowitz (Ed.), *Advances in experimental social psychology* (Vol. 19, pp. 81–124). New York: Academic.

Nadler, A., Fisher, J. D., & Ben-Itzhak, S. (1983). With a little help from my friend: Effects of single or multiple act aid as a function of donor and task characteristics. *Journal of Personality and Social Psychology, 44,* 310–321.

Nadler, A., Fisher, J. D., & Streufert, S. (1974). The donor's dilemma: Recipient's reactions to aid from friend or foe. *Journal of Applied Social Psychology, 4,* 265–275.

Nadler, A., Fisher, J. D., & Streufert, S., (1976). When helping hurts: Recipient's level of self esteem and donor-recipient similarity as determinants of recipient's reactions to being helped. *Journal of Personality, 44,* 392–409.

Nadler, A., & Halabi, S. (2006). Intergroup helping as status relations: Effects of status stability, identification, and type of help on receptivity to high status group's help. *Journal of Personality and Social Psychology, 91,* 97–110.

Nadler, A., Halabi, S., & Harpaz-Gorodeisky, G. (2009). Intergroup helping as status organizing processes: Creating, maintaining, and challenging status relations through giving, seeking, and receiving help. In S. Demoulin, J. P. Leyens, & J. F. Dovidio (Eds.), *Intergroup misunderstandings: Impact of divergent social realities* (pp. 311–331). Washington, DC: Psychology Press.

Nadler, A., Harpaz-Gorodeisky, G., & Ben-David, Y. (2009). Defensive helping: Threat to group identity, ingroup identification, status stability, and common group identity as determinants of intergroup helping. *Journal of Personality and Social Psychology, 97*(5), 823–834.

Nadler, A., Lewinstein, E., & Rahav, G. (1991). Acceptance of retardation and help seeking: Correlates of help seeking preferences of mothers and fathers of retarded children. *Mental Retardation, 29*(1), 17–23.

Nadler, A., Maler, S., & Friedman, A. (1984). Effects of helper's sex, subject's androgyny, and self evaluation on males' and females' willingness to seek and receive help. *Sex Roles, 10,* 327–340.

Nadler, A., Mayseless, O., Peri, N., & Chemerinski, A. (1985). Effects of self esteem and ability to reciprocate on help seeking behavior. *Journal of Personality, 53,* 23–36.

Nadler, A., & Porat, I. (1978). When names do not help: Effects of anonymity and locus of need attributions on help seeking behavior. *Personality and Social Psychology Bulletin, 4,* 624–628.

Nadler, A., & Saguy, T. (2004). Trust building and reconciliation between adversarial groups: A social psychological perspective. In H. Langholtz & C. E. Stout (Eds.), *The psychology of diplomacy* (pp. 29–47). New York: Praeger.

Nadler, A., Sheinberg, L., & Jaffe, Y. (1981). Coping with stress by help seeking: Help seeking and receiving behaviors in male paraplegics. In C. Spielberger, I. Sarason, & N. Milgram (Eds.), *Stress and anxiety* (Vol. 8, pp. 375–386). Washington, DC: Hemisphere.

Oliner, S. P., & Oliner, P. M. (1988). *The altruistic personality: Rescuers of Jews in Nazi Europe.* New York: Free Press.

Omoto, A. M., & Snyder, M. (1995). Sustained helping without obligation: Motivation, longevity of service and perceived attitude change among AIDS volunteers. *Journal of Personality and Social Psychology, 68*(4), 671–686.

Omoto, A. M., & Snyder, M. (2002). Considerations of community: The context and process of volunteerism. *American Behavioral Scientist, 45,* 846–867.

Omoto, A. M., & Snyder, M. (2009). Influences of psychological sense of community on voluntary helping and prosocial action. In S. Stürmer & M. Snyder (Eds.), *The psychology of prosocial behavior: Group processes, intergroup relations, and helping* (pp. 223–243). Oxford, UK: Wiley-Blackwell.

Omoto, A. M., Snyder, M., & Martino, S. C. (2000). Volunteerism and the life course: Investigating age-related agendas for action. *Basic and Applied Social Psychology, 22,* 181–197.

Penner, L. A. (2002). The causes of sustained volunteerism: An interactionist perspective. *Journal of Social Issues, 58,* 447–468.

Penner, L. A., Dovidio, J. F., Piliavin, J. A., & Schroeder, D. A. (2005). Prosocial behavior: Multilevel perspectives. *Annual Review of Psychology, 56,* 365–392.

Penner, L. A., & Finkelstein, M. A. (1998). Dispositional and structural determinants of volunteerism. *Journal of Personality and Social Psychology, 74,* 525–537.

Penner, L. A., Fritzsche, B. A., Craiger, J. P., & Freifeld, T. R. (1995). Measuring the prosocial personality. In J. Butcher & C. D. Spielberger (Eds.), *Advances in personality assessment* (Vol. 10, pp. 147–163). Hillsdale, NJ: Erlbaum.

Penner, L. A., & Orom, H. (2009). Enduring goodness: A person by situation perspective on prosocial behavior. In M. Mikulincer & P. Shaver (Eds.), *Prosocial emotions motives and behavior* (pp. 55–72). Washington, DC: Psychology Press.

Piliavin, J. A. (2003). Doing well by doing good: Benefits for the benefactor. In C. L. M. Keyes & J. Haidt (Eds.), *Flourishing: The positive personality and the life well lived* (pp. 227–247). Washington, DC: American Psychological Association.

Piliavin, J. A. (2009). Volunteering across the life span: Doing well by doing good. In S. Stürmer & M. Snyder (Eds.), *The psychology of prosocial behavior: Group processes, intergroup relations, and helping* (pp. 157–172). Oxford, UK: Wiley-Blackwell.

Piliavin, J. A., Dovidio, J. F., Gaertner, S. L., & Clark, R. D. (1981). *Emergency intervention.* New York: Academic.

Piliavin, I. M., Rodin, J., & Piliavin, J. A. (1969). Good Samaritanism: An underground phenomenon? *Journal of Personality and Social Psychology, 13,* 289–299.

Piliavin, J. A., & Unger, R. K. (1985). The helpful but helpless female: Myth or reality? In V. O. O'Leary, R. K. Unger, & B. S. Wallston (Eds.), *Women, gender, and social psychology* (pp. 149–186). Hillsdale, NJ: Erlbaum.

Pratkanis, A. R., & Turner, M. E. (1996). The proactive removal of discriminatory barriers: Affirmative action as effective help. *Journal of Social Issues, 52*(4), 111–132.

Reicher, S. D., Cassidy, C., Wolpert, I., Hopkins, N., & Levine, M. (2006). Saving Bulgaria's Jews: An analysis of social identity and the mobilisation of social solidarity. *European Journal of Social Psychology, 36,* 49–72.

Reicher, S.D., Haslam, A. (2009). Beyond help: A social psychology of collective solidarity and social cohesion. In S. Stürmer & M. Snyder (Eds.), *The psychology of prosocial behavior: Group processes, intergroup relations, and helping* (pp. 290-309). Oxford, UK: Wiley-Blackwell.

Robinson, J. L., Zahn-Waxler, C. J., & Emde, R. N. (2001). Relationship context as a moderator of sources of individual differences in empathic development. In R. Emde & J. Hewitt (Eds.), *Infancy to early childhood: Genetic and environmental influences on developmental change* (pp. 257–268). London: Oxford University Press.

Rogoff, B. (2003). *The cultural nature of human development.* New York: Oxford University Press.

Rosenhan, D. L. (1970). The natural socialization of altruistic autonomy. In J. Macaulay & L. Berkowitz (Eds.), *Altruism and helping behavior: Social psychological studies of some antecedents and consequences* (pp. 251–268). New York: Academic Press.

Ross, A. S., & Braband, J. (1973). Effect of increased responsibility on bystander intervention: II. The cue value of a blind person. *Journal of Personality and Social Psychology, 25,* 254–258.

Rudolph, U., Roesch, S. C., Greitemeyer, T., & Weiner, B. (2004). A meta-analytic review of help giving and aggression from an attributional perspective. *Cognition and Emotion, 18,* 815–848.

Rushton, J. P. (1975). Generosity in children: Immediate and long term effects of modeling, preaching, and moral judgment. *Journal of Personality and Social Psychology, 31,* 459–466.

Rushton, J. P., Fulker, D. W., Neale, M. C., Nias, D. K. B., & Eysenck, H. J. (1986). Altruism and aggression: The heritability of individual differences. *Journal of Personality and Social Psychology, 50,* 1192–1198.

Rutkowski, G. K., Gruder, C. L., & Romer, D. (1983). Group cohesiveness, social norms, and bystander intervention. *Journal of Personality and Social Psychology, 44,* 545–552.

Ryan, A. M., Patrick, H., & Shim, S. (2005). Differential profiles of students identified by their teacher as having avoidant, appropriate, or dependent help-seeking tendencies in the classroom. *Journal of Educational Psychology, 97,* 275–285.

Ryan, R. M., & Deci, E. L. (2001). On happiness and human potentials: A review of research on hedonic and eudaimonic well-being. *Annual Review of Psychology, 52,* 141–166.

Saucier, D. A., Miller, C. T., & Doucet, N. (2005). Differences in helping whites and blacks: A meta-analysis. *Personality and Social Psychology Bulletin, 9,* 2–16.

Schaller, M., & Cialdini, R. B. (1988). The economics of empathic helping: Support for a mood management motive. *Journal of Experimental Social Psychology, 24,* 163–181.

Schneider, M. E., Major, B., Luhtanen, R., & Crocker, J. (1996). Social stigma and the potential costs of assumptive help. *Personality and Social Psychology Bulletin, 22,* 201–209.

Schuster, M. A., Stein, B. D., Jaycox, L. H., Collins, R. L., Marshall, G. N., Elliott, M. N., et al. (2001). A national survey of stress reactions after the September 11, 2001, terrorist attacks. *New England Journal of Medicine, 345,* 1507–1512.

Schwartz, S. H., & Gottlieb, A. (1976). Bystander reactions to a violent theft: Crime in Jerusalem. *Journal of Personality and Social Psychology, 34,* 1188–1199.

Schwartz, S. H., & Howard, J. A. (1982). Helping and cooperation: A self-based motivational model. In V. J. Derlega & J. Grzelak (Eds.), *Cooperation and helping behavior: Theories and research* (pp. 327–353). New York: Academic.

Schwartz, S. H. & Howard, J.A. (1984). Internalized values as motivators of altruism. In E. Staub, D. Bar-Tal, J. Karylowski, & J. Reykowski (Eds.), *Development and maintenance of prosocial behavior* (pp. 229–255). New York: Plenum.

Sechrist, G., & Milford, L. (2007). The influence of social consensus information on intergroup helping behavior. *Basic and Applied Social Psychology, 29*(4), 365–374.

Shaver, P., Mikulincer, M., & Shemesh-Iron, M. (2009). A behavioral systems perspective on prosocial behavior. In M. Mikulnicer & P. Shaver (Eds.), *Prosocial emotions motives and behavior* (pp. 73–93). Washington, DC: Psychology Press.

Shell, R., & Eisenberg, N. (1992). A developmental model of recipients' reactions to aid. *Psychological Bulletin, 111,* 413–433.

Sidanius, J., & Pratto, F. (1999). *Social dominance: An intergroup theory of social hierarchy and oppression.* Cambridge, UK: Cambridge University Press.

Simpson, J. A., Rholes, W. S., & Nelligan, J. S. (1992). Support seeking and support giving within couples in an anxiety-provoking situation: The role of attachment styles. *Journal of Personality and Social Psychology, 62,* 434–446.

Skitka, L. J. (1999). Ideological and attributional boundaries on public compassion: Reactions to individuals and communities affected by a natural disaster. *Personality and Social Psychology Bulletin, 25,* 793–808.

Smith, K. D., Keating, J. P., & Stotland, E. (1989). Altruism reconsidered: The effect of denying feedback on a victim's status to empathic witnesses. *Journal of Personality and Social Psychology, 57,* 641–650.

Snyder, M., Clary, E. G., & Stukas, A. A. (2000). The functional approach to volunteerism. In J. M. Olson & G. R. Maio (Eds.), *Why we evaluate: Functions of attitudes* (pp. 365–393). Mahwah, NJ: Erlbaum.

Sprafkin, J. N., Liebert, R. M., & Poulous, R. W. (1975). Effects of a prosocial televised example on children's helping. *Journal of Personality and Social Psychology, 48,* 35–46.

Staub, E. (1971). Helping a person in distress: The influence of implicit and explicit "rules" of conduct on children and adults. *Journal of Personality and Social Psychology, 17,* 137–144.

Staub, E. (1974). Helping a distressed person: Social, personality, and stimulus determinants. In L. Berkowitz (Ed.), *Advances in experimental social psychology* (Vol. 7, pp. 293–341). New York: Academic.

Staub, E., & Vollhardt, J. (2008). Altruism born of suffering: The roots of caring and helping after victimization and other trauma. *American Journal of Orthopsychiatry, 78,* 267–280.

Steblay, N. M. (1987). Helping behavior in rural and urban environments: A meta-analysis. *Psychological Bulletin, 102,* 346–356.

Stewart-Williams, S. (2007). Altruism among kin vs. non-kin: Effects of cost of help and reciprocal exchange. *Evolution and Human Behavior, 28,* 193–198.

Stocks, E. L., Lishner, D. A., & Decker, S. K. (2009). Altruism or psychological escape: Why does empathy promote prosocial behavior. *European Journal of Social Psychology, 39*(5), 649–665.

Stouffer, S. A., Lumsdaine, A. A., Lumsdaine, M. H., Williams, R. M., Jr., Smith, M. B., Janis, I. L., et al. (Eds.). (1949). *The American soldier: Combat and its aftermath* (Vol. 2). Oxford, UK: Princeton University Press.

Stürmer, S., & Snyder, M. (2009). Helping "us" versus "them": Towards a group-level theory of helping and altruism within and across group boundaries. In S. Stürmer & M. Snyder (Eds.), *The psychology of prosocial behavior: Group processes, intergroup relations, and helping* (pp. 33–58). Oxford, UK: Wiley-Blackwell.

Stürmer, S., Snyder, M., Kropp, A., & Siem, B. (2006). Empathy-motivated helping: The moderating role of group membership. *Personality and Social Psychology Bulletin, 32,* 943–956.

Stürmer, S., Snyder, M., & Omoto, A. M. (2005). Prosocial emotions and helping: The moderating role of group membership. *Journal of Personality and Social Psychology, 85,* 532–546.

Taylor, J., & Turner, R. J. (2001). A longitudinal study of the role and significance of mattering to others for depressive symptoms. *Journal of Health and Social Behavior, 42,* 309–324.

Tessler, R. C., & Schwartz, S. H. (1972). Help seeking, self-esteem, and achievement motivation: An attributional analysis. *Journal of Personality and Social Psychology, 21*(3), 318–326.

Todorov, T. (2001). *The fragility of goodness.* London: Weidenfeld & Nicolson.

Trivers, R. (1985). *Social evolution.* Menlo Park, CA: Benjamin/Cummings.

Tsang, J. (2006). Gratitude and prosocial behavior: An experimental test of gratitude. *Cognition and Emotion, 20,* 138–148.

Tsang, J. (2007). Gratitude for small and large favors: A behavioral test. *Journal of Positive Psychology, 3,* 157–167.

Turner, J. C., & Reynolds, K. J. (2001). The social identity perspective in inter-group relations: Theories, themes, and controversies. In R. Brown & S. Gaertner (Eds.), *Intergroup processes* (pp. 133–153). Oxford, UK: Blackwell.

Twenge, J. M., Baumeister, R. F., DeWall, C. N., Ciarocco, N. J., & Bartels, J. M. (2007). Social exclusion decreases prosocial behavior. *Journal of Personality and Social Psychology, 92*(1), 56–66.

van Leeuwen, E. (2007). Restoring identity through outgroup helping: Beliefs about international aid in response to the December 2004 tsunami. *European Journal of Social Psychology, 37,* 661–671.

van Leeuwen, E., & Tauber, S. (2009). The strategic side of outgroup helping. In S. Stürmer & M. Snyder (Eds.), *The psychology of prosocial behavior: Group processes, intergroup relations, and helping* (pp. 81–99). Oxford, UK: Wiley-Blackwell.

Van Vugt, M., & Park, J. H. (2009). The tribal instinct hypothesis: Evolution and the social psychology of intergroup relations. In S. Stürmer & M. Snyder (Eds.), *The psychology of prosocial behavior: Group processes, intergroup relations, and helping* (pp. 13–32). Oxford, UK: Wiley-Blackwell.

Van Vugt, M., & van Lange, P. A. M. (2006). Psychological adaptations for prosocial behavior: The altruism puzzle. In M. Schaller, J. A. Simpson, & D. T. Kenrick (Eds.), *Evolution and social psychology* (pp. 237–261). New York: Psychology Press.

Veroff, J. B. (1981). The dynamics of help-seeking in men and women: A national survey study. *Psychiatry, 44,* 189–200.

Vollhardt, J. R. (2009). Altruism born of suffering and prosocial behavior following adverse life events: A review and conceptualization. *Social Justice Research, 22*(1), 53–97.

Wayment, H. (2004). It could have been me: Vicarious victims and disaster-focused distress. *Personality and Social Psychology Bulletin, 30,* 515–528.

Webley, P., & Lea, S. E. G. (1993). The partial unacceptability of money in repayment for neighborly help. *Human Relations, 46,* 65–76.

Weiner, B. (1993). On sin versus sickness: A theory of perceived responsibility and social motivation. *American Psychologist, 48,* 957–965.

Weiner, B. (2006). *Social motivation, justice, and the moral emotions: An attributional approach.* Mahwah, NJ: Erlbaum.

Weiner, B., Perry, R. P., & Magnusson, J. (1988). An attributional analysis of reactions to stigmas. *Journal of Personality and Social Psychology, 55*(5), 738–748.

Weiss, H. M., & Knight, P. A. (1980). The utility of humility: Self-esteem, information search, and problem-solving efficiency. *Organizational Behavior and Human Performance, 25,* 216–223.

Westmaas, J. L., & Silver, R. C. (2001). The role of attachment in responses to victims of life crises. *Journal of Personality and Social Psychology, 80,* 425–438.

Wills, T. A. (1991). Similarity and self-esteem in downward comparison. In J. Suls & T. A. Wills (Eds.), *Social comparison: Contemporary theory and research* pp. 51-74). Hillsdale, NJ: Erlbaum.

Wills, T. A., & DePaulo, B. M. (1991). Interpersonal analysis of the help seeking process. In C. R. Snyder & D. R. Forsyth (Eds.), *Handbook of social and clinical psychology* (pp. 350–375). Elmsford, NY: Pergamon.

Weinstein, N., DeHaan, C.R., & Ryan, R.M. (2010). Attributing autonomous vs. introjected motivation to helpers and the recipient experience: Effects on gratitude, attitudes and well being. *Motivation and Emotion, 34,* 418-431.

Worchel, S. W., Wong, F. Y., & Scheltema, K. E. (1989). Improving intergroup relations: Comparative effects of anticipated cooperation and helping on attraction for an aid giver. *Social Psychology Quarterly, 52,* 213–219.

Yinon, Y., & Landau, M. O. (1987). On the reinforcing value of helping behavior in a positive mood. *Motivation and Emotion, 11,* 83–93.

Antisocial Behavior in Individuals and Groups
An Empathy-Focused Approach

Emanuele Castano

Abstract

In this chapter a broadened perspective on antisocial behavior is proposed, which includes not only what is customarily considered antisocial behavior (e.g., aggression, theft, bullying) but also prejudice and discrimination toward outgroup members. This broadening is balanced by a narrowing of the causal factors that are considered, with an exclusive focus on empathy, or lack thereof, as the psychological dimension underlying the diverse types of antisocial behavior. It is argued that antisocial behavior is facilitated by low levels of dispositional empathy, but also by social psychological processes that actively curtail empathic reaction to others (us *versus* them distinction, dehumanization). The discussion of empathy as a thread common to a variety of antisocial behaviors also serves as a bridge between the personality and social psychological literature.

Keywords: antisocial behavior, aggression, offending, criminality, prejudice, discrimination, empathy, perspective-taking

Introduction

Recognizing the emotion of a fellow human being and experiencing that emotion as a consequence of such recognition is arguably one of the greatest idiosyncrasies of being human. Perhaps this situation is not *uniquely* human, but it certainly is what we would mention as an important milestone in our evolutionary history. As Hoffman (2000) wrote, "empathy is the spark of human concern for others, the glue that makes social life possible" (p. 3).

If empathy is central to our social existence, then a lack thereof is likely to hinder it. In this chapter I attempt to make the case that much of what we understand to be antisocial behavior is the consequence, among other things, of either an incapacity to experience empathy, or of the emergence of social practices, structures, and institutions that prevent us from experiencing empathy toward other human beings. The first claim, that antisocial behavior is the consequence of an incapacity to experiencing empathy, looks at dispositional empathy: empathy

as an individual difference that begins to develop very early in life, primarily in the form of distress at the suffering and pain of others, and evolves into the capacity to recognize distress in others. It includes the elaboration of an appropriate emotional response to that distress, which requires the cognitive capacity of taking another person's perspective. These steps can be thwarted by biological and neurological deficiencies (Decety & Ickes, 2009) as well as by poor socialization and rearing practices (Eisenberg, 2005; Hoffman, 1963, 2000; Krevans & Gibbs, 1996; Staub, 1994). Emotionality and the empathy level of caregivers, particularly the mother, affect the child's capacity to develop levels of empathy that are adequate to foster prosocial, and to inhibit antisocial, behavior (Eisenberg, 2005). In the first two sections of this chapter, I review evidence that antisocial behavior is associated with low dispositional empathy.

The second claim is that we *learn* when and toward whom to experience empathy, and that in this case, too, a lack of empathy can and indeed does lead to antisocial behavior. Signs of empathic feelings can be observed among nonhuman animals (Preston & DeWaal, 2002), and humans can certainly experience empathy for nonhuman creatures, such as puppies, bunnies, and even less cute animals or plants. However, it is toward human beings that our evolutionary history has made us particularly prone to empathic feelings because of the advantages of being sensitive to the needs of our offspring, and because we are social animals for whom cooperation with others is functional to survival and reproduction (Caporael, 1997; deWaal, 2005).

Not surprisingly, therefore, the very building blocks of empathy such as mimicry, emotional contagion, and the mirroring of the experience of another person, seem to be fairly ubiquitous and automatic processes (Lamm, Meltzoff, & Decety, 2010; Rizzolatti & Craighero, 2004). It is equally clear, however, that we also have at our disposal cognitive processes that can prevent an empathic response. This capacity is courtesy of the enhanced cognitive control exerted by the prefrontal cortex: empathic responses are automatically prepared, but the prefrontal cortex inhibits actual response. When the prefrontal cortex is damaged, a compulsive imitation of gestures and complex actions occurs (L'hermitte, Pillon, & Serdan, 1986). This curtailing is an important, adaptive feature, and not only for British subjects in Victorian times. For, if we were to react with empathic feelings to each and every situation that has the potential to elicit such feelings, we would soon be exhausted (Maslach & Jackson, 1982). Furthermore, in a host of contexts, such as those in which medical personnel find themselves, automatic empathic reaction would not only be detrimental for the person experiencing it (e.g., emotional burnout), but also for the patients. Recent fMRI findings show that, when visually presented with body parts being pricked by needles, control participants show activation in areas involved in self-other distinctions (dorsolateral and medial prefrontal cortex) and the *pain matrix* (Derbyshire, 2000), but physicians who practice acupuncture activate only the former (Cheng et al. 2007; see also Decety, Yang, & Cheng, 2010).

In the above example, empathy needs to be reduced for positive consequences to ensue, but there are a variety of contexts characterized by a curtailing of empathy toward others that result in antisocial behavior. By "contexts," I refer to the interplay between social structures and institutions on the one hand, and psychological processes on the other—particularly the process of social categorization. Not all others are created equal, of course. Outgroup members, however defined, are perceived and treated differently than ingroup members, as extensive theoretical and empirical work shows (Brewer, 1979; Yzerbyt, Castano, Leyens, & Paladino, 2000). Stereotyping, prejudice, and the exclusion of outgroup members from the moral community and the scope of justice are interpreted here as foremost examples of antisocial behavior. "Here in America you cannot see the suffering, the desolation, the pain of the Iraqi people," the Associated Press journalist Scheherezade Faramarzi told my undergraduate class earlier this year while describing the Iraq War. "News gives you no opportunity to feel empathy for them." In the third section of this chapter, I review the literature and highlight the role that curtailing empathy toward outgroup members plays in discriminatory behavior toward them.

I would like to think that this chapter is unusual in at least a couple of ways. First, it covers material (specifically in the second and third sections) that is not typically discussed in handbook chapters on antisocial behavior. Normally, when we think about antisocial behavior, prejudice, discrimination, and collective violence do not come to mind. My attempt to expand our understanding of what antisocial behavior is has at least one scientific and one political motive. First, I believe that considering the similarity in the proximal antecedents of behaviors that psychologists have traditionally put in different classes will inform and improve psychological theory. Integration, even when not immediately creating a new research paradigm, is valuable.

Second, I think that the societal discourse that considers the murder of a single person an unspeakable act, but often overlooks the murder of hundreds of thousands as a necessary evil, needs to be challenged. This societal discourse is mirrored in our scientific discourse through the separation of fields of inquiry that I mentioned above. Textbooks almost always separate chapters on antisocial behavior, prejudice, and intergroup relations. Although I do not devote many words to an explicit discussion of an integration, the chapter itself, by identifying and discussing empathy as a common mediator for a larger definition of antisocial behavior, partly makes a case for it.

The perspective that I take in this chapter has at least one disadvantage. What you are about to read is far from being a comprehensive account of antisocial behavior. I have not included discussions of impulsivity, labeling theory, and criminal subculture, or of other factors that research has shown to be connected to antisocial behavior. For those areas, I urge you to read the excellent review by Geen (1998), which discusses the impact of social learning, frustration, norms, and other factors—and to consult one of the handbooks of antisocial behavior for a more comprehensive review of its possible causes (e.g., Stoff, Breiling, & Maser, 1997). In this chapter, I discuss empathy, or lack thereof, as a predictor of antisocial behavior, which I understand in a much broader sense than is customarily the case.

I should also say that my focus on empathy is the consequence of my belief that a great deal of antisocial behavior has to do with *disconnectedness*. Davis (2004) puts it clearly: "[Empathy is] the psychological process that at least temporarily unites the separate social entities of self and other" (p. 20). It is the broken connection between the self and the other, between the ingroup and the outgroup, that I see as an important precursor of antisocial behavior.

Before reviewing evidence of the relation between empathy and antisocial behavior, I discuss how this chapter attempts to combine personality and social psychological research in a meaningful manner, and offer a brief definition of empathy.

Person, Situation

In spite of sharing the most prestigious scientific journals and at least one prominent Society (the Society for Personality and Social Psychology), personality and social psychologists have long diverged on their answer to the foremost question in our field: What influences human behavior?

There is a long tradition, going back to ancient Greece throughout European intellectual history, in which human behavior is primarily conceived of as stemming from traits, or dispositions. What these are, however, is disputed. The most traditional view in personality theory and research, which can be traced back to Allport (1937), views traits as organized hierarchically in layers of increasing abstractness, at the top of which reside five or seven dimensions (Costa & McCrae, 1992; Digman, 1990; Goldberg, 1993). These dimensions, or global traits (e.g., conscientiousness, agreeableness), are thought to be determined by both environment and biology (Caspi, Roberts, & Shiner, 2005; Krueger, South, Johnson, & Iacono, 2008), and are considered to be relatively stable over the life span (Roberts & DelVecchio, 2000) and to be related to a variety of consequential life outcomes (for a recent review, see Ozer & Benet-Martinez, 2006).

A broader, and quite radically different, view of personality has been proposed by Mischel (1968, 1973), who criticizes trait theory's reduction of personality to a set of highly abstract dimensions that impact behavior mostly independently of situational context. Mischel's starting point in his original contribution (1968) was investigating the rather weak empirical evidence for cross-situational stability of behavior, which led him to elaborate a view of personality as a system rather than simply a collection of abstract traits. This perspective, which calls for an integration of many of psychology's subfields, provides a bridge between what he identifies as two distinct approaches to personality, namely, the dispositional and the processing approaches (Mischel & Shoda, 2008). These ideas were later elaborated in the cognitive-affective processing system (CAPS), a metatheory in which behavior is not seen as caused by either traits as traditionally conceived or by the environment, but rather as the outcome of complex interactions between a set of predispositions, a variety of cognitive-affective units (expectancies, affects, etc.), and the specific circumstances in which the person finds herself (and her subjective understanding of such circumstances) (Mischel & Shoda, 1995; see also Mendoza-Denton & Ayduk, chapter 18, this volume). Behavioral stability, according to Mischel, is to be found in the *if. . . then. . .* behavioral signatures not *across* but rather *within* different situations.

The foremost evidence in support of Mischel's view is concerned with, quite fittingly to the purpose of this chapter, aggression among children at the Wediko summer camp.[1] These data show that aggressive behavior varied widely, yet systematically, from one situation to another, with some children displaying aggression specifically (if not exclusively) in interaction with peers, while others did so in interaction with adults, for instance when given a warning (Shoda, Mischel, & Wright, 1994). This unique data yields strong support for a view of behavior as stemming from the interaction of individual characteristics (what Mischel calls a "personality system") and the specific context as encoded and interpreted by the perceiver.

Data like this, however, is unique. Research on the empathy-antisocial behavior relation stemming from the personality tradition has conceptualized empathy as a trait in the traditional way. Social psychological research—focusing on the impact of the situation—has either inferred empathy (or lack thereof) as playing a role in the context at hand, or measured it as a state. The bulk of this chapter reviews this evidence, with the primary aim of making the case for empathy as a critical mediating factor on antisocial behavior. I will return to the question of integration of person and situation variables in the concluding section, when outlining the directions for future research.

What Is Empathy?

As is customary, the impressive amount of research on empathy has not led to a common definition, but rather to a variety of understandings of what is meant by empathy. One important distinction is between affective empathy and cognitive empathy. *Affective empathy* refers to the extent to which a person experiences emotions in response to another person's expression of an emotional state. Some authors distinguish, within this affective response, between empathy (an emotional response evoked by the affective state or situation of the other person) and sympathy (an emotional response, elicited by the emotional state or situation of the other person, that is not identical to the other's emotion and involves feelings of concern or sorrow for the other person) (Miller & Eisenberg, 1988).

Cognitive empathy, conversely, refers to the understanding of what another person is experiencing, to putting oneself in the other person's shoes. Although what is meant by empathy can and in some cases does make a difference, by and large, when referring to empathy without further discussion, I mean both an understanding of the emotional state of another as well as some sharing of that emotional state or concern/sorrow for the person (akin to sympathy). In considering empathy as inextricably composed of affect and cognition, I concur with most empathy researchers (e.g., Davis, 1983; Hoffman, 1982), and certainly with S. Feshbach (1978), who described empathy as encompassing three components: (1) a cognitive ability to discriminate affective cues in others, (2) a capacity to assume the perspective of another person, and (3) emotional responsiveness to the experience of emotions.

Dispositional Empathy and Antisocial Behavior

> Individuals who vicariously experience the negative reactions of others that occur because of their own aggressive behavior may be less inclined to continue their aggression or to aggress in future interactions.
> *Miller and Eisenberg* (1988, p. 324)

As I hinted at above, the link between empathy and antisocial behavior around which this chapter revolves is ultimately about connectedness. The greater a person's capacity, or readiness, to establish a connection with other human beings (the greater the empathy), the lesser the chances that she will engage in behavior that disregards and disrupts such a connection (antisocial behavior). This section is devoted to establishing whether this conjecture is supported by psychological research. I review evidence that comes from studies that have investigated a variety of populations, varying from young children to adult inmates, have operationalized empathy in several ways, and have looked at different indicators of antisocial behavior. Is empathy an inhibitor of antisocial behavior?

A good starting point to begin answering this question is a meta-analysis by Miller and Eisenberg (1988). While the authors recognize that antisocial behavior may be the consequence of deficits in both cognitive and affective empathy, the meta-analysis focused on *affective* empathy. In the various studies included in the meta-analysis, empathy was measured in different ways: (1) a picture/story assessment of empathy, in which participants, typically children, are presented with narratives/pictures depicting a person in emotion-eliciting situations and asked what they feel (see N. D. Feshbach & Roe, 1968); (2) self-reports/questionnaires, typically the Mehrabian and Epstein (1972) scale, which does not differentiate between various affective types of empathy; (3) facial/gestural indexes of empathy; (4) experimental inductions of empathy; and (5) empathy training.

Antisocial behavior measures ranged from peer or teacher ratings of aggressive attitudes to aggression measured in experimental settings, and also included measures of externalizing behaviors—namely, negative behaviors that are expressed outwardly and are likely to directly affect other people and society at large (e.g., threatening, fighting, general disobedience). The results of the meta-analysis showed that while empathy tended to correlate negatively with aggression and antisocial/externalizing behavior, it was only when it was measured through questionnaires that the correlation was reliable. This might have been due to the fact that it is dispositional empathy that it is the most reliable predictor of these kinds of behavior, or to a development-related confound, for the studies that assessed empathy via a questionnaire tended to have adults, adolescents and school-age children, as opposed to the studies that used the other methods, which tended to use younger children. In fact, a reliable negative correlation between aggression and empathy also appeared when the latter was measured with the picture/story method, if studies using preschoolers were eliminated from the analyses.

Since correlations between self-report measures that are relatively transparent in their goals may tell us more about the person's response style and self-presentation than about the extent of the relation between the two concepts being measured, it is important to note that in the 15 samples in which empathy was measured via a questionnaire, the measures of aggression were not, with one exception, self-report measures, but ranged from teachers' ratings of peer-directed physical and verbal aggression (Bryant, 1982) to the administration of shocks in a learning task (Gaines, Kirwin, & Gentry, 1977). One example of the latter is a milestone study by Mehrabian and Epstein (1972), in which participants were asked to punish with electric shock another participant (in actuality a confederate) every time he provided a wrong answer. The mean intensity of all the shocks administered was used as measure of aggressive behavior, while empathy was assessed via a questionnaire that focused on affective empathy, built ad hoc for the experiment—to become one of the most widely used self-report measures of empathy. The immediacy of the victim was also manipulated. In one condition, the victim was fully visible, while in the other condition, he was hidden. Results showed that empathic tendency alone is not sufficient to inhibit aggressive behavior, but when it is combined with immediacy of the victim, it has an inhibitory effect.

Several studies have been conducted since Miller and Eisenberg's (1988) meta-analysis, and yielded further support for the proposed empathy-antisocial link. Richardson, Hammock, Smith, Gardner, and Signo (1994) investigated the effect of empathy on self-report as well as behavioral measures of aggression in a series of studies. In a first study they found perspective-taking as well as empathic concern (Interpersonal Reactivity Index, IRI, Davis, 1983) to be negatively correlated to some subscales of the Buss-Durkee Hostility Inventory (Buss & Durkee, 1957), to other measures of conflict management with friends and siblings, and to a conflict tactics scale (Steinmetz, 1977). In a second study, instructing students to empathize with another participant with whom they engaged in a competitive task led to a decrease in aggression (lower electric shocks) compared to participants who did not receive such instructions. In a third study, they were able to show that the perspective-taking subscale of the IRI (but not the empathic concern subscale) moderated responses in moderate-threat situations, with high perspective-takers responding less aggressively (measured by the degree of offensiveness of messages sent to another participant) than their low perspective-taking counterparts (see also Richardson, Green, & Lago, 1998).

Similar moderating effects of empathy were found in an excellent study conducted by Giancola (2003), which investigated the effect of alcohol consumption on aggression (in this case, as well, using the administration of electric shocks to, allegedly, another participant) and used the empathic concern and perspective-taking subscales of the IRI as a measure of empathy. Alcohol led to increased aggression among low empathy males (particularly at low levels of provocation), but not among high empathy males. Importantly, the moderating effect of empathy emerged using either of the IRI subscales, yielding support for the idea that while cognitive and affective aspects of empathy can be distinguished, they may well operate jointly in inhibiting antisocial behavior. Other studies, using different measures of empathy, have also found the same negative relationship with aggression, both physical and verbal. Sergeant et al. (2006), for example, found that Empathic Quotient (Baron-Cohen et al., 2003) scores correlated negatively with physical and verbal aggression, as well as with anger and hostility, among both heterosexual and homosexual males.

The relation between aggression and empathy has also long been documented with young children (N. D. Feshbach & Feshbach, 1969), but I focus here on more recent studies. Hastings, Zahn-Waxler, Robinson, Usher, and Bridges (2000) conducted one of the few longitudinal studies assessing the effect of concern for others (a composite measure that included empathic and sympathetic reaction to others in distress) on externalizing behavior, and were able to show that higher levels of concern at age 4–5 predicted a decrease in both stability and severity of externalizing problems at age 6–7. Another study by Strayer and Roberts (2004) reached similar conclusions. The authors assessed physical and verbal aggression using Lenrow's (1965) Puppet Procedure with a group of 5-year-olds, and compiled empathy scores for the same using a variety of indicators ranging from the children's reaction to stimuli to ratings by teachers, parents and friends. This elaborate measure of empathy revealed a very strong correlation with physical (-.48) as well as verbal (-.37) aggression. This study is noteworthy in two respects. First, the measure of empathy is not self-reported, but a composite of different methods and sources. Second, and related to the first point, it allows for the causal claim between empathy and aggression, both because of the longitudinal character of the study, and because aggression was measured in response to a specific situation that occurred at the end of the study.

Aggression researchers have also noted the importance, particularly when working with children and youth, to assess not only the degree of aggressive behavior, but its persistence. Carrasco, Barker, Tremblay, and Vitaro (2006) assessed self-reports of physical aggression, theft, and vandalism once per year in a multiyear longitudinal study that also included, in one year, a measure of empathy amid other personality dimensions. The results showed that boys with a persistent (as compared to low-declining) trajectory in physical aggression and vandalism (but not theft) showed lower levels of empathy.

Research has also investigated the impact of empathy on specific forms of aggression, such as relational aggression, proactive/reactive aggression, and bullying. Relational aggression is defined as harming others through purposeful manipulation of and damage to interpersonal relationships (see Crick & Grotpeter, 1995). In a sample of college-age individuals, Loudin, Loukas, and Robinson (2003) found that perspective-taking was negatively correlated with relationally aggressive behavior among both males and females, but empathic concern only correlated with such a behavior in men.

In addition to varying in the form that it takes, aggression can also vary in terms of its genesis. Baron and Richardson (1994) proposed a distinction between proactive and reactive aggression. Proactive aggression is thought to be characterized by little emotional intensity (Hubbard et al., 2002) and is aimed at attaining a goal, rather than as a response to threat or goal blocking, which characterize reactive aggression. Thus, Mayberry and Espelage (2007) argued that the former should be related to higher levels of cognitive empathy/perspective-taking, but to lower levels of affective empathy. In a study with a large sample of middle schoolers, however, they found no systematic differences between these two forms of aggression. On the empathic concern and perspective-taking subscales of the IRI, they found a difference between those showing aggression in general and those who did not. As in other research studies reviewed here, this effect was very clear for males, but less so for females, who displayed a difference between aggression and nonaggression only on the perspective-taking measure.

A very specific kind of antisocial behavior, which can have profound consequences for its victims, is bullying (Geffner, Loring, & Young, 2001). This, too, has been shown to be related to empathy. Attitudes toward bullying correlated negatively with empathic concern (measured with the Olweus' Empathic Responsiveness Questionnaire, ERQ; Olweus & Endresen, 1998) among 13- to 16-year-olds (Endresen & Olweus, 2001). And in a large study using middle school students, Mayberry and Espelage (2007) found that students involved in bullying others reported lower levels of empathy as compared to those not involved. Similarly, Nickerson, Mele, and Princiotta (2008) found that students who were classified as defenders of the victim on the basis of their response to a hypothetical bullying scenario (Participant Role Descriptions, PRD, Salmivalli et al., 1996) scored higher on empathy (ERQ) as compared to those who were classified as observers. Most recently, Jolliffe and Farrington (2011) provide further evidence using a large sample of English teenagers, and show that the negative relation between affective empathy and bullying remains, at least for males, even when controlling for impulsivity, verbal fluency, and socioeconomic status (SES) and other variables.

Programs to Reduce Aggression

Consistent with the findings reviewed above, showing that empathy (either in its affective or cognitive component) is associated with lower degrees of antisocial behavior, empathy emerges as an important mediating factor in programs aimed at reducing aggression among children and youth (Battistich et al., 1991, 1997; N. D. Feshbach & Feshbach, 1982, N. Feshbach, 1979). One such program is PATH (Promoting Alternative Thinking Strategies), in which elementary school teachers provide lessons on topics such as self-control, emotions, and problem solving. Findings from longitudinal studies show that PATH is effective in enhancing empathy and diminishing externalizing behavior (Greenberg, Kusche, Cook, & Quamma, 1995). McMahon and Washburn (2003) investigated the impact of *Second Step: A Violence Prevention Program* (Committee for Children, 1997) among African American students ages 11–14, in two inner-city schools, and found that increases in empathy from pretest to posttest (Bosworth & Espelage, 1995) predicted less aggressive behavior at posttest (Orpinas & Frankowski, 2001). Jagers et al. (2007) assigned youth (grades 5–7) randomly to a classroom social-development intervention, a school/family community intervention, or a control condition, and found that either interventions, as compared to the control condition, led to a reduction in self-reported violent behavior, and that this effect was mediated by their measure of empathic concern. Importantly, the longitudinal character of this study offers greater reassurance than can be obtained from most studies using cross-sectional designs with regard to causality.

Empathy and Offending

In the evidence reviewed so far linking empathy and antisocial behavior, the latter was measured in a variety of ways, ranging from self-reports, to teachers' ratings, to electric shocks given in an experimental setting. An important subcategory of antisocial behavior is what can be classified as offending behavior. What characterizes this kind of behavior is that it is punishable with imprisonment, and it is thus important to establish whether empathy plays a role with regard to this specific subset of antisocial behavior.

In early work on offending, the link with empathy can already be found, and, with some exceptions (e.g., Hudak, Andre, & Allen, 1980), findings from research in the 1960s and 1970s have tended to support the existence of a negative relation between offending and cognitive empathy (Deardorff, Finch, Kendall, Lira, & Indrisano, 1975; Hogan, 1969; Hoppe & Singer, 1976; Kurtines & Hogan, 1972) and, to a lesser extent, affective empathy (Eysenck & McGurk, 1980). Empirical investigations of this link continued over three decades, with studies becoming more sophisticated in their measurement of empathy, often distinguishing between cognitive and affective empathy. Thirty-five of these studies were recently included in a meta-analysis by Jolliffe and Farrington (2004). These studies were characterized by the fact that empathy was measured through self-reports, official records of delinquent/criminal behavior had been used, and a standard measure of effect size could be computed. Results confirmed a negative relation, with a moderate effect size, between empathy (particularly cognitive) and offending, and that violent offenders showed lower empathy (both types) than nonviolent offenders.[2]

A few years later, the same authors conducted a study that investigated predictors of specific kinds of criminal behavior (Jolliffe & Farrington, 2007). To this end, they measured offending by self-reports and used the Basic Empathy Scale (BSE; Jolliffe & Farrington, 2006), which assesses both affective and cognitive empathy. Overall, the results of this study showed the expected negative relation between empathy and offending, with an effect size of -.24. This effect is driven primarily by the affective empathy subscale of the BSE, but in general both

kinds of empathy show the same type of relations with the various subcategories of offense. Gender, however, makes quite a difference, with the relationship holding much more clearly for males than for females. Gender interacted with type of offense in predicting whether or not empathy was implicated, with empathy negatively predicting offenses such as vandalism, fighting, and serious theft among males (but not females) while predicting only the specific *theft from a person* category of offense among females (see Loudin, Loukas, & Robinson, 2003 for a discussion on aggression in males *versus* females).

Offenses that included violence were related, negatively, to empathy, for both males and females, although in this category only affective empathy differed between those who reported violent offenses and those who did not. This result is consistent with findings of an investigation into the close relationships of African American delinquents (Marcus & Gray, 1998), in which frequency of offending moderated the strength of the association between empathy and offending, with the relation emerging only at a high frequency of offending. This relation, among men, accounted for the result described above. Among men, low empathy was no longer specifically associated to violence once frequency was taken into account.

Researchers have also turned their attention to investigating empathy in the context of white-collar crimes. Cohen (2010) reports findings of two studies in which empathic concern but not perspective-taking (Davis, 1980) shows a unique, negative relation with many of the seven unethical negotiation strategies (e.g., misrepresentation, inappropriate information gathering; Lewicki, Saunders, & Barry, 2007).[3] These studies represent an interesting new direction that will help provide a more accurate picture of antisocial behavior in our society, and hopefully contribute to changing the belief that antisocial behavior is primarily found among low-SES, marginalized populations.

Given the nature of this *Handbook*, I have looked at antisocial behavior and offending that is not associated with psychopathology. After all, only a minority of offending (at least of the offending that results in a conviction) is carried out by individuals who can be diagnosed with a psychopathological condition. Nonetheless, it is important to mention psychopathy because its very diagnosis (Hare, 1991, 2003) includes both low empathy (with the broader criterion of emotional callousness) and the presence of antisocial tendencies (e.g., criminal versatility).

(See Costanzo, Hoyle, & Leary, chapter 23, this volume, for discussion of personality, social psychology, and psychopathology.) A review of this literature is beyond the scope of this chapter (for several detailed accounts see the *Handbook of Antisocial Behavior*, Stoff, Breiling, & Maser, 1997), but a few findings that look at the building blocks of empathy are worth mentioning. Psychopathic individuals (compared to controls) display reduced electrodermal responses specifically to distress cues (Blair, Jones, Clark, & Smith, 1997), and reduced recognition of the fearful expression of others (Blair, Colledge, Murray, & Mitchell, 2001; for a review, see Marsh & Blair, 2008). Both of these are important steps in the development of empathy, and their inhibition is likely to interfere with moral socialization (Eisenberg, 2002; Hoffman, 1994), thus facilitating antisocial behavior. As Blair notes, "individuals with the developmental disorder of psychopathy [. . .] fail to respond appropriately to specific expressions. In psychopathic individuals, the processing of other individuals' sadness and fear is particularly affected. This leads to a failure in socialization. The psychopathic individual does not learn to avoid actions that cause harm to others" (Blair, 2003, p. 567).[4]

I began this section asking whether the role of empathy as an inhibitor of antisocial behavior is consistent with available empirical evidence. After reviewing the substantial literature on this relation, I think it is safe to conclude that this is indeed the case. From the early meta-analysis by Miller and Eisenberg (1988), to the most recent studies on different kinds of aggression, bullying, and offending behavior, empathy emerged as an important inhibiting factor. Furthermore, programs aiming at reducing antisocial behavior have also shown that empathy plays a mediational role. In the next section we continue our review of the effects of dispositional empathy, but we focus on a different class of antisocial behavior: prejudice.

Dispositional Empathy, Ideological Attitudes, and Prejudice

Social and personality psychology have proposed several perspectives to account for the emergence of prejudice (Brown, 1995; see also Tropp & Molina, chapter 22, this volume). One such perspective sees prejudice as stemming from characteristics of the individual, typically associated with rearing and early socialization practices. In this section I review evidence that a lack of empathy might impact prejudicial attitudes through the development of specific ideological attitudes.

Among the most well-known correlates of prejudicial attitudes is the authoritarian personality dimension (Adorno et al., 1950). While social psychologists have long criticized Adorno's work on methodological and theoretical grounds (Brown, 1995), authoritarianism has enjoyed a comeback in recent years, primarily as a consequence of Altemeyer's work and the development of the Right Wing Authoritarianism (RWA) scale measuring the dimensions of conventionalism, authoritarian aggression, and authoritarian submission. RWA as measured by the homonymous scale has been found to predict quite reliably negative attitudes toward minorities and stigmatized groups and to prejudice in general (Altemeyer, 1998, 1996; Van Hiel & Mervielde, 2005).

Over the past two decades, the authoritarian submission dimension of RWA has been complemented by the work of Sidanius, Pratto, and colleagues on social dominance theory (Sidanius, 1993; Pratto, Sidanius, and Levin, 2006), which was also accompanied by a scale to measure social dominance orientation (SDO; Pratto et al., 1994). As with RWA, SDO is not as stable as one would expect if it were a personality trait (e.g., Guimond, Dambrun, Michinov, & Duarte; 2003) and is better conceived as a measure of a social, ideological attitude.[5] As the name suggests, SDO measures a preference for a world in which social groups are organized hierarchically, with some groups dominating others, or equal, where no groups exert power over other groups.

Such preferences appear to be recognized and rewarded by the societal system—with high SDO individuals doing well in hierarchy-enhancing roles (e.g., students majoring in business) and low SDO individuals performing better on hierarchy-attenuating roles (e.g., sociology majors) (van Laar, Sidanius, Rabinowitz, & Sinclair, 1999). The measures are also related to policy preferences: people who score high on SDO are more likely to support policies that support inequality between groups (Sidanius, Pratto, & Bobo, 1996). While noting that both of these correlates of SDO have obvious conceptual links with empathy, most important to our concerns here is the fact that SDO predicts explicit (e.g., Whitley, 1999) as well as implicit (Pratto & Shih, 2000) prejudicial attitudes (for a review, see Sibley & Duckitt, 2008).

While RWA and SDO tend to correlate, their effect on prejudice has been shown to be driven by two different motives. A view of the world as a dangerous place enhances RWA, while seeing the world as a competitive jungle leads to SDO

(Duckitt, 2001, 2006). Accordingly, negativity toward drug dealers was predicted exclusively by RWA, while SDO predicted negativity to unemployed persons. Feminists, however, who represent a threat but are also a dominated group, are denigrated by both high SDO and high RWA individuals.

Attachment, Ideological Attitudes, and Prejudice

The antecedents of RWA and SDO are theorized to be grounded in two socialization processes, punitive and unaffectionate socialization, respectively. Cross-cultural data has provided some support for the link between these socialization practices and prejudice, mediated by RWA and SDO (Duckitt, 2001). Punitive and unaffectionate practices have been linked to social behavior by developmental psychology working on Hoffman's (1963) and Staub's (1979) insights, and one of the mediating factors between socialization and behavior has been found to be a child's empathy (Krevans & Gibbs, 1996; Janssens & Gerris, 1992) and sympathy (Spinrad et al., 1999; for a review, see Eisenberg, Fabes, & Spinrad, 2006). Furthermore, such practices have been linked to the development of an insecure attachment style (Bowlby, 1999) which, in turn, has been found to correlate negatively with empathy and positively with SDO and RWA.

Empathy, sympathy, and perspective-taking have been found to be lower among adolescents with insecure attachment style (Laible, Carlo, & Roesch, 2004; Markiewicz, Doyle, & Brendgen, 2001). Waters, Hay, and Richters (1986) reported that the empathy level of 3.5-year-old children was related to earlier attachment to their mothers, with insecure attachment styles leading to lower empathy (see also Van der Mark, van Ijzendoorn, & Bakermans-Kranenburg; 2002; Mikulincer & Shaver, chapter 19, this volume).

Although the relationship between attachment, SDO, and RWA has been investigated to a much lesser extent, a few studies have found a pattern consistent with the overall picture that is emerging from what is outlined above. Weber and Federico (2007) measured two types of insecure attachment styles, anxious and avoidant (Ainsworth, Blehar, Waters, & Wall, 1978; Bowlby, 1969,1982), using Brennan, Clark, and Shavers's (1998) measure, as well as the tendency to perceive the world as a competitive jungle and as a dangerous place, before assessing participants' RWA and SDO. What they found was that the greater the participants' (undergraduate students in a North American university) anxiety and avoidance scores, the greater their RWA and SDO. This pattern was mediated by the *competitive jungle* and *dangerous world* worldviews, in a manner largely consistent with Duckitt's (2001) dual-process model regarding the origins of RWA and SDO. Anxious attachment style predicted more strongly the dangerous world worldview, which in turn affected RWA (but not SDO); avoidant style predicted more strongly the competitive jungle worldview, which in turn predicted SDO (but not RWA).

From Lack of Empathy to Prejudice

The research reviewed above has provided evidence of the links between socialization practices and attachment, attachment style and empathy, attachment style and ideological attitudes (RWA and SDO), and ideological attitudes and prejudice. The next piece of the puzzle is the relationship between empathy and prejudice. Evidence for this relation was recently provided in two studies by Bäckström and Björklund (2007), using Swedish high school students as samples. In a first study, they measured participants' SDO (Pratto et al., 1994) and used the IRI (Davis, 1980) to assess empathy (*minus* the personal distress subscale), and used several measures of prejudice tapping both classic and modern racism (e.g., McConahay's 1986), as well as specific forms of prejudice such as prejudice against homosexuality. Using structural equation modeling, they then demonstrated that empathy had both a direct and an indirect negative effect on prejudice. The indirect effect was through SDO. The greater the empathy, the lower the SDO scores, the lower the level of prejudice. As expected, the greater the empathy, the lower the prejudice.

A second study replicated the same pattern, with the addition of RWA. Empathy, in addition to its direct and indirect (via SDO) effects on prejudice, also affected prejudice through RWA. The higher the empathy, the lower the RWA, and the lower the RWA, the lower the level of prejudice. Importantly, the only exogenous variable in the model also behaved in a manner consistent with the overall picture that is emerging regarding empathy, prejudice, and the other variables discussed in this section: gender. The difference between males and females with respect to their level of prejudice was primarily due to their differences in empathy.[6]

The second section of this chapter looked at how dispositional empathy is associated with antisocial behavior toward other individuals; this third section also looked at dispositional empathy, but focused on its relation to prejudicial attitudes and discrimination toward outgroup members. Here I attempted to put together a puzzle, the pieces of which are different psychological findings in areas as disparate as socialization and attachment, ideology, and prejudice. Given the scarcity of comprehensive research the conclusion can only be preliminary, but the overall picture suggests that empathy, which is affected by early socialization practices and attachment styles, affects prejudice both directly and indirectly, through ideological attitudes. The next section concerns itself with the link between empathy and prejudicial attitudes and discrimination, but looks at empathy as moderated by the social categorization processes.

US, Them, and Empathy

One of the most well-established findings in social psychological research on group processes and intergroup relations is the ingroup bias: the tendency to favor the ingroup over the outgroup in terms of resource allocation, social judgment, and behavior (Brewer, 1979; Hewstone, Rubin, & Willis, 2002). It is Henri Tajfel and his colleagues who first set out to understand the minimal conditions under which this bias emerges. In a milestone series of studies, Tajfel, Billig, Bundy, and Flament (1971) showed that a categorization of individuals into two groups (the ingroup and the outgroup) based on minimal criteria (such as preference for one abstract painter over another) is sufficient to elicit preference for the ingroup, for instance, in the allocation of resources. Tajfel and colleagues interpreted these findings as evidence that, because individuals derive part of their identity from their membership in social groups, social-categorization (us vs. them) results in the need to establish and maintain a positive distinctiveness of the ingroup.

These ideas developed into social identity theory (Tajfel & Turner, 1979) and later into self-categorization theory (J. C. Turner, Hogg, Oakes, Reicher, & Wetherell, 1987), which elaborates on how the process of social categorization affects social perception, judgment, and behavior. According to this view, stereotyping and prejudice are not to be understood as stemming from the characteristics of the individual (such as ideology or other personality traits), but, rather, as a consequence of the "us versus them" distinction.[7]

Now, let us return to our main concern. As noted above, Davis (2004) defines empathy as "the psychological process that at least temporarily unites the separate social entities of self and other" (p. 20). This unity should not be considered equivalent to a confusion between the self and the other (Batson,

1987; Decety & Jackson, 2004), which would be detrimental to empathy. Nonetheless, a commonality of experience is a fundamental component of empathy, and I argue that when entities are being explicitly excluded by the (collective) self, such as in the case of the *us versus them* distinction, empathy toward them might be curtailed. There exists evidence that this might be the case.

Mimicry (the imitation of facial expression or other gestures), which has been shown to be higher among high (vs. low) perspective-takers (Chartrand & Bargh, 1999) and a building-block of empathy (Iacoboni, 2008), is more likely to occur with members of the ingroup as opposed to the outgroup (McHugo & Smith, 1996; Philippot, Yabar, Bourgeois, 2007; Yabar, Johnston, Miles, & Peace, 2006), and research shows an ingroup advantage in emotion recognition (Elfenbein & Ambady, 2002). It would seem that the very possibility of empathy toward outgroup members, as compared to ingroup members, might be curtailed at very early stages of perception: we may learn *not* to engage in the very processes that are conducive to empathy when perceiving outgroup members. In fact, individuals display greater empathy (measured through a variety of physiological indicators and evaluations) in response to pleasant and unpleasant pictures depicting ingroup, as compared to outgroup, members (Brown, Bradley, & Lang, 2006), and vicarious emotions can be felt on behalf of ingroup members, but to a much lesser extent on behalf of outgroup members (e.g., Dumont, Yzerbyt, Wigboldus, & Gordjin, 2003; Mackie, Devos, & Smith, 1999). Recent findings more directly show that the pain of outgroup members may not be processed in the same way as the pain of ingroup members. Xuo, Wang, and Han (2009) found lower neural activity in the anterior cingulate cortex, which is part of the affective division of the pain matrix, when participants (Chinese and Caucasians) viewed painful stimuli applied to the face of outgroup, as compared to ingroup members. Avenanti, Sirigul, and Aglioti (2010) found convergent evidence, by looking at corticospinal inhibition, as opposed to activation of the pain matrix. Corticospinal inhibition is an indication that a resonant activation of pain representations is present. In their study, in which white and black participants looked at painful stimuli applied to either a black or white hand, corticospinal inhibition was found only for ingroup pain, suggesting the absence of sensorimotor contagion for the outgroup targets. Of interest, this inhibition correlated with a measure of the racial Implicit Association

Test (IAT): participants with higher implicit ingroup preference presented greater differences in the corticospinal reactivity to ingroup and outgroup models' pain.

This tendency to experience less empathy toward outgroup members, to have an eye-to-eye experience with them, may prevent recognition of their individuality, thus contributing to stereotyping and prejudice. Social scientists and practitioners in a variety of fields, such as those operating in conflict-resolution and multicultural education workshops, have long recognized this possibility.

In workshops aimed at reducing conflict between Israelis and Palestinians, moderators encouraged participants to learn to take the perspective of the other via role-taking (e.g., Rouhana & Kelman, 1994; see also Fisher, 1994; Shechtman & Basheer, 2005), and in a workshop conducted with the two ethnic groups in Sri Lanka that have been engaged in a decade-long struggle, prosocial behavior toward the outgroup went hand-in-hand with increased empathy toward it (Malhotra & Liyanage, 2005). In the "jigsaw classroom" (Aronson & Patnoe, 1997), interdependence among children of different racial and ethnic groups is created by having them work cooperatively.

Typically, empathy is not specifically measured in these studies, but Fisher (1994) noted that participants in these workshops report feeling more empathy toward outgroup members, and Aronson and Bridgeman (1979) argue that it is increased empathy that is responsible for the improvement in intergroup relations that is typically observed in the jigsaw studies. Furthermore, Bridgeman (1981) observed increased role-taking capacity among children who underwent a similar program. These claims are consistent with results from developmental studies showing that changes in the capacity for role-taking among children go hand in hand with a reduction in prejudicial attitudes. A longitudinal study by Doyle and Aboud (1995) investigated white children's prejudice toward blacks and native Indians, from age 6 to 9, and found that a decrease in prejudice was associated developmentally, among other things, with the perception that different perspectives may exist.

In most of the programs reviewed above it is difficult to separate the effect of empathy induction, perspective-taking or role-play from other factors in reducing stereotypes, prejudice, and negative intergroup attitudes. A host of experimental studies, however, have focused on perspective-taking/role-play and on inducing empathic feelings, and can

thus provide some more specific insights. After reviewing each of these two lines of research, I conclude this section with evidence that the single most important strategy in reducing prejudice, namely intergroup contact, does so in part through enhancing empathy toward the outgroup.

Role-Playing and Perspective-Taking

Imagine going through the usual daily activities, but sitting in a wheelchair: going to work, shopping, hugging your child, cooking dinner, and so forth. Think of the different perspective you would have on the world, being just a few feet lower; think of the many obstacles that you would encounter, such as a step that is too high for your wheelchair to mount, or a door too narrow for you to pass through. If you do this exercise just for ten minutes or so, it is likely that your empathy for people in wheelchairs will increase.

A variation on this exercise was carried out forty years ago in a study by Clore and Jeffery (1972), who had student participants traveling around campus in a wheelchair or watching somebody else doing it. Subsequently, they measured the participants' experienced empathy during the experience (e.g., compassionate, concerned) as well as attitudes toward the disabled. What they observed was that both role-playing conditions led to enhanced feelings of empathy and more positive attitudes toward disabled people. Furthermore, attitudes were also significantly affected by the manipulation four months later. Although no mediational analysis is reported, the authors favored an interpretation in terms of affective empathy for the change of attitudes.

An even more dramatic manipulation was used by Pacala, Boult, Bland, and O'Brien (1995), in an experiment aimed at investigating how to improve attitudes toward the elderly among medical students. The manipulation used was the aging game, in which participants play the role of an elderly person in a 90-minute long exercise: they wear "earplugs to simulate hearing loss, heavy socks to simulate pedal edema, and popcorn kernels in their shoes to simulate the discomfort of arthritis" (Pacala et al., 1995, p. 48). Compared to a control group, the game led to an improvement of attitudes toward the elderly, albeit a direct measure of empathy revealed only a trend in the expected directions.

Several studies looked at children, particularly in a school context, and investigated how role-play and perspective-taking manipulations affected intergroup attitudes. In a study by Weiner and Wright (1973), two groups of white children in third grade were randomly assigned to either an experimental or a control group. The experimental group was further divided into two groups, the Orange and Green groups, which were alternatively assigned as superior or inferior from day one to day two of the study. At day 3 and after a week, results showed that the experimental group was significantly more likely to desire a picnic with a group of black children and held less-prejudiced beliefs when compared to controls.

A series of other studies conducted primarily in the 1970s and 1980s, and looking at the effect of role-playing on racial attitudes, were reviewed in a meta-analysis conducted by McGregor (1993). The manipulation of role-play in these studies varied from dramatization (physically acting out an unfamiliar role) to forced-compliance (writing an essay supporting a position one opposes) to value-discrepancy (pinpointing discrepancies between values and behaviors) to simulation games (Chapman, 1974), but all studies included a measure of racist attitude change.

In one study included in this meta-analysis, three groups of children who initially had equally strong preferences for whites *over* blacks received, over a 6-week period, either training in Piagetan tasks (e.g., conservation of number, superordinate classification, and two- and three-dimensional perspective training), on role-taking (e.g., putting oneself in the place of others), or no training at all (Hohn, 1973). Results showed that both types of training led to significant reduction in the prowhite bias, compared to the control condition. Furthermore, the training also positively affected a behavioral measure, in which children assigned a black or a white character to either a positive or a negative situation. In another study reviewed in McGregor (1993) a variety of behavioral differential and interaction measures and a sociometric indicator were taken to assess racial prejudice among high school students. Then, after receiving a 3-week treatment (one of which consisted of a racial role-playing group) or no treatment, measures were taken anew. Racial role-playing led to positive changes in several categories, particularly on the sociometric choice.

All in all, across 29 findings, McGregor (1993) found a significant effect of role-playing, with an average effect size of .42. While no mediational analyses were presented to show that it was indeed an increase in empathy that led to the reduction in racist attitudes, this result suggests that role playing is indeed an effective strategy.

More recently, Galinsky and Moskowitz (2000) investigated the effects on stereotyping of simply looking at the world through the eyes of an outgroup member. These authors sought to investigate whether the benefits of stereotype-suppression evidenced by Macrae, Bodenhausen, Milne, and Jetten (1994) could be achieved while at the same time avoiding the paradoxical effect of enhanced stereotype accessibility later in time.

In a first study, they presented participants with a photo of an elderly man and asked them to write an essay describing a day in his life. Instructions varied between conditions, asking participants to either suppress their stereotypic preconceptions or to take the perspective of the individual in the picture when writing their essays (*imagine a day in the life of this individual as if you were that person, looking at the world through his eyes and walking through the world in his shoes*). A third condition gave no specific instructions. Participants then completed a lexical decision task aimed at measuring the accessibility of negatively valenced, stereotypical traits of the elderly, and finally wrote another essay about another elderly man. Both essays were evaluated for stereotypicality and valence. Results showed that while both suppression and perspective-taking instructions led to diminished stereotypical content, perspective-taking was the most effective strategy in augmenting the positive content in the description of the elderly man. Importantly, the lexical decision task measure revealed that suppression instructions led to hyperaccessibility of the stereotype (rebound effect), while perspective-taking did not differ from the control condition.

Two studies replicated this pattern of findings, and showed that perspective-taking decreased stereotypical ratings of the outgroup as a whole and led to an enhanced overlap between the representation of the outgroup and the self (Galinsky & Moskowitz, 2000; Study 2); in addition, perspective-taking decreased ingroup bias by improving the evaluation of the outgroup (Study 3). The self-outgroup overlap mediated the effect of the perspective-taking manipulation on stereotypical ratings of the elderly, thus suggesting that perspective-taking diminished stereotyping by extending to the outgroup the positive view that individuals have of the self. Consistently, Galinsky and Ku (2004) found that the enhanced attitudes toward the elderly following perspective-taking were evident only for individuals with high self-esteem (either based on traits or experimentally enhanced).

These findings suggest that individuals develop more positive attitudes toward outgroup members

Similar findings were obtained by R. N. Turner, Hewstone, and Voci (2007) in a study examining attitudes toward South Asians among white British undergraduates. In this study too, cross-group friendship had a positive impact on willingness to self-disclose to a hypothetical Asian friend, and this, in turn, impacted attitudes toward Asians via, among other mediators, empathic feelings toward Asian people.

Swart, Hewstone, Christ, and Voci (under review) investigated the effect of cross-group friendships among black high-school students in South Africa, and found that the higher the number of outgroup friends and the amount of time spent with them (cross-group friendships), the greater the level of affective empathy toward the outgroup. In turn, high affective empathy meant more positive attitudes toward the outgroup, fewer negative action tendencies, and greater perceived outgroup variability. Related cross-sectional research by the same authors showed that, although some differences emerged in the overall model, and in whether empathy mediated the effect of friendships partially or fully, the pattern held for both white (privileged minority) and black (underprivileged majority) groups (see also Myers, Hewstone, & Cairns, 2009; Swart et al., in press; but see Vorauer & Sasaki, 2009, for the possible ironic effects of empathic induction in intergroup contexts).

The specific reasons why empathy is doing the mediating are not well understood, and not much discussed either. As I argued earlier, it is the very process of social categorization and the exclusion of outgroups from the (collective) self that might be responsible for curtailing empathy. When outgroup members' identity as such is not salient anymore (Brewer & Miller, 1988), the other is perceived as a human being and empathic feelings are now free to emerge. For contact with specific members to generalize to the outgroup as a whole, however, we know that the social identity of the individuals with whom contact occurs must be kept salient (Brown & Hewstone, 2005; Hewstone & Brown, 1986). In other words, the contact must be intergroup in character. If this occurs, empathy may translate to the group level. Once we see eye-to-eye with members of the outgroup it may be more difficult to revert back to holding prejudiced attitudes toward their group as a whole. This possibility was discussed by Hoffman (2000), who proposes that empathizing with members of another group does not require the breakdown of group boundaries, but rather the simple recognition that there is shared emotionality between the ingroup and the outgroup.

An additional mechanism through which empathy may exert its positive effect is the self-other overlap discussed above. The empathy elicited by positive contact with members of an outgroup whose collective identity is salient may lead to increased overlap in the representation of the self and of the outgroup, which in turn reduces the likelihood of prejudice toward it. Consistently, R. N. Turner, Hewstone, Voci, and Vonofakou (2008) found that the relationship between extended contact (knowing ingroup members who have outgroup friends; Wright et al., 1997) with a minority and attitude toward that minority was partly mediated by the degree to which the outgroup was assumed to overlap with the self.

Given what we have discussed above with regard to the mediating role of empathy in reducing prejudice and promoting positive intergroup relations, it could be expected that empathy might also be doing some of the work in the results obtained within the framework of the dual identity model, a combination of the common ingroup identity model (Gaertner & Dovidio, 2000) and the mutual differentiation model (Hewstone & Brown, 1986). The dual identity model suggests that one way to reduce intergroup bias is by creating a superordinate identity without denying the lower levels of identity, that is, the ingroup and outgroup identity. To my knowledge, no empirical evidence exists testing the mediational role of empathy toward the outgroup on the effect of the creation of a supraordinate, common identity, but given that the creation of such a common identity elicits a rapprochement of the self-image with that of the outgroup, it is reasonable to assume that empathy may be playing a role here as well.

Dehumanization

> The degradation imposed on the prisoners was not a matter of cruelty, but a necessary process. For those operating the gas chambers not to be overwhelmed by distress, victims had to be reduced to subhuman objects beforehand.
> *Primo Levi* (1981)

I argued above that the process of social categorization, in its *us versus them* instantiation, curtails empathy toward *them*. Here I argue that in addition to the cognitive exclusion itself, the dehumanization of the outgroup may further prevent empathy, and thus facilitate antisocial behavior toward its members. Not only is the person or group rejected from the ingroup, but they are denied membership in the most inclusive ingroup of all, that is, humanity.

Dehumanization has long been considered an important precursor of collective violence. From the dehumanization of Jews in the years preceding World War II (Nazi propaganda termed them *bacilli, rats, poisonous mushrooms*) to that of the enemy in the training of soldiers (*Japes, Gooks, Hajis*), there is considerable anecdotal evidence and theorizing in support of the view that dehumanizing others is an important step in promoting violence toward them, and perhaps a necessary step for lethal violence (Staub, 1992). Perceiving another person as human activates empathetic reactions that would make it difficult to mistreat him or her without risking personal distress. Once the other is dehumanized, however, such self-sanctions for mistreatment can be disengaged (Bandura, 1990).

Rigorous empirical research is less readily available, but several studies exist that support such a claim. Struch and Schwartz (1989) investigated the role of dehumanization of ultraorthodox Jews in Israel by nonultraorthodox Jews, and found that the effect of perceived conflict on desire to aggress the ultraorthodox was mediated by two measures of dehumanization (perceived value dissimilarity and trait inhumanity). Bandura, Underwood, and Fromson (1975), using a Milgram-like paradigm, found that merely overhearing an experimenter referring to students who were (allegedly) to be subjected to electric shocks as "animals" (as opposed to "nice," or to a control condition) led participants to give increasingly higher shocks to them. McAlister, Bandura, and Owen (2006) compared support for military force against Iraq before and after the 9/11 attacks, and found that dehumanization (of both the terrorists and unspecified "enemy rulers") was one of the mediators leading to the enhanced support for such an attack.

Dehumanization also occurs as a consequence of violence, most likely to justify the violence a posteriori. Across three studies conducted in the United States and the UK, Leidner, Castano, Zaiser, and Giner-Sorolla (2010) investigated the role of dehumanization in predicting demands for justice in the context of the torturing and murdering of Iraqi prisoners by U.S. or UK military personnel, as compared to the same actions carried out by outgroup military personnel. They found that when the perpetrator was the ingroup, participants who scored high on ingroup glorification tendencies (Roccas et al., 2006) demanded less justice (punishment for the perpetrators and reparations to the victims), and that this effect was mediated by dehumanization of the Iraqis. Similar effects were found by Castano

and Giner-Sorolla (2006), also across the United States and the U.K. In three studies they showed that ingroup responsibility for the death of large numbers of outgroup members led to greater infrahumanization (Leyens et al., 2000) of the victims. For instance, in one study British participants read about the fate of Australian Aborigines as either being quasi-exterminated at the hands of their own ancestors, or weathering the arrival of the British without too many negative consequences. The former group ended up infrahumanizing the Aborigines to a much greater extent.

This research provides indirect evidence supporting the main claim of this chapter, namely that lack of empathy plays an important role in the emergence of antisocial behavior, such as violence toward others. In fact, I argue that dehumanization is the ultimate exclusion of the other, in which empathy is not only unlikely (it is difficult to take the perspective of a nonhuman being) and nonadvisable (mistrust and fear), but also impossible (disgust and other emotions are felt instead of empathic concerns). Some of these findings are informative in a more direct manner, for they touch on the perception of the other as a sentient being.

Castano and Giner-Sorolla's (2006) measure of dehumanization, called infrahumanization, was proposed by Leyens and colleagues to refer to a phenomenon whereby the capacity to experience certain kind of emotions, namely sophisticated and cognitively complex emotions such as nostalgia, guilt, and humiliation is denied to certain others (i.e., outgroup). These emotions are also considered uniquely human, thus leading to the interpretation of such a denial of emotions as infrahumanization (Leyens et al., 2000). In Castano and Giner-Sorolla (2006), the specific ways in which the victims of the ingroup were dehumanized was by diminishing the alleged depth of their emotional life: when the ingroup was responsible for outgroup deaths, outgroup members were perceived as being less able to experience secondary emotions. Similarly, in the study mentioned above by Leidner et al. (2010), beyond explicit dehumanization, the minimization of the emotional suffering of family members of tortured and murdered prisoners led to a lesser demand for justice. To the extent that empathy, at least affective empathy, is experienced in reaction to another person's display of (typically negative) emotion, these results are telling. By perceiving others as incapable of experiencing certain emotions, or simply by perceiving them as experiencing emotions less deeply (minimization of their expected suffering),

Eisenberg, N., & Lennon, R. (1983). Sex differences in empathy and related capacities. *Psychological Bulletin, 94,* 100–131.

Elfenbein, H. A., & Ambady, N. (2002). Is there an in-group advantage in emotion recognition? *Psychological Bulletin, 128,* 243–249.

Endresen, I. M., & Olweus, D. (2001). Self-reported empathy in Norwegian adolescents: Sex differences, age trends, and relationship to bullying. In A. C. Bohart & D. J. Stipek (Eds.), *Constructive and destructive behavior: Implications for family, school, and society* (pp. 147–165). Washington, DC: American Psychological Association.

Eysenck, S. B., & McGurk, B. J. (1980). Impulsiveness and venturesomeness in a detention center population. *Psychological Reports, 47,* 1299–1306.

Feshbach, N. (1979). Empathy training: A field study in affective education. In S. Feshbach & A. Fraczek (Eds.), *Aggression and behavior change: Biological and social processes.* (pp. 234–249). New York: Praeger.

Feshbach, N. D. (1988). Television and the development of empathy. *Applied Social Psychology Annual, 8,* 261–269.

Feshbach, N. D., & Feshbach, S. (1969). The relationship between empathy and aggression in two age groups. *Developmental Psychology, 1,* 102–107.

Feshbach, N. D., & Feshbach, S. (1982). Empathy training and the regulation of aggression: Potentialities and limitations. *Academic Psychology Bulletin, 4,* 399–413.

Feshbach, N. D., & Roe, K. (1968). Empathy in six- and seven-year-olds. *Child Development, 39,* 133–145.

Feshbach, S. (1978). The environment of personality. *American Psychologist, 33,* 447–455.

Fisher, R. (1994). General principles for resolving intergroup conflict. *Journal of Social Issues, 50,* 47–66.

Gaertner, S. L., & Dovidio, J. F. (2000). *Reducing intergroup bias: The common ingroup identity model.* New York: Psychology Press.

Gaines, T., Kirwin, P. M., & Gentry, W. D. (1977). The effect of descriptive anger expression, insult, and no feedback on interpersonal aggression, hostility, and empathy motivation. *Genetic Psychology Monographs, 95,* 349–367.

Galinsky, A. D., & Ku, G. (2004). The effects of perspective-taking on prejudice: The moderating role of self-evaluation. *Personality and Social Psychology Bulletin. 30,* 594–604.

Galinsky, A. D., & Moskowitz, G. B. (2000). Perspective-taking: Decreasing stereotype expression, stereotype accessibility, and in-group favoritism. *Journal of Personality and Social Psychology, 78,* 708–724.

Geen, R. G. (1998). Aggression and antisocial behavior. In D. T. Gilbert, S. T. Fiske, & L. Gardner (Eds.), *The handbook of social psychology* (4th ed., Vol. 2, pp. 317–356). New York: McGraw-Hill.

Geffner, R. A., Loring, M., & Young, C. (Eds.). (2001). *Bullying behavior: Current issues, research, and interventions.* Binghamton, NY: Haworth Maltreatment and Trauma Press/ Haworth Press.

Giancola, P. R. (2003). The moderating effects of dispositional empathy on alcohol-related aggression in men and women. *Journal of Abnormal Psychology, 112,* 275–281.

Goldberg, L. R. (1993). The structure of phenotypic personality traits. *American Psychologist, 48,* 26–34.

Greenberg, M. T., Kusche, C. A., Cook, E. T., & Quamma, J. P. (1995). Promoting emotional competence in school-aged children: The effects of the PATHS curriculum. *Development and Psychopathology, 7,* 117–136.

Guimond, S., Dambrun, M., Michinov, N., & Duarte, S. (2003). Does social dominance generate prejudice? Integrating individual and contextual determinants of intergroup cognitions. *Journal of Personality and Social Psychology, 84,* 697–721.

Haney, C., Banks, C., & Zimbardo, P. (1973). Interpersonal dynamics in a simulated prison. *International Journal of Criminology and Penology, 1,* 69–97.

Hare, R. D. (1991). *The Hare Psychopathy Checklist-Revised.* North Tonawanda, NY: Multi-Health Systems.

Hare, R. D. (2003). *Manual for the Revised Psychopathy Checklist* (2nd ed.). Toronto, ON, Canada: Multi-Health Systems.

Hastings, P. D., Zahn-Waxler, C., Robinson, J., Usher, B., & Bridges, D. (2000). The development of concern for others in children with behavior problems. *Developmental Psychology, 36,* 531–546.

Hermans, E. J., Putman, P., & van Honk, J. (2006). Testosterone administration reduces empathetic behavior: A facial mimicry study. *Psychoneuroendocrinology, 31,* 859–866.

Hersh, S. M. (2004, May 10). Torture at Abu Ghraib: American soldiers brutalized Iraqis; How far up does the responsibility go? *The New Yorker.* Retrieved from http:// www.newyorker.com/archive/2004/05/10/040510fa_fact.

Hewstone, M. (2009). Living apart, living together? The role of intergroup contact in social integration. *Proceedings of the British Academy, 162,* 243–300.

Hewstone, M., & Brown, R. J. (Eds.). (1986). *Contact and conflict in intergroup encounters.* Oxford, UK: Blackwell.

Hewstone, M., Rubin, M., & Willis, H. (2002). Intergroup bias. *Annual Review of Psychology, 53,* 575–604.

Hoffman, M. L. (1963). Parent discipline and the child's consideration for others. *Child Development, 34,* 573–588.

Hoffman, M. L. (1982). Development of prosocial motivation: Empathy and guilt. In N. Eisenberg-Berg (Ed.), *Development of prosocial behavior* (pp. 281–313). New York: Academic Press.

Hoffman, M. L. (1994). Discipline and internalization. *Developmental Psychology, 30,* 26–28.

Hoffman, M. L. (2000). *Empathy and moral development: Implications for caring and justice.* New York: Cambridge University Press.

Hogan, R. (1969). Development of an empathy scale. *Journal of Consulting and Clinical Psychology, 33,* 307–316.

Hohn, R. L. (1973). Perceptual training and its effect on racial preferences of kindergarten children. *Psychological Reports, 32,* 435–441.

Hoppe, C. M., & Singer, R. D. (1976). Overcontrolled hostility, empathy, and egocentric balance in violent and nonviolent psychiatric offenders. *Psychological Reports, 39,* 1303–1308.

Hovland, C. I., & Weiss, W. (1951). The influence of source credibility on communication effectiveness. *Public Opinion Quarterly, 15,* 635–650.

Hubbard, J. A., Smithmyer, C. M., Ramsden, S. R., Parker, E. H., Flanagan, K. D., Dearing, K. F., et al. (2002). Observational, physiological, and self-report measures of children's anger: Relations to reactive versus proactive aggression. *Child Development, 73,* 1101–1118.

Hudak, M. A., Andre, J., Allen, R. O. (1980). Delinquency and social values: Differences between delinquent and nondelinquent adolescents. *Youth and Society, 11,* 353–368.

Iacoboni, M. (2008). Mesial frontal cortex and super mirror neurons. *Behavioral and Brain Sciences, 31,* 30.

Insko, C. A., Schopler, J., Graetz, K. A., & Drigotas, S. M. (1994). Interindividual-intergroup discontinuity in the prisoner's dilemma game. *Journal of Conflict Resolution, 38,* 87–116.

Jagers, R. J., Morgan-Lopez, A. A., Howard, T., Browne, D. C., & Flay, B. R. (2007). Mediators of the development and prevention of violent behavior. *Prevention Science, 8,* 171–179.

Janssens, J. M. A. M., & Gerris, J. R. M. (1992). Child rearing, empathy, and prosocial development. In J. M. A. M. Janssens & J. R. M. Gerris (Eds.), *Child rearing: Influence on prosocial and moral development* (pp. 57–77). Amsterdam, Netherlands: Swets & Zeitlinger.

Jolliffe, D., & Farrington, D. P. (2004). Empathy and offending: A systematic review and meta-analysis. *Aggression and Violent Behavior, 9,* 441–476.

Jolliffe, D., & Farrington, D. P. (2006). Development and validation of the Basic Empathy Scale. *Journal of Adolescence, 29,* 589–611.

Jolliffe, D., & Farrington, D. P. (2007). Examining the relationship between low empathy and self-reported offending. *Legal and Criminological Psychology, 12,* 265–286.

Jolliffe, D., & Farrington, D. P. (2011). Is low empathy related to bullying after controlling for individual and social background variables? *Journal of Adolescence 34,* 59–71.

Karacanta, A., & Fitness, J. (2006). Majority support for minority out-groups: The roles of compassion and guilt. *Journal of Applied Social Psychology, 36,* 2730–2749.

Killen, M., & Smetana, J. G. (Eds.). (2006). *Handbook of moral development.* Mahwah, NJ: Erlbaum.

Krevans, J., & Gibbs, J. C. (1996). Parents' use of inductive discipline: Relations to children's empathy and prosocial behavior. *Child Development, 67,* 3263–3277.

Krueger, J., & Rothbart, M. (1988). Use of categorical and individuating information in making inferences about personality. *Journal of Personality and Social Psychology, 55,* 187–195.

Krueger, R. F., South, S., Johnson, W., & Iacono, W. (2008). The heritability of personality is not always 50%: Gene–environment interactions and correlations between personality and parenting. *Journal of Personality, 76,* 1485–1521.

Kunda, Z., & Oleson, K. C. (1995). Maintaining stereotypes in the face of disconfirmation: Constructing grounds for subtyping deviants. *Journal of Personality and Social Psychology, 68,* 565–579.

Kunda, Z., & Oleson, K. C. (1997). When exceptions prove the rule: How extremity of violence determines the impact of deviant examples on stereotypes. *Journal of Personality and Social Psychology, 72,* 965–979.

Kurtines, W., & Hogan, R. (1972). Sources of conformity in unsocialized college students. *Journal of Abnormal Psychology, 80,* 49–51.

Laible, D. J., Carlo, G., & Roesch, S. C. (2004). Pathways to self-esteem in late adolescence: The role of parent and peer attachment, empathy, and social behaviours. *Journal of Adolescence, 27,* 703–716.

Lamm, C., Meltzoff, A. N., & Decety, J. (2010). How do we empathize with someone who is not like us? *Journal of Cognitive Neuroscience,* Epub ahead of print.

Lanzetta, J. T., & Englis, B. G. (1989). Expectations of cooperation and competition and their effects on observers' vicarious emotional responses. *Journal of Personality and Social Psychology, 56,* 543–554.

Laurenceau, J. P., Barrett, L. F., & Pietromonaco, P. R. (1998). Intimacy as an interpersonal process: The importance of self-disclosure, partner disclosure, and perceived partner responsiveness in interpersonal exchanges. *Journal of Personality and Social Psychology, 74,* 1238–1251.

Leidner, B., Castano, E., Zaiser, E., & Giner-Sorolla, R. (2010). Ingroup glorification, moral disengagement, and justice in the context of collective violence. *Personality and Social Psychology Bulletin, 36,* 1115–1129.

Lenrow, P. B. (1965). Studies of sympathy. In S. S. Tomkins & C. E. Izard (Eds.), *Affect, cognition and personality.* (pp. 264–293). New York: Springer.

Levi, P. (1981). *Se questo è un uomo* [If this is a man]. Torino, Italy: Einaudi.

Lévi-Strauss, C. (1955). *Tristes tropiques.* Paris: Librairie Plon.

Lewicki, R. J., Barry, B., & Saunders, D. M. (2007). *Essentials of negotiation* (4th ed.). Boston: McGraw-Hill/Irwin.

Leyens, J.-P., Paladino, P. M., Rodriguez-Torres, R., Vaes, J., Demoulin, S., Rodriguez-Perez, A., et al. (2000). The emotional side of prejudice: The attribution of secondary emotions to ingroups and outgroups. *Personality and Social Psychology Review, 4,* 186–197.

L'hermitte, F., Pillon, B. & Serdan, M. (1986). Human autonomy and the frontal lobes: Part I. Imitation and utilization behavior: A neurological study of 75 patients. *Annals of Neurology, 19,* 326–334.

Loudin, J. L., Loukas, A., & Robinson, S. (2003). Relational aggression in college students: Examining the roles of social anxiety and empathy. *Aggressive Behavior, 29,* 430–439.

Mackie, D. M., Devos, T., & Smith, E. R. (1999). Intergroup emotions: Explaining offensive action tendencies in an intergroup context. *Journal of Personality and Social Psychology, 79,* 602–616.

Macrae, C. N., Bodenhausen, G. V., Milne, A. B., & Jetten, J. (1994). Out of mind but back in sight: Stereotypes on the rebound. *Journal of Personality and Social Psychology, 67,* 808–817.

Malhotra, D., & Liyanage, S. (2005). Long-term effects of peace workshops in protracted conflicts. *Journal of Conflict Resolution, 49,* 908–924.

Maner, J. K., Luce, C. L., Neuberg, S. L., Cialdini, R. B., Brown, S., & Sagarin, B. J. (2002). The effects of perspective taking on motivations for helping: Still no evidence for altruism. *Personality and Social Psychology Bulletin, 28,* 1601–1610.

Marcus, R. F., & Gray, L., Jr. (1998). Close relationships of violent and nonviolent African American delinquents. *Violence and Victims, 13,* 31–46.

Markiewicz, D., Doyle, A. B., & Brendgen, M. (2001). The quality of adolescents' friendships: Associations with mothers' interpersonal relationships, attachments to parents and friends, and prosocial behaviors. *Journal of Adolescence, 24,* 429–445.

Marsh, A. A., & Blair, R. J. R. (2008). Deficits in facial affect recognition among antisocial populations: A meta-analysis. *Neuroscience and Behavioral Reviews, 32,* 454–465.

Maslach, C, & Jackson, S. E. (1982). Burnout in health professions: A social psychological analysis. In G. Sanders & J. Suls (Eds.), *Social psychology of health and illness.* (pp. 227–254). Hillsdale, NJ: Erlbaum.

Mayberry, M. L., & Espelage, D. L. (2007). Associations among empathy, social competence, and reactive/proactive aggression subtypes. *Journal of Youth and Adolescence, 36,* 787–798.

McAlister, A. L., Bandura, A., & Owen, S. V. (2006). Mechanisms of moral disengagement in support of military force: The impact of Sept. 11. *Journal of Social and Clinical Psychology, 25,* 141–165.

(1974) discussed the role of responsive mothering in minimizing the splitting of the self into good versus bad me. Erikson (1950) conceptualized personality development in terms of resolving a series of social and interpersonal crises throughout the life span. And, most notably in his seminal work on attachment theory, Bowlby argued that the need to attach to significant others is innate and serves a survival function, discussing how parents' responsivity (or its lack thereof) to the child's attachment needs has a lifelong impact on the child's personality.

Against the backdrop of this rich tradition of thinking about the inherently interpersonal nature of personality, a second influential tradition in personality science has historically rested on the bedrock assumption that personality dispositions supersede contexts, relationships, and situations (see Fleeson, chapter 3, this volume; Mischel & Shoda, 2008). In the words of Gilbert and Malone (1995), this tradition "construes skin as a special boundary that separates one set of 'causal forces' from another. On the sunny side of the epidermis are the external or situational forces that press inward on the person, and on the meaty side are the internal or personal forces that exert pressure outward" (p. 21). This approach, in other words, distinguishes the forces on behavior that are the result of personality from the forces on behavior arising from the situation or the environment, and are thus the concern of social psychology. For example, most people would be expected to be joyous at a party with one's friends, and good cheer here may not tell us much about a person's dispositional cheeriness. On the other hand, if a person is consistently of good cheer across a number of different contexts, even when the situation does not necessarily call for it, we would have a case for saying that the person is indeed a cheery kind of person.

Based on the lexical hypothesis (Allport & Odbert, 1936)—the idea that language encodes the important dimensions of personality—this approach has focused on empirically reducing, principally through factor analysis, the large number of personality descriptors in language down to a discrete number of core components. Today, the "Big Five" taxonomy of personality—open-mindedness, conscientiousness, extraversion, agreeableness, and neuroticism—probably enjoys the widest recognition and acceptance resulting from these efforts (for review, see John & Srivastava, 1999). Recent investigations in this area have sought to prove the universality of these five dimensions for describing human personality (e.g., McCrae & Allik, 2002),

and to link these personality descriptors to their genetic markers (e.g., McCrae et al., 2000).

And yet, to the degree the other people inevitably fall on the sunny side of the epidermis, this approach is difficult to reconcile with the tenets of the social constructivist (i.e., social interactional, interpersonal, symbolic interactionist) approaches to personality. Perhaps sensing a growing trend toward the innate and biological in the search for the roots of personality, Gergen (1990) lamented, "It is as if we have at our disposal a rich language for characterizing rooks, pawns, and bishops but have yet to discover the game of chess. How can we redefine qualities of self in such a way that their derivation from the whole is made clear? " (p. 594) Gergen suggested not only that people need to be understood within their social networks, but that there may be nothing *to* understand about personality and self outside of social interactions. This view echoes Sullivan's own assertion that "No such thing as the durable, unique, individual personality is ever clearly justified. For all I know every human being has as many personalities as he has interpersonal relations" (Sullivan, 1950/1964, p. 220). According to this view, people are but the unique confluence of their various social relationships, in the same way that the nexus along which laser beams meet, while readily identifiable, is composed only of the beams themselves.

The notion that there is no such thing as personality outside of our social relationships and interactions is a challenging proposition to those interested in personality, not only because it contradicts empirical evidence suggesting long-term stability in people's temperament through life (e.g., Caspi & Silva, 1995), but also because, at a certain level, it *feels* wrong. In other words, we have a strong intuition that there surely exist stable individual qualities that characterize people across time and situations (Bem & Allen, 1974; Mischel, 1973). Nevertheless, the social constructivist message that we are fundamentally shaped by our relationships strikes a chord of truth, and the fact that this notion has been with psychology for over a century is testament to its utility and importance.

Recall Gergen's (1990) challenge: *How can we redefine qualities of self in such a way that their derivation from the whole is made clear?* Our primary goal in this chapter is to address this challenge, attempting to reaffirm the existence of personality at the same time that we incorporate social constructivist principles into the conceptualization thereof. In line with many of the chapters in this

Handbook, this task requires that we reconsider the traditional dichotomy between personality psychology as concerned with "internal" forces on behavior and social psychology as concerned with the "external" forces on behavior. We are certainly not the first to challenge this dichotomy (see, e.g., Kitayama & Cohen, 2007; Malle, 1999; Mischel & Shoda, 1995; Turner, Reynolds, Haslam, & Veentra, 2006), and we use insights from this research to conceptualize the bidirectional influence of people and social interactions.

More specifically, we adopt a framework borne out of the central tenet of cultural psychology that context and person are coconstitutive, or "make each other up" (Shweder, 1990). This framework, the cultural cognitive-affective processing system (C-CAPS; Mendoza-Denton, Ayduk, Shoda & Mischel, 1997; Mendoza-Denton & Mischel, 2007), is introduced here in light of recent theory and research suggesting that the roots of culture are *themselves* to be found in social interaction (Tomasello, Carpenter, Call, Behne, & Moll, 2005; Tomasello & Herrmann, 2010)—an insight that allows the framework to bear directly on the relationship between social interaction and personality. The framework suggests, and we will aim to show, that social interaction influences personality on multiple levels—from the dyad to the peer group to the community to the culture, and that the direction of influence is reciprocal as well.

We offer this framework within an exciting empirical literature, principally within the field of social cognition, arguing for two related points. The first is that there is predictable situational specificity in people's behavior: that is, behavior does vary across situations, yet does so in systematic and reliable ways (e.g., Ayduk & Gyurak, 2008; Fleeson, 2004; Shoda, Mischel, & Wright, 1994). The second point is that the "active ingredients" of situations—the psychologically meaningful triggers of behavior in a given situation (Mischel & Shoda, 1995)—tend to be social interactional in nature: that is, to detect the systematicity and reliability with which people's behavior changes across situations, it is often critical to categorize situations along the interpersonal dimension (Baldwin, 1992; English & Chen, 2007; Fournier, Moskowitz, & Zuroff, 2008, 2009).

Searching for Stability in Behavioral Inconsistency Across Situations

In the 1985 movie *Back to the Future*, one of the characters that provokes both sympathy and laughs is George McFly. He is, in a word, a pushover: he has trouble asserting himself at the dinner table with his own family, and is continuously humiliated and bullied at work by his supervisor Biff. We return to George McFly later, but we note for now that this depiction of McFly reveals one of our fundamental assumptions about people. It is the assumption that people will carry similar qualities from one situation (e.g., the dinner table) to the next (e.g., the office). It does not strike us as implausible that McFly is quiet, shy, and unassertive across contexts, and we often expect and assume such cross-situational consistency in the people that we ourselves interact with every day (Bem & Allen, 1974). This sense of consistency gives us a feeling of knowing people—of being able to understand and describe the underlying attributes that are characteristic of the person, rather than attributable to other people or to the social interaction they happen to be in.

Nevertheless, research over the past century has convincingly shown that cross-situational variability is at least as impressive as cross-situational consistency (Borkenau, Riemann, Spinath, & Angleitner, 2006; Fleeson, 2004; Fournier, Moskowitz, & Zuroff, 2008, 2009; Hartshorne & May, 1928; Mischel, 1968; Mischel & Peake, 1982; Zayas & Shoda, 2007). Although attempts at resolving cross-situational inconsistency historically pitted sources of consistency against sources of variability, revolving around whether to interpret behavioral variability across situations as "noise" or "signal" (see Epstein, 1979; Mischel & Peake, 1982; Moskowitz, 1988), the emerging consensus is that cross-situational consistency and variability are both stable and important expressions of the personality system (Fleeson, 2004; Fournier et al., 2008; see Fleeson, chapter 3, this volume).

An examination of the evidence for stability and predictability in the variability of people's behavior across situations reveals much about the social embeddedness of personality. In the section that follows, we first provide evidence that such stable variability exists, and importantly, that such variability tends to revolve around the *interpersonal dimension*. This feature of person-situation interactions provides a base for understanding the coconstitution of person and social interaction.

One of the first tests of the hypothesis that behavioral variability across situations is stable was conducted by Shoda et al. (1994), who, within the context of a summer camp setting, recorded and analyzed the behavior of children as it unfolded in vivo over the course of a summer. Among the first issues to tackle was *how to classify the camp situations into meaningful categories.* Probably the most intuitive way to do so would be according to setting type—for example cabin time, story time, or breakfast. As it turned out, however, interviews with the camp counselors as well as the children themselves yielded a different kind of grouping. Rather than grouping situations nominally—that is, according to the physical setting or activity type, the natural groupings tended to emerge around interpersonal themes. The situation "types" are worth repeating here: *when a peer approached sociably, when a peer teased or threatened, when an adult approached sociably, when an adult warned,* and *when an adult punished.*

In contrast to the prediction that variability across situations is noise that only adds error to the measurement of personality and must be removed either through aggregation or denser data measurement (e.g., Epstein, 1979; see also Moskowitz, 1988), the data showed that when grouping situations along these interpersonal dimension, the camp counselees' *if... then...* profiles were both distinctive and stable. Figure 18.1 presents example profiles of two of the children at the camp, children #9 and #28 (from Shoda et al., 1994). In these figures, the children's *if... then...* profile stability is seen in the similarity of the profiles represented by the dotted and the solid lines, which summarize the data from nonoverlapping samples of situations.

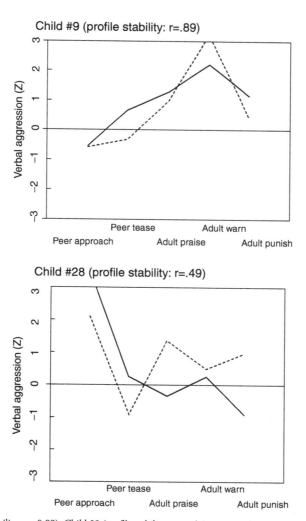

Fig.18.1 Child 9 (profile stability: r = 0.89). Child 28 (profile stability: r = 0.49). Reprinted with permission from Shoda et al. (1994).

Recognizing that people are of course more likely to be aggressive when provoked than when approached sociably, it is of note that the data here represent z-scores. That is, the data were standardized within situations, thus showing how much each child differed from the population mean within that situation. Shoda and colleagues termed these graphical depictions "behavioral signatures" to underline both the behavioral variability across situations as well as the uniqueness and stability of these patterns.

Mischel and Shoda (1995) drew a distinction between "nominal" and "psychological" situations to clarify the importance of the individual's own perspective and construal of a situation in determining his/her response to it (see also Fleeson, 2007). Notably, in Shoda et al. (1994) the "active ingredients" of the situations turned out to be social interactional in nature. This provides us with the first clue that to unlock the coherence that lies underneath surface-level variability across situations, it is necessary to take into account people's interpersonal interactions.

More recently, Fournier and colleagues (2008, 2009) have argued that the interpersonal circumplex model (Wiggins, 1980; Wiggins, Phillips, & Trapnell, 1989) may be especially useful in the search for situation-behavior contingencies (such as if . . . then . . . signatures) because this model can serve as an organizational framework for both behavior and situations. The interpersonal circumplex represents one of the most rigorous efforts to empirically derive a classificatory framework for personality based on the interpersonalist tradition of Cooley, Mead, and Sullivan. This is because the adjectives and dimensions used to characterize personality are inherently interpersonal, always thought to operate specifically in relation to other people. This model organizes interpersonal behavior along two orthogonal dimensions, agency and communion. At the poles of the agency axis are dominance and submission, while communion is anchored by agreeable versus quarrelsome behavior. Wiggins and Trapnell (1996) found that the dimensions of agency and communion underlie an impressive host of classificatory schemes for human behavior, including, for example, individualism/collectivism in cross-cultural psychology (e.g., Triandis & Suh, 2002), status versus reciprocal alliances in evolutionary psychology (Buss, 1991), and the division of social roles into instrumental versus communal (Parsons & Bales, 1955). Although the two factors of the Big Five taxonomy, extraversion and agreeableness, conceptually map on to the dimensions of agency and communion, there is an important difference in that the Big Five taxonomy posits three additional independent factors to characterize personality (neuroticism, open-mindedness, conscientiousness). In the interpersonal circumplex, by contrast, variability in personality results solely from different combinations of the agentic and communal dimensions: for example, a person that combines high agency and high communion would be classified as gregarious-extraverted, but a person that combines high agency and low communion would be arrogant-calculating (a person such as George McFly would likely be unassured-submissive, characterized principally by low agency).

While the classification of behavior along the interpersonal dimension is inherent to the circumplex model, the genius of Fournier et al. (2008) lies in their recognition that just as the model can characterize actors, so can it characterize actors' *interactants*. The researchers conducted a study in which participants recorded their own behavior along the interpersonal circumplex in relation to the four different combinations of behavior for other people along the circumplex—quarrelsome-dominant (QD), quarrelsome-submissive (QS), agreeable-dominant (AD), and agreeable-submissive (AS). The results yielded evidence both for mean interindividual differences in behavior (e.g., some people were, in general, more quarrelsome than others) as well as evidence for the intraindividual stability of signatures (the latter was accomplished by examining the stability of the cross-situational patterning of a given person's behavior when splitting that person's data in half over many iterations, a strategy similar to that used by Shoda and colleagues in 1994). Beyond noting the importance of this research in moving toward an integration of trait and signature perspectives (see also Mischel & Shoda, 2008; Fleeson, 2004), the critical point here is that the *if . . . then . . .* profiles examined by these researchers can be *simultaneously* characterized both as "personality signatures" and as de facto interpersonal interactions. As such, the work of Fournier and colleagues allows for a true integration of a (person-by-situation) interactionist perspective with an interpersonalist perspective where "interpersonal relationships *are* the situation" (Wiggins & Trobst, 1999, p. 655, italics in original).

Although the interpersonal dimension is not necessarily the only way to categorize situations (see, e.g., Bem & Funder, 1978; Fleeson, 2007; Ten Berge & De Raad, 1999; Zayas & Shoda, 2009), research in the social-cognitive tradition consistently

Then they were asked to evaluate the quality of their research ideas. Those who were primed with the negative Zajonc face evaluated their research ideas more poorly than those in the control condition, who were not exposed to this prime.

Baldwin (1999) integrates these findings by explicitly linking relational schemas to variability in behavior across situations. He writes,

> People display an *if . . . then* "behavioral signature" from one situation to the next, such as "If he is in an achievement situation, he is dominant; however, if he is with a romantic partner, he is submissive." The relational schema approach reinforces the point that this cross-situational variability is coherent, psychologically meaningful, and derived from *if . . . then . . .* outcome expectancies [Mischel, 1973], particularly expectancies regarding the environmental contingencies of valued interpersonal goals. (p. 130–131)

In the relational schema approach, then, people have many relational schemas—every relationship provides people with a specific set of psychological situations. While this is of course reminiscent of Sullivan's (1950/1964) own statement, "for all I know every human being has as many personalities as he has interpersonal relations," (p. 220)—Baldwin's conception differs importantly in underscoring the *stability* of people's relational schemas within a dynamic, CAPS-like system.

Transference and the Relational Self

The social-cognitive model of transference (for reviews, see Andersen, Saribay, & Kooji, 2008; Chen & Andersen, 2008) has proven to be a powerful theoretical and empirical tool to demonstrate the processes that explain why people's lives tend to be characterized by recurrent patterns of interpersonal interactions (à la Sullivan). The model is based on the basic assumption that we have significant-other (S-O) schemas that are stored in memory. These significant-other representations tend to be chronically accessible (due to extensive prior contact with the S-O) and are therefore readily applied to understand new people when they resemble the S-O (hence, when the S-O representation is *applicable* to the new people). In other words, transference occurs when a significant-other schema is activated (by chronic accessibility and applicability) and applied to a new person.

The basic transference paradigm that examines this process empirically combines idiographic and nomothetic approaches. In the idiographic component of the paradigm, which takes place first,

participants generate descriptors of an S-O. In the nomothetic component, which follows several weeks later, participants are given descriptions of a series of new target people, one of whom shares some of the traits of the S-O that the participant had generated in the first session. They are then asked to make confidence judgments about the traits of the new person that weren't included in the target's description but which were part of the S-O representation. A common finding in this context is that perceivers go beyond the information given about the new target person—they "fill in the gaps" by making inferences about the new person—based on the accessible S-O representation (e.g., Andersen, Glassman, Chen, & Cole, 1995; Hinkley & Andersen, 1996). In addition to such memory and inference effects, perceivers also transfer representation-derived affect onto the new target person—they tend to like new people who resemble their positively toned significant others, and dislike those who resemble their negatively toned significant others, for example, and show more pleasant facial expressions when learning about the former than the latter targets (Andersen, Reznik, & Manzella, 1996).

Representation-derived motivational tendencies (approach-avoidance) are also readily transferred, as people seek to approach new people resembling positive S-Os and avoid those resembling negative S-Os (Andersen et al., 1996). In turn, they expect targets resembling their positively-toned S-Os to like and accept them more than those resembling their negatively toned S-Os (Andersen et al., 1996). Even more importantly for the idea that personality is shaped by social interaction, transference processes also influence the working self-concept that is accessible at any given point in time. That is, S-O representations are intricately tied to *self-when-with-the-other* representations (in a way very similar to the notion of interpersonal scripts in the work on relational schemas). Hence, when people encounter new people resembling S-Os, their working self-concept tends to change in a way that overlaps with their self-representations that are linked with S-O schemas (Hinkley & Andersen, 1996). Furthermore, the working self-concept tends to be more positive when transference is occurring with respect to a positive than a negative S-O.

In summary, Andersen and colleagues' work persuasively argues that one "becomes" the person he/she typically is when with this S-O—making the self inherently relational (see Andersen & Chen, 2002, for review). This phenomenon can explain how we can be both stable in our personality and also reliably different with different people (see Andersen & Chen, 2002, and Andersen & Thorpe, 2009, for detailed discussions). That is, on the one hand, we tend to exhibit different aspects of ourselves in interpersonal situations to the extent that they activate different S-O representations. This explains the cross-situational variability of behavior. On the other hand, we tend to have same kinds of behaviors, emotions, and working self-concept across interpersonal situations to the extent that they are functionally similar in activating the same S-O representation. This explains why our personality remains reliably stable when we find ourselves in the same kind of psychological situation (and hence, why the *if . . . then . . .* signatures are stable).

Rejection Sensitivity

Rejection sensitivity (RS) has been defined as a generalized dynamic to anxiously expect, readily perceive, and intensely react to rejection (Downey & Feldman, 1996). Originally developed to account for the psychological legacy of rejection within close or intimate relationships (Downey & Feldman, 1996; Feldman & Downey, 1994; see Ayduk & Gyurak, 2008, and Romero-Canyas, Downey, Berenson, Ayduk, & Kang, 2010a, for reviews), the construct has since been applied to rejection based on race (Chan & Mendoza-Denton, 2008; Mendoza-Denton, Downey, Purdie, Davis, & Pietrzak, 2002), sexual orientation (Pachankis, Goldfried, & Ramrattan, 2008), and gender (Mendoza-Denton, Shaw-Taylor, Chen, & Chang 2009). The general cognitive-affective course of the dynamic (expectations→perceptions →reactions) is shared by all of these constructs. Nevertheless, the differences among them are illustrative of the ways in which personality dynamics are manifested differently depending on the type of social interaction at hand.

IF . . . THEN . . . SIGNATURES OF
THE RS DYNAMIC

People high in RS have high levels of anxiety and concern about abandonment and expectations of rejection. People low in RS, by contrast, are relatively unconcerned about rejection and expect acceptance. Nevertheless, the RS model specifically proposes that there is situational specificity to the activation of such expectations; that is, it conforms to an *if . . . then . . .* pattern, whereby *if* the interpersonal situation has to do with the possibility of rejection,

then the dynamic becomes activated (see Ayduk & Gyurak, 2008, for a similar argument). Examples of such situations include asking someone out for a date, or asking to borrow someone's class notes. This situational specificity, which is built into the assessment of RS, is important because it underscores how changes in the interpersonal environment can determine whether the dynamic becomes activated. For example, Downey, Mougios, Ayduk, London, and Shoda (2004) found that high RS individuals show a startle blink response (denoting activation of the defensive motivational system; Lang, Bradley, & Cuthbert, 1990) more strongly than low RS individuals while viewing artwork that depicted scenes of social isolation, rejection, and alienation. However, this was not the case while viewing artwork that was negative in tone, but nonrepresentational (hence, unrelated to social rejection). The startle response is an uncontrolled physiological threat response that, despite being "internal," is sensitive to interpersonal cues, and is particularly activated in situations that communicate rejection for people high in RS.

Other studies document the situational specificity of high RS individuals' aggression and hostility. For example, Ayduk, Downey, Testa, Yen, and Shoda (1999) had participants who differed in their levels of RS participate in an ostensible online "get to know you" task with a confederate. Although no participants ended up being able to meet their purported partner, half were told that they could not continue because of a computer malfunction, and half were told that their partner did not in fact want to continue. Only the high RS participants in the intentional condition showed the expected negative effects of rejection, reporting greater emotional reactivity and reacting with retaliatory hostility. Importantly, however, no differences in RS were found in the computer malfunction condition. Similar specificity for high RS individuals' aggression was found in a separate study in which participants were given an opportunity to punish their rejector by allocating to him/her more spicy hot sauce (Ayduk, Gyurak, & Luerssen, 2008).

Of note, the empirical evidence suggests that high RS people are not more aggressive than low RS people overall (Ayduk & Gyurak, 2008). Rather, the *if . . . then . . .* signature for aggression in RS is such that in the presence of psychological features that signal rejection, high RS individuals become reliably more aggressive than low RS individuals, but given the possibility of securing acceptance, high RS people are in fact *more* accommodating in their behavior (Ayduk, May, Downey, & Higgins, 2003), engaging in self-silencing and ingratiation (Romero-Canyas et al., 2010b; Purdie & Downey, 2000, Ayduk et al., 2003). Figure 18.2 illustrates this *if . . . then . . .* signature (from Ayduk & Gyurak, 2008). The pattern is directly applicable to our understanding of real-world puzzles in surface-level behavioral inconsistencies, such as the fawning suitor who showers a potential partner with flowers and chocolates but then becomes physically abusive as the relationship goes on.

REJECTION SENSITIVITY BASED ON OTHER ASPECTS OF SOCIAL IDENTITY

Research on RS shows that an important "active ingredient" for differentiating among situations seems to be whether, when interpersonal acceptance is at stake, it is because of a characteristic that is unique to us (e.g., our appearance, see Park, 2007), or because of a characteristic that we share with others, such as our race, our gender, or our sexual orientation.

Based on this insight, Mendoza-Denton and colleagues (2002) extended the RS construct to understand the psychological legacy of stigmatization and discrimination based on status characteristics. Focusing initially on race, the race-based rejection sensitivity model (RS-race) recalls the question by Gordon Allport (1954, p. 138): "what would happen to your personality if you heard it said over and over that you were lazy and of inferior blood?" The current analysis suggests that a complete understanding of the psychological legacy of stigmatization requires an appreciation of context, of person, and of social interactions.

The differences between the original RS model (hereafter called *RS-personal* to reflect its domain specificity) and the RS-race model are illustrative of the ways that C-CAPS dynamics are sensitive to the subtleties of social interaction—in this case, who rejects you, and for what reason. Race-based rejection sensitivity shares the broad characteristics of the general RS-dynamic. Reflecting the different social interactions around which personal and race-based rejection revolve, however, both the trigger features and the outcomes to which these two dynamics have been related are different.

Whereas the trigger features for RS-personal are interpersonal situations that might trigger rejection for personal reasons, RS-race is more likely to be triggered in interpersonal situations where prejudice and discrimination might be relevant—such as when a security guard begins stopping people after an alarm sounds, or at a busy restaurant when a waitress might be deciding whom to serve (Mendoza-Denton et al., 2002). These instances are social situations in which people, even if they are secure in their acceptance within their personal relationships, might be particularly attuned to discrimination based on their stigmatized social identity. Building on research suggesting that discrimination is experienced as rejection (Branscombe, Schmitt, & Harvey, 1999), within the RS-race model prior experiences of race-based exclusion, mistreatment, or discrimination can lead people to develop racism-specific anxious rejection expectations. An important distinction with RS-personal is that anxious expectations of race-based rejection can develop out of the realization that *others'* experiences with discrimination

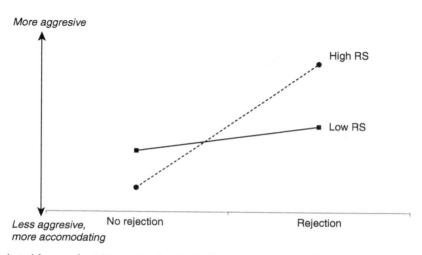

Fig. 18.2 Psychological features of social interaction. Reprinted with permission from Ayduk and Gyurak (2008).

might be relevant to the self as a member of the same social category.

The original formulation of RS-race focused specifically on African Americans, and the resulting RS-race questionnaire revealed, as expected, greater mean levels as well as greater within-group variability in RS-race among African Americans as compared to either European Americans or Asian Americans. It is theoretically important to note, however, that Asian Americans' lower scores on the measure for African Americans does not mean that this latter group does not experience race-based rejection. In fact, research consistently shows that Asian Americans experience as much discrimination as other minority groups (Cheryan & Monin 2005; Crocker & Lawrence, 1999; Oyserman & Sakamoto, 1997; Greene, Way, & Pahl, 2006). The difference, rather, lies in the *types of interpersonal situations* where such discrimination happens. In the case of African Americans, a roadblock where police are randomly pulling people over might activate race-based rejection concerns (Mendoza-Denton et al., 2002), whereas for Asian Americans, asking a store clerk who just mumbled something to repeat what s/he just said might activate the dynamic (Chan & Mendoza-Denton, 2008). In sum, the *if . . . then . . .* profiles of RS-race for different groups reflect the social interactional contexts in which rejection is likely to unfold.

Further illustrating that individual and cultural differences can arise not only from differences in the availability of CAUs, but also from the distinctive organization among these CAUs, different manifestations of RS have been linked to different *outcomes*. As we have noted, RS-personal has been tied to difficulties in personal relationships, including relationship hostility (Ayduk et al., 1999, 2008) and breakups (Downey, Freitas, Michaelis, & Khouri, 1998), as well as depression (Ayduk, Downey, & Kim, 2001). RS-race among African Americans, by contrast, has been specifically linked to adjustment difficulties in institutions with a historical legacy of race-based discrimination, both in terms of belonging (Mendoza-Denton & Page-Gould, 2008; Mendoza-Denton, Goldman-Flythe, Pietrzak, Downey, & Aceves, 2010) and goal attainment (e.g., academic achievement; Mendoza-Denton et al., 2002; 2008). Consistent with a literature on the self-protective properties of stigma (Crocker & Major, 1989), RS-race among African Americans is unrelated to self-esteem. Yet, among Asian Americans, RS-race is unrelated to academic achievement, but

uniquely predicts internalizing symptomatology (self-esteem, depression, and anxiety) even after controlling for RS-personal (Chan & Mendoza-Denton, 2008).

This outcome difference in RS-race between Asian Americans and African Americans may be reflective of social interactional forces as well. For African Americans, a powerful collective act—the civil rights movement—may have been a catalyst not only to make available, but to ensure the chronic accessibility of, prejudice as an explanation for negative outcomes, paving the way for protected self-esteem (see Twenge & Crocker, 2002, for historical data supporting this view). Asian Americans, by contrast, have not had a similarly powerful and widespread collective consciousness-raising movement. Thus, discounting of negative outcomes as a socially shared coping strategy for discrimination may not be as widespread in this group. Cognitive-affective dynamics thus reflect sociohistorical forces: African Americans, *if* experiencing rejection from an outgroup member, may *then* not attribute the outcome to themselves (and thus suffer no drop in self-esteem) as a result of a culturally shared set of cognitions recognizing prejudice as a source of negative outcomes. Asian Americans, *if* discriminated against, may *then* in fact feel responsible for the negative outcome, and suffer decreases in self-esteem.

In recent research, Pachankis et al. (2008) have further shown the specificity of the rejection sensitivity dynamic—its attunement to social dynamics—in their investigation of rejection sensitivity on the basis of sexual orientation among gay men. This manifestation of group-based RS shares features of RS-personal in that the dynamic develops out of painful personal experiences of parental rejection specifically related to one's sexual identity, which then affect future interactions through internalized homophobia.

As the examples above show, the specifics of RS dynamics, both in terms of trigger features and outcomes, reflect the social interactional history of the individual—interactions with parents, as well as symbolic interactions through the influence of culture via shared values or beliefs. Researchers interested in assessment face a difficult choice between being able to develop context-free measures of dispositions that can apply to many people across many different contexts, or developing contextualized assessments that take into account the importance of social-interactional history, but

self: Strategic self-regulation for coping with rejection sensitivity. *Journal of Personality and Social Psychology, 79,* 776–792.

Baldwin, M. W. (1992). Relational schemas and the processing of social information. *Psychological Bulletin, 112,* 461–484.

Baldwin, M. W. (1999). Relational schemas: Research into social-cognitive aspects of interpersonal experience. In D. Cervone & Y. Shoda (Eds.), *The coherence of personality: Social-cognitive bases of consistency, variability, and organization* (pp. 127–154). New York: Guilford.

Baldwin, M. W., & Baccus, J. R. (2003). An expectancy-value approach to self-esteem. In S. J. Spencer, S. Fein, M. P. Zanna, & J. M. Olson (Eds.), *Motivated social perception: The Ontario Symposium* (Vol. 9, pp. 171–194). Mahwah, NJ: Erlbaum.

Baldwin, M. W., Carrell, S. E., & Lopez, D. F. (1993). Priming relationship schemas: My advisor and the Pope are watching me from the back of my mind. *Journal of Experimental Social Psychology, 26,* 435–454.

Baldwin, M. W., Fehr, B., Keedian, E., Seidel, M., & Thomson, D. (1993). An exploration of the relational schemata underlying attachment styles: Self-report and lexical decision approaches. *Personality and Social Psychology Bulletin, 19,* 746–754.

Baldwin, M. W., & Keelan, J. P. R. (1999). Interpersonal expectations as a function of self-esteem and sex. *Journal of Social and Personal Relationships, 16,* 822–833.

Baldwin, M. W., & Sinclair, L. (1996). Self-esteem and "if . . . then" contingencies of interpersonal acceptance. *Journal of Personality and Social Psychology, 71,* 1130–1141.

Banaji, M. R., Hardin, C., & Rothman, A. J. (1993). Implicit stereotyping in person judgment. *Journal of Personality and Social Psychology, 65,* 272–281.

Baumeister, R. F., & Leary, M. R. (1995). The need to belong: Desire for interpersonal attachments as a fundamental human motivation. *Psychological Bulletin, 117,* 497–529.

Bedell, P. (1997). Resilient women: Risk and protective factors in the lives of female offenders. Unpublished Master's Thesis. Vermont College of Norwich University, Norwich, VT.

Bem, D. J., & Allen, A. (1974). On predicting some of the people some of the time: The search for cross-situational consistencies in behavior. *Psychological Review, 81,* 506–520.

Bem, D. J., & Funder, D. C. (1978). Predicting more of the people more of the time: Assessing the personality of situations. *Psychological Review, 85,* 485–501.

Borkenau, P., Riemann, R., Spinath, F. M., & Angleitner, A. (2006). Genetic and environmental influences on person x situation profiles. *Journal of Personality, 74,* 1451–1479.

Bowlby, J. (1969). *Attachment and loss: Vol. I. Attachment.* New York: Basic Books.

Bowlby, J. (1973). *Attachment and loss: Vol. II. Separation: Anxiety and anger.* New York: Basic Books.

Bowlby, J. (1980). *Attachment and loss: Vol. III. Loss: Sadness and depression.* New York: Basic Books

Branscombe, N. R., Schmitt, M. T., & Harvey, R. D. (1999). Perceiving pervasive discrimination among African Americans: Implications for group identification and well-being. *Journal of Personality and Social Psychology, 77,* 135–149.

Buss, D. M., (1987). Selection, evocation, and manipulation. *Journal of Personality and Social Psychology, 53,* 1214–1221.

Buss, D. M. (1991). Evolutionary personality psychology. *Annual Review of Psychology, 41,* 459–491.

Campbell, J. D. (1990). Self-esteem and clarity of the self-concept. *Journal of Personality and Social Psychology, 59,* 538–549.

Carpenter, M., Nagell, K., & Tomasello, M. (1998). Social cognition, joint attention, and communicative competence from 9 to 15 months of age. *Monographs of the Society of Research in Child Development, 63,* 1–143.

Caspi, A., & Silva, P. A. (1995). Temperamental qualities at age three predict personality traits in young adulthood. *Child Development, 66,* 486–498.

Cervone, D. (2005). Personality architecture: Within-person structures and processes. *Annual Review of Psychology, 56,* 423–452.

Chan, W. Y., & Mendoza-Denton, R. (2008). Status-based rejection sensitivity among Asian Americans: Implications for psychological distress. *Journal of Personality, 76,* 1317–1346.

Chen, S., & Andersen, S. M. (2008). The relational self in transference: Intrapersonal and interpersonal consequences in everyday social life. In J. V. Wood, A. Tesser, & J. G. Holmes (Eds.), *The self and social relationships.* (pp. 231–253). New York: Psychology Press.

Cheng, C., Chiu, C., Hong, Y., & Cheung, J. S. (2001). Discriminative facility and its role in the perceived quality of interactional experiences. *Journal of Personality, 65,* 765–785.

Chiu, C., Hong, Y., Mischel, W., & Shoda, Y. (1995). Discriminative facility in social competence: Conditional versus dispositional encoding and monitoring-blunting of information. *Social Cognition, 13,* 49–70.

Cheryan, S., & Monin, B. (2005). "Where are you really from?" Asian Americans and identity denial. *Journal of Personality and Social Psychology, 89,* 717–730.

Cooley, C. H. (1902). *Human nature and the social order.* New York: Scribner's.

Cousins, S. D. (1989). Culture and self-perception in Japan and the United States. *Journal of Personality and Social Psychology, 56,* 124–131.

Crocker, J., & Knight, K. M. (2005). Contingencies of self-worth. *Current Directions in Psychological Science, 14,* 200–203.

Crocker, J., & Lawrence, J. S. (1999). Social stigma and self-esteem: The role of contingencies of worth. In D. A. Prentice & D. T. Miller (Eds.), *Cultural divides: Understanding and overcoming group conflict* (pp. 364–392). Thousand Oaks, CA: Sage.

Crocker, J., & Major, B. (1989). Social stigma and self-esteem: The self-protective properties of stigma. *Psychological Review, 96,* 608–630.

Downey, G., & Feldman, S. (1996). Implications of rejection sensitivity for intimate relationships. *Journal of Personality and Social Psychology, 70,* 1327–1343.

Downey, G., Freitas, A. L., Michealis, B., & Khouri, H. (1998). The self-fulfilling prophecy in close relationships: Do rejection sensitive women get rejected by romantic partners? *Journal of Personality and Social Psychology, 75,* 545–560.

Downey, G., Mougios, V., Ayduk, O., London, B. E., & Shoda, Y. (2004). Rejection sensitivity and the defensive motivational system: Insights from the startle response to rejection cues. *Psychological Science, 15,* 668–673.

Dutton, D. G., & Browning, J. J. (1988). Concern for power, fear of intimacy, and aversive stimuli for wife assault, In G. Hotaling, D. Finkelhor, J. T. Kirkpatrick, & M. A. Straus (Eds.), *Family abuse and its consequences: New directions in research* (pp.130–175). Newbury Park, CA: Sage.

Dutton, D. G., Saunders, K., Staromski, A., & Bartholomew, K. (1994). Intimacy anger and insecure attachment as precursors of abuse in intimate relationships. *Journal of Applied Social Psychology, 24,* 145–156.

English, T., & Chen, S. (2007). Culture and self-concept stability: Consistency across and within contexts among Asian- and European-Americans. *Journal of Personality and Social Psychology, 93,* 478–490.

Epstein, S. (1979). The stability of behavior: I. On predicting most of the people much of the time. *Journal of Personality and Social Psychology, 37,* 1097–1126.

Erikson, E. (1950). *Childhood and society.* New York: Norton.

Feldman, S., & Downey, G. (1994). Rejection sensitivity as a mediator of the impact of childhood exposure to family violence on adult attachment behavior. *Development and Psychopathology, 6,* 231–247.

Fiske, S. T. (2004). Social beings: A core motives approach to social psychology. Hoboken, NJ: Wiley.

Fleeson, W. (2004). Moving personality beyond the person-situation debate: The challenge and the opportunity of within-person variability. *Current Directions, 13,* 83–87.

Fleeson, W. (2007). Situation-based contingencies underlying trait-content manifestation in behavior. *Journal of Personality, 75,* 825–861.

Fournier, M. A., Moskowitz, D. S., & Zuroff, D. C. (2008). Integrating dispositions, signatures, and the interpersonal domain. *Journal of Personality and Social Psychology, 94,* 531–545.

Fournier, M. A., Moskowitz, D. S., & Zuroff, D. C. (2009). The interpersonal signature. *Journal of Research in Personality, 43,* 155–162.

Geertz, C. (1973). The interpretation of cultures: Selected essays. New York: Basic Books.

Gergen, K. J. (1990). Social understanding and the inscription of self. In J. W. Stigler, R. A. Shweder, & G. Herdt (Eds.), *Cultural psychology: Essays on comparative human development* (pp.569–607). Cambridge, UK: Cambridge University Press.

Gergen, K. J. (1993). Belief as relational resource. *International Journal for the Psychology of Religion, 3,* 231–235.

Gilbert, D. T., & Malone, P. S. (1995). The correspondence bias. *Psychological Bulletin, 117,* 21–38.

Goff, P. A., Steele, C. M., & Davies, P. G. (2008). The space between us: Stereotype threat and distance in interracial contexts. *Journal of Personality and Social Psychology, 94,* 91–107.

Gottman, J. M. (1998). Psychology and the study of the marital processes. *Annual Review of Psychology, 49,* 169–197.

Gottman, J. M., & Levenson, R. W. (1999). How stable is marital interaction over time? *Family process, 38,* 159–165.

Greene, M. L., Way, N., & Pahl, K. (2006). Trajectories of perceived adult and peer discrimination among black, Latino, and Asian American adolescents: Patterns and psychological correlates. *Developmental Psychology, 42,* 218–238.

Hardin, C. D., & Conley, T. D. (2001). A relational approach to cognition: Shared experience and relationship affirmation in social cognition. In G. B. Moskowitz (Ed.), *Cognitive social psychology: The Princeton Symposium on the Legacy and Future of Social Cognition (pp. 3-17).* Hillsdale, NJ: Erlbaum.

Hardin, C. D., & Higgins, E. T. (1996). Shared reality: How social verification makes the subjective objective. In E. T. Higgins & R. M. Sorrentino (Eds.), *Handbook of motivation and cognition: The interpersonal context* (Vol. 3, pp. 28-84). New York: Guilford.

Harris, L. M., Gergen, K. J., & Lannamann, J. W. (1986). Aggression rituals. *Communication Monographs, 53,* 252–265.

Harris, L. M., & Sadeghi, A. R. (1987). Realizing: How facts are created in human interaction. *Journal of Social and Personal Relationships, 4,* 481–495

Hartshorne, H., & May, M. A. (1928). *Studies in deceit.* Oxford, UK: Macmillan.

Henderson, A. J. Z., Bartholomew, K., & Dutton, D. G. (1997). He loves me; he loves me not: Attachment and separation resolution of abused women. *Journal of Family Violence, 12,* 169–191.

Higgins, E. T. (1996). Knowledge activation: Accessibility, applicability, and salience. In E. T. Higgins & A. W. Kruglanski (Eds.), *Social psychology: Handbook of basic principles* (pp. 133–168). New York: Guilford.

Higgins, E. T., Rholes, W. S., & Jones, C. R. (1977). Category accessibility and impression formation. *Journal of Experimental Social Psychology, 13,* 141–154.

Hinkley, K., & Andersen, S. M. (1996). The working self-concept in transference: Significant-other activation and self change. *Journal of Personality and Social Psychology, 71,* 1279–1295.

Hinton, G. E., McClelland, J. L., & Rumelhart, D. E. (1986). Distributed representations. In D. E. Rumelhart & J. L. McClelland (Eds.), *Parallel distributed processing: Explorations in the microstructures of cognition: Vol. 1. Foundations* (pp. 77–109). Cambridge, MA: MIT Press/Bradford Books.

Horberg, E. J., & Chen, S. (2010). Significant others and contingencies of self-worth: Activation and consequences of relationship-specific contingencies of self-worth. *Journal of Personality and Social Psychology, 98,* 77–91.

Horney, I. C. (1937). *The neurotic personality of our time.* New York: Norton.

James, W. (1890). *The principles of psychology* (Vol. 1). Cambridge, MA: Harvard University Press.

John, O. P., & Srivastava, S. (1999). The Big Five trait taxonomy: History, measurement, and theoretical perspectives. In L. Pervin & O. John (Eds.), *Handbook of personality: Theory and research* (pp. 102–138). New York: Guilford.

Kammrath, L., Mendoza-Denton, R., & Mischel, W. (2005). Incorporating *if . . . then . . .* signatures in person perception: Beyond the person-situation dichotomy. *Journal of Personality and Social Psychology, 88,* 605–613.

Kashima, Y. (2001). Culture and social cognition: Toward a social psychology of cultural dynamics. In D. Matsumoto (Ed.), *The handbook of culture and psychology* (pp. 325–360). New York: Oxford University Press.

Kitayama, S. (2002). Culture and basic psychological processes—toward a system view of culture: Comment on Oyserman et al. (2002). *Psychological Bulletin, 128,* 89–96.

Kitayama, S., & D. Cohen, D. (Eds.). (2007). *Handbook of cultural psychology.* New York: Guilford.

Klein, M. (1974). *Love, guilt, and reparation, and other works, 1921–1925.* New York: Free Press.

Kraus, M. W., & Chen, S. (2010). Facial feature resemblance elicits the transference effect. *Psychological Science, 21,* 518–522.

Lang, P. J., Bradley, M. M., & Cuthbert, B. N. (1990). Emotion, attention, and the startle reflex. *Psychological Review, 97,* 377–395.

Linton, R. (1936). *The study of man: An introduction.* New York: Appleton-Century.

Malle, B. F. (1999). How people explain behavior: A new theoretical framework. *Personality and Social Psychology Review, 3,* 23–48.

McCrae, R. R., & Allik, J. (. (2002). *The five-factor model of personality across cultures*. New York: Kluwer Academic/Plenum.

McCrae, R. R., Costa, P. T., Ostendorf, F., Angleitner, A., Hrebickova, M., Avia, M. D., et al. (2000). Nature over nurture: Temperament, personality, and life span development. *Journal of Personality and Social Psychology, 78,* 173–186.

Mead, G. H. (1934). *Mind, self, and society: From the standpoint of a social behaviorist*. Chicago: University of Chicago Press.

Mendoza-Denton, R., Ayduk, O. N., Shoda, Y., & Mischel, W. (1997). Cognitive-affective processing system analysis of reactions to the O. J. Simpson criminal trial verdict. *Journal of Social Issues, 53,* 563–581.

Mendoza-Denton, R., Downey, G., Purdie, V. J., Davis, A., & Pietrzak, J. (2002). Sensitivity to status-based rejection: Implications for African American students' college experience. *Journal of Personality and Social Psychology, 83,* 896–918.

Mendoza-Denton, R., Goldman-Flythe, M., Pietrzak, J., Downey, G., & Aceves, M. J. (2010). Group-value ambiguity: Understanding the effects of academic feedback on minority students' self-esteem. *Social Psychological and Personality Science, 1,* 127–135.

Mendoza-Denton, R., & Hansen, N. (2007). Networks of meaning: Intergroup relations, cultural worldviews, and knowledge activation principles. *Social and Personality Psychology Compass, 1,* 68–83.

Mendoza-Denton, R., & Mischel, W. (2007). Integrating system approaches to culture and personality: The cultural cognitive-affective processing system (C-CAPS). In S. Kitayama & D. Cohen (Eds.), *Handbook of cultural psychology* (pp. 175–195). New York: Guilford.

Mendoza-Denton, R., & Page-Gould, E. (2008). Can cross-group friendships influence minority students' well being at historically white universities? *Psychological Science, 19,* 933–939.

Mendoza-Denton, R., Park, S., & O'Connor, A. (2007). Toward a science of the social perceiver. In G. Downey, Y. Shoda, & D. Cervone (Eds.), *Persons in context: Building a science of the individual* (pp. 211–225). New York: Guilford.

Mendoza-Denton, R., Shaw-Taylor, L., Chen, S., & Chang, E. (2009). Ironic effects of explicit gender prejudice on women's test performance. *Journal of Experimental Social Psychology, 45,* 275–278.

Mischel, W. (1968). *Personality and assessment*. New York: Wiley.

Mischel, W. (1973). Toward a cognitive social learning reconceptualization of personality. *Psychological Review, 80,* 252–283.

Mischel, W., & Peake, P. K. (1982). Beyond déjà vu in the search for cross-situational consistency. *Psychological Review, 89,* 730–755.

Mischel, W., & Shoda, Y. (1995). A cognitive-affective system theory of personality: Reconceptualizing situations, dispositions, dynamics, and invariance in personality structure. *Psychological Review, 102,* 246–268.

Mischel, W., & Shoda, Y. (1999). Integrating dispositions and processing dynamics within a unified theory of personality: The cognitive affective personality system (CAPS). In L. Pervin & 0. John, (Eds.), *Handbook of personality: Theory and research* (pp. 197–218). New York: Guilford.

Mischel, W., & Shoda, Y. (2008). Toward a unifying theory of personality: Integrating dispositions and processing dynamics within the cognitive-affective processing system. In O. P.

John, R. W. Robins, & L. A. Pervin (Eds.), *Handbook of personality psychology* (3rd ed., pp. 208–241). New York: Guilford.

Moskowitz, D. S. (1988). Cross-situational generality in the laboratory: Dominance and friendliness. *Journal of Personality and Social Psychology, 54,* 829–839.

Murray, S. L., Griffin, D. W., Rose, P., & Bellavia, G. M. (2003). Calibrating the sociometer: The relational contingencies of self-esteem. *Journal of Personality and Social Psychology, 85,* 63–84.

Nisbett, R. E., & Cohen, D. (1996). *Culture of honor: The psychology of violence in the South*. Boulder, CO: Westview.

Obeyeskere, G. (1981). *Medusa's hair: An essay on personal symbols and religious experience*. Chicago, IL: University of Chicago Press.

O'Hearn, R. E., & Davis, K. E. (1997). Women's experience of giving and receiving emotional abuse. *Journal of Interpersonal Violence, 12,* 375–391.

Over, H., & Carpenter, M. (2009). Eighteen-month-old infants show increased helping following priming with affiliation. *Psychological Science, 20,* 1189–1193.

Oyserman, D., & Sakamoto, I. (1997). Being Asian American: Identity, cultural constructs, and stereotype perception. *Journal of Applied Behavioral Science, 33,* 435–453.

Pachankis, J. E., Goldfried, M. R., & Ramrattan, M. E. (2008). Extension of the rejection sensitivity construct to the interpersonal functioning of gay men. *Journal of Consulting and Clinical Psychology, 76,* 306–317.

Park, L. E. (2007). Appearance-based rejection sensitivity: Implications for mental and physical health, affect, and motivation. *Personality and Social Psychology Bulletin, 33,* 490–504.

Park, L. E. (2010). Responses to self-threat: Linking self and relational constructs with approach and avoidance motivation. *Social and Personality Psychology Compass, 4,* 201–221.

Parsons, T., & Bales, R. F. (1955). *Family, socialization, and interaction process*. Glencoe, IL: Free Press.

Pinel, E. C. (1999). Stigma consciousness: The psychological legacy of social stereotypes. *Journal of Personality and Social Psychology, 76,* 114–128.

Purdie, V., & Downey, G. (2000). Rejection sensitivity and adolescent girls' vulnerability to relationship-centered difficulties. *Child Maltreatment, 5,* 338–349.

Read, S. J., & Miller, L. C. (1998). *Connectionist models of social reasoning and social behavior*. Mahwah, NJ: Erlbaum.

Revenstorf, D., Vogel, B., Wegener, C., Halweg, K., & Schindler, L. (1980). Escalation phenomena in interaction sequences: An empirical comparison of distressed and nondistressed couples. *Behavior Analysis and Modification, 2,* 97–116.

Romero-Canyas, R., Downey, G., Berenson, K., Ayduk, O, & Kang, J. N. (2010a). Rejection Sensitivity and the rejection-hostility link in romantic relationships. *Journal of Personality, 78,* 119–148.

Romero-Canyas, R., Downey, G., Reddy, K. S., Rodriguez, S., Cavanaugh, T., & Pelayo, R. (2010b). Paying to belong: When does rejection trigger ingratiation? *Journal of Personality and Social Psychology, 99,* 802–823.

Searle, J. (1995). *The construction of social reality*. New York: Free Press.

Shoda, Y., LeeTiernan, S., & Mischel, W. (2002). Personality as a dynamical system: Emergency of stability and distinctiveness from intra- and interpersonal interactions. *Personality and Social Psychology Review, 6,* 316–325.

Shoda, Y., & Mischel, W. (1993). Cognitive social approach to dispositional inferences: What if the perceiver is a cognitive social theorist? *Personality and Social Psychology Bulletin, 19,* 574–585.

Shoda, Y., Mischel, W., & Wright, J. C. (1994). Intra-individual stability in the organization and patterning of behavior: Incorporating psychological situations into the idiographic analysis of personality. *Journal of Personality and Social Psychology, 67,* 674–687.

Shweder, R. A. (1990). Cultural psychology—what is it? In J. W. Stigler, R. A. Shweder, & G. Herdt (Eds.), *Cultural psychology: Essays on comparative human development* (pp. 1–43). Cambridge, UK: Cambridge University Press.

Stryker, S. (2002). Traditional symbolic interactionism, role theory, and structural symbolic interactionism. In J. H. Turner (Ed.), *Handbook of sociological theory* (pp. 211–231). New York: Kluwer Academic/Plenum.

Suh, E. M. (2002). Culture, identity consistency, and subjective well-being. *Journal of Personality and Social Psychology, 83,* 1378–1391.

Sullivan, H. S. (1950/1964). The illusion of personal individuality. In H. S. Sullivan, *The fusion of psychiatry and social science* (pp. 198–226). New York: Norton.

Sullivan, H. S. (1953). *The interpersonal theory of psychiatry.* New York: Norton.

Swann, W. B., Jr., Hixon, J. G., & de la Ronde, C. (1992). Embracing the bitter "truth": Negative self-concepts and marital commitment. *Psychological Science, 3,* 118–121.

Ten Berge, M. A., & De Raad, B. (1999). Taxonomies of situations from a trait psychological perspective: A review. *European Journal of Personality, 13,* 337–360.

Tomasello, M., Kruger, A., & Ratner, H. (1993) Cultural learning. *Behavioral and Brain Sciences, 16,* 495–552.

Tomasello, M., & Herrmann, E. (2010). Ape and human cognition: What's the difference? *Current Directions in Psychological Science, 19,* 3–8.

Tomasello, M., Carpenter, M., Call, J., Behne, T., & Moll, H. (2005). Understanding and sharing intentions: The ontogeny and phylogeny of cultural cognition. *Behavioral and Brain Sciences, 28,* 675–691.

Triandis, H. C., & Suh, E. M. (2002). Cultural influences on personality. *Annual Review of Psychology, 53,* 133–160.

Triandis, H. C., Lambert, W. W., Berry, J. W., Lonner, W., Heron, A., Brislin, R. W., et al. (1980). *Handbook of cross-cultural psychology.* Boston, MA: Allyn & Bacon.

Turner, J. C., Reynolds, K. J., Haslam, S. A., & Veenstra, K. E. (2006). Reconceptualizing personality: Producing individuality by defining the personal self. In T. Postmes & J. Jetten (Eds.), *Individuality and the group: Advances in social identity* (pp. 11–36). London: Sage.

Twenge, J. M., & Crocker, J. (2002). Race and self-esteem: Meta-analyses comparing whites, blacks, Hispanics, Asians, and American Indians and comment on Gray, Little, and Hafdahl (2000). *Psychological Bulletin, 128,* 371–408.

Wiggins, J. S. (1980). Circumplex models of interpersonal behavior. In L. Wheeler (Ed.). *Review of personality and social psychology* (Vol. 1, pp. 265–294). Beverly Hills, CA: Sage.

Wiggins, J. S., Phillips, N., & Trapnell, P. D. (1989). Circular reasoning about interpersonal behavior: Evidence concerning some untested assumptions underlying diagnostic classification. *Journal of Personality and Social Psychology, 56,* 296–305.

Wiggins, J. S., & Trapnell, P. D. (1996). A dyadic-interactional perspective on the five-factor model. In J. S. Wiggins (Ed.), *The five-factor model of personality: Theoretical perspectives* (pp. 88–162). New York: Guilford.

Wiggins, J. S., & Trobst, K. K. (1999). The fields of interpersonal behavior. In L. Pervin & 0. John, (Eds.), *Handbook of personality: Theory and research* (pp. 653–670). New York: Guilford.

Woodward, A. L. (1998). Infants selectively encode the goal object of an actor's reach. *Cognition, 69,* 1–34.

Woodward, A. L. (1999). Infants' ability to distinguish between purposeful and non-purposeful behaviors. *Infant Behavior and Development, 22,* 145–160.

Word, C., Zanna, M., & Cooper, J. (1974). The non-verbal mediation of self-fulfilling prophecies in interracial interaction. *Journal of Experimental Social Psychology, 10,* 109–120.

Wright, J. C., & Mischel, W. (1988). Conditional hedges and the intuitive psychology of traits. *Journal of Personality and Social Psychology, 55,* 454–469.

Zayas, V., & Shoda, Y. (2007). Predicting preferences for dating partners from past experiences of psychological abuse: Identifying the psychological ingredients of situations. *Personality and Social Psychology Bulletin, 33,* 123–138.

Zayas, V., & Shoda, Y. (2009). Three decades after the personality paradox: Understanding situations. *Journal of Research in Personality, 43,* 280–281.

Zayas, V., Shoda, Y., & Ayduk, O. N. (2002). Personality in context: An interpersonal systems perspective. *Journal of Personality, 70,* 851–900.

experimental settings and daily social life, and can have varying effects on cognitions and behaviors (e.g., Baldwin et al., 1996; Collins & Read, 1994; Shaver, Collins, & Clark, 1996). Indeed, we have shown that positive effects of contextual priming of security-enhancing representations are found even among chronically insecure people (e.g., Mikulincer, Gillath, et al., 2001; Mikulincer & Shaver, 2001). Thus, adult attachment theory does not assert that a person's current attachment orientation must mirror or match his or her attachment orientations with parents during childhood. Rather, the current orientation is a complex amalgam of historical and contemporary contextual factors, which enable the "reworking" of mental representations of self and attachment figures in relation to changing social experiences and new relationships (Davila & Cobb, 2004; Simpson, Rholes, Campbell, & Wilson, 2003).

Attachment-system functioning can be affected by a partner's behavior. For example, the partner can be a source of threat and therefore trigger attachment-system activation (e.g., by threatening abandonment or violence). Moreover, a person's relational cognitions and behaviors depend not only on the functioning of his or her attachment system but also on the partner's behavior. Indeed, several studies have shown that both partners' attachment orientations contribute uniquely to the prediction of both partners' relationship satisfaction (e.g., Brennan & Shaver, 1995; Collins & Read, 1990). In addition, other studies, using observational techniques, diary keeping, and narrative accounts, have revealed that a person's attachment orientation has differential effects on relational emotions, cognitions, and behaviors depending on the partner's attachment style (e.g., Collins & Feeney, 2000; Simpson, Rholes, & Nelligan, 1992).

In other words, attachment theory is a prime example of "person by situation" approaches to human behavior. The person in this case includes an innate attachment behavioral system, attachment-related working models of self and others, procedural knowledge implicit in attachment strategies, and associative neural networks connecting these strategies with the appraisal of social situations, including interaction partners' behaviors. The situation consists of a relationship partner's responses, social and cultural rules for certain kinds of interactions, and other relevant contextual cues that affect the appraisal of social transactions and alter the functioning of the attachment system. The complexities of this process stem from the fact that major parts of the "person" component were originally based on variations in the availability and responsiveness of primary caregivers in threatening situations (an important category of social "situations"), and major parts of the "situation" component are shaped by the person's attachment style, which can affect both the perception of the situation and a partner's own social behavior.

Conceptualizing Behavioral Systems

For the purpose of illustration, we will focus here on five behavioral systems: attachment, exploration, caregiving, sex, and power. We will describe their normative parameters (goals, triggers, primary strategies) and the major individual differences in their functioning, conceptualized in terms of hyperactivation and deactivation.

The Attachment Behavioral System

According to Bowlby (1973, 1980, 1982), one of the earliest behavioral systems to appear in human development is the attachment system, whose inferred biological function is to protect a person (especially during infancy and early childhood) from danger by assuring that the person maintains proximity to caring and supportive others—the person's attachment figures. Bowlby thought the need to seek and maintain proximity to attachment figures evolved biologically because of children's prolonged dependence on "stronger and wiser" others, usually parents, who can defend children from predators and other dangers while supporting their gradual development of knowledge and skills. Although the attachment system is most important and most visible during the early years of life, Bowlby (1988) claimed it is active across the life span and is frequently manifested in the seeking of support and love from relationship partners.

The main goal of the attachment system is to sustain a sense of safety or security (called "felt security" by Sroufe & Waters, 1977), based on beliefs that the world is generally safe, that one is competent and lovable, and that key people will be available and supportive in times of need. This system is activated by events that threaten the sense of security, such as encounters with actual or symbolic threats and noticing that an attachment figure is not sufficiently near, interested, or responsive. In such cases, a person is automatically motivated to seek and reestablish actual or symbolic proximity to an attachment figure (the system's primary strategy). These bids for proximity persist until protection and security are attained. The attachment system is then deactivated, and the person can calmly and coherently return to other activities.

We can observe the activation of the attachment system when an infant drops whatever it is doing (e.g., playing with interesting toys) and seeks comfort and support from a caregiver when a noise is heard or a stranger enters the room (Ainsworth et al., 1978). The same kind of activation occurs in the minds of adults when they encounter conscious or unconscious threats. For example, we (Mikulincer, Gillath, & Shaver, 2002) conducted experiments in which we subliminally presented threatening words (e.g., failure, separation) to adults and then assessed indirectly (by measuring reaction times in a word-identification task or a Stroop color-naming task) whether names of attachment figures became mentally available for processing following the threat. It turned out that the names of a person's attachment figures did become more available following unconscious exposure to threatening words, but the same words had no effect on the mental availability of names of people, even familiar ones, who were not viewed as attachment figures. That is, mental representations of attachment figures tended to be automatically activated when comfort, protection, or support was perceived to be needed.

In adults, the primary attachment strategy does not necessarily require overt proximity-seeking, although such behavior is often evident. It can also involve the internal activation of comforting mental representations of attachment figures (Mikulincer & Shaver, 2004, 2007b). These cognitive representations can create a sense of safety and security and help a person deal successfully with threats without requiring physical proximity to an actual person. Interestingly, internal activation of these representations seems not only to reduce distress but also causes a person to feel and be more like one of his or her supportive attachment figures—through a process of conscious or unconscious identification (Mikulincer & Shaver, 2004).

Across several experimental studies, we have consistently found that priming thoughts of a supportive attachment figure (which we call "security priming"; Mikulincer & Shaver, 2007b) has positive effects on a person's mood, mental health, compassionate and prosocial feelings and behaviors, and tolerance toward outgroup members (e.g., Mikulincer, Hirschberger, et al., 2001; Mikulincer & Shaver, 2001; Mikulincer, Shaver, Gillath, & Nitzberg, 2005; Mikulincer, Shaver, & Horesh, 2006). Similar positive effects of security priming on self-concepts, appraisals of romantic partners,

and openness to new information have been documented (e.g., Baccus, Baldwin, & Packer, 2004; Green & Campbell, 2000; Rowe & Carnelley, 2006).

Another developmental change in attachment-system functioning concerns the selection of primary attachment figures (those toward whom proximity seeking is directed). During infancy, one or both parents, grandparents, older siblings, or daycare workers are likely to serve as attachment figures. Ainsworth (1973) reported that infants she observed tended to seek proximity to their primary caregiver when tired or ill, and Heinicke and Westheimer (1966) found that infants were more easily soothed by their primary caregivers than by other consoling adults. During adolescence and adulthood, other relationship partners often become targets of proximity seeking and bids for emotional support, including close friends and romantic partners (e.g., Fraley & Davis, 1997; Hazan & Zeifman, 1999). Teachers and supervisors in academic settings or therapists in clinical settings can also serve as real or potential sources of comfort and support. Moreover, groups, institutions, and symbolic personages (e.g., God) can be used mentally as attachment figures (Granqvist & Kirkpatrick, 2008; Granqvist, Mikulincer, & Shaver, 2010). In our studies, we have found, for example, that the actual presence of a supportive relationship partner in different kinds of relationships (romantic, leader-follower, intragroup, and therapeutic) has long-term influences on a person's attachment security and more general psychological well-being and mental health (e.g., Davidovitz, Mikulincer, Shaver, Ijzen, & Popper, 2007; Gur, 2006; Lavi, 2007; Rom & Mikulincer, 2003).

Besides these normative processes related to attachment security and insecurity, there are major individual differences in tendencies to hyperactivate or deactivate the attachment system. Partly because of their clinical significance, these individual differences have received more research attention than the normative functioning of the system (see Mikulincer & Shaver, 2007a, for a review). The two major dimensions of attachment insecurity—anxious attachment (or hyperactivation) and avoidant attachment (or deactivation)—can be reliably measured with self-report questionnaires or structured interviews (Crowell, Fraley, & Shaver, 2008). Across hundreds of studies, anxious attachment in adolescents and adults has been associated with increased emotionality, vigilance regarding partner availability and commitment, jealousy, hurt feelings, self-doubts, intrusiveness, and even coercive violence. Avoidant attachment has been associated with suppression of feelings, denial of vulnerability and hurt feelings, lack of self-disclosure, sexual infidelity, and lack of compassion. Thus, the same concepts that are used to understand the attachment behavioral system as an innate motivational system can also be used to characterize important individual differences in attachment behavior (see also Simpson & Winterheld, chapter 20, this volume).

The Exploration Behavioral System

In their discussions of the attachment behavioral system as it expresses itself in infancy, Bowlby (1982) and Ainsworth (1967) recognized that infants possess an innate propensity to explore and play, and they viewed normal exploratory behavior as dependent on a secure relationship with an attachment figure. In emphasizing the motivation to explore, Bowlby and Ainsworth were attuned to other prominent theorists of their time (e.g., Berlyne, 1960; Harlow, 1955; Piaget, 1953; White, 1959), who viewed infants and children as intrinsically motivated to explore and learn about the world, even at the cost of temporarily distancing themselves from attachment figures. Bowlby (1982) attributed this motivation, which Harlow (1955) called an "exploratory drive," to an innate exploration behavioral system. His conception resembled that of White (1959), who used the term "effectance motivation," seeing evidence of this form of motivation in curiosity, exploratory play, mastery of skills, and investment in school and work activities. He thought that acting on this motivation produced feelings of efficacy, which in 1965 he called "joy in being a cause" (p. 203).

The primary strategy of the exploration system, seeking new information about oneself and the world, is activated whenever a person encounters novel situations, objects, or people or experiences novel internal states that contradict or challenge existing knowledge and working models. In Piaget's (1953) terms, the new information cannot be easily assimilated to existing schemas, so one must work to accommodate (change, develop) the schemas. The exploration system can also be activated by environmental affordances (Gibson, 1977) which provide opportunities to learn new skills and gain expertise in a specific field (e.g., in a college major). The exploratory system is deactivated when the desired knowledge or skill set is acquired, resulting in a temporary sense of competence and mastery.

Successful cycles of activation and deactivation of the exploration system cause a person to perceive him- or herself as efficacious and worthy of admiration or respect, another source of self-esteem (or self-efficacy; Bandura, 1986). People with a history of positive exploratory experiences can approach novel, ambiguous, or complex situations, internal states, or new information with confidence that they can effectively manage the new material and tasks. They can open themselves to new experiences and information, be more tolerant of ambiguity and temporarily violated expectations, and actively seek out situations that challenge their current knowledge or skills and allow the broadening and building of new competencies.

However, when the primary exploration strategy fails to accomplish the system's goal, due to personal shortcomings or environments that inhibit or frustrate exploratory attempts, a person is forced to adopt secondary strategies, just as happens in the attachment domain. As with all behavioral systems, we contend, the major secondary strategies are hyperactivation and deactivation. Hyperactivation of the system is characterized by engagement in exploratory activities even in situations where no exploration is needed and, instead, rapid decisions and actions are required, and by difficulties in deactivating the system once new information is acquired and digested. As a result, a hyperactivated person may endlessly acquire new information without feeling comfortable engaging the environment and may remain in a state of ambivalence and indecision that prevents him or her from making a decision or taking a confident course of action. Moreover, because of past negative experiences with exploration, hyperactivation arouses doubts and worries about one's ability to explore and master new tasks and environments, thereby reducing self-esteem and strengthening fear of failure.

In contrast, deactivation of the exploration system is characterized by inhibition and avoidance of exploratory activities and defensive evasion of situations or internal states that might activate the system. Such deactivation is manifested in cognitive closure, intolerance of ambiguity and novelty, and preference for known stimuli and environments over complex or novel ones. When people who habitually rely on deactivating strategies are encouraged by circumstances to engage in exploration, they may nevertheless experience boredom and lack of interest, and they may often dampen exploratory efforts before a sense of mastery and competence is achieved.

The Caregiving Behavioral System

According to Bowlby (1982), humans are born with a capacity to develop empathy and compassion for others and care for them when they are in need. He attributed this set of activities, focusing initially on parents' responses to children's expressions of need, to a caregiving behavioral system. This system presumably emerged over the course of evolution because it increased humans' inclusive fitness (Hamilton, 1964) by increasing the survival and reproduction chances of people who responded to the needs of others with whom they shared genes (children, siblings, close family members, and members of extended families and genetically related larger groups, such as small tribes). Today, through educational elaboration of caregiving tendencies (e.g., socializing children to view all human beings as members of a single family), the caregiving system may be activated by genuine concern for anyone in need. Although most people probably care more, and more easily, for others with whom they are closely related, either psychologically or genetically, most people's caregiving motives and behaviors can be applied more widely to all suffering human beings and even to members of other species (see Castano, chapter 17, this volume). Of course, many other motives, prejudices, and attitudes also affect caregiving in particular circumstances, as is true for any other prosocially oriented motive or value.

The goal of the caregiving system is assumed to be the reduction of other people's suffering, protecting them from harm, and fostering their healthy growth and development (e.g., Collins, Guichard, Ford, & Feeney, 2006; George & Solomon, 2008; Kunce & Shaver, 1994; Shaver, Mikulincer, & Shemesh-Iron, 2009). The triggers that activate the caregiving system include (1) realizing that another person is confronting danger, stress, or discomfort and is either openly seeking help or would clearly benefit from it; and (2) realizing that another person has an opportunity to master new skills or achieve important goals and either needs help in taking advantage of the opportunity or seems eager to talk about it or to be validated for making an effort (Collins et al., 2006). Once one's caregiving system is activated, a person calls on a repertoire of behaviors that might promote the other's welfare (the system's primary strategy). This repertoire includes showing interest in the other's problems or goals, affirming the other's competence or potential, expressing love and affection, providing advice and instrumental aid as needed, not interfering with the person's own problem-solving or exploratory efforts, and admiring and applauding his or her successes (Collins et al., 2006; Feeney & Collins, 2004).

A key element of the caregiving system's primary strategy is what Batson (2009) called empathic concern, which involves taking the other's perspective in order to help him or her reduce suffering or pursue growth. According to Collins et al. (2006), empathic concern includes sensitivity and responsiveness, the two aspects of parenting that have been emphasized as contributing to a child's secure attachment. Sensitivity includes attunement to, and accurate interpretation of, another's signaled or communicated needs, and responding appropriately and helpfully to the person's support-seeking behavior (George & Solomon, 2008). Responsiveness includes validating a troubled person's needs and feelings; respecting his or her beliefs and values; and helping the person feel understood and cared for (Reis & Shaver, 1988).

When the caregiving system functions well, it benefits the person being cared for by solving a problem, increasing the person's sense of safety and security, or bolstering his or her growth and development (Collins et al., 2006). Appropriate care also benefits the support provider, even though its primary goal is to benefit the other. It promotes an inner sense of what Erikson (1993) called "generativity"—a sense that one is more than an isolated self and is able to contribute importantly to others' welfare. Generativity includes positive feelings about one's own efficacy and goodness, confidence in one's social skills, and heightened feelings of love for and connection with other people (Mikulincer, Shaver, & Gillath, 2009). In addition, these benefits tend to enhance the quality of two people's or a person's and a group's relationship (e.g., Collins & Feeney, 2000).

Although we assume that everyone is born with the potential to provide care, the quality of care provided by a particular individual in a particular situation can be impaired by worries that dampen or conflict with sensitivity and responsiveness. It can also be impaired by problems in emotion regulation, which can cause a caregiver to allow feelings of uncertainty, emotional contagion from a suffering other, or self-doubts about efficacy to feel overwhelmed. Batson (2009) and other researchers (e.g., Eisenberg, 2009) call this reaction personal distress. Collins et al. (2006) summarized research findings on this general topic, finding that caregiving can be disrupted or impaired by social skill deficits, depletion of psychological resources, lack of a desire to help, and egoistic motives that interfere with accurate empathy and genuine other-oriented concern.

Table 19.1 Examples of Hyperactivation and Deactivation Scale Items for Each Behavioral System

System	Hyperactivation	Deactivation
Caregiving	• When helping people, I often worry that I won't be as good at it as other people are • When I'm unable to help a person who is in distress, I feel worthless • I sometimes try to help others more than they actually want me to	• When I see people in distress, I don't feel comfortable jumping in to help • I sometimes feel that helping others is a waste of time • I often don't pay much attention to other people's discomfort or distress
Sex	• I worry about not being "good enough" in bed • I need a lot of reassurance regarding my sexual performance • Being sexually desirable is extremely important to me	• During sexual activity, I sometimes feel uninvolved and uninterested • I often find it hard to experience pleasure during sexual activity • I feel comfortable responding to my partner's sexual needs (R)
Exploration	• I get frustrated if I can't master new material perfectly • Often, my intense desire to learn or master something new gets in the way of mastering it • Often, thinking I'm not as good as other people interferes with my ability to learn something new	• Being exposed to new material often bores me or leaves me indifferent • I tend to lose interest in a conversation if the topic under discussion is something I know little about • When I have leisure time, I prefer to do familiar things rather than learning about or exploring something new
Power	• I feel anxious in situations where I have little control over other people and their actions • In an argument or disagreement, my strong desire to fight back makes it difficult for me to consider other possible responses • It's hard for me to stop arguing, even when the other person has conceded	• I tend to relinquish important goals if their attainment requires confronting other people • I tend to avoid attacking, even if it's a matter of self-defense • I'd rather let others win an argument, even when I know I'm right

Note: R designates a reverse-scored item.

Shaver et al., 2011). Factor analyses conducted in the United States and Israel, and in English and Hebrew, yielded the intended two factors for each set of items, and the low correlations between the hyperactivation and deactivation scores for each scale indicate that the two strategies are roughly independent, as in the ECR measure of attachment style. These scales have good test-retest reliability, and their validity is indicated by high correlations between self-reports and relationship partner reports. This correspondence implies that the self-reports concern, at least in part, social behaviors that can be observed by relationship partners. We have also examined the convergent validity of each of the new scales by correlating them with preexisting self-report measures tapping various aspects of exploration,

caregiving, sex, and power. In general, the findings indicate that hyperactivation scores are associated with preexisting measures tapping intense but anxious activation of the targeted behavioral tendency, and deactivation scores are associated with inhibition of the tendency. For example, Shaver et al. (2011) found that hyperactivation scores of the Power Behavioral System Scale were associated with reports of physical aggression, verbal aggression, outbursts of anger, hostility, risk for violent behavior, abusive behavior in intimate relationships, angry rumination, and problems in controlling anger. In addition, power hyperactivation was associated with reports of conflict-escalating behavior during conflicts, greater vengeance and less forgiveness following others' transgressions, and higher levels of aggression and violence in response to driving-related and other provocations.

In contrast, power deactivation was associated with measures of submissiveness, self-abasement, lack of assertiveness, avoidance and giving up during interpersonal conflicts, a tendency to withdraw in response to interpersonal transgressions, and higher levels of internalized anger, avoidance, and surrender in response to provocations (Shaver et al., 2011). Interestingly, both hyperactivation and deactivation are associated with lower scores on scales measuring feelings of dominance and power expression, implying that these secondary orientations are, as intended, alternative ways of coping with lack of power, just as attachment anxiety and avoidance are two ways of coping with, or reacting to, frequent failure to attain a sense of felt security (Shaver et al., 2011).

Psychological Correlates of Individual Differences in Behavioral-System Functioning

Bowlby (1982) believed that individual differences in the functioning of behavioral systems have important implications for mental health, psychological functioning, and social adjustment. First, because the cycle of behavioral-system activation and deactivation can elicit strong emotions (e.g., fear in the face of danger during attachment-system activation; curiosity and excitement in the presence of a novel object or an attractive sexual partner; relief after attaining a sense of attachment security or reaching orgasm), individual differences in the functioning of these systems can affect moods and the experience and regulation of emotions. Second, because experiences of behavioral-system activation are likely to be encoded and stored in memory schemas or working models, individual differences in behavioral-system functioning should be manifested in the ways people think about themselves and others. Third, because the optimal functioning of a behavioral system has adaptive advantages, suboptimal functioning can erode a person's mental health and life satisfaction. In this section, we briefly review research on the ways in which these individual differences, measured with self-report scales, are correlated with emotion regulation, mental representations of self and others, and mental health. We place more emphasis on attachment anxiety and avoidance, as measured by the ECR and other self-report scales, because they have been more thoroughly studied than the hyperactivation and deactivation of the other behavioral systems.

Attachment and Emotion Regulation

According to attachment theorists (Cassidy & Kobak, 1988; Mikulincer & Shaver, 2003), secondary attachment strategies can bias emotion regulation and alter, obstruct, or suppress the experience and expression of emotions. The deactivating strategies used by avoidant individuals are intended to defuse or suppress negative emotions, because these emotions can activate unwanted attachment-related needs and are viewed as signs of weakness or vulnerability incompatible with the desire for self-reliance. Unlike avoidant people, anxiously attached people tend to perceive negative emotions as congruent with their goal of attachment-system hyperactivation (Mikulincer & Shaver, 2003). As a result, people who score high on attachment anxiety tend to generate and intensify negative emotional states that activate the attachment system (e.g., fear, anxiety, distress) and emphasize a person's weaknesses, incompetence, and neediness (e.g., sadness, shame, guilt). This strategy can create a self-perpetuating or -amplifying cycle of distress, maintained by ruminative thoughts even after a threat subsides.

These tendencies have been extensively documented in empirical studies of attachment insecurities and ways of coping with stressful events (see Mikulincer & Florian, 1998; Shaver & Mikulincer, 2002, for reviews). In these studies, higher avoidance scores are associated with higher scores on measures of coping by distancing, and higher scores on attachment anxiety are associated with higher scores on measures of emotion-focused coping.

Attachment strategies are also manifested in the ways people cope with threats (see Mikulincer & Shaver, 2007a, for a review). For example, Fraley and Shaver (1997) examined the role of secondary attachment strategies in the suppression of separation-related thoughts. Participants wrote continuously about whatever thoughts and feelings they were experiencing while being asked to suppress thoughts about their romantic partner leaving them for someone else. Attachment anxiety was associated with poorer ability to suppress separation-related thoughts, as indicated by more frequent thoughts of breaking up after the suppression task and higher skin conductance during the task. In contrast, more avoidant individuals were better able than less avoidant ones, not only to stop thinking about separation, but also to reduce the intensity of their autonomic responses to these painful thoughts. Fraley, Garner, and Shaver (2000) found that these avoidant defenses act in a *preemptive* manner by holding attachment-related material out of awareness right from the moment of first encountering it.

In a series of studies examining the experience of death anxiety (e.g., Mikulincer & Florian, 2000; Mikulincer, Florian, & Tolmacz, 1990), anxious individuals were found to intensify death concerns and keep death-related thoughts active in memory. In contrast, avoidant individuals tended to suppress death concerns and dissociate their conscious claims from their unconscious (but still measurable) anxiety. Although avoidance was related to low levels of self-reported fear of death, it was also related to heightened death anxiety measured by the Thematic Apperception Test.

Attachment-related biases in emotion regulation were also notable in Mikulincer and Orbach's (1995) study of emotional memories. Anxious individuals quickly accessed negative emotional memories and then had difficulty controlling the spread of activation from one negative emotional memory to another. In contrast, avoidant individuals had poor access to negative emotional memories, and those that were recalled were rather shallow.

Attachment and Mental Representations of Self and Others

According to attachment theory, attachment insecurities, mainly along the anxiety dimension, seem to converge into negative representations of the self (Mikulincer & Shaver, 2007a). Indeed, as compared with secure people, anxiously attached people report lower self-esteem (e.g., Bartholomew & Horowitz, 1991), view themselves as less competent and efficacious than their peers (e.g., Cooper, Shaver, & Collins, 1998), and possess less optimistic expectations about their ability to cope with stressful events (e.g., Cozarelli, Sumer, & Major; 1998). For example, Cozarelli et al. (1998) found that more anxiously attached women undergoing an abortion reported lower levels of self-efficacy for coping with the abortion beforehand and lower self-esteem several months afterward.

Secondary attachment strategies also tend to defensively bias insecure people's working models of self (e.g., Bowlby, 1988; Main, 1990). Whereas hyperactivating strategies negatively bias anxious people's sense of self-esteem, thereby increasing a self-relevant source of distress, deactivating strategies favor defensive processes of self-enhancement and self-inflation, thereby increasing a sense of self-reliance. Mikulincer (1998a) exposed people to various kinds of threatening and neutral situations, and assessed self-appraisals following the manipulations.

Participants with an avoidant attachment style made more explicit and implicit positive self-appraisals following threatening, as compared with neutral, situations. In contrast, anxiously attached participants reacted to threat with self-devaluation, making more explicit and implicit negative self-appraisals following threatening than neutral conditions.

Attachment insecurities also influence or are related to the mental representation of others. Numerous studies have shown that people who score high on anxiety or avoidance hold less positive views of human nature, use less positive terms when describing relationship partners, perceive relationship partners as less supportive, have more negative expectations concerning their partners' behavior and tend to explain their partner's hurtful behavior in more negative ways (see Mikulincer & Shaver, 2007a, for a review).

Secondary attachment strategies are also likely to bias person perception. For example, avoidant individuals, who want to maintain distance from others and view themselves as strong and perfect, are likely to emphasize distinctiveness, uniqueness, and devaluation of others. In contrast, anxiously attached people, who want to be loved and accepted, are likely to increase their sense of connectedness and belongingness and favor a false sense of consensus. Indeed, Mikulincer, Orbach, and Iavnieli (1998) found that whereas anxious individuals were more likely than their secure counterparts to perceive others as similar to themselves and to exhibit a false consensus bias in trait and opinion descriptions, avoidant individuals were more likely than secure ones to perceive others as dissimilar to them and to exhibit a false distinctiveness bias.

Attachment and Mental Health

Bowlby (1988) viewed secondary attachment strategies as risk factors that reduce resilience in times of stress and contribute to emotional problems and poor adjustment. Indeed, many studies have shown that self-reports of attachment anxiety are associated with global distress, depression, anxiety, eating disorders, substance abuse, conduct disorders, and severe personality disorders (see Mikulincer & Florian, 1998; Mikulincer & Shaver, 2007a, for reviews). For avoidance, the findings are more complex. On the one hand, a host of studies yielded no significant associations between avoidant attachment and self-report measures of global distress (see Mikulincer & Shaver, 2007a, for a review). On the other hand, several studies indicate that avoidant attachment is associated with particular patterns of emotional and behavioral problems, such as a pattern of depression characterized by perfectionism, self-punishment, and self-criticism (e.g., Zuroff & Fitzpatrick, 1995), somatic complaints (e.g., Mikulincer, Florian, & Weller, 1993), a hostile view of other people (e.g., Mikulincer, 1998b), substance abuse and conduct disorders (e.g., Cooper et al., 1998), and schizoid and avoidant personality disorders (e.g., Brennan & Shaver, 1998).

In addition, studies that focus on highly demanding and distressing events reveal that avoidant attachment is related to higher levels of reported distress. For example, Berant, Mikulincer, and Florian (2001) and Berant, Mikulincer, and Shaver (2008) assessed mothers' reactions to the birth of an infant with a congenital heart defect and found that avoidance, as assessed at the time of the initial diagnosis of the infant's disorder, was the most potent predictor of maternal distress one and seven years later.

It seems that avoidant attachment may help a person remain balanced and stable under fairly normal circumstances, when the level of stress is low. But under more demanding conditions, these people's avoidant coping strategies may collapse, causing avoidant individuals to exhibit high levels of distress and emotional problems (see Costanzo, Hoyle, & Leary, chapter 23, this volume). Indeed, Mikulincer, Dolev, and Shaver (2004) showed that the addition of a demanding cognitive task, which had previously been shown to interfere with mental suppression (e.g., Wegner, Eber, & Zanakos, 1993), impaired avoidant individuals' ability to block the activation of attachment-related worries and negative self-views. Under a low cognitive load, avoidant individuals were able to suppress thoughts related to a painful romantic relationship breakup. But when a cognitive load was imposed (a secondary but demanding cognitive task), avoidant individuals experienced a strong rebound of previously suppressed thoughts about the painful separation and heightened activation of negative self-representations.

Exploring the Psychological Correlates of Other Behavioral Systems

In our research program (Doron, 2009; Mikulincer, Birnbaum, & Shaver, 2009; Shaver et al., 2009; Shaver et al., 2011), we have begun to explore the psychological correlates of individual differences in the functioning of the caregiving, sex, exploration, and power systems. These preliminary findings indicate that hyperactivation or deactivation of each of these systems, like attachment anxiety and avoidance,

are associated with problems in the regulation of emotions, impulses, and goal-directed actions and put a person at risk for emotional problems and maladjustment.

Using the self-report scales described above (each one in a different sample), we found that hyperactivated forms of caregiving, sex, exploration, and power, like attachment anxiety, were associated with deficits in emotion-regulation, self-regulation, and social skills. The deficits were reflected in lower scores on scales measuring self-control, negative mood regulation, and social skills and higher scores on scales measuring rumination, threat appraisal, emotional intensity, and interpersonal problems. Deactivated forms of caregiving, sex, exploration, and power were associated with lower scores on negative mood regulation and social skills and with more interpersonal problems.

Our findings also reveal that hyperactivation and deactivation interfere with behavioral system functioning and are therefore inversely correlated with measures of positive psychological states. For example, both hyperactivation and deactivation of caregiving, sex, exploration, and power are associated with lower self-esteem, mastery, coherence, optimism, and psychological well-being. Moreover, these secondary strategies, like attachment insecurities, are associated with greater psychological distress and negative affectivity and with heightened levels of anxiety, depression, and other emotional problems.

In additional studies, we gathered preliminary data showing that hyperactivation and deactivation of each behavioral system impairs actual caregiving, sexual, exploratory, or power-related behavior. Here, due to space limitations, we provide examples concerning only the caregiving and power systems.

With respect to the caregiving system, Shaver et al. (2009) videotaped mothers and their preschool children while the children attempted to solve increasingly difficult puzzles. Two independent judges, blind with respect to the mothers' CSS scores, rated the hyperactivating mothers as more distressed and less helpful when interacting with their children, and rated mothers scoring higher on deactivated caregiving as less warm and less helpful during the puzzle-solving task. In another study, Shaver et al. (2009) randomly designated one partner in a dating couple as the "caregiver," and the other partner was asked to disclose a personal problem that would be discussed with the "caregiver" while the couple was videotaped. Two independent judges who were blind to the CSS scores of the and criminality, and intergroup aggression (see Mikulincer & Shaver, 2007a, for a review).

Using the Power Behavioral System scale, Shaver et al. (2011) found that attachment anxiety was moderately associated with both hyperactivation and deactivation of the power system. That is, people who worry about being loved, accepted, and esteemed by others (anxious attachment) can score high on both secondary power strategies. Thus, the external façade of submissiveness and passivity that characterizes power system deactivation may mask attachment-related anxieties that can make sudden hyperactivation of the power system more likely under certain conditions (Bartholomew & Allison, 2006).

With regard to avoidant attachment, Shaver et al. (2011) found a moderate association with hyperactivation of the power system. This hyperactivation was also noted by Mikulincer (1998b), who found that avoidantly attached adults were aroused physiologically and attributed hostile intent to a hurtful other even when the other's negative behavior was unintentional. Rholes, Simpson, and Orina (1999) videotaped dating couples while the female partner was waiting for an upcoming painful task and found that avoidant attachment in the male partner was associated with hostility toward his partner (coded from video-recordings). Thus, although avoidant individuals are rarely comfortable describing themselves as needy or angry, they nevertheless can react with hostility and hatred.

In a recent series of studies, we found that attachment insecurities bias not only the functioning of the power system but also the psychological benefits of its optimal functioning. For example, Mikulincer and Shaver (2011) found that attachment anxiety weakens the link between the sense of power and an approach or promotion motivational orientation. Specifically, they found that participants who were asked to recall a particular incident in which they had power over one or more other people (power priming) were more optimistic and more likely to prefer a riskier plan than participants in a neutral priming condition mainly when they scored relatively low on attachment anxiety. These effects of power priming were not significant when attachment anxiety was relatively high. Mikulincer and Shaver (2011) also found that experimentally priming the sense of power led to more objectification of another person (e.g., perception of the other as an object to be used instrumentally for personal need satisfaction) and less empathy mainly when participants scored relatively high on avoidant attachment.

All of the reviewed findings illustrate the various ways in which individual differences in attachment system functioning can affect other behavioral systems. Bowlby (1982) began his theorizing by portraying attachment security as a "secure base for exploration," which suggested that the attachment system is primary, comes first in development, and forms either a solid or shaky foundation for the functioning of other behavioral systems. However, changes in the functioning of the other systems (e.g., failure to learn new skills and then doubting one's competence and value; volunteering to help others and becoming more self-confident as a result) can feed back on attachment security. At present we know little about the extent to which other behavioral systems affect the attachment system, but Gillath, Mikulincer, Birnbaum, and Shaver (2008) provided initial evidence for effects of sexual arousal on attachment security and caregiving inclinations. In four studies, heterosexual adults were subliminally primed with either neutral pictures or photographs of naked members of the opposite sex and were asked to describe their willingness or unwillingness to self-disclose, become psychologically intimate, deal constructively with interpersonal conflicts, and sacrifice for a partner. The results indicated that activating the sexual system moved people, on average, in the direction of greater self-disclosure and intimacy—tendencies usually associated with attachment security. Moreover, subliminal sexual priming, as compared with neutral priming, produced a stronger tendency to sacrifice for a partner and more constructive handling of conflicts, presumably reflecting a more caring attitude toward close relationship partners.

Perhaps priming people with a sense of caring for others might increase momentary attachment security—for example, by strengthening a person's sense of connectedness. We have preliminary evidence for such effects in cases where anxious people become more secure as a result of volunteering to help others (Gillath, Shaver, et al., 2005). Future research should explore more systematically the ways in which other behavioral systems shape the functioning of the attachment system. It should also examine reciprocal relations between caregiving, power, exploration, and sex. We also need more research on the mediators of these effects. The preliminary findings we reviewed here suggest that, at least in adults, different behavioral systems are intertwined, such that activation of one has effects on the others, and individual differences in one tend to be correlated with individual differences in the others. But there is still a great deal that we do not understand about the mechanisms.

How Are Behavioral Systems Associated with Personality?

When considering interrelations among the attachment, exploration, caregiving, sexual, and power systems, it is natural to wonder whether all of them are affected or explained by innate temperaments or personality traits. It is certainly logically possible that hyperactivated and deactivated forms of social behavior are mere reflections of individual differences in biological predispositions or broadband traits. In fact, several studies, extensively reviewed by Mikulincer and Shaver (2007a), have indicated that attachment anxiety is associated with the Big Five neuroticism trait (sometimes called emotional instability) and with measures of the behavioral inhibition system (BIS; Carver & White, 1994), and avoidant attachment is associated with lower scores on the Big Five extraversion and agreeableness traits and with measures of the behavioral activation system (BAS), relations between the attachment variables and relevant correlates remain significant when other personality variables are controlled.

Moreover, using the new behavioral system scales, Shaver et al. (2009), Shaver et al. (in press), Shaver and Mikulincer (2006), and Doron (2009) found similar associations in the caregiving, sex, exploration, and power domains. In addition, deactivated exploration was associated with lower scores on Big Five openness to experience, hyperactivated power was associated with lower scores on agreeableness, and hyperactivated sexuality was associated with lack of conscientiousness.

Moreover, using the evidence so far suggests that these correlations are lower than .50, implying that broad personality traits explain no more than 25% of the variance in behavioral system scores. Moreover, Mikulincer and Shaver (2007a) reviewed many studies showing that attachment measures frequently outperform broadband personality measures in predicting emotions, social cognitions, and social behavior, using both concurrent and longitudinal research designs. In addition, several researchers have controlled for neuroticism, general anxiety, self-esteem, or measures of BIS and BAS and still obtained theoretically predicted effects of attachment anxiety and avoidance (see Mikulincer & Shaver, 2007a, for a review). Attachment effects are never fully, and usually not even partially, explained by alternative personality constructs. Similar findings have been reported by Shaver et al. (2009), Shaver et al. (in press), Mikulincer et al. (2009), and Doron (2009) in studies of the psychological correlates of individual differences in the functioning of the caregiving, sex, exploration, and power systems. Moreover, using functional magnetic resonance imaging, Gillath, Bunge, et al. (2005) found different patterns of regional brain activation associated with neuroticism and attachment anxiety.

Beyond these indications of discriminant validity, there is nothing in the reigning conceptualization of the Big Five personality traits that would have generated the huge and coherent body of research findings generated over the past 25 years by Bowlby's attachment theory (see Cassidy & Shaver, 2008, for reviews). Attachment theory is more concerned than most broadband trait theories with psychodynamic processes, and it is more firmly rooted in evolutionary biology and developmental psychology. The Big Five trait model is, by comparison, mainly descriptive, not at all psychodynamic, and not very well rooted in evolutionary biology. Thus, in our opinion, attachment theory and its associated measures and research findings are scientifically fruitful and important whether or not individual differences in behavioral system functioning turn out to overlap to some extent, and for reasons not yet fully understood, with global personality traits.

What are the Origins of Individual Differences in Behavioral System Functioning?

This is an important question that needs to be answered if we are to pursue a more complete behavioral systems approach to personality. To date, unfortunately, we have no direct evidence concerning the sources of individual differences in the exploration, caregiving, sexual, and power systems, because we have only recently created assessment tools and begun to examine their construct validity. However, extensive research has been conducted on the sources of individual differences in attachment system functioning. We will review this research briefly here, in hopes that it will serve as a guide for future research on the other behavioral systems.

According to Bowlby (1973, 1982), individual differences in the functioning of a behavioral system are shaped by the history of positive and negative outcomes of system activation in various situations and environments across the life span, beginning very early in childhood. With regard to the attachment system, Ainsworth et al. (1978) proposed that attachment patterns are shaped by interactions with one's attachment figures during infancy. In the earliest studies of

Monographs of the Society for Research in Child Development, 50, 66–104.

Main, M., & Solomon, J. (1990). Procedures for identifying infants as disorganized/disoriented during the Ainsworth strange situation. In M. T. Greenberg, D. Cicchetti, & M. Cummings (Eds.), *Attachment in the preschool years: Theory, research, and intervention* (pp. 121–160). Chicago: University of Chicago Press.

Maslow, A. H. (1954). *Motivation and personality.* New York: Harper.

McCrae, R. R., & Costa, P. T. (1990). *Personality in adulthood.* New York: Guilford.

Mikulincer, M. (1997). Adult attachment style and information processing: Individual differences in curiosity and cognitive closure. *Journal of Personality and Social Psychology, 72,* 1217–1230.

Mikulincer, M. (1998a). Adult attachment style and affect regulation: Strategic variations in self-appraisals. *Journal of Personality and Social Psychology, 75,* 420–435.

Mikulincer, M. (1998b). Adult attachment style and individual differences in functional versus dysfunctional experiences of anger. *Journal of Personality and Social Psychology, 74,* 513–524.

Mikulincer, M, Birnbaum, G., & Shaver, P. R. (2009). *The Sexual Behavioral System Scale—Development and validity.* Unpublished manuscript.

Mikulincer, M., Dolev, T., & Shaver, P. R. (2004). Attachment-related strategies during thought suppression: Ironic rebounds and vulnerable self-representations. *Journal of Personality and Social Psychology, 87,* 940–956.

Mikulincer, M., & Florian, V. (1998). The relationship between adult attachment styles and emotional and cognitive reactions to stressful events. In J. A. Simpson & W. S. Rholes (Eds.), *Attachment theory and close relationships* (pp. 143–165). New York: Guilford.

Mikulincer, M., & Florian, V. (2000). Exploring individual differences in reactions to mortality salience: Does attachment style regulate terror management mechanisms? *Journal of Personality and Social Psychology, 79,* 260–273.

Mikulincer, M., Florian, V., & Tolmacz, R. (1990). Attachment styles and fear of personal death: A case study of affect regulation. *Journal of Personality and Social Psychology, 58,* 273–280.

Mikulincer, M., Florian, V., & Weller, A. (1993). Attachment styles, coping strategies, and posttraumatic psychological distress: The impact of the Gulf War in Israel. *Journal of Personality and Social Psychology, 64,* 817–826.

Mikulincer, M., Gillath, O., Halevy, V., Avihou, N., Avidan, S., & Eshkoli, N. (2001). Attachment theory and reactions to others' needs: Evidence that activation of the sense of attachment security promotes empathic responses. *Journal of Personality and Social Psychology, 81,* 1205–1224.

Mikulincer, M., Gillath, O., Sapir-Lavid, Y., Yaakobi, E., Arias, K., Tal-Aloni, L., et al. (2003). Attachment theory and concern for others' welfare: Evidence that activation of the sense of secure base promotes endorsement of self-transcendence values. *Basic and Applied Social Psychology, 25,* 299–312.

Mikulincer, M., Gillath, O., & Shaver, P. R. (2002). Activation of the attachment system in adulthood: Threat-related primes increase the accessibility of mental representations of attachment figures. *Journal of Personality and Social Psychology, 83,* 881–895.

Mikulincer, M., Hirschberger, G., Nachmias, O., & Gillath, O. (2001). The affective component of the secure base schema: Affective priming with representations of attachment security. *Journal of Personality and Social Psychology, 81,* 305–321.

Mikulincer, M., & Orbach, I. (1995). Attachment styles and repressive defensiveness: The accessibility and architecture of affective memories. *Journal of Personality and Social Psychology, 68,* 917–925.

Mikulincer, M., Orbach, I., & Iavnieli, D. (1998). Adult attachment style and affect regulation: Strategic variations in subjective self-other similarity. *Journal of Personality and Social Psychology, 75,* 436–448.

Mikulincer, M., & Shaver, P. R. (2001). Attachment theory and intergroup bias: Evidence that priming the secure base schema attenuates negative reactions to out-groups. *Journal of Personality and Social Psychology, 81,* 97–115.

Mikulincer, M., & Shaver, P. R. (2003). The attachment behavioral system in adulthood: Activation, psychodynamics, and interpersonal processes. In M. P. Zanna (Ed.), *Advances in experimental social psychology* (Vol. 35, pp. 53–152). New York: Academic.

Mikulincer, M., & Shaver, P. R. (2004). Security-based self-representations in adulthood: Contents and processes. In W. S. Rholes & J. A. Simpson (Eds.), *Adult attachment: Theory, research, and clinical implications* (pp. 159–195). New York: Guilford.

Mikulincer, M., & Shaver, P. R. (2007a). *Attachment in adulthood: Structure, dynamics, and change.* New York: Guilford.

Mikulincer, M., & Shaver, P. R. (2007b). Boosting attachment security to promote mental health, prosocial values, and inter-group tolerance. *Psychological Inquiry, 18,* 139–156.

Mikulincer, M., & Shaver, P. R. (2011). Attachment, anger, and aggression. In P. R. Shaver & M. Mikulincer (Eds.), *Human aggression and violence: Causes, manifestations, and consequences* (pp. 241-257). Washington, DC: American Psychological Association.

Mikulincer, M., Shaver, P. R., & Gillath, O. (2009). A behavioral systems perspective on compassionate love. In L. Underwood, S. Sprecher, & B. Fehr (Eds.), *The science of compassionate love: Research, theory, and application.* Malden, MA: Blackwell.

Mikulincer, M., Shaver, P. R., Gillath, O., & Nitzberg, R. A. (2005). Attachment, caregiving, and altruism: Boosting attachment security increases compassion and helping. *Journal of Personality and Social Psychology, 89,* 817–839.

Mikulincer, M., Shaver, P. R., & Horesh, N. (2006). Attachment bases of emotion regulation and posttraumatic adjustment. In D. K. Snyder, J. A. Simpson, & J. N. Hughes (Eds.), *Emotion regulation in families: Pathways to dysfunction and health* (pp. 77–99). Washington, DC: American Psychological Association.

Mikulincer, M., Shaver, P. R., Sapir-Lavid, Y., & Avihou-Kanza, N. (2009). What's inside the minds of securely and insecurely attached people? The secure-base script and its associations with attachment-style dimensions. *Journal of Personality and Social Psychology, 97,* 615–633.

Mikulincer, M., & Sheffi, E. (2000). Adult attachment style and cognitive reactions to positive affect: A test of mental categorization and creative problem solving. *Motivation and Emotion, 24,* 149–174.

Murray, H. A. (1959). Preparations for the scaffold of a comprehensive system. In S. Koch (Ed.), *Psychology: A study of a science* (Vol. 3, pp. 7–54). New York: McGraw-Hill.

O'Connor, T. G., & Croft, C. M. (2001). A twin study of attachment in preschool children. *Child Development, 72,* 1501–1511.

Parker, G. A. (1974). Assessment strategy and the evolution of fighting behavior. *Journal of Theoretical Biology, 47,* 223–243.

Piaget, J. (1953). *Origins of intelligence in the child*. London: Routledge.

Reis, H. T., & Shaver, P. R. (1988). Intimacy as an interpersonal process. In S. Duck (Ed.), *Handbook of research in personal relationships* (pp. 367–389). London: Wiley.

Rholes, W. S., Simpson, J. A., & Orina, M. (1999). Attachment and anger in an anxiety-provoking situation. *Journal of Personality and Social Psychology, 76,* 940–957.

Rom, E., & Mikulincer, M. (2003). Attachment theory and group processes: The association between attachment style and group-related representations, goals, memories, and functioning. *Journal of Personality and Social Psychology, 84,* 1220–1235.

Rowe, A. C., & Carnelley, K. B. (2006). *Long lasting effects of repeated priming of attachment security on views of self and relationships.* Paper presented in the 13th European Conference on Personality, Athens, Greece.

Ryan, R. M., & Frederick, F. (1997). On energy, personality, and health: Subjective vitality as a dynamic reflection of well-being. *Journal of Personality, 65,* 529–565.

Schachner, D. A., & Shaver, P. R. (2004). Attachment dimensions and sexual motives. *Personal Relationships, 11,* 179–195.

Schmitt, D. E., et al. (2003). Are men universally more dismissing than women? Gender differences in romantic attachment across 62 cultural regions. *Personal Relationships, 10,* 307–331.

Schmitt, D. E., Alcalay, L., Allensworth, M., Allik, I. U., Ault, L., Austers, I., et al. (2004). Patterns and universals of adult romantic attachment across 62 cultural regions: Are models of self and of other pancultural constructs? *Journal of Cross-Cultural Psychology, 35,* 367–402.

Shaver, P. R., Collins, N. L., & Clark, C. L. (1996). Attachment styles and internal working models of self and relationship partners. In G. J. O. Fletcher & J. Fitness (Eds.), *Knowledge structures in close relationships: A social psychological approach* (pp. 25–61). Mahwah, NJ: Erlbaum.

Shaver, P. R., & Hazan, C. (1993). Adult romantic attachment: Theory and evidence. In D. Perlman & W. Jones (Eds.), *Advances in personal relationships* (Vol. 4, pp. 29–70). London: Kingsley.

Shaver, P. R., & Mikulincer, M. (2002). Attachment-related psychodynamics. *Attachment and Human Development, 4,* 133–161.

Shaver P. R., & Mikulincer, M. (2006). Conceptualization and operationalization of individual differences in the functioning of the sexual behavioral system. Paper presented at the International Association for Relationship Research Biannual Conference, Crete, Greece.

Shaver, P. R., & Mikulincer, M. (2008). Augmenting the sense of security in romantic, leader-follower, therapeutic, and group relationships: A relational model of psychological change. In J. P. Forgas & J. Fitness (Eds.), *Social relationships: Cognitive, affective, and motivational processes* (pp. 55–74). New York: Psychology Press.

Shaver, P. R., Mikulincer, M., Alonso-Arbiol, I., & Lavy, S. (2010). Assessment of adult attachment across cultures: Conceptual and methodological considerations. In P. Erdman, K.-M. Ng, & S. Metzger (Eds.), *Attachment: Expanding the cultural connections*. New York: Routledge/Taylor & Francis.

Shaver, P. R., Mikulincer, M., & Shemesh-Iron, M. (2009). A behavioral-systems perspective on prosocial behavior. In M. Mikulincer & P. R. Shaver (Eds.), *Prosocial motives, emotions, and behavior: The better angels of our nature*. Washington DC: American Psychological Association.

Shaver, P. R., Segev, M, & Mikulincer, M. (2011). A behavioral-systems perspective on power and aggression. In P. R. Shaver & M. Mikulincer (Eds.), *Human aggression and violence: Causes, manifestations, and consequences* (pp. 71-87). Washington, DC: American Psychological Association.

Simpson, J. A., Collins, W. A., Tran, S., & Haydon, K. C. (2007). Attachment and the experience and expression of emotions in romantic relationships: A developmental perspective. *Journal of Personality and Social Psychology, 92,* 355–367.

Simpson, J. A., Rholes, W. S., Campbell, L., & Wilson, C. L. (2003). Changes in attachment orientations across the transitions to parenthood. *Journal of Experimental Social Psychology, 39,* 317–331.

Simpson, J. A., Rholes, W. S., & Nelligan, J. S. (1992). Support seeking and support giving within couples in an anxiety-provoking situation: The role of attachment styles. *Journal of Personality and Social Psychology, 62,* 434–446.

Simpson, J. A., Rholes, W. S., & Phillips, D. (1996). Conflict in close relationships: An attachment perspective. *Journal of Personality and Social Psychology, 71,* 899–914.

Sprecher, S., & Cate, R. M. (2004). Sexual satisfaction and sexual expression as predictors of relationship satisfaction and stability. In J. H. Harvey, A. Wenzel, & S. Sprecher (Eds.), *Handbook of sexuality in close relationships* (pp. 235–256). Mahwah, NJ: Erlbaum.

Sroufe, L. A., & Waters, E. (1977). Attachment as an organizational construct. *Child Development, 48,* 1184–1199.

Steele, H, & Steele, M. (Eds.). (2008). *Clinical applications of the Adult Attachment Interview.* New York: Guilford.

Thibault, J. W., & Kelley, H. H. (1959). *The social psychology of groups.* New York: Wiley.

Tracy, J. L., Shaver, P. R., Albino, A. W., & Cooper, M. L. (2003). Attachment styles and adolescent sexuality. In P. Florsheim (Ed.), *Adolescent romance and sexual behavior: Theory, research, and practical implications* (pp. 137–159). Mahwah, NJ: Erlbaum.

van IJzendoorn, M. (1995). Adult attachment representations, parental responsiveness, and infant attachment: A meta-analysis on the predictive validity of the Adult Attachment Interview. *Psychological Bulletin, 117,* 387–403.

van IJzendoorn, M. H., & Sagi-Schwartz, A. (2008). Cross-cultural patterns of attachment: Universal and contextual dimensions. In J. Cassidy & P. R. Shaver (Eds.), *Handbook of attachment: Theory, research, and clinical applications* (2nd ed.). New York: Guilford.

Waters, H. S., & Waters, E. (2006). The attachment working models concept: Among other things, we build scriptlike representations of secure base experiences. *Attachment and Human Development, 8,* 185–198.

Wegner, D. M., Erber, R., & Zanakos, S. (1993). Ironic processes in the mental control of mood and mood-related thoughts. *Journal of Personality and Social Psychology, 65,* 1093–1104.

White R. W. (1959). Motivation reconsidered: The concept of competence. *Psychological Review, 66,* 297–333.

White R. W. (1965). The experience of efficacy in schizophrenia. *Psychiatry, 28,* 199–211.

Zuroff, D. C., & Fitzpatrick, D. K. (1995). Depressive personality styles: Implications for adult attachment. *Personality and Individual Differences, 18,* 253–365.

Person-by-Situation Perspectives on Close Relationships

Jeffry A. Simpson *and* Heike A. Winterheld

Abstract

In this chapter, we review theories and research that have adopted interactional (person-by-situation) approaches to the study of relationships. We first discuss interactional thinking within social and personality psychology, highlighting the fundamental ways in which individuals and situations intersect. We then review three major theoretical models that are exemplars of person-by-situation frameworks and have important implications for interpersonal processes: the cognitive-affective processing system (CAPS) model (Mischel & Shoda, 1995), interdependence theory (Kelley & Thibaut, 1978), and attachment theory (Bowlby, 1969, 1973, 1980). Following this, we explain how and why different person-by-situation approaches have expanded our understanding of individuals within relationships, focusing on romantic relationships. We spotlight programs of research on self-esteem and dependency/ risk regulation, promotion versus prevention orientations, and diathesis-stress models based in attachment theory. These lines of inquiry have documented that certain types of situations elicit unique reactions in people who have specific dispositional strengths (e.g., high self-esteem, greater attachment security) or vulnerabilities (e.g., low self-esteem, greater attachment insecurity). Collectively, this research confirms that one cannot predict or understand how individuals think, feel, or behave in relationships without knowing the relational context in which they are embedded. We conclude by identifying new directions in which interactional-based thinking might head, focusing on how functional strategies can further our understanding of person-by-situation effects.

Keywords: person-by-situation models, close relationships, cognitive-affective processing system (CAPS) model, attachment theory, dependency/risk regulation model, interdependence theory

Person-by-Situation Perspectives on Close Relationships

> Every psychological event depends upon the state of the person and at the same time on the environment, although their relative importance is different in different cases.
>
> *Kurt Lewin* (1936, p. 12)

Kurt Lewin was the founder of several disciplines in psychology, including social and industrial/organizational psychology. He was, however, much more than a founding father. Lewin was a broad-minded visionary who, with the development of field theory (Lewin, 1948), wanted to explain how forces that

reside both within individuals and in their immediate environments motivate people to act in their everyday lives. Thirty years after his famous dictum that behavior cannot be understood unless one considers both who a person is and the environment in which he or she is embedded, psychologists remained embroiled in debates about what explained more variance in social behavior—the dispositions that people have, or the situations in which they find themselves (see Mischel, 1968; Wicker, 1969). The basic answer, of course, was sketched in Lewin's writings decades earlier. The central theme of this chapter echoes one of Lewin's deepest insights: To fully understand *how and why* individuals behave as they do, one must discern who they are as people (e.g., their traits, dispositions, values, attitudes), the types of situations to which they are responding, and how these variables sometimes combine (statistically interact) to influence how individuals think, feel, and behave.

In this chapter, we discuss several theories and programs of research in the relationship sciences that have adopted interactional (person-by-situation) approaches to the study of social behavior. As we shall see, some excellent examples of how person-by-situation models can advance our understanding of how and why people behave the way they do already exist in the relationships literature. One of the primary reasons for this is that relationship partners are often the most salient and important "feature of the environment" to which individuals respond in many significant social situations. Most of our attention, therefore, will focus on person-by-situation models and effects that pertain to close relationships.

The chapter is divided into four major sections. In the first section, we briefly overview "interactional" thinking within social and personality psychology, highlighting different approaches to the study of personality and social behavior and discussing how individuals and situations can intersect (Snyder & Ickes, 1985). In the second section, we discuss three major theoretical models that are exemplars of person-by-situation frameworks and have important implications for the study of dispositions within dyadic contexts: the cognitive-affective processing system (CAPS) model (Mischel & Shoda, 1995), interdependence theory (Kelley & Thibaut, 1978), and attachment theory (Bowlby, 1969, 1973, 1980). Each of these theories addresses how certain personality traits or individual differences are likely to *combine* with certain situations to jointly predict how people think, feel, and behave.

In the third section, we review how different person-by-situation approaches have extended our understanding of individuals within relationships, placing special emphasis on romantic relationships. Specifically, we review research on self-esteem and dependency/risk regulation processes (Murray, Holmes, & Griffin, 2000) along with recent research on how promotion and prevention orientations (Higgins, 1998) operate in different interpersonal contexts. We then turn to a long-standing program of research by Simpson, Rholes, and their colleagues that has tested a series of diathesis-stress predictions associated with attachment theory. Each of these programs of research has confirmed that certain

types of situations elicit certain kinds of responses in people who possess certain dispositional strengths (e.g., high self-esteem, greater attachment security) or vulnerabilities (e.g., low self-esteem, greater attachment insecurity). Collectively, these programs of research indicate that one can neither predict nor understand how individuals think, feel, and behave without knowing the specific social situations that individuals are confronting and how they perceive and interpret each situation. We conclude the chapter by suggesting new directions in which interactional-based thinking might head, accentuating the promise of functional strategies for furthering our understanding person-by-situation effects (Snyder & Cantor, 1998).

Interactional Perspectives in Psychology

Social and personality psychology have rather distinct historical origins (Jones, 1985), partly because each field began with different missions and goals. Social psychology started as an enterprise that sought to understand how factors external to individuals affect the way in which they think, feel, and behave. Gordon Allport (1968, p. 3), for example, defined social psychology as the "attempt to understand and explain how the thoughts, feelings, and behavior of individuals are influenced by the actual, imagined, or implied presence of others." Personality psychology, on the other hand, wanted to determine how forces that reside *within* individuals guide their behavior over time and in different situations. Being both a social and a personality psychologist, Allport (1937, p. 48) also offered a foundational definition of personality, referring to it as "the dynamic organization within the individual of those psychophysical systems that determine his [*sic*] unique adjustments to his environment."

One feature that these two definitions share is what Lewin (1948) addressed in field theory—the principle forces that impel people to *move* through the life space. Social and personality psychology both address how and why individuals are motivated to think, feel, and behave in response to forces, with personality psychology placing emphasis on forces that reside within individuals (e.g., traits, needs, motives, desires), and with social psychology focusing on forces that lie outside a person but within their local environment (e.g., social norms and roles, situational presses and expectations, other people). However, Lewin also believed that personality traits should affect what people attend to, perceive, interpret, remember, and react to in different social situations. Personality, in other words, should often play a role in determining the meaning and potential impact that certain situations have on individuals who possess certain traits or dispositions. This is why Lewin developed and used manipulation checks in studies; he understood that persons and situations were inextricably connected in more profound ways than many people assumed. Today, the premise that behavior is the result of characteristics of both the person and the situation is almost universally accepted (see Snyder & Cantor, 1998; Snyder & Ickes, 1985). This is especially true in the field of interpersonal relationships, where relationship partners are often the most prominent and important "feature" in the environments of most individuals. Moreover, the effects of some personality traits (e.g., agreeableness) are not witnessed unless individuals are in situational contexts that are relevant to the expression of their traits (e.g., those that allow agreeable people to cooperate with others).

Historically, three major strategies have been used to investigate how personality and social situations dovetail to guide how individuals think, feel, and behave: the dispositional strategy, the interactional strategy, and the situational strategy (Snyder & Ickes, 1985). The oldest strategy, the dispositional one, reveals how specific traits or dispositions impact how individuals think, feel, and behave both over time and in different social settings. This strategy was used in early research on trait constructs such as the authoritarian personality (Adorno, Frenkel-Brunswik, Levinson, & Sanford, 1950), the need for social approval (Crowne & Marlowe, 1960), and Machiavellianism (Christie & Geis, 1970). One cardinal feature of the dispositional strategy is that it identifies individuals who regularly and consistently display certain social behaviors that presumably reflect the influence of the trait(s) being studied (Snyder & Ickes, 1985). Although the dispositional approach has generated many interesting and important findings (see Snyder & Ickes, 1985), it has distinct limitations. For example, the dispositional strategy tends to be atheoretical and, in some cases, tautological (e.g., evidence for possessing the trait of extraversion is sometimes inferred from the fact that certain people talk more than others). It also focuses heavily on whether and how certain dispositions impact how people think, feel, and behave to the relative neglect of important situational factors. For this reason, studies based solely on the dispositional strategy tend to explain relatively little variance in most social behaviors.

Realizing that most dispositional constructs, including virtually all personality traits (Mischel,

1968) and attitudes (Wicker, 1969), account for approximately 10% of the variance in most behaviors, psychologists returned to Lewin and began using what is now known as the interactional strategy. In addition to Lewin's seminal writings, the seeds of the interactional strategy were evident in other early lines of work, including Murray's (1938) model of needs and motives, Kelly's (1955) theory of personal constructs, and Neisser's (1967) cognitive research, which inspired the motivated cognition movement (Endler, 1982). Consistent with Lewin, each of these theorists claimed that dispositions should influence how people perceive and interpret the meaning of certain social situations, depending on their current needs and motivational states. This explains why the interactional strategy considers both dispositional *and* situational information when specifying when and why certain traits should or should not be moderated by (statistically interact with) certain types of situations, resulting in consistent and predictable *context-dependent* patterns of thought, feeling, and action.

Within the past two decades, a hybrid discipline of personality and social psychology has emerged in several subareas of both fields. For example, interactional strategies have been successfully applied to the study of prosocial behavior (e.g., Carlo, Eisenberg, Troyer, Switzer, & Speer. 1991); dominance, conformity, and dissent within groups (e.g., Maslach, Santee, & Wade, 1987); stress reactions (e.g., Davis & Matthews, 1996); intrinsic and extrinsic motivation (e.g., Thompson, Chaiken, & Hazelwood, 1993); alcohol use (e.g., Hull & Young, 1983); self-concept and social behavior (e.g., Brown & Smart, 1991); resistance to persuasion (e.g., Zuwerink & Devine, 1996); obedience to authority figures (e.g., Blass, 1991); perceptions of social support (e.g., Lakey, McCabe, Fisicaro, & Drew, 1996); and intimacy and self-disclosure (e.g., Shaffer, Ogden, & Wu, 1987). When dispositions and situations are both properly measured and modeled, up to 80% of the variance in behavior can be explained (Snyder & Cantor, 1998).

There are different types of moderating variables in the interactional strategy, two of which are particularly relevant to this chapter: (1) strong versus weak situations, and (2) precipitating versus nonprecipitating situations. *Strong situations* have clear and distinct norms, rules, or expectations that specify how individuals should behave in the situation (e.g., appropriate behavior at funerals, or when the national anthem is being played). These highly role-governed situations reduce the influence that most dispositions have on behavior, suppressing the effects of individual difference variables. *Weak situations*, in contrast, involve fewer rules, norms, or expectations regarding how one ought to behave in the situation (e.g., a party at a friend's house, an initial encounter with a stranger in a waiting room). As a consequence, weak situations allow dispositions to exert greater influence on behavior because situational forces are ambiguous or largely absent. Person-by-situation interaction effects are, therefore, more likely to emerge when a disposition is relevant to the situation being investigated and when the situation is neither too strong nor too weak.

The second major moderating variable in the interactional strategy is whether situations are precipitating or nonprecipitating. *Precipitating situations* shift the cause of a behavior to a particular disposition, which then alters, amplifies, or mutes how an individual responses to it. For example, certain classes of situations (e.g., a rowdy party) may lead certain individuals (e.g., extraverts) to act on their schemas (working models) associated with extraversion, leading them to think, feel, and behave in a more boisterous and lively manner. Precipitating situations, which are also known as "situational moderating variables," operate when: (1) features of the situation are theoretically relevant to the disposition; (2) the situation makes the schema(s) underlying the disposition salient guides to behavior; and (3) the situation is not too strong and permits different types or degrees of responding, depending on whether an individual scores high, moderate, or low on the disposition.

The third major investigative approach is the situational strategy (Snyder & Ickes, 1985). This strategy attempts to explain consistencies and regularities in social behavior by examining how people with different dispositional tendencies select, alter, or manipulate the social situations that affect their daily lives. The situational strategy is actually a dynamic version of the interactional strategy, but one that considers the reciprocal nature of situations and dispositions (Snyder & Ickes, 1985). Thus, this strategy addresses not only how situations affect dispositions, but how dispositions shape the micro and macro environments in which people live. Within the study of relationships, the situational strategy has confirmed that individual differences associated with self-monitoring affect how high and low self-monitors choose friends as activity partners (Snyder, Gangestad, & Simpson, 1983) and evaluate prospective romantic partners (Snyder, Berscheid, & Glick, 1985). Other research has demonstrated that

certain personality traits systematically affect the choice of long-term mates (Buss, 1984), which in turn affect long-term relationship outcomes (Caspi & Herbener, 1990).

Major Interactional Theories

Given the compelling logic of interactional approaches, one might expect they would be found in many domains across psychology. While they have informed the study of several important topics in psychology (see above), interactional strategies are not as prevalent as one might anticipate. There are several reasons for this. To begin with, a considerable amount of research in social and personality psychology has not been grounded in broad theoretical frameworks that specify how and why certain situations should have *precipitating* effects on certain people. This problem has been compounded by the fact that, unlike personality traits, we still do not have a good taxonomy or understanding of the fundamental types of social situations that regularly influence individuals and their lives (for an important exception, see Kelley et al., 2003; see also Reis & Holmes, chapter 4, this volume). Fortunately, some major relationship-based theories have incorporated both person and situation variables, making the relationships field an exemplar of how the interactional approach can be applied to generate novel and important insights into person-by-situation effects. This has been facilitated by recent advances in data analytic methods (see Kenny, Kashy, & Cook, 2006), which now allow researchers to design and test person-by-situation models much more easily than before. For example, the development of new repeated-measures techniques for diary studies now permits researchers to follow individuals across time as they (and potentially their partners) move through a range of different situations (e.g., Bolger & Romero-Canyas, 2007).

In this section, we highlight three major theories. We first discuss Mischel and Shoda's (1995) CAPS model of dispositions in relation to situations. This general model is one of the most prominent and best exemplars of how person-by-situation approaches can be fruitfully adopted to expand our understanding of when, how, and why certain situations reveal patterning and consistency in social behavior among certain people. We then turn to two other major theories, both of which have deep interpersonal roots: interdependence theory (Thibaut & Kelley, 1959; Kelley & Thibaut, 1978) and attachment theory (Bowlby, 1969, 1973, 1980). These theories offer more specific predictions about how certain dispositions should interface with certain types of situations to generate unique patterns of thought, feeling, and action. As we shall see, relationship partners are very important and salient features of the individual's "social environment" according to these theories. This, in turn, introduces some interesting complications in that: (1) each partner's dispositions (e.g., traits, motives, needs, desires) become an important element of the other partner's immediate situation/environment; (2) the dispositions of *both* partners must be taken into consideration; and (3) the *beliefs* that individuals have about their partner's needs and dispositions may determine what happens, independent of whether or not these beliefs reflect the partner's actual needs or dispositions.

The Cognitive-Affective Processing System (CAPS) Model

Traditional personality approaches have been based on the assumption that people's dispositional characteristics remain stable across different situations and contexts. Research, however, has not always supported this assumption. People's behavior in relation to nearly all traits varies considerably across contexts and situations (Mischel, 1968). To determine whether individual differences in behaviors are generated by transitory situational factors or by people's enduring personality characteristics, researchers often statistically average trait-related behaviors across many situations. This averaging process reveals the extent to which people differ in their overall level of trait-related behavior, but it does not allow for situation-specific predictions, that is, for predictions that address when, where, and why patterns of behavior differ (Mischel, Shoda, & Mendoza-Denton, 2002). An average summary score for a person's level of agreeableness, for example, might reveal that a highly agreeable person is more accommodating than other people across different contexts (e.g., when negotiating a business deal with a client, when negotiating vacation plans with his/her spouse). However, it does not identify important exceptions to this person's global action tendencies, such as situations in which he/she responds in less obliging or more confrontational ways (e.g., during specific types of conflict with a romantic partner, during difficult negotiations with specific people).

To generate predictions that move beyond understanding overall average differences in behavior, Mischel and Shoda (1995) proposed the cognitive-affective processing system (CAPS) model (see also Mendoza-Denton & Ayduk, chapter 18, this volume). Instead of treating situational variability as noise that conceals the true stability and consistency of personality across situations, the CAPS model assumes that intraindividual variability of behavior across situations and different contexts may reflect an enduring yet dynamic personality system, one that incorporates rather than ignores the impact of situations (see also Cervone, 2004).

The CAPS model focuses on situations as they are perceived and understood by individuals (cf. Kelly, 1955), and it attempts explain *why* situations exert different effects on different people. The model proposes that people have mental representations, or cognitive-affective units (CAUs), that exist within a large network of associations and constraints known as CAPS networks. CAUs form the stable units of personality and contain people's construals, goals, expectations, beliefs, and emotions with respect to situations, others, and the self. They also contain self-regulatory standards, competencies, plans, and strategies (Mischel & Shoda, 1995). Once activated (or inhibited), CAUs guide how people interpret or construe an encountered situation or person, and they automatically activate cognitive, emotional, and behavioral responses to that situation or person. Each individual has a relatively stable activation network among the units within the system, reflecting his/her social (e.g., early caregiving experiences, culture) and biological (e.g., temperament, genes) history and background.

One key assumption of the CAPS model is that mental representations have conditional qualities—"*if . . . then properties,*" such as *if* I encounter X . . . *then* I will do Y. According to Mischel (1999), every person has a unique *if . . . then . . .* profile, which constitutes his/her *behavioral signature.* Empirical evidence supports this premise. Shoda, Mischel, and Wright (1994), for example, observed children's behavior in various naturalistic situations and found that children's *if . . . then . . .* profiles were distinct and stable across time. Moreover, Chen (2003) has shown that the more familiar individuals are with someone, the more others are thought of in conditional terms. People also think conditionally about themselves. If a person identifies a situation that is linked to one of his/her behaviors in an "*if . . . then . . .*" manner, the behavior is more likely to occur. For example, a highly anxious person who perceives his/her partner's fishing trip with friends as abandonment or neglect is more likely to display clingy or angry behaviors.

The CAPS model, therefore, suggests a reconceptualization of personality traits as specific *if . . . then . . .* behavioral profiles, which specify what a given individual will do in specific situations. According to the model, individual differences can emerge in two ways. First, people differ in the accessibility of their schemas and the situational cues that activate their schemas. In a given situation, different schemas should become activated for different people, leading them to perceive different aspects of the same situation or to interpret the same situation in different ways. For example, a partner's "ambiguous" comment about one's appearance before a formal event might be construed as rejection by one individual, but as a neutral comment by another individual. Different schemas can also become activated for different individuals when meeting a particular person. For instance, when individuals encounter new people who resemble significant others from the past that activate schemas of them, these schemas tend to evoke *if . . . then . . .* profiles that lead individuals to respond to new people as they would with prior significant others (e.g., parents; Andersen & Chen, 2002). Second, the pattern of linkages and strength of associations between situations and behaviors that have been established over time should differ from one person to another. Even if two people share the same view of a given situation (e.g., interpreting a partner's ambiguous remark as rejection), their *behavioral* responses might differ considerably. One person, for instance, might respond with anger or hostility, whereas the other might react with silence or withdrawal. To predict behavior, therefore, researchers must determine: (1) how a person construes the situation (which is influenced by his/her schemas and their degree of accessibility), and (2) the person's specific situation-behavior linkage (i.e., his/her *if . . . then . . .* profile) (Shoda et al., 1994).

In general, the CAPS model emphasizes regularities in within-person cognitive, emotional, and behavioral responses in particular contexts. The assumption that different cognitive-affective representations can be activated in different situations allows for the existence of seemingly contradictory traits in the same person (Fleeson, 2001, 2004). For example, fearful-avoidant individuals (who have negative views of themselves and others) might display dismissive behavioral tendencies in one situation, but anxious-ambivalent qualities (e.g., clingy behavior or neediness) in another situation. In addition, identifying certain *if . . . then . . .* profiles allows researchers to capture important exceptions to

people's global behavioral tendencies and to pinpoint which situations typically elicit or inhibit trait-relevant behaviors. For example, given their negative expectations regarding the responsiveness of others, people who score high on attachment avoidance should be reluctant to enter certain social situations. Consistent with the CAPS perspective, Beck and Clark (2009) have found that avoidant persons tend to sidestep social situations that provide information about others' evaluations of them (i.e., socially diagnostic situations), but enjoy socializing with others in *nondiagnostic* social situations that do not provide information about whether others like them. In addition, Zaki, Bolger, and Ochsner (2008) have documented that trait affective empathy (an individual's tendency to experience others' emotions) predicts empathic accuracy (an individual's tendency to accurately assess others' emotions), but only in certain interpersonal situations (when others express these emotions clearly).

Given that each partner constitutes a significant part of the other person's immediate situation or environment in most close relationships, the CAPS model can also be applied to dyadic contexts. To the extent that a person's "situation" consists largely of his/her partner's behavior, the interpretation and psychological experience of the situation (i.e., the partner's behavior) should be influenced by the individual's CAPS network, which in turn should influence his/her behavioral response to the partner. The partner then interprets and experiences this response through his/her own CAPS network, from which another behavioral response flows. The behavior of an individual, therefore, emerges from the *interaction* between the individual and his/her situation, which consists primarily of the behavior displayed by his/her partner.

Zayas, Shoda, and Ayduk (2002) have adapted Lewin's famous equation to close relationship contexts. The behavior of one partner (B_1) emerges from the interaction between his/her dispositional characteristics (P_1) and the situational input (i.e., his/her partner's behavior, B_2), such that $B_1 = f(P_1, B_2)$. The behavior of the second partner can be conceptualized similarly: $B_2 = f(P_2, B_1)$. Hence, if an individual's immediate environment consists mainly of his/her partner's behavior, E_1 becomes a function of the individual's own behavior (B_1) and his/her partner's characteristics (P_2). The partner then interprets and responds (B_2) to the individual's initial behavior, so that $E_1 = f(P_2, B_1)$ and $E_2 = f(P_1, B_2)$. As partners interact across time, the "interlocking" of their respective CAPS systems should create a dyadic system, within which the dispositional characteristics of each individual are embedded and from which each individual's behaviors, as well as the unique behavioral patterns of the dyad, gradually emerge (Zayas et al., 2002). As partners interact more often and spend more time together, attention to and encoding of the partner's behavior increases. For this reason, the situational input for one's own behavior increases in psychological significance over time, leading to stable and predictable *interaction signatures* of relationships. If, for instance, an individual's partner consistently criticizes him/her for having a drink with dinner, this might repeatedly activate a specific subset of the individual's CAPS network ("*If* I have a drink . . . *then* X criticizes me), triggering a particular response such as defensiveness. Over time, the thoughts and emotions in the individual's CAPS network related to this particular situation will become more accessible, and the behavior (defensiveness) might be triggered by minimal input on part of the partner (e.g., even a "glance" by the partner when one has a drink elicits defensiveness).

People's dispositional characteristics also predispose them to select, evoke, or manipulate certain situations (Buss, 1987), including the partner and his/her behavior. This, in turn, may amplify or sustain these dispositional characteristics. For example, if an individual's behavior is consistent over time (e.g., s/he always withdraws during relationship conflicts), the individual's *partner* will be repeatedly exposed to situations that activate the same thoughts and emotions within his/her relevant CAUs (e.g., "*if* there is conflict, *then* he/she pulls away and we grow apart"). This, in turn, should generate specific behavioral responses in the partner (e.g., approach behavior to try to reestablish intimacy). This behavioral response may then serve as a situational trigger for the other person, who is likely to experience his/her partner's approach behavior as threatening, resulting in even more withdrawal, thereby perpetuating or exacerbating the cycle. Because the patterns and associations among cognitions and affects within CAPS networks also reflect the impact of individuals' social and genetic backgrounds, the CAPS model is consistent with interpersonal theories such as attachment theory (Bowlby, 1969, 1973, 1980) and interdependence theory (Kelley & Thibaut, 1978; Thibaut & Kelley, 1959).

In sum, the CAPS model is a broad person-by-situation framework that explains how situations may interact with personality traits or individual differences to improve our ability to predict and understand certain trait-behavior linkages. According to the CAPS model, personality reflects stable patterns of behavior that result from certain trait-situation pairings and are activated in certain situations. One limitation of the CAPS model is that it does not explain why, from an ontogenetic standpoint, certain situations should come to trigger certain patterns of thoughts, feelings, or behaviors in certain people. Other theories are needed to explain when, how, and why certain situations should elicit the cardinal personality signatures of people who have certain traits. This is where major interpersonal theories such as interdependence theory and attachment theory make important contributions to our understanding of person-by-situation effects.

Interdependence Theory

Interdependence theory, which was developed by two of Lewin's students (Thibaut & Kelley, 1959; Kelley & Thibaut, 1978), is one of the major theories within social psychology that directly addresses how people and their environments interact, resulting in specific behavioral decisions. According to interdependence theory, when two people decide what to do in a given situation, their choices should depend on: (1) the type of situation the partners are in, and (2) each partner's needs, motives, and/or dispositions in relation to the other. The specific type of situation that two people find themselves in should affect how they are dependent on each other and how they can thus influence each other's outcomes in the situation (i.e., their degree of *inter*dependence). The interpersonal dispositions/orientations of each partner (e.g., each partner's interpersonally relevant traits, motives, values, attitudes, and beliefs) should also guide how each partner perceives, interprets, and makes decisions about what to do in the situation. In other words, the dispositions of *each* partner should be "functionally relevant" to how each partner thinks, feels, and acts, depending on the features of the situation at hand (Holmes, 2002).

One of the main obstacles to studying persons and situations has been identifying the fundamental dimensions on which social situations differ (see also Reis & Holmes, chapter 4, this volume). In fact, one of the primary limitations of Mischel and Shoda's (1995) CAPS model is that it does not provide a "theory of situations" capable of specifying *why* certain personality traits are activated by exposure to certain situations (Holmes, 2002). On the person side, we have a fairly good taxonomy of the major personality traits (e.g., the Big Five) and several basic interpersonal orientations (e.g., attachment styles, self-esteem). On the situation side, however, a solid taxonomy of situations remains elusive, partly because there are a multitude of possible situations that differ on myriad dimensions. Kelley et al. (2003) have recently used interdependence theory to identify approximately 20 "prototypical situations" that have unique outcome patterns and distinct qualities. Some of these prototypical situations (e.g., those involving principles of exchange, investment, threat, trust) should be systematically associated with important relationship processes and outcomes, and they are encountered on a regular basis.

Figure 20.1 depicts one common relationship-relevant situation known as "mutual exchange with profit" (see Holmes, 2002). The values in each cell reflect each person's (each partner's) level of satisfaction or dissatisfaction with each behavioral choice, with each partner having two options from which to choose. In the hypothetical example shown in Figure 20.1, if both partners select option 1 (both decide to clean the house), each partner benefits by 10 points because the house gets cleaned while the couple enjoys spending time together. This cooperative choice entails a reciprocal exchange in which each partner shares equally in the largest total benefits in any of the four cells (i.e., the partners share 20 points). One or both partners may, however, be drawn to option 2 (not cleaning the house), which would yield 5 additional points (15) if the other partner chooses option 1 (cleans the house by himself/herself) and, in doing so, receives no benefits (or perceives costs if s/he feels treated unfairly). This "exchange" situation pits motives to cooperate against motives to maximize personal gains, and it

is one of a handful of fundamental relationship-relevant situations (see Kelley et al., 2003, for other situations).

Each of the 20 fundamental situations identified by Kelley et al. (2003) varies on six situation dimensions (Holmes, 2002). As shown in Table 20.1, the first situation dimension is the *degree of interdependence*, which is indexed by the extent to which each partner can influence the quality (goodness) of his or her partner's outcomes in the situation. The greater the potential for influence, the more interdependent partners are in that situation. Relationships in which partners are more interdependent over many different situations tend to be closer because partners have stronger and more frequent impact on each other across different life domains (Kelley et al., 1983). The second dimension is the *mutuality of dependence*, which reflects the degree to which partners have equal versus unequal power over each other in the situation. Greater mutuality of dependence reflects more equal power in the situation, whereas less mutuality signifies more unequal power. The third dimension, *correspondence of outcomes*, represents the extent to which each partner has similar versus conflicting initial interests in the situation before any negotiation occurs. More correspondent situations are easier to resolve because the initial behavioral choice that is best for one partner is also likely to be best for the other partner, with little if any need for compromise. The fourth dimension, the *basis of control*, reflects the degree to which partners can control each other's outcomes in the situation by using exchange principles (e.g., by making promises or threats) or coordinating their activities (e.g., when one partner begins dinner, and the other performs the next logical steps). The fifth dimension, the *temporal structure* of decision-making, reflects how soon decisions will have consequences for one or both partners once a decision has been made. Some decisions have immediate consequences (e.g., deciding to have life-altering surgery), whereas the full effects of others take years to unfold (e.g., deciding to have children). The sixth dimension, the *degree of uncertainty*, represents the extent to which partners are uncertain about the long-term outcomes of a decision due to incomplete information or lack of knowledge. In more uncertain situations, for example, partners cannot predict whether their current decisions will or will not result in the outcomes they anticipated or hoped for.

Each of the six situation dimensions listed in Table 20.1 has a "function of rule," and each one is relevant to a particular set of interpersonal dispositions.

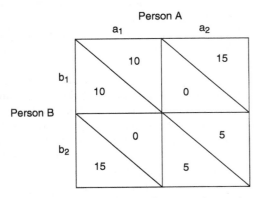

Fig. 20.1 Mutual exchange with profit situation (reprinted with permission from Holmes, 2002)

Table 20.1 Dimensions of Situations and Interpersonal Dispositions (reprinted with permission from Holmes, 2002)

Dimension of Situation	Function of Rule	Interpersonal Disposition
1. Degree of interdependence 2. Mutuality of interdependence	Increase or decrease dependence on partner	Avoidance of interdependence/ Comfort with dependence
3. Correspondence of outcomes	Promote prosocial or self-interested goals	Cooperative/competitive Responsive/unresponsive
	Expectations about partner's goals	Anxiety about responsiveness/ Confidence or trust
4. Basis of control	Control through Exchange (promise/threat) or Coordination (initiative/follow)	Dominant/submissive Assertive/passive
5. Temporal structure	Promote immediate or distant goal striving	Dependable/unreliable Loyal/uncommitted
6. Degree of uncertainty	Cope with incomplete information or uncertain future	Need for certainty/openness Optimism/pessimism

For example, in situations that differ in the degree of interdependence, the functional (i.e., operative) decision rule is whether to increase or decrease dependence on the partner in the situation. Which decision is made should depend on the degree to which one or both partners are dispositionally inclined to avoid interdependence (as is true of avoidantly attached people) or to embrace it (as is true of securely attached people). In situations that differ in mutuality of interdependence, the functional rule is to promote either prosocial goals or self-interested goals. Which decision is made should depend on the degree to which one or both partners have a cooperative versus competitive orientation or a responsive versus unresponsive orientation toward other people, especially the partner. In situations that differ in correspondence of outcomes, the functional rule centers on expectations of the partner's goals or what the partner wants to achieve. Thus, decisions should hinge on the degree to which individuals are concerned about whether their partners are sufficiently responsive to them and/or how much confidence or trust they can place in their partners. In situations that differ in the basis of control, the functional rule involves whether control of the partner's outcomes occurs through exchange or coordination tactics. Which decision is made should depend on the degree to which one or both partners are dominant versus submissive or assertive versus passive. In situations that differ in temporal structure, the functional rule is to facilitate either immediate or distant goal-striving. The decision followed should hinge on the degree to which one or both partners are dependable versus unreliable or loyal versus uncommitted to each other. Finally, in situations that vary in degree of uncertainty, the functional rule is how to deal with incomplete information or unknown future events. The decision that is made should depend on the degree to which one or both partners has a high need for certainty, is open to new experiences, or is optimistic about future events.

In sum, for each of the six situation dimensions, specific interpersonal dispositions, including interpersonally relevant personality traits and relationship orientations, should become salient and guide how people construe certain situations and how they make decisions when in them. Put another way, situations differ in the extent to which they are "relevant" to certain dispositions and are likely to elicit their expression (Holmes, 2002). People who prefer autonomy and emotional independence in relationships, for instance, should dislike or feel uncomfortable in situations that pull for greater interdependence. Such situations should activate the relationship-relevant schemas and working models of these individuals, which should in turn motivate them to behave in ways that *decrease* their dependence on their partners, especially in situations that might foster greater interdependence. Preferences for autonomy and emotional independence, however, should not become activated and guide thoughts, feelings, and behavior in other situations.

Attachment Theory

Bowlby (1969, 1973, 1980) began formulating attachment theory after observing the deleterious effects that long-term caregiver/child separations had on the emotional and physical well-being of children. He conjectured that the need to form attachment bonds with primary caregivers is an innate, biologically based tendency that was selected during evolutionary history because it increased the probability of surviving the many perils of childhood. Indeed, the tendency to seek physical and psychological proximity to attachment figures (e.g., primary caregivers, romantic partners) is one of the central tenets of attachment theory. According to Bowlby (1969, 1973), virtually all children and adults are motivated to seek some form of contact with their attachment figures, especially when they are distressed, threatened, or feel overwhelmed (Kobak & Duemmler, 1994).

The earliest attachment research focused on relationships between young children and their mothers. Ainsworth, Blehar, Waters, and Wall (1978) identified three types of infant/caregiver relationships: secure, avoidant, and anxious-resistant. When upset, children who have a secure relationship with their mothers glean comfort from her presence and actively use her to regulate and reduce negative affect when it arises. Avoidant children, by comparison, do not express their needs for proximity to their mothers by directly seeking contact when they become distressed. Rather, avoidant children turn away from their mothers to regulate and dissipate negative affect and utilize other coping strategies (e.g., distraction). Avoidant behavior may be an evolved strategy to suppress emotions, needs, or actions that are unwanted, dysfunctional, or were associated with painful rejections from past attachment figures. It also allows children (and perhaps adults) to not put excessive demands on their attachment figures, who may be unwilling or unable to invest more in the relationship and might otherwise terminate it (Main, 1981).

Children who have anxious-resistant attachment relationships also do not use their mothers as a source of comfort when they are distressed. Instead of avoiding their caregivers, however, anxious children cling to their mothers, remain distressed even after establishing contact with them, and do not resume normal activities such as exploration. These behaviors suggest that anxious children are hypersensitive to separations from their caregivers, despite the fact that they do not seem to receive sufficient "felt security" from them. Anxious behavior could

reflect an evolved strategy designed to express emotions, needs, or actions intensely in order to attract and retain the attention of inconsistent, poorly motivated, or inattentive caregivers (Main, 1981).

As individuals grow and develop, relationship experiences become encoded in working models (schemas), which explain much of the continuity and stability witnessed in personality and social behavior across development (Bowlby, 1973). Working models are cognitive structures that encompass an individual's cumulative experiences in and perceptions of earlier attachment relationships (Collins, Guichard, Ford, & Feeney, 2004). They contain episodic, semantic, and affective information about prior relationships and interpersonal events including: (1) rules about the emotions and thoughts one has about relationship partners; (2) guidelines for how to interpret and regulate emotional experiences in relationships; (3) beliefs and values about relationships and relationship-based experiences; (4) expectations about what future relationships and relationship experiences ought to be like; and (5) memories and emotions linked to past relationships. Working models guide behavior and affective experiences in relationships, and they provide a cognitive/emotional context through which new relationship information is filtered, interpreted, and usually assimilated.

Conceptually analogous attachment patterns and corresponding behaviors have also been documented in adults (see Mikulincer & Shaver, 2007a; also chapter 19, this volume). In adults, attachment patterns (known as "attachment styles") exist within a 2-dimensional space defined by the continuously distributed, relatively orthogonal dimensions of attachment anxiety and avoidance (Brennan, Clark, & Shaver, 1998; Simpson, Rholes, & Phillips, 1996). Within this framework, greater attachment security is indicated by lower scores on both the anxiety and avoidance dimensions. Individuals who score high on attachment anxiety worry about losing their partners, yearn to achieve greater felt security, and are hypervigilant to signs that their partners could be pulling away from them (Mikulincer & Shaver, 2003). Those who score high on attachment avoidance worry about losing their independence and autonomy, yearn to maintain control in their relationships, and use deactivating strategies when dealing with threatening events. As Kobak and Sceery (1988) have discussed, highly secure persons openly acknowledge distress when it arises and turn to significant others for comfort and emotional support to dissipate negative affect. Highly avoidant

Diathesis-Stress and Attachment Styles

According to attachment theory, specific types of situations should activate certain working models, depending on an individual's attachment history. Bowlby (1973, 1988) hypothesized that diathesis-stress effects should emerge in certain stressful interpersonal contexts, with greater attachment insecurity often acting as the diathesis (the personal vulnerability) and with stress being indexed by how an individual responds to a potentially taxing situation (e.g., feeling afraid, ill, or fatigued, experiencing relationship conflict) or a difficult life event (e.g., having a baby, experiencing a major relationship breakup or loss). Greater attachment security, on the other hand, should buffer people from all but the most extreme of stressful events (Mikulincer & Florian, 1998). Securely attached people have positive and benevolent working models of themselves and others, and they typically utilize constructive, problem-focused coping strategies when they become distressed. These assets should serve as an "inner resource" (Mikulincer & Shaver, 2007b; also chapter 19, this volume), permitting highly secure people to take advantage of the attributes and resources that other people—especially their attachment figures—are able and willing to offer.

How an individual reacts to a specific life stressor should depend on his or her relationship history, which presumably has shaped his/her working models. As discussed earlier, highly anxious individuals have received inconsistent or unpredictable care from past attachment figures, especially when they were upset and needed comforting (Cassidy & Berlin, 1994). Given these experiences, anxious individuals worry about losing their attachment figures in adulthood, crave more felt security, and are vigilant to detecting even trivial signs that their partners might be pulling away from them (Mikulincer & Shaver, 2003). They should, therefore, be bothered by—and their working models should become activated in—situations that threaten or call into question the quality, stability, or permanence of their primary relationships. Accordingly, stressful situations that center on relationship issues (e.g., unresolved relationship conflicts, the long-term absence of partners, discouragement of closeness by partners) should elicit the *relational signatures*—the prototypical emotional, cognitive, and behavioral tendencies—that define attachment anxiety (Simpson & Rholes, 2012).

Highly avoidant individuals have been rejected and rebuffed by prior attachment figures, especially when they were distressed and needed support (Crittenden & Ainsworth, 1989). As a consequence,

they have learned to be independent and self-reliant, which explains why they strive to retain autonomy and control in relationships. One way to achieve these goals is to avoid or exit situations that might require engaging in activities that could undermine their independence, autonomy, or control in relationships. Giving or receiving emotional forms of care and support ought to be one such situation (Bowlby, 1973). Highly avoidant people, therefore, should be particularly bothered by—and their working models should be activated in—situations that involve giving or receiving support, being emotionally intimate, or having to express personal emotions. These types of situations, in other words, should elicit the prototypical emotional, cognitive, and behavioral features that are the hallmarks of avoidant attachment (Simpson & Rholes, 2012).

Highly secure individuals have received good, consistent, and predictable care from past attachment figures, especially when they were upset (Bowlby, 1973). During adulthood, therefore, secure individuals do not worry about relationship loss or their partners wanting to become emotionally closer to them. To the contrary, secure people want to develop greater closeness and intimacy with their partners (Mikulincer, 1998), which is facilitated by their use of constructive, problem-focused coping strategies. When most chronic or acute stressors are encountered, the benevolent working models of secure people should become activated (Mikulincer & Shaver, 2007b). Unlike their insecure counterparts, secure people should turn to their attachment figures openly and directly in order to solve their problems, quell their negative emotions, and move forward with their plans and goals.

During the past two decades, several studies have documented theoretically meaningful attachment style by situation effects (for reviews, see Mikulincer & Shaver, 2003, 2007a; chapter 19, this volume). Some of the most programmatic work on this topic has been conducted by Simpson, Rholes, and their colleagues (see Simpson & Rholes, 2012), who have spent 20 years testing attachment diathesis-stress effects in situations that, according to attachment theory, activate the working models of secure, anxious, or avoidant people. This body of work has focused on the unique role that different sources of stress assume in eliciting the quintessential features—the relational signatures—of attachment security, anxiety, and avoidance.

The first study in this program of research explored how adult romantic attachment styles moderate support-giving and support-seeking in romantic couples when one partner is waiting to engage in an "anxiety-provoking" task. Simpson, Rholes, and Nelligan (1992) unobtrusively videotaped dating couples while the female partner was waiting to do an activity that, she was told, made most people feel anxious. While she waited to do the stressful task (which never occurred), her male partner waited with her, believing that he was going to do a different, nonstressful activity. After the study, observers rated how distressed and how much support each female partner sought and how much support her male partner offered. Securely and avoidantly attached partners differed considerably in the amount of support they sought or gave, depending on how distressed the female partner was during the waiting period. If women were less distressed, they sought less support from their male partners, regardless of their attachment styles. If, however, women were more securely attached, they sought more support if they were more distressed, but less support if they were less distressed. Conversely, avoidant women sought *less* support if they were more distressed and more support if they were less distressed. Securely attached men provided more support if their partners were more distressed (regardless of the woman's attachment style), whereas avoidant men offered less support, especially when their partners were more distressed. Similar effects have been documented when the support-giving and support-receiving roles are reversed (i.e., when men wait to do a stressful task with their nonstressed female partners; Simpson, Rholes, Oriña, & Grich, 2002). Thus, corroborating specific person-by-situation predictions derived from attachment theory, highly avoidant people are not poorer support-seekers and support-providers in general; rather, they are deficient only when they or their partners are upset and support-seeking or giving is clearly required. Similarly, highly secure people do not always seek or provide greater support; they do so primarily when they or their partners are distressed and direct emotional support truly needs to be sought or provided.

The second study in this line of research examined how relationship-based sources of stress affect the display of different conflict resolution tactics, depending on each partner's attachment style. Simpson, Rholes, and Phillips (1996) randomly assigned dating couples to discuss either a major or a minor unresolved problem in their relationship. Each couple was then videotaped as the partners tried to resolve the problem as best they could. The discussions were then coded by observers. Consistent with attachment theory, more anxiously attached individuals reacted less positively toward their partners, but only when they were trying to resolve a *major* problem that posed a more serious threat to their relationship. For example, highly anxious individuals who discussed a major problem displayed greater distress and more discomfort during their discussions, and they reported feeling more anger and hostility toward their partners. At the end of their discussions, they perceived their partners and relationships less positively in terms of the amount of love, commitment, mutual respect, openness, and supportiveness in the relationship. Highly anxious women who discussed a major problem had discussions that were rated as lower in quality. Thus, consistent with specific person-by-situation predictions gleaned from attachment theory, highly anxious people do not think, feel, or behave in a less functional manner in all conflict situations; they do so mainly in stressful situations that call into question the permanence, stability, or quality of their close relationships. Less anxious (i.e., more secure) individuals, by comparison, respond in a more functional manner, particularly when dealing with major relationship conflicts.

We have also investigated how attachment to one's parents (measured by the Adult Attachment Interview; AAI) is related to the types of caregiving that "work best" in calming secure, anxious, and avoidant people when they are upset. Simpson, Winterheld, Rholes, and Oriña (2007) had both partners in romantic relationships complete the AAI. One week later, each couple was videotaped trying to resolve the most important current problem in their relationship. After the study, observers rated each discussion for the degree to which: (1) emotional, instrumental, and physical caregiving behaviors were displayed; (2) care recipients appeared calmed by their partner's caregiving attempts; and (3) each partner appeared distressed during the discussion. Individuals who had more secure representations of their parents were rated as more calmed if their partners gave them emotional care, especially if they were distressed during the discussion. Conversely, individuals who had more avoidant representations of their parents were more calmed by instrumental caregiving behaviors from their partners, especially if they were distressed. Thus, as anticipated by attachment theory, securely attached people benefit more from emotional forms of support (which they most likely received earlier in life), but chiefly when they are distressed. Avoidant people, in contrast, benefit more from instrumental support (which they probably received to some degree during childhood), but principally when they are upset. This indicates that avoidant people do benefit from certain forms of support, particularly those that may not threaten their sense of independence and autonomy. When secure and avoidant individuals are less distressed, however, they are both receptive to alternate forms of caregiving.

What are highly anxious people thinking and feeling in relationship-threatening situations that might explain why their relationships tend to be so turbulent and unstable? To address this question, Simpson, Ickes, and Grich (1999) had dating couples try to infer what their partners were thinking and feeling (from a videotape of their interaction) as both partners rated and discussed slides of attractive opposite-sex people who ostensibly were interested in meeting and dating new people on campus. This task was designed to be a relationship-threatening one, particularly for highly anxious people. In this relationship-threatening context, highly anxious individuals were better at inferring the relationship-threatening thoughts and feelings that their partners were actually having about the attractive opposite-sex stimulus persons during the rating and evaluation task. Highly anxious people, in other words, got more directly "into the heads" of their partners in this situation, showing signs of cognitive hypervigilance. Less anxious (more secure) persons, however, were less empathically accurate in this situation. If they were more empathically accurate, highly anxious individuals also perceived that their relationships were less stable and they felt more threatened and distressed during the rating and discussion task. They also reported sharp declines in feelings of closeness to their partners following the task. And highly anxious individuals who more accurately inferred their partner's threatening thoughts and feelings were more likely to have broken up with their partners 4 months later. In sum, this study confirms that highly anxious people "get into the heads" of their partners and accurately infer the relationship-threatening thoughts and feelings that their partners are having precisely when what they value the most—their relationships—could be in jeopardy. Highly anxious people are not more empathically accurate than other people in general; they are more accurate mainly in situations that threaten their relationships.

Most recently, we have investigated how people with different attachment styles remember their own behavior during attachment-relevant discussions with their romantic partners. Simpson, Rholes, and Winterheld (2010) had couples engage in two videotaped discussions of major, unresolved conflicts in their relationship. Immediately after the discussions, each partner reported how supportive and emotional distant s/he had been in the discussions. One week later, each partner returned to the lab and was asked to recall how supportive and emotionally distant s/he had been one week earlier. Highly avoidant individuals remembered being less supportive one week later, but only if they were distressed during the original discussions. Highly anxious individuals remembered being less emotionally distant, but only if they were distressed during the discussions. These memory biases are consistent with the cardinal needs and goals of highly avoidant and highly anxious people. Avoidant people want to limit intimacy and maintain control and autonomy in their relationships, so they remember themselves as being less supportive, particularly during difficult conversations with their partners. Anxious people, in contrast, desire greater felt security, so they remember themselves as being less emotionally distant (emotionally closer), particularly if their conversations were difficult.

Our program of research has also investigated how attachment styles are associated with reactions to chronically stressful life events. One such event is the transition to parenthood. Accordingly, we examined how the experience of having a first baby impacts the marital satisfaction of partners who have different attachment styles (Rholes, Simpson, Campbell, & Grich, 2001). Consistent with predictions, if highly anxious women enter the transition to parenthood perceiving less support from their husbands, they experience significant declines in marital satisfaction across the first 6–7 months of the transition. If, however, they enter parenthood perceiving greater spousal support, they do not report declines. Mediation analyses indicated that highly anxious women who enter the transition period perceiving less spousal support experience larger drops in perceived spousal support from the prenatal period to 6 months postpartum, which in turn predicts larger pre-to-postpartum declines in their marital satisfaction. Attachment avoidance was not related to marital changes, which is understandable given that avoidant people place less importance on the quality of their relationships.

Bowlby (1988) hypothesized that anxiously attached mothers who enter the transition to parenthood harboring doubts about the supportiveness of their partners should also experience postpartum increases in depressive symptoms. He reasoned that the perception of insufficient partner support should be tied to deeper and more pervasive concerns about possible relationship loss, especially among highly anxious people. If, however, highly anxious mothers enter the transition feeling well supported by their partners, they should be buffered from experiencing depressive symptoms. Bowlby (1988) also conjectured that the connection between (1) higher anxiety in combination with more doubts about the partner's supportiveness and (2) increases in depression should be mediated by (3) the degree to which these new mothers perceive declines in partner support during the first few months postpartum. Simpson, Rholes, Campbell, Tran, and Wilson (2003) found each of these effects in anxiously attached first-time mothers.

Our program of work has also tested how people with different attachment styles respond to less taxing yet still stressful daily events in their relationships. Campbell, Simpson, Boldry, and Kashy (2005) had both partners in dating relationships complete daily diaries for 14 consecutive days. After the diary period, each couple was videotaped trying to resolve the most contentious unresolved problem that arose during the diary period. Highly anxious individuals perceived greater daily conflict in their relationships, significantly more than their partners did. They also reported that daily conflicts were more detrimental to the future of their relationships. Moreover, on days when they perceived greater relationship-based conflict, highly anxious individuals believed that their partners had a more negative outlook on their relationship and its future, a view that typically was *not* shared by their partners. When partners discussed the most serious conflict in the lab after the diary phase, highly anxious individuals both reported and were rated as being more distressed, regardless of how positively their partners behave toward them (rated by observers) during their discussion. Less anxious (more secure) individuals exhibited the opposite pattern of effects in both the diary and the lab portions of this study.

Viewed in its entirety, this long-standing program of research (see Simpson & Rholes, 2012) has documented that certain types of stressful situations have powerful and unique effects on people who have different attachment styles. Our work has examined the way in which relationship partners think, feel, *and* behave in a variety of situations, including lab-based conflict and support interactions, lab-based relationship-threatening discussions, major life transitions, and everyday life stressors. Across these different social contexts, avoidant people are not always unsupportive, withdrawn, or uncooperative with their relationship partners; rather, these defining features of avoidance are elicited by certain types of stressful situations (e.g., feeling pressure to give or receive support, to become more intimate, to share deep emotions). Likewise, anxious people are not always clingy, demanding, or prone to engaging in dysfunctional conflict resolution tactics; instead, the cardinal features of anxiety are evoked by certain types of stressful situations (e.g., those that pose a threat to the stability or quality of their relationships). And secure people are not always supportive, nondepressed, or inclined to display functional conflict resolution tactics; the defining features of security are witnessed primarily in stressful situations that activate their positive working models and constructive interpersonal tendencies.

Future Directions

In this chapter, we have highlighted how and why the adoption of a person-by-situation or "interactionist" approach to the study of relationships can yield novel and deeper insights into important relationship dynamics, above and beyond what can be provided by adopting an exclusively trait or an exclusively situational approach. Although several interactionist programs of research currently exist within the relationships field, person-by-situation perspectives are by no means the norm. In fact, there are several prominent domains of theory and research with in both personality and social psychology that could benefit from the application of interactionist frameworks. Some long-standing lines of research might be enriched and expanded by infusing what we know about certain individual differences into extant social psychological theories and models. Other significant lines of research could be extended and refined by incorporating the functional meaning of different types of situations into personality-based theories and models.

With respect to how individual differences might inform major social psychological theories and models, let's return to interdependence theory. This comprehensive theory, which focuses on how relationship partners make decisions about what to do given the payoffs associated with doing different activities with or without the partner, has not systematically examined whether and how people who score high versus low on certain trait-like measures (e.g., self-esteem, neuroticism, attachment insecurity) perceive and respond to certain types of situations differently (see Kelley et al., 2003). For example, when deciding what to do in situations that could reveal whether the current partner really

Kelley, H. H., & Thibaut, J. W. (1978). *Interpersonal relationships: A theory of interdependence.* New York: Wiley.

Kelly, G. A. (1955). *The psychology of personal constructs.* New York: Norton.

Kenny, D. A., Kashy, D. A., & Cook, W. L. (2006). *Dyadic data analysis.* New York: Guilford.

Kobak, R. R., & Duemmler, S. (1994). Attachment and conversation: Toward a discourse analysis of adolescent and adult security. In K. Bartholomew & D. Perlman (Eds.), *Advances in personal relationships: Vol. 5. Attachment processes in adulthood* (pp. 121–149). London: Kingsley.

Kobak, R. R., & Sceery, A. (1988). Attachment in late adolescence: Working models, affect regulation, and representations of self and others. *Child Development, 59,* 135–146.

Lakey, B., McCabe, K. M., Fisicaro, S. A., & Drew, J. B. (1996). Environmental and personal determinants of support perceptions: Three generalizability studies. *Journal of Personality and Social Psychology, 70,* 1270–1280.

Levine, J. M., Higgins, E. T., & Choi, H. S. (2000). Development of strategic norms in groups. *Organizational Behavior and Human Decision Processes, 82,* 88–101.

Lewin, K. (1936). *A dynamic theory of personality.* New York: McGraw-Hill.

Lewin, K. (1948). *Resolving social conflicts: Selected papers on group dynamics.* New York: Harper.

Main, M. (1981). Avoidance in the service of attachment: A working paper. In K. Immelmann, G. Barlow, M. Main, & L. Petrinovich (Eds.), *Behavioral development: The Bielefeld interdisciplinary project* (pp. 651–693). New York: Cambridge University Press.

Malloy, T. E., & Kenny, D. A. (1986). The social relations model: An integrative method for personality research. *Journal of Personality, 54,* 199–225.

Manian, N., Papadakis, A. A., Strauman, T. J., & Essex, M. (2006). The development of children's ideal and ought self-guides: Parenting, temperament, and individual differences in guide strength. *Journal of Personality, 74,* 1619–1646.

Maslach, C., Santee, R. T., & Wade, C. (1987). Individuation, gender role, and dissent: Personality mediators of situational forces. *Journal of Personality and Social Psychology, 53,* 1088–1093.

Mikulincer, M. (1998). Adult attachment style and individual differences in functional versus dysfunctional experiences of anger. *Journal of Personality and Social Psychology, 74,* 513–524.

Mikulincer, M., & Florian, V. (1998). The relationship between adult attachment styles and emotional and cognitive reactions to stressful events. In J. A. Simpson & W. S. Rholes (Eds.), *Attachment theory and close relationships* (pp. 143–165). New York: Guilford.

Mikulincer, M., Gillath, O., & Shaver, P. R. (2002). Activation of the attachment system in adulthood: Threat-related primes increase the accessibility of mental representations of attachment figures. *Journal of Personality and Social Psychology, 83,* 881–895.

Mikulincer, M., & Shaver, P. R. (2003). The attachment behavioral system in adulthood: Activation, psychodynamics, and interpersonal processes. In M. P. Zanna (Ed.), *Advances in experimental social psychology* (Vol. 35, pp. 53–152). New York: Academic.

Mikulincer, M., & Shaver, P. R. (2007a). *Attachment in adulthood: Structure, dynamics, and change.* New York: Guilford.

Mikulincer, M., & Shaver, P. R. (2007b). Boosting attachment security to promote mental health, pro-social values, and inter-group tolerance. *Psychological Inquiry, 18,* 139–165.

Mischel, W. (1968). *Personality and assessment.* New York: Wiley.

Mischel, W. (1999). Personality coherence and dispositions in a cognitive-affective personality system (CAPS) approach. In D. Cervone & Y. Shoda (Eds.), *The coherence of personality: Social-cognitive bases of consistency, variability, and organization* (pp. 37–60). New York: Guilford.

Mischel, W., & Shoda, Y. (1995). A cognitive-affective system theory of personality: Reconceptualizing situations, dispositions, dynamics, and invariance in personality structure. *Psychological Review, 102,* 246–268.

Mischel, W., Shoda, Y., & Mendoza-Denton, R. (2002). Situation-behavior profiles as a locus of consistency in personality. *Current Directions in Psychological Science, 11,* 50–54.

Molden, D. C., Lee, A. Y., & Higgins, E. T. (2008). Motivations for promotion and prevention. In J. Shah & W. Gardner (Eds.), *Handbook of motivation science* (pp. 169–187). New York: Guilford.

Molden, D. C., Lucas, G. M., Finkel, E. J., Kumashiro, M., & Rusbult, C. E. (2009). Perceived support for promotion-focused and prevention-focused goals: Associations with well-being in unmarried and married couples. *Psychological Science, 20,* 787–793.

Murray, H. A. (1938). *Explorations in personality: A clinical and experimental study of fifty men of college age.* Oxford, UK: Oxford University Press.

Murray, S. L., Holmes, J. G., & Collins, N. L. (2006). Optimizing assurance: The risk regulation system in relationships. *Psychological Bulletin, 132,* 641–666.

Murray, S. L., Holmes, J. G., & Griffin, D. W. (1996a). The benefits of positive illusions: Idealization and the construction of satisfaction in close relationships. *Journal of Personality and Social Psychology Bulletin, 70,* 79–98.

Murray, S. L., Holmes, J. G., & Griffin, D. W. (1996b). The self-fulfilling nature of positive illusions in romantic relationships: Love is not blind, but prescient. *Journal of Personality and Social Psychology, 71,* 1155–1180.

Murray, S. L., Holmes, J. G., & Griffin, D. W. (2000). Self-esteem and the quest for felt security: How perceived regard regulates attachment processes. *Journal of Personality and Social Psychology, 78,* 478–498.

Murray, S. L., Holmes, J. G., MacDonald, G., & Ellsworth, P. C. (1998). Through the looking glass darkly? When self-doubt turns into relationship insecurities. *Journal of Personality and Social Psychology, 75,* 1459–1480.

Murray, S. L., Rose, P., Bellavia, G., Holmes, J. G., & Kusche, A. (2002). When rejection stings: How self-esteem constrains relationship-enhancement processes. *Journal of Personality and Social Psychology, 83,* 556–573.

Neisser, U. (1967). *Cognitive psychology.* New York: Appleton-Century-Crofts.

Rholes, W. S., Simpson, J. A., Campbell, L., & Grich, J. (2001). Adult attachment and the transition to parenthood. *Journal of Personality and Social Psychology, 81,* 421–435.

Sarason, I. G., Sarason, B. R., & Shearin, E. N. (1986). Social support as an individual difference variable: Its stability, origins, and relational aspects. *Journal of Personality and Social Psychology, 50,* 845–855.

Sassenberg, K., Kessler, T., & Mummendey, A. (2003). Less negative = more positive? Social discrimination as avoidance or approach. *Journal of Experimental Social Psychology, 39,* 48–58.

Shaffer, D. R., Ogden, J. K., & Wu, C. (1987). Effects of self-monitoring and prospect of future interaction on self-disclosure reciprocity during the acquaintance process. *Journal of Personality, 55,* 75–96.

Shah, J. (2003). The motivational looking glass: How significant others implicitly affect goal appraisals. *Journal of Personality and Social Psychology, 85,* 424–439.

Shah, J., Higgins, E. T., & Friedman, R. S. (1998). Performance incentives and means: How regulatory focus influences goal attainment. *Journal of Personality and Social Psychology, 74,* 285–293.

Shah, J. Y., Brazy, P. C., & Higgins, E. T. (2004). Promoting us vs. preventing them: Regulatory focus and the manifestations of intergroup bias. *Personality and Social Psychology Bulletin, 30,* 433–446.

Shoda, Y., Mischel, W., & Wright, J. C. (1994). Intra-individual stability in the organization and patterning of behavior: Incorporating psychological situations into the idiographic analysis of personality. *Journal of Personality and Social Psychology, 65,* 1023–1035.

Simpson, J. A. (2007). Foundations of interpersonal trust. In A. W. Kruglanski & E. T. Higgins (Eds.), *Social psychology: Handbook of basic principles* (2nd ed., pp. 587–607). New York: Guilford.

Simpson, J. A., Ickes, W., & Grich, J. (1999). When accuracy hurts: Reactions of anxious-ambivalent dating partners to a relationship-threatening situation. *Journal of Personality and Social Psychology, 76,* 754–769.

Simpson, J. A., & Rholes, W. S. (1994). Stress and secure base relationships in adulthood. In K. Bartholomew & D. Perlman (Eds.), *Advances in personal relationships: Vol. 5. Attachment processes in adulthood* (pp. 181–204). London: Kingsley.

Simpson, J. A., & Rholes, W. S. (2012). Adult attachment orientations, stress, and romantic relationships. In P. G. Devine, A. Plant, J. Olson, & M. Zanna (Eds.), *Advances in experimental social psychology, Vol. 45.* New York: Elsevier.

Simpson, J. A., Rholes, W. S., Campbell, L., Tran, S., & Wilson, C. L. (2003). Adult attachment, the transition to parenthood, and depressive symptoms. *Journal of Personality and Social Psychology, 84,* 1172–1187.

Simpson, J. A., Rholes, W. S., & Nelligan, J. S. (1992). Support-seeking and support-giving within couple members in an anxiety-provoking situation: The role of attachment styles. *Journal of Personality and Social Psychology, 62,* 434–446.

Simpson, J. A., Rholes, W. S., Oriña, M. M., & Grich, J. (2002). Working models of attachment, support giving, and support seeking in a stressful situation. *Personality and Social Psychology Bulletin, 28,* 598–608.

Simpson, J. S., Rholes, W. S., & Phillips, D. (1996). Conflict in close relationships: An attachment perspective. *Journal of Personality and Social Psychology, 71,* 899–914.

Simpson, J. A., Rholes, W. S., & Winterheld, H. A. (2010). Attachment working models twist memories of relationship events. *Psychological Science, 21,* 252–259.

Simpson, J. A., Winterheld, H. A., Rholes, W. S., & Oriña, M. M. (2007). Working models of attachment and reactions to different forms of caregiving from romantic partners. *Journal of Personality and Social Psychology, 93,* 466–477.

Snyder, M., Berscheid, E., & Glick. P. (1985). Focusing on the exterior and the interior: Two investigations of the initiation of personal relationships. *Journal of Personality and Social Psychology, 48,* 1427–1439.

Snyder, M., & Cantor, N. (1998). Understanding personality and social behavior: A functionalist strategy. In D. T. Gilbert, S. T. Fiske, & G. Lindzey (Eds.), *Handbook of social psychology* (4th ed., pp. 635–679). New York: McGraw-Hill.

Snyder, M., Gangestad, S., & Simpson, J. A. (1983). Choosing friends as activity partners: The role of self-monitoring. *Journal of Personality and Social Psychology, 45,* 1061–1072.

Snyder, M., & Ickes, W. (1985). Personality and social behavior. In G. Lindzey & E. Aronson (Eds.), *Handbook of social psychology* (3rd ed., pp. 883–947). New York: Random House.

Sroufe, L. A., & Waters, E. (1977). Attachment as an organizational construct. *Child Development, 48,* 1184–1199.

Thibaut, J. W., & Kelley, H. H. (1959). *The social psychology of groups.* New York: Wiley.

Thompson, E. P., Chaiken, S., & Hazelwood, J. D. (1993). Need for cognition and desire for control as moderators of extrinsic reward effects: A person x situation approach to the study of intrinsic motivation. *Journal of Personality and Social Psychology, 64,* 987–999.

Wicker, A. W. (1969). Attitudes versus actions: The relationship of verbal and overt behavioral responses to attitude objects. *Journal of Social Issues, 25,* 41–78.

Winterheld, H. A. (2008). *Regulatory focus and social support: A dyadic perspective.* Unpublished dissertation: University of Minnesota, Minneapolis, MN.

Winterheld, H. A., & Simpson, J. A. (2011). *Seeking security or growth: A regulatory focus perspective on motivations in romantic relationships. Journal of Personality and Social Psychology.*

Zaki, J., Bolger, N., & Ochsner, K. (2008). It takes two: The interpersonal nature of empathic accuracy. *Psychological Science, 19,* 399–404.

Zayas, V., Shoda, Y., & Ayduk, O. N. (2002). Personality in context: An interpersonal systems perspective. *Journal of Personality, 70,* 851–900.

Zuwerink, J. R., & Devine, P. G. (1996). Attitude importance and resistance to persuasion: It's not just the thought that counts. *Journal of Personality and Social Psychology, 70,* 931–944.

Personality Influences on Group Processes
The Past, Present, and Future

Craig D. Parks

Abstract

This chapter addresses the role of personality traits in group decision-making and performance processes. I begin with a review of the history of interaction between group and personality researchers to show that, at one time, the domains went hand in hand. Methodological concerns in the 1950s, however, led group researchers to move away from personality, resulting in a piecemeal approach to personality influences in groups. Following this historical analysis, I review modern work in conflict, group performance, group decision-making, and group maintenance, with a key theme being that although there are few systematic studies of traits in groups, there is in fact quite a bit of isolated work being done. I conclude with a discussion of the barriers to increased collaboration between the two camps, why such collaboration is important for both, and some ideas about what a person x situation interaction within a group might reflect.

Keywords: group decision-making, social dilemmas, group task performance, group membership

Within the field of groups research, much emphasis is currently placed on the idea that groups are an information-processing unit: Information enters the unit via group member knowledge and expertise, and/or introduction by an external source; the information is examined by group members as to its relevance and value for the group task; it is then integrated somehow; and a decision or action is produced (Hinsz, Tindale, & Vollrath, 1997). Consideration of groups in this light bears marked similarity to analyses of how individuals deal with social information, and indeed, groups researchers are now investigating a number of information-processing-type phenomena, like memory analogues (e.g., Austin, 2003), selective information processing (Wittenbaum, Hollingshead, & Botero, 2004), and group-level emotions (Mackie, Silver, & Smith, 2004). In this way, researchers are able to tackle the larger question of to what extent individual-level phenomena are influential when people are aggregated and must take collective action.

Seemingly absent in this work is a consideration of the role of individual differences in group performance. Indeed, as one looks across the relatively recent history of groups research, it is difficult to find much evidence that individual differences have been systematically tested as an influence on group output. One might well conclude that research on groups has evolved independently from research on individual differences. Such a conclusion would not be completely correct, but unfortunately would have some basis in truth.

In this chapter, I review work and ideas that are seated at the intersection of group process and individual difference research. We will see that, while we do have some good evidence that individual differences can influence group outcomes, there are a number of potentially fruitful research questions that have so far gone largely unasked. This work has progressed largely piecemeal, and one of my primary goals is to highlight the gaps in our knowledge. We will look at how personality research has contributed to our understanding of group performance, group decision-making, and group maintenance. Our focus will be on four general types of group situations: conflict, task performance, decision-making, and group maintenance. The first three follow from McGrath's (1984) circumplex model of group task type (and I address his fourth major type, idea generation, in the section on decision-making), and group maintenance is an important aspect of group functioning that cuts across all task types. Note that I will not address the role of social identity, or more accurately the interplay of social identity and personality, in group performance. This is not because social identity is an unimportant variable in modeling of groups. Far from it. Rather, social identity affects enough of the processes that we will discuss that a thorough treatment of the topic would make this chapter unduly large.

Before discussing the actual group processes, it is useful to ask why there is not a more collaborative history between the two subdisciplines. As we will see shortly, in the early days of social psychology, groups researchers also wrote on personality traits, and vice versa. Why did this not continue? Is it just happenstance that things ended up as they are today? The answer, not surprisingly, is no. That groups researchers have not given careful study to personality variables, and vice versa, is predictable from historical developments in each area.

A Brief History of the Groups–Individual Differences Interface

It was not always the case that group and individual difference research were separated. A basic tenet of some early theories of personality was that the social groups to which one belongs are primal influences on personality development (e.g., Lewin, 1935; see also Krech & Crutchfield, 1948). In their early model of cooperative processes, May and Doob (1937) noted that the model was only applicable to those with "normal" personalities, and that systematic research on cooperation by people with unusual sets of traits was necessary. Lippitt and White (1943), in their classic study of styles of leadership within groups of children, were careful to equate the groups on a number of personality variables. Lewin (1939, 1944), who was a prominent personality theorist before moving into the study of groups, argued that natural groups offer an excellent venue for studying both normal and abnormal personality characteristics, and for learning how to induce changes in personality. Early organizational

psychologists had suggested that the content of personality in adults was in part shaped by the nature of the work group to which the person belonged (Hughes, 1928; Merton, 1940). Finally, Sherif (1948), in his overview of social psychology, suggested that personality traits would likely affect a plethora of group-related phenomena (e.g., formation of ingroups and outgroups, amount and nature of interaction among group members, expression of prejudice), and that expression of a particular trait would be influenced by one's ingroups, one's roles within such groups, the extent to which one is entrusted with responsibilities by other group members, and the nature of group goals. At the end of the 1940s, then, the notion that groups research and personality research go hand in hand was well established.

A decade later, however, Thibaut and Kelley (1959) described a detailed model of interpersonal group processes with no reference at all to personality characteristics. Their model was instead oriented primarily around principles of conditioning, and was quickly characterized as a strict stimulus-response approach to groups (see Berger & Lambert, 1968).[1] A little later, Steiner (1966, 1972) presented his ideas on group productivity, again with no reference to the potential impact of personality variables; he argued that the individual-level factors that affect group performance are the person's skills and abilities and knowledge base relevant to the task. As these two sets of theorists together provide the framework for most contemporary research on groups, that personality-based factors would seem underrepresented in today's literature is not surprising. The question then becomes, what produced such a rapid shift in the zeitgeist?

I suggest that personality as a predictor variable got caught in the cross fire that was produced when post–World War II researchers searched for better methods for researching groups. The twin solutions, generated during the 1950s, were not designed to incorporate traits into the research plan. These solutions, specifically, were the application of behaviorist principles, and conception of the group as a productivity system.[2]

Behaviorism

Early modern research into groups, which is usually taken to have started with Shaw's (1932) comparison of individual and group problem-solving, was all over the place in terms of both methodology and findings. Preexisting groups were sometimes studied in their natural settings, and sometimes brought

respondents with nine three-option choice tasks, each structured as our "Situation A-B-C" example above. The person's orientation is indicated if they make at least six choices that are of the same motivation. This method has proven to have good test-retest reliability over as much as six months (van Lange & Semin-Goossens, 1998).

Though there is some evidence that SVO may have a genetic basis (Rushton, Fulker, Neale, Nias, & Eysenck, 1986), it is generally thought to result from some social learning process. Knight, Dubro, and Chao (1985) showed that individualistic children, regardless of age, perform more poorly on memory tasks than do other children, and suggested that the application of learned behavior-outcome associations will be partly a function of cognitive capability. Knight and Kagan (1981) found American girls more frequently individualistic than boys, and attributed this to the children having learned that deviation from social standards (in this case, the American emphasis on individualism) is less acceptable for females than for males. Related to this, McClintock and Keil (1983) summarized a series of cross-cultural studies of children in which the point at which regular cooperative behavior occurs is predictable from the culture's degree of emphasis on cooperation, suggesting that socialization has some influence on SVO. In studies of adults, van Lange and colleagues (van Lange, Otten, De Bruin, & Joireman, 1997) showed that, relative to individualists and competitors, cooperators are more likely to show a secure attachment style. This is an important relationship from a social learning standpoint, because attachment style is assumed to result directly from past interaction experiences. Van Lange et al. also found cooperators to have come from larger families; the logic here is that such families provide more opportunities to experience conflict and conflict resolution. Taken as a whole, this research suggests that one's SVO is a function of one's social experiences, filtered through one's cognitive capabilities and cultural standards.

Social value orientation seems to influence cooperative behavior by operating on perceptions of the situation and of how others' actions are interpreted. Regarding the situation, individualists and competitors tend to view mixed-motive situations in terms of power: To compete means that one is strong, whereas cooperation reflects weakness and an unwillingness to stand up to others. By contrast, cooperators see the situation in terms of intelligence. Cooperation is the smart thing to do because it produces quality outcomes in the long run, whereas competition is an unintelligent strategy because it leads to short-term gain, but long-term loss (Liebrand, Jansen, Rijken, & Suhre, 1986). In terms of the actions of others, the key issue is the speed with which the other person performs a behavior that is in response to the actor. How quickly does Other respond to selfishness with selfishness, or to cooperation with cooperation? A quick response seems to strengthen the influence of SVO on behavior, as competitors are especially competitive, and cooperators especially cooperative, with those who immediately imitate their actions (Parks & Rumble, 2001). Different levels of SVO, then, produce different outlooks on the nature of a mixed-motive interaction.

Social value orientation has also been extensively studied within the realm of negotiation. The general finding is that SVO matters only when negotiators are relatively resistant to making concessions. When this is the case, prosocial negotiators approach the situation as a problem to be solved and with low levels of contentiousness; as a result, they are more successful than proself negotiators (De Dreu, Weingart, & Kwon, 2000). More recent work indicates that negotiations among prosocial individuals benefit from use of reciprocation, but negotiations among proself individuals are harmed by reciprocation (Olekalns & Smith, 2003), and that prosocial negotiators are sensitive to the orientations of other negotiators and adjust their approaches accordingly, but proself negotiators are not (Weingart, Brett, Olekalns, & Smith, 2007).

Social value orientation has been studied extensively since its introduction in the mid-1960s (see Messick & McClintock, 1968), and meta-analysis of these data reveal a medium-effect relationship between SVO and cooperation (Balliet, Parks, & Joireman, 2009). Social value orientation also predicts behavior in other interpersonal situations, such as close relationships (van Lange, Agnew, Harinck, & Steemers, 1997) and support for charitable endeavors (van Lange, Bekkers, Schuyt, & van Vugt, 2007), to name just two.

"Big Five" Traits

Not surprisingly, researchers have wondered whether Big Five traits might also predict cooperative behavior, as most of the five lend themselves to some predictions about how they might relate to cooperation. The greatest amount of work has been done on agreeableness, and these studies clearly show a direct relationship between degree of agreeableness and frequency of cooperation (e.g., Graziano, Habashi,

Sheese, & Tobin, 2007; Graziano, Jensen-Campbell, & Hair, 1996; Jensen-Campbell, Graziano, & Hair, 1996; Koole, Jager, van den Berg, Vlek, & Hofstee, 2001; Ross, Rausch, & Canada, 2003). An important effect that emerges from this body of work is the finding that low-agreeable individuals are more likely to favor power-based solutions to the mixed-motive task (Graziano et al., 1996; Jensen-Campbell et al., 1996) and to favor more aggressive negotiation tactics (V. F. Wood & Bell, 2008) than high-agreeable individuals. In fact, high-agreeable individuals are generally unsuccessful at securing satisfying negotiated outcomes, as are extraverts, though this effect is mitigated somewhat if the person has high aspirations (Barry & Friedman, 1998). Related to this, negotiators often try to infer, from the opponent's behavior, the extent to which that person is agreeable (Morris, Larrick, & Su, 1999). As we just noted, cognitions about power are also a distinguishing factor for the different types of SVO. Finally, some negotiation theorists have begun looking at unmitigated communion (UC; Fritz & Helgeson, 1998) as a trait predictor that is distinct from agreeableness. Someone who is high on UC has a high level of concern for, and anxiety about, relationships, but a low level of concern for self. The negotiation work suggests that high-UC individuals will make unusually large concessions in order to avoid stressing the relationship (Amanatullah, Morris, & Curhan, 2008).

There exists a small amount of work on other of the Big Five. Specifically, there is some evidence that extraversion and cooperation are inversely related (Graziano, Feldesman, & Rahe, 1985; Koole et al., 2001; Ross et al., 2003), though questions have been raised about exactly how extraversion influences cooperation (Wolfe & Kasmer, 1988). There seems to be no systematic work on openness, conscientiousness, or neuroticism within mixed-motive contexts, though one could argue that each might affect mixed-motive choice: A high-conscientious person might be especially attuned to group-level needs; an open person might be flexible in terms of responding to the choices of others; a neurotic person might be concerned with how others perceive his/her choices. Broader study of the Big Five within mixed-motive settings would be valuable.

Individual-Group Discontinuity

A special kind of conflict situation is individual-group discontinuity, or the tendency for interactions between two groups to be more hostile and competitive than analogous interaction between two individuals (Insko & Schopler, 1998). While a number of different explanations have been offered for the phenomenon (e.g., maintenance of a schema that characterizes groups as less trustworthy than individuals, perceived pressure to benefit one's group as much as possible), less attention has been paid to whether different traits might predict to what extent one expects group-level interaction to be contentious. However, some work has been done on the role of dispositional proneness to guilt in the existence of the discontinuity. In general, this work suggests that the discontinuity effect is especially prominent in those who are prone to guilt, seemingly because such people are concerned about meeting their obligations to their ingroup when in a group interaction situation, a concern labeled by researchers as "group morality." Low guilt-prone individuals, on the other hand, are more concerned with interpersonal civility or "individual morality" (politeness, fairness, reciprocation), and so behave with consideration to all regardless of the situation (e.g., Pinter et al., 2007). Along these lines, Ketelaar and Au (2003) found that people who failed to cooperate in an individual-level interaction, and then reported feeling guilty about their actions, subsequently became more cooperative relative to those who did not report feeling guilty, even if the next action was delayed by as much as a week. Ketelaar and Au did not specifically assess guilt proneness, but it was measured via self-report, and it is possible that this report reflected a general proclivity toward feeling guilty. Certainly their results are consistent with the notions of individual and group morality.

Summary

Studies of the role of personality in at least some types of cooperative interpersonal behavior are many and have provided important insight into resolution of mixed-motive situations. The reader will have noticed, however, that this section is slanted toward research on social dilemma situations. With the exception of SVO, attempts to assess the contribution of personality traits to negotiation behavior are few. This is not a unique insight. Twenty-five years ago, Lewicki and Litterer (1985) lamented the dearth of studies of personality influences on negotiation behavior. Unfortunately, nothing has changed, and the discipline is still in need of programmatic study of the issue.

It is also worth noting that there have been few attempts to discover the limits of trait influence on cooperation. Integration of a person-situation framework into this area has been called for in the past (van Lange, 2000), but such work is only just getting under way (Graziano et al., 2007). This is unfortunate, because past studies have provided tantalizing glimpses into what those limits might be. For example, van Lange and Liebrand (1991) found that people with a competitive SVO would nonetheless be completely cooperative if they knew the Other was a truly nonexploitative individual, like a priest. Thus, while they could take maximum advantage of this person, the competitors recognized that to do so was simply wrong, and they refrained. This is admittedly a rather extreme stimulus person, but it raises the question of how much more typical the person would have to be before personality begins to influence choice. And, at the other end, how mundane does the situation have to be before choice is driven only by traits? These are issues that simply have not been explored.

Task Groups

Integration of personality characteristics into the study of task-performing groups coincides with the growth, in the 1980s, of interest in groups by organizational psychologists. This attraction encouraged study of trait influences for two reasons. First, personality traits, and more general individual differences, have long been of interest to those trying to understand workplace behavior. Consider, for example, the ever-debated question of what combination of characteristics makes for a good leader. (See van Knippenberg, chapter 27, this volume.) Second, organizational researchers were quick to distinguish between a "group," or mere collection of individuals, and a "team," which is a set of people who have an interpersonal dynamic (Hackman, 1987). Part of this dynamic is the ability of group members to work together, and such a concern demands that personality traits be part of the mix. As well, while organizational psychologists largely retained the group-as-system approach, at the same time they saw practical limitations to that framework, in that managers of work groups finally have to be concerned with both the quantity and quality of what is coming out of the group (Ilgen, 1999). Both of these have to be influenced by individual differences among workers; it thus makes sense to consider such differences when studying task groups.

A group, not being an actual organism, cannot have a personality, so the impact of personality on group performance is assumed to occur through the range of levels of a trait across group members.

As we shall see, with some traits maximal benefit is derived from having trait homogeneity across group members, but for other traits heterogeneity is preferred.

The Big Five

The Big Five have received far and away the most attention in the prediction of group performance. Two meta-analyses executed almost simultaneously found both agreeableness and conscientiousness to predict level of group performance (Bell, 2007; Peeters, van Tuijl, Rutte, & Reymen, 2006). That these two are important is, on the surface, readily explainable: High-conscientious people would realize that the group needs to produce quality output in a timely fashion, while high-agreeable people would be easy to get along with. However, these two analyses reported somewhat different dynamics regarding how the trait manifests itself. Bell found the minimum level of agreeableness within the group to be (positively) predictive of performance, but Peeters et al. found its mean (positive) and variability (negative) to be the key indicators. Bell is thus arguing that the group is only as good as its least agreeable member, while Peeters and colleagues would say that the group needs its members to have about the same levels of agreeableness, and that the mean level needs to be high. Regarding conscientiousness, both found the mean level to be (positively) predictive, but Peeters et al. found that its variability is (negatively) predictive as well. Further, Bell also found openness to experience to be predictive, but Peeters et al. did not. Why the two analyses produced different patterns of results is almost certainly due to different standards for inclusion of studies in the database; whether those differences represent predictive factors, or simple chance variation, needs investigation.

More recently, researchers have argued that different types of tasks require different combinations and levels of Big Five traits. This notion is termed *group personality composition* (GPC) and has been supported through both meta-analysis of prior work (Halfhill, Sundstrom, Lahner, Calderone, & Nielsen, 2005) and observation of real groups in the field (Halfhill, Nielsen, & Sundstrom, 2008). In general, this research suggests that, in some situations, one needs to be most concerned with the minimal level of a trait within the group; in other situations, it is the mean level that needs attention; and in still others the variance is most crucial. For example, Halfhill et al. (2008) found that mean levels of agreeableness and conscientiousness best predicted group performance, as did variation (inversely) in conscientiousness, but minimum levels of both traits predicted observer perceptions of the group's performance. (As real task groups are often evaluated by a superior, observer perceptions are an important consideration.) Along these same lines, some have argued that any analysis of personality influences on group performance needs to distinguish between led and self-managed groups, as there is some evidence that extraversion is more important than agreeableness in leaderless groups (e.g., Humphrey, Hollenbeck, Meyer, & Ilgen, 2007).

Theorists have also investigated potential connections between Big Five traits and entire organizations. The idea here is that the organization (which is ultimately one gigantic task group) will attract and recruit individuals, especially subgroup leaders, of a particular type, and members who are not of that type will migrate out. The long-term result will be an organization that is quite homogeneous. Data do support this idea (e.g., Giberson, Resick, & Dickson, 2005).

Finally, researchers have begun studying how Big Five dimensions relate to group member response to group failure. The best evidence suggests that, if failure can be attributed to particular members, others attend to the failing member's perceived level of conscientiousness before deciding whether to help or punish that person (Taggar & Neubert, 2004, 2008). The decision may also be influenced by the perceiver's levels of extraversion and agreeableness (Jackson & LePine, 2003), though at present these connections are only weakly established.

Trust

Trust has also been studied in regard to its role in task group performance, though the current state of knowledge is not nearly as thorough as that for trust and mixed-motive behavior. This may be because the impact of trust on group performance is proving to be complicated, as there is little evidence for a direct link between the two. Instead, trust seems to have indirect effects on group performance, affecting such variables as team member motivation (Dirks, 1999), knowledge sharing (Quigley, Tesluk, Locke, & Bartol, 2007), willingness to critique individual member contributions (Langfred, 2004), and commitment to the group (Costa, Roe, & Taillieu, 2001), and mediating the link between interpersonal conflict and group performance (Rispens, Greer, & Jehn, 2007). It is worth noting that this research is characterized by the same lack of consistency in operational definitions of trust as we saw in the work on mixed-motive choice. As well, no research has yet been conducted on how task group members deal with differing levels of trust across members, and how those differences impact overall group performance. Clearly there is much more that needs to be done.

Un(der)studied Traits

The narrow focus on the Big Five appears to have diverted attention away from other traits that might also help explain group performance. There are a host of data sets that identify potentially important traits that have not, to date, been followed up: The 16PF dimensions of dominance (Davies & Kanaki, 2006) and emotional stability (van der Zee, Atsma, & Brodbeck, 2004); narcissism (Campbell, Bush, Brunell, & Shelton, 2005); self-reliance (Daus & Joplin, 1999); and optimism (Watson, Chemers, & Preiser, 2001), to name a few. As well, some theorists have argued for the need to study particular traits in connection to group performance, but those arguments have so far fallen by the wayside. For example, DeMatteo, Eby, and Sundstrom (1998) suggested that need for achievement might be an important influence on a group member's contribution to the group product, but no one seems to have formally tested this idea. Similarly, Keinen and Koren (2002) argued for the need to study the performance of groups composed of different mixtures of Type A and B individuals, but again, no one seems to have responded to their call. There is thus quite a bit of room for personality researchers with interest in group performance to pursue new ideas.

Sport Groups

A special type of performing group is a sport team. Despite their unusual dynamic and circumstances, sport teams have a number of features in common with general task groups: They are small; consist of members who have special expertise for the task; aggregate individual efforts into a single output; and can be affected by interpersonal aspects. It is thus reasonable to ask whether phenomena that occur in regular task groups also manifest themselves in sport teams, and sport-team researchers have looked into how personality traits impact the dynamics and performance of the team.

A dominant trait in this literature is "sport-confidence" (Vealey, Hayashi, Garner-Holman, & Giacobbi, 1998). It is treated as having both trait and state components, and is alternately defined as

decide for themselves when there is sufficient agreement as to the proper course of action. Determination of consensus is an overall understudied phenomenon, but in general this work shows that the "majority wins" idea dominates (Ladbury & Hinsz, 2009), even though a "2/3-majority wins" rule is a better descriptor of what actually happens within a group (Stasser, 1999). The question then arises, do people with particular levels of certain traits favor more or less stringent rules for consensus?

Research directed toward this question is especially sparse. The only study that seems to have directly investigated it suggests that, collectively, groups in which the mean levels of extraversion, openness, and agreeableness are high contain members who are more likely to adhere to an assigned decision rule, and groups in which the mean levels are low contain members who are more likely to deviate and create their own rule (Sager & Gastil, 2006). However, there are some other questions suggested by research on individual decision-makers that deserve attention. For example, are people with particular traits more likely to demand unanimity than others? This is important because there is usually no need for all group members to concur—majority rules typically lead to appropriate group decisions (Hastie & Kameda, 2005), and there is no evidence that intragroup relations are necessarily harmed by some members disagreeing with the chosen action, as people will usually accept a negative decision if they feel they were allowed to fully express and justify their preference (e.g., Tyler, Degoey, & Smith, 1995). As achievement of unanimity is more effortful and time-consuming, there is usually no good reason to apply this rule instead of majority.[7] The motivations of a person who demands it anyway are thus an interesting psychological issue. One can imagine a number of traits that might plausibly encourage someone to want complete agreement before committing the group to a position: dominance, authoritarianism, and neuroticism, to name just three. Yet no studies of this issue seem to have been conducted. This represents yet another potentially fruitful line of inquiry that hopefully will be initiated soon.

RISK

A long-standing issue within the study of group decision-making is how group members reach consensus on risky alternatives. The basic premise is that the group decision will exaggerate the prevailing preference across individuals: The consensus will more strongly favor taking the risk if the members were generally inclined toward risk, and will more strongly favor caution if members were inclined toward caution. While no one has as yet examined how personality traits might influence group risk decisions, there is an emerging literature on trait influences on individual risk decisions that is readily applicable to group questions. For example, Soane and Chmiel (2005) found that people who are low-neurotic, high-conscientious, and high-agreeable are consistently risk averse, whereas different combinations of these traits described people whose risk tolerance was more situation specific. More generally, people who have a propensity to take risks have a Big Five profile of extraversion and openness, combined with low levels of conscientiousness, agreeableness, and neuroticism (Nicholson, Soane, Fenton-O'Creevy, & Willman, 2005). Uncertainty orientation may also predict risk tolerance, with UOs being more favorably disposed to risk than COs (Sorrentino, Hewitt, & Raso-Knott, 1992). As well, decision theorists have discussed whether risk propensity might itself be a trait. While some researchers have developed scales to measure this presumed trait (Meertens & Lion, 2008) others have presented data questioning whether the trait does indeed exist (Li & Liu, 2008). Regardless, it is clear that we should know what will happen when people with different combinations of these traits must work together to reach consensus.

Summary

There are many intriguing connections between personality traits and elements of group decision-making. As we have seen, this work has proceeded piecemeal, and the lack of systematicity has left some rather large holes in our knowledge base. As we still do not have a very good understanding of how group members reach consensus, systematic research to fill these holes and to flesh out the possible connections would be fruitful indeed.

Group Maintenance

A sometimes-overlooked, but important, aspect of understanding groups is the process by which group members maintain as an entity. Maintenance is not an issue for ad hoc groups that are assembled to accomplish just one task, but for intact, ongoing groups, keeping group members satisfied and committed is critical.

Cohesion

Cohesion generally refers to a sense of attraction to one's fellow group members, and a feeling that the group is an important part of one's self-concept (Hogg, 1993). Cohesion is a fundamental component of any ongoing group, as members who do not see the group as personally valuable will usually not be motivated to continue participating in it. Accordingly, some researchers have asked whether personality contributes to cohesion. An important finding from this work is that widespread diversity in traits across members is harmful to cohesion, as such breadth often leads to formation of subgroups organized around the traits (e.g., "We are the introverted ones, and they are the extraverted ones"; Molleman, 2005), especially if the trait in question is conscientiousness (Rico, Molleman, Sanchez-Manzares, & Van der Vegt, 2007). At the individual level, high-agreeable individuals are especially likely to feel cohesive with other members (O'Neill & Kline, 2008), and cohesion seems to be fostered by the presence of an extravert, as extraverts are especially good at providing the social and emotional input that attracts members to the group (Barry, Stewart, Neubert, & Mount, 1998; van Vianen & De Dreu, 2001), though this basic effect seems to be moderated by a host of task characteristics. Interestingly, introverts are generally dissatisfied with groups that contain people more extraverted than they (Peeters, Rutte, van Tuijl, & Reymen, 2006), which suggests that a possible technique for enhancing cohesion—inclusion of a member who is especially outgoing—could backfire, if the rest of the members are more introverted. Along these same lines, high-conscientious people are typically dissatisfied with their group experience if some other members are low-conscientious, even if the group's performance was of good quality (Gevers & Peeters, 2009). This may be a function of high-conscientious individuals often lacking the interpersonal skills needed to work cooperatively with others (Witt, Burke, Barrick, & Mount, 2002)—perhaps such individuals simply want to get the job done, and are attracted to a group not because it offers a pleasant climate, but because the specific combination of abilities within the group represents an effective tool for accomplishing the group task. Indeed, van Vianen and De Dreu (2001) have argued that studies of personality influences on cohesion must distinguish between task cohesion (attraction to a group because of the set of abilities within the group) and social cohesion (attraction because the environment will be interpersonally enjoyable) in order to fully understand those influences.

Resolution of Relational Conflict

Within intact groups, it is not uncommon for particular members to develop negative interpersonal relationships with each other. The members may disagree over how the group is evolving; one member may be less satisfied with a recent group performance than another member; or the two may simply dislike each other. How the conflict is managed and resolved can have substantial impact on the group's ability to perform, as well as its long-term well-being (De Dreu & Weingart, 2003). As such, researchers are interested in understanding how relational conflict develops, and some have asked whether particular personality traits play a role in its development and management. Regarding development of conflict, the evidence is spare. Baron (1989) found that Type A individuals and low self-monitors were relatively likely to experience conflict with group members of lower status (though not with members of equal status). More generally, Mount and colleagues (Mount, Barrick, & Stewart, 1998) showed that conscientious, emotionally stable, and agreeable individuals are best-suited for group tasks that require interaction among group members. Whether this is because such people are especially adept at avoiding conflicts is unclear; though, in group settings, agreeable individuals are sensitive to interpersonal relations, considerate of others, and tend to favor collaboration (Moberg, 2001), so it seems likely that at least those individuals have a talent for avoiding and defusing conflict. Conversely, those who are low on emotional stability, extraversion, and/or agreeableness tend to be especially adversely affected by interpersonal conflict, to the point where it can threaten their well-being (Dijkstra, van Dierendonck, Evers, & De Dreu, 2005). At the collective level, the mean level of agreeableness within the group is a good predictor of the frequency of relational conflict, with the two being inversely related (Varela, Burke, & Landis, 2008).

More work has been done on whether different traits predict how one prefers to manage a relational conflict. In a thorough analysis, Antonioni (1999) examined favored strategies associated with each of the Big Five and found that extraverts favor integration (creation of a novel solution to the conflict) or domination (imposition of a solution); agreeable people prefer integration or avoidance (failure to deal directly with the conflict and letting it die on its own); open and conscientious people both prefer integration; and neurotics favor avoidance. As well, agreeable people and neurotics each explicitly dislike domination, and extraverts, open people, and conscientious people all dislike avoidance. Two other styles of resolution, compromise (identification of a middle ground) and obliging (acceptance of the other party's wishes), did not seem to be favored or expressly disliked by any class of individuals. Later work (Park & Antonioni, 2007) has added a level of complexity to these patterns, demonstrating that the trait-strategy relationship can be moderated by the other person's behaviors. As we noted earlier, Graziano and colleagues (Graziano et al., 1996) showed that low-agreeable individuals are more willing to employ domination-like solutions than are high-agreeable people, though both groups consider the tactic less desirable than avoidance or a negotiated solution (Graziano et al. did not distinguish between integration and compromise).

Integration of New Members

Another aspect of group maintenance is the process by which new members are taught the formal and informal norms of the group. A few studies have investigated whether particular traits relate to the ease with which the new member acquires the normative information. This research shows that new members who are extraverts, who are open, or who have a high need for control are especially likely to seek feedback on the propriety of their behaviors, and to take the initiative to build relationships (e.g., Wanberg & Kammeyer-Mueller, 2000). Emotional stability is an important trait for new members who are trying to simultaneously maintain connections to another group (Luijters, van der Zee, & Otten, 2006). As well, there is some indirect evidence that dispositional trust may affect the socialization process, in that group members may consider new members of questionable trustworthiness until the socialization process is complete (Moreland & Levine, 2002). However, a direct analysis of how differences in dispositional trust affect one's interaction with new members has not yet been conducted. There is also some evidence that socialization is more readily accomplished in diverse rather than homogeneous groups (Arrow, 1998), but this work has focused strictly on demographic diversity. Whether this principle holds for diversity of individual differences is an open question. Finally, there is some work from the cross-cultural literature on assimilation that suggests the need to look further into Big Five traits and new member socialization.

Some of these studies address a trait labeled "flexibility," which has characteristics of both openness and agreeableness, and show that high-flexible people more easily assimilate into a new cultural group than low-flexible people (Bakker, van der Zee, & van Oudenhoven, 2006), while others support the importance of extraversion in successful assimilation (Ying & Han, 2006).

Usually, new members are either self-selected or assigned to the group by some authority. However, an emerging interest in this research area is in the process by which potential new members are identified and recruited by existing group members, a process referred to as "brokerage." Simply put, a broker is a group member who attempts to bring together people unfamiliar to each other, and thereby expand a social network (Burt, 2005). While the concept has long been a topic of interest within sociology and management science, only recently have researchers become interested in the psychological dynamics of brokerage, one reason being that the bringing together of unacquainted, yet similar, individuals into one group can strengthen the cohesion within that group. The question of primary interest is whether particular types of people are more or less likely to serve as brokers, and personality traits have been brought into this discussion. Self-monitoring is an obvious trait to investigate here, as high and low self-monitors differ considerably on the breadth of their social networks (e.g., Flynn, Reagans, Amanatullah, & Ames, 2006), and indeed, self-monitoring does seem to predict brokerage. In fact, high self-monitors will take on the task of connecting not only their own acquaintances who are unknown to each other, but also bring acquaintances of their acquaintances into the group (Oh & Kilduff, 2008). As social network dynamics are also affected by other traits, like extraversion and neuroticism (e.g., S. G. B. Roberts, Wilson, Fedurek, & Dunbar, 2008), it is worth asking whether these traits might also predict a person's willingness to bring new, similar individuals into the group.[8]

Summary

Cohesion, management of relational conflict, and integration of new group members, all critical to successful maintenance of an ongoing group, all seem to be affected by particular traits of existing members. Not surprisingly, Big Five traits seem to be important for all three of these phenomena, but self-monitoring, Type A/Type B, and trust have all also been identified as traits of potential predictive value. Additional insights may be gained by looking to the literature on cultural assimilation, as researchers there are interested in whether personality can predict an individual's successful assimilation into a new culture, a process that may be similar to the joining of a new task or social group.

Where do we go from Here?

By now the reader has realized that we know a lot of little things about the contribution of personality traits to group phenomena. There exist both a number of holes in the fabric of our knowledge, and a need for some organizing frameworks to help us make sense out of what we do know. How can these goals be accomplished?

First, we must encourage greater collaboration between personality and groups researchers. This may seem an obvious statement, but clearly it is not yet happening, so there is worth in pointing this out. Intellectually it is not difficult, as both sets of researchers speak the same language and are largely interested in the same issues—a recent survey of personality and social psychologists by Tracy, Robins, and Sherman (2009) found that of 35 topics of study of potential interest to social and/or personality psychologists, 26 of them were selected at statistically equal rates by members of the two subdisciplines. The hurdle seems to be largely methodological. Tracy et al. (2009) examined the methodologies used by social and personality psychologists, and found a significant positive correlation between the frequency with which one employs research designs that involve collecting data on some aspect of a group and the extent to which one considers oneself a social psychologist, but no correlation when the question was the extent to which one considers oneself a personality researcher; in fact, the correlation was in the negative direction. While over 80% of social psychologists reported group-oriented data collection as a regular tool in their kit, less than two-thirds of personality psychologists claimed it, with its popularity among this group comfortably ahead of only study of special-case populations such as twins, animals, and single subjects, and barely ahead of the use of patients as subjects. On the other hand, social psychologists reported using longitudinal and cross-sectional designs far less frequently than did personality psychologists.

The differences do not stop at mere research tools. As noted above, the two groups agreed on 26 of 35 topics as being of interest; however, only one

possibly groupish topic, judgment and decision-making, fell in this set. The other groups topics (intergroup processes, social influence, social roles) were chosen statistically more frequently by social researchers than by personality researchers. (The other general areas in which there was divergence were attitudes and person perception, both more popular with social psychologists, and health psychology and development, both favored more by personality psychologists.) These differences stand out even more when one learns that Tracy et al.'s primary point was that there is much more overlap between the personality and social fields than is commonly thought. Clearly the overlap does not extend to the study of groups.

Are these differences coincidental or purposeful? It may be that social psychologists disdain the study of personality development because they are not skilled in longitudinal designs, or it may be that there is just no interest in undertaking such research. While my inference throughout this chapter has been that it is the latter, once again we can look to the Tracy et al. data for information, in particular their findings on the stereotypes held of personality and social psychologists. Three such stereotypes are relevant for our purposes: Personality researchers are thought to rely heavily on self-reports and qualitatively analyzed narrative data, and social psychologists are seen as not terribly worried about construct validity. That all of these beliefs are shown to be wrong by Tracy et al.'s objective data illustrates, I would argue, the crux of the problem. The debates about the value of self-reports and narrative analysis as data collection tools are long-standing and ongoing (see Soto, John, Gosling, & Potter, 2008, for recent evidence on the usefulness of self-reports), and while no one would presumably argue that lack of concern about construct validity is acceptable, at the same time it needs to be recognized that there are hurdles to the study of real-world groups—it is illegal, for example, to observe a deliberating jury, and it is unlikely the members of any board of directors would allow observation of their discussion of high-level matters—and so groups researchers often have to rely on laboratory analogues of these scenarios. Well-crafted analogues can and should be engaging, and will produce interpretable and insightful data. So, for example, detailed mock trials, developed from actual court transcripts, have been created. (And, it should be remembered, any subject pool member who is a registered voter has the potential to be sitting on a jury next week.) Are the stakes as high for the mock jury as they are for

scales in a longitudinal twin study. *Journal of Personality and Social Psychology, 97,* 142–155.

Bolin, A. U., & Neuman, G. A. (2006). Personality, process, and performance in interactive brainstorming groups. *Journal of Business and Psychology, 20,* 565–585.

Bond, M. H., & Shiu, W. Y.-F. (1997). The relationship between a group's personality resources and the two dimensions of its group process. *Small Group Research, 28,* 194–217.

Bonner, B. L. (2000). The effects of extroversion on influence in ambiguous group tasks. *Small Group Research, 31,* 225–244.

Bradshaw, S. D., Stasson, M. F., & Alexander, D. (1999). Shyness and group brainstorming: Effects on productivity and perception of performance. *North American Journal of Psychology, 1,* 267–276.

Burt, R. S. (2005). *Brokerage and closure.* New York: Oxford University Press.

Burt, R. S., Jannotta, J. E., & Mahoney, J. T. (1998). Personality correlates of structural holes. *Social Networks, 20,* 63–87.

Camacho, L. M., & Paulus, P. B. (1995). The role of social anxiousness in group brainstorming. *Journal of Personality and Social Psychology, 68,* 1071–1080.

Campbell, W. K., Bush, C. P., Brunell, A. B., & Shelton, J. (2005). Understanding the social costs of narcissism: The case of the tragedy of the commons. *Personality and Social Psychology Bulletin, 31,* 1358–1368.

Carron, A. V., Shapcott, K. M., & Burke, S. M. (2008). Group cohesion in sport and exercise: Past, present and future. In M. R. Beauchamp & M. A. Eys (Eds.), *Group dynamics in exercise and sport psychology* (pp. 117–139). New York: Routledge.

Chase, M. A., Feltz, D. L., & Lirgg, C. D. (2003). Sources of collective and individual efficacy of collegiate athletes. *International Journal of Sport and Exercise Psychology, 1,* 180–191.

Costa, A. C., Roe, R. A., & Taillieu, T. (2001). Trust within teams: The relation with performance effectiveness. *European Journal of Work and Organisational Psychology, 10,* 225–244.

Couch, L. L., & Jones, W. H. (1997). Measuring levels of trust. *Journal of Research in Personality, 31,* 319–336.

Crott, H. W., & Werner, J. (1994). The norm-information-distance model: A stochastic approach to preference change in group interaction. *Journal of Experimental Social Psychology, 30,* 68–95.

Daus, C. S., & Joplin, J. R. W. (1999). Survival of the fittest: Implications of self-reliance and coping for leaders and team performance. *Journal of Occupational Health Psychology, 4,* 15–28.

Davies, M. F., & Kanaki, E. (2006). Interpersonal characteristics associated with different team roles in work groups. *Journal of Managerial Psychology, 21,* 638–650.

De Dreu, C. K. W., Beersma, B., Stroebe, K., & Euwema, M. C. (2006). Motivated information processing, strategic choice, and the quality of negotiated agreement. *Journal of Personality and Social Psychology, 90,* 927–943.

De Dreu, C. K. W., Nijstad, B. A., & van Knippenberg, D. (2008). Motivated information processing in group judgment and decision making. *Personality and Social Psychology Review, 12,* 22–49.

De Dreu, C. K. W., & Weingart, L. R. (2003). Task versus relationship conflict, team performance, and team member satisfaction: A meta-analysis. *Journal of Applied Psychology, 88,* 741–749.

De Dreu, C. K. W., Weingart, L. R., & Kwon, S. (2000). Influence of social motives on integrative negotiation: A meta-analytic review and test of two theories. *Journal of Personality and Social Psychology, 78,* 889–905.

DeMatteo, J. S., Eby, L. T., & Sundstrom, E. (1998). Team-based rewards: Current empirical evidence and directions for future research. *Research in Organizational Behavior, 20,* 141–183.

Dennis, A. R., & Williams, M. L. (2005). A meta-analysis of group size effects in electronic brainstorming: More heads are better than one. *International Journal of e-Collaboration, 1,* 24–42.

Deutsch, M. (1958). Trust and suspicion. *Journal of Conflict Resolution, 2,* 265–279.

Deutsch, M. (1960). Trust, trustworthiness and the F-Scale. *Journal of Abnormal and Social Psychology, 61,* 138–140.

DeYoung, C. G., Peterson, J. B., & Higgins, D. M. (2002). Higher-order factors of the Big Five predict conformity: Are there neuroses of health? *Personality and Individual Differences, 33,* 533–552.

Dijkstra, M. T. M., van Dierendonck, D., Evers, A., & De Dreu, C. K. W. (2005). Conflict and well-being at work: The moderating role of personality. *Journal of Managerial Psychology, 20,* 87–104.

Dirks, K. T. (1999). The effects of interpersonal trust on work group performance. *Journal of Applied Psychology, 84,* 445–455.

Fallon, J. D., Avis, J. M., Kudisch, J. D., Gornet, T. P., & Frost, A. (2000). Conscientiousness as a predictor of productive and counterproductive behaviors. *Journal of Business and Psychology, 15,* 339–349.

Flynn, F. J., Reagans, R. E., Amanatullah, E. T., & Ames, D. R. (2006). Helping one's way to the top: Self-monitors achieve status by helping others and knowing who helps whom. *Journal of Personality and Social Psychology, 91,* 1123–1137.

Fritz, H. L., & Helgeson, V. S. (1998). Distinctions of unmitigated concern from communion: Self-neglect and overinvolvement with others. *Journal of Personality and Social Psychology, 75,* 121–140.

Fukuyama, F. (1995). Trust: The Social Virtues and the Creation of Prosperity. New York: Free Press.

Furnham, A., & Yazdanpanahi, T. (1995). Personality differences and group versus individual brainstorming. *Personality and Individual Differences, 19,* 73–80.

Gallo, P. S., & McClintock, C. G. (1965). Cooperation and competitive behavior in mixed motive games. *Journal of Conflict Resolution, 9,* 68–78.

Gevers, J. M. P., & Peeters, M. A. G. (2009). A pleasure working together? The effects of dissimilarity in team member conscientiousness on team temporal processes and individual satisfaction. *Journal of Organizational Behavior, 30,* 379–400.

Giberson, T. R., Resick, C. J., & Dickson, M. W. (2005). Embedding leader characteristics: An examination of homogeneity of personality and values in organizations. *Journal of Applied Psychology, 90,* 1002–1010.

Grabitz-Gniech, G. (1971). Some restrictive conditions for the occurrence of psychological reactance. *Journal of Personality and Social Psychology, 19,* 188–196.

Graziano, W. G., Feldesman, A. B., & Rahe, D. F. (1985). Extraversion, social cognition, and the salience of aversiveness in social encounters. *Journal of Personality and Social Psychology, 49,* 971–980.

Graziano, W. G., Habashi, M. M., Sheese, B. E., & Tobin, R. M. (2007). Agreeableness, empathy, and helping: A person x situation perspective. *Journal of Personality and Social Psychology, 93,* 583–599.

Graziano, W. G., Jensen-Campbell, L. A., & Hair, E. C. (1996). Perceiving interpersonal conflict and reacting to it: The case for agreeableness. *Journal of Personality and Social Psychology, 70,* 820–835.

Hackman, J. R. (1987). The design of work teams. In J. W. Lorsch (Ed.), *Handbook of organizational behavior* (pp. 315–342). Englewood Cliffs, NJ: Prentice-Hall.

Halfhill, T. R., Nielsen, T. M., & Sundstrom, E. (2008). The ASA framework: A field study of group personality composition and group performance in military action teams. *Small Group Research, 39,* 616–635.

Halfhill, T. R., Sundstrom, E., Lahner, J., Calderone, W., & Nielsen, T. M. (2005). Group personality composition and group effectiveness: An integrative review of empirical research. *Small Group Research, 36,* 83–105.

Harms, P. D., Roberts, B. W., & Wood, D. (2007). Who shall lead? An integrative personality approach to the study of antecedents of status in informal social organizations. *Journal of Research in Personality, 41,* 689–699.

Hastie, R., & Kameda, T. (2005). The robust beauty of majority rules in group decisions. *Psychological Review, 112,* 494–508.

Heisler, J. M., & Crabill, S. L. (2006). Who are "stinkybug" and "Packerfan4"? Email pseudonyms and participants' perceptions of demography, productivity, and personality. *Journal of Computer-Mediated Communication, 12,* 114–135.

Hertel, G., Schroer, J., Batinic, B., & Naumann, S. (2008). Do shy people prefer to send e-mail? Personality effects on communication media preferences in threatening and nonthreatening situations. *Social Psychology, 39,* 231–243.

Hewlin, P. F. (2009). Wearing the cloak: Antecedents and consequences of creating facades of conformity. *Journal of Applied Psychology, 94,* 727–741.

Hinsz, V. B., Tindale, R. S., & Vollrath, D. A. (1997). The emerging conceptualization of groups as information processors. *Psychological Bulletin, 121,* 43–64.

Hodson, G., & Sorrentino, R. M. (2003). Uncertainty orientation in the group context: Categorization effects on persuasive message processing. *Journal of Social Psychology, 143,* 291–312.

Hogg, M. A. (1993). Group cohesiveness: A critical review and some new directions. *European Review of Social Psychology, 4,* 85–111.

Hogg, M. A. (2008). Personality, individuality, and social identity. In F. Rhodewalt (Ed.), *Personality and social behavior* (pp. 177–196). New York: Psychology Press.

Hughes, E. C. (1928). Personality types and the division of labor. *American Journal of Sociology, 33,* 754–768.

Humphrey, S. E., Hollenbeck, J. R., Meyer, C. J., & Ilgen, D. R. (2007). Trait configurations in self-managed teams: A conceptual examination of the use of seeding for maximizing and minimizing trait variance in teams. *Journal of Applied Psychology, 92,* 885–892.

Ilgen, D. R. (1999). Teams embedded in organizations: Some implications. *American Psychologist, 54,* 129–139.

Insko, C. A., & Schopler, J. (1998). Differential distrust of groups and individuals. In C. Sedikides, J. Schopler, & C. A. Insko (Eds.), *Intergroup cognition and intergroup behavior* (pp. 75–108). Mahwah, NJ: Erlbaum.

Jackson, C. L., & LePine, J. A. (2003). Peer responses to a team's weakest link: A test and extension of LePine and Van Dyne's model. *Journal of Applied Psychology, 88,* 459–475.

James, W. (1907/1975). *Pragmatism.* Cambridge, MA: Harvard University Press.

Jensen-Campbell, L. A., Graziano, W. G., & Hair, E. C. (1996). Personality and relationships as moderators of interpersonal conflict in adolescence. *Merrill-Palmer Quarterly, 42,* 148–164.

Jones, G. R., & George, J. M. (1998). The experience and evolution of trust: Implications for cooperation and teamwork. *Academy of Management Review, 23,* 531–546.

Judge, T. A., Bono, J. E., Ilies, R., & Gerhardt, M. W. (2002). Personality and leadership: A qualitative and quantitative review. *Journal of Applied Psychology, 87,* 765–780.

Karau, S. J., & Elsaid, A. M. M. K. (2009). Individual differences in beliefs about groups. *Group Dynamics, 13,* 1–13.

Keinen, G., & Koren, M. (2002). Teaming up Type As and Bs: The effects of group composition on performance and satisfaction. *Applied Psychology: An International Review, 51,* 425–445.

Kelly, G. A. (1955). *The psychology of personal constructs.* New York: Norton.

Ketelaar, T., & Au, W. T. (2003). The effects of feelings of guilt on the behaviour of uncooperative individuals in repeated social bargaining games: An affect-as-information interpretation on the role of emotion in social interaction. *Cognition and Emotion, 17,* 429–453.

Kimmerle, J., Cress, U., & Hesse, F. W. (2007). An interactional perspective on group awareness: Alleviating the information-exchange dilemma (for everybody?). *International Journal of Human-Computer Studies, 65,* 899–910.

Kirchler, E., & Davis, J. H. (1986). The influence of member status differences and task type on group consensus and member position change. *Journal of Personality and Social Psychology, 51,* 83–91.

Klein, M. H. (1967). Compliance, consistent conformity, and personality. *Journal of Personality and Social Psychology, 5,* 239–245.

Knight, G. P., Dubro, A. F., & Chao, C.-C. (1985). Information processing and the development of cooperative, competitive, and individualistic social values. *Developmental Psychology, 21,* 37–45.

Knight, G. P., & Kagan, S. (1981). Apparent sex differences in cooperation-competition: A function of individualism. *Developmental Psychology, 17,* 783–790.

Komorita, S. S., & Parks, C. D. (1995). Intergroup relations: Mixed-motive interaction. *Annual Review of Psychology, 46,* 183–207.

Komorita, S. S., & Parks, C. D. (1996). *Social dilemmas.* Boulder, CO: Westview.

Koole, S. L., Jager, W., van den Berg, A. E., Vlek, C. A. J., & Hofstee, W. K. B. (2001). On the social nature of personality: Effects of extraversion, agreeableness, and feedback about collective resource use on cooperation in a resource dilemma. *Personality and Social Psychology Bulletin, 27,* 289–301.

Kramer, R. M. (1999a). Trust and distrust in organizations: Emerging perspectives, enduring questions. *Annual Review of Psychology, 50,* 569–598.

Kramer, R. M. (1999b). Stalking the sinister attribution error: Paranoia inside the lab and out. *Research in Negotiation in Organizations, 7,* 59–91.

Kramer, R. M., & Cook, K. S. (2004). Trust and distrust in organizations: Dilemmas and approaches. In R. M. Kramer & K. S. Cook (Eds.), *Trust and distrust in organizations* (pp. 1–18). New York: Russell Sage.

Kray, L. J., Thompson, L., & Lind, E. A. (2005). It's a bet! A problem-solving approach promotes the construction of contingent agreements. *Personality and Social Psychology Bulletin, 31,* 1039–1051.

Krech, D., & Crutchfield, R. S. (1948). *Theory and problems of social psychology.* New York: McGraw-Hill.

Ladbury, J. L., & Hinsz, V. B. (2009). Individual expectations for group decision processes: Evidence for overestimation of majority influence. *Group Dynamics, 13,* 235–254.

Langfred, C. W. (2004). Too much of a good thing? Negative effects of high trust and individual autonomy in self-managing teams. *Academy of Management Journal, 47,* 385–399.

Laughlin, P. R. (1999). Collective induction: Twelve postulates. *Organizational Behavior and Human Decision Processes, 80,* 50–69.

Lewicki, R. J., & Litterer, J. A. (1985). *Negotiation.* Homewood, IL: Irwin.

Lewin, K. (1935). *A dynamic theory of personality.* New York: McGraw-Hill.

Lewin, K. (1939). Field theory and experiment in social psychology: Concepts and methods. *American Journal of Sociology, 44,* 868–897.

Lewin, K. (1944). Constructs in psychology and psychological ecology. *University of Iowa Studies of Child Welfare, 20,* 23–27.

Li, S., & Liu, C.-J. (2008). Individual differences in a switch from risk-averse preferences for gains to risk-seeking preferences for losses: Can personality variables predict the risk preferences? *Journal of Risk Research, 11,* 673–686.

Liebrand, W. B. G., Jansen, R. W. T. L., Rijken, V. M., & Suhre, C. J. M. (1986). Might over morality: Social values and the perception of other players in experimental games. *Journal of Experimental Social Psychology, 22,* 203–215.

Lippitt, R., & White, R. (1943). The "social climate" of children's groups. In R. Barker, J. Kounin, & H. Wright (Eds.), *Child behavior and development* (pp. 405–508). New York: McGraw-Hill.

Luijters, K., van der Zee, K. I., & Otten. S. (2006). Acculturation strategies among ethnic minority workers and the role of intercultural personality traits. *Group Processes and Intergroup Relations, 9,* 561–575.

Mackie, D. M., Silver, L. A., & Smith, E. R. (2004). Intergroup emotion: Emotion as an intergroup phenomenon. In L. Z. Tiedens & C. W. Leach (Eds.), *The social life of emotions* (pp. 227–245). New York: Cambridge University Press.

Mann, R. D. (1959). A review of the relationships between personality and performance in small groups. *Psychological Bulletin, 56,* 241–270.

Manzo, L. G., Silva, J. M., & Mink, R. (2001). The Carolina Sport Confidence Inventory. *Journal of Applied Sport Psychology, 13,* 260–274.

May, M. A., & Doob, L. W. (1937). *Competition and cooperation.* New York: Social Science Research Council.

Mayer, R. C., Davis, J. H., & Schoorman, F. D. (1995). An integrative model of organizational trust. *Academy of Management Review, 20,* 709–734.

McClintock, C. G., & Keil, L. J. (1983). Social values: Their definition, their development, and their impact upon human decision making in settings of outcome interdependence. In

H. H. Blumberg, A. P. Hare, V. Kent, & M. Davies (Eds.), *Small groups and social interaction* (Vol. 2, pp. 123–143). London: Wiley.

McGrath, J. E. (1984). *Groups: Interaction and performance.* Englewood Cliffs, NJ: Prentice-Hall.

Meertens, R. M., & Lion, R. (2008). Measuring an individual's tendency to take risks: The risk propensity scale. *Journal of Applied Social Psychology, 38,* 1506–1520.

Merton, R. K. (1940). Bureaucratic structure and personality. *Social Forces, 18,* 560–568.

Messick, D. M., & McClintock, C. G. (1968). Motivational bases of choice in experimental games. *Journal of Experimental Social Psychology, 4,* 1–25.

Miller, M. D., & Brunner, C. C. (2008). Social impact in technologically-mediated communication: An example of online influence. *Computers in Human Behavior, 24,* 2972–2991.

Moberg, P. J. (2001). Linking the strategy to the five-factor model: Theoretical and empirical foundations. *International Journal of Conflict Management, 12,* 47–68.

Molleman, E. (2005). Diversity in demographic characteristics, abilities, and personality traits: Do faultlines affect team functioning? *Group Decision and Negotiation, 14,* 173–193.

Moreland, R. L., & Levine, J. M. (2002). Socialization and trust in work groups. *Group Processes and Intergroup Relations, 5,* 185–201.

Morris, M. W., Larrick, R. P., & Su, S. K. (1999). Misperceiving negotiation counterparts: When situationally determined bargaining behaviors are attributed to personality traits. *Journal of Personality and Social Psychology, 77,* 52–67.

Mount, M. K., Barrick, M. R., & Stewart, G. L. (1998). Five-factor model of personality and performance in jobs involving interpersonal interactions. *Human Performance, 11,* 145–165.

Nicholson, N., Soane, E., Fenton-O'Creevy, M., & Willman, P. (2005). Personality and domain-specific risk taking. *Journal of Risk Research, 8,* 157–176.

Nord, W. R. (1969). Social exchange theory: An integrative approach to social conformity. *Psychological Bulletin, 71,* 174–208.

Oh, H., & Kilduff, M. (2008). The ripple effect of personality on social structure: Self-monitoring origins of network brokerage. *Journal of Applied Psychology, 93,* 1155–1164.

Olekalns, M., & Smith, P. L. (2003). Testing the relationships among negotiators' motivational orientations, strategy choices, and outcomes. *Journal of Experimental Social Psychology, 39,* 101–117.

O'Neill, T. A., & Kline, T. J. B. (2008). Personality as a predictor of teamwork: A business simulator study. *North American Journal of Psychology, 10,* 65–78.

Osborn, A. (1953). *Applied imagination.* New York: Scribner's.

Park, H.-J., & Antonioni, D. (2007). Personality, reciprocity, and strength of conflict resolution strategy. *Journal of Research in Personality, 41,* 110–125.

Parks, C. D. (1994). The predictive ability of social values in resource dilemmas and public good games. *Personality and Social Psychology Bulletin, 20,* 431–438.

Parks, C. D., & Nelson, N. L. (1999). Discussion and decision: The interrelationship between initial preference distribution and group discussion content. *Organizational Behavior and Human Decision Processes, 80,* 87–101.

Parks, C. D., & Rumble, A. C. (2001). Elements of reciprocity and social value orientation. *Personality and Social Psychology Bulletin, 27,* 1301–1309.

Paulhus, D. L., & Morgan, K. L. (1997). Perceptions of intelligence in leaderless groups: The dynamic effects of shyness and acquaintance. *Journal of Personality and Social Psychology, 72,* 581–591.

Peeters, M. A. G., Rutte, C. G., van Tuijl, H. F. J. M., & Reymen, I. M. M. J. (2006). The Big Five personality traits and individual satisfaction with the team. *Small Group Research, 37,* 187–211.

Peeters, M. A. G., van Tuijl, H. F. J. M., Rutte, C. G., & Reymen, I. M. M. J. (2006). Personality and team performance: A meta-analysis. *European Journal of Personality, 20,* 377–396.

Pena, J., Walther, J. B., & Hancock, J. T. (2007). Effects of geographic distribution on dominance perceptions in computer-mediated groups. *Communication Research, 34,* 313–331.

Penrod, S., & Hastie, R. (1980). A computer simulation of jury decision making. *Psychological Review, 87,* 133–159.

Pinter, B., Insko, C. A., Widlschut, T., Kirchner, J. L., Montoya, R. M., & Wolf, S. T. (2007). Reduction of interindividual-intergroup discontinuity: The role of leader accountability and proneness to guilt. *Journal of Personality and Social Psychology, 93,* 250-265.

Quigley, N. R., Tesluk, P. E., Locke, E. A., & Bartol, K. M. (2007). Multilevel investigation of the motivational mechanisms underlying knowledge sharing and performance. *Organization Science, 18,* 71–88.

Rice, L., & Markey, P. M. (2009). The role of extraversion and neuroticism in influencing anxiety following computer-mediated interactions. *Personality and Individual Differences, 46,* 35–39.

Rico, R., Molleman, E., Sanchez-Manzanares, M., & Van der Vegt, G. S. (2007). The effects of diversity faultlines and team task autonomy on decision quality and social integration. *Journal of Management, 33,* 111–132.

Rispens, S., Greer, L. L., & Jehn, K. A. (2007). It could be worse: A study on the alleviating roles of trust and connectedness in intragroup conflicts. *International Journal of Conflict Management, 18,* 325–344.

Roberts, B. W., Wood, D., & Smith, J. L. (2005). Evaluating five-factor theory and social investment perspectives on personality trait development. *Journal of Research in Personality, 39,* 166–184.

Roberts, S. G. B., Wilson, R., Fedurek, P., & Dunbar, R. I. M. (2008). Individual differences and personal social network size and structure. *Personality and Individual Differences, 44,* 954–964.

Roccas, S., Sagiv, L., Schwartz, S. H., & Knafo, A. (2002). The Big Five personality factors and personal values. *Personality and Social Psychology Bulletin, 28,* 789–801.

Ross, S. R., Rausch, M. K., & Canada, K. E. (2003). Competition and cooperation in the five-factor model: Individual differences in achievement orientation. *Journal of Psychology: Interdisciplinary and Applied, 137,* 323–337.

Rouse, S. V., & Haas, H. A. (2003). Exploring the accuracies and inaccuracies of personality perception following internet-mediated communication. *Journal of Research in Personality, 37,* 446–467.

Rule, B. G., & Sandilands, M. L. (1969). Test anxiety, confidence, commitment, and conformity. *Journal of Personality, 37,* 470–467.

Rushton, J. P., Fulker, D. W., Neale, M. C., Nias, D. K. B., & Eysenck, H. J. (1986). Altruism and aggression: The heritability of individual differences. *Journal of Personality and Social Psychology, 50,* 1192–1198.

Sager, K. L., & Gastil, J. (2006). The origins and consequences of consensus decision making: A test of the social consensus model. *Southern Communication Journal, 71,* 1–24.

Sanna, L. J., & Parks, C. D. (1997). Group research trends in social and organizational psychology: Whatever happened to intragroup research? *Psychological Science, 8,* 261–267.

Segerstrom, S. C. (2007). Optimism and resources: Effects on each other and on health over 10 years. *Journal of Research in Personality, 41,* 772–786.

Shaw, M. E. (1932). A comparison of individuals and small groups in the rational solution of complex problems. *American Journal of Psychology, 44,* 491–504.

Sherif, M. (1948). *An outline of social psychology.* New York: Harper and Brothers.

Shuper, P. A., & Sorrentino, R. M. (2004). Minority versus majority influence and uncertainty orientation: Processing persuasive messages on the basis of situational expectancies. *Journal of Social Psychology, 144,* 127–147.

Skinner, B. F. (1953). *Science and human behavior.* New York: Free Press.

Smith, R. E., Smoll, F. L., Cumming, S. P., & Grossbard, J. R. (2006). Measurement of multidimensional sport performance anxiety in children and adults: The Sport Anxiety Scale-2. *Journal of Sport and Exercise Psychology, 28,* 479–501.

Snyder, M., & Monson, T. C. (1975). Persons, situations, and the control of social behavior. *Journal of Personality and Social Psychology, 32,* 637–644.

Soane, E., & Chmiel, N. (2005). Are risk preferences consistent? The influence of decision domain and personality. *Personality and Individual Differences, 38,* 1781–1791.

Sorrentino, R. M., Hewitt, E. C., & Raso-Knott, P. A. (1992). Risk-taking in games of chance and skill: Informational and affective influences on choice behavior. *Journal of Personality and Social Psychology, 62,* 522–533.

Sorrentino, R. M., & Roney, C. J. R. (2000). *The uncertain mind.* Philadelphia: Psychology Press.

Soto, C. J., John, O. P., Gosling, S. D., & Potter, J. (2008). The developmental psychometrics of Big Five self-reports: Acquiescence, factor structure, coherence, and differentiation from ages 10 to 20. *Journal of Personality and Social Psychology, 94,* 718–737.

Stasser, G. (1999). A primer of social decision scheme theory: Models of group influence, competitive model-testing, and prospective modeling. *Organizational Behavior and Human Decision Processes, 80,* 3–20.

Stasser, G., & Titus, W. (1985). Pooling of unshared information in group decision making: Biased information sampling during discussion. *Journal of Personality and Social Psychology, 48,* 1467–1478.

Steiner, I. D. (1966). Models for inferring relationships between group size and potential group productivity. *Behavioral Science, 11,* 273–283.

Steiner, I. D. (1972). *Group process and productivity.* New York: Academic.

Steiner, I. D., & Vannoy, J. S. (1966). Personality correlates of two types of conformity behavior. *Journal of Personality and Social Psychology, 4,* 307–315.

(e.g., stating support for minority advancement while indicating that minorities are inexperienced or not qualified), thereby perpetuating a tendency to see themselves as nonprejudiced. Relatedly, work by Sears and colleagues on symbolic racism (e.g., Sears & Kinder, 1985; Sears & Henry, 2005) proposes that white individuals have negative attitudes toward racial minorities due to processes of family and societal socialization, at the same time as they generally support egalitarian principles in society. At times, these potential discrepancies intersect and lead to a "principle implementation gap," whereby individuals who endorse egalitarianism often do not support social policy that is consonant with such ideology (Sears & Funk, 1991; Sears & Jessor, 1996). Although there are important distinctions among these models, one commonality is that they focus principally on how dominant group members respond to racial minorities, rather than exploring more generally how and why groups develop prejudices toward each other.

Specifying Sources of Prejudice

In an important and pertinent theoretical article, Duckitt (1992) conducted a historical analysis of prejudice research that reveals how different theoretical perspectives make partial and complementary contributions to our understanding of the development and nature of prejudice. According to Duckitt (1992), numerous processes lead to prejudice including (1) universal psychological processes and motivations that build in a human propensity for prejudice (e.g., social categorization, social identification); (2) individual and ideological bases of prejudice (e.g., authoritarianism, political ideology); and (3) processes focusing on social and structural dynamics of prejudice (e.g., resource conflict, group-based disparities in power and status). We briefly review processes relevant to each category in the sections that follow.

Human Propensities for Prejudice: Social Identities and Self-Categorization

Arguably one of the most influential social psychological theories within intergroup relations is social identity theory (SIT; Tajfel, 1981; Tajfel & Turner, 1986; J. C. Turner, 1999). The theoretical engine of SIT is that people value social identities because they can potentially derive a positive sense of self from their group memberships, and that realizing this potential is a function of how favorably their group compares relative to other relevant groups.

SOCIAL IDENTITY THEORY

As a reaction to other theories that focus on historical and political contexts that define intergroup relations (see Sherif, 1966; Bobo, 1999), SIT researchers were motivated to investigate group relations in a "sterile" environment—void of historical and political factors—to examine psychological, and potentially universal, processes that underlie intergroup prejudice. They observed that the mere categorization of individuals into social groups—artificial or natural categories—motivates a need for positive distinctiveness, whereby individuals seek to identify and highlight the favorable and unique attributes of their group in comparison with other groups (see Tajfel, 1981; Tajfel & Turner, 1986). A primary explanatory mechanism here is that individuals strive for positive distinctiveness of their social groups, which often results in attitudes or behaviors favoring their own groups over other groups.

Research from the social identity perspective has further revealed that we tend to assume greater similarities between ourselves and other ingroup members, while perceiving greater differences between ourselves and outgroup members (Wilder, 1984). Indeed, even in the absence of long-standing conflicts between groups, we tend to evaluate our own groups more positively, and allocate more resources to our own groups, compared to how we evaluate and treat other groups (see Bourhis, Sachdev, & Gagnon, 1994; Tajfel, Billig, Bundy, & Flament, 1971). Moreover, we tend to take on the norms, behaviors, and attitudes of our groups, as we become increasingly motivated to promote the group's welfare and serve as good representatives for the group (see Hogg, 2003).

SELF-CATEGORIZATION THEORY

While social identity theory (SIT; Tajfel & Turner, 1986) focuses on intergroup relations and the biases that can result from group memberships, it does not elucidate the cognitive processes by which people come to identify themselves as members of social groups. As an extension of SIT, self-categorization theory (SCT; J. C. Turner, Hogg, Oakes, Reicher, & Wetherell, 1987) argues that people categorize information about themselves from the individual level (e.g., I like apple pie) to the group level (e.g., I am an American) as a function of the interactive forces of the environment and the individual's predispositions. Although the social environment exerts a strong influence on whether people identify themselves as individuals or as group members (see J. C. Turner & Onorato, 1999), people do have the capacity to change their self-categorizations across social contexts depending on the salience and accessibility of different self-attributes and social groups. Those social groups to which we often turn tend to be those that are more cognitively accessible and "on top of the mind" when we interact with others and seek meaning in our social worlds.

J. C. Turner and colleagues (1987) have also argued that there is a functional antagonism between individual and group levels of self-categorization, such that the more a person thinks of herself as a unique individual, the less she will be inclined to think of herself as a group member. However, the rigidity of this distinction between individual and group aspects of self has been challenged by other theoretical approaches highlighting the interplay between these levels, as our understandings of group memberships are influenced by our personal experiences as group members and the personal meanings we attach to them (see Deaux, 1993; Deaux & Perkins, 2001). Nonetheless, what is central for the present discussion is that when people categorize themselves as group members, they begin to think and act as group members, and become especially motivated to promote the interests and norms of their groups (see Hogg & Abrams, 1988).

Individual and Ideological Bases of Prejudice

While the cognitive and motivational processes outlined by social identity research may be common factors underlying intergroup prejudice, there are also many predictors of prejudice that are likely to vary across individuals. Although these tend to be conceptualized as personality variables, it is important to note that individual differences can develop over time through a person's experiences within social structures and institutions, such as familial, political, and economic systems. That is, social structures and institutions—be they large or small—have the capacity to impact and transform the psychology of individuals (e.g., see R. E. Lane, 1991; 2000).

AUTHORITARIAN PERSONALITY

As one well-known example, conceptions of the authoritarian personality (Adorno et al., 1950; Fromm, 1941) propose that individuals' early socialization experiences can predispose them to adopt a hierarchical orientation such that they hold authority figures in high regard and tend to denigrate those individuals or groups that are perceived to be weaker or lower in status. More specifically, individuals who

grow up in strict, rule-abiding, and disciplinary households are believed to be susceptible to adherence to strong authority figures and more likely to tolerate or even support the mistreatment of "weaker" and "nontraditional" groups. Thus, early childhood experiences (e.g., submission to strict parental authority) sow the seeds for a particular type of personality (i.e., authoritarian), which makes one prone to belligerence toward weak or deviant groups.

Almost since its initial development, authoritarian personality theory was met with considerable critique within the social science community. Criticisms varied but generally included concerns such as limitations associated with empirically testing the effects of early childhood socialization retrospectively, and the biased phrasing of questions that would induce agreement. More recent work by Altemeyer (1981, 1988) has sought to deal with these measurement issues, creating a reliable and well-validated scale to assess right-wing authoritarianism rooted in submission to authority and punitiveness toward deviants. However, ideological biases persist in the measurement of authoritarianism, such that the construct is often paired with political conservatism (e.g., Ray & Furnham, 1984). To be sure, political conservatism is often associated with higher prejudice scores, and at times it has been described as a motivated approach to seeing the world akin to other individual difference characteristics (see Jost, Glaser, Kruglanski, & Sulloway, 2003). Nonetheless, debates continue regarding whether political conservatism necessarily entails the endorsement of prejudice toward other groups (see Jost et al. 2009), and perhaps for this reason, greater research attention has focused on ideological variables based in psychological processes that are likely to motivate prejudice (e.g., Altemeyer, 1988; Jost & Banaji, 1994; Sidanius & Pratto, 1999).

Ideology is a particularly complex and slippery construct (Jost, 2006; Jost, Federico, Napier, 2009). Within political science, sociology, and social psychology there have been wide-ranging definitions attempting to converge on the essence of ideology (see Adorno et al., 1950; Apter, 1964; Converse, 1964; R. E. Lane, 1962; Rokeach, 1968). Social structures and institutions have "charges" (i.e., particular perspectives and/or suggested ways of being) that imbue their populations—to a greater or lesser degree—with a set of shared social representations (see Moscovici, 1988) that may be called *ideology*. Ideology has the capacity to inform and guide individual attitudes and behavior, and these in turn have the capability—in aggregate—to influence structures and social institutions (see mutual constitution; e.g., Shweder, 1990). Thus, ideology is not a static construct; it evolves as a function of the interplay between individuals and institutions.

While there is no clear consensus on a definition, Jost et al. (2009) suggest "that ideology is shared, that it helps to interpret the social world, and that it normatively specifies good and proper ways of addressing life's problems" (p. 309). In this regard, ideologies make explicit the *shared* values and beliefs of specific groups. These shared values and beliefs provide ways of interpreting the world and provide a "moral compass" as to how to navigate the world.

It is inevitably the case, however, that there are competing ideologies and groups that are well entrenched in their own philosophical perspectives. It is these "points of contact" between ideological perspectives where there is potential for tension and conflict—where psychological processes associated with ideology inform intergroup relations. We now turn to exploring key themes and theoretical perspectives that emphasize ideology to understand intergroup relations. In particular, we will discuss social dominance theory (Sidanius, 1993) and system justification theory (Jost & Banaji, 1994) in the sections that follow as examples of social psychological theories that highlight the importance of ideology in intergroup relations.

SOCIAL DOMINANCE THEORY

Social dominance theory (SDT; Sidanius, 1993; Sidanius & Pratto, 1999) argues that most, if not all, modern industrialized nations are defined by status- and power-based group hierarchies. That is, a common theme in most societies is a social hierarchy in which certain groups are at the top and others are at the bottom. Status and power hierarchies are concretized by the unequal distribution of positive resources (e.g., higher levels of education, greater home ownership, more access to health care) in which the dominant group members obtain more than subordinate group members. These trends are coupled with an unequal distribution of negative resources (e.g., higher imprisonment rates, increased mortality rates) through which subordinate groups are more adversely affected than dominant groups. Overall, SDT seeks to understand prejudice through the synthesis of sociostructural factors and person-level factors (see Hodson, 2009, for a related argument).

Specifically, Sidanius and colleagues (1993) argue that social hierarchies are maintained through "legitimizing myths" that act as ideological scaffolding maintaining the status quo. For example, hierarchy-enhancing myths work to ensure that social hierarchies are part of the (conscious or unconscious) language that individuals employ while interacting in society (e.g., racism, xenophobia). Conversely, hierarchy-attenuating myths promote egalitarian values and social equality (e.g., meritocracy, affirmative action). As societies vary in the proportion of hierarchy-enhancing and hierarchy-attenuating myths they espouse, they correspondingly vary in the relative stability of social hierarchies inherent in their communities.

Moreover, social dominance theory proposes that, as individuals go from infancy to adulthood to an advanced age, their position corresponds with a certain level of power in society. Similarly, arbitrary group differentiations—such as those based in ethnicity, race, or religion—are typically stratified within the hierarchical system. Sidanius and Pratto (1999; see also Pratto et al., 1994) further contend that individuals from high status groups are more likely to endorse group-based hierarchies than individuals from low status groups. However, this does not mean that individuals from low status groups will never support group-based hierarchies; indeed, individuals from low status groups may do so, even when it would appear to work against their own and their group's self-interest. Thus, social dominance theory accounts for power differentials through ideological mechanisms—such as legitimizing myths—and through individual-level endorsement of those status-based hierarchies (i.e., social dominance orientation).

Social dominance orientation (SDO; Pratto et al., 1994) is an individual difference variable assessing endorsement of hierarchical group relations and structural inequality (Sidanius, 1993; Sidanius & Pratto, 1999). Research within the social dominance framework shows there are interactions between person-level factors (i.e., levels of SDO) and situation-level factors (e.g., schools, workplaces). For example, Haley and Sidanius (2005) investigate the person-by-situation congruence as it applies to social organizations (e.g., work environments) and show how an individual's sociopolitical attitudes (e.g., SDO) should be compatible with their institutional environment. Hierarchy-enhancing organizations (e.g., police forces) are usually comprised of individuals with antiegalitarian beliefs, whereas hierarchy-attenuating organizations (e.g., human rights organizations) are usually comprised of individuals with relatively democratic beliefs.

The "sorting" of people into particular social environments may be reinforced by the extent to which (1) individuals choose to be in contexts that give them opportunities to act on their orientations (e.g., self-selection), and (2) the social context affords individuals high or low in SDO opportunities to behave in a manner consistent with their orientations (e.g., institutional selection and socialization). Self-selection involves processes by which people opt into certain environments, such as how a college student selects a major or a recent graduate selects her first job (Sidanius, Pratto, Sinclair, & van Laar, 1996). All things being equal, individuals tend to select environments that are compatible with their sociopolitical views. Similarly, institutions recruit and select individuals whose values appear congruent with the institutional culture, and socialization practices within institutions further fuel the compatibility between individuals' sociopolitical attitudes and the environment in which they find themselves (see also Newcomb, 1943).

Moreover, individuals who experience congruence between their sociopolitical values and the institutional culture are especially likely to enjoy a good amount of success. For example, van Laar, Sidanius, Rabinowitz, and Sinclair (1999) demonstrated individuals who have congruence between their college major (e.g., business) and sociopolitical attitudes (e.g., high SDO) tend to benefit from relatively high levels of academic achievement. By contrast, when individuals are a "poor fit" for their institutions (e.g., high SDO individuals in egalitarian environments) there is a greater likelihood of personal dissatisfaction, and disidentification and exit from the institution.

SYSTEM JUSTIFICATION THEORY

Work by Jost and colleagues (1994, 2004) on system justification focuses specifically on why subordinate group members willingly accept and, arguably, promote the group hierarchies inherent within social institutions. This perspective emphasizes the role that ideologies play in forming a "false consciousness" among subordinate groups such that members of these groups work to support the social hierarchy by accepting and even promoting group disparities. Thus, rather than react against the system that oppresses them, subordinate group members often work to promote and maintain such systems by such acts as outgroup favoritism. System justification theory emphasizes how ideology works to legitimize group-based power and status asymmetries, by promoting the perceptions that both high and low status groups deserve their lots in life. High status group members benefit from such ideologies because they maintain the status quo and ensure their privileged status; however, for low status group members, these ideological perspectives ensure their unprivileged status in society.

Although somewhat related, system justification theory (SJT) and social dominance theory (SDT) are distinct on several key issues. For instance, SDT argues that there are individual differences in support for group-based social hierarchies, whereas SJT does not propose any such individual differences and focuses solely on ideological structures that justify the system. Additionally, SDT distinguishes between hierarchy-enhancing and hierarchy-attenuating beliefs, whereas SJT emphasizes only those beliefs that maintain social hierarchies.

SDT also distinguishes between various forms of discrimination, in the forms of individual, institutional, and behavioral asymmetry, while SJT focuses primarily on behavioral asymmetry whereby low status group members favor the high status outgroup. Nonetheless, what these perspectives share in common is a focus on how ideologies and belief systems provoke behavioral and attitudinal responses toward other groups.

Social and Structural Dynamics of Prejudice

Moreover, due to the significance of the group-based hierarchies described above, there are likely to be a range of social and structural dimensions that instigate and perpetuate prejudice between groups. In particular, decades of work have shown that people are likely to develop prejudice and hostility toward other groups to the extent that they are perceived as posing a threat to one's own group (Sumner, 1906; Levine & Campbell, 1972; Sherif, 1966). Threats to one's group may be perceived and defined in a number of ways, such as against oneself as a group member in cross-group interaction (e.g., Stephan & Stephan, 1985), or when one becomes aware of negative stereotypes surrounding one's group membership (e.g., Steele, 1997). Yet perhaps the most commonly studied forms of threat in studies of prejudice involve structural relations between groups, such as those that involve (perceived or actual) conflicts in group interests and competition over material and social resources (e.g., Blumer, 1958; Bobo, 1999; Levine & Campbell, 1972; Quillian, 1995; see also Stephan & Stephan, 2000).

RECATEGORIZATION AND SUPERORDINATE GROUP IDENTITIES

Alternatively, a process of *recategorization* may also emerge, whereby members of initially distinct groups come to recognize their shared membership in a superordinate category that includes both groups (Gaertner & Dovidio, 2000). Gaertner, Dovidio, and their colleagues have conducted numerous studies in laboratory and field settings showing the benefits of recategorization for improving intergroup attitudes (e.g., Gaertner & Dovidio, 2000; Gaertner, Mann, Murrell, & Dovidio, 1989; Gaertner, Rust, Dovidio, Bachman, & Anastasio, 1994; Gaertner, Dovidio, & Bachman, 1996). When recategorization occurs, attitudes toward former outgroup members become more positive due to the same categorization processes that govern other forms of ingroup bias.

Depending on the relative salience of subgroup and superordinate categories, however, categorization at the superordinate level can be difficult to maintain, or may not always be successfully achieved when groups come into contact (Hornsey & Hogg, 2000; Dovidio, Gaertner & Saguy, 2009). For example, groups may not always agree on the characteristics that define the superordinate category (Mummendey & Wenzel, 1999). Moreover, due to asymmetries in status, characteristics of all groups may not be adequately represented at the superordinate level (Devos & Banaji, 2005), such that members of lower status groups may feel as if they are being subsumed within the broader social category (Hornsey & Hogg, 2000).

Additional empirical work supporting this perspective is well grounded in social dominance theory (Sidanius, 1993; Sidanius & Pratto, 1999). This perspective contends that the distribution of material and symbolic resources are largely guided by group-based status and power asymmetries, such that those who have greater status and power are motivated to maintain the status quo. In contexts of ethnic relations in diverse nations, one of the ways in which this group power asymmetry is concretized is through the domains of national identity in which the dominant group feels more "ownership" over the nation than subordinate groups. This tendency is revealed in trends such as higher levels of national identity for dominant group members (e.g., European Americans) compared to subordinate group members (e.g., African Americans) and a stronger positive association between ethnic identity and national identity for dominant group members compared to members of subordinate groups (see Sidanius, Feshbach, Levin, & Pratto, 1997; Sidanius & Petrocik, 2001; Staerkle, Sidanius, Green, & Molina, 2005; Staerkle, Sidanius, Green, & Molina, 2010).

As nations become increasingly diverse, one of the growing concerns is how to manage cultural diversity (Deaux, 2006; Fredrickson, 1999; Hollinger, 1995; Plaut, 2002; Prentice & Miller, 1999) and ensure that the positive effects of diversity are preserved (Page, 2007) while potential negative repercussions are diminished (e.g., Maalouf, 2003; Putnam, 2007). A central question, then, is how to create a sense of common, shared identity among people of diverse backgrounds that differ in power and status. Does a formation of "one-ness" require attenuation of subgroup loyalties (Schlesinger, 1998), recognition of valued subgroup identities (Huo & Molina, 2006), and/or salience of both national and ethnic identities (Hornsey & Hogg, 2000)?

Assimilation perspectives typically argue that an immigrant's ethnic ties decrease over time (e.g., generations) while ties to nation are simultaneously forming and growing (for reviews see Alba & Nee, 2003; Gordon, 1964; Portes & Rumbaut, 2006). Such perspectives are not without debate (see Rumbaut, 1999) and may be presented in one of several ways (see Suarez-Orozco, 2002). For example, in "classic" assimilationist approaches, ethnic loyalties are supplanted by national loyalties that typically have little, if any, resemblance to one's own customs, traditions, and beliefs. This version of assimilation argues that (old) ethnic loyalties are "melted away"—or in harsher terms, "obliterated"—and replaced by (new) national ties (Fredrickson, 1999; Gordon, 1964). In "revised" assimilationist approaches, ethnic loyalties and the beliefs, traditions, and norms associated with ethnicities "melt" into the national identity and redefine the content of the nation (Alba & Nee, 2003; see also LaFromboise et al., 1993). In this revised version, national identity is organic and evolves as a synthesis of many cultures and ideas such that identification with the nation serves to simultaneously reinforce ethnic ties.

Other variations propose that assimilation is a likely process for only a subset of groups. One variation is the *black exceptionalism hypothesis* (Sears & Savalei, 2006), which suggests that new immigrant groups such as Asians and Latinos will assimilate much as old European immigrants (e.g., Irish, Italian) did, while blacks have and will continue to remain relatively unincorporated into the American tapestry. The rationale here is that the black experience in America has been rather unique and severe in historical terms (e.g., slavery, Jim Crow), which has resulted in greater group consciousness and lower national attachment among blacks compared to other ethnic minority groups.

Another variation is referred to as *segmented assimilation* (Zhou, 1999) and focuses on the second generation and its economic incorporation into American society. The author argues that children of first-generation immigrants may follow three lines: (1) individuals integrate into the middle class and their ethnicities wane over time; (2) individuals may become part of the poorer social classes; or (3) individuals may have economic success and deliberately retain their ethnic identities. This variant allows for new immigrant groups to follow an "old European" immigrant account of full assimilation, a black nonintegration account, or an integration into American society while simultaneous maintenance of ethnic group identity.

While there are varied models of assimilation, as discussed above, psychological research in this area suggests that people's strategies for balancing ethnic and national identities may follow a range of trajectories not fully captured by assimilation approaches (Berry, 2001). That is, assimilation may not be sufficient to account for the range of psychological experiences and perspectives of diverse groups in a shared society (Sears & Savalei, 2006). In particular, racial and ethnic group identities may be highly valued and enhancing parts of an individual's self-concept (Huo & Molina, 2006; C. Taylor, 1994), such that any attempts to diminish loyalty to these groups would likely be interpreted as a threat (Branscombe et al., 1999; Hornsey & Hogg, 2000). Such trends are supported both by theoretical and empirical work in the social identity theory tradition (Tajfel & Turner, 1986; J. C. Turner et al., 1987) as well as work in political philosophy arguing that recognition of valued (sub-)group identities is one of the cornerstones of multiculturalism (e.g., Kymlicka, 1996; C. Taylor, 1994).

Hornsey and Hogg (2000) have therefore proposed that both superordinate (e.g., national) and subgroup (e.g., racial or ethnic) identities be maintained as dual identities (see also Hewstone, Rubin, & Willis, 2002; Gaertner & Dovidio, 2000). Specifically, these authors show that when superordinate identities are emphasized without recognition of subgroup identities, members of subgroups may experience this as an identity threat and in turn react with increased prejudice toward the dominant group; by contrast, when the valued subgroup identity is recognized in tandem with the superordinate identity, members of subgroups are likely to experience this as validation and report lower prejudice toward the dominant group (Hornsey & Hogg, 2000). Similar findings have been observed by Huo and Molina (2006), who show that among members of racial and ethnic minority groups, perceptions of subgroup respect—namely, recognition of one's valued subgroup by other members of the superordinate group—are related to more positive affect toward the superordinate group (e.g., Americans) and more trust in the justice system. While dominant and subordinate groups may both value integration (Zagefka & Brown, 2002), dominant group members tend to prefer representations that focus principally on the superordinate category, whereas subordinates tend to prefer dual identity representations (see Dovidio, Gaertner, & Kafati, 2000). Nonetheless, current perspectives emphasize the importance of recognizing both superordinate and subgroup identities in recategorization, in the hopes of maximizing the potential for prejudice reduction and positive relations between these groups.

THE ROLE OF CROSS-GROUP FRIENDSHIP IN INTERGROUP CONTACT

Recent work on intergroup contact has also pointed to the special role that cross-group friendships may play in prejudice reduction. In a pioneering paper, Pettigrew (1997) showed how the close affective ties generated by cross-group friendships could lead to greater intergroup liking and identification with outgroup members, which in turn fed into more positive feelings toward the outgroup as a whole. He analyzed cross-sectional survey responses from participants in seven different European nations, in which they were asked to state whether they had any friends of a different culture, nationality, race, ethnicity, or social class, and to complete several measures of intergroup prejudice. Pettigrew (1997) observed that having cross-group friendships was consistently and significantly associated with lower intergroup prejudice among participants across national contexts—and particularly for such affective prejudice measures as feelings of sympathy and admiration for the outgroup. By contrast, less intimate contact with outgroup members, such as coworkers or neighbors, yielded far smaller effects (see also Hamberger & Hewstone, 1997).

Wright, Aron, and their colleagues (Wright, Aron & Tropp, 2002; Wright, Brody, & Aron, 2005;

Wright & van der Zande, 1999) similarly propose that greater closeness to individual outgroup members corresponds with lower prejudice toward the whole outgroup through the mechanism of including the outgroup in the self. According to the authors' broader self-expansion model (see Aron & McLaughlin-Volpe, 2001; Brody, Wright, Aron, & McLaughlin-Volpe, 2008), people have an appetitive interest in outgroups, and especially in relations with outgroup members that would allow them to expand the self by incorporating a broader range of resources, perspectives, and identities that will help them to navigate the world. While noting that we may at times experience concern about being rejected, these authors further propose that we should be especially drawn to outgroup members who are quite different from ourselves, as they offer the greatest opportunities for self-expansion (Brody et al., 2008).

By virtue of including outgroup members in the self through the formation of cross-group friendships, we become inclined to give our outgroup friends (and other members of that friend's group) the same kinds of psychological benefits we normally reserve for ourselves and members of our own group. Cross-group friendships can lead us to make more positive attributions for outgroup members' intentions and behaviors (Joseph, Weatherall, & Stringer, 1997; Wright et al., 2002), and to become more concerned about the outgroup's welfare (Aron & McLaughlin-Volpe, 2001). In an early test of these ideas, McLaughlin-Volpe and her coauthors (2002) asked participants to report how many interactions they had had with outgroup members (quantity of contact), and how close they felt to the outgroup member with whom they had the closest relationship (quality of contact), along with reporting their feelings toward outgroup members in general. Greater numbers of cross-group interactions were associated with more positive feelings toward outgroup members, but only among those who reported having close cross-group relationships.

Similar findings have been observed in an experimental study by Wright and his colleagues (Wright, Aron, & Tropp, 2002; Wright, Brody, & Aron, 2005; Wright & van der Zande, 1999), which provided initial evidence for the causal effects of cross-group friendship on prejudice reduction. White female participants were randomly paired with either a same-ethnic partner (white) or a cross-ethnic partner (Latina or Asian) for four sessions over a period of 8 weeks, during which they engaged in a range of friendship-building activities. Participants reported feelings of closeness to the partner following each testing session, and after the final session, participants completed measures of intergroup outcomes, ostensibly as part of a separate study. White participants paired with a same-race and cross-race partner both developed strong feelings of closeness to their partners over the testing sessions. However, compared to those paired with a same-race partner, those paired with a cross-race partner showed less prejudiced responses, being less likely to cut university funding for ethnic minority organizations supporting the partner's ethnic group.

Recent meta-analytic investigations have yielded similar patterns of results (see Pettigrew & Tropp, 2006; Davies, Tropp, Aron, Pettigrew, & Wright, in press), such that cross-group friendships—and particularly those assessed with behavioral indicators of intimacy—typically show greater reductions in prejudice than other contact studies. Taken together with other recent findings (e.g., Aberson, Shoemaker, & Tomolillo, 2004; Binder et al., 2009; Eller & Abrams, 2004; Levin, van Laar, & Sidanius, 2003; Paolini, Hewstone, Cairns, & Voci, 2004), there is now a growing consensus that intergroup contact typically reduces prejudice, yet it is perhaps most effective for reducing prejudice when it involves close cross-group friendships.

This work largely supports Pettigrew's (1998) contention that *friendship potential* is an important factor for realizing the potential of intergroup contact to reduce prejudice, as it is typified by extensive and repeated equal status contact across a range of social contexts, which over time encourages greater degrees of shared experience, self-disclosure, and other kinds of friendship-building processes. There is also other evidence to suggest that situational features such as institutional support, cooperation, common goals, and equal status can facilitate positive contact experiences, and in turn, promote the development of cross-group friendships. For example, when students from different racial backgrounds participate cooperatively in shared school activities, they become more likely to choose each other as best friends (Hallinan & Teixeira, 1987; Patchen, 1982). Additionally, when children from different ethnolinguistic groups are educated in classes where their languages have equal status sanctioned by the school, they can become more likely to choose children from the other group as friends (Aboud & Sankar, 2007; Wright & Tropp, 2005). Such positive effects of cross-group friendships may also be cumulative over time, such that students with more cross-race friends during their high school years have a greater tendency to form cross-group friendships in college (e.g., Stearns et al., 2009).

We now have ample evidence to support the important role that friendship contact can play in prejudice reduction. Yet we still know relatively little about how cross-group friendships are experienced or navigated by the individuals involved. Some recent work suggests that self-disclosure and perceived partner responsiveness can promote greater intimacy in cross-group friendships (see Shelton, Trail, West, & Bergsieker, 2010; R. N. Turner et al., 2007). In addition, individuals can vary in the extent to which they are willing to engage with members of other groups. For example, people who score highly on "openness to experience" may be more likely to seek out contact opportunities (Jackson & Poulsen, 2005), as part of a broader orientation toward trying out new cultural experiences (McCrae & Costa, 1997). Compared to those low in openness to experience, people high in openness to experience also tend to score lower on authoritarianism (Hodson, Hogg, & MacInnis, 2009), such that their positive contact may be more likely to translate into lowered prejudice and the formation of cross-group friendships. At the same time, other work shows that positive contact is often most effective in shifting intergroup attitudes among people who are least inclined toward relationships with outgroup members, such as those high in social dominance orientation and authoritarianism (Dhont & van Hiel, 2009; Hodson, 2008; Hodson, Harry, & Mitchell, 2009), and low in support for diversity (Adesokan, van Dick, Ullrich, & Tropp, in press). Thus, although some may be initially less drawn toward intergroup contact or less inclined to develop friendships with outgroup members, positive outcomes of contact can still be achieved even among those most resistant to cross-group relationships.

Nonetheless, an enduring structural barrier to the formation of cross-group friendships involves societal patterns of segregation (Orfield & Lee, 2007). Segregation can inhibit people's opportunities to develop friendships across group boundaries both through lack of opportunity (see Pettigrew, 1998; Wagner, Christ, Pettigrew, Stellmacher, & Wolf, 2007), and through disrupting communication between potential friends when contact does occur (Vorauer & Sakamoto, 2006). Studies with children and adolescents suggest that they are generally more likely to choose same-race than cross-race friends (Dubois & Hirsch, 1990; Hallinan & Teixeira, 1987), although they become more likely

to report cross-race friendships when there is a greater representation of students from other races in their schools (Hallinan & Smith, 1985; Joyner & Kao, 2000; Khmelkov & Hallinan, 1999).

There is also other evidence to suggest that cross-group friendships can be more difficult to sustain over time than same-race friendships. Cross-group friendships typically decrease during the transition from childhood to adolescence (Asher, Singleton, & Taylor, 1982; Dubois & Hirsch, 1990), such that children become even more likely to have greater numbers of same-race than cross-race friends as they grow older (Aboud, Mendelson, & Purdy, 2003). This may be because parents and peers are important sources of information that can either encourage or discourage interactions across group boundaries (Aboud, 2005; Aboud & Sankar, 2007; Edmonds & Killen, 2009; Fishbein, 1996). It may well be for these reasons that cross-group ties are more vulnerable and harder to maintain than same-group ties (Reagans, 1998), and why people may resegregate voluntarily even when there are opportunities for intergroup contact (Clack, Dixon, & Tredoux, 2005; Rogers, Hennigan, Bowman, & Miller, 1984; Schofield, 1978; Tatum, 1997).

Anxiety Reduction Through Intergroup Contact

Such trends suggest that, whether due to societal segregation or social messages, people often experience a great deal of uncertainty and anxiety about navigating relationships across group lines (Stephan & Stephan, 1985; Stephan, Stephan, & Gudykunst, 1999), and these tendencies can curb their willingness to forge cross-group friendships. Indeed, people often anticipate being rejected in intergroup encounters, which can curb their interest or willingness to participate in intergroup contact (see Shelton & Richeson, 2005; Tropp & Bianchi, 2006). Moreover, individuals may vary in the extent to which they are chronically aware of their group membership (Pinel, 1999) and expect to be rejected by others on the basis of group membership (Mendoza-Denton et al., 2002), which could further contribute to anxieties about cross-group interactions.

Researchers have therefore begun to examine the roles that anxiety and other psychological processes play in intergroup encounters, and how these processes may be transformed through intergroup contact. Reviewing much of the recent work in this area, Trawalter, Richeson, and Shelton (2009) suggest that anxious responses to cross-group

Conclusion

In this chapter, we have reviewed a range of perspectives concerning individual and contextual factors that contribute to creating and reducing intergroup prejudice. Prior work has typically favored a focus either on the individual or on the social context in predicting prejudice and its reduction (see Hodson, 2009), yet emerging theory and research offers great potential for the convergence of these approaches. Future intergroup research should therefore pursue the joint exploration of psychological motivations and experiences of individuals and features of the broader social context that may fuel or influence individuals' motivations and experiences. Such a multifaceted, contextual approach would not only enable us to develop a more nuanced understanding of intergroup encounters, but would also serve to inform the strategies we use to reduce prejudice, diminish intergroup threat and anxiety, and build the capacity for empathy and positive relations between groups.

References

Aberson, C., Shoemaker, C., & Tomolillo, C. (2004). Implicit bias and contact: The role of interethnic friendships. *Journal of Social Psychology, 144,* 335–347.

Aboud, F. E. (2005). The development of prejudice in childhood and adolescence. In J. F. Dovidio, P. Glick, & L. A. Rudman (Eds.), *On the nature of prejudice: Fifty years after Allport* (pp. 310–326). Malden, MA: Blackwell.

Aboud, F. E., Mendelson, M. J., & Purdy, K. T. (2003). Cross-race peer relations and friendship quality. *International Journal of Behavioral Development, 27*(2), 165–173.

Aboud, F. E., & Sankar, J. (2007). Friendship and identity in a language-integrated school. *International Journal of Behavioral Development, 31,* 445–453.

Adesokan, A., van Dick, R., Ullrich, J., & Tropp, L. R. (in press). Diversity beliefs as a moderator of the contact-prejudice relationship. *Social Psychology.*

Adorno, T. W., Frenkel-Brunswik, E., Levinson, D. J., & Sanford, R. N. (1950). *The authoritarian personality.* New York: Harper & Row.

Alba, R., & Nee, V. (2003). *Remaking the American mainstream: Assimilation and contemporary immigration.* Cambridge, MA: Harvard University Press.

Allport, G. W. (1954). *The nature of prejudice.* Reading, MA: Addison-Wesley.

Altemeyer, B. (1981). *Right-wing authoritarianism.* Winnipeg: University of Manitoba Press.

Altemeyer, B. (1988). *Enemies of freedom: Understanding right-wing authoritarianism.* San Francisco: Jossey-Bass.

Apter, D. E. (1964). *Ideology and discontent.* New York: Free Press.

Arkin, R. M., Carroll, P. J., & Oleson, K. C. (2010). Commentary: The end of the beginning. In R. M. Arkin, K. C. Oleson, & J. P. Carroll (Eds.), *Handbook of the uncertain self* (pp. 444–448). New York: Psychology Press.

Aron, A., & McLaughlin-Volpe, T. (2001). Including others in the self: Extensions to own and partner's group memberships. In C. Sedikides & M. Brewer (Eds.), *Individual self, relational self, collective self* (pp. 89–108). New York: Psychology Press.

Aronson, E., & Gonzalez, A. (1988). Desegregation, jigsaw, and the Mexican-American experience. In P. A. Katz & D. A. Taylor (Eds.), *Eliminating racism: Profiles in controversy* (pp. 301–314). New York: Plenum.

Asher, S. R., Singleton, L. C., & Taylor, A. R. (1982). *Acceptance versus friendship: A longitudinal study of racial integration.* Paper presented at the annual meeting of the American Educational Research Association, New York.

Batson, C. D., Polycarpou, M. P., Harmon-Jones, E., Imhoff, H. J., Mitchener, E. C., Bednar, L. I., et al. (1997). Empathy and attitudes: Can feeling for a member of a stigmatized group improve feelings toward the group? *Journal of Personality and Social Psychology, 72* (1), 105–118.

Baumeister, R. F., & Leary, M. R. (1995). The need to belong: Desire for interpersonal attachments as a fundamental human motivation. *Psychological Bulletin, 117,* 497–529.

Berry, J. W. (2001). A psychology of immigration. *Journal of Social Issues, 57,* 615–631.

Bettencourt, B. A., Brewer, M. B., Croak, M. R., & Miller, N. (1992). Cooperation and the reduction of intergroup bias: The role of reward structure and social orientation. *Journal of Experimental Social Psychology, 28*(4), 301–319.

Binder, J., Zagefka, H., Brown, R., Funke, F., Kessler, T., Mummendey, A., et al. (2009). Does contact reduce prejudice or does prejudice reduce contact? A longitudinal test of the contact hypothesis amongst majority and minority groups in three European countries. *Journal of Personality and Social Psychology, 96*(4), 843–856.

Blalock, H. M. (1967). *Toward a theory of minority-group relations.* New York: Wiley.

Blascovich., J., Mendes, W. B., Hunter, S. B., Lickel, B., & Kowai-Bell, N. (2001). Perceiver threat in social interactions with stigmatized others. *Journal of Personality and Social Psychology, 80,* 253–267.

Blumer, H. (1958). Race prejudice as a sense of group position. *Pacific Sociological Review, 1,* 3–7.

Bobo, L. (1988). Group conflict, prejudice, and the paradox of contemporary racial attitudes. In P. A. Katz & D. A. Taylor (Eds.), *Eliminating racism: Profiles in controversy* (pp. 85–114). New York: Plenum.

Bobo, L. (1999). Prejudice as group position: Microfoundations of a sociological approach to racism and race relations. *Journal of Social Issues, 55,* 445–472.

Bonilla-Silva, E. (2003). *Racism without racists: Color-blind racism and the persistence of racial inequality in the United States.* Lanham, MD: Rowman & Littlefield.

Bourhis, R. Y., Sachdev, I., & Gagnon, A. (1994). Intergroup research with the Tajfel matrices: Methodological notes. In M. P. Zanna and J. M. Olson (Eds.), *The psychology of prejudice: The Ontario symposium* (pp. 209–232). Hillsdale, NJ: Erlbaum.

Branscombe, N. R., Ellemers, N., Spears, R., & Doosje, B. (1999). The context and content of social identity threat. In N. Ellemers, R. Spears, & B. Doosje (Eds.), *Social identity: Context, commitment, and content* (pp. 35–58). Oxford, UK: Blackwell.

Brewer, M. B. (1991). The social self: On being the same and different at the same time. *Personality and Social Psychology Bulletin, 17* (5), 475–482.

Brewer, M. B. (1999). The psychology of prejudice: Ingroup love or outgroup hate? *Journal of Social Issues, 55* (3), 429–444.

Brewer, M. B., & Brown, R. J. (1998). Intergroup relations. In D. T. Gilbert, S. T. Fiske, & G. Lindzey (Eds.), *The handbook of social psychology* (4th ed., Vol. 2, pp. 554–594). New York: McGraw-Hill.

Brewer, M. B., & Kramer, R. M. (1985). The psychology of intergroup attitudes and behavior. *Annual Review of Psychology, 36*, 219–243.

Brewer, M. B. & Miller, N. (1984). Beyond the contact hypothesis: Theoretical perspectives on desegregation. In N. Miller & M. B. Brewer (Eds.), *Groups in contact: The psychology of desegregation* (pp. 291–302). Orlando, FL: Academic.

Brody, S. Wright, S. C., Aron, A., & McLaughlin-Volpe, T. (2008). Compassionate love for individuals in other social groups. In B. Fehr, S. Sprecher, & L. Underwood (Eds.), *The science of compassionate love* (pp. 283–308). Malden, MA: Wiley.

Brown, R., Eller, A., Leeds, S., & Stace, K. (2007). Intergroup contact and intergroup attitudes: A longitudinal study. *European Journal of Social Psychology, 37*, 692–703.

Brown, R., & Hewstone, M. (2005). An integrative theory of intergroup contact. *Advances in Experimental Social Psychology, 37*, 255–343.

Brown, R., Maras, P., Masser, B., Vivian, J., & Hewstone, M. (2001). Life on the ocean wave: Testing some intergroup hypotheses in a naturalistic setting. *Group Processes and Intergroup Relations, 4*, 81–97.

Brown, R., Vivian, J., & Hewstone, M. (1999). Changing attitudes through intergroup contact: The effects of group membership salience. *European Journal of Social Psychology, 29*, 741–764.

Butz, D. A., & Plant, E. A. (2006). Perceiving outgroup members as unresponsive: Implications for approach-related emotions, intentions, and behavior. *Journal of Personality and Social Psychology, 91*(6), 1066–1079.

Carroll, P. J., Arkin, R. M., Seidel, S. D., & Morris, J. (2009). The relative importance of needs among traumatized and non-traumatized samples. *Motivation and Emotion, 33*, 373–386.

Clack, B., Dixon, J., & Tredoux, C. (2005). Eating together apart: Patterns of segregation in a multi-ethnic cafeteria. *Journal of Community and Applied Psychology, 15*, 1–16.

Cohen, E. G. (1982). Expectation states and interracial interaction in school settings. *Annual Review of Sociology, 8*, 209–235.

Converse, P. E. (1964). The nature of belief systems in mass publics. In D. E. Apter (Ed.), *Ideology and discontent* (pp. 206–261). New York: Free Press.

Cook, S. W. (1984). Cooperative interaction in multiethnic contexts. In N. Miller & M. B. Brewer (Eds.), *Groups in contact: The psychology of desegregation* (pp. 155–185). Orlando, FL: Academic.

Cook, S.W., & Sellitz, C. (1955) Some factors which influence the attitudinal outcomes of personal contact. *International Social Science Bulletin, 7*, 51–58.

Crandall, C. S., Eshelman, A., & O'Brien, L. (2002). Social norms and the expression and suppression of prejudice: The struggle for internalization. *Journal of Personality and Social Psychology, 82*, 359-378.

Davies, K., Tropp, L. R., Aron, A., Pettigrew, T. F., & Wright, S. C. (in press). Cross-group friendships and intergroup attitudes: A meta-analytic review. *Personality and Social Psychology Review*.

Deaux, K. (1993). Reconstructing social identity. *Personality and Social Psychology Bulletin, 19*, 4–12.

Deaux, K. (2006). *To be an immigrant*. New York: Russell Sage.

Deaux, K., & Perkins, T. S. (2001). The kaleidoscope self. In C. Sedikides & M. B. Brewer (Eds.), *Individual self, relational self, collective self* (pp. 299–313). Philadelphia: Psychology Press.

Devine, P. G., & Vasquez, K. A. (1998). The rocky road to positive intergroup relations. In J. L. Eberhardt & S. T. Fiske (Eds.), *Confronting racism: The problem and the response* (pp. 234–262). Thousand Oaks, CA: Sage.

Devos, T., & Banaji, M.R. (2005). American = white? *Journal of Personality and Social Psychology, 88*(3), 447–466.

Dhont, K. & Van Hiel, A. (2009). We must not be enemies: Interracial contact and the reduction of prejudice among authoritarians. *Personality and Individual Differences, 46*, 172–177.

Dovidio, J. F., Brigham, J. C., Johnson, B. T., & Gaertner, S. L. (1996). Stereotyping, prejudice, and discrimination: Another look. In C. N. Macrae, C. Stangor, & M. Hewstone (Eds.), *Stereotypes and stereotyping* (pp. 276–322). New York: Guilford.

Dovidio, J. F., & Gaertner, S. L. (1998). On the nature of contemporary prejudice: The causes, consequences, and challenges of aversive racism. In J. L. Eberhardt & S. T. Fiske (Eds.), *Confronting racism: The problem and the response* (pp. 3–32). Thousand Oaks, CA: Sage.

Dovidio, J. F., Gaertner, S. L., & Kafati, G. (2000). Group identity and intergroup relations: The common ingroup identity model. In S. Thye, E. Lawler, M. Macy, & H. Walker (Eds.), *Advances in group processes* (pp. 1–35). Stamford, CT: JAI Press.

Dovidio, J. F., Gaertner, S. L., & Saguy, T. (2009). Commonality and the complexity of "we": Social attitudes and social change. *Personality and Social Psychology Review, 13*, 3–20.

Dovidio, J. F., Glick, P., & Rudman, L. A. (Eds.). (2005). *On the nature of prejudice: Fifty years after Allport*. Malden, MA: Blackwell.

DuBois, D. L., & Hirsch, B. J. (1990). School and neighborhood friendship patterns of blacks and whites in early adolescence. *Child Development, 61*, 524–536.

Duckitt, J. (1992). Psychology and prejudice: A historical analysis and integrative framework. *American Psychologist, 47*(10), 1182–1193.

Edmonds, C., & Killen, M. (2009). Do adolescents' perceptions of parental racial attitudes relate to their intergroup contact and cross-race relationships? *Group Processes and Intergroup Relations, 12*, 5–21.

Eggins, R. A., Haslam, S. A., & Reynolds, K. J. (2002). Social identity and negotiation: Subgroup representation and superordinate consensus. *Personality and Social Psychology Bulletin, 28*, 887–899.

Eller, A., & Abrams, D. (2004). Come together: Longitudinal comparisons of Pettigrew's reformulated intergroup contact model and the common ingroup identity model in Anglo-French and Mexican-American contexts. *European Journal of Social Psychology, 34*, 229–256.

Ensari, N. K., & Miller, N. (2002). The out-group must not be so bad after all: The effects of disclosure, typicality, and salience on intergroup bias. *Journal of Personality and Social Psychology, 83*, 313–329.

Esses, V. M., Dovidio, J. F., Jackson, L. M., & Armstrong, T. L. (2001). The immigration dilemma: The role of perceived group competition, ethnic prejudice, and national identity. *Journal of Social Issues, 57,* 389–412.

Esses, V. M., Wagner, U., Wolf, C., Preiser, M., & Wilbur, C. J. (2006). Perceptions of national identity and attitudes towards immigrants and immigration in Canada and Germany. *International Journal of Intercultural Relations, 30,* 685–696.

Fishbein, H. D. (1996). *Peer prejudice and discrimination: Evolutionary, cultural, and developmental dynamics.* Boulder, CO: Westview.

Fiske, S. T., Cuddy, A. J. C., Glick, P., & Xu, J. (2002). A model of (often mixed) stereotype content: Competence and warmth respectively follow from perceived status and competition. *Journal of Personality and Social Psychology, 82*(6), 878–902.

Fiske, S. T., & Neuberg, S. L. (1999). The continuum model: Ten years later. In S. Chaiken & Y. Trope (Eds.), *Dual-process theories in social psychology* (pp. 231–254). New York: Guilford.

Fiske, S. T., Xu, J., Cuddy, A. C., & Glick, P. (1999). (Dis) respecting versus (dis)liking: Status and interdependence predict ambivalent stereotypes of competence and warmth. *Journal of Social Issues, 55*(3), 473–489.

Forbes, H. D. (1997). *Ethnic conflict: Commerce, culture, and the contact hypothesis.* New Haven, CT: Yale University Press.

Fossett, M. A., & Kielcolt, J. (1989). The relative size of minority populations and whites' racial attitudes. *Social Science Quarterly, 70,* 820–835.

Foster, D., & Finchilescu, G. (1986). Contact in a "non-contact" society: The case of South Africa. In M. Hewstone & R. Brown (Eds.), *Contact and conflict in intergroup encounters* (pp. 119–136). Oxford, UK: Blackwell.

Fredrickson, G. M. (1999). Models of American ethnic relations: A historical perspective. In D. A. Prentice & D. T. Miller (Eds.), *Cultural divides: Understanding and overcoming group conflict* (pp. 23–34). New York: Russell Sage.

Frey, F. E., & Tropp, L. R. (2006). Being seen as individuals versus as group members: Extending research on metaperception to intergroup contexts. *Personality and Social Psychology Review, 10,* 265–280.

Fromm, E. (1941). *The fear of freedom.* London, UK: Routledge.

Gable, S. L., & Strachman, A. (2008). Approaching social rewards and avoiding social punishments: Appetitive and aversive social motivation. In J. Y. Shah & W. Gardner (Eds.), *Handbook of motivation science* (pp. 561-575). New York: Guilford.

Gaertner, S. L., & Dovidio, J. F. (2000). *Reducing intergroup bias: The common ingroup identity model.* Ann Arbor, MI: Taylor & Francis.

Gaertner, S. L., Dovidio, J. F., & Bachman, B. A. (1996). Revisiting the contact hypothesis: The induction of a common ingroup identity. *International Journal of Intercultural Relations, 20,* 271–290.

Gaertner, S. L., Mann, J., Murrell, A., & Dovidio, J. F. (1989). Reducing intergroup bias: The benefits of recategorization. *Journal of Personality and Social Psychology, 57,* 239–249.

Gaertner, S. L., Rust, M. C., Dovidio, J. F., Bachman, B. A., & Anastasio, P. A. (1994). The contact hypothesis: The role of a common ingroup identity on reducing intergroup bias. *Small Groups Research, 25,* 224–249.

Galinsky, A. D., & Moskowitz, G. B. (2000). Perspective-taking: Decreasing stereotype expression, stereotype accessibility, and in-group favoritism. *Journal of Personality and Social Psychology, 78* (4), 708–724.

Gordon, M. M. (1964). *Assimilation in American life: The role of race, religion, and national origins.* New York: Oxford University Press.

Green, C. W., Adams, A. F., & Turner, C. W. (1988). Development and validation of the School Interracial Climate Survey. *American Journal of Community Psychology, 16,* 241–259.

Haley, H., & Sidanius, J. (2005). Person-organization congruence and the maintenance of group-based social hierarchy: A social dominance perspective. *Group Processes and Intergroup Relations, 8,* 187–203.

Hallinan, M. T., & Smith, S. S. (1985). The effects of classroom racial composition on students' interracial friendliness. *Social Psychology Quarterly, 48,* 3–16.

Hallinan, M. T., & Teixeira, R. A. (1987). Opportunities and constraints: Black-white differences in the formation of interracial friendships. *Child Development, 58,* 1358–1371.

Hamberger, J., & Hewstone, M. (1997). Inter-ethnic contact as a predictor of blatant and subtle prejudice: Tests of a model in four West European nations. *British Journal of Social Psychology, 36,* 173–190.

Hewstone, M. (2003). Intergroup contact: Panacea for prejudice? *Psychologist, 16,* 352–355.

Hewstone, M., & Brown, R. (Eds.). (1986). *Contact and conflict in intergroup encounters.* Oxford, UK: Blackwell.

Hewstone, M., Rubin, M., & Willis, H. (2002). Intergroup bias. *Annual Review of Psychology, 53,* 575–604.

Hodson, G. (2008). Interracial prison contact: The pros for (social dominant) cons. *British Journal of Social Psychology, 47,* 325–351.

Hodson, G. (2009). The puzzling person-situation schism in prejudice research. *Journal of Research in Personality, 43,* 247–248.

Hodson, G., Harry, H., & Mitchell, A. (2009). Independent benefits of contact and friendship on attitudes toward homosexuals among authoritarians and highly identified heterosexuals. *European Journal of Social Psychology, 35,* 509–525.

Hodson, G., Hogg, S. M., & MacInnis, C. C. (2009). The role of "dark personalities" (narcissism, Machiavellianism, psychopathy), Big Five personality factors, and ideology in explaining prejudice. *Journal of Research in Personality, 43,* 686–690.

Hogg, M. A. (2003). Social identity. In M. Leary & J. P. Tangey (Eds.), *Handbook of self and identity* (pp. 462–479). New York: Guilford.

Hogg, M. A. (2010). Human groups, social categories, and collective self: Social identity and the management of self-uncertainty. In R. M. Arkin, K. C. Oleson, & P. J. Carroll (Eds.), *Handbook of the uncertain self* (pp. 401–420). New York: Psychology Press.

Hogg, M. A., & Abrams, D. (1988). *Social identifications: A social psychology of intergroup relations and group processes.* London and New York: Routledge and Kegan Paul.

Hollinger, D. (1995). *Post-ethnic America.* New York: Basic Books.

Hornsey, M. J., & Hogg, M. A. (2000). Subgroup relations: A comparison of mutual intergroup differentiation and common ingroup identity models of prejudice reduction. *Personality and Social Psychology Bulletin, 26*(2), 242–256.

Horowitz, D. (2000). *Ethnic groups in conflict.* Berkeley and Los Angeles: University of California Press.

Huo, Y. J., & Molina, L. E. (2006). Is pluralism a viable model of diversity? The benefits and limits of subgroup respect. *Group Processes and Intergroup Relations, 9,* 359–376.

Islam, M. R., & Hewstone, M. (1993). Dimensions of contact as predictors of intergroup anxiety, perceived out-group variability, and out-group attitude: An integrative model. *Personality and Social Psychology Bulletin, 19,* 700–710.

Jackson, J. W., & Poulsen, J. R. (2005). Contact experiences mediate the relationship between five-factor model personality traits and ethnic prejudice. *Journal of Applied Social Psychology, 35,* 667–685.

Johnson, D. W., Johnson, R. T., & Maruyama, G. (1984). Goal interdependence and interpersonal-personal attraction in heterogeneous classrooms: A meta-analysis. In N. Miller & M. B. Brewer (Eds.), *Groups in contact: The psychology of desegregation* (pp. 187–212). Orlando, FL: Academic.

Joseph, S., Weatherall, K., & Stringer, M. (1997). Attributions for unemployment in Northern Ireland: Does it make a difference what your name is? *Irish Journal of Psychology, 18*(3), 341–348.

Jost, J. T. (2006). The end of the end of ideology. *American Psychologist, 61*(7), 651–670.

Jost, J. T., & Banaji, M. (1994). The role of stereotyping in system justification and the production of false consciousness. *British Journal of Social Psychology, 33,* 1–27.

Jost, J. T., & Banaji, M. R., Nosek, B. A. (2004). A decade of system justification theory: Accumulated evidence of the conscious and unconscious bolstering of the status quo. *Political Psychology, 25,* 881–920.

Jost, J. T., Federico, C. M., & Napier, J. L. (2009). Political ideology: Its structure, function, and elective affinities. *Annual Review of Psychology, 60,* 307–337.

Jost, J., Glaser, J., Kruglanski, A. W., & Sulloway, F. J. (2003). Political conservatism as motivated social cognition. *Psychological Bulletin, 129,* 339–375.

Joyner, K., & Kao, G. (2000). School racial composition and adolescent racial homophily. *Social Science Quarterly, 81,* 810–825.

Kalev, A., Dobbin, F., & Kelly, E. (2006). Best practices or best guesses? Assessing the efficacy of corporate affirmative action and diversity policies. *American Sociological Review, 71*(4), s589–617.

Khmelkov, V. T., & Hallinan, M. T. (1999). Organizational effects on race relations in schools. *Journal of Social Issues, 55*(4), 627–645.

Kramer, R. M., & Messick, D. M. (1998). Getting by with a little help from our enemies: Collective paranoia and its role in intergroup relations. In C. Sedikides, J. Schopler, & C. A. Insko (Eds.), *Intergroup cognition and intergroup behavior* (pp. 233–255). Mahwah, NJ: Erlbaum.

Kramer, R. M., & Wei, J. (1999). Social uncertainty and the problem of trust in social groups: The social self in doubt. In T. Tyler, R. M. Kramer, & O. P. John (Eds.), *The psychology of the social self* (pp. 145–168). Mahwah, NJ: Erlbaum.

Kurzban, R., & Neuberg, S. (2005). Managing ingroup and outgroup relationships. In D. M. Buss (Ed.), *The handbook of evolutionary psychology* (pp. 653–675). Hoboken, NJ: Wiley.

Kymlicka, W. (1996). *Multicultural citizenship.* Oxford, UK: Oxford University Press.

Landis, D., Hope, R. O., & Day, H. R. (1984). Training for desegregation in the military. In M. B. Brewer & N. Miller (Eds.), *Groups in contact: The psychology of desegregation* (pp. 258–278). Orlando, FL: Academic.

LaFromboise, T., Coleman, H., & Gerton, J. (1993). Psychological aspects of bicultural competence: Evidence and theory. *Psychological Bulletin, 114,* 395–412.

Lane, K. A., Banaji, M. R., Nosek, B. A., & Greenwald, A. G. (2007). Understanding and using the Implicit Association Test: IV. Procedures and validity. In B. Wittenbrink & N. Schwarz (Eds.), *Implicit measures of attitudes: Procedures and controversies (pp. 59–102).* New York: Guilford.

Lane, R. E. (1962). *Political ideology.* Oxford, UK: Free Press.

Lane, R. E. (1991). *The market experience.* Cambridge, UK: Cambridge University Press.

Lane, R. E. (2000). *The loss of happiness in market democracies.* New Haven, CT: Yale University Press.

Lee, Y. T., McCauley, C., Moghaddam, F., & Worchel, S. (2004) (Eds.). The psychology of ethnic and cultural conflict. Westport, CT: Praeger.

Leary, M. R., Tambor, E. S., Terdal, S. K., & Downs, D. L. (1995). Self-esteem as an interpersonal monitor: The sociometer hypothesis. *Journal of Personality and Social Psychology, 68,* 518–530.

Lee, Y. T., McCauley, C., Moghaddam, F., & Worchel, S. (Eds.). (2004). *The psychology of ethnic and cultural conflict.* Westport, CN: Praeger.

Levin, S., van Laar, C., & Sidanius, J. (2003). The effects of ingroup and outgroup friendships on ethnic attitudes in college: A longitudinal study. *Group Processes and Intergroup Relations, 6,* 76–92.

Levine, R. A., & Campbell, D. T. (1972). *Ethnocentrism: Theories of conflict, ethnic attitudes, and group behavior.* New York: Wiley.

Longshore, D., & Wellisch, J. (1981). *The impact of the Emergency School Aid Act on human relations in desegregated elementary schools.* Paper presented at the annual meeting of the American Sociological Association.

Maalouf, A. (2000). *In the name of identity: Violence and the need to belong.* New York: Penguin.

Mallett, R., K., Huntsinger, J. R., Sinclair, J. R., & Swim, J. K. (2008). Seeing through their eyes: When majority group members take collective action on behalf of an outgroup. *Group Processes and Intergroup Relations, 11* (4), 451–470.

Mallett, R. K., & Wilson, T. D. (2010). Increasing positive intergroup contact. *Journal of Experimental Social Psychology, 46,* 382–387.

Maslow, A. (1962). *Toward a psychology of being.* Princeton, NJ: Van Nostrand.

Maslow, A. H. (1943). A theory of human motivation. Psychological Review, 50, 370-396.

McCrae, R. R., & Costa, P. T. (1997). Conceptions and correlates of openness to experience. In R. Hogan, J. A. Johnson, & S. R. Briggs (Eds.), *Handbook of personality psychology* (pp. 825–847). Orlando, FL: Academic.

McLaughlin-Volpe, T., Aron, A., Wright, S. C., & Reis, H. T. (2002). *Intergroup social interaction and intergroup prejudice: Quantity versus quality.* Unpublished manuscript.

Mendoza-Denton, R., Downey, G., Purdie, V. J., Davis, A., & Pietrzak, J. (2002). Sensitivity to status-based rejection: Implications for African American students' college experience. *Journal of Personality and Social Psychology, 83,* 896–918.

Mendoza-Denton, R., Page-Gould, E., & Pietrzak, J. (2006). Mechanisms for coping with status-based rejection expectations. In S. Levin & C. van Laar (Eds.), *Stigma and group inequality: Social psychological perspectives* (pp. 151–169). Mahwah, NJ: Erlbaum.

Migacheva, K., & Tropp, L. R. (2010, June). *Learning goals as a way to promote positive intergroup contact.* Paper presented at the biennial meeting of the Society for the Psychological Study of Social Issues, New Orleans.

Migacheva, K., Tropp, L. R., & Crocker, J. (2011). Focusing beyond the self: Goal orientations in intergroup relations. In L. R. Tropp & R. Mallett (Eds.), *Moving beyond prejudice reduction: Pathways to positive intergroup relations* (pp. 91-115). Washington, DC: American Psychological Association.

Miller, N. (2002). Personalization and the promise of contact theory. *Journal of Social Issues, 58,* 387–410.

Miller, N., Brewer, M. B., & Edwards, K. (1985). Cooperative interaction in desegregated settings: A laboratory analogue. *Journal of Social Issues, 41*(3), 63–79.

Miller, N., & Harrington, H. J. (1995). Social categorization and intergroup acceptance: Principles for the design and development of cooperative learning teams. In R. Hertz-Lazarowitz & N. Miller (Eds.), *Interaction in cooperative groups* (pp. 203–227). New York: Cambridge University Press.

Molden, D. C., Lee, A. Y., & Higgins, E. T. (2008). Motivations for promotion and prevention. In J. Y. Shah & W. L. Gardner (Eds.), *Handbook of motivation science* (pp. 169–187). New York: Guilford.

Molina, L. E., & Wittig, M. A. (2006). Relative importance of contact conditions in explaining prejudice reduction in a classroom context: Separate and equal? *Journal of Social Issues, 62*(3), 489–509.

Molina, L. E., Wittig, M. A., & Giang, M. T. (2004). Mutual acculturation and social categorization: A comparison of two perspectives on intergroup bias. *Group Processes and Intergroup Relations, 7*(3), 239–265.

Moscovici, S. (1988). Notes toward a description of social representations. *European Journal of Social Psychology, 18* (3), 211–250.

Mummendey, A., Otten, S., Berger, U., & Kessler, T. (2000). Positive-negative asymmetry in social discrimination: Valence of evaluation and salience of categorization. *Personality and Social Psychology Bulletin, 26*(10), 1258–1270.

Mummendey, A., & Wenzel, M. (1999). Social discrimination and tolerance in intergroup relations: Reactions to intergroup difference. *Personality and Social Psychology Review, 3,* 158–174.

Murphy, G. (1958). *Human potentialities.* New York: Basic Books.

Nagda, B. A. (2006). Breaking barriers, crossing borders, building bridges: Communication processes in intergroup dialogues. *Journal of Social Issues, 62,* 553–576.

Newcomb, T. M. (1943). *Personality and social change.* New York: Dryden.

Orfield, G., & Lee, C. (2007). *Historic reversals, accelerating resegregation, and the need for new integration strategies.* A report of the Civil Rights Project, UCLA.

Page, S. E. (2007). *The difference: How the power of diversity creates better groups, firms, schools, and societies.* Princeton, NJ: Princeton University Press.

Page-Gould, E., Mendoza-Denton, R., Alegre, J. M., & Siy, J. O. (2010). Understanding the impact of cross-group friendship on interactions with novel outgroup members. *Journal of Personality and Social Psychology, 98,* 775–793.

Page-Gould, E., Mendoza-Denton, R., & Tropp, L. R. (2008). With a little help from my cross-group friend: Reducing anxiety in intergroup contexts through cross-group friendship. *Journal of Personality and Social Psychology, 95,* 1080–1094.

Paolini, S., Hewstone, M., Cairns, E., & Voci, A. (2004). Effects of direct and indirect cross-group friendships on judgments of Catholics and Protestants in Northern Ireland: The mediating role of an anxiety-reduction mechanism. *Personality and Social Psychology Bulletin, 30,* 770–786.

Parker, J. H. (1968). The interaction of negroes and whites in an integrated church setting. *Social Forces, 46*(3), 359–366.

Patchen, M. (1982). *Black–white contact in schools.* West Lafayette: Purdue University Press.

Pettigrew, T. F. (1991). Toward unity and bold theory: Popperian suggestions for two persistent problems of social psychology. In C. W. Stephan, W. F. Stephan, & T. F. Pettigrew (Eds.), *The future of social psychology* (pp. 13–27). New York: Springer-Verlag.

Pettigrew, T. F. (1997). Generalized intergroup contact effects on prejudice. *Personality and Social Psychology Bulletin, 23,* 173–185.

Pettigrew, T. F. (1998). Intergroup contact theory. *Annual Review of Psychology, 49,* 65–85.

Pettigrew, T. F., & Tropp, L. R. (2005). Allport's intergroup contact hypothesis: Its history and influence. In J. F. Dovidio, P. Glick, & L. Rudman (Eds.), *On the nature of prejudice: Fifty years after Allport* (pp. 262–277). Malden, MA: Blackwell.

Pettigrew, T. F., & Tropp, L. R. (2006). A meta-analytic test of intergroup contact theory. *Journal of Personality and Social Psychology, 90*(5), 751–783.

Pettigrew, T. F., & Tropp, L. R. (2008). How does intergroup contact reduce prejudice? Meta-analytic tests of three mediators. *European Journal of Social Psychology, 38,* 922–934.

Pettigrew, T. F., & Tropp, L. R. (2011). *When groups meet: The dynamics of intergroup contact.* New York: Psychology Press.

Pettigrew, T. F., Wagner, U., & Christ, O. (2010). Population ratios and prejudice: Modeling both contact and threat effects. *Journal of Ethnic and Migration Studies, 36,* 635–650.

Phinney, J. S., Horenczyk, G., Liebkind, K., & Vedder, P. (2001). Ethnic identity, immigration, and well-being: An interactional perspective. *Journal of Social Issues, 57,* 493–510.

Pinel, E. C. (1999). Stigma consciousness: The psychological legacy of social stereotypes. *Journal of Personality and Social Psychology, 76,* 114–128.

Pinel, E. C. (2002). Stigma consciousness in intergroup contexts: The power of conviction. *Journal of Experimental Social Psychology, 38,* 178–185.

Plant, E. A., & Devine, P. G. (2003). The antecedents and implications of interracial anxiety. *Personality and Social Psychology Bulletin, 29,* 790–801.

Plant, E. A., & Devine, P. G. (2008). Interracial interactions: Approach and avoidance. In A. J. Elliot (Ed.), *Handbook of approach and avoidance motivation* (pp. 571–584). New York: Psychology Press.

Plaut, V. C. (2002). Cultural models of diversity in America: The psychology of difference and inclusion. In R.A. Shweder, M. Minow, & H. R. Markus (Eds.), *Engaging cultural differences: The multicultural challenge in liberal democracies* (pp. 365–395). New York: Russell Sage.

Portes, A., & Rumbaut, R. G. (2006). *Immigrant America: A portrait.* Berkeley and Los Angeles: University of California Press.

Pratto, F., Sidanius, J., Stallworth, L., & Malle, B. (1994). Social dominance orientation: A personality variable predicting social and political attitudes. *Journal of Personality and Social Psychology, 67,* 741–763.

Prentice, D. A., & Miller, D. T. (1999). *Cultural divides: Understanding and overcoming group conflict*. New York: Russell Sage.

Putnam, R. D. (2007). E pluribus unum: Diversity and community in the twenty-first century. *Scandinavian Journal of Political Studies, 30,* 137–174.

Quillian, L. (1995). Prejudice as a response to perceived group threat: Population composition and anti-immigrant and racial prejudice in Europe. *American Sociological Review, 60,* 586–611.

Ray, J, & Furnham, A. (1984). Authoritarianism, conservatism, and racism. *Ethnic and Racial Studies, 7,* 406–412.

Reagans, R. (1998). Differences in social difference: Examining third party effects on relational stability. *Social Networks, 20,* 143–157.

Riordan, C. (1978). Equal-status interracial contact: A review and revision of the concept. *International Journal of Intercultural Relations, 2,* 161–185.

Riordan, C., & Ruggiero, J. (1980). Producing equal-status interracial interaction: A replication. *Social Psychology Quarterly, 43,* 131–136.

Robinson, J. W., & Preston, J. D. (1976). Equal status contact and modification of racial prejudice: A reexamination of the contact hypothesis. *Social Forces, 54,* 911–924.

Rogers, M., Hennigan, K., Bowman, C., & Miller, N. (1984). Intergroup acceptance in classroom and playground settings. In N. Miller & M. B. Brewer (Eds.), *Groups in contact: The psychology of desegregation* (pp. 187–212). Orlando, FL: Academic.

Rokeach, M. (1968). *Beliefs, attitudes, and values*. San Francisco: Jossey-Bass.

Rothwell, J. T. (2009). *Trust in diverse, integrated cities: A revisionist perspective*. Unpublished paper, Woodrow Wilson School of Public and International Affairs, Princeton University.

Rumbaut, R. G. (1999). Assimilation and its discontents: Ironies and paradoxes. In C. Hirschman, P. Kasinitz, & J. DeWind (Eds.), *The handbook of international migration: The American experience* (pp. 172–195). New York: Russell Sage.

Schlesinger, A. M. (1998). *The disuniting of America: Reflections on a multicultural society* (Rev. ed.). New York: Norton.

Schofield, J. W. (1978). School desegregation and intergroup attitudes. In D. Bar-Tal & L. Saxe (Eds.), *Social psychology of education: Theory and research* (pp. 330–363). Washington, DC: Halsted.

Schofield, J. W., & Eurich-Fulcer, R. (2001). When and how school desegregation improves intergroup relations. In R. Brown & S. L. Gaertner (Eds.), *Blackwell handbook of social psychology: Intergroup processes* (pp. 475–494). Malden, MA: Blackwell.

Schofield, J., W., & Sagar, H. A. (1979). The social context of learning in an interracial school. In R. Rist (Ed.), *Inside desegregated schools* (pp. 155–199). San Francisco, CA: Academic.

Schuman, H., Steeh, C., Bobo, L., & Krysan, M. (1997). *Racial attitudes in America: Trends and interpretations*. Cambridge, MA: Harvard University Press.

Sears, D. O., & Funk, C. L. (1991). The role of self-interest in social and political attitudes. In M. P. Zanna (Ed.), *Advances in Experimental Social Psychology* (Vol. 24, pp. 2–91). New York: Academic.

Sears, D. O., & Henry, P. J. (2005). Over thirty years later: A contemporary look at symbolic racism. In M. P. Zanna (Ed.), *Advances in experimental social psychology* (Vol. 37, pp. 95–150). San Diego, CA: Academic.

Sears, D. O. & Jessor, T. (1996). Whites' racial policy attitudes: The role of white racism. *Social Science Quarterly, 77,* 751–759.

Sears, D. O., & Kinder, D. R. (1971). Racial tensions and voting in Los Angeles. In W. Z. Hirsch (Ed.), *Los Angeles: Viability and prospects for metropolitan leadership* (pp. 51–88). New York: Praeger.

Sears, D. O., Kinder, D. R. (1985). Whites' opposition to busing: On conceptualizing group conflict. *Journal of Personality and Social Psychology, 48*(5), 1148–1161.

Sears, D. O., & Savalei, V. (2006). The political color line in America: Many "peoples of color" or black exceptionalism? *Political Psychology, 27*(6), 895–924.

Shelton, J. N., & Richeson, J. A. (2005). Intergroup contact and pluralistic ignorance. *Journal of Personality and Social Psychology, 88,* 91–107.

Shelton, J. N., Richeson, J. A., & Vorauer, J. D. (2006). Threatened identities and interethnic interactions. *European Review of Social Psychology, 17,* 321–358.

Shelton, J. N., Trail, T. E., West, T. V., & Bergseiker, H. B. (2010). From strangers to friends: The interpersonal process of intimacy in developing interracial friendships. *Journal of Social and Personal Relationships, 27,* 71–90.

Sherif, M. (1966). *Group conflict and cooperation*. London: Routledge and Kegan Paul.

Sherif, M., Harvey, O. J., White, J. B., Hood, W. R., & Sherif, C. W. (1961). *Intergroup conflict and cooperation: The Robbers Cave experiment*. Norman: University of Oklahoma Book Exchange.

Shweder, R. A. (1990). Cultural psychology—what is it? In J. W. Stigler, R. A. Shweder, & G. Herdt (Eds.), *Cultural Psychology: Essays on comparative human development* (pp. 1–46). Cambridge, UK: Cambridge University Press.

Sidanius, J. (1993). The psychology of group conflict and the dynamics of oppression: A social dominance perspective. In S. Iyengar & W. J. McGuire (Eds.), *Explorations in political psychology* (pp. 183–219). Durham, NC: Duke University Press.

Sidanius, J., Feshbach, S., Levin, S., & Pratto, F. (1997). The interface between ethnic and national attachment: Ethnic pluralism or ethnic dominance? *Public Opinion Quarterly, 61,* 102–133.

Sidanius, J., & Petrocik, J. R. (2001). Communal and national identity in a multiethnic state: A comparison of three perspectives. In R. D. Ashmore & L. Jussim (Eds.), *Social identity, intergroup conflict, and conflict reduction* (pp. 101–129). London: Oxford University Press.

Sidanius, J., & Pratto, F. (1999). *Social dominance: An intergroup theory of hierarchy and oppression*. New York: Cambridge University Press.

Sidanius, J., Pratto, F., Sinclair, S., & van Laar, C. (1996). Mother Teresa meets Genghis Khan: The dialectics of hierarchy-enhancing and hierarchy-attenuating career choices. *Social Justice Research, 9,* 145–170.

Staerkle, C., Sidanius, J., Green, E., & Molina, L. E. (2005). Ethnic minority-majority asymmetry attitudes towards immigrants across 11 nations. *Psicologia Politica, 30,* 7–26.

Staerkle, C., Sidanius, J., Green, E., & Molina, L. E. (2010). National and ethnic identity of minorities and majorities across twelve national contexts. *Political Psychology, 31,* 491–519.

Stearns, E., Buchmann, C., & Bonneau, K. (2009). Interracial friendships in the transition to college: Do birds of a feather flock together once they leave the nest?. *Sociology of Education, 82*, 173-195.

Steele, C. M. (1997). A threat in the air: How stereotypes shape intellectual identity and performance. *American Psychologist, 52*, 613–629.

Stephan, W. G., & Stephan, C. W. (1985). Intergroup anxiety. *Journal of Social Issues, 41*, 157–175.

Stephan, W. G., & Stephan, C. W. (2000). An integrated threat theory of prejudice. In S. Oskamp (Ed.), *Reducing prejudice and discrimination* (pp. 23–45). Mahwah, NJ: Erlbaum.

Stephan, W. G., & Stephan, C. W. (2005). Intergroup relations program evaluation. In J. F. Dovidio, P. Glick, & L. Rudman (Eds.), *On the nature of prejudice: Fifty years after Allport* (pp. 431–446). Malden, MA: Blackwell.

Stephan, W. G., Stephan, C. W., & Gudykunst, W. B. (1999). Anxiety in intergroup relations: A comparison of anxiety/uncertainty management theory and integrated threat theory. *International Journal of Intercultural Relations, 23*, 613–628.

Suarez-Orozco, M. M. (2002). Everything you ever wanted to know about assimilation but were afraid to ask. In R. A. Shweder, M. Minow, & H. R. Markus (Eds.), *Engaging cultural differences: The multicultural challenge in liberal democracies* (pp. 19–42). New York: Russell Sage.

Sumner, W. G. (1906). *Folkways*. Boston: Ginn.

Tajfel, H. (1981). *Human groups and social categories*. Cambridge: Cambridge University Press.

Tajfel, H., Billig, M. G., Bundy, R. P., & Flament, C. (1971). Social categorization and intergroup behaviour. *European Journal of Social Psychology, 1*, 149-178.

Tajfel, H., & Turner, J.C. (1979). An integrative theory of intergroup conflict. In W. G. Austin & S. Worchel (Eds.), *The social psychology of intergroup relations*. Monterey, CA: Brooks/Cole.

Tajfel, H., & Turner, J. C. (1986). The social identity theory of intergroup behaviour. In S. Worchel & W. G. Austin (Eds.), *Psychology of intergroup relations* (pp. 7–24). Oxford: Brooks/Cole.

Tatum, B. D. (1997). *Why are all the black kids sitting together in the cafeteria?* New York: Basic Books.

Taylor, C. (1994). The politics of recognition. In A. Gutmann (ed.), *Multiculturalism: Examining the politics of recognition* (pp. 25–73). Princeton, NJ: Princeton University Press.

Taylor, M. (1998). How white attitudes vary with the racial composition of local populations: Numbers count. *American Sociological Review, 63*, 512–535.

Trawalter, S., Richeson, J. A., & Shelton, J. N. (2009). Predicting behavior during interracial interactions: A stress and coping approach. *Personality and Social Psychology Review, 13*, 243–268.

Tropp, L. R. (2003). The psychological impact of prejudice: Implications for intergroup contact. *Group Processes & Intergroup Relations, 6*, 131-149.

Tropp, L. R. (2006). Stigma and intergroup contact among members of minority and majority status groups. In S. Levin & C. van Laar (Eds.), *Stigma and group inequality: Social psychological perspectives* (pp. 171–191). Mahwah, NJ: Erlbaum.

Tropp, L. R. (2008). The role of trust in intergroup contact: Its significance and implications for improving relations between groups. In U. Wagner, L. R. Tropp, G. Finchilescu, & C. Tredoux (Eds.), *Improving intergroup relations: Building on the legacy of Thomas F. Pettigrew* (pp. 91–106). Malden, MA: Blackwell.

Tropp, L. R., & Bianchi, R. A. (2006). Valuing diversity and interest in intergroup contact. *Journal of Social Issues, 62*(3), 533–551.

Tropp, L. R., & Bianchi, R. A. (2007). Interpreting references to group membership in context: Feelings about intergroup contact depending on who says what to whom. *European Journal of Social Psychology, 37*(1), 153–170.

Turner, J. C. (1999). Some current issues in research on social identity and self-categorization theories. In N. Ellemers, R. Spears, & B. Doosje (Eds.), *Social identity: Context, commitment, content* (pp. 6-34). Oxford, UK: Blackwell.

Turner, J. C., Hogg, M. A., Oakes, P. J., Reicher, S. D., & Wetherell, M. S. (1987). Rediscovering the social group: A self-categorization theory. Cambridge, MA: Blackwell.

Turner, J. C., & Onorato, R. S. (1999). Social identity, personality, and the self-concept: A self- categorization perspective. In T. R. Tyler, R. M. Kramer, & O. P. John (Eds.), *The psychology of the social self* (pp. 11–46). Mahwah, NJ: Erlbaum.

Turner, R. N., Hewstone, M., & Voci, A. (2007). Reducing explicit and implicit outgroup prejudice via direct and extended contact: The mediating role of self-disclosure and intergroup anxiety. *Journal of Personality and Social Psychology, 93*, 369–388.

Uslaner, E. M. (2011). Trust, diversity, and segregation. *Comparative Sociology, 10*, 221–247.

Van Laar, C., Sidanius, J., Rabinowitz, J., & Sinclair, S. (1999). The three r's of academic achievement: Reading, 'riting, and racism. *Personality and Social Psychology Bulletin, 25*, 139–151.

Van Oudenhoven, J. P., Groenewoud, J. T., & Hewstone, M. (1996). Cooperation, ethnic salience, and generalization of interethnic attitudes. *European Journal of Social Psychology, 26*, 649–661.

Verkuyten, M. (2009). Support for multiculturalism and minority rights: The role of national identification and out-group threat. *Social Justice Research, 22*, 31–52.

Vescio, T. K., Sechrist, G. B., & Paolucci, M. P. (2003). Perspective taking and prejudice reduction: The mediational role of empathy arousal and situational attributions. *European Journal of Social Psychology, 33*, 455–472.

Voci, A., & Hewstone, M. (2003). Intergroup contact and prejudice toward immigrants in Italy: The mediational role of anxiety and the moderational role of group salience. *Group Processes and Intergroup Relations, 6*, 37–54.

Vorauer, J. D. (2006). An information search model of evaluative concerns in intergroup interaction. *Psychological Review, 113*, 862–886.

Voruaer, J., & Sakamoto, Y. (2009). I thought we could be friends, but . . . Systematic miscommunication and defensive distancing as obstacles to cross-group friendship formation. *Psychological Science, 17*, 326–331.

Vorauer, J., & Sasaki, S. J. (2009). Helpful only in the abstract? Ironic effects of empathy in intergroup interaction. *Psychological Science, 20*, 191–197.

Wagner, U., Christ, O., Pettigrew, T. F., Stellmacher, J., & Wolf, H. (2006). Prejudice and minority proportion: Contact instead of threat effects. *Social Psychology Quarterly, 69*(4), 380–390.

Walker, I., & Crogan, M. (1998). Academic performance, prejudice, and the jigsaw classroom: New pieces to the puzzle. *Journal of Community and Applied Social Psychology, 8*, 381–393.

Whitley, B. E. (1999). Right-wing authoritarianism, social dominance orientation, and prejudice. *Journal of Personality and Social Psychology, 77*, 126–134.

Wilder, D. A. (1984). Intergroup contact: The typical member and the exception to the rule. *Journal of Experimental Social Psychology, 20,* 177–194.

Wilder, D. A. (1993). The role of anxiety in facilitating stereotypic judgments of outgroup behavior. In D. M. Mackie & D. L. Hamilton (Eds.), *Affect, cognition and stereotyping: Interactive processes in group perception* (pp. 87–109). San Diego, CA: Academic Press

Wilder, D. A., & Shapiro, P. (1989). Effects of anxiety on impression formation in a group context: An anxiety-assimilation hypothesis. *Journal of Experimental Social Psychology, 25,* 481–499.

Wildschut, T., & Insko, C. A. (2007). Explanations of interindividual-intergroup discontinuity: A review of the evidence. *European Review of Social Psychology, 18,* 175–211.

Williams, R. M., Jr. (1947). *The reduction of intergroup tensions.* New York: Social Science Research Council.

Wittig, M. A., & Molina, L. (2000). Moderators and mediators of prejudice reduction. In S. Oskamp (Ed.), *Reducing prejudice and discrimination* (pp. 295–318). Mahwah, NJ: Erlbaum.

Wright, S. C., Aron, A., & Tropp, L. R. (2002). Including others (and groups) in the self: Self-expansion and intergroup relations. In J. P. Forgas & K. D. Williams (Eds.), *The social self: Cognitive, interpersonal, and intergroup perspectives* (pp. 343–363). Philadelphia: Psychology Press.

Wright, S. C., Brody, S. A., & Aron, A. (2005). Intergroup contact: Still our best hope for reducing prejudice. In C. S. Crandall & M. Schaller (Eds.), *The social psychology of prejudice: Historical perspectives.* (pp. 115–142). Seattle: Lewinian Press.

Wright, S. C., & Lubensky, M. E. (2009). The struggle for social equality: Collective action versus prejudice reduction. In S. Demoulin, J. Leyens, & J. F. Dovidio (Eds.), *Intergroup misunderstandings: Impact of divergent social realities* (pp. 291–310). New York: Psychology Press.

Wright, S. C., & Tropp, L. R. (2005). Language and intergroup contact: Investigating the impact of bilingual instruction on children's intergroup attitudes. *Group Processes and Intergroup Relations, 8,* 309–328.

Wright, S. C., & van der Zande, C. C. (1999). *Bicultural friends: When cross-group friendships cause improved intergroup attitudes.* Paper presented at the annual meeting of the Society for Experimental Social Psychology, St. Louis, MO.

Yarrow, M. R., Campbell, J. D., & Yarrow, L. J. (1958). Acquisition of new norms: A study of racial desegregation. *Journal of Social Issues, 14*(1), 8–28.

Yzerbyt, V., & Demoulin, S. (2010). Intergroup relations. In S. T. Fiske, D. T. Gilbert, & G. Lindzey (Eds.), *Handbook of social psychology* (5th ed., pp. 1024-1083). Hoboken, NJ: Wiley.

Zagefka, H., & Brown, R. (2002). The relationship between acculturation strategies, relative fit, and intergroup relations: Immigrant-majority relations in Germany. *European Journal of Social Psychology, 32,* 171–188.

Zhou, M. (1999). Segmented assimilation: Issues, controversies, and recent research on the new second generation. In C. Hirschman, P. Kasinitz, & J. DeWind (Eds.), *The handbook of international migration: The American experience* (pp. 196–211). New York: Russell Sage.

PART 3

Life Domains

Personality, Social Psychology, and Psychopathology
Reflections on a Lewinian Vision

Philip R. Costanzo, Rick H. Hoyle, *and* Mark R. Leary

Abstract

In this chapter, we first consider the historical and conceptual roots of the tripartite, but at times rocky, marriage of the fields of personality, social, and abnormal psychology. After briefly describing the hopes of early 20th-century scholars to array the study of normal and abnormal behavior, thought, and feeling on the same conceptual continua, we call for the rekindling of these conjunctive hopes. Indeed, we argue that with the advent of current cross-cutting developments in cognitive, socioemotional, and biological perspectives in the broader domain of the behavioral sciences, that the time is ripe for rearranging the marriage among these fields. In order to provide a conceptual frame for such a conjunctive effort, we return to Lewinian field theory and its definition of forces of locomotion in the life space as a particularly notable way to put the examination of normal and abnormal psychology in the same theoretical space. By addressing some critical ideational themes in the domains of personality and social psychology, we attempt to illustrate the overlap of these themes with the ideas and questions of scholars of abnormal behavior. Of course, in deploying a Lewinian model our analyses turn to the dynamics of person x environment interactions in the regions of the life space. In doing so we define the phenomena of meaning-making and the multiple "worldview" existential models in social and personality psychology as the forces constituting the primary dynamics defining the permeability of adaptive regions of the "life space" or phenomenal field. We illustrate these dynamics by detailed consideration of human adaptation in two critical regions or domains of life experience in the behavioral field: the domain of regulatory transactions and the domain of acceptance, social affection, and relationships. While these domains certainly do not exhaust all regions of the life space, we argue that they are particularly pertinent for parsing continua of normal-to-abnormal adaptation and conjoining the nature of psychopathology with the everyday struggles of personal and social significance to all humans. We conclude our analysis by rather unabashed advocacy, not specifically for the model we explore, but for scholarship that is aimed at developing models that link the normal to what we refer to as the abnormal or psychopathological. As humans, the cloths of our selves and our environments are made from common as well as individually unique fibers. We conclude that to disambiguate how such fibers are woven together to frame the forces driving our travels from blissful adaptation to painful maladjustment should be a primary agenda for our interconnected sciences of human behavior.

Keywords: psychopathology, adaptation, life space, Lewinian field theory, belongingness, self-regulation, social acceptance, abnormal behavior, worldviews, meaning-making, P x E interaction, normal-abnormal continua, social construction, belief restoration

Introduction: Preliminary Considerations and a bit of Relevant History

There are many reasons, both intellectual and historical, that scholars who are interested in psychopathology are (or should be) intensely interested in those areas of personality and social psychology that probe phenomena that are relevant to understanding and treating emotional and behavioral problems. There are also many intellectual and historical reasons why the study of psychopathology should be of the utmost interest to scholars of personality and social behavior. In this chapter we discuss the underlying threads of connection that weave these fields of psychology together in their search for an understanding of factors giving rise to the diversity of human behavior, feeling, and thought.

At the outset of this chapter, we should be clear that we do not intend or pretend to redefine psychopathological manifestations in new terms, nor do we envision ourselves as rewriting the diagnostic descriptions provided by the *Diagnostic and Statistical Manual, 5th edition* (*DSM-V*). Our goals are considerably more modest. We propose an underlying set of core processes and domains of adaptation on which personality and social psychologists focus a good deal of their theoretical and empirical attention. We then seek to link these to the process dimensions that are critical to both theorists and researchers of psychopathology and to treatment and prevention specialists. As we shall see, these dimensions are shared by personality and social psychology on one hand and by clinical, counseling, and other areas interested in psychological disorder on the other. This should not come as a surprise to the historically informed reader. The history of basic theory and research on individual differences and on social processes shares a lineage with the history of theory and practice in the domain of mental health and illness (see Brehm, 1976; Hill & Weary 1983; Kowalski & Leary, 2000; Ruble, Costanzo, & Oliveri, 1992). In this context, it is worth remembering that it was not until needs for assessment and intervention of returning servicemen and women following World War II, that the field of clinical psychology in the United States fully staked a claim to the study of psychopathology and mental illness as a separate domain of knowledge bridging behavioral science and practice (Watson, 1953; see also Pettigrew & Cherry, chapter 2, this volume).

Indeed, from the early to mid-20th century, personality, social, and abnormal psychologists shared a single APA sponsored research journal, the *Journal of Abnormal and Social Psychology* (*JASP*). Perusing the issues of this journal as far back as the 1920s and forward to its "closing date" in 1965 is quite an instructive exercise. The topics of the review papers, theoretical expositions, and research reports are quite diverse, including case histories of multiple personalities; personality-based factors guiding memory, perception, and interaction; and the social dynamics relating to distinctions between what were referred to as abnormal and normal patterns of reaction to myriad stimuli and circumstances. Many of the articles "crossed over" the issues pertinent to all of these subfields. For example, one quite interesting paper (Wells, 1926) examined the relationship of values to the acquisition of disordered behavior. In another (Slotkin, 1942), the social interactive phenomena associated with schizophrenia are considered along with individually variant patterns of adaptation to such interactive phenomena. In one particularly compelling paper by Albert Pepitone and colleague (Pepitone & Wilpizeski, 1960), laboratory-induced social rejection was found to result in attributional ""defenses" to protect the person from declines in both positive affect and esteem. The authors linked the failure of these attributional defenses to buffer the effects of social rejection to the natural occurrence of depression and dysphoric states.

The Pepitone article is used here only to illustrate the early to mid-20th century overlap of the basic social psychology of "normal" behavior with the study of psychopathological consequences that might issue from the failure of adaptive response patterns characterizing that normal behavior. In the 44 years of *JASP*, articles of this variety are liberally sprinkled among the published papers.

In 1965, *JASP* split into two separate journals—the *Journal of Abnormal Psychology* (*JAP*) and the *Journal of Personality and Social Psychology* (*JPSP*). Interestingly, *JAP* was actually the original journal founded by Morton Prince in 1906. It was through his vision, prompted by the changing societal conditions brought about by World War 1, that Prince later expanded *JAP* into a periodical that explicitly included social psychology (i.e., *JASP*). One could argue that the transformation of the everyday social and personal processes brought about by the massive war and the international realignments it presaged was a metaphor for the transformation of "normal" behavioral processes into extreme forms of adaptation that might be referred to as psychopathology. For Prince, it was abundantly clear that a full account of abnormal behavior and states of mind could not be ventured without an understanding of normal adaptive personal and social processes. In turn, in an even stronger sense, he believed that a science of normal social behavior, emotion, and thought would be woefully incomplete without an understanding of the abnormalities that could arise from extreme personal vulnerabilities and extreme environmental stresses and demands. Put succinctly, the creation of *JASP* was an intellectual statement by Prince that arrayed the normal and abnormal in human behavior on a continuous dimension rather than as categorical strangers.

This vision is also clearly reflected in Daniel Katz's final editorial for *JASP* at the time that it was divided into two journals. Katz regarded the division as a bow to the necessities brought about by specialization, the expansion of psychology, and the effects of these changes on the increasing number of scholarly contributions submitted. He also noted that the articles published in *JASP* had become subject to specialty-based reading depending on the subfield of the reader. So, Prince's hope that *JASP* would serve as a unifying force intermingling the scholarship concerning normal and abnormal behavior was fading rapidly in the mid-1960s. In his editorial, Katz lamented this splitting of the scholarly turf of social psychology and psychopathology (Katz regarded personality as a subcomponent of social psychology—a view of some controversy). Katz wrote: "to divide the generic area of social psychology into two parts on the basis of the distinction between normal and abnormal processes scarcely contributes to the theoretical understanding of human behavior" (Katz, 1965, p. 591). Thus, Katz considered the generic area of social psychology as a resource and basic field for the study of psychopathology. Prince, however, regarded the study of social psychology as being appropriately advanced by the intellectual questions and findings of abnormal psychology. In an initial 1921 editorial creating *JASP* as an integrated journal, he and his coeditor, Floyd Allport, noted that "social psychology because it is interested more deeply than any other branch in the forces underlying human conduct has been able to profit, in a peculiar way, by the discoveries of psycho-pathology [*sic*]" (Allport & Prince, 1921).

Whether it is the case that social psychological principles and models of normal behavior, feeling, and emotion are at the base of our understanding of psychopathology, or the case that the study of psychopathology is a prime origin for understanding the true theoretical significance of social psychology,

the value of inquiry at their conjunctive borders seems indisputable. In either direction of contribution one could argue convincingly that the original suppositions of scholars such as Prince, Allport, and Katz that the fields were inextricably bound and would be lessened in scope and general impact by separation into independent domains of inquiry were and remain highly defensible.

We raise this bit of history to contextualize the thrust of this chapter. Envisioning the study of normal and abnormal behavior as continuous dimensions of adaptive processes is certainly not a new idea (see Brehm & Smith, 1976; Weary & Mirels, 1982; Snyder & Forsyth, 1991; Leary & Maddux, 1987; Strauman, Costanzo, Merrill, & Jones, 2010). What has changed over the last 50 years that makes this an ideal time to capitalize on such a linkage is ironically the product of the symbolic and real partitioning of abnormal and personality/social psychology into separate fields of inquiry in the mid-1960s. The relatively separate pursuit of the study of normal behavior and psychopathology and the specialization that this entailed over the past 50 years has facilitated the growth of these separate domains. Limits on the scope of theory and conceptualization produced myriad testable hypotheses and minitheories that allowed for the rapid sorting of fruitful and nonfruitful directions for research.

Undoubtedly, these separated fields developed in concert as the larger field of psychology witnessed several revolutions of central process dimensions. For example, the dominant impact that reinforcement theory had on the constructions of psychological process from the 1930s through the early 1960s had profound effects on both clinical and personality/social psychology. Personality traits indexing sensitivity to or locus of reinforcement became a subject for the study of individual differences (Rotter, 1966). Reinforcement theories of attitude formation and change as well as social interaction and exchange also became prominent parts of social psychology at this time (see Shaw & Costanzo, 1982). Learning-based models of both psychopathology and psychotherapy in clinical psychology emerged in this very fruitful period of growth for reinforcement theory perspectives. Indeed, psychopathology was preferentially relabeled in some quarters as "behavior disorders," and both operant and classical reinforcement theory approaches provided the term "behavior therapy" to describe models of psychotherapy that were based on learning theory (see for examples, Wolpe, 1958, 1969; Bandura, 1969; Ullman & Krasner, 1975).

The cognitive revolution emerging in the mid-1960s greatly affected theory-building and research in each domain as well. Terms such as "schema," "accessibility," and "information processing" were as likely to find their way into the clinic as the social psychology laboratory. (see Beck, 1976; Beck, Rush, & Emery, 1979; Hollon & Garber, 1990). They were also as likely to be seen as mediators of social behavior as they were of individual differences and personality (Humphreys & Revelle, 1984). With the emergence of enhanced interest in the "self" running parallel to the cognitive revolution, scholars of both normal and abnormal behavior became intrigued by models identifying self-concept, self esteem, and the downside of self-disintegration and its psychopathological manifestations as central components of adaptation (see for examples Linville, 1987; Baumeister, 1991; Curtis, 1991; Deaux, 1992; Leary, 2004).

In this period of primacy for cognitive phenomena, behavior therapy slowly morphed into cognitive behavior therapy. At the same time, texts, articles, and even entire journals appeared featuring the study of social cognition, social information processing. individual differences in cognitive style, cognitive theories of personality, and so on (see Higgins, 1992, for a discussion). These selected illustrations are interesting because, while in most ways, the study of psychopathology and the study of "normal behavior" simultaneously overlapped in their guiding theoretical orientations, they were infrequently connected in the direct study of related phenomena.

The recent upswing of research and method advance in the study of genetic and neural processes in the past decade has brought forward biologically based conceptions of both control systems and mediators of social, affective, and psychopathological adaptations (Charney & Nestler, 2004; Cozolino, 2010; Lambert & Kinsley, 2010; Zorumski & Rubin, 2005; Lieberman, 2010). In these recent advances the interconnections and dimensional nature of normality-abnormality have become more evident. Neural accounts of inhibition/disinhibition or impulsivity/reflectivity, for examples, have often directly linked the normal to the abnormal consequences of these processes (Lubow & Weiner 2010). Similarly, the study of gene–environment interactions as they affect the emergence of personal characteristics as well as social and emotional proclivities further illustrates the dimensional ties between normal and abnormal adaptations (Caspi, Harriri, Holmes, Uher, & Moffitt 2010).

These historical developments in the field of psychology at large serve as an important backdrop for a renewal of Morton Prince's vision of a unified science of social and abnormal psychology. The intent of this chapter is to offer a beginning formulation that might facilitate that unification. We will not present a proposal to merge the fields formally, but rather a proposal to create the kind of common conceptual framework that might encourage the active and collaborative exchange of knowledge and models between scholars of normal and abnormal behavior.

Where is the Personality in all of this?

Although the above narrative mentions the field of personality as a third partner discipline bridging normal and abnormal behavior, and although personality has a prominent place in the conceptual analysis we propose, its historical role as a discipline has been frequently overshadowed by both clinical psychology and social psychology. Like Katz, a contingent of social psychologists over the years has viewed personality psychology as a subfield of social psychology—that component dealing with individual variations from the central tendencies generated by social and environmental influences. Indeed, for some social psychologists, individual variation has its main role of providing error estimates for the situationally driven effects of experimentally manipulated social and contextual variables. (see Barenbaum & Winter, 2003, and Funder & Faust, 2010, for discussions of the place of personality in social psychology).

From the standpoint of abnormal psychology, however, personality theory and research has often constituted the "guts" of models of psychopathology. Indeed, in some older schools of thought (like psychoanalysis), the dynamics of personality functioning were conceived of as the originating forces in the generation of psychopathology. For the first half of the 20th century, personality models and theories were overwhelmingly put forward by clinical and abnormal psychologists, and these perspectives were often linked to intervention strategies predicated on the propositions of those theories (see for example White, 1948). The study and measurement of individual differences has constituted a rather separate tradition of research in personality and generally derived from the advances of methodologists and psychometricians.

One positive consequence of the 1965 split of *JASP* into *JAP* and *JPSP* is that it conferred a visible identity on personality psychologists, particularly those who were neither social nor abnormal psychologists. Despite the existence of journals in the domain of personality, such as the *Journal of Personality* (which ironically was founded by William MacDougal, the author of the first American textbook in social psychology), the presence of the term "personality" in the title of a top-tier APA journal gave the field of personality a boost of visibility. Nevertheless, the reality was that the primary contributors to *JPSP* happened to be social psychologists—and that persists until the present day.

Given the dominion that both abnormal and social psychology have had over the study of personality, the split of *JASP* fostered a demarcation line between research devoted to the understanding of normal behavior and abnormal behavior, with scholars of personality also following this line of demarcation. Indeed, even in today's academic world, personality researchers who were not trained as either social or clinical psychologists are relatively rare.

In the formulation presented below, we are most concerned with traversing the normal/abnormal distinction with conceptualizations of both personality and social processes. Any model of psychopathology requires a joint focus on individuals as vulnerable or resilient actors and situations as contexts that induce vulnerability or resilience.

The Lewinian Equation: Setting the Conceptual Framework

Although we might well begin anew in designing a framework for the conjunction of personality and social psychology with the study of psychopathology, Kurt Lewin (1935, 1943) has done a great deal of the intellectual heavy lifting underlying our approach to the conjunction. It is informative that while Lewin is regarded as the father of experimental social psychology, one finds accounts of his theory and perspective in volumes on personality theory as well. Although not a "psychopathologist," Lewin provided the groundwork for the development of a model for examining relative personal and environmental influences on maladaptive behavior. He built his theory by metaphorically relating behavioral phenomena to concepts extant in physics and mathematics. He likened the behavioral field to the force fields that are central to physical theory. In the case of human behavior, Lewin considered the field to be the "life space" in which individuals exist and develop and used mathematical concepts from topology to illustrate the individual's "locomotion" or movement within the field of behavior. The field or life space becomes more articulated and differentiated with

development and experience. This process of differentiation leads to the formation of differentially accessible regions, each containing goals relating to one or another domain of life. This differential accessibility of distinct goal regions was referred to as "permeability." The greater the permeability of the region, the more attracted the person would be to that region, and conversely, the less permeable the region, the more repulsed the person would be. For example, for some people, positive relational goals may be contained in less permeable regions of the life space because of either personal predilections or environmental demands. In these instances, the person would display impeded "locomotion" and greater tension or negative arousal in the domain of relationships. In Lewin's model, the individual is seen as using various processes to reduce tension and keep the field in an equilibrated state.

One of the primary strategies for establishing equilibrium is to "construct" meanings that simultaneously reduce tension and permit locomotion to important goal regions of the life space. To provide a concrete example, the extent of repulsion to relational goal regions could be regulated by mental constructions or worldviews that characterize human beings and human environments as fair and just places within which secure attachment to others is attainable. The experiential disconfirmation of these adaptive (but perhaps illusory) constructions creates a tension that drives people to alter their behaviors, feelings, and emotions in such a way that the equilibrium of the life space is restored and the perceived permeability of this important goal region is increased. From the standpoint of psychopathology, these restorative steps might unfortunately include self-denigration (for example, "the world is fair and just, but I am unworthy of it") or the denigration of particular others or categories of others (for example, "the world is fair and just, but teachers are unfair to their students") or even a redefinition of the field in such a way that regions are further segmented into permeable and less permeable subregions (for example, "the world is a safe place as long as I don't go on elevators"). These reformulated constructions often restore equilibrium at the expense of altering if not misinterpreting reality or one's own efficacy within that reality.

This set of propositions concerning adjustments that individuals make in their perceptions of the field of behavior allows a powerful model of parsing the continuum from adaptive to maladaptive constructions and thus the continuum from normality to psychopathology. In Lewin's formulation, behavior or locomotion through the field is viewed as the interactive product of the chronic experientially acquired attributes of the Person and the exigencies in the current Environment confronting that Person at a moment in time. It should be noted that Lewin's deceptively simple Behavior = Person x Environment formula gains complexity when advances in modern social and personality science are brought to bear on the equation. The biological versions of individual difference variation that have recently emerged permit rather palpable definitions of what one might characterize as vulnerability or proneness to disordered behavior, feeling, and thinking. The "field" or ENVIRONMENT of which Lewin spoke in the 1940's and 1950s now is populated by many constructs in modern social psychology. While Lewin viewed the important components of the environmental field as those constructed by the person (the phenomenal field), contemporary social psychologists have spent a good deal of their research effort on figuring out both how and by what set of processes the field is constructed and identifying the primary dimensions or domains of behavior along which constructions of the field significantly vary.

The Behavioral Field: Some Critical Components

Lewin's P x E behavioral field encompasses all internal and external factors operating on an individual's psychological responses, but we focus here on two broad and critical components. One of these is a set of generic beliefs systems and life perspectives that provide a sense of existential definition and purpose to individuals (what Lewin might view as belief-anchored principles of "construction"). The second component consists of domains of personal adaptation or interpersonal life that are prominent goals within the "regions" of the behavioral and social field. Presumably, some domains are more important than others both for understanding human behavior generally and for understanding the causes of emotional and behavioral problems, and we focus on two that we believe are particularly important and that serve as useful exemplars of the dimensional (vs. categorical) nature of psychopathology. They are also widely recognized as important domains among scholars of both normal and abnormal behavior.

Specifically, we focus on:

1. *Regulatory forces*—those dimensions, traits, and environmental characteristics that index the

controllability of the field to the actor. These forces link together the components of the field or the personal characteristics of actors that impinge on efficacy and goal-seeking. Processes of self-regulation have been primary concerns of personality, social, clinical, and developmental psychologists over the last 75 years. These processes have worn a number of labels and have been linked to a wide variety of phenomena connecting normal to abnormal adaptation (see also Norem, chapter 12, this volume).

2. *Inclusionary/exclusionary interpersonal forces*—those dimensions that involve the degree to which people feel that they are socially valued and accepted as opposed to devalued and rejected. These include exposure to field arrays that connote rejection and acceptance, or that provide socially evaluative feedback. These relational phenomena are not only primary determinants of felt security and the quality of people's lives, but they are also central to the construction and experience of "self" and the sense of identity. However, the components of identity and self-conception influenced by these interpersonal forces are ones that enable us to feel a sense of self as "belonging" as distinguished from those that enable an experience of self as powerful and efficacious. Environments vary in the degree to which they enable a positive image of the social self, and people vary in their chronic sense of their own social value as well as their own self-perceived social and personal potency.

As we proceed through the next three sections of this chapter, we will consider each of the components described as critical to our Lewinian analysis of normal-to-abnormal dimensions. Our first task will be to describe the manner in which worldviews serve to establish what Lewin referred to as the "permeability" of regions of the field to the person. That is, meaning-making principles and beliefs are ones that enable or inhibit our locomotion in the life space. As such, we engage in multiple adaptive and maladaptive constructions to maintain and defend the meanings and beliefs that govern our sense of purpose and stability.

The life space itself is composed of multiple domains, but as we have noted, we will focus on only two domains or regions of the field that relate to self-regulation (control) and social acceptance (belongingness), because these domains encompass multiple other adaptive phenomena and are two of the most relevant for linking personality and social psychology to the study of abnormal behavior and psychopathology. Of course, we would not be the first to propose that *agency* and *communion*, or *individual autonomy* and *social connection* are at the heart of human adaptation (see Bakan, 1966; Triandis, 1995, Costanzo, 1992; Abele & Wojciszke, 2007, for examples). Both our capacity and our opportunities to attach to others as well as to approach our individual goals define much of the terrain of most formulations of mental health. It is these dimensions along with our needs to maintain a consistent and confirmable set of ideologies of the nature of life and society that emboldens us to manage the demands in the field and to tolerate the consequences when we fail to manage either social or personal demands. Psychopathology can be defined as people's incapacity to manage the fields of behavior that they confront either because of environmental pressures or chronic personal attributes.

In this respect, we can conceive of the properties inherent in Lewin's E term as exposing individuals to circumstances that induce either vulnerabilities or resiliencies in persons (Ps). Among personality researchers traits and chronic individual styles or patterns frequently constitute the origin of the specific vulnerabilities, However, Lewin's equation and notion of "permeability" implies that individuals varying greatly in vulnerability might each be affected by environments strongly conveying properties of resilience or vulnerability.

From the standpoint of Lewin's Person term, some persons find many interpersonal fields as self-threatening and thus possess a vulnerability to such events as rejection or regulatory failure that might occasion avoidance of either social interaction or attempts at self-regulation. To the extent that such extreme varieties of interpersonal avoidance would be associated with psychopathology, Lewin's model provides for a simple yet elegant algorithm for the interplay between the person and environment resulting in psychopathological states, behaviors, and feelings.

On the Person side of Lewin's formula, one is confronted with the possibility of a nearly infinite array of dimensions on which individuals might vary in vulnerability. Much of personality research has been directed at "economizing" that array by redefining either "blends" of attributes such as latent constructs (Bagozzi, 1994), candidate genetic predispositions (Caspi et al., 2010), or N-numbered dimensional models such as the Big Five (McCrae, 1992; McCrae & Costa, 1987) to limit what might be regarded as pivotal dimensions of individual

differences. This limitation of dimensions of personal variation becomes particularly critical if one is attempting to employ Lewin's equation as a parsimonious model for understanding psychopathology.

Below, we begin our field-based analyses of vulnerability and resilience by considering the role of meaning and *worldviews* in defining the ease with which people move to different environments and different domains and regions of the field. We follow with sections depicting the particulars of personality and social research and theory on regulation and belongingness as prime sources of adaptive and maladaptive locomotion through the field of behavior. It is our intent to describe those P x E interactions in these domains that are involved in generating psychological vulnerabilities and psychopathological adjustments. In our concluding section, we discuss how, given our model of adaptive demand and field-based vulnerability, it is critical for scholars of human psychology to link the study of normal and abnormal manifestations of human adjustment and to place them on a continuum that links personality and social psychology to the research and development of clinical science and practice in psychology.

Psychopathology and Constructions of Meaning and Purpose

Historically, personality and social psychologists have identified the domain of human transactions relating to "sense-making" as a primary aspect of Lewin's phenomenal field. Despite the many developments in the field of social psychology since Lewin's touchstone theorizing, the process of construction has remained at the forefront of theories of both social behavior and of the definitions of personal consistencies and traits (see Burke, 2006). Along with the importance of construction as a general process in social psychological theory, the challenges of everyday and lifelong coping have been indexed in social psychology by multiple existential "facts of life." These "facts" provide for both meaning and purpose as well as doubt and uncertainty about the goals and values we seek (see Pyszynski, Greenberg, Koole, & Solomon, 2010, for an illuminating review of existential issues or "facts of life" pertinent to coping and its challenges).

Indeed, one could argue convincingly that the intellectual center of social psychology inheres in its illumination of the power of situational meanings in driving both the struggles of everyday living and the management of our ultimate life goals. Whether one is deploying social psychology's research and theory to explore the parameters of the cognitive and implicit unconscious, inherent biases of attribution, strivings for consistency, desires for autonomy and freedom, the aversion of self-awareness, justifications of status quo systems, the distortive influences that define our relational liaisons, distortions of personal power and control, our "totalitarian egos," or the salience of our awareness of our mortality, among many other phenomena driving phenomenalistic and situational meanings, social psychologists continuously, even if implicitly, revisit the Lewinian invention of the diversely constructed phenomenal field. As we locomote through that field, existential challenges to coping and their differential magnitude (perhaps indexed by the concept of regional permeability) array persons on a dimension of normal to abnormal. Each of us can occupy any point on that continuum depending on the relationship of personal attributes and environmental presses at any moment in time or persistently through large swatches of time and existence. Thus, for example, the depressed individual is not a separated version of humanity whose characteristics and existential demands are peculiar to the rank-and-file "normals" among us.

As we painfully know, many if not all of us can range into the territory of depression—sometimes in mild and "normal" forms and other times in severe vegetative, excruciating forms. Further, it is clear that while we all can range into this depressive territory, some of us go to visit it a good deal more frequently than others of us, stay there longer, and suffer more profoundly for it . A primary point that we wish to make in our analysis (and later on we express it as a major assumption underlying our approach) is that the principles of the P x E dynamics underlying short acute trips into depression, sadness, and a sense of lowered purpose are the very same principles of coping that take us on long and perhaps deep, despairing, and lifelong journeys into that territory. It should be clear that we seek not to trivialize profound phenomena like depression or serious psychopathology more generally, but to humanize it by linking it to the pervasive struggles of coping we all are challenged by as we negotiate the meanings in our lives and the purposes to which we set our goals and valued end-states. Whether our meaning-making beliefs in such end-states as justice, fairness, consistency, or the value of self (to name just a few relevant worldviews from social psychology's storehouse of many) are illusions or "truths" of human existence, our success or failure in sustaining these illusions or believed truths is, in our formulation, at the heart of coping and constitutes the signature processes of both healthy and psychopathological coping.

Vulnerability-Inducing Environments: Social Psychology

Given the perspective on the pivotal nature of meaning constructions offered above, scholars of social psychology have made one of the most compelling aspects of laboratory inductions or simulations of environmental qualities the manipulation of situational meanings. The primary task of laboratory experimentation in social psychology is the creation of contextual arrangements that encapsulate shared situational definitions. These "creations," in the ideal case, serve as instances of situations and phenomenal demands that humans confront in the actual environment (Wilson, Aronson, & Carlsmith, 2010). Frequently, theories and hypotheses in social psychology are concerned with these meaning-based constructions as markers of the remnants of social evolutionary endowments (see Kenrick, 1994; Kenrick, Nieuweboer, & Buunk, 2010; Neuberg, Kenrick, & Schaller 2010; also see Gangestad, chapter 7, this volume). Further, these constructions are linked to both motive systems and the demands for adaptation. As we shall see below, constructed environments that permit the inference of centrally important phenomenal features of the field such as justice/fairness, control/efficacy, order/consistency, belongingness, safety, self-centrality, and so on are at the core of adaptive behavioral accommodations and can either block or enable movement in the behavioral field.

A repeated proposition of many theories in social psychology is that, when field-embedded meanings are absent or ambiguous, restorative motives arise to either reconstruct the field or to distort the existing field as one containing these requisite features. The underlying premise of such "restorative distortion" in social psychology is that the retention (or creation) of adaptive ideological visions of the environment frequently take precedence over getting it "right" in a single instance of disconfirming evidence. Thus, for example, observing a victim suffer for no apparent reason has been found to lead to the denigration of the innocent victim rather than leading to the adoption of a view that might imply the capriciousness of justice in human society (Lerner, Ross, & Miller, 2002). Indeed one who lives within a system in which innocent victims are plentiful and in which the norm of justice is frequently violated might form explicit or implicit impressions of the unjustly treated as perpetually deserving of their fate.

This can lead to persistent group-based beliefs that might be considered to be a "social pathology" (i.e., beliefs supporting discrimination, torture, and even genocide in extreme cases; see Jost, 2004).

With regard to our effort to examine the social psychological component of psychopathology, it should be clear that people sometimes turn such ideologically restorative distortions against themselves, either nonconsciously or consciously. Mental disorders associated with symptoms of self-loathing, self-injurious behavior and habits, depressive cognitions and feelings, suicidal ideation, and so on can be theoretically considered to be a consequence of repeated exposure to circumstances that threaten "adaptive" field constructions that the world is an orderly, benign, just, or "loving" place. As discussed above, these processes of construction can be employed to provide an account for states of affect, disorders of behavior, and distortions of thought that are associated with psychopathology (see for example Valiente et al., 2010; Abramson, Metalsky, & Alloy, 1989).

To provide a compelling example from the literature on psychopathology, one might consider the alterations that occur in conventional beliefs and expectations following intense and traumatic victimization. Individuals are left in the psychological quandary of either abandoning the adaptive construction that the world is a safe place or assuming that somehow they are at fault and the cause of their own victimization. Beyond this cognitive and conceptual challenge, victims of trauma often make "unthinking" and nonconscious behavioral accommodations that render them more vulnerable to revictimization—an extreme effect of a confirmatory bias (see Van der Kolk et al., 1996, or Janoff-Bulman, 1989, for descriptions of this phenomenon).

As Van De Kolk (2004) noted:

Traumatic events such as family and social violence, rapes and assaults, disasters, wars, accidents, and predatory violence may temporarily or permanently alter the organism's response to its environment. While people have evolved to be enormously resourceful and capable of surviving and overcoming extreme experiences, certain events, particularly if they occur early in the life cycle, can overwhelm the capacity of the organism to cope with stress and permanently alter the perception of danger and the regulation of internal homeostasis. (p. 319)

In addition, studies of the effects of extreme early childhood trauma illustrate the spread of these effects to the domain of human attachment and bonding in children and adolescents (see Cicchetti & Lynch, 1995). In essence, exposure to trauma is viewed as disrupting one's internal homeostasis, self-regulatory capacity, and relationship expectancies. This work on trauma and its wake is a clear example of a meaning-based or existential breakdown. As we have noted, such disconfirmations of the common assumptions rendering the world as orderly, safe, just, and fair, for examples, can render regions of the behavioral field as less permeable, and thus the adaptive constructions that "grease" the field of behavior are altered by such intense experiences.

While social psychologists have developed multiple models, theories, and research projects to test the degree to which assumptions about the orderliness and safety of the world promote adaptive behavior, few of these approaches have yet been brought to bear on the study of pathological trauma. Further, social psychologists have infrequently referred to the literature on trauma-based readjustments in expectation to extend their particular approaches in the direction of clinical application. Lerner's (1978) just world hypothesis; Jost's (Jost & Banaji, 1994) notion of system justification; and Solomon, Greenberg, and Pyszczynski's (1991) theory of terror management and mortality salience are only a few of the myriad approaches in social psychology that point to adaptive worldviews. The trauma-based scholarship of clinical researchers illustrates the extreme survival-based utility of such constructions and the psychopathological manifestations that result from extreme disconfirmations of "status quo" beliefs. Although various traumatic social events have been analyzed through the lenses of these theories—events such as adaptation following 9/11, reactivity to natural disasters, and personal encounters with extreme torture—little connection has been made between the social psychological significance of purposive constructions and the literature on reactive psychopathology. By employing a model, derived from Lewin's field theory, that arrays purposive belief systems as the sets of processes that serve to calibrate P's entry into the adaptive regions of the field, we may be able to conceptualize this conjunction of subdisciplines in an overarching perspective. While each of these social psychological approaches and other similar approaches have been applied to the circumstances of depression, deflated self-esteem, and the like, the theories and the research based on them have not truly benefited from the enormous amount of descriptive and empirical work that has been the products of scholars of psychopathology. Similarly, it is exceedingly rare for scholars of psychopathology to cite social psychological theories and research regarding adaptive worldviews to advance understanding of where a "normal" response to environmental priming of disregulatory beliefs is transformed into a chronic abnormal adaptation that might be referred to as "psychopathology."

Personal Vulnerability: Worldviews, Self-Views, and Personality

The Lewinian formula that we have adopted as an orienting framework for this chapter proposed that behavior (and its associated cognitions and emotions) is a function of the interaction between field forces (or the constructed environment) and personal predilections. This P x E formula, while simple and obvious on the surface, creates complexities of theory and research when applied to psychopathology. We have introduced the preliminary conceptual components of the environmental term in the P x E formula as it pertains to psychopathological states and constructions. However, we also made clear that it is the "phenomenal field" rather than the material environment that has the most profound effect on adaptation. Personality and individual differences when partnered with the eliciting properties of the field occasion behavioral orientations, emotional inclinations, and cognitive constructions that favor or inhibit adaptation. In this sense, it is as at least as important to examine the aspects of personal orientation and individual differences in specific vulnerabilities as it is to parse situational impacts when examining models of psychopathological functioning.

One of the most compelling categories of individual differences and personality is comprised of the many constructs that index variability in self-views, worldviews, and personal meanings and expectations. These personality attributes often parallel the social psychological models probing the priming of "status quo" conceptions of the environment. Individual differences in a priori conceptions of the world as fair, just, rejecting, or orderly have much to do with our resilience and vulnerability to threats and challenges (see, for examples, Rubin & Peplau, 1975; Mikulincer & Florian, 2010; Hafer & Gosse, 2010). Depending on one's extremity on these ideological attributes, the phenomenal field can appear to block some goal strivings and enable others. The same environmental array can seem to some to occasion fear or anxiety while appearing neutral or even secure to others. In most instances, however, personality differences in beliefs and expectations can only alter the perception of the phenomenal field within its material limits. For example, few would view floods or famines as occasions for optimistic interpretations and constructions of the field despite their trait-like tendencies to infuse situations with positive meanings. On the other hand, the environments that human beings face are typically considerably more ambiguous in their structure and meaning than are obvious material disasters. For example, whether a particular smile on the part of an associate connotes amusement, derision, love, or seductive motives is open to interpretive construction. To the extent that ideological beliefs and traits provide chronic interpretive guides for resolving the ambiguities of social meaning, they become prominent parts of people's meaning-making apparatus. Ideological traits provide for efficient and rapid resolutions of ambiguity—even if the specific nature of those resolutions is personally painful. As we shall see in the section on the domain of belongingness and social acceptance below, in the interpersonal world individual differences in chronic views concerning acceptance, warmth, and safety provide clarity about the meaning of multiple and generally ambiguous interactive cues. Furthermore, a chronic philosophical stance that supports beliefs in the agonistic nature of human beings can have self-confirming properties. As such, individuals prone to see the interpersonal world as an unfriendly place are likely to view many interactive cues as sustaining that belief. Again, while this is certainly painful, such ideological beliefs do reduce the ambiguous qualities of interpersonal exchange and provide a familiar clarity about the nature of the environments we confront. These interpretive and meaning-promoting personal consistencies are, of course, a critical aspect of the adaptive apparatus that renders people vulnerable to psychopathological behaviors, thoughts, and feelings. As noted earlier, these meaning-making processes determine the difficulty of entering various regions and domains of the field. Chronic beliefs that the world is a hostile unwelcoming place, or an uncontrollable place, or an unjust place, for examples, impede people's capacity to enter these regions of the adaptive field and are likely to result in maladaptive constructions that redefine the field of behavior or the self in ways that promote continuing distress. Again, considering the case of traumatic disorders from the literature of psychopathology (see Van der Kolk, 2004; Janoff-Bulman, 1989),

subject to the drawing-down of their capacity to exert control over the influence of the immediate environment. Capacity for control could have been drawn down prior to entering a given environment or the immediate environment might itself be a source of multiple demands on the capacity to self-regulate. In either case, the features of environments described earlier exert a stronger influence on self-regulation. Reductions in the capacity for control result, in part, from the exercise of self-regulation repeatedly within a relatively short span of time (Baumeister, Bratslavsky, Muraven, & Tice, 1998). In such cases, even people who generally are adept at self-regulation may struggle. To the extent that the reduced capacity persists, the adverse effects of the environment on self-regulation may be prolonged, resulting in symptoms such as those described earlier. Environments also vary in the extent to which they allow for the exercise of control (Cantor, 1994). Environments low on this quality are particularly problematic for individuals high in the motivation to control their behavior. Conversely, individuals not accustomed to or expecting to control events and outcomes would find such environments comfortable in their consistency with expectation.

Weak situations increase the expression of dispositions (Caspi & Moffit, 1993). Thus, to the extent that people are dispositionally inclined toward poor self-regulation, weak situations put them in a vulnerable state. Weak situations are those that offer little or no information about appropriate or desirable behavior. Absent such information, people are left to behave in ways that reflect their dispositional tendencies. If those tendencies are adaptive for self-regulation, then weak situations do not increase vulnerability; however, if, as in the case of, for instance, impulsivity, those tendencies are maladaptive, vulnerability is increased (c.f., DeWall, Baumeister, Schurtz, & Gaillot, 2010). In the absence of cues or contingencies in the immediate environment that facilitate self-regulation when it is required, the individual is left to his or her own devices and falters.

Such a formulation is particularly important in the case of addictive behavioral systems. Individuals temperamentally and neurologically disposed to increased impulsivity and decreased inhibitory function are subject to succumbing to addictive substances and classes of behavior that take on addictive qualities (as in the case of eating disorders). Weak environments, or even more pronouncedly, "disinhibiting" environmental conditions amplify the effects of addictive vulnerabilities on deviant addictive behaviors (e.g., Lynam et al., 2000). Such environments may be developmentally disparate. For example, adolescents are particularly confronted with peer influences encouraging impulsive and rule-breaking behaviors (Dishion, Spracklen, Andrews, & Patterson, 1996). Those whose biological or personality attributes dispose them to disinhibition are likely to encounter not only experimental substance use during this period, but are likely to be triggered to eventual addictive use even in the absence of social cues. Furthermore, the same impulsivity that engenders this reactivity to substances also brings with it comorbid consequences in areas bearing on behavior control (e.g., Keenan, Loeber, Zhang, Stouthamer-Loeber, & Van Kammen, 1995). Thus, addictive substance use is associated with multiple antisocial disorders of behavior. This cascading effect of regulatory vulnerability is thus a critical aspect of multiple behavior disorders.

With further development of research and theory in the domain of self-regulation among personality and social psychologists, our understanding of the dimensions of psychopathology that derive from disregulatory process should also be advanced. Some recent examples of this work are evident in the perspective offered by regulatory focus theory (Higgins, 1997, 1998). In that model the proneness to seek control via goal promotion and goal prevention are each seen as characteristics of both people and of environments. The "regulatory fit" between the person and environment (Higgins, 2000) is a critical factor in the distinction between adaptive and maladaptive behavior—between the "normal" and the psychopathological. This perspective is inherently Lewinian in its major thrust and illustrates the P x E contingencies that render the normal-to-the-pathological a dimensional rather than categorical distinction in the domain of self-regulation.

P × E Vulnerabilities for Psychological Difficulties Associated with Interpersonal Rejection

A pervasive issue in the study of human behavior has involved the primary forces that motivate people to do what they do. Even researchers who do not study motivation per se have assumptions about the basic processes that motivate people's actions, and journals in personality, social, and clinical psychology are rife with motivational constructs that invoke motives, needs, and desires involving, for example, cognitive consistency, approval, achievement, control, power, felt security, meaning, acceptance, self-esteem, understanding, self-verification, terror management, uniqueness, self-actualization, and so on (see Norem, chapter 12, this volume).

These motivational constructs have provided one of the few rallying points for those interested in interpersonal processes, individual differences, and psychopathology. Social psychologists have considered how these motives are instigated by and play out in interpersonal contexts; personality psychologists have examined the nature, sources, and implications of individual differences in the strength of these motives; and clinical psychologists and others interested in psychological problems have explored how these motives may lead to dysfunctional behavior and how the failure to satisfy them can create emotional and behavioral problems.

Although others might disagree, there is good reason to suspect that, of the panoply of motives that have been studied, the motive for social acceptance and belonging is among the most basic social motives (Baumeister & Leary, 1995; Leary & Allen, 2011; Williams, 2007). That is, if we step back and ask which of the motives listed above exerts the strongest and most pervasive influence on the largest number of social behaviors in the greatest number of interpersonal contexts, a strong case can be made that it is the motive to be accepted, as opposed to rejected, by other people. Throughout evolutionary history, being accepted as group members, friends, and relational partners has been vitally important because our hominid ancestors were unlikely to survive and reproduce without the benefit of supportive relationships and cooperative groups. Thus, natural selection favored those who were concerned about acceptance and behaved in ways that promoted their inclusion in social groups and relationships. As a result, human beings are not only highly social animals in the sense of living in groups, but they also possess a strong drive to form and maintain an array of relationships and group memberships.

Oddly, social psychologists did not fully appreciate the centrality of social acceptance in understanding social behavior for many years. (We find it curious that other motives that seem far less important to human behavior and well-being, such as the desire for cognitive consistency, received far more attention.) But, in fact, little of the content of social psychology makes much sense unless we assume that people are motivated to foster and maintain relationships with other people. People's concerns about social acceptance permeate much, if not most, of what they do and influence the dynamics of most interpersonal encounters. When people fret over their physical appearance, seek membership in groups of various kinds, conform to social norms, manage the impressions that they convey of themselves to other people, foster and enhance close relationships, seek to be successful, and strive for status, they are influenced, at least in part, by concerns with promoting their value and acceptance by other people. And, even when people are not focused on seeking acceptance, they usually pursue whatever goals are prepotent in ways that do not jeopardize their acceptance by other people.

Furthermore, concerns with acceptance also relate strongly to people's emotional lives (Leary, Koch, & Hechenbleikner, 2001). People experience hurt feelings when they do not perceive that others adequately value having relationships with them (Feeney, 2005; Leary & Leder, 2010), feel socially anxious when they think that others will form impressions of them that may undermine their social acceptance (Leary, 2010), become embarrassed when they project social images that might compromise their relational value, and feel guilty when their acceptance may be eroded by others' views of their ethical behavior (even if they know that they didn't actually do anything wrong). Over time, feeling inadequately accepted can lead to deep-seated loneliness, and depression, and influence people's self-images and self-esteem (Leary et al., 2001).

Given that concerns with social acceptance and rejection pervade social life and underlie a great deal of human behavior and emotion, we should not be surprised that problems with real, anticipated, and imagined acceptance also set the stage for an array of emotional and behavioral problems. As we will see, some of these problems stem from dysfunctional means of seeking acceptance, whereas others reflect sequelae of rejection and people's efforts to cope with it. Our model of P x E vulnerabilities suggests that the problems that people experience that stem from issues of acceptance and rejection can be construed in terms of situational and person variables that increase people's vulnerabilities for experiencing rejection, along with their vulnerabilities for problems that stem from rejection. We first examine features of situations that heighten people's vulnerability to dysfunctional effects of rejection and then discuss personality attributes that are associated with vulnerability.

Environmental Vulnerabilities

Everyone occasionally encounters situations in which they feel inadequately accepted, if not downright rejected. What these situations have in common is that they lead people to perceive that their relational value is low or declining—that is, that other people value having relationships with them less than the person desires. The question, from the standpoint of our P x E model of vulnerability, is what features of the social environment and of persons cause people to perceive that their relational value is low, thus triggering a vulnerability for psychological difficulties.

Typically, the word *rejection* connotes being avoided, excluded, or ostracized by people who know the individual personally and who, in most cases, have an existing relationship with him or her. So, when children are rejected by their peers or neglected by their parents, people are rejected by romantic partners or ostracized by family members, people are denied admission into or expelled from a group, or individuals are betrayed by friends or lovers, they take the rejection quite personally, as well they should. These situations render people vulnerable to dysfunctional responses both because they sever important social connections and because they raise broader questions about one's desirability as a partner, friend, group member, or social participant. Yet being rejected by those who do not know us personally can also lead to dysfunctional emotional and behavioral responses. And, even when people are not explicitly shunned, avoided, or excluded, but rather others simply do not show interest in or seek them out, people may experience strong negative emotions, show decreased self-esteem, and behave in maladaptive ways.

For example, people who are the targets of prejudice and discrimination feel devalued and rejected. Whether others' reactions are based on race, ethnicity, age, gender, socioeconomic class, or other social categories, many of the negative effects of prejudice and discrimination are essentially effects of being devalued and rejected (Kessler, Mickelson, & Williams, 1999; Sellers & Shelton, 2003). People who possess visible stigmas (such as deformities or skin lesions) or who are known to be ill (with HIV or cancer, for example) likewise feel devalued and rejected (Kleck & Strenta, 1980). Similarly, immigrants often feel inadequately accepted by the residents of the new country. Often, the response reflects indifference rather than disapproval or animosity, although there are certainly instances in which residents of the new country are openly disparaging and rejecting (Wiley, Perkins, & Deaux, 2008; Tartakovsky, 2007). In addition, people who have suffered serious damage to their public

reputations—such as the married politician who is known to have fathered a child with another woman, or the celebrity whose serious indiscretions are caught on videotape—presumably feel widely dismissed by the population at large. Situations that involve failure—or even inadequate success—are also troubling, fueled in part by implications of the failure for people's relational value to others. Students who fail, employers who botch important projects, people who go through foreclosure or bankruptcy, and workers who lose their jobs have increased vulnerability to psychological problems because, in addition to whatever practical consequences these events have, they are often viewed as diminishing the person's relational value and undermining their social connections.

Social situations that undermine relational value can make people vulnerable to at least three kinds of psychological problems. The emotional implications are most immediate and pronounced, and research has documented the effects of rejection episodes on depression, hurt feelings, loneliness, and hostility (Leary et al., 2001). For example, children who are rejected by their peers, people who experience long-term ostracism, and spouses whose marriages break up are all unusually prone to depression (Cole & Carpentieri, 1990).

When people perceive that they are being rejected, they sometimes experience a great deal of anger that, when unmodulated, can explode into violence (Leary, Twenge, & Quinlivan, 2006; Twenge, Baumeister, Tice, & Stucke, 2001). Rejected lovers sometimes attack their partners or ex-partners, ostracized students shoot or otherwise harm their classmates, and fired workers may return to exact retribution on employers and coworkers (Leary, Kowalski, Smith, & Phillips, 2003). Although it may seem paradoxical that people would attack those whom they want to accept them (violence is rarely a good way to endear oneself to others), research suggests that aggression is most likely when people perceive that the rejection was unfair, that there is little likelihood of repairing the relationship, and that other relational opportunities exist (Richman & Leary, 2009; see also Maner, DeWall, Baumeister, & Schaller, 2007).

Furthermore, because rejections are so distressing, people exert a great deal of effort into assuring that they are accepted, sometimes to the point of engaging in actions that are harmful to themselves or others. For example, people who are highly dependent or insecurely attached may subvert their own needs and desires in order to please friends, romantic partners, group members, and others so as to minimize the possibility of being disliked or rejected (Hazan & Shaver, 1990). Research shows that such behaviors corrode well-being over time, as in the case of self-silencing in which people censor themselves so as to not harm a relationship (Harper, Dickson, & Welsh, 2006).

Personality Vulnerabilities

Every normal person suffers emotionally from important rejections, and most people have at some point behaved maladaptively to avoid rejection or in response to a rejection episode. Although these situations decenter and distress people to varying degrees, most people cope successfully over time. However, some people are more sensitive to the effects of interpersonal rejection than others and, in fact, may experience more subjective rejection because of the ways in which they construe social events. Thus, a full understanding of the impact of vulnerability to the pernicious effects of rejection requires, as Lewin suggested, attention to both P and E influences that increase vulnerability.

Four categories of personality variables are associated with greater vulnerability to the dysfunctional effects of rejection. First, people who are more strongly motivated to be accepted (or to avoid rejection) presumably worry more about rejection, try to behave in ways that promote their relational value even at cost to themselves, and react strongly when signs of rejection are detected. For example, people who are high in the need to belong, fear of negative evaluation, or attachment anxiety may be highly motivated to avoid all rejections and, thus, react more often and more strongly when they perceive that their relational value is low (Leary & Kelly, 2009; McClure, Lydon, Baccus, & Baldwin, 2010).

Second, the ways in which people construe others' behaviors, and particularly the degree to which they perceive others as rejecting can make some people prone to experience rejection. For example, people who are high in rejection sensitivity (Downey & Feldman, 1994) anxiously expect that others will not adequately accept them, and these expectations increase the likelihood that they will interpret others' reactions as rejecting (Ayduk, Downey, Testa, & Yen, 1999). Similarly, people who are low in trait self-esteem or highly depressed interpret neutral and ambiguous reactions from other people as expressing rejection (Koch, 2002; Nezlek, Kowalski, Leary, Blevins, & Holgate, 1997). People who are particularly conscious of how others might respond to their possession of a stigma (Pinel,

1999) or their membership in a socially devalued group (Mendoza-Denton, Purdie, Downey, & Davis, 2002) are also at greater risk for pernicious effects of relational devaluation.

Third, individual differences in people's interpersonal styles set some people up for rejection. People who lack certain social skills may mismanage their interactions with other people in ways that make interactions with them awkward and uncomfortable, leading others to avoid dealing with them except when necessary (Butler, Doherty, & Potter, 2007). In addition, people who do not possess attributes that are generally valued in interaction partners—such as being a good conversationalist, having a pleasant disposition or pleasing sense of humor, showing an interest in other people, possessing useful abilities and skills, and so on—will not be actively sought as relational partners and group members as frequently or concertedly as people who possess such attributes (Amstutz & Kaplan, 1987; Eastwick & Finkel, 2008; Park & Killen, 2010). A good deal of research shows, for example, that people tend to avoid those who are depressed and do not interact with them in a warm or accepting manner (Joiner & Metalsky, 1995).

Finally, individual differences in people's tendencies to experience a variety of negative emotions may predispose them to react strongly when they perceive that their relational value is not as high as they desire. For example, people who are prone to depression, hurt feelings, or loneliness may respond more strongly to a particular episode of rejection than people who are less inclined to feel depressed, hurt, or lonely (Kelly, 2001; Leary & Springer, 2000).

The Complexity of P × E Effects

According to our P × E model of psychological vulnerability, vulnerability to dysfunctional responses to interpersonal rejection are increased by situational features that lead people to experience low relational value and are greater for people whose personal characteristics predispose them to experience, perceive, and react to such situations. Lewin's model implies a multiplicative relationship between personal and environmental influences that has been fashioned into interactionist models in personality and social psychology. Although interactionism is widely accepted, often implicitly, as the way that person and environmental factors influence behavior, the data sometimes tell a different story.

At times, situational and personality vulnerabilities do, in fact, interact in a statistical sense such that situational rejections have different effects depending on people's personal dispositions, and personal dispositions manifest differently depending on the features of the situation. For example, mild episodes of rejection may have little or no effect on people who score high in self-esteem or low in rejection-sensitivity, but very strong effects on people who are low in self-esteem or high in rejection sensitivity (Kelly, 2001; Nezlek et al., 1997).

However, often the effects of personal and environment influences are simply additive. Changes in situational parameters intensify people's reactions, and people who score high versus low on relevant personality variables differ in the strength of their reactions, but situational and dispositional factors do not interact statistically (Buckley, Winkel, & Leary, 2004; Kelly, 2001).

Contemporary versions of interactionism go beyond simple interactive effects of P and E, and these can also be seen in reactions to rejection. For example, personality variables may be associated with different interpersonal styles whose function appears to be to reduce the possibility of rejection, but those styles may, in fact, increase the probability of rejection. For example, people who are socially anxious worry unduly about being accepted by others, and they may avoid certain interpersonal encounters and be reticent when in them to forestall rejection (DePaulo, Epstein, & LeMay, 1990). Yet, their reluctance to interact might lower their relational value to others and paradoxically decrease acceptance. Then, of course, the person is particularly troubled by others' disinterest. Similarly, people who are dispositionally high in rejection sensitivity may react strongly to perceived rejection in ways that undermine their relationships, such as by behaving aggressively (Downey, Freitas, Michaelis, & Khouri, 1998). In these instances, P and E interact to increase vulnerability via a chain of events in which they mutually influence each other.

In another pattern, a chronic pattern of rejection may lead to relatively stable changes in people's personalities. The person who is widely accepted increases in confidence, self-esteem, and opportunities to develop social skills, whereas the person who feels generally devalued loses confidence, self-esteem, and adaptive social abilities. These divergent personalities then respond differently to situations that connote low relational value, leading to yet greater differences in their vulnerability to negative effects of rejection.

The interplay of environment and person variables on psychological vulnerability that we have described here with respect to interpersonal rejection apply equally to other antecedents of psychological problems and to other types of difficulties.

Conclusions

At the outset of this chapter, we stated our intention of linking together the scholarship of social and personality psychologists with that of clinical researchers concerned with an understanding of maladaptive behaviors and psychopathology. As we noted, the history of the study of human adaptation from these fields has had a number of both empirical and conceptual interconnections. In presenting these connections, first through the eyes of foundational scholars such as Morton Prince and Floyd Allport and subsequently through tracing an abbreviated history of shared overarching conceptual models employed by scholars of normal and abnormal behavior during the 20th century, we stated our opinion that it is time to once again join together the research and theory of abnormal and normal behavior under a shared rubric. In doing so we made a claim and assumption that abnormal behaviors/ psychopathology are continuously arrayed on the same dimensions as are "normal" behaviors and psychological adaptation. What should be implicitly clear from the analyses that followed these initial claims and statements is that this dimensional "hookup" of the normal and abnormal in human behavior requires an overarching model or theory flexible enough to encompass both normality and abnormality. Through the years, both social and personality psychology have advanced by positing a wide array of models and hypotheses that account for distinct personally and environmentally caused variations in behavior, cognition, and feeling. In like manner, scholars of psychopathology have explored the causes and correlates of various maladaptive categories of behavior. While each set of scholars would occasionally venture into the disciplinary " life space" of the other, this had been typically done with the intent of poaching an idea here or there or a newly discovered process that might encompass the phenomena studied by scholars of both abnormal and normal behavior. These included the importation of concepts like attributional bias or notions of cognitive load, trait-like habits of control, or conceptions of attachment anxieties from social and personality psychology to abnormal psychology.

Likewise personality and social psychologists also from time to time "poached" concepts developed by scholars of abnormal psychology to help in their conceptions of models of "normal" adaptation. Concepts such as ego depletion or psychological defense or unconscious distortion were imported from scholars of psychopathology by scholars studying adaptation in everyday "normal" life. Obviously those of us working in each of these fields do not begrudge these poachings at all. It is always a pleasure when one's ideas and pet models are generalized to account for a wider range of behaviors and human conditions that constituted their original targets of understanding. However what has not happened since the heyday of omnibus theories of personality is the use of overarching conceptual models to define the dynamics of behavioral continua ranging from the normal to the abnormal in human experience. While we haven't advocated for the return of competing wholly encased theoretical perspectives on human behavior, we do believe that scholars of normal and abnormal behavior need to work to develop shared ways of conceiving of human adaptation in its various manifestations.

In the analysis we offered in this chapter we employed such a flexible conceptual framework. Lewin's approach originated in the foundational years of experimental social psychology. However its flexibility in defining processes of adaptation through the concepts of life space, field forces and person x environment interactions allows for it to serve as a touchstone perspective for the placement of normal and abnormal behavior on continua undergirded by the same conceptual architecture. We do believe that in the upcoming decades the advances that might be realized in the understanding of human adaptation more generally and psychopathological adaptation in particular will be best realized by the self-conscious development of flexible conceptual models that allow the integration of human psychological processes from the everyday to the exceptional to be an achievable goal. Our use of Lewinian field theory conceptions constitutes one example of the application of a flexible overarching perspective to the linked study of normal and abnormal behavior. In the current scholarly landscape of the behavioral sciences, we believe that the growing need to integrate newly emerging knowledge in the neural and biological sciences with knowledge derived from the sciences of personality and social psychology will "force" the integration of the normal and the abnormal and will result in the creation of models that explain both under the same rubric.

In the meantime, it is our hope that the analysis we have provided above of what we consider to be field driven behavior in the important domains of regulation/control and acceptance/rejection will offer a view that illustrates the utility of overarching conceptions of the nature of human adaptation. It is our hope that the analysis presented serves to encourage personality and social psychologists to think beyond the particulars of separate processes to the characterization of the human condition in all its glory and all its pain. This actually was Morton Prince's vision. However over the past 90 years since that vision was first put forward in the founding of the *Journal of Abnormal and Social Psychology* much has been learned about the nature of personality and social behavior. Perhaps this advanced state of knowledge can, at last, promote the realization of Prince's wise vision. We also hope that the Lewinian analyses we provided of the seminal roles of "field forces," "regulation," and "belongingness" in human adaptation to life's circumstances can serve as a model for other conceptual conjunctions of researchers of "normal" and "abnormal" behavior.

References

Abele A. E., Wojciszke B. (2007) Agency and communion from the perspective of self versus others. *Journal of Personality and Social Psychology, 93*(5), 751–763.

Abramson L. Y., Metalsky, G. I., & Alloy, L. B. (1989). Hopelessness depression: A theory-based subtype of depression. *Psychological Review, 96,* 358–372.

Amstutz, D. K. & Kaplan, M. F. (1987). Depression, physical attractiveness, and interpersonal acceptance. *Journal of Social and Clinical Psychology, 5,* 365–377.

Ayduk, O., Downey, G., Testa, A., & Yen, Y. (1999). Does rejection elicit hostility in rejection sensitive women? *Social Cognition, 17,* 245–271.

Bagozzi, R. (1994). A general approach to representing multifaceted personality constructs: Application to state self-esteem. *Structural equation modeling, 1,* 35–67.

Bandura, A. (1969). *Principles of behavior modification.* New York: Holt.

Barenbaum, N., & Winter, D. (2003). Personality. In D. K. Fredheim (Ed.) *Handbook of psychology: History of psychology* (pp. 177–197). New York: Wiley.

Bargh, J. A., Gollwitzer, P. M., Lee-Chai, A. Y., Barndollar, K., & Troetschel, R. (2001). The automated will: Nonconscious activation and pursuit of behavioral goals. *Journal of Personality and Social Psychology, 81,* 1014–1027.

Baumeister, R. (1999). *Escaping the self.* New York: Basic Books.

Baumeister, R.F., Bratslavsky, E., Muraven, M., & Tice, D.M. (1998). Ego depletion: Is the active self a limited resource? *Journal of Personality and Social Psychology, 74,* 1252–1265.

Baumeister, R. F., & Leary, M. R. (1995). The need to belong: Desire for interpersonal attachments as a fundamental human motivation. *Psychological Bulletin, 117,* 497–529.

Beck, A. T. (1976). *Cognitive therapy and emotional disorders.* New York: International Universities Press.

Beck, A. T., Rush, A. J., Shaw, B. F., & Emery, G. (1979). *Cognitive therapy of depression.* New York: Guilford.

Benassi, V. A., Sweeney, P. D., & Dufour, C. L. (1988). Is there a relationship between locus of control orientation and depression? *Journal of Abnormal Psychology, 97*, 357–367.

Brehm, S. S. (1976). *The application of social psychology to clinical practice.* Washington, DC: Hemisphere Press.

Brehm, S. S., & Smith, T. W. (1986). Social psychological approaches to psychotherapy and behavior change. In S. L. Garfield & A. E. Bergin (Eds.) *Handbook of psychotherapy and behavior change* (3rd ed., pp. 69–115). New York: Wiley.

Briere, J., & Rickards, S. (2007). Self-awareness, affect regulation, and relatedness: Differential sequels of childhood versus adult victimization experiences. *Journal of Nervous and Mental Disease, 195*, 497–503.

Buckley, K. E., Winkel, R. E., & Leary M. R. (2004). Reactions to acceptance and rejection: Effects of level and sequence of relational evaluation. *Journal of Experimental Social Psychology, 40*, 14-28.

Burke, P. (2006). *Contemporary social psychological theories.* Stanford, CA.: Stanford University Press.

Buss, A. H. (1980). *Self-consciousness and social anxiety.* San Francisco: Freeman.

Butler, J. C., Doherty, M. S., & Potter, R. M. (2007). Social antecedents and consequences of interpersonal rejection sensitivity. *Personality and Individual Differences, 43*, 1376–1385.

Cantor, N. (1994). Life task problem solving: Situational affordances and personal needs. *Personality and Social Psychology Bulletin, 20*, 235–243.

Caspi A., & Moffitt T. E. (1993). When do individual differences matter? A paradoxical theory of personality coherence. *Psychological Inquiry, 4*, 247–271.

Caspi, A., Hariri, A. R., Holmes, A., Uher, R., & Moffitt, T. E. (2010). Genetic sensitivity to the environment: The case of the serotonin transporter gene and its implications for studying complex diseases and traits. *American Journal of Psychiatry, 167*(5), 509–527.

Charney, D., & Nestler, E. J. (2004). *Neurobiology of mental illness.* New York: Oxford.

Cicchetti, D., & Lynch, M. (1995). Failures in the expectable environment and their impact on individual development: The case of child maltreatment. In D. Cicchetti & D. J. Cohen (Eds.), *Developmental psychopathology, Volume 2. Risk, disorder, and adaptation* (pp. 71). New York: Wiley.

Cole, D. A., & Carpentieri, S. (1990). Social status and the comorbidity of child depression and conduct disorder. *Journal of Consulting and Clinical Psychology, 58*, 748–757.

Cozolino, L. J. (2010). *The neuroscience of psychotherapy: Healing the social brain.* New York: Norton.

Curtis, R. D. (1991) *The relational self: Theoretical convergences in psychoanalysis and social psychology.* New York: Guilford.

Deaux, K. (1992). Focusing on the self: Challenges to self definition and their consequences for mental health. In D. Ruble, P. Costanzo, & M. Oliveri (Eds.) *The social psychology of mental health.* New York: Guilford.

DePaulo, B. M., Epstein, J. A., & LeMay, C. S. (1990). Responses of the socially anxious to the prospect of interpersonal evaluation. *Journal of Personality, 48*, 623–640.

DeWall, C. N., Baumeister, R. F., Schurtz, D. R., & Gaillot, M. T. (2010). Acting on limited resources: The interactive effects of self-regulatory depletion and individuals differences. In R. H. Hoyle (Ed.), *Handbook of personality and self-regulation* (pp. 243–262). Malden, MA: Blackwell.

Dishion, T. J., Spracklen, K. M., Andrews, D. W., & Patterson, G. R. (1996). Deviancy training in male adolescents friendships. *Behavior Therapy, 27*, 373–390.

Downey, G., & Feldman, S. I. (1996). Implications of rejection sensitivity for intimate relationships. *Journal of Personality and Social Psychology, 70*, 1327–1343.

Downey, G., Feldman, S., & Ayduk, O. (2000). Rejection sensitivity and male violence in romantic relationships. *Personal Relationships, 7*, 45–61.

Downey, G., Freitas, A. L., Michaelis, B., & Khouri, H. (1998). The self-fulfilling prophecy in close relationships: Rejection sensitivity and rejection by romantic partners. *Journal of Personality and Social Psychology, 75*, 545–560.

Duval, S., & Wicklund, R. (1972). *A theory of objective self-awareness.* New York: Academic.

Eastwick, P. W., & Finkel, E. J. (2008). Sex differences in mate preferences revisited: Do people know what they initially desire in a romantic partner? *Journal of Personality and Social Psychology, 94*, 245–264.

Feeney, J. (2005). Hurt feelings in couple relationships: Exploring the role of attachment and perceptions of personal injury. *Personal Relationships, 12*, 253–272.

Fejfar, M. C., & Hoyle, R. H. (2000). Effect of private self-awareness on negative affect and self-referent attribution: A quantitative review. *Personality and Social Psychology Review, 4*, 132–142.

Fitzsimons, G. M., & Bargh, J. A. (2003). Thinking of you: Nonconscious pursuit of interpersonal goals associated with relationship partners. *Journal of Personality and Social Psychology, 84*, 148–164.

Frazier, P. (2003). Perceived control and distress following sexual assault: A longitudinal test of a new model. *Journal of Personality and Social Psychology, 84*, 1257–1269.

Funder, D., & Faust, L. (2010). Personality in social psychology. In S. Fiske, D. Gilbert, & G. Lindzey (Eds.), *Handbook of social psychology* (5th ed., pp. 668–697). Hoboken, NJ: Wiley.

Govern, J. M., & Marsch, L. A. (2001). Development and validation of the situational self-awareness scale. *Consciousness and Cognition, 10*, 366–378.

Hafer, C. L., & Gosse, L. (2010). Preserving the belief in a just world: When and for whom are different strategies preferred? In D. R. Bobocel, A. C. Kay, M. P. Zanna, & J. M. Olson (Eds.), *The psychology of justice and legitimacy: The Ontario symposium* (Vol. 11, pp. 79–102). New York: Psychology Press.

Harper, M. S., Dickson, J.W., & Welsh, D. P. (2006). Self-silencing and rejection sensitivity in adolescent romantic relationships. *Journal of Youth and Adolescence, 35*, 459–467.

Hazan, C., & Shaver, P. R. (1990). Love and work: An attachment theoretical perspective. *Journal of Personality and Social Psychology, 59*, 270–280.

Heatherton, T. F., & Baumeister, R. F. (1991). Binge eating as escape from self. *Psychological Bulletin, 110*, 86–108.

Higgins, E. T. (1992). Social cognition as social science: How social action creates social meaning. In D. Ruble, P. Costanzo, & M. Oliveri (Eds.), *The social psychology of mental health.* New York: Guilford.

Higgins, E. T. (1997). Beyond pleasure and pain. *American Psychologist, 52*, 1280–1300.

Higgins, E. T. (1998). Promotion and prevention: Regulatory focus as a motivational principle. In M. P. Zanna (Ed.), *Advances in Experimental Social Psychology* (Vol. 30, pp. 1–46). New York: Academic.

Higgins, E. T. (2000). Making a good decision: Value from fit. *American Psychologist, 5,* 1217–1230.

Hill, M. G., & Weary, G. (1983). Perspectives on the *Journal of Abnormal and Social Psychology:* How it began and how it was transformed over the years. *Journal of Social and Clinical Psychology, 1,* 4–14.

Hollon, S., & Garber, J. (1990). Cognitive therapy for depression. *Personality and Social Psychology Bulletin, 16*(1), 58–73.

Humphreys, M.S ., & Revelle, W. (1984). Personality, motivation, and performance: A theory of the relationship between individual differences and information processing. *Psychological Review, 91,* 153–184.

Ingram, R. E. (1990). Self-focused attention in clinical disorders: Review and a conceptual model. *Psychological Bulletin, 107,* 156–176.

Janoff-Bulman, R. (1989). Assumptive worlds and the stress of traumatic events: Applications of the schema construct. *Social Cognition, 7,* 113–136.

Joiner, T. E., & Metalsky, G. I. (1995). A prospective test of an integrative interpersonal theory of depression: A naturalistic study of college roommates. *Journal of Personality and Social Psychology, 69,* 778–788.

Jost, J. T., & Banaji, M. R. (1994). The role of stereotyping in system-justification and the production of false consciousness. *British Journal of Social Psychology, 33,* 1–27.

Kanfer, F. H. (1970). Self-regulation: Research, issues, and speculation. In C. Neuringer & J. L. Michael (Eds.), *Behavior modification in clinical psychology* (pp. 178–220). New York: Appleton-Century-Crofts.

Katz, D. (1964) Editorial. *Journal of Abnormal and Social Psychology, 69*(6), 591–593.

Keenan, K., Loeber, R., Zhang, Q., Stouthamer-Loeber, M., & Van Kammen, W. B. (1995). The influence of deviant peers on the development of boys' disruptive and delinquent behavior: A temporal analysis. *Development and Psychopathology, 7,* 715–726.

Kelly, K. M. (2001). Individual differences in reactions to *rejection.* In M. R. Leary (Ed.), *Interpersonal rejection.* New York: Oxford University Press.

Kenrick, D. T. (1994). Evolutionary social psychology: From sexual selection to social cognition. In M. P. Zanna (Ed.), *Advances in Experimental Social Psychology* (Vol. 26, pp. 75–121). San Diego, CA: Academic.

Kenrick, D.T., Nieuweboer, S., & Buunk, A.P. (2010). Universal mechanisms and cultural diversity: Replacing the blank slate with a coloring book. In M. Schaller, A. Norenzayan, S. Heine, T. Yamagishi, & T. Kameda (Eds.), *Evolution, culture, and the human mind* (pp. 257–271). Mahwah, NJ: Erlbaum.

Kessler, R. C., Mickelson, K. D., & Williams, D. R. (1999). The prevalence, distribution, and mental health correlates of perceived discrimination in the United States. *Journal of Health and Social Behavior, 40,* 208–230.

Kleck, R. E., & Strenta, A. (1980). Perceptions of the impact of negatively valued physical characteristics on social interaction. *Journal of Personality and Social Psychology, 39,* 861–873.

Kowalski, R. M., & Leary M. R. (2003). *Key readings in social-clinical psychology .* New York: Psychology Press.

Lambert, K. G., & Kinsley, C. H. (2010) *Clinical neuroscience: Psychopathology and the brain.* New York: Oxford University Press.

Leary, M. R. (2004). *The curse of the self: Self-awareness, egotism, and the quality of human life.* New York: Oxford University Press.

Leary, M. R. (2010). Social anxiety as an early warning system: A refinement and extension of the self-presentational theory of social anxiety. In S. G. Hofman & P. M. DiBartolo (Eds.), *Social phobia and social anxiety: An integration* (2nd ed.). New York: Allyn & Bacon.

Leary, M. R., & Allen, A. B. (2011). Belonging motivation: Establishing, maintaining, and repairing relational value. In D. Dunning (Ed.), *Social motivation.* Philadelphia: Psychology Press.

Leary, M. R., & Kelly, K. M. (2009). Belonging motivation. In M. R. Leary & R. H. Hoyle (Eds.), *Handbook of individual differences in social behavior.* New York: Guilford.

Leary, M. R., & Leder, S. (2009). The nature of hurt feelings: Emotional experience and cognitive appraisals. In A. Vangelisti (Ed.), *Feeling hurt in close relationships.* New York: Cambridge University Press.

Leary, M. R., Koch, E., & Hechenbleikner, N. (2001). Emotional responses to interpersonal rejection. In M. R. Leary (Ed.), *Interpersonal rejection* (pp. 145–166). New York: Oxford University Press.

Leary, M. R., Kowalski, R. M., Smith, L., & Phillips, S. (2003). Teasing, rejection, and violence: Case studies of the school shootings. *Aggressive Behavior, 29,* 202–214.

Leary, M. R., & Maddux, J. E. (1987). Progress toward a viable interface between social and clinical-counseling psychology. *American Psychologist, 42,* 904–911.

Leary, M. R., Twenge, J. M., & Quinlivan, E. (2006). Interpersonal rejection as a determinant of anger and aggression. *Personality and Social Psychology Review, 10,* 111–132.

Lerner, M. J. (1980). *The belief in a just world a fundamental delusion: Perspectives in social psychology.* New York: Plenum.

Lerner, M. J., & Miller, D. T. (1978). Just world research and the attribution process: Looking back and ahead. *Psychological Bulletin, 85,* 1030–1051.

Lerner, M. J., Ross, M., & Miller, D. T. (2002). *The justice motive in everyday life.* New York: Cambridge University Press.

Lewin, K. (1935). *A dynamic theory of personality.* New York: McGraw-Hill

Lewin, K. (1943). Defining the "Field at a Given Time." *Psychological Review.* 50, 2

Lieberman, M. (2010). Social cognitive neuroscience. In S. Fiske, D. Gilbert, & G. Lindzey. (Eds.), *Handbook of social psychology* (pp. 143–193). New York: Wiley.

Lewinsohn, P. M., Steinmetz, J. L., Larson, D. W., & Franklin, J. (1981). Depression-related cognitions: Antecedent or consequence? *Journal of Abnormal Psychology, 90,* 213–219.

Lubow, R., & Weiner, I. (2010*). Latent inhibition: Neuroscience applications and schizophrenia.* New York : Cambridge University Press.

Lynam, D. R., Caspi, A., Moffitt, T. E., Wikström, P. O., Loeber, R., & Novak, S. P. (2000). The interaction between impulsivity and neighborhood context on offending: The effects of impulsivity are stronger in poorer neighborhoods. *Journal of Abnormal Psychology, 109,* 563–574.

Magnusson, D., & Öhman, A. (Eds.). (1987). *Psychopathology: An interactional perspective.* New York: Academic.

Maner, J. K., DeWall, C. N., Baumeister, R. F., & Schaller, M. (2007). Does social exclusion motivate interpersonal reconnection? Resolving the "porcupine problem." *Journal of Personality and Social Psychology, 92,* 42–55.

McClure, M. J., Lydon, J. E., Baccus, J. R., & Baldwin, M. W. (2010). A signal detection analysis of chronic attachment anxiety at speed dating: Being unpopular is only the first part of the problem. *Personality and Social Psychology Bulletin, 36,* 1024–1036.

McCrae, R. R. & Costa, P. T., Jr. (1987). Validation of the five-factor model of personality across instruments and observers. *Journal of Personality and Social Psychology, 52*(1), 81–90.

McCrae, R. R., & John, O. P. (1992). An introduction to the five-factor model and its applications. *Journal of Personality, 60*(2), 175–215.

McGuire, W. J., & McGuire, C. V. (1982). Significant others in self-space: Sex differences and developmental trends in the social self. In J. Suls (Ed.), *Psychological perspectives on the self* (Vol. 1, pp. 71–96). Mahwah, NJ: Erlbaum.

McKenzie, K. S., & Hoyle, R. H. (2008). The Self-Absorption Scale: Reliability and validity in non-clinical samples. *Personality and Individual Differences, 45,* 726–731.

Mendoza-Denton, R., Purdie, V., Downey, G., & Davis, A. (2002). Sensitivity to status-based rejection: Implications for African-American students' college experience. *Journal of Personality and Social Psychology, 83,* 896–918.

Mikulincer, M., & Florian, V. (2000). Exploring individual differences in reactions to mortality salience: Does attachment style regulate terror management mechanisms? *Journal of Personality and Social Psychology, 79*(2), 260–273.

Nesse, R. (1998). Emotional disorders in evolutionary perspective. *British Journal of Medical Psychology, 71,* 397–415.

Neuberg, S., Kenrick, D., & Schaller, M. (2010). Evolutionary social psychology. In S. Fiske, D. Gilbert, & G. Lindzey. (Eds.), *Handbook of social psychology* (5th ed., pp. 761–796). New York: Wiley.

Nezlek, J. B., Kowalski, R. M., Leary, M. R., Blevins, T., & Holgate, S. (1997). Personality moderators of reactions to interpersonal rejection: Depression and trait self-esteem. *Personality and Social Psychology Bulletin, 23,* 1235–1244.

Pepitone, A., & Wilpizeski, C. (1960). Some consequences of experimental rejection. *Journal of Abnormal and Social Psychology, 60*(3), 359–364.

Pinel, E. C. (1999). Stigma consciousness: The psychological legacy of social stereotypes. *Journal of Personality and Social Psychology, 76,* 114–128.

Prince, M., & Allport, F. (1921). Editorial announcement. *Journal of Abnormal and Social Psychology, 1*(1), 1–5.

Pyszczynski, T., & Greenberg, J. (1987). Self-regulatory perseveration and the depressive self-focusing style: A self-awareness theory of reactive depression. *Psychological Bulletin, 102,* 122–138.

Pyszczynski, T., Greenberg, J., Koole, S., & Solomon, S. (2010). Experimental existential psychology: Coping with the facts of life. In S. Fiske, D. Gilbert, & G. Lindzey (Eds.), *Handbook of social psychology* (5th ed., pp. 724–760). New York: Wiley.

Richman, L. S, & Leary, M. R. (2009). Reactions to discrimination, stigmatization, ostracism, and other forms of interpersonal rejection: A dynamic, multi-motive model. *Psychological Review, 116,* 365–383.

Rotter, J. B. (1966). Generalized expectancies of internal versus external control of reinforcements. *Psychological Monographs, 80,* 1–28 (Whole No. 609).

Rubin, Z., & Peplau, L.A. (1975). Who believes in a just world? *Journal of Social Issues, 31*(3), 65–90.

Sarason, E. G., Sarason, B. R., & Pierce, G. R. (1990). Anxiety, cognitive interference, and performance. *Journal of Social Behavior and Personality, 5,* 1–18.

Sellers, R. M., & Shelton, J. N. (2003). The role of racial identity in perceived racial discrimination. *Journal of Personality and Social Psychology, 84,* 1079–1092.

Shafran, R., & Mansell, W. (2001). Perfectionism and psychopathology: A review of research and treatment. *Clinical Psychology Review, 21,* 879–906.

Shah, J. (2003). Automatic for the people: How representations of significant others implicitly affect goal pursuit. *Journal of Personality and Social Psychology, 84,* 661–681.

Shaw, M. E, & Costanzo, P. (1982). *Theories of social psychology.* New York: McGraw-Hill.

Shaw, M. E., Strother, S. C., McFarlane, A. C., Morris, P., Anderson, J., Clark, C. R., et al. (2002). Abnormal functional connectivity in posttraumatic stress disorder. *NeuroImage, 15*(3): 661–674.

Skinner, E. A. (1996). A guide to constructs of control. *Journal of Personality and Social Psychology, 71,* 549–570.

Slotkin, J. S. (1942). The nature and effects of social interaction in schizophrenia. *Journal of Abnormal and Social Psychology, 37*(3), 345–368.

Snyder, C. R., & Forsyth, D. R. (1991). *Handbook of social and clinical psychology.* New York: Pergamon.

Solomon, S., Greenberg, J., & Pyszczynski, T. (1991). A terror management theory of social behavior: The psychological functions of self-esteem and cultural worldviews. In M. P. Zanna (Ed.), *Advances in experimental social psychology* (Vol. 24, pp. 93–159). San Diego, CA: Academic.

Strauman, T., Costanzo, P., Merril, K., & Jones, N. (2010). The applications of social psychology to clinical psychology. In E. T. Higgins & A. W. Kruglanski (Eds.), *Social psychology: A handbook of basic principles.* New York: Guilford.

Tartakovsky, E. (2007). A longitudinal study of acculturative stress and homesickness: High-school adolescents immigrating from Russia and Ukraine to Israel without parents. *Social Psychiatry and Psychiatric Epidemiology, 42,* 485–494.

Thompson, S. C., Sobolew-Shubin, A., Galbraith, M. E., Schwankovsky, L., & Cruzen, D. (1993). Maintaining perceptions of control: Finding perceived control in low-control circumstances. *Journal of Personality and Social Psychology, 64,* 293–304.

Twenge, J. M., Baumeister, R. F., Tice, D. M., & Stucke, T. S. (2001). If you can't join them, beat them: Effects of social exclusion on aggressive behavior. *Journal of Personality and Social Psychology, 81,* 1058–1069.

Ullmann, L. P., & Krasner, L. (1975). *A psychological approach to abnormal behavior.* Englewood Cliffs, NJ: Prentice-Hall.

Valiente, C., Espinosa, R., Vázquez, C., Cantero, D., & Fuentenebro, F. (2010). World assumptions in psychosis: Do paranoid patients believe in a just world? *Journal of Nervous and Mental Disease, 198*(11), 892–806.

van der Kolk, B. A., Pelcovitz, D., Roth, S., Mandel, F. S., McFarlane, A., & Herman, J.L. (1996). Dissociation, somatization, and affect dysregulation: The complexity of adaptation to trauma. *American Journal of Psychiatry, 153*(7), 83–93.

van der Kolk, B. (2004). The psychobiology of PTSD. In J. Panksepp (Ed.), *A textbook of biological psychiatry* (pp. 319–344). Hoboken, NJ: Wiley-Liss.

Verdejo-García, A., Lawrence, A. J., & Clark, L. (2008). Impulsivity as a vulnerability marker for substance-use disorders: Review of findings from high-risk research, problem gamblers, and genetic association studies. *Neuroscience and Biobehavioral Reviews, 32,* 777–810.

Watson, R. (1953). A brief history of clinical psychology. *Psychological Bulletin, 5*(5), 321–346.

Wells, F. L. (1926). Value psychology and the affective disorders with special reference to regression. *Journal of Abnormal and Social Psychology, 21*(2), 135–148.

Wiley, S., Perkins, K., & Deaux, K. (2008) Through the looking glass: Ethnic and generational patterns of immigrant identity. *International Journal of Intercultural Relations, 32,* 385–398.

Williams, K. D. (2007). Ostracism. *Annual Review of Psychology, 58,* 425–452.

Wilson, T., Aronson, E., & Carlsmith, K. (2010). The art of laboratory experimentation, In S. Fiske, D. Gilbert, & G. Lindzey (Eds.), *The handbook of social psychology* (5th ed., pp. 52–81). New York: Wiley.

Wolpe, J. (1958). *Psychotherapy by reciprocal inhibition.* Stanford, CA: Stanford University Press.

Wolpe, J. (1969). *The practice of behavior therapy.* New York : Pergamon.

Zorumski, C. F., & Rubin, E. H. (2005). *Psychopathology in the genome and neuroscience era.* Washington, DC: American Psychiatric Association.

Individual and Societal Well-Being

Shigehiro Oishi

Abstract

This chapter highlights the contributions that have been made by personality and social psychology, respectively and together, to the science of well-being. Since its humble beginning in the 1930s, the science of well-being has grown to become one of the most vibrant research topics in psychological science today. The personality tradition of well-being research has shown that it is possible to measure well-being reliably, that self-reported well-being predicts important life outcomes, and that well-being has nontrivial genetic origins. The social psychology tradition has illuminated that there are various cultural meanings of "well-being," that responses to well-being questions involve multiple cognitive processes, that happiness is experienced often in relationship contexts, and that it is possible to improve one's well-being. Finally, there are recent methodological integrations of the personality and social psychology perspectives that delineate person-situation interactions and gene–environment interactions.

Keywords: subjective well-being, happiness, measurement, cognitive processes, motivational processes, genes, culture

The goal of this chapter is to provide an overview of research on individual and societal well-being (the well-being of individuals and society). In doing so, I hope to highlight the major contributions that traditional personality and social psychology perspectives, respectively and together, have made to the literature on well-being (see Table 24.1 for a summary). The traditional personality perspective is characterized by a profound concern with measurement and construct validity issues (e.g., Cattell, 1943; Cronbach & Meehl, 1955) and a simultaneous interest in the whole person (Allport, 1937, 1961; H. A. Murray, 1938; see also Fleeson, chapter 3, this volume). Without the establishment of construct validity and the development of measurement tools, it would have been impossible to build the science of well-being we have today. Without the interest in the whole person, important within-person variations in well-being would not have

been discovered. A traditional social psychology perspective is characterized by a deep concern with the situational effects and mediating variables (e.g., Darley & Latané, 1968; Festinger, 1954). This perspective helped advance our understanding of extraneous effects on and cognitive processes involved in well-being judgments. I will first define the concept of well-being that I use in this chapter and review the most frequently used scales in well-being research. Second, I will summarize contributions from each tradition, followed by recent findings that have integrated personality and social psychology perspectives.

I will use the term "well-being" in the most inclusive sense, namely as the state of "being well" (Kitayama & Markus, 2000), either referring to individuals or societies. In contrast, I will use the term "individual well-being," or "subjective well-being" (used interchangeably with individual

Table 24.1 A Summary of Representative Personality and Social Psychology Approaches to Subjective Well-Being

Research Focus	
Personality Approach	Social Psychology Approach
Measurement Issues	Cognitive Processes
Construct Validation	Situation/Mood Effects
Genetic Contributions	Relational Context
Intra-Individual Variation	Cultural Context
Ecological Validity	Internal Validity

Integrative Approaches
Gene-Environment Interaction
Integrative Hedonic Adaptation Theory
Value-as-a-Moderator Model

well-being), when specifically referring to the cognitive evaluation of life as a whole and/or affective experiences (Diener, Suh, Lucas, & Smith, 1999). In other words, individual and subjective well-being refers to individuals' subjective evaluation of how well they feel their life is going. Finally, I will use the term "societal well-being," or the well-being of society, when specifically referring to the collective state of "being well" (see Oishi, 2010, for various concepts of well-being).

The Measurement of Individual Well-Being: A Brief History

There have been numerous attempts to measure the different conceptions of individual well-being. In 1934, Hartman investigated for the first time, to my knowledge, the temporal stability of individual well-being (or happiness in this case), as well as self-informant agreement of happiness among college students. He used the following item: "If you compare yourself with others of the same sex and age, how would you rate your own *general happiness*? Hartman found that the single-item measure of happiness was highly stable over a one month period, $r = .70$. In addition, he showed that participants' self-reported happiness was reliably correlated with the average of four friends' ratings of the participants' happiness, $r = .34$.

During the 1930s and 1940s, similar efforts to establish the scientific inquiry into subjective well-being were attempted by several others (e.g., Jasper, 1930; Washburne, 1941). However, the study of subjective well-being did not gain momentum in

mainstream psychology. This was partially because behaviorism was dominant in psychology at that time. According to behaviorism (e.g., J. B. Watson, 1913), a construct had to be measured objectively, and any study based on self-reports was mistrusted. The objective assessment of subjective well-being is so difficult, however, that even Henry Murray, the genius who had successfully measured implicit motives such as need for affiliation gave up and declared that "Aristotle's assertion that the only rational goal of goals is happiness has never been successfully refuted as far as we know, but, as yet, no scientist has ventured to break ground for a psychology of happiness" (H. A. Murray & Kluckhohn, 1948, p. 13). With the cognitive revolution of the 1960s and 1970s in psychology, however, subjective phenomena such as happiness and love finally became acceptable research topics.

In the 1960s and 1970s, three types of single-item measures dominated large-scale national and international surveys on subjective well-being (see A. Campbell, 1981; A. Campbell, Converse, & Rodgers, 1976; Gurin, Veroff, & Feld, 1960 for reviews on this literature): (1) a general life satisfaction item (e.g., "All things considered, how satisfied are you with your life as a whole these days?"), (2) Cantril's (1965) Ladder item ("Where on the ladder would you say you personally stand at the present time?"), and (3) a happiness item (e.g., Taking all things together, would you say you are 1 = *very happy*, 2 = *quite happy*, 3 = *not very happy*, 4 = *not at all happy*).

In addition, Bradburn (1969) developed the Affect Balance Scale to assess both positive and negative affective aspects of well-being. Sample items included "Did you feel particularly excited or interested in something?" "Proud because someone complimented you on something you had done?" The Affect Balance Scale has been used in several large international surveys, including the World Values Survey. Furthermore, two widely used measures of eudaimonic well-being1, the Purpose in Life Test (PIL; Crumbaugh & Maholick, 1964), and the Life Regard Index (LRI; Battista & Almond, 1973) were developed in the 1960s and 1970s (see Steger et al., 2006 for critique). In the area of gerontology, several multi-item measures that assess older adults' subjective sense of well-being were developed around this time. For instance, Neugarten, Havighurst, and Tobin (1961) developed the Life Satisfaction Index A. Lawton (1975) developed the Philadelphia Geriatric Center Morale Scale to measure older individuals' perceived sense of their own aging, agitation, and lonely dissatisfaction. These two scales are still widely used in gerontology and life span developmental psychology (Pinquart & Sörensen, 2000).

In the 1980s, several multi-item scales of individual well-being were developed for more general populations. Diener and colleagues (Diener, Emmons, Larsen, & Griffin, 1985) developed the 5-item Satisfaction with Life Scale (SWLS) to measure a general sense of life satisfaction. Ryff (1989) also created the 84-item psychological well-being scale that consists of six subscales (autonomy, self-acceptance, positive relations, growth, purpose in life, and environmental mastery). Ryff constructed this scale to capture human potentials and the maturity of personality expressed by theorists such as Carl Rogers and Abraham Maslow. Whereas the SWLS asks directly how satisfied respondents are with their lives, Ryff's scale assesses the respondents' perception of the degree to which they are autonomous, self-accepting, loving, and so forth. In addition, D. Watson, Clark, and Tellegen (1988) developed the Positive and Negative Affect Schedule (PANAS) in order to measure both positive and negative affect (PA and NA).

In the 1990s and 2000s, additional influential scales were developed. Lyubomirsky and Lepper (1999) developed the 4-item Subjective Happiness Scale. Cummins, McCabe, Romeo, and Gullone (1994) devised the Comprehensive Quality of Life scale, which includes many specific life domains. Several other scales were created to assess eudaimonic aspects of well-being. For instance, Steger et al. (2006) devised the 10-item Meaning of Life scale to measure the presence of meaning in life and the active pursuit of meaning in life. Ryan and Frederick (1997) created the 7-item Subjective Vitality Scale to encompass physical and mental aliveness and vigor. Finally, numerous researchers now use brain activities (Urry et al., 2004), hormone levels (e.g., Adam, Hawkley, Kudielka, & Cacioppo, 2006), and facial expressions (e.g., Harker & Keltner, 2001) as proxies to well-being. With the development of diverse measures, the field of individual well-being has progressed since the mid-1980s (see Diener, Suh, Lucas, & Smith, 1999; Ryan & Deci, 2001; Ryff & Singer, 1998, for reviews). More recently, psychologists have also delved into the investigation of societal well-being, namely the questions such as "What is happy society?" and "What predicts the well-being of society?" (see Diener, Lucas, Schimmack, & Heliwell, 2009; Oishi & Schimmack, 2010).

The Contributions of Personality Psychology to the Science of Well-Being

Personality psychologists have consistently been concerned with measurement and construct validity issues (e.g., D. T. Campbell & Fiske, 1959; Cattell, 1943; Cronbach, & Meehl, 1955; Thorndike, 1936). According to Cattell (1943), Thorndike gave differential psychologists in the 1930s and 1940s reason for optimism by stating that "whatever exists, exists in some quantity, and can therefore ultimately be measured" (p. 559). Earlier efforts to measure happiness by Jasper (1930), Hartman (1934), and Washburne (1941) reflect Thorndike's optimism. However, Hartman and his contemporaries did not yet have the concept of construct validity and an appreciation for demonstrating nomological networks through a program of research.

Construct Validity

The construct validity concept proposed by Cronbach and Meehl (1955) was ambitious in that its demonstration requires not just a one-to-one association between a measure and a criterion (e.g., a correlation between Test A scores and behavior B), but also a large set of associations and lack of associations, or nomological network. In other words, a one-shot study is not sufficient to demonstrate construct validity; rather it takes a series of programmatic research and "a rigorous chain of inference" (Cronbach & Meehl, 1955, p. 291) to demonstrate a nomological network and construct validity. Cronbach and Meehl state, "It is ordinarily necessary to evaluate construct validity by integrating evidence from many different sources. . . . An attempt to identify any one criterion measure or any composite as *the* criterion aimed at is, however, usually unwarranted" (p. 285).

Whereas Cronbach and Meehl (1955) did not offer concrete strategies to show construct validity, D. T. Campbell and Fiske (1959) provided a tangible roadmap for construct validity via a multitrait-multimethod matrix. First, monotrait-heteromethod correlations should be significantly different from zero (e.g., self-reported life satisfaction should be significantly correlated with informant-reported life satisfaction). Second, monotrait-heteromethod correlations should be higher than heterotrait-heteromethod correlations (e.g., the self-informant correlation on life satisfaction should be higher than the correlation between self-reported life satisfaction and informant-reported self-esteem). Third, monotrait-heteromethod correlations should be higher than heterotrait-monomethod correlations (e.g., self-informant correlation on life satisfaction should be higher than the correlation between self-reported life satisfaction and self-reported self-esteem). Finally, the pattern of correlations among traits should be similar between monomethod and heteromethods (e.g., if life satisfaction was significantly associated with self-esteem but not with narcissism in self-reports, then life satisfaction should also be associated with self-esteem but not with narcissism in informant reports).

Over the last two decades, significant effort was made to establish the construct validity via a nomological network or multitrait-multimethod matrix. Diener, Smith, and Fujita (1995), for example, used the multitrait-multimethod approach to investigate the structure of affect. Lucas, Diener, and Suh (1996) used a similar approach to demonstrate convergent and discriminant validity of life satisfaction, positive affect, optimism, and self-esteem. Steger and colleagues (2006) also used this approach to establish convergent and discriminant validity of meaning in life. These programs of construct validation research laid a firm foundation for further research on predictors of individual well-being.

Latent Trait

In addition to the exemplary programs of construct validity in subjective well-being, the idea of "hypothetical construct" (Cronbach & Meehl, 1955, p. 284) and latent ability/trait (Lord, 1952; Samejima, 1969) that are central to the personality tradition are visible in various programs of research in well-being. Below I summarize representative well-being research that demonstrates the appreciation of latent trait models and various sophisticated statistical techniques. Structural equation modeling (SEM), for instance, was adapted by well-being researchers early and used to examine structural relations among various well-being constructs (e.g., Allen, Bentler, & Gutek, 1985; Chirkov, Ryan, Kim, & Kaplan, 2003; Diener, Smith, Fujita, 1995; Grob et al., 1996; Keyes, Shmotkin, & Ryff, 2002; Schimmack, 2008; Schimmack, Bockenholt, & Reisenzein, 2002; Vitterso & Nilsen, 2002). SEM has been used to test various important theoretical questions in well-being research. For example, Schimmack and colleagues (2002) showed that the latent link between extraversion and hedonic balance (PA – NA) was positive, and that the link between neuroticism and hedonic balance was negative in the United States, Germany, Mexico, Japan, and Ghana. Interestingly, the latent association between hedonic balance and life satisfaction was larger among Americans and Germans than among Mexicans, Japanese, and Ghanaians. Similarly, SEM has been used to provide unique insights into long-debated issues such as the relative contribution of trait and state to well-being. Eid and Diener (2004), for example, used the multistate-multitrait-multiconstruct model (an extension of SEM) to decompose variance due to measurement error, trait life satisfaction and occasion-specific mood. They found that roughly 74% of reliable interindividual differences in self-reported life satisfaction was due to trait life satisfaction, and 16% was due to occasion-specific mood.

Likewise, item response theory (IRT) has been utilized to determine the measurement properties of various well-being scales. For instance, Baker, Zevon, and Rounds (1994) used IRT to examine differences in item information between positive and negative affect. Baker and colleagues found that the 31-item negative affect scale they used did not capture individuals who were very low in trait negative affect very well and best gathered information about individuals who were quite high in trait negative affect. The amount of information obtained by the 21-item positive affect scale was more evenly distributed, peaking around individuals with the mean level of trait positive affect. Furthermore, Reise, Widaman, and Rugh (1993) introduced IRT to test cross-cultural equivalence of measurement, which has been used in cross-cultural investigations of subjective well-being (e.g., Oishi, 2006).

A typological, as opposed to dimensional, approach such as latent class analysis has also been shown to be fruitful. Eid and Diener (2001) used a multigroup latent class analysis, and found that 83% of Australian and American college students belonged to the "class" who deemed all positive emotions desirable, whereas only 9% of Chinese and 32% of Taiwanese students belonged to this class. There was also a "class" unique to Chinese, in which respondents deemed all positive emotions undesirable. Vitterso, Biswas-Diener, and Diener (2005) used the mixed Rasch model (which combines IRT and latent class analysis) in their investigation of cross-cultural comparison in life satisfaction. Although Norwegians' and Greenlanders' raw scores in the Satisfaction with Life Scale (Diener et al., 1985) did not differ, Norwegians were higher in latent life satisfaction once the raw scores were transformed to interval scales via IRT. This discrepancy was explained in part by the different frequency of the "class" that used extreme ends of the scale (Greenlanders were overrepresented in this class). These latent class analyses demonstrated important within-nation differences in response patterns, including culture-specific "class," and clarified observed differences.

Finally, the traditional latent trait view has resulted in active programs of research in the behavioral genetics of subjective well-being. Tellegen, Lykken, Bouchard, Wilcox, Segal, and Rich (1988), for example, used twins reared together and apart and found that the intraclass correlation for the well-being subscale of the Multidimensional Personality Questionnaire was .64 for monozygotic (MZ) twins reared apart, whereas it was only .23 for dizygotic (DZ) twins reared together. Tellegen and colleagues estimated that 48% of variance in well-being could be explained by genes. Lykken and Tellegen (1996) later reanalyzed the data, corrected for reliability of the well-being scale, and reported the revised estimated heritability coefficient of .80.

Other researchers' heritability estimates of subjective well-being tend to be closer to Tellegen et al.'s (1988) initial estimate than their later 1996 estimate. For instance, using a large sample of twins from the Netherlands, Stubbe, Posthuma, Boomsma, and De Geus (2005) found a heritability coefficient of .38 for the Satisfaction with Life Scale scores. Roysamb, Harris, Magnus, Vitterso, and Tambs (2002) found in a Norwegian sample of twins the heritability estimate to be .54 for women and .46 for men. Furthermore, Gatz, Pedersen, Plomin, Nesselroade, and McClearn (1992) found very low heritability estimates in a sample of Swedish twins reared together and apart. The intraclass correlation was .22 for the MZ twins reared apart, .51 for the MZ twins reared together, -.01 for DZ twins reared apart, and .30 for the DZ twins reared together on the entire Center for Epidemiological Studies Depression (CES-D) Scale (yielding a heritability coefficient of only .16). In the well-being subscale of CES-D (e.g., "I was happy," "I enjoyed life"), the intraclass correlation was .03 for MZ reared apart, .21 for MZ twins reared together, .03 for DZ twins reared apart, and .26 for DZ twins reared together (yielding a heritability coefficient of .00). It is important to keep in mind, however, that heritability estimates vary across different measures and samples. A major contribution of behavioral genetic research on subjective well-being is that it clarified two major sources of individual differences in subjective well-being, genetics and environments.

Intraindividual Variation

As described above, one major tradition in personality psychology is characterized by its concern with

measurement, construct validity, and latent traits. Whereas the approaches presented so far have focused on "variables," several pioneers in personality psychology were deeply concerned with the whole person. Allport (1937) famously advocated the study of individuality as a central topic in personality psychology. Later Allport (1961) elaborated the idiographic approach by declaring, "The problem of individuality, then, is not how John's intelligence or dominance compares with these same qualities abstracted from other people but how John's intelligence is related to his dominance, to his values, to his conscience, and to everything else in his personality" (p. 10).

Another pioneer in personality psychology, Henry Murray, was also concerned with the whole person as evidenced in his 1938 *Explorations in Personality*. He stated the goals of his investigation as follows:

> Man is to-day's great problem. What can we know about him and how can it be said in words that have clear meaning? What propels him? With what environmental objects and institutions does he interact and how? What occurrences in his body are most influentially involved? What mutually dependent processes participate in his differentiation and development? What courses of events determine his pleasures and displeasures? And finally, by what means can he be intentionally transformed? (p. 3).

To answer these fundamental questions about individuality, H. A. Murray and his collaborators collected an enormous amount of information for each of their participants, using diverse methods including interviews, intelligence tests, laboratory experiments, galvanic skin responses, musical preferences, as well as the Thematic Apperception Test (TAT).

In the spirit of the ideographic approach proposed by Allport and Murray, Wessman and Ricks (1966) investigated the daily moods of 25 Radcliffe students and 18 Harvard students. All of the participants completed a survey of daily moods at night for 6 weeks. In addition, the 18 Harvard student participants provided all kinds of information, including questionnaire responses to the Minnesota Multiphasic Personality Inventory (MMPI), the Rorschach test, the TAT, and intensive clinical interviews. Wessman and Ricks analyzed not only the mean level of daily moods, but also the variability of mood (e.g., fluctuation, oscillation). They examined the patterns of daily affective experiences along with situation factors such as positive academic feedback and menstruation, dispositional factors such as trait depression measured by the MMPI and helplessness assessed by the TAT, and life history such as past academic failure and sibling conflicts. Like H. A. Murray (1938), Wessman and Ricks also included several case studies (e.g., Cage, an unhappy man), making their investigation both qualitative and quantitative. In many respects, Wessman and Ricks's work is truly impressive in its depth and represents an ideal research program on subjective well-being. Furthermore, their main findings stood the later empirical examinations with much larger sample sizes:

> The happier men were found to be optimistic in their expectations and possessed high self-esteem and self-confidence. Particularly there was ample evidence of their success and satisfaction in interpersonal relationships. They possessed what is hypothetically termed ego-strength and a satisfying sense of identity. There was excellent organization and direction to their lives, with a distinct sense of continuity and purpose and the necessary mastery of themselves and interpersonal situations to attain their goals. (p. 106)

The spirit of the idiographic approach is also evident in the Grant Study, the longitudinal study of 94 Harvard graduates over 30 years. The original sample was 268 Harvard students, who were interviewed by a psychiatrist for eight hours when they were still in college in 1940. In addition to the extensive interviews on family background and career aspiration, they completed various psychological and cognitive tests, extensive physical examinations, and physiological measures (e.g., EEG). From 1950 to 1952, all of the original participants were reinterviewed and completed the TAT and other projective tests. In 1970, 30 years after the original assessment, 94 participants of the original sample were interviewed by Vaillant, the psychoanalyst and the longtime director of the Grant Study. At the time of the 30 years follow-up, participants who possessed mature defense mechanisms (e.g., sublimation) were rated by independent judges as happier and better adjusted than those who used immature defense mechanisms (e.g., denial; Vaillant, 1977). Although Vaillant (1977) reported some quantitative analyses of the Grant Study like this, most analyses were qualitative. He emphasized the "whole person" approach by famously stating that "when describing the adaptive maneuvers of these men, I was repeatedly reminded that their lives were 'too human for science, too beautiful for numbers, too sad for diagnosis, and too immortal for bound journals.' Human beings need science. But science never does human beings justice" (p. 11).

Whereas Allport and Murray's approach to the whole person centered on qualitative methods such as the coding of free, open-ended responses (e.g., the TAT, letters, interviews), Raymond Cattell's approach to the whole person was highly quantitative, centering on a highly sophisticated data analytic technique called P-technique factor analysis (Cattell, 1952; Cattell, Cattell, & Rhymer, 1947). Whereas the traditional factor analysis was based on correlations or covariance derived at the level of a sample (e.g., correlations among 20 items among 200 students, or a 20 × 20 correlation or covariance matrix derived from 200 students), Cattell created the P-technique factor analysis, which is based on correlations or covariance at the level of an individual (e.g., correlations among 20 items that were assessed over 100 occasions, or a 20 × 20 correlation or covariance matrix derived from 100 occasions). He advocated its application in personality and clinical psychology to discover fundamental dimensions in covariation within one person. Because of the labor-intensive analysis involved, Cattell's approach did not flourish right away. However, with the greater availability of computers beginning in the 1970s, the P-technique factor analysis became a powerful tool in person-centered personality research. For instance, Zevon and Tellegen (1982) used P-technique factor analysis to investigate individual differences in the within-person factor structure of affect. Twenty-three college students completed a 61-item mood scale for 90 consecutive days. P-factor analyses revealed clear independent positive and negative affect factors for 21 out of the 23 participants. Using P-factor analysis, D. Watson, Clark, and Tellegen (1984) replicated Zevon and Tellegen's findings with 18 Japanese college students (see also Feldman, 1995; Scollon, Diener, Oishi, & Biswas-Diener, 2005).

Besides Cattell's P-factor-analytic tradition, several researchers interested in within-person variability in well-being have used spectral analysis to discover cyclical patterns. For instance, Larsen (1987) analyzed daily fluctuations of mood ratings provided by college students using spectral analysis. He found that individuals high in affect intensity showed faster cycles of mood changes than those low in affect intensity. Larsen and Kasimatis (1990) further examined weekly mood cycles and found that individuals high in novelty seeking and sensation seeking did not conform to the weekly cyclical changes in moods. More recently, Ram and colleagues (2005) combined IRT, P-factor analysis, and spectral analysis; the results showed individual differences in deviation from weekly cycles in moods. Recent advancements in dynamic factor analysis now make it easier for psychologists who are interested in the "whole person" and intraindividual variability and changes to empirically examine individuality (e.g., McArdle, 2009; Molenaar, 2004; Boker & Nesselroade, 2002).

Goals and Motives

Henry Murray's (1938) interest in the "whole person" is best reflected in his ideas of needs and presses. In the area of subjective well-being, Emmons, Little, and Cantor put goals and needs to the center stage of research in the 1980s. Emmons (1986), Little (1983), and Cantor et al. (1987) all argued that individuals' goals, personal projects, and life tasks reflect not only their personality but also their environments, roles, and developmental stages. For instance, the probability of success and perceived importance of personal strivings were shown to be associated with daily positive affect and global life satisfaction (Emmons, 1986).

In the tradition of H. A. Murray, McClelland, and Vaillant, McAdams also investigated the role of implicit motives in well-being. For example, McAdams and Vaillant (1982) found that implicit need for intimacy measured at age 30 predicted income, enjoyment of job, and marital enjoyment at age 47. More recently, McAdams, Reynolds, Lewis, Patten, and Bowman (2001) have analyzed personal narratives and found that individuals high in self-reported well-being tended to use transformative narratives (i.e., bad things turning good), whereas those low in self-reported well-being tended to use contamination narratives (i.e., good things turning bad).

King and her colleagues extended earlier goal research, which tended to focus on short-term goals, to long-term goals. These included wishes and possible selves. When participants were asked to write "three wishes," for example, those who wrote about undoing something they had done were less satisfied with their lives and more depressed (King & Broyles, 1997). In another study, King, Richards, and Stemmerich (1998) found that individuals who were working on personal goals related to their worse fears were less satisfied with their lives and more depressed than those who were not working on the personal goals that were directly related to their worse fears. Interestingly, the degree to which individuals' short-term goals were associated with their life goals was unrelated to life satisfaction or depression.

In the 1990s, Deci, Ryan, Kasser, Sheldon and colleagues also began their active program of research on well-being using self-determination theory. Through numerous studies they showed that self-determination (e.g., intrinsic motivation) is a key component to well-being. For example, they found that the pursuit of intrinsic goals (e.g., personal growth, autonomy, enhancement of others and communities) provided people with a deep sense of satisfaction, whereas the pursuit of extrinsic goals (e.g., financial success, physical attractiveness, and social reputation) did not provide people with such satisfaction (e.g., Kasser & Ryan, 1993; see Ryan & Deci, 2001; Sheldon, 2004, for review).

In addition to various main effects, the moderating role of goals and needs on subjective well-being have been conveyed. For instance, Emmons (1991) found that individuals who were striving for achievement reported more intense positive emotions when they experienced positive events related to achievement than when they experienced positive events unrelated to achievement. Likewise, individuals who were striving for affiliation and intimacy reported experiencing more intense positive emotions when they experienced positive events relevant to interpersonal relationships than when they experienced positive events irrelevant to interpersonal issues. Similarly, Brunstein, Schultheiss, and Grässman (1998) showed that congruence between implicit motives and explicit goals was associated with positive emotional experiences; individuals high in implicit need for affiliation were happier if they had explicit goals related to affiliation than if they had not.

There are many other important motivational and cognitive constructs that have received research attention in the context of well-being. For instance, Schwartz and colleagues (Schwartz, Ward, Monterosso, Lyubomirsky, White, & Lehman, 2002) have created a self-report scale that measures maximizing versus satisficing tendencies and showed that maximizing is negatively associated with life satisfaction and subjective happiness, and positively associated with depression and regret. They found that maximizing was associated with more frequent use of upward social comparisons, which was previously found to be associated with less happiness (Lyubomirsky & Ross, 1997). Likewise, Iyengar, Wells, and Schwartz (2006) found that college seniors who were maximizers found better paying jobs than did those who were satisficers, yet they were less satisfied with their job after graduation than the satisficers. Thus, it appears that the motivation to maximize their return on whatever decisions they are making has a negative impact when it comes to subjective well-being. Lyubomirsky and Ross (1999) also demonstrated that happy people are more motivated to justify their decisions than are unhappy people in the context of college applications. Namely, happy people (those high in the Subjective Happiness Scale) showed the typical postdecision dissonance reduction (increasing the liking of the school they got into and chose to attend), whereas unhappy students did not show the typical postdecision dissonance reduction. Finally, in a series of studies, Robinson, Tamir, and colleagues have shown that categorization speeds can tell us a great deal about happy and unhappy people (see Robinson, 2004; Clore & Robinson, chapter 13, this volume for review). Thus, there are various motivational and cognitive factors such as maximizing versus satisficing, social comparison, and categorization speed that can play a significant role in predicting individuals' subjective well-being.

In summary, enormous contributions have been made to the science of well-being by researchers who follow the personality tradition. These range from the establishment of sound measurement tools (e.g., Diener et al., 1985) to the discovery of the structure of well-being (e.g., Diener et al., 1995; Schimmack, 2008), to the partition of trait and state well-being (e.g., Eid & Diener, 2004), to the attention to the whole person (e.g., McAdams & Vaillant, 1982). Despite such major contributions to the science of well-being, the personality tradition is not without its flaws. One major weakness of this approach is its heavy reliance on correlational designs. Although longitudinal designs are increasingly used, experimental methods are rarely used. This makes causal mechanisms in well-being unclear. Another weakness of the personality approach so far has been its relative lack of attention to judgment processes involving well-being measures. A. Campbell (1981), the pioneering survey researcher of quality of life, explicated that in order for responses to well-being questions to be meaningful, three conditions have to be met: (1) "all the countless experiences people go through from day to day add to . . . global feelings of well-being," (2) "these feelings remain relatively constant over extended periods," and (3) that "people can describe them with candor and accuracy" (p. 23)." Personality psychologists tend to be content with psychometric information (e.g., reliability) and tend not to question the assumptions regarding how participants form responses to well-being questions.

The Contributions of Social Psychology to the Science of Well-Being

Copious contributions have also been made to the science of well-being by researchers who follow the social psychology tradition. Unlike many personality psychologists, social psychologists have questioned the basic assumptions regarding well-being judgments and demonstrated several ways in which extraneous conditions affect well-being judgments (e.g., Schwarz & Strack, 1999). In addition, many researchers have illuminated the effect of life events on well-being (e.g., Brickman, Coates, & Janoff-Bullman, 1978). Furthermore, other social psychologists have delineated the relational and cultural contexts of well-being (Gable, Reis, & Downey, 2003; Kitayama & Markus, 2000), created new interventions (Pennebaker, 1997), and provided practical advice to increase happiness (Hsee, Hastie, & Chen, 2008). Below I will review some of the representative findings from each of these lines of research.

Cognitive Processes Underlying Self-Reports

Schwarz (1999) decomposed how respondents form answers to survey questions into several specific processes (see Robinson & Clore, 2002; Clore & Robinson, chapter 13 in this volume). Expanding on A. Campbell's (1981) assumptions, Schwarz argued that responses to survey and typical personality questions would change sometimes dramatically depending on how questions are asked. First, respondents have to understand the question asked. For instance, if the question reads "how satisfied are you with your life these days?" the interpretation of "these days" could make a difference. Some might interpret that to mean this week, while others could interpret it to mean the last few months. Second, respondents must interpret the response formats. For instance, some researchers ask respondents to indicate how often they experienced various emotions during the past few weeks using a format such as 1 = *never*, 2 = *rarely*, 3 = *sometimes*, 4 = *often*, 5 = *almost always*, while other researchers ask respondents to indicate how intensely they felt various emotions using a format such as 1 = *not at all*, 2 = *slightly*, 3 = *moderately*, 4 = *strongly*, and 5 = *very strongly*. Yet other researchers ask respondents to indicate the absolute frequency of emotional experiences (e.g., "how many times did you feel happy?"). In addition to the interpretation issues (e.g., some respondents might interpret their anger experience once a week as "often," whereas others might it as "rarely"), the response formats change the answers to important theoretical questions. For instance, when the vague quantifiers (e.g., "never," "rarely" "sometimes") were used, the frequency of positive emotions was uncorrelated with the frequency of negative emotions ($r = -.04$). However, the frequency of positive emotions was highly positively associated with the frequency of negative emotions ($r = .58$, $p < .01$) among the same sample when absolute frequencies (e.g., once, twice) were used (Schimmack, Oishi, Diener, & Suh, 2000, Study 1).

Besides the interpretation of question meaning and response formats, the context of questions has been shown to affect respondents' answers to well-being questions. For instance, Strack, Martin, and Schwarz (1988) showed that the preceding question could affect responses to well-being questions. When participants first answered a question regarding dating satisfaction, followed by a general happiness question, the response to the dating question was highly correlated with "general happiness" ($r = .55$, $p < .01$). In contrast, when participants answered the question regarding dating satisfaction after the general happiness question, the size of the correlation was significantly smaller ($r = .16$). Furthermore, in the conversation norm condition, in which participants were told that "Now we would like to learn about two areas of life that may be important for people's overall well-being: (a) happiness with dating, and (b) happiness in general" (p. 434), dating happiness was only moderately correlated with general happiness, although the question regarding dating happiness was asked first ($r = .24$). Thus, when the dating question was asked first, and when participants were not told to separate the dating domain from life in general, participants who were satisfied with their dating life reported higher levels of life satisfaction than those who were dissatisfied with their dating life. When the dating question was asked after the general life satisfaction question, participants who were satisfied with their lives were not necessarily those who were satisfied with dating. If indeed the preceding question and conversation norms could radically change responses to well-being questions, it would seem questionable that well-being questions are valid measures. A recent meta-analysis on item-order effects on well-being judgments, however, has shown that the item-order effect is relatively small in effect size (average weighted $d = .18$, or $r = .09$; Schimmack & Oishi, 2005). Taken collectively, then, although preceding questions *can* drastically change responses to

well-being questions, it is also important to note that the typical effect size for item-order effects on judgments is not large.

The item-order effects are often interpreted by the accessibility effect (Wyer & Srull, 1989 for review). When respondents answer well-being questions, the concept that is accessible at the time of judgments (e.g., dating when the preceding question was about dating) has a disproportional influence. The accessible concept can also affect well-being judgments by providing the standards for the judgments. For instance, when participants were primed with a recent positive event, they evaluated their current life as more satisfying than those who were primed with a recent negative event. In contrast, however, when participants were primed with a positive event that happened a long time ago, these respondents evaluated their current lives as less satisfying than those who were primed with a negative event that happened a long time ago (Strack, Schwarz, & Gschneidinger, 1985). In this case the negative event that happened a long time ago provided the anchor point in participants' evaluation of current life (e.g., "compared to back then, my life now is pretty good").

Mood Effects

In addition to judgment effects, Schwarz and Strack (1999) have shown various extraneous mood effects on well-being judgments. For instance, German participants who were contacted after the German soccer team beat Chile in the World Cup reported higher levels of well-being than those who were contacted before the game (17.4 vs. 14.3 on a 20-point scale, Schwarz et al., 1987). Respondents who answered the well-being questions in a pleasant office reported higher levels of life satisfaction than those who answered the same questions in an unpleasant office. Similarly, participants who were contacted on a sunny day reported higher levels of happiness and life satisfaction than participants who were contacted on a rainy day (Schwarz & Clore, 1983). Interestingly, however, when participants were asked about the weather before the happiness and life satisfaction questions, there was no effect of weather on well-being judgments. Based on these findings, Schwarz and Strack argued that responses to the well-being questions are susceptible to weather and the preceding question; global life satisfaction judgments fluctuate as widely as daily mood (see, however, Eid & Diener, 2004; Schimmack & Oishi, 2005, for evidence for stability of well-being reports).

Other Judgmental Biases

Kahneman and his colleagues have demonstrated that global reports of well-being are vulnerable to various judgmental biases. For instance, participants in Fredrickson and Kahneman's (1993) experiment watched short films (about 35 seconds) and long films (about 100 seconds) and evaluated their affect continuously while watching these films. At the end, they gave an overall evaluation of the films. Participants did not take into account duration of pleasant experiences, as the overall evaluation of the short and long pleasant films was not different. Furthermore, Fredrickson and Kahneman found that the peak (highest) pleasantness rating and the end rating predicted overall evaluation, while the duration of being in a pleasant mood did not. Similarly, participants in Kahneman, Fredrickson, Schreiber, and Redelmeier (1993) were asked to put their hand in water at 14°C for 60 seconds in one trial. In the other trial, they were asked to put their hand in water at 14°C for 60 seconds and then 30 seconds at 15°C. Logically speaking, participants had less pain in the first trial than in the second trial. When asked later, however, more participants preferred the second trial to the first trial. Participants in this study also attended less to the duration of being in pain and used the end experience as a heuristic for the overall evaluation (see also Diener, Wirtz, & Oishi, 2001).

Other studies that have measured both online experiences and retrospective reports have consistently found significant discrepancies between online experiences and retrospective reports. For instance, Mitchell, Thompson, Peterson, and Cronk (1997) found that cyclists reported much more positive evaluation of their 3-week cycling trip after the trip was over than they did during the trip. Similarly, Wirtz, Kruger, Scollon, and Diener (2003) found that after the spring break, college students evaluated their spring break trip much more positively afterward than they did during the break. Furthermore, Wirtz and colleagues showed that the students' overall evaluation of the trip was predicted by their pretrip expectations.

Hedonic Adaptation

Whereas the social psychological research on well-being summarized so far has focused on cognitive processes and the effects of subtle manipulations (e.g., item-order, standard of comparison, misattribution), there are several programs of research that have explored the ways in which significant life events affect well-being judgments. One of the most famous studies in subjective well-being is Brickman et al.'s (1978) research on lottery winners and accident victims (see also Suh, Diener, & Fujita, 1996). Brickman and colleagues selected those who won a major lottery some time between one month and 12 months before the study was conducted. Similarly, they carefully selected accident victims who had been injured during the same period of time (one month to 12 months before the study was conducted). Because winning a major lottery and having a serious injury are among the most extraordinary life events, lay people might assume that these major life events would profoundly affect well-being judgments. With regard to current happiness ("how happy are you at this stage of your life? 0 = *not at all* and 5 = *very much*), lottery winners were indeed significantly happier than were the accident victims (*M*s = 4.00 vs. 2.96). However, lottery winners were no more happy than the participants in the control group (i.e., nonlottery winners), who were matched with the lottery winners in terms of residential areas (*M* = 3.82). As one might expect, the accident victims were less happy with their lives than those in the control group (*F* = 7.16, *p* < .01). Interestingly, however, when participants rated their enjoyment of mundane activities (e.g., talking with a friend, watching TV), lottery winners reported enjoying these activities *less* than the control participants did (*M*s = 3.33 vs. 3.82, *F* = 7.05, *p* < .01). Further, the accident victims reported enjoying daily activities only marginally less than did the control group (*M*s = 3.48 vs. 3.82, *F* = 3.14, *p* = .08). Based on these findings, Brickman and colleagues proposed the theory of the hedonic treadmill, which captures adaptation processes even to major life events. Although adaptation to a serious accident was not strong (paraplegic and quadriplegic patients were still substantially less happy than the control participants and the lottery winners), adaptation to winning the lottery was fairly robust (see also Lucas, Clark, Georgellis, & Diener, 2003; Lehman, Wortman, & Williams, 1987, for long-lasting effects of losing a spouse or child on well-being). As theorized by Brickman and colleagues, it appears that a major positive event like winning the lottery sets a higher standard of comparison when evaluating life in general and makes mundane daily activities less enjoyable. The surprisingly small effect of these major life events has inspired several prominent lines of research in contemporary social psychology.

Gilbert, Wilson, and their colleagues have demonstrated that people overestimate the power of life events on their well-being in numerous experiments in and outside of the laboratory (see also Schkade & Kahneman, 1998). For instance, Gilbert and colleagues (Gilbert, Pinel, Wilson, Blumberg, & Wheatley, 1998) asked assistant professors at the University of Texas (forecasters) to estimate on a 1–7 point scale how happy they would be if they learned they were granted or denied tenure. These researchers also contacted the professors who were granted tenure (positive experiencers) and those who were denied tenure (negative experiencers) at the University of Texas. On average, the current assistant professors predicted that they would be quite happy if they learned of their tenure (M = 5.90 on the 7-point scale) and not so happy if they learned of the denial of the tenure (M = 3.42). These predictions were wrong in both cases. The current assistant professors (forecasters) overestimated the happiness of those who did get tenure (Ms = 5.90 vs. 5.24, F = 4.14, p < .05). Conversely, the current assistant professors underestimated the happiness of those who did not get tenure (Ms = 3.42 vs. 4.71, F = 4.36, p < .05). Wilson, Wheatley, Meyers, Gilbert, and Axsom (2000) extended their original findings to a college football game, in which students, like assistant professors in Gilbert et al. (1998), overestimated the effect of the win or loss of their college team on their happiness. Interestingly, Wilson and colleagues demonstrated that students who were asked to think about other mundane activities (e.g., school work, leisure time activities) as well as the target game showed much smaller affective forecasting errors. In other words, attention to the target event was a key cause of affective forecasting error and when attention is distributed to various daily activities, affective forecasting errors can be substantially reduced.

More recently, Wilson, Gilbert, and colleagues turned their research attention to the adaptation issue originally raised by Brickman et al. (1978). Wilson and Gilbert (2008) hypothesized that hedonic adaptation can be conceptualized by the following steps: attention, reaction, explanation, and adaptation (thus, it is called the AREA model). People pay attention and react to a new event, but once they find a satisfactory explanation as to why this event happened, they are more likely to adapt to the event. Thus, the effect of this life event will be weakened. For instance, when Jane Smith, an assistant professor, has just found out about her promotion to associate professor, she is likely to react very strongly. However, as she learns the reasons why she got the promotion (e.g., a strong letter written by a prominent scholar in her field), she is likely to adapt

to the promotion. Based on this observation, Wilson and Gilbert hypothesized that by creating uncertainty regarding why a positive event happened, it would be possible to delay the adaptation process and prolong the positive feeling. Indeed, in a series of clever experiments, they confirmed their hypothesis.

Close Relationships and Well-Being

When the nationally representative sample of American participants were asked to nominate two of the most important domains in life, 55% of the respondents nominated "a happy marriage" (A. Campbell, Converse, & Rodgers, 1976). The second and the third most frequently nominated domains were "a good family life" (36% of the respondents) and "being in good health" (35%). Indeed, when A. Campbell and colleagues predicted global well-being from satisfaction with various life domains, satisfaction with family life was the strongest predictor, followed by marital satisfaction, and financial satisfaction. These findings have been replicated many times in various samples (e.g., Antonucci, Fuhrer, & Jackson, 1990; Diener & Seligman, 2002; Ryff & Singer, 1998). A recent meta-analysis (Heller, Watson, & Ilies, 2004) also showed that marital satisfaction was strongly associated with life satisfaction (i.e., a weighted average correlation coefficient of .42; cf., with $r = .35$ for the job satisfaction-life satisfaction correlation, and $r = .28$ for the health satisfaction-life satisfaction correlation; see also Schimmack & Lucas, 2007).

With their characteristic attention to processes, social psychologists have also shown that positive illusions (see S. L. Murray, Holmes, & Griffin, 2003, for review), accommodation (Rusbult et al., 1991), and responsiveness (Reis, Clark, & Holmes, 2004), among others predict the quality of close relationships and emotional well-being. Gable, Reis, and Downey (2003), for instance, found that both actual positive behaviors by partners and the (erroneous) perception that partners engaged in positive behaviors toward them were positively associated with participants' daily moods and relationship satisfaction, whereas actual negative behaviors by partners and the (erroneous) perception that partners engaged in negative behaviors were negatively associated with daily moods and relationship satisfaction. Rusbult et al. (1991) identified that accommodation, or the willingness to inhibit an impulse to react destructively, when a partner engaged in a negative behavior, was reciprocal, and predicted satisfaction, commitment, and investment in a romantic relationship. Laurenceau, Barrett, and Pietromonaco (1998) demonstrated that when participants' self-disclosure was reciprocated by the partner's self-disclosure, participants felt a greater degree of intimacy toward the partner. This process was in part mediated by perceived responsiveness of the partner. Similarly, Lemay, Clark, and Feeney (2007) found that individuals who are responsive to their partner's needs perceived that their partner was also responsive to their needs. Furthermore, the mutual projection of responsiveness predicted satisfaction with the relationship. Most intense human emotions occur in the context of close relationships (Berscheid & Reis, 1998). We feel happy, sad, and angry, often because of someone else. Close relationship researchers remind subjective well-being researchers that well-being cannot be understood outside of close relationship contexts.

The Cultural Psychology of Well-Being

Another major contribution of social psychology to the science of well-being is that of cultural psychology (see Diener et al., 2003; Mesquita & Leu, 2007; Tov & Diener, 2007; also Adams, chapter 8, this volume). Kitayama and Markus (2000) asked the fundamental question regarding the meaning of well-being and demonstrated multiple forms of well-being across cultures. Among middle- and upper-middle-class North Americans, for example, "being well" often means being able to take care of themselves. A major task in this cultural context is to help one another feel autonomous and feel good about the self via mutual praising and encouragement. Among East Asians, "being well" often means being connected to others. A major task in this cultural context, then, is to be sensitive to significant others' needs, to sympathize with one another, and to fulfill the requirements of one's roles. Consistent with these cultural differences, general happiness was strongly associated with pride among Americans, whereas it was strongly associated with *fureai*, or friendly feeling among Japanese (e.g., Kitayama, Markus, & Kurokawa, 2000; Kitayama, Mesquita, & Karasawa, 2006). Similarly, pride loaded on the positive mood factor along with other positive emotions among European Americans and Hispanic Americans, whereas it loaded on both positive and negative moods among Asian Americans, Japanese, and Indians (Scollon et al., 2005). More recently, Tsai and colleagues found that the ideal positive emotion entailed high activation (e.g., excitement) among North Americans, whereas it entailed low activation (e.g., calm) among East Asians (Tsai, Louie, Chen, & Uchida, 2007; Tsai, Miao, & Seppala, 2007).

These findings show that the meanings of "being well" and "positive" emotion differ across cultures.

Moreover, numerous studies have shown that the predictors of well-being are different across cultures. For instance, the satisfaction of basic needs (e.g., financial satisfaction) had a stronger link with life satisfaction in poor nations than in wealthy nations (Diener & Diener, 1995). Similarly, self-esteem has a greater association with life satisfaction in individualist nations than in collectivist nations (Diener & Diener, 1995). The frequency of emotional experiences was more strongly associated with life satisfaction in individualist nations than in collectivist nations (Suh, Diener, Oishi, & Triandis, 1998). In addition, the type of motivation predictive of life satisfaction was also different across cultures. For instance, Japanese college students who were pursuing their goals to make their family and friends happy became more satisfied with their lives over time as they achieved their goals than Japanese who were not pursuing their goals to make their family and friends happy (Oishi & Diener, 2001). In contrast, American college students who were pursuing their goals for themselves became more satisfied with their lives over time as they achieved their goals than other Americans who were not pursuing their goals for themselves. Likewise, among Americans, pursuing goals with an avoidant mindset was negatively associated with life satisfaction, whereas it was not negatively associated with life satisfaction among Koreans and Russians, where avoiding negative evaluations is deemed important (Elliot, Chirkov, Kim, & Sheldon, 2001). Recently, Uchida and colleagues (2008) showed that social support was associated with life satisfaction to the extent that it supported self-esteem among Americans, whereas it was associated with life satisfaction above and beyond self-esteem among Japanese and Filipinos. In addition to various cross-cultural variations, several researchers have shown within-nation variations in subjective well-being as well. For instance, Plaut, Markus, and Lachman (2002) found that autonomy is high in many states in New England and Mountain West, and low in Eastern South Central states (e.g., Alabama, Mississippi). In other words, autonomy-based well-being is more pronounced in New England and Mountain West (where there is a historical tradition for independence) than elsewhere in the United States.

Intervention Studies

In addition to basic research, personality and social psychologists have increasingly delved into intervention studies of well-being (see Emmons, 2008; King, 2008, for reviews). Pennebaker has pioneered the writing intervention (see Pennebaker, 1997; Smyth, 1998, for a summary), and its success has opened the door for a later generation of social psychologists to put their theories into interventions. In Pennebaker's intervention studies, participants in the experimental condition typically write about the topic (e.g., personal trauma) and those in the control condition typically write about a mundane topic (e.g., what they did yesterday) for 15 to 30 minutes for 3 to 5 consecutive days. Those in the experimental condition typically experienced reduced self-reported distress, and most impressively improved immune functioning and fewer doctor visits. King (2001) showed that writing about the best possible selves resulted in a higher level of self-reported well-being. Interestingly, however, Lyubomirsky, Sousa, and Dickerhoof (2006) found that thinking privately rather than writing about the three happiest experiences resulted in higher levels of life satisfaction 4 weeks later.

Emmons and McCullough (2003, Study 1) put college students randomly into one of the three conditions for 10 weeks: the gratitude listing condition, writing about a hassle condition, and writing about a neutral life event condition. They found that students in the gratitude condition reported higher levels of life satisfaction, more optimism, and fewer physical symptoms during the 10-week period than those in the hassle and neutral life event condition. Seligman, Steen, Park, and Peterson (2005) conducted one of the most ambitious intervention studies to date with over 500 participants and up to 6-month follow-ups on their happiness and depression. Participants were randomly assigned to one of six conditions: (1) writing a letter of gratitude and delivering the letter, (2) writing three good things in life every night for one week, (3) writing their best qualities every night for one week, (4) using their signature strengths in a new way every day for one week, (5) identifying their strengths and using them for one week, and (6) control group (writing about early memories every night for one week). Seligman and colleagues found the gratitude visit intervention to be the most powerful intervention right after the experiment. The effect of the gratitude visit, however, disappeared after the first three months. Although the three good things intervention and the using signature strengths intervention did not result in noticeable gain immediately after the experiment was over, its effect was evident 6 months later. In short, recent intervention studies are clearly

promising. However, a diverse array of populations, dependent variables, and measurement instruments would be desirable, as well as explorations of which interventions are most beneficial and why.

There are several other important findings that can be directly applied to interventions. Van Boven and Gilovich (2003), for instance, found that experiential purchases (e.g., concerts, travel) made people happier than material purchases (e.g., a TV, clothing). Likewise, Dunn, Aknin, and Norton (2008) found that individuals who spend more of their income on others were happier than those who spend less of their income on others. Most strikingly, Dunn and colleagues found that participants who were randomly assigned to spend money on others were happier later than those who were assigned to spend money on themselves. These findings suggest that it may be wise to spend money on experiential purchases or on others rather than on materials for ourselves.

Based on findings from the judgment and decision-making literature, Hsee, Hastie, and Chen (2008) have also proposed specific strategies, hedonomics, to increase happiness. For instance, based on the utility function of the prospect theory, Hsee and colleagues suggested that we separate two good outcomes (e.g., dining and watching a movie) as opposed to combining them into one event. Because the effect of a gain has the marginal utility function (concaved at a higher end, and therefore, after a certain point, more gain does not add much to the total utility), it is better to have two separate moderate gains than one intense gain. Hsee and colleagues also noted affective forecasting errors regarding material purchases occur because people do not think about the consumption experience during the acquiring stage (i.e., they only imagine how nice this big screen T.V. will look in their family room, while ignoring all other daily activities). Like Wilson and colleagues' affective forecasting study (2000), Hsee et al. recommend that people imagine day-to-day consumption experiences during the purchase. In addition, Hsee and colleagues emphasize that many purchase situations are joint-evaluation conditions, where people are comparing one product against others. For instance, when people purchase a TV, they compare many models that differ on multiple dimensions, and their decision is highly dependent on which dimension they weigh most heavily. The consumption phase, however, is not a joint-evaluation condition but is a single-evaluation condition (you will be watching the one TV you bought, not comparing your TV with another model). During the acquisition phase, Hsee and colleagues recommend that we keep in mind that a consumption situation is often single-evaluation, not a joint-evaluation. In short, many of the judgment and decision research findings have practical implications for happiness, making hedonomics a promising research enterprise for the future.

In sum, numerous contributions have been made to the science of well-being by researchers from the social psychology tradition. They range from delineating various meanings of "well-being" (Kitayama & Markus, 2000) to discovering cognitive processes and biases involving well-being judgments (Kahneman, 1999; Schwarz & Strack, 1999) and hedonic adaptation (Brickman et al., 1978; Wilson & Gilbert, 2008), to delineating relational contexts of well-being (Gable et al., 2003), to creating new interventions (Pennebaker, 1997) and providing practical advice (Hsee et al., 2008). One major weakness of social psychology tradition has been its relative lack of attention to individual differences, and its lopsided attention to situation factors over person factors. Because of their near-exclusive focus on cognitive and situation factors, social psychology models typically fail to provide much information regarding how individuals' personality, dispositions, and genetics play a role.

The Contributions of Personality *and* Social Psychology to the Science of Well-Being

Many pioneers in personality and social psychology, such as William McDougal, Floyd Allport, Kurt Lewin, Gordon Allport, and Henry Murray, were interactionists because they took into account both personal and situational factors in their theorizing (see Oishi, Kesebir, & Snyder, 2009, for review). Both McDougal (1908/1921) and H. A. Murray (1938), for instance, theorized important dispositions (instincts and needs, respectively) and situations that elicit particular behavioral tendencies. F. Allport's (1924) textbook of social psychology, for example, includes many chapters on personality dispositions as well as genetics. Kurt Lewin and Gordon Allport wrote influential books both in personality (Lewin's 1935 *A Dynamic Theory of Personality*; Allport's 1937 *Personality: A Psychological Interpretation*) and social psychology (Lewin's 1948 *Resolving Social Conflicts*; Allport's 1954 *Nature of Prejudice*). Despite the initial close connection, personality and social psychologies went on divergent paths. In his famous APA presidential address, Lee Cronbach (1957) lamented the separation of experimental and correlational psychologies as follows: "It is now commonplace for a student to get his PhD in experimental psychology without graduate training in test theory or developmental psychology, and the student of correlational branches can avoid experimental psychology only a little less completely" (p. 672). Social psychology became a research enterprise based largely on laboratory experiments, while personality psychology remained an enterprise based largely on correlational methods. This historical divergence culminated in the bitter person-situation debate in the 1970s and the 1980s (e.g., Diener & Larsen, 1984; Epstein, 1979; Kenrick & Funder, 1988; Mischel, 1968; Mischel & Peake, 1982; Nisbett & Ross, 1980). After the person-situation debate subsided, various integrative models have been proposed (e.g., Fleeson, 2001; Funder & Colvin, 1991; Mischel & Shoda, 1995). Although prototypical personality psychologists are still very different from prototypical experimental social psychologists, there are many hybrid personality-social psychologists and there is much hybrid personality-social psychology research (see Tracy, Robins, & Sherman, 2009, for an excellent review). I will next summarize some representative examples of the integrative approach in the area of well-being.

Methodological Integration

The research summarized in the "Intraindividual Variation" section above, in particular Wessman and Ricks's (1966) intense study of 25 Radcliffe and 18 Harvard students, has illuminated both person and situation factors in understanding individual well-being. Similarly, many daily diary and experience sampling studies of well-being have delineated various types of person-situation interactions in predicting subjective well-being, including the selection of particular situations (Diener, Larsen, & Emmons, 1984; Emmons, Larsen, & Diener, 1986; Mehl, Vazire, Holleran, & Clark, 2010), affective reactions and experiences in particular situations (e.g., Cote & Moscowitz, 1998; Diener & Larsen, 1984; Nezlek & Plesko, 2003; Oishi, Diener, Scollon, & Biswas-Diener, 2004; Suls, Martin, & David, 1998; D. Watson et al., 1984), and memory of particular emotional events (Oishi, Schimmack, Diener, Kim-Prieto, Scollon, & Choi, 2007). For instance, Crocker, Sommers, and Luhtanen (2002) followed college seniors who had applied for graduate school and found a main effect of admission outcomes (obviously happier after the acceptance, more sad after the rejection), but also an interaction between

important social context (see Cacioppo, Fowler, & Christakis, 2009, for an exception). For instance, Fowler and Christakis (2008) have shown that happiness is distributed in social networks such that it reaches out to three degrees of separation. Their research demonstrates that a person's happiness is related to the happiness of their friends, their friends' friends, and their friends' friends' friends. It will be crucial to examine the effects of social networks and whether there are individual and/or cultural difference variables that moderate the social network effect on individual well-being.

Finally, although the results of intervention studies (Emmons, 2008; Seligman et al., 2005) and suggestions made by hedonomics (Hsee et al., 2008) are truly impressive, very few studies have investigated whether a particular intervention or cognitive strategy will work better for some individuals or cultural groups than others. As applied well-being research matures, it is important to keep in mind potential individual and cultural differences in application.

Summary and Conclusion

The goal of this chapter was to review the contributions that have been made by personality and social psychology, respectively and together, to the science of well-being. Considering that the science of well-being was once deemed impossible (H. A. Murray & Kluckhohn, 1948), the contributions made by personality and social psychology to the science of well-being have been truly extraordinary. Since its humble beginning in the 1930s (Hartmann, 1934; Jasper, 1930), the science of well-being has grown to become one of the most vibrant research topics in psychological science today largely due to the solid measurements, creative methodologies, sophisticated data analytic techniques, and attention paid to cognitive processes as well as to relational and cultural contexts by contemporary personality and social psychologists.

The personality tradition of well-being research has shown that it is possible to measure well-being reliably (Diener et al., 1985; D. Watson et al., 1988), that self-reported well-being converges with informant reports (Lucas et al., 1996), that self-reported well-being predicts important life outcomes (Lyubomirsky et al., 2005), and that well-being has nontrivial genetic origins (Tellegen et al., 1988). The personality tradition of well-being research has also shown that there are individual differences in patterns of well-being over time (Larsen, 1987; Zevon & Tellegen, 1982); that different types of

goals, needs, and narratives are strongly associated with the levels and patterns of well-being (Emmons, 1986; McAdams & Vaillant, 1982); and that maximizing, social comparison, and categorization speeds all reliably predict the levels of well-being (Lyubomirsky & Ross, 1997; Robinson et al., 2004; Schwartz et al., 2002).

The social psychology tradition has illuminated that there are various cultural meanings of "well-being" (Kitayama & Markus, 2000), that responses to well-being questions involve multiple cognitive processes (Kahneman, 1999), that the effects of life events are often short-lived (Brickman et al., 1978; Wilson & Gilbert, 2008), that happiness is experienced often in relationship contexts (Gable et al., 2003), and that it is possible to improve one's well-being (Hsee et al., 2008; Lyubomirsky et al., 2006).

Finally, there are recent methodological integrations of the personality and social psychology perspectives that delineate person-situation interactions (Crocker et al., 2002; Diener et al., 1984) and gene–environment interactions (Caspi et al., 2003; Riemann et al., 1998). The integration of the two approaches can also be seen by the well-being research that has combined correlational and experimental methods (e.g., Lucas & Baird, 2004; Tamir, 2005). Thus, there are theoretical integrations of personality and social psychological perspectives, as seen in the value-as-moderator model (Oishi et al., 1999) and the revised hedonic treadmill theory of well-being (Diener et al., 2006).

As summarized above, the integrative approach of personality *and* social psychology has been successful. I believe that future developments in the science of well-being are likely to take place when the united personality and social psychology approach is further integrated into economics, anthropology, sociology, political science, biology, and neuroscience. Although I emphasize the benefits of the integrative approach, it is important to note that the integrative approach is not necessarily superior to the traditional personality and social psychology approaches, respectively. Because the integrative approach focuses on person-situation interactions and reveals the complexity of well-being, it often lacks the parsimony and elegance of the traditional main effect approach to theorizing and research in well-being. It should also be acknowledged that several influential programs of research in well-being would not have been produced unless they were grounded firmly in respective personality and social psychology traditions. For instance, the P-technique factor analytic approach to the structure of well-being (e.g., Zevon & Tellegen, 1982) and the behavioral genetic research on well-being (e.g., Lykken & Tellegen, 1996) would not have emerged without the firm grounding in the traditional personality perspective. Alternatively, Wilson and Gilbert's (2008) AREA model of hedonic adaptation and Hsee et al.'s (2008) hedonomics would not have been born without the stable foundation in traditional experimental social psychology.

In conclusion, I hope many personality and social psychologists will take the integrative, hybrid approach. But, I also understand that the hybrid approach may not be for everyone. The traditional personality approach suits some, while the traditional social approach suits others, and the hybrid approach suits yet other psychologists. In the end, this review shows that there are divergent yet meaningful ways of "being" a personality, a social, or a personality-social psychologist in the science of well-being.

Acknowledgment

I would like to thank Selin Kesebir, Felicity Miao, and Patrick Seder for their comments on an earlier version of this paper.

Notes

[1] Eudaimonic well-being is the idea of well-being originally advocated by Aristotle. Eudaimonia is often translated as a life well lived. Aristotle argued that individuals could achieve eudaimonia only if they engage in virtuous activities. Although eudaimonic well-being researchers emphasize the distinction between eudaimonic and hedonic well-being (and indeed Aristotle distinguished amusement from eudaimonia), Aristotle saw them as interrelated. For instance, Aristotle stated in book 1 of the *Nicomachean Ethics*: "virtuous actions must be pleasurable in themselves" (Thomson, 1953, p. 79).

References

Adam, E. K., Hawkley, L. C., Kudielka, B. M., & Cacioppo, J. T. (2006). Day-to-day dynamics of experience-cortisol associations in a population-based sample of older adults. *Proceedings of the National Academy of Sciences, USA, 103,* 17058–17063.

Allen, H. M., Jr., Bentler, P. M., & Gutek, B. A. (1985). Probing theories of individual well-being: A comparison of quality-of-life models assessing neighborhood satisfaction. *Basic and Applied Social Psychology, 6,* 181–203.

Allport, F. H. (1924). *Social psychology.* Boston: Houghton Mifflin.

Allport, G. W. (1937). *Personality: A psychological interpretation.* New York: Holt.

Allport, G. W. (1954). *The nature of prejudice.* Reading, MA: Addison-Wesley.

Allport, G. W. (1961). *Patterns and growth in personality.* New York: Holt, Rinehart, and Winston.

Antonucci, T.C., Fuhrer, R., & Jackson, J. S. (1990). Social support and reciprocity: A cross-ethnic and cross-national perspective. *Journal of Social and Personal Relationships, 7,* 519–530.

Baker, J. G., Zevon, M. A., & Rounds, J. B. (1994). Differences in positive and negative affect dimensions: Latent trait analysis. *Personality and Individual Differences, 17,* 161–167.

Battista, J., & Almond, R. (1973). The development of meaning in life. *Psychiatry, 36,* 409–427.

Berscheid, E., & Reis, H. T. (1998). Attraction and close relationships. In D. T. Gilbert, S. T. Fiske, & G. Lindzey (Eds.), *The handbook of social psychology* (4th ed., Vol. 2, pp. 193–281). Boston: McGraw-Hill.

Boker, S. M., & Nesselroade, J. R. (2002). A method for modeling the intrinsic dynamics of intra-individual variability: Recovering the parameters of simulated oscillators in multiwave data. *Multivariate Behavioral Research, 37,* 127–160.

Bolger, N., Davis, A., & Rafaeli, E. (2003). Diary methods: Capturing life as it is lived. *Annual Review of Psychology, 54,* 579–616.

Bolger, N., & Zuckerman, A. (1995). A framework for studying personality in the stress process. *Journal of Personality and Social Psychology, 69,* 890–902.

Bradburn, N. M. (1969). *The structure of psychological well-being.* Chicago, IL: Aldine.

Brunstein, J. C., Schultheiss, O. C., & Grässman, R. (1998). Personal goals and emotional well-being: The moderating role of motive dispositions. *Journal of Personality and Social Psychology, 75,* 494–508.

Cacioppo, J. T., Fowler, J. H., & Christakis, N. A. (2009). Alone in the crowd: The structure and spread of loneliness in a large social network. *Journal of Personality and Social Psychology, 97,* 977–991.

Campbell, A. (1981). *The sense of well-being in America: Recent patterns and trends.* New York: McGraw-Hill.

Campbell, A., Converse, P. E., & Rodgers, W. L. (1976). *The quality of American life: Perceptions, evaluations, and satisfactions.* New York: Russell Sage.

Campbell, D. T., & Fiske, D. W. (1959). Convergent and discriminant validation by the multitrait-multimethod matrix. *Psychological Bulletin, 56,* 81–105.

Cantor, N., Norem, J. K., Niedenthal, P. M., Langston, C. A., & Brower, A. M. (1987). Life tasks, self-concept ideals, and cognitive strategies in a life transition. *Journal of Personality and Social Psychology, 53,* 1178–1191.

Cantril, H. (1965). *The pattern of human concern.* New Brunswick, NJ: Rutgers University Press.

Caspi, A., Sudgen, K., Moffitt, T. E., Taylor, A., Craig, I. W., Harrington, H., et al. (2003). Influence of life stress on depression: Moderation by a polymorphism in the 5-HTT gene. *Science, 301,* 386–389.

Cattell, R. B. (1943). The description of personality: I. Foundations of trait measurement. *Psychological Review, 50,* 559–594.

Cattell, R. B. (1952). The three basic factor-analytic research designs—their interrelations and derivatives. *Psychological Bulletin, 49,* 499–520.

Cattell, R. B., Cattell, A. K. S., & Rhymer, R. M. (1947). P-technique demonstrated in determining psycho-physiological source traits in a normal individual. *Psychometrika, 12,* 267–288.

Chirkov, V., Ryan, R. M., Kim, Y., & Kaplan, U. (2003). Differentiating autonomy from individualism and independence: A self-determination theory perspective on internalization of cultural orientations and well-being. *Journal of Personality and Social Psychology, 84,* 97–109.

Cote, S., & Moskowitz, D. S. (1998). On the dynamic covariation between interpersonal behavior and affect: Prediction from neuroticism, extraversion, and agreeableness. *Journal of Personality and Social Psychology, 75,* 1032–1046.

Cronbach, L. J. (1957). The two disciplines of scientific psychology. *American Psychologist, 12,* 671–684.

Cronbach, L. J., & Meehl, P. E. (1955). Construct validity in psychological tests. *Psychological Bulletin, 52,* 281–302.

Crocker, J. Sommers, S. R., & Luhtanen, K. K. (2002). Hopes dashed and dreams fulfilled: Contingencies of self-worth and graduate school admissions. *Personality and Social Psychology Bulletin, 28,* 1275–1286.

Crumbaugh, J. C., & Maholick, L. T. (1964). An experimental study in existentialism: The psychometric approach to Frankl's concept of noogenic neurosis. *Journal of Clinical Psychology, 20,* 200–207.

Cummins, R. A., McCabe, M. P., Romeo, Y., & Gullone, E. (1994). The Comprehensive Quality of Life Scale (ComQol): Instrument development and psychometric evaluation on college staff and students. *Educational and Psychological Measurement, 54,* 372–382.

Darley, J. M., & Latané, B. (1968). Bystander intervention in emergencies: Diffusion of responsibility. *Journal of Personality and Social Psychology, 8,* 377–382.

Dawes, R. M., & Messick, D. M. (2000). Social dilemmas. *International Journal of Psychology, 35,* 111–116.

Diener, E., & Diener, M. (1995). Cross-cultural correlates of life satisfaction and self-esteem. *Journal of Personality and Social Psychology, 68,* 653–663.

Diener, E., Diener, M., & Diener, C. (1995). Factors predicting the subjective well-being of nations. *Journal of Personality and Social Psychology, 69,* 851–864.

Diener, E., Emmons, R. A., Larsen, R. L., & Griffin, S. (1985). The Satisfaction with Life Scale. *Journal of Personality Assessment, 49,* 71–75.

Diener, E., & Larsen, R. J. (1984). Temporal stability and cross-situational consistency of affective, behavioral, and cognitive responses. *Journal of Personality and Social Psychology, 47,* 871–883.

Diener, E., Larsen, R. J., & Emmons, R. A. (1984). Person × Situation interactions: Choice of situations and congruent response models. *Journal of Personality and Social Psychology, 47,* 580–592.

Diener, E., Lucas, R. E., Schimmack, U., & Helliwell, J. (2009). *Well-being for public policy.* New York: Oxford University Press.

Diener, E., Lucas, R. E., & Scollon, C. N. (2006). Beyond the hedonic treadmill: Revising the adaptation theory of well-being. *American Psychologist, 61,* 305–314.

Diener, E., Oishi, S., Lucas, R.E. (2003). Personality, culture, and subjective well-being: Emotional and cognitive evaluations of life. *Annual Review of Psychology, 54,* 403–425.

Diener, E., Smith, H., & Fujita, F. (1995). The personality structure of affect. *Journal of Personality and Social Psychology, 69,* 130–141.

Diener, E., Suh, E. M., Lucas, R. E., & Smith, H. (1999). Subjective well-being: Three decades of progress. *Psychological Bulletin, 125,* 276–302.

Diener, E., Wirtz, D., & Oishi, S. (2001). End effects of rated quality of life: The James Dean effect. *Psychological Science, 12,* 124–128.

Dunn, E. W., Aknin, L. B., & Norton, M. I. (2008). Spending money on others promotes happiness. *Science, 319,* 1687–1688.

Durkheim, E. (1897/1951). *Suicide: A study in sociology* (J. A. Spaulding & G. Simpson, Trans.). New York: Free Press.

Eid, M., & Diener, E. (2001). Norms for experiencing in different cultures: Inter- and intranational differences. *Journal of Personality and Social Psychology, 81,* 869–885.

Eid, M., & Diener, E. (2004). Global judgments of subjective well-being: Situational variability and long-term stability. *Social Indicators Research, 65,* 245–277.

Elliot, A. J., Chirkov, V. I., Kim, Y., & Shelodn, K. M. (2001). A cross-cultural analysis of avoidance (relative to approach) personal goals. *Psychological Science, 6,* 505–510.

Emmons, R. A. (1986). Personal strivings: An approach to personality and subjective well-being. *Journal of Personality and Social Psychology, 51,* 1058–1068.

Emmons, R. A. (2008). Gratitude, subjective well-being, and the brain. In M. Eid & R. J. Larsen (Eds.), *The science of subjective well-being* (pp. 469–489). New York: Guilford.

Emmons, R. A., Diener, E., & Larsen, R. J. (1986). Choice and avoidance of everyday situations and affect congruence: Two models of reciprocal interactionism. *Journal of Personality and Social Psychology, 51,* 815–826.

Epstein, S. (1979). The stability of behavior: I. On predicting most of the people much of the time. *Journal of Personality and Social Psychology, 37,* 1097–1126.

Feldman, L. A. (1995). Valence focus and arousal focus: Individual differences in the structure of affective experience. *Journal of Personality and Social Psychology, 69,* 153–166.

Festinger, L. (1954). A theory of social comparison processes. *Human Relations, 7,* 117–140.

Fleeson, W. (2001). Toward a structure- and process-integrated view of personality: Traits as density distributions of states. *Journal of Personality and Social Psychology, 80,* 1011–1027.

Fowler, J. H., & Christakis, N. A. (2008). Dynamic spread of happiness in a large social network: Longitudinal analysis over 20 years in the Framingham Heart Study. *British Medical Journal, 337,* a2338.

Fredrickson, B. L., & Kahneman, D. (1993). Duration neglect in retrospective evaluations of affective episodes. *Journal of Personality and Social Psychology, 65,* 45–55.

Fujita, F., & Diener, E. (2005). Life satisfaction set point: Stability and change. *Journal of Personality and Social Psychology, 88,* 158–164.

Funder, D. C., & Colvin, C. R. (1991). Explorations in behavioral consistency: Properties of persons, situations, and behaviors. *Journal of Personality and Social Psychology, 60,* 773–794.

Gable, S. L., Reis, H. T., & Downey, G. (2003). He said, she said: A quasi-signal detection analysis of daily interactions between close relationship partners. *Psychological Science, 14,* 100–105.

Gatz, M., Pederson, N. L, Plomin, R., & Nesselroade, J. R. (1992). Importance of shared genes and shared environments for symptoms of depression in older adults. *Journal of Abnormal Psychology, 101,* 701–708.

Gilbert, D. T., Pinel, E. C., Wilson, T. D., Blumberg, S. J., & Wheatley, T. P. (1998). Immune neglect: A source of durability bias in affective forecasting. *Journal of Personality and Social Psychology, 75,* 617–638.

Grob, A., Little, T. D., Wanner, B., Wearing, A. J., & Euronet. (1996). Adolescents' well-being and perceived control across 14 sociocultural contexts. *Journal of Personality and Social Psychology, 71,* 785–795.

Gurin, G., Veroff, J., & Feld, S. (1960). *Americans view their mental health.* New York: Basic Books.

Harker, L. A., & Keltner, D. (2001). Expressions of positive emotion in women's college yearbook pictures and their relationship to personality and life outcomes across adulthood. *Journal of Personality and Social Psychology, 80,* 112–124.

Hartmann, G. W. (1934). Personality traits associated with variations in happiness. *Journal of Abnormal and Social Psychology, 29,* 202–212.

Headey, B., & Wearing, A. (1989). Personality, life events, and subjective well-being: Toward a dynamic equilibrium model. *Journal of Personality and Social Psychology, 57,* 731–739.

Heller, D., Watson, D., & Ilies, R. (2004). A role of person versus situation in life satisfaction: A critical examination. *Psychological Bulletin, 130,* 574–600.

Higgins, E. T. (1990). Personality, social psychology, and person-situation relations: Standards and knowledge activation as a common language. In L. A. Pervin (Ed.), *Handbook of personality: Theory and research* (pp. 301–338). New York: Guilford.

Hsee, C. K., Hastie, R., & Chen, J. (2008). Hedonomics: Bridging decision research with happiness research. *Perspectives on Psychological Science, 3,* 224–243.

Inglehart, R., Foa, R., Peterson, C., & Welzel, C. (2008). Development, freedom, and rising happiness: A global perspective (1981–2007). *Perspectives on Psychological Science, 3,* 264–285.

Iyengar, S. S., Wells, R. E., & Schwartz, B. (2006). Doing better but feeling worse: Looking for the "best" job undermines satisfaction. *Psychological Science, 17,* 143–150.

Jasper, H. H. (1930). The measurement of depression-elation and its relation to a measure of extroversion-introversion. *Journal of Abnormal and Social Psychology, 25,* 307–318.

Kahneman, D. (1999). Objective happiness. In D. Kahneman, E. Diener, & N. Schwarz (Eds.), *Well-being: The foundations of hedonic psychology* (pp. 3–25). New York: Russell Sage.

Kahneman, D., Fredrickson, B. L., Schreiber, C. A., & Redelmeier, D. A. (1993). When more pain is preferred to less: Adding a better end. *Psychological Science, 4,* 401–405.

Kang, S.-M., Shaver, P. R., Sue, S., Min, K.-H., & Jing, H. (2003). Culture-specific patterns in the prediction of life satisfaction: Roles of emotion, relationship quality, and self-esteem. *Personality and Social Psychology Bulletin, 29,* 1596–1608.

Kasser, T., & Ryan, R. M. (1993). A dark side of the American dream: Correlates of financial success as a central life aspiration. *Journal of Personality and Social Psychology, 65,* 410–422.

Kenrick, D. T., & Funder, D. C. (1988). Profiting from controversy: Lessons from the person-situation debate. *American Psychologist, 43,* 23–34.

Keyes, C. L. M., Shmotkin, D., & Ryff, C. D. (2002). Optimizing well-being: The empirical encounter of two traditions. *Journal of Personality and Social Psychology, 82,* 1007–1022.

King, L. A. (2001). The health benefits of writing about life goals. *Personality and Social Psychology Bulletin, 27,* 798–807.

King, L. A. (2008). Interventions for enhancing subjective well-being: Can we make people happier and should we? In M. Eid & R. J. Larsen (Eds.), *The science of subjective well-being* (pp. 431–448). New York: Guilford.

King, L. A., & Broyles, S. J. (1997). Wishes, gender, personality and well-being. *Journal of Personality, 65,* 49–76.

King, L. A., Richards, J. H., & Stemmerich, E. (1998). Daily goals, life goals, and worst fears: Means, ends, and subjective well-being. *Journal of Personality, 66,* 713–744.

Kitayama, S., & Markus, H. R. (2000). The pursuit of happiness and the realization of sympathy: Cultural patterns of self, social relations, and well-being. In E. Diener & E. M. Suh (Eds.), *Culture and subjective well-being* (pp. 113–160). Cambridge, MA: MIT Press.

Kitayama, S., Markus, H. R., & Kurokawa, M. (2000). Culture, emotion, and well-being: Good feelings in Japan and the United States. *Cognition and Emotion, 14,* 93–124.

Kitayama, S., Mesquita, B., & Karasawa, M. (2006). Cultural affordances and emotional experience: Socially engaging and disengaging emotions in Japan and the United States. *Journal of Personality and Social Psychology, 91,* 890–903.

Kwan, V. S. Y., Bond, M. H., & Singelis, T. M. (1997). Pancultural explanations for life satisfaction: Adding relationship harmony to self-esteem. *Journal of Personality and Social Psychology, 73,* 1038–1051.

Larsen, R. J. (1987). The stability of mood variability: A spectral analytic approach to daily mood assessments. *Journal of Personality and Social Psychology, 52,* 1195–1204.

Larsen, R. J., & Kasimatis, M. (1990). Individual differences in entrainment of mood to the weekly calendar. *Journal of Personality and Social Psychology, 58,* 164–171.

Laurenceau, J., Barrett, L. F., & Pietromonaco, P. R. (1998). Intimacy as an interpersonal process: The importance of self-disclosure, partner disclosure, and perceived partner responsiveness in interpersonal exchanges. *Journal of Personality and Social Psychology, 74,* 1238–1251.

Lawton, M. P. (1975). The Philadelphia Geriatric Center Morale Scale: A revision. *Journal of Gerontology, 30,* 85–89.

Lehman, D. R., Wortman, C. B., & Williams, A. F. (1987). Long-term effects of losing a spouse or child in a motor vehicle crash. *Journal of Personality and Social Psychology, 52,* 218–231.

Lemay, E. P., Jr., Clark, M. S., & Feeney, B. C. (2007). Projection of responsiveness to needs and the construction of satisfying communal relationships. *Journal of Personality and Social Psychology, 92,* 834–853.

Lewin, K. (1935). *A dynamic theory of personality.* New York: McGraw-Hill.

Lewin, K. (1948). *Resolving social conflicts: Selected papers on group dynamics.* New York: Harper.

Little, B. R. (1983). Personal projects: A rationale and method for investigation. *Environment and Behavior, 15,* 273–309.

Lord, F. (1952). A theory of test scores. *Psychometric Monographs, 7,* 84.

Lucas, R. E. (2005). Time does not heal all wounds: A longitudinal study of reaction and adaptation to divorce. *Psychological Science, 16,* 945–950.

Lucas, R. E., & Baird, B. M. (2004). Extraversion and emotional reactivity. *Journal of Personality and Social Psychology, 86,* 473–485.

Lucas, R. E., Clark, A. E., Georgellis, Y., & Diener, E. (2003). Reexamining adaptation and the set point model of happiness: Reactions to changes in marital status. *Journal of Personality and Social Psychology,84,* 527–539.

Lucas, R. E., Clark, A. E., Georgellis, Y., & Diener, E. (2004). Unemployment alters the set point for life satisfaction. *Psychological Science,15,* 8–13.

Lucas, R. E., Diener, E., & Suh, E. (1996). Discriminant validity of well-being measure. *Journal of Personality and Social Psychology, 71,* 616–628.

Lykken, D., & Tellegen, A. (1996). Happiness is a stochastic phenomenon. *Psychological Science, 7,* 186–189.

Lyubomirsky, S., King, L., & Diener, E. (2005). The benefits of frequent positive affect: Does happiness lead to success? *Psychological Bulletin, 131,* 803–855.

Lyubomirsky, S., & Lepper, H. (1999). A measure of subjective happiness: Preliminary reliability and construct validation. *Social Indicators Research, 46,* 137–155.

Lyubomirsky, S., & Ross, L. (1997). Hedonic consequences of social comparison: A contrast of happy and unhappy people. *Journal of Personality and Social Psychology, 73,* 1141–1157.

Lyubomirsky, S., & Ross, L. (1999). Changes in attractiveness of elected, rejected, and precluded alternatives: A comparison of happy and unhappy individuals. *Journal of Personality and Social Psychology, 76,* 988–1007.

Lyubomirsky, S., Sousa, L., Dickerhoof, R. (2006). The costs and benefits of writing, talking, and thinking about life's triumphs and defeats. *Journal of Personality and Social Psychology, 90,* 692–708.

McAdams, D. P., Reynolds, J., Lewis, M., Patten, A. H., & Bowman, P. J. (2001). When bad things turn good and good things turn bad: Sequences of redemption and contamination in life narrative and their relation to psychosocial adaptation in midlife adults and in students. *Personality and Social Psychology, 27,* 474–485.

McAdams, D. P., & Vaillant, G. E. (1982). Intimacy motivation and psychosocial adjustment: A longitudinal study. *Journal of Personality Assessment, 46,* 586–593.

McArdle, J. J. (2009). Latent variable modeling of differences and changes with longitudinal data. *Annual Review of Psychology, 60,* 577–605.

Mehl, M. R., Vazire, S., Holleran, S. E., & Clark, C. S. (2010). Eavesdropping on happiness: Well-being is related to having less small talk and more substantive conversations. *Psychological Science, 21,* 539-541.

Mesquita, B., & Leu, J. (2007). The cultural psychology of emotion. In S. Kitayama, & D. Cohen (Eds.), *Handbook of cultural psychology* (pp. 734–759). New York: Guilford.

Mischel, W. (1968). *Personality and assessment.* New York: Wiley.

Mischel, W., & Peake, P. K. (1982). Beyond déjà vu in the search for cross-situational consistency. *Psychological Review, 89,* 730–755.

Mischel, W., & Shoda, Y. (1995). A cognitive-affective system theory of personality: Reconceptualizing situations, dispositions, dynamics, and invariance in personality structure. *Psychological Review, 102,* 246–268.

Mitchell, T. R., Thompson, L., Peterson, E., & Cronk, R. (1997). Temporal adjustments in the evaluation of events: The "rosy view." *Journal of Experimental Social Psychology, 33,* 421–448.

Molenaar, P. C. M. (2004). A manifesto on psychology as idiographic science: Bringing the person back into scientific psychology—this time forever. *Measurement: Interdisciplinary Research and Perspectives, 2,* 201–218.

Murray, H. A. (1938). *Explorations in personality: A clinical and experimental study of fifty men of college age.* New York: Oxford University Press.

Murray, H. A., & Kluckhohn, C. (1948). Outline of a conception of personality. In C. Kluckhohn & H. A. Murray (Eds.), *Personality in nature, society, and culture* (pp. 3–32). New York: Knopf.

Murray, S. L., Holmes, J. G., & Griffin, D. W. (2003). Reflections on the self-fulfilling effects of positive illusions. *Psychological Inquiry, 14,* 289–295.

Neugarten, B. L., Havighurst, R. J., & Tobin, M. A. (1961). The measurement of life satisfaction. *Journal of Gerontology, 16,* 134–143.

Nesselroade, J. R (2002). Elaborating the differential in differential psychology. *Multivariate Behavioral Research, 37,* 543–561.

Neiss, M. B., Sedikides, C., & Stevenson, J. (2006). Genetic influences on level and stability of self-esteem. *Self and Identity, 5,* 247–266.

Nezlek, J. B., & Plesko, R. M. (2003). Affect-and self-based models of relationships between daily events and daily well-being. *Personality and Social Psychology Bulletin, 29,* 584–596.

Nisbett, R. E., & Ross, L. (1980). *Human inference: Strategies and shortcomings of social judgment.* Englewood Cliffs, NJ: Prentice-Hall.

Norem, J. K., & Cantor, N. (1986). Defensive pessimism: Harnessing anxiety as motivation. *Journal of Personality and Social Psychology, 51,* 1208–1217.

Norem, J. K., & Illingworth, K. S. S. (1993) Strategy dependent effects of reflecting on self and tasks: Some implications of optimism and defensive pessimism. *Journal of Personality and Social Personality, 65,* 822–835.

Oishi, S. (2000). Goals as cornerstones of subjective well-being: Linking individuals and cultures. In E. Diener & E. M. Suh (Eds.), *Cross-cultural psychology of subjective well-being* (pp.87–112). Boston: MIT Press.

Oishi, S. (2006). The concept of life satisfaction across cultures: An IRT analysis. *Journal of Research in Personality, 41,* 411–423.

Oishi, S. (2010). Culture and well-being: Conceptual and methodological issues. In E. Diener, J. F. Helliwell, & D. Kahneman, (Eds.), *International differences in well-being.* New York: Oxford University Press.

Oishi, S., & Diener, E. (2001). Goals, culture, and subjective well-being. *Personality and Social Psychology Bulletin, 27,* 1674–1682.

Oishi, S., Diener, E., Choi, D.W., Kim-Prieto, C., & Choi, I. (2007). The dynamics of daily events and well-being across cultures: When less is more. *Journal of Personality and Social Psychology, 93,* 685–698.

Oishi, S., Diener, E., Scollon, C. N., & Biswas-Diener, R. (2004). Cross-situational consistency of affective experiences across cultures. *Journal of Personality and Social Psychology, 86,* 460–472.

Oishi, S., Diener, E., Suh, E., & Lucas, R. E. (1999). Value as a moderator in subjective well-being. *Journal of Personality, 67,* 157–184.

Oishi, S., Kesebir, S., & Diener, E. (in press). Income inequality and happiness. *Psychological Science.*

Oishi, S., Kesebir, S., & Snyder, B. H (2009). Sociology: A lost connection in social psychology. *Personality and Social Psychology Review, 13,* 334–353.

Oishi, S., Rothman, A., J., Snyder, M., Su, J., Zehm, K., Hertel, A. W., et al. (2007). The socio-ecological model of pro-community action: The benefits of residential stability. *Journal of Personality and Social Psychology, 93,* 831–844.

Oishi, S., & Schimmack, U. (2010). Culture and well-being: A new inquiry into the psychological wealth of nations. *Perspectives on Psychological Science, 5,* 463–471.

Oishi, S., Schimmack, U., & Colcombe, S. (2003). The contextual and systematic nature of life satisfaction judgments. *Journal of Experimental Social Psychology, 39,* 232–247.

Oishi, S., Schimmack, U., & Diener, E. (2001). Pleasures and subjective well-being. *European Journal of Personality, 15,* 153–167.

Oishi, S., Schimmack, U., Diener, E., Kim-Prieto, C., Scollon, C. N., & Choi, D, W. (2007). The value-congruence model of memory for emotional experiences: An explanation for cultural differences in emotional self-reports. *Journal of Personality and Social Psychology, 93,* 897–905.

Olson, J. M., Vernon, P. A., Harris, J. A., & Jang, K. L. (2001). The heritability of attitudes: A study of twins. *Journal of Personality and Social Psychology, 80,* 845–860.

Pennebaker, J. W. (1997). Writing about emotional experiences as a therapeutic process. *Psychological Science, 8,* 162–166.

Pinquart, M., & Sörensen, S. (2000). Influences of socioeconomic status, social network, and competence on subjective well-being in later life: A meta-analysis. *Psychology and Aging, 15,* 187–224.

Ram, N., Chow, S.-M., Bowles, R. P., Wang, L., Grimn, K., Fujita, F., & Nesselroade, J. R. (2005). Examining interindividual differences in cyclicity of pleasant and unpleasant affects using spectral analysis and item response modeling. *Psychometrika, 70,* 773–790.

Reis, H. T., Clark, M. S., & Holmes, J. G. (2004). Perceived partner responsiveness as an organizing construct in the study of intimacy and closeness. D. J. Mashek, & A. P. Aron (Eds.), *Handbook of closeness and intimacy* (pp. 201–225). Mahwah, NJ: Erlbaum.

Reise, S. P., Widaman, K. F., & Pugh, R. H. (1993). Confirmatory factor analysis and item response theory: Two approaches for exploring measurement invariance. *Psychological Bulletin, 114,* 552–566.

Riemann, R., Angleitner, A., Borkenau, P., & Eid, M. (1998). Genetic and environmental sources of consistency and variability in positive and negative mood. *European Journal of Personality, 12,* 345–364.

Robinson, M.D. (2004). Personality as performance: Categorization tendencies and their correlates. *Current Directions in Psychological Science, 13,* 127–129.

Robinson, M. D., & Clore, G. L. (2002). Belief and feeling: Evidence for an accessibility model of emotional self-report. *Psychological Bulletin, 128,* 934–960.

Roysamb, E., Harris, J. R., Magnus, P., Vitterso, J., & Tambs, K. (2002). Subjective well-being: Sex-specific effects of genetic and environmental factors. *Personality and Individual Differences, 32,* 211–223.

Rusbult, C. E., Verette, J., Whitney, G. A., Slovik, L. F., & Lipkus, I. (1991). Accommodation processes in close relationships: Theory and preliminary empirical evidence. *Journal of Personality and Social Psychology, 60,* 53–78.

Ryan, R. M., & Deci, E. L. (2001). On happiness and human potentials: A review of research on hedonic and eudaimonic well-being. *Annual Review of Psychology, 52,* 141–166.

Ryan, R. M., & Frederick, C. M. (1997). On energy, personality, and health: Subjective vitality as a dynamic reflection of well-being. *Journal of Personality, 65,* 529–565.

Ryff, C. D. (1989). Happiness is everything, or is it? Exploration on the meaning of psychological well-being. *Journal of Personality and Social Psychology, 57,* 1069–1081.

Ryff, C. D., & Singer, B. (1998). The contours of positive human health. *Psychological Inquiry, 9,* 1–28.

Samejima, F. (1969). Estimation of latent ability using a response pattern of graded scores. *Psychometrika Monograph Supplement, 34,* 100.

Schimmack, U. (2008). The structure of subjective wellbeing. In M. Eid and R. J. Larsen (Eds.) *The science of subjective well-being* (pp. 97–123). New York: Guilford.

Schimmack, U., Bockenholt, U., & Reisenzein, R. (2002). Response styles in affect ratings: Making a mountain out of a molehill. *Journal of Personality Assessment, 78,* 461–483.

Schimmack, U., & Lucas, R. E. (2007). Marriage matters: Spousal similarity in life satisfaction. *Schmollers Jahrbuch, 127,* 1–7.

Schimmack U., & Oishi, S. (2005). Chronically accessible versus temporarily accessible sources of life satisfaction judgments. *Journal of Personality and Social Psychology, 89,* 395–406.

Schimmack, U., Oishi, S., Diener, E., & Suh, E. (2000). Facets of affective experiences: A framework for investigations of trait affect. *Personality and Social Psychology Bulletin, 26,* 655–668.

Schimmack, U., Radhakrishnan, P., Oishi, S., Dzokoto, V., & Ahadi, S. (2002). Culture, personality, and subjective well-being: Integrating process models of life satisfaction. *Journal of Personality and Social Psychology, 82,* 582–593.

Schkade, D. A., & Kahneman, D. (1998). Does living in California make people happy? A focusing illusion in judgments of life satisfaction. *Psychological Science, 9,* 340–346.

Schwartz, B., Ward, A., Monterosso, J., Lyubomirsky, S., White, K., & Lehman, D. R. (2002). Maximizing versus satisficing: Happiness is matter of choice. *Journal of Personality and Social Psychology, 83,* 1178–1197.

Schwarz, N. (1999). Self-reports: How the questions shape the answers. *American Psychologist, 54,* 93–105.

Schwarz, N., & Strack, F. (1999). Reports of subjective well-being: Judgmental processes and their methodological implications. In D. Kahneman, E. Diener, & N. Schwarz (Eds.), *Well-being: The foundations of hedonic psychology* (pp. 61–84). New York: Russell Sage.

Scollon, C. N., & Diener, E. (2006). Love, work, and changes in extraversion and neuroticism over time. *Journal of Personality and Social Psychology, 91,* 1152–1165.

Scollon, C. N., Diener, E., Oishi, S., & Biswas-Diener, R. (2005). An experience sampling and cross-cultural investigation of the relation between pleasant and unpleasant affect. *Cognition and Emotion, 19,* 27–52.

Seligman, M. E. P., Steen, T. A., Park, N., & Peterson, C. (2005). Positive psychology progress: Empirical validation of interventions. *American Psychologist, 60,* 410–421.

Sheldon, K. M. (2004). *Optimal human being: An integrated multi-level perspective.* Mahwah, NJ: Erlbaum.

Smyth, J. M. (1998). Written emotional expression: Effect sizes, outcome types, and moderating variables. *Journal of Consulting and Clinical Psychology, 66,* 174–184.

Snyder, M. (1993). Basic research and practical problems: The promise of a "functional" personality and social psychology. *Personality and Social Psychology Bulletin, 19,* 251–264.

Snyder, M. (2009). In the footsteps of Kurt Lewin: Practical theorizing, action research, and the psychology of social action. *Journal of Social Issues, 65,* 225–245.

Spotts, E. L., Lichtenstein, P., Pedersen, N., Neiderhiser, J. M., Hansson, K., Cederblad, M., et al. (2005). Personality and marital satisfaction: A behavioral genetic analysis. *European Journal of Personality, 19,* 205–227.

Steger, M. F., Frazier, P., Oishi, S., & Kaler, M. (2006). The Meaning in Life Questionnaire: Assessing the presence of and search for meaning in life. *Journal of Counseling Psychology, 53,* 80–93.

Strack, F., Martin, L. L., & Schwarz, N. (1988). Priming and communication: Social determinants of information use in judgments of life satisfaction. *European Journal of Social Psychology, 18,* 429–442.

Strack, F., Schwarz, N., & Gschneidinger, E. (1985). Happiness and reminiscing: The role of time perspective, affect, and mode of thinking. *Journal of Personality and Social Psychology, 49,* 1460–1469.

Stubbe, J. H., Posthuma, D., Boomsma, D. I., & De Geus, E. J. C. (2005). Heritability of life satisfaction in adults: A twin-family study. *Psychological Medicine, 35,* 1581–1588.

Suh, E. M. (2002). Culture, identity consistency, and subjective well-being. *Journal of Personality and Social Psychology, 83,* 1378–1391.

Suh, E., Diener, E., & Fujita, F. (1996). Events and subjective well-being: Only recent events matter. *Journal of Personality and Social Psychology, 70,* 1091–1102.

Suh, E., Diener, E., Oishi, S., & Triandis, H. C. (1998). The shifting basis of life satisfaction judgments across cultures: Emotions versus norms. *Journal of Personality and Social Psychology, 74,* 482–493.

Suls, J., Martin, R., & David, J. P. (1998). Person-environment fit and its limits: Agreeableness, neuroticism, and emotional reactivity to interpersonal conflicts. *Personality and Social Psychology Bulletin, 24,* 88–98.

Tamir, M. (2005). Don't worry, be happy? Neuroticism, trait-consistent affect regulation, and performance. *Journal of Personality and Social Psychology, 89,* 449–461.

Tellegen, A., Lykken, D. T., Bouchard, T. J., Wilcox, K. J., Segal, N. L., & Rich, S. (1988). Personality similarity in twins reared apart and together. *Journal of Personality and Social Psychology, 54,* 1031–1039.

Tesser, A. (1993). The importance of heritability in psychological research: The case of attitudes. *Psychological Review, 100,* 129–142.

Thomson, J. A. K. (1953). *The ethics of Aristotle: The* Nicomachean Ethics. London: Penguin.

Thorndike, E. L. (1936). The value of reported likes and dislikes for various experiences and activities as indications of personal traits. *Journal of Applied Psychology, 20,* 285–313.

Tidwell, M. O., Reis, H. T., & Shaver, P. R. (1996). Attachment, attractiveness, and social interaction: A diary study. *Journal of Personality and Social Psychology, 71,* 729–745.

Tov, W., & Diener, E. (2007). Culture and subjective well-being. In S. Kitayama, & D. Cohen (Eds.), *Handbook of cultural psychology* (pp. 691–713). New York: Guilford.

Tracy, J. L., Robins, R. W., & Sherman, J. W. (2009). The practice of psychological science: Searching for Cronbach's two streams in social-personality psychology. *Journal of Personality and Social Psychology, 96,* 1206–1225.

Tsai, J. L., Louie, J. Y., Chen, E. E., & Uchida, Y. (2007). Learning what feelings to desire: Socialization of ideal affect through children's storybooks. *Personality and Social Psychology Bulletin, 33,* 17–30.

Tsai, J. L., Miao, F. F., & Seppala, E. (2007). Good feelings in Christianity and Buddhism: Religious differences in ideal affect. *Personality and Social Psychology Bulletin, 33,* 409–421.

Uchida, Y., Kitayama, S., Mesquita, B., Reyes, J. A. S., & Morling, B. (2008). Is perceived emotional support beneficial? Well-being and health in independent and interdependent cultures. *Personality and Social Psychology Bulletin, 34,* 741–754.

Urry, H. L., Nitschke, J. B., Dolski, I., Jackson, D. C., Dalton, K. M., Mueller, C. J., et al. (2004). Making a life worth living: Neural correlates of well-being. *Psychological Science, 15,* 367–372.

Vaillant, G. E. (1977). *Adaptation to life.* Boston, MA: Little, Brown.

Van Boven, L., & Gilovich, T. (2003). To do or to have? That is the question. *Journal of Personality and Social Psychology, 85,* 1193–1202.

Vittersø, J., Biswas-Diener, R., & Diener, E (2005). The divergent meanings of life satisfaction: Item response modeling of the Satisfaction with Life Scale in Greenland and Norway. *Social Indicators Research, 74,* 327–348.

Vittersø, J., & Nilsen, F. (2002). The conceptual and relational structure of subjective well-being, neuroticism, and extraversion: Once again, neuroticism is the important predictor of happiness. *Social Indicators Research, 57,* 89–118.

Washburne, J. N. (1941). Factors related to the social adjustment of college girls. *Journal of Social Psychology, 13,* 281–289.

Watson, J. B. (1913). Psychology as the behaviorist views it. *Psychological Review, 20,* 158–177.

Watson, D., Clark, L. A., & Tellegen, A. (1984). Cross-cultural convergence in the structure of mood: A Japanese replication and a comparison with U.S. findings. *Journal of Personality and Social Psychology, 47,* 127–144.

Watson, D., Clark, L. A., & Tellegen, A. (1988). Development and validation of brief measures of positive and negative affect: The PANAS scales. *Journal of Personality and Social Psychology, 54,* 1063–1070.

Wessman, A. E., & Ricks, D. F. (1966). *Mood and personality.* New York: Holt, Rinehart, & Winston.

Wilson, T. D., & Gilbert, D. T. (2008). Explaining away: A model of affective adaptation. *Perspectives on Psychological Science, 5,* 370–386.

Wilson, T. D., Wheatley, T. P., Meyers, J. M., Gilbert, D. T., & Axsom, D. (2000). Focalism: A source of durability bias in affective forecasting. *Journal of Personality and Social Psychology, 78,* 821–836.

Wirtz, D., Kruger, J., Scollon, C. N., & Diener, E. (2003). What to do on spring break? The role of predicted, online, and remembered experience in future choice. *Psychological Science, 14,* 520–524.

Wyer, R. S., Jr., & Srull, T. K. (1989). *Memory and cognition in its social context.* Hillsdale, NJ: Erlbaum.

Zevon, M. A., & Tellegen, A. (1982). The structure of mood change: An idiographic/nomothetic analysis. *Journal of Personality and Social Psychology, 43,* 111–122.

Multiculturalism
Cultural, Social, and Personality Processes

Verónica Benet-Martínez

Abstract

This chapter discusses the psychological and societal processes involved in the phenomenon of multiculturalism. An emphasis is placed on reviewing and integrating relevant findings and theories stemming from cultural, personality, and social psychology. The chapter includes sections devoted to defining multiculturalism at the individual, group, and societal level, discussing the links between acculturation and multiculturalism, how to best operationalize and measure multicultural identity, the issue of individual differences in multicultural identity, and the possible psychological and societal benefits of multiculturalism. The chapter concludes with a discussion of future challenges and needed directions in the psychological study of multiculturalism.

Keywords: multiculturalism, multicultural, biculturalism, bicultural, diversity, intercultural, bicultural identity integration, identity

Multiculturalism is a fact of life for many people. The global increase in intercultural contact due to factors such as immigration, speed of travel and communication, and international corporate presence is difficult to ignore. Undoubtedly, multiculturalism and globalization influence how people see themselves and others, and how they organize the world around them. Take, for instance, U.S. President Barack Hussein Obama. Obama straddles countries and cultures (Hammack, 2010). The son of a Kenyan and an American, he studied the Quran in his youth and as an adult he was baptized. His multicultural background enables him to speak the language of a globalized world, in which people of diverse origins encounter each other and negotiate common meaning across shrinking cultural divides (Saleh, 2009). Obama exemplifies the word "multiculturalism" as a biracial individual from a multicultural family who has lived in various countries; also, several of his key advisors have also lived outside the United States (Bartholet & Stone, 2009), and almost half of his cabinet are racial or ethnic minorities

(Wolf, 2009). In fact, in his inaugural speech, Obama stated that multiculturalism is a national strength (Obama, 2009), and since then, he has deliberately set out to select a diverse cabinet, based on the premise that multicultural individuals have insights, skills, and unique psychological experiences that contribute to society (Nguyen & Benet-Martínez, 2010).

The prevalence and importance of multiculturalism has long been acknowledged in psychology (e.g., Hermans & Kempen, 1998; LaFromboise, Coleman, & Gerton, 1993), yet the phenomenon has been investigated empirically only in the last decade or so. However, the study of multiculturalism has exciting and transformative implications for social and personality psychology, as the issue of how individuals develop a sense of national, cultural, ethnic, and racial group membership becomes particularly meaningful in situations of cultural clashing, mixing, and integration (Baumeister, 1986; Deaux, 2006; Phinney, 1999). Furthermore, the individual and contextual factors that influence how an individual makes sense of his/her multicultural experiences provide personality psychologists with another window through which to study individual differences in identity and self-concept. In fact, as Phinney (1999) eloquently said, "increasing numbers of people find that the conflicts are not between different groups but between different cultural values, attitudes, and expectations *within themselves*" (p. 27, italics added).

The study of multiculturalism also affords unique methodological tools to social and personality psychologists. By virtue of having two or more cultures that can be independently manipulated, multicultural individuals give researchers a quasi-experimental design ideal for the study of how culture affects behavior (Hong, Morris, Chiu, & Benet-Martínez, 2000). In addition, previously identified cross-cultural differences can be replicated in experiments with multicultural individuals without the confounding effects (i.e., differences in SES, translation issues) that often characterize cross-national comparisons (Ramirez-Esparza, Gosling, Benet-Martínez, Potter, & Pennebaker, 2006; Sanchez-Burks et al., 2003).

With the increase of cultural diversity in academic, political, and media spheres, empirical research on multiculturalism has finally begun to appear in social and personality psychology journals. The main goal of this chapter is to review and integrate this research and propose an agenda for future studies. However, because multiculturalism issues are quite new to empirical social and personality psychology, this chapter also includes sections devoted to defining the constructs of multiculturalism and multicultural identity, summarizing the relevant work from the field of acculturation studies, and discussing how to best operationalize and measure multiculturalism (see also Hong, Wan, No, & Chiu, 2007).

Defining Multiculturalism: Individual, Intergroup, and Societal Levels

Who is multicultural? There are many definitions of multiculturalism, ranging from general (i.e., based on demographic characteristics) to psychologically specific conceptualizations (e.g., cultural identifications or orientations). Broadly speaking, those who are mixed-race and mixed-ethnic, those who have lived in more than one country (such as expatriates, international students, immigrants, refugees, and sojourners), those reared with at least one other culture in addition to the dominant mainstream culture (such as children of immigrants or colonized people), and those in intercultural relationships may all be considered multicultural (Berry, 2003; Padilla, 2006).[1] In the United States alone, multicultural individuals may include the 13% who are foreign-born, the 34% who are nonwhite, and the 20% who speak a language other than English at home (U.S. Census Bureau, 2006). High numbers of multicultural individuals (10% of the population by some estimates) can also be found in other nations where migration is strong (e.g., Canada, Australia, western Europe, Singapore) or where there is a history of colonization (e.g., Hong Kong).

Psychologically, there is no commonly agreed definition of multiculturalism. Loosely speaking, multiculturalism can be defined as the experience of having been exposed to and having internalized two or more cultures (Hong et al., 2000; Nguyen & Benet-Martínez, 2007).[2] More specifically, multicultural individuals are those who display multicultural competence, that is, display cultural behaviors such as language use, choice of friends, media preferences, value systems, and so forth, that are representative of two or more cultures (LaFromboise et al., 1993). Multicultural individuals are also those who self-label (e.g., "I am multicultural") or for whom group self-categorization (e.g., "I am American" and "I am Chinese"; "I am Chinese-American") reflects their cultural pluralism. Relatedly, multicultural *identity* is the condition of having attachments with and loyalties toward these different cultures (Benet-Martínez & Haritatos, 2005). Lastly, multicultural individuals can also be those who report acculturation attitudes supportive of an integration or biculturalism strategy (Berry, 2003; e.g., endorsing the statement "I prefer to have both national and ethnic friends").

Note then that multicultural identity is only one component (although perhaps the most important one) of the more complex and multidimensional notion of multiculturalism. That is, an individual who has been exposed to and has learned more than one culture is a multicultural person, but only when this individual expresses an attachment with these cultures can we say that the individual has a multicultural identity. This is because acquisition of knowledge from a new culture does not always produce identification with that culture (Hong et al., 2007). Thus multicultural identity involves a significant degree of identification with more than one culture; however, it does not presuppose similar degrees of identification with all the internalized cultures. Lastly, having a multicultural identity involves following the norms of more than one culture, or at least being cognizant of them (see later section on variations in multicultural identity); this premise is supported by social identity research showing that individuals who identify strongly (vs. weakly) with a culture are more likely to follow that culture's norms (Jetten, Postmes, & McAuliffe, 2002), and that for these individuals cultural norms have greater impact on behavioral intentions than personal attitudes (Terry, Hogg, & White, 1999).

Societal and Intergroup Levels

As described in Nguyen and Benet-Martínez (2010), the terms "multicultural" and "bicultural" are typically used to describe individuals, but they can also be used to describe nations and states (e.g., bicultural and bilingual Quebec, where Anglo- and Francophone cultures coexist), institutions and policies (e.g., multicultural education), and groups (e.g., multicultural teams). Although the term is recent, the concept of biculturalism dates back to the origins of modern Canada (1774, when British authorities allowed French Canadians full use of their language, system of civil law, and freedom to practice their Roman Catholicism). Biculturalism should not be confused with bilingualism (having fluency in two languages), although these terms are conceptually related since often (but not always) bicultural individuals and institutions are also bilingual (Grosjean, 1996; Lambert, 1978).[3]

Multicultural ideology and policies advocate that society and organizations should include and equally value distinct cultural groups (Fowers & Richardson, 1996). Although the term "multiculturalism" is typically used to acknowledge the presence of the distinct cultures of immigrant groups, sometimes it can also be applied to acknowledge the presence of indigenous peoples in colonized nations. One assumption behind the multicultural ideology is that public acceptance and recognition of one's culture and opportunities for multicultural interactions are crucial for self-worth and well-being (Burnet, 1995). Support for this argument is found in counseling (Sue & Sue, 2003), education (Banks & Banks, 1995), corporate (Plaut, Thomas, & Goren, 2009), and developmental contexts (Berry, Phinney, Sam, & Vedder, 2006; Yip, Seaton, & Sellers, 2006).

Multiculturalism has been formally adopted as an official policy in nations such as Canada, Australia, and the Netherlands, for reasons that vary from country to country. Multicultural policies influence the structures and decisions of governments to ensure that political and economic resources are allocated equitably to all represented cultural groups. Examples of government-endorsed multicultural policies are dual citizenship, government support for media outlets (e.g., newspapers, television, radio) in minority languages, support for cultural minority holidays, celebrations, and community centers, establishment of official multilingual policies, and acceptance of traditional and religious codes of dress and behavior in the public sphere (e.g., work, school).

Not all minority groups are perceived to deserve multicultural policies equally. Typically, multicultural recognition and rights are more easily given to "involuntary" groups (colonized people, descendents of slaves, refugees) than to immigrants. Supposedly, these immigrants would have waived their demands and rights by voluntary leaving their country of origin. In other words, multicultural policies tend to be less supported in relation to immigrant groups than in relation to involuntary minorities (Verkuyten, 2007). In fact, work closely examining multicultural attitudes and their effects from both the minority and majority perspectives reveals some interesting moderating factors (see Verkuyten, 2007, and Berry, 2006, for excellent reviews). For instance, minorities (e.g., Turkish, Moroccan in the Netherlands) are more likely to endorse multiculturalism than members of an ethnic majority group (e.g., Dutch). Cross-national data on multiculturalism validates this finding (Deaux, Reid, Martin, & Bikmen, 2006; Schalk-Soekar, 2007; Verkuyten & Martinovic, 2006; Wolsko et al., 2006). Further, in-group identification is positively related to endorsement of multiculturalism for minority individuals, while this link is negative among majority individuals (Verkuyten & Martinovic, 2006). The fact that multiculturalism appeals more to ethnic minority groups than to majority group members is not surprising, given that the gains of this policy are more obvious to the former group (Berry, 2006; Berry & Kalin, 1995; Verkuyten & Thijs, 1999). Studies have also found that minorities' endorsement of multiculturalism is linked to positive ingroup evaluation, while for majorities endorsement of multiculturalism is related to positive outgroup views (Verkuyten, 2005). Lastly, endorsement of multiculturalism is positively associated to self-esteem for both minority and majority individuals who identify strongly with their ethnic group (Verkuyten, 2009). This suggests that multicultural recognition provides a normative context in which both majorities and minorities with high levels of ethnic identification can feel good about themselves (Verkuyten & Thijs, 2004).

A promising line of research conducted by Van der Zee and colleagues (e.g., Van der Zee, Atsma, & Brodbeck, 2004; Van der Zee & Van der Gang, 2007) has been examining the interactive role between individual factors such as personality (i.e., traits related to multicultural effectiveness, Van der Zee & Van Oudenhoven, 2000) and social identity, and contextual pressures in how individuals respond to situations involving cultural diversity. This work has shown, for instance, that individuals high in extraversion and initiative respond more favorably to intercultural situations, but these differences disappear under threat (Van der Zee & Van der Gang, 2007). This finding suggests that the link between social traits and success in culturally diverse contexts is not driven by a special ability to deal with the potential threat of cultural differences but rather by the social stimulation afforded by culturally diverse situations. The study also showed that individual differences in neuroticism are linked to reactions toward cultural diversity only under conditions of threat. Given the increasingly global nature of today's workforce, this work promises to be very informative with regard to which competencies minority and majority members need to possess to facilitate constructive intercultural interactions.

Not surprisingly, multiculturalism is a controversial issue in some societies. Some political segments within the United States and some European nations view multiculturalism as a policy that promotes group stereotyping and negative outgroup feelings and undermines national unity, social integration, and even security (Huntington, 2004). Alternatives to multiculturalism propone, explicitly or implicitly, policies supportive of "monoculturalism" (normative cultural unity or homogeneity), "assimilation" (the belief that cultural minorities should abandon their original culture and adopt the majority culture), or "nativism" (return to the original settlers' cultural traits—e.g., English, Protestantism, and American liberalism in the case of the United States). Underlying these views is the belief that the majority-based macroculture is substantive (i.e., essential), foundational (i.e., original and primary), and that it provides the moral center for society; the legitimacy of this macroculture thus is always prior to the social phenomenon that may potentially shape it.

Unfortunately, most popular discussions in favor/ against multiculturalism involve an implicit dichotomization of complex political and psychological issues: opposition between universalism and particularism, between unity and fragmentation, between right and left (Hartman & Gerteis, 2005). Recent

multiculturalism theory departs from this aforementioned unidimensional space and makes a distinction between the social and the cultural dimensions, thereby identifying three distinct types of multicultural ideologies: cosmopolitanism, fragmented pluralism, and interactive pluralism (Hartman & Gerteis, 2005). A review of each these three multiculturalism approaches reveals issues and constructs that are highly relevant to social psychology, and the study social identity and intergroup dynamics in particular. For instance, the *cosmopolitan* approach recognizes the social value of diversity, but it is skeptical about the obligations and constraints that group membership and societal cohesion can place on individuals (Hartman & Gerteis, 2005). In a way, this approach defends cultural diversity to the extent it supports and facilitates individual rights and freedoms (Bilbeny, 2007). Thus, the cosmopolitan approach supports a strong macrosocial boundary and weak internal groups and emphasizes the permeability of cultural group membership and boundaries (Hollinger, 1995). Here cultural group qualities are neutralized rather than negated (as in the assimilationist approach), and policies are to ensure that every individual is free to choose her or his place in the ethnic mosaic. An example of this type of "weak" group identification is the white ethnic identity of many Americans who self-identify as "Irish American" or "Italian American." Note that these group affiliations do not imply adopting a separatist identity or even strong identity, because there is no societal pressure to choose between this and other forms of cultural/ethnic identifications, and also because there is nothing about being "Irish" that is particularly in tension with being "American" (Hartman & Gerteis, 2005).

The *fragmented pluralism* approach, on the other hand, endorses weaker macrosocial boundaries but very strong internal groups and boundaries given that cultural group membership is seen as essential rather than partial and voluntaristic (Young, 2000). Structurally, this approach is the most opposite to assimilation. In fragmented pluralism the focus is on the recognition and maintenance of group rights and distinctive group cultures (e.g., separate institutions or practices), and the state is seen mainly as a tool for cohesion given its role as a force mediating between different group claims and value systems, which at times may be divergent or in some cases directly opposed. The phenomenon of "segmented assimilation" described by the sociologists Portes and Rumbaut (2001), can be seen as evidence for the existence of fragmented pluralism in the United

States: Assimilation into mainstream society by immigrants and their descendents is uneven due to the fact that different groups are available to which the immigrants may assimilate into (e.g., majority culture middle class, urban underclass) and to the fact that these different groups afford different opportunities to the immigrant groups. Lastly, the *interactive pluralism* approach, like the fragmented pluralism view, also prioritizes the role of groups, but it mainly stresses groups-in-interaction. This approach sees group interactions as essential, not only because group interactions facilitate societal cohesion and harmony but also because from these interactions a new and constantly redefined macroculture emerges (Alexander, 2001; Taylor, 2001). That is, social boundaries and moral order are produced in a democratic manner through the interaction of groups, and as cultural groups and their interactions change, the nature of the macroculture itself changes. Because this dynamic and more complex macroculture represents the complexity and reality of *all* groups, it is thus is more easily recognized and valued by all. This view contrasts with cosmopolitanism or fragmented pluralism, where the macroculture tends to be thinner and essentially procedural in nature.

The above constructs (macro- and group-culture) and processes (group interaction, permeability of cultural group membership and boundaries, procedural vs. substantive views of macroculture) are highly relevant to some well-known social psychological work. For instance, work on the common group identity model (Gaertner, Dovidio, Nier, Ward, & Baker, 1999), social identity complexity (Roccas & Brewer, 2002), group identity dimensionality (Roccas, Sagiv, Schwartz, Halevy, & Eidelson, 2008), procedural justice (Huo, 2003), and system justification theory (Jost & Banaji, 1994) speaks to some of the issues and processes underlying the above multiculturalism modes. However, the psychological validity, viability, and consequentiality of each of the models of multiculturalism reviewed above remains untested; this is an important gap that social psychology is in an ideal position to fill, given its theoretical and methodological richness.

Acculturation and Multiculturalism

Multiculturalism and acculturation are tightly intertwined, with multi/biculturalism being one of four outcomes of the acculturation process. Traditional views of acculturation (the process of learning or adapting to a new culture) asserted that to acculturate means to assimilate—that is, adopting the new or dominant culture requires rejecting one's ethnic or original culture (Gordon, 1964). In other words, acculturation originally was conceptualized as a unidimensional, one-directional, and irreversible process of moving toward the new mainstream culture and away from the original ethnic culture (Trimble, 2003). However, a wealth of acculturation studies conducted in the last 25 years (see Sam & Berry, 2006, for a review), supports acculturation as a bidimensional, two-directional, multidomain complex process, in which assimilation into the mainstream culture is not the only way to acculturate. In other words, equating acculturation with assimilation is simply inaccurate.

The bidimensional model of acculturation is based on the premise that acculturating individuals have to deal with two central issues, which comprise the two cultural orientations of acculturation (Berry, 2003): (1) the extent to which they are motivated or allowed to retain identification and involvement with the culture of origin, now the nonmajority, ethnic culture; and (2) the extent to which they are motivated or allowed to identify with and participate in the mainstream, dominant culture. The negotiation of these two central issues results in four distinct acculturation positions (see left side of Figure 25.1): assimilation (involvement and identification with the dominant culture only), integration/biculturalism (involvement and identification with both cultures), separation (involvement and identification with the ethnic culture only), or marginalization (lack of involvement and identification with either culture; see Rudmin, 2003, for a thorough discussion of this strategy). Empirical work on the these four acculturation attitudes or strategies reveals that, at least at the individual level, the most common strategy used by immigrant and cultural minorities is integration/biculturalism, followed by separation, assimilation, and marginalization (Berry et al., 2006; Sam & Berry, 2006). Further, there is now robust evidence supporting the psychometric validity of the multidimensional model of acculturation and its advantages over unidimensional models in predicting a wide array of outcomes (Flannery, Reise, & Yu, 2001; Ryder, Allen, & Paulhus, 2000).

Cross-national acculturation studies have found a zero or even positive association between national/mainstream identity and ethnic identity in settler countries such as the United States ($r = .15$), Canada (.09), or New Zealand (.32), which have a long tradition of immigration (see Table 4.1 in Phinney,

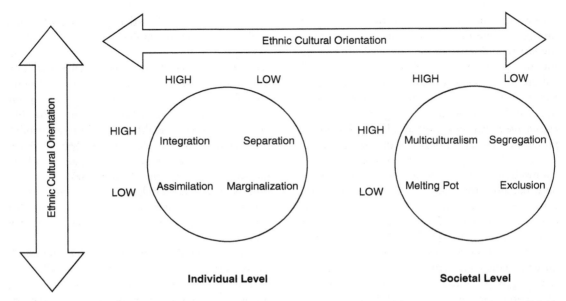

Fig. 25.1 Acculturation and multiculturalism at the individual versus societal levels. Adapted from Berry (2003) and reprinted from Nguyen and Benet-Martínez (2010).

Berry, Vedder, & Liebkind, 2006). However, this association is often moderately negative in nonsettler countries such as France (-.13), Germany (-.28), and the Netherlands (-.27) (Phinney et al., 2006). This pattern of associations speaks to the prevalence of multicultural identities across countries, which may result from the interaction of two factors: the climate of the receiving country (e.g., settler vs. nonsettler) and the predominant immigrant group (e.g., Turkish in Europe vs. Asian and Latin groups in the settler societies).

CULTURAL FRAME-SWITCHING
Additional support for the idea that individuals can simultaneously hold two or more cultural orientations is provided by recent sociocognitive experimental work showing that multicultural individuals shift between their different cultural orientations in response to cultural cues, a process called *cultural frame-switching* (CFS; Hong et al., 2000; Verkuyten & Pouliasi, 2006).

Multicultural individuals' ability to engage in CFS has been documented in multiple behavioral domains such as attribution (Benet-Martínez, Leu, Lee, & Morris, 2002; Cheng, Lee, & Benet-Martínez, 2006; Hong et al., 2000; Verkuyten & Pouliasi, 2002), personality self-views (Ramirez-Esparza, Gosling, Benet-Martínez, & Pennebaker, 2006; Ross, Xun, & Willson, 2002; Verkuyten & Pouliasi, 2006), ethnic identity (Verkuyten & Pouliasi, 2002), emotional experience (Perunovic, Heller, & Rafaeli,

2007), self-construals (Gardner, Gabriel, & Lee, 1999; Kemmelmeier & Cheng, 2004; Lechuga, 2008), values (Fu, Chiu, Morris, & Young, 2007; Verkuyten & Pouliasi, 2006), cooperation (Wong & Hong, 2005), autobiographical memory (Bender & Ng, 2009), and decision-making (Briley, Morris, & Simonson, 2005) among others. Further, the existence of dual dynamic culture-specific meaning systems among multiculturals has been demonstrated both at the explicit (Pouliasi & Verkuyten, 2007) and implicit level (Devos, 2006).

Note that CFS is not merely a knee-jerk response to cultural cues. In order for a particular cultural cue to influence behavior, the relevant cultural schemas have to be cognitively *available* (i.e., the individual has internalized values, norms, attitudes, and emotional associations relevant to that culture), cognitively *accessible* (the schemas have been recently activated by explicit or implicit contextual cues), and *applicable* to the situation (Hong et al., 2000; Hong, Benet-Martínez, Morris, & Chiu, 2003).[4]

Although CFS is often unconscious and automatic (like a bilingual individual switching languages depending on the audience), it does not always have to be. Individuals going through acculturation may to some extent manage the CFS process by controlling the accessibility of cultural schemas. For instance, immigrants desiring to adapt quickly to the new culture often surround themselves with symbols and situations that prime the meaning system of the host culture. Conversely, immigrants and expatriates desiring to keep alive their original ways of thinking and feeling— that is, desiring to maintain the accessibility of constructs from their home culture, often surround themselves with stimuli priming that culture (e.g., ethnic food, art, and music) (Sedikides, Wildschut, Routledge, Arndt & Zhou, 2009). These active processes of priming oneself may help multicultural individuals in their ongoing effort to negotiate and express their cultural identities (Hong et al., 2000).

The CFS processes described above can also be understood as a form of multicultural "identity performance" (Wiley & Deaux, 2011). Identity performance involves "the purposeful expression (or suppression) of behaviors relevant to those norms conventionally associated with a salient social identity" (Klein, Spears, & Reicher, 2007, p. 30). According to this framework, multicultural individuals do not passively react to cultural cues; rather they actively manage their identity presentation in response to the type of audience and macrocontext (e.g., presence of members from one culture or the other, or both), and the categorization (e.g., low vs. high status) and treatment received by this audience, thus behaving in ways designed to elicit recognition or confirmation of their important identities (Barreto, Spears, Ellemers, & Shahinper, 2003; Wiley & Deaux, 2011). For instance, some research shows that when Asian American individuals are in situations where their "Americanness" is being questioned (because of their appearance, race, language, or norms), they react to American cues with behaviors that assert and reinforce "American" identity practices—for example, by listing more U.S. television shows and advertising an American lifestyle (Cheryan & Monin, 2005). Interestingly, none of these reactions seems to bring higher identification and pride with American culture or lower identification and pride with being Asian; this would support the identity performance view that CFS and behaviors such as the above involve strategic identity presentations rather than fundamental changes in identity evaluation and meaning. In short, multicultural identities are expressed differently depending on the opportunities afforded (and denied) by a given context, including other people's (actual and anticipated) evaluations, expectations, and behaviors (see Figure 1 in Wiley & Deaux, 2011).

ACCULTURATION DOMAINS AND LEVELS

Lastly, it is important to point out that the acculturation perspective does not presuppose that multicultural individuals internalize and use their different cultures globally and uniformly (Nguyen & Benet-Martínez, 2010). Acculturation changes can take place in many different domains of life: language use or preference, social affiliation, communication style, cultural identity and pride, and cultural knowledge, beliefs, and values (Zane & Mak, 2003); and acculturation changes in some of these domains may occur independently of changes in other components. For instance, a Japanese American bicultural individual may endorse Anglo-American culture behaviorally and linguistically and yet be very Japanese (ethnic culture) in terms of her/ his values and attitudes. Similarly, a Mexican American bicultural individual can behave in ways that are predominantly Mexican (e.g., speak mostly Spanish, live in a largely Mexican neighborhood) and yet display great pride in and attitudinal attachment to American culture. In fact, some recent acculturation work suggests that, independently of how much the mainstream culture is internalized and practiced, some immigrants and their descendents adhere to the ethnic cultural values even more strongly than members of their home country, probably because they can become gradually "encapsulated" within the norms and values of an earlier era in their homeland, (Kim-Jo, Benet-Martínez, & Ozer, 2010; Kosmitzki, 1996). What might drive this *cultural encapsulation* phenomenon? First, when immigrant groups arrive to a new country, they bring with them the values and norms of their home culture *at that time*. As time passes, the home culture may undergo change (e.g., modernization, globalization), but immigrants continue to transmit this original cultural values and norms they brought with them (Matsumoto, 2000). Second, as immigrants' multicultural contacts with both the majority and other minority members increase, cultural clash and the possibility of cultural assimilation (particularly for their children) become more real; therefore, reactive (conscious or unconscious) behaviors, motives, or cognitive associations that reflect higher salience and strengthening of the original home culture may arise in response (ethnic cultural reaffirmation effect; Bond & Yang, 1982; Kosmitzki, 1996).

The drivers and outcomes of acculturation (and its multiculturalism mode) are not constant but rather dynamic and vary across time and local and national contexts (Schwartz & Unger, 2010). As seen above, these forces may operate differently depending on the immigrant group and receiving society. Lastly, it is important to acknowledge that acculturation is simultaneously interpersonal, intrapersonal (see this chapter's section on individual differences in multicultural identity), and contextually influenced (Schwartz & Unger, 2010).

Thus far, the discussion of acculturation has been at the individual level, but acculturation is also tied to multiculturalism at the societal level. As depicted in the right side of Figure 25.1, at the societal level, there are also four strategies corresponding to the four individual acculturation strategies (Berry, 2003). Countries with public policies that promote the assimilation of acculturating individuals are described as melting pots. Those that encourage separation are referred to as segregationist, and those that promote marginalization are labeled exclusionary (see also previous section, where I reviewed assimilation views and three possible multiculturalism approaches described by Hartman & Gerteis, 2005). Most importantly, national policies supporting the integration/biculturalism strategy are considered multicultural (Ward & Masgoret, 2008). For example, Canada's multicultural policies encourage ethnic and cultural groups to maintain, develop, and share their cultures with others as well as to accept and interact with other groups (Berry, 1984). Although acculturating individuals by and large prefer the bicultural or integration strategy, in reality, most host countries are melting pots, encouraging the assimilation of acculturating individuals into the dominant culture (Van Oudenhoven, Ward, & Masgoret, 2006). Consequently, when national policies and dominant groups' acculturation attitudes do not match with acculturating individuals' strategies, conflicts and problems in intergroup relations may arise (Bourhis, Moïse, Perreault, & Senécal, 1997; Jasinskaja-Lahti, Liebkind, Horenczyk, & Schmitz, 2003). Thus, public policies regarding acculturation and multiculturalism undoubtedly can affect intercultural relations within a country, especially as changing global migration patterns diversify many nations around the world.

Multicultural Identity: Operationalization and Measurement

Psychological acculturation, and the narrower constructs of biculturalism and multiculturalism have been operationalized and measured in a variety of ways, including unidimensional scales, bidimensional scales (e.g., median-split, addition, multiplication, and subtraction methods), direct measures of acculturation strategies, cultural identification question(s), or simple demographic questions. An exhaustive review of the available instruments and theoretical and psychometric issues involved in measuring biculturalism (and acculturation) is beyond the scope of this paper (see Arends-Tóth & van de Vijver, 2006; Zane & Mak, 2003; for excellent reviews). Accordingly, I provide instead a practical and brief summary of the available approaches and their pros and cons.

Early attempts at measuring biculturalism relied on bipolar, single-dimension scales that explicitly or implicitly reflected a unidirectional view of acculturation. In this framework, low scores or the starting point of the scale typically reflected separation, and high scores or the other end of the scale reflected assimilation, with biculturalism being tapped by middle scores or the midpoint of the scale (e.g., Cuéllar, Harris, & Jasso, 1980; Rotheram-Borus, 1990; Suinn, Rickard-Figueroa, Lew, & Vigil, 1987). These unidimensional scales should be avoided because they equate involvement and identification with one culture to a lack of involvement and identification with the other culture. In addition, these scales confound biculturalism and marginalization. For example, a scale item may be "Whom do you associate with?" and the response choices may be labeled with 1 = *mostly individuals from the ethnic culture*, 2 = *individuals from both the ethnic and dominant cultures equally*, 3 = *mostly individuals from the dominant culture*. A bicultural individual would select "2" because he/she has many friends from both cultures, but a marginalized individual may also select "2" but because his/her lack of socialization with members from each culture is similar.

With the increased adoption of the bidimensional model of acculturation came an increase in the number of bidimensional scales, where involvement with ethnic and dominant cultures is measured in two separate multi-item scales. With this method, biculturalism can be operationalized in different ways. Typically, bicultural individuals are those who have scores above the median (e.g., Ryder et al., 2000; Tsai, Ying, & Lee, 2000) or midpoint (e.g., Donà & Berry, 1994) on both cultural orientations. More recently, cluster analyses (e.g., Lee, Sobal, & Frongillo, 2003) and latent class analyses (e.g., Stevens, Pels, Vollebergh, & Crijnen, 2004) have also been used to create categories of acculturation strategies, including the integration or bicultural strategy. This typological approach allows researchers to differentiate bicultural individuals from other acculturating types (assimilated, separated, or marginalized) but does not provide a biculturalism score. Other, nontypological ways of operationalizing biculturalism when using bidimensional scales are to add the two cultural orientation subscale scores (e.g., Cuéllar, Arnold, & Maldonado, 1995) or combine them into an interaction term (Birman, 1998) so that low and high scores represent low and high level of biculturalism respectively. One caveat of these last two methods is the difficulty in differentiating between individuals who have medium scores on both cultural scales and those who score very high on one scale and low on the other. Lastly, some researchers have used a method where scores on the two cultural orientation scales are subtracted from another, so that scores close to zero denote biculturalism (Szapocznik, Kurtines, & Fernandez, 1980). This approach is not recommended because, like unidimensional measurement, it makes bicultural and marginalized individuals indistinguishable from each other. Obviously, two key advantages of these multidimensional approaches are that the cultures of interest (e.g., ethnic, mainstream, and religious cultures), regardless of their number, can be independently assessed, and that their measurement can be tailored to particular acculturating groups (e.g., mixed-race individuals, sojourners, etc.).[5]

Some researchers prefer to measure the acculturation strategies directly (e.g., Berry, Kim, Power, Young, & Bujaki, 1989). These instruments typically include four scales with statements capturing favorable attitudes toward the integration (biculturalism), assimilation, separation, and marginalization strategies. Because each individual receives a score on each of these acculturation strategies, a bicultural individual would be someone whose highest score is on the integration subscale. This widely used approach has some advantages over traditional acculturation scales (e.g., it allows us to measure the construct of biculturalism *attitudes* directly) but it suffers from some nontrivial conceptual and psychometric limitations (e.g., low score reliabilities, lack of scale independence; see Kang, 2006; Rudmin, 2003; Schwartz & Zamboanga, 2008; Zane & Mak, 2003; for reviews).

When time or reading levels are compromised, researchers may choose to measure biculturalism with one or two questions. For instance, bicultural individuals can be those who self-identify with a hyphenated label (e.g., Persian-American) rather than an ethnic (e.g., Persian) or a national (e.g., American) label, those who endorse the label "bicultural" (vs. "monocultural"), or those who score above the midpoint on two single items stating "I feel/am U.S. American" and "I feel/am Chinese"

(e.g., Benet-Martínez & Haritatos, 2005). Lastly, I should warn against the common practice of using demographic variables such as generational status, legal residence, or linguistic ability and preference, as a proxy for psychological acculturation (e.g., Buriel, Calzada, & Vasquez, 1982). As mentioned earlier, bicultural involvement and identification can occur at different rates for different life domains, for different individuals, and for different cultural groups, and demographic variables seem to be poor to modest predictors of these changes (Phinney, 2003; Schwartz, Pantin, Sullivan, Prado, & Szapocznik, 2006).

Individual Differences in Multicultural Identity

> I had been rowing back and forth, in a relentless manner, between two banks of a wide river. Increasingly, what I wanted was to be a burning boat in the middle of the water, visible to both shores yet indecipherable in my fury.
> *lê thi diem thúy* (2003)

> I am not half of anything. My identity has no boundaries, nor do my experiences. Because I am bicultural, it does not mean that I'm lacking anything. On the contrary, I like to think that I have the best of both worlds. I like to think that I have more.
> *Livingston* (2003)

As the above quotes show, the process of negotiating multiple cultural identities is complex and multifaceted. A careful review of the early (and mostly qualitative) work on this topic in the acculturation (e.g., Padilla, 1994; Phinney & Devich-Navarro, 1997) and popular (e.g., Chavez, 1994; O'Hearn, 1998) literatures reveals that multicultural individuals often talk about their multiple cultural attachments in complicated ways, including both positive and negative terms. Multiculturalism can be associated with feelings of pride, uniqueness, and a rich sense of community and history, while also bringing to mind identity confusion, dual expectations, and value clashes. Further, multicultural individuals often deal differently with the implications of cultural and racial stereotypes and the pressures for loyalties and certain behaviors coming from their different cultural communities (LaFromboise et al., 1993). An important issue, then, is how particular personality dispositions, contextual pressures, and acculturation and demographic variables impact the process of multicultural identity formation and the meanings associated with this experience.

Although most acculturating individuals use the integration/biculturalism strategy (Berry et al., 2006), research on acculturation has almost exclusively focused on individual differences *across* acculturation strategies rather than *within* acculturation strategies. Yet, not all bicultural individuals are alike. Early theoretical work on this issue is worth reviewing, even if briefly. In a seminal review of the biculturalism phenomenon, LaFromboise et al. (1993) described two biculturalism modes: *alternation* and *fusion*. Alternating bicultural individuals switch their behaviors in response to situational cultural demands, whereas fused bicultural individuals are oriented to a third emerging culture that is distinct from each of their two cultures (e.g., Chicano culture). Birman (1994) expanded on LaFromboise et al.'s (1993) framework to describe four types of bicultural individuals: *blended* (i.e., fused), *instrumental* (individuals behaviorally oriented to both cultures but identified with neither), *integrated* (individuals behaviorally oriented to both cultures but identified with only their ethnic culture), and *explorers* (behaviorally oriented to the dominant culture but identified with only their ethnic culture). Phinney and Devich-Navarro's (1997) qualitative and quantitative study sought to empirically integrate Berry's (2003), LaFromboise et al.'s (1993), and Birman's (1994) conceptual models of biculturalism. This study identified two bicultural types which were given labels similar to those in LaFromboise et al.'s study: *blended biculturals*— whose narratives emphasized identification with a combination of the two cultures more than with each culture separately, and *alternating biculturals*— who emphasized situational differences in how they saw themselves culturally.

These researchers are credited with calling attention to the experience of biculturalism and for advancing this area of research; however, a conceptual limitation of the above typologies is their confounding of identity and behavioral markers. Specifically, whereas the labels "blended" and "fused" refer to identity-related aspects of the bicultural experience (e.g., seeing oneself as Asian American or Chicano), the label "alternating" refers to the behavioral domain, that is, the ability to engage in cultural frame-switching (Benet-Martínez et al., 2002). Naturally, individuals' subjective experience of their bicultural identity and their bicultural behavior/competencies do not have to map onto each other (Roccas & Brewer, 2002; Boski, 2008). For instance, a bicultural individual may have a blended or *fused* identity (e.g., someone who

is sees him/herself as a product of both Jewish and American cultures and accordingly identifies as Jewish American) and also *alternate* (between speaking mainstream English and Yiddish depending on the context; i.e., frame-switch). Thus researchers should be aware that the two labels "blended" and "alternating" do not tap different types of bicultural individuals but rather different components of the bicultural experience (i.e., identity in the case of "fused" and behaviors in the case of "alternating").

BICULTURAL IDENTITY INTEGRATION (BII)
After an extensive review and synthesis of the empirical and qualitative acculturation and multiculturalism literature, Benet-Martínez et al. (2002) proposed the theoretical construct of BII as a framework for investigating individual differences in bicultural identity organization. BII captures the degree to which "biculturals perceive their mainstream and ethnic cultural identities as compatible and integrated vs. oppositional and difficult to integrate" (Benet-Martínez et al., 2002, p. 9). As an individual difference variable, BII thus focuses on bicultural individuals' subjective perceptions of managing dual cultural identities (i.e., how they cognitively and affectively organize this experience). The emphasis here is on *subjective* (i.e., the perception and experience of) cultural overlap and compatibility because, as was found in a study of over 7,000 acculturating adolescents in 13 countries, objective differences between ethnic and host cultures do not seem to relate to adjustment (Berry et al., 2006).

Bicultural individuals with high BII tend to see themselves as part of a hyphenated culture (or even part of a combined, emerging "third" culture), and find the two cultures largely compatible and easy to integrate. Bicultural individuals with low BII, on the other hand, tend to see themselves as living "in-between cultures" and report seeing the two cultures as largely conflictual and disparate. Interestingly, high and low BIIs have consistently emerged as similar in their endorsement of Berry's integrative acculturation strategy (Benet-Martínez, Lee, & Leu, 2006; Benet-Martínez et al., 2002) and in basic demographic variables such as years spent in the United States and age of migration; however, compared with high BIIs, low BIIs tend to be less proficient in English and less identified with American culture. This pattern underscores competence in the host, majority culture as a key component of BII.

In summary, bicultural individuals high and low on BII identify with both mainstream (e.g., American) and ethnic (e.g., Chinese) cultures but differ in their ability to create a synergistic, integrated cultural identity. Although no construct in the existing literature captures all the nuances of BII, a few acculturation and ethnic minority theorists have discussed particular acculturation experiences and outcomes that seem to relate (if only partially) to the identity integration versus opposition continuum defined by BII. Examples of these constructs are: "identity synthesis" (Schwartz, 2006), "blendedness" (Padilla, 1994; Phinney & Devich-Navarro, 1997), versus "cultural homelessness" (Vivero & Jenkins, 1999), and "oppositional identities" (Cross, 1995; Ogbu, 1993).

In their first study of BII, Benet-Martínez and her colleagues (Benet-Martínez et al., 2002) demonstrated the psychological relevance of this individual difference variable by showing that variations in BII moderate the process of cultural frame-switching. Specifically, Chinese-American biculturals high on BII (those who perceive their cultural identities as compatible) exhibited culturally congruent behavior when presented with external cues associated with one of their cultural backgrounds (e.g., made stronger external attributions to an ambiguous social event after being primed with Chinese icons, and made stronger internal attributions to the same event after seeing American icons). However, Chinese-American biculturals low on BII (those who perceive their cultural identities to be in opposition), behaved in *non*culturally congruent ways when exposed to these same cues. Specifically, low BIIs exhibited Chinese-congruent behaviors (i.e., external attributions) in response to American cues and American-congruent behaviors (internal attributions) in response to Chinese cues. In other words, low BIIs exhibited a type of "behavioral reactance" that the sociocognitive literature describes as a contrast or reverse priming effect (Dijksterhuis et al., 1998).

The above contrastive attributional responses displayed by biculturals with low levels of BII have since then been replicated (Cheng, Lee, & Benet-Martínez, 2006; Zou, Morris, & Benet-Martínez, 2008), and a recent study shows these effects also in the domain of personality self-views (Mok & Morris, 2009). As discussed in Benet-Martínez et al. (2002), the prime-inconsistent behavior of low BIIs is supported by academic and popular depictions of cultural clash (e.g., Ogbu, 2008; Roth, 1969), where inner cultural conflict is often described as leading to behavioral and/or affective "reactance" against the cultural expectations embedded in particular situations. For instance, in Roth's novel, the conflicted bicultural protagonist finds himself feeling and acting particularly Jewish when traveling to the Midwest, and feeling/acting conspicuously American when visiting Israel.[6]

Research on BII reports a positive association between BII and (1) psychological well-being, even after controlling for trait neuroticism (Chen, Benet-Martínez, & Bond, 2008; Downie et al., 2004); (2) creative performance (Cheng, Sanchez-Burks, & Lee, 2008); (3) having larger and more richly interconnected social networks (Mok, Morris, Benet-Martínez, & Karakitapoglu-Aygun, 2007); (4) higher perceived similarity between one's minority and majority cultural ingroups (Miramontez, Benet-Martínez, & Nguyen, 2008); and (6) preference for culturally blended persuasive appeals (Lau-Gesk, 2003).

Recent work on BII has also shown that BII is not a unitary construct, as initially suggested in earlier work (e.g., Benet-Martínez et al., 2002). Instead, BII seems to involve two relatively independent psychological constructs, *cultural harmony* versus conflict and *cultural blendedness* versus distance, each representing unique and separate aspects of the dynamic intersection between mainstream and ethnic cultural identities within bicultural individuals (Benet-Martínez & Haritatos, 2005). Cultural harmony versus conflict captures the degree of harmony versus tension or clash felt between the two cultural orientations (e.g., "I find it easy to balance both Chinese and American cultures" vs. "I feel caught between the two cultures"). Cultural blendedness versus distance, on the other hand, captures the degree of overlap versus dissociation or compartmentalization perceived between the two cultural orientations (e.g., "I feel part of a combined culture" vs. "I am simply a Chinese who lives in the United states"). (See Table 2 in Benet-Martínez & Haritatos [2005] for original items and their factor structure, and Table 25.1 in this chapter for the newly expanded Bicultural Identity Integration Scale—Version 2: BIIS-2.)

The relative psychometric independence of BII's components of cultural harmony and blendedness (correlations between the two scales range between .30 and .40) suggests that these two constructs are formative—that is, causal—rather than reflective (i.e., effect) indicators of BII (Bollen & Lennox, 1991). That is, rather than a latent construct with two resulting dimensions (cultural harmony and blendedness), BII should perhaps be understood as emerging or resulting from (rather than leading to) variations in cultural blendedness and harmony (see

Table 25.1 Bicultural Identity Integration Scale–Version 2 (BIIS-2; Huynh & Benet-Martínez, 2011)

BICULTURAL HARMONY VS. CONFLICT ITEMS:

I find it easy to harmonize _____ and American cultures.

I rarely feel conflicted about being bicultural.

I find it easy to balance both _____ and American cultures.

I do not feel trapped between the _____ and American cultures.*

I feel torn between _____ and American cultures. (R)

I feel that my _____ and American cultures are incompatible. (R)

Being bicultural means having two cultural forces pulling on me at the same time. (R)

I feel conflicted between the American and _____ ways of doing things. (R) *

I feel like someone moving between two cultures. (R) *

I feel caught between the _____ and American cultures. (R) *

BICULTURAL BLENDEDNESS VS. COMPARTMENTALIZATION ITEMS:

I feel _____ and American at the same time.

I relate better to a combined _____-American culture than to _____ or American culture alone.

I cannot ignore the _____ or American side of me.

I feel _____-American.*

I feel part of a combined culture.*

I find it difficult to combine _____ and American cultures. (R)

I do not blend my _____ and American cultures. (R)

I am simply a(n) _____ who lives in North America. (R) *

I keep _____ and American cultures separate. (R) *

Note:
* Original items from the BIIS-1 (Benet-Martínez & Haritatos, 2005). R = Reverse score these items. The BIIS-2 can be used with any ethnic minority culture and adapted to any host culture.

Figure 25.2). Thus, behaviors, attitudes, and feelings described by cultural researchers under the rubric of low BII (e.g., the feelings of tension and incompatibility reported in the first quote opening this section of the chapter) may in fact be largely capturing the resulting phenomenology of the more basic experience of cultural conflict and/or cultural distance.

Cultural harmony and blendedness are each associated with different sets of personality, performance-related, and contextual antecedents (Benet-Martínez & Haritatos, 2005), which explains the very different phenomenological experiences of biculturalism in the existing literature. Specifically, as indicated by path analyses (see Figure 1 in Benet-Martínez & Haritatos, 2005), lack of cultural blendedness (i.e., cultural distance) is predicted by the personality trait of close-mindedness (i.e., low openness to experience), low levels of bicultural competence (particularly with regard to the mainstream culture), experiencing strains in the linguistic domain (e.g., being self-conscious about one's accent), and living in a community that is not culturally diverse (see also Miller, Kim, & Benet-Martínez, 2011). Perhaps low openness makes acculturating individuals perceive ethnic and mainstream cultures more rigidly, both in terms of their "essential" defining characteristics and the boundaries between them; it may also make them less permeable to new cultural values and lifestyles. Such attitudes may lead to the belief that one's two cultural identities cannot "come together" and must

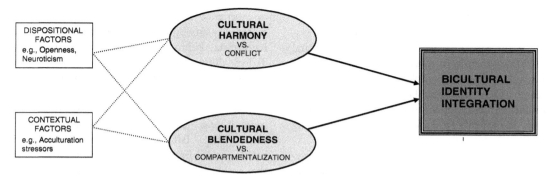

Fig. 25.2 High versus low levels of Bicultural Identity Integration result from variations in cultural harmony and cultural blendedness (adapted from Benet-Martínez & Haritatos, 2005).

remain separate. Also, the perception that one has a noticeable accent and that one's cultural background is uncommon in the local environment function as chronic and explicit reminders of the bicultural's unique status as cultural minority and also accentuate perceptions of cultural difference. Aside from these antecedents, cultural distance may also be related to the need for optimal distinctiveness (Brewer, 1991). Specifically, some biculturals may choose to keep their ethnic and mainstream identities separate in an effort to affirm both their intragroup (ethnic) similarity and intergroup (American) differentiation (Benet-Martínez & Haritatos, 2005). That is, biculturals low on cultural blendedness may be keeping ethnic (e.g., Chinese) and American cultures separate to affirm their strong ties to their Chinese culture while also differentiating themselves from the mainstream American cultural group. Lastly, cultural distance may be related to seeing one's two cultures as being very different from each other (Ward & Kennedy, 1993). To the extent that perceptions of difference may be accentuated in the early stages of mainstream culture acquisition (e.g., experience of cultural shock), one could speculate that, as biculturals' exposure to and competence in the mainstream culture increases, perceptions of cultural distance would decrease.

Low cultural harmony (i.e., conflict), on the other hand, is largely predicted by having a neurotic disposition, and experiencing discrimination and strained intercultural relations (e.g., being told that one's behavior is "too American" or "ethnic"—see Figure 1 in Benet-Martínez & Haritatos, 2005; Miller, Kim, & Benet-Martínez, 2011). Perhaps for biculturals high on neuroticism, switching cognitive and behavioral frames in response to different cultural cues (i.e., CFS; Hong et al., 2000) brings

feelings of confusion regarding one's ability to maintain consistent, recognizable self-identities. Also, it is likely that the acculturation strains of discrimination and strained intercultural relations create a strong discrepancy between explicit and implicit attitudes toward each culture. In other words, if a bicultural individual consciously identifies with and values both mainstream Anglo/American and ethnic cultures but also experiences prejudice and rejection from members of one or both of these groups, feelings of anger and distress may create internal discrepancy and attitudinal ambivalence (Van Hook & Higgins, 1988).

In summary, it seems that cultural blendedness is particularly linked to performance-related personal and contextual challenges (e.g., trait of openness, linguistic fluency, living in a culturally diverse enclave), while cultural harmony is linked to factors that are largely intra- and interpersonal in nature (e.g., emotional stability, lack of social prejudice and rejection). All in all, this work underscores the importance of adding an individual differences perspective in understanding the bicultural experience, and the consequentiality of personality factors in the acculturation domain (Ozer & Benet-Martínez, 2006). These patterns of relationships also suggest that variations in BII, far from being purely subjective identity representations, are psychologically meaningful experiences linked to specific contextual pressures and dispositional factors (see Figure 25.2).[7]

As mentioned earlier, much of the research on BII has found that individuals with low levels of conflict (high BII) are better adjusted and more effective in a variety of domains. However, some research also indicates that those with low levels of BII are more cognitively complex (Benet-Martínez et al., 2006). This suggests that conflicting cultural identities may have positive cognitive benefits. Perhaps, inner cultural conflict leads to more systematic and careful processing of cues from cultural situations, which in turn leads to cultural representations that are more complex and nuanced. Other researchers have also argued that the more severe the cultural conflict experienced, the greater the need to engage in more effortful and complex sense-making (Tadmor, Tetlock, & Peng, 2009).

Future work on BII should identify the behavioral domains associated with biculturals' feelings of conflict (e.g., clashes in work values, marriage practices, gender roles, etc.), as well as the types of contexts associated with biculturals' feelings of distance and compartmentalization (e.g., home vs. work, relatives vs. friends, etc.). Second, BII research should be integrated with theory on the benefits and costs of social identity complexity (Brook, Garcia, & Fleming, 2009; Roccas & Brewer, 2002; Settles, 2004). Second, because bicultural identities contain multiple elements including self-categorization, and importance and meaning attached to each identity, a bicultural individual may perceive blendedness on some of these elements (e.g., self-categorization), but not on others (e.g., importance), and harmony on some elements (e.g. meaning), but conflict on others. A full understanding of BII will require systematic investigation of these various careful identity elements (Wiley & Deaux, 2011).

Variation in BII and personality dispositions seem to be key individual difference variables in predicting bicultural identity structure and bicultural experiences, but there are other relevant variables. Hong and colleagues (Chao, Chen, Roisman, & Hong, 2007; No, Hong, Liao, Lee, Wood, & Chao, 2008) have shown that Asian American biculturals who hold essentialist beliefs about race— that is, believe race is an essentialist entity reflecting biological essence, unalterable, and indicative of abilities and traits—have more difficulties (i.e., longer latencies) in cultural frame-switching behavior, display stronger emotional reactivity when talking about bicultural experiences, and identify less with the host culture. The researchers have argued that essentialist race beliefs give rise to perception of less permeability between racial and cultural group boundaries, thus impeding an integration of experiences with both their ethnic and host cultures. Future research should examine how essentialist beliefs about race and culture as well as BII (particularly the blendedness vs. distance component) relate to cognitive constructs such low openness

to experience, need for closure, and low integrative complexity among acculturating individuals (Kosic, Kruglanski, Pierro, & Mannetti, 2004; Tadmor & Tetlock, 2006).

Given the changing and often lifelong nature of acculturation experiences, future studies examining the interplay between individual differences in personality (e.g., openness, neuroticism), bicultural identity (e.g., BII), and racial/cultural essentialist beliefs should be examined in longitudinal studies that are also sensitive to dynamic political/economic factors. Studies on cultural transitions such as repatriation among sojourners and immigrants (Sussman, 2000, 2002; Tsuda, 2003), for instance, reveal a complex pattern of identity shifts and adjustment outcomes that are driven by both psychological (e.g., self-concept clarity, strength of home and host culture identities) and sociopolitical factors (e.g., economic and political situation in home country). Similarly, work on transnationalism (Mahalingam, 2006), supports the temporal and dynamic nature of what Levitt and Schiller (2004) call immigrants' "ways of being," (actual social relations and practices that individuals engage in) and "ways of belonging" (practices that signal or enact an identity demonstrating a conscious connection to a particular group). Future work on individual differences in multicultural identity can also benefit tremendously from recent theorizing on social identity development. Relying on recent intergroup models as well as on developmental (i.e., neo-Piagetian) and social cognitive frameworks, Amiot and colleagues (Amiot, de la Sabionnière, Terry, & Smith, 2007) have recently proposed a four-stage model that explains the specific processes by which multiple social identities develop intraindividually and become integrated within the self over time. Their theoretically rich model also specifies the factors that facilitate and hinder these identity change processes, as well as the consequences associated with identity integration.

Group Differences in Multiculturalism
Multicultural individuals may belong to one of the following five groups based on the voluntariness, mobility, and permanence of contact with the dominant group: immigrants, refugees, sojourners, ethnic minorities, and indigenous people (Berry, Kim, Minde, & Mok, 1987). Immigrants arrive in the host country voluntarily and usually with the intention to stay, whereas refugees arrive in the host country by force or due to lack of other alternatives. Like immigrants, sojourners, such as expatriates and

international students, also arrive in the host country voluntarily, but their stay is usually temporary. Ethnic minorities and indigenous people are those born in the host country, but indigenous people differ from ethnic minorities in that the host country and culture was involuntarily imposed on them (e.g., via colonization or military occupation). The ethnic minority group may be divided into second-generation individuals (whose parents are immigrants or refugees) and third- or later-generation individuals (whose parents were born in the host country; Padilla, 2006). Many mixed-race or mixed-ethnic individuals are also multicultural, regardless of their acculturating group status (Padilla, 2006).

One can speculate about possible group-level differences among the groups mentioned above with regard to their levels of BII due to their group's history in the host country, their relations with members of the dominant group, the current political and socioeconomic situation, and other structural variables (Nguyen & Benet-Martínez, 2010). For instance, often immigrants and sojourners choose to migrate to the host country for economic or educational opportunities, and some may even have the option of returning to their native countries; thus, relative to the other groups, this type of multicultural individual may be more focused on opportunities and less focused on cultural issues. Consequently, cultural differences may not necessarily be internalized or translated into the experience of cultural identity conflict or distance. Conversely, refugees and indigenous people are often forced into contact with the dominant culture, and the involuntary nature of this contact (e.g., refugees may want to return to their native countries, but this is not possible due to conflicts between the host and native countries or within their native countries) magnifies cultural differences and identity conflict. Relatedly, African Americans, with their history of involuntary slavery and expatriation, may also experience more cultural identity conflict and distance than other groups. Lastly, there are reasons to think that feelings of cultural conflict may also be common among mixed-heritage individuals and second-generation individuals (at least relative to immigrants and sojourners). Mixed-race and mixed-ethnic individuals are often given (implicit or explicit) messages suggesting that they are not "enough" of one culture or the other (Root, 1998). Likewise, second-generation ethnic minorities are sometimes considered not "ethnic" enough by both their parents and dominant culture peers

with regard to certain cultural "markers" (e.g., ethnic language fluency) while also not being considered part of the mainstream culture (Padilla, 2006).

In addition to the voluntariness of contact and group expectations, variables such as generational status and cultural socialization may also play a role in BII, particularly the experience of cultural distance. Immigrants first learn their ethnic culture in their native country and later learn the dominant culture in the host country, thus their competencies and associations with each culture may be more compartmentalized and situation-specific (i.e., high cultural distance) compared to other groups. This dissociation may also occur among second-generation ethnic minorities for whom dominant and ethnic cultures are largely relegated to the public (e.g., work) and private (e.g., home) spheres, respectively. However, other second- and later-generation ethnic minorities (e.g., Chicano individuals) may be reared with a blend of both cultures, and thus the structure and experience of their identities may be more blended (i.e., low cultural distance). How these processes work for 1.5-generation individuals (immigrant children who moved to another country early and thus are socialized early into the host country culture) relative to first- and later-generation individuals remains to be explored.

All in all, notice that the above propositions focus on the relative level of perceived cultural distance or conflict across groups—that is, I do not assert that some groups perceive cultural distance or conflict while others do not.

Psychological and Societal Consequences of Multiculturalism

What impact, if any, does multiculturalism have on individuals and the larger society? The issue of whether multiculturalism is beneficial is often theoretically and empirically debated. Some researchers contend that the integration/biculturalism strategy, as compared to the other three acculturation strategies (separation, assimilation, marginalization), is the most ideal, leading to greater benefits in all areas of life (e.g., Berry, 1997; Phinney, Horenczyk, Liebkind, & Vedder, 2001). However, others have argued that this is not always the case, because the process of dealing with two cultures and acquiring two behavioral repertoires places a burden on the individual and can lead to stress, isolation, identity confusion, and hindered performance (e.g., Gordon, 1964; Rudmin, 2003; Vivero & Jenkins, 1999). For instance, when examining the links between biculturalism and *adjustment*, some researchers have found positive associations (e.g., Szapocznik & Kurtines, 1980; Ward & Kennedy, 1994), but others have found no link or a negative one (e.g., Burnam, Hough, Karno, Escobar, & Telles, 1987; Rotheram-Borus, 1990). In other words, findings have been mixed with regard to the direction and magnitude of these associations (Myers & Rodriguez, 2003; Rogler, Cortes, & Malgady, 1991).

A recent meta-analysis suggests that the above seemingly contradictory findings may be attributable to the ways in which biculturalism has been measured (Nguyen & Benet-Martínez, 2011; see also the review of measurement issues in this chapter). Across the 83 studies and 23,197 participants, biculturalism was found to have a significant and positive relationship with both psychological adjustment (e.g., life satisfaction, positive affect, self-esteem) and sociocultural adjustment (e.g., academic achievement, career success, social skills, lack of behavioral problems). Further, this biculturalism-adjustment link was significantly stronger than the association between each cultural orientation (dominant or ethnic) and adjustment. Interestingly, the magnitude of the biculturalism-adjustment association was moderated by the type of acculturation scales used (see Figure 25.3). When only studies using direct measures of acculturation strategies were included (i.e., Berry's scales), the relationship was weak to moderate (*r* = .21). However, when only studies using unidimensional scales were included, the relationship was strong (*r* = .54). Finally, when only studies using bidimensional scales were used (i.e., biculturalism measured via scores above the median or midpoint on both cultural orientations, the addition method, the multiplication method, or cluster or latent class analysis), the relationship between biculturalism and adjustment was even stronger (r = .70). In other words, biculturalism is related to better adjustment, but this relationship is best detected when biculturalism is measured bidimensionally. This is not perhaps not surprising given the point made earlier about how unidimensional acculturation scales can potentially confound biculturalism and marginalization.

The results from the above meta-analysis clearly invalidate early accounts of bicultural individuals as "marginal" and stumped between two worlds (Gordon, 1964), and they also suggest important future research directions for social and personality psychologists studying increasingly diverse samples, such as examining the role that social context may play in this biculturalism-adjustment relationship,

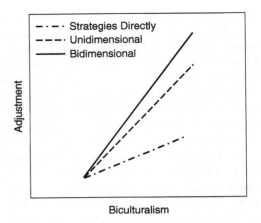

Fig. 25.3 Effect size of the biculturalism-adjustment relationship by type of acculturation scale (Nguyen & Benet-Martínez, 2011).

or understanding individual differences in biculturalism that can moderate the biculturalism-adjustment relationship (e.g., Chen et al., 2008).

The positive relationship between multiculturalism and adjustment may be due to the competencies and flexibility (social and cognitive) that multicultural individuals acquire in the process of learning and using two cultures (Benet-Martínez, Lee, & Leu, 2006; Leung, Maddox, Galinsky, & Chiu, 2008). Specifically, by virtue of their frequent experiences attending to, processing, and reacting to different sociocultural contexts, multicultural individuals process and organize sociocultural information in more cognitively complex ways than monoculturals (Benet-Martínez et al., 2006). These competencies may make bicultural individuals more adept at adjusting to various people or situations in either of their cultures and possibly in other cultures. In addition, this flexibility may buffer them from the psychological or sociocultural maladjustment that they might have otherwise suffered as a result of challenging acculturation experiences. It is possible that being oriented to only one culture rather than both has some adjustment costs, resulting from rejection from or lack of belongingness with members of the other culture (Roccas, Horenczyk, & Schwartz, 2000; Rogler et al., 1991; Ross, Xun, Wilson, 2002). In short, involvement with two or more cultures (vs. the cultural relinquishing that characterizes assimilation or separation) in all likelihood facilitates the acquisition of cognitive and social skills as well as wider behavioral repertoires and competencies which, in turn, buffer multicultural individuals against the psychological maladjustment (e.g., anxiety, loneliness) or sociocultural challenges (e.g., interpersonal conflicts, intercultural miscommunication) that can often characterize the acculturation experience (Padilla, 2006).

It is also possible that better adjusted individuals (e.g., those with higher self-esteem) find it easier to be bicultural or are able to use resources, which would otherwise be used to cope with maladjustment, to participate in both cultures and to interact with people from either culture, thus becoming more bicultural. The biculturalism-adjustment relationship may also be due to a third variable, such as the dominant group's attitudes toward acculturation. For example, a host country with multicultural policies and a dominant group that is accepting and nondiscriminatory toward acculturating individuals may allow for acculturating individuals to become bicultural as well as to attain high levels of adjustment.

In examining and understanding the outcomes of multiculturalism at the individual level, it is important to note that multiculturalism is not necessarily an individual choice; groups and intergroup relations also play a role. For example, an individual may favor the integration/biculturalism strategy, but if he/she is never accepted into mainstream society or consistently encounters discrimination, then the integration/biculturalism strategy may not be possible or even adaptive. Similarly, if one lives in a community without same-ethnic individuals, then assimilation may be adaptive. Although more research is needed to determine causality among intergroup relations, multiculturalism, and adjustment, public policies facilitating multilingual education, racial/cultural diversity in schools and other organizations, and the prohibition of disparate treatment for different groups, may influence an individual's ability to become multicultural, and in turn, his/her psychological and social well-being.

Multiculturalism may also have significant implications for greater national success and improved national functioning (Berry, 1998; Schwartz, Montgomery, & Briones, 2006). In children and adolescents, multiculturalism is positively related to greater academic achievement (Farver, Bhadha, & Narang, 2002; Régner & Loose, 2006). These educationally successful students may be able to contribute a great deal to society when they become adults. In the workplace, multicultural individuals may also contribute to organizational success, especially when it comes to international business negotiations, management of culturally diverse teams, and expatriate assignments, because their multicultural competence may generalize to intercultural competence (Bell & Harrison, 1996; Brannen &

Thomas, 2010; Thomas & Inkson, 2004). In addition, they have skills (e.g., multilingualism, cultural frame-switching, intercultural sensitivity) that are crucial in our increasingly globalized world; thus, multicultural individuals are ideal cultural mediators for intercultural conflicts and miscommunications within communities, nations, and internationally (see introductory point about President Obama).

More generally, it has been found that individuals with more extensive multicultural experiences, such as multicultural individuals, have greater cognitive complexity (Benet-Martínez et al., 2006), integrative complexity (Tadmor & Tetlock, 2006; Tadmor, Tetlock, & Peng, 2009), and creativity (Leung, Maddux, Galinsky, & Chiu, 2008; Maddux & Galinsky, 2009; Simonton, 1997), which are necessary for innovation and progress. The sociologist Gouldner (1985) argued that when a person draws on more than one line of thought, he/she can escape the control of any one of them; this person can toggle between the two (or more) ways of thinking and also forge new understandings. Biculturals, because of their experiences moving between cultural systems, may have richer associations with a single concept than monocultural persons, and they may have greater tolerance for ambiguity because they are comfortable with situations in which one basic idea may have different nuances depending on the community they inhabit at the time (Benet-Martínez et al., 2006).

If the experience of managing different systems of thought (e.g., different sets of cultural norms, belief systems, contextual cues, and languages) leads to richer and more complex associations among biculturals, it is not surprising to find that the general cognitive benefits described above are not restricted to multiculturals. Research in psycholinguistics shows that some of these cognitive benefits also appear in individuals who speak more than one language (Bialystock, 1999; Costa, Hernandez, Costa-Faidella, & Sebastian-Galles, 2009; Lambert, 1978). Recently, Crisp and Turner (2011) have outlined a theoretical model that specifies the antecedent conditions and cognitive processes through which perceiving multiple identities, *in oneself and others*, can lead to generalized cognitive flexibility. Drawing from the literatures on multiculturalism, bilingualism, creativity, cognitive development, multiple social categorization, self-categorization, minority influence, political ideology, and social identity complexity, Crisp and Turner posit that (1) exposure to diversity, particularly diversity defined by meaningful incongruent multiple identities (e.g., female engineer, male midwife) leads to (2) a systematic process of cognitive restructuring that can temporarily trigger, and over time develop, divergent thought and a more generalized flexibility in category use, and (3) that can have observable effects across a wide range of intra- (e.g., creativity, cognitive complexity) and interpersonal (e.g., prejudice, stereotyping) domains. In sum, social policies promoting multiculturalism and social diversity may benefit *all* individuals *and* society at large.

New Directions

> One and one don't necessarily add up to two.
> Cultural and racial amalgams create a third, wholly indistinguishable category where origin and home are indeterminate.
> *O'Hearn* (1998, p. xiv)

The possibility of being oriented to an *emergent third culture* has important implications for research on multiculturalism, and future acculturation theory and research will likely incorporate these effects (Nguyen & Benet-Martínez, 2010). The currently accepted bidimensional model of acculturation with ethnic and dominant cultural orientations might be replaced by a tridimensional model, where the third cultural orientation is a culture that emerges from the integrating of two interacting cultures—for example, Chicano culture in the United States (Flannery et al., 2001). Moreover, this tridimensional model might be more applicable to later-generation individuals and those who identify with a global international culture (Chen et al., 2008) than either the unidimensional or bidimensional model of acculturation. As of yet, no study has examined a third cultural orientation or compared a tridimensional model to the other models.

Understanding how emerging *global cultures* and multicultural spaces that integrate elements from local and foreign cultures influence psychological processes is of paramount importance (Chen et al., 2008; Chiu & Cheng, 2007; Nguyen, Huynh, & Benet-Martínez, 2010). The coexistence of symbols and ideas representing different cultural traditions in the same physical space is increasingly common (e.g., Starbucks cafés or McDonald's restaurants placed in traditional, and sometimes even historic, buildings throughout Europe and Asia). A recent study sought to examine how the copresence of images from seemingly distinctive cultures in the same space affects cognition (Chiu, Mallorie, Keh, & Law, 2009). This study presented monocultural Chinese and European American individuals with

single and joint presentation of icons from American and Chinese cultures. Chinese participants in the joint Chinese-American icon presentation condition attributed more characteristically Chinese attributes and behaviors to a Chinese target person than Chinese participants in the single presentation condition. Similarly, European American participants in the joint Chinese-American presentation condition attributed more characteristically Western attributes and behaviors to an American target. Contrary to the common expectation that the salience of one's culture will diminish with globalization, these results show that a globalized environment that includes symbols from multiple distinctive cultures may draw people's attention to their heritage culture as a way to bring coherence and structure to the situation (see also Chiu & Cheng, 2007). Future studies are needed however to examine these effects among multicultural individuals, for whom culturally mixed situations in all likelihood do not represent a threat or mismatch with their sense of self.

The above results from Chiu et al.'s (2009) study with Chinese and American monoculturals may be informative regarding the perceived incompatibility between cultural orientations that characterizes biculturals with low levels of BII (Benet-Martínez & Haritatos, 2006) and the contrast effects often obtained with this group of biculturals. Recall that low levels of cultural blendedness and cultural harmony are linked to cognitive rigidity (i.e., low openness to experience) and neuroticism respectively. These dispositions may make biculturals more prone to experience rumination and cognitive epistemic needs, such as need for closure, when facing quickly changing and ambiguous cultural situations, a common feature of the acculturation experience. In other words, perhaps the mere presence of a single clear cultural cue makes a bicultural low in BII ruminate about his/her two cultures (e.g., compare them), resulting in a simultaneous activation of both cultures very similar to the one achieved by the joint cultural images used in Chiu et al.'s (2009) study. This joint cultural activation, in turn, may elicit need for closure, or the desire to bring structure over the situation by focusing on and reinforcing a single cultural affiliation. But which of the two cultural identities, you may ask? The contrast effects repeatedly found in studies with low BIIs show that it would be the *other* culture, that is, the one not being initially primed or activated. Perhaps as suggested by Mok and Morris (2009), for these conflicted biculturals, following the lead of a particular cultural cue feels like leaving the other part of the cultural self behind, so they affirm that other identity to restore equilibrium in the bicultural identities and regain control over the self and the situation.

Lastly, future work should examine how much the psychology of having multiple national, ethnic, or racial identities applies to the *intersection of other types of cultures* and identities (Nguyen & Benet-Martínez, 2010). Professional, generational, and geographic cultures are some examples, but social class and religion are also relevant (Cohen, 2009). For example, an individual from the southern region of the United States living in the northern region of the United States may be bicultural. A culture of honor, which justifies violence in defense of one's reputation, is relatively prevalent in the South but not the North; therefore, southern white males living in the North may have to adapt to the norms in the North and negotiate those two cultures (Cohen, Nisbett, Bowdle, & Schwarz, 1996). Sexual minorities, such as gay/lesbian individuals, may also be bicultural, considering that they negotiate and move between gay/lesbian culture and mainstream heterosexual culture (Fingerhut, Peplau, & Ghavami, 2005). Furthermore, the pair of cultures to which "biculturalism" refers need not be within the same category. For example, engineering is a male-dominated occupation; therefore, women engineers may also be considered bicultural because they must negotiate their identities as women and as nontraditional engineers (Cheng et al., 2008; Sacharin, Lee, & Gonzalez, 2009; Settles, 2004). In addition, multicultural experiences and identity negotiations emerge when individuals find themselves living and working in contexts where SES levels and favored religion are very different from the ones attached to self—for example, low SES students attending private colleges and universities, or Muslims living in highly secular societies (Verkuyten & Yildiz, 2007). I believe that the identity structures and processes discussed in this chapter (e.g., cultural frame-switching, BII) may also apply to these other types of identities, but research on this kind of identity intersectionality is desperately needed (Cole, 2009).

Multiculturalism and Globalization: Implications for Social-Personality Psychology

The need for both social and personality psychology to respond to the theoretical and methodological questions posed by the growing phenomenon of multiculturalism cannot be overestimated. In their sampling and design choices, social and personality researchers (including those who do cultural work) have often implicitly assumed that culture is a stable, uniform influence, and that nations and individuals are culturally homogeneous. But rapid globalization, continued massive migration, and the resulting demographic changes have resulted in social spaces (schools, homes, work settings) that are culturally diverse, and in the growing number of individuals who identify with, and live in more than one culture (Hong et al., 2000). Current and future cultural studies need to move beyond traditional between-group cultural comparisons and develop theoretical models and methodologies that capture the multiplicity and malleability of cultural meaning *within* individuals. Some recent studies have taken this approach in examining the interplay between personality dispositions and psychosocial processes such as acculturation (Ryder et al., 2000), multicultural attitudes (Van der Zee et al., 2004), bicultural identity structure (Benet-Martínez & Haritatos, 2005), and bilingualism (Chen et al, 2008; Ramirez-Esparza et al., 2006).

Future cultural research can also benefit from exciting methodological advances. Because cultural, social, and personality processes operating at the individual level may not replicate at the cultural level and vice versa (see Tables 3–4 in Benet-Martínez, 2007), researchers can use multilevel modeling and latent-class techniques to deal with these complexities (e.g., Eid & Diener, 2001; see also Christ, Sibley, & Wagner, chapter 10, this volume). These underused techniques have the potential of fostering a fruitful synergy between the fields of personality and social psychology—which have provided a wealth of information regarding individual- and group-level characteristics (e.g., traits and values, majority/minority status)—and the fields of anthropology or sociology, which are very informative regarding culture-level phenomena (e.g., economy, religion, and many other key demographic factors).

In addition, although many studies have established that cultural forces influence social behavior and personality (i.e., culture→person effects), almost no attention has been given to the processes by which individual factors in turn influence culture (person→culture effects) (but see Adams, chapter 8, this volume). Evidence from recent studies shows, for instance, that our personalities shape the cultural contexts in which we live by influencing both micro- (e.g., personal spaces, music preferences, content and style of personal Web pages, etc.; Gosling et al., 2002; Rentfrow & Gosling, 2003; Vazire & Gosling, 2004) and macro- (e.g., political orientation, social activism, etc.; Jost et al., 2003) cultural elements.

Lastly, to the extent that social and personality psychology can be seen as two distinct (but relatively similar) "cultures" within psychology (Funder & Fast, 2010; Tracy, Robins, & Sherman, 2009), and that the research reviewed here attests to the adjustment benefits of having two cultures and integrating them with oneself, I want to argue that social and personality psychology would benefit from being more blended. Although there is some evidence that this integration exists already at the institutional level (e.g., *Journal of Personality and Social Psychology*, Society for Personality and Social Psychology), the blending and integration of questions, methods, and theories from the two subdisciplines is less obvious at the individual (i.e., researcher) level. This is unfortunate given that, as shown with the studies linking multiculturalism and multilingualism with general cognitive benefits, the integration of social and personality psychologies could lead to research that is more innovative, multifaceted, and significant.

Concluding Comments

Researchers and practitioners have acknowledged the importance of multiculturalism, and noted its consequences for how we conceptualize culture, optimal psychological functioning, and identity development (e.g., Arnett, 2002, 2008; Hermans & Kempen, 1998). Recently, multiculturalism has also taken center stage in popular culture. Earlier, it was mentioned that President Obama is undoubtedly multicultural and that biculturalism may refer to cultures other than ethnic cultures. At the 2009 Radio and Television Correspondents' Dinner, John Hodgman, a humorist and actor famous for his role in Apple's Mac vs. PC commercials, delivered a speech on biculturalism and hybridity, and identified Obama as being of two worlds: the world of "nerds" and the world of "jocks" (C-SPAN, 2009). Like a nerd, Obama values science, objectivity, and the questioning of the status quo, and like a jock, Obama is likable, confident, and fun to be around. As mentioned earlier, bicultural individuals often experience the external pressure of not having or representing "enough" of one culture or another. In line with this, Hodgman questioned Obama's authenticity as a nerd and tested him on his nerdiness. Although delivered as a humorous speech, it accurately highlights the bicultural experience, particularly the expectations and possible strains related to that experience.

Humor aside, as Verkuyten eloquently said, "Multiculturalism is concerned with complex issues that involve many questions and dilemmas. There are promises and there are important pitfalls . . . Multiculturalism is about the delicate balance between recognizing differences and developing meaningful communalities, between differential treatment and equality, between group identities and individual liberties" (Verkuyten, 2007, p. 294). Undoubtedly, there are different kinds of diversity and thus different forms of multicultural policies and theories will perhaps develop to accommodate differences in history, group representation, political structure, and resources. Above all, multiculturalism is indisputably *a fact* of life, and it is our collective duty to maximize its individual and collective benefits. Through exposure to and internalization of different cultures, minority and majority individuals can experience different ways of learning, viewing, and reacting to the world. This experience makes these individuals' cultural identities more complex and layered and enriches their cognitive and behavioral repertoires. Research mentioned earlier shows that these psychological processes lead to higher cognitive complexity and more creative and tolerant thinking. These attributes are an indispensable skill in our global world.

Acknowledgments

Veronica Benet-Martínez is an ICREA (Catalan Institute of Advanced Studies) professor at Pompeu Fabra University. She can be reached at veronica. benet@upf.edu. This chapter benefited greatly by the ideas and suggestions provided by Angela-MinhTu Nguyen. Some sections of this chapter include revised and updated material from Nguyen and Benet-Martínez (2010).

Notes

[1] For the sake of simplicity and consistency, in this chapter I favor the broader term "multicultural" or "multiculturalism" over the term "bicultural." Regardless of the term used, I always refer to individuals and societies who position themselves between two (or more) cultures and incorporate this experience (i.e., values, knowledge, and feelings associated to each of these identities and their intersection) into their sense of who they are.

[2] Hong et al. (200) define culture as a loosely organized network of knowledge that is produced, distributed, and reproduced among a collection of interconnected people. This "loose" view of culture contrasts with the "systemic" view (e.g., Greenfield, 2000; Markus & Kitayama, 1991; Triandis, 1996), which sees culture as a coherent system of meanings with an identifiable central theme around which all cultural meanings are organized (e.g., independence vs. interdependence).

[3] See Lambert (1992) for a review of his ambitious research program on the social psychology of bilingualism. Decades of research by Lambert and collaborators debunked the idea that

having two linguistic systems within one's brain divides a person's cognitive resources and reduces efficiency of thought and language. Instead, Lambert's work provided strong evidence for cognitive, educational, and social advantages to being bilingual.

[4] Note that behaviors differing across cultural groups can also be understood from this framework. Specifically, according to the "culture-as-situated-cognition" perspective (Oyserman, Sorensen, Reber, Chen, & Sannum, 2009), cross-cultural differences in behavior are due to cross-national differences in the likelihood that particular mind-sets will be cued at a particular moment in time. Institutions, media, folklore, and practices within each culture drive the types of cues and their ubiquity, and thus the mind-sets that will be more frequently cued.

[5] A recent meta-analysis of the aggregate reliability of three well-known bidimensional acculturation instruments found that variability in the reliability estimates was associated with scale length, gender, and ethnic composition of the samples, and that this pattern of association was different for ethnic and mainstream culture orientations (Huynh, Howell, & Benet-Martínez, 2009).

[6] BII is typically conceptualized as a relatively stable individual difference tapping a bicultural's overall feelings and perceptions regarding the compatibility and integration of his/her dual cultural orientations; however, like most other individual difference constructs, BII should also be seen as an emerging from the interaction of the person and his/her audience, and thus as also malleable and reactive (Wiley & Deaux, 2011).

[7] A recent study has shown that BII is a construct also applicable to the multiracial experience (Cheng & Lee, 2009). This study also established the malleability of BII: a manipulation inducing recall of positive multiracial experiences resulted in an increase of both blendedness and harmony, while recall of negative multiracial experiences resulted in decreases.

References

Alexander, J. (2001). Theorizing the "modes of incorporation." *Sociological Theory, 19,* 237–249.

Amiot, C. E., de la Sablonniere, R., Terry, D. J., & Smith, J. R. (2007). Integration of social identities in the self: Toward a cognitive-developmental model. *Personality and Social Psychology Review, 11,* 364–388.

Arends-Tóth, J. V., & van de Vijver, F. J. R. (2006). Assessment of psychological acculturation. In D. L. Sam & J. W. Berry (Eds.), *Cambridge Handbook of Acculturation Psychology* (pp. 142–160). Cambridge, UK: Cambridge University.

Arnett, J. J. (2002). The psychology of globalization. *American Psychologist, 57,* 774–783.

Arnett, J. J. (2008). The neglected 95%: Why American psychology needs to become less American. *American Psychologist, 63,* 602–614.

Banks, J. A., & Banks, C. M. (1995). *Handbook of research on multicultural education.* New York: Macmillan.

Barreto, M., Spears, R., Ellemers, N., & Shahinper, K. (2003). Who wants to know? The effect of audience on identity expression among minority group members. *British Journal of Social Psychology, 42,* 299–318.

Bartholet, J., & Stone, D. (2009, January 17). *A team of expatriates. Newsweek.* Retrieved from http://www.newsweek.com/id/180207

Baumeister, R. (1986). *Identity: Cultural change and the struggle for self.* New York: Oxford University.

Bell, M. P., & Harrison, D. A. (1996). Using intra-national diversity for international assignments: A model of bicultural competence and expatriate adjustment. *Human Resource Management Review, 6,* 47–74.

Bender, & Ng, (2009). Dynamic biculturalism: Socially connected and individuated unique selves in a globalized world. *Social and Personality Psychology Compass, 3,* 199.

Benet-Martínez, V. (2007). Cross-cultural personality research: Conceptual and methodological issues. In R.W. Robins, R.C. Fraley, & R. Krueger (Eds.), *Handbook of research methods in personality psychology* (pp. 170-190). New York, NY: Guildford Press.

Benet-Martínez, V., & Haritatos, J. (2005). Bicultural identity integration (BII): Components and psychosocial antecedents. *Journal of Personality, 73,* 1015–1050.

Benet-Martínez, V., Lee, F., & Leu, J. (2006). Biculturalism and cognitive complexity: Expertise in cultural representations. *Journal of Cross-Cultural Psychology, 37,* 386–407.

Benet-Martínez, V., Leu, J., Lee, F., & Morris, M. (2002). Negotiating biculturalism: Cultural frame switching in biculturals with oppositional versus compatible cultural identities. *Journal of Cross-Cultural Psychology, 33,* 492–516.

Berry, J. W. (1984). Multicultural policy in Canada: A social psychological analysis. *Canadian Journal of Behavioural Science, 16,* 353–370.

Berry, J. W. (1997). Immigration, acculturation, and adaptation. *Applied Psychology: An International Review, 46,* 5–34.

Berry, J. W. (1998). Social psychological costs and benefits of multiculturalism: A view from Canada. *Trames, 2,* 209–233.

Berry, J. W. (2003). Conceptual approaches to acculturation. In K. M. Chun, P. B. Organista, & G. Marín (Eds.), *Acculturation: Advances in theory, measurement, and applied research* (pp. 17–37). Washington, DC: American Psychological Association.

Berry, J. W. (2006). Attitudes towards immigrants and ethnocultural groups in Canada. *International Journal of Intercultural Relations, 30,* 719–734.

Berry, J. W., & Kalin, R. (1995). Multicultural and ethnic attitudes in Canada: Overview of the 1991 survey. *Canadian Journal of Behavioural Science, 27,* 301–320.

Berry, J. W., Kim, U., Minde, T., & Mok, D. (1987). Comparative studies of acculturative stress. *International Migration Review, 21,* 491–511.

Berry, J. W., Kim, U., Power, S., Young, M., & Bujaki, M. (1989). Acculturation attitudes in plural societies. *Applied Psychology: An International Review, 38,* 185–206.

Berry, J. W., Phinney, J. S., Sam, D. L. & Vedder, P. (2006). Immigrant youth: Acculturation, identity, and adaptation. *Applied Psychology: An International Review, 55,* 303–332.

Bialystok, E. (1999). Cognitive complexity and attentional control in the bilingual mind. *Child Development, 70,* 636–644.

Bilbeny, N. (2007). *La identidad cosmopolita: Los límites del patriotismo en la era global.* Barcelona, Spain: Kairós.

Birman, D. (1994). Acculturation and human diversity in a multicultural society. In E. J. Trickett, R. J. Watts & D. Birman (Eds.), *Human diversity: Perspective on people in context* (pp. 261–284). San Francisco, CA: US: Jossey-Bass.

Birman, D. (1998). Biculturalism and perceived competence of Latino immigrant adolescents. *American Journal of Community Psychology, 26,* 335–354.

Bollen, K., & Lennox, R. (1991). Conventional wisdom on measurement: A structural equation perspective. *Psychological Bulletin, 110,* 305–314.

Bond, M. H., & Yang, K. (1982). Ethnic affirmation versus cross-cultural accommodation: the variable impact of questionnaire language on Chinese bilingual from Hong Kong. *Journal of Cross-Cultural Psychology, 13*, 169–185.

Boski, P. (2008). Five meanings of integration in acculturation research. *International Journal of Intercultural Relations, 32*, 142–153.

Bourhis, R. Y., Moïse, L. C., Perreault, S., & Senécal, S. (1997). Towards an interactive acculturation model: A social psychological approach. *International Journal of Psychology, 32*, 369–386.

Brannen, M. Y., & Thomas, D. C. (2010). Bicultural individuals in organizations: Implications and opportunity. *International Journal of Cross-Cultural Management, 10*, 5–16.

Brewer, M. B. (1991). The social self: On being the same and different at the same time. *Personality and Social Psychology Bulletin, 17*, 475–482.

Briley, D. A., Morris, M. W., & Simonson, I. (2005). Cultural chameleons: Biculturals, conformity motives, and decision making. *Journal of Consumer Psychology, 15*, 351–362.

Brook, A. T., Garcia, J., & Fleming, M. A. (2008). The effects of multiple identities on psychological well-being. *Personality and Social Psychology Bulletin, 34*, 1588–1600.

Buriel, R., Calzada, S., & Vasquez, R. (1982). The relationship of traditional Mexican American culture to adjustment and delinquency among three generations of Mexican American male adolescents. *Hispanic Journal of Behavioral Sciences, 4*, 41–55.

Burnam, M. A., Hough, R. L., Karno, M., Escobar, J. I., & Telles, C. A. (1987). Acculturation and lifetime prevalence of psychiatric disorders among Mexican Americans in Los Angeles. *Journal of Health and Social Behavior, 28*, 89–102.

Burnet, J. (1995). Multiculturalism and racism in Canada. In J. Hjarno (Ed.), *Multiculturalism in the Nordic societies* (pp. 43–50). Copenhagen: TemaNord.

C-SPAN. (2009). 2009 Radio and Television Correspondents' Dinner. Retrieved June 28, 2009, from http://www.c-spanvideo.org/program/287153-1.

Chao, M., Chen, J., Roisman, G., & Hong, Y. (2007). Essentializing race: Implications for bicultural individuals' cognition and physiological reactivity. *Psychological Science, 18*, 341–348.

Chavez, D. (1994). *Face of an angel*. New York: Farrar, Straus, and Giroux.

Chen, S. X., Benet-Martínez, V., & Bond, M. H. (2008). Bicultural identity, bilingualism, and psychological adjustment in multicultural societies: Immigration-based and globalization-based acculturation. *Journal of Personality, 76*, 803–838.

Cheng, C., Lee, F., & Benet-Martínez, V. (2006). Assimilation and contrast effects in cultural frame-switching: Bicultural Identity Integration (BII) and valence of cultural cues. *Journal of Cross-Cultural Psychology, 37*, 742–760.

Cheng, C.-Y., & Lee, F. (2009). Multiracial identity integration: Perceptions of conflict and distance among multiracial individuals. *Journal of Social Issues, 65*, 51 – 68.

Cheng, C.-Y., Sanchez-Burks, J., & Lee, F. (2008). Connecting the dots within: Creative performance and identity integration. *Psychological Science, 19*, 1178–1184.

Cheryan, S., & Monin, B. (2005). Where are you *really* from? Asian Americans and identity denial. *Journal of Personality and Social Psychology, 89*, 717–730.

Chiu, C. Y., & Cheng, S. Y. (2007). Toward a social psychology of culture and globalization: Some social cognitive consequences of activating two cultures simultaneously. *Social and Personality Psychology Compass, 1*, 84–100.

Chiu, C. Y., Mallorie, L., Keh, H., & Law, W. (2009). Perceptions of culture in multicultural space: Joint presentation of images from two cultures increases in-group attribution of culture-typical characteristics. *Journal of Cross-Cultural Psychology, 40*, 282–300.

Cohen, A. B. (2009). Many forms of culture. *American Psychologist, 3*, 194–204.

Cohen, D., Nisbett, R. E., Bowdle, B. R., & Schwarz, N. (1996). Insult, aggression, and the southern culture of honor: An "experimental ethnography." *Journal of Personality and Social Psychology, 70*, 945–960.

Cole, E. R. (2009). Intersectionality and research in psychology. *American Psychologist, 63*, 170–180.

Costa, A., Hernández, M., Costa-Faidella J., Sebastián-Gallés, N. (2009). On the Bilingual advantage in conflict processing: Now you see it, now you don't. *Cognition, 113*, 135–149. Crisp, R. J. & Turner, R. N. (2011). Cognitive adaptation to the experience of social and cultural diversity. *Psychological Bulletin, 137*, 242-266.

Cross, W. E. (1995). Oppositional identity and African American youth: Issues and prospects. In W. D. Hawley (Ed.), *Toward a common destiny: Improving race and ethnic relations in America* (pp. 185–204). San Francisco: Jossey-Bass.

Cuéllar, I., Arnold, B., & Maldonado, R. (1995). Acculturation Rating Scale for Mexican Americans—II: A revision of the original ARSMA scale. *Hispanic Journal of Behavioral Sciences, 17*, 275–304.

Cuéllar, I., Harris, L. C., & Jasso, R. (1980). An acculturation scale for Mexican American normal and clinical populations. *Hispanic Journal of Behavioral Sciences, 2*, 199–217.

Deaux, K. (2006). *To be an immigrant*. New York: Russell Sage.

Deaux, K., Reid, A., Martin, D., & Bikmen, N. (2006). Ideologies of diversity and inequality: Predicting collective action in groups varying in ethnicity and immigrant status. *Political Psychology, 27*, 123–146.

Devos, T. (2006). Implicit bicultural identity among Mexican American and Asian American college students. *Cultural Diversity and Ethnic Minority Psychology, 12*, 381–402.

Dijksterhuis, A., Spears, R., Postmes, T., Stapel, D. A., Koomen, W., van Knippenberg, A., et al. (1998). Seeing one thing and doing another: Contrast effects in automatic behavior. *Journal of Personality and Social Psychology, 75*, 862–871.

Donà, G., & Berry, J. W. (1994). Acculturation attitudes and acculturative stress of Central American refugees. *International Journal of Psychology, 29*, 57–70.

Downie, M., Koestner, R., ElGeledi, S., & Cree, K. (2004). The impact of cultural internalization and integration on well-being among tricultural individuals. *Personality and Social Psychology Bulletin, 30*, 305–314.

Eid, M., & Diener, E. (2001). Norms for experiencing emotions in different cultures: Inter- and intranational differences. *Journal of Personality and Social Psychology, 81*, 869–885.

Farver, J. A. M., Bhadha, B. R., & Narang, S. K. (2002). Acculturation and psychological functioning in Asian Indian adolescents. *Social Development, 11*, 11–29.

Fingerhut, A. W., Peplau, L. A., & Ghavami, N. (2005). A dual-identity framework for understanding lesbian experience. *Psychology of Women Quarterly, 29*, 129–139.

Flannery, W. P., Reise, S. P., & Yu, J. (2001). An empirical comparison of acculturation models. *Personality and Social Psychology Bulletin, 27*, 1035–1045.

Fowers, B. J., & Richardson, F. C. (1996). Why is multiculturalism good? *American Psychologist, 51*, 609–621.

Fu, H.-Y., Chiu, C.-Y., Morris, M. W., Young, M. (2007). Spontaneous inferences from cultural cues: Varying responses of cultural insiders and outsiders. *Journal of Cross-Cultural Psychology, 38,* 58–75.

Funder, D., & Fast, L. (2010). Personality in social psychology. In S. T. Fiske, D. T. Gilbert, & G. Lindzey (Eds.), *The handbook of social psychology* (pp. 668-697), 5th ed. Hoboken, NJ: Wiley.

Gaertner, S. L., Dovidio, J. F., Nier, J. A., Ward, C. W., & Banker, B. S. (1999). Across cultural divides: The value of a superordinate identity. In D. A. Prentice & D. T. Miller (Eds.), *Cultural divides: Understanding and overcoming group conflict* (pp. 173–212). New York: Russell Sage.

Gardner, W. L., Gabriel, S., & Lee, A. Y. (1999). "I" value freedom, but "we" value relationships: Self-construal priming mirrors cultural differences in judgment. *Psychological Science, 10,* 321–326.

Gordon, M. M. (1964). *Assimilation in American life.* New York: Oxford University Press.

Gosling, S. D., Ko, S. J., Mannarelli, T., & Morris, M. E. (2002). A room with a cue: Judgments of personality based on offices and bedrooms. *Journal of Personality and Social Psychology, 82,* 379–398.

Gouldner, A. (1985). *Against fragmentation.* New York: Oxford University Press.

Greenfield, P. M. (2000). Three approaches to the psychology of culture: Where do they come from? Where can they go? *Asian Journal of Social Psychology, 3,* 223–240.

Grosjean, P. (1996). Living with two languages and two cultures. In I. Parasnis (Ed.), *Cultural and language diversity and the deaf experience* (pp. 20–37). Cambridge, UK: Cambridge University Press.

Hammack, P. L. (2010). The political psychology of personal narrative: The case of Barack Obama. *Analyses of Social Issues and Public Policy, 10,* 182-206.

Hartmann, D., & Gerteis, J. (2005). Dealing with diversity: Mapping multiculturalism in sociological terms. *Sociological Theory, 23,* 218–240.

Hermans, H. J. M., & Kempen, H. J. G. (1998). Moving cultures: The perilous problem of cultural dichotomies in a globalizing society. *American Psychologist, 53,* 1111–1120.

Hollinger, D. A. (1995). *Postethnic America: Beyond multiculturalism.* New York: Basic Books.

Hong, Y. Y., Benet-Martínez, V., Chiu, C. Y., & Morris, M. W. (2003). Boundaries of cultural influence: Construct activation as a mechanism for cultural differences in social perception. *Journal of Cross-Cultural Psychology, 34,* 453–464.

Hong, Y., Chan, G., Chiu, C., Wong, R. Y. M., Hansen, I. G., Lee, S., et al. (2003). How are social identities linked to self-conception and intergroup orientation? The moderating effect of implicit theories. *Journal of Personality and Social Psychology, 85,* 1147–1160.

Hong, Y. Y., Morris, M. W., Chiu, C. Y., & Benet-Martínez, V. (2000). Multicultural minds: A dynamic constructivist approach to culture and cognition. *American Psychologist, 55,* 709–720.

Hong, Y., Wan, C., No, S., & Chiu, C. (2007). Multicultural identities. In S. Kitayama & D. Cohen (Eds.), *Handbook of cultural psychology.* (pp. 323–345). New York: Guilford.

Huntington, S. P. (2004). *Who are we? The challenges to America's national identity.* New York: Simon & Schuster.

Huo, Y. J. (2003). Procedural justice and social regulation across group boundaries: Does subgroup identity undermine relationship-based governance? *Personality and Social Psychology Bulletin, 29,* 336–348.

Huynh, Q.-L., & Benet-Martínez, V. (2011). *Bicultural Identity Integration Scale—Version 2: Development and Validation.* Manuscript in preparation.

Huynh, Q.-L., Howell, R. T., & Benet-Martínez, V. (2009). Reliability of bidimensional acculturation scores: A meta-analysis. *Journal of Cross-Cultural Psychology, 40,* 256–274.

Jasinskaja-Lahti, I., Liebkind, K., Horenczyk, G., & Schmitz, P. (2003). The interactive nature of acculturation: Perceived discrimination, acculturation attitudes and stress among young ethnic repatriates in Finland, Israel, and Germany. *International Journal of Intercultural Relations, 27,* 79–97.

Jetten, J., Postmes, T., & McAuliffe, B. (2002). "We're all individuals": Group norms of individualism and collectivism, levels of identification and identity threat. *European Journal of Social Psychology, 32,* 189–207.

Jost, J. T., & Banaji, M. R. (1994). The role of stereotyping in system-justification and the production of false consciousness. *British Journal of Social Psychology, 33,* 1–27.

Jost, J. T., Glaser, J., Kruglanski, A. W., & Sulloway, F. (2003). Political conservatism as motivated social cognition. *Psychological Bulletin, 129,* 339–375.

Kang, S.-M. (2006). Measurement of acculturation, scale formats, and language competence: Their implications for adjustment. *Journal of Cross-Cultural Psychology, 37,* 669–693.

Kemmelmeier, M., & Cheng, B.Y. (2004). Language and self-construal priming: a replication and extension in a Hong Kong sample. *Journal of Cross-Cultural Psychology 35,* 705–712.

Kim-Jo, T., Benet-Martínez, V., & Ozer, D. (2010). Culture and conflict resolution styles: The role of acculturation. *Journal of Cross-Cultural Psychology, 41,* 264–269.

Klein, O., Spears, R., & Reicher, S. (2007). Social identity performance: Extending the strategic side of SIDE. *Personality and Social Psychology Review, 11,* 1–18.

Kosic, A., Kruglanski, A. W., Pierro, A., & Mannetti, L. (2004). The social cognitions of immigrants' acculturation: Effects of the need for closure and reference group at entry. *Journal of Personality and Social Psychology, 86,* 796–813.

Kosmitzki, C. (1996). The reaffirmation of cultural identity in cross-cultural encounters. *Personality and Social Psychology Bulletin, 22*(3), 238–247.

LaFromboise, T., Coleman, H. L., & Gerton, J. (1993). Psychological impact of biculturalism: Evidence and theory. *Psychological Bulletin, 114,* 395–412.

Lambert, W. E. (1978). Cognitive and socio-cultural consequences of bilingualism. *Canadian Modern Language Review, 34,* 537–547.

Lambert, W. E. (1992). Challenging established views on social issues: The power and limitations of research. *American Psychologist, 47,* 533–542.

Lau-Gesk, L. G. (2003). Activating culture through persuasion appeals: An examination of the bicultural consumer. *Journal of Consumer Psychology, 13,* 301–315.

Lê, T. D. T. (1998). California palms. In O'Hearn, C. C. (Ed.), *Half and half: Writers on growing up biracial and bicultural.* New York: Pantheon

Lê, T. D. T. (2003). *The gangster we are all looking for.* New York: Random House.

Lechuga, J. (2008). Is acculturation a dynamic construct? *Hispanic Journal of Behavioral Sciences, 30,* 324–339.

Lee, S.-K., Sobal, J., & Frongillo, E. A. (2003). Comparison of models of acculturation: The case of Korean Americans. *Journal of Cross-Cultural Psychology, 34,* 282–296.

Leung, A. K.-Y., Maddux, W. W., Galinsky, A. D., & Chiu, C. Y. (2008). Multicultural experience enhances creativity: The when and how. *American Psychologist, 63,* 169–181.

Levitt, P., & Schiller, N. (2004). Conceptualizing simultaneity: A transnational social field perspective on society. *International Migration Review, 37,* 595–629.

Livingston, K. (2003). *My half identity.* Bilingual/Bicultural Family Network. Retrieved from http://www.biculturalfamily.org/

Maddux, W. W., & Galinsky, A. D. (2009). Cultural borders and mental barriers: The relationship between living abroad and creativity. *Journal of Personality and Social Psychology, 96,* 1047–1061.

Mahalingam, R. (2006). *Cultural psychology of immigrants.* Mahwah, NJ: Erlbaum.

Markus, H. R., & Kitayama, S. (1991). Culture and the self: Implications for cognition, emotion, and motivation. *Psychological Review, 98,* 224–253.

Matsumoto, D. (2000). *Culture and psychology.* Belmonte: Wadsworth/Thomson Learning.

Miller, M.J., Kim, J., & Benet-Martinez, V. (2011). Validating the Riverside Acculturation Stress Inventory (RASI). *Psychological Assessment, 23,* 300-310.

Miramontez, D. R., Benet-Martínez, V., & Nguyen, A.-M. D. (2008). Bicultural identity and self/group personality perceptions. *Self and Identity, 7,* 430–445.

Mok, A., Morris, M., Benet-Martínez, V., & Karakitapoglu-Aygun, Z. (2007). Embracing American culture: Structures of social identity and social networks among first-generation biculturals. *Journal of Cross-Cultural Psychology, 38,* 629–635.

Mok, A., & Morris, M. W. (2009). Cultural chameleons and iconoclasts: Assimilation and reactance to cultural cues in biculturals' expressed personalities as a function of identity conflict. *Journal of Experimental Social Psychology, 45,* 884–889.

Myers, H. F., & Rodriguez, N. (2003). Acculturation and physical health in racial and ethnic minorities. In K. M. Chun, P. B. Organista, & G. Marin (Eds.), *Acculturation: Advances in theory, measurement, and applied research* (pp. 163–185). Washington, DC: American Psychological Association.

Nguyen, A.-M. D, & Benet-Martínez, V. (2010). Multicultural Identity: What it is and why it matters. In R. Crisp (Ed.), *The psychology of social and cultural diversity* (pp. 87-114). Hoboken, NJ: Wiley-Blackwell.

Nguyen, A.-M. D., & Benet-Martínez, V. (2007). Biculturalism unpacked: Components, individual differences, measurement, and outcomes. *Social and Personality Psychology Compass, 1,* 101–114.

Nguyen, A.-M. D., & Benet-Martínez, V. (2011). *Biculturalism is linked to adjustment: A meta-analysis.* Manuscript submitted for publication.

Nguyen, A.-M. D., Huynh, Q., & Benet-Martínez, V. (2010). *Glocalization and cultural reaffirmation.* Poster presented at the annual meeting of the Society of Personality and Social Psychologists, Las Vegas, NV.

No, S., Hong, Y., Liao, H.-Y., Lee, K., & Wood, D., & Chao, M. M. (2008). Lay theory of race affects and moderates Asian Americans' responses toward American culture. *Journal of Personality and Social Psychology, 95,* 991-1004.

O'Hearn, C. C. (1998). *Half and half: Writers on growing up biracial and bicultural.* New York: Pantheon.

Obama, B. H. (2009, January 21). Inaugural address. Retrieved July 8, 2009, from http://www.whitehouse.gov/blog/inaugural-address/

Ogbu, J. U. (1993). Differences in cultural frame of reference. *International Journal of Behavioral Development, 16,* 483–506.

Ogbu, J. U. (2008). *Minority status, oppositional culture, and schooling.* New York: Routledge.

Oyserman, D., Sorensen, N., Reber, R., Chen, S. X., & Sannum, P. (2009). Connecting and separating mindsets: Culture as situated cognition. *Journal of Personality and Social Psychology, 97,* 217–235.

Ozer, D. J., & Benet-Martinez, V. (2006). Personality and the prediction of consequential outcomes. *Annual Review of Psychology, 57,* 401–421.

Padilla, A. M. (1994). Bicultural development: A theoretical and empirical examination. In R. G. Malgady & O. Rodriguez (Eds.), *Theoretical and conceptual issues in Hispanic mental health* (pp. 20–51). Melbourne, FL: Krieger.

Padilla, A. M. (2006). Bicultural social development. *Hispanic Journal of Behavioral Sciences, 28,* 467–497.

Perunovic, W. Q. E., Heller, D., & Rafaeli, E. (2007) Within-person changes in the structure of emotion: The role of cultural identification and language. *Psychological Science, 18,* 607–613.

Phinney, J. S. (1999). An intercultural approach in psychology: Cultural contact and identity. *Cross-Cultural Psychology Bulletin, 33,* 24–31.

Phinney, J. S. (2003). Ethnic identity and acculturation. In K. M. Chun, P. B. Organista, & G. Marin (Eds.), *Acculturation: Advances in theory, measurement, and applied research* (pp. 63–81). Washington, DC: American Psychological Association.

Phinney, J., Berry, J. W., Vedder, P., & Liebkind, K. (2006). The acculturation experience: Attitudes, identities, and behaviors of immigrant youth. In J. W. Berry, J. S. Phinney, D. L. Sam, & P. Vedder (Eds.), *Immigrant youth in transition: Acculturation, identity, and adaptation across national contexts* (pp. 71-116). Mahwah, NJ: Erlbaum.

Phinney, J. S., & Devich-Navarro, M. (1997). Variations in bicultural identification among African American and Mexican American adolescents. *Journal of Research on Adolescence, 7,* 3–32.

Phinney, J. S., Horenczyk, G., Liebkind, K., & Vedder, P. (2001). Ethnic identity, immigration, and well-being: An interactional perspective. *Journal of Social Issues, 57,* 493–510.

Plaut, V. C., Thomas, K. M., & Goren, M. J. (2009). Is multiculturalism or colorblindness better for minorities? *Psychological Science, 4,* 444-446.

Portes, A., & Rumbaut, R. G. (2001). *Legacies: The story of the immigrant second generation.* New York: Russell Sage.

Pouliasi, K., & Verkuyten, M. (2007). Networks of meaning and the bicultural mind: A structural equation modeling approach. *Journal of Experimental Social Psychology, 43,* 955–963.

Ramirez-Esparza, N., Gosling, S., Benet-Martínez, V., Potter, J. & Pennebaker, J. (2006). Do bilinguals have two personalities? A special case of cultural frame-switching. *Journal of Research in Personality, 40,* 99–120.

Régner, I., & Loose, F. (2006). Relationship of sociocultural factors and academic self-esteem to school grades and school disengagement in North African French adolescents. *British Journal of Social Psychology, 45,* 777–797.

Rentfrow, P. J., & Gosling, S. D. (2003). The do re mi's of everyday life: The structure and personality correlates of music preferences. *Journal of Personality and Social Psychology, 84,* 1236-1256.

Roccas, S., & Brewer, M. B. (2002). Social identity complexity. *Personality and Social Psychology Review, 6,* 88–107.

Roccas S., Horenczyk G., Schwartz S. (2000). Acculturation discrepancies and well-being: the moderating role of conformity. *European Journal of Social Psychology, 30,* 323–334.

Roccas, S., Sagiv, L., Schwartz, S. H., Halevy, N., & Eidelson, R. (2008). Towards a unifying model of identification with groups: Integrating theoretical perspectives. *Personality and Social Psychology Review, 12,* 280–306.

Rogler, L. H., Cortes, D. E., & Malgady, R. G. (1991). Acculturation and mental health status among Hispanics: Convergence and new directions for research. *American Psychologist, 46,* 585–597.

Root, M. P. P. (1998). Experiences and processes affecting racial identity development: Preliminary results from the biracial sibling project. *Cultural Diversity and Mental Health, 4,* 237–247.

Ross, M., Xun, W. Q. E., & Wilson, A. E. (2002). Language and the bicultural self. *Personality and Social Psychology Bulletin, 28,* 1040–1050.

Roth, P. (1969). *Portnoy's complaint.* New York: Random House.

Rotheram-Borus, M. J. (1990). Adolescents' reference-group choices, self-esteem, and adjustment. *Journal of Personality and Social Psychology, 59,* 1075–1081.

Rudmin, F. W. (2003). Critical history of the acculturation psychology of assimilation, separation, integration, and marginalization. *Review of General Psychology, 7,* 3–37.

Ryder, A. G., Alden, L. E., & Paulhus, D. L. (2000). Is acculturation unidimensional or bidimensional? A head-to-head comparison in the prediction of personality, self-identity, and adjustment. *Journal of Personality and Social Psychology, 79,* 49–65.

Sacharin, V., Lee, F., & Gonzalez, R. (2009). Identities in harmony? Gender-work identity integration moderates frame-switching in cognitive processing. *Psychology of Women Quarterly, 3,* 275–284.

Saleh, N. (2009, January 29). The world's first global president. *Miller-Mccune.* Retrieved from http://www.miller-mccune.com/politics/the-world%27s-first-global-president-960.

Sam, D. L., & Berry, J. W. (2006). *Cambridge handbook of acculturation psychology.* Cambridge, UK: Cambridge University Press.

Sanchez-Burks, J., Lee, F., Choi, I., Nisbett, R., Zhao, S., & Koo, J. (2003). Conversing across cultures: East-West communication styles in work and nonwork contexts. *Journal of Personality and Social Psychology, 85,* 363–372.

Schalk-Soekar, S. (2007). *Multiculturalism: A stable concept with many ideological and political aspects.* Tilburg, The Netherlands: University of Tilburg.

Schwartz, S. J. (2006). Predicting identity consolation from self-construction, eudaimonistic self-discovery, and agentic personality. *Journal of Adolescence, 29,* 777–793.

Schwartz, S. J., Montgomery, M. J., & Briones, E. (2006). The role of identity in acculturation among immigrant people: Theoretical propositions, empirical questions, and applied recommendations. *Human Development, 49,* 1–30.

Schwartz, S. J., Pantin, H., Sullivan, S., Prado, G., & Szapocznik, J. (2006). Nativity and years in the receiving culture as markers of acculturation in ethnic enclaves. *Journal of Cross-Cultural Psychology, 37,* 345–353.

Schwartz, S. J., & Unger, J. (2010). Biculturalism and context: What is biculturalism, and when it is adaptive? Commentary on Mistry and Wu. *Human Development, 53,* 26–32.

Schwartz, S. J., & Zamboanga, B. L. (2008). Testing Berry's model of acculturation: A confirmatory latent class approach. *Cultural Diversity and Ethnic Minority Psychology, 14,* 275–295.

Sedikides, C., Wildschut, T., Routledge, C., Arndt, J., & Zhou, X. (2009). Buffering acculturative stress and facilitating cultural adaptation: Nostalgias as a psychological resource. In R. S. Wyer Jr., C.-Y. Chiu, & Y.-Y. Hong (Eds.), *Understanding culture: Theory, research and application* (pp. 351–368). New York, NY: Psychology Press.

Settles, I. H. (2004). When multiple identities interfere: The role of identity centrality. *Personality and Social Psychology Bulletin, 30,* 487–500.

Simonton, D. K. (1997). Foreign influence and national development: The impact of open milieus on Japanese civilization. *Journal of Personality and Social Psychology, 72,* 86–94.

Stevens, G. W. J. M., Pels, T. V. M., Vollebergh, W. A. M., & Crijnen, A. A. M. (2004). Patterns of psychosocial acculturation in adult and adolescent Moroccan immigrants living in the Netherlands. *Journal of Cross-Cultura Psychology, 35,* 689–704.

Sue, D. W., & Sue, F. (2003). *Counseling the culturally diverse: Theory and practice* (4th ed.). New York: Wiley.

Suinn, R. M., Rickard-Figueroa, K., Lew, S., & Vigil, P. (1987). The Suinn-Lew Asian Self-Identity Acculturation Scale (SL-ASIA). *Educational and Psychological Measurement, 47,* 401–407.

Sussman, N. M. (2000). The dynamic nature of cultural identity throughout cultural transitions: Why home is not so sweet. *Personality and Social Psychology Review, 4,* 355–373.

Sussman, N. M. (2002). Testing the cultural identity model of the cultural transition cycle: Sojourners return home. *International Journal of Intercultural Relations 26,* 391–408.

Szapocznik, J. & Kurtines, W. (1980). Acculturation, biculturalism, and adjustment among Cuban Americans. In A. M. Padilla (Ed.), *Psychological dimensions on the acculturation process: Theory, models, and some new findings* (pp. 139–159). Boulder, CO: Westview.

Tadmor, C. T., & Tetlock, P. E. (2006). Biculturalism: A model of the effects of second-culture exposure on acculturation and integrative complexity. *Journal of Cross-Cultural Psychology, 37,* 173–190.

Tadmor, C. T., Tetlock, P. E., & Peng, K. (2009). Acculturation strategies and integrative complexity: The cognitive implications of biculturalism. *Journal of Cross-Cultural Psychology, 40,* 105–139.

Taylor, C. (2001). Democracy, inclusive and exclusive. In R. Madsen, W. M. Sullivan, A. Swidler, & S. M. Tipton (Eds.), *Meaning and modernity: Religion, polity, and the self* (pp. 181–194). Berkeley: University of California Press.

Terry, D. J., Hogg, M. A., & White, K. M. (1999). The theory of planned behaviour: Self-identity, social identity and group norms. *British Journal of Social Psychology, 38,* 225–244.

Thomas, D. C., & Inkson, K. (2004). *Cultural intelligence: People skills for global business.* San Francisco: Berrett-Koehler.

Tracy, J. L., Robins, R. W., & Sherman, J. W. (2009). The practice of psychological science: Searching for Cronbach's two streams in social-personality psychology. *Journal of Personality and Social Psychology, 96,* 1206–1225.

Triandis, H. C. (1996). The psychological measurement of cultural syndromes. *American Psychologist, 51,* 407–415.

Trimble, J. E. (2003). Introduction: Social change and acculturation. In K. M. Chun, P. B. Organista, & G. Marín (Eds.),

Acculturation: Advances in theory, measurement, and applied research (pp. 3–13). Washington, DC: American Psychological Association.

Tsai, J. L., Ying, Y.-W., & Lee, P. A. (2000). The meaning of "being Chinese" and "being American": Variation among Chinese American young adults. *Journal of Cross-Cultural Psychology, 31,* 302–332.

Tsuda, T. (2003). *Strangers in the ethnic homeland: Japanese Brazilian return migration in transnational perspective.* New York: Columbia University Press.

U.S. Census Bureau. (2006). Retrieved March 18, 2008, from http://www.census.gov

Van der Zee, K. I., Atsma, N., & Brodbeck, F. C. (2004). The influence of social identity and personality on outcomes of cultural diversity in teams. *Journal of Cross-Cultural Psychology, 35,* 283–303.

Van der Zee, K. I., & Van der Gang, I. (2007). Personality, threat, and affective responses to cultural diversity. *European Journal of Personality, 21,* 453–470.

Van der Zee, K. I., & Van Oudenhoven, J. P. (2000). Psychometric qualities of the Multicultural Personality Questionnaire: A multidimensional instrument of multicultural effectiveness. *European Journal of Personality, 14,* 291–309.

Van Hook, E., & Higgins, E. T. (1988). Self-related problems beyond the self-concept: Motivational consequences of discrepant self-guides. *Journal of Personality and Social Psychology, 55,* 625–633.

Van Oudenhoven, J. P., Ward, C., & Masgoret, A.M. (2006). Patterns of relations between immigrants and host societies. *International Journal of Intercultural Relations, 30,* 637–651.

Vazire, S., & Gosling, S. D. (2004). E-perceptions: Personality impressions based on personal websites. *Journal of Personality and Social Psychology, 87,* 123–132.

Verkuyten, M. (2005). Ethnic group identification and group evaluation among minority and majority groups: Testing the multiculturalism hypothesis. *Journal of Personality and Social Psychology, 88,* 121–138.

Verkuyten, M. (2007). Social psychology and multiculturalism. *Social and Personality Psychology Compass, 1,* 1–16.

Verkuyten, M. (2009). Self-esteem and multiculturalism: An examination among ethnic minority and majority groups in the Netherlands. *Journal of Research in Personality, 43,* 419–427.

Verkuyten, M., & Martinovic, B. (2006). Understanding multicultural attitudes: The role of group status, identification, friendships, and justifying ideologies. *International Journal of Intercultural Relations, 30,* 1–18.

Verkuyten, M. & Pouliasi, K. (2002). Biculturalism among older children: Cultural frame switching, attributions, self-identification, and attitudes. *Journal of Cross-Cultural Psychology, 33,* 596–609.

Verkuyten, M., & Pouliasi, K., (2006) Biculturalism and group identification: The mediating role of identification in cultural frame-switching. *Journal of Cross-Cultural Psychology, 37,* 312–326.

Verkuyten, M., & Thijs, J. (1999). Multiculturalism among minority and majority adolescents in the Netherlands. International *Journal of Inter-cultural Relations, 26,* 91–108.

Verkuyten, M., & Thijs, J. (2004). Global and ethnic self-esteem in school context: Minority and majority groups in the Netherlands. *Social Indicators Research, 67,* 253–281.

Verkuyten, M., & Yildiz, A. A. (2007). National (dis)identification and ethnic and religious identity: A study among Turkish-Dutch Muslims. *Personality and Social Psychology Bulletin, 33,* 1448–1462.

Vivero, V. N., & Jenkins, S. R. (1999). Existential hazards of the multicultural individual: Defining and understanding "cultural homelessness." *Cultural Diversity and Ethnic Minority Psychology, 5,* 6–26.

Ward, C., & Kennedy, A. (1993). Where's the culture in cross-cultural transition? Comparative studies of sojourners adjustment. *Journal of Cross-Cultural Psychology, 24,* 221–249.

Ward, C., & Kennedy, A. (1994). Acculturation strategies, psychological adjustment, and sociocultural competence during cross-cultural transitions. *International Journal of Intercultural Relations, 18,* 329–343.

Ward, C., & Masgoret, A.M. (2008). Attitudes toward immigrants, immigration, and multiculturalism in New Zealand: A social psychological analysis. *International Migration Review, 42,* 227–248.

Wiley, S., & Deaux, K. (2011). The bicultural identity performance of immigrants. In A. E. Azzi, X. Chryssochoou, B. Klandermans, & B. Simon (Eds.), *Identity and participation in culturally diverse societies: A multidisciplinary perspective* (pp. 49–68). Chichester, West Sussex, UK: Wiley-Blackwell.

Wolf, R. (2009, April 20). Most diverse Cabinet in history still incomplete. *USA Today.* Retrieved from http://www.usatoday.com/news/washington/2009-04-19-cabinet_N.htm

Wolsko, C., Park, B., Judd, C. M., & Wittenbrink, B. (2006). Considering the Tower of Babel: Correlates of assimilation and multiculturalism among ethnic minority and majority groups in the United States. *Social Justice Research, 19,* 277–306.

Wong, R. Y.-M., & Hong, Y.-Y. (2005). Dynamic influences of culture on cooperation in the Prisoner's Dilemma. *Psychological Science, 16,* 429–434.

Yip, T., Seaton, E. K., & Sellers, R. M. (2006). African American racial identity across the lifespan: Identity status, identity content, and depressive symptoms. *Child Development, 77,* 1504–1517.

Young, I. M. (2000). *Inclusion and democracy.* Oxford: Oxford University Press.

Zane, N., & Mak, W. (2003). Major approaches to the measurement of acculturation among ethnic minority populations: A content analysis and an alternative empirical strategy. In K. M. Chun, P. B. Organista, & G. Marín (Eds.), *Acculturation: Advances in theory, measurement, and applied research* (pp. 39–60). Washington, DC: American Psychological Association.

Zou, X., Morris, M., & Benet-Martinez, V. (2008). Identity motives and cultural priming: Cultural (dis)identification in assimilative and contrastive responses. *Journal of Experimental Social Psychology, 44,* 1151–1159

Personality and Social Contexts as Sources of Change and Continuity Across the Life Span

Abigail J. Stewart *and* Kay Deaux

Abstract

This chapter provides a framework designed to address how individual persons respond to changes and continuities in social systems and historical circumstances at different life stages and in different generations. We include a focus on systematic differences among the people who experience these changes in the social environment—differences both in the particular situations they find themselves in and in their personalities. Using examples from research on divorce, immigration, social movement participation, and experiences of war, we make a case for an integrated personality and social psychology that extends the analysis across time and works within socially and historically important contexts.

Keywords: divorce, ethnicity, generation, identity change, immigration, life span, political activism, social identity, social movements, women's movement

As persistently and tenaciously as psychologists attempt to isolate variables of interest, remove them from their messy contexts, and subject them to detailed analysis, a full understanding of both how people change and how they stay the same across the life span requires a different approach. Personality psychologists have worked hard to identify stable individual traits that provide a sense of personal continuity over time and consistency to behavior, and social psychologists have invested considerable energy and ingenuity to construct laboratory-based settings that capture the essence of social processes and behavior. Although these efforts have provided rich understanding of many important aspects of human behavior, we believe the task of understanding how people both change and remain the same across different life stages and many different situations requires a broader perspective. In this chapter, we begin with a framework designed to address how individual persons respond to changes and continuities in social systems and historical circumstances at different life stages (Stewart & Healy, 1989).

We add to this framework a focus on systematic differences among the people who experience these changes in the social environment—differences both in the particular situations they find themselves in and in their personalities.

"Personalities" in this analysis are defined not only by trait dimensions, but also in terms of cognitive styles, values, and social and political attitudes. An important aspect of these various elements of persons is the degree to which they change over time, and how they foster change or enhance continuity within the individual. Some traits—for example, "Big Five" traits—are defined as relatively stable over long periods (Costa & McCrae, 1994; McCrae & Costa, 2008). Yet even they have been shown to change on average over the life span (Roberts & Mroczek, 2008; Srivastava, John, Gosling, & Potter, 2003). Perhaps more interesting from our perspective is evidence that these five traits differ in the degree to which they foster change and continuity. Thus, individuals who are high in extraversion seek out social interaction while those who are low in it avoid such contact (Park, Sher, Wood, & Krull, 2009). Equally, individuals who are high in "openness to experience," which is correlated with sensation-seeking and a felt need for new experiences, seek out novel situations (Aluja, Garcia, & Garcia, 2003; McCrae & Costa, 1997). In short, people high in both of these traits pursue experiences that in turn have the potential to change them. Similarly, people high in authoritarianism, system justification, or social dominance orientation, view existing social hierarchies positively, and therefore are inclined toward maintenance of the status quo and continuity (Jost, Glaser, Kruglanski, & Sulloway, 2003). We include within our concept of personality the idea of social identities, that is, those definitions of self that reflect a self-categorization and association with others who share membership and meanings associated with those group memberships (Deaux, Reid, Mizrahi & Ethier, 1995). Social identities can play an important role in influencing how people define and respond to continued and changed social circumstances. For example, women who had strongly identified with their occupational roles during World War II employment responded with resentment to the demand that they leave the labor force after the war, while other less-identified women were more accepting of the change (Ginzberg & Associates, 1966; Yohalem, 1978; Stewart & Malley, 2004). Similarly, identification with a particular group can be intensified by some events (e.g., among women, the women's movement; among African Americans, the civil rights movement), and that newly intensified social identity may both reflect a personal transformation and become a force for continuity in subsequent years—driving personal and political commitments and behaviors over time (Cole & Stewart, 1996; Cole, Zucker, & Ostrove, 1998; Franz & McClelland, 1994; Franz, 1994).

Social identity and self-categorization theories focus most often on the situationally induced salience of social identities and generally assume, at least implicitly, considerable flexibility and change over time in the choice of what identity is salient and what characteristics may define any particular identity. "Social contexts" from these perspectives often consist of a set of carefully constructed manipulations of events, aimed at demonstrating how the salience of a particular identity will influence behavioral outcomes. For example, particular social identities or personalities may be threatened (Pronin, Steele, & Ross, 2004; Shih, Bonam, Sanchez, & Peck, 2007; Steele, 1997); the token status of a particular identity may be highlighted (Sekaquaptewa & Thompson, 2002); and social, economic, and political threats can elicit authoritarian and aggressive responses (Bonnano & Jost, 2006; see also Doty, Peterson, & Winter, 1991) Some investigators within the social identity tradition have recently offered more interactive models that consider the bidirectional influence between the enactment of a social identity and the social context, a welcome development that allows a more integrated perspective on individual and context, although the time frame for such analyses is still quite limited (Klein, Spears, & Reicher, 2007; Wiley & Deaux, 2010).

In addition to theories that emphasize group identification and self-categorization, personality psychologists are often interested in a notion of identity that is broader and overlaps with the notion of a self. Erikson (1963), for example, argued that identifications with groups, roles and social locations, as well as with traits and ideologies, develop by early adulthood into a relatively coherent and stable structure that he viewed as an individual's personal "identity." In his account, that identity, like any integrative structure, should be relatively resistant to change in itself and becomes a force for continuity in the person's behavior over time. At the same time, a persistent integrative structure must be capable of adaptation (e.g., to changed circumstances, roles, etc.) if it is to endure across the life span. Therefore, this integrated identity should enable incremental change over the life span, while fostering an experience of continuity at the same time (see also Crocker & Canevello, chapter 11, this volume).

Theorists working from these notions of identity often define social contexts quite broadly, to focus on outside-of-the-laboratory settings and events that influence daily life. This broader scope can include the routine daily encounters with people in one's neighborhood or the persuasive advertisements on television; more often they include singular, dramatic events such as war, winning a lottery, the election of a black president, or the devastation caused by a hurricane or other natural disaster. Some of these social events or situations are expected to influence immediate responses, but are not expected to have long-term effects on a person's life. That is, they may create vivid temporary circumstances without significantly altering the people who are facing those difficulties. Other events may be so substantial, or include the accumulation over time of so many modest changes, that some or most individuals who experience them are transformed in fundamental ways. Finally, some contexts are themselves relatively stable over time; these can include the natural environment within a particular location, traditional cultural practices, and social structures such as gender, race, and social class relations within a particular culture. The obligation to analyze the impact of these macro elements is often handed over to sociologists and historians (also see Pettigrew & Cherry, chapter 2, this volume). It is our belief, however, that we as personality and social psychologists can profit from greater consideration of the ways in which these macro factors influence change and continuity in human lives. We need, then, a theoretical framework that includes attention to the many ways that different aspects of both persons and social contexts foster both change and continuity over time if we are to do justice to understanding lives.

We use the framework offered by Stewart and Healy (1989) as a starting point, as it incorporates aspects of the person and social contexts and additionally adopts a life span perspective. Stewart and Healy argue that many background assumptions about the way the world works—ranging from cognitive perspectives such as a belief in a just world and system justification to more temperamental traits such as optimism or pessimism—arise early in childhood and are based loosely on background social conditions among other things. Individuals who grow up under difficult conditions, for example, may be more likely to develop pessimistic outlooks even though temperament may dispose them in a more optimistic direction. Equally, broadly based social conditions may influence whole generations (toward or away from mistrust of government, for example), but more personal experiences can counter or amplify generational effects. These traits and beliefs tend to be relatively stable and resistant to change from an early age.

By early adulthood, a person's identity, constructed out of many social experiences of fitting in and not fitting in to situations and groups, begins to confer some conscious consistency or sense of coherence over time, while incorporating alterations and additions (e.g., as a new interest is integrated in midlife, or a career change or divorce occurs). When large-scale social change coincides with this period of conscious identity-formation, background assumptions from childhood may be altered quite dramatically, and the resulting identity may actually form around the unique generational experience, as happened in the Great Depression (Elder, 1974). Similar coalescence is associated with the "greatest generation," which survived the 1930s depression and fought World War II (Stewart & Malley, 2004), and the generation influenced by student movements in the 1960s and 1970s in the United States (Cole & Stewart, 1996; Franz & McClelland, 1994) and Europe (Passerini, 1996), as well as by the Cultural Revolution in China (Braungart & Braungart, 1994). There may, then, be generational differences in the degree to which personality and identity development is largely a matter of highly individual personal experiences or widely shared and consciously recognized cohort experiences (Stewart, 2003). Features of identity are accordingly both shaped by social experiences and act as motivators for individuals' subsequent behavior.

Finally, throughout adulthood social behaviors are outcomes that can be relatively stable over the life course and tied to traits (e.g., friendliness or risk-taking). Alternatively, these outcomes may be tied to particular developmental periods, such as political protest activism, which peaks in adolescence; or life review, which peaks in late life). Outcomes can also be dependent on more immediate situations, as when altruistic or obedient behavior is tied to strong situational demands for action. These latter behaviors can be influenced at any stage of the life span but only reshape adult personality when they are the result of relatively powerful, dramatic and intense experiences (e.g., war) or suddenly and dramatically changed social conditions that challenge previous assumptive frameworks or identities. In this chapter we examine events that may appear to originate in personal life (events such as filing for divorce, moving a family, joining a demonstration or the military), but also can be considered in their broader social contexts. These contexts may represent gradual or incremental change (as in shifting demographic patterns of immigration or societal rates of divorce) or may exemplify sudden change (as in the case of wars or natural disasters). Our goal is to shed light on how these different kinds of changes relate to changes within persons. All of these personal-social changes can influence individuals at all stages of life. Parental divorce, for example, can influence children's ideas about intimacy and conflict in relationships, while sudden immersion into armed conflict can shape their view of external danger and the value of security. At the same time, changes in the external context can have powerful shaping influences on adolescents' formation of conscious identities, and on older adults' opportunities and remade selves.

Changing Family Context: The Impact of Divorce

Divorce is an example of a personal life change that has consequences both for people who seek it and for those around them (their spouses, children, other family members, friends and coworkers). Moreover, it is affected by legal and normative circumstances in the larger social environment (Dillon, 1993). Psychological research on the consequences of divorce for both adults and children has assessed fairly narrow effects. Most of the literature on children has focused on two issues: the short-term impact of divorce on adjustment, and the long-term impact on adult relationship formation and adjustment (see Amato & Keith, 1991; Chase-Lonsdale & Hetherington, 1990; Emery, 1988; Furstenberg & Cherlin, 1991; Furstenberg & Teitler, 1994; Wallerstein, 1991; Wallerstein & Blakeslee, 1989). An underlying assumption of much of this research is that exposure first to an "intact" family structure followed by its dissolution must create doubt in a child's mind about the stability and reliability of relationships and families. Thus, the "assumptive framework" that a child is developing about this domain of human experience differs from the one developed by a child exposed to a family structure that endures throughout her or his childhood (see, e.g., Janoff-Bulman, 1991).

Some scholars have raised serious questions about whether this way of framing "divorce" is adequate (Hetherington, 1979; Stewart, Copeland, Chester, Malley, & Barenbaum, 1997). Is divorce conceptualized best as a discrete change in the family environment, marked by parental separation and legitimated and symbolized by legal divorce? Or as a much more protracted parental conflict that both predates and follows the divorce? Or as protracted exposure to two people with different parenting values or styles that are evident before and after the divorce? Some researchers have also pointed out that for some children parental separation and divorce are followed by changes in custody, parental remarriage, and the acquisition of step-parents and step-siblings (Hetherington & Arasteh, 1988; Stewart et al., 1997). Each of these changes may be associated with conflict or happiness, improvements or declines in material comfort and security, greater or lesser access to reliable adult guidance. According to this view, parental divorce is far from a single discrete event, nor is it homogeneous in its character across families or over time within a child's experience. Therefore, the inferences a child might draw from it—about the difficulty or fragility of relationships, or about the attractiveness of establishing and maintaining them—might be quite different. That said, the underlying assumption even of these researchers is that children use their experiences of family stability or instability to form expectations about how relationships and households work. Differences in experience should yield different expectations. Interestingly, despite the fact that most research in this domain is based on this sort of reasoning, much of the research has focused not on these expectations but instead on two outcomes: adjustment (mental health) and adult relationship formations. Perhaps not surprisingly, the effects in these two areas are inconsistent, contested, and mostly modest. If researchers focused more on how children's early exposure to changes in family structure affects their beliefs and expectations about the durability and reliability of relationships and families, the yield might be greater. For example, Franklin, Janoff-Bulman, and Roberts (1990) found that college students whose parents had divorced did not differ in their general trust or optimism for the future and for themselves, but they did differ in their optimism about the likely success of their future marriages. In turn, it may be that these expectations are important mediators between the actual family changes children experience, and both mental health and relationship behavior.

It is important to note that the social meaning of divorce in most parts of the United States has changed dramatically over the past 60 years (see Amato & Keith, 1991; Gerstel, 1987; Kitson & Raschke, 1981). In 1950 divorce was a rare and stigmatized event defined by an adversarial legal process. By 1970 it was far more common and was increasingly "no-fault"; by 1990 divorce was frequent, carried little or no social stigma in most places, and children's interests were often separately protected by courts. In short, the social and legal context of divorce in the United States must be considered part of understanding its impact. The impact of a rare and stigmatized event is likely to be greater and different than the impact of a common and socially accepted event, even if in both cases the event entails some real and felt personal loss. Moreover, changes in the rate of divorce may have consequences for normative changes across long marriages. Kasen, Chen, Sneed, Crawford, and Cole (2006) found that marital conflict declined over 20 years for women born during the baby boom, but women from an earlier birth cohort reported no such decline. They argue that the decline may result from two factors: women in high-conflict marriages divorcing more in the baby boom cohort; and women in that generation having more egalitarian marriages in which conflict declines over time within it. Thus, the allegedly private worlds of both marriage and divorce may be shown to have changed in response to changes in social norms.

At a much more personal level, divorce is not experienced in the same way by children and adults within the same family. Stewart et al. (1997) found that the adults in their sample of families with school-age children, studied within six months of the parents' physical separation, had most often been engaged in a fairly protracted process of making the decision to divorce. The physical separation was in an important sense the end of a process of emotional disentanglement and choice that parents worked to conceal from the children (not always successfully, of course). For children, the point of physical separation (usually the father moving out of the family home) was most often accompanied by an "announcement" by the parents, and triggered an emotional process of reaction and adaptation (except in cases where children had guessed what was going on). In this way households often contain (at least) two generations with quite different psychological relationships to both personal and social events. Although these generations may be in close connection in their process of reacting to an event, they have quite different standpoints and those different standpoints affect their relations with each other and the impact of the events. A final comment on reactions to divorce: it has been noted frequently that divorce is experienced very differently by children whose parents never engaged in open conflict and those who did (Amato & Keith, 1991; Block, Block, & Gjerde, 1986; Stewart et al., 1997). When conflict has been open, divorce is more often both an intelligible "solution" and a relief. When it has been completely hidden, it can be more difficult for the children to understand and accept as necessary. This difference should alert us to the fact that events that appear to be "the same" may differ psychologically in crucial ways.

Finally, what do we know about divorce and adults? In this case, researchers have been much more inclined to consider personality or dispositional predictors of divorce, and indeed a few have been identified. For example, men high in power motivation have higher rates of relationship dissolution in general (with or without benefit of marriage; Stewart et al., 1997; Stewart & Chester, 1982; Stewart & Rubin, 1976; Winter & Barenbaum, 1985). They also have more conflict in their

relationships than do other men. This connection to relationship conflict and dissolution does not hold for women high in power motivation, who appear to find greater benefit in maintaining relationships than in either dissolving them or increasing the level of conflict in them. So here we see adult personality as a source of both continuity (for women) and change (for men) in relationships.

Considerable evidence suggests that divorce can be the occasion for significant personal growth in adults (Riessman, 1990; Stacey, 1990, 1991; Stewart et al., 1997). Many individuals, particularly women, report that divorce benefits them by enabling them to develop new parts of themselves, parts that had been constrained or hampered by limiting relationships. Bursik (1991) compared the change over time in ego development of women who showed a process of adjustment in well-being over one year with those who did not. Those women who adjusted during this period also showed significant increases in ego development; those who did not adapt well to the divorce showed no change. There is, then, not only evidence that for adults some personality characteristics foster divorce, but also evidence that successfully coping with a major life stressor can foster adult personality change.

Finding some specific benefits of divorce for women underscores the importance of consideration of social structural factors including, but not limited to, gender. As another example, Barrett (2003) considers the claim of a weaker negative impact of divorce on African American adults in comparison with European Americans. She demonstrates, in a carefully controlled study, that African Americans actually show larger negative mental health effects at the point of legal divorce, but lesser ones at the point of separation. She suggests that within the African American community separation may be viewed as less final than it is for most European Americans, and therefore as less distressing. In contrast, European Americans generally view separation as the beginning of an inevitable process of dissolution. Thus the difference may lie both in the timing and the social meanings of these particular events, rather than in the overall severity of their impact.

The importance of economic factors in postdivorce adjustment is highlighted in a study by McHenry and McKelvey (2003). Using national survey data, they found that even after controlling for education and time since divorce, white women were significantly higher in economic well-being after divorce and more likely to be remarried than were black women. Thus, structural variables such as gender, race, and class, which are also implicated in research on children's adjustment (e.g., Wolchik et al., 1993), are generally important contextual factors in the impact of divorce on personality.

In sum, we note that although the literature on divorce has rarely linked social level changes in marital and family norms to outcomes for the individuals who experience it, this might be a valuable avenue to pursue, in accord with the logic of Stewart and Healy's (1989) model. Second, the concept of "generation" has only rarely been specifically identified as applying to divorce in the sense that divorcing households contain two generations with quite different psychological relationships to the events (see Stewart et al., 1997). It might be fruitful to tie this notion of generation to others more common in the literature, e.g., both birth cohort (link between time of birth and social events), and generations with respect to immigration. Finally, developmental factors (such as age of parental divorce) have been examined and sometimes found to be important features of children's responses to divorce. However, these factors have mostly been examined in terms of adjustment and well-being rather than the kinds of outcomes pointed to by the model, such as background assumptions about relationships and families (for young children) and identities (for adolescents). It would be particularly valuable for research on the long-term impact of divorce to include more attention to these kinds of outcomes.

Immigration as Psychological Context: Historical Events and Family Dynamics

A second domain that we have chosen to illustrate the interplay of personality and social context is immigration (see Deaux, 2006), with a particular emphasis on differences between generations in the events that they confront and the ways in which they cope with their changed circumstances. Generation has multiple meanings, and the interpretation of the concept speaks both to different social and historical contexts in which the individual actor plays his or her role and to immediate family circumstances—as illustrated above in the case of divorce, in which the context for development and change is different for children and adults in the same family. In this section of the chapter, we (1) unpack the concept of generation; (2) discuss key aspects of the immigration process, including motivations to emigrate and conditions of arrival; and (3) explore the interdependencies between personality and social factors, as they are moderated by demographic factors such as generation and ethnicity.

Two Forms of Generational Analysis

The traditional immigration literature has generally ignored or conflated what Telles and Ortiz (2008) have shown to be an important distinction between two types of generational analysis. In the first, which they term historical or family generation, the question is how waves of immigrants differ across historical time periods. This use of generation would be similar to the discussion in the previous section, in which children are compared to their parents (or grandparents) and one looks at how members of each generation, now differing in age, differ on some specific characteristics or orientations. Alternatively, to the extent the data are available, one might compare people across historical time periods, attempting to keep other factors such as age constant, as for example when one compares West Indian immigrants who arrived in the United States in different decades of the 20th century (Model, 2009).

A second form of generational analysis is referred to as "generation-since-immigration" (Telles & Ortiz, 2008). In this case, the time period is held constant while comparisons are made between people, ideally similar in age, who differ in the number of generations they are removed from the original immigrant experience. Thus, people of the same age might be immigrants themselves, might be the children of parents who immigrated, or might need to look back to their grandparents to connect to the original move from one country to another. This second form of analysis is only possible when a country has an ongoing history of immigration, such that multiple generations live in a common situation within the same historical time period. The United States, which has had continuous immigration in large numbers ever since the mid-1960s, currently satisfies those conditions, especially for particular ethnic groups in certain parts of the country, for example, Mexican Americans in southern California (Telles & Ortiz, 2008).

For our purposes, the distinction between these two forms of generational analysis is important because different explanatory factors tend to be invoked in explaining any observed generational differences. In the historical or family generation analysis of immigration, the causal focus tends to be on the social, economic, and historical conditions that have varied across time, thus accounting for variations in the behavioral patterns and outcomes of immigrant groups who experience the different contexts. These are social contextual factors writ large, more likely to be in the domain of sociologists, economists, and historians, but also amenable to psychological consideration as the Stewart and Healy (1989) analysis of feminist generations has shown.

A generation-since-immigration analysis, the second form delineated by Telles and Ortiz (2008), to a large extent keeps historical time period constant and looks instead at the immediate context and the social circumstances that immigrants encounter. If age is also kept constant, biological and developmental factors can be constrained and the emphasis shifts much more squarely to the personality and social psychological factors that contribute to observed differences in attitudes and behaviors. Telles and Ortiz (2008) provide striking evidence of the difference in the two generational perspectives in their analysis of educational attainment of Californians of Mexican ancestry. While a historical generational analysis shows progress across generations, a generation-since-immigration analysis indicates that there is a leveling off and even a decline in later generations. Although the causal factors for this pattern are tentative, there is some suggestion that experiences with discrimination are relevant to the outcomes. For personality and social psychologists, the dynamics of these processes, as they develop differently for people who represent different generations of immigrant ancestry, provide fertile ground for exploration.

To illustrate the role of personality and social factors in the immigrant experience, and in particular the variations in that experience that are associated with generational status, we consider two general areas: what motivates a person to emigrate, and what economic and social conditions affect occupational and psychological outcomes.

Motivations to Leave

One aspect of immigration concerns the conditions and precipitating factors by which people choose to leave their country of origin and move to a new location. This question can be addressed from a number of vantage points, representing various levels of conceptual analysis. In a demographic analysis of generation as historical context, the focus is on broad-gauged features of both the sending and the receiving societies that characterize the push and pull factors for immigration (see Massey, 1999). These factors include the economic and political conditions in both countries and the existence of social networks and previously established communities, as well as political events that may create a flow of refugees from one country to another. Here the emphasis is clearly on social context as the major determinant, though at a scale rarely incorporated by social and personality theorizing.

Some sociological analyses have considered more individualized circumstances as determinants of decisions to migrate. Kandel and Massey (2002), for example, looked at perceptions of community, finding that the motivations of children in areas of Mexico that have a high rate of out-migration are significantly related to the extent to which members of their immediate social network have previously moved to the United States. Model (2009), in an analysis of West Indian immigration, argues that selectivity of the immigrant population, specifically more education and higher motivation, can account for subsequent success rates in the destination country.

Although Model's claim for higher motivation rests on outcome, rather than independent assessment of motivation levels, it is a widely shared assumption within the immigration field that those who emigrate are in some way more motivated than those who do not. The empirical evidence for this assumption is in fact quite limited, but there is some indication that people who express the desire to emigrate are higher in both achievement and power motivation than those who are less inclined to move (Boneva & Frieze, 2001).

A more interactional analysis of motivations to migrate, which nicely illustrates the interdependence of person and social context, is represented in the work of Tartakovsky and Schwartz (2001), who considered the degree of fit between individual values (e.g., self-development, preservation, and materialism) and the predominant values of possible destination countries. In their study Russian Jews who placed a higher value on self-development and materialism preferred Germany or the United States as destinations, whereas those Jews for whom traditionalism and preservation were a primary concern were more likely to emigrate to Israel.

Conditions of Arrival

Once arrived in the destination country, immigrants are immersed in a new social context, one that introduces a new set of economic and social conditions and that requires the person to develop strategies to adapt to and negotiate with the new circumstances. From our perspective, the interplay of person and situation is both complex in its form and central to the analysis.

ECONOMIC CONDITIONS

The economic opportunities that exist in a country, together with the human capital possessed by the immigrant group, have been a central focus of immigration scholars. In a recent analysis of immigration, Richard Alba (2009) argued that the successful integration and upward mobility of earlier generations of immigrants to the United States, such as Italians and Jews, was due in large part to an expanding postwar economy that opened up new opportunities for education and employment, thus allowing these former immigrants to enter the mainstream without displacing previously dominant white majority members. Similarly, he argues, the future integration of current waves of nonwhite immigrants will be facilitated by the retirement of a large baby-boom generation that will open up jobs to other populations. Demography in this sense becomes destiny, as the full weight of explanation is carried by economic conditions encountered by different historical generations of immigrants.

The effects of economic conditions on individual behavior, however, require that there be some fit between the kinds of opportunities that are available and the resources and skills that individuals have to take advantage of those opportunities. A changing job picture, for example a shift from manual labor and blue-collar factory jobs to positions that require higher levels of education and training, will differentially affect immigrant groups that differ in these human capital factors. Thus the flow of young immigrants from Mexico and Central America, most often with limited educational backgrounds, is likely to persist only as long as large numbers of low-level jobs are available in the United States.

A reverse example of lack of fit was found by Tang and her colleagues (2007) in a study of outcomes of female Chinese immigrants to Canada. In this instance, in large part because of Canada's policy of favoring high-skilled workers, the women were highly educated and had held high-status occupations in China. In Canada, several years after they had immigrated, almost all of these women were either unemployed or severely underemployed relative to their skills. Not surprisingly, the consequence of this lack of fit between individual resources and societal opportunity was significant rates of psychological distress and negative affect.

SOCIAL CONDITIONS

The context of arrival for an immigrant is defined not only by economic conditions and opportunities, but also by the social conditions, consisting both of the attitudes and reactions of the native-born majority and of the support and networks offered by the ethnic ingroup.

Views of immigrants have changed over time, vary between regions of a country, and differ as a function of the target group. In the United States, over the past century, attitudes toward immigrants have shown numerous shifts. In the 1920s and 1930s, for example, attitudes were quite negative; by midcentury they became much more favorable, only to drop again at the end of the century (Lapinski, Peltola, Shaw, & Yang, 1997. Similar shifts can be seen in Europe, with anti-immigrant sentiment increasing during the latter years of the 20th century (Pettigrew, 1998). Ethnic group differences can also be found within these more general patterns. In general, Asian immigrants rank relatively high in the racial hierarchy, have higher rates of intermarriage and less residential segregation than other immigrant groups, and are characterized more favorably in attitudinal surveys. Other contemporary immigrant groups experience less favorable climates. Within New York City, for example, Afro-Caribbean immigrants report significantly more discrimination than do Latino immigrants, who in turn report more discrimination than do immigrants from China or from Russia (Kasinitz, Mollenkopf, Waters, & Holdaway, 2008). Specific comparisons between attitudes toward Latino and either Russian or Dutch immigrants show that people are more negative and more anxious about the arrival of the former than of the latter groups (Brader, Valentino, & Suhay, 2008). The consequences of these attitudinal variations for the lives of immigrants are substantial. Each encounter of daily life may be shaped by the attitudes held by those with whom one interacts, and the development of goals, options, and beliefs about the future will be shaped accordingly.

Consideration of both ethnic and generational differences by Deaux and her colleagues (Deaux et al., 2007; Wiley, Perkins, & Deaux, 2008) has shown that even when age and historical period are held constant, significant psychological and behavior differences appear between first- and second-generation immigrants. Assessment of the correspondence between measures of private and public regard for one's group, for example, a way of thinking about the degree to which the "looking-glass self" is a common experience, shows differences for both ethnicity and generation. Asian students show a high correspondence between these two perspectives on the value of one's ethnic group and that association does not change between generations. For black immigrant groups, in contrast (and to a slightly lesser degree, Latino immigrant groups), relatively high correspondence in the first generation is contrasted with independence of the two perspectives in the second generation. One explanation of these findings is that black and Latino immigrants encounter more hostility and discrimination in the United States than do immigrants from Asian countries; consequently, one way of coping with these experiences, which are likely to have happened more often to second-generation than to first-generation immigrants, is to disregard what is believed to be a negative evaluation by others when making evaluations of one's ethnic group membership.

This distinction between first- and second-generation immigrants, and specifically Afro-Caribbean immigrants, has behavioral consequences as well. As Deaux et al. (2007) found, the impact of stereotype threat on academic performance is affected; while first-generation immigrants are immune to the effects of stereotype threat (and in fact perform better in threat as compared to no threat conditions), second-generation immigrants show the decline in performance previously demonstrated for native-born African American participants.

The attitudes and behaviors of the outgroup are one important element of the social context for immigrants; but also critical is the nature of ingroup networks that create a greater or lesser degree of social support. One of the characteristics of current immigration to the United States, in contrast to that experienced by immigrants in the mid-20th century, is the existence of sizable communities of ethnic cohorts, already well established and with developed networks. As Massey (1999) and others have noted, the first wave of immigrants arrive in a country with no social and economic resources to draw on. In what Massey terms "cumulative causation," costs and risks of migration are reduced for each subsequent generation of migrants because the community can provide support, information, and connections to jobs and housing. In a recent historical generational analysis of West Indian migration to the United States, Canada, England, and Amsterdam, Model (2009) argues that those who choose to emigrate are generally better educated and more motivated than those who do not emigrate, echoing earlier arguments about dispositional characteristics of

immigrants. However, looking across time periods, Model also finds some decline in the occupational and financial success of later generations of immigrants, an outcome that she attributes to lesser selectivity in subsequent generations. Less educated and less motivated people can more easily immigrate, she argues, in part because the barriers to immigration are essentially lower; that is, the preexisting communities in the new country reduce the challenges and require less motivation to accomplish the task.

In another analysis of West Indian immigration, Foner (2003) points to the differences between West Indian migrants to New York versus London. In the United States, black immigrants arrive to preexisting communities of native-born African Americans and an established racial hierarchy, one that, for better or worse, gives them a certain invisibility to the larger community. In contrast, black immigrants to England are a distinct minority group in an otherwise primarily white community, a condition that was particularly true during the 1950s when the Caribbean immigration to England was at its peak and Southeast Asian migration was still relatively small. These two different contexts set up different social conditions in which immigrant groups and individuals need to develop ways of coping and negotiating their lives.

Some destinations not only provide an ethnic cohort, sometimes a multigenerational community of people who have similar backgrounds and cultural experiences, but also are characterized by a broader immigrant base. New York City, for example, has been referred to as a "majority minority city" because the proportion of native-born whites is a minority within the city (Kasinitz, Mollenkopf, & Waters, 2002). Similarly, immigrants constitute the majority in Los Angeles (though ethnic diversity of the total population is less in Los Angeles than in New York). Such differences in community composition are more than demographic data summaries: these numbers mark distinctly different psychological environments in which issues of ingroup boundaries and self-definition are both variable and crucial. In New York, for example, a second-generation youth may identify him or herself as a "New Yorker" whose peer group includes people from a variety of ethnic groups who share not past tradition but current practices (Kasinitz, Mollenkopf, & Waters, 2002).

An Intersectional Analysis of Immigration Experience

The previous examples of ethnicity, when combined with a consideration of generational differences, suggest how complicated the territory of immigration research can be. Even the concept of generation, which has been considered from two different analytic perspectives, can be further subdivided. For example, demographers have long recognized the importance of age of arrival in their analysis of the outcomes of immigration. The first move in this direction was the introduction of the concept of a 1.5 generation, positioned between first generation (those who are born in another country) and second generation (those whose parents were born in another country but who themselves were born in the new country). The 1.5 generation typically refers to children who were born in a foreign country but who immigrated to the new country before the age of 12, thus experiencing most of their adolescence and high school education in the adopted country. A more finely divided categorization system offered by Rumbaut (2004) considers seven distinct periods of first-generation immigration, ranging from those who arrive in early childhood to those who arrive in late adulthood. Using common demographic outcomes, Rumbaut (2004) reports differences in educational attainment, language proficiency, and encounters with the criminal justice system. The causal mechanisms are typically unspecified and unexplored in these demographic analyses, but the space for investigation by developmental, personality, and social psychologists is great.

In a more psychological analysis of outcomes that might relate to age of arrival, Milstein, Lucić, Galek, and Flannelly (n.d.) hypothesized curvilinear relationships between age at arrival (younger than 6, 6 to 12, and older than 12) and a variety of measures of psychological well-being (e.g., anxiety, self-esteem), making the assumption that the middle-age children would experience the most conflict between pressures from family and peer cultures. Consistent with their predictions, the children who emigrated to the United States between ages 6 and 12 had the lowest level of self-esteem and the highest level of anxiety, compared to those who were either younger or older at time of arrival. We know of no other studies that have explored these more psychological outcomes as a function of age of arrival, but the possibilities for empirical work are exciting, particularly as they might be encompassed by some of the theoretical premises of the Stewart and Healy (1989) model.

As Stewart and Healy (1989) show, the impact of a particular event or set of circumstances is expected to differ, depending on the age at which the social event is experienced. Consider differences even within a single immigrant family, for example, a family of four consisting of parents in their early 30s with a young teenager and a second child under 5 years of age. According to the Stewart and Healy framework, the different ages of family members would predispose them to different experiences and challenges of immigration. For the adults, in early or mature stages of adulthood, the move would be framed in terms of opportunities and life choices, realized in labor market participation and perhaps in terms of anticipated educational opportunities for their children. The adolescent, in contrast, might be beginning to work through issues of personal identity that would now include an immigrant, or hyphenated American identity, among other elements. Equally, the process of immigration is likely to influence the shape of the teenager's identification with the country of origin and with the new identity category "immigrant." For the young child, fundamental values and assumptive frameworks about the world in general would still be the major focus. To the extent that immigration coincided with increased family stress and conflict, it might actually disrupt an earlier sense of a predictable and safe environment. Alternatively, in some families a relatively ready acceptance of the family in the receiving country and parents' and siblings' presence throughout the immigration process might provide a stable and secure context that is the most salient source of expectations about the world.

Another point that Rumbaut (2004) makes about the differences in age of arrival is that ethnic groups often differ. As an example, immigrants to the United States from Mexico and Guatemala are on average younger than are immigrants from Russia and China. Thus a comparison of ethnic immigrant groups, keeping current age constant, might mask differences that are due to the life stage they were in when they first came to the country, an important psychological factor that could easily be ignored in a straightforward demographic comparison. Ethnic differences can also be seen in the patterns of parent-child relationships in immigrant families (Fuligni, Tseng, & Lam, 1999)—in this case, not varying by generation but only by ethnic background. Generally these investigators find that Asian and Latino adolescents have a stronger sense of family obligation than do immigrants with European backgrounds, a psychological variable that has measurable effects on providing assistance to one's family and feeling obligated to provide help in the future. Stewart and Healy (1989) argue that there are individual differences in the disposition to pass on the values and traditions of the previous generation, but also that experiences of generational discontinuity disrupt that disposition. To the extent that teenagers feel that the parental generation's values and traditions are useless because of changed social traditions, the impulse to pass on those values and traditions may decline. That decline in turn can foster intrafamilial distance or conflict (Portes & Rumbaut, 2001; Suárez-Orozco & Suárez-Orozco, 2001).

In sum, the analysis of the interplay of person and social factors in the immigration setting necessarily must include a recognition of the intersectional aspects of key demographic variables. In addition to generation, ethnicity, and age, gender also is likely to be a key factor (see Deaux & Bikmen, 2010). Particularly when considered in terms of the immediate family context, where the balance of power between partners may shift as opportunity structures and forms of contact with the outgroup can differ for men and women, gender is an important moderating factor in the analysis of behavior. The interplay between the person and the social context that is contained within these various demographic categories is a prime example of the need for a framework, such as that offered by Stewart and Healy (1989), that can take both person factors and social-historical context into account.

Seeking Social Change: Personality and Social Movement Experience

A considerable literature across disciplines describes the precursors and sequelae of social movement activity (see Duncan, chapter 31, this volume). Much of this literature focuses on the social-level factors that lead to the development of successful and unsuccessful movements for social change. Additionally, however, investigators have asked what moves individuals to take part in social movements and what are the consequences of social movement participation for the later lives of those involved. This literature has been relatively self-conscious about the issue of life stage at the time of social movement participation; much less often has it examined the impact of important social movements in the social environment for people of all ages. Thus, the impact of social movements has been examined most often only from the perspective of activists—nearly always a tiny minority of the population affected by large social movements (e.g., the women's movement, the civil rights movement, and the antiwar movement of the late 1960s/early 1970s).

Psychologists paid little attention to social movement participation before the student movements of the 1960s, partly because many of those movements did not attract mass public support and perhaps partly because they did not interest the predominantly white, male, middle- and upper-class scholars of that period. (The labor movement is a striking example of a movement that did attract significant public support, and still psychologists did not study the impact of labor movement activism on individuals.) However, in research on 1960s student activists, we learned that their parents' activism in the 1930s had been consequential in their own development (Block, Haan, & Smith, 1973; Rothman & Lichter, 1982). We know nothing, except from memoirs and historians, about the psychological significance of political and social movement activism for that generation of adult activists themselves, but the fact that the impulse to participate in social movement politics persisted across generations suggests that there were important effects. Moreover, later studies have shown that activists from the 1960s generation tended to have children who were activists in their own time (Duncan & Stewart, 1995). In short, there is reason to believe that even when social movements do not have demonstrable effects on the larger society, the experience of participation in them affects the individuals who engage in them, as well as their offspring.

Some social movements lead individuals to address a particular social issue; then there is significant change in the social context, and the movement must adapt to the changed circumstances. The movement in opposition to the Vietnam War took that shape. Many young people participated in some activity opposing the war at some point and many more observed and cared about the activism of others (Stewart, Settles, & Winter, 1998, refer to these as "engaged observers"). When the war did end, participants understood the meaning of their activism differently, some believing that the activism was effective in bringing an end to the war and others concluding that it had been ineffective. This issue of political efficacy has been identified as one important consequence of social movement participation; most evidence suggests that participation generally fosters both political efficacy and further political participation in later adulthood (Cole & Stewart, 1996; Cole, Zucker, & Ostrove, 1998; Fendrich & Lovoy, 1988; McAdam, 1988, 1989). Thus, even though a social movement may "end," the individual activist is likely to view the political arena as personally relevant in the future (Cole & Stewart, 1996; Duncan, 1999; Stewart, Settles, & Winter, 1998).

The social movement activism of the 1960s and 1970s was strongly associated with youth, and specifically with college students. This association is much less marked for the long-term and earlier civil rights movement. In the 1940s, 1950s, and early 1960s the prime movers in the civil rights movement included adults of all ages (Branch, 1988; Marable, 1984; Stewart, 1999). However, Freedom Summer in 1964 initiated a new phase of the movement that specifically engaged young adults. Some of our earliest and most detailed understanding of the impact of civil rights participation comes from research focused largely on white students who engaged in this phase of the struggle (e.g., McAdam, 1989). It is regrettable that we have so little data from the previous period, when it would have been much more feasible to examine the psychological significance of participating in the movement at different ages. We do have some memoirs, biographies, and case studies, however, that are important sources of information both about people's motivation to engage in the civil rights movement, and the impact on them of doing so (Barnard, 1990; Stalvey, 1970; Stewart, 1999).

Careful comparisons of young activists and sympathetic nonactivists (e.g., those who applied but did not participate in Freedom Summer) suggest that participation in the civil rights movement did not alter activists' political attitudes or opinions (Franz & McClelland, 1994; McAdam, 1989). However, as adults those who participated were less likely than their sympathizing counterparts to pursue conventional work and family lives and were less focused on traditional indicators of "success," such as income (Fendrich & Lovoy, 1988; Flacks, 1988; McAdam, 1989; Franz & McClelland, 1994). It is, of course, difficult to know whether these different outcomes are the consequence of their activist experience or of their less conventional values and attitudes as young adults, or both.

Although there is little explicit work on the impact of movements on people of varying ages, social movement scholars have recognized the way in which social movements can create "generations" within a society. Thus, individuals who have been powerfully influenced by a particular social movement—whether or not they were activists in it—may come to identify strongly with their age peers. Like Stewart and Healy (1989), most of these scholars draw on the theoretical account of Karl

Mannheim (1952), who proposed that some generations are defined by the way that a particular age cohort experiences disruptive social changes (which are often accompanied by social movements). These historically defined generations in turn become a part of the political and social landscape with consequences for generations that precede and follow them. Thus, the generation of adults in the late 1940s and 1950s ("the Silent Generation") was defined in contrast to the depression and war generations; and the generation of adults in the late 1970s and 1980s ("GenX") in the United States were defined substantially in contrast to the baby boomers who came of age in the 1960s and early 1970s (Strauss & Howe, 1991). The "Greatest Generation" and the Baby Boom operate then to define others' experience as well as their own. Social movement scholars have noticed that during some periods protest movement activists view their movement as based in unique generational experience. This process of generational identification happens most often in the context of social movements when activism is strongly concentrated in young adults, such as the student movements in Europe, the United States, and Japan in 1968 (Kurlansky, 2004; Passerini, 1996), and the revolutions in Eastern Europe and China in 1989 (Braungart & Braungart, 1994). This identification with a generation may have consequences of its own that alter or amplify the impact of the social movement itself. Thus, though many student activists in the 1960s were focused on particular political goals (e.g., civil rights for African Americans, ending the war in Vietnam, access to legal abortion), nonetheless their identification with their generation may have broadened their focus to include the need to end inequalities of various kinds, and to reject material values and goals. This broader focus in turn may partially account for their tendency as adults to concentrate in relatively lower-paid human service occupations (Fendrich & Lovoy, 1988; Franz & McClelland, 1994; Nassi, 1981; Whalen & Flacks, 1989).

It appears, then, that if individuals engage in social movement activism during their youth, there is likely to be considerable long-term impact on their personal, vocational, and political lives. One cause of that impact may be core values that led them into social protest activism in the first place; another may be their identification with their age peers and construction of a generational identity; and a third may be the experience of political efficacy. There is some evidence for all of these possibilities. In addition, it is possible, as Stewart and

Healy (1989) would suggest, that it is critical that these individuals were young adults at the time—that is, at a time in their lives when they were actively engaged in a process of self-definition and identity formation. The identity they formed may have provided a politicized self-understanding that in turn provides consistent motivation for continued political participation. This possibility is best addressed by research that compares generations or cohorts that were of different ages when exposed to particular social movements.

One social movement that has been studied relatively extensively is the "second wave" women's movement that took place in the late 1960s and 1970s in the United States. The impact of the movement on women's (and men's) lives, as well as on social institutions in the United States (e.g., the family, the workplace and the public sphere) has been documented by historians, sociologists, demographers, and economists (see, e.g., Blau DuPlessis & Snitow, 1998; Enke, 2007; Epstein, 2009; Goldin, 2006; Rosen, 2000). Establishing a precise causal account is generally impossible in the context of changes occurring in so many domains and over such a long period, but there is agreement that social life in the United States before and after the women's movement was profoundly different. The historian Rosen (2000) describes her experience asking students in the 1980s what they knew about the conditions for women before the women's movement. Shocked by their lack of awareness, "I began to cover the blackboard with short catch phrases that reflected some of the ordinary but invariably painful female experiences that the women's movement had excavated and exposed to public view. . . . What stunned me was that the changes in women's lives had been so deep, so wide-ranging, so transformative" (p. xiii). Many changes occurred in the legal and policy domain, including the end of sex-segregated job advertisements, recognition of sexual harassment as a phenomenon in the workplace, legalization of contraceptive availability to various age groups, and legal protection from sex discrimination in a range of areas (Epstein, 2009; Pedriana, 2004).

In a thorough analysis of precisely what changed in women's lives (as opposed to policy and law), the economist Goldin (2006) argues that changes in control of fertility, human capital investment (education), marriage and childbearing age, labor force participation, and wages were all part of a "quiet revolution that transformed women's employment, education, and family" (p. 1). Rates of women's pursuit of higher education and the labor force participation of mothers of young children both increased substantially. As women's economic independence increased, so did rates of childlessness and divorce. Thus not only were women's lives changed, but so were the social institutions of work and family.

Though an economist herself, Goldin (2006) points to some possible psychological processes that were behind these large-scale changes. For example, expectations regarding future work, social norms concerning women's family and career, and factors accounting for women's life satisfaction all gradually shifted over successive years. Some of the changes were preconditions for others, such as college majors, professional school enrollment, and occupational change. Goldin cites evidence that "Young women in their late teens during the 1970s upwardly revised their expectations of being in the paid labor force when they were older" (p. 9). She notes that this shift in expectations "may have been enabled" by the "resurgence of feminism . . . and the women's liberation movement . . . [which] supported their challenging older ways and outmoded norms" (p. 9, note 29). She further speculates that increased contraceptive availability (especially "the pill") increased women's control over their fertility, and that women were able to create identities around lifetime careers, as well as families.

In addition to this evidence of the changed circumstances of women's lives associated with the women's movement, social attitudes about women's roles changed as well. For example, the sociologists Mason and Lu (1988) showed that both men's and women's attitudes toward women's family roles were more "profeminist" in 1985 than in 1977. In a more recent review Huddy, Neely, and Lafay (2000) examined support for improvement in "women's status in society" as assessed in national polls in the 1970s, 1980s, and 1990s. They show that fewer than 50% of both men and women supported improvements in women's status in 1970 and 1971; by the end of the decade the rate was about two-thirds for both. By 1994 the rates were 78% of women and 71% of men. In short, considerable evidence indicates that there was more support after the women's movement than before for women's efforts to increase their educational and occupational accomplishments and general status in society.

What have psychologists contributed to our understanding of the consequences of the second wave women's movement for women's lives? First, some of the research on the impact of experiences of activism has focused on the women's movement. Cole and Stewart (1996), for example, examined the impact of participation in the women's movement in later life for black and white women who had attended the University of Michigan in the late 1960s and early 1970s. They found that women who reported that they had been active in the movement during college (a majority of both the black and white subsamples) were also more politically active in middle age and higher in midlife social responsibility. In an analysis of women who had been publicly recognized student activists (not merely self-described ones), Cole, Zucker, and Ostrove (1998) showed that this high level of activism was associated in middle age not only with higher levels of political efficacy and collectivism, but also with higher levels of feminist consciousness and identity. Stewart, Settles, and Winter (1998) differentiated between women who were activists and both nonparticipants and "engaged observers," or women who were interested in and informed about the movement, but not activists themselves. They found that activists were more likely than both engaged observers and nonparticipants to be politically active in middle age. However, engaged observers and activists were equally likely to report that the movement had an impact on their lives, and to have well-developed political attitudes. Interestingly, in one sample Stewart, Settles, and Winter (1998) were able to assess the type of impact that different movements had on women's lives. Forms of impact in this case included consequences for their worldview or political understanding, indirect effects through intimate others (e.g., the impact of war on brothers and husbands), and direct effects on their own personal lives. Participation in the women's movement differed from participation in the civil rights and antiwar movements in that women reported that it had a much greater impact on their personal lives.

Duncan and Stewart (2000) examined a sample of women who had participated in the 1992 March on Washington for Reproductive Rights. Taking advantage of the age heterogeneity in the sample, they assessed generational differences among activists in that protest and found that the women who "came of age" during the period of the second wave women's movement (like those studied in the research described above) were more likely to identify with the label "feminist" than women from older or younger cohorts. The impact of the women's movement in politicizing women's collective identification with women, and influencing personality

development, has been examined in several other studies. Using five samples of college-educated women, Duncan and Agronick (1995) confirmed the hypothesis that the movement had a greater impact on women who were young adults at the height of the women's movement than on women who were middle-aged at the time. Although the younger cohort generally attached much greater significance to the movement, women in both cohorts who found meaning in the women's movement were more likely to have attained higher educational and career outcomes, and to be assertive and self-confident in midlife. Thus, the impact of the movement was similar for both cohorts of women who were affected by it, but the impact was more widely felt—as expected—for the young adults. In a study focused on personality development, Agronick and Duncan (1998) compared women who reported that the women's movement had a substantial impact on them with those who did not. They found that felt impact of the women's movement was associated with higher levels of dominance, self-acceptance, empathy, psychological-mindedness and achievement via independence.

Zucker and Stewart (2007) tested a different hypothesis with multiple cohorts. Using a sample of three generations of alumnae from the University of Michigan (women who graduated in the early 1950s, 1970s, and 1990s), they found that the women in the youngest cohort—born after the second wave, and with the gains of the women's movement as part of their background environment of rearing—were more likely than older women to report that they held feminist beliefs as children. Thus, as Stewart and Healy (1989) predict, feminist ideology had become part of their "assumptive world." Studying only contemporary young women, Aronson (2008) reported that young adult women have incorporated independence and self-development into their notions of being adults—ideas not associated with adult femininity before the women's movement. Consistent with these findings, meta-analytic assessment of patterns of self-assessed agency and communion show that women's agency has increased over time, while there has been little change in communal orientation for either women or men between the mid-1970s and the mid-1990s (Twenge, 1997).

Some research has documented the role that negative stereotypes of feminists has played in the development of this younger generation of women (see, e.g., Buschman & Lenart, 1996). Second wave feminists, for example, were found to associate the women's movement with empowerment and liberation, while younger feminists reported having to overcome negative images before embracing the identity (Horne, Mathews, Detrie, Burke, & Cook (2001).

Stewart (1994) approached the question of age at the time of encounter with feminism in a very different way: with three case studies of women drawn from the same cohort. She showed that the meaning of the women's movement was actually different for each woman, despite their shared cohort. For example, one of the three, even though she was a young adult at the time of the women's movement, came to college with a strong distaste for the traditional female role and experienced the women's movement as confirming and supporting her preexisting worldview. It was important to her, but not transformative. In contrast, for a second woman who had married and become a mother right after college, the women's movement offered a transformative vision both of the social world and of her own life, in much the way Stewart and Healy predicted for young adults forming identities. Finally, a third woman, who was also exposed to the women's movement at the time that she was a young mother, saw it as a remote and irrelevant phenomenon. More than a decade later, in the context of her divorce and career changes, feminism suddenly became a central focus of her reading and thinking and revolutionized her perspective. These three women of the same generation actually encountered feminism in a serious way at three different life stages (in childhood, young adulthood, and middle age), and its impact was very much in line with the Stewart and Healy model of impact at those three different times in the life span. Thus, a person's *chronological age* at a particular moment (1970, for example) is much less important than her *psychological life stage*, or age at the time of the impact of an important social event. Moreover, some events are likely to have substantial impact at the time they happen but are unlikely to have lingering effects on individuals as they age, while others (like the women's movement) remain culturally available for years.

Evidence across studies suggests that social movements have substantial consequences for identity, personality, cognitive perspective, and later behavior. More importantly for our argument, the evidence also suggests that the age or life stage of an individual at the time is an important context shaping different effects, with the effects stronger and more pervasive if individuals were adolescents or young adults at the time of their involvement.

Finally, though participation in social movements has been a major focus of research on their effects, it would clearly be valuable to examine their impact across generations, not only among activists but among people of all ages at that time, and in the children of those who experience transformative social changes or strong continuities over time.

Catastrophes of Human and Natural Origin

We have considered several different forms of change that result from the interplay of personality and social context. Each of the cases described so far includes, to a large extent, a choice made by an individual or a small group of people (e.g., a decision to seek a divorce, a decision to move to another country, a decision to participate in a social movement). At the same time, each of these behaviors is shaped by the existing social context, in ways both recognized and not. The understanding and experience of divorce is influenced by the existing social norms and the frequency of divorce in the society; the likelihood and ease of immigration is affected by one's knowledge of others who have made the move and by the policies and economic conditions of both country of origin and country of destination; and participation in social movements has a reciprocal relationship with the political conditions of a society at a given time and place.

Other events clearly originate at the social or natural level, such as wars, economic depressions, hurricanes and earthquakes. In this case, the individual does not choose whether or not to engage in the event, but rather decides how to respond to it. Although these events often affect the entire population in some way, they typically do not have uniform effects. Consequently, psychologists have taken advantage of these often tragic circumstances to study the general impact of large-scale social changes, not only as they affect the population at large but also in terms of their effects on particular groups and on individuals, both as general processes and occasionally as a function of age at the time of the event. Although these studies do exist, we believe that psychologists could make more extensive use of these opportunities to increase our understanding of personality continuity and change as a function of the intersection of individuals' life stage and these events.

The General Impact of War

War is unquestionably a major life stressor for everyone exposed to it, whether soldier or civilian. In a meta-analysis of 72 studies assessing the impact of exposure to war and 5 other types of events (bereavement, illness, injury, disasters, and violence), Sundin and Horowitz (2003) found that exposure to war produced the largest impact on people. Nevertheless, most studies of the impact of World War II have focused only on immediate psychological sequelae for soldiers, including post-traumatic stress disorder (PTSD; Magruder & Yeager, 2009). A few recent studies of these veterans have focused on the long-term impact of their war experience on mental health, marital and family relationships, work lives, and physical health and mortality, typically emphasizing the cost of war experience to individual lives (Dirkzwager, Bramsen, & Ploeg, 2001; Elder, Clipp, Brown, Martin, & Friedman, 2009; Elder, Shanahan, & Clipp, 1994).

Elder and his colleagues (Elder, Shanahan, & Clipp, 1994; Lee, Vaillant, Torrey, & Elder, 1995; MacLean & Elder, 2007) have considered the differential impact of the timing of military experience during wartime as well as exposure to combat. They consistently find that combat exposure is a strong predictor of negative outcomes; somewhat less consistent findings point to more benign effects for men who were younger (those in their teens and early twenties) in comparison with those who were older (usually early thirties) at the time of their war experience. The emphasis in this research has been on the life and career disruptive aspects of wartime experience for older men, though Stewart and Healy's model might point us to consider that men in their early thirties also have well-developed identities and are therefore expected to be more resistant to change than younger men. Considerably less research has focused on the impact of war on those who remain at home: women, children, and older men. However, historians have debated the impact of World War II on American women's labor force participation, and some research suggests that wartime work experience was a powerful force in creating an enduring occupational identity for women (Anderson, 1981; Chafe, 1990; Hartmann, 1982). Stewart and Malley (2004) argue that in addition the experience of independent coping during this period supported women's development of confidence in their own capacities.

Some longitudinal projects studied the American generation that was most directly affected by World War II as young adults (e.g., the Stanford-Terman data; Elder, Shanahan, & Clipp, 1997; the Grant Study; see Lee, Vaillant, Torrey, & Elder, 1995; and the Berkeley Guidance and Berkeley and Oakland Growth Studies; see Clausen, 1993), but few investigations have considered how the war may have mattered differently for different kinds of individuals. In a handful of studies, prewar personalities had been assessed and investigators were able to examine differential responses to war experiences as a function of personality. In a study of lifelong mortality risk in the same sample, Elder, Clipp, Brown, Martin, and Friedman (2009) found that prewar mental health and personality variables did not predict early mortality, while overseas duty, service in the Pacific theater, and combat exposure did (see also Elder, Shanahan, & Clipp, 1997). Across many studies combat exposure has been identified as a significant factor in postwar adjustment after World War II and little evidence was generated from that research suggesting that prewar personality factors were consequential for postwar sequelae. For that reason, research on veterans of later wars has also focused on combat exposure (Foy & Card, 1987; Green, Grace, Lindy, Gleser, & Leonard, 1990). We note, though, that the World War II–related datasets available to assess the impact of personality as a moderator of the impact of combat exposure (or other experiences) included only limited data on personality, and also only included limited data on wartime experience. Contemporary research on veterans includes more extensive assessments of personality and wartime experiences and holds the promise of identifying somewhat more nuanced understanding of the impact of war on soldiers. Schnurr, Friedman, and Rosenberg (1993) examined prewar personalities in a sample of Dartmouth graduates who participated in the Vietnam War and found that those men with more introverted and withdrawn prewar personalities, when exposed to combat, were more likely to develop PTSD symptoms. Civilians exposed to, but not participating in, war can also show negative effects. Bramsen, Dirkzwager, and Van Der Ploeg (2000), for example, were able to replicate the Schnurr et al. (1993) findings in a sample of civilian peacekeepers who were exposed to traumatic violence as part of their roles.

The central importance of combat exposure to all of these findings has been recognized as indicating that both soldiers and civilians in zones of open conflict face massive stressors that, in the case of PTSD, overwhelm the coping capacities of those who experience the stress. In line with these findings, Zeidner and Ben-Zur (1993) examined the different coping strategies used by a large sample of Israeli civilians faced with the threat of SCUD missile attacks during the Persian Gulf War. They found fairly strong evidence of coping patterns linked with gender stereotypes (women reporting higher levels of social support seeking and emotional expression than men; men reporting higher levels of denial). At the same time, both women and men reported using both emotion-focused and problem-focused coping strategies, suggesting that in crises like war people may tend to mobilize all coping strategies even if to different degrees according to cultural norms. In this study, emotion-focused coping was associated with distress, while problem-focused coping was not, suggesting that the passive role often associated with exposure to combat and danger in war is particularly problematic. In a study of Yugoslav civilians affected by air attacks a year earlier, Lecic-Tosevski, Gavrilovic, Knezevic, and Priebe (2003) found that personality traits assessed before the attacks predicted intrusive or avoidance symptoms following them. Individuals with "detached" personalities before the attacks were more likely to experience intrusive symptoms after the attacks. While we do not yet have a well-developed understanding of the role of personality in war responses, there is strong evidence that personality characteristics are not associated with combat exposure itself, but are related to the postexposure responses. We must pursue the leads we have, not only so we can develop a fuller understanding of people's reactions to extreme situations like war, but also more differentiated responses to those suffering aftereffects of exposure to war.

Some research has considered the impact of war exposure on children who live in war zones, looking at children's psychological stress symptoms, as well as at aggression and the kinds of expectations these children develop about safety, security, and the trustworthiness of other people (Leavitt & Fox, 1993; Qouta, Punamaki, & El Sarraj, 2008; Sagi-Schwartz, 2008). Though not animated specifically by Stewart and Healy's theory, this research confirms the importance of social context—including both violence and the family environment within a violent context—in shaping children's expectations about the world. Cummings, Goeke-Morey, Schermerhorn, Merrilees, and Cairns (2009) have offered an adaptation of Bronfenbrenner's ecological model of development (1986) aimed at the study of children's responses to political violence of all kinds. They stress the importance of simultaneously and comparatively examining different political conflicts, as well as different family environments, and children's different responses. Comparative studies of children who are similar in ethnicity and economic and educational resources in the family, but who grow up in settings that differ in terms of violence, would provide valuable evidence to clarify precisely how exposure to community violence and war have the effects on children that they do. In addition, we know little about how children with different temperaments or personalities respond to war exposure, though it seems likely that some children are more highly attuned to and anxious about these experiences, and some may be particularly vulnerable to angry and aggressive responses. It is important for us to understand more about these potentially different reactions as we cope with more and more children who have been raised in areas of substantial intergroup violence and war.

The Impact of Particular War Experiences: The Holocaust and Internment

The events surrounding World War II also served as an impetus for the study of the effects of other experiences during wartime periods, such as the Holocaust and the internment of Japanese Americans. Many early studies confirmed that survivors of these experiences suffer from high rates of PTSD symptoms, but later studies with more careful approaches to sampling and measurement found less consistent evidence of any particular "survivor syndrome" (see Baranowsky, Young, Johnson-Douglas, Williams-Keeler, & McCarrey, 1998; Ozer, Best, Lipsey, & Weiss, 2003; and Shmotkin & Lomranz, 1998, for reviews). One difficulty in this literature is the designation of appropriate comparison groups, though some have been suggested, such as Jewish immigrants from Europe to the United States, Israel, or Canada who were not concentration camp survivors (Leon, Butcher, Kleinman, Goldberg, & Almagor, 1981) and Jews who had immigrated at other times and were not in Europe at the time of the Holocaust (Shmotkin & Lomranz, 1998). The person's age at the time of their traumatic experience has not been a particular focus of this work. However, van der Hal-van Raalte, van Ijzendoorn, and Bakermans-Kranenberg (2008) studied post-traumatic stress in a sample of older adults who had survived the Holocaust as children and found that survivors who had adopted a strong "sense of coherence" (an orientation to life that develops over the life span and aims toward problem-solving and adaptation to changed circumstances) were buffered from the continued impact in old age of severe traumatic experience during the war. In contrast, the survivors who scored low in coherence were higher in post-traumatic symptoms.

Because the sense of coherence was assessed long after the Holocaust it is impossible to know whether survivors differed in personality resources before the Holocaust. It is an important priority both to understand whether these personality resources matter in children exposed to traumatic experiences, and whether they can be enhanced after traumatic exposure in childhood.

Many studies of the impact of the Holocaust on individuals have considered the intergenerational "transmission" of the traumatic experience and the nature of the family dynamics in households headed by survivors of the Holocaust and other traumatic experiences during war (see especially Danieli, 1998). Although there is considerable debate about whether second- (and third-) generation effects on mental health exist (see, e.g., Baranowsky et al., 1998; Leon et al.,1981; Sigal & Weinfeld, 1989), there is greater agreement that the families of Holocaust survivors have some common features that are (on average) different from comparison households. These include a constrained communication pattern involving a sense that there is an important and painful past experience in one or more parents' lives; that the parents prefer not to talk about that experience; and that it is important to develop survival skills (see, e.g., Baranowsky et al., 1998; Prince, 1985; Sigal & Weinfeld, 1989). In a study of the children of Holocaust survivors without a comparison group, Wiseman (2008) found high levels of reported loneliness and "failed intersubjectivity"; she argues that the sense of not being understood and not understanding the experience of another is at the heart of the family dynamic in these families. These kinds of features might be expected to shape the childhood expectations about social relationships, safety and security, even if they might not generate mental health problems or the "transmission of trauma." It is important, then, for studies of intergenerational effects to focus not only on potential outcomes for mental health, but on beliefs, values, and expectations, as well as relational and survival skills.

Parallel studies have been conducted on the impact of internment camps in the United States during World War II, particularly for Japanese Americans. The deprivation of civil rights, property and resources, and freedom was consequential not only for adults who were interned but also for their children, including both those who were interned with their parents and the later offspring of previously interned parents. The issue of family dynamics has been a major focus of this research, in contrast to the emphasis on mental health outcomes and PTSD that characterizes research on the active participants in warfare. Nagata (1993, 1998), for example, found some key differences in the family lives reported by Japanese Americans born after the war, depending on whether their parents had been interned or not. Familial communication was one important difference: although the internment was mentioned in families of internees, it was not discussed freely or openly. Interestingly, when parents did discuss their experience they rarely expressed negative feelings about it or described negative features of the camps. Children formed a view of the experience as secret, suspecting there was much more to know than they were told. In addition, children of internees expressed lower self-esteem, and more shame than those whose parents were not interned, but they also developed a stronger interest in their ethnic heritage and ethnic identity. In a follow-up analysis, Nagata, Trierweiler, and Talbot (1999) found that children who had never been interned themselves reported this pattern of painful silence within the family and strong ethnic identity more than those children who were themselves interned with their parents as infants or small children. The authors draw directly on Stewart and Healy's theorizing to suggest that even this very early direct exposure to the internment shaped the worldviews of young internees. They suggest in addition that perhaps the sense of a shared experience—even with a small child—mitigates the isolation and separation between the generations (also reported by Wiseman, 2008, for Holocaust survivors' families). Nagata and Cheng (2003) collected parallel data from the parents directly. Consistent with results from the children, the parents reported both greater silence about the internment experience and a wish to spare their children from exposure to knowledge of it, in comparison with noninterned parents. Interestingly, though, they reported much higher overall rates of discussing the internment with their children than the children did, perhaps reflecting their wishes or intentions rather than their actual behavior.

Nagata (1999) analyzed the experiences of three young women who were interned with their families at different ages (12, 20, and 23). Consistent with Stewart and Healy's theory, she argues that the internment experience had some age-related effects; for example, the association entirely with her ethnic group during the internment enhanced the ethnic identification of the youngest girl. Equally, the older girls felt more able to build skills and knowledge they cared about during the internment, and thus viewed it as an experience they could shape and that did not merely shape them. Finally, does personality matter in post-traumatic family dynamics? It seems plausible that parents with different temperaments and dispositions might address the task of parenting after social trauma differently, but the literature reveals little along these lines.

Although the literature on social trauma like the Holocaust and the internment is relatively extensive, it has relied heavily on clinical rather than community samples and has focused more on post-traumatic mental health than on other psychological outcomes. Findings about family dynamics in post-trauma households across these two experiences are so similar that they suggest an important direction for research. Do parents who have survived more individual-directed traumas (e.g., sexual abuse or other forms of violence) create the same kinds of households, with a weighty silence and sense of secrecy dominating interactions? Are there differences—for example in the implications for ethnic identity, or for expression of guilt and anger—in the households of survivors of social traumas that affect an entire group, which may thereby feel implicated (e.g., in being Jewish or Japanese American) and ones that are much more individual or not targeted at a group to which other family members belong (e.g., sexual abuse, rape, or violence)?

Other Traumatic Events

Unfortunately, there is no shortage of traumatic events in our contemporary world, and consequently we can point to multiple sites where one might instructively consider the interplay of person and context when high-impact events are unanticipated but must be dealt with in some fashion. The recent earthquakes in Haiti, Chile, New Zealand, and Japan are vivid examples; the ramifications of the 9/11 attack in the United States and similar strikes in Madrid and in London are additional instances. Hurricane Katrina and its aftermath in New Orleans is yet another example. In many of these cases, it is too early to look for substantial research that might serve as a case study for the kind of analysis we are proposing here. However, some published work concerning Katrina and 9/11 has emerged. In both of these cases, large populations were affected by the events; at the same time, both cases also illustrate the ways in which events have an uneven impact on the population, creating quite different situations for members of some groups

than for others. In the case of 9/11, for example, one can look to the impact of the event on the resident Arab and Muslim populations in particular, who because of their assumed similarity with the perpetrators, had distinctive post-9/11 experiences. For many members of the Arab and Muslim communities, the aftermath was a complicated mix, including both widespread discrimination at individual and institutional levels as well as new opportunities for self-definition and collective action on behalf of their communities (Cainkar, 2009). Similarly, as a consequence of residential housing patterns, predominantly black and poor neighborhoods in New Orleans were the site of much more serious and long-lasting consequences than were more upscale neighborhoods.

Concluding Thoughts

Our analysis of personality and contexts across the life span provides a distinctive framework for the kinds of issues that this *Handbook* addresses. We have in many respects defined our task quite broadly: On the personality side we include not only trait dimensions, but also cognitive styles, values, political attitudes, and social identities; on the social side, we consider immediate situations but we focus too on broad social contexts and events that dramatically influence people's lives, such as war, divorce, and natural disasters. Further, our basic model is one that demands consideration of a historical time line, whose influence is to be discerned in the interplay of personal development and historical circumstance.

This perspective on personality and social psychology has implications both for theoretical conceptions and for methodological choices. At a conceptual level, the influence of personality and social factors on each other is complex; causal direction cannot be automatically assumed, and the possibilities for change must be taken into account. Often, discussions of the relationship between these two have been represented as a P × S interaction, probably deriving from the previously dominant analysis of variance framework in which two main effects can also contribute to (or be submerged by) a more significant interaction effect. While that idea still has utility, we would argue that more complicated models are also needed to account for the role that persons and contexts play as they are joined across the life course. The two components are at times not easily disentangled as people operate in their lived environment—environments that may, in Lewinian terms, be more a subjective life space than a set of conditions that can be specifically characterized in general terms. Further, when we extend our thinking beyond a specific point in time to a longer sequence of actions and events, the need to consider bidirectionality and mutual causation becomes apparent. Situations can affect and change persons; but persons, in their choices to enter or avoid situations, or to interpret them to fit their own schema, can also alter the nature of those situations.

Another clear implication of our model is that we need to incorporate some kinds of developmental thinking into our social and personality models. The same event occurring with people who may be equivalent on some measure of personality will not necessarily have the same impact or yield the same outcome at different points in the life span. Social psychologists have typically been uninterested in variations in behavior as a function of age, most often finessing the question by concentrating on readily available college students. Personality psychologists have also tended to emphasize patterns that can be viewed as more or less "universal," at least among adults. We argue here for paying attention to the different tasks and dynamics associated with particular life stages into our studies of the connections between personality and social contexts. This call for more developmental thinking has methodological implications as well. Certainly it would be helpful if we had more longitudinal studies in our storeroom. Longitudinal studies, used more often by developmental psychologists and personality psychologists than by social psychologists, are often systematically planned to include a defined set of measures over a specified period of time. Yet it is also possible, we suggest, to develop more serendipitous strategies for building a longitudinal data base. When unexpected events occur at the societal level, it would be possible for ingenious investigators to look to past data bases to find measures that could serve as appropriate "before" assessments, to then be followed up with new data collections that would use comparable measures on a similar population. Equally, collecting new data from a cross-section of age groups would provide the basis for longitudinal assessment of different patterns of change for people who experience changes at different times in their lives. Such strategies would give us valuable information about the effect of large events on a broad spectrum of society, including, if the data allowed, information about the interplay of personality and social factors.

Certainly statistical models have a role to play in this longitudinal framework. Indeed, if statistical models unconsciously guide our theorization, we might look to the emergence of path analysis and structural equation modeling, as well as multilevel modeling (see Christ, Sibley, & Wagner, chapter 10, this volume) as guides for the next generation of personality-social theorizing, playing a role comparable to that of analysis of variance and regression in earlier generations. Implicit in our message is also a call (hardly original on our part) to expand and diversify the participant pool of our research. Variables such as age, gender, class, ethnicity, and generation all make a difference—not in and of themselves, but as markers for particular kinds of experiences that influence thought and action.

In this chapter we have argued that in some research areas psychologists have already been building the kind of rich and integrative understanding that our framework allows. We hope that personality and social psychologists working in other areas will be inspired to incorporate explicit attention to all of the elements we have considered here—personality, social and personal life changes, developmental stages, and historical periods—and that they will find the combination greater and more generative than the sum of its parts.

Acknowledgments

We would like to thank Nicola Curtin and Nicky Newton for helpful comments on an earlier version of the manuscript.

References

Agronick, G. S., & Duncan, L. E. (1998). Personality and social change: Individual differences, life path, and importance attributed to women's movement. *Journal of Personality and Social Psychology, 74*(6), 1545–1555.

Alba, R. (2009). *Blurring the color line: The new chance for a more integrated America.* Cambridge, MA: Harvard University Press.

Aluja, A., Garcia, O., & Garcia, L.F. (2003). Relationships among extraversion, openness to experience, and sensation seeking. *Personality and Individual Differences, 35*(3), 671-680.

Amato, P. R., & Keith, B. (1991). Parental divorce and adult well-being: A meta-analysis. *Journal of Marriage and the Family, 55,* 43–58.

Anderson, K. (1981). *Wartime women: Sex roles, family relations, and the status of women during World War II.* Westport, CT: Greenwood.

Aronson, P. (2008). The markers and meanings of growing up: Contemporary young women's transition from adolescence to adulthood. *Gender and Society, 22,* 56–82.

Barnard, H. F. (Ed.). (1990). *Outside the magic circle: The autobiography of Virginia Foster Durr.* Tuscaloosa: University of Alabama Press.

Baranowsky, A. B., Young, M., Johnson-Douglas, S., Williams-Keeler, L., & McCarrey, M. (1998). PTSD transmission: A review of secondary traumatization in Holocaust survivor families. *Canadian Psychology, 39*(4), 247–256.

Barrett, A. E. (2003). Race differences in the mental health effects of divorce. *Journal of Family Issues, 24,* 995–1010.

Blau DuPlessis, R., & Snitow, A. (Eds.). (1998). *The feminist memoir project: Voices from women's liberation.* New York: Three Rivers Press.

Block, J. H., Block, J., & Gjerde, P. F. (1986). The personality of children prior to divorce: A prospective study. *Child Development, 57,* 827–840.

Block, J. H., Haan, N., & Smith, M. B. (1973). Socialization correlates of student activism. *Journal of Social Issues, 25,* 143–177.

Boneva, B. S., & Frieze, I. H. (2001). Toward a concept of a migrant personality. *Journal of Social Issues, 57*(3), 477–491.

Bonnano, G. A., & Jost, J. T. (2006). Conservative shift among high exposure survivors of the September 11th terrorist attacks. *Basic and Applied Social Psychology, 28,* 311–323.

Brader, T., Valentino, N. A., & Suhay, E. (2008). What triggers public opposition to immigration? Anxiety, group cues, and immigration threat. *American Journal of Political Science, 52,* 959–978.

Bramsen, I., Dirkzwager, A. J., & Van Der Ploeg, H. M. (2000). Predeployment personality traits and exposure to trauma as predictors of posttraumatic stress symptoms: A prospective study of former peacekeepers. *American Journal of Psychiatry, 157*(7), 11115–11159.

Branch, T. (1988). *Parting the waters: America in the King years, 1954–1963.* New York: Simon & Schuster.

Braungart, R. G., & Braungart, M. M. (1994). Political attitudes and behaviour of Chinese youth: Interpretations of the 1989 Beijing uprising. *Politics and the Individual, 4*(1), 1–29.

Bronfenbrenner, U. (1986). Ecology of the family as a context for human development: Research perspectives. *Developmental Psychology, 22*(6), 723-742.

Bursik, K. (1991). Adaptation to divorce and ego development in adult women. *Journal of Personality and Social Psychology, 60,* 300–306.

Buschman, J. K., & Lenart, S. (1996). "I am not a feminist, but . . ." College women, feminism, and negative experiences. *Political Psychology, 17*(1), 58–75.

Cainkar, L. A. (2009). *Homeland insecurity: The Arab American and Muslim American experience after 9/11.* New York: Russell Sage.

Chafe, W. H. (1990). World War II as a pivotal experience for American women. In M. Dietrich & D. Fischer-Hornung (Eds.), *Women and war: The changing status of American women from the 1930s to the 1950s* (pp. 21–34). New York: St. Martin's.

Chase-Lonsdale, P. L., & Hetherington, E. M. (1990). The impact of divorce on life-span development: Short and long term effects. In D. L. Featherman & R. Lerner (Eds.), *Life span development and behavior* (Vol. 10, pp. 105–151). Hillsdale, NJ: Erlbaum.

Clausen, J. A. (1993). *American lives: Looking back at the children of the Great Depression.* New York: Free Press.

Cole, E. R., & Stewart, A. J. (1996). Meanings of political participation among black and white women: Political identity and social responsibility. *Journal of Personality and Social Psychology, 71,* 130–140.

Cole, E. R., Zucker, A. N., & Ostrove, J. M. (1998). Political participation and feminist consciousness among women activists of the 1960s. *Political Psychology 19*(2), 341–379.

Costa, P. T., Jr., & McCrae, R. R. (1994). Set like plaster? Evidence for the stability of personality. In T. F. Heatherton & J. L. Weinberger (Eds.), *Can personality change?* (pp. 21–40). Washington, DC: American Psychological Association.

Cummings, E. M., Goeke-Morey, M. C., Schermerhorn, A. C., Merrilees, C. E., & Cairns, E. (2009). Children and political violence from a social ecological perspective: Implications from research on children and families in Northern Ireland. *Clinical Child and Family Psychology Review, 12,* 16–38.

Danieli, Y., (Ed.). (1998). *International handbook of multigenerational legacies of trauma.* New York: Plenum.

Deaux, K. (2006). *To be an immigrant.* New York: Russell Sage.

Deaux, K., & Bikmen, N. (2010). Immigration and power. In A. Guinote & T. Vescio (Eds.), *The social psychology of power* (pp. 381–407). New York: Guilford.

Deaux, K., Bikmen, N., Gilkes, A., Ventuneac, A., Joseph, Y., Payne, Y., et al. (2007). Becoming American: Stereotype threat effects in Afro-Caribbean groups. *Social Psychology Quarterly, 70,* 384–404.

Deaux, K., Reid, A., Mizrahi, K. & Ethier, K.A. (1995). Parameters of social identity. *Journal of Personality and Social Psychology, 68*(2), 280-91.

Dillon, M. (1993). *Debating divorce: Moral conflict in Ireland.* Lexington: University of Kentucky Press.

Dirkzwager, A. J. E., Bramsen, I., & Van der Ploeg, H. M. (2001). The longitudinal course of posttraumatic stress disorder symptoms among aging military veterans. *Journal of Nervous and Mental Disease, 189*(12), 846–853.

Doty, R., Peterson, B., & Winter, D. G. (1991). Threat and authoritarianism in the United States, 1978–1987. *Journal of Personality and Social Psychology, 61,* 629–640.

Duncan, L. E. (1999). Motivation for collective action: Group consciousness as a mediator of personality, life experiences, and women's rights activism. *Political Psychology, 20*(3), 611–635.

Duncan, L. E., & Agronick, G. S. (1995). The intersection of life stage and social events: Personality and life outcomes. *Journal of Personality and Social Psychology, 69*(3), 558–568.

Duncan, L. E., & Stewart, A. J. (1995). Still bringing the Vietnam War home: Sources of contemporary student activism. *Personality and Social Psychology Bulletin, 21,* 914–924.

Duncan, L. E., & Stewart, A. J. (2000). A generational analysis of women's rights activists. *Psychology of Women Quarterly, 24,* 297–308.

Elder, G. (1974). *Children of the Great Depression: Social change and life experience.* Chicago, IL: Free Press.

Elder, G. H., Jr., Clipp, E. C., Brown, J. S., Martin, L. R., & Friedman, H. S. (2009). The lifelong mortality risks of World War II experiences. *Research on Aging, 31*(4), 391–412.

Elder, G. H., Jr., Shanahan, M. J., & Clipp, E. C. (1994). When war comes to men's lives: Life-course patterns in family, work, and health. *Psychology and Aging, 9*(1), 5–16.

Elder, G. H., Jr., Shanahan, M. J., & Clipp, E. C. (1997). Linking combat and physical health: The legacy of World War II in men's lives. *American Journal of Psychiatry, 154*(3), 330–336.

Emery, R. E. (1988). *Marriage, divorce, and children's adjustment.* Newbury Park, CA: Sage.

Enke, A. (2007). *Finding the movement: Sexuality, contested space, and feminist activism.* Durham, NC: Duke University Press.

Epstein, C. F. (2009). Reflections on women and the law in the USA. *International Social Science Journal, 59*(191), 17–26.

Erikson, E. (1963). *Identity: Youth and crisis.* New York: Norton.

Fendrich, J. M., & Lovoy, K. L. (1988). Back to the future: Adult political behavior of former student activists. *American Sociological Review, 53*, 780–784.

Flacks, R. (1988). *Making history: The radical tradition in American life*. New York: Columbia University Press.

Foner, N. (2000). *From Ellis Island to JFK: New York's two great waves of immigration*. New York: Russell Sage.

Foner, N. (2003). Immigrants and African Americans: Comparative perspectives on the New York experience across time and space. In J. Reitz (Ed.), *Host societies and the reception of immigrants* (pp. 45-71). LaJolla, CA: Center for Comparative Immigration Studies.

Foy, D. W., & Card, J. J. (1987). Combat-related posttraumatic stress disorder etiology: Replicated findings in a national sample of Vietnam era men. *Journal of Clinical Psychology, 43*, 28–31.

Franklin, K. M., Janoff-Bulman, R., & Roberts, J. E. (1990). Longterm impact of parental divorce on optimism and trust: Changes in general assumptions or narrow beliefs? *Journal of Personality and Social Psychology, 59*, 743–755.

Franz, C. E. (1994). Reconstituting the self: The role of history, personality, and loss in one woman's life. In C. E. Franz & A. J. Stewart (Eds.), *Women creating lives: Identities, resilience, and resistance* (pp. 213–226). Boulder, CO: Westview.

Franz, C. E., & McClelland, D. C. (1994). Lives of women and men active in the social protests of the 1960s: A longitudinal study. *Journal of Personality and Social Psychology, 66*(1), 196–205.

Fuligni, A., Tseng, V., & Lam, M. (1999). Attitudes towards family obligations among American adolescents with Asian, Latin American, and European backgrounds. *Child Development, 70*, 1030–1044.

Furstenberg, F. F., & Cherlin, A. (1991). *Divided families*. Cambridge, MA: Harvard University Press.

Furstenberg, F. F., & Teitler, J. O. (1994). Reconsidering the effects of marital disruption: What happens to children of divorce in early adulthood? *Journal of Family Issues, 15*, 173–190.

Gerstel, N. (1987). Divorce and stigma. *Social Problems, 34*(2), 172–186.

Ginzberg, E., & Associates. (1966). *Educated American women: Life styles and self-portraits*. New York: Columbia University Press.

Goldin, C. (2006). The quiet revolution that transformed women's employment, education, and family. *AEA Papers and Proceedings, 96*(2), 1–21.

Green, B. L., Grace, M. C., Lindy, J. D., Gleser, G. C., & Leonard, A. (1990). Risk factors for PTSD and other diagnoses in a general sample of Vietnam veterans. *American Journal of Psychiatry, 147*, 729–733.

Hartmann, S. (1982). *The home front and beyond: American women in the 1940s*. Boston: Twayne.

Hetherington, E. M. (1979). Divorce: A child's perspective. *American Psychologist, 34*, 851–858.

Hetherington, E. M., & Arasteh, J. D. (Eds.). (1988). *Impact of divorce, single parenting, and stepparenting on children*. Hillsdale, NJ: Erlbaum.

Horne, S., Mathews, S., Detrie, P., Burke, M., & Cook, B. (2001). Look it up under "F": Dialogues of emerging and experienced feminists. *Women and Therapy, 23*(2) 5–18.

Huddy, L., Neely, F. K., & Lafay, M. R. (2000). The polls— trends: Support for the women's movement. *Public Opinion Quarterly, 64*, 309–350.

Janoff-Bulman, R. (1991). Understanding people in terms of their assumptive worlds. In D. Ozer, J. M. Healy Jr., & A. J. Stewart (Eds.), *Perspectives in personality: Self and emotion* (Vol. 3, pp. 99–116). London: Kingsley.

Jost, J. T., Glaser, J., Kruglanski, A. W., & Sulloway, F. J. (2003). Political conservatism as motivated social cognition. *Psychological Bulletin, 129*(3), 339–375.

Kandel, W., & Massey, D. S. (2002). The culture of Mexican migration: A theoretical and empirical analysis. *Social Forces, 80*, 981–1004.

Kasen, S., Chen, H., Sneed, J., Crawford, T., & Cohen, P. (2006). Social role and birth cohort influences on gender-linked personality traits in women: A 20-year longitudinal analysis. *Journal of Personality and Social Psychology, 91*, 944–958.

Kasinitz, P., Mollenkopf, J., & Waters, M. C. (2002). Becoming American/becoming New Yorkers: Immigrant incorporation in a majority minority city. *International Migration Review, 36*, 1020–1036.

Kasinitz, P., Mollenkopf, J. H., Waters, M. C., & Holdaway, J. (2008). *Inheriting the city: The children of immigrants come of age*. New York and Cambridge, MA: Russell Sage and Harvard University Press.

Kitson, G. C., & Raschke, H. J. (1981). Divorce research: What we know: what we need to know. *Journal of Divorce, 4*(3), 1–37.

Klein, O., Spears, R., & Reicher, S. (2007). Social identity performance: Extending the strategic side of SIDE. *Personality and Social Psychology Bulletin, 11*, 28–45.

Kurlansky, M. (2004). *1968: The year that rocked the world*. New York: Ballantine.

Lapinski, J. S., Peltola, P., Shaw, G., & Yang, A. (1997). Trends: Immigrants and immigration. *Public Opinion Quarterly, 61*, 356–383.

Leavitt, L. A., & Fox, N. A. (Eds.). (1993). *The psychological effects of war and violence on children*. Hillsdale, NJ: Erlbaum.

Lecic-Tosevski, D., Gavrilovic, J., Knezevic, G., & Priebe, S. (2003). Personality factors and posttraumatic stress: Associations in civilians one year after air attacks. *Journal of Personality Disorders, 17*(6), 537–549.

Lee, K. A., Vaillant, G. E., Torrey, W. C., & Elder, G. H., Jr. (1995). A 50-year prospective study of the psychological sequelae of World War II combat. *American Journal of Psychiatry, 152* (4), 516–522.

Leon, G. R., Butcher, J. N., Kleinman, M., Goldberg, A., & Almagor, M. (1981). *Journal of Personality and Social Psychology, 41*(3), 503–516.

MacLean, A., & Elder, G. H., Jr. (2007). Military service in the life course. *Annual Review of Sociology, 33*, 175–196.

Magruder, K. M., & Yeager, D. E. (2009). The prevalence of PTSD across war eras and the effect of deployment on PTSD: A systematic review and meta-analysis. *Psychiatric Annals, 39* (8), 778–789.

Mannheim, K. (1952). The problem of generations. *Essays on the sociology of knowledge* (pp. 276–322). London: Routledge and Kegan Paul.

Marable, M. (1984). *Race, reform, and rebellion: The second reconstruction in black America, 1945–1982*. Jackson: University Press of Mississippi.

Mason, K. O., & Lu, Y.-H. (1988). Attitudes toward women's familial roles: Changes in the United States, 1977–1985. *Gender and Society, 2*(1), 39–57.

Massey, D. S. (1999). Why does immigration occur? A theoretical synthesis. In C. Hirschman, P. Kasinitz, & J. DeWind

(Eds.), *The handbook of international migration: The American experience* (pp. 34-52). New York: Russell Sage.

McAdam, D. (1988). *Freedom summer.* New York: Oxford University Press.

McAdam, D. (1989). The biographical consequences of activism. *American Sociological Review, 54,* 744–760.

McCrae, R. R., & Costa, P. T., Jr. (1997). Conceptions and correlates of openness to experience. In R. Hogan, J. A. Johnson, & S. R. Briggs (Eds.), *Handbook of personality psychology* (pp. 825–847). San Diego, CA: Academic.

McCrae, R. R., & Costa, P. T., Jr. (2008). The five-factor theory of personality. In O. P. John, R. W. Robins, & L. A. Pervin (Eds.), *Handbook of personality psychology: Theory and research* (pp. 159–181). New York: Guilford.

McHenry, P. C., & McKelvey, M. W. (2003). The psychosocial well-being of black and white mothers following marital dissolution: A brief report of a followup study. *Psychology of Women Quarterly, 27,* 31–36.

Milstein, G., Lucić, L., Galek, K., & Flannelly, K. J. (n. d.). *Immigrant identity development and well-being: Enculturation, context of migration, and acculturation.* Unpublished manuscript, New York: City University of New York.

Model, S. (2009). *West Indian migrants: A black success story?* New York: Russell Sage.

Nagata, D. K. (1993). *Legacy of injustice: Exploring the cross-generational impact of the Japanese American internment.* New York: Plenum.

Nagata, D. K. (1998). Intergenerational effects of the Japanese American internment. In Y. Danieli (Ed.), *International handbook of multigenerational legacies of trauma* (pp. 125–140). New York: Plenum.

Nagata, D. K. (1999). Expanding the internment narrative: Multiple layers of Japanese American women's experience. In M. Romero & A. J. Stewart (Eds.), *Women's untold stories: Breaking silence, talking back, voicing complexity* (pp. 71–82). New York: Routledge.

Nagata, D. K., & Cheng, W. J. Y. (2003). Intergenerational communication of race-related trauma by Japanese American former internees. *American Journal of Orthopsychiatry, 73,* 266–278.

Nagata, D. K., Trierweiler, S. J., & Talbot, R. (1999). Long-term effects of internment during early childhood on third-generation Japanese Americans. *American Journal of Orthopsychiatry, 69*(1), 19–29.

Nassi, A. J. (1981). Survivors of the sixties: Comparative psychosocial and political development of former Berkeley student activists. *American Psychologist, 36,* 753–761.

Ozer, E. J., Best, S. R., Lipsey, T. L., & Weiss, D. S. (2003). Predictors of posttraumatic stress disorder and symptoms in adults: A meta-analysis. *Psychological Bulletin, 129,* 52–73.

Park, A., Sher, K. J., Wood, P. J., & Krull, J. L. (2009). Dual mechanisms underlying accentuation of risky drinking via fraternity/sorority affiliation: The role of personality, peer norms, and alcohol availability. *Journal of Abnormal Psychology, 118*(2), 241–255.

Passerini, L. (1996). *Autobiography of a generation: 1968.* Middletown, CT: Wesleyan University Press.

Pedriana, N. (2004). Help wanted NOW: Legal resources, the women's movement, and the battle over sex-segregated job advertisements. *Social Problems, 51*(2), 182–201.

Pettigrew, T. F. (1998). Reactions toward the new minorities in Europe. *Annual Review of Sociology, 24,* 77–103.

Portes, A., & Rumbaut, R. G. (2001). *Legacies: The story of the immigrant second generation.* Berkeley: University of California Press and New York: Russell Sage.

Prince, R. M. (1985). *The legacy of the Holocaust: Psychohistorical themes in the second generation.* Ann Arbor, MI: UMI Research Press.

Pronin, E. Steele, C., & Ross, L. (2004). Identity bifurcation in response to stereotype threat: Women and mathematics. *Journal of Experimental Social Psychology, 40*(2), 152–168.

Qouta, S., Punamaki, R.-L., & El Sarraj, E. (2008). Child development and family mental health in war and military violence: The Palestinian experience. *International Journal of Behavioral Development, 32*(4), 310–321.

Riessman, C. W. (1990). *Divorce talk: Women and men make sense of personal relationships.* New Brunswick, NJ: Rutgers University Press.

Roberts, B. W., & Mroczek, D. (2008). Personality trait change in adulthood. *Current Directions in Psychological Science, 17,* 31–35.

Rosen, R. (2000). *The world split open: How the modern women's movement changed America.* New York: Penguin.

Rothman, S., & Lichter, S. R. (1982). *Roots of radicalism: Jews, Christians, and the New Left.* New York: Oxford University Press.

Rumbaut, R. (2004). Ages, life stages, and generational cohorts: Decomposing the immigrant first and second generations in the United States. *International Migration Review, 38,* 1160–1205.

Sagi-Schwartz, A. (2008). The well-being of children living in chronic war zones: The Palestinian-Israeli case. *International Journal of Behavioral Development, 32*(4), 322–336.

Schnurr, P. P., Friedman, M. J., & Rosenberg, S. D. (1993). Preliminary MMPI scores as predictors of combat-related PTSD symptoms. *American Journal of Psychiatry, 150*(3), 479–483.

Sekaquaptewa, D., & Thompson, M. (2002). The differential effects of solo status on members of high- and low-status groups. *Personality and Social Psychology Bulletin, 28*(5), 694–707.

Shih, M., Bonam, C., Sanchez, D. T., & Peck, C. (2007). The social construction of race: Biracial identity and vulnerability to stereotypes. *Cultural Diversity and Ethnic Minority Psychology, 13,* 125–133.

Shmotkin, D., & Lomranz, J. (1998). Subjective well-being among Holocaust survivors: An examination of overlooked differentiation. *Journal of Personality and Social Psychology, 75*(1), 141–155.

Sigal, J. J., & Weinfeld, M. (1989). *Trauma and rebirth: Intergenerational effects of the Holocaust.* New York: Praeger.

Srivastava, S., John, O. P., Gosling, S. D., & Potter, J. (2003). Development of personality in early and middle adulthood: Set like plaster or persistent change? *Journal of Personality and Social Psychology, 84*(5), 1041–1053.

Stacey, J. (1990). *Brave new families.* New York: Basic Books.

Stacey, J. (1991). Backward toward the postmodern family: Reflections on gender, kinship, and class in the Silicon Valley. In A. Wolfe (Ed.), *America at century's end* (17–34). Berkeley and Los Angeles: University of California Press.

Stalvey, L. M. (1970). *The education of a WASP.* New York: William Morrow.

Steele, C. M. (1997). A threat in the air: How stereotypes shape intellectual identity and performance. *American Psychologist, 52,* 613–629.

Suárez-Orozco, C., & Suárez-Orozco, M. M. (2001). *Children of immigration.* Cambridge, MA: Harvard University Press.

Stewart, A. J. (1994). The women's movement and women's lives: Linking individual development and social events. In A. Lieblich & R. Josselson (Eds.), *Exploring identity and gender: The narrative study of lives* (Vol. 2, pp. 230–250). Thousand Oaks, CA: Sage.

Stewart, A. J. (1999). "I've got to try to make a difference": A white woman in the civil rights movement. In M. Romero & A. J. Stewart (Eds.), *Women's untold stories* (pp. 195–211). New York: Routledge.

Stewart, A. J. (2003). 2002 Carolyn Sherif Award Address: Gender, race, and generation in a midwest high school: Using ethnographically informed methods in psychology. *Psychology of Women Quarterly, 27,* 1–11.

Stewart, A. J., & Chester, N. L., (1982). Sex differences in human motives: Achievement, affiliation and power. In A. J. Stewart (Ed.), *Motivation and society* (pp. 172–218). San Francisco: Jossey-Bass.

Stewart, A. J., Copeland, A. P., Chester, N. L., Malley, J. E., & Barenbaum, N. L. (1997). *Separating together: How divorce transforms families.* New York: Guilford.

Stewart, A. J., & Healy, J. M., Jr. (1989). Linking individual development and social changes. *American Psychologist, 44,* 30–42.

Stewart, A. J., & Malley, J. E. (2004). Women of "the greatest generation." In C. Daiute & C. Lightfoot (Eds.), *Narrative analysis: Studying the development of individuals in society* (pp. 223–244). Thousand Oaks, CA: Sage.

Stewart, A. J., & Rubin, Z. (1976). The power motive in dating couples. *Journal of Personality and Social Psychology, 34,* 305–309.

Stewart, A. J., Settles, I. H., & Winter, N. J. G. (1998). Women and the social movements of the 1960s: Activists, engaged observers, and nonparticipants. *Political Psychology, 19,* 63–94.

Strauss, W., & Howe, N. (1991). *Generations: The history of America's future, 1584 to 2069.* New York: William Morrow.

Sundin, E. C., & Horowitz, M. J. (2003). Horowitz's Impact of Event Scale evaluation of 20 years of use. *Psychosomatic Medicine, 65,* 870–876.

Tang, T. N., Oatley, K., & Toner, B. B. (2007). Impact of life events and difficulties on the mental health of Chinese immigrant women. *Journal of Immigrant and Minority Health, 9,* 281–290.

Tartakovsky, E., & Schwartz, S. H. (2001). Motivation for emigration, values, well-being, and identification among young Russian Jews. *International Journal of Psychology, 36,* 88–99.

Telles, E. E., & Ortiz, V. (2008). *Generations of exclusion: Mexican Americans, assimilation, and race.* New York: Russell Sage.

Twenge, J. M. (1997). Changes in masculine and feminine traits over time: A meta-analysis. *Sex Roles, 36,* 305–325.

Van der Hal-van Raalte, E. A. M., van Ijzendoorn, M. H., & Bakermans-Kranenberg, M. J. (2008). Sense of coherence moderates late effects of early childhood Holocaust exposure. *Journal of Clinical Psychology, 64*(12), 1352–1367.

Wallerstein, J. S. (1991). The long-term effects of divorce on children: A review. *Journal of the American Academy of Child and Adolescent Psychiatry, 30,* 349–360.

Wallerstein, J. S., & Blakeslee, S. (1989). *Second chances.* New York: Ticknor & Fields.

Whalen, J., & Flacks, R. (1989). *Beyond the barricades: The sixties generation grows up.* Philadelphia, PA: Temple University Press.

Wiley, S., & Deaux, K. (2010). The bicultural performance of immigrants. In A. Azzi, X. Chryssochoou, B. Klandermans, & B. Simon (Eds.), *Identity and participation in culturally diverse societies: A multidisciplinary perspective* (pp. 49–68). Chichester, West Sussex, UK; and Malden, MA: Wiley-Blackwell.

Wiley, S., Perkins, K., & Deaux, K. (2008). Through the looking glass: Ethnic and generational patterns of immigrant identity. *International Journal of Intercultural Relations, 32,* 385–398.

Winter, D. G., & Barenbaum, N. (1985). Responsibility and the power motive in women and men. *Journal of Personality, 53,* 335–355.

Wiseman, H. (2008). On failed intersubjectivity: Recollections of loneliness experiences in offspring of Holocaust survivors. *American Journal of Orthopsychiatry, 78*(2), 350–358.

Wolchik, S. A., Ramirez, R., Sandler, I. N., Fisher, J. L., Organista, P. B., & Brown, C. (1993). Inner-city, poor children of divorce: Negative divorce-related events, problematic beliefs, and adjustment problems. *Journal of Divorce and Remarriage, 19*(1/2), 1–20.

Yohalem, A. (1978). *The careers of professional women: Commitment and conflict.* Montclair, NJ: Allanheld, Osmun.

Zeidner, M., & Ben-Zur, H. (1993). Coping with a national crisis: The Israeli experience with the threat of missile attacks. *Personality and Individual Differences, 14*(1), 209–224.

Zucker, A., & Stewart, A. J. (2007). Growing up and growing older: Feminism as a context for women's lives. *Psychology of Women Quarterly, 31,* 137–145.

Leadership
A Person-in-Situation Perspective

Daan van Knippenberg

Abstract

Leadership research has a long history from both personality psychological and social psychological perspectives, but integrated treatment of these person-situation influences is surprisingly scarce. To sketch the contours of such an integrated approach, I first outline the personality approach to leadership effectiveness and then move on to an alternative to straightforward conceptualizations of leader personality-leadership effectiveness linkages: a person-in-situation perspective that sees leadership effectiveness as a function of the interaction between leader personality and situation (task, follower, and context characteristics) and that incorporates insights form social psychological, behavior-in-situation research in leadership. Although the person-in-situation perspective is far less developed than probably it should be, there are indicators that it holds more promise for our understanding of leadership effectiveness than more one-sided approaches. I aim to capture what can be concluded on the basis of the evidence so far as well as present an associated research agenda for the further development of this perspective on the interface of the personality and social psychology of leadership.

Keywords: leadership, personality, trait activation, five-factor model, transformational leadership, charismatic leadership, social identity, social exchange

Most if not all social groupings are characterized by a leadership structure, and leadership in principle has huge potential to affect these social groupings (Cartwright & Zander, 1968; Chemers, 2001). It is not surprising then that leadership research has a long history in psychology and the social and behavioral sciences more generally. The main question driving this research is, and always has been, what makes leaders effective in mobilizing and motivating followers—what gives leaders the influence to motivate followers to work to collective ends? (Bass, 1990; van Knippenberg, van Knippenberg, De Cremer, & Hogg, 2004; Yukl & van Fleet, 1994). Leadership research has an equally long history of trying to understand leadership effectiveness as a function of leader personality and individual differences. Indeed, the notion that there is something unique in the personality of great leaders that

distinguishes them from the rest of us mere mortals seems to hold great intuitive appeal. Also at a more mundane level there is a long-standing tradition in research and practice (i.e., leadership selection) working from the proposition that certain personality traits and individual differences better position one for effective leadership than others (Judge, Piccolo, & Kosalka, 2009).

In somewhat of an uncomfortable counterpoint to this long-standing tradition, leadership research has an almost equally long history of concluding that the personality and individual difference approach to leadership effectiveness is not very successful (Bass, 1990; Bono & Judge, 2004; Stogdill, 1948; Yukl, 2002). The conclusion that the personality approach holds little promise always looms in the shadows (cf. House & Aditya, 1997), and indeed there are a range of theories and approaches that emphasize situational influence on—the social psychology of—leadership. These situational approaches are not without their shortcomings and limitations either, however (Chemers, 2001; Yukl & Van Fleet, 1994), and, rather than prioritize the one over the other, the more constructive way forward would seem to be to develop more sophisticated models of the relationship between leader personality and leadership effectiveness that take situational influences into account and thus capture the personality psychology as well as the social psychology of leadership.

In this chapter I explore the potential of a person-in-situation approach to leadership that highlights the notion that the relationship between leader personality and leadership effectiveness is contingent on characteristics of the situation—the task, the followers, team and organizational characteristics, and so forth. While a contingency approach is far from new to the leadership arena (e.g., Fiedler, 1967; House, 1971), contingency approaches to leadership have focused on leadership behavior or style much more than on leader personality, and the person-in-situation approach to leadership is more of a terra incognita than even many in the field of leadership would realize. Moreover, many of the "behavior-in-situation" approaches to leadership effectiveness have also enjoyed only modest success at best, so the issue clearly is more complex than "just" linking personality to the "right" behavior.

In considering the potential of a person-in-situation approach to leadership, I use a perspective that argues that situations can "bring out" the influence of individual personality and dispositions as well as "override" this influence (Mischel, 1977; Tett & Burnett, 2003). As a note upfront, I limit this analysis to personality and individual differences as dispositions to perceive, think, and behave in certain ways, and exclude such traits as abilities (e.g., cognitive intelligence, emotional intelligence) and demographics and physical characteristics (e.g., gender, height) that are sometimes understood to be part of the trait approach to leadership but involve different conceptual bases.

To set the stage for the current analysis, I first review the personality (trait) approach to leadership, both to establish its modest success in predicting leadership effectiveness and to identify the personality and individual difference variables that might hold the greater promise in trying to understand leadership effectiveness. I then move on to review the person-in-situation approach more generally and outline what it would mean for leadership research before I review published empirical work

on leader personality and individual differences from the person-in-situation perspective as well as social psychological, behavior-in-situation perspectives that provide building blocks for an integrative personality-situation perspective on leadership.

Personality and Leadership Effectiveness: A Review in Broad Strokes

A complicating factor in reviewing the leadership literature is that researchers have focused on a wide variety of potential indicators of leadership effectiveness that arguably all may reflect some aspect of leadership effectiveness. Psychological research in leadership is concentrated around work contexts (i.e., leadership in organizations, leadership of work groups) and it is no surprise that follower performance—either individual or as a team or organization—typically is seen as the most important indicator of leadership effectiveness (e.g., Kaiser, Hogan, & Craig, 2008; see also Day & Schleicher, chapter 28, this volume). More specific performance-related outcomes like creativity (e.g., Hirst, van Dick, & van Knippenberg, 2009) and innovation (Eisenbeiss, van Knippenberg, & Boerner, 2008) may also be considered from this perspective as indicators of effective leadership. Even so, research has more often than not relied on evaluative ratings of leadership and of the leader-follower relationship (e.g., leader-member exchange, or LMX; Graen & Uhl-Bien, 1995) as indicators of leadership effectiveness. While a case can be made that such subjective perceptions may set the stage for leader influence and effectiveness in terms of follower performance (e.g., Giessner & van Knippenberg, 2008; cf. van Knippenberg & van Knippenberg, 2005), there also is compelling evidence that such subjective ratings may reflect perceivers' beliefs about what is good leadership as much as objective evidence of good leadership (Lord & Maher, 1991). That is, perceivers' judgment of an individual's leadership qualities may be driven as much by the extent to which the individual's characteristics match the perceivers' (implicit) beliefs about the attributes of a good leader (e.g., in terms of gender or behavioral style) as by actual objective indicators of the individual's leadership qualities. It is somewhat unfortunate, then, that evidence for the relationship between personality and leadership effectiveness derives more from subjective indicators of effectiveness than from more objective indicators (Judge, Bono, Ilies, & Gerhardt, 2002). Moreover, this difference between objective and subjective indicators of leadership effectiveness also points to the possibility that inconsistent findings may be attributed to differences in the criteria for leadership effectiveness involved (Lord & Hall, 1992).

In addition, there is a tendency for research in personality and leadership to focus on the relationship between personality and leadership behavior or style rather than leadership effectiveness. Much of this research seems to be guided by the notion that certain forms of leadership are particularly effective (e.g., transformational and charismatic leadership) and therefore it is particularly interesting to study their determinants, even to the extent that the research problem is framed as being about the relationship between leader personality and charismatic-transformational leadership rather than leadership effectiveness (e.g., House & Howell, 1992). While it makes perfect sense to consider certain leadership behavior or style as explaining the relationship between personality and leadership effectiveness, effectiveness of any given leadership behavior or style cannot be assumed in the context of a particular study. Studies of the personality and individual difference determinants of leadership that do not include measures of leadership effectiveness thus at best can only provide circumstantial evidence regarding the personality-effectiveness relationship.

An illustration of this point is found in a study by House, Spangler, and Woycke (1991) on presidential charisma. These researchers found that personality (more on this below) predicted charisma and presidential effectiveness, but also that personality and charisma independently predicted effectiveness—the relationship between personality and presidential effectiveness could not be attributed to leader charisma. Again, a focus on leader behavior is obvious in the study of leadership and personality, because the enacted leadership—the actual behavior of the leader vis-à-vis followers—would be what explains the relationship between leader personality and leadership effectiveness in terms of influence on followers. In order to determine this, however, researchers need to test a mediation model in which personality is related to effectiveness via its influence on leader behavior (cf. Baron & Kenny, 1986; Edwards & Lambert, 2007). This is an approach that is taken less often than one would like in research in personality and leadership, and our ability to draw conclusions about the relationship between personality and leadership effectiveness likewise suffers.

A related complication in this respect is that many studies of personality and leadership have actually focused on leadership emergence—being perceived to be a leader in a group without a formal leader—rather than leadership effectiveness. Whereas to a certain extent leader emergence and leadership effectiveness might reflect similar influences—the (attributed) possession of leadership qualities—emergence of an individual as a leader in a formally leaderless group should not be equated with effectiveness in influencing followers of an individual in a formal leadership position (Judge et al., 2002; Lord, De Vader, & Alliger, 1986). The core concern of leadership research is with leadership effectiveness and not with leadership emergence, and accordingly the present review prioritizes studies of leadership effectiveness over those of leadership emergence.

Another issue that may have worked to make progress in personality and leadership slower than one would like is that the field has suffered from a true proliferation of personality and individual difference variables, some of which are highly idiosyncratic to leadership research (e.g., Fiedler, 1967) or at least partly overlapping content-wise (e.g., dominance, authoritarianism, and attitude toward delegation; Ashour & England, 1972). A big improvement in this respect, though not without drawbacks, has been the more recent focus on personality as captured by the five-factor model of personality, colloquially referred to as the Big Five (e.g., Goldberg, 1990; Macrae & Costa, 1997). The five-factor model of personality carries the not too modest claim of capturing the universal structure of personality and providing a description of personality that is more or less comprehensive. The big improvement from a leadership perspective is that many of the seemingly related and overlapping but differently labeled personality constructs investigated in earlier years can be traced back to the same "higher-order" Big Five factor (Judge et al., 2002). A more extensive discussion regarding the relationship between the Big Five and leadership effectiveness follows below, but for now I will use the introduction of the Big Five to leadership research as a reference point for a review of research on the personality–leadership effectiveness relationship before the Big Five, more contemporary research on the Big Five and leadership, and recent research that explores the influence of personality and individual difference factors probably less easily captured by the Big Five.

Before the Big Five: Rise and Fall of the Trait Perspective

In a concise review capturing the essence of the personality and leadership literature, Judge et al. (2002)

trace back research in personality and leadership to as early as 1904. They note that in the first 50 years or so of psychological research in leadership the so-called trait perspective, which included not only personality but also traits reflecting ability rather than personality, such as intelligence, was the dominant and to many researchers obvious perspective on leadership. As the evidence regarding the relationship between personality and leadership was amassing, however, reviews of the personality-leadership relationship emerged that concluded that the evidence for personality predictors of leadership was disappointing and inconsistent (Mann, 1959; Stogdill, 1948), and this has seemed to be the favored conclusion ever since for many reviewers of the field (e.g., Bass, 1990; Yukl, 2002).

These early studies concerned a wide variety of personality variables—or at least a wide variety of labels and measures for these variables. This is a common and serious problem in research in personality where the use of different construct names and measures often obscures the high conceptual and empirical overlap between constructs. As a consequence, scientific progress is hampered. Accordingly, an important contribution to making sense of the role of personality in human behavior is to identify the communalities and differences between personality constructs to better integrate the diversity of studies available. The influential review of Mann (1959) did exactly this by identifying over 350 different measures (including measures of intelligence) and grouping these into seven dimensions: extraversion, dominance, masculinity, interpersonal sensitivity, adjustment, and conservatism, as well as the nonpersonality variable of intelligence. In evaluating the evidence for the personality-leadership linkage along each of these six personality dimensions, Mann's conclusions emphasized the low correlations between personality and leadership typically observed, and thus contributed to a disenchantment with the trait approach to leadership.

While Mann's conclusion reflected poorly on the role of personality in leadership, Lord et al. (1986) revisited these conclusions and argued that they tended to be misrepresented and overstated. Rather than a narrative review of the literature, Lord et al. conducted a meta-analysis to quantitatively integrate findings from different studies (using Mann's review as a starting point and updating where possible). Their conclusion was that a significant positive relationship existed between leadership and the personality variables dominance ($r = .13$) and masculinity ($r = .34$; intelligence was the strongest predictor of

leadership; also see Judge, Colbert, & Ilies, 2004). Arguably, however, with only two out of six personality dimensions related to leadership and a quite modest relationship for dominance in particular, one may wonder to what extent Mann's conclusions were not dead-on. Another key point to highlight here, and also underscored by Lord et al., is that these findings concern leadership perceptions or emergence rather than indicators of the effectiveness of formal leaders. In combination, then, based on these findings of what can be seen as the mainstream of research in leadership and personality "before the Big Five," the conclusion seems warranted that there was no convincing evidence of an important role of personality in leadership effectiveness.

A somewhat separate stream of leader personality research revolved around a perspective that understands personality in terms of needs—need for power, need for affiliation, and need for achievement (McClelland, 1975; McClelland & Atkinson, 1976; Winter, 1973) in combination with individuals' disposition to be socially responsible (labeled activity inhibition or responsibility). An influential proposition within this perspective is that leadership can be understood as flowing from a leadership motive profile (McClelland, 1975, 1985). This profile would be formed by a combination of moderate-to-high need for power, low need for affiliation, and high activity inhibition (i.e., which presumably reflects the use of power for social rather than personal goals). Individuals possessing this personality profile (as compared with not possessing this profile) would be more likely to be effective leaders. The rationale for this proposition is that people high in need for power would be interested in influence on others—indeed, would actively engage in attempts to gain influence, which is a necessary requirement for leadership. Low need for affiliation—that is, low concern with having good relationships with others—would be important because a desire to be liked by others associated with high need for affiliation would restrain leaders in making important but difficult decisions that would not be appreciated by others. High activity inhibition—high self-control, high social responsibility—would be important, because it would mean that the individual would be more likely to use his or her influence to achieve organizational ends rather than personal desires.

Tests of the leadership motive perspective (e.g., Winter, 1991) are heavily compromised by methodological concerns. McClelland and Boyatsis (1982), for instance, find that having the leader motive profile versus not having it (i.e., scoring differently on the three dimensions) predicts leadership success in achieving promotions (but only for nontechnical managers). Note that promotions need not reflect leader effectiveness in mobilizing and motivating followers. Also note that much of this support revolves around one and the same AT&T dataset. Moreover support is far from consistent (e.g., Cornelius & Lane, 1984; Winter, 1987). The most important problem with the leadership motive profile approach is that the classification of individuals as either possessing or not possessing the profile on the basis of three scores obscures the contribution of each of the three dimensions to the influence of the profile. Conceptually the profile is an interactive effect of three variables, but statistically it is not tested as such (cf. Baron & Kenny, 1986). As a result, we cannot conclude that all three variables contribute to the presumed influence of the profile, and any conclusions based on leadership motive profile research are tentative at best.

In apparent recognition of this problem, a number of researchers did look at the different components of the motive profile separately (but not at the implied three-way interaction). Most telling perhaps in this respect is a study of presidential leadership, by Spangler and House (1991), which found that the motive profile did not predict any outcomes above and beyond the scores on the separate dimensions and moreover found that the need for power x activity inhibition interaction implied by the motive profile did not predict any of the outcomes of interest either. In the previous section, I already mentioned the research by House et al. (1991), who found that leader need for power and activity inhibition were positively related to both leader charisma and leader performance. Inconsistent with the leadership motive profile perspective, however, need for affiliation was unrelated to charisma or performance (the interactions implied by the motive profile were not tested), and other studies similarly disappointed in their evidence for the role for needs/motives in leadership effectiveness (e.g., Harms, Roberts, & Wood, 2007). In another study that did involve the test of one of the implied interactions, De Hoogh et al. (2005b) used separate measures of the needs for power, affiliation, and achievement, as well as a measure of responsibility (cf. activity inhibition) in a study of charismatic leadership and follower positive work attitude (i.e., an indicator of leadership effectiveness). Feeding into the methodological concerns with the power motive approach, De Hoogh et al. did observe positive relationships between need for power and charismatic leadership

(but not follower work attitude) and responsibility and follower attitude (but not charisma), but did not observe reliable relationships for need for affiliation or for the need for power x responsibility interaction implied by the leadership motive profile. A test of the full need for power x need for affiliation x responsibility interaction that represents the leader power motive was not reported. One reading of the De Hoogh et al. study, then, is that, while showing some evidence for the role of leader need for power, it suggests that a more proper test of the relationship between the leadership motive factors and personality essentially shows that the leadership motive profile proposition is not supported. Note that evidence for the implied mediation model—personality influencing effectiveness via charismatic leadership—was not obtained. In view of such evidence, then, a state of the science assessment would suggest that the leadership motive profile approach holds little promise for our understanding of leadership effectiveness.

Probably partly as the result of a disenchantment from the trait approach, the field shifted its emphasis to the study of leader behavioral style (i.e., how the leader typically behaves). Much of this research was inspired by the notion that leadership style could largely be captured along two dimensions, task-oriented leadership or initiating structure and relations-oriented leadership or consideration (Stogdill & Coons, 1957), whereas a second stream of research focused on participative leadership, the extent to which leaders were autocratic in their behavior and decisions or more democratic in consulting and listening to their subordinates (e.g., Vroom & Yetton, 1973). When it turned out that the behavioral approach like the trait approach did a poor job in capturing leadership effectiveness (but see Judge, Piccolo, & Ilies, 2004), the emphasis shifted to contingency approaches that aimed to model the effectiveness of different behavioral styles as a function of task, situational, and follower characteristics (e.g., Fiedler, 1964; House, 1971; Kerr & Jermier, 1978; Vroom & Yetton, 1973). These contingency approaches had their own personality-ish twist in Fiedler's (1964, 1967) propositions regarding the role of the leader's least preferred coworker (LPC) score.

Fiedler proposed that a leader's evaluation of his or her least preferred coworker ever—the leader's LPC score—is a key determinant of leadership effectiveness. The extent to which the situation is favorable (captured by a combination of task and follower characteristics) would determine whether low LPC leaders (unfavorable or very favorable conditions) or high LPC leaders (conditions ranging from moderately unfavorable to moderately favorable) would be more effective. What exactly LPC captures other than leaders' evaluation of their least liked coworker (i.e., not necessarily subordinate) is not clear, however, but it is clear that Fielder saw LPC as predictive of the extent to which the leader is task-oriented (low LPC) or relationship-oriented (high LPC) even to the extent that LPC can be seen as a proxy for leadership style. In this respect, Rice (1978) concluded that LPC is best understood as representing the extent to which the leader values a task-oriented versus relationship-oriented leadership style. Viewed this way, the LPC approach can be seen as falling into one of the traps of research in personality and individual differences. The more a trait is conceptualized in a narrow and specific way, the more it might be predictive of the outcomes it is tailored to predict (cf. Fishbein & Ajzen, 1975), but the less insightful these relationships are and the lower the generalizability of insights to other domains. If LPC should be understood as the disposition to display task-oriented or relationship-oriented leadership, it should come as no surprise if it predicts such leadership. In terms of adding value to our understanding of leadership beyond a focus on leadership styles, it would seem to have limited value. Moreover, as with other contingency theories, empirical support ultimately disappointed, and in combination with the conceptual criticism on the LPC measure this spelled the end of the field's interest in leader LPC.

In sum, then, on the basis of the research reviewed so far, the conclusion would seem justified that there is little evidence for the importance of leader personality in leadership effectiveness. At least in part, this could be attributed to a proliferation of personality and individual difference variables with very little attempt at integration (House & Aditya, 1997; cf. Mann, 1959) as well as to a tendency in early research to focus more on leadership emergence than leadership effectiveness (Lord et al., 1986). In a sense following up on Mann's more qualitative attempt, the introduction of the Big Five to the field of leadership made an important contribution in terms of providing a focus and higher-order framework, and thus in addressing the former problem. In addition, evidence for the relationship with leadership effectiveness in addition to such leadership perceptions as emergence and leadership behavior has also been accumulating, addressing the latter issue. The field maintained its openness to the

personality perspective also for different reasons: the social psychological, behavior-in-situation contingency theories of leadership too lacked empirical support. Indeed, unlike the mainstream of personality research, these behavior-in-situation approaches were relegated to the history of leadership research and I will not discuss them further here, but rather refer interested readers to older reviews (e.g., Yukl & Van Fleet, 1994). Moreover, the limited success of the contingency approaches set aside, even if one can convincingly determine that certain leadership behavior is effective within certain context, one would still like to determine the origins of the behavior, and leader personality would be an obvious candidate to investigate.

Enter the Big Five: Reinvigorating the Trait Perspective

The five-factor model of personality provides a structure to capture a large range of personality variables identified in research in personality and to group these under five higher-order factors (Digman, 1990; Goldberg, 1990; Macrae & Costa, 1997; see also Fleeson, chapter 3 in this volume). These five factors—the Big Five—are extraversion, conscientiousness, openness to experience, agreeableness, and emotional stability (also known by its flip-side label neuroticism). These factors represent continuous variables, not types, and are more or less independent of each other. More extraverted (as opposed to more introverted) people are more sociable, outgoing, active, and assertive, and tend to experience more positive affect. Conscientiousness reflects the disposition to be industrious, achievement-oriented, and sensitive to obligations and responsibilities. Openness to experience captures the tendency toward autonomy, nonconformity, and imagination. More agreeable people are more trusting, caring, and gentle, and more focused on harmonious relationships. Emotional stability or neuroticism captures the disposition toward poor emotional judgment and negative affect such as insecurity, anxiety, and hostility (i.e., low emotional stability, high neuroticism).

As noted in the previous, one of the key contributions of the Big Five is that it allows researchers to group personality variables that go under different labels and associated measurement under the same higher-order Big Five factor. In a meta-analysis of the Big Five and leadership Judge et al. (2002) for instance addressed dominance and sociability as aspects of extraversion, achievement-orientation, and dependability as aspects of conscientiousness, and self-esteem and locus of control as aspects of emotional stability, and in their qualitative review they note that leader self-confidence (cf. De Cremer & van Knippenberg, 2004), the only trait to systematically emerge across the qualitative reviews discussed by Judge et al., can be grouped under the factor emotional stability. While this inclusive approach focused on broad categories is not without its critics either—indeed, it is criticized for being too inclusive and neglecting important within-factor differences (e.g., Hough, 1992; also see Block, 1995)—it does seem to have become the dominant approach to personality in research in personality, social, and organizational psychology, including in the job performance domains leadership is expected to influence (Barrick & Mount, 1991; Hurtz & Donovan, 2000; cf. Judge, Heller, & Mount, 2002). Research in leadership and personality is no exception.

Judge et al. (2002) conducted a meta-analysis to capture the relationships between the Big Five factors and leadership emergence and effectiveness. Their findings show that all Big Five dimensions are positively correlated with leadership effectiveness (i.e., when focusing on emotional stability rather than neuroticism) and with the exception of agreeableness to leader emergence (with significant correlations ranging from .16 to .33). A more stringent regression test showed that extraversion and openness to experience are positively related to both emergent leadership and leadership effectiveness, while emotional stability is positively related to effectiveness only, and conscientiousness is positively related to emergence only. In this analysis, agreeableness was related to neither emergence nor effectiveness. The Judge et al. results thus supports the conclusion that there are reliable relationships between at the very least (i.e., contingent on whether conclusions are based on correlations or regression evidence) some Big Five dimensions and leadership effectiveness. Critics would probably argue with the size of these relationships and with the fact that findings are primarily based on subjective leadership perceptions rather than objective (performance) evidence, but the Judge et al. findings seem at the very least to support the conclusion that further engagement with the Big Five and leadership is worthy of research efforts.

When the 1960s and 1970s contingency approaches to leadership effectiveness did not make good on their promise, the field shifted its emphasis among others to what still is one of the major emphases in leadership research today, charismatic and transformational leadership. Charismatic and transformational leadership are highly related concepts. Indeed, theories of charismatic and transformational leadership overlap as much as different theories of transformational leadership or different theories of charismatic leadership (Kirkpatrick & Locke, 1996; van Knippenberg & Hogg, 2003). Accordingly, I will refer here to transformational leadership, which is the more commonly evoked label in research in (Big Five) personality traits and leadership, but take this to apply to charismatic leadership as well.

Transformational leadership is proposed to capture a particularly motivating and inspiring form of leadership, comprising such aspects as the communication of an inspiring vision and of high performance expectations as well as great personal commitment (e.g., personal sacrifices; role modeling) in pursuit of these visions of excellence (Bass, 1985; Burns, 1978; Conger & Kanungo, 1987; House, 1977; Shamir, House, & Arthur, 1993). From a conceptual point of view, a particularly troublesome aspect of transformational leadership research is that there is no clear definition of what constitutes transformational leadership and that many attempts to capture the essence of transformational leadership rely heavily on its proposed outcomes. Transformational leadership often seems to be more or less defined as particularly effectively leadership (e.g., Bass, 1985; Bass & Riggio, 2006; Conger & Kanungo, 1987; Shamir et al., 1993). This is problematic for the study of leadership effectiveness, where leadership and effectiveness should be defined and operationalized independently from each other (i.e., otherwise, the effectiveness of transformational leadership is literally established by definition). For most practical purposes, transformational leadership seems to be more or less defined by its measurement in subjective ratings in questionnaires, which unfortunately also suffer from operationalizations in part in terms of leadership's perceived effectiveness (e.g., ratings of the extent to which the leader motivates one to accomplish more than one expected to accomplish).

Meta-analytic evidence largely relying on surveys with subjective ratings of leadership effectiveness (i.e., which may inflate relationships) suggests that transformational leadership is indeed positively related to leadership effectiveness (Judge & Piccolo, 2004; Lowe, Kroeck, & Sivasubramaniam, 1996). There is also meta-analytic evidence that transformational leadership is more effective than its nontransformational counterpart transactional leadership (leadership based on contingent rewards and interventions inspired by suboptimal performance to promote high performance and prevent poor performance), but the contingent reward aspect of transactional leadership appears to be sometimes as effective as transformational leadership (Judge & Piccolo, 2004). The proposition that transformational leadership is a particularly effective form of leadership has also inspired research in the (Big Five) personality trait predictors of transformational leadership. This research is captured by two meta-analyses by Judge and Bono (2000; Bono & Judge, 2004). Findings from the more recent Bono and Judge analysis show that all Big Five dimensions are positively related to transformational leadership, although correlations are modest, ranging from .13 (conscientiousness) to .24 (extraversion). (In addition, contingent reward was positively associated with emotional stability, extraversion, and agreeableness, although correlations were even more modest here; all < .18). As before, however, these leader behaviors should not be equated with leadership effectiveness, and evidence of the relationship between personality and leader behavior cannot be assumed to generalize to leadership effectiveness.

In combination, then, these meta-analytical integrations of the empirical evidence support the conclusion that at least some of the Big Five personality traits are positively related to leadership effectiveness, and suggest that this relationship might be explained by the relationship between the Big Five dimensions and transformational leadership. This is not to say, however, that no traits other than the Big Five have been studied since the introduction of the five-factor model to the leadership field or that no other potentially mediating variables have been considered. In the following, I first review evidence that can be directly linked to the Big Five perspective and then move on to review evidence that in a sense goes "beyond" the five-factor model.

First, there are two concepts that are sometimes discussed in trait-like terms, but that ultimately are treated as psychological variables predicted by the Big Five, leadership self-efficacy and motivation to lead. Seminal work by Bandura (1986, 1997) has established that an important influence in motivation and goal-directed behavior is self-efficacy, the expectation that one is able to execute a certain act, complete a certain course of action, or achieve a certain goal—a self-evaluation of one's capabilities. Without sufficient levels of self-efficacy in relation to a certain target, it would make little sense to the individual to undertake efforts to achieve that target. In principle, the concept of self-efficacy may be

applied to any behavioral domain, including leadership, and research in leadership self-efficacy has done exactly that (Anderson, Krajweski, Griffin, & Jackson, 2008; Paglis & Green 2002; Singer, 1991). The rationale to expect leadership self-efficacy to play a role in leadership effectiveness is that leaders with higher leadership self-efficacy would be more likely to proactively engage with the leadership role, attempt to influence followers, and so forth. Tests of the relationship between leadership self-efficacy and indicators of leadership effectiveness corroborate this proposition (Chemers, Watson, & May, 2000; Hoyt, Murphy, Halverson, & Watson, 2003; Paglis & Green, 2002).

This has inspired researchers to explore the role of leadership self-efficacy in mediating the relationship between (Big Five) personality traits and leadership effectiveness, and indeed there is some evidence that emotional stability, extraversion, conscientiousness, and openness to experience predict leadership self-efficacy (Chan & Drasgow, 2001), and thus leadership effectiveness (Ng, Ang, & Chan, 2008). Chan and Drasgow introduce a further step in this proposed mediating chain through the concept of motivation to lead, an individual difference factor proposed to predict leadership potential (presumably a proxy for leadership effectiveness; cf. Hendricks & Payne, 2007). Chan and Drasgow provide evidence of Big Five influences on motivation to lead (also see Harms et al., 2007) as well as of the influence of individual differences in individualism-collectivism (Triandis, 1995) mediated by leadership self-efficacy. Tentatively, we may thus conclude that leadership self-efficacy and motivation to lead may help explain the relationship between Big Five factors and leadership effectiveness in that the Big Five may influence leadership self-evaluation and motivation and thus inspire more proactive and persistent engagement with the leadership role.

Another thing to note in reference to leadership self-efficacy and motivation to lead is that these are sometimes discussed as individual differences variables (e.g., Chan & Drasgow, 2001), which carries the personality-like specter of chronic stability. Yet, leadership self-efficacy has also been shown to be contingent on contextual influences (Paglis & Green, 2002) and self-efficacy more generally is seen as a variable with both trait (i.e., stable) and state (i.e., variable) aspects (Judge, Locke, & Durham, 1997). Accordingly, motivation to lead as a variable contingent on leadership self-efficacy should likewise be at least partly state-like. Probably then, leadership self-efficacy and motivation to lead are better understood as mediating psychological states that may help explain the influence of leader personality than as traits in and of themselves.

While reliance on the Big Five offered great advantages to a field in need of consolidation rather than further construct proliferation, the five-factor model is no silver bullet either. There are personality and individual difference variables that are less easily captured by the Big Five, or that deserve attention as more specific aspects of personality, that may be highly relevant to leadership—indeed, that sometimes may be more proximal to the leadership process. More recently, research has started to explore such factors against the backdrop of the dominant Big Five perspective in leadership and personality.

Rubin, Munz, and Bommer (2005) showed that leaders higher in positive affectivity—the disposition to experience positive affective states (i.e., moods, emotions)—were rated as more transformational. While positive affectivity arguably could be seen as an aspect of extraversion, the interest value of the particular focus on affective disposition lies in the fact that it points to another mediating mechanism not discussed so far. Research in leadership and emotions suggests that leader displays of positive affect may feed into leadership effectiveness because they may contribute to attributions of charismatic and transformational leadership (Bono & Ilies, 2006; Damen, van Knippenberg, & van Knippenberg, 2008b) and may add to leaders' persuasiveness in motivating follower performance (Damen, van Knippenberg, & van Knippenberg, 2008a). Leaders' display of affect and emotion could thus also provide a viable avenue for research exploring the mechanisms through which leader personality may affect leadership effectiveness. Conversely, a specific focus on leader positive and negative affectivity as aspects of personality may add to our understanding of the role of personality in leadership effectiveness, as these may be the personality aspects that are most directly linked to leader affective displays (cf. van Knippenberg, van Knippenberg, Van Kleef, & Damen, 2008).

Research in charismatic and transformational leadership in particular emphasizes the role of leaders as proactive change agents. This seems to fit well with the notion of proactive personality—the individual disposition toward proactive behavior targeted at effective change in the environment rather than more reactively adapting to it (Bateman & Crant, 1993). Bateman and Crant (1993; Crant and Bateman, 2000) show that proactive personality predicted ratings of charismatic and transformational leadership above and beyond Big Five dimensions, and Deluga (1998a) adds to this that proactive personality also predicts perceived presidential performance. As one might have come to expect by now, however, correlations were modest.

Inspired by a growing concern with derailing leadership, leadership research is increasingly attuned to the need for ethical, moral, and socially responsible leadership (cf. Rus, van Knippenberg, & Wisse, 2010). Taking this issue on from a personality perspective, De Hoogh and Den Hartog (2008) focused on leader social responsibility, a personality characteristic consisting of such aspects as moral standards and concern for others, as a predictor of ethical and despotic leadership. They found that leader social responsibility predicted ethical leadership behavior (positively) and despotic leadership (negatively) which in turn predicted perceptions of team effectiveness and subordinate optimism. The implied mediation model (i.e., leader social responsibility predicts leadership effectiveness through its influence on leader behavior) was not tested, however, and simple correlations showed no relationship between leader social responsibility and effectiveness, raising doubts about the importance of leader social responsibility in leadership effectiveness.

Ever since the rise of the contingency perspective in leadership research, has research in leader behavior and leadership effectiveness been attuned to the moderating influence of the situation (i.e., task, followers, context). It is perhaps somewhat odd, then, that the vast majority of studies in leadership and personality have been concerned with unmoderated relationships. Obviously, the very point of this chapter is that leadership and personality are better understood from this person-in-situation perspective, but before we address this issue, there is a last individual difference variable to discuss that has been argued to deal with this issue in a different way—by capturing leaders' responsiveness to the social context: self-monitoring. Self-monitoring refers to the disposition to observe, regulate, and control the public appearance of the self (Snyder, 1974, 1987), and cannot be "reduced" to an aspect of the Big Five (i.e., extraversion would be the most likely candidate; Gangestad & Snyder, 2000). High self-monitoring individuals are concerned with how they are perceived by others and with the ways in which they may change their presentation to change these perceptions. Thus, self-monitoring may help people to present a more favorable and appropriate image of the self to others—that is, an image that is responsive to the situation and more specifically to the "audience" in question. Self-monitoring may thus help build social relations and increase influence over others. Moreover, as argued in leadership categorization theory and the implicit leadership theory perspectives on leadership (e.g., Eagly & Karau, 2002; Lord & Maher, 1991; Meindl, Dukerich, & Ehrlich, 1985), leadership in part is in the eye of the beholder, and those able to project the "right" image may as a result gain clout as a leader (Gardner & Avolio, 1998; Meindl, 1995; Reicher & Hopkins, 2003; van Knippenberg & Hogg, 2003; cf. Leary, Robertson, Barnes, & Miller, 1986). Self-monitoring may thus be positively related to leadership emergence and effectiveness. Moreover, because of its association with responsiveness to the social context (i.e., behavioral flexibility), self-monitoring may be a leader trait that predicts emergence and effectiveness across situations (Zaccaro, Foti, & Kenny, 1991), and that thus may yield stronger and more reliable relationships with leadership effectiveness than personality variables that are associated less with behavioral flexibility.

Zaccaro et al. put this proposition to the test in a study of emergent leadership across four tasks that differed in terms of the leadership behavior that would be most appropriate. Self-monitoring was expected to be related to leadership emergence through the display of appropriate leadership behaviors. For two of the four tasks, self-monitoring was related to both leader emergence and task-appropriate leadership behavior (but the mediation model implied was not tested). Although not speaking to behavior flexibility, but following the same underlying logic, Sosik and Dworakivsky (1998) showed that self-monitoring was positively related to charismatic leadership, and Warech, Smither, Reilly, Millsa, and Reilly (1998) complemented these findings with evidence of an association between self-monitoring and ratings of leadership effectiveness. Day, Schleicher, Unckless, and Hiller (2002) integrated the empirical evidence for the relationship between self-monitoring and leader emergence meta-analytically and established a positive correlation. The observed correlation was quite modest, however ($r = .21$), and not larger than those for the Big Five observed by Judge et al. (2002), which would have been expected if the presumed behavioral flexibility of high self-monitoring leaders renders them more responsive to the social context than any of the Big Five factors presumably would. It would thus seem that a focus on self-monitoring cannot substitute for an account of the influence of

the situation. Part of the problem here might be that high self-monitoring does not actually imply that one is able to present an "effective" image with high credibility, and perceptions of inauthentic impression management may reflect negatively on leadership perceptions (Sosik, Avolio, & Jung, 2002).

Taking stock, then, can we conclude that after the field's disenchantment from the trait perspective recent developments in the field of personality have reinvigorated this perspective? Some no doubt would answer this question with a definite yes (e.g., Judge et al., 2009) and in view of the empirical evidence that has been amassing we can conclude that at least in terms of research activity it is. More pessimistic assessors of the field might argue, however, that as the evidence is accumulating, it becomes increasingly clear that the relationship between personality and leadership effectiveness is modest at best—significant, but perhaps not too relevant to our understanding of leadership. To a certain extent, this seems to be a bit of a debate about whether the glass is half full or half empty. There is something, but is it enough to make us academically happy? While I would not argue with the legitimacy of that question, I contend that the more important and more interesting question is: Can we do better? My answer is, yes, we can, by taking a person-in-situation approach to leadership effectiveness. Such a perspective does not deny the value of a focus on leader personality, but rather views the role of leader personality as best understood in context, where situational influences (i.e., characteristics of the task, followers, and the context) are proposed to possess both the capacity to enhance and to attenuate the relationship between leader personality and leadership effectiveness.

Leadership as Person-in-Situation: A Review and Research Model

The essence of a person-in-situation perspective on leadership is the notion that situational influences affect the relationship between leader personality and leadership effectiveness—in statistical terms, leadership effectiveness is a function of person x situation interactions. Situation here is understood to refer to characteristics of the task, follower(s), and the group and organizational context in which the leadership process is enacted. The rationale to look for such person x situation interactions is the notion that the modest relationships between personality and effectiveness reported in, for instance, many meta-analyses may not reflect modest relationships across the board, but rather substantial variability in the strength of these relationships. The key, then, is to distinguish situations in which leader personality may be hardly related to leadership effectiveness from situations in which the relationship between personality and effectiveness is substantial. This implies two obvious and related questions: what would be the conceptual rationale to expect such personality x situation interactions, and whether there is evidence for such interactions.

In the following sections, I review evidence concerning the role of the situation in the leader personality-effectiveness relationship to answer the latter question and in that sense assess the promise of the person-in-situation perspective on leadership effectiveness. First, however, to address the former question I discuss the person-in-situation approach more generally to outline how contextual influences may both enhance and attenuate the relationship between personality and outcomes of interest, and outline how this may be applied to leadership.

Person-in-Situation: Activation, Inhibition, and Effectiveness

Personality reflects the disposition to think, feel, and act in certain ways. The qualification inherent in the concept of disposition is key to the person-in-situation perspective in leadership, organizational behavior, and personality and social psychology in general. Disposition does not imply that the individual always thinks, feels, and acts in that particular way—it merely means that the individual is more inclined to do so than others scoring lower on the aspect of personality in question. Thus, given that people do not always act according to their dispositions, a key question in understanding the influence of personality on behavior is what stimulates people to follow, or not follow, their dispositional tendencies—when is people's personality actually expressed in their behavior? This question assumes center-stage in the person-in-situation perspective.

One influential answer to this question lies in the notion of *situation strength* (Mischel, 1973, 1977; Snyder & Ickes, 1985; Weiss & Adler, 1984). Situation strength refers to the extent to which the situation is clear on what is appropriate and inappropriate behavior within the context of the situation and thus in a sense "enforces" certain behavior. Strong situations are associated with clear situational cues or norms for behavior and invite people to behave in a relatively uniform way. A more extreme example of such a situation would be marching soldiers, who are trained to march in a way that is described carefully and in detail to ensure maximum

uniformity of behavior. In such a strong situation, there is little if any room for the expression of individual dispositions. The very strength of such a situation would override or inhibit the influence of personality on individuals' behavior. Weak situations, in contrast, are characterized by the absence of behavioral cues and norms to guide and dictate behavior. They are less clear on what is expected or appropriate, and leave far more degrees of freedom for individuals to behave as they see fit. As a result, they allow for, and indeed may invite, the expression of individual differences. The situation strength perspective thus suggests that to the extent that we are able to capture the strength of the situation, we are able to predict the degree to which personality will influence behavior.

Building on the situation strength perspective, the more recent trait activation theory (Tett & Burnett, 2003; Tett & Guterman, 2000) is gaining substantial clout in organizational psychology. In addition to situation strength, Tett and Burnett (2003) propose the notion of *situation trait relevance*. A situation has trait relevance to the extent that "it is thematically connected by the provision of cues, responses to which (or lack of responses to which) indicate a person's standing on the trait" (p. 502). Trait relevant cues lead to *trait activation*, the result being the expression of the trait in question. Extraversion, for instance, is a "social" trait—it captures behavioral tendencies in social interaction. In nonsocial situations there would typically be no trait relevant cues to activate an individual's extraverted disposition. Social interaction, in contrast, may provide such cues and thus evoke different responses from more introverted and more extraverted individuals.

Tett and Burnett propose that both situation strength and situation trait relevance are important to trait expression. While strong situations may inhibit trait expression, weak situations will only invite the expression of a trait to the extent that the situation contains trait relevant cues to activate the trait. The trait activation perspective thus suggests that to predict the extent to which personality expresses itself in behavior, we need to capture both the strength of the situation and situation trait relevance. Strictly speaking then, trait expression is function of a personality trait x situation trait relevance x situation strength interaction. All other things being equal, however, conceiving of personality trait expression as a function of trait x strength and trait x trait relevance interactions also is consistent with trait activation theory.

Trait activation is not the end of the story, however. It may answer the question of when personality traits are expressed in individuals' behavior, but it says little about the effects of the behavior. That is, personality expression should not be equated with behavioral effectiveness. The fact that a situation invites the expression of a trait does not mean that the expression of the trait is effective in achieving desired outcomes (Tett & Burnett, 2003; cf. Deluga, 1998a). In understanding and predicting "beyond behavior" therefore, we need not only theories of trait activation but also of the contingencies of behavioral effectiveness in producing the outcomes of interest. As of yet, the emerging person-in-situation perspective in leadership deals with the former much more than with the latter, and later in this chapter I will argue that in addressing the latter question the integration of the personality and social psychology of leadership should fully materialize.

What does all this mean for leader personality and leadership effectiveness? There is no reason why the notions of situation strength, situation trait relevance, and trait activation would not directly apply to leadership (De Hoogh, Den Hartog, & Koopman, 2005b; Ng et al., 2008). The relationship between leader personality and leader behavior can thus be understood as a function of situation strength and situation trait relevance. Leader personality should have little influence on leader behavior in strong situations or in situations with low trait relevance. In contrast, leader personality should have substantial relationships with leader behavior in weak situations with high trait relevance. Leader behavior should not be equated with leadership effectiveness,

however, and models of leader personality and leadership effectiveness should capture both situational influences in terms of strength and relevance, and in terms of the contingencies of the effectiveness of the leadership behavior associated with the personality trait in question. Figure 27.1 provides a graphic representation of the leadership model implied by this perspective, in which the emphasis is on situational influences in terms of situation strength, situation trait relevance, and situational contingencies of trait expression effectiveness ("situation behavioral appropriateness"). This model is an application of trait activation theory to leadership and I hasten to add that I claim credits for neither trait activation theory (Tett & Burnett, 2003) nor for the insight that it holds great potential in its application to leadership (De Hoogh et al., 2005b; Ng et al., 2008).

In the following sections, I review what leadership research has on offer in this respect. This review relies on the same "temporal" division as the review of the leader personality-effectiveness relationship presented in the previous section, using the rise of the Big Five perspective in leadership research as an artificial watershed. In reviewing this evidence, I will discuss studies in the trait activation terms displayed in Figure 27.1. Note, however, that this represents my reading of these studies from the perspective of trait activation and effectiveness, and not the authors'. With two exceptions (De Hoogh et al., 2005b; Ng et al., 2008), these studies have not been designed from the perspective of trait activation theory—or another clearly articulated person-in-situation perspective for that matter

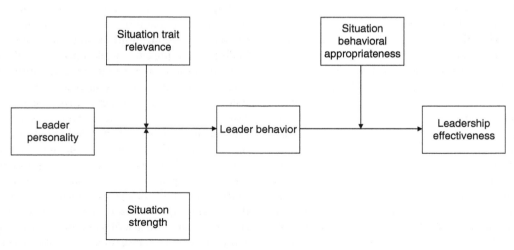

Fig. 27.1 A Trait Activation Model of leadership effectiveness (building on Tett & Burnett, 2003).

(e.g., Diener, Larsen, & Emmons, 1984). Thus, I review the evidence as the available evidence for leader personality x situation interactions and not in an evaluation of a trait activation perspective on personality and leadership or of any other theoretical perspective on person-in-situation leadership.

Person-in-Situation: Before the Big Five

Unfortunately, earlier research on situational influences on the relationship between leader personality and leadership comes with a methodological disclaimer. In statistical-methodological terms, the person-in-situation perspective describes interactions between personality variables and situational characteristics, or put differently a moderator role for situational variables in the personality-leadership relationship (e.g., Baron & Kenny, 1986). In view of our current understanding of such interactions/moderated relationships, it may be hard to imagine, but much of the earlier work in the field does not assess the influence of the situation in statistically appropriate ways. Rather than testing statistical interactions, conclusions were often based on a comparison of results for subsamples, concluding that the situation exerts an influence because the personality-leadership relationship is statistically significant in the one situation but not in the other (e.g., Cornelius & Lane, 1984; McClelland & Boyatzis, 1982). The problem with this approach is that significance is an arbitrary (even if consensually agreed on) dichotomy, and the fact that a relationship is significant in the one situation but nonsignificant in the other does not preclude the possibility that they are otherwise virtually identical. Absent appropriate tests of statistical moderation (cf. Baron & Kenny, 1986), such findings are tentative at best and probably should not be taken as evidence at all. Reviewing this evidence thus is primarily instructive in terms of capturing the evolution of our understanding.

The original trait perspective on leadership was not prone to consider person x situation interactions. Indeed, the behavioral contingency theories that focused on situational moderators of the effectiveness of leadership styles probably were the main influence for research in leadership and personality to consider situational influences, and not necessarily with much theoretical consideration. Some of the more visible research in situational influences on the personality-effectiveness relationship was conducted within the "needs" tradition. Earlier research in this tradition does not lend itself well as evidence, however, due to the absence of tests of statistical

interactions (McClelland & Boyatsis, 1982) or due to the use of difference scores to capture person-situation match (Winter, 1987) which is equally problematic from a methodological perspective (Edwards, 1994).

In later research, Fodor and Riordan (1995) focused on the moderating influence of group conflict on the relationship between leader need for power, leader behavior, and follower self-esteem. They argued that group conflict thwarts fulfillment of the need for power and thus leads to stress that disrupts the functioning of leaders with a high need for power (i.e., conflict as a trait relevant cue, but as frustrating rather than facilitating). While Fodor and Riordan found some support for the predicted person x situation interaction in measures of leader behavior, the proposed interaction was not supported for the variable that would be most indicative of leadership effectiveness, follower self-esteem. In a related vein, De Hoogh et al. (2005a) found that the nature of the organization—for profit or voluntary—interacted with leader need for power and responsibility in predicting charisma, albeit not as expected based on leadership motive profile propositions, but not in predicting effectiveness in terms of follower attitudes. If anything, then, this sheds further doubts on the leadership motive profile approach.

Person-in-Situation: Big Five and Beyond

Like earlier Big Five leadership research, person-in-situation studies relying on the five-factor model have focused on transformational/charismatic leadership and leadership self-efficacy. Ployhart, Lim, and Chan (2001) studied the relationship between the Big Five and transformational leadership in more or less challenging performance contexts. They argued that transformational leadership and therefore also its personality predictors, are more important in more challenging performance contexts, implicitly arguing for the trait-relevance of challenges. In partial support of predictions, results showed that transformational leadership in more challenging contexts was predicted by openness to experience and extraversion, whereas in less challenging contexts it was predicted by extraversion and emotional stability. Lim and Ployhart (2004) tested a related model and proposed that all Big Five dimensions except conscientiousness would predict transformational leadership regardless of performance context, but that performance context would moderate the relationship between transformational leadership and performance (i.e., contexts would not differ in their trait relevance, but in the effectiveness of behavioral trait expression). Contrary to predictions, regression analysis only found support for the proposed relationship between emotional stability and transformational leadership and relationships between leadership and performance did not differ between contexts. Engaging with similar notions of challenge, De Hoogh et al. (2005b) focused on the Big Five as predictors of charismatic leadership as a function of environmental dynamism. They argued that charismatic leaders are more likely to emerge (i.e., act charismatic) and be effective in times of crisis, turbulence, and uncertainty and that accordingly Big Five dimensions that dispose leaders to act charismatically should be activated by a dynamic, turbulent environment. Predictions for the relationship with charismatic leadership were confirmed for openness to experience, agreeableness, and conscientiousness, and charismatic leadership was more positively related to perceptions of leader effectiveness in dynamic environments. Extraversion was not related to charismatic leadership, however, and emotional stability was negatively related to charismatic leadership in dynamic environments. The implied mediation model (i.e., Big Five predicts effectiveness through charismatic leadership) was not tested.

Even so, a noteworthy aspect of the De Hoogh et al. study is that it implies that trait relevance cannot be equated with trait effectiveness. While environmental dynamism was associated with greater perceived effectiveness of charismatic leadership as well as with more positive relations between openness to experience and charismatic leadership (i.e., consistent with a model in which trait expression and effectiveness go hand in hand), agreeableness and emotional stability actually went at the expense of charismatic leadership when charismatic leadership was more effective, suggesting a model in which trait expression goes hand in hand with lower trait effectiveness. Also speaking to this issue are findings from a Howell and Avolio (1993) study of locus of control as a predictor of transformational leadership. Locus of control captures individual differences in the belief that what happens to the individual is under the individual's control (internal locus) or externally caused (external locus; Rotter, 1966), and is closely aligned with emotional stability (Judge et al., 1997). Howell and Avolio found that more internal locus of control was associated with higher ratings on the three dimensions of transformational leadership distinguished (charisma, individualized consideration, intellectual stimulation; Bass, 1985). They also studied the extent to which the team climate was supportive of innovation as a situational moderator of the relationship between transformational leadership and performance, expecting that this relationship would be stronger under high support for innovation. This prediction was confirmed for two of the dimensions of transformational leadership, but the reverse pattern was observed for charisma. Howell and Avolio also observed that for charisma and individualized consideration the relationship with locus of control was stronger under conditions of low support for innovation. These findings too point to the possibility that traits may express themselves more in leadership behavior under conditions where the behavior is less effective (a negative relationship between individualized consideration and performance was obtained under low support for innovation). As findings for charisma suggest, however, trait activation and trait effectiveness can also go hand in hand.

These findings underscore the importance of separate treatment of trait expression and trait effectiveness. Indeed, they hint at the possibility that part of the issue with the modest relationships between personality and effectiveness may lie in the fact that personality may sometimes be more predictive of leadership when that leadership is less effective. One of the challenges to the person-in-situation perspective on leadership thus would seem to be to establish when the one and when the other obtains.

Ng et al. (2008) worked from a trait activation perspective in their study of the relationship of extraversion, emotional stability, and conscientiousness with perceptions of leadership effectiveness. Ng et al. proposed that the influence of these personality factors on leadership effectiveness may be understood from their relationship with leadership self-efficacy. Extraversion, emotional stability, and conscientiousness were all expected to be positively related to leadership self-efficacy and thus to feed into leadership effectiveness, and this hypothesis was confirmed. With increasing job demands, however, task demands would assume center-stage and leadership self-efficacy would be less contingent on personality. That is, job demands are proposed to be a situational influence that inhibits trait activation and the expression of personality in leadership self-efficacy and thus in leadership effectiveness. This moderated mediation model (cf. Edwards & Lambert, 2007) was confirmed. Job autonomy, in contrast, with its associated decision latitude and discretion on the job, was proposed to create a weak situation and activate personality's expression in leadership self-efficacy and thus in leadership effectiveness. This moderated mediation model was confirmed for emotional stability and conscientiousness, but the relationship between extraversion and effectiveness was mediated by leadership self-efficacy regardless of job autonomy. Job demands and job autonomy are variables that are strongly aligned with the underlying logic of trait activation theory, and from that perspective it is promising to see that these predictions received such consistent support.

When the leadership field lost its faith in the 1960s and 1970s contingency approaches to leadership effectiveness, a perspective that arose in addition to the focus on charismatic-transformational leadership and that is still influential today is the social exchange perspective (Dansereau, Graen, & Haga, 1975). This perspective, captured under the label of leader-member exchange (LMX), focuses on leader-follower relationship quality, and understands this in terms of the quality of social exchange. Social exchange theory (Homans, 1958) describes how the quality of human relationships can be captured by the extent to which relationship partners exchange material and immaterial (e.g., friendship) goods in a spirit of mutual trust and to mutual satisfaction. LMX theory understands leader-follower relationships in these terms, and predicts that higher LMX (i.e., social exchange relationship quality) leads to more favorable outcomes including those that are typically understood as indicators of leadership effectiveness (Graen & Uhl-Bien, 1995; Schriesheim, Castro, & Cogliser, 1999). The LMX framework tends to be well supported, albeit largely in research with subjective indicators of leadership effectiveness (Gerstner & Day, 1997; Ilies, Nahrgang, & Morgeson, 2007).

A long-standing proposition in the study of interpersonal relationships is that similarity attracts—more similar people get along better (Byrne, 1971). Applied to leadership and personality, leaders should be able to build better relationships with followers that are more similar to them in personality. Within the trait activation theory framework, this is perhaps best understood in terms of trait effectiveness—the expression of a trait is more effective in engendering positive perceptions and responses from the other party when the other party is inclined toward similar behavior. In support of this logic, Deluga (1998b) found that leader-follower conscientiousness similarity predicted follower performance. A recent study by Nahrgang, Morgeson, and

Ilies (2009), however, provides some important qualifications to the conclusion invited by the Deluga findings. Nahrgang et al. focused on leader extraversion and agreeableness (i.e., the "social" Big Five dimensions) and observed that leader-follower extraversion similarity did not predict relationship quality. Leader-follower similarity in agreeableness did, but not in the way proposed by the similarity/attraction hypothesis. Follower perceptions of relationship quality were lowest when both the leader and the follower were low on agreeableness and higher when the leader was high on agreeableness regardless of follower agreeableness. Thus, it was not similarity leading to attraction—indeed, similarity in low agreeableness was associated with the worse relationship (i.e., presumably because both parties tend to behave rather unpleasantly in interaction). Rather, leader agreeableness fed into favorable follower perceptions (i.e., presumably because of the leader's pleasant interaction style), especially when it was most needed (i.e., when the follower is disagreeable), suggesting that there are asymmetries in the effects of leader-follower personality combinations that are not captured by the similarity-attraction principle. Nahrgang et al. (2009) also identified time as a moderator of the influence of leader personality on leader-follower relationships. Based on LMX theory, they predicted that personal characteristics (i.e., personality) would be important early on in relationship development, but not later on when more work-specific variables would be more influential (i.e., leader and follower performance). This prediction was supported for leader agreeableness (and follower extraversion), suggesting that the effectiveness of trait expression diminishes as more task-relevant information enters the relationship.

Recently, leadership research has also started to explore the influence of leaders' learning orientation. Learning orientation refers to individuals' disposition to try to achieve mastery (i.e., develop their competence and skills) in the activities they undertake (Dweck, 1986; Dweck & Legett, 1988). More learning-oriented individuals are more attuned to opportunities for learning and development and more willing to invest in learning and development, and less discouraged by challenges and setbacks (Button, Mathieu, & Zajac, 1996). For leadership this implies that leaders with a stronger learning orientation should be more motivated to improve their leadership skills and thus ultimately their effectiveness given that circumstances provide opportunities for learning. DeRue and Wellman (2009) established this very point, demonstrating that developmental challenges help leadership skill acquisition up to a point and that leaders with a stronger learning orientation are more able to benefit from such challenges (also see Heslin & Latham, 2004). The focus on learning orientation and related constructs is only just emerging, but might hold particular promise—more on this in the next section.

In sum, there is clear evidence that situational factors influence the relationship of leader personality with leader behavior and leadership effectiveness. These studies of person x situation interactions are quite diverse in focus and conceptual angle, however, and one would be hard put to argue that they present a clear picture of the personality-effectiveness relationship. Part of the problem here might be that most of these studies are not driven by a broader theory of person-situation interactive influences that would help organize studies under an overarching umbrella (i.e., as I have tried to do in the current review with the reconceptualizations in terms of trait activation theory). Even so, these studies are valuable in identifying what a conceptual framework for the person-in-situation study of leadership effectiveness should look like and which questions it should be able to address. In the following, I outline the contours of such a conceptual framework and an agenda for the research required to develop the framework.

Toward a Person-in-Situation Model of Leader Personality and Effectiveness

In defining the shape that a person-in-situation model of leader personality and leadership effectiveness should take, a good start is to identify what is currently lacking or most needed. The review in the previous section suggests that perhaps the most important issue to take into consideration is that trait activation is not the same as trait effectiveness. This suggests at least two issues to address in this respect, the first more methodological, the second conceptual.

First, these findings lend further strength to the more general argument that the tendency of much leadership and personality research to study leader behavior or style as the ultimate outcome of interest rather than leadership effectiveness is problematic, because the linkage with effectiveness cannot be assumed. If the bottom line for leadership research is leadership effectiveness, research in leader personality should study leadership effectiveness and not limit itself to presumed proxies of leadership effectiveness such as charismatic and transformational leadership. In a related vein, it is surprising to see

how many studies of personality and leadership that do assess both intermediate and outcome variables do not test the implied mediation model (i.e., personality predicting outcomes via its relationship with the intermediate variables). Another obvious call to arms thus is to develop and test mediation models that link personality to effectiveness outcomes through intermediate psychological and behavioral processes, both to establish a relationship between personality and effectiveness and to develop theory about mediating processes (for a showcase example of how this may be done, see Ng et al., 2008).

Second, it implies that part of the reason for the modest success of the trait approach in leadership may lie in the fact that the expression of traits does not necessarily result in behavior that is appropriate to the situation. A successful person-in-situation perspective on leadership should therefore be able to capture both the contingencies of trait expression and the contingencies of trait effectiveness—or put differently, identify the traits that are associated with situation behavioral appropriateness. Personality can only be expected to have substantial relationships with leadership effectiveness when the situation invites its expression in leadership *and* when this trait expression is appropriate to the circumstances. That is, to understand the influence of personality in situation, we need to understand the influence of behavior in situation. Importantly, to determine the contingencies of behavioral effectiveness leadership research can rely on a rich research tradition in the social psychology of leadership. The realization that trait expression and trait effectiveness cannot be equated and may each have their own contingencies thus invites an integration of personality and social psychological research in leadership that brings the field an important step closer to more broad-ranging models of leadership effectiveness. Indeed, whereas personality approaches to leadership can be criticized for being underdeveloped in terms of their understanding of the effectiveness of (personality-based) behavior in situation, social psychological approaches can be criticized for treating leader behavior as a "given" and generally being mute as to the origins of the leader behavior studied.

The trait activation model of leadership effectiveness displayed in Figure 27.1 is useful in structuring the relevant situational influences in terms of where they intervene in the leadership process and to identify the different steps in which situational influences need to be taken into consideration. It also has the advantage of being consistent with a more general person-in-situation model, which helps leadership research to benefit from insights from nonleadership research (cf. Ng et al., 2008). In short, it identifies the elements of a good person-in-situation model of leadership. The challenge for future research, however, is to put more flesh on these bones and to provide a conceptually grounded account of the situational influences (i.e., follower, task, and context) that shape situation strength, situation trait relevance, and situation behavioral appropriateness in the process from leader personality to leadership effectiveness. Situation strength and situation trait relevance have been the domain of person-in-situation approaches to leadership, whereas situation behavioral appropriateness has been the domain of social psychological behavior-in-situation approaches. While this points to the obvious value of an integration of personality psychological and social psychological research in leadership, it also points to a challenging disconnect: it may not be so obvious how to establish links between personality traits and leadership behavior that has been shown to be situationally appropriate. In this respect, I highlight two issues: first, the conceptual limitations of the five-factor model; second, social psychological perspectives on leadership that have so far not been linked to personality at all.

As to the first, the five-factor model that seems to have become somewhat of a "gold standard" in research in leadership and personality comes with a caveat. The five-factor model holds the far-ranging claim of capturing human personality. Obviously, this is a great and valuable starting point in studying the influence of personality in any domain. A disadvantage of the five-factor model is that it is an inductively generated taxonomy rather than a theory. It provides a description of personality rather than a theory to understand personality and its influence on cognition, affect, and behavior, and there is no underlying theory distinguishing different aspects of personality. This makes it more challenging to develop theory about relationships with outcome variables. Leadership is no exception in this respect, as researchers by necessity have to rely on a combination of common sense and earlier findings as "empirical arguments" (which cannot replace theory; Sutton & Staw, 1995). Whereas it makes perfect sense to continue developing our understanding of the relationship between the Big Five dimensions and leadership on the basis of the assumption that the Big Five capture a lot of the variation in personality, there thus is also a strong case to be made to develop our understanding of leadership and personality on the basis of perspectives that have stronger conceptual grounding even when they are more narrowly defined—especially when part of the task the field is facing is establishing a link with behavior-in-situation approaches that were not limited in their conceptual development by the descriptive constraints of the five-factor model.

Interestingly and importantly, there is a growing research interest in two perspectives on individual differences in goal-directed behavior that seem better attuned than the Big Five to the kind of situations in which leadership processes are typically enacted and that are also associated with well-developed theoretical frameworks: goal orientation and self-regulatory focus. Leadership ultimately is a goal-directed process. The essence of leadership is influencing followers to some end pursued by the leader, and probably the most convincing indicators of leadership effectiveness are those capturing followers' behavior directed to achieving those ends. Accordingly, a potentially very useful way of conceiving of leader personality in relation to leadership effectiveness is in terms of dispositions relevant to self-regulation in goal-directed behavior. Both the goal orientation framework proposed by Dweck (1986; Dweck & Leggett, 1988) and the self-regulatory focus framework proposed by Higgins (1987, 1996, 1997) provide conceptual accounts of such differences (see also Norem, chapter 12, this volume). The goal-orientation framework distinguishes two motivational orientations underlying goal-directed behavior in achievement situations, learning orientation and performance orientation. Learning orientation was already addressed in the previous section. Performance orientation captures individuals' dispositions to focus on realizing a favorable impression of their abilities and performance, either in terms of proving their qualities by performing well (performance-approach orientation) or in terms of avoiding appearing to be a poor performer by staying clear of challenging performance situations (performance-avoidance orientation; Elliot & Church, 1997; VandeWalle, 1997). While the study of leader goal-orientation is only just taking off (DeRue & Wellman, 2009; Heslin & Latham, 2004), there is evidence in the DeRue and Wellman study as well as in research outside the leadership domain (Hirst, van Knippenberg, & Zhou, 2009) that goal orientations and situational influences interact in predicting behavioral outcomes. Given the links between the notion of challenges in the DeRue and Wellman study and the proposition regarding the greater importance of leadership in uncertain and dynamic environments (e.g., De Hoogh et al., 2005b), there seems to be ample scope for the integration of goal-orientations into the broader framework of person-in-situation leadership models. Self-regulatory focus captures dispositional differences in the motivation to pursue certain ends in terms of the motivation to approach gains—a promotion focus—and the motivation to avoid losses—a prevention focus (Higgins, 1987, 1996, 1997). These different self-regulatory foci are associated with specific cognitive and affective processes and therefore with specific outcomes. Promotion focus is, for instance, associated with a more risk-taking and open-minded gain-oriented style than prevention focus, and therefore has been proposed to be more predictive of transformational leadership (Brockner & Higgins, 2001; Kark & Van-Dijk, 2007). Research in regulatory focus is also increasingly exploring the contingencies of the effects of promotion and prevention focus such as greater sensitivity to positive (promotion focus) or negative (prevention focus) feedback (Van-Dijk & Kluger, 2004) and greater sensitivity to leader visions emphasizing the realization of positive outcomes (promotion focus) or the prevention of negative outcomes (prevention focus; Stam, van Knippenberg, & Wisse, 2010a). As with goal-orientation, research in leadership and regulatory focus is still in its infancy. Given its more proximal nature to goal-directed behavior than the Big Five, however, regulatory focus may provide an important angle in further developing person-in-situation models of leadership.

A second challenge in linking the personality psychology and the social psychology of leadership is that some of the better-supported social psychological perspectives may not have obvious linkages to the personality dimensions primarily studied in personality approaches to leadership. This might mean that leadership characteristics associated with leadership effectiveness cannot easily be traced back to leader personality—or at least not to the personality dimensions more typically studied in leadership research. In the previous section, I discussed the contemporary perspective on charismatic-transformational leadership and LMX. Probably the third main stream of research rising from the ashes of the contingency theories of leadership (i.e., in addition to research in charismatic-transformational leadership and LMX) is what I would group under the heading leadership categorization theories (cf. van Knippenberg & Hogg, 2003).

The label *leadership categorization theory* is primarily associated with the seminal work of Lord (e.g., Lord & Maher, 1991), but also applies to research in implicit leadership theories (Eden & Leviatan, 1975), the romance of leadership (Meindl et al., 1985), and role congruity theory of gender and leadership (Eagly & Karau, 2002). What these theories have in common is the proposition that at least to a certain extent leadership is in the eye of the beholder. Beliefs about leadership—whether the observer is aware of these beliefs or not—color individuals' perception of leadership, and lead individuals to see "better" leadership when a (potential) leader matches their implicit beliefs about leadership. Such implicit leadership theories or leader prototypes (i.e., mental representations capturing the ideal-type of a leader) help explain, for instance, individuals' tendency to overly attribute (changes in) team or organizational performance to leadership (Lord, 1977; Meindl et al., 1985) or to see more leadership qualities in male than in female leaders (Eagly & Karau, 2002).

Because perceptions of good leadership presumably set the stage for future leader influence (cf. van Knippenberg & Hogg, 2003), the implication of leadership categorization theories is that leaders may gain influence over followers to the extent that they can convey an image of themselves that matches followers' implicit beliefs or prototypes of good leadership (Meindl, 1995; cf. Reicher & Hopkins, 2003). Clearly, there are constraints to leaders' ability to do so—it is impossible for female leaders to perfectly match a leader prototype that favors being male—but to the extent that such characteristics are open to social construction, we may inquire about the personality predictors of leaders' ability to present themselves in ways that would allow them to gain clout with followers through leadership categorization processes. I discussed earlier how self-monitoring would be a personality predictor to focus on in this respect but how research has so far not really supported this notion, presumably because self-monitoring captures motivation more than ability to convey images of the self that connect with followers. More sophisticated, situation-sensitive developments of this perspective may provide clearer linkages between leader personality and leader categorization processes.

The social identity theory of leadership (Hogg & van Knippenberg, 2003; van Knippenberg & Hogg, 2003) is a fourth, more recently established perspective, that is in part related to leadership categorization theories. The social identity perspective emphasizes the group membership, and thus social identity (Tajfel & Turner, 1986; Turner, Hogg, Oakes, Reicher, & Wetherell, 1987), that leaders and followers share, and that forms a basis for followers' responses to leadership. To the extent that followers identify with the collective (i.e., group, team, organization, nation), followers are proposed to be more open to the influence of leaders that are perceived to be group prototypical—to embody the social identity of the group, representing what group members have in common and what distinguishes the group from other groups (Hogg, 2001). That is, it is the group prototype and not an abstracted leader prototype (cf. Lord & Maher, 1991) that is proposed to provide the frame of reference for responses to leadership the more followers identify with the collective (Hogg, 2001). From the perspective of an integrated person-situation perspective on leadership, an important question arising from this perspective is what leaders can do to convey their group prototypicality (cf. Reicher & Hopkins, 2003) and, following from this, which personality factors, if any, are related to leaders' ability to do so.

The social identity perspective also identifies a second main influence on leadership effectiveness—leader group-serving behavior—which is also highlighted in some theories of charismatic leadership (Conger & Kanungo, 1987; De Cremer & van Knippenberg, 2002). One important reason why leader group prototypicality feeds into leadership effectiveness is that it instills trust in leaders' motivation to pursue the collective's interest. To the extent that trust in leader group-orientedness cannot be based on leader group prototypicality, leadership effectiveness will be contingent on actual indicators of leader group-oriented behavior, such as leader self-sacrifice on behalf of the collective (van Knippenberg & van Knippenberg, 2005). This, then, raises the question what leads leaders to behave in group-serving ways (Rus et al., 2010). Of particular relevance to the present discussion, it raises the question of whether there are personality and individual difference factors that play a role here. Potentially, these are more readily found in factors that directly speak to individuals' disposition to look beyond their own self-interest such as individualist-collectivistic orientation (or idiocentrism-allocentrism; Triandis, Leung, Villareal, & Clack, 1985) and social value orientation (Messick & McClintock, 1968) than in the Big Five.

A final perspective I would highlight here is that on leader fairness (van Knippenberg, De Cremer, & van Knippenberg, 2007) and related perspectives on leader ethics and morality (e.g., Brown, Treviño, & Harrison, 2005). Research in social and organizational justice goes back more than 40 years, but only relatively recently has it started to explicitly connect with leadership, noting that leaders often are primary sources of decisions associated with fairness experiences both in terms of the outcome of the decision (distributive fairness) and in terms of the way the decision was reached and communicated (procedural and interactional justice; Colquitt, Conlon, Wesson, Porter, & Ng, 2001). While many of the complexities of leader fairness likely still need to be uncovered, we are safe in concluding that leader fairness feeds into leadership effectiveness (van Knippenberg et al., 2007). Accordingly, in the spirit of the current discussion we may ask about the personality determinants of leader fairness (as well as leader ethical/moral conduct). Again, it is not obvious that the more persuasive answers lie within the five-factor model.

Another important issue to note here, almost as an aside even though it may be of primary importance, is that personality is not the only cause of leader behavior (e.g., Rus et al., 2010). Studies of the determinants of leader behavior have almost exclusively emphasized personality, but leader behavior can also be influenced by situational factors. There is for instance evidence that transformational leadership (Dvir, Eden, Avolio, & Shamir, 2002) and leader fairness (Skarlicki & Latham, 1996) can be developed in training, and Rus et al. (2010) show that, contingent on the extent to which being a leader is central to their identity, leaders are more likely to behave in self-serving ways if other leaders are perceived to do so. In that sense, the obviously, albeit for instructive purposes deliberately, missing aspect in Figure 27.1 are situational influences that directly feed into leader behavior: the social psychology of the determinants of leader behavior. This is a perspective that is more or less missing from leadership research, but the present analysis would identify it as one of the key areas of interest for future research to complement research on the personality determinants of leader behavior.

To recap then, we still know very little about person x situation interactions in leadership and far less than we probably should know for a more broad-ranging person-in-situation perspective integrating personality and social psychological approaches to leadership. Even so, the research to date has been very important in defining the contours of the much-needed person-in-situation model of leadership effectiveness. The biggest challenges

I identify in this respect are, first, bridging the personality perspective that is dominated by the five-factor model and the social psychological perspective in which the more promising findings might less obviously be linked to the Big Five, and, second, developing the social psychology of the determinants of leader behavior.

Before moving on to some final words in concluding this chapter, I first sidestep to one particular situational influence that a person-in-situation model of leadership should incorporate—follower personality. This discussion of follower personality is to underscore the potential value that the trait activation perspective may also have in developing this part of the model and to highlight the fact that on the follower side too an integrated personality-social psychology of leadership is required.

Follower Personality-in-Situation

Clearly, the emphasis in research on personality and leadership has been on leader personality. Follower personality also plays a role in leadership effectiveness, however, and I consider here whether the person-in-situation perspective would also be instrumental in developing our understanding of the role of followers in leadership effectiveness. The same leader characteristic may have different effects for different followers, and follower characteristics thus act as moderators of the relationship between leader characteristics and leadership effectiveness (e.g., van Knippenberg et al., 2007). Follower personality in that sense is a subset of this category of situational contingencies of leadership effectiveness.

Perhaps in line with people's understanding of the differences between leader and follower roles (cf. van Gils, van Quaquebeke, & van Knippenberg, 2010), research in the role of follower personality has focused on a set of personality and individual difference variables that only partly overlaps with those studied in research in leader personality. Obvious overlap is found in the study of Big Five dimensions and related variables that may be understood as more specific aspects of the Big Five dimensions or as closely aligned constructs. Earlier, I mentioned work by Deluga (1998b) and Nahrgang et al. (2009) on follower extraversion, agreeableness, and conscientiousness as predictors of leader-follower relationship quality (also see Phillips & Bedeian, 1994), and their interactions with leader personality and time in relationship.

Day and Crain (1992) and Hui, Law, and Chen (1999) focused on follower negative affectivity as a

predictor of leader-follower relationship quality. Negative affectivity is the disposition to experience negative affect and is related to neuroticism (i.e., low emotional stability). This research found that there was a negative relationship between negative affectivity and relationship quality. Speaking more directly to a person-in-situation perspective, some of this research also addressed the moderating role of follower negative affectivity in responses to leadership. Skarlicki, Folger, and Tesluk (1999) showed that negative affectivity and agreeableness moderated the relationship between leader fairness and retaliative behavior (i.e., undesirable behavior in response to perceived unfair treatment). They found that the relationship between (un)fairness and retaliation was stronger for followers with higher negative affectivity and lower agreeableness. Tepper, Duffy, Henle, and Lambert (2006) similarly found that leader fairness was more impactful for followers with higher negative affectivity. In a related vein, Epitropaki and Martin (2005) presented evidence that transformational leadership was more positively related to follower identification for followers with higher negative affectivity.

In combination, these findings would support the conclusion that follower negative affectivity (cf. low emotional stability) renders it more important (i.e., in terms of leadership effectiveness) that the leader engages in positive acts of leadership (fairness, transformational leadership) and refrains from negative acts. Where responses to leader fairness are concerned, there is some evidence that this conclusion may hold more generally for follower negative dispositions (cf. Skarlicki et al.'s findings for low agreeableness). Judge, Scott, and Ilies (2006) showed that leader fairness is more impactful for followers high in trait hostility. One reading of these findings is from a trait activation perspective, where followers with tendencies to respond negatively (i.e., low agreeableness and high negative affectivity and trait hostility) are more likely to react to leader fairness (i.e., where fairness presumably is the norm and unfairness the salient deviation from that norm). Brennan and Skarlicki (2004) found, however, that leader interactional fairness was more impactful for followers with lower hostility and higher self-discipline (cf. conscientiousness), so clearly the final word on this has not been said. Epitropaki and Martin also focused on follower positive affectivity, which is related to extraversion. They found that the relationship between transformational leadership and identification was weaker for followers higher in positive affectivity. Moreover, the Skarlicki et al.

(1999) findings for agreeableness can of course also be read as saying that leader fairness is less impactful for more agreeable followers. Tentatively, then, we might also propose that follower positive dispositions render leadership effectiveness less contingent on the extent to which the leader engages in positive acts of leadership and refrains from negative acts. Studies by De Cremer (2003) and De Hoogh and Den Hartog (2009) can also be interpreted through this lens. De Cremer looked at follower self-esteem, a factor closely aligned with emotional stability (Judge et al., 1997), as a moderator of responses to leader fairness, and found that followers lower in self-esteem were more sensitive to leader fairness (cf. Vermunt, van Knippenberg, van Knippenberg, & Blaauw, 2001). De Hoogh and Den Hartog studied follower locus of control and emotional stability, two closely associated factors that, like self-esteem, capture follower self-evaluation (Judge et al., 1997). They found that leader charisma was associated with low follower burnout for followers with an external locus of control (i.e., low self-evaluation), and autocratic leadership associated with high burnout for followers low on emotional stability (i.e., low self-evaluation). These studies too thus support the conclusion that followers with more positive dispositions are less sensitive to the positive and negative acts of leadership.

As noted earlier, self-regulatory focus has been studied more as a follower characteristic than as a leader characteristic. Stam et al. (2010a, 2010b) demonstrate regulatory fit effects in responses to leader visionary appeals. Regulatory fit refers to the extent to which situational cues correspond with individual's regulatory focus. Regulatory fit (vs. misfit) is associated with stronger effects of regulatory focus—a proposition that aligns well with a trait activation interpretation. Specifically, Stam et al. showed that follower promotion focus and prevention focus moderate the extent to which followers are more inspired by promotion-oriented or prevention-oriented visionary appeals (Stam et al., 2010a) or by appeals that are geared to stimulate (vs. not stimulate) the formation of a promotion-oriented (ideal) image of the self (Stam et al., 2010b). De Cremer, Mayer, van Dijke, Schouten, and Bardes (2009) focused on follower regulatory focus as a moderator of responses to leader self-sacrificial behavior. They argued that self-sacrifice is prevention-oriented and that therefore leader self-sacrifice is more effective in engendering cooperative behavior for followers with a prevention focus. Results supported this prediction. This finding too lends itself well to a trait activation interpretation.

There is a strong tradition in leadership research in understanding leadership effectiveness in terms of the mediating and moderating influence of follower self-concept and identity (Shamir et al., 1993; Lord, Brown, & Freiberg, 1999; van Knippenberg & Hogg, 2003). Core to this perspective is a focus on follower self-construal, the extent to which an individual conceives of the self in terms of uniquely defining characteristics that distinguish self from other individuals or more in terms of an extended sense of self that incorporates others and captures shared social identity (van Knippenberg et al., 2004). As discussed above, the social identity model of leadership (Hogg & van Knippenberg, 2003; van Knippenberg & Hogg, 2003) in particular proposes that follower self-construal (i.e., social identification) is a key moderator of responses to leadership.

While self-construal in this perspective is primarily understood as a state and not as a trait, there are trait-like counterparts of self-construal, and these have received some attention in leadership research. One of these is individuals' cultural orientation in terms of individualism (or idiocentrism) versus collectivism (or allocentrism), which presumably at least in part reflects the disposition to conceive of the self in collective terms (i.e., "we"; collectivism, allocentrism) or in individualizing terms (i.e., "I"; individualism, idiocentrism; Triandis, 1995). Transformational leadership as compared with transactional leadership is more focused on the collective interest and on the self-interest, and accordingly, one would expect follower self-construal to moderate the effectiveness of transformational and transactional leadership (van Knippenberg & Hogg, 2003). This is exactly the pattern of results Walumbwa and Lawler (2003; Walumbwa, Lawler, & Avolio, 2007) obtained for individual differences in collectivism-individualism (cf. Jung & Avolio, 1999). Moreover, Walumbwa et al. showed that this was further moderated by the cultural context, with the combination of transformational leadership and follower collectivistic orientation yielding more positive outcomes in countries with a collectivistic culture, and the combination of transactional leadership and follower individualistic orientation yielding more positive outcomes in countries with a more individualistic culture. These findings are highly consistent with a trait activation interpretation, where leadership style and cultural context are seen as providing trait relevant cues.

Related are findings reported by De Cremer and Alberts (2004) for the moderating role of follower need to belong in the effectiveness of leader procedural fairness. Need to belong captures the disposition to seek social affiliations (Baumeister & Leary, 1995) and thus presumably is a proxy for the desire to identify with collectives. Procedural fairness reflects the leader's appraisal of the follower (i.e., higher procedural fairness indicating that the follower is held in higher regard; Koper, van Knippenberg, Bouhuijs, Vermunt, & Wilke, 1993), and this would be of greater concern to followers with a stronger need to belong (cf. stronger identification with the group; Tyler, 1999). De Cremer and Alberts's (2004) finding that leader fairness was more effective for followers with a higher need to belong supports this line of reasons. Again, leadership can be interpreted here as a trait relevant cue. Moreover, these findings contribute to establishing stronger linkages between fairness and social identity perspectives on leadership (Lind, Kray, & Thompson, 2001; Ullrich, Christ, & van Dick, 2009; van Knippenberg & Hogg, 2003).

A quite different perspective, so far unique to a focus on follower personality, is that in terms of dispositional differences in follower epistemic motivation—the disposition to carefully process information and form well-grounded judgments and decisions (Kruglanski & Webster, 1996). Dispositional differences in epistemic motivation are captured under different labels and with different measurement, but the underlying logic remains the same: some individuals are more likely to pay careful attention and to carefully consider information, while others prefer swift closure over extended elaboration of information and options. In leadership research, there are two applications of this perspective. First, from a social identity theory of leadership perspective, Pierro, Cicero, Bonaiuto, van Knippenberg, and Kruglanski (2005, 2007) argued and showed that followers with a higher need for closure (i.e., lower epistemic motivation) are more inclined to rely on their group memberships in making sense of the world. As a consequence, leadership effectiveness is more contingent on the extent to which the leader is perceived to be group prototypical for followers with higher need for closure. In trait activation terms, this is consistent with an interpretation that leader group prototypicality is a more trait relevant cue for followers with a higher need for closure, and this is indeed what Pierro et al. found. Because epistemic motivation has not only trait but also state aspects, this perspective can also be generalized to situational moderators of leadership effectiveness, and this is exactly what Cicero, Pierro, and van Knippenberg (2007, 2010) did in studies of follower stress and

follower role ambiguity as moderators of the influence of leader group prototypicality.

Second, from the perspective that dispositional differences in epistemic motivation capture careful consideration of information versus quick-and-dirty judgment formation, Van Kleef et al. (2009) predicted that follower personal need for structure (i.e., reflecting low epistemic motivation) moderates the effectiveness of leader displays of happiness versus anger. The tendency of followers with low epistemic motivation to form quick-and-dirty judgments was expected to express itself primarily in their reliance on their first affective-evaluative responses to the leader (i.e., which are more favorable for happy than for angry leaders), so that they would perform better with a happy leader. Followers with high epistemic motivation, in contrast, were expected to carefully consider what the leader's emotional display meant and to rely primarily on their conclusions regarding the information conveyed about task performance (i.e., where anger suggests a greater need for improvement than happiness) and thus to perform better with an angry leader. These predictions were confirmed. In trait activation terms, the psychological perceptions of leader and task feedback are trait relevant cues, and Van Kleef's et al. mediation evidence is consistent with this interpretation.

From the perspective of leadership research, leader personality is clearly the main attraction and not follower personality. Even so, it is important to note that follower personality does moderate the effectiveness of different leader characteristics and behavior, and does so in ways that can be meaningfully understood from a trait activation perspective, where leadership provides the trait relevant cues. The logic underlying the leader person-in-situation model displayed in Figure 27.1 can thus be fruitfully extended to identify the situational moderator role of follower personality, and this speaks to the value and consistency of the trait activation perspective adopted here. This brief sidestepping to consider follower personality was merely meant, however, to extend the invitation to consider this too from a person-in-situation perspective, and one in which the leader—including leader personality—is considered as situation. Ultimately, however, leader personality assumes center-stage in the current analysis, and this is what I focus the concluding section on.

Conclusion

It would seem that to many people, academics and practitioners alike, there is just too much intuitive appeal in the notion that leader personality plays an important role in leadership effectiveness to give up on it even when research findings are often less consistent and less supportive of this strong role of personality than one would like. Recent social psychological perspectives, in comparison, seem to receive more consistent support. Even so, it is important to recognize that these perspectives typically treat leader behavior as a given, as if questions regarding the origins of leader behavior are not part of our quest for understanding leadership effectiveness. Absent social psychological analyses of the determinants of leader behavior, which are very scarce (Rus et al., 2010; cf. Fielding & Hogg, 1997), personality analyses developed from a person-in-situation perspective would still seem to be an obvious contender to address these questions and thus advance our understanding of leadership effectiveness. Conversely, social psychological analysis of leadership are more developed, and more successful in their understanding of the situational contingencies governing leader behavior-leadership effectiveness linkages. One clear conclusion of this chapter therefore is that broad-ranging models of leadership that cover both the effectiveness and the origins of leadership can only be integrative models of the personality and social psychology of leadership.

This conclusion should not be understood as a claim that there is strong support for this person-in-situation perspective, however. We have only started to scratch the surface in this respect and most of the work still needs to be done. Rather, my proposition is that when we more consistently and systematically explore integrative personality-social psychological perspectives on leadership, we will be more successful in developing our understanding of leadership effectiveness. The bottom line of this chapter thus, first and foremost, is a research call to arms.

References

Anderson, D. W., Krajewski, H. T., Griffin, R. D., & Jackson, D. N. (2008). A leadership self-efficacy taxonomy and its relation to effective leadership. *Leadership Quarterly, 19*, 595–608.

Ashour, A. S., & England, G. (1972). Subordinates assigned level of discretion as a function of leader's personality and situational variables. *Journal of Applied Psychology, 56*, 120–123.

Bandura, A. (1986). *Social foundations of thought and action: A social-cognitive theory*. Englewood Cliffs, NJ: Prentice-Hall.

Bandura, A. (1997). *Self-efficacy: The exercise of self-control*. New York: Freeman.

Baron, R. M., & Kenny, D. A. (1986). The moderator-mediator distinction in social psychological research: Conceptual, strategic, and statistical considerations. *Journal of Personality and Social Psychology, 51*, 1173–1182.

Barrick, M. R., & Mount, M. K. (1991). The Big Five personality dimensions and job performance: A meta-analysis. *Personnel Psychology, 44*, 1–26.

Bass, B. M. (1985). *Leadership and performance beyond expectations*. New York: Free Press.

Bass, B. M. (1990). *Bass and Stogdill's handbook of leadership* (3rd ed.). New York: Free Press.

Bass, B. M., & Riggio, R. E. (2006). *Transformational leadership*. Mahwah, NJ: Erlbaum.

Bateman, T. S., & Crant, J. M. (1993). The proactive component of organizational behavior. *Journal of Organizational Behavior, 14*, 103–118.

Baumeister, R. F., & Leary, M. R. (1995). The need to belong: Desire for interpersonal attachments as a fundamental human motivation. *Psychological Bulletin, 117*, 497–529.

Block, J. (1995). A contrarian view of the five-factor approach to personality description. *Psychological Bulletin, 117*, 187–215.

Bono, J. E., & Ilies, R. (2006). Charisma and emotional contagion: Toward understanding the role of positive emotions in leadership. *Leadership Quarterly, 17*, 317–334.

Bono, J. E. & Judge, T. A. (2004). Personality and transformational and transactional leadership: A meta-analysis. *Journal of Applied Psychology, 89*, 901–910.

Brennan, A., & Skarlicki, D. P. (2004). Personality and perceived justice as predictors of survivors' reactions following downsizing. *Journal of Applied Social Psychology, 34*, 1306–1328.

Brockner, J., & Higgins, E. T. (2001). Regulatory focus theory: Implications for the study of emotions at work. *Organizational Behavior and Human Decision Processes, 86*, 35–66.

Brown, M. E., Treviño, L. K., & Harrison, D. A. (2005). Ethical leadership: A social learning theory perspective for construct development. *Organizational Behavior and Human Decision Processes, 97*, 117–134.

Burns, J. M. (1978). *Leadership*. New York: Harper & Row.

Button, S. B., Mathieu, J. E., & Zajac, D. M. (1996). Goal orientation in empirical research: A conceptual and empirical foundation. *Organizational Behavior and Human Decision Processes, 67*, 26–48.

Byrne, D. (1971). *The attraction paradigm*. New York: Academic.

Cartwright, D., & Zander, A. (Eds.). (1968). *Group dynamics: Research and theory* (3rd ed.). London: Tavistock.

Cicero, L., Pierro, A., & van Knippenberg, D. (2007). Leader group prototypicality and job satisfaction: The moderating role of job stress and team identification. *Group Dynamics, 11*, 165–175.

Cicero, L., Pierro, A., & van Knippenberg, D. (2010). Leadership and uncertainty: how role ambiguity affects the relationship between leader group prototypicality and leadership effectiveness: The moderating role of role ambiguity. *British Journal of Management*.

Chan, K.-Y., & Drasgow, F. (2001). Toward a theory of individual differences and leadership: Understanding the motivation to lead. *Journal of Applied Psychology, 86*, 481–498.

Chemers, M. M. (2001). Leadership effectiveness: An integrative review. In M. A. Hogg & R. S. Tindale (Eds.), *Blackwell handbook of social psychology: Group processes* (pp. 376–399). Oxford, UK: Blackwell.

Chemers, M. M., Watson, C. B., & May, S. (2000). Dispositional affect and leadership effectiveness: A comparison of self-esteem, optimism, and efficacy. *Personality and Social Psychology Bulletin, 26*, 267–277.

Colquitt, J. A., Conlon, D. E., Wesson, M. J., Porter, C. O., & Ng, K. Y. (2001). Justice at the millennium: A meta-analytic review of 25 years of organizational justice research. *Journal of Applied Psychology, 86,* 425–445.

Conger, J. A., & Kanungo, R. N. (1987). Towards a behavioral theory of charismatic leadership in organizational settings. *Academy of Management Review, 12,* 637–647.

Cornelius, E. T., III, & Lane, F. B. (1984). The power motive and managerial success in a professionally oriented service industry organization. *Journal of Applied Psychology, 69,* 32–39.

Crant, J. M., & Bateman, T. S. (2000). Charismatic leadership viewed from above: The impact of proactive personality. *Journal of Organizational Behavior, 14,* 103–118.

Damen, F., van Knippenberg, B., & van Knippenberg, D. (2008a). Affective match: Leader emotional displays, follower positive affect, and follower performance. *Journal of Applied Social Psychology, 38,* 868–902.

Damen, F., van Knippenberg, D., & van Knippenberg, B. (2008b). Leader affective displays and attributions of charisma: The role of arousal. *Journal of Applied Social Psychology, 38,* 2594–2614.

Dansereau, F., Graen, G., & Haga, W. J. (1975). A vertical dyad linkage approach to leadership within formal organizations: A longitudinal investigation of the role making process. *Organizational Behavior and Human Performance, 13,* 46–78.

Day, D. V., & Crain, E. C. (1992). The role of affect and ability in initial exchange quality perceptions. *Group and Organization Management, 17,* 380–397.

Day, D. V., Schleicher, D. J., Unckless, A. L., & Hiller, N. J. (2002). Self-monitoring personality at work: A meta-analytic investigation of construct validity. *Journal of Applied Psychology, 87,* 390–401.

De Cremer, D. (2003). Why inconsistent leadership is regarded as procedurally unfair: The importance of social self-esteem concerns. *European Journal of Social Psychology, 33,* 535–550.

De Cremer, D., & Alberts, H. J. E. M. (2004). When procedural fairness does not influence how positive I feel: The effects of voice and leader selection as a function of belongingness need. *European Journal of Social Psychology, 34,* 333–344.

De Cremer, D., Mayer, D. M., van Dijke, M., Schouten, B. C., & Bardes, M. (2009). When does self-sacrificial leadership motivate prosocial behavior? It depends on followers' prevention focus. *Journal of Applied Psychology, 94,* 887–899.

De Cremer, D., & van Knippenberg, D. (2002). How do leaders promote cooperation? The effects of charisma and procedural fairness. *Journal of Applied Psychology, 87,* 858–866.

De Cremer, D., & van Knippenberg, D. (2004). Leader self-sacrifice and leadership effectiveness: The moderating role of leader self-confidence. *Organizational Behavior and Human Decision Processes, 95,* 140–155.

De Hoogh, A. H. B., & Den Hartog, D. N. (2008). Ethical and despotic leadership, relations with leader's social responsibility, top management team effectiveness and subordinates' optimism: A multi-method study. *Leadership Quarterly, 19,* 297–311.

De Hoogh, A. H. B., & Den Hartog, D. N. (2009). Neuroticism and locus of control as moderators of the relationship of charismatic leadership and autocratic leadership with burnout. *Journal of Applied Psychology, 94,* 1058–1067.

De Hoogh, A. H. B., Den Hartog, D. N., & Koopman, P. L. (2005a). Linking the Big Five factors of personality to charismatic and transactional leadership: Perceived dynamic work environment as a moderator. *Journal of Organizational Behavior, 26,* 839–865.

De Hoogh, A. H. B., Den Hartog, D. N., Koopman, P. L., Thierry, H., Van den Berg, P. T., Van der Weide, J. G., et al. (2005b). Leader motives, charismatic leadership, and subordinates' work attitude in the profit and voluntary sector. *Leadership Quarterly, 16,* 17–38.

Deluga, R. J. (1998a). American presidential proactivity, charismatic leadership, and rated performance. *Leadership Quarterly, 9,* 265–291.

Deluga, R. J. (1998b). Leader-member exchange quality and effectiveness ratings. *Group and Organization Management, 2,* 189–216.

DeRue, D. S., & Wellman, N. (2009). Developing leaders via experience: The role of developmental challenge, learning orientation, and feedback availability. *Journal of Applied Psychology, 94,* 859–875.

Diener, E., Larsen, R. J., & Emmons, R. A. (1984). Person x situation interactions: Choice of situations and congruence response models. *Journal of Personality and Social Psychology, 47,* 580–592.

Digman, J. M. (1990). Personality structure: The emergence of the five-factor model. *Annual Review of Psychology, 41,* 417–440.

Dvir, T., Eden, D., Avolio, B. J., & Shamir, B. (2002). Impact of transformational leadership on follower development and performance: A field experiment. *Academy of Management Journal, 45,* 735–744.

Dweck, C. S. (1986). Motivational processes affecting learning. *American Psychologist, 41,* 1040–1048.

Dweck, C. S., & Legett, E. L. (1988). A social-cognitive approach to motivation and personality. *Psychological Review, 95,* 256–273.

Eagly, A. H., & Karau, S. J. (2002). Role congruity theory of prejudice toward female leaders. *Psychological Review, 109,* 573–598.

Eden, D., & Leviatan, V. (1975). Implicit leadership theory as a determinant of the factor structure underlying supervisory behavior. *Journal of Applied Psychology, 60,* 736–741.

Edwards, J. R. (1994). The study of congruence in organizational behavior research: Critique and a proposed alternative. *Organizational Behavior and Human Decision Processes, 58,* 51–100.

Edwards, J. R., & Lambert, L. S. (2007). Methods for integrating moderation and mediation: A general analytic framework using moderated path analysis. *Psychological Methods, 12,* 1–22.

Elliot, A. J., & Church, M. A. (1997). A hierarchical model of approach and avoidance achievement motivation. *Journal of Personality and Social Psychology, 72,* 218–232.

Eisenbeiss, S. A., van Knippenberg, D., & Boerner, S. (2008). Transformational leadership and team innovation: Integrating transformational leadership and team climate models. *Journal of Applied Psychology, 93,* 1438–1446.

Epitropaki, O., & Martin, R. (2005). The moderating role of individual differences in the relation between transformational/transactional leadership perceptions and organizational identification. *Leadership Quarterly, 16,* 569–589.

Fiedler, F. E. (1964). A contingency model of leadership effectiveness. In L. Berkowitz (Ed.), *Advances in experimental social psychology* (Vol. 1, pp. 149–190) New York: Academic.

Fiedler, F. E. (1967). *A theory of leadership effectiveness.* New York: McGraw-Hill.

Fielding, K. S., & Hogg, M. A. (1997). Social identity, self-categorization, and leadership: A field study of small interactive groups. *Group Dynamics: Theory, Research, and Practice, 1,* 39–51.

Fishbein, M., & Ajzen, I. (1975). *Belief, attitude, intention, and behavior: An introduction to theory and research.* Reading, MA: Addison-Wesley.

Fodor, E. M., & Riordan, J. M. (1995). Leader power motive and group conflict as influences on leader behavior and group member self-affect. *Journal of Research in Personality, 29*, 418–431.

Gangestad, S. W., & Snyder, M. (2000). Self-monitoring: Appraisal and reappraisal. *Psychological Bulletin, 126*, 530–555.

Gardner, W. L., & Avolio, B. J. (1998). The charismatic relationship: A dramaturgical perspective. *Academy of Management Review, 23*, 32–58.

Gerstner, C. R., & Day, D. V. (1997). Meta-analytic review of leader-member exchange theory: Correlates and construct issues. *Journal of Applied Psychology, 82*, 827–844.

Giessner, S. R., & van Knippenberg, D. (2008) "License to fail": Goal definition, leader group prototypicality, and perceptions of leadership effectiveness after leader failure. *Organizational Behavior and Human Decision Processes, 105*, 14–35.

Goldberg, L. R. (1990). An alternative "description of personality": The Big-Five factor structure. *Journal of Personality and Social Psychology, 59*, 1216–1229.

Graen, G. B., & Uhl-Bien, M. (1995). Relationship-based approach to leadership: Development of leader-member exchange (LMX) theory of leadership over 25 years: Applying a multi-level multi-domain approach. *Leadership Quarterly, 6*, 219–247.

Harms, P. D., Roberts, B. W., & Wood, D. (2007). Who shall lead? An integrative personality approach to the study of the antecedents of status in informal social organizations. *Journal of Research in Personality, 41*, 689–699.

Hendricks, J. W., & Payne, S. C. (2007). Beyond the Big Five: Leader goal orientation as a predictor of leadership effectiveness. *Human Performance, 20*, 317–343.

Heslin, P. A., & Latham, G. P. (2004). The effect of upward feedback on managerial behavior. *Applied Psychology: An International Review, 53*, 23–37.

Higgins, E. T. (1987). Self-discrepancy: A theory relating self and affect. *Psychological Review, 94*, 319–340.

Higgins, E. T. (1996). The "self digest": self-knowledge serving self-regulatory functions. *Journal of Personality and Social Psychology, 71*, 1062–1083.

Higgins, E. T. (1997). Beyond pleasure and pain. *American Psychologist, 52*, 1280–1300.

Hirst, G., van Dick, R., & van Knippenberg, D. (2009). A social identity perspective on leadership and employee creativity. *Journal of Organizational Behavior, 30*, 963–982.

Hirst, G., van Knippenberg, D., & Zhou, J. (2009). A multi-level perspective on employee creativity: Goal orientation, team learning behavior, and individual creativity. *Academy of Management Journal, 52*, 280–293.

Hogg, M. A. (2001). A social identity theory of leadership. *Personality and Social Psychology Review, 5*, 184–200.

Hogg, M. A., & van Knippenberg, D. (2003). Social identity and leadership processes in groups. *Advances in Experimental Social Psychology, 35*, 1–52.

Homans, G. C. (1958). Social behavior as exchange. *American Journal of Sociology, 63*, 597–606.

Hough, L. (1992). The "Big Five" personality variables-construct confusion: Description versus prediction. *Human Performance, 5*, 139–155.

House, R. J. (1971). A path-goal theory of leader effectiveness. *Administrative Science Quarterly, 16*, 321–339.

House, R. J. (1977). A 1976 theory of charismatic leadership. In J. G. Hunt & L. L. Larson (Eds.), *Leadership: The cutting edge.* (pp. 189–207). Carbondale: Southern Illinois University Press.

House, R. J., & Aditya, R. N. (1997). The social scientific study of leadership: Quo vadis? *Journal of Management, 23*, 409–473.

House, R. J., & Howell, J. M. (1992). Personality and charismatic leadership. *Leadership Quarterly, 3*, 81–108.

House, R. J., Spangler, W. D., & Woycke, J. (1991). Personality and charisma in the U.S. presidency: A psychological theory of leader effectiveness. *Administrative Science Quarterly, 36*, 364–396.

Howell, J. M., & Avolio, B. J. (1993). Transformational leadership, transactional leadership, locus of control, and support for innovation: key predictors of consolidated-business-unit performance. *Journal of Applied Psychology, 78*, 891-902.

Hoyt, C. L., Murphy, S. E., Halverson, S. K., & Watson, C. B. (2003). Group leadership: Efficacy and effectiveness. *Group Dynamics: Theory, Research, and Practice, 7*, 259–274.

Hui, C., Law, K. S., & Chen, Z. X. (1999). A structural equation model of the effects of negative affectivity, leader-member exchange, and perceived job mobility on in-role and extra-role performance: A Chinese case. *Organizational Behavior and Human Decision Processes, 77*, 3–21.

Hurtz, G. M., & Donovan, J. J. (2000). Personality and job performance: The Big Five revisited. *Journal of Applied Psychology, 85*, 869–879.

Ilies, R., Nahrgang, J. D., & Morgeson, F. P. (2007). Leader-member exchange and citizenship behavior: A meta-analysis. *Journal of Applied Psychology, 92*, 269–277.

Judge, T. A., & Bono, J. E. (2000). Five-factor model of personality and transformational leadership. *Journal of Applied Psychology, 85*, 751–765.

Judge, T. A., Bono, J. E., Ilies, R., & Gerhardt, M. (2002). Personality and leadership: A qualitative and quantitative review. *Journal of Applied Psychology, 87*, 765–780.

Judge, T. A., Colbert, A. E., & Ilies, R. (2004). Intelligence and leadership: A quantitative review and test of theoretical propositions. *Journal of Applied Psychology, 89*, 542–552.

Judge, T. A., Heller, D., & Mount, M. K. (2002). Five-factor model of personality and job satisfaction: A Meta-analysis. *Journal of Applied Psychology, 87*, 530–541.

Judge, T. A., Locke, E. A., & Durham, C. C. (1997). The dispositional causes of job satisfaction: A core self-evaluations approach. *Research in Organizational Behavior, 19*, 151–188.

Judge, T. A., & Piccolo, R. (2004). Transformational and transactional leadership: A meta-analytic test of their relative validity. *Journal of Applied Psychology, 89*, 755–768.

Judge, T. A., Piccolo, R. F., & Ilies, R. (2004). The forgotten ones? A re-examination of consideration, initiating structure, and leadership effectiveness. *Journal of Applied Psychology, 89*, 36–51.

Judge, T. A., Piccolo, R. F., & Kosalka, T. (2009). *The bright side and dark side of leader traits: A review and theoretical extension of the leader trait paradigm.* Working paper, University of Florida.

Judge, T. A., Scott, B. A., & Ilies, R. (2006). Hostility, job attitudes, and workplace deviance: Test of a multilevel model. *Journal of Applied Psychology, 91*, 126–138.

Jung, D. I., & Avolio, B. (1999). Effects of leadership style and followers' cultural values on performance under different task structure conditions. *Academy of Management Journal, 42,* 208–218.

Kaiser, R. B., Hogan, R., & Craig, S. B. (2008). Leadership and the fate of organizations. *American Psychologist, 63,* 96–110.

Kane, T. D., Zaccaro, S. J., Tremble, T. R., Jr., & Masuda, A. D. (2002). An examination of the leader's regulation of groups. *Small Group Research, 33,* 65–120.

Kark, R., & Van Dijk, D. (2007). Motivation to lead, motivation to follow: The role of the self-regulatory focus in leadership processes. *Academy of Management Review, 32,* 500–528.

Kerr, S., & Jermier, J. M. (1978). Substitutes for leadership: Their meaning and measurement. *Organizational Behavior and Human Performance, 22,* 375–403.

Kirkpatrick, S. A., & Locke, E. A. (1996). Direct and indirect effects of three core charismatic leadership components on performance and attitudes. *Journal of Applied Psychology, 81,* 36–51.

Koper, G., van Knippenberg, D., Bouhuijs, F., Vermunt, R., & Wilke, H. (1993). Procedural fairness and self-esteem. *European Journal of Social Psychology, 23,* 313–325.

Kruglanski, A. W., & Webster, D. M. (1996). Motivated closing of the mind: "Seizing" and "freezing." *Psychological Review, 103,* 263–283.

Leary, M. R., Robertson, R. B., Barnes, B. D., & Miller, R. S. (1986). Self-presentations of small group leaders: Effects of role requirements and leadership orientation. *Journal of Personality and Social Psychology, 51,* 742–748.

Lim, B.-C., & Ployhart, R. E. (2004). Transformational leadership: Relations to the five-factor model and team performance in typical and maximum contexts. *Journal of Applied Psychology, 89,* 610–621.

Lind, E. A., Kray, L., & Thompson, L. (2001). Primacy effects in justice judgments: Testing predictions from fairness heuristic theory. *Organizational Behavior and Human Decision Processes, 85,* 189–210.

Lord, R. G. (1977). Functional leadership behavior: Measurement and relation to social power and leadership perceptions. *Administrative Science Quarterly, 22,* 114–133.

Lord, R. G., Brown, D. J., & Freiberg, S. J. (1999). Understanding the dynamics of leadership: The role of follower self-concepts in the leader/follower relationship. *Organizational Behavior and Human Decision Processes, 78,* 1–37.

Lord, R. G., De Vader, C. L., & Alliger, G. M. (1986). A meta-analysis of the relation between personality traits and leadership perceptions: An application of validity generalization procedures. *Journal of Applied Psychology, 71,* 402–410.

Lord, R. G., & Hall, R. J. (1992). Contemporary views of leadership and individual differences. *Leadership Quarterly, 3,* 137–157.

Lord, R. G., & Maher, K. J. (1991). *Leadership and information processing: Linking perceptions and performance.* Boston, MA: Unwin Hyman.

Lowe, K. B., Kroeck, K. G., & Sivasubramaniam, N. (1996). Effectiveness correlates of transformational and transactional leadership: A meta-analytic review of the MLQ literature. *Leadership Quarterly, 7,* 385–425.

Mann, R. D. (1959). A review of the relationships between personality and performance in small groups. *Psychological Bulletin, 56,* 241–270.

McCrea, R. R., & Costa, P. T., Jr. (1997). Personality trait structure as a human universal. *American Psychologist, 52,* 509–516.

McClelland, D. C. (1975). *Power: The inner experience.* New York: Irvington.

McClelland, D. C. (1985). *Human motivation.* Glenview, IL: Scott, Foresman.

McClelland, D. C., & Atkinson, J. W. (1976). *The achievement motive.* New York: Irvington.

McClelland, D. C., & Boyatsis, R. E. (1982). Leadership motive pattern and long-term success in management. *Journal of Applied Psychology, 67,* 737–743.

Meindl, J. R. (1995). The romance of leadership as a follower-centric theory: A social constructionist approach. *Leadership Quarterly, 6,* 329–341.

Meindl, J. R., Ehrlich, S. B., & Dukerich, J. M. (1985). The romance of leadership. *Administrative Science Quarterly, 30,* 78–102.

Messick, D. M., & McClintock, C. G. (1968). Motivational basis of choice in experimental games. *Journal of Experimental Social Psychology, 4,* 1–25.

Mischel, W. (1973). Toward a cognitive social learning reconceptualization of personality. *Psychological Review, 80,* 252–283.

Mischel, W. (1977). The interaction of person and situation. In D. Magnusson & N. S. Endler (Eds.), *Personality at the crossroads: Current issues in interactional psychology,* (pp. 333–352). Hillsdale, NJ: Erlbaum.

Nahrgang, J. D., Morgeson, F. P., & Ilies, R. (2009). The development of leader-member exchanges: Exploring how personality and performance influence leader and member relationships over time. *Organizational Behavior and Human Decision Processes, 108,* 256–266.

Ng, K.-Y., Ang, S., & Chan, K.-Y. (2008). Personality and leader effectiveness: A moderated mediation model of leadership self-efficacy, job demands, and job autonomy. *Journal of Applied Psychology, 93,* 733–743.

Paglis, L. L., & Green, S. G. (2002). Leadership self-efficacy and managers' motivation for leading change. *Journal of Organizational Behavior, 23,* 215–235.

Phillips, A. S., & Bedeian, A. G. (1994). Leader-follower exchange quality: The role of personal and interpersonal attributes. *Academy of Management Journal, 37,* 990–1001.

Pierro, A., Cicero, L., Bonaiuto, M., van Knippenberg, D., & Kruglanski, A. W. (2005). Leader group prototypicality and leadership effectiveness: The moderating role of need for cognitive closure. *Leadership Quarterly, 16,* 503–516.

Pierro, A., Cicero, L., Bonaiuto, M., van Knippenberg, D., & Kruglanski, A. W. (2007). Leader group prototypicality and resistance to organizational change: The moderating role of need for closure and team identification. *Testing, Psychometrics, Methodology in Applied Psychology, 14,* 27–40.

Ployhart, R. E., Lim, B.-C., & Chan, K.-Y. (2001). Exploring relations between typical and maximum performance ratings and the five factor model of personality. *Personnel Psychology, 54,* 809–843.

Reicher, S., & Hopkins, N. (2003). On the science and art of leadership. In D. van Knippenberg & M. A. Hogg (Eds.), *Leadership and power: Identity processes in groups and organizations* (pp. 197–209). London: Sage.

Rice, R. W. (1978). Construct validity of the least preferred co-worker score. *Psychological Bulletin, 85,* 1199–1237.

Rotter, J. B. (1966). Generalized expectancies for internal versus external locus of control of reinforcement. *Psychological Monographs: General and Applied, 80.*

Rubin, R. S., Munz, D. C., & Bommer, W. H. (2005). Leading from within: The effects of emotion recognition and personality on transformational leadership behavior. *Academy of Management Journal, 48,* 845–858.

Rus, D., van Knippenberg, D., & Wisse, B. (2010). Leader self-definition and leader self-serving behavior. *Leadership Quarterly, 21,* 509–529.

Schriesheim, C. A., Castro, S. L., & Cogliser, C. C. (1999). Leader-member exchange (LMX) research: A comprehensive review of theory, measurement, and data-analytic practices. *Leadership Quarterly, 10,* 63–113.

Shamir, B., House, R., & Arthur, M. B. (1993). The motivational effects of charismatic leadership: A self-concept based theory. *Organization Science, 4,* 577–594.

Singer, M. (1991). The relationship between employee sex, length of service and leadership aspirations: A study from valence, self-efficacy, and attribution perspectives. *Applied Psychology: An International Review, 40,* 417–436.

Skarlicki, D. P., Folger, R., & Tesluk, P. (1999). Personality as a moderator in the relationship between fairness and retaliation. *Academy of Management Journal, 42,* 100–108.

Skarlicki, D. P., & Latham, G. P. (1996). Increasing citizenship behavior within a labor union: A test of organizational justice theory. *Journal of Applied Psychology, 81,* 161–169.

Snyder, M. (1974). The self-monitoring of expressive behavior. *Journal of Personality and Social Psychology, 30,* 526–537.

Snyder, M. (1987). *Public appearances/private realities: The psychology of self-monitoring.* New York: Freeman.

Snyder, M., & Ickes, W. (1985). Personality and social behavior. In G. Lindzey & E. Aronson (Eds.), *The handbook of social psychology* (Vol. 2, pp. 883–974). New York: Random House.

Sosik, J. J., Avolio, B. J., & Jung, D. I. (2002). Beneath the mask: Examining the relationship of self-presentation attributes and impression management to charismatic leadership. *Leadership Quarterly, 13,* 217–242.

Sosik, J. J., & Dwarokivsky, A. C. (1998). Self-concept based aspects of charismatic leadership: More than meets the eye. *Leadership Quarterly, 9,* 503–526.

Spangler, W. D., & House, R. J. (1991). Presidential effectiveness and the leadership motive profile. *Journal of Personality and Social Psychology, 60,* 439–455.

Stam, D., van Knippenberg, D., & Wisse, B. (2010a). The role of regulatory fit in visionary leadership. *Journal of Organizational Behavior, 31,* 499–518.

Stam, D., van Knippenberg, D., & Wisse, B. (2010b). Focusing on followers: The role of regulatory focus and possible selves in visionary leadership. *Leadership Quarterly, 21,* 457–468.

Stogdill, R. M. (1948). Personal factors associated with leadership: A survey of the literature. *Journal of Psychology, 25,* 35–71.

Stogdill, R. M., & Coons, A. E. (1957). *Leader behavior: Its description and measurement.* Columbus, OH: Bureau of Business Research.

Sutton, R. I., & Staw, B. M. (1995). What theory is not. *Administrative Science Quarterly, 40,* 371–384.

Tajfel, H., & Turner, J. C. (1986). The social identity theory of intergroup behavior. In S. Worchel & W. Austin (Eds.), *Psychology of intergroup relations* (pp. 7–24). Chicago: Nelson-Hall.

Turner, J. C., Hogg, M. A., Oakes, P. J., Reicher, S. D., & Wetherell, M. S. (1987). *Rediscovering the social group: A self-categorization theory.* Oxford, UK: Blackwell.

Tepper, B. J., Duffy, M. K., Henle, C. A., & Lambert, L. S. (2006). Procedural injustice, victim precipitation, and abusive supervision. *Personnel Psychology, 59,* 101–123.

Tett, R. P., & Burnett, D. D. (2003). A personality trait-based interactionist model of job performance. *Journal of Applied Psychology, 88,* 500–517.

Tett, R. J., & Guterman, H. A. (2000). Situation trait relevance, trait expression, and cross-situational consistency: Testing a principle of trait activation. *Journal of Research in Personality, 34,* 397–423.

Triandis, H. C. (1995). *Individualism and collectivism.* Boulder, CO: Westview.

Triandis, H. C., Leung, K., Villareal, M., & Clack, F. (1985). Allocentric vs. idiocentric tendencies: Convergent and discriminant validation. *Journal of Research in Personality, 19,* 395–415.

Tyler, T. R. (1999). Why people cooperate with organizations: An identity-based perspective. *Research in Organizational Behavior, 21,* 201–246.

Ullrich, J., Christ, O., & van Dick, R. (2009). Substitutes for procedural fairness: Prototypical leaders are endorsed whether they are fair or not. *Journal of Applied Psychology, 94,* 235–244.

VandeWalle, D. (1997). Development and validation of a work domain goal orientation instrument. *Educational and Psychological Measurement, 8,* 995–1015.

Van-Dijk, D., & Kluger, A. N. (2004). Feedback sign effect on motivation: Is it moderated by regulatory focus? *Applied Psychology: An International Review, 53,* 113–135.

van Gils, S., van Quaquebeke, N., & van Knippenberg, D. (2010). The X-factor: On the relevance of implicit leadership and followership theories for leader-member exchange (LMX) agreement. *European Journal of Work and Organizational Psychology, 19,* 333–363.

Van Kleef, G. A., Homan, A. C., Beersma, B., van Knippenberg, D., van Knippenberg, B., & Damen, F. (2009). Searing sentiment or cold calculation? The effects of leader emotional displays on team performance depend on follower epistemic motivation. *Academy of Management Journal, 52,* 562–580.

van Knippenberg, B., & van Knippenberg, D. (2005). Leader self-sacrifice and leadership effectiveness: The moderating role of leader prototypicality. *Journal of Applied Psychology, 90,* 25–37.

van Knippenberg, D., De Cremer, D., & van Knippenberg, B. (2007). Leadership and fairness: The state of the art. *European Journal of Work and Organizational Psychology, 16,* 113–140.

van Knippenberg, D., & Hogg, M. A. (2003). A social identity model of leadership effectiveness in organizations. *Research in Organizational Behavior, 25,* 243–295.

van Knippenberg, D., van Knippenberg, B., De Cremer, D., & Hogg, M. A. (2004). Leadership, self, and identity: A review and research agenda. *Leadership Quarterly, 15,* 825–856.

van Knippenberg, D., van Knippenberg, B., van Kleef, G. A., & Damen, F. (2008). Leadership, affect, and emotions. In N. Ashkanasy & C. Cooper (Eds.), *Research companion to emotions in organizations* (pp. 465–475). Cheltenham, UK: Elgar.

Vermunt, R., van Knippenberg, D., van Knippenberg, B., & Blaauw, E. (2001). Self-esteem and outcome fairness: Differential importance of procedural and outcome considerations. *Journal of Applied Psychology, 86,* 621–628.

Vroom, V. H., & Yetton, P. W. (1973). *Leadership and decision making.* Pittsburgh, PA: University of Pittsburgh Press.

Walumbwa, F. O., & Lawler, J. J. (2003). Building effective organizations: Transformational leadership, collectivist orientation, work-related attitudes, and withdrawal behaviors in three emerging economies. *International Journal of Human Resource Management, 14,* 1083–1101.

Walumbwa, F. O., Lawler, J. J., & Avolio, B. J. (2007). Leadership, individual differences, and work-related attitudes: A cross-cultural investigation. *Applied Psychology: An International Review, 56,* 212–230.

Warech, M. A., Smither, J. W., Reilly, R. R., Millsap, R. E., & Reilly, S. P. (1998). Self-monitoring and 360-degree ratings. *Leadership Quarterly, 9,* 449–473.

Weiss, H. M., & Adler, S. (1984). Personality and organizational behavior. *Research in Organizational Behavior, 6,* 1–50.

Winter, D. G. (1973). *The power motive.* New York: Free Press.

Winter, D. G. (1987). Leader appeal, leader performance, and the motive profiles of leaders and followers: A study of American presidents and elections. *Journal of Personality and Social Psychology, 52,* 196–202.

Winter, D. G. (1991). A motivational model of leadership: Predicting long-term management success from TAT measures of power motivation and responsibility. *Leadership Quarterly, 2,* 67–80.

Yukl, G. (2002). *Leadership in organizations* (5th ed.). New York: Prentice Hall.

Yukl, G., & Van Fleet, D. D. (1994). Theory and research on leadership in organizations. In H. C. Triandis, M. P. Dunnette, & L. M. Hough (Eds.), *Handbook of industrial and organizational psychology,* (2nd ed., Vol. 4, pp. 769–827). Palo Alto, CA: Consulting Psychologists Press.

Zaccaro, S. J., Foti, R. J., & Kenny, D. A. (1991). Self-monitoring and trait-based variance in leadership: An investigation of leader flexibility across multiple group situations. *Journal of Applied Psychology, 76,* 308–315.

Work and Organizations
Contextualizing Personality and Social Psychology

David V. Day *and* Deidra J. Schleicher

Abstract

This chapter addresses the relevance of personality and social psychology to the central life domain of work and organizations. We begin with a general discussion of how the field of organizational psychology is distinct from, yet has been informed by, theory and research in personality and social psychology, distinguishing between horizontal and vertical theory borrowing in this regard. We then summarize research on four key organizational topics that have particularly strong theoretical and empirical records for integrating across personality and social psychology: person-environment fit, job attitudes, leadership, and teams. Within each of these organizational research areas we discuss examples of horizontal and vertical theory borrowing as well as new theoretical frameworks with the potential to contribute to the fields of personality and social psychology.

Keywords: Work and organizations, organizational psychology, organizational behavior, theory borrowing, personality, person-environment fit, leadership, teams, job attitudes, multilevel theory

Introduction

Work occupies a central role in the lives of many people—whether we like it or not! For those sufficiently skilled or otherwise fortunate to be employed in these challenging times, the overall amount of time spent in work-related activities can comprise as much as a quarter of our adult lives and perhaps even half of our waking lives. Much of this time spent working is "at work." That is, work occurs in organizational contexts while we are engaged in activities with bosses, colleagues, and coworkers. For this reason, work and organizations can be considered a key life domain in which personality and social psychology are important and interrelated considerations.

There are additional concerns that make the context of work a compelling one to examine with regard to personality and social psychology. In most organizations there are issues of status and hierarchy—and power—to deal with. And as noted, most work contexts are interpersonal in nature. It is also

the case that people can strongly identify with their job and organization, and also draw great personal and professional meaning from their work. Thus, not only do people spend a good part of their lives at work and in organizational settings, but it is also an important domain in terms of their respective identities and overall well-being. Work and work-related concerns matter in organizational psychology in ways that influence theory and research in the field (Johns, 2006).

For all of these reasons, we will examine the context of work and organizations in ways that illuminate how perspectives in personality and social psychology are linked (or should be) in this important life domain. We will also examine how certain topics within the broad field of organizational psychology have been informed by theory and research in personality and social psychology. We begin with a brief overview of the interrelated fields of work psychology, industrial and organizational psychology, and organizational behavior. We then discuss a so-called balance-of-trade deficit between the respective fields of organizational and personality and social psychology. This will be followed by a review of four core areas in work and organizations that have been informed and strengthened by theory and research in personality and social psychology, concluding with recommendations on how this noted trade deficit might be better balanced in the future.

Organizational Psychology Defined

A core discipline in the broader field of work and organizations is *organizational psychology* (traditionally labeled industrial-organizational psychology; see www.siop.org; Kozlowski, in press). Organizational psychology is based on a scientist-practitioner model in which basic principles of psychology are studied and applied in work-related contexts, with the overarching goal to enhance human well-being and performance in such contexts. In this chapter, we will use the term *organizational psychology* more broadly to reflect the discipline and literature base concerned with applying psychological principles to work and organizations. This includes work done in the similar disciplines of *work psychology* (the term that is more widely used in Europe; www.eawop.org); *occupational psychology* (used mainly in Britain); and *organizational behavior*, which is one division (www.obweb.org) of a much larger academic-oriented Academy of Management.

Researchers have identified four persistent historical themes in the development of organizational psychology in the United States (Zickar & Gibby, 2007): (1) emphasis on productivity, (2) emphasis on quantification, (3) focus on selection and differential psychology, and (4) interplay between science and practice. Many of these themes also apply to organizational psychology outside of the United States, although it has been observed that the boundaries of organizational (or occupational) psychology in Britain generally "have been wider and more permeable" than in North America, especially in terms of influences from psychoanalytic and ergonomic perspectives (Warr, 2007, p. 103). Perhaps the biggest difference according to Warr (2007) is the long-standing interest in the welfare of working people in European-based work psychology, especially with regard to mental health issues. In Britain, many of the early influential contributors to occupational psychology had medical backgrounds, which was not the case in the United States. The lack of a mental health focus in the United States may also be due in part to less permeable boundaries between organizational and clinical psychology (e.g., stringent membership and licensing requirements across various divisions of the American Psychological Association).

Within and across these various themes, as well as looking at the general discipline more globally, the field of organizational psychology is quite diverse in terms of topics of theory and research. These include both so-called micro topics that pertain mainly to personnel psychology and human resource management (e.g., measurement and testing, selection, training, performance appraisal) and more macro topics (e.g., motivation, leadership, attitudes, group behavior, team effectiveness), although this is somewhat of an arbitrary distinction. The foundation of organizational psychology is grounded firmly in individual differences, but one of the major developments occurring over the previous decade is an increased interest in groups, teams, and other larger collectives of individuals. As we review later in the chapter, this trend has shaped the theory-building and research efforts of those studying topics related to work and organizations.

There are some important implications of organizational psychology that distinguish it from the fields of personality and social psychology. Because of the scientist-practitioner orientation, there is a pervasive concern not only with obtaining statistical significance in research but also in demonstrating practical significance. This manifests itself in heightened concerns with regard to the effect sizes associated with research results in organizational psychology (Dunnette, 1990) and also with a clear articulation of the practical implications of noted findings. Another way of stating this is that applied researchers are keen to demonstrate the "so what?" aspect of their work. This goes to the core of the field's collective identity as being devoted to issues relevant to applied psychology. Considered as either a special life domain or a contextualized lens by which to view theory and research, the field tends to maintain a greater concern for potential application than the more basic issues addressed in social and personality psychology.

One purpose of this brief overview is to introduce different facets of the diverse field of organizational psychology and to illustrate that it has its own identity, purpose and goals, literature, and even tools and methods; that is, it is more than merely applied social psychology. To fully make that claim in a convincing manner it needs to have its own theories; but does it? There was a time not so long ago when it was commonly said that what is published in the *Journal of Personality and Social Psychology* will show up in the *Journal of Applied Psychology* five years later applied to organizational phenomena. Although we will elaborate on why this state of affairs is changing, a pertinent question remains unanswered: Why are there many examples of personality and social psychological theories subsequently applied to organizational issues but a relative shortage of examples of theories developed in organizational psychology that are used in personality and social psychology? What is the reason for the noted trade deficit when it comes to theory in these respective fields? Is it simply because of the general tendency for knowledge to flow from basic to applied scientific audiences? Overall, how might there be greater theoretical reciprocation between organizational and personality and social psychology?

Organizational Psychology and the Practice of Theory Borrowing

Although it is not admitted explicitly—at least not usually—there is ongoing tension between researchers in the respective fields of organizational and personality and social psychology. The source of this tension stems from perceptions of the scientific orientation of researchers and the source of theory in the respective fields. In particular, there is the belief or perception that those in social psychology are theory originators whereas researchers in organizational psychology are mainly "applicationists" (in the pejorative sense). In short, there are the real scientists who develop theory and test basic hypotheses generated from personality and social psychology theory and the other folks who use this theory to explain phenomena in work and organizations. Again, this is often an implicit tension but it goes directly to values-based beliefs as to the relative merits of basic versus applied sciences. Instead of arguing the relative merits of each perspective, we will elaborate on the potential underlying reasons for the friction. But most assuredly it is not because those in the organizational psychology domain are less ambitious or insightful than our social psychology colleagues—at least that is not how those of us in the organizational psychology part of the equation see it!

Whetten and colleagues have recently elaborated on the practice of "theory borrowing" in the organizational sciences (Whetten, Felin, & King, 2009). The practice is prevalent, and the observation is not a new one. In discussing the influence of social psychology approximately 20 years ago, it was noted that there was a so-called trade deficit between organizational psychology and more basic fields such as

personality and social psychology, and in particular, social cognition (Ilgen & Klein, 1989). Nonetheless, there are valid reasons for this practice of theory borrowing, including that (1) organizational phenomena are best considered through a multidisciplinary lens; (2) there is an applied focus to the work and organizations discipline, and (3) it ultimately enhances the quality of theory-based scholarship because "systematically applying a theory in different settings improves the theory's explanatory power by delineating its boundaries, or scope conditions" (Whetten et al., 2009, p. 539).

What is a new observation is the distinction Whetten et al. (2009) drew between horizontal and vertical theory borrowing. Horizontal borrowing involves applying a theory at the same level of analysis but in a new (e.g., organizational) context. One example of this practice is the use of equity theory principles (Adams, 1965) to demonstrate the relevance and potential importance of organizational justice (Greenberg, 1987), especially with regard to how employees perceive workplace practices in terms of fairness (Folger & Greenberg, 1985). Vertical borrowing on the other hand involves applying concepts formulated at one level of analysis to a different level, typically from an individual level to that of a group or organization. An example of this type of borrowing is the application of identity and self-concepts to forge an understanding of organizational identity (albeit mainly as a metaphor). It is possible to borrow theory at both the horizontal and vertical levels simultaneously, as theory linking social identity with individual and group motivation has proposed (Ellemers, de Gilder, & Haslam, 2004). As a result, in some cases it is a fuzzy distinction in terms of whether it is either horizontal or vertical theory borrowing. In the case of social identity theory it could be an example of horizontal borrowing at the individual level but vertical borrowing at the group or organizational level.

Although the preceding may help justify or at least rationalize the practice of theory borrowing, it does not say much about the nature of the theory-based trade imbalance between the respective fields of organizational and social psychology. This is where we see things changing as those in organizational psychology elaborate and build multilevel and cross-level theories of individuals and broader contexts such as groups and organizations. This is a notable advance because individuals are inherently nested within workgroups and broader organizations. Until relatively recently, there has been a dearth of multilevel theory and suitable analytical tools to handle issues of data nonindependence that arise from these nesting issues. There have been significant contributions made in organizational psychology that have the potential to enhance greater theory borrowing from researchers in personality and social psychology.

Attention to levels-of-analysis issues in organizational research began to form in the mid-1980s (Rousseau, 1985), developing in sophistication through the 1990s (Chan, 1998; House, Rousseau, & Thomas-Hunt, 1995; Klein, Dansereau, & Hall, 1994; Morgeson & Hofmann, 1999), and reaching a critical mass with the publication of a highly influential book on multilevel theory, research, and methods (Klein & Kozlowski, 2000). Developments continue to be made on relevant conceptual frameworks and statistical approaches (e.g., Bliese & Hanges, 2004; Chen, Bliese, & Mathieu, 2005). Although the respective content, comprehensiveness, and sophistication of these contributions are varied, they have broadened our appreciation for the importance of understanding (1) the meaning of constructs at various levels of aggregation, (2) the types of empirical evidence needed for each construct type, and (3) the appropriate methods for testing multilevel and cross-level effects.

In the following sections we review several key research areas in work and organizations. The organizational psychology literature is too large to review comprehensively here, so we instead present four key domains that illustrate examples of horizontal and vertical theory borrowing as well as new theoretical frameworks with the potential to contribute to the fields of personality and social psychology. In this regard, we have focused on four topics that have particularly strong theoretical and empirical records for integrating across personality and social psychology: person-environment fit, job attitudes, leadership, and teams.

Review of Select Areas in Organizational Psychology

Person-Environment Fit

We begin our review of specific work and organizations research domains with the topic of person-environment fit. Because the construct of fit involves the interaction between the person and aspects of the environment, it is the work and organizations domain in which integrated personality and social psychology approaches should most naturally be present. Also, fit can be considered an umbrella area for several more specific research domains within work and organizations, including employee attraction/recruitment and

selection, the prediction of job performance (particularly by personality), work attitudes, socialization, and employee retention. In fact, the concept of person-environment fit has been described as "so pervasive as to be one of if not the dominant conceptual forces in the field" (Schneider, 2001, p. 142).

Often referred to generally as person-environment fit (or simply *fit*), the construct as used in organizational psychology refers to congruence between the person (i.e., employee) and aspects of the environment (i.e., the vocation or occupation, organization, group or team, job, or supervisor; Kristof, 1996; Kristof-Brown, Zimmerman, & Johnson, 2005). The key focus is on whether aspects of the person "fit in" with those of the occupation, organization, work group, supervisor, or the demands of the job. A fundamental property of person-environment fit theory is that the person and the environment are conceptualized on commensurate dimensions (Edwards, Caplan, & Harrison, 1998). These dimensions might include skills, needs, preferences, values, personality traits, goals, or attitudes (Kristof-Brown et al., 2005). When the dimensions of fit are conceptualized exclusively as demographic variables, the research focus has been termed "relational demography" in the organizational literature (e.g., Tsui & O'Reilly, 1989), such as Heilman's influential work on gender in organizations (e.g., Heilman & Parks-Stamm, 2007; Heilman & Okimoto, 2007; Lyness & Heilman, 2006). Nonetheless, fit typically concerns deeper-level characteristics (e.g., values, personality) rather than more surface-level demographic variables. Research has demonstrated that although demographic variables initially influence behavior in organizations in significant ways, over time it is the deeper-level characteristics that prove most important in determining individual and organizational outcomes (Harrison, Price, & Bell, 1998). Nonetheless, this distinction can become murky when demographic characteristics such as gender or ethnicity correlate with personal values and values-based behavior such as with transformational leadership (Eagly, Johannesen-Schmidt, & van Engen, 2003).

According to the attraction-selection-attrition model (Schneider, 1987; Schneider, Goldstein, & Smith, 1995), employees often show congruence between their personality or values and those of the organization, because these personal characteristics would in part determine who applies to the organization (attraction), who is selected into the organization (selection), and who remains with versus leaves the organization (attrition). Thus, in many cases, individuals share the characteristics and values of the organization to which they belong (Kristof, 1996; Trevino, 1986). Nonetheless, there is also variability across employees with regard to the congruence between employee and organizational characteristics, and this has given rise to a large research area on the topic of fit. The theoretical assumption is that individuals will be most successful and happy in organizations that share their characteristics and values (Chatman, 1989); in other words, individual differences in fit should determine the important outcomes of job performance, satisfaction, and employee retention. The empirical literature has largely supported these assumptions. For example, a recent meta-analysis (Kristof-Brown et al., 2005) based on 172 studies and 836 effect sizes demonstrated significant links between several types of fit (person-organization, person-group, person-job, and person-supervisor) and both pre-entry (applicant attraction, intent to hire, job acceptance, job offer) and post-entry (attitudes, performance, strain, tenure, withdrawal behaviors) criteria. Some of the strongest meta-analytic effects were found for person-job fit ($r = -.46$ with intent to quit and .67 with intent to hire), person-organization fit ($r = -.35$ with intent to quit and .65 with organizational satisfaction), person-group fit ($r = -.22$ with intent to quit and .42 with coworker satisfaction), and person-supervisor fit ($r = -.12$ with perception of politics and .46 with supervisor satisfaction).

Given the theoretical and practical importance of fit, substantial research has been directed toward understanding the essential elements of the fit equation. It should be noted that some of this research that we review predates the introduction of the fit term to the literature. Indeed, various forms of person-environment interaction have been prevalent in the field for almost 100 years (see Ekehammer, 1974; Lewin, 1935; Parsons, 1909; Pervin, 1968). Whether or not it was specifically labeled as fit, such research has been undertaken in an effort to identify the important elements of the person (as they fit with the demands of the job and other aspects of the organizational context) that impact outcomes of importance to organizations.

The proliferation of concepts, measures, and analytic approaches has made fit a somewhat elusive construct (Judge & Ferris, 1992; Kristof-Brown et al., 2005). Two conceptual debates within the person-environment fit literature that are particularly germane to our review concern (1) what the most relevant dimensions of fit are, and (2) whether fit should be conceptualized as complementary or supplementary (Muchinsky & Monahan, 1987). With regard to fit dimensions, the fit construct has been assessed using numerous dimension types including skills, preferences, values, and personality traits. The two most common of these have been values and personality, spawning debates about the relative merits of these dimensions. For example, Chatman (1991) argued for values as the most important basis for person-organization fit, because values are enduring characteristics of both individuals and organizations. On the other hand, Ryan and Kristof-Brown (2003) have argued that personality traits are more stable, proximal to behavior, and visible in others' behavior than are values, and thus personality traits should be fundamental dimensions of fit. For this reason, as well as the general goals of this chapter, we focus our review primarily on the personality aspects of fit. But as an interesting aside, we note that in recent years social dominance theorists (see e.g., Sidanius & Pratto, 2001) have extended these fit dimensions to sociopolitical attitudes, arguing that a similar person-organization fit exists for people's anti-egalitarianism beliefs and their organizational environments. A growing body of research supports this claim, showing that hierarchy-enhancing organizations (e.g., police forces) tend to be populated by those with anti-egalitarian beliefs whereas hierarchy-attenuating organizations (e.g., civil liberties organizations) tend to be populated by those with more egalitarian beliefs (see Haley & Sidanius, 2005). This is a relevant example of researchers in social psychology broadening and building on a mainstream theory in organizational psychology.

Another debate in the organizational literature is whether fit is best conceptualized as complementary or supplementary (Muchinsky & Monahan, 1987). The supplementary conceptualization of fit addresses the extent to which the individual and the environment are *similar* and therefore rooted in theories of interpersonal attraction (Byrne, 1971) as well as the attraction-selection-attrition model (Schneider, 1987; Schneider, Goldstein, & Smith, 1995). The complementary approach to fit assesses the extent to which individual characteristics *fill a gap* in the current environment or the other way around (i.e., the extent to which the environment fulfills an individual need). Whereas the complementary notion of fit has dominated the person-job fit literature (Edwards, 1991), the supplementary fit concept has been more prevalent in the person-organization fit literature (Chatman, 1989; 1991).

In the remainder of our section on fit, we focus mainly on personality-related issues in the person-environment equation. Because there has been substantially more personality research on complementary forms of fit, especially the critical topic of person-job fit, this will be the first stream of research reviewed below (*personality as predictor*). The second stream of research (*personality as motivation*) moves beyond personality traits as merely descriptive and predictive devices to work that views them as theoretical constructs that are imbued with motivational force. Both the first and second research streams tend to adopt complementary views of fit with regard to personality in the context of work and organizations. Whereas the first stream of research views personality from the perspective of how it can fill a gap or a need in the job, the second stream broadens to include a consideration of how the job (and other aspects of the environment) can fill a need within the individual. In the third section (*trait activation theory*), we examine an important theory in the organizational psychology literature that takes a more comprehensive approach to both the person and situation sides of the fit equation; one firmly grounded in the personality and social psychology literatures. Much of the work reviewed in these three sections represents examples of horizontal theory borrowing (Whetten et al., 2009) from personality and social psychology. We will conclude this section by examining one example of vertical theory borrowing regarding the concept of *collective personality*.

PERSONALITY AS PREDICTOR

Personality structure, processes, and individual differences are major areas of theoretical and research interest in psychology (see Fleeson, chapter 3, this volume). Thus, it is somewhat surprising that personality had fallen out of favor among organizational psychologists in the second half of the 20th century, only to see a remarkable resurgence beginning around 1990. An area of particular interest is identifying stable personality predictors of job performance. This would fall under the "demands-abilities" type of person-job fit (Edwards, 1991), wherein a match is sought between demands of the job and characteristics of the person who would fill the job. This is an important issue because of the field's overarching interest in predicting and improving performance in work-related contexts; however, it is also somewhat misleading because identifying stable dispositional predictors of job performance does little to improve individual performance,

although it is helpful in employee selection. Being able to predict with any degree of certainty those person(s) who will be more likely to perform more effectively in a given job is a topic that has been at the core of organizational psychology since its origins (Katzell & Austin, 1992), but one that can be considered more of practical than theoretical importance (Taylor & Russell, 1939).

The interest in personality as a predictor of job performance almost completely disappeared following what was seen as a highly critical review of the use of personality measures for employment decisions (Guion & Gottier, 1965). Although it was later revealed that the critical comments of Guion and Gottier had been taken out of context and widely misinterpreted in an overly pessimistic manner (Day & Silverman, 1989), it was not until the introduction and acceptance of the *five-factor model of personality* (Digman, 1990; Goldberg, 1990; McCrae & Costa, 2003) that the field changed in a dramatic way in its view of the merits of personality for employee selection.

In the same year (1991) and in the same journal (*Personnel Psychology*), two separate meta-analytic reviews were published on the relationship between personality and job performance, both using the five-factor model as an integrative personality framework (Barrick & Mount, 1991; Tett, Jackson, & Rothstein, 1991). The respective reviews reported evidence of systematic relationships between various personality factors and measures of job performance. But what is "befuddling" (Goldberg, 1993, p. 31) is that whereas Barrick and Mount reported a corrected correlation of .23 for conscientiousness and .06 for agreeableness, Tett et al. reported a corrected correlation of .18 for conscientiousness and 0.33 for agreeableness. If there is any systematic relation in these results linking personality with job performance as Goldberg claims, we agree with others who claim that "it's a systematic relation that is difficult to see" (Doris, 2002, p. 68).

Despite the inconsistency and overall weak effect sizes, personality research related to selection or job performance exploded in popularity. Between 1986 and 1992 there were fewer than 10 studies published or presented in each of those years on these topics; however, by 2005 there were over 40 per year (Morgeson et al., 2007). Why such strong interest in a relatively mundane and atheoretical area? One reason may be because of the applied interest in improving selection processes in organizations. But after more than 10 years of research on the topic of personality as a predictor of job performance, there are those in the field who still believe the reported effect sizes—even after correcting them for a host of statistical artifacts—are "not very impressive" (Morgeson et al., 2007, p. 693). This has created a backlash urging the reconsideration of the use of personality tests in personnel selection contexts. There is the additional point that there is little theory in any of this outside of the benefits of using a parsimonious structural model to organize personality measures.

Although it has not attracted nearly the amount of organizational research attention as the five-factor model, *self-monitoring personality* has also been shown to be a predictor of practically meaningful outcomes in the domain of work and organizations. The notion of a self-monitoring personality and its measurement was first introduced by Snyder (1974) and subsequently revised (Gangestad & Snyder, 2000; Snyder & Gangestad, 1986). At its fundamental core, self-monitoring theory proposes that there are individual differences in the extent to which people are oriented toward and engage in expressive control in social situations. Those who are relatively high self-monitors tend to be responsive to social and interpersonal cues for situationally appropriate attitudes and behavior (i.e., "performances"; Gangestad & Snyder, 2000, p. 530). Those who are low self-monitors use their own attitudes, emotions, and dispositions as guides for their behavior. Although there has been considerable debate on this issue, it has been argued that self-monitoring personality is a discrete class variable in that there are no meaningful distinctions to be made at moderate levels of the construct (Gangestad & Snyder, 1985); someone is either a high or a low self-monitor as determined by the respective score on the Self-Monitoring Scale.

There are probably dozens of such specialty personality constructs and measures with potential relevance to work and organizations; however, self-monitoring personality has proved to be especially potent in predicting a wide range of work-related outcomes, no doubt because of the social and interpersonal nature of organizational settings. A meta-analysis evaluating the effects of self-monitoring personality at work (Day, Schleicher, Unckless, & Hiller, 2002) demonstrated that self-monitoring was positively related to job performance—especially subjective ratings of performance—as well as leadership. But as the theory predicts, self-monitoring is negatively correlated with organizational commitment. The implications are that high self-monitors are especially effective in domains where impression management and expressive control

are important (job performance ratings, leadership) but are likely to "jump ship" for better opportunities when available (low commitment). These results illustrate specific ways in which personality and social psychology are integrated in the work and organizations literature.

Beyond a purely predictive role for self-monitoring personality, researchers have attempted to better understand some of the processes underlying the noted superior effectiveness of high self-monitors in work contexts. Mehra, Kilduff, and Brass (2001) adopted a structuralist perspective to examine hypothesized differences between high and low self-monitors in terms of how they create and potentially benefit from social networks in organizations. Specifically, it was hypothesized that high self-monitors would be more likely to occupy central positions in work-related social networks and that this network centrality would be related to job performance. Results provided support for both of these hypothesized effects, and also demonstrated that self-monitoring personality directly predicted job performance (i.e., network position only partially mediated the relationship between SM and job performance). These findings suggest that stable dispositional effects associated with self-monitoring personality are predictive of job performance and that part of this effect is associated with how high self-monitors are motivated and better able to create central network positions for themselves, which sociological theorists have argued is important for career advancement (Burt, 1992).

The organizational psychology research on self-monitoring personality provides a good example of horizontal theory borrowing (Whetten et al., 2009) in terms of adopting concepts developed for advancing basic knowledge and using them to test theoretically grounded predictions in a specialized (work) context. This would be considered "appropriate" theory borrowing in that the way self-monitoring theory is thought to operate is identical across the respective basic and applied contexts (Morgeson & Hofmann, 1999; Rousseau, 1985).

PERSONALITY AS MOTIVATION

It is possible to conceptualize personality traits as not merely descriptive but as also being imbued with motivational force (see Norem, chapter 12, this volume). Although traits have long been considered as needs or drives (e.g., Allport, 1951; Murray, 1938), only recently has the organizational research returned to this view. As Tett and Burnett (2003) have noted, these attempts to vitalize personality traits with motivational force have heightened "appreciation for them as theoretical—not just descriptive—constructs" (p. 500). This renewed appreciation for the motivational force of personality traits in organizational research has had (and should continue to have) two important implications for personality research in the more applied literature. First, the "demands-abilities" form of person-job fit (where the attributes of the employee fulfill the demands of the job; Edwards, 1991) has been the dominant theoretical lens through which the relevance of personality to behavior in work contexts has been examined. The other form of complementary fit, "needs-supplies" fit (Edwards, 1991; Kristof-Brown et al., 2005), has been largely neglected in research on personality. This concerns the extent to which individual needs are met by environmental resources (i.e., how well are employees' needs, desires, or preferences met by their jobs or organizations). Although this theoretical view has strongly influenced the study of job attitudes, it has not been widely applied to the study of personality in organizations. Allowing employees the opportunity to express their traits via demands of the job or aspects of the organizational context is seen as intrinsically rewarding in the sense that it fulfills specific individual needs (Murray, 1938; Tett & Burnett, 2003). Thus, renewed recognition of the motivational force of personality traits may stimulate research in which individual needs are being met by the environment, as opposed to the other way around. Interestingly, Kristof-Brown et al. (2005) demonstrated in their meta-analysis on various forms of person-environment fit that the needs-supplies form of fit usually had a much greater impact on individual attitudes and behaviors than did the demands-abilities form of fit.

Viewing personality traits as having motivational force also helps us understand *why* personality may lead to enhanced job performance. General agreement has emerged that the distal measures of personality such as the five-factor model link to work behavior through proximal motivational constructs (Kanfer, 1991; McCrae & Costa, 1996; Mount & Barrick, 1995). However, unlike personality, an accepted framework has not existed in the organizational psychology literature for measuring such motivational constructs. As Barrick, Stewart, and Piotrowski (2002) have noted, "a broadly applicable theory of work motivation requires the identification of a limited number of basic goals that regulate human behavior in the workplace" (p. 43). Wiggins and Trapnell (1996) and Hogan (1996; Hogan & Shelton,

1998) have proposed two broad motivational intentions underlying social interactions, motives that have relevance for understanding behavior in work and organization contexts. Building on concepts from evolutionary biology, anthropology, and sociology, as well as socioanalytic theory (Hogan, 1996), researchers have suggested that individuals strive to *get along* and to *get ahead* (also referred to as striving for communion and striving for status [agency], respectively; Bakan, 1966; Barrick et al., 2002). Communion striving (getting along) represents actions directed toward obtaining acceptance in personal relationships and getting along with others. Status striving (getting ahead) represents actions directed toward obtaining power and dominance within a status hierarchy. Barrick et al. (2002) added a third primary motivation to this taxonomy, *accomplishment striving*, to capture the fact that tasks in organizations can be performed without social interaction.

In an empirical study, Barrick et al. (2002) confirmed the link between these primary motives and both the five-factor model of personality and job performance. Specifically, agreeableness, extraversion, and conscientiousness were found to be the personality factors fundamentally associated with striving for communion, striving for status, and striving for accomplishment, respectively. In addition, striving for status and striving for accomplishment mediated the effects of extraversion and conscientiousness on ratings of sales performance. Finding that proximal motives can mediate the relationship between more distal personality variables and work behaviors sets a fruitful and more theoretically rich agenda for future research examining the relationship between personality and work behavior. The next section reviews an important theory in the organizational literature that can help explain why only some traits and motives are relevant in some situations, and it does so using a trait perspective firmly grounded in the personality literature.

TRAIT ACTIVATION THEORY

Building on early work by Murray (1938) and Allport (1951), trait activation theory (Tett & Burnett, 2003; Tett & Guterman, 2000) applies interactionist principles from personality and social psychology to clarify how individual traits come to be expressed as work-related behavior and how such behavior becomes valued as job performance. Trait activation theory posits four key axioms. The first is that traits are manifested as expressive work behaviors only as responses to trait-relevant situational cues. Such cues are considered to fall into three broad and interrelated categories: task, social, and organizational. Situation trait relevance is a qualitative feature of situations that is essentially trait-specific. Notably, it provides a direct answer to the longstanding quest for an all-encompassing taxonomy of situational characteristics by describing situations on the basis of the traits themselves. Just as the five-factor model offers a useful framework for organizing diverse traits (e.g., Costa & McCrae, 1992; Goldberg, 1992), trait activation theory offers a parallel framework for organizing diverse situations.

The second axiom is that trait expression is dependent not only on the relevance of the situation but also on the strength of the situation. Situation strength is the degree to which a situation motivates everyone to respond the same way (Mischel, 1973). A strong situation overrides the effects of individual differences in behavioral propensities. Thus, traits are evident as differences among individuals' behavior only to the degree that the situation is weak. Trait relevance therefore is a qualitative feature of the situation, whereas situation strength is more quantitative, capturing the intensity of the situation. Differences among individuals on a particular trait will be evident to the degree that the situation (1) offers cues to express that trait and (2) is not so strong as to demand that everyone respond the same way.

The third axiom in trait activation theory stipulates that trait-expressive work behavior is distinct from job performance, with the latter being delineated as valued work behavior. Trait-expressive work behavior may be rated by others positively, negatively, or neutrally, depending on the degree to which it is perceived to meet task, social, or organizational demands. The demands at each level that serve as cues for trait expression also serve as reference points for behavioral evaluation as performance. In trait activation theory, separating work behavior from job performance (i.e., as valued behavior) is critical to understanding trait-performance linkages because the processes underlying trait expression are fundamentally different from those underlying performance appraisal (i.e., observer judgments).

The fourth and final axiom is that trait expression entails two parallel, motivational reward systems. Building on the needs model of personality traits (e.g., Murray, 1938), intrinsic reward derives from trait expression (i.e., as need fulfillment) and extrinsic reward derives from the reactions of others to one's trait expressions. Thus, person-situation fit is maximized when intrinsic and extrinsic rewards are aligned: People want to work on tasks with other

people and in organizations where they are rewarded for being themselves. By the same token, fit will be poor in situations lacking cues relevant to the person's dispositions and, even worse, when such cues are present but invite negative reactions from others when acted on (what are called "distracters"; Tett & Burnett, 2003).

These axioms of trait activation theory have been supported empirically (Tett & Guterman, 2000) and extended to an assessment center context (Haaland & Christiansen, 2002; Lievens, Tett, & Schleicher, 2009). The assessment center is a comprehensive approach to assessing candidates for purposes of selection or development, in which candidate evaluations are made on multiple dimensions across multiple simulation exercises (Spychalski, Quinones, Gaugler, & Pohley, 1997; Thornton & Rupp, 2005). The application of trait activation theory to assessment centers has resulted in an improved theoretical understanding of what factors stimulate candidate behaviors in assessment center exercises as well as useful practical recommendations for how such exercises might be better designed to more fully elicit relevant behavior.

Trait activation theory provides a useful framework for synthesizing and integrating much of what we have reviewed above in terms of the extant personality research in the context of work and organizations. The theory offers critical and theoretically grounded insights into which traits will be relevant to performance under which task, social, and organizational conditions, and most importantly, why these traits would be relevant. As such, it represents horizontal and vertical theory borrowing of interactionist principles from personality and social psychology that goes beyond viewing personality traits in descriptive terms and only for purposes of prediction.

COLLECTIVE PERSONALITY

This final section examines an example of vertical theory borrowing with regard to conceptualizing, measuring, and testing the effects of collective personality. What does it mean to say that a team or organization has a "personality?" Is that a potentially meaningful construct? Clearly if by "personality" one means a stable dispositional characteristic that is at least partly a function of heredity then the answer must be no. But if it describes behavioral regularities, habits, and routines of a collective then perhaps it is possible to claim that "collective personality" is a meaningful scientific construct (and apart from Carl Jung's use of this term). That is the approach taken by Hofmann and Jones (2005) in examining potential relationships between leadership, collective personality, and organizational performance (profit and profit variability). Personality was conceptualized and measured using the five-factor model with individual employees rating the "typical behavior" displayed in their respective stores. These ratings were aggregated to the store level and evaluated using metrics such as intraclass correlations and other indexes of within-group agreement in ratings (Bliese, 2000). The evidence suggested that aggregating personality ratings to the store level was appropriate; thus, these overall scores were used to denote collective personality around the five-factor model.

In addition, the collective personality construct was considered to be functionally isomorphic (Morgeson & Hofmann, 1999) with the behavioral routines associated with individual personality. That is, they produce the same outcomes in terms of "regularized, consistent patterns of behavior that can be observed and described by others" (Hofmann & Jones, 2005, p. 510). One difference is that whereas individual personality is inherently an intrapersonal construct, collective personality is an interpersonal phenomenon that manifests itself through interactions among members of the collective. For that reason it was also expected that the leadership of the collective would matter in terms of which particular types of interactions (e.g., conscientious, extroverted, agreeable, open, emotionally stable) were modeled and reinforced. In other words, the particular approach of the leader (transformational or passive) would be significantly related to the particular type of personality at the collective level.

After controlling for store activity and other types of leadership, results supported the hypotheses that transformational leadership was significantly related to the collective personality factors of openness to experience, agreeableness, extraversion, and conscientiousness. Also as expected, passive leadership had negative relationships with all of the collective personality factors, including emotional stability. Finally, collective personality was shown to be related to profit variability over time (but not to overall store profit) in predictable ways. Taken together, Hofmann and Jones (2005) suggest that collective personality should be considered as part of an integrated model including individual personality within team contexts that has at its center "the shared norms and expectations that, through social control, result in collective behavioral regularities" (p. 519). This example of vertical theory borrowing proved to be a rich source of insight as to how personality might emerge at a collective level, shaped through social control (i.e., leadership) and predictive of meaningful organizational outcomes.

Job Attitudes

Perhaps more than any other area in organizational research, the influence of social psychology is readily apparent in the domain of job attitudes, an area of central importance to both the science and practice of work and organizations. Although attitudes have been applied and studied in a number of different disciplines (e.g., political science, marketing, as well as organizational psychology), their ontological home is generally recognized as social psychology (see Ajzen, chapter 15, this volume). It is social psychologists who first noted and systematically examined attitudes (early examples include Allport, 1935, and Newcomb, 1946) and the bulk of more basic research on the nature of attitudes continues to emanate from social psychology. This research in turn has provided a large empirical and theoretical foundation from which organizational researchers could draw in helping to understand and measure attitudes at work. Since the early 1900s, thousands of studies on job attitudes have been published (Lawler, 1970).

This interest in the study of work attitudes has continued to present day in large part due to their practical relevance in organizations. This relevance is based in the use of attitudes as both predictors (i.e., antecedents) and criteria (i.e., outcomes). In terms of job attitudes as predictors, it has been recognized that employees' attitudes have important implications for their behavior. Organizations care about job performance and employee retention, so there is understandable interest in concepts that have potential to predict these outcomes. Because job attitudes have been shown to predict important work outcomes, they have become important criteria against which organizations judge the value of interventions or proposed policies. It is this practical relevance that has supported ongoing interest in job attitudes research within organizational psychology for nearly a century.

The seminal work on attitudes in social psychology has helped address key questions regarding how job attitudes should be conceptualized. For example, most researchers in the field agree on a tripartite conceptualization of attitudes (e.g., Breckler, 1984; Rosenberg & Hovland, 1960), wherein attitudes comprise the separate components of affect (i.e., how the individual *feels* about the attitude object), cognition (i.e., how the individual *thinks* about the attitude object), and behavior (i.e., how the individual *behaves toward* the attitude object). Some organizational researchers (e.g., Hulin & Judge, 2003) have debated whether or not this three-component model applies to all job attitudes, suggesting that some may have only one component, or some may have more than three components. As will become clear when we review the separate job attitudes literature below, it is not easy to see all three components in some of the job attitudes popular in the organizational literature. Nonetheless, there has been some empirical support for this three component model (see Breckler, 1984), and it continues to be a popular way to conceptualize attitudes. In addition, we argue later that greater attention of researchers to the multiple components of attitudes might improve our understanding of job attitudes and their relationships to key organizational outcomes.

SPECIFIC WORK ATTITUDES

Applying the definition of attitude typically used in the social psychology literature (see Albarracin, Johnson, & Zanna, 2005; Eagly & Chaiken, 1993) to the domain of work and organizations, job attitudes reflect employees' relatively stable evaluative dispositions toward referents such as the organization, their supervisor, or the job itself. These vary in intensity and favorability and tend to guide an employee's responses to these targets. A number of specific types of work attitudes have been studied by researchers. There are multiple work attitudes because although all entail an evaluation of aspects of the organizational context, specific work attitudes vary with regard to both the target of evaluation (e.g., job, organization) and the dimensions believed to be important in the favorability assessment. Rather than borrowed from the social psychology literature, these specific work attitudes arose out of practical organizational needs. Many were studied because of a hypothesized link with productivity, which has been identified as one of the four persistent themes in American organizational psychology (Zickar & Gibby, 2007). The most popular of these specific work attitudes include job satisfaction, organizational commitment, job involvement, employee engagement, and perceived organizational support. Each of these is briefly reviewed below, followed by a discussion of how perspectives from personality and social psychology have shed light on our understanding of these job attitudes.

Research on job attitudes began with *job satisfaction*. Not only is it the most popular work attitude,

no other construct in all of organizational psychology has been studied more than job satisfaction (Brief, 1998; Cranny, Smith, & Stone, 1992; Spector, 1997). Despite this popularity, the answer to the question of what job satisfaction is turns out to be surprisingly complex. There have been two basic approaches to defining job satisfaction, and most of the extant definitions can be classified under one or both of these general definitions (see Weiss, 2002). The first approach is based on job satisfaction as an affective reaction or emotional state. For example, Locke (1969) defined job satisfaction as a positive emotional state resulting from an employee's perception that his or her job allowed for the expression and fulfillment of her values. Similarly, Cranny et al. (1992) defined job satisfaction as an emotional state resulting from an employee's comparison of actual and desired job outcomes. The second approach involves characterizing job satisfaction as an *attitude* rather than (and distinct from) an emotional state. In line with the tripartite model of attitudes (Rosenberg & Hovland, 1960), this perspective still allows for an affective component to job satisfaction—as all attitudes could consist of affective, cognitive, and behavioral components—but views job satisfaction more generally as a tripartite evaluation of one's job. This latter more encompassing approach has become the most accepted one in the more recent literature (e.g., Brief, 1998; Hulin & Judge, 2003; Miner, 1992; Weiss, 2002); it also represents the perspective taken in this chapter.

Although it has not been studied nearly as frequently as job satisfaction, there have been thousands of published studies on the topic of *organizational commitment*. Research on this work attitude began in the 1950s with attempts to understand the causes of voluntary turnover, which is a very costly problem for organizations. Prior to the 1970s, organizational commitment was defined in many ways; however, one prominent definition was the strength of employee's identification with and involvement in his or her organization (Porter, Steers, Mowday, & Boulian, 1974). A more contemporary definition that better reflects the attitudinal components of commitment is provided by Solinger, Olffen, and Roe (2008): "[O]rganizational commitment is an attitude of an employee *vis-a-vis* the organization, reflected in a combination of affect (emotional attachment, identification), cognition (identification and internalization of its goals, norms, and values), and action readiness (a generalized behavioral pledge to serve and enhance the organization's interests)" (p. 80). Organizational commitment is typically studied as a multidimensional construct corresponding to affective (an employee's emotional link to the organization), continuance (an employee's assessment of whether she should remain with the organization from a cost-benefit perspective relative to the availability of other alternatives), and normative (an employee's feeling of obligation to the organization and that staying is the "right" thing to do) forms of commitment (Meyer & Allen, 1990).

With regard to *job involvement*, definitions of this attitude have varied over the years (Keller, 1997). Lodahl and Kejner (1965) defined it as "the internalization of values about the goodness of work" (p. 24). Another definition that captures the general idea of job involvement was offered by Kanungo (1982) and reiterated by Elloy, Everett, and Flynn (1991) as "a generalized cognitive state of psychological identification with the job" (p. 162). These represent only a sample of the many definitions of job involvement in the academic literature; however, most of these definitions have included a measure of the degree of psychological involvement one is experiencing with one's current job, with aspects of one's job, or with work in general (Keller, 1997).

Employee engagement is a recent addition to the organizational research literature and as such there is less accumulated scientific knowledge on this job attitude. We mention it here because it appears to be gaining in popularity with researchers and has been embraced enthusiastically by practitioners (see Macey & Schneider, 2008a). Employee engagement has become a "buzzword" of sorts in organizations, presumably because of its role as a sort of amalgam of several related job attitudes (i.e., job satisfaction, organizational commitment, and job involvement). Some have suggested that it represents an evolution of these prior job attitudes (Macey & Schneider, 2008a) because of its espoused potential to predict important organizational outcomes (e.g., employee retention and performance; Harter, Schmidt, & Hayes, 2002) and possibly provide a competitive advantage at the organizational level (Macey & Schneider, 2008b). Theoretical work on the notion of employee engagement began with research defining engagement as the extent to which employees feel able to express their real or authentic selves at work (Kahn, 1990). The conceptualization of employee engagement continues to undergo revisions (Macey & Schneider, 2008a; Thomas, 2007) and has been suggested to comprise affective as well as attitudinal and behavioral components, or what

Macey and Schneider (2008a) term "state" and "behavioral" engagement, respectively. Nonetheless, other researchers have questioned whether employee engagement is simply "old wine in a new bottle" (e.g., Griffin, Parker, & Neal, 2008; Newman & Harrison, 2008).

As originally defined by Eisenberger and colleagues (Eisenberger & Fasolo, 1990; Eisenberger, Huntington, Hutchison, & Sowa, 1986; Rhoades & Eisenberger, 2002), *perceived organizational support* refers to employees' global beliefs about the degree to which their organization values their work and cares for them. In a sense the unique aspect of this particular job attitude is that it represents an employee's view of the organization's view toward this employee. This is typically the result of employees perceptions based on organizational actions and policies, including social-emotional benefits (e.g., approval, respect, caring, and concern) and economic or tangible benefits (e.g., wages, benefits, and training and development opportunities). Perceived organizational support is one side of the relationship that exists between the organization and the employee. It is how the employee sees the employer supporting or contributing to his or her well-being.

INTEGRATING PERSONALITY AND SOCIAL PSYCHOLOGY INTO THE STUDY OF WORK ATTITUDES

A review of the job attitudes literature suggests that an integrated approach to this domain exists at an empirical but perhaps not a theoretical level. Although extensive meta-analyses have been conducted on antecedents of various job attitudes revealing that both social and personality factors are important determinants, an integrated approach has not carried over to the theoretical work in the area. This failure is perhaps not surprising given the relative dearth of theoretical development on job attitudes in general. Nonetheless, there are two notable exceptions, both of which emanate from organizational research and provide theoretical models of job attitudes in general (as opposed to specific work attitudes): social information processing theory and affective events theory. We first review this theoretical work below, followed by a brief summary of the empirical work, and conclude this section with new directions that illustrate a better integration of personality and social psychology in the study of job attitudes.

Social information processing theory (Salancik & Pfeffer, 1978) was developed to explain how work attitudes develop. Prior to this theory, researchers generally accepted the idea that more objective factors such as the nature of the work, promotion opportunities, pay, and such were the primary determinants of work attitudes. Social information processing theory proposed that the social context and particularly the informational cues provided by the social context influence the development and maintenance of work attitudes. Job attitudes are not formed in response to objective aspects of the job or as a result of conscious, rational decision-making processes, but rather are formed largely as a result of the cues individuals receive from their network of coworkers, the consequences of past choices, items stored in memory, as well as signals that emanate directly from the attitude object itself (i.e., task, object, or person).

Social information processing theory has received substantial empirical attention and has been applied to research in a variety of contexts. Although findings from these studies have generally been supportive, most of this work has tested specific aspects of the theory rather than the full model. In addition, although it is clear how this theory advances our understanding of the important social determinants of job attitudes beyond merely the objective job characteristics, there is no attempt to incorporate the role of individual differences (e.g., personality) into this model of attitude development.

Affective events theory (Weiss & Cropanzano, 1996) is a process model of how emotions (or affect) are thought to influence job performance and the development of job attitudes (also see Forgas, 1995, for a description of the related affective infusion model). Affective events theory does not claim that emotions are the sole cause of work attitudes; rather, it suggests that work events and the corresponding emotions can affect short-term job attitudes, while long-term work attitudes are more likely to be the product of cognitive judgments or more conscious decisions and deliberation. For example, when employees are exposed to an event (e.g., workplace problems, duties, and demands) they first experience an emotion. This emotional reaction is a subconscious primary appraisal that is either positive or negative. With a longer delay, employees begin to think more about the experience in an analytic way. Nonetheless, the initial response is an emotional and reflexive one that does not require much time, effort, or thought. This theory has received fairly consistent empirical support in the literature (Thoreson, Kaplan, Barsky, Warren, & de Chermont, 2003). Given that affective events theory includes both features of the work environment and dispositions as antecedents of work attitudes, it comes

closer to an integrated personality and social approach to understanding work attitudes.

In terms of the empirical work conducted on specific job attitudes, meta-analyses have assumed that there are two general categories of job attitude antecedents: (1) aspects of the social context (job, organization, supervisor, coworkers) and (2) aspects of the individual. Results have revealed that both categories are indeed important antecedents. For example, meta-analyses on *job satisfaction* indicate that job characteristics (autonomy, feedback, job complexity, skill variety, task identity, and task significance), organizational climate, and constraints are important contextual antecedents of job satisfaction (Bowling & Hammond, 2008; Carr, Schmidt, Ford, & DeShon, 2003; Parker et al., 2003; Podaskoff, LePine, & LePine, 2007; Rhoades & Eisenberger, 2002), as are alternative work arrangements such as telecommuting, wherein employees perform work tasks somewhere other than a central workplace for some portion of their work schedule (Bailey & Kurland, 2002; Feldman & Gainey, 1997). Results of a meta-analysis (Gajendran & Harrison, 2007) suggested that telecommuting was positively associated with job satisfaction through its effects on greater perceived autonomy, reduced work-family conflict, and higher relationship quality with one's supervisor.

There has also been considerable interest in the role that individual difference variables play in job satisfaction (e.g., Bowling, Beehr, Wagner, & Libkuman, 2005; Judge, Heller, & Mount, 2002). This has been especially true with regard to affective disposition, including the general propensity to be satisfied or happy in life or on the job (Judge & Hulin, 1993; Staw, Bell, & Clausen, 1986) as well as positive and negative affectivity (Brief, Butcher, & Roberson, 1995; Connolly & Viswesvaran, 2000; Thoresen et al., 2003). Other person-based antecedents of job satisfaction that have been studied include the personality factors associated with the five-factor model. Meta-analyses examining the link between these characteristics and job satisfaction (Bowling, 2007; Judge, Heller, & Mount, 2002; Podaskoff, MacKenzie, & Bommer, 1996; Thoresen et al., 2003) have revealed the strongest relationships for conscientiousness, extraversion, and neuroticism (negatively related), with a weaker relationship for agreeableness and generally no relationship for openness to experience. Beyond the five-factor model, meta-analyses have also documented positive relationships between job satisfaction and internal locus of control, self-esteem, and self-efficacy (Bowling, 2007). There has even been research showing that one's level of job satisfaction may be at least partially genetically determined (Arvey, Bouchard, Segal, & Abraham, 1989).

Similar meta-analytic relationships have been found for *organizational commitment*, including the importance of job characteristics, aspects of the climate, and constraints/hindrances versus support (Carr et al., 2003; Cooper-Hakim & Viswesvaran, 2005; Mathieu & Zajac, 1990; Podsakoff et al., 2007; Rhoades & Eisenberger, 2002). Regarding personality variables, negative and positive affect (Thoresen et al., 2003) and the factors of conscientiousness, extraversion, and neuroticism have been meta-analytically related to organizational commitment (Podsakoff et al., 1996; Thoresen et al., 2003), along with work ethic (Cooper-Hakim & Viswesvaran, 2005; Mathieu & Zajac, 1990). In addition, altruism is positively related to organizational commitment (Organ & Ryan, 1995; Podsakoff et al., 1996), whereas self-monitoring personality is negatively related to organizational commitment (Day, et al., 2002).

Regarding antecedents of *job involvement* that have been studied meta-analytically, the most important contextual determinants appear to be aspects of the climate (e.g., professionalism) and support from coworkers and the organization (Carr et al., 2003; Rhoades & Eisenberger, 2002). The strongest personality predictors of job involvement include one's work ethic (Cooper-Hakim & Viswesvaran, 2005) and self-monitoring personality (Day et al., 2002), both of which are positively related to job involvement. Finally, regarding the attitude of *perceived organizational support* (POS), meta-analyses suggest that organizational rewards, pay and promotion, and job security are strong positive determinants of POS (Rhoades & Eisenberger, 2002), whereas job or organizationally related politics and stressors are negatively related to POS (Viswesvaran, Sanchez, & Fisher, 1999). There also appears to be meta-analytic evidence of a link between employees' personality and their relative level of espoused POS (Rhoades & Eisenberger, 2002).

There is also a significant yet largely untapped role for both person and social factors as moderators of the link between job attitudes and important outcomes such as job performance and employee retention. Using the example of job satisfaction, Judge, Thoresen, and Bono's (2001) meta-analysis showed an overall positive correlation of .30 between satisfaction and job performance. Although this is a relatively sizable correlation for applied organizational research, Judge and colleagues suggested that

more research is needed to uncover potential moderators of this relationship, including social and contextual variables (e.g., performance-reward contingency, job characteristics), individual differences (e.g., need for achievement, work centrality, self-concept), characteristics of the attitude (e.g., cognitive accessibility), and study design characteristics (e.g., aggregation, level of analysis). These are all likely candidates to contribute to a better understanding of why and when job attitudes predict behavior in organizations; however, we feel that those moderators based on theoretical developments in personality or social psychology are likely to be most promising in this regard. We will next review a few of these potential new directions and promising research streams.

It was the *compatibility principle* of attitude theory first proposed in the social psychology literature (Ajzen & Fishbein, 1977, 1980; see also Ajzen, chapter 15, this volume) that led Harrison, Newman, and Roth (2006) to propose and test the possibility of a global or overall job attitude. The compatibility principle essentially states that to maximize the relationship between attitudes and criteria, the attitude and criterion have to be at similar levels of abstraction. That is, narrow attitudes should better predict narrow behaviors and broad attitudes should better predict broader categories of behavior. It is typically broader criteria such as performance and withdrawal (incorporating lateness, tardiness, and turnover) that organizational researchers are most interested in predicting from attitudes; thus, Harrison et al. (2006) argued that a global job attitude should be better at predicting these than the individual attitudes of job satisfaction, organizational commitment, and so forth. They also argued that combining organizational commitment and job satisfaction into an overall job or work attitude is feasible, given these constructs' nomological and definitional similarity. Harrison et al. demonstrated via meta-analysis that a global job attitude construct was quite useful for predicting variables consisting of integrated measures of performance (contextual and task) and withdrawal (tardiness, absenteeism, and turnover). Continued research employing the compatibility principle with the study of job attitudes promises to make both theoretical and practical contributions to job attitude measurement and its use as a predictor.

An additional example involves the work on job attitude strength (Schleicher, Watt, & Greguras, 2004). These authors questioned a relatively simplistic approach to job attitudes typically employed in the organizational literature that ignores the likelihood that not all employees possess similarly strong (i.e., consistent, crystallized, impactful; Krosnick & Petty, 1995) attitudes (Fazio & Zanna, 1978). One indicator of attitude strength is the consistency between the *affective and cognitive components* of an attitude, termed affective-cognitive consistency. For example, in the context of job satisfaction, an employee might think that her job provides a fair amount of compensation (cognitive satisfaction), yet still not like the job (affective satisfaction). Affective-cognitive consistency has been found to moderate the predictive validity of attitude scales (Kraus, 1995; Norman, 1975), with higher consistency associated with stronger attitude-behavior relations. Applying this to the realm of job attitudes, Schleicher et al. (2004) found that affective-cognitive consistency in employees' job satisfaction attitudes significantly moderated the relationship between job satisfaction and job performance ($r = .57$ vs. $-.03$ for those employees high vs. low in affective-cognitive consistency; replicated in a second sample, $r = .54$ and $-.11$, respectively). This previously unexamined quality of job attitudes may in part explain why the majority of prior research (e.g., Iaffaldano & Muchinsky, 1985; Petty, McGee, & Cavendar, 1984) has not found larger overall correlations between job satisfaction and performance. This prior research reveals an implicit assumption that all employees hold similarly strong attitudes toward their jobs. Continued research regarding the strength of job attitudes is likely to prove fruitful in terms of reaching a better understanding of what particular conditions enhance the ability of job attitudes to predict employee behaviors.

Both of these examples illustrate how application of attitude theory from social psychology can help resolve important and long-standing unanswered questions in the job attitudes literature (e.g., Are global or facet measures of job attitudes better? Why isn't job satisfaction more strongly related to job performance?). As such, they represent aspects primarily of horizontal theory borrowing (Whetten et al., 2009). It is noteworthy that neither the compatibility principle nor affective-cognitive consistency would be considered recent developments in attitude theory. One wonders how much more quickly our understanding of job attitudes would progress if organizational researchers stayed better informed of current work on attitudes in social psychology.

Leadership

There is probably no more controversial topic in organizational psychology than leadership (Day, in press; see also van Knippenberg, chapter 27, this volume). Despite nearly a century of scientific, mainly psychological, research, there still are claims that the leadership field is "curiously unformed" (Hackman & Wageman, 2007, p. 43). The pessimistic sentiments regarding leadership can be traced to issues such as the lack of a standard operational definition of the construct, an overly narrow focus of study, and the tendency to theorize about leadership in ways that make it too esoteric for nonacademics to appreciate.

Despite these concerns, leadership research continues to be an area of keen interest in organizational psychology; however, this does not appear to be the case in social psychology. From January 2008 through December 2010, only one article was published in the *Journal of Personality and Social Psychology* (published monthly) with either the term *leader* or *leadership* in the title (i.e., Maner & Mead, 2010). In that same time period, there were 37 articles published in the *Journal of Applied Psychology* (published bi-monthly) that included one or both of these terms in the title. This is a remarkable historical shift given that the origins of leadership research in the late 1930s and early 1940s was dominated by social psychology researchers (Day & Zaccaro, 2007) and that the foundation of modern leadership studies can be traced to early social psychology research on interpersonal influence processes (Back, 1951; French, 1956). Although there appear to be social psychologists researching areas with leadership implications such as power and influence, the empirical study of leadership is presently dominated by those with backgrounds in work and organizations. The sheer volume of available leadership theory and research precludes a comprehensive review in this chapter (interested readers please consult Bass, 2008; Day, in press; and van Knippenberg, chapter 27, this volume). Instead, we will focus on a few dominant themes and theoretical perspectives that have particular relevance for personality and social psychology.

PERSONALITY AND LEADERSHIP

This leadership approach is also known as the trait approach and is one of the oldest historically. Because of its importance to the leadership field and particular relevance to personality psychology, it will be reviewed briefly here; however, a more detailed treatment of the topic can be found in chapter 27 of this volume (van Knippenberg). Although personality-based approaches to leadership had fallen out of favor until recently, there are two particular developments—one methodological and one theoretical—that have worked in concert to reinvigorate interest in leadership and personality (Day, in press). The methodological advance is meta-analysis and the theoretical development is the previously discussed five-factor model of personality. These two important advances were used by researchers to estimate the relationship between personality as measured by the five-factor model and the outcomes of leadership emergence (perceptions of a leader) and leadership effectiveness (performance of a leader). Results aggregated across 222 effects and 73 independent samples indicated that extraversion was the most consistent correlate of leadership across settings and criterion categories, and that conscientiousness, openness, and emotional stability all demonstrated nonzero relationships with leadership (Judge, Bono, Ilies, & Gerhardt, 2002). Only agreeableness was found to be unrelated to either emergence or leadership effectiveness.

From these results Judge et al. (2002) concluded that their findings "provide strong evidence in favor of the trait approach" (p. 776). Despite this assertion, we agree with one prominent leadership scholar who maintains that traits simply are not enough for understanding leadership (Bass, 2008). Traits may play an important role—especially in terms of shaping followers' perceptions (Lord, De Vader, & Alliger, 1986)—but they provide little insight into the interpersonal processes that are at the heart of leadership. For this reason, we next examine a leadership theory that emphasizes the role of interpersonal processes in the interactions between leaders and followers and the development of their mutual relationship.

LEADER-MEMBER EXCHANGE (LMX)

The origins of LMX can be traced to theory on social exchange and power (Blau, 1964), especially in terms of subjective, relationship-oriented interactions between leaders and followers (i.e., horizontal theory borrowing). What distinguishes LMX from other leadership theories is its focus on the leader-follower dyadic relationship characterized by an exchange of socioemotional resources, mutual trust, and long-term commitments. A fundamental tenet of LMX theory is that leaders develop different exchange relationships with their followers and develop high-quality relationships with just a few due to limited resources (Graen & Uhl-Bien, 1995). Thus, the level of analysis is on the dyad rather than the individual characteristics, behavior, or followers' perceptions of the leader. It is the quality of this exchange that has been shown to predict various

outcomes such as follower performance, satisfaction with supervision, organizational commitment, and turnover intentions (Gerstner & Day, 1997).

Central to LMX theory is the notion of role-making in terms of the extent that a leader allows followers the discretion to negotiate their respective roles (Dansereau, Graen, & Haga, 1975; Graen & Cashman, 1975). From this perspective it is clear how core processes of social psychology contribute to the quality of interpersonal (leadership) exchange that is developed and the latitude that a follower is given to establish a favorable organizational role. This illustrates an important point: Because leaders develop potentially different exchange qualities with followers, there can be differential power relations among followers reporting to the same leader. In short, all followers are not created as equals and some have greater informal—and possibly formal—power as a result of a more favorable relationship with the leader. For these reasons (among others) it is important to know how LMX forms and potentially changes over time.

In a recent investigation into the development of LMX, researchers examined how leader and follower personality shape the initial exchange quality and how leader and follower performance affect changes in exchange quality over time (Nahrgang, Morgeson, & Ilies, 2009). Using multilevel growth modeling techniques, results from 69 leaders and 330 followers suggested that leaders do form differentiated relationships with followers, LMX develops quickly and then stabilizes, leader agreeableness and follower extraversion influence exchange quality ratings at the initial interaction, and the leader and member performance influence the LMX development over time (cross-level moderation).

From these and other findings it is clear that LMX has numerous implications for theory and research in personality and social psychology. At the heart of LMX is the interpersonal relationship that develops between someone in a more powerful organizational position (leader) with someone in a less powerful position (follower). Results across numerous studies suggest that establishing a high-quality exchange with one's leader is associated with positive follower effects (Gerstner & Day, 1997) as well as to the leader and organization in the form of followers' citizenship and prosocial behaviors (Ilies, Nahrgang, & Morgeson, 2007). From this literature it can be concluded that relationships between leaders and followers matter and provide another line of evidence regarding the value of relationship science. As Berscheid (1999) noted, relationship science "is clearly essential to the further development of social psychology" (p. 262), and we argue that attention to work relationships should play a key role in that further development. Organizational researchers can contribute to this goal by focusing more on how LMX quality develops and changes over time rather than focusing solely on the antecedents of or outcomes associated with exchange quality level. Personality and social psychology researchers can benefit from LMX theory and research given that everyday relationships often develop between people of differential status and power. Thus, LMX theory offers the possibility of greater reciprocity between the respective fields of organizational and social psychology in enhancing our understanding of interpersonal relationships.

TRANSFORMATIONAL, CHARISMATIC, AND SELF-SACRIFICIAL LEADERSHIP

Beginning in the 1980s, researchers and theorists began to focus on the emotional and symbolic aspects of leadership (see van Knippenberg, chapter 27, this volume, for more background on the personality bases of transformational and charismatic leadership). Collectively, the emergence of transformational, charismatic, and visionary leadership theories define what has been termed the New Leadership School (Bryman, 1992). What these particular theories have in common is a focus on how leaders inspire followers through rhetoric and symbolism in ways that appeal to their values and emotions to put the needs of the group or organization over their personal self-interests. The major contributors in developing the New Leadership School include Bass (1985; Bass & Riggio, 2006) and House (1977; House & Shamir, 1993; House, Spangler, & Woycke, 1991). Although these theories have had a tremendous impact in helping to resurrect leadership as a relevant domain for empirical research (Day, in press), there are unresolved difficulties in terms of perpetuating overly heroic and leader-centric perspectives of leadership in addition to conceptual and empirical ambiguities regarding the degree of construct similarity (Yukl, 1999).

Although there are points of relevance in each of these theories with regard to research and theory in social psychology (e.g., affect, identification), the origins are more strongly grounded in political science (Burns, 1978) and sociology (Weber, 1924/1947). Nonetheless, research on transformational and charismatic leadership provided "indirect and nontrivial attention" to the more delineated construct of self-sacrificial leadership (Choi & Mai-Dalton, 1999,

p. 397). Both transformational and charismatic leaders were thought to exhibit, and encourage in others, behaviors that involve foregoing personal interests and privileges for the betterment of collective welfare (Choi & Yoon, 2005). In particular, this type of altruistic leadership is thought to involve self-sacrifice in at least three fundamental areas (Choi & Mai-Dalton, 1998): (1) *division of labor* (taking on arduous tasks and assuming responsibility for failures), (2) *distribution of rewards* (foregoing legitimate future organizational rewards), and (3) *exercise of power* (foregoing resources and privileges that have already been awarded).

There are several reasons to believe that self-sacrificial leadership has the potential to inform and be informed further by theory and research in personality and social psychology. One way is through reorienting the fundamental perspective away from the leader to the followers in terms of their attributions (Choi & Mai-Dalton, 1998; Choi & Yoon, 2005), self-esteem (De Cremer, van Knippenberg, van Dijke, & Bos, 2006), and prosocial behavior (e.g., cooperation; De Cremer, Mayer, van Dijke, Schouten, & Bardes, 2009). Research has also demonstrated that followers' collective identification (De Cremer et al., 2006) and preventive self-regulatory focus (De Cremer et al., 2009) moderate relationships between leader self-sacrifice and follower outcomes. A follower-centered approach to leadership builds on the work of other scholars (Lord & Brown, 2004; Lord, Brown, & Freiberg, 1999) in recognizing that it is not the leader's behavior that results directly in relevant outcomes. Instead, it is the interpretation that followers attach to leader behavior that is most important. Furthermore, the research of De Cremer and colleagues, in particular, has demonstrated that followers' identification and regulatory focus serve as contingencies in predicting these outcomes of interest.

This represents a major shift in the leadership field to fostering a more inclusive approach that elevates followers as a focus of leadership research to higher standing on par with personality, behavior, and other personal attributes and characteristics usually associated with the leader. Although it has been recognized for some time that effective leadership involves an interaction of the leader, followers, and the situation (Gibb, 1954; McGrath, 1962), much of the theoretical and empirical focus has been on the leader first, the situation second, and followers a distant third. Enhancing the focus on the followers is long overdue if for no other reason that it is the followers or subordinates that produce the desirable organizational effects that are generally attributed to their leaders (Lord & Brown, 2004).

TEAM LEADERSHIP

It has been noted that whereas leadership has important implications for enhancing team effectiveness, most of the relevant theory and research does not address explicitly leadership in team settings (Kozlowski & Ilgen, 2006). Instead, the focus traditionally has been more on general processes in a relatively context-free manner. But as teams have become a more central domain of organizational research (as reviewed in the next section) there has been increasing interest in advancing and testing team-centric leadership approaches. As a result of the surging interest in teams and how to lead them (e.g., Hackman, 2002) there is a wealth of relatively new theory and data such that some commentators have predicted that "team leadership as a discipline appears to be on the cusp of some truly significant breakthroughs" (Day, Gronn, & Salas, 2006, p. 211). Rather than attempting to review every theoretical approach to team leadership, we will focus on just three that illustrate different forms and types of theory borrowing.

In general, team leadership has been conceptualized along three different levels of analysis: individual, interpersonal (or shared), and collective. Each level has its own unique theoretical foundation and as a result a different orientation to the notion of theory borrowing. It is important to recognize that this is not a competitive analysis in that there is no right or wrong—or better or worse—approach to team leadership. Indeed, because of the dynamic nature of leadership processes in teams it is entirely possible for all three approaches to operate if not simultaneously than certainly in a complementary fashion.

A prominent team leadership approach at the individual level is based on an attempt to understand what is it that leaders do, also called *functional leadership theory* (Morgeson, DeRue, & Peterson, 2009; Zaccaro, Rittman, & Marks, 2001). The origins of functional leadership theory can be traced to work conducted on leadership training for the U.S. Civil Service Commission (McGrath, 1962). The essence of the approach is conceptualized in terms of the leader as completer. That is, the primary leadership function is "*to do, or get done, whatever is not being adequately handled for group needs*" (McGrath, 1962, p. 5, italics in original). An important implication of this definition is that someone need not

hold a formal leadership role to serve as a team leader: Anyone can recognize gaps in the needs of a team and attempt to handle them. In conceptualizing leadership in a more inclusive manner it also recognizes that whereas there may be just one formal team leader (*the* leader) there can be multiple leaders across the life span of the team or during a team performance episode (Marks, Mathieu, & Zaccaro, 2001). As a result, anyone can be a leader in the team even if only for a fleeting moment by serving to fulfill a critical team function, such as providing feedback, managing team boundaries, or solving team problems (Morgeson et al., 2009). Conceptually, this approach considers leadership to be a more ample rather than scarce resource available to teams and organizations.

The origins of the McGrath's (1962) conceptualization of functional team leadership can be found in early literature on group dynamics as well as studies of management and supervision in large industrial organizations. As such, it is probably not completely accurate to say that the theory was borrowed from social psychology as much as it was the result of integration of small group research with the emerging fields of management, leadership, and administration. Nonetheless, the level of analysis was comparable, so this likely could be considered horizontal theory borrowing. But a more important and interesting aspect of this work can be found in this observation by McGrath: "These and other studies make it clear that real-life organizations are not composed of the leaders and the led. Rather, most large groups contain a number of echelons of leaders, each having mutual, interactive influence upon the other" (1962, p. 22). Eschewing the notion of echelon, this is an apt description of a shared approach to team leadership.

Research on the topic of *shared leadership* grew out of interest in self-managed work teams in which the group members take responsibility for their shared work and operate without a formally appointed leader (Manz & Sims, 1980, 1987). A reasonable question to ponder is, if there is no formally appointed leader, then how will vital leadership functions like setting direction or building commitment occur in a team? The answer from the perspective of those interested in shared leadership is that it will be taken on as a shared responsibility across some or all of the individual team members. In this way shared leadership is defined as a "dynamic, interactive influence process among individuals in groups for which the objective is to lead one another to the achievement of group or organizational goals or both" (Pearce & Conger, 2003, p. 1). Given the emphasis on an interactive influence process it is clear that there are social psychological origins at work in the forms of power and social influence (French & Raven, 1958), social systems theory (Katz & Kahn, 1978), social exchange (Blau, 1964; Homans, 1958), and early conceptualizations of mutual, peer-based leadership (Bowers & Seashore, 1966). Any theory borrowing involved in the development of shared leadership theory would appear to be horizontal in nature.

Recent work has advanced an even more collective perspective on team leadership by incorporating principles from multilevel theory (Klein & Kozlowski, 2000) to integrate issues of team development and adaptation with team learning as emergent group phenomena (Kozlowski & Bell, 2008). Although such approaches can incorporate the guidance of a formal team leader, an important role of the leader is to help the team develop in ways that it takes on more responsibility for its own learning, leadership, and performance (Kozlowski, Watola, Jensen, Kim, & Botero, 2009). What Kozlowski and colleagues call *adaptive team leadership* others have termed collective *leadership capacity* in teams (Day, Gronn, & Salas, 2004). Because the basic concepts at issue (e.g., learning, adaptation, leadership) are considered to be properties of the collective team as social actor, this would be considered a form of vertical theory borrowing (Whetten et al., 2009). That is, the focus is on the global properties of the team rather than shared, emergent properties of the team members. A question going forward to the next section on teams and teamwork is whether there is opportunity for the multilevel and collective aspects of the organizational field to reciprocate theoretically with personality and social psychology.

Teams and Teamwork

"Human history is largely a story of people working together in groups to explore, achieve, and conquer" (Kozlowski & Ilgen, 2006, p. 77). Indeed, teams of people working together for a common purpose is as old as our history as a species and increasingly has become the hallmark of effective organizations (Hackman, 2002). From its origins in small group research within social psychology (e.g., Shaw, 1976; Steiner, 1972; see also Parks, chapter 21, this volume), there has been a trend toward greater theoretical and empirical attention on what constitutes effective teams and teamwork. This increased attention is partly attributable to how work has been restructured around teams as a way to better use

organizational resources and "enable more rapid, flexible, and adaptive responses to the unexpected" (Kozlowski & Ilgen, 2006, p. 77). Additional evidence of this dramatic shift from individual contributors to teams has been documented with regard to how knowledge is created. In a review of nearly 20 million scholarly papers and more than two million patents over five decades, it was shown that teams have replaced solo authors as the dominant source of new knowledge production across a variety of fields including the social sciences (Wuchty, Jones, & Uzzi, 2007).

The ascendancy of teams and teamwork as a focus of research and theory goes beyond their popular organizational use. It also reflects a focus—especially among those in the work and organizations field—on multilevel issues and emergent phenomena in broader collectives (Kozlowski & Klein, 2000; Marks et al., 2001). As such, it represents an especially relevant area to appreciate how both horizontal and vertical theory borrowing contribute to advancing research and enhancing theory building (Whetten et al, 2009).

TEAM EFFECTIVENESS

Similar to the individual level a fundamental concern of team-oriented researchers is with performance. Although the outcome of a team's actions (i.e., performance) is an important criterion in team research, more often researchers refer to and consider team effectiveness. The latter is a more holistic term encompassing whether the team performed to complete its task and also how the team interacts (e.g., team processes) in achieving its outcome (Salas, Sims, & Burke, 2005). Thus, processes such as teamwork are focal areas of concern in team research.

From their review of the teamwork literature, a purported "Big Five" was proposed in terms of a set of requisite teamwork components required for task completion (i.e., team performance) regardless of the type of type of task examined (Salas et al., 2005). The proposed teamwork components are: (1) *team leadership*, in that the failure of a team leader to guide and structure team experiences in coordinating adaptive action often results in ineffective team performance; (2) *mutual performance monitoring*, in terms of keeping track of others' work while carrying out one's own; (3) *backup behavior*, which can take the form of providing feedback and coaching, assisting a teammate in performance a task, and completing a task for an overloaded or overwhelmed teammate; (4) *adaptability*, or recognizing deviations from expected action and adjusting actions appropriately; and (5) *team orientation*, or an attitude of focusing on the overall welfare and functioning of the team over individual needs or performance. The five factors are interdependent in that something like team orientation is proposed to enhance team effectiveness through team members' willingness to engage in mutual performance monitoring.

Although it is sensible to view teamwork as an important antecedent of team effectiveness, it is probably better considered as part of a broader system. An influential organizing heuristic for understanding team effectiveness as a process model—termed the *input-process-output* framework—was proposed initially as a way to help organize the research literature on small groups (McGrath, 1964). Inputs take the form of team composition as well as various types of resources at individual, team, and organizational levels (Kozlowski & Ilgen, 2006). Processes are activities such as teamwork that team members undertake to combine their resources to address task demands but can also be conceptualized as cognitive, affective, and motivational emergent states (e.g., team mental models, team cohesion, collective efficacy) that build over time as the team members interact and the team develops (Marks et al., 2001). Outputs can take the form of evaluations of team performance, assessments of whether the needs of the team and its members were met, as well as evidence of the willingness to remain as a team member (Hackman, 1987). The basic input-process-output framework has been expanded more recently to address issues of feedback cycles and process/outcome mediators that are thought to more accurately reflect the dynamic nature of team performance episodes (Ilgen, Hollenbeck, Johnson, & Jundt, 2005).

A meta-analysis of the literature on teamwork processes (LePine, Piccolo, Jackson, Mathieu, & Saul, 2008) identified 10 relatively narrow processes (mission analysis, goal specification, strategy formation, monitoring progress, system monitoring, team monitoring, coordination, conflict management, motivation, and affect management) that can be explained empirically by the higher-order factors of transition, action, and interpersonal processes (Marks et al., 2001). These teamwork processes were found to have moderately positive relationships with team performance and member satisfaction, and the results shown to be similar across process dimensions regardless of level of dimension specificity.

Another recent meta-analytic study focused on the role of collective cognitive processes (i.e., team cognition) in the input-process-output framework and as a central driver of team performance (DeChurch & Mesmer-Magnus, 2010). Results across 65 studies and 231 effects demonstrated that team cognition explains incremental variance in team effectiveness beyond what is predicted by behavioral processes and motivational states. Taken together, the results suggest that there is a cognitive foundation to teamwork and that not all types of cognition have the same effect on teamwork. In particular, between-study moderators on performance effects were associated with the nature of emergence as well as the form and content of cognition. Because these moderators further illustrate important aspects of multilevel research as well as different forms of theory borrowing, we will elaborate on them in the following section.

COGNITIVE UNDERPINNINGS OF EFFECTIVE TEAMWORK

In what might be considered a classic example of vertical theory borrowing, it was proposed that groups act as information processing entities defined as "the degree to which information, ideas, or cognitive processes are shared . . . among group members and how this sharing of information affects both individual- and group-level outcomes" (Hinsz, Tindale, & Vollrath, 1997, p. 43). Others have conceptualized this kind of group-level effect as an emergent property through bottom-up processes, and that emergence can be qualitatively distinct in terms of composition or compilation processes (Kozlowski & Klein, 2000). *Composition* is based on the assumption of construct isomorphism in which phenomena are identical as they emerge across levels. *Compilation* is at the other end of this emergence continuum and describes cases in which higher level processes take on a completely different form from those at lower levels.

There are two different perspectives on team cognition that illustrate these distinct types of emergent properties. The first is the notion of *team mental models* (Cannon-Bowers, Salas, & Converse, 1993) in which team members develop a shared understanding of key elements of their performance environment and thus are able to work together effectively without the need for detailed communication. Because a shared mental understanding of the situation is thought to emerge across members of the team in a way that would enhance agreement or perceptual congruence within teams, this would be considered an example of a compositional process. In comparison, *team transactive memory* (Austin, 2003) is a cognitive framework that addresses the knowledge held uniquely by team members as well as a collective awareness of "who knows what." Because team members are thought to hold complementary task or team knowledge, this type of group cognition can be considered to be an example of a compilation process. Transactive memory is an irreducible system operating at the group level that relies on a distribution of specializations among group members (Wegner, 1995).

The relevance of this distinction between these two forms of team cognition has both theoretical as well as empirical implications. At the theoretical level, it shows how vertical theory borrowing can take isomorphic (convergent) forms across levels as well as nonisomorphic (patterned) forms. Thus, researchers need to pay careful attention to their construct meanings and be clear on those meanings as theories are borrowed from individual levels and applied to group/team or organizational levels. In terms of empirical implications, the results reported by DeChurch and Mesmer-Magnus (2010) demonstrated stronger effects for compilation emergence of team cognition (transactive memory) than composition emergence (shared mental models) on behavioral processes and team performance indicators. From these findings the authors concluded that patterned knowledge is more highly related to process and performance than its isomorphic counterpoint. In other words, the nature of emergence is an important consideration in the ultimate predictive capacity of multilevel constructs.

It has been noted recently that team effectiveness is a truly multidisciplinary area of research including cognitive, military, and human factors, and clinical psychologists as well those from the organizational and social psychology disciplines (Salas, Goodwin, & Burke, 2009). Although this multidisciplinary nature makes teams an exciting and dynamic area of study, it also poses challenges in terms of integrating theory and research in a cross-disciplinary manner. Given the intense focus on building and testing multilevel theories—including those related to teams and teamwork—by many in the work and organizations field, it poses a unique opportunity for reciprocal theory borrowing. Because teams provide the kind of interpersonal context in which to conceptualize, model, and test core aspects of personality and social psychology, we believe that this provides for some very interesting possibilities with regard to future collaborations between organizational and personality and social psychology researchers. For example, one of the critical research questions posed by Salas and Wildman (2009) as a future research need in the teams area is greater attention to how and why team composition matters. This would not only involve an incorporation of personality at the individual and team level (Driskell, Goodwin, Salas, & O'Shea, 2006) but also potentially examining cultural values such as collectivism (Bell, 2007). These (and other) key areas are topics in which personality and social psychology researchers hold a great deal of expertise.

Unfortunately, from our perspective as organizational psychologists we do not see the same level of interest among those in personality and social psychology in attempting to better understand, predict, and control those factors that contribute to effective teams and teamwork. A general exception to this rule can be found in the work on socially situated cognition (Smith & Semin, 2004), distributed social cognition (Smith & Collins, 2009), and situated social influence (Mason, Conrey, & Smith, 2007). These approaches all adopt a more contextualized lens involving multiple sources and targets that also recognize the dynamic nature of many processes studied in personality and social psychology. It is interesting that Mason et al. sharply criticize the field of social psychology on this issue:

> What our field has often failed to do is to contextualize our robust microlevel understanding of social influence processes by explicitly situating those processes in a social situation involving multiple individuals, interacting over time, linked in social networks of friendship and influence. (p. 296)

They then comment that the lack of social psychologists' participation in embedding social influence in broader contexts has resulted in researchers using "simplistic, empirically inaccurate models of influence processes" (p. 296). Of course, organizational theorists and researchers have been developing and testing for years the kinds of dynamic, multilevel models that Mason and colleagues describe (see also Christ, Sibley & Wagner, chapter 10, this volume). Furthermore, most would agree that part (but not all) of the construct of leadership involves the kinds of contextualized social influence processes that social psychologists apparently have generally failed to consider. This is an ideal space where theory borrowing from the organizational field can help to inform and even accelerate research on socially situated constructs of interest to personality and social psychology researchers.

Conclusions

We opened this chapter with a brief overview of why work and organizations make up a special life domain with particular relevance and meaning to many people. It is not merely a context in which personality and social psychology theories and principles are applied. Rather, work and organizations constitute a domain where personality, interpersonal behavior, social relations, power and influence, and other relevant topics can be studied "in the wild" (Hutchins, 1995). Organizations are inherently interpersonal in nature and often involve dealing with issues associated with conflict, status, hierarchy, and power. Of course a challenge is being able to study such things with the equivalent methodological rigor available in a laboratory setting. Field experiments and quasi-experimentation in organizational settings are possible and offer reasonable—although often more difficult—alternatives to lab experiments. Nonetheless, a point we hoped to make was in illustrating the critical impact that context has in organizational theory and research, and context can be difficult to simulate in the lab.

Despite its importance, context is not always clearly defined or sufficiently recognized even by those in the organizational field. In a recent treatise on the "essential impact" of context on organizational concerns, Johns (2006) defined context as "situational opportunities and constraints that affect occurrence and meaning" of constructs as well as the functional relations between variables (p. 386). According to Johns, context operates in ways that can restrict the range of measurements, change the causal direction between variables, reverse signs, prompt curvilinear effects, and threaten validity. In other words, context potentially changes the very nature of what is studied, which can require modifications to existing theory or the development of altogether new theories.

Context can be manifested in a number of different ways, but one with particular relevance for this chapter is that context can serve as a cross-level effect (Johns, 2006). Specifically, contextual variables at one level of analysis can affect variables at another level, typically in a top-down manner such that higher-level contextual factors (e.g., organizational climate) have direct effects on lower-level variables (e.g., individual work attitudes) or moderate relationships between lower-level effects (Kozlowski & Klein, 2000; Mowday & Sutton, 1993). As noted in the section on teams and teamwork in this chapter, there are also emergent properties or states to consider in collectives that form as

a result of bottom-up, interactive processes that are shaped and constrained by higher-level contextual factors.

The focus on context and levels of analysis (e.g., multilevel models, cross-level effects) in the organizational domain could serve as both a potential threat and opportunity with regard to its relevance for those with interests mainly in personality and social psychology. In terms of a potential threat, this could further divide scholars working in the respective fields of organizational and personality or social psychology. But instead of a "basic" versus "applied" divide that has been the case historically, the new divide would be between those who theorize and research issues at a single level, devoid of interest in context, and those who place levels of analysis and context as integral concerns to theory and research. This point was made especially clear by Kozlowski and Klein (2000):

> There is increasing recognition that the confines of single-level models—*a legacy of primary disciplines that undergird organizational science*—need to be broken. A meaningful understanding of the phenomena that comprise organizational behavior necessitates approaches that are more integrative, that cut across multiple levels, and that seek to understand phenomena from a combination of perspectives. There is a solid theoretical foundation for a broadly applicable levels perspective, for an expanding, empirically based research literature, and for progress toward the development of new and more powerful analytic tools. A levels perspective offers a paradigm that is distinctly organizational. (p. 77, italics added)

Although a levels perspective could be a distinctly organizational science, there is no reason why it must be so. At the core of personality and social psychology are both intrapersonal and interpersonal phenomena. Because of this inherent multilevel nature, researchers in personality and social psychology should be concerned with issues of levels and context (e.g., Smith & Semin, 2004; see also Christ et al., chapter 10, this volume). With regard to the noted trade (i.e., theory) deficit between the fields of organizational and personality and social psychology, one area in which this might begin to change is with greater attention to the levels perspective noted by Kozlowski and Klein (2000). In line with this recommendation, Mason et al. (2007) have called for "cross-disciplinary conceptual integration" as a means of addressing the general lack of contextualization in personality and social psychology. It is our hope that such concerns will capture the scientific imagination of those in the field of personality and social psychology such that they are motivated to engage in theory borrowing from organizational research and in doing so not only foster greater rapprochement between the fields but also help forge a sounder science of individuals and how they interact and interrelate in important life domains.

References

Adams, J. S. (1965). Inequity in social exchange. *Advances in Experimental Social Psychology, 2,* 267–299.

Ajzen, I., & Fishbein, M. (1977). Attitude-behavior relations: A theoretical analysis and review of empirical literature. *Psychological Bulletin, 84,* 888–918.

Ajzen, I., & Fishbein, M. (1980). *Understanding attitudes and predicting social behavior.* Englewood Cliffs, NJ: Prentice-Hall.

Albarracin, B. T., Johnson, B. T., & Zanna, M. P. (2005). *The handbook of attitudes.* New York: Routledge.

Allport, G. W. (1935). Attitudes. In C. Murchison (Ed.), *Handbook of social psychology* (pp. 798–884). Worchester, MA: Clark University Press.

Allport, G. W. (1951). *Personality: A psychological interpretation.* London: Constable.

Arvey, R. D., Bouchard, T. J., Segal, N. L., & Abraham, L. M. (1989). Job satisfaction: Environmental and genetic components. *Journal of Applied Psychology, 74,* 187–192.

Austin, J. R. (2003). Transactive memory in organizational groups: The effects of content, consensus, specialization, and accuracy on group performance. *Journal of Applied Psychology, 88,* 866–878.

Back, K. W. (1951). Influence through social communication. *Journal of Abnormal and Social Psychology, 46,* 9–23.

Bailey, D. E., & Kurland, N. B. (2002). A review of telework research: Findings, new directions and lessons for the study of modern work. *Journal of Organizational Behavior, 23,* 383–400.

Bakan, D. (1966). *The duality of human existence: Isolation and communion in Western man.* Boston: Beacon.

Barrick, M. R., & Mount, M. K. (1991). The Big Five personality dimensions and job performance: A meta-analysis. *Personnel Psychology, 44,* 1–26.

Barrick, M. R., Stewart, G. L., & Piotrowski, M. (2002). Personality and job performance: Test of the mediating effects of motivation among sales representatives. *Journal of Applied Psychology, 87,* 43–51.

Bass, B. M. (1985). *Leadership and performance beyond expectations.* New York: Free Press.

Bass, B. M. (2008). *The Bass handbook of leadership: Theory, research, and managerial applications* (4th ed.). New York: Free Press.

Bass, B. M., & Riggio, R. E. (2006). *Transformational leadership* (2nd ed.). Mahwah, NJ: Erlbaum.

Bell, B. S. (2007). Deep-level composition variables as predictors of team performance A meta-analysis. *Journal of Applied Psychology, 92,* 595–615.

Berscheid, E. (1999). The greening of relationship science. *American Psychologist, 54,* 260–266.

Blau, P. M. (1964). *Exchange and power in social life.* New York: Wiley.

Bliese, P. D. (2000). Within-group agreement, non-independence, and reliability: Implications for data aggregation and analysis. In K. J. Klein & S. W. J. Kozlowski (Eds.), *Multilevel theory, research, and methods in organizations: Foundations, extensions, and new directions* (pp. 349–381). San Francisco: Jossey-Bass.

Bliese, P. D., & Hanges, P. J. (2004). Being too liberal and too conservative: The perils of treating grouped data as though they were independent. *Organizational Research Methods, 7,* 400–417.

Bowers, D. G., & Seashore, S. E. (1966). Predicting organizational effectiveness with a four-factor theory of leadership. *Administrative Science Quarterly, 11,* 238–263.

Bowling, N. A. (2007). Is the job satisfaction–job performance relationship spurious? A meta-analytic examination. *Journal of Vocational Behavior, 71,* 167–185.

Bowling, N. A., Beehr, T. A., Wagner, S. H. & Libkuman, T. M. (2005). Adaptation-level theory, opponent process theory, and dispositions: An integrated approach to the stability of job satisfaction. *Journal of Applied Psychology, 90,* 1044–1053.

Bowling, N. A., & Hammond, D. G. (2008). A meta-analytic examination of the construct validity of the Michigan Organizational Assessment Questionnaire Job Satisfaction Subscale. *Journal of Vocational Behavior, 73,* 63–77.

Breckler, S. J. (1984). Empirical validation of affect, behavior, and cognition as distinct components of attitude. *Journal of Personality and Social Psychology, 47,* 1191–1205.

Brief, A. P. (1998). *Attitudes in and around organizations.* Thousand Oaks, CA: Sage.

Brief, A. P., Butcher, A. H., & Roberson, L. (1995). Cookies, disposition, and job-attitudes—the effects of positive mood-inducing events and negative affectivity on job-satisfaction in a field experiment. *Organizational Behavior and Human Decision Processes, 62,* 55–62.

Bryman, A. (1992). *Charisma and leadership in organizations.* Newbury Park, CA: Sage.

Burns, J. M. (1978). *Leadership.* New York: Harper & Row.

Burt, R. S. (1992). *Structural holes: The social structure of competition.* Cambridge, MA: Harvard University Press.

Byrne, D. (1971). *The attraction paradigm.* New York: Academic.

Cannon-Bowers, J. A., Salas, E., & Converse, S. A. (1993). Shared mental models in expert team decision making. In N. J. Castellan Jr. (Ed.), *Individual and group decision making: Current issues* (pp. 221–246). Hillsdale, NJ: Erlbaum.

Carr, J. Z., Schmidt, A. M., Ford, J. K., & DeShon, R. P. (2003). Climate perceptions matter: A meta-analytic path analysis relating molar climate, cognitive and affective states, and individual level work outcomes. *Journal of Applied Psychology, 88,* 605–619.

Chan, D. (1998). Functional relations among constructs in the same content domain at different levels of analysis: A typology of composition models. *Journal of Applied Psychology, 83,* 234–246.

Chatman, J. A. (1989). Improving interactional organizational research: A model of person-organization fit. *Academy of Management Review, 14,* 333–349.

Chatman, J. A. (1991). Matching people and organizations: Selection and socialization in public accounting firms. *Administrative Science Quarterly, 36,* 459–484.

Chen, G., Bliese, P. D., & Mathieu, J. E. (2005). Conceptual framework and statistical procedures for delineating and testing multilevel theories of homology. *Organizational Research Methods, 8,* 375–409.

Choi, Y., & Mai-Dalton, R. R. (1998). On the leadership function of self-sacrifice. *Leadership Quarterly, 9,* 475–501.

Choi, Y., & Mai-Dalton, R. R. (1999). The model of followers' responses to self-sacrificial leadership: An empirical test. *Leadership Quarterly, 10,* 397–421.

Choi, Y., & Yoon, J. (2005). Effects of leaders' self-sacrificial behavior and competency on followers' attribution of charismatic leadership among Americans and Koreans. *Current Research in Social Psychology, 11,* 51–69.

Connolly, J. J., & Viswesvaran, C. (2000). The role of affectivity in job satisfaction: A meta-analysis. *Personality and Individual Differences, 29,* 265–281.

Cooper-Hakim, A., & Viswesvaran, C. (2005). The construct of work commitment: Testing an integrated framework. *Journal of Applied Psychology, 131,* 241–259.

Costa, P. T., Jr., & McCrae, R. R. (1992). *Revised NEO personality inventory (NEO PI-R) and NEO five-factor inventory (NEO FFI) professional manual.* Odessa, FL: Psychological Assessment Resources.

Cranny, C. J., Smith, P. C. & Stone, E. F. (1992). *Job satisfaction: How people feel about their jobs and how it affects their performance.* New York: Lexington.

Dansereau, F., Jr., Graen, G., & Haga, W. J. (1975). A vertical dyad linkage approach to leadership within formal organizations: A longitudinal investigation of the role making process. *Organizational Behavior and Human Performance, 13,* 46–78.

Day, D. V. (in press). Leadership. In S. W. J. Kozlowski (Ed.), *The Oxford handbook of organizational psychology.* New York: Oxford University.

Day, D. V., Gronn, P., & Salas, E. (2004). Leadership capacity in teams. *Leadership Quarterly, 15,* 857–880.

Day, D. V., Gronn, P., & Salas, E. (2006). Leadership in team-based organizations: On the threshold of a new era. *Leadership Quarterly, 17,* 211–216.

Day, D. V., Schleicher, D. J., Unckless, A. L., & Hiller, N. J. (2002). Self-monitoring personality at work: A meta-analytic investigation of construct validity. *Journal of Applied Psychology, 87,* 390–401.

Day, D. V., & Silverman, S. B. (1989). Personality and job performance: Evidence of incremental validity. *Personnel Psychology, 42,* 25–36.

Day, D. V., & Zaccaro, S. J. (2007). Leadership: A critical historical analysis of the influence of leader traits. In L. L. Koppes (Ed.), *Historical perspectives in industrial and organizational psychology* (pp. 383–405). Mahwah, NJ: Erlbaum.

DeChurch, L. A., & Mesmer-Magnus, J. R. (2010). The cognitive underpinnings of effective teamwork: A meta-analysis. *Journal of Applied Psychology, 95,* 32–53.

De Cremer, D., Mayer, D. M., van Dijke, M., Schouten, B. C., & Bardes, M. (2009). When does self-sacrificial leadership motivate prosocial behavior? It depends on followers' prevention focus. *Journal of Applied Psychology, 94,* 887–899.

De Cremer, D., van Knippenberg, D., van Dijke, M., & Bos, A. E. R. (2006). Self-sacrificial leadership and follower self-esteem: When collective identification matters. *Group Dynamics: Theory, Research, and Practice, 10,* 233–245.

Digman, J. M. (1990). Personality structure: Emergence of the five-factor model. *Annual Review of Psychology, 41,* 417–440.

Doris, J. M. (2002). *Lack of character: Personality and moral behavior.* Cambridge, UK: Cambridge University Press.

Driskell, J. E., Goodwin, G. F., Salas, E., & O'Shea, P. G. (2006). What makes a good team player? Personality and team

effectiveness. *Group Dynamics: Theory, Research, and Practice, 5,* 111-123.

Dunnette, M. D. (1990). Blending the science and practice of industrial and organizational psychology: Where are we and where are we going? In M. D. Dunnette & L. M. Hough (Eds.), *Handbook of industrial and organizational psychology* (2nd ed., Vol. 1, pp. 1–27). Palo Alto, CA: Consulting Psychologists.

Eagly, A. H. & Chaiken, S. (1993). The impact of attitudes on memory: An affair to remember. *Psychological Bulletin, 125,* 64–86.

Eagly, A. H., Johannesen-Schmidt, M. C., & van Engen, M. L. (2003). Transformational, transactional, and laissez-faire leadership styles: A meta-analysis comparing men and women. *Psychological Bulletin, 129,* 569–591.

Edwards, J. R. (1991). Person-job fit: A conceptual integration, literature review, and methodological critique. In C. L. Cooper (Ed.), *International review of industrial and organizational psychology* (Vol. 6, pp. 283–357). Chichester, UK: Wiley.

Edwards, J. R., Caplan, R. D., & Harrison, R. V. (1998). Person-environment fit theory: Conceptual foundations, empirical evidence, and directions for future research. In C. L. Cooper (Ed.), *Theories of organizational stress* (pp. 28–67). Oxford, UK: Oxford University Press.

Eisenberger, R., & Fasolo, P. (1990). Perceived organizational support and employee diligence, commitment, and innovation. *Journal of Applied Psychology, 75,* 51–60.

Eisenberger, R., Huntington, R., Hutchison, S., & Sowa, D. (1986). Perceived organizational support. *Journal of Applied Psychology, 71,* 500–507.

Ekehammar, B. (1974). Interactionism in personality from a historical perspective. *Psychological Bulletin, 81,* 1026–1048.

Ellemers, N., de Gilder, D., & Haslam, S. A. (2004). Motivating individuals and groups at work: A social identity perspective on leadership and group performance. *Academy of Management Review, 29,* 459–478.

Elloy, D. F., Everett, J. E., & Flynn, W. R. (1991). An examination of the correlates of job involvement. *Group and Organizational Studies, 16,* 160–177.

Fazio, R. H., & Zanna, M. P. (1978). Attitudinal qualities relating to the strength of the attitude-behavior relationship. *Journal of Experimental Social Psychology, 14,* 398–408.

Feldman, D. C., & Gainey, T. W. (1997). Patterns of telecommuting and their consequences: Framing the research agenda. *Human Resource Management Review, 7,* 369–388.

Folger, R. G., & Greenberg, J. (1985). Procedural justice: An interpretive analysis of personnel systems. *Research in Personnel and Human Resources Management, 3,* 141–183.

Forgas, J. P. (1995). Mood and judgment: The affect infusion model (AIM). *Psychological Bulletin, 117,* 39–66.

French, J. R. P. (1956). A formal theory of social power. *Psychological Review, 63,* 181–194.

French, J. R. P., & Raven, B. H. (1958). Legitimate power, coercive power, and observability in social influence. *Sociometry, 21,* 83–97.

Gajendran, R. S., & Harrison, D. A. (2007). The good, the bad, and the unknown about telecommuting: Meta-analysis of psychological mediators and individual consequences. *Journal of Applied Psychology, 92,* 1524–1541.

Gangestad, S. W., & Snyder, M. (1985). "To carve nature at its joints": On the existence of discrete classes in personality. *Psychological Review, 92,* 317–349.

Gangestad, S. W., & Snyder, M. (2000). Self-monitoring: Appraisal and reappraisal. *Psychological Bulletin, 126,* 530–555.

Gerstner, C. R., & Day, D. V. (1997). Meta-analytic review of leader-member exchange theory: Correlates and construct issues. *Journal of Applied Psychology, 82,* 827–844.

Gibb, C. A. (1954). Leadership. In G. Lindzey (Ed.), *Handbook of social psychology* (Vol. 2, pp. 877–920). Cambridge, MA: Addison-Wesley.

Goldberg, L. R. (1990). An alternative "description of personality": The Big-Five factor structure. *Journal of Personality and Social Psychology, 59,* 1216–1229.

Goldberg, L. R. (1992). The development of markers for the Big-Five factor structures. *Psychological Assessment, 4,* 26–42.

Goldberg, L. R. (1993). The structure of phenotypic personality traits. *American Psychologist, 48,* 26–34.

Graen, G. B., & Cashman, J. F. (1975). A role making model of leadership in formal organizations. In J. G. Hunt & L. L. Larson (Eds.), *Leadership frontiers* (pp. 143–165). Kent, OH: Kent State University.

Graen, G. B., & Uhl-Bien, M. (1995). Relationship-based approach to leadership: Development of leader-member exchange (LMX) theory of leadership over 25 years: Applying a multi-level multi-domain perspective. *Leadership Quarterly, 6,* 219–247.

Greenberg, J. (1987). A taxonomy of organizational justice theories. *Academy of Management Review, 12,* 9–22.

Griffin, M. A., Parker, S. K., & Neal, A. (2008). Is behavioral engagement a distinct and useful construct? *Industrial and Organizational Psychology: Perspectives on Science and Practice, 1,* 48–51.

Guion, R. M., & Gottier, R. F. (1965). Validity of personality measures in personnel selection. *Personnel Psychology, 18,* 135–164.

Haaland, S. & Christiansen, N. D. (2002). Implications of trait-activation theory for evaluating the construct validity of assessment center ratings. *Personnel Psychology, 55,* 137–163.

Hackman, J. R. (1987). The design of work teams. In J. Lorsch (Ed.), *Handbook of organizational behavior* (pp. 315–342). New York: Prentice Hall.

Hackman, J. R. (2002). *Leading teams: Setting the stage for great performances.* Boston: Harvard Business School.

Hackman, J. R., & Wageman, R. (2007). Asking the right questions about leadership. *American Psychologist, 62,* 43–47.

Haley, H., & Sidanius, J. (2005). Person-organization congruence and the maintenance of group-based social hierarchy: A social dominance perspective. *Group Processes and Intergroup Relations, 8,* 187–203.

Harrison, D. A., Newman, D. A., & Roth, P. L. (2006). How important are job attitudes? Meta-analytic comparisons of integrative behavioral outcomes and time sequences. *Academy of Management Journal, 49,* 305–325.

Harrison, D. A., Price, K. H., & Bell, M. P. (1998). Beyond relational demography: Time and the effects of surface- and deep-level diversity on work group cohesion. *Academy of Management Journal, 41,* 96–107.

Harter, J. K., Schmidt, F. L., & Hayes, T. L. (2002). Business-unit-level relationship between employee satisfaction, employee engagement, and business outcomes: A meta-analysis. *Journal of Applied Psychology, 87,* 268–279.

Heilman, M. E., & Parks-Stamm, E. J. (2007). Gender stereotypes in the workplace: Obstacles to women's career progress. In S. J. Correll (Ed.), *Social psychology of gender: Advances in group processes* (Vol. 24, pp. 47–78). Amsterdam and Oxford: Elsevier, JAI Press.

Heilman, M. E., & Okimoto, T. G. (2007). Why are women penalized for success at male tasks? The implied communality deficit. *Journal of Applied Psychology, 92,* 81–92.

Hinsz, V. B., Tindale, R. S., & Vollrath, D. A. (1997). The emerging conceptualization of groups as information processors. *Psychological Bulletin, 121,* 43–64.

Hofmann, D. A., & Jones, L. M. (2005). Leadership, collective personality, and performance. *Journal of Applied Psychology, 90,* 509–522.

Hogan, R. (1996). A socioanalytic perspective on the five-factor model. In J. S. Wiggins (Ed.), *The five-factor model of personality* (pp. 163–179). New York: Guilford.

Hogan, R., & Shelton, D. (1998). A socioanalytic perspective on job performance. *Human Performance, 11,* 129–144.

Homans, G. C. (1958). Social behavior as exchange. *American Journal of Sociology, 63,* 597–606.

House, R., Rousseau, D. M., & Thomas-Hunt, M. (1995). The meso paradigm: A framework for the integration of micro and macro organizational behavior. *Research in Organizational Behavior, 17,* 71–114.

House, R. J. (1977). A 1976 theory of charismatic leadership. In J. G. Hunt & L. L. Larson (Eds.), *Leadership: The cutting edge* (pp. 189–207). Carbondale: Southern Illinois University.

House, R. J., & Shamir, B. (1993). Towards an integration of transformational, charismatic, and visionary theories of leadership. In M. M. Chemers & R. Ayman (Eds.), *Leadership: Perspectives and research directions* (pp. 81–107). New York: Academic.

House, R. J., Spangler, W. D., & Woycke, J. (1991). Personality and charisma in the U.S. presidency: A psychological theory of leader effectiveness. *Administrative Science Quarterly, 36,* 364–396.

Hulin, C. L., & Judge, T. A. (2003). Job attitudes. In W. C. Borman, D. R. Ilgen, & R. J. Klimoski (Eds.), *Handbook of psychology: Industrial and organizational psychology* (Vol. 12, pp. 255–276). Hoboken, NJ: Wiley.

Hutchins, E. (1995). *Cognition in the wild.* Cambridge, MA: MIT.

Iaffaldano, M. T., & Muchinsky, P. M. (1985). Job satisfaction and job performance: A meta-analysis. *Psychological Bulletin, 97,* 251–273.

Ilgen, D. R., Hollenbeck, J. R., Johnson, M., & Jundt, J. (2005). Teams in organizations: From I-P-O models to IMOI models. *Annual Review of Psychology, 56,* 517–543.

Ilgen, D. R., & Klein, H. J. (1989). Organizational behavior. *Annual Review of Psychology, 40,* 327–351.

Ilies, R., Nahrgang, J. D., & Morgeson, F. P. (2007). Leader-member exchange and citizenship behaviors: A meta-analysis. *Journal of Applied Psychology, 92,* 269–277.

Johns, G. (2006). The essential impact of context on organizational behavior. *Academy of Management Review, 31,* 386–408.

Judge, T. A., Bono, J. E., Ilies, R., & Gerhardt, M. W. (2002). Personality and leadership: A qualitative and quantitative review. *Journal of Applied Psychology, 87,* 765–780.

Judge, T. A., & Ferris, G. R. (1992). The elusive criterion of fit in human resource staffing decisions. *Human Resource Planning, 15,* 47–67.

Judge, T. A., Heller, D., & Mount, M. K. (2002). Five-factor model of personality and job satisfaction: A meta-analysis. *Journal of Applied Psychology, 87,* 530–541.

Judge, T. A., & Hulin, C. L. (1993). Job satisfaction as a reflection of disposition: A multiple source causal analysis. *Organizational Behavior and Human Decision Processes, 56,* 388–421.

Judge, T. A., Thoresen, C. J., & Bono, J. E. (2001). The job satisfaction–job performance relationship: A qualitative and quantitative review. *Psychological Bulletin, 127,* 376–407.

Kahn, W. A. (1990). Psychological conditions of personal engagement and disengagement at work. *Academy of Management Journal, 33,* 692–724.

Kanfer, R. (1991). Motivation theory and industrial and organizational psychology. In M. D. Dunnette & L. M. Hough (Eds.), *Handbook of industrial and organizational psychology* (pp. 75–170). Palo Alto, CA: Consulting Psychologists.

Kanungo, R. N. (1982). Measurement of job and work involvement. *Journal of Applied Psychology, 67,* 341–349.

Katz, D., & Kahn, R. L. (1978). *The social psychology of organizations* (2nd ed.). New York: Wiley.

Katzell, R. A., & Austin, J. T. (1992). From then to now: The development of industrial-organizational psychology in the United States. *Journal of Applied Psychology, 77,* 803–835.

Keller, R. T. (1997). Job involvement and organizational commitment as longitudinal predictors of job performance: A study of scientists and engineers. *Journal of Applied Psychology, 82,* 539–545.

Klein, K. J., Dansereau, F., & Hall, R. J. (1994). Levels issues in theory development, data collection, and analyses. *Academy of Management Review, 19,* 105–129.

Klein, K. J., & Kozlowski, S. W. J. (Eds.). (2000). *Multilevel theory, research, and methods in organizations: Foundations, extensions, and new directions.* San Francisco: Jossey-Bass.

Kozlowski, S. W. J. (Ed.). (in press). *The Oxford handbook of industrial and organizational psychology.* New York: Oxford University.

Kozlowski, S. W. J., & Bell, B. S. (2008). Team learning, development, and adaptation. In V. I. Sessa & M. London (Eds.), *Work group learning: Understanding, improving, and assessing how groups learn in organizations* (pp. 15–44). New York: Erlbaum.

Kozlowski, S. W. J., & Ilgen, D. R. (2006). Enhancing the effectiveness of work groups and teams (Monograph). *Psychological Science in the Public Interest, 7,* 77–124.

Kozlowski, S. W. J., & Klein, K. J. (2000). A multilevel approach to theory and research in organizations: Contextual, temporal, and emergent processes. In K. J. Klein & S. W. J. Kozlowski (Eds.), *Multilevel theory, research and methods in organizations: Foundations, extensions, and new directions* (pp. 467–511). San Francisco: Jossey-Bass.

Kozlowski, S. W. J., Watola, D. J., Jensen, J. M., Kim, B. H., & Botero, I. C. (2009). Developing adaptive teams: A theory of dynamic team leadership. In E. Salas, G. F. Goodwin & C. S. Burke (Eds.), *Team effectiveness in complex organizations: Cross-disciplinary perspectives and approaches* (pp. 113–155). New York: Routledge.

Kraus, S. J. (1995). Attitudes and the prediction of behavior: A meta-analysis of the empirical literature. *Personality and Social Psychology Bulletin, 21,* 58–75.

Kristof, A. L. (1996). Person-organization fit: An integrative review of its conceptualizations, measurement, and implications. *Personnel Psychology, 49,* 1–49.

Kristof-Brown, A. L., Zimmerman, R. D., & Johnson, E. C. (2005). Consequences of individuals' fit at work: A meta-analysis of person-job, person-organization, person-group, and person-supervisor fit. *Personnel Psychology, 58,* 281–342.

Krosnick, J. A., & Petty, R. E. (1995). Attitude strength: An overview. In R. E. Petty & J. A. Krosnick (Eds.), *Attitude strength: Antecedents and consequences* (pp. 1–24). Mahwah, NJ: Erlbaum.

Lawler, E. E. (1970). Job attitudes and employee motivation: Theory, research, and practice. *Personnel Psychology, 23,* 223–237.

LePine, J. A., Piccolo, R. F., Jackson, C. L., Mathieu, J. E., & Saul, J. R. (2008). A meta-analysis of teamwork processes: Tests of a multidimensional model and relationships with team effectiveness criteria. *Personnel Psychology, 61,* 273–307.

Lewin, K. (1935). *Dynamic theory of personality.* New York: McGraw-Hill.

Lievens, F., Tett, R. P., & Schleicher, D. J. (2009). Assessment centers at the crossroads: Toward a reconceptualization of assessment center exercises. *Research in Personnel and Human Resources Management, 28,* 99–152.

Locke, E. A. (1969). What is job satisfaction? *Organizational Behavior and Human Performance, 4,* 309–336.

Lodahl, T. M., & Kejner, M. (1965). The definition and measurement of job involvement. *Journal of Applied Psychology, 49,* 24–33.

Lord, R. G., & Brown, D. J. (2004). *Leadership processes and follower self-identity.* Mahwah, NJ: Erlbaum.

Lord, R. G., Brown, D. J., & Freiberg, S. J. (1999). Understanding the dynamics of leadership: The role of follower self-concepts in the leader/follower relationship. *Organizational Behavior and Human Decision Processes, 78,* 167–203.

Lord, R. G., De Vader, C. L., & Alliger, G. M. (1986). A meta-analysis of the relation between personality traits and leadership perceptions: An application of validity generalization procedures. *Journal of Applied Psychology, 71,* 402–409.

Lyness, K. S., & Heilman, M. E. (2006). When fit is fundamental: Performance evaluation and promotions of upper-level female and male managers. *Journal of Applied Psychology, 91,* 777–785.

Macey, W. H., & Schneider, B. (2008a). The meaning of employee engagement. *Industrial and Organizational Psychology: Perspectives on Science and Practice, 1,* 3–30.

Macey, W. H., & Schneider, B. (2008b). Engaged in engagement: We are delighted we did it. *Industrial and Organizational Psychology: Perspectives on Science and Practice, 1,* 76–83.

Maner, J. K., & Mead, N. L. (2010). The essential tension between leadership and power: When leaders sacrifice group goals for the sake of self-interest. *Journal of Personality and Social Psychology, 99,* 482–497.

Manz, C. C., & Sims, H. P., Jr. (1980). Self-management as a substitute for leadership: A social learning theory perspective. *Academy of Management Review, 5,* 361–367.

Manz, C. C., & Sims, H. P., Jr. (1987). Leading workers to lead themselves: The external leadership of self-managing work teams. *Administrative Science Quarterly, 32,* 106–129.

Marks, M. A., Mathieu, J. E., & Zaccaro, S. J. (2001). A temporally based framework and taxonomy of team processes. *Academy of Management Review, 26,* 356–376.

Mason, W. A., Conrey, F. R., & Smith, E. R. (2007). Situating social influence processes: Dynamic, multidirectional flows of influence within social networks. *Personality and Social Psychology Review, 11,* 279–300.

Mathieu, J. E., & Zajac, D. (1990). A review and meta-analysis of the antecedents, correlates, and consequences of organizational commitment. *Psychological Bulletin, 108,* 171–194.

McCrae, R. R., & Costa, P. T., Jr. (1996). Toward a new generation of personality theories: Theoretical contexts for the five-factor model. In J. S. Wiggins (Ed.), *The five-factor model of personality* (pp. 51–87). New York: Guilford.

McCrae, R. R., & Costa, P. T., Jr. (2003). *Personality in adulthood: A five-factor theory* (2nd ed.). New York: Guilford.

McGrath, J. E. (1962). *Leadership behavior: Some requirements for leadership training.* Washington, DC: U.S. Civil Service Commission, Office of Career Development.

McGrath, J. E. (1964). *Social psychology: A brief introduction.* New York: Holt, Rinehart, and Winston.

Mehra, A., Kilduff, M., & Brass, D. J. (2001). The social networks of high and low self-monitors: Implications for workplace performance. *Administrative Science Quarterly, 46,* 121–146.

Meyer, J. P. & Allen, N. J. (1990). Affective and continuance commitment to the organization: Evaluation of measures and analysis of concurrent and time-lagged relations. *Journal of Applied Psychology, 75,* 710–720.

Miner, J. B. (1992). *Industrial-organizational psychology.* New York: McGraw-Hill.

Mischel, W. (1973). Toward a cognitive social learning reconceptualization of personality. *Psychological Review, 80,* 252–283.

Morgeson, F. P., Campion, M. A., Dipboye, R. L., Hollenbeck, J. R., Murphy, K. R., & Schmitt, N. (2007). Reconsidering the use of personality tests in personnel selection contexts. *Personnel Psychology, 30,* 683–729.

Morgeson, F. P., DeRue, D. S., & Peterson, E. (2010). Leadership in teams: A functional approach to understanding leadership structures and processes. *Journal of Management, 36,* 5–39.

Morgeson, F. P., & Hofmann, D. A. (1999). The structure and function of collective constructs: Implications for multilevel research and theory development. *Academy of Management Review, 24,* 249–265.

Mount, M. K., & Barrick, M. R. (1995). The Big Five personality dimensions: Implications for research and practice in human resource management. *Research in Personnel and Human Resources Management, 13,* 153–200.

Mowday, R. T., & Sutton, R. I. (1993). Organizational behavior: Linking individuals and groups to organizational contexts. *Annual Review of Psychology, 44,* 195–229.

Muchinsky, P. M., & Monahan, C. J. (1987). What is person-environment congruence? Supplementary versus complementary models of fit. *Journal of Vocational Behavior, 31,* 268–277.

Murray, H. (1938). *Explorations in personality.* New York: Oxford University.

Nahrgang, J. D., Morgeson, F. P., & Ilies, R. (2009). The development of leader-member exchanges: Exploring how personality and performance influence leader and member relationships over time. *Organizational Behavior and Human Decision Processes, 108,* 256–266.

Newcomb, T. M. (1946). The influence of attitude climate upon some determinants of information. *Journal of Abnormal and Social Psychology, 41,* 291–302.

Newman, D. A., & Harrison, D. A. (2008). Been there, bottled that: Are state and behavioral work engagement new and useful construct "wines"? *Industrial and Organizational Psychology: Perspectives on Science and Practice, 1,* 31–35.

Norman, R. (1975). Affective-cognitive consistency, attitudes, conformity, and behavior. *Journal of Personality and Social Psychology, 32,* 83–91.

Organ, D. W., & Ryan, K. (1995). A meta-analytic review of attitudinal and dispositional predictors of organizational citizenship behaviors. *Personnel Psychology, 48,* 775–802.

Parker, C. P., Baltes, B. B., Young, S. A., Huff, J. W., Altmann, R. A., Lacost, H. A., et al. (2003). Relationships between psychological climate perceptions and work outcomes: A meta-analytic review. *Journal of Organizational Behavior, 24,* 389–416.

Podaskoff, N. P., LePine, J. A., & LePine, M. A. (2007). Differential challenge stressor–hindrance stressor relationships with job attitudes, turnover intentions, turnover, and withdrawal behavior: A meta-analysis. *Journal of Applied Psychology, 92,* 438–454.

Podaskoff, P. M., MacKenzie, S. B., & Bommer, W. H. (1996). Meta-analysis of the relationships between Kerr and Jermier's substitutes for leadership and employee job attitudes, role perceptions, and performance. *Journal of Applied Psychology, 81,* 380–399.

Porter, L. W., Steers, R. M., Mowday, R. T., Boulian, P. V. (1974). Organizational commitment, job satisfaction, and turnover among psychiatric technicians. *Journal of Applied Psychology, 59,* 603–609.

Parsons, F. (1909). *Choosing a vocation.* Boston: Houghton-Mifflin.

Pearce, C. L., & Conger, J. A. (2003). All those years ago: The historical underpinnings of shared leadership. In C. L. Pearce & J. A. Conger (Eds.), *Shared leadership: Reframing the hows and whys of leadership* (pp. 1–18). Thousand Oaks, CA: SAGE.

Pervin, L. A. (1968). Performance and satisfaction as a function of individual-environment fit. *Psychological Bulletin, 69,* 56–68.

Petty, M. M., McGee, G. W., & Cavender, J. W. (1984). A meta-analysis of the relationships between individual job satisfaction and individual performance. *Academy of Management Review, 9,* 712–721.

Rhoades, L. & Eisenberger, R. (2002). Perceived organizational support: A review of the literature. *Journal of Applied Psychology, 87,* 698–714.

Rosenberg, M. J., & Hovland, C. 1. (1960). Cognitive, affective, and behavioral components of attitude. In M. J. Rosenberg, C. I. Hovland, W. J. McGuire, R. P. Abelson, & W. J. Brehm (Eds.), *Attitude organization and change: An analysis of consistency among attitude components* (pp. 1–14). New Haven, CT: Yale University.

Rousseau, D. M. (1985). Issues of level in organizational research: Multi-level and cross-level perspectives. *Research in Organizational Behavior, 7,* 1–37.

Ryan, A. M., & Kristof-Brown, A. L. (2003). Personality's role in person-organization fit: Unresolved issues. In M. R. Barrick & A. M. Ryan (Eds.), *Personality and work* (pp. 262–288). San Francisco, CA: Jossey-Bass.

Salancik, G. R. & Pfeffer, J. (1978). A social information processing approach to job attitudes and task design. *Administrative Science Quarterly, 23,* 224–253.

Salas, E., Goodwin, G. F., & Burke, C. S. (Eds.). (2009). Team effectiveness in complex organizations: Cross-disciplinary perspectives and approaches. New York: Routledge.

Salas, E., Sims, D. E., & Burke, C. S. (2005). Is there a "Big Five" in teamwork? *Small Group Research, 36,* 555–599.

Salas, E., & Wildman, J. L. (2009). Ten critical research questions: The need for new and deeper explorations. In E. Salas, G. F. Goodwin & C. S. Burke (Eds.), *Team effectiveness in complex organizations: Cross-disciplinary perspectives and approaches* (pp. 525–546). New York: Routledge.

Schleicher, D. J., Watt, J. D., Greguras, G. J. (2004). Reexamining the job satisfaction-performance relationship: The complexity of attitudes. *Journal of Applied Psychology, 89,* 165–177.

Schneider, B. (1987). The people make the place. *Personnel Psychology, 40,* 437–453.

Schneider, B. (2001). Fits about fit. *Applied Psychology: An International Review, 50,* 141–152.

Schneider, B., Goldstein, H. W., & Smith, D. B. (1995). The ASA framework: An update. *Personnel Psychology, 48,* 747–773.

Shaw, M. E. (1976). *Group dynamics: The psychology of small group behavior* (2nd ed.). New York: McGraw-Hill.

Sidanius, J. & Pratto, F. (2001). *Social dominance: An intergroup theory of social hierarchy and oppression.* Cambridge: Cambridge University Press.

Smith, E. R., & Collins, E. C. (2009). Contextualizing person perception: Distributed social cognition. *Psychological Review, 116,* 343–364.

Smith, E. R., & Semin, G. R. (2004). Socially situated cognition: Cognition in its social context. *Advances in Experimental Social Psychology, 36,* 53–117.

Snyder, M. (1974). Self-monitoring of expressive behavior. *Journal of Personality and Social Psychology, 30,* 526–537.

Snyder, M., & Gangestad, S. W. (1986). On the nature of self-monitoring: Matters of assessment, matters of validity. *Journal of Personality and Social Psychology, 51,* 125–139.

Solinger, O. N., Olffen, W. V., & Roe, R. A. (2008). Beyond the three-component model of organizational commitment. *Journal of Applied Psychology, 93,* 70–83.

Spector, P. E. (1997). *Job satisfaction: Application, assessment, causes, and consequences.* Thousand Oaks, CA: Sage.

Spychalski, A. C., Quinones, M. A., Gaugler, B. B., & Pohley, K. A. (1997). A survey of assessment center practices in organizations in the United States. *Personnel Psychology, 50,* 71–90.

Staw, B. M., Bell, N. E., & Clausen, J. A. (1986). Stability in the midst of change: A dispositional approach to job attitudes. *Journal of Applied Psychology, 70,* 469–480.

Steiner, I. D. (1972). *Group process and productivity.* New York: Academic.

Taylor, H. C., & Russell, J. T. (1939). The relationship of validity coefficients to the practical effectiveness of tests in selection. *Journal of Applied Psychology, 23,* 565–578.

Tett, R. P., & Burnett, D. D. (2003). A personality trait-based interactionist model of job performance. *Journal of Applied Psychology, 88,* 500–517.

Tett, R. P., & Guterman, H. A. (2000). Situation trait relevance, trait expression, and cross-situational consistency: Testing a principle of trait activation. *Journal of Research in Personality, 34,* 397–423.

Tett, R. P., Jackson, D. N., & Rothstein, M. (1991). Personality measures as predictors of job performance: A meta-analytic review. *Personnel Psychology, 44,* 703–742.

Thomas, C. H. (2007). A new measurement scale for employee engagement: Scale development, pilot test, and replication. *Academy of Management Proceedings,* 1–6.

Thoresen, C. J., Kaplan, S. A., & Barsky, A. P., Warren, C. R., de Chermont, K. (2003). The affective underpinnings of job perceptions and attitudes: A meta-analytic review and integration. *Psychological Bulletin, 129,* 914–945.

Thornton, G. C., III, & Rupp, D. E. (2005). *Assessment centers in human resources management.* Mahwah, NJ: Erlbaum.

Trevino, L. K. (1986). Ethical decision making in organizations: A person-situation interactionist model. *Academy of Management Review, 11,* 601–617.

Tsui, A. S., & O'Reilly, C. A., III. (1989). Beyond simple demographic effects: The importance of relational demography in superior-subordinate dyads. *Academy of Management Journal, 32,* 402–423.

Viswesvaran, C., Sanchez, J. I., & Fisher, J. (1999). The role of social support in the process of work stress: A meta-analysis. *Journal of Vocational Behavior, 54,* 314–334.

Warr, P. (2007). Some historical developments in I-O psychology outside the United States. In L. L. Koppes (Ed.), *Historical perspectives in industrial and organizational psychology* (pp. 81–107). Mahwah, NJ: Erlbaum.

Weber, M. (1924/1947). *The theory of social and economic organization* (T. Parsons & A. M. Henderson, Trans.). New York: Oxford University.

Wegner, D. M. (1995). A computer network model of human transactive memory. *Social Cognition, 13,* 319–339.

Weiss, H. M. (2002). Deconstructing job satisfaction: Separating evaluations, beliefs, and affective experiences. *Human Resource Management Review, 12,* 173–194.

Weiss, H. M. & Cropanzano, R. (1996). Affective events theory: A theoretical discussion of the structure, causes, and consequences of affective experiences at work. *Research in Organizational Behavior, 18,* 1–74.

Whetten, D. A., Felin, T., & King, B. G. (2009). The practice of theory borrowing in organizational studies: Current issues and future directions. *Journal of Management, 35,* 537–563.

Wiggins, J. S., & Trapnell, P. D. (1996). A dyadic-interactional perspective on the Five-Factor Model. In J. S. Wiggins (Ed.), *The five-factor model of personality: Theoretical perspectives* (pp. 88–162). New York: Guildford.

Wuchty, S., Jones, B. F., & Uzzi, B. (2007, May 18). The increasing dominance of teams in the production of knowledge. *Science, 316,* 1036–1038.

Yukl, G. (1999). An evaluation of conceptual weaknesses in transformational and charismatic leadership theories. *Leadership Quarterly, 10,* 285–305.

Zaccaro, S. J., Rittman, A. L., & Marks, M. A. (2001). Team leadership. *Leadership Quarterly, 12,* 451–483.

Zickar, M. J., & Gibby, R. E. (2007). Four persistent themes throughout the history of I-O psychology in the United States. In L. L. Koppes (Ed.), *Historical perspectives in industrial and organizational psychology* (pp. 61–80). Mahwah, NJ: Erlbaum.

A Person x Intervention Strategy Approach to Understanding Health Behavior

Alexander J. Rothman *and* Austin S. Baldwin

Abstract

In this chapter, we suggest that an integration of perspectives from personality and social psychology (i.e., a person x intervention strategy framework) provides a rich context in which to explore more precise specifications of the mediators and moderators that guide health behavior and decision-making. To that end, we first discuss how conceptualizations of moderated mediation and mediated moderation can enrich theory and serve to enumerate specific principles to guide the development and dissemination of more effective health behavior interventions. Second, we review research from four different literatures that rely on a similar person x intervention strategy framework—that is, the effectiveness of an intervention strategy depends on the degree to which it matches features of the target person—to examine evidence for the processes that mediate the effect of this moderated intervention approach. Finally, we describe how a more systematic analysis of the interplay between mediating and moderating processes can stimulate advances in theory, intervention research, and practice of health behavior.

Keywords: health behavior, intervention matching, mediation, moderation

Despite continuing awareness that the behavioral choices people make have a dramatic effect on rates of morbidity and mortality, data both in the United States and across the world continue to paint a discouraging picture and pose a vexing problem for researchers and practitioners (e.g., Mokdad, Marks, Stroup, & Gerberding, 2004). For example, the explosive growth in rates of obesity in the United States over the past 20 years (Flegal, Carroll, Ogden, & Curtin, 2010; Ogden et al., 2006) reflect patterns of poor dietary choices combined with insufficient rates of physical activity . There is little doubt that the factors that shape people's health behaviors are complex and reflect the operation of systems at the individual, interpersonal, and structural level. For example, people's eating habits are affected by structural features of the environment in which they live (e.g., Brownell & Horgan, 2004; French et al., 2001), interpersonal interactions with friends and

strangers (e.g., Christakis & Fowler, 2007), and the intrapsychic and biological systems that regulate experiences of satiety and enjoyment (e.g., Blundell et al., 2005; Wardle & Carnell, 2009). Given the complexity of the factors that regulate people's health behavior, theoretical models are needed that provide a framework that can not only integrate these empirical observations, but also leverage them to generate a set of principles that guide practice.

As investigators develop and test basic principles regarding the determinants of people's health practices, it is essential that we capitalize on the findings that emerge from this work and enable them to inform the design and evaluation of intervention strategies to promote healthy behavior (Glanz & Bishop, 2010; Michie, Rothman, & Sheeran, 2007; Rothman & Salovey, 2007). The specification of theoretical principles provides important guidance to behavioral intervention design as these principles specify the constructs that need to be altered in order to promote healthy behavior. Thus, careful consideration must be given to the degree of correspondence between an intervention strategy and the theoretical principles on which it is grounded (Michie & Prestwich, 2010). Yet, the transition from theory to practice has not proven to be seamless and is often constrained by the nature of the information provided by the theory (Rothman, 2004). Theories that specify constructs that predict behavior provide necessary but not sufficient information to guide intervention design. Conceptualized within the framework of a mediational model that is comprised of links between an intervention and a construct (i.e., mediator) and between a construct and an outcome, a theory that provides guidance regarding only the determinants of behavior can inform only the latter portion of the mediational model (i.e., the relation between the putative mediator and an outcome). In order to design an effective intervention strategy, investigators need guidance regarding how to affect change in the targeted construct (i.e., the first portion of the mediational model) and information about in which settings and for which types of people the construct is likely to be particularly important (Jeffery, 2004; Rothman, 2004). Framed somewhat more broadly, the successful interplay between theory and practice rests on the accurate specification of the mediators and moderators that guide health behavior and health decision-making.

Basic principles in both social and personality psychology have provided an important theoretical foundation for understanding the psychological processes that regulate people's health practices. In social psychology, a substantial number of models have been proposed that delineate the psychological states that guide people's behavior (e.g., health belief model; Rosenstock, Strecher, & Becker, 1988; precaution adoption process model; Weinstein, 1988; protection motivation theory; Maddux & Rogers, 1983; social cognitive theory; Bandura, 1986; theory of planned behavior; Ajzen, 1991; theory of reasoned action; Ajzen & Fishbein, 1980; transtheoretical model of behavior change; Prochaska et al., 1992; for a review and comparison of different models, see Conner & Norman, 2005; Salovey et al., 1998; Sutton, 2002; Weinstein, 1993). Although these models may differ in the specific constructs thought to be most closely associated with behavior, they are all grounded on the assumption that the constructs identified in a given model represent mechanisms that may facilitate or inhibit

healthy behavioral practices. Thus, the mechanisms serve as the targets for interventions designed to promote behavior change.

However, the implication of many of these models is that the mechanisms that facilitate or inhibit healthy behavior change (i.e., the targets for intervention) are assumed to be constant across people and time, and interventions guided by these models have generally assumed a "one size fits all" approach to intervention design. This state of affairs reflects the fact that these models provide a rich description of factors that could serve as mediators of behavior change, but are largely silent regarding factors that delimit the influence of these putative mediators (i.e., moderators). Thus, investigators are given limited theoretical guidance regarding the applicability of basic principles across people or settings. One exception to this perspective are stage models of behavior change (e.g., precaution adoption process model, or PAPM; Weinstein, 1988; transtheoretical model of behavior change, or TTM; Prochaska et al., 1992), which propose that the factors that facilitate behavior depend on where people are in the behavior change process, providing investigators with the opportunity to develop intervention strategies that match a person's stage. Yet, even these models are limited in the degree to which the linkages between mediators and moderators are specified.

The observation that individual differences in personality prospectively predict rates of morbidity and mortality (Martin et al., 2007; Hampson et al., 2006; Friedman et al., 1995; Lahey, 2009) has led to the emergence of models that delineate the linkages between personality and health. However, identifying a clear, direct effect of personality on health behavior has proven to be elusive (Christensen, 2004; Smith, 2006). One reason for this is because the effect of personality on health is likely to occur through multiple systems; yet there has been considerable interest in the premise that specific personality traits serve to promote or inhibit healthy behavior (Bogg & Roberts, 2004; Booth-Kewley & Vickers, 1994). Within this framework, personality serves as a risk- or protective-factor depending on the trait and the behavioral outcome in question. In contrast to social psychological models of health behavior, models of personality and health provide a rich description of who engages in a particular pattern of behavior, but offers limited guidance regarding mechanisms that could serve as targets for intervention.

Some investigators have begun to specify predictions regarding the psychological states–typically derived from social psychological models of health behavior such as TPB (Ajzen, 1991)—that underlie the association between traits and behavior, and these efforts can be roughly categorized into two approaches (e.g., Conner et al., 2009; De Bruijn et al., 2009; Rhodes, 2006). In one case, personality is construed as a determinant of the beliefs (e.g., attitudes toward the behavior; self-efficacy) that, in turn, operate as more proximal predictors of behavior, whereas in the other case, personality is thought to alter the manner or degree to which beliefs affect behavior (e.g., amplifying or minimizing the effect of intention on behavior). For instance, people who score high on conscientiousness may engage in healthy behavior because they tend to hold more favorable attitudes about the behavior (an instance of the first approach) and/or because they are better able to translate their intentions to act into actual behavior (an instance of the second approach).

We think that integrating the perspectives afforded by both a social and a personality-based analysis of health behavior is a promising strategy as, taken together, these approaches provide a more complete theoretical roadmap for intervention design than either on its own. The psychological processes specified in models of health behavior provide investigators with a list of potential targets for intervention (e.g., social cognitive theory suggests that self-efficacy should be targeted)—mediating processes that could be altered strategically to increase healthy behavior and decrease unhealthy behavior—and, in some cases, guidance regarding strategies that could be use to elicit change. An individual difference perspective affords the opportunity to consider the operation of these processes in a more refined manner as it introduces the question as to whether and/or when these processes operate in a consistent manner across people. For example, to the extent that people who are low in conscientiousness have difficulty translating their intentions into behavior, they should particularly benefit from an intervention strategy that focuses on that aspect of the behavior change process (e.g., Conner et al., 2009). To the extent that investigators are encouraged to consider systematically factors that may moderate the impact of different intervention strategies on behavior and behavioral decision-making, they have adopted the analytic framework of the person x situation (P x S) perspective that has fruitfully informed our understanding of behavior in a myriad of domains (Mischel & Shoda, 1995; Snyder & Ickes, 1985; Snyder & Cantor, 1998). In the present case, however, the emphasis is on the experience

afforded by an intervention strategy as the defining aspect of the situation. Thus, we propose person x intervention strategy (P x IS) as a modified label for this framework to capture the emphasis on intervention strategies.

To date, although investigators have not always characterized their work this way, there are several lines of research on intervention strategies to promote healthy behavior that could be categorized under the heading of a P x IS approach. Research on message framing, message tailoring, stage models, and treatment matching have all examined the premise that the effectiveness of a specific intervention strategy depends on the degree to which it fits with or corresponds to features of the target person. For example, research on message framing has shown that messages that emphasize the costs of not engaging in a health behavior (e.g., not getting a mammogram) are more effective for people who are dispositionally sensitive to negative outcomes, whereas messages that emphasize the benefits of engaging in a health behavior (e.g., getting a mammogram) are more effective for people who are dispositionally sensitive to positive outcomes (Rothman & Updegraff, 2011). Although these four different programs of research share several features, there have been limited attempts to examine them as a whole and, in particular, to discern whether they rely on a shared set of underlying psychological processes. We believe that drawing comparisons across these different lines of research will help to elucidate the degree to which these P x IS approaches rely on similar mediational processes. Moreover, given that the effectiveness of these intervention strategies is predicated on the status of individual-level moderators such as personality, this analysis provides an opportunity to better specify the interdependence of mediators and moderators, an approach that can be grounded in emerging conceptual and statistical work on mediated moderation and moderated mediation (Muller et al., 2005).

In this chapter, we examine these issues in the following manner. First, we examine the emerging perspectives on the interplay between mediation and moderation and its implications for specifying and testing theory-based intervention strategies. In particular, we address how the conceptual frameworks afforded by mediated moderation and moderated mediation can be used by investigators to guide the design, application, and dissemination of interventions to promote healthy behavior. Second, we review and compare how different research programs that are grounded on a P x IS framework have approached specifying and testing the psychological processes that are predicted to underlie these moderated intervention effects. Finally, we consider how a more focused analysis of the interplay between mediation and moderation—mediated moderation and moderated mediation—could provide a generative framework to guide future work in this area that could inform both theory and practice.

Forging a Tighter Connection Between Mediation and Moderation

As investigators work to specify how, where, and for whom a particular phenomenon occurs, they are striving to delineate the parameters that mediate (how) and moderate (where, for whom) the observed outcome. Mediators describe the processes through which an intervention influences an observed outcome and thus their status is affected by the intervention (i.e., Independent Variable [IV]→Mediator) and, in turn, the mediators affect the status of the outcome (i.e., Mediator→Dependent Variable [DV]). Moderators are constructs independent of the intervention that affect the magnitude and, at times, the direction of the effect the intervention has on the outcome (i.e., the observed outcome is a function of an interaction between the moderator and the intervention). To date, the literature has emphasized differentiating between moderators and mediators (see Baron& Kenny, 1986; Kraemer et al., 2008; MacKinnon, 2008). One unintended consequence of this emphasis is that investigators tend to focus on either mediators or moderators and too rarely examine how mediators can provide insights about moderators and vice versa.

To the extent that mediators and moderators are the building blocks of theory, engaging the interplay between mediators and moderators is at the heart of developing, testing, and refining theory (McGuire, 1989; Rothman, 2004). For example, specifying the mediational process that underlies the effect of an intervention on an outcome provides a framework for generating hypotheses regarding potential moderators as it enables investigators to generate hypotheses about factors that might augment or impair the underlying process. And in a similar manner, evidence that an intervention works only for certain people or in certain situations is in essence a clue that the underlying process is affected by some aspect of the moderating factor and thus provides a framework for generating hypotheses about mediational processes that might operate differentially across types of people or situations. In order to pursue these hypotheses, however, investigators need an analytic framework that can guide their work. The emergence of statistical techniques that allow investigators to test models that simultaneously engage both mediation and moderation provides this framework (e.g., Fairchild & MacKinnon, 2009; Muller et al., 2005; Preacher, Rucker, & Hayes, 2007). With these models of mediated moderation and moderated mediation, investigators have a conceptual and statistical framework to guide a program of research that affords better specification of interventions and theory. It is to these two models that we turn.

Mediated Moderation

Imagine a situation where an intervention strategy (e.g., the delivery of a loss-framed message about dental care and dental health) elicits a behavioral outcome (e.g., greater rates of flossing), but the magnitude of this effect is contingent on a baseline characteristic of the target population (e.g., people's sensitivity to negative outcomes). In this case, one would report that the benefit of providing a loss-framed appeal is moderated by people's sensitivity to negative outcomes (Mann et al., 2004). Although the interaction between the person-level characteristic and the intervention strategy is evidence of moderation, it does not address the question of mediation—that is, why do people who are more sensitive to negative outcomes respond more favorably to a loss-framed appeal? Mediated moderation provides a framework for articulating and testing the mediational process that underlies the observed moderated effect and allows investigators to answer questions regarding what processes lead to the observed moderated treatment effect (see Mueller et al., 2005 for a detailed description of the underlying statistical issues).

Figure 29.1 provides a graphical representation of an intervention effect (Path A) that is moderated and the two paths (B and C) that would comprise the underlying mediational process. In specifying the underlying mediational process one can distinguish between two distinct ways in which the moderator affects the impact of the intervention on behavior. In one case, the moderated treatment effect may reflect the fact that the moderator alters the intervention's ability to affect the status of a putative mediator (see Figure 29.1a, Option I). For example, it could be that when the tone of a loss-framed message does not match a person's dispositional style that person does not feel sufficiently engaged or interested in the health issue (which, in turn, would guide that person's behavior). In this

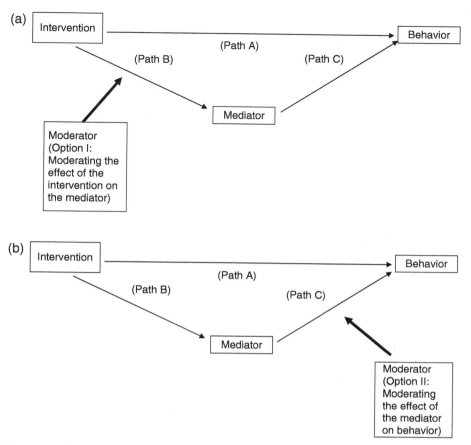

Fig. 29.1 Understanding the interplay between moderators and mediators: (a) Moderating the effect of the intervention on the mediator, (b) Moderating the effect of the mediator on the outcome.

case, the reason why the intervention led to behavior change for some people and not others can be attributed to the intervention strategy's differential ability to elicit change in the mediator (Path B). Moreover, given that the moderator in this example did not alter the relation between the putative mediator and the outcome (Path C), the investigator can assume that if an intervention strategy could be designed that elicits interest or engagement among people who are not particularly sensitive to negative outcomes, it would be effective. In the end, evidence that the moderator's influence is localized to the path linking the intervention and the mediator (Path B) should indicate to investigators that they are faced with *an intervention challenge*. We characterize this as an intervention issue because the investigator is faced with the need to identify and design a new intervention strategy that can elicit a change in the mediator for the group or setting who are currently unaffected. In fact, investigators have found that gain-framed appeals are an effective way

to promote behavior change for people who are not sensitive to negative outcomes. The observation that messages are more effective when the frame matches a person's dispositional sensitivity to negative or positive outcomes is an excellent illustration of how different intervention strategies delivered strategically to particular people may utilize the same mediational process.

Alternatively, the moderated treatment effect may reflect the fact that the moderator altered the relation between the putative mediator and the behavioral outcome (see Figure 29.1b, Option II). Although the intervention strategy elicits a change in the mediator for everyone (i.e., regardless of their standing on the moderator, people who received the framed message feel engaged with or interested in the issue), the manner with which change in the putative mediator (e.g., greater engagement) translates into change in behavior (Path C) depends on the moderator. In this situation, investigators are confronted with *a theoretical challenge* as the predicted relation between the mediator and the outcome does not hold across setting or group. We characterize this as a theoretical issue because the data indicate that investigators need a more complex set of theoretical principles to describe how the determinants of a behavior vary across groups of people or settings. To move forward, refinements must be made to the theoretical model that can account for variation in the underlying process and these refinements will, in turn, provide a basis for designing new interventions. For instance, investigators may find that an intervention strategy is needed that targets a different set of behavioral determinants, or alternatively an intervention strategy is needed to target factors that otherwise inhibit the influence of the initial hypothesized mediator on the outcome.

Distinguishing between these two variations of mediated moderation should prove to be particularly useful for investigators because it serves to highlight the specific theoretical and practical challenges that need to be addressed in future work.

Moderated Mediation

With mediated moderation, investigators are able to test why an intervention may have worked for some people or in some settings but not for or in others. The focus is on delineating a single mediational path (as illustrated in Figure 29.1). However, it is possible that an intervention strategy affects the behavior of all members of the target population (i.e., there is a direct effect of the intervention on a behavioral outcome; see Path A, Figure 29.2), but the process underlying this effect differs across people.[1] The premise that the specific mediational path that links an intervention and an outcome depends on the status of a moderator is what is captured by tests of moderated mediation. Traditionally, investigators have assumed that an intervention operates through a single, consistent mediational path (although that path might involve several mediational steps) and thus have structured their research designs and statistical analyses to test that path. The advent of moderated mediation provides investigators with a framework within which to not only conceptualize but also test hypotheses regarding mediational paths that operate systematically for specific groups of people or in specific settings.

Under what conditions might moderated mediation be a plausible outcome? One likely candidate would be an intervention with multiple components, where classes of individuals might be differentially responsive to different facets of the intervention. This might be particularly germane for investigators who are testing an intervention

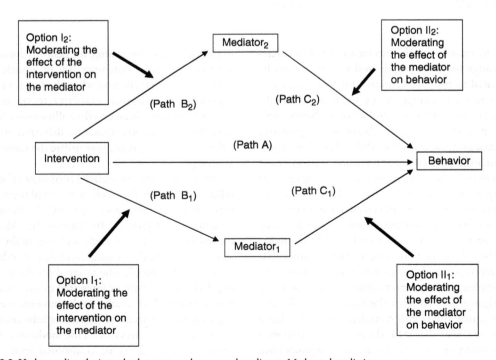

Fig. 29.2 Understanding the interplay between moderators and mediators: Moderated mediation.

that is grounded in a stage model of health behavior (e.g., TTM; Prochaska & Velicer, 1997; or PAPM; Weinstein, 1988). A stage model assumes that people at different stages in the behavior change process are responsive to a particular set of determinants and thus an intervention strategy must be stage-matched to be effective (see Weinstein, Rothman, & Sutton, 1998, for a conceptual overview of stage models). For example, Weinstein (1988) proposes that different strategies should be directed at people who know about a health problem but have not yet decided whether to act (Stage 1) and people who have decided to act but have not yet taken action (Stage 2). Imagine that an intervention was designed to include intervention strategies that target the needs of people in both of these stages. In this case, there would be aspects of the intervention that would both match and mismatch the needs of people at each of the two stages. For people who are undecided (i.e., Stage 1), the stage-matched aspect of the intervention strategy would elicit a change in the putative mediator (illustrated by $Mediator_1$ in Figure 29.2) which in turn would elicit a transition to the next stage, Stage 2. The stage-mismatched aspect of the intervention strategy would be expected to elicit no change in the second mediator for people in Stage 1. For people who have decided to act (i.e., Stage 2), the stage-matched aspect of the intervention strategy would elicit a change in the putative mediator, which in this case would be $Mediator_2$ (see Figure 29.2) and change in this mediator would, in turn, elicit a transition to the next stage, Stage 3. The stage-mismatched aspect of the intervention strategy would be expected to elicit no change in the first mediator for people in Stage 2. The development of appropriate strategies for testing predictions derived from stage models has proven to be challenging for investigators (see Herzog, 2008). Moderated mediation may provide a useful guide for developing new ways to approach and test these questions.

Within a moderated mediation framework, investigators can also distinguish among several different patterns of results that may have unique implications for both theory and practice. In one case, the moderator may target the links between the intervention strategy and the putative mediators (e.g., Paths B_1 and B_2 in Figure 29.2). Here the nature of the impact of the intervention is predicated on the differential influence it has on the mediators—what we will term *selective influence*. However, the relation between the two mediators and the outcome is consistent across all levels of the moderator. As we noted in our discussion of mediated moderation, this pattern of findings would be indicative of *an intervention challenge*.

In the other case, the moderator may target the links between the putative mediators and the outcome (e.g., Paths C_1 and C_2 in Figure 29.2). Here the intervention is observed to have a similar influence on the two mediators regardless of a person's status on the moderator (i.e., stage). Instead the impact of the intervention is predicated on the differential predictive power of the two mediators—what we will term *selective prediction*. As we noted in our discussion of mediated moderation, this pattern of findings would be indicative of *a theoretical challenge*. However, a more precise understanding of the specific constructs that guide behavior for different classes of people will also have important implications for intervention design as it will help investigators target the application of different intervention strategies.

Implications for Current Intervention Approaches

Mediated moderation and moderated mediation provide conceptual and statistical frameworks for thinking about the interplay between mediators and moderators. Although these frameworks are clearly applicable to intervention strategies that are predicated on matching the intervention to a particular person or classes of people, investigators have yet to capitalize on these connections. Questions regarding the mediational processes that may underlie the effect of matched intervention strategies have tended to focus narrowly on tests of mediation and, in doing so, may miss opportunities to capture how the factors that specify the match between the intervention and the person may have implications for how the intervention strategy ultimately elicits changes in the targeted outcome. With this perspective in mind, we now turn to a review of four different approaches that investigators have used to develop matched intervention strategies and the evidence that has accrued regarding underlying mediational processes. After considering the state of these literatures, we will return to models of mediated moderation and moderated mediation and their implications for future work in this area.

Matching Intervention Strategies to People: an Overview of Different Approaches

Health-related matching interventions provide information, strategies, or treatment approaches that are targeted to a specific group of people, or tailored to individuals based on characteristics that are specific to the individual. For example, as previously mentioned, various studies have shown that framing health information in terms of what people stand to gain by engaging in healthy behaviors (i.e., gain-framed messages) is more effective in changing behavior for people who are dispositionally oriented toward attaining positive outcomes, whereas framing information in terms of what people stand to lose by failing to engage in healthy behaviors proves to be more effective in changing the behavior of people who are dispositionally oriented toward avoiding negative outcomes (e.g., Cesario, Grant, & Higgins, 2004; Latimer et al., 2008; Mann, Sherman, & Updegraff, 2004). Given that people vary in their preferences about a variety of health-related behaviors, such as whether they walk, bike, or swim to get their exercise, or whether it is important that the doctor they see has "good bedside manner" or not, the idea of matching health-related interventions to specific individuals or groups seems to have considerable intuitive appeal. Moreover, there is evidence that this approach can be an effective way to change people's beliefs and behaviors across a wide range of health-related contexts (e.g., Cesario, Grant, & Higgins, 2004; Christensen, Moran, Lawton, Stallman, & Voigts, 1997; Kreuter, Bull, Clark, & Oswald, 1999; Weinstein, Lyon, Sandman, & Cuite, 1998). The effectiveness of a matching approach to health-related interventions rests on the notion that some intervention strategies will work best for some types of people, whereas different intervention strategies will work best for others—what we have labeled a P x IS approach. Underlying this premise is the assumption that a "matched" intervention strategy is a more effective way to alter the mechanism or mediator targeted by the intervention to promote behavior.

Although these diverse approaches to matching are based on a similar P x IS framework, they have largely arisen in separate research literatures. As a consequence, it is currently unclear whether there is a core set of mediating processes that might explain why a diverse set of matching interventions, across a wide range of behaviors and contexts, are effective. By examining a diverse set of findings that rest on a similar framework, we can elucidate patterns of similarities and differences in the evidence for mediational processes thought to underlie the effect of different matching interventions. These patterns may also reveal associations between mediational mechanisms and the moderators or classes of moderators that are used to specify the match between intervention and the target person. Taken together,

this analysis should provide a basis for synthesizing the findings across these literatures in a way that moves work on matched interventions forward.

We identified empirical studies that tested some type of matching intervention in a health domain. Specifically, we reviewed interventions that involved matching messages to different types of behavioral construals (i.e., message framing), different personality traits, and specific individuals (i.e., message tailoring, message framing), as well as interventions designed to match to people at different stages of behavior change or to deliver treatments to patients with different treatment preferences. Within each literature, we focused on papers that met two criteria: first, the paper addressed a health-related matching effect, and second, the paper proposed a mediating process through which the matching effect is thought to occur. Our goal was not to conduct an exhaustive review of the respective literatures, but instead to identify papers within each literature where the authors explicitly attempted to elucidate the proposed mediating processes. The number of these exemplar papers varied across the different literatures.

Our review of the evidence for mediational processes proposed in each literature was guided by four criteria. First, we determined whether there was empirical evidence for the proposed mediational pathways. Specifically, we looked for evidence that the matching intervention produces an effect on the proposed mediating variable (an IV-MV relation), evidence of a relation between the mediator and the dependent variable (an MV-DV relation), and for evidence that the proposed mediating variable accounts for the matching effect on the dependent variable (an IV-MV-DV relation).

Second, we distinguished between two types of evidence for mediation: measurement-of-mediation evidence and moderation-of-process evidence (see Spencer, Zanna, & Fong, 2005, for a detailed discussion of the differences among different approaches to mediation). In short, measurement-of-mediation evidence exists when the proposed MV is measured, and that measured variable is used in a test of the indirect effect of the IV on the DV. In contrast, moderation-of-process evidence exists when the effect of the IV on the DV occurs only under conditions in which the mediating process is likely to occur. This approach is conceptually similar to the framework underlying mediated moderation, but the mediating variable is not measured. Instead, the evidence for mediation is based on a series of logical arguments and experimental manipulations to create the expected conditions.

The primary strength of the measurement-of-mediation approach is that the entire mediational pathway is measured and can be subjected to a statistical test to assess the indirect effect through the MV. The primary weakness of this approach is that the MV-DV relation is correlational, even in randomized interventions where the IV-MV and IV-DV relations are causal (Bullock, Green, & Ha, 2010). Although study design can address the temporal precedent limitation of correlational data, there is always the possibility that another, unmeasured variable is causing the effect evident in the correlation. The primary strength of the moderation-of-process evidence is that conditions under which the process is thought to occur can be experimentally manipulated, and thus causal claims about the process can be made. As Spencer et al. (2005) note, this strength rests on the quality and coherence of the underlying theoretical arguments. The primary weakness of this approach is that because the MV is not measured, it is impossible to subject the mediational pathway to a statistical test to assess the indirect effect, and thus it remains unclear whether the matched intervention is affecting the proposed mediating process or some other process that is also unmeasured.

Third, we differentiated between evidence that is based on interventions to which people have been randomized and evidence that is based on nonexperimental matching. For example, consider the hypothesis that patients who prefer a doctor who has a "good bedside manner" will have better treatment outcomes when they are treated by a physician who has good interpersonal skills. The question could be addressed by randomizing patients with varying preferences for physician-style to physicians with varying degrees of interpersonal skill (randomized matching) or by examining treatment outcomes of patients who happen to see physicians who either do or do not match their preferred style (nonrandomized matching). The limitations of drawing causal inferences from nonrandomized matching are the same as with any type of nonrandomized design. In addition, the limitations of drawing causal inferences about the relation between the MV and the DV are also still present in a randomized matching intervention. However, in a randomized matching intervention, causal inferences can be drawn about the effect of the matching on the proposed mediational process and outcomes.

Finally, we differentiated between evidence of a mediational effect on people's beliefs, and evidence that demonstrated an effect on people's behavior.

Although a mediational effect on people's beliefs, attitudes, or behavioral intentions may provide compelling evidence for a theoretical principle, in the domain of health and illness, the ultimate value of delineating the mediational processes of a matching intervention rests on the ability of the processes to explain people's behavior.

In reviewing the exemplar papers from each literature, there were four different (but not mutually exclusive) processes that were offered as putative mediators of matched interventions. These four classes of processes echo those that were proposed by McGuire (1968) in his classic examination of the interplay between personality and persuasion. Specifically, investigators have emphasized the acquisition of information (learning), the evaluation and construal of information (perception, consistency), and the utility of information (function).

First, a variety of investigators have suggested that compared to nonmatched interventions, matched interventions elicit greater attention among the intervention recipients and more thorough processing of the relevant information (Kreuter, Bull, Clark, & Oswald, 1999; Oenema, Tan, & Brug, 2005; Ruiter, Kessels, Jansma, & Brug, 2006; Updegraff, Sherman, Luyster, & Mann, 2007). It is thought that these forms of enhanced cognitive processing result in behavior change because it increases the likelihood that the information communicated in the intervention is encoded and, over time, will remain salient and accessible in people's minds. Second, some investigators have suggested that matching interventions evoke biased (i.e., more favorable) cognitive processing from recipients (Adams, Norman, Hovell, Sallis, & Patrick, 2009; Carmack Taylor et al., 2006; Kreuter, Bull, Clark, & Oswald, 1999; Pinto, Lynn, Marcus, DePue, & Goldstein, 2001; Rothman, Martino, Bedell, Detweiler, & Salovey, 1999). In other words, people are more likely to construe and evaluate matched information more favorably and these responses will guide subsequent behavior. Third, investigators have suggested that when intervention material "fits" people's motivational and self-regulatory orientations it is easier for them to process, and this sense of fluency leads people to feel right or good about the message or treatment, which in turn increases the emphasis or weight placed on the intervention material (Cesario, Grant, & Higgins, 2004; Christensen, 2000; Christensen, Moran, Lawton, Stallman, & Voigts, 1997; Latimer, Rivers, Rench, Katulak, Hicks, Hodorowski, et al., 2008; Sherman, Mann, Updegraff, 2006; Spiegel, Grant-Pillow, & Higgins, 2004). Fourth, investigators have suggested that some types of matching interventions work because the information provided meets people's specific needs (e.g., the right kind of information) based on what stage they find themselves in a behavior change process (Adams et al., 2009; Carmack Taylor et al., 2006; Pinto et al., 2001; Weinstein, Lyon, Sandman, & Cuite, 1998). Thus, people are more likely to change their behavior when they receive information (or treatment) that is most relevant to them at a given point in time. Our review will focus on the existing evidence for these four processes as putative mediators of matched interventions.

Message Framing

The content of health messages and communications can be framed in terms of what people stand to gain by engaging in a health behavior (a gain-framed message) or in terms of what people stand to lose if they fail to engage in a health behavior (a loss-framed message). In order to determine how and when gain- and loss-framed messages should be used, investigators have worked to enumerate the personal and situational factors that moderate the impact of each frame. In particular, two general perspectives have emerged regarding *when* loss- and gain-framed messages are maximally effective. One view has emphasized how people's construal of the targeted health behavior as risky and uncertain versus safe and certain moderates the impact of framed appeals (Rothman & Salovey, 1997; Rothman et al., 2008). The other view has emphasized how people's dispositional sensitivity to favorable or unfavorable outcomes moderates the impact of framed appeals (Mann, Sherman, & Updegraff, 2004). In both cases, research has emphasized that a gain- or loss-framed appeal will be maximally effective when it matches people's underlying construal of the issue at hand (Rothman & Updegraff, 2011).

MATCHING FRAMES TO THE PERCEPTION OF THE BEHAVIOR

A great deal of attention has been paid to how differences in how people perceive a health behavior moderate the effectiveness of framed appeals. In particular, investigators have focused on differences in how people construe the risk or uncertainty posed by engaging in the behavior (Rothman & Salovey, 1997; Rothman et al., 2008). From this perspective, gain-framed messages are thought to be most effective in changing behaviors that are construed to pose minimal risk (e.g., preventive behaviors like using sunscreen), whereas loss-framed messages are thought to be most effective in changing behaviors

that are construed to pose some risk (e.g., detection behaviors like cancer screening; for a recent review, see Rothman & Updegraff, 2011). However, little attention has been paid to the mediational processes that would explain why matching framed messages to how people construe the behaviors produces behavior change. We identified two papers that proposed and tested a mediational process to explain the effect of matching framed messages to different types of behaviors (Gerend, Shephard, & Monday, 2008; Rothman et al., 1999). In both cases, the authors proposed that when a framed message matched the perceived riskiness of the behavior, it would result in a form of biased cognitive processing such that people would think more positively about the message and the advocated behavior, and would perceive a heightened sense of susceptibility to the health problem. In addition, the matching of message frames in the studies reported in both papers was done experimentally.

In both studies, there was evidence for an IV-MV-DV relation, and in both cases this relation was tested using a measurement-of-mediation approach. Specifically, matched framed messages led to more favorable thoughts and attitudes about the behavior (i.e., screening for gum disease; Rothman et al., 1999) and to a heightened sense of susceptibility to the relevant health threat (i.e., human papillomavirus; Gerend et al., 2008). However, in both studies, evidence for mediation was limited to conditions that revealed a loss-framed advantage (i.e., when a behavior screened for a health problem, Rothman et al., 1999; when uncertainty was high, Gerend et al., 2008). Although the evidence is limited to two studies, it suggests the possibility that the effect of matching loss-framed messages with behaviors that are construed as risky is mediated by these cognitive processes, whereas the match between gain-framed messages and non-risky/certain behaviors may be mediated by another process that was not specified or tested. However, it is important to note that in both studies, the mediational effects were evident only when people's behavioral intentions were the outcome variable.

MATCHING FRAMES TO PERSONALITY

A second line of research on message framing has emphasized matching the delivery of framed health messages so that the tone or the emphasis of the message matches people's underlying dispositional tendencies. For example, people differ in the extent to which they are dispositionally oriented toward or sensitive to the attainment of positive outcomes or the avoidance of negative outcomes (Carver & White, 1994; Higgins, 2000). These dispositional tendencies are predicted to affect how people respond to gain- and loss-framed information. Specifically, gain-framed messages (i.e., what people stand to gain by engaging in a health behaviors) should be particularly effective for people who are oriented toward attaining positive outcomes, whereas loss-framed messages (i.e., what people stand to lose if they fail to engage in a health behaviors) should be particularly effective for those who are oriented toward avoiding negative outcomes.

A number of papers were identified that tested the mediating processes thought to underlie matching framed messages to personality traits. Three of the papers (Cesario, Grant, & Higgins, 2004; Latimer et al., 2008; Spiegel, Grant-Pillow, & Higgins, 2004) dealt with individual differences in regulatory focus (Higgins, 2000), and two papers (Sherman, Mann, & Updegraff, 2006; Updegraff, Sherman, Luyster, & Mann, 2007) dealt with individual differences in a related construct, behavioral inhibition and behavioral activation (BIS/BAS; Carver & White, 1994).[2] Specifically, the authors of these studies tested the theoretically based hypothesis that people with a predominant promotion focus (BAS orientation) would find messages emphasizing accomplishment of positive outcomes, and framed in terms of pursuing those goals eagerly, to be more persuasive than messages emphasizing the possibility of experiencing negative outcomes and framed in terms of working vigilantly to prevent these outcomes. The opposite pattern of results has been hypothesized for those with a predominant prevention focus (BIS orientation). The matching effects reported in all the studies we have identified for review in this section were examined in randomized experiments.

The studies reported in these papers have addressed three different processes thought to underlie matching message content to dispositional differences in people's orientation to valenced outcomes. First, it has been proposed that this type of matching creates a "proper fit," leading people to feel right about the message, and it is this feeling right that mediates this matching effect (Cesario et al., 2004; Latimer et al., 2008; Spiegel et al., 2004). Second, it has been proposed that this type of matching effect leads to greater attention and message scrutiny (Updegraff et al., 2007). Third, matching to personality is thought to evoke a form of biased cognitive processing that leads people to feel a heightened sense of self-efficacy and greater

intention to change their behavior (Sherman et al., 2006). The evidence for all three explanations will be reviewed.

There is evidence that matching message content to people's predominant motivational orientation leads to a subjective sense of feeling right that mediates the matching effect (i.e., an IV-MV-DV relation). However, in the studies reported by Cesario et al. (2004) and Spiegel et al. (2004), the subjective sense of feeling right was never measured. Instead, evidence of mediation was inferred based on a moderation-of-process approach. For example, Cesario et al. (2004) experimentally manipulated whether people had an alternative explanation for their feelings due to "proper fit," and found that providing people with an alternative explanation for feeling right attenuated the hypothesized effect of "proper fit" on their evaluation of the messages. In other words, the experience of "proper fit" on people's evaluation of the message only occurred when they could not attribute their feelings to something else.

Latimer et al. (2008) tested the feeling right hypothesis using a measurement-of-mediation approach. Specifically, they found that people who were given messages about physical activity that matched their predominant motivational orientation reported more positive feelings (i.e., greater satisfaction) about engaging in the behavior. Moreover, they demonstrated that the positive feelings that resulted from the matching mediated the effect on the amount of physical activity people engaged in. The studies reported by Cesario et al. (2004) demonstrated the mediational effect on people's message evaluations and beliefs, whereas the studies reported by Spiegel et al. (2004) and Latimer et al. (2008) demonstrated the mediational effect on people's fruit and vegetable intake and physical activity levels, respectively. Taken together, these findings suggest that there is good evidence for the explanation that "proper fit," leads to a subjective sense of feeling right that mediates the matching effect.

There is also evidence of an IV-MV-DV relation for the explanation that matching message content to people's predominant motivational orientation elicits more thorough processing of the message. Specifically, Updegraff et al. (2007) demonstrated that people pay more attention to messages that are matched to their personality than to those that are mismatched by showing that people's evaluations of the messages were more sensitive to the strength of the message content when they were matched. Furthermore, they demonstrated with a measurement-of-mediation approach that people's evaluation of the messages mediated the effect of matching on their attitude toward flossing (the focal health behavior), but there was no consistent evidence of mediation when flossing behavior was the focal outcome. In another study examining the cognitive processes that are elicited when messages are matched to personality, Sherman et al. (2006) found that matched messages about flossing led to heightened perceptions of self-efficacy and greater intention to floss. Moreover, using a measurement-of-mediation approach, both self-efficacy and behavioral intention were found to mediate the effect of matching on people's flossing behavior over a 7-day period. Although it is not clear that the greater attention people pay to the messages has a direct relation to their behavior, there is some evidence that the effect matching framed messages has on people's behavior is mediated by the thoughts elicited by the message. Taken together, it may be that the greater attention that people pay to matched framed messages and the feeling of "fit" that they elicit represent a set of psychological experiences that are antecedent to the beliefs that have been shown to predict behavior directly.

Message Tailoring

Over the past two decades, tailored message interventions has emerged as a primary intervention strategy for health communication and health behavior change researchers (for reviews, see Noar, Benac, & Harris, 2007; Skinner, Campbell, Rimer, Curry, & Prochaska, 1999). Tailored messages contain health information that has been customized to address a specific person's demographic, psychosocial, and/or behavioral characteristics. For example, in a tailored message intervention designed to help people to quit smoking, each person would first provide information specific to their cessation efforts such as their primary reasons for wanting to quit, particular challenges they anticipate when trying to quit, and the primary situation in which they smoke. The messages and information each person subsequently receives is then tailored based on the information they provided (e.g., strategies are provided that address their specific reasons for quitting, barriers to quitting, and the situations where they typically smoke). In contrast to a personality-based matching strategy where messages are matched to a certain class of person and everyone who shares that trait receives the same message, tailored messages provide information that is typically matched on multiple dimensions (e.g., reasons to change behavior, strategies to change behavior, relevant demographics) with the resulting combination of information being matched (i.e., tailored) to each specific person (see Kreuter & Wray, 2003, for a comparison of different approaches to targeting or tailoring messages). Given the level of individualization that tailored messages provide, it could be argued that tailored interventions are the most extreme form of a message matching intervention.

Investigators who have considered the mediating processes that might underlie the effect that tailored message interventions have on people's behavior have primarily focused on the premise that the high degree of personal relevance of the message should elicit greater attention to and more thorough processing of the message (e.g., Bull, Holt, Kreuter, Clark, & Scharff, 2001; Kreuter et al., 1999; Oenema et al., 2005; Ruiter et al., 2006) and more favorable cognitive responses to the message (e.g., Kreuter et al., 1999; Oenema et al., 2005). In fact, there is substantial evidence that compared to nontailored messages (i.e., standardized messages that provide each person with the same information), tailored messages are perceived to be more personally relevant (Brug, Steenhuis, van Assema, & de Vries, 1996; Oenema et al., 2005; Skinner et al., 2002), are more likely to catch people's attention (Brug et al., 1996; Kreuter et al., 1999; Ruiter et al., 2006), are more likely to be read and remembered (Brug et al., 1996; Bull et al., 2001; Skinner, Strecher, & Hospers, 1994), and are considered more interesting (Brug et al., 1996; Kreuter et al., 1999; Oenema et al., 2005). But the extent to which these cognitive responses mediate the effect of tailored messages on behavior is not clear as there are surprisingly few studies that have formally tested the full mediating process (IV-MV-DV). For example, Ruiter and colleagues (2006) demonstrated that people divert more attention and cognitive resources to tailored materials than to nontailored materials through measures of brain activity and reaction time. However, there was no mediational test to determine if the greater attention paid to the materials led to behavior change (or intention to change), and thus it is unclear whether greater cognitive attention is integral to the effect of tailored messages on behavior or whether it is epiphenomenal.

We did identify two exemplar papers that have explicitly tested a mediating process that might underlie a tailored message effect (Kreuter et al., 1999; Oenema et al., 2005). In both studies, the authors proposed that tailored messages elicit biased (i.e., more favorable) cognitive responses, and in both studies, the tailoring interventions were examined experimentally. Kreuter and colleagues (1999) provided evidence of an IV-MV relation such that tailored materials about weight loss led to more favorable thoughts about the materials than did nontailored materials. In addition, there was some evidence of an MV-DV relation. Specifically, among people who received tailored materials, more favorable thoughts about the materials were associated with greater immediate intention to change weight loss-related behaviors and greater self-reported behavior change one month later. However, no direct effect of the tailoring intervention on behavior (an IV-DV relation) was reported, and thus no formal statistical test of mediation was conducted. Yet, the evidence from this study suggests the possibility that tailored materials affect behavior by eliciting more favorable cognitive responses.

Oenema and colleagues (2005) demonstrated that tailored materials about nutrition were perceived as more personally relevant, individualized, and interesting than nontailored materials (IV-MV relations). Moreover, there was evidence that judgments of both personal relevance and individualization mediated the effect of tailoring on intention to change fat intake, intention to change vegetable intake, and self-rated fat intake, and the perceived interestingness of the materials also mediated the effect of tailoring on intention to change fat intake (IV-MV-DV relations). The findings from both of these studies (Kreuter et al., 1999; Oenema et al., 2005) are consistent with previous findings that tailored messages elicit certain cognitive responses (e.g., Brug et al., 1996), but go beyond most of the existing evidence by providing evidence that certain types of cognitive processing elicited by tailored materials do mediate the effect of this intervention strategy on people's intentions and behavior.

Stage Matching

Some theoretical models of behavior change assume that people's decisions to change their health behaviors or adopt precautionary behaviors progresses through a series of stages (Prochaska & Velicer, 1997; Weinstein, 1988). For example, people who smoke must first recognize that smoking is a threat to their own health, they must then decide that the threat is sufficient to motivate them to quit smoking, and finally they must decide whether they can quit smoking and how they are going to do it. Moreover, stage models are predicated on the assumption that each stage represents a unique decision point and that there is a unique set of factors that regulate the transition between each stage. Interventions guided by stage models assume that people will be more likely to progress through the stages and change their behavior when they are provided an intervention that is matched to their current stage. For example, people who are in a stage characterized by their indecision about whether to change their behavior should be influenced more by an intervention that highlights the risk of a health threat and its relevance to them than by an intervention that specifies exactly how people might take action (e.g., where to get a vaccine, what pharmacological products are available to aid smoking cessation). Because stage models rest on the strong assumption that interventions are more effective when they address people's stage-specific needs, evidence for a stage process requires a comparison of stage-matched and stage-mismatched intervention strategies (Herzog, 2008; Weinstein, Rothman, et al., 1998). This approach is distinct from that used to evaluate tailored intervention strategies, which relies on research designs that are structured to provide comparisons between a tailored intervention message and a standardized intervention message.

The factors that mediate a stage-matched intervention are the specific factors thought to underlie the transitions from stage to stage. For example, one stage-based model of behavior change, the PAPM (Weinstein, 1988), assumes that when people shift from being undecided about whether to change their behavior to having decided to change their behavior, this transition is mediated by an increased understanding about why the behavior should be changed (e.g., increased perceptions of the relevant health risk). Yet, when people progress to actually changing their behavior, that transition is mediated by an increased confidence in how the behavior can be changed. Thus, the putative mediating variable changes across different stage transitions. We identified one paper based on the PAPM that specified stage-specific processes as mediators of stage movement and measured changes in the mediating variables (Weinstein, Lyon, Sandman, & Cuite, 1998).

The majority of stage-based interventions have been derived from another stage model, the transtheoretical model of behavior change (Prochaska & Velicer, 1997). The TTM assumes that people progress through a series of five stages (precontemplation, contemplation, preparation, action, and maintenance) and that stage progressions are mediated by shifts in cognitive processes (e.g., consciousness raising, self-reevaluation), behavioral processes (e.g., reinforcement management, stimulus control), beliefs about the behavior (i.e., pros and cons of changing behavior), and self-efficacy to change.

However, the model has been criticized for not specifying the processes that mediate each separate stage transition sufficiently (Herzog, 2008). Although various studies based on the TTM have measured constructs that might serve as mediators of stage transitions (e.g., Quinlan & McCaul, 2000; Rakowski et al., 1998), very few have tested whether changes in these variables mediate the effect of the TTM-based intervention on behavior. We identified three papers that reported mediational tests in TTM-guided interventions; one in the domain of sun protective behaviors (Adams et al., 2009) and two in the domain of physical activity (Carmack Taylor et al., 2006; Pinto et al., 2001).

In a test of a PAPM-based intervention, Weinstein, Lyon and colleagues (1998) hypothesized that people who are undecided about changing their behavior need information about the relevant health risk, whereas people who have decided to change but have not yet acted need information about how they can take action. In the context of testing homes for radon gas, they demonstrated evidence of an IV-MV relation such that people who were randomized to receive information that was matched to their current stage reported greater changes in and less need for stage-relevant information than those who were randomized to receive information that was mismatched to their stage. There was also evidence that the matching intervention influenced people's stage movement and ordering of radon tests (IV-DVs). Although the proposed mediators (perceived risk, information about how to test) were measured, there was no evidence reported that the change in the mediating variables affected stage movement or test ordering (MV-DVs). Thus, mediation was not assessed through a measurement-of-mediation approach; instead, evidence for mediation was based on a moderation-of-process approach (e.g., presenting people with risk information was more effective when people were undecided about testing than when people had already decided).

Regarding the evidence for mediation in interventions based on the TTM, all three studies (Adams et al., 2009; Carmack Taylor et al., 2006; Pinto et al., 2001), using a measurement-of-mediation approach, reported that the stage-based intervention influenced the proposed mediating processes. Specifically, people who received a stage-based intervention reported positive changes in the perceived pros and cons of sun protective behaviors (Adams et al., 2009), and positive changes in behavioral and cognitive processes relevant to physical activity, in

the perceived pros of physical activity (Carmack Taylor et al., 2006; Pinto et al., 2001), and in physical activity self-efficacy (Pinto et al., 2001). However, evidence for the effect of these mediating variables on behavioral outcomes was more elusive. Carmack Taylor et al. (2006) reported that the putative mediators had no effect on physical activity, and Pinto et al. (2001) found that some of the behavioral processes and perceived pros of physical activity had a limited effect on people's readiness to change behavior (i.e., stage transition). Only Adams et al. (2009) showed clear evidence that the changes in perceived pros and cons resulted in changes in sun protective behaviors.[3]

Based on this review of exemplar papers, there is some limited evidence that changes in the processes associated with a particular stage of behavior change mediates the effect of stage-matched interventions. However, the evidence from the TTM-based studies is limited by the fact that none specified exactly which processes (e.g., change in pros and cons, self-efficacy) mediate each specific stage transition (e.g., contemplation to preparation, preparation to action). More specified mediational predictions along these lines are necessary in order to understand the unique value that a stage-based approach to behavior change might have (see Weinstein, Lyon, et al., 1998). Also, given that stage-based matching interventions are grounded in a particular set of theoretical models, for clarity of presentation we have considered meeting people's specific stage-based needs as a process that is different from processes thought to underlie other matching interventions. Yet, it is possible that providing people with information or strategies that are most appropriate for their stage of behavior change not only addresses their stage-based needs, but also elicits a pattern of responding that has been observed in other matching interventions: more thorough processing of the information, more favorable responses to the information and a sense that the intervention "feels right." In other words, stage-matched interventions may work for the same reasons that many other matching interventions work. To our knowledge, no empirical evidence exists that can definitively speak to this possibility. We will return to this issue later in the chapter.

Patient x Treatment Matching

When people are faced with a health threat, such as discovering that they have a disease or illness that could potentially prove fatal, they can engage in strategies to avoid or minimize the threat or to actively confront it (see Suls & Fletcher, 1985). Regarding people's approaches to managing this type of threat, reliable individual differences exist in the types of strategies people prefer. For example, when faced with the threat posed by a chronic illness, some people prefer detailed information about the illness and its treatment (i.e., active coping), whereas others prefer to know minimal information (i.e., avoidant coping; Levinson, Kao, Kuby, & Thisted, 2005; Swenson, Buell, Zettler, White, Ruston, & Lo, 2004). Patient x treatment matching occurs when patients are provided a treatment (or treatment context) that matches with their preferred mode of coping.

One context in which patient x treatment matching has been operationalized and evaluated is the degree to which there is a match between what chronic illness patients and their physicians believe about the patient's role in health care and the patient's control over health outcomes. The evidence suggests that when patients and their physicians agree on what the patient's role should be (i.e., active or passive), patients report greater satisfaction with care and trust in their physician (Krupat, Bell, Kravitz, Thom, & Azari, 2001) and greater treatment adherence (Cvengros, Christensen, Hillis, & Rosenthal, 2007; Cvengros, Christensen, Cunningham, Hillis, & Kaboli, 2009). For example, patients who desire an active role in their health care and treatment are a better "match" for physicians who share the same belief about patients' roles, whereas patients who prefer a more passive (or avoidant) role are a better "match" for physicians who believe that patients should be more passive and physicians more directive. Yet, conclusions drawn from these particular studies of patient x treatment matching are limited by the fact that the matching of patients and physicians was not randomized. Moreover, the processes that might mediate this type of matching effect have not been examined.

In a related line of work that was motivated by research on person x situation interactions (e.g., Mischel & Shoda, 1995), researchers designed randomized interventions to help patients cope with surgery by matching patients who differ in their preference for health-relevant information with interventions that differ in their coping focus (i.e., avoidance or direct; Martelli, Auerbach, Alexander, & Mercuri, 1987; Miller & Mangan, 1983). The evidence from these interventions suggests that patients tend to be less anxious and adapt better after surgery when the type of information given to

them before the surgery matches their preference. Specifically, patients who initially indicate that they desire information cope better when they are given detailed information about the procedure and are directed to engage in direct coping; low-information patients cope better when they are given minimal information about the procedure and engage in avoidant forms of coping (Martelli et al., 1987; Miller & Mangan, 1983). The evidence for the effectiveness of this type of patient x treatment matching intervention is compelling, particularly given that these were randomized interventions. Yet, the processes that mediate this type of matching effect were not examined.

We did identify one paper that examined a potential mediating process of patient x treatment matches. Christensen et al. (1997) proposed that patients' perceptions of control mediate the effect of matching a treatment-style to a patient's preferences and examined this possibility using a measurement-of-mediation approach. In a study of patients with end stage renal disease (ESRD), patients who reported a preference for active involvement in their treatment (similar to high-information patients) reported lower levels of control when assigned to a clinic-based hemodialysis treatment. Compared to hemodialysis that is done at home, where the patient takes a very active role in running dialysis equipment and monitoring medication, clinic-based hemodialysis is a relatively passive treatment because clinic staff does all the monitoring. Thus, the relatively passive treatment afforded by clinic-run dialysis provides a mismatch for people who desire active involvement and this was shown to lead to lower levels of perceived control (IV-MV). In turn, the lower levels of perceived control mediated the negative association between patients' desire for involvement and behavioral adherence to the treatment regimen (IV-MV-DV). Although this analysis does provide evidence of mediation on a behavioral outcome, conclusions about mediation drawn from these data are limited by the fact that patients were not randomized to the treatment setting (i.e., clinic or home).

The data reported by Christensen et al. (1997) suggest a plausible mediating process through which patient x treatment matches are effective, but it is not readily evident why patients who desire less control would experience a heightened sense of control in a treatment context that affords passivity, as the perceptions of control mediational path would suggest. It could be that perceptions of control might mediate the effect observed for patients who desire more active control and another mediational process may be needed to explain the treatment-matching effect for those who desire less control (i.e., a case of moderated mediation). Alternatively, it may be that patient x treatment matching effects are best explained as a case of "proper fit," where the match produces a sense of "feeling right" (see Cesario et al., 2004) or greater satisfaction (see Latimer et al., 2008) that mediates the effect on people's behavior. For people who desire more control over their treatment, the experience of "fit" may elicit a heightened sense of control. For people who desire less control over their treatment, the experience of "fit" may be marked by a different set of beliefs, such as how content or satisfied they are with the treatment. To date, however, the mediational processes that explain this type of matching effect have not been well specified, and the empirical evidence to date has been derived from nonrandomized matches. Thus, before definitive conclusions can be drawn about the mediational processes that underlie patient x treatment matches, as well as differences and similarities with other types of matching effects, additional conceptual and empirical work is needed.

What Processes Underlie Matching Interventions? An Initial Synthesis

In our review of the relevant literatures, the evidence for four different mediational processes of health-related matching interventions was examined. First, evidence from interventions that involved message tailoring or matching message content to personality indicated that matched interventions elicit greater attention to and more thorough processing of the intervention material. However, across both literatures, there was no clear evidence that the increased attention and processing actually mediated the effect of the matching intervention on people's behavior. Second, evidence from three separate literatures indicated that matched interventions elicit more favorable thoughts and beliefs than do nonmatched interventions. Moreover, there was some evidence that the more favorable thoughts and beliefs mediate the effect of tailored messages and messages matched to people's personality on behavior. Third, evidence from interventions that matched messages to people's personality indicated that exposure to a matched intervention elicits a subjective experience of "proper fit," which mediates the effect of the intervention on people's behavior. Finally, there was some evidence from stage-matched interventions that providing information that meets people's stage-based needs, as specified by particular stage models, can mediate the effect of the matched intervention on behavior.

Given the state of the evidence across these different research literatures, is there a core set of mediational processes that underlie matching interventions? First, consistent with the prevailing models of health behavior (Rothman & Salovey, 2007), it appears that cognitions (i.e., thoughts and beliefs) that are evoked by matched interventions play an important mediating role in the effect of matched interventions on people's behavior. Specifically, matching interventions that elicit biased cognitive responses to the message (i.e., more favorable thoughts and beliefs about the advocated behavior) may be more likely to elicit the intended effect on people's behavior than interventions that do not. However, we did not find any evidence that the increased attention and processing that can result from matched interventions had a direct influence on people's behavior. Why might this be the case? It might be that increased attention and processing is epiphenomenal—it results from matched interventions but simply does not affect behavior. Perhaps more likely, however, is that the effect that increased attention has on behavior is conditional on other factors. In particular, the mediated effect of increased attention may be moderated by the quality of the information presented in the intervention. Greater message scrutiny may be beneficial when the message content is compelling (e.g., elicits favorable thoughts and beliefs), but may be detrimental when the message content is easily denigrated or counterargued (see Updegraff et al., 2007). Although this more elaborate process is plausible, the research designs and measurement strategies that investigators have utilized to date have been unable to test these hypotheses directly.

Second, it appears that the sense of "proper fit" that matched interventions can elicit may also play a critical role in mediating the effect of the intervention on behavior. Although the evidence for "proper fit" as a mediational process was limited to a particular set of studies that matched messages to different personality types, it is possible that this process may generalize to other types of matching intervention effects. For example, in addition to evoking more favorable thoughts and beliefs about the advocated behavior, individually tailored message interventions might also evoke an independent, subjective sense that the message "feels right." In addition, it seems plausible that patient x treatment matching interventions also evoke a subjective sense that the matched treatment approach "feels right" and this experience could help account for the effect on treatment adherence behavior. Although no studies in these respective literatures have been designed to test these hypotheses, we think that future work in these areas would benefit from testing whether matched interventions evoke a subjective sense of "feeling right."

Third, it appears that fulfilling people's stage-based needs can mediate the effect of a stage-matched intervention on people's behavior. What remains unclear, however, is whether meeting a person's stage-based needs is a mediational process that is distinct from the other processes offered to explain the effect of matched interventions. For example, if a woman who is undecided about whether she should get an annual mammogram receives information that emphasizes the likelihood of getting breast cancer and the effectiveness of regular mammograms in reducing breast cancer mortality (as opposed to information emphasizing how to get a mammogram), she would be receiving a stage-matched intervention. It seems plausible that under those conditions, she might think more favorably about the information than about information that was mismatched to her stage, and given that she is undecided about screening, this intervention might be more likely to evoke a subjective sense that the information provided "feels right." Thus, it may be that the provision of stage-matched intervention is effective because it elicits biased cognitive processing and a subjective sense of "feeling right"—the two mediational paths that have been the primary focus of other lines of research. From this perspective, what a stage-based approach provides is guidance regarding how to operationalize the match between a message and a person. The extent to which stage-based approaches operate through these other mediational paths is an important question for future research.

Does the current state of the science suggest a core set of mediational processes that underlie the effect of matched intervention strategies? Although the empirical evidence available is not sufficient to answer this question definitively, it does provide investigators a clear roadmap for future research. In particular, given the pattern of findings observed across different approaches to developing matched interventions, we believe that theoretical progress will come if investigators prioritize testing multiple mediating processes within a single study. For example, it seems quite plausible that both cognitive processes (e.g., biased cognitive responses) and

subjective or affective processes (e.g., sense of "feeling right") independently, but simultaneously, mediate the effect matched interventions have on behavior. Other combinations of multiple mediators might be worth considering as well. As we indicated earlier, matched interventions may lead to increased attention that temporally precedes some form of biased cognitive processing in a sequential mediational path. This sequence of mediational paths may prove to be a more accurate reflection of the underlying process than considering both processes independently or simultaneously. Research designs will need to be constructed carefully in order to capture this temporal sequence.

Reaffirming the Link Between Mediators and Moderators: A Road Forward

As we noted at the outset of this chapter, research on the mediational processes that underlie the effect of matched intervention strategies is fundamentally a question about the interplay between moderation (i.e., the features that specify whether an intervention strategy is a match) and mediation (i.e., the mechanism through which the matched strategy works). Yet, the theoretical and the empirical analysis of these mediating processes have paid strikingly limited attention to the role of the moderator and its implications for mediation. In particular, to what extent does the parameter (e.g., personality, stage of change) on which the matched intervention is based affect the process through which the intervention affects behavior? We believe that greater consideration of the interplay between mediation and moderation (i.e., mediated moderation and moderated mediation) could provide a productive framework for moving forward in this area.

What implications might arise from focusing on moderated mediation and mediated moderation? One issue that becomes apparent is that investigators are encouraged to consider two different classes of matching effects. In one case, the effect of a matched intervention strategy is captured by a single mediational route through which matching—regardless of the underlying nature of the match—affects behavior. For example, the effect of a gain-framed message that is a match for a person with a high BAS score and the effect of a loss-framed message that is a match for a person with a high BIS score are both assumed to operate through the same set of underlying mechanisms. This perspective is best represented by models of mediated moderation (see Figure 29.1). Although the specific mediational route might involve multiple mediators that operate in parallel or in sequence, the model is structured to capture the distinction between interventions that do and do not match a feature of a person. What is important to note from this perspective is that the specific characteristics of the moderator that defines the match between the intervention and the person do not affect the mediational process.

In the other case, more than one mediational route is needed to capture the effect of a matched intervention strategy. Here the characteristics of the moderator that are used to define the match between the intervention and the person determine the nature of the underlying mediational process. This perspective is best represented by models of moderated mediation (see Figure 29.2), where at least two distinct mediational routes are specified. Stage-matched interventions may provide the clearest case for the possibility of moderated mediation. With stage-matched interventions, the mediator that is affected by the intervention is predicated on the process that is specified to underlie each stage transition. For example, within the framework of the PAPM (Weinstein, 1988), changes in perceptions of personal vulnerability are predicted to mediate the effect of an intervention matched for a person in the undecided stage, whereas changes in perceptions of self-efficacy are predicted to mediate the effect of an intervention matched for a person in the decided stage. Although stage models provide the clearest example of moderated mediation, this framework could underlie other forms of intervention matching. For example, to the extent that the effect of matching the affective tone of messages to people's BIS sensitivities and the effect of matching the affective tone of messages to people's BAS sensitivities can be attributed to different mediational paths, it would be a case of moderated mediation. Research designs are needed that will allow investigators to distinguish between these two classes of matching effects and thereby better specify the underlying mediational process.

Another benefit of thinking more carefully about moderation is that it may lead investigators to think more precisely about the relative effects of matching and mismatching intervention strategies. In particular, is the observed advantage for matched intervention strategies due to the beneficial effects of intervention matching, the detrimental effects of intervention mismatching, or both? Comparisons between matched and mismatched interventions have typically not included a control group, which would be needed in order to differentiate between these different effects. One exception to this rule

was a study of patient x treatment matching by Cvengros et al. (2009). What is particularly striking about the findings from this study is that the investigators observed that a matched intervention performed no better than control, but a mismatched intervention performed worse than control. Although one must be cautious in concluding too much from a single study, in some situations it could be the case that it is more important to avoid providing a mismatched intervention strategy than to optimize the fit or match of the intervention strategy. One implication of this observation is that investigators will need to be more explicit about how they conceptualize the difference between a matched and a mismatched intervention. Do matching and mismatching interventions represent two discrete categories or do they represent two ends of a single bipolar dimension? If the latter conceptualization proves to be more accurate, investigators will need to be able to operationalize variability in the degree to which an intervention matches a person and to structure tests of how this variability alters the effects reviewed in this chapter.

When investigators think about mediational processes they typically focus on processes elicited by the intervention that facilitate the desired outcome (e.g., heightening perceptions of self-efficacy leads to increased behavior change). Yet, mediational paths can involve both facilitating and inhibiting processes. It may be that there are aspects of the intervention that promote the desired outcome and aspects of the intervention that undermine the desired outcome. Where appropriate, investigators should assess both classes of putative mediators. For example, it could be the case that a matched intervention strategy triggers a mediational process that facilitates a behavioral outcome (e.g., it promotes greater feelings of self-efficacy), whereas a mismatched intervention strategy triggers a distinct mediational process that inhibits a behavioral outcome (e.g., it promotes feelings of concern or confusion). Better specification of these mediational paths will provide investigators with a clearer and more comprehensive understanding of why their interventions are and are not working.

Finally, considering the interplay between mediators and moderators may also encourage investigators to think through how the effects of intervention matching might unfold over time. In his classic analysis of the effects of personality on persuasion, McGuire (1968) delineated how the moderating effect of certain personality traits varied depending on the specific phase of the persuasion process (e.g., reception vs. yielding). Research on intervention matching might similarly benefit from greater attention to different phases of not only the persuasion process, but also the behavior change process (Rothman & Salovey, 2007). For example, there may be value in differentiating between people whose beliefs about the behavior must change before they would choose to take action and those who merely need encouragement or a prompt in order to act on their beliefs. Rothman and Updegraff (2011) have suggested that the mediational processes underlying message framing effects may differ depending on whether people need to be persuaded or prompted in order to act. In particular, the experience of "feeling right" may be sufficient to elicit action among people who only need to be prompted, but insufficient for people who need to be persuaded that action is needed.

To date, research on intervention matching has tended to focus on a single behavioral outcome (e.g., a vaccination) or a cumulative behavioral outcome (e.g., treatment adherence). However, many important health behaviors involve an ongoing series of behavioral decisions (e.g., dietary behavior, physical activity), and people's responses to and experiences with the behavior may be an important determinant of sustained behavior change (Rothman et al., 2004; Rothman, Sheeran, & Wood, 2009). Investigators may want to consider how matched intervention strategies affect not only the decision to initiate a behavior, but also the decision to maintain a pattern of behavior over time. For example, certain classes of matched interventions such as message tailoring might be particularly well suited to helping people recognize and attend to outcomes afforded by the behavior that are personally relevant and meaningful, which, in turn, heightens people's satisfaction with the new pattern of behavior (e.g., Baldwin, Rothman, Hertel, Keenan, & Jeffery, 2009; Baldwin, Rothman, & Jeffery, 2009). Evidence has emerged in the domains of diet, physical activity, and smoking cessation that perceived satisfaction with a new behavior is an important determinant of sustained behavior change (Baldwin et al., 2006; Finch et al., 2005; Hertel et al., 2008). Moreover, the degree to which matched interventions lead people to infer that the behavior in question "feels right" for them, they may be more inclined to respond favorably to the experiences afforded by the behavior and pay less attention to those aspects of the behavior that are unpleasant. In a similar manner, to the extent that matched interventions lead people to construe behaviors as being in line with their own personal

goals, people may find it easier to transform a new pattern of behavior into a habit. According to Wood and Neal (2007), personal goals can work synergistically with behaviors to form and support habits by encouraging people to create or seek out environments that support the behavior.

Throughout this chapter our analysis has focused on different way investigators have utilized a P x IS approach to promote healthy behavior. However, the conclusions that we have drawn regarding the state of the evidence in the health domain and the emerging research questions we have identified may be applicable to other domains of research that are similarly predicated on a P x S framework. In particular, there is little reason to believe that the limitations that we have identified regarding research on health behavior will prove to be unique to this domain. Yet, the degree to which the principles identified in this paper regarding mediational mechanisms and the hypothesized linkages between mediators and moderators generalize across substantive domains is a question worthy of future study. In this chapter, we examined the pattern of findings obtained across four lines of work within the domain of health behavior that share an underlying conceptual framework, but are traditionally treated as distinct research literatures. This comparison process proved to be quite productive as it served to not only clarify the strengths and weaknesses of different research programs but also generate a new series of hypotheses regarding potential differences between different approaches to operationalizing the match between a person and an intervention strategy. The opportunity to draw comparisons across substantive research domains is likely to prove at least as generative, providing investigators the opportunity to delineate a core set of psychological processes that underlie all forms of P x S matches.

Final Thoughts

The translation of theory into practice requires the development of theoretical models that not only specify how constructs *can* influence each other when they are observed in an isolated setting (i.e., does manipulating one construct elicit change in another construct?), but also what *does* happen when the relation between those constructs is observed in a more complex social environment (cf. Mook, 1983). The transition from a focus on what can happen to what does happen is analogous to the movement from a focus on mediational process alone to a focus on the interplay between mediators and moderators, as understanding what does happen is predicated on identifying the factors (i.e., features of people, settings, behaviors) that regulate the strength and direction of different mediational paths. This transition has proven to be a challenge for models of health behavior and as a result has constrained the manner in which these models have been able to inform the development and dissemination of effective intervention strategies (Rothman, 2004; Weinstein & Rothman, 2005; Rothman, 2009).

As we noted at the outset of this chapter, social psychological models of health behavior have uniformly emphasized the specification of constructs that can predict health behaviors (i.e., potential targets for intervention), but have provided limited guidance as to when or for whom these constructs are most likely to be important. On the other hand, models of personality and health behavior have emphasized identifying which aspects of a person's personality are associated with different health practices (i.e., who is likely to perform a particular behavior), but have provided limited guidance as to the processes that underlie the relation between personality and behavior. Thus, these two approaches provide complementary frameworks for understanding people's health behavior and, taken together, have the potential to provide a roadmap for the integration of process (i.e., mediators) and context (i.e., moderators) and the development of models that are able to specify not only what can happen, but also what does happen.

In the present chapter, we have examined research programs that have focused on developing and testing intervention strategies designed to match features of individuals or classes of individuals. The P x IS approach that underlies these research programs provides a useful framework for understanding the interplay between mediators and moderators. Yet, investigators working within these different programs of research have not capitalized on the opportunities afforded by this work to delineate whether and, if so, how aspects of people's personality and background affect the processes that are hypothesized to regulate people's health practices. We believe that the advent of new methods for conceptualizing and testing the linkages between mediators and moderators (i.e., mediated moderation, moderated mediation) will help investigators recognize these opportunities and provide them with the tools to take advantage of them. The theoretical advances that are likely to emerge from this work should provide a foundation for designing, testing, and disseminating new intervention methods.

With the development of models that more formally describe how differences in personality affect the processes that guide health behavior, investigators may find it easier to expand these models to accommodate other classes of moderators. In particular, these models may offer a roadmap for how to integrate into these models advances in our understanding of the role played by moderators that operate at different levels of analysis such as those at the biological and genetic level of analysis. For example, there is an emerging body of empirical evidence that genetic differences moderate how people respond to both dietary behavior and physical activity protocols (e.g., Bouchard & Rankinen, 2001; Ukkola & Bouchard, 2004). Given that people's responses to new behavioral practices affect their willingness and ability to continue the behavior, theoretical models are needed that can specify how genetic factors regulate the operation of the psychological processes that guide behavior (Bryan, Hutchison, Seals, & Allen, 2007; Dishman, 2008). These models may also provide insights into the degree to which the observed moderating influence of differences in personality can be localized to underlying differences in biology. In either case, these models will continue to provide investigators with innovative ways to approach the delivery of intervention strategies that can be matched to the individual in order to maximize their effectiveness.

Notes

[1] Moderated mediation does not necessitate that there be a moderated treatment effect on the outcome. The extent to which there is an intervention by moderator interaction depends on the relative strength of the two underlying mediational paths (Muller et al., 2005).

[2] Investigators have also tested the impact of health messages designed to match personality traits that are not oriented toward sensitivity to valenced outcomes. For example, a series of studies have examined the effectiveness of matching messages to differences in people's health locus of control (Williams-Piehota, Schneider, Pizarro, Moward, & Salovey, 2004), need for cognition (Williams-Piehota, Schneider, Pizarro, Moward, & Salovey, 2003), or preferred coping style (Williams-Piehota, Pizarro, Schneider, Moward, & Salovey, 2005). Although these studies have largely demonstrated the effectiveness of matching health messages to personality, these studies have not focused on mediating processes (for an overview of this line of work, see Latimer, Katulak, Mowad, & Salovey, 2005).

[3] Because none of these three studies compared a stage-matched intervention to a stage-mismatched intervention, any conclusions drawn from these studies regarding the validity of a stage-based approach is limited.

References

Adams, M. A., Norman, G. J., Hovell, M. F., Sallis, J. F., & Patrick, K. (2009). Reconceptualizing decisional balance in an adolescent sun protection intervention: Mediating effects and theoretical interpretations. *Health Psychology, 28,* 217–225.

Ajzen, I. (1991). The theory of planned behavior. *Organizational Behavior and Human Decision Processes, 50,* 179–211.

Ajzen, I. & Fishbein, M. (1980). *Understanding attitudes and predicting social behavior.* Englewood Cliffs, NJ: Prentice Hall.

Baldwin, A. S., Rothman, A. J., Hertel, A. W., Linde, J. A., Jeffery, R. W., Finch, E. A., et al. (2006). Specifying the determinants of behavior change initiation and maintenance: An examination of self-efficacy, satisfaction, and smoking cessation. *Health Psychology, 25,* 626–634.

Baldwin, A. S., Rothman, A. J., Hertel, A. W., Keenan, N. K., & Jeffery, R. W. (2009). Longitudinal associations between people's cessation-related experiences and their satisfaction with cessation. *Psychology and Health, 24,* 187–201.

Baldwin, A. S., Rothman, A. J., & Jeffery, R. W. (2009). Satisfaction with weight loss: Examining the longitudinal covariation between people's weight-loss-related outcomes and experiences and their satisfaction. *Annals of Behavioral Medicine, 38,* 213–224.

Bandura, A. (1986). *Social foundations of thought and action: A social cognitive theory.* Englewood Cliffs, NJ: Prentice Hall.

Baron, R. M., & Kenny, D. A. (1986). The moderator-mediator variable distinction in social psychological research: Conceptual, strategic, and statistical considerations. *Journal of Personality and Social Psychology, 51,* 1173–1182.

Blundel, J. E., Stubbs, R. J., Golding, C., Croden, F., Alam, R., Whybrow, S., et al. (2005). Resistance and susceptibility to wait gain: Individual variability in response to a high-fat diet. *Physiology and Behavior, 86,* 614–622.

Bogg, T., & Roberts, B. W. (2004). Conscientiousness and health-related behaviors: A meta-analysis of the leading behavioral contributors to mortality. *Psychological Bulletin, 130,* 887–919.

Booth-Kewley, S., & Vickers, R. R. (1994). Associations between major domains of personality and health behavior. *Journal of Personality, 62,* 281–298.

Bouchard, C., & Rankinen, T. (2001). Individual differences in response to regular physical activity. *Medical Science and Sports Exercise, 33,* S446–S451.

Brownell, K. D., & Horgen, K. B. (2004). *Food fight: The inside story of the food industry, America's obesity crisis, and what we can do about it.* New York: McGraw-Hill.

Brug, J., Steenhuis, I., van Assema, P., & de Vries, H. (1996). The impact of computer-tailored nutrition intervention. *Preventive Medicine, 25,* 236–242.

Bryan, A., Hutchison, K. E., Seals, D. R., & Allen, D. L. (2007). A transdisciplinary model integrating genetic, physiological, and psychological correlates of voluntary exercise. *Health Psychology, 26,* 30–39.

Bull, F. C., Holt, C. L., Kreuter, M. W., Clark, E. M., & Scharff, D. (2001). Understanding the effects of printed health education materials: Which features lead to which outcomes? *Journal of Health Communication, 6,* 265–279.

Bullock, J. G., Green, D. P., & Ha, S. E. (2010). Yes, but what's the mechanism? (Don't expect an easy answer). *Journal of Personality and Social Psychology, 98,* 550–558.

Carmack Taylor, C. L., DeMoor, C., Smith, M. A., Dunn, A. L., Basen-Engquist, K., Nielsen, I., Pettaway, C., Sellin, R., Massey, P., & Gritz, E. R. (2006). Active for Life after cancer: A randomized trial examining a lifestyle physical activity program for prostate cancer patients. *Psycho-Oncology, 15,* 847–862.

Carver, C. S., & White, T. L. (1994). Behavioral inhibition, behavioral activation, and affective responses to impending reward and punishment: The BIS/BAS scales. *Journal of Personality and Social Psychology, 67,* 319–333.

Cesario, J., Grant, H., & Higgins, E. T. (2004). Regulatory fit and persuasion: Transfer from "feeling right." *Journal of Personality and Social Psychology, 86,* 388–404.

Christakis, N. A., & Fowler, J. H. (2007). The spread of obesity in a large social network over 32 years. *New England Journal of Medicine, 357,* 370–379.

Christensen, A. J. (2000). Patient x treatment context interaction in chronic disease: A conceptual framework for the study of patient adherence. *Psychosomatic Medicine, 62,* 435–443.

Christensen, A.J. (2004). *Patient adherence with treatment regimens: Bridging the gap between behavioral science and biomedicine.* New Haven, CT: Yale University Press.

Christensen, A. J., Moran, P. J., Lawton, W. J., Stallman, D., & Voigts, A. L. (1997). Monitoring attention style and medical regimen adherence in hemodialysis patients. *Health Psychology, 16,* 256–262.

Conner, M., Grogan, S., Fry, G., Gough, B., & Higgins, A. R. (2009). Direct, mediated, and moderated impacts of personality variables on smoking initiation in adolescents. *Psychology and Health, 24,* 1085–1104.

Conner, M., & Norman, P. (Eds.). (2005). *Predicting health behaviour: Research and practice with social cognition models* (2nd ed.). Buckingham, UK: Open University Press.

Cvengros, J. A., Christensen, A. J., Cunningham, C., Hillis, S. L., & Kaboli, P. J. (2009). Patient preferences for and reports of provider behavior: Impact of symmetry on patient outcomes. *Health Psychology, 28,* 660–667.

Cvengros, J. A., Christensen, A. J., Hillis, S. L., & Rosenthal, G. E. (2007). Patient and physician attitudes in the health care context: Attitudinal symmetry predicts patient satisfaction and adherence. *Annals of Behavioral Medicine, 33,* 262–268.

de Bruijn, G.-J., Brug, J., & van Lenthe, F. J. (2009). Neuroticism, conscientiousness, and fruit consumption: Exploring mediator and moderator effects in the theory of planned behavior. *Psychology and Health, 24,* 1051–1069.

Dishman, R. K. (2008). Gene-physical activity interactions in the etiology of obesity: Behavioral considerations. *Obesity, 16,* S60–S65.

Fairchild, A.J., & MacKinnon, D.P. (2009). A general model for testing mediation and moderation effects. *Prevention Science, 10,* 87–99.

Finch, E. A., Linde, J. A., Jeffery, R. W., Rothman, A. J., King, C. M., & Levy, R. L. (2005). The effects of outcome expectations and satisfaction on weight loss and maintenance: Correlational and experimental analyses. *Health Psychology, 24,* 608–616.

Flegal, K.M., Carroll, M.D., Ogden, C.L., & Curtin, L.R. (2010). Prevalence and trends in obesity among US adults, 1999-2008. *Journal of the American Medical Association, 303,* 235-241.

French, S. A., Jeffery, R. W., Story, M., Breitlow, K. K., Baxter, J. S., Hannan, P., et al. (2001). Pricing and promotion effects on low-fat vending snack purchases: The CHIPS study. *American Journal of Public Health, 91,* 112–117.

Friedman, H. S., Tucker, J. S., Schwartz, J. E., Martin, L. R., Tomlinson-Keasey, C., Wingard, D. L., et al. (1995). Childhood conscientiousness and longevity: Health behaviors and cause of death. *Journal of Personality and Social Psychology, 68,* 696–703.

Gerend, M. A., Shephard, J. E., & Monday, K. A. (2008). Behavioral frequency moderates the effects of message framing on HPV vaccine acceptability. *Annals of Behavioral Medicine, 35,* 221–229.

Glanz, K., & Bishop, D. B. (2010). The role of behavioral science theory in development and implementation of public health interventions. *Annual Review of Public Health, 31,* 399–418.

Hampson, S. E., Goldberg, L. R., Vogt, T. M., & Dubanoski, J. P. (2006). Forty years on: Assessments of children's personality traits predict self-reported health behaviors and outcomes at midlife. *Health Psychology, 25,* 57–64.

Hertel, A. W., Finch, E., Kelly, K., King, C., Lando, H., Linde, J., et al. (2008). The impact of outcome expectations and satisfaction on the initiation and maintenance of smoking cessation: An experimental test. *Health Psychology, 27,* S197–S206.

Herzog, T. A. (2008). Analyzing the transtheoretical model using the framework of Weinstein, Rothman, and Sutton (1998): The example of smoking cessation. *Health Psychology, 27,* 548–556.

Higgins, E. T. (2000). Making a good decision: Value from fit. *American Psychologist, 55,* 1217–1230.

Jeffery, R. W. (2004). How can health behavior theory be made more useful for intervention research? *International Journal of Behavioral Nutrition and Physical Activity, 1,* 10.

Kraemer, H. C., Kiernan, M., Essex, M., & Kupfer, D. J. (2008). How and why criteria defining moderators and mediators differ between the Baron & Kenny and MacArthur approaches. *Health Psychology, 27,* S101–S108.

Kreuter, M. W., Bull, F. C., Clark, E. M., & Oswald, D. L. (1999). Understanding how people process health information: A comparison of tailored and nontailored weight-loss materials. *Health Psychology, 18,* 487–494.

Kreuter, M. W., & Wray, R. J. (2003). Tailored and targeted health communication: Strategies for enhancing information relevance. *American Journal of Health Behavior, 27,* S227–S232.

Krupat, E., Bell, R. A., Kravitz, R. L., Thom, D., & Azari, R. (2001). When physicians and patients think alike: Patient-centered beliefs and their impact on satisfaction and trust. *Journal of Family Practice, 50,* 1057–1062.

Lahey, B. B. (2009). Public health significance of neuroticism. *American Psychologist, 64,* 241–256.

Latimer, A. E., Katulak, N. A., Mowad, L., & Salovey, P. (2005). Motivating cancer prevention and early detection behaviors using psychologically tailored messages. *Journal of Health Communication, 10,* 137–155.

Latimer, A. E., Rivers, S. E., Rench, T. A., Katulak, N. A., Hicks, A., Hodorowski, J. K., et al. (2008). A field experiment testing the utility of regulatory fit messages for promoting physical activity. *Journal of Experimental Social Psychology, 44,* 826–832.

Levinson, W., Kao, A., Kuby, A., & Thisted, R. A. (2005). Not all patients want to participate in decision making: A national study of public preferences. *Journal of General Internal Medicine, 20,* 531–535.

MacKinnon, D. P. (2008). *Introduction to statistical mediation analysis.* New York: Erlbaum.

MacKinnon, D. P., Fairchild, A. J., & Fritz, M. S. (2007). Mediation analysis. *Annual Review of Psychology, 58,* 593–614.

Maddux, J. E., & Rogers, R. W. (1983). Protection motivation and self-efficacy: A revised theory of fear appeals and attitude change. *Journal of Experimental Social Psychology, 19,* 469–479.

Mann, T., Sherman, D., & Updegraff, J. (2004). Dispositional motivations and message framing: A test of the congruency hypothesis in college students. *Health Psychology, 23,* 330–334.

Martelli, M. F., Auerbach, S. M., Alexander, J., & Mercuri, L. G. (1987). Stress management in the health care setting: Matching interventions with patient coping styles. *Journal of Consulting and Clinical Psychology, 55,* 201–207.

Martin, L. R., Friedman, H. S., & Schwartz, J. E. (2007). Personality and mortality risk across the life span: The importance of conscientiousness as a biopsychosocial attribute. *Health Psychology, 26,* 428–436.

McGuire, W. J. (1968). Personality and susceptibility to social influence. In Borgatta, E. F. & Lambert, W. W. (Eds.), *Handbook of personality theory and research* (pp. 1130–1187). Chicago: Rand McNally.

McGuire, W. J. (1989). A perspectivist approach to the strategic planning of programmatic scientific research. In B. Gholson, W. R. Shadish Jr., R. A. Neimeyer, & A. C. Houts (Eds.), *Psychology of science: Contributions to metascience* (pp. 214–245). New York: Cambridge University Press.

Michie, S., & Prestwich, A. (2010). Are interventions theory based? Development of a theory coding scheme. *Health Psychology, 29,* 1–8.

Michie, S., Rothman, A. J., & Sheeran, P. (2007). Current issues and new direction in psychology and health: Advancing the science of behavior change. *Psychology and Health, 22,* 249–253.

Miller, S. M., & Mangan, C. E. (1983). Interacting effects of information and coping styles in adapting to gynecological stress: Should the doctor tell all? *Journal of Personality and Social Psychology, 45,* 223–236.

Mischel, W., & Shoda, Y. (1995). A cognitive-affective system theory of personality: Reconceptualizing situations, dispositions, dynamics, and invariance in personality structure. *Psychological Review, 102,* 246–268.

Mokdad, A. H., Marks, J. S., Stroup, D. F., & Gerberding, J. L. (2004). Actual causes of death in the United States, 2000. *Journal of the American Medical Association, 291,* 1238–1245.

Mook, D. G. (1983). In defense of external invalidity. *American Psychologist, 38,* 379–387.

Muller, D., Judd, C. M., & Yzerbyt, V. Y. (2005). When moderation is mediated and mediation is moderated. *Journal of Personality and Social Psychology, 89,* 853–863.

Noar, S. M., Benac, C. N., & Harris, M. S. (2007). Does tailoring matter? Meta-analytic review of tailored print health behavior change interventions. *Psychological Bulletin, 133,* 673–693.

Oenema, A., Tan, F., & Brug, J. (2005). Short-term efficacy of a web-based computer tailored nutrition intervention: Main effects and mediators. *Annals of Behavioral Medicine, 29,* 54–63.

Ogden, C.L., Carroll, M.D., Curtin, L.R., McDowell, M.A., Tabak, C.J., & Flegal, K.M. (2006). Prevalence of overweight and obesity in the United States, 1999-2004. *Journal of the American Medical Association, 295,* 1549-1555.

Pinto, B. M., Lynn, H., Marcus, B. H., DePue, J., & Goldstein, M. G. (2001). Physician-based activity counseling: Intervention effects on mediators of motivational readiness for physical activity. *Annals of Behavioral Medicine, 23,* 2–10.

Preacher, K.J., Rucker, D.D., & Hayes, A.F. (2007). Addressing moderated mediation hypotheses: Theory, methods, and prescriptions. *Multivariate Behavioral Research, 42,* 185-227.

Prochaska, J. O., DiClemente, C. C., & Norcross, J. C. (1992). In search of how people change: Applications to addictive behaviors. *American Psychologist, 47,* 1102–1114.

Prochaska, J. O., & Velicer, W. F. (1997). The transtheoretical model of health behavior change. *American Journal of Health Promotion, 12,* 38–48.

Quinlan, K. B., & McCaul, K. D. (2000). Matched and mismatched interventions with young adult smokers: Testing a stage theory. *Health Psychology, 19,* 165–171.

Rakowski, W., Ehrich, B., Goldstein, M. G., Rimer, B. K., Pearlman, D. N. Clark, M. A., et al., (1998). Increasing mammography among women aged 40–74 by use of a stage-matched, tailored intervention. *Preventive Medicine, 27,* 748–756.

Rhodes, R. E. (2006). The built-in environment: The role of personality and physical activity. *Exercise and Sport Sciences Reviews, 34,* 83–88.

Rosenstock, I. M., Strecher, V. J., & Becker, M. H. (1988). Social learning theory and the health belief model. *Health Education Quarterly, 15,* 175–183.

Rothman, A. J. (2004). Is there nothing more practical than a good theory? Why innovations and advances in health behavior change will arise if interventions are more theory-friendly. *International Journal of Behavioral Nutrition and Physical Activity, 1,* 11.

Rothman, A. J. (2009). Capitalizing on opportunities to nurture and refine health behavior theories. *Health Education and Behavior, 26,* 150S–155S.

Rothman, A. J., Baldwin, A., & Hertel, A. (2004). Self-regulation and behavior change: Disentangling behavioral initiation and behavioral maintenance. In K. Vohs & R. Baumeister (Eds.), *The handbook of self-regulation* (pp. 130–148). New York: Guilford.

Rothman, A. J., Martino, S. C., Bedell, B. T., Detweiler, J. B., & Salovey, P. (1999). The systematic influence of gain- and loss-framed messages on interest in and use of different types of health behavior. *Personality and Social Psychology Bulletin, 25,* 1355–1369.

Rothman, A. J., & Salovey, P. (1997). Shaping perceptions to motivate healthy behavior: The role of message framing. *Psychological Bulletin, 121,* 3–19.

Rothman, A. J., & Salovey, P. (2007). The reciprocal relation between principles and practice: Social psychology and health behavior. In A. Kruglanski and E. T. Higgins (Eds.), *Social psychology: Handbook of basic principles* (2nd ed., pp. 826–849). New York: Guilford.

Rothman, A. J., Sheeran, P., & Wood, W. (2009). Reflective and automatic processes in the initiation and maintenance of food choices. *Annals of Behavioral Medicine* (Special Issue), *38,* S4–S17.

Rothman, A. J., & Updegraff, J. A. (2011). Specifying when and how gain- and loss-framed messages motivate healthy behavior: An integrated approach. In G. Keren (Ed.), *Perspectives on framing* (pp.257–278). New York: Psychology Press.

Rothman, A. J., Wlaschin, J., Bartels, R., Latimer, A., & Salovey, P. (2008). How persons and situations regulate message framing effects: The study of health behavior. In A. Elliot (Ed.), *Handbook of approach and avoidance motivation.* (pp. 475–486). Mahwah, NJ: Erlbaum.

Ruiter, R. A. C., Kessels, L. T. E., Jansma, B. M., & Brug, J. (2006). Increased attention for computer-tailored health communications: An event-related potential study. *Health Psychology, 25,* 300–306.

Salovey, P., Rothman, A. J., & Rodin, J. (1998). Health behavior. In D. T. Gilbert, S. T. Fiske, & G. Lindzey (Eds.), *The handbook of social psychology* (4th ed., Vol. 2, pp. 633–683). Boston: McGraw-Hill.

Sherman, D. K., Mann, T., & Updegraff, J. A. (2006). Approach/avoidance motivation, message framing, and health behavior: Understanding the congruency effect. *Motivation and Emotion, 30,* 165–169.

Skinner, C. S., Campbell, M. K., Rimer, B. K., Curry, S., & Prochaska, J. O. (1999). How effective is tailored print communication? *Annals of Behavioral Medicine, 21,* 290–298.

Skinner, C. S., Schildkraut, J. M., Berry, D., Calingaert, B., Marcom, P. K., Sugarman, J., et al. (2002). Pre-counseling education materials for brca testing: Does tailoring make a difference? *Genetic Testing, 6,* 93–105.

Skinner, C. S., Strecher, V. J., & Hospers, H. (1994). Physicians' recommendations for mammography: Do tailored messages make a difference? *American Journal of Public Health, 84,* 43–49.

Smith, T.W. (2006). Personality as risk and resilience in physical health. *Current Directions in Psychological Science, 15,* 227-231.

Snyder, M., & Cantor, N. (1998). Understanding personality and social behavior: A functionalist strategy. In D. T. Gilbert, S. T. Fiske, & G. Lindzey (Eds.), *The handbook of social psychology* (4th ed., pp. 635-679). New York: Oxford University Press.

Snyder, M., & Ickes, W. (1985). Personality and social behavior. In G. Lindzey & E. Aronson (Eds.), *Handbook of social psychology: Vol. 2. Special fields and applications* (3rd ed., pp. 883–948). New York: Random House.

Spencer, S. J., Zanna, M. P., & Fong, G. T. (2005). Establishing a causal chain: Why experiments are often more effective than mediational analyses in examining psychological processes. *Journal of Personality and Social Psychology, 89,* 845–851.

Spiegel, S., Grant-Pillow, H., & Higgins, E. T. (2004). How regulatory fit enhances motivational strength during goal pursuit. *European Journal of Social Psychology, 34,* 39–54.

Suls, J., & Fletcher, B. (1985). The relative efficacy of avoidant and nonavoidant coping strategies: A meta-analysis. *Health Psychology, 4,* 249–288.

Sutton, S. (2002). Using social cognition models to develop health behaviour interventions: Problems and assumptions. In D. Rutter & L. Quine (Eds.), *Changing health behaviour: Intervention and research with social cognition models* (pp. 193–208). Buckingham: Open University Press.

Swenson, S. L., Buell, S., Zettler, P., White, M., Ruston, D. C., & Lo, B. (2004). Patient-centered communication: Do patients really prefer it? *Journal of General Internal Medicine, 19,* 1069–1079.

Ukkola, O., & Bouchard, C. (2004). Role of candidate genes in the responses to long-term overfeeding: Review of findings. *Obesity Review, 5,* 3–12.

Updegraff, J. A., Sherman, D. K., Luyster, F. S., & Mann, T. L. (2007). The effects of message quality and congruency on perceptions of tailored health communications. *Journal of Experimental Social Psychology, 43,* 249–257.

Wardle J., & Carnell, S. (2009). Appetite is a heritable phenotype associated with adiposity. *Annals of Behavioral Medicine, 38,* 25–30.

Weinstein, N. D. (1988). The precaution adoption process. *Health Psychology, 7,* 355–386.

Weinstein, N. D. (1993). Testing four competing theories of health-protective behavior. *Health Psychology, 12,* 324–333.

Weinstein, N. D., Lyon, J. E., Sandman, P., & Cuite, C. (1998). Experimental evidence for stages of health behavior change: The precaution adoption process model applied to home radon testing. *Health Psychology, 17,* 445–453.

Weinstein, N. D., & Rothman, A. J. (2005). Revitalizing research on health behavior theories. *Health Education Research, 20,* 294–297.

Weinstein, N. D., Rothman, A. J., & Sutton, S. R. (1998). Stage theories of health behavior: Conceptual and methodological issues. *Health Psychology, 17,* 290–299.

Williams-Piehota, P., Pizarro, J., Schneider, T. R., Mowad, L., & Salovey, P. (2005). Matching health messages to monitor-blunting coping styles to motivate screening mammography. *Health Psychology, 24,* 58–67.

Williams-Piehota, P., Schneider, T. R., Pizarro, J., Mowad, L., & Salovey, P. (2003). Matching health messages to information-processing styles: Need for cognition and mammography utilization. *Psychology and Health, 19,* 407–423.

Williams-Piehota, P., Schneider, T. R., Pizarro, J., Mowad, L., & Salovey, P. (2004). Matching health messages to health locus of control beliefs for promoting mammography utilization. *Psychology and Health, 19,* 407–423.

Wood, W., & Neal, D. T. (2007). A new look at habits and the habit-goal interface. *Psychological Review, 114,* 843–863.

Forensic Personality and Social Psychology

Saul Kassin *and* Margaret Bull Kovera

Abstract

Forensic psychology is a term used to describe a broad range of research topics and applications that address human behavior in the legal system. Personality and social psychologists are among those who have contributed to our understanding of individual differences in performance (e.g., among liars and lie detectors, crime suspects, witnesses, and jurors) and situational influences (e.g., effects of training on lie detection, the false evidence ploy on false confessions, police feedback on eyewitnesses, and inadmissible testimony on jurors) as well as the role that psychologists have played within the legal system. In this chapter, we discuss how individual difference and situational variables contribute to the reliability of different types of evidence (e.g., confessions, eyewitnesses, alibis) introduced in court as well as how jurors make decisions about the evidence presented at trial.

Keywords: deception detection, confessions, eyewitnesses, juries, forensic psychology

Forensic psychology is a term used to describe a broad and growing range of research topics and applications that address human behavior in the legal system. In recent years, forensic psychologists have participated as scientists, trial consultants, advocates, critics, expert witnesses, and policy advisors. In so doing, they conduct their research not only in university-based laboratories but in police stations, courtrooms, prisons, and other legal settings.

Trained in the principles and methods of basic psychology, forensic psychology researchers study a wide range of issues—such as perception and memory processes as they influence eyewitness identifications and testimony; the processes of persuasion as they apply to police interrogations and the confessions they produce; cognitive development as it applies to the testimony, accuracy, and suggestibility of preschoolers and other children; adolescent brain development and its link to various metrics of legal competence; personality testing as it applies to the criminal profiling of serial bombers, rapists, arsonists, and other offender types; the use of the polygraph and other measures of bodily arousal as lie detector tests; and person perception and group dynamics as they apply to how jurors and juries make decisions.

Personality and social psychologists in particular have made substantial contributions to our understanding of the legal system, addressing broad and varied issues (Brewer & Williams, 2005). For example, researchers have examined whether police can tell when someone is lying and how they can make these judgments more accurately (Vrij, 2008); how juries make decisions in civil lawsuits (Bornstein, Wiener, Schopp, & Wilborn, 2008); how juries react to a battle of opposing experts in the courtroom (Levett & Kovera, 2008, 2009); how people evaluate claims of sexual harassment within different legal frameworks (Wiener et al, 2002); which personal attitudes and values are associated with support for the death penalty (Butler & Moran, 2007; Miller & Hayward, 2008); the perceived links between race and criminality (Eberhardt, Goff, Purdie, & Davies, 2004); the reasons why some people seek revenge in their sentencing decisions (Carlsmith & Darley, 2008); the dispositional and situational causes of prison abuse (Carnahan & McFarland, 2007; Haney & Zimbardo, 2009; Reicher & Haslam, 2006); and which types of procedures lead people to see a process as fair and just (Blader & Tyler, 2003; Skitka, 2009). This research is vitally important because the commonsense notions of judges, lawyers, and laypeople do not comport with much of what personality and social psychologists have discovered (Borgida & Fiske, 2007). For example, courts still harbor misconceptions about the nature of eyewitness memory (Wells & Quinlivan, 2009).

This chapter overviews basic research and recent developments in selected areas of forensic personality and social psychology. First, we discuss police investigations and the collection of testimonial evidence from suspects, informants, and eyewitnesses. Next we describe various aspects of the courtroom trial—namely, the selection of a jury, the presentation of evidence previously collected, the biasing influences of nonevidentiary sources of information, and the processes and outcomes of jury deliberations. Finally, we discuss various questions concerning science, common sense, and the role that forensic personality and social psychology plays in the legal system.

It is noteworthy that much of the research described in this chapter is more deeply rooted in social psychology than in personality theory. It is clear that personality traits and other bases of individual differences do contribute to juror decision-making, vulnerability to making false confessions, and other legally relevant behaviors. But forensic psychology researchers are often motivated not only to understand human behavior in the legal system but to identify procedures or interventions that will improve the quality of justice. Perhaps because of this practical social policy goal, researchers tend to design studies to identify situational factors that influence legally relevant behaviors—precisely because these situational factors are more amenable to systemic change than are individual differences in legal actors. Sometimes the pressure to focus on situational variables is explicit, as in the area of eyewitness identification research, wherein a leading scholar called on others to refocus their research efforts on identifying procedure variables that could be controlled by the criminal justice system in an effort to increase eyewitness accuracy (Wells, 1978). These applied concerns have produced a body of research that emphasizes the role of situational

variables in behavior to the relative neglect of personality variables or person x situation interactions.

Evidence

Whenever a serious crime is committed, detected, and reported to police, an evidence-gathering process is set into motion. Crime scene investigators collect available physical evidence from fingerprints, shoeprints, tire tracks, hairs, fibers, bloodstains, and other biological traces. If the crime resulted in death, an autopsy is conducted. In all cases, police interview witnesses and other persons of interest in an effort to develop a theory of what happened, how it happened, and why—and, most important, to identify suspects for interrogation. As part of this process, police must often determine whether the witnesses and suspects they interview are telling the truth or lying. How accurate are these judgments?

Deception Detection

People are surprisingly inept at deception detection (for reviews, see Bond & DePaulo, 2006; Granhag & Stromwall, 2004; see also Uleman & Saribay, chapter 14, this volume). There are several reasons for this problem—including the fact that people exhibit a truth bias, tending to take others' self-reports at face value; that people often lack the motivation to discern the truth; that lie detection is an inherently difficult and subtle task, lacking a single diagnostic cue such as Pinocchio's growing nose; and that liars often use deliberate behavioral countermeasures to conceal their deception; that liars often embed their deception within otherwise truthful narratives; and that social perceivers seldom receive useful feedback about their judgments and therefore cannot learn from their mistakes (Vrij, 2008).

Over the years, researchers have identified the social perception tendencies that impair lie detection performance, including the tendency to rely on visual behavioral cues that do not signal deception (DePaulo et al., 2003; Zuckerman, DePaulo, & Rosenthal, 1981). People are more accurate when they are instructed to focus on telltale cues of the body and voice than on the face (DePaulo, Lassiter, & Stone, 1982), when they report having based their judgments more on vocal cues than on visual information (Anderson et al., 1999), and when they are presented with audio recordings of liars and truth tellers rather than videotapes (Kassin, Meissner, & Norwick, 2005). In a survey of 2,500 adults in 63 countries, Bond and others found that more than 70% believed that liars tend to avert direct eye contact—a cue that is not supported by the research.

Similarly, most of Bond et al.'s survey respondents believed that people squirm, stutter, fidget, and groom themselves when they lie—also cues not supported by the research (The Global Deception Research Team, 2006).

A second problem, particularly in a high stakes forensic context, is that people assume that the way to spot a liar is to detect signs of anxiety and stress leakage. Yet in important real life situations (for example, at a high stakes poker table, the security screening area of an airport, or a police interrogation room) truth tellers are also likely to exhibit signs of stress (Bond & Fahey, 1987). For this reason, researchers have been seeking alternative approaches. One promising alternative behavioral cue rests on the observation that lying requires greater cognitive effort than telling the truth; hence social perceivers should focus on behavioral cues that betray effort (Vrij, 2008).

At present, forensically relevant research on human lie detection is focused on two sets of issues—involving, respectively, the personal and situational factors that influence deception detection performance. The first issue concerns the question of whether certain individuals are uniquely talented in their lie-detection skills—either as a function of their exposure to special training, experience, or intuitive abilities. The second issue concerns the question of whether lie detection performance is influenced by the circumstances of an encounter or the types of interview strategies that are used.

TRAINING TO DETECT DECEPTION

In *Criminal Interrogations and Confessions*, an influential manual on interrogation first published in 1962 and now in its fourth edition, Inbau, Reid, Buckley, and Jayne (2001) advise police investigators (1) to ask a series of special "behavior provoking questions" that elicit answers supposedly diagnostic of guilt and innocence (e.g., "Do you know who did take the money?" "What do you think should happen to the person who took the money?"), and then (2) to observe changes in the suspect's verbal and nonverbal behavior (e.g., eye contact, pauses, posture, fidgety movements) that betray whether he or she is telling the truth or lying. For a person who is under suspicion, an investigator's judgment at this stage becomes a pivotal choice point, determining whether the suspect is interrogated or sent home.

Based on one published study, Inbau et al. (2001) claim that training in the Reid technique produces an exceedingly high, 85% level of accuracy (this claim is explicitly made in John E. Reid and Associates training sessions) in differentiating truthful accounts from those that are deceptive. Yet the study is seriously flawed, and the results are grossly out of step with basic social psychology. In that study, Horvath, Jayne, and Buckley (1994) selected 60 interview tapes from the Reid collection, the ground truths of which could not be established with certainty. Then they edited the tapes, showed these edited tapes to four experienced in-house staff members of John E. Reid and Associates, and concluded from their judgments that the Reid technique produced high levels of accuracy (no comparison group of untrained or lay evaluators was included). Yet in laboratories all over the world, research has consistently shown that most of the demeanor cues touted by the Reid technique do not empirically discriminate between truth-telling and deception (DePaulo et al., 2003).

Evaluations of the Reid approach to lie detection have not produced impressive results. Vrij, Mann, and Fisher (2006) had some subjects but not others commit a mock crime they were motivated to deny. All subjects were then interviewed using the Reid technique. Responses to the behavior provoking questions did not significantly distinguish between truth tellers and liars in the predicted manner (e.g., the liars were not more anxious or less helpful). In principle, it is reasonable to expect that special questions can be developed to that would discriminate between truthful and deceptive suspects, in part because innocent people are more likely than perpetrators to waive their rights to silence, to counsel, and to a lineup—cooperative acts that may betray the fear that accompanies innocence rather than guilt (Kassin, 2005). Currently, however, there is no empirical support for the diagnostic value of the questions advocated in the Reid technique.

There is also no evidence that the verbal and nonverbal cues that police are often trained to observe reliably differentiate between liars and truth tellers. For example, Kassin and Fong (1999) randomly trained some college students but not others in the use of the behavioral symptoms cited by the Reid technique. All students then watched videotaped interviews of mock suspects, some of whom committed one of four mock crimes; others of whom did not. Upon questioning, all suspects denied their involvement. Observers could not reliably differentiate between the two groups of suspects. In fact, those who underwent training were significantly less accurate, more confident, and more biased toward seeing deception. Using these same taped interviews, Meissner and Kassin (2002) tested experienced samples of police detectives and found that they exhibited these same erroneous and biased tendencies. Police frequently make erroneous prejudgments of guilt with confidence (e.g., Elaad, 2003; Garrido, Masip, & Herrero, 2004; Leach, Talwar, Lee, Bala, & Lindsay, 2004). In fact, recent studies suggest that the behavioral cues that Reid-trained police are taught to use are highly consistent with common sense (Masip, Herrero, Garrido, & Barba, 2010).

ARE THERE INDIVIDUAL "WIZARDS" OF LIE DETECTION?

Three aspects of lie detection performance can be distinguished: overall judgment accuracy, response bias, and confidence. Focused on accuracy, researchers have long sought to identify individual and group differences in deception detection ability. Clearly, the distribution of lie detection accuracy scores suggests that some individuals are intuitively and consistently more accurate than others (Ekman, O'Sullivan, & Frank, 1999). Although some social perceivers are better than others at distinguishing truths and lies, a review of the literature indicates that individual differences are small (Bond & DePaulo, 2008). Focusing on professional expertise, Ekman and O'Sullivan (1991) found that U.S. Secret Service agents were somewhat more accurate than judges, psychiatrists, police investigators, and other groups. Prisoners are also more accurate than others (Hartwig, Granhag, Strömwall, & Andersson, 2004).

In the most recent—and controversial—effort to identify individuals with special lie detection abilities, O'Sullivan and Ekman (2004) tested approximately 13,000 people from all walks of life, using parallel tasks, and reported having identified 15 "wizards" of lie detection who achieved at least an 80% level of accuracy in two or three parallel tests. Recently, however, C. Bond and Uysal (2007) challenged both the poorly controlled procedures through which these test scores were derived and the statistical significance of the so-called wizards (for a rejoinder, see O'Sullivan, 2007). With regard to methods, it appears that O'Sullivan and Ekman (2004) collected much of their data at lie detection workshops they had conducted, that the tests were often self-scored by subjects, and that follow-up stimulus tests were often mailed to subjects and taken without supervision. As for the results, Bond and Uysal (2007) argued that the small number of high-performers who emerged from the testing were

statistical flukes, that the number did not statistically exceed chance expectations in light of the thousands of subjects tested and the criterion set for wizardry. In a more recent effort to identify experts, G. Bond (2008) tested 234 law enforcement professionals and college students, tested subjects in a controlled setting, and adopted a more stringent criterion (80% accuracy on four different tests, each administered twice). Using this procedure, two "experts" emerged whose performance were unlikely to have been achieved by chance. Clearly, more research is needed on this issue.

SITUATIONAL INFLUENCES ON LIE-DETECTION PERFORMANCE

As some researchers have focused on individual differences and the lessons potentially to be learned from top performers, others have sought to improve police lie detection performance—either through the use of emerging brain imaging technologies (e.g., Kozel et al., 2005) or by developing new approaches to interviewing that can increase the diagnosticity of human truth and lie judgments (Colwell, Hiscock, & Memon, 2002). In one line of research, interviewers made more accurate judgments by withholding crime details while questioning suspects, a strategy that traps guilty liars in discernible inconsistencies when these facts are later disclosed (Hartwig, Granhag, Strömwall, & Vrij, 2005). Interviewers who are trained in this "strategic disclosure" technique thus become more accurate in their judgments (Hartwig, Granhag, Strömwall, & Kronkvist, 2006). In a second line of research, Vrij, Fisher, Mann, and Leal (2006) theorized that lying is more effortful than telling the truth, so interviewers should tax a suspect's cognitive load and attend to cues that betray effort. Hence, when interviewers had truth tellers and liars recount their stories in reverse chronological order, they became more accurate in their ability to distinguish between the truthful and deceptive accounts (Vrij, Mann, Fisher, Leal, Milne, & Bull, 2008). People are also better at discriminating truths and lies when asked to determine if a speaker "has to think hard" than when asked the more direct question, "Is the person lying?" (Landström, Granhag, & Hartwig, 2005).

Police Interrogations and Confessions

There is no evidence more powerful than confession. U.S. courts typically exclude a confession from evidence if it was extracted by physical force; deprivation of food, sleep, or other biological needs;

threats of punishment or harm; promises of immunity or leniency; or without properly notifying the suspect of his or her *Miranda* rights (Kamisar, LaFave, & Israel, 2003). Thus, the modern American police interrogation has become a psychologically oriented process of influence (for an historical overview, see Leo, 2008; for social psychological perspectives on interrogation, see Davis & O'Donahue, 2004; Kassin, 1997; Kassin & Wrightsman, 1985; Zimbardo, 1967).

How do police get suspects to confess? Before describing specific techniques, it is important to note that police interrogation is by definition a guilt-presumptive process—a theory-driven social interaction led by an authority figure who holds a strong a priori belief about the target and who measures success by the ability to extract an admission from that target. Does this presumption influence the way police conduct interrogations, perhaps leading them to adopt a questioning style that confirms their beliefs? Modeled after the classic biased hypothesis-testing experiment by Snyder and Swann (1978), and other similar studies (for reviews, see Nickerson, 1998; Snyder, 1992; Snyder & Stukas, 1999), Kassin, Goldstein, and Savitsky (2003) investigated whether presumption of guilt shapes the conduct of student interrogators, their suspects, and ultimately the judgments made by neutral observers. In Phase I, participants who were assigned to be suspects stole $100 as part of a mock theft or engaged in a related but innocent act, after which they were interviewed via headphones from a remote location. Serving as investigators, students who conducted the interviews were led to believe either that most suspects are guilty or that most are innocent. The sessions were audiotaped and followed by postinterrogation questionnaires given to all participants. In Phase II, observers who were blind to the manipulations in Phase I listened to the taped interviews, judged the suspects as guilty or innocent, and rated their impressions of both suspects and investigators.

Overall, investigators who were led to expect guilt rather than innocence asked more guilt-presumptive questions, used more techniques, exerted more pressure to get a confession, and made innocent suspects sound more anxious and defensive to observers. They were also more likely to believe that the suspects were guilty. Condition-blind observers who later listened to the tapes also perceived suspects in the guilty-expectations condition as more likely to have committed the mock crime. The presumption of guilt thus set into motion a process of behavioral confirmation, shaping the interrogator's behavior, the suspect's behavior, and ultimately the judgments of neutral observers. The most pressure-filled sessions, as rated by all participants, occurred when interrogators who presumed guilt were paired with suspects who were innocent. In these sessions, interrogators who presumed guilt saw the innocent suspect's plausible denials as proof of a guilty person's resistance—and redoubled their efforts to elicit a confession. Using a similar laboratory methodology, other researchers have replicated these results (Hill, Memon, & McGeorge, 2008).

Legally prohibited from eliciting confessions through violence, physical discomfort, threats of harm, or promises of leniency, observational studies have confirmed that modern police interrogation is a psychologically oriented process (Soukara, Bull, Vrij, Turner, & Cherryman, 2009). In a recent survey, police investigators estimated that the mean length of interrogation is 1.6 hours and that the tactics most frequently used were to physically isolate suspects from family and friends, typically in a small private room; identifying contradictions in the suspects' accounts; trying to establish rapport to gain suspects' trust; confronting suspects with evidence of their guilt; and appealing to their self-interests (Kassin et al., 2007).

Numerous training manuals advise police in how to extract confessions from suspects. In the technique recommended by the most influential manual (Inbau et al., 2001), interrogation consists of a multistep process that is essentially reducible to an interplay of three processes (Kassin, 1997, 2005; Kassin & Gudjonsson, 2004): *isolation,* which increases stress, discomfort, and the suspect's desire to escape the situation; *confrontation,* in which the interrogator strongly accuses the suspect of the crime, sometimes citing real or fictitious evidence to bolster the claim; and *minimization,* in which a sympathetic interrogator morally justifies or excuses the crime, leading the suspect to infer he or she will be treated with leniency upon confessing.

DISPOSITIONAL RISK FACTORS

Some suspects are dispositionally more vulnerable to influence than others and at greater risk for false confessions. Individuals with personality traits that render them prone to *compliance* in social situations are especially vulnerable because of their eagerness to please others and a desire to avoid confrontation, particularly with those in authority (Gudjonsson, 2003). Individuals who are prone to *suggestibility*—whose memories can be altered by misleading questions and negative feedback—are also more likely to confess under interrogation. Similarly, people who are also highly anxious, fearful, depressed, delusional, or otherwise psychologically disordered are often at a heightened risk to confess under pressure (Gudjonsson, 2003).

Youth is another substantial risk factor for false confessions. Statistics show that more than 90 percent of juveniles whom police seek to question waive their *Miranda* rights to silence and a lawyer (Grisso, 1981). The presence of a parent, guardian, or other "interested adult"—which many states require to protect young suspects—does not lower this waiver rate, as adults often urge their youths to cooperate with police (Oberlander & Goldstein, 2001). Juveniles represent a disproportionate number of the population of false confessors. In a database of 125 proven false confessions, 33% of the cases involved juveniles, most of whom had confessed to a murder (Drizin & Leo, 2004). Adolescents are not only more compliant and suggestible than adults but also their decision-making is characterized by an "immaturity of judgment"—a pattern of behavior characterized by impulsivity, a focus on immediate gratification, and a diminished capacity in future orientation and perceptions of risk (Owen-Kostelnik, Reppucci, & Meyer, 2006). To the adolescent not fully focused on long-term consequences, confession may thus serve as an expedient way out of a stressful situation.

People who are intellectually impaired are also at risk in the interrogation room. At least 22% of exonerees in their sample of false confessions were diagnosable with mental retardation, as measured by conventional IQ tests (Drizin & Leo, 2004). This result is not surprising. Most people who are mentally retarded cannot comprehend their rights, leading some researchers to describe the *Miranda* warnings delivered to low IQ individuals as "words without meaning" (Cloud, Shepherd, Barkoff, & Shur, 2002). People who are intellectually impaired also exhibit an acquiescence response bias that leads them to say "yes" to a whole range of questions—even when an affirmative response is incorrect, inappropriate, or absurd (Finlay & Lyons, 2002). They are also highly suggestible, as measured by the degree to which they are influenced by leading and misleading questions (Gudjonsson, 2003).

Psychopathology may also put people at risk in an interrogation setting. Depressed mood is linked to a susceptibility to provide false confession to police (Gudjonsson, Sigurdsson, Asgeirsdottir, & Sigfusdottir, 2006). Multiple exposures to unpleasant or traumatic life events also were significantly associated with self-reported false confessions during interrogation (Gudjonsson, Sigurdsson, Asgeirsdottir, & Sigfusdottir, 2007). Most mentally disordered offenders exhibited insufficient understanding of *Miranda*, particularly when the warnings required increased levels of reading comprehension (Rogers, Harrison, Hazelwood, & Sewell, 2007). Finally, offenders with mental illness self-reported a 22% lifetime false confession rate (Redlich, 2007; also see Redlich, Summers, & Hoover, 2010)—notably higher than the 12% found in samples of prison inmates without mental illness (Sigurdsson & Gudjonsson, 1996).

SITUATIONAL RISK FACTORS

At the broadest level, situational variation in people's tendency to confess is evident in that confession rates vary across countries, indicating the role of institutional and cultural influences. For example, suspects detained for questioning in the United States confess at a rate 40 to 45 percent; in England the figure is closer to 60 percent. In Japan, where few restraints are placed on police, and where social norms favor confession as a response to transgressions and shame, more than 90 percent of defendants confess.

Within the United States, anecdotal evidence from DNA exonerations suggests that certain interrogation tactics, though legal, put innocent people at risk to confess. One potentially problematic tactic is the *false evidence ploy*—in which police bolster their accusations by telling suspects that there is incontrovertible evidence of their guilt (e.g., a fingerprint, blood or hair sample, eyewitness identification, or failed lie-detector test)—even if such evidence does not exist. Can this sort of deception lead people to feel so trapped that they confess to crimes they did not commit? Although the U.S. Supreme Court has sanctioned the false evidence ploy (*Frazier v. Cupp*, 1969), empirical research warns of the risk (see Kassin et al., 2010).

In self-report surveys, actual suspects state that they confessed because they perceived themselves to be trapped by the evidence (Gudjonsson & Sigurdsson, 1999; Moston, Stephenson, & Williamson, 1992). Laboratory experiments showing that false evidence causes innocent people to confess to prohibited acts they did not commit—and may even lead them to internalize the belief in their own culpability. In the first such study, experimenters accused college students typing on a keyboard of causing the computer to crash by pressing a key they were instructed to avoid (Kassin & Kiechel, 1996). Despite their innocence and initial denials, participants were asked to sign a confession. In some sessions but not others, a confederate said she witnessed the subject hit the forbidden key. This false evidence nearly doubled the number of students who signed a written confession. This effect replicates even when the confession was said to bear a financial consequence or future commitment of time (e.g., Horselenberg, Merckelbach, & Josephs, 2003; Redlich & Goodman, 2003) and even among informants who are pressured to report on a confession allegedly made by another person (Swanner, Beike, & Cole, 2010). Using a completely different paradigm, Nash and Wade (2009) used digital editing software to fabricate video evidence of participants in a computerized gambling experiment "stealing" money from the "bank" during a losing round. Presented with this false evidence, all participants confessed and most internalized the belief in their own guilt.

Across the history of basic psychology, it has been clear that misinformation renders people vulnerable to manipulation from a host of influences. Classic experiments have shown that the presentation of false information via confederates, witnesses, counterfeit test results, bogus norms, false physiological feedback, and the like, can substantially alter people's visual perceptions and judgments, beliefs, behaviors, emotional states, feelings of physical attraction, self-assessments, memories for observed and experienced events, and even certain medical outcomes—as seen in studies of the well-known placebo effect (Benedetti, 2009; Price, Finniss, & Benedetti, 2008). American courts permit the false evidence ploy on the assumption that it does not induce false confessions, but scientific evidence of human malleability in the face of misinformation is broad and pervasive. There is no reason to believe that innocents inside an interrogation room are immune to this effect (for a review, see Kassin et al., 2010).

A second problematic tactic is *minimization*, the process by which interrogators offer moral justification or face-saving excuses, minimizing the crime and making confession seem like a cost-effective solution. Interrogators are trained to suggest to suspects that their actions were spontaneous, accidental, provoked, peer-pressured, or otherwise justifiable by external factors. By design, minimization tactics lead people to infer by pragmatic implication (Harris & Monaco, 1978; Hilton, 1995) that they will be treated with leniency if they confess even when no explicit promises are made (Kassin & McNall, 1991).

To measure the behavioral effects of minimization on confessions, Russano, Meissner, Farchet, and Kassin (2005) paired participants with a confederate for a problem-solving study and instructed them to work alone on some trials and jointly on others. In a guilty condition, the confederate sought help on an individual problem, inducing the participant to violate the experimental rule; in the innocent condition, the confederate did not make this request. The experimenter soon "discovered" the similarity in their solutions, separated the participant and confederate, and accused the participant of cheating. The experimenter tried to get the participant to sign an admission by promising leniency (research credit in exchange for a return session without penalty), making minimizing remarks ("I'm sure you didn't realize what a big deal it was"), using both tactics, or using no tactics. As predicted, the confession rate was higher among guilty subjects than innocent, when leniency was promised than when it was not, and when minimization was used than when it was not. Compared to the no-tactics condition, minimization increased not only the rate of true confessions from the guilty (from 46% to 81%) but false confessions from the innocent as well (from 6% to 18%).

THE PHENOMENOLOGY OF INNOCENCE

There is an additional factor, not a disposition per se but rather a situation-based state of mind that can prove problematic: the phenomenology of innocence. On the basis of anecdotal and research evidence, Kassin (2005) suggested the ironic hypothesis that *innocence* itself may put *innocents* at risk. People who stand falsely accused believe that truth and justice will prevail and that their innocence will become transparent to investigators, juries, and others. Often failing to realize that they are suspects not witnesses, they cooperate fully with police by waiving their rights and speaking freely to defend themselves. Although mock criminals vary their disclosures according to whether the interrogator seems informed about the evidence, innocents are uniformly forthcoming—regardless of how informed the interrogator seems to be (Hartwig et al., 2005).

Four out of five suspects in a sample of live and videotaped interrogations waived their rights and submitted to questioning—and people who had no prior record of crime were the most likely to do so (Leo, 1996), suggesting that innocents in particular are at risk to waive their rights. In a controlled laboratory setting, some participants, but not others, committed a mock theft of $100 (Kassin & Norwick, 2004). Upon questioning, participants who were innocent were more likely to sign a waiver than those who were guilty. Afterward, most innocent subjects said that they waived their rights precisely because they were innocent: "I did nothing wrong," "I had nothing to hide." In short, *Miranda* warnings may not adequately protect the citizens who need it most—those accused of crimes they did not commit.

SITUATIONAL AND DISPOSITIONAL RISK FACTORS AS SUFFICIENT

The reasons why people confess to crimes they did not commit are numerous and multifaceted (Kassin & Gudjonsson, 2004). In some cases, the individual is so dispositionally naive, compliant, suggestible, delusional, anxious, or otherwise impaired that little interrogative pressure is required to produce a false confession. In these instances, clinical testing and assessment may be useful in determining whether an individual suspect is prone to confess. At other times, however, normal adults who are not overly naive, impaired, or disordered—confess to crimes they did not commit as a way of coping with the stress of police interrogation. Human beings can often be profoundly manipulated by figures of authority and other aspects of their surroundings and induced to behave in ways that are detrimental to themselves and others. In short, it is clear that both personal and situational risk factors may be sufficient, and neither is necessary, to increase the risk of a false confession.

Alibi Evidence

An alibi is a form of witness who tells a story, accompanied by some means of proof, which places a suspect at the time of the crime in another place, making it impossible for him or her to have committed the crime. An alibi may place the defendant in any other setting (e.g., at home, at work, or in a public place) and engaged in any other activity (e.g., sleeping, working, recreating), and the corroborating proof that is offered may consist of physical evidence (e.g., surveillance camera footage, ATM receipts) or person evidence (e.g., sworn testimony from friends, family members, or strangers). What makes alibis important is that they often contradict the state's incriminating evidence—forcing juries to choose between the conflicting accounts.

Innocent people who were convicted but later exonerated by DNA often presented alibis and prosecutors often cited "weak alibis" as proof of guilt (Olson & Wells, 2004). There are two reasons why people cannot be trusted to assess a defendant's

denials with accuracy. One is the now familiar phenomenon described earlier that people are poor judges of truth and deception. In one two-part study, college students committed one of four mock crimes, which they found to be moderately stressful: breaking and entering a locked office building, shoplifting in a local gift shop, vandalizing a building by chalking it with graffiti, or breaking into someone's personal computer account (Kassin & Fong, 1999). Afterward, a security officer apprehended and brought them to the laboratory for questioning. Others innocently reported to the same crime scenes, at which point they too were apprehended and brought for questioning. All participants were preinstructed to deny involvement if questioned and all were issued an incentive to be judged innocent by their questioner. During the interviews, which were videotaped, all suspects denied their guilt, offering alibis that were true (among those who were innocent) or false (among those who committed the mock crimes). In a second part of the study, other participants watched the tapes and judged the mock suspects. Participants were unable to differentiate between suspects whose alibis were true and false.

In a follow-up study using the same tapes, police could not distinguish between true and false alibis (Meissner & Kassin, 2002). In studies conducted in Sweden, researchers separately interviewed each member of truth-telling pairs and lying pairs of suspects about their alibis for a lunch that they did or did not have together. Replicating past research, they found that lay observers could only modestly distinguish between the truthful and deceptive alibis on the basis of these interviews. Interestingly, the problem stemmed from the fact that observers most frequently cited "consistency within pairs of suspects" as a basis for their judgments. Yet the lying pairs, forewarned that they would be interviewed, fabricated alibis with consistent details (Granhag, Strömwall, & Jonsson, 2003; Strömwall, Granhag, & Jonsson, 2003).

There is a second reason for concern over the way in which juries are likely to use alibi evidence. As a general rule, most people, when they are not alone, spend most of their time with family, friends, and acquaintances—precisely the kinds of defense-interested parties that may elicit skepticism from juries. Attribution theory predicts that jurors would discount the testimony of alibi witnesses who provide friendly support for defendants with whom they have a positive relationship. At the same time, research described earlier shows that people often do not discount what others say even when it is logically appropriate to do so (Jones, 1990). To test these propositions in the context of alibi evidence, mock jurors watched a trial involving a defendant who was positively identified by an eyewitness but whose innocence was supported by an alibi who was either a relative or a stranger (Lindsay, Lim, Marando, & Cully, 1986). As indicated by a lowered conviction rate, jurors were influenced by the stranger but not by the relative. In a second study, mock jurors heard testimony from a witness who corroborated or failed to corroborate the defendant's account that he was at home during an armed robbery for which he was identified (Culhane & Hosch, 2004). Jurors were significantly influenced by the alibi when it was the defendant's neighbor ("Yes, I saw him working in his yard from 5:00 to 7:30") but not when it was his girlfriend ("Yes, he was with me at his home from 5:00 on"). Other studies as well have shown that jurors see alibis as more or less credible depending on their relationship to the defendant (Hosch et al., 2011).

In an effort to understand what constitutes a strong and believable alibi to social perceivers, Olson and Wells (2004) proposed a taxonomy consisting of two dimensions: (1) whether the proof comes in the form of physical or personal evidence, and (2) the extent to which the alibi is easy or difficult to fabricate. To test this model, they presented participants, instructed to play the role of detectives, with brief descriptions of crimes followed by the alibis of three suspects. In all cases, participants rated the credibility of the alibis—which varied in the nature of the physical evidence (none; easy to fabricate; difficult to fabricate) and the person evidence (none; motivated familiar other; nonmotivated familiar other; nonmotivated stranger). Overall, the results supported the proposed taxonomy—though there were also two noteworthy findings. One was that participants were generally skeptical of alibis, yielding a mean believability score of only 7.4 out of 10 even in the strongest condition containing difficult to fabricate physical evidence (e.g., the defendant's presence on a timed and dated security camera) and difficult to fabricate person evidence (e.g., a store clerk). Second, participants were more likely to believe physical evidence than person evidence— even when the physical evidence was easy to fabricate (e.g., a cash receipt). This latter result more specifically confirms that social perceivers are inherently skeptical of human alibis that are familiar to a defendant—even when not motivated by familiarity, friendship, and personal interest.

Eyewitness Identifications

Mistaken eyewitness identifications, like false confessions, contribute to the prevalence of wrongful convictions. Inaccurate identification of innocent suspects are a factor in 50–90% of wrongful convictions, depending on the sample of cases examined, making it the single most frequent cause of this error (Garrett, 2008; Wells et al., 1998). In several DNA exoneration cases, multiple witnesses had mistakenly identified the innocent defendant as the person whom they saw committing a crime (e.g., Wells et al., 1998).

Wells (1978) identified two broad categories of variables that influence witness accuracy: Estimator variables and system variables. Estimator variables are factors that are present during the crime, including characteristics of the crime, the witness (including individual difference variables), and the perpetrator. Research on estimator variables provides information that allows police officers, prosecutors, judges, expert witnesses, and jurors to postdict the likelihood that witnesses will make accurate identifications given particular witnessing conditions. System variables are characteristics of the identification procedure that actors in the criminal justice system can control, such as instructions to the witness, the method of presenting lineup members to the witness, and whether the lineup administrator knows which lineup member is the suspect. Research on system variables not only provides information that assists legal decision-makers postdict witness accuracy but also provides evidence to support changes in the policies and procedures that govern the collection of eyewitness identification evidence. Because situational variables are more easily inferred from police reports and witness testimony and they are more likely to be modifiable by the justice system, research on these variables is more plentiful than research on personality influences on eyewitness accuracy.

ESTIMATOR VARIABLES

A number of factors associated with the witnessing conditions, the witness, and the perpetrator allow legal decision-makers to postdict the accuracy of eyewitness identifications. Perpetrators who conceal their hairlines with a bandana, baseball cap, or hoody are more difficult for witnesses to identify than those whose hairlines are fully visible (Cutler, 2006; Cutler, Penrod, & Martens, 1987a). Other alterations of appearance—the addition of glasses, changed hair, or advancing age— also increase the difficulty of the witness's identification task (Read, 1995; Read,

Tollestrup, Hammersley, McFadzen, & Christensen, 1990). But perpetrators need not alter their appearance for their characteristics to influence the accuracy of witness identifications. For example, the race and ethnicity of the victim and the perpetrator interact to influence the accuracy of witness identifications. Witnesses are more likely to correctly identify perpetrators with whom they share racial or ethnic group membership than perpetrators who are members of a different racial or ethnic group, a phenomenon known as the own-race bias or the cross-race effect (Meissner & Brigham, 2001; Platz & Hosch, 1988). Conversely, witnesses are more likely to mistakenly identify innocent suspects when the perpetrator and the witness come from different racial or ethnic groups than when they come from the same group. This bias does not appear to be the result of individual differences in witness prejudice but instead may be the result of decreased practice in differentiating among other race faces (Meissner & Brigham, 2001).

The level of stress that witnesses experience can vary depending on the circumstances of the crime that is witnessed. When witnesses fear for their lives because the perpetrator is threatening them with physical harm, stress levels will be high. It is also possible to witness a crime while lacking knowledge that a crime is being committed, with the witness learning only later that it will be necessary for them to identify the perpetrator. Field studies of the effects of stress on the accuracy of eyewitness identifications have produced mixed results (Behrman & Davey, 2001; Valentine, Pickering, & Darling, 2003), and laboratory studies can be problematic because it is unethical to induce in the lab the high levels of stress actual witnesses experience in life-threatening situations.

Researchers ethically manipulated extreme stress in one experimental study in the context of a military survival-training program that was designed to teach military personnel to endure high-stress interrogations (Morgan et al., 2004). Participants underwent high-stress interrogation, a low-stress interrogation, or both types of interrogations after which they attempted to identify their interrogators from photo-arrays. When the interrogator was present in the photo-array, personnel made more correct identifications of interrogators from low-stress interviews than from high-stress interrogations. The stressfulness of the interrogations did not affect the rate of mistaken identifications from target-absent photo-arrays. A meta-analysis of the effects of stress on eyewitness identification accuracy confirmed these findings; high stress negatively influenced the accuracy of correct identifications but did not significantly affect mistaken identifications (Deffenbacher, Bornstein, Penrod, & McGorty, 2004).

In addition to increasing witness stress, the presence of a weapon can draw the attention of the witness to the weapon and away from other features of the perpetrator that might later assist the witness in identifying the culprit. A meta-analysis testing the effects of weapon presence on identification accuracy revealed that the presence of a weapon decreased the ability of witnesses to make an accurate identification (Steblay, 1992). Weapon effects are exacerbated when the weapon is a gun or when witnesses participate in a live situation that manipulates the presence of an object that could be construed as a weapon (e.g., a syringe; Maas & Kohnken, 1989). Children are also susceptible to the weapon focus effect (Davies, Smith, & Blincoe, 2008; Pickel, Narter, Jameson, & Lenhardt, 2008). In addition to drawing witnesses' attention because they pose a threat, weapons that are unusual for a particular setting (e.g., a gun at a baseball game; Pickel, 1999) are more memorable than weapons that are expected given the crime setting (e.g., scissors at a hair salon; Pickel, 1998), suggesting that threat and typicality both contribute to the weapon focus effect (Hope & Wright, 2007).

The length of time that a witness views a perpetrator's face (exposure duration) or that passes between the witnessed event and the identification attempt (retention interval) also affects witness accuracy. Longer exposure durations and shorter retention intervals are both associated with improved witness memory. These findings have been replicated across paradigms, including facial recognition paradigms in which participants are exposed to a series of target faces and then when watching a series of test faces must indicate whether those faces were seen previously in the target phase (Laughery, Alexander, & Lane, 1971), laboratory simulation paradigms (Cutler, Penrod, O'Rourke, & Martens, 1986; Memon, Hope, & Bull, 2003), field studies (Krafka & Penrod, 1985), and archival studies of actual crimes (Behrman & Davey, 2001; Klobuchar, Steblay, & Caligiuri, 2006; Valentine et al., 2003). Meta-analysis confirms that exposure duration is positively correlated with correct identifications and that longer exposures reduce mistaken identifications. Conversely, longer retention intervals reduce correct identification and increase mistaken identifications (Shapiro & Penrod, 1986).

SYSTEM VARIABLES

The identification procedure is similar to an experiment in which the lineup administrator is testing whether the suspect and the perpetrator are the same person (Wells & Luus, 1990). Just as there are characteristics of experiments that allow for stronger conclusions (e.g., experimenters who are blind to conditions, stimulus materials and instructions that do not create demand characteristics), features of the identification task may also allow for stronger inferences that the suspect is indeed the perpetrator. The most commonly researched features are lineup composition, instructions to the witness, the method of presenting the lineup members to the witness, and whether the lineup administrator knows which lineup member is the suspect.

Lineup Composition

If an administrator selects fillers for a photo array or lineup that do not resemble the perpetrator (e.g., the perpetrator is light-skinned and all the fillers are dark-skinned), the lineup composition may signal to the witness which lineup member is the suspect. Administrators generally use one of two methods to select fillers for identification tasks. In the "match-to-suspect" method, administrators select fillers that resemble the suspect. Alternatively, administrators may match the fillers to the witness's description of the perpetrator (i.e., the match-to-description method). Fillers chosen using this method must have any characteristic that witnesses mention in their descriptions but may vary on any feature that is omitted.

Photo arrays constructed using the match-to-description method of choosing lineup fillers increase correct identifications and decrease mistaken identifications compared to matched-to-suspect photo arrays. Witnesses were more likely to mistakenly identify innocent suspects when the fillers were matched to the suspect than when they were matched to the culprit (Clark & Tunnicliff, 2001), a variation on the match-to-description method that is only possible in laboratory experiments in which the culprit's identity is known. In another study, researchers constructed individual photo arrays for each witness to a staged theft that varied in whether the fillers matched the suspect, matched the witness's description of the perpetrator, or mismatched the witness's description as well as whether the perpetrator was present in the lineup (Wells, Rydell, & Seelau, 1993). When the culprit was present, witnesses made more correct identifications from arrays in which the fillers were matched

to the witnesses' descriptions of the perpetrator than from those in which the fillers were matched to the suspect—who in this case is also the perpetrator. There were no differences in correct identifications obtained from arrays in which the fillers were matched or mismatched to description. For target-absent arrays, witnesses made more false identifications from arrays in which the fillers mismatched the description than from either the suspect-matched or description-matched arrays. In sum, the match-to-description arrays produced the best mix of correct and false identifications.

Lineup Instructions

The lineup administrator provides instructions to witnesses about how they are to approach the identification task and these instructions have the potential to communicate the lineup administrator's hypothesis to the witness. For example, instructions may indicate to the witness that the administrator believes that the perpetrator is one of the lineup members or that the administrator expects the witness to make a choice from the lineup (i.e., make a positive identification). In contrast, instructions could warn the witness that the perpetrator may not be one of the lineup members. When this type of warning is present, witnesses are less likely to make a positive identification than when the instructions suggest that the perpetrator is in the lineup (Cutler, Penrod, & Martens, 1987b; Malpass & Devine, 1981). A meta-analysis of the effects of biased lineup instructions on witness accuracy suggested that biased instructions increase false identifications but do not affect rates of correct identifications (Steblay, 1997). Although in his qualitative reanalysis of the studies contained in the meta-analysis, Clark (2005) questioned the meta-analytic findings regarding correct identifications, concluding instead that biased instructions also increase correct identifications. However, the authors of both the quantitative and qualitative reviews agree that biased instructions increase the likelihood of mistaken identifications (Clark, 2005; Steblay, 1997).

Lineup Presentation

Lineup administrators most frequently present lineup members or photos from a photospread to witnesses simultaneously; the witness then indicates whether the perpetrator is among the lineup members or depicted in one of the photos (Wolgater, Malpass, & McQuiston, 2004). An alternative method of presenting lineup members consists of presenting each lineup member sequentially to witnesses, with the witnesses judging whether each lineup member is the perpetrator and continuing to the next lineup member only when they judge that it is not (Wells et al., 1998). A meta-analysis of laboratory research comparing identifications made from sequential and simultaneous lineups suggests that witnesses are less likely to make both correct and mistaken identifications from a sequential lineup than from a simultaneous lineup but that the reduction in correct identifications is much smaller than the reduction in mistaken identifications (Steblay, Dysart, Fulero, & Lindsay, 2001). This pattern of results may be the result of a shift in criterion for choosing between the two lineups, with witnesses more likely to make a positive identification (i.e., a choice) from a simultaneous lineup (Meissner, Tredoux, Parker, & MacLin, 2005).

Based on these findings and others, some researchers have argued for policy reform, advocating that sequential lineup presentation become standard operating procedure (Wells, Malpass, Lindsay, Fisher, Turtle, & Fulero, 2000). Others have argued that the science examining the sequential superiority effect is not yet developed enough to support a shift in policy, especially because the psychological mechanisms underlying the benefits of sequential lineups are not yet understood (McQuiston-Surrett, Malpass, & Tredoux, 2006). The sequential lineup, as it has been implemented in research, contains a variety of features in addition to sequential presentation such as backloading of pictures (i.e., the witness does not know how many photos will be presented) and the stopping rule (i.e., the identification task is over when the witness has identified a photo as the perpetrator or all the photos have been exhausted). It remains unclear if one or several of these features are necessary to produce the sequential superiority effect.

Lineup Administration

Because the lead officer on a case is usually the person who serves as the administrator of a lineup or photospread, lineup administrators typically know which lineup member is the suspect. Just as experimenters who know the hypothesis of their studies are at risk of communicating it to their research participants (Rosenthal, 2002), knowledge of the suspect's identity provides the opportunity for lineup administrators to communicate, purposively or inadvertently, to witnesses who the suspect is. Indeed, when lineup administrators know which lineup member is the suspect and have sufficient contact with the participant to communicate that information to the witness, witnesses are more likely

to choose the suspect from a lineup than when the administrator conducts a double-blind lineup (e.g., neither the administrator nor the witness knows which lineup member is the suspect; Greathouse & Kovera, 2009; Phillips, McAuliff, Kovera, & Cutler, 1999). Other variables that bias witnesses toward making a positive identification from the lineup seem to increase the influence of nonblind lineup administration. Nonblind administration is especially likely to produce suspect identifications when the procedure also contains biased instructions and simultaneous presentation of lineup members (Greathouse & Kovera, 2009).

Some practitioners have questioned the utility of both double-blind lineup administration and sequential presentation of lineup members based on the results of a field study commissioned by the Illinois legislature in which researchers randomly assigned the identification procedures that police were to use when conducting a lineup (Mecklenburg, 2006). Specifically, police officers conducted either single-blind, simultaneous lineups or double-blind, sequential lineups. Witnesses were more likely to identify suspects and less likely to identify fillers from single-blind simultaneous lineups, a result that some have promoted as an indictment of both double-blind administration and sequential presentation (Mecklenburg, Bailey, & Larson, 2008). This assessment appears premature given that the field study confounded the manipulation of lineup presentation and double-blind administration, precluding strong inferences about the effects of either variable (Schacter et al., 2008). Also, filler identifications may be differentially recorded depending on whether the officers are aware of who the fillers in the lineup are, with uncertain identifications of fillers registered as a nonidentification when the police officer knows who the suspect and fillers are but as an identification when the officer is unsure of whether the member identified is a suspect or a filler (Wells, 2008). These methodological concerns have caused commentators to warn against using these data in support of public policy (Ross & Malpass, 2008; Schacter et al., 2008; Steblay, 2008; Wells, 2008).

POSTDICTORS OF WITNESS ACCURACY
There is also a class of variables that legal decision-makers can use to postdict witness accuracy. These variables—witness confidence, witness description accuracy, witness consistency, and identification speed—are not characteristics of the witnessed event nor are they characteristics of the identification task that are under the control of actors in the criminal

justice system. Nevertheless, these variables are often used to evaluate the potential accuracy of a witness's identification, with varying degrees of research support for that use.

Witness Confidence

Although U.S. case law specifically instructs judges to consider witness confidence when determining whether an identification task was suggestive (*Manson v. Braithwaite*, 1977) and allows judges to instruct jurors to consider witness confidence when determining how much weight they should give to an eyewitness identification (*United States v. Telfaire*, 1978), there is limited empirical support for the notion that witness confidence is strongly related to identification accuracy. One meta-analysis found that there is a relatively small relationship between witness confidence and accuracy but that the relationship was much stronger for choosers (i.e., those witnesses who made a positive identification from the lineup) than for nonchoosers (Sporer, Penrod, Read, & Cutler, 1995). Optimal viewing conditions also produce stronger confidence-accuracy correlations than do less optimal conditions (Bothwell, Deffenbacher, & Brigham, 1987).

Witness confidence is malleable, which is one reason why it may not be more strongly related to identification accuracy. Feedback that confirms the accuracy of witness identifications increases the confidence of witnesses, whether the feedback comes from administrators (Bradfield, Wells, & Olson, 2002) or from cowitnesses (Luus & Wells, 1994). In addition to altering witness confidence, feedback about the identification also changes witnesses' reports of the conditions under which they viewed the crime in both laboratory (Bradfield et al., 2002) and archival studies (Wright & Skagerberg, 2007). A meta-analysis revealed that the postidentification feedback effect on confidence is rather large ($d = .79$) and although the feedback effects on witness reports of witnessing conditions are somewhat smaller, they are robust (Douglass & Steblay, 2006). Given that judges are to evaluate the reliability of an identification based on whether the witness had a good view of the perpetrator, how much attention the witness paid to the perpetrator, and witness confidence (Manson v. Braithwaite, 1977), it is troublesome that feedback has the potential to taint all of these criteria (Wells & Quinlivan, 2009).

Witness Description Accuracy and Consistency

Although defense attorneys intuitively believe that their clients must be innocent if witnesses' descriptions of the perpetrators do not match the physical characteristics possessed by their clients, there is limited empirical evidence to support this view (Susa & Meissner, 2008). For example, in one field study, a target attempted to deposit obviously altered money orders at a bank and tellers provided descriptions and attempted identifications of the target later that same day (Pigott, Brigham, & Bothwell, 1990). The accuracy of the descriptions was not significantly related to identification accuracy.

Similarly, trial attorneys are trained to elicit inconsistencies in witness testimony and use those inconsistencies to later impeach the witness's credibility. Although it is relatively easy to extract inconsistent statements from witnesses given that they are interviewed many times during an investigation, the few studies that have examined whether these inconsistencies predict witness identification accuracy find that they do not (Fisher & Cutler, 1996).

Identification Speed

Witnesses who identify a lineup member relatively quickly tend to be more accurate than those who make an identification after a longer deliberation process. Although some studies suggest that those witnesses who make an identification within 10 to 12 seconds are more accurate than those who take more time to make an identification (Dunning & Perretta, 2002), other studies failed to support this 10 to 12 second cutoff while providing support for the general principle that quicker identification speeds are related to increased identification accuracy (Weber, Brewer, Wells, Semmler, & Keast, 2004). Archival studies of real crime also support the premise that identification speed and accuracy are related (Valentine et al., 2003). In this study of 600 identification procedures, witnesses whom police officers described to be fast choosers were more likely to choose the suspect from the lineup than were witnesses whom police described to be slow or average choosers. Although there are methodological limitations of this archival research (e.g., the investigators' knowledge of the suspect's identity could have influenced their judgments of identification speed), the findings are consistent with the findings from laboratory studies that do not suffer these limitations.

In summary, there are a variety of factors that influence the accuracy of eyewitness identifications (Cutler & Kovera, 2010). In their attempts to identify factors that affect the reliability of eyewitness identifications, researchers have focused on features of witnessed events and procedures that investigators use to elicit identifications from witnesses. Although individual differences in witnesses can be conceptualized as features of the witnessing condition, research on individual differences is relatively rare. There are a few studies showing that elderly witnesses and children make more false identifications than young adult witnesses (e.g., Lindsay, Pozzulo, Craig, Lee, & Corber, 1997; Searcy, Bartlett, & Memon, 2000). Some individual difference variables—such as witness race—have been examined in situational context to the extent that race effects are found in combination with perpetrator race, with witnesses making more accurate identifications when witness and perpetrator race are the same rather than different (Meissner & Brigham, 2001). There are practical reasons why individual difference research in this area is uncommon. Legal decision-makers are unlikely to have access to individual difference information about witnesses other than demographic information, especially as experts called to testify on issues of eyewitness identification rarely interview witnesses in the course of evaluating case materials (Cutler & Kovera, 2010). Thus, individual differences in personality or processing style are unlikely to prove helpful in postdicting eyewitness accuracy. In addition, individual differences in eyewitness behavior do not provide information about how to reduce rates of false identifications, a goal of eyewitness researchers.

Trial by Jury

In the American criminal justice system, the trial is just the tip of an iceberg. Once a crime is committed, detected, and reported, investigating police gather evidence from suspects, eyewitnesses, and others. If there is sufficient evidence to make an arrest, prosecuting and defense lawyers begin a lengthy process known as "discovery," often leading defendants to plead guilty as part of a settlement. In cases that go to trial, sentencing, prison, parole decisions, and the processes of appeal typically follow a conviction. The criminal justice apparatus is extensive and complex. So is the civil justice system, where plaintiffs and defendants oppose each other to resolve financial disputes. Yet through it all, the trial—the central adjudicative event—is the heart and soul of the system, motivating parties to gather evidence and negotiate a settlement and later forming the basis for sentencing and appeals decisions. For this reason, forensic personality and social psychologists have focused a great deal of attention on the processes of a trial by jury.

Jury Selection

When defendants are charged with a crime or plaintiffs sue to recover damages from defendants because they believe the defendants have done them harm, juries are constituted to hear the evidence in the case and determine whether the defendants are guilty of the crimes with which they are charged or whether the defendants are liable for the harm that plaintiffs have suffered. To form a jury, the court calls community members to the courthouse to form a pool of potential jurors, called the *venire*. In a pretrial proceeding known as *voir dire*, the judge and the attorneys representing both parties in the dispute question the venirepersons to determine whether they hold biases that would prevent them from being fair and impartial jurors. The process of jury selection is really one of deselection, in which prospective jurors are removed from the jury panel through one of two mechanisms. Challenges for cause are exercised when the attorney convinces the judge that the venireperson is biased and are unlimited in number. An attorney may also eliminate venirepersons without stating reasons for their excusal using peremptory challenges; these challenges are limited in number and may not be used to remove jurors because of their race (*Batson v. Kentucky*, 1986) or gender (*J.E.B. v. Alabama*, 1994).

Traditional attorney-conducted jury selection generally consists of attorneys using their naive theories of attitudes and personality, stereotypes, and knowledge of litigation folklore to choose which jurors to challenge (Fulero & Penrod, 1990a; 1990b). Attorneys often believe that jurors who share similarities with their clients will be better able to empathize with the clients and therefore will return more favorable verdicts (Kerr, Hymes, Anderson, & Weathers, 1995). There may be situations in which attorneys believe that jurors will view a demographically similar defendant who has committed heinous crimes as a black sheep who does not reflect the values of their shared in-group and will consequently attempt to distance themselves from the defendant, making similar jurors undesirable (Marques, Abrams, Paz, & Martinez Taboada, 1998). Thus, folklore can lead attorneys to have competing hypotheses about the desirability of a single juror, bringing into question the effectiveness of traditional jury selection. Indeed, jurors excluded using peremptory challenges render similar verdicts to the juries actually seated in those cases (Zeisel & Diamond, 1978); attorneys rely on the same characteristics to exclude venirepersons that college students do and were more likely to accept jurors who opposed their position than favored their side (Olczak, Kaplan, & Penrod, 1991); and the attitudes of juries seated by attorneys in actual felony trials were no different from the attitudes of juries composed of the first 12 venirepersons or 12 who were randomly chosen (Johnson & Haney, 1994).

SCIENTIFIC JURY SELECTION

Social scientists conducted the first scientific jury selection in the early 1970s when they used social science methods to help attorneys defending anti-war activists select a jury (Schulman, Shaver, Coleman, Enrich, & Christie, 1973). The scientists used community surveys to identify demographic characteristics and attitudes that were correlated with potential jurors' biases against the defendants. Based on the results of these surveys, the scientists developed profiles of jurors who would be favorable to the defense, and the defense attorneys used these profiles when deciding how to use their peremptory challenges. Since that first case, researchers have conducted a substantial number of studies in an attempt to identify demographic, personality, and attitudinal predictors of jury verdicts.

Demographic variables are weak and inconsistent predictors of verdict (Diamond, 2006). Although the majority of studies find no effect of juror demographics on verdicts, there are some situations in which demographics are reliable predictors of verdicts. For example, blacks are more likely than whites to hold anti–death penalty attitudes that would exclude them from serving on juries in capital trials (Fitzgerald & Ellsworth, 1984; Haney, Hurtado, & Vega, 1994). Gender predicts verdict but generally only in cases in which women are disproportionately likely to be the victims, including child sexual abuse (Bottoms & Goodman, 1994; Kovera, Gresham, Borgida, Gray, & Regan, 1997; Kovera, Levy, Borgida, & Penrod, 1994; Quas, Bottoms, Haegerich, & Nysse-Carris, 2002), rape (Brekke & Borgida, 1988; Wenger & Bornstein, 2006), intimate partner violence (Feather, 1996; Kern, Libkuman, & Temple, 2007) and sexual harassment (Blumenthal, 1998). Men are also more influential and less prone to being influenced than women during jury deliberations (Golding, Bradshaw, Dunlap, & Hodell, 2007).

Personality traits do not fare much better than demographic variables as predictors of verdict. For example, tendencies toward belief in a just world sometimes predict victim-blaming and sometimes predict punitiveness toward defendants (Gerbasi, Zuckerman, & Reis, 1977; Moran & Comfort, 1982). Extraverts are more likely than introverts to acquit criminal defendants (Clark et al., 2007). But the only personality trait that consistently predicts verdict across a variety of cases is authoritarianism, the behavioral tendency to respect authority and convention and to punish those who do not do the same (Adorno, Frenkel-Brunswik, Levinson, & Sanford, 1950). Authoritarians are more likely than people who are low in authoritarianism to convict defendants (Narby, Cutler, & Moran, 1993) and sentence them more harshly (Bray & Noble, 1978; Butler & Moran, 2007), especially when the trait is measured using one of the scales designed to measure authoritarianism in a legal context (Kravitz, Cutler, & Brock, 1993).

Even combinations of demographic and personality variables do not explain more than 10% of the variance in juror verdicts according to several studies (Moran & Comfort, 1982; Visher, 1987). Attitudes are somewhat better predictors of attitudes, especially when those attitudes are closely linked to case issues. The Juror Bias Scale (JBS; Kassin & Wrightsman, 1983) consists of items measuring laypersons' beliefs about reasonable doubt and the probability that defendants committed the crimes with which they are charged and predicts convictions in some criminal trials. Although refinements of the JBS improved its predictive validity (Lecci & Myers, 2002; Myers & Lecci, 1998), substantial variance in verdicts remained unexplained by the scale. Most recently, researchers have augmented items from the JBS with items assessing beliefs about conviction proneness, confidence in the justice system, cynicism toward the defense, racial bias, social justice, and innate criminality to form the Pretrial Juror Attitude Questionnaire, which predicted verdicts in a variety of criminal trials even after controlling for mock jurors' scores on the JBS and a legal authoritarianism scale (Lecci & Myers, 2008).

Case-specific attitudes are stronger predictors of verdict than are general measures of juror bias. In civil cases, jurors who favor tort reform are more likely to prefer defense verdicts than are jurors who oppose tort reform (Moran, Cutler, & DeLisa, 1994), and beliefs that there is a litigation crisis predict verdicts in civil cases (Vinson, Costanzo, & Berger, 2008). Attitudes toward drugs predict ratings of defendant guilt in drug trafficking cases (Moran, Cutler, & Loftus, 1990), and jurors with favorable attitudes toward psychiatrists and the insanity defense are more inclined toward verdicts of not guilty by reason of insanity (Cutler, Moran, & Narby, 1992; Skeem, Louden, & Evans, 2004). Attitudes toward the death penalty not only predict verdicts in capital cases (Allen, Mabry, & McKelton, 1998; O'Neil, Patry, & Penrod, 2004) but also predict verdicts of impaneled jurors in felony trials, irrespective of whether those trials were capital cases (Moran & Comfort, 1986). Thus, among demographic characteristics, personality traits, and attitudes, attitudes are the strongest, most reliable predictors of verdict.

BIAS IN JURY SELECTION

A primary purpose of jury selection is the identification of biased jurors and either their removal or rehabilitation (Crocker & Kovera, 2010); yet there is bias in the choice of jurors to remove from service. Prosecutors are more likely to excuse black venirepersons than are defense attorneys (Clark et al., 2007; Rose, 1999), suggesting that race plays a role in whom attorneys choose to challenge. In a jury selection simulation, attorneys who had a choice between excluding a black or a white venireperson were more likely to exclude the black venireperson, irrespective of the other characteristics that were paired with the two potential jurors (Sommers & Norton, 2007). Attorneys in this study were skilled at providing race-neutral reasons to support their choices (Sommers & Norton, 2007), providing an explanation for why appeals of verdicts based on racially biased exclusion of prospective jurors are unlikely to be successful (Gabbidon, Kowal, Jordan, Roberts, & Vincenzi, 2008).

The voir dire process may also create bias in jurors. In capital cases, the court must determine whether jurors hold attitudes toward the death penalty that would interfere with their ability to follow the law and their impartial evaluation of the evidence (*Wainwright v. Witt*, 1985). Jurors who survive this death qualification process are more likely to convict defendants (Cowan, Thompson, & Ellsworth, 1984). Just watching a death qualification procedure makes already death-qualified jurors more conviction prone (Haney, 1980). Attorneys' expectations about jurors' attitudes change the questions that they ask during voir dire (Crocker, Kennard, Greathouse, & Kovera, 2009), influence attorneys' evaluations of the attitudes that venirepersons hold even after extended voir dire questioning (Greathouse, Crocker, Kennard, Austin, & Kovera, 2009), and ultimately change the trial-relevant attitudes that jurors hold (Greathouse et al., 2009).

Other Procedural Issues in Jury Decision-Making

Voir dire is the legal procedure that is used to seat an unbiased jury but how many unbiased jurors are needed on a jury to ensure good decision-making? And what decision rule should jurors use to determine a verdict? Should they come to a unanimous decision to ensure a just verdict or is some form of majority all that is needed?

JURY SIZE

In a series of important decisions, the U.S. Supreme Court has held that a six-person jury is of sufficient size for determining a defendant's guilt in noncapital cases (*Williams v. Florida*, 1970) but that a jury of five community members is too small (*Ballew v. Georgia*, 1978). Thus, these decisions established six persons as the minimum number of jurors required to make a jury. But do juries of 6 make similar decisions as juries consisting of 12? A meta-analysis of the studies that have examined the effect of jury size on decision-making found that 12-person juries deliberated longer, had more accurate recall of the evidence, generated more arguments about the evidence, and represented more diverse constituencies than 6-person juries (Saks & Marti, 1977). One study found that on average jurors' contributions to deliberations were the same whether they were on a 6-member or a 12-member jury (Hastie, Penrod, & Pennington, 1983), so the sheer number of people on the 12-person versus 6-person juries may explain the difference in deliberation length. However, juries with more diverse members tend to discuss a wider range of issues (Sommers, 2006). Finally, 12-person juries provide a greater opportunity for jurors holding a minority position on the jury to have at least one ally. Although the *Williams* court argued that what matters is the proportional size of the minority, the meta-analysis of jury size studies showed that 12-person juries were more likely to hang than 6-person juries, suggesting that it is easier for those holding minority viewpoints to hold fast to their positions when they have another person who shares their views.

DECISION RULE

About the same time the U.S. Supreme Court was considering the issue of jury size, it also made several rulings about the appropriateness of nonunanimous decision rules and ultimately ruled that nonunanimous decisions were constitutional in some circumstances (*Johnson v. Louisiana*, 1972). So although the Court also held that six-person juries must use a unanimous decision rule (*Burch v. Louisiana*, 1979), all states require unanimity in capital trials, and many states require that juries reach unanimity in criminal felony trials, nonunanimous decisions are allowed in less serious cases. The nonunanimous decision rule does reduce the number of hung juries (Kalven & Zeisel, 1966; Padawer-Singer, Singer, & Singer, 1977), but does the failure to require unanimity reduce the quality of jury decisions?

There are drawbacks to a nonunanimous decision rule. When juries are required to deliberate to a unanimous verdict, minority viewpoints are more thoroughly vetted than when only a five out of six majority needs to be reached (Hans, 1978). The decision rule also affects juries' decision-making processes; nonunanimous juries took votes earlier in deliberation, spent a greater proportion of the deliberation voting rather than discussing the evidence, were more likely to employ normative influence processes against other jurors, and were more verdict-driven than unanimous juries (Hastie et al., 1983). In general, unanimous juries were more likely to hang but also took more time considering the evidence and were more satisfied, suggesting that the benefits of nonunanimous juries (e.g., fewer hung juries) may not outweigh the drawbacks (Hastie et al., 1983).

Evidentiary Issues in Jury Decision-Making

Juries are charged with evaluating complex evidence and arriving at a fair verdict. Some critics have expressed concern about whether jurors are up to the tasks before them. Do jurors give too much weight to DNA evidence? Are jurors unduly influenced by evidence that the defendant confessed to the charged crimes, especially when there is evidence that the confession was coerced? Given the unreliability of eyewitness identifications, are jurors sensitive to the factors that influence their accuracy? Can jurors identify the methodological flaws that may be present in scientific or expert evidence? A body of jury simulation research now exists that addresses these questions (Devine, Clayton, Dunford, Seying, & Pryce, 2001).

There is no question that physical evidence— especially DNA evidence—impresses jurors (Lieberman, Carrell, Miethe, & Krauss, 2008). Despite jurors' positive views of physical evidence and courts' concerns that jurors may overvalue physical evidence, Bayesian analyses of jurors' decisions about blood and enzyme types—which compare jurors' judgments to the normative judgments that would be made if jurors were to accurately apply statistics to their evaluations—suggest that jurors provide too little weight to this information when rendering verdicts (Smith, Penrod, & Otto, 1996). Generally, jurors undervalue probabilistic evidence (Faigman & Baglioni, 1988; Schklar &

Diamond, 1999). Jurors are sensitive to variations in physical evidence; when there was a higher probability that other members of the population other than the defendant matched the physical evidence, jurors were less likely to judge the defendant to be guilty (Smith et al., 1996). However, jurors are also influenced by how easily they can generate examples of matches other than the defendant even when the probability of other matches remains constant (Koehler, 2001; Koehler & Macchi, 2004).

Confessions are another powerful form of evidence against a defendant, more persuasive than either eyewitness or character testimony (Kassin & Neumann, 1997). Although jurors will discount confessions that police elicit by threatening physical harm and punishment, their verdicts are not sensitive to the ability of promises of leniency to elicit false confessions even though such promises do affect their perceptions of the voluntariness of the confession (Kassin & Wrightsman, 1980). Jury deliberations and judicial instructions do not improve their sensitivity to factors that increase the likelihood of false confessions (Kassin & Wrightsman, 1981). Even when jurors believe that a confession is involuntary (e.g., produced through threat of physical harm) and that the confession did not influence their decisions, they are more likely to find a defendant guilty than are jurors who do not hear evidence of the involuntary confession (Kassin & Sukel, 1997). Laypeople also perform poorly when asked to identify which confessions—both those generated in the laboratory and provided by convicted inmates—were true versus false (Kassin et al., 2005). The perspective of viewers of false confessions influences their ability to consider situational influences on the elicitation of a confession. Videotapes that focused on the suspect minimized the effects of situational pressures on jurors' evaluations (Lassiter & Irvine, 1986) and videotapes that contained both the interrogator and the suspect improved reliance on situational cues to coercion (Lassiter, Geers, Munhall, Handley, & Beers, 2001; Lassiter, Ware, Ratcliff, & Irvin, 2009; Ware, Lassiter, Patterson, & Ransom, 2008).

Despite the large body of evidence that eyewitness identifications are often unreliable, eyewitness evidence exerts a powerful influence on juror decisions (Loftus, 1980). Moreover, jurors are insensitive to the estimator variables that influence identification accuracy, including weapon focus, viewing conditions, retention interval, and stressfulness (Cutler, Penrod, & Dexter, 1990; Cutler, Penrod, & Stuve, 1988). They are also insensitive to variations in system variables, such as biased instructions and simultaneous versus sequential presentation, but are somewhat sensitive to bias in the choice of fillers for the lineup (Devenport, Stinson, Cutler, & Kravitz, 2002). In contrast, variations in witness confidence do influence jurors' evaluations of eyewitness reliability (Cutler et al., 1988, 1990), even though witness confidence is only weakly related to witness accuracy (Sporer et al., 1995) and easily mutated in response to feedback (Douglass & Steblay, 2006).

Another form of evidence that has been extensively studied is expert evidence. Early studies focused on whether expert testimony on a variety of topics (e.g., battered women, child sexual abuse, eyewitness identifications, rape) influenced juror judgments (e.g., Brekke & Borgida, 1988; Fox & Walters, 1986; Kovera et al., 1994, 1997; Schuller, 1992; Schuller & Cripps, 1998). Expert evidence has a greater impact on jurors' decisions when it is presented toward the beginning of the trial (Brekke & Borgida, 1988; Schuller & Cripps, 1998) and when experts concretely tie their testimony to the case facts (Brekke & Borgida, 1988; Fox & Walters, 1986; Kovera et al., 1997; Schuller, 1992). Expert evidence also educates jurors, sensitizing them to factors affecting the reliability of other types of evidence (e.g., Cutler, Dexter, & Penrod, 1989; Cutler, Penrod, & Dexter, 1989; Kovera et al., 1997). An underlying assumption of all of these studies is that expert evidence should influence juror judgments.

More recently, researchers have begun to examine whether jurors have the ability to evaluate the quality of expert evidence, recognizing that courts admit research that varies in its scientific validity and reliability (Kovera & McAuliff, 2000). Jury simulation studies suggest that jurors are insensitive to low construct validity (Kovera, McAuliff, & Hebert, 1999), nonblind experimenters (McAuliff, Kovera, & Nunez, 2009), or confounds (McAuliff et al., 2009). Jurors are sometimes sensitive to the absence of control groups in research presented at trial (McAuliff & Kovera, 2008; McAuliff et al. 2009). Neither cross-examination (Kovera et al., 1997) nor opposing experts (Levett & Kovera, 2008; 2009) help jurors recognize the flaws in the research underlying expert testimony.

Very little research has explored the role of personality in evaluations of different types of evidence, with the exception of studies looking at the role of need for cognition (Cacioppo & Petty, 1982) in jurors' decisions. Need for cognition is an individual difference in people's desire and motivation to engage in deliberative and effortful cognitive processes. Although differences in need for cognition did not affect jurors' abilities to differentiate among true and false confessions (Lassiter, Slaw, Briggs, & Scanlan, 1992), they do play a role in how jurors evaluate other forms of evidence. Low need for cognition jurors were less likely to find a defendant liable when the defense expert presented anecdotal evidence than when he did not, whereas high need for cognition jurors were unaffected by the presentation of anecdotal evidence (Bornstein, 2004). High need for cognition jurors were more sensitive to the absence of a control group in the evidence presented by an expert than were low need for cognition jurors (McAuliff & Kovera, 2008) yet cross-examination helped low need for cognition jurors notice flaws in expert evidence but had no effect on the judgments of high need for cognition jurors (Salerno & McCauley, 2009).

Nonevidentiary Issues in Jury Decision-Making

Although jurors are supposed to base their decisions on the evidence presented at trial, there are times when information that is not evidence influences their decisions. Because of rules governing the admissibility of evidence, not all case-relevant information is admissible in court, including information on the defendant's prior criminal record, evidence obtained through illegal searches, information about the defendant's character or reputation). Jurors are sometimes exposed to this extra-evidentiary information through pretrial publicity about the case or because the information is inappropriately revealed during the course of the trial. In addition to extra-evidentiary information that comes to jurors through external sources, jurors have their own principles and values that guide their decisions in everyday life. During a trial, jurors are supposed to abdicate these personally held beliefs and make decisions based on the evidence and the law even if their principles are at odds with the law. Can jurors ignore extra-evidentiary information, whether it come from external or internal sources, when making trial decisions?

PRETRIAL PUBLICITY
Pretrial publicity negatively affects both pretrial and postdeliberation judgments of defendant guilt (Otto, Penrod, & Dexter, 1994; Ruva, McAvoy, & Bryant, 2007; Steblay, Besirevic, Fulero, & Jimenez-Lorente, 1999). Information from the media influences juror judgments even when the media is only

topically related to the case but does not include any case-specific prejudicial information (Greene & Wade, 1988; Kovera, 2002). A meta-analysis revealed that pretrial publicity exerts a small to medium effect on juror judgments across a wide variety of participants, settings, cases, facts, and research methods (Steblay et al., 1999).

There are several procedural safeguards that are intended to remedy the effects of pretrial publicity on juror judgments: extended voir dire, judicial admonishments to ignore pretrial publicity, delays of the trial (i.e., continuances), and changes of venue to a location in which there is less publicity or at least publicity that is less prejudicial (American Bar Association, 2003). When there is significant potential that pretrial publicity has biased the venire, judges may give attorneys increased latitude in questioning jurors—known as extended voir dire—so that they may better ferret out bias in the jury pool. It is unlikely that extended voir dire will successfully correct for pretrial publicity effects. Jurors are less likely to report their bias in court, as opposed to in a community survey outside the court context (Chrzanowski, 2005). Jurors' reports about whether they can remain impartial and ignore pretrial publicity are unrelated to their perceptions of defendant guilt (Costantini & King, 1980/1981; Kerr, Kramer, Carroll, & Alfini, 1991; Moran & Cutler, 1991), yet it is these self-reports that the courts use to determine whether jurors are biased (Posey & Dahl, 2002). Moreover, although mock jurors participating in an extended voir dire were less likely to convict than were mock jurors who participated in a standard voir dire, extended voir dire did not reduce prejudicial effects of PTP on juror judgments. Judicial instructions to disregard the PTP are similarly ineffective at reducing PTP effect (Fein, McCloskey, & Tomlinson, 1997; Kramer, Kerr, & Carroll, 1990). In one study, a continuance reduced the influence of PTP regarding facts of the case but not PTP that aroused negative emotions (Kramer et al., 1990). Thus, changes of venue remain the best remedy for the effects of prejudicial PTP, even in highly publicized cases like the prosecution of Timothy McVeigh in the Oklahoma City bombing case (Studebaker et al., 2000).

INADMISSIBLE EVIDENCE

Judges may rule some trial-relevant information to be inadmissible at trial if they deem the information to be unreliable or overly prejudicial. Even if the information has been ruled inadmissible, it is possible for a jury to hear it. For example, witnesses may make statements in their testimony that contain inadmissible evidence. An attorney will object to the statement and the judge will rule it inadmissible, admonishing the jury to disregard the evidence. There is no question that inadmissible evidence, once presented in court, influences jurors' judgments in a manner consistent with the evidence (Steblay, Hosch, Culhane, & McWethy, 2006). That is if the inadmissible evidence supports the prosecution, then jurors who hear that information are more likely to convict than those who do not; if the inadmissible evidence supports the defense, then jurors become less likely to convict.

Are there any variables that moderate the effects of inadmissible information on juror judgments? Judicial admonitions to disregard the inadmissible evidence are often not effective at minimizing the effects (Kassin & Sukel, 1997; Wissler & Saks, 1985); however, the effects of the instruction to disregard are dependent on a number of other factors, such as the assumed relevance of the information the jurors are asked to exclude (Steblay et al., 2006). To test the "just verdict hypothesis," mock jurors read a transcript of a double-murder trial with weak evidence, leading only 24 percent to vote guilty (Kassin & Sommers, 1997). Three other groups read the same case except that the state's evidence included a wire-tapped phone conversation in which the defendant confessed to a friend. In all cases, the defense lawyer objected to the disclosure. When the judge ruled to admit the tape into evidence, the conviction rate increased considerably to 79 percent, but when the judge excluded the tape and instructed jurors to disregard it, their reaction depended on the reason for the tape's being excluded. When told to disregard the tape because it was barely audible and could not be trusted, participants delivered the same 24 percent conviction rate as in the no-tape control group, as they should. However, when jurors were told to disregard the item because it had been illegally obtained, 55 percent voted guilty. Despite the judge's warning, these latter participants were unwilling to ignore testimony they saw as highly relevant merely because of a legal "technicality." Additional studies indicate that jurors in this situation may comply with a judge's instruction to disregard when the technicality involves a *serious* violation of the defendant's rights (Fleming, Wegener, & Petty, 1999) and that the process of deliberation increases compliance, which minimizes the bias (London & Nunez, 2000).

JURY NULLIFICATION

Judges instruct jurors that they are to make a decision based on the evidence provided at trial and the laws that the judge describes to them. Yet juries also have the right to ignore the law if they find that defendants are guilty according to the law but acted in a manner that is consistent with the morals and values of the community (Horowitz & Willging, 1991). Jurors' attitudes may conflict with the law when they believe that a defendant's behavior meets the legal definition of a crime but that any reasonable person would have acted similarly in a comparable situation or that the defendant's actions were understandable or principled (Finkel, 1995). Euthanasia is the prototypical example of a crime in which jurors' sentiments and attitudes may lead jurors' to nullify the law (Horowitz, Kerr, Park, & Gockel, 2006; Meissner, Brigham, & Pfeifer, 2003); the behavior meets the legal definition of a crime but if jurors believe that the defendant's intent was to end the victim's suffering, jurors may feel compelled to nullify the law. Jurors may also nullify even when they believe the defendant's actions were wrong but believe that the punishment that the defendant will receive is not proportionate to the crime (Horowitz & Willging, 1991; Niedermeier, Horowitz, & Kerr, 1999).

Judges are not required to instruct jurors on their right to nullify the law but when they do, nullification instructions can alter jury verdicts (Horowitz, 1988). In one study, Horowitz (1985) found that the nullification instructions used in Maryland did not produce different verdicts than did standard jury instructions but that radical nullification instructions that explicitly informed jurors of their nullification rights caused them to acquit the defendant more frequently when the defendant was deserving of sympathy. When the defendant was charged with drunk driving, however, and therefore not deserving of sympathy, jurors were more likely to convict when they received the radical nullification instruction.

Science, Common Sense, and the Role of Forensic Psychology in the Courts

Increasingly, personality and social psychologists are called to serve as consultants on matters of policy and practice, as expert witnesses in cases involving credibility assessment, eyewitness identifications, repressed memories, police-induced confessions, race discrimination in jury selection, pretrial publicity biases, the death penalty, and other areas of forensic research. In most instances, the goal of such testimony is to provide fact finders with information about general causation principles that may have relevance to the particulars of an individual

case. Hence, the eyewitness expert would educate the jury about stress, race, weapon focus, and other factors that can influence the accuracy of eyewitness perception and memory; the confession expert would describe the dispositional and situational factors known to increase the risk that innocent people might confess. In neither instance would the expert offer an opinion as to the accuracy of a particular witness or innocence of a particular confessor.

Are psychologists permitted to testify as such in court? In many states, the so-called *Frye* test (1923) demands that to be admissible expert testimony must conform to generally accepted principles within a discipline (*Frye v. United States*, 1923). The Federal Rules of Evidence (FRE), codified in 1975, broadened the emphasis by stating that expert testimony is admissible if the expert is qualified, if the testimony is reliable, and if the testimony would assist the jury. In *Daubert v. Merrell Dow Pharmaceuticals* (1993), the U.S. Supreme Court urged trial judges to serve as even more active gatekeepers of scientific evidence by ascertaining for themselves whether an expert proffers information that is scientific according to such criteria as being testable, falsifiable, peer reviewed, reliable, valid, and generally accepted.

As these criteria indicate, the psychological research literature becomes worthy of presentation in an American courtroom only if the courts determine that it can be trusted—*and that it will assist the jury*. To assess the value of a psychological expert to a jury, of course, it is necessary to determine what lay people know—about perception, memory, decision-making, obedience to authority, and various forms of social influence—as a matter of common knowledge, in the absence of expert testimony. Across a range of substantive domains, this has been achieved through surveys of lay people as well as mock jury studies designed to assess the degree to which people are sensitive to factors associated with a particular behavior. In the edited volume *Psychological Science in Court: Beyond Common Knowledge*, Borgida and Fiske (2007) note that in a number of areas, the psychological science outright contradicts intuitive commonsense beliefs about human behavior. Thus, the findings from forensic personality and social psychology have great potential for educating fact finders about human behavior in legal domains.

Conclusion

In recent years, personality and social psychologists have made substantial contributions in an effort to identify and solve a range of problems within the legal system. In this chapter, we reviewed research concerning police investigations and the collection of testimonial evidence from suspects, alibis, and eyewitnesses as well as various aspects of the courtroom trial—such as jury selection, the influences of evidentiary and nonevidentiary sources of information, and the processes and outcomes of jury deliberations.

It is clear that personality traits and other individual-based characteristics account for differences in deception detection, vulnerability to making false confessions, juror decision-making, and other legally relevant behaviors. It is also clear that many forensic psychologists have testified as experts to inform courts and policy-makers about these personological variables. Determined to identify procedures or interventions that will improve the quality of justice, however, a good deal of the research in this area has focused instead on situational variables, practical "system variables" that are amenable to reform—such as the methods that are used to interrogate crime suspects, obtain identifications from eyewitnesses, or select jurors for trial who are fair and impartial. In both domains, forensic personality and social psychology has made significant contributions.

References

Adorno, T., Frenkel-Brunswik, E., Levinson, D., & Sanford, N. (1950). *The authoritarian personality.* New York: Harper.

Allen, M., Mabry, E., & McKelton, D. (1998). Impact of juror attitudes about the death penalty on juror evaluations of guilt and punishment: A meta-analysis. *Law and Human Behavior, 22,* 715–731.

American Bar Association (2003). *Model rules of professional conduct* (5th ed.). Chicago, IL: Center for Professional Responsibility (American Bar Association).

Anderson, D. E., DePaulo, B. M., Ansfield, M. E., Tickle, J. J., & Green, E. (1999). Beliefs about cues to deception: Mindless stereotypes or untapped wisdom? *Journal of Nonverbal Behavior, 23,* 67–89.

Ballew v. Georgia, 435 U.S. 223 (1978).

Batson v. Kentucky, 476 U.S. 79 (1986).

Behrman, B. W., & Davey, S. L. (2001). Eyewitness identification in actual criminal cases: An archival analysis. *Law and Human Behavior, 25,* 475–491.

Benedetti, F. (2009). *Placebo effects: Understanding the mechanisms in health and disease.* New York: Oxford University Press.

Blader, S. L., & Tyler, T. R. (2003). A four-component model of procedural justice: Defining the meaning of a "fair" process. *Personality and Social Psychology Bulletin, 29,* 747–758.

Blumenthal, J. A. (1998). The reasonable woman standard: A meta-analytic review of gender differences in perceptions of sexual harassment. *Law and Human Behavior, 22,* 33–57.

Bond, C. F., & DePaulo, B. M. (2006). Accuracy of deception judgments. *Personality and Social Psychology Review, 10,* 214–234.

Bond, C. F., & DePaulo, B. M. (2008). Individual differences in judging deception: Accuracy and bias. *Psychological Bulletin, 134,* 477–492.

Bond, C. F., & Fahey, W. E. (1987). False suspicion and the misperception of deceit. *British Journal of Social Psychology, 26,* 41–46.

Bond, C. F., & Uysal, A. (2007). On lie detection "wizards." *Law and Human Behavior, 31,* 109–115.

Bond, G. D. (2008). Deception detection expertise. *Law and Human Behavior, 32,* 339–351.

Borgida, E., & Fiske, S. T. (Eds.). (2007). *Psychological science in court: Beyond common sense.* Oxford, UK: Blackwell.

Bornstein, B. H. (2004). The impact of different types of expert scientific testimony on mock jurors' liability verdicts. *Psychology, Crime, and Law, 10,* 429–446.

Bornstein, B. H., Wiener, R. L., Schopp, R., & Willborn, S. L. (Eds.). (2008). *Civil juries and civil justice: Psychological and legal perspectives.* New York: Springer.

Bothwell, R. K., Deffenbacher, K. A., & Brigham, J. C. (1987). Correlation of eyewitness accuracy and confidence: Optimality hypothesis revisited. *Journal of Applied Psychology, 72,* 691–695.

Bottoms, B. L., & Goodman, G. S. (1994). Perceptions of children's credibility in sexual assault cases. *Journal of Applied Social Psychology, 24,* 702–732.

Bradfield, A. L., Wells, G. L., & Olson, E. A. (2002). The damaging effect of confirming feedback on the relation between eyewitness certainty and identification accuracy. *Journal of Applied Psychology, 87,* 112–120.

Bray, R. M., & Noble, A. M. (1978). Authoritarianism and decisions of mock juries: Evidence of jury bias and group polarization. *Journal of Personality and Social Psychology, 36,* 1424–1430.

Brekke, N., & Borgida, E. (1988). Expert psychological testimony in rape trials: A social-cognitive analysis. *Journal of Personality and Social Psychology, 55,* 372–386.

Brewer, N., & Williams, K. D. (Eds.). (2005). *Psychology and law: An empirical perspective.* New York: Guilford.

Burch v. Louisiana, 99 S. Ct. 1623 (1979).

Butler, B., & Moran, G. (2007). The impact of death qualification, belief in a just world, legal authoritarianism, and locus of control on venirepersons' evaluations of aggravating and mitigating circumstances in capital trials. *Behavioral Sciences and the Law, 25,* 57–68.

Carlsmith, K. M., & Darley, J. M. (2008). Psychological aspects of retributive justice. *Advances in Experimental Social Psychology, 40,* 193–236.

Carnahan, T., & McFarland, S. (2007). Revisiting the Stanford Prison Experiment: Could participant self-selection have led to the cruelty? *Personality and Social Psychology Bulletin, 33,* 603–614.

Chrzanowski, L. M. (2005). *Rape? Truth? And the media: Laboratory and field assessments of pretrial publicity in a real case.* Unpublished doctoral dissertation, City University of New York.

Clark, J., Boccaccini, M. T., Caillouet, B., & Chaplin, W. F. (2007). Five factor model personality traits, jury selection, and case outcomes in criminal and civil cases. *Criminal Justice and Behavior, 34,* 641–660.

Clark, S. E. (2005). A re-examination of the effects of biased lineup instructions in eyewitness identification. *Law and Human Behavior, 29,* 395–342.

Clark, S., & Tunnicliff, J. L. (2001). Selecting lineup foils in eyewitness identification experiments: Experimental control and real-world simulation. *Law and Human Behavior, 25,* 199–216.

Cloud, M., Shepherd, G. B., Barkoff, A. N., & Shur, J.V. (2002). Words without meaning: The Constitution, confessions, and mentally retarded suspects. *University of Chicago Law Review, 69*, 495–624.

Colwell, K., Hiscock, C. K., & Memon, A. (2002). Interviewing techniques and assessment of statement credibility. *Applied Cognitive Psychology, 16*, 287–300.

Costantini, E., & King, J. (1980/1981). The partial juror: Correlates and causes of prejudgment. *Law and Society Review, 15*, 9–40.

Cowan, C. L., Thompson, W. C., & Ellsworth, P. C. (1984). The effects of death qualification on jurors: Predisposition to convict and on the quality of deliberation. *Law and Human Behavior, 8*, 53–79.

Crocker, C. B., Kennard, J. B., Greathouse, S. M., & Kovera, M. B. (2009, March). *An investigation of attorneys' questioning strategies during voir dire*. Paper presented at the meeting of the American Psychology-Law Society, San Antonio, TX.

Crocker, C. B., & Kovera, M. B. (2010). The effects of rehabilitative voir dire on juror bias and decision making. *Law and Human Behavior, 34*, 212–226.

Culhane, S. E., & Hosch, H. M. (2004). An alibi witness' influence on mock jurors' verdicts. *Journal of Applied Social Psychology, 34*, 1604–1616.

Cutler, B. L. (2006). A sample of witness, crime, and perpetrator characteristics affecting eyewitness identification accuracy. *Cardozo Public Law, Policy, and Ethics Journal, 4*, 327–340.

Cutler, B. L., Dexter, H. R., & Penrod, S. D. (1989). Expert testimony and jury decision making: An empirical analysis. *Behavioral Sciences and the Law, 7*, 215–225.

Cutler, B. L., & Kovera, M. B. (2010). *Evaluating eyewitness identification*. New York: Oxford University Press.

Cutler, B. L., Moran, G. P., & Narby, D. J. (1992). Jury selection in insanity defense cases. *Journal of Research in Personality, 26*, 165–182.

Cutler, B. L., Penrod, S. D. & Dexter, H. R. (1990). Juror sensitivity to eyewitness identification evidence. *Law and Human Behavior, 14*, 185–191.

Cutler, B. L., Penrod, S. D., & Martens, T. K. (1987a). The reliability of eyewitness identification: The role of system and estimator variables. *Law and Human Behavior, 11*, 223–238.

Cutler, B. L., Penrod, S. D., & Martens, T. K. (1987b). Improving the reliability of eyewitness identification: Putting context into context. *Journal of Applied Psychology, 72*, 629–637.

Cutler, B. L., Penrod, S. D., O'Rourke, T. E., & Martens, T. K. (1986). Unconfounding the effects of contextual cues on eyewitness identification accuracy. *Social Behaviour, 1*, 113–134.

Cutler, B. L., Penrod, S. D., & Stuve, T. E. (1988). Juror decision making in eyewitness identification cases. *Law and Human Behavior, 12*, 41–55.

Daubert v. Merrell Dow Pharmaceuticals, Inc., 509 U.S. 579, 113 S. Ct. 2786 (1993).

Davies, G. M., Smith, S., & Blincoe, C. (2008). A "weapon focus" effect in children. *Psychology, Crime, and Law, 14*, 19–28.

Davis, D., & O'Donahue, W. (2004). The road to perdition: Extreme influence tactics in the interrogation room. In W. O'Donohue (Eds.), *Handbook of forensic psychology* (pp. 897–996). San Diego: Academic.

Deffenbacher, K. A., Bornstein, B. H., Penrod, S. D., & McGorty, E. K. (2004). A meta-analytic review of the effects of high stress on eyewitness memory. *Law and Human Behavior, 28*, 687–706.

DePaulo, B. M., Lassiter, G. D., & Stone, J. I. (1982). Attentional determinants of success at detecting deception and truth. *Personality and Social Psychology Bulletin, 8*, 273–279.

DePaulo, B. M., Lindsay, J. J., Malone, B. E., Muhlenbruck, L., Charlton, K., & Cooper, H. (2003). Cues to deception. *Psychological Bulletin, 129*, 74–112.

Devenport, J. L., Stinson, V., Cutler, B. L., & Kravitz, D. A. (2002). How effective are the cross-examination and expert testimony safeguards? Jurors' perceptions of the suggestiveness and fairness of biased lineup procedures. *Journal of Applied Psychology, 87*, 1042–1054.

Devine, D. J., Clayton, L. D., Dunford, B. B., Seying, R., & Pryce, J. (2001). Jury decision making: 45 years of empirical research on deliberating groups. *Psychology, Public Policy, and Law, 7*, 622–727.

Diamond, S. S. (2006). Beyond fantasy and nightmare: A portrait of the jury. *Buffalo Law Review, 54*, 717–763.

Douglass, A. B., & Steblay, N. (2006). Memory distortion in eyewitnesses: A meta-analysis of the post-identification feedback effect. *Applied Cognitive Psychology, 20*, 859–869.

Drizin, S. A., & Leo, R. A. (2004). The problem of false confessions in the post-DNA world. *North Carolina Law Review, 82*, 891–1007.

Dunning, D., & Perretta, S. (2002). Automaticity and eyewitness accuracy: A 10- to 12-second rule for distinguishing accurate from inaccurate positive identifications. *Journal of Applied Psychology, 87*, 951–962.

Eberhardt, J. L., Goff, P. A., Purdie, J. A., & Davies, P. G. (2004). Seeing black: Race, crime, and visual processing. *Journal of Personality and Social Psychology, 87*, 876–893.

Ekman, P., & O'Sullivan, M. (1991). Who can catch a liar? *American Psychologist, 46*, 913–920.

Ekman, P., O'Sullivan, M., & Frank, M. G. (1999). A few can catch a liar. *Psychological Science, 10*, 263–266.

Elaad, R. (2003). Effects of feedback on the overestimated capacity to detect lies and the underestimated ability to tell lies. *Applied Cognitive Psychology, 17*, 349–363.

Faigman, D. L., & Baglioni, A. J. (1988). Bayes' theorem in the trial process: Instructing jurors on the value of statistical evidence. *Law and Human Behavior, 12*, 1–17.

Feather, N. T. (1996). Domestic violence, gender, and perceptions of justice. *Sex Roles, 35*, 507–519.

Fein, S., McCloskey, A. L., & Tomlinson, T. M. (1997). Can the jury disregard that information? The use of suspicion to reduce the prejudicial effects of pretrial publicity and inadmissible testimony. *Personality and Social Psychology Bulletin, 23*, 1215–1226.

Fleming, M. A., Wegener, D. T., & Petty, R. E. (1999). Procedural and legal motivations to correct for perceived judicial biases. *Journal of Experimental Social Psychology, 35*, 186–203.

Finlay, W., & Lyons, E. (2002). Acquiescence in interviews with people who have mental retardation. *Mental Retardation, 40*, 14–29.

Finkel, N. J., (1995). *Commonsense justice: Jurors' notions of the law*. Cambridge, MA: Harvard University Press.

Fisher, R. P., & Cutler, B. L. (1996). The relation between consistency and accuracy of eyewitness testimony. In G. M. Davies, S. Lloyd-Bostock, M. McMurran, & C. Wilson (Eds.), *Psychology and law: Advances in research* (pp. 21–2800). Berlin: De Gruyter.

Fitzgerald, R., & Ellsworth, P. C. (1984). Due process vs. crime control: Death qualification and jury attitudes. *Law and Human Behavior, 8*, 31–51.

Fox, S. G., & Walters, H. A. (1986). The impact of general versus specific expert testimony and eyewitness confidence upon mock juror judgment. *Law and Human Behavior, 10,* 215–228.

Frazier v. Cupp, 394 U.S. 731 (1969).

Frye v. United States, 293 F. 1013 (D.C. Cir. 1923).

Fulero, S. M., & Penrod, S. D. (1990a). Attorney jury selection folklore: What do they think and how can psychologist help? *Forensic Reports, 3,* 233–259.

Fulero, S. M., & Penrod, S. D. (1990b). The myths and realities of attorney jury selection folklore and scientific jury selection: What works? *Ohio Northern University Law Review, 17,* 229–253.

Gabbidon, S. L., Kowal, L. K., Jordan, K. L., Roberts, J. L., & Vincenzi, N. (2008). Race-based peremptory challenges: An empirical analysis of litigation from the U. S. Courts of Appeals, 2002–2006. *American Journal of Criminal Justice, 33,* 59–68.

Garrett, B. (2008). Judging innocence. *Columbia Law Review, 108,* 55–142.

Garrido, E., Masip, J., & Herrero, C. (2004). Police officers' credibility judgments: Accuracy and estimated ability. *International Journal of Psychology, 39,* 254–275.

Gerbasi, K. C., Zuckerman, M., & Reis, H. T. (1977). Justice needs a new blindfold: A review of mock jury research. *Psychological Bulletin, 84,* 323–345.

Global Deception Research Team (2006). A world of lies. *Journal of Cross-Cultural Psychology, 37,* 60–74.

Golding, J. M., Bradshaw, G. S., Dunlap, E. E., & Hodell, E. C. (2007). The impact of mock jury gender composition on deliberations and conviction rates in a child sexual assault trial. *Child Maltreatment, 12,* 182–190.

Granhag, P. A., Strömwall, L. A., & Jonsson, A.-C. (2003). Partners in crime: How liars in collusion betray themselves. *Journal of Applied Social Psychology, 33,* 848–868.

Greathouse, S. M., Crocker, C. B., Kennard, J. B., Austin, J., & Kovera, M. B. (2009). Do attorney expectations influence the voir dire process? Unpublished manuscript, John Jay College, City University of New York.

Greathouse, S. M., & Kovera, M. B. (2009). Instruction bias and lineup presentation moderate the effects of administrator knowledge on eyewitness identification. *Law and Human Behavior, 33,* 70–82.

Greene, E., & Wade, R. (1988). Of private talk and public print: General pre-trial publicity and juror decision-making. *Applied Cognitive Psychology, 2,* 123–135.

Grisso, T. (1981). *Juveniles' waiver of rights: Legal and psychological competence.* New York: Plenum.

Gudjonsson, G. H. (2003). *The psychology of interrogations and confessions: A handbook.* Chichester, UK: Wiley.

Gudjonsson, G. H., & Sigurdsson, J. F. (1999). The Gudjonsson Confession Questionnaire-Revised (GCQ-R): Factor structure and its relationship with personality. *Personality and Individual Differences, 27,* 953–968.

Gudjonsson, G. H., Sigurdsson, J. F., Asgeirsdottir, B. B., & Sigfusdottir, I. D. (2006). Custodial interrogation, false confession, and individual differences: A national study among Icelandic youth. *Personality and Individual Differences, 41,* 49–59.

Gudjonsson, G. H., Sigurdsson, J. F., Asgeirsdottir, B. B., & Sigfusdottir, I. D. (2007). Custodial interrogation: What are the background factors associated with claims of false confession to police? *Journal of Forensic Psychiatry and Psychology, 18,* 266–275.

Haney, C. (1984). On the selection of capital juries: The biasing effects of the death-qualification process. *Law and Human Behavior, 8,* 121–132.

Haney, C., Hurtado, A., & Vega, L. (1994). Modern death qualification: New data on its biasing effects. *Law and Human Behavior, 18,* 619–633.

Haney, C., & Zimbardo, P. G. (2009). Persistent dispositionalism in interactionist clothing: Fundamental attribution error in explaining prison abuse. *Personality and Social Psychology Bulletin, 35,* 807–814.

Hans, V. P. (1978). *The effects of the unanimity requirement on group decision processes in simulated juries.* Unpublished doctoral dissertation, University of Toronto.

Harris, R. J., & Monaco, G. E. (1978). Psychology of pragmatic implication: Information processing between the lines. *Journal of Experimental Psychology: General, 107,* 1–22.

Hartwig, M., Granhag, P. A., Strömwall, L. A., & Andersson, L. O. (2004). Suspicious minds: Criminals' ability to detect deception. *Psychology, Crime, and Law, 10,* 83–95.

Hartwig, M., Granhag, P. A., Strömwall, L. A., & Vrij, A. (2005). Detecting deception via strategic disclosure of evidence. *Law and Human Behavior, 29,* 469–484.

Hartwig, M., Granhag, P. A., Strömwall, L. A., & Kronkvist, O. (2006). Strategic use of evidence during police interviews: When training to detect deception works. *Law and Human Behavior, 30,* 603–619.

Hastie, R., Penrod, S. D., & Pennington, N. (1983). *Inside the jury.* Cambridge, MA: Harvard University Press.

Hill, C., Memon, A., & McGeorge, P. (2008). The role of confirmation bias in suspect interviews: A systematic evaluation. *Legal and Criminological Psychology, 13,* 357–371.

Hilton, D. J. (1995). The social context of reasoning: Conversational inference and rational judgment. *Psychological Bulletin, 118,* 248–271.

Hope, L., & Wright, D. (2007). Beyond unusual? Examining the role of attention in the weapon focus effect. *Applied Cognitive Psychology, 21,* 951–961.

Horowitz, I. A. (1985). The effect of jury nullification instructions on verdicts and jury functioning in criminal trials. *Law and Human Behavior, 9,* 25–36.

Horowitz, I. A. (1988). Jury nullification: The impact of judicial instructions, arguments, and challenges on jury decision making. *Law and Human Behavior, 12,* 439–453.

Horowitz, I. A., Kerr, N. L., Park, E. S., & Gockel, C. (2006). Chaos in the courtroom reconsidered: Emotional bias and juror nullification. *Law and Human Behavior, 30,* 163–181.

Horowitz, I. A., & Willging, T. E. (1991). Changing views of jury power, *Law and Human Behavior, 15,* 165–182.

Horselenberg, R., Merckelbach, H., & Josephs, S. (2003). Individual differences and false confessions: A conceptual replication of Kassin and Kiechel (1996). *Psychology, Crime, and Law, 9,* 1–18.

Horvath F., Jayne B. C., & Buckley J. P. (1994). Differentiation of truthful and deceptive criminal suspects in behavior analysis interviews. *Journal of Forensic Science, 39,* 793–807.

Hosch, H. M., Culhane, S. E., Jolly, K. W., Chavez, R. M., & Shaw, L. H. (2011). Effects of an alibi witness's relationship to the defendant on mock jurors' judgments. *Law and Human Behavior, 35,* 127–142.

Inbau, F. E., Reid, J. E., Buckley, J. P., & Jayne, B. C. (2001). *Criminal interrogation and confessions* (4th ed.). Gaithersberg, MD: Aspen.

J.E.B. v. Alabama ex rel. T. B., 114 S. Ct. 1419 (1994).

Johnson, C., & Haney, C. (1994). Felony voir dire: An exploratory study of its content and effect. *Law and Human Behavior, 18,* 487–506.

Johnson v. Louisiana, 406 U.S. 356 (1972).

Jones, E. E. (1990). *Interpersonal perception.* New York: Freeman.

Kalven, H., Jr., & Zeisel, H. (1966). *The American jury.* Boston: Little, Brown.

Kamisar, Y., LaFave, W. R., Israel, J. H., & King, N. J. (2003). *Modern criminal procedure* (10th ed.). St. Paul, MN: West Publishing.

Kassin, S. M. (1997). The psychology of confession evidence. *American Psychologist, 52,* 221–233.

Kassin, S. M. (2005). On the psychology of confessions: Does *innocence* put *innocents* at risk? *American Psychologist, 60,* 215–228.

Kassin, S. M., Drizin, S. A., Grisso, T., Gudjonsson, G. H., Leo, R. A., & Redlich, A. D. (2010). Police-induced confessions: Risk factors and recommendations. *Law and Human Behavior, 34,* 3–38.

Kassin, S. M., & Fong, C. T. (1999). "I'm innocent!" Effects of training on judgments of truth and deception in the interrogation room. *Law and Human Behavior, 23,* 499–516.

Kassin, S. M., Goldstein, C. J., & Savitsky, K. (2003). Behavioral confirmation in the interrogation room: On the dangers of presuming guilt. *Law and Human Behavior, 27,* 187–203.

Kassin, S. M., & Gudjonsson, G. H. (2004). The psychology of confession evidence: A review of the literature and issues. *Psychological Science in the Public Interest, 5,* 35–69.

Kassin, S. M., & Kiechel, K. L. (1996). The social psychology of false confessions: Compliance, internalization, and confabulation. *Psychological Science, 7,* 125–128.

Kassin, S. M., Leo, R. A., Meissner, C. A., Richman, K. D., Colwell, L. H., Leach, A.-M., et al. (2007). Police interviewing and interrogation: A self-report survey of police practices and beliefs, *Law and Human Behavior, 31,* 381–400.

Kassin, S. M., & McNall, K. (1991). Police interrogations and confessions: Communicating promises and threats by pragmatic implication. *Law and Human Behavior, 15,* 233–251.

Kassin, S. M., Meissner, C. A., & Norwick, R. J. (2005). "I'd know a false confession if I saw one": A comparative study of college students and police investigators. *Law and Human Behavior, 29,* 211–227.

Kassin, S. M., & Neumann, K. (1997). On the power of confession evidence: An experimental test of the "fundamental difference" hypothesis. *Law and Human Behavior, 21,* 469–484.

Kassin, S. M, & Norwick, R. (2004). Why people waive their Miranda rights: The power of innocence. *Law and Human Behavior, 28,* 211–221.

Kassin, S. M., & Sommers, S. R. (1997). Inadmissible testimony, instructions to disregard, and the jury: Substantive versus procedural considerations. *Personality and Social Psychology Bulletin, 23,* 1046–1054.

Kassin, S. M., & Sukel, H. (1997). Coerced confessions and the jury: An experimental test of the "harmless error" rule. *Law and Human Behavior, 21,* 27–46.

Kassin, S. M., & Wrightsman, L. S. (1980). Prior confessions and mock juror verdicts. *Journal of Applied Social Psychology, 10,* 133–146.

Kassin, S. M., & Wrightsman, L. S. (1981). Coerced confessions, judicial instruction, and mock juror verdicts. *Journal of Applied Social Psychology, 11,* 489–506.

Kassin, S. M., & Wrightsman, L. S. (1983). The construction and validation of a juror bias scale. *Journal of Research in Personality, 17,* 423–442.

Kassin, S. M., & Wrightsman, L. S. (1985). Confession evidence. In S. Kassin & L. Wrightsman (Eds.), *The psychology of evidence and trial procedure* (pp. 67–94). Beverly Hills, CA: Sage.

Kern, R., Libkuman, T. M., & Temple, S. L. (2007). Perceptions of domestic violence and mock jurors' sentencing decisions. *Journal of Interpersonal Violence, 22,* 1515–1535.

Kerr, N. L., Hymes, R. W., Anderson, A. B., & Weathers, J. E. (1995). Defendant-juror similarity and mock juror judgments. *Law and Human Behavior, 19,* 545–567.

Kerr, N. L., Kramer, G. P., Carroll, J. S., & Alfini, J. J. (1991). On the effectiveness of voir dire in criminal cases with prejudicial pretrial publicity: An empirical study. *American University Law Review, 40,* 665–701.

Klobuchar, A., Steblay, N., & Caligiuri, H. (2006). Improving eyewitness identifications: Hennepin County's blind sequential lineup project. *Cardozo Public Law, Policy, and Ethics Journal, 4,* 381–413.

Koehler, J. J. (2001). When are people persuaded by DNA match statistics? *Law and Human Behavior, 25,* 493–513.

Koehler, J. J., & Macchi, L. (2004). Thinking about low-probability events: An exemplar-cuing theory. *Psychological Science, 15,* 540–546.

Kovera, M. B. (2002). The effects of general pretrial publicity on juror decisions: An examination of moderators and mediating mechanisms. *Law and Human Behavior, 26,* 43–72.

Kovera, M. B., Gresham, A. W., Borgida, E., Gray, E., & Regan, P. C. (1997). Does expert testimony inform or influence juror decision-making? A social cognitive analysis. *Journal of Applied Psychology, 82,* 178–191.

Kovera, M. B., Levy, R. J., Borgida, E., & Penrod, S. D. (1994). Expert witnesses in child sexual abuse cases: Effects of expert testimony and cross-examination. *Law and Human Behavior, 18,* 653–674.

Kovera, M. B., & McAuliff, B. D. (2000). The effects of peer review and evidence quality on judge evaluations of psychological science: Are judges effective gatekeepers? *Journal of Applied Psychology, 85,* 574–586.

Kovera, M. B., McAuliff, B. D., & Hebert, K. S. (1999). Reasoning about scientific evidence: Effects of juror gender and evidence quality on juror decisions in a hostile work environment case. *Journal of Applied Psychology, 84,* 362–375.

Kozel, F., Johnson, K., Mu, Q., Grenesko, E., Laken, S., & George, M. (2005). Detecting deception using functional magnetic resonance imaging. *Biological Psychiatry, 58,* 605–613.

Krafka, C., & Penrod, S. (1985). Reinstatement of context in a field experiment on eyewitness identification. *Journal of Personality and Social Psychology, 49,* 58–69.

Kramer G. P., Kerr, N. L., & Carroll, J. S. (1990). Pretrial publicity, judicial remedies, and jury bias. *Law and Human Behavior, 14,* 409–438.

Kravitz, D. A., Cutler, B. L., Brock., P. (1993). Reliability and validity of the original and revised Legal Attitudes Questionnaire. *Law and Human Behavior, 17,* 661–667.

Landström, S., Granhag, P. A., & Hartwig, M. (2005). Witnesses appearing live vs. on video: How presentation format affect observers' perception, assessment, and memory. *Applied Cognitive Psychology, 19,* 913–933.

Lassiter, G. D., Geers, A. L., Munhall, P. J., Handley, I. M., & Beers, M. J. (2001). Videotaped confessions: Is guilt in the eye of the camera? *Advances in Experimental Social Psychology, 33*, 189–254.

Lassiter, G. D., & Irvine, A. A. (1986). Videotaped confessions: The impact of camera point of view on judgments of coercion. *Journal of Applied Social Psychology, 16*, 268–276.

Lassiter, G. D., Slaw, R. D., Briggs, M. A., & Scanlan, C. R. (1992). The potential for bias in videotaped confessions. *Journal of Applied Social Psychology, 22*, 1838–1851.

Lassiter, G. D., Ware, L. J., Ratcliff, J. J., & Irvin, C. R. (2009). Evidence of the camera perspective bias in authentic videotaped interrogations: Implications for emerging reform in the criminal justice system. *Legal and Criminological Psychology, 14*, 157–170.

Laughery, K. R., Alexander, J. F., & Lane, A. B. (1971). Recognition of human faces: Effects of target exposure time, target position, and type of photograph. *Journal of Applied Psychology, 59*, 490–496.

Leach, A. M., Talwar, V., Lee, K., Bala, N., & Lindsay, R. C. L. (2004). Intuitive lie detection and children's deception by law enforcement officials and university students. *Law and Human Behavior, 28*, 661–685.

Lecci, L., & Myers, B. (2002). Examining the construct validity of the original and revised JBS: A cross-validation of sample and method. *Law and Human Behavior, 26*, 455–463.

Lecci, L., & Myers, B. (2008). Individual differences in attitudes relevant to juror decision making: Development and validation of the Pretrial Juror Attitude Questionnaire (PJAQ). *Journal of Applied Social Psychology, 38*, 2010–2038.

Leo, R. A. (1996). Inside the interrogation room. *Journal of Criminal Law and Criminology, 86*, 266–303.

Leo, R. A. (2008). *Police interrogation and American justice.* Cambridge, MA: Harvard University Press.

Levett, L. M., & Kovera, M. B. (2008). The effectiveness of opposing expert witnesses for educating jurors about unreliable expert evidence. *Law and Human Behavior, 32*, 363–374.

Levett, L. M., & Kovera, M. B. (2009). Psychological mediators of the effects of opposing expert testimony on juror decisions. *Psychology, Public Policy, and Law, 15*, 124–148.

Lieberman, J. D., Carrell, C. A., Miethe, T. D., & Krauss, D. A. (2008). Gold versus platinum: Do jurors recognize the superiority and limitations of DNA evidence compared to other types of forensic evidence? *Psychology, Public Policy, and Law, 14*, 27–62.

Lindsay, R. C. L., Lim, R., Marando, L., & Cully, D. (1986). Mock-juror evaluations of eyewitness testimony: A test of metamemory hypotheses. *Journal of Applied Social Psychology, 16*, 447–459.

Lindsay, R. C. L., Pozzulo, J. D., Craig, W., Lee, K., & Corber, S. (1997). Simultaneous lineups, sequential lineups, and showups: Eyewitness identification decisions of adults and children. *Law and Human Behavior, 21*, 391–404.

Loftus, E. F. (1980). Impact of expert psychological testimony on the unreliability of eyewitness identification. *Journal of Applied Psychology, 65*, 9–15.

London, K., & Nunez, N. (2000). The effect of jury deliberations on jurors' propensity to disregard inadmissible evidence. *Journal of Applied Psychology, 85*, 932–939.

Luus, C. A. E., & Wells, G. L. (1994). The malleability of eyewitness confidence: Co-witness and perseverance effects. *Journal of Applied Psychology, 79*, 714–723.

Maass, A., & Kohnken, G. (1989). Eyewitness identification: Simulating the "weapon effect." *Law and Human Behavior, 13*, 397–408.

Malpass, R. S., & Devine, P. G. (1981). Eyewitness identification: Lineup instructions and the absence of the offender. *Journal of Applied Psychology, 66*, 482–489.

Manson v. Braithwaite, 432 U.S. 98 (1977).

Marques, J. M., Abrams, D., Paez, D., & Martinez-Taboada, C. (1998). The role of categorization and in-group norms in judgments of groups and their members. *Journal of Personality and Social Psychology, 75*, 976–988.

Masip, J., Herrero, C., Garrido, E., & Barba, A. (2010). Is the Behaviour Analysis Interview just common sense? *Applied Cognitive Psychology, 5.*

McAuliff, B. D., & Kovera, M. B. (2008). Juror need for cognition and sensitivity to methodological flaws in expert evidence. *Journal of Applied Social Psychology, 38*, 385–408.

McAuliff, B. D., Kovera, M. B., & Nunez, G. (2009). Can jurors recognize missing control groups, confounds, and experimenter bias in psychological science? *Law and Human Behavior, 33*, 247–257.

McQuiston-Surrett, D. E., Malpass, R. S., & Tredoux, C. G. (2006). Sequential vs. simultaneous lineups: A review of methods, data, and theory. *Psychology, Public Policy, and Law, 12*, 137–169.

Mecklenburg, S. H. (2006). *Report to the legislature of the state of Illinois: The Illinois pilot program on double-blind, sequential lineup procedures.* Retrieved on June 10, 2008, from http://www.chicagopolice.org/IL%20Pilot%20on%20Eyewitness%20ID.pdf

Mecklenburg, S. H., Bailey, P., & Larson, M. (2008). The Illinois Field Study: A significant contribution to understanding real world eyewitness identification issues. *Law and Human Behavior, 32*, 22–27.

Meissner, C. A., & Brigham, J. C. (2001). Thirty years of investigating the own race bias in memory for faces: A meta-analytic review. *Psychology, Public Policy, and Law, 7*, 3–35.

Meissner, C. A., Brigham, J. C., & Pfeifer, J. E. (2003). Jury nullification: The influence of judicial instruction on the relationship between attitudes and juridic decision making. *Basic and Applied Social Psychology, 25*, 243–254.

Meissner, C. A., & Kassin, S. M. (2002). "He's guilty!": Investigator bias in judgments of truth and deception. *Law and Human Behavior, 26*, 469–480.

Meissner, C. A., Tredoux, C. G., Parker, J. F., & MacLin, O. H. (2005). Eyewitness decisions in simultaneous and sequential lineups: A dual-process signal detection theory analysis. *Memory and Cognition, 33*, 783–792.

Memon, A., Hope, L., & Bull, R. (2003). Exposure duration: Effects on eyewitness accuracy and confidence, *British Journal of Psychology, 94*, 339–354.

Miller, M. K., & Hayward, R. D. (2008). Religious characteristics and the death penalty. *Law and Human Behavior, 32*, 113–123.

Moran, G., & Comfort, J. C. (1982). Scientific juror selection: Sex as a moderator of demographic and personality predictors of impaneled felony juror behavior. *Journal of Personality and Social Psychology, 43*, 1052–1063.

Moran, G., & Comfort, J. C. (1986). Neither "tentative" nor "fragmentary": Verdict preference of impaneled felony jurors as a function of attitude toward capital punishment. *Journal of Applied Psychology, 71*, 146–155.

Moran, G., & Cutler, B. L. (1991). The prejudicial impact of pretrial publicity. *Journal of Applied Social Psychology, 21*, 345–367.

Moran, G., Cutler, B. L., & De Lisa, A. (1994). Attitudes toward tort reform, scientific jury selection, and juror bias: Verdict inclination in criminal and civil trials. *Law and Psychology Review, 18*, 309–328.

Moran, G., Cutler, B. L., & Loftus, E. F. (1990). Jury selection in major controlled substance trials: The need for extended voir dire. *Forensic Reports, 3*, 331–348.

Morgan, C. A., III, Hazlett, G., Doran, A., Garrett, S., Hoyt, G., Thomas, P., et al. (2004). Accuracy of eyewitness memory for persons encountered during exposure to highly intense stress. *International Journal of the Law and Psychiatry, 27*, 265–279.

Moston, S., Stephenson, G. M., & Williamson, T. M. (1992). The effects of case characteristics on suspect behaviour during questioning. *British Journal of Criminology, 32*, 23–40.

Myers, B., & Lecci, L. (1998). Revising the factor structure of the Juror Bias Scale: A method for the empirical evaluation of theoretical constructs. *Law and Human Behavior, 22*, 239–256.

Narby, D. J., & Cutler, B. L. (1994). Effectiveness of voir dire as a safeguard in eyewitness cases. *Journal of Applied Psychology, 79*, 724–729.

Nash, R. A., & Wade, K. A. (2009). Innocent but proven guilty: Eliciting internalized false confessions using doctored-video evidence. *Applied Cognitive Psychology, 23*, 624–637.

Nickerson, R. S. (1998). Confirmation bias: A ubiquitous phenomenon in many guises. *Review of General Psychology, 2*, 75–220.

Niedermeier, K. E., Horowitz, I. A., & Kerr, N. L. (1999). Informing jurors of their nullification powers: A route to a just verdict or judicial chaos. *Law and Human Behavior, 23*, 331–351.

Oberlander, L. B., & Goldstein, N. E. (2001). A review and update on the practice of evaluating Miranda comprehension. *Behavioral Sciences and the Law, 19*, 453–471.

Olczak, P. V., Kaplan, M. F., & Penrod, S. (1991). Attorney's lay psychology and its effectiveness in selecting jurors: Three empirical studies. *Journal of Social Behavior and Personality, 6*, 431–452.

Olson, E. A., & Wells, G. L. (2004). What makes a good alibi? A proposed taxonomy. *Law and Human Behavior, 28*, 157–176.

O'Neil, K. M., Patry, M. W., & Penrod, S. D. (2004). Exploring the effects of attitudes toward the death penalty on capital sentencing verdicts. *Psychology, Public Policy, and Law, 10*, 443–470.

O'Sullivan, M. (2007). Unicorns or Tiger Woods: Are lie detection experts myths or rarities? A response to "On lie detection 'Wizards'" by Bond and Uysal. *Law and Human Behavior, 31*, 117–123.

O'Sullivan, M., & Ekman, P. (2004). The wizards of deception detection. In P. A. Granhag & L. A. Strömwall (Eds.), *Deception detection in forensic contexts*. Cambridge, UK: Cambridge University Press.

Otto, A. L., Penrod, S., & Dexter, H. R. (1994). The biasing effects of pretrial publicity on juror judgments. *Law and Human Behavior, 18*, 453–469.

Owen-Kostelnik, J., Reppucci, N, D. & Meyer, J. D. (2006). Testimony and interrogation of minors: Assumptions about maturity and morality. *American Psychologist, 61*, 286–304.

Padawer-Singer, A. M., Singer, A. N., & Singer, R. L. (1977). Legal and social-psychological research in the effects of pre-trial publicity on juries, numerical makeup of juries, non-unanimous verdict requirements. *Law and Psychology Review, 3*, 71–79.

Phillips, M. R., McAuliff, B. D., Kovera, M. B., & Cutler, B. L. (1999). Double-blind photoarray administration as a safeguard against investigator bias. *Journal of Applied Psychology, 84*, 940–951.

Pickel, K. L. (1998). Unusualness and threat as possible causes of the "weapon focus." *Memory, 6*, 277–295.

Pickel, K. L. (1999). The influence of context on the "weapon focus" effect. *Law and Human Behavior, 23*, 299–311.

Pickel, K. L., Narter, D. B., Jameson, M. M., & Lenhardt, T. T. (2008). The weapon focus effect in child eyewitnesses. *Psychology, Crime, and Law, 14*, 61–72.

Pigott, M. A., Brigham, J. C., & Bothwell, R. K. (1990). A field study of the relationship between quality of eyewitnesses' descriptions and identification accuracy. *Journal of Police Science and Administration, 17*, 84–88.

Platz, S. J., & Hosch, H. M. (1988). Cross-racial/ethnic eyewitness identification: A field study. *Journal of Applied Social Psychology, 18*, 972–984.

Posey, A. J., & Dahl, L. M. (2002). Beyond pretrial publicity: Legal and ethical issues associated with change of venue surveys. *Law and Human Behavior, 26*, 107–125.

Price, D. D., Finniss, D. G., & Benedetti, F. (2008). A comprehensive review of the placebo effect: recent advances and current thought. *Annual Review of Psychology, 59*, 565–590.

Quas, J. A., Bottoms, B. L., Haegerich, T. M., & Nysse-Carris, K. L. (2002). Effects of victim, defendant, and juror gender on decisions in child sexual assault cases. *Journal of Applied Social Psychology, 32*, 1993–2021.

Read, J. D. (1995). The availability heuristic in person identification: The sometimes misleading consequences of enhanced contextual information. *Applied Cognitive Psychology, 9*, 91–122.

Read, J. D., Tollestrup, P., Hammersley, R., McFadzen, E., & Christensen, A. (1990). The unconscious transference effect: Are innocent bystanders ever misidentified? *Applied Cognitive Psychology, 4*, 3–31.

Redlich, A. D. (2007). Double jeopardy in the interrogation room: Young age and mental illness. *American Psychologist, 62*, 609–611.

Redlich, A. D., Alicia, A. E., & Hoover, S. (2010). Self-reported false confessions and false guilty pleas among offenders with mental illness. *Law and Human Behavior, 34*, 79–90.

Redlich, A. D., & Goodman, G. S. (2003). Taking responsibility for an act not committed: Influence of age and suggestibility. *Law and Human Behavior, 27*, 141–156.

Reicher, S. D., & Haslam, S. A. (2006). Rethinking the psychology of tyranny: The BBC prison study. *British Journal of Social Psychology, 45*, 1–40.

Rogers, R., Harrison, K. S., Hazelwood, L. L., & Sewell, K. W. (2007). Knowing and intelligent: A study of Miranda warnings in mentally disordered defendants. *Law and Human Behavior, 31*, 401–418.

Rose, M. R. (1999). The peremptory challenge accused of race or gender discrimination? Some data from one county. *Law and Human Behavior, 23*, 695–702.

Rosenthal, R. (2002). Covert communications in classrooms, clinics, courtrooms, and cubicles. *American Psychologist, 57*, 839–849.

Ross, S. J., & Malpass, R. M. (2008). Moving forward: Responses to "Studying eyewitness investigations in the field." *Law and Human Behavior, 32*, 16–21.

Russano, M. B., Meissner, C. A., Narchet, F. M., & Kassin, S. M. (2005). Investigating true and false confessions within a novel experimental paradigm. *Psychological Science, 16*, 481–486.

Ruva, C. L., McEvoy, C., & Bryant, J. B. (2007). Effects of pretrial publicity and jury deliberation on juror bias and source memory errors. *Applied Cognitive Psychology, 21*, 45–67.

Saks, M. J., & Marti, M. W. (1997). A meta-analysis of the effects of jury size. *Law and Human Behavior, 21*, 451–467.

Salerno, J. M., & McCauley M. R. (2009). Mock jurors' judgments about opposing scientific experts: Do cross-examination, deliberation, and need for cognition matter? *American Journal of Forensic Psychology, 27*, 37–60.

Schacter, D., Dawes, R., Jacoby, L. L., Kahneman, D., Lempert, R., Roediger, H. L., et al. (2008). Policy forum: Studying eyewitness investigations in the field. *Law and Human Behavior, 32*, 3–5.

Schklar, J., & Diamond, S. S. (1999). Juror reactions to DNA evidence: Errors and expectancies. *Law and Human Behavior, 23*, 159–184.

Schuller, R. A. (1992). The impact of battered woman syndrome evidence on jury decision-processes. *Law and Human Behavior, 16*, 597–620.

Schuller, R. A., & Cripps, J. (1998). Expert evidence pertaining to battered women: The impact of gender of expert and timing of testimony. *Law and Human Behavior, 22*, 17–31.

Schulman, J., Shaver, P., Colman, R., Emrich, B., & Christie, R. (1973, May). Recipe for a jury. *Psychology Today*, 37–84.

Searcy, J. H., Bartlett, J. C., & Memon, A. (2000). Influence of post-event narratives, lineup conditions, and individual differences on false identification by young and older eyewitnesses. *Legal and Criminological Psychology, 5*, 219–235.

Skeem, J. L., Louden, J. E., & Evans, J. (2004). Venirepersons's attitudes toward the insanity defense: Developing, refining, and validating a scale. *Law and Human Behavior, 28*, 623–648.

Smith, B. C., Penrod, S. D., Otto, A. L., & Park, R. C. (1996). Jurors' use of probabilistic evidence. *Law and Human Behavior, 20*, 49–82.

Sommers, S. R. (2006). On racial diversity and group decision making: Identifying multiple effects of racial composition on jury deliberations. *Journal of Personality and Social Psychology, 90*, 597–612.

Sommers, S. R., & Norton, M. I. (2007). Race-based judgments, race-neutral justifications: Experimental examination of peremptory use and the Batson challenge procedure. *Law and Human Behavior, 31*, 261–273.

Shapiro, P. N., & Penrod, S. (1986). Meta-analysis of facial identification studies. *Psychological Bulletin, 100*, 139–156.

Sigurdsson, J. F., & Gudjonsson, G. H. (1996). The psychological characteristics of "false confessors." A study among Icelandic prison inmates and juvenile offenders. *Personality and Individual Differences, 20*, 321–329.

Skitka, L. J. (2009). Exploring the "lost and found" of justice theory and research. *Social Justice Research, 22*, 98–116.

Snyder, M. (1992). Motivational foundations of behavioral confirmation. *Advances in Experimental Social Psychology, 25*, 67–114.

Snyder, M., & Stukas, A. (1999). Interpersonal processes: The interplay of cognitive, motivational, and behavioral activities in social interaction. *Annual Review of Psychology, 50*, 273–303.

Snyder, M., & Swann, W. B., Jr. (1978). Hypothesis-testing processes in social interaction. *Journal of Personality and Social Psychology, 36*, 1202–1212.

Sommers, S. R. (2006). On racial diversity and group decision making: Identifying multiple effects of racial composition on jury deliberations. *Journal of Personality and Social Psychology, 90*, 597–612.

Sommers, S. R., & Norton, M. I. (2007). Race-based judgments, race-neutral justifications: Experimental examination of peremptory use and the Batson challenge procedure. *Law and Human Behavior, 31*, 261–273.

Soukara, S., Bull, R., Vrij, A., Turner, M., & Cherryman, J. (2009). What really happens in police interviews of suspects: Tactics and confessions. *Psychology, Crime and Law, 15*, 493–506.

Sporer, S. L., Penrod, S., Read, D., & Cutler, B. (1995). Choosing, confidence, and accuracy: A meta-analysis of the confidence-accuracy relation in eyewitness identification studies. *Psychological Bulletin, 118*, 315–327.

Steblay, N. M. (1992). A meta-analytic review of the weapon focus effect. *Law and Human Behavior, 16*, 413–424.

Steblay, N. M. (1997). Social influences in eyewitness recall: A meta-analytic review of lineup instruction effects. *Law and Human Behavior, 21*, 283–297.

Steblay, N. K. (2008). Commentary on "Studying eyewitness investigations in the field": A look forward. *Law and Human Behavior, 32*, 11–15.

Steblay, N. M., Besirevic, J., Fulero, S. M., & Jimenez-Lorente, B. (1999). The effects of pretrial publicity on juror verdicts: A meta-analytic review. *Law and Human Behavior, 23*, 219–235.

Steblay, N. M., Dysart, J., Fulero, S., & Lindsay, R. C. L. (2001). Eyewitness accuracy rates in sequential and simultaneous line-up presentations: A meta-analytic comparison. *Law and Human Behavior, 25*, 459–474.

Steblay, N., Hosch, H. M., Culhane, S. E., & McWethy, A. (2006). The impact on juror verdicts of judicial instruction to disregard inadmissible evidence: A meta-analysis. *Law and Human Behavior, 30*, 469–492.

Strömwall, L. A., Granhag, P. A., & Jonsson, A.-C. (2003). Deception among pairs: "Let's say we had lunch and hope they will swallow it!" *Psychology, Crime, and Law, 9*, 109–124.

Studebaker, C. A., Robbennolt, J. L., Penrod, S. D., Pathak-Sharma, M. K., Groscup, J. L., & Devenport, J. L. (2002). Studying pretrial publicity effects: New methods for improving ecological validity and testing external validity. *Law and Human Behavior, 26*, 19–41.

Susa, K. J., & Meissner, C. A. (2008). Eyewitness descriptions, accuracy of. In B. L. Cutler (Ed.), *Encyclopedia of Psychology and Law*. Thousand Oaks, CA: Sage.

Swanner, J. K., Beike, D. R., & Cole, A. T. (2010). Snitching, lies and computer crashes: An experimental investigation of secondary confessions. *Law and Human Behavior, 34*, 53–65.

United States v. Telfaire, 469 F. 2d 552, 558–59 (1978).

Valentine, T., Pickering, A., & Darling, S. (2003). Characteristics of eyewitness identifications that predict the outcome of real lineups. *Applied Cognitive Psychology, 17*, 969–993.

Vinson, K. V., Costanzo, M. A., & Berger, D. E. (2008). Predictors of verdict and punitive damages in high-stakes civil litigation. *Behavioral Sciences and the Law, 26*, 167–186.

Visher, C. A. (1987). Juror decision making: The importance of evidence. *Law and Human Behavior, 11*, 1–17.

Vrij, A. (2008). *Detecting lies and deceit: Pitfalls and opportunities*. Chichester, UK: Wiley.

Vrij A., Mann S., & Fisher, R. (2006). An empirical test of the Behaviour Analysis Interview. *Law and Human Behavior, 30*, 329–345.

Vrij, A., Fisher, R., Mann, S., & Leal, S. (2006). Detecting deception by manipulating cognitive load. *Trends in Cognitive Sciences, 10*, 141–142.

Vrij, A., Mann, S., Fisher, R., Leal, S., Milne, R., & Bull, R. (2008). Increasing cognitive load to facilitate lie detection: The benefit of recalling an event in reverse order. *Law and Human Behavior, 32*, 253–265.

Wainwright v. Witt, 469 U.S. 412 d 841 (1985).

Ware, L. J., Lassiter, G. D., Patterson, S. M., & Ransom, M. R. (2008). Camera perspective bias in videotaped confessions: Evidence that visual attention is a mediator. *Journal of Experimental Psychology: Applied, 14*, 192–200.

Weber, N., Brewer, N., Wells, G. L., Semmler, C., & Keast, A. (2004). Eyewitness identification accuracy and response latency: The unruly 10–12 second rule. *Journal of Experimental Psychology: Applied, 10*, 139–147.

Wells, G. L. (1978). Applied eyewitness-testimony research: System variables and estimator variables. *Journal of Personality and Social Psychology, 36*, 1546–1557.

Wells, G. L. (2008). Field experiments on eyewitness identification: Towards a better understanding of pitfalls and prospects. *Law and Human Behavior, 32*, 6–10.

Wells, G. L., & Luus, C. A. E. (1990). Police lineups as experiments: Social methodology as a framework for properly conducted lineups. *Personality and Social Psychology Bulletin, 16*, 106–117.

Wells, G. L., Malpass, R. S., Lindsay, R. C. L., Fisher, R. P., Turtle, J. W., & Fulero, S. M. (2000). From the lab to the police station: A successful application of eyewitness research. *American Psychologist, 55*, 581–598.

Wells, G. L., & Quinlivan, D. S. (2009). Suggestive eyewitness identification procedures and the Supreme Court's reliability test in light of eyewitness science: 30 years later. *Law and Human Behavior, 33*, 1–24.

Wells, G. L., Rydell, S. M., & Seelau, E. P. (1993). On the selection of distracters for eyewitness lineups. *Journal of Applied Psychology, 78*, 835–844.

Wells, G. L., Small, M., Penrod, S., Malpass, R. S., Fulero, S. M., & Brimacombe, C. A. E. (1998). Eyewitness identification procedures: Recommendations for lineups and photospreads. *Law and Human Behavior, 22*, 1–39.

Wenger, A. A., & Bornstein, B. H. (2006). The effects of victim's substance use and relationship closeness on mock jurors' judgments in an acquaintance rape case. *Sex Roles, 54*, 547–555.

Wiener, R. L., Hackney, A., Kadela, K., Rauch, S., Seib, H., Warren, L., et al. (2002). The fit and implementation of sexual harassment law to workplace evaluations. *Journal of Applied Psychology, 87*, 747–764.

Williams v. Florida, 399 U.S. 78 (1970).

Wissler, R. L., & Saks, M. J. (1985). On the inefficacy of limiting instructions: When jurors use prior conviction evidence to decide on guilt. *Law and Human Behavior, 9*, 37–48.

Wogalter, M. S., Malpass, R. S., & McQuiston, D. E. (2004). A national survey of police on preparation and conduct of identification lineups. *Psychology, Crime, and Law, 10*, 69–82.

Wright, D. B., & Skagerberg, E. M. (2007). Post-identification feedback affects real eyewitnesses. *Psychological Science, 18*, 172–178.

Zeisel, H., & Diamond, S. S., (1978). The effect of peremptory challenges on jury and verdict: An experiment in a federal district court. *Stanford Law Review, 30*, 491–531.

Zimbardo, P. G. (1967, June). The psychology of police confessions. *Psychology Today, 1*, 17–20, 25–27.

The Psychology of Collective Action

Lauren E. Duncan

Abstract

Personality and social psychology research on motivation for collective action is reviewed and integrated into a model presented in Figure 31.1. The personality work effectively identifies correlates of collective action without necessarily providing explanations of motivation. The social psychological work provides convincing motives for collective action but downplays individual difference variables. The integration of these two traditions addresses these gaps and allows for a deeper, more complex understanding of the phenomenological experience of the development of group consciousness and links to collective action. Promising areas for potential future research are discussed.

Keywords: activism, collective action, group consciousness, politicized collective identity, relative deprivation, stratum consciousness, nigrescence, personality, motivation, feminism

Introduction

The question of why people become involved in collective action has been the subject of ongoing interest in psychology. This chapter reviews and integrates the personality and social psychological literatures on motivation for participation in collective action. Research on collective action by personality psychologists historically used individual differences in personality characteristics and life experience variables to explain involvement in collective action (e.g., Block, Haan, & Smith, 1973). This tradition, while allowing psychologists to identify personality characteristics that distinguished activists from nonactivists, did not explain *why* these individual differences in personality characteristics were associated with collective action. Research on collective action by social psychologists was rooted in theories of social identity, relative deprivation, and resource mobilization theory (see van Zomeren, Postmes, & Spears, 2008, for a meta-analysis and review) and provided obvious motives for individual participation in collective action. However, this tradition downplayed individual difference variables.

Integrating individual difference variables into the study of motivation for collective action allows a deeper, more complex understanding of this motivation and can explain why some group members develop group consciousness and become politically active whereas others do not.

This chapter combines the work on collective action in personality and social psychology by integrating four social psychological theories into a schematic model presented by Duncan (1995, 1999). This model posits group consciousness variables (from social psychology) as mediating the relationships between individual difference variables (from personality psychology) and participation in collective action and provides a compelling motive for this participation (see Figure 31.1). In this model, group consciousness is used as an overarching term that encompasses social psychological variables related to group identification and common fate, critical analysis of a group's position in society, and a collective orientation toward redressing power imbalances between groups.

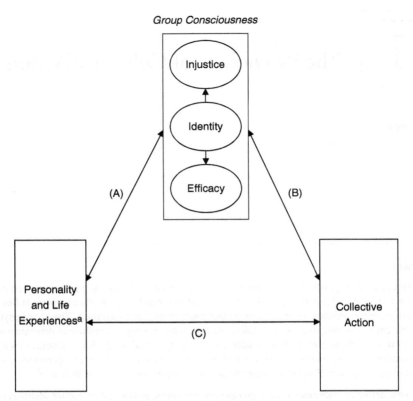

Fig. 31.1 Integrated model of personality and social psychological theories of collective action.
ᵃ Some personality and life experience variables are hypothesized to moderate Path B.

Figure 31.1 illustrates two paths to collective action, direct (Path C) and indirect (Path B). It integrates the research in personality and social psychology on collective action by showing how individual difference variables contribute to group consciousness (Path A) and how group consciousness, in turn, can motivate collective action (Path B). Research suggests that these indirect paths may be taken most often when basic needs are met, and there are no immediate, life-disrupting crises threatening a particular group (e.g., during "movements of affluence"; Kerbo, 1982; see, also, Duncan, 1999; Duncan & Stewart, 2007). The figure also suggests that personality and life experiences can directly affect behavioral outcomes (Path C), which is most likely to occur when there is little time to articulate a coherent ideological reason for action (e.g., during "movements of crisis"; see Kerbo, 1982, and Duncan, 1999). Reciprocal effects are also possible in this model. That is, this model acknowledges that group consciousness can develop and personality can change as a result of participating in collective action. For example, Agronick and Duncan (1998) found that between the ages of 28 and 43,

women showed increased dominance, self-acceptance, empathy, psychological mindedness, and achievement via independence, as measured by the California Psychological Inventory, as a result of their participation in the Women's Movement (reversed path C).

Research in social psychology is largely concerned with Path B, whereas the research in personality psychology is largely concerned with Paths A and C. In the remainder of this chapter, I review four social psychological models of group consciousness, three of which elucidate the phenomenological experience of group consciousness on an individual level. I then review and integrate the personality research on collective action with the social psychological work, ending with a discussion of some promising avenues for future research.

Social Psychological Models of Group Consciousness and Collective Action

Social psychological models dominate current psychological research on collective action (see, e.g., the December 2009 issue of the *Journal of Social Issues*). For example, findings culled from 69 published social psychological studies utilizing 182 independent samples were reviewed and organized in a meta-analysis by van Zomeren et al. (2008), who found that the literature could be organized into three broad domains, which examined the effects on collective action of: (1) perceived injustice, (2) identity, and (3) efficacy variables. They tested a model of collective action (referred to as SIMCA, or social identity model of collective action) that showed that identity was related to collective action, and that perceived injustice and perceived efficacy mediated the relationship between identity and collective action. In the meta-analysis, collective action was operationalized as attitudinal support for protest, protest intentions, or behaviors aimed at redressing the cause of the group's disadvantage (e.g., signing a petition, attending a demonstration). An overview of perceived injustice, identity, and efficacy variables is provided below.

Perceived Injustice

Van Zomeren et al. identified two developments in the relative deprivation literature relevant to collective action. First, they noted that perceptions of injustice based on group memberships rather than individual characteristics were more likely to be related to collective action (Smith & Ortiz, 2002). Second, relative deprivation researchers began distinguishing between *cognitive* measures of injustice (i.e., perceptions of unfairness or discrimination; e.g., Corning & Myers, 2002; Kawakami & Dion, 1993) and *affective* measures of injustice (i.e., dissatisfaction, fraternal resentment, group-based anger; or perceptions and feelings of relative deprivation; e.g., Gill & Matheson, 2006; van Zomeren, Spears, Fischer, & Leach, 2004). Based on the argument that group-based emotions (e.g., anger) bridged the relationship between appraisals and specific action tendencies (van Zomeren et al., 2004; Yzerbyt, Dumont, Wigboldus, & Gordijn, 2003), van Zomeren et al. (2008) hypothesized that affective measures of injustice would be better predictors of collective action than would cognitive measures. In the meta-analysis, cognitive injustice was operationalized as perceptions of procedural and distributive fairness, and affective injustice was operationalized as relative deprivation. Van Zomeren et al. found that affective measures of injustice were indeed more powerful predictors of collective action than cognitive ones. In an analysis of a subset of data containing injustice, efficacy, and identity variables, they found that injustice mediated the relationship between identity and collective action.

Perceived Efficacy

In the 1970s, sociologists argued that collective action could not be predicted by individual perceptions or feelings of deprivation; rather, social movement organizations were essential in mobilizing groups of people to action (McCarthy & Zald, 1977). Central to this approach was the notion, taken from economics, that people were rational actors who acted to maximize gains and minimize costs. In short, according to this approach, people would engage in collective action when the expected benefits for such action outweighed the costs (McCarthy & Zald, 1977). In psychology, Klandermans (1984) argued that on the individual level, a key aspect of the cost/benefit analysis was an evaluation of the effectiveness of a particular action. That is, the perceived efficacy of a particular action affected the likelihood of an individual engaging in that action.

Other psychological research emphasized the importance of group efficacy, or the belief that through collective action, one's group could make change (Drury & Reicher, 2005; Gurin, Miller, & Gurin, 1980; Mummendey, Kessler, Klink, & Mielke, 1999). In their meta-analysis, van Zomeren et al. (2008) operationalized efficacy as a political or group-based sense of control, influence, or effectiveness to change a group-related problem, specifically excluding measures of cost/benefit analyses (which I argue is better conceptualized as moderating the relationship between group consciousness and collective action). They found that perceived efficacy was related to collective action. In addition, in a subset of data containing injustice, efficacy, and identity variables, perceived efficacy mediated the relationship between identity and collective action.

Social Identity

Theories of social identity (Tajfel, 1978; Tajfel & Turner, 1979) emphasized the importance for individual well-being of maintaining a positive evaluation of one's group. Collective action was posited as one way in which members of low-status groups in society could maintain positive evaluations of their groups in societies that devalued them. Note that this observation was relevant for groups with impermeable boundaries, under situations that were seen as illegitimate and unstable. Under these conditions, group identification was seen as a potential predictor of collective action.

Simon and colleagues (Simon et al., 1998; Simon & Klandermans, 2001; Stürmer & Simon, 2004) argued that a *politicized* group identity (i.e., identification with a social movement organization) was essential to predict collective action. Simon et al. (1998) found that identification with the gay movement, rather than the wider social group (gay people), was important for predicting collective action and intentions to act. In their meta-analysis, van Zomeren et al. (2008) operationalized *nonpoliticized* group identities in two ways: as (1) the cognitive centrality of the group identity, and (2) attachment or affective commitment to the disadvantaged group. Further, *politicized* identity was operationalized as cognitive centrality or affective commitment to a social movement organization or as an activist. Van Zomeren et al. found that politicized identities were better direct predictors of collective action than nonpoliticized identities. In addition, in a subset of data containing injustice, efficacy, and identity variables, the relationship between identity and collective action was mediated by perceived injustice and perceived efficacy. They argued that possessing a politicized group identity exposed individuals to group-based perceptions and emotions (e.g., injustice and efficacy), which would then lead to collective action.

Simon and Klandermans (2001) emphasized the role of power struggles in collective action. In the case of politicized collective identity, "group members should intentionally engage, as a mindful and self-conscious collective (or as representative thereof), in such a power struggle knowing that it is the wider, more inclusive societal context in which this struggle takes place and needs to be orchestrated accordingly" (p. 323). Similar to sociological constructs of collective identities, this work emphasized the notion that groups struggling for power do it in a context whereby they attempt to persuade wider society of the justness of their cause. Subašić, Reynolds, and Turner (2008) elaborated this idea by arguing that social change can only occur when the minority garners the support of the "silent majority."

This recent work is extremely useful in organizing and modeling social psychological efforts to understand collective action. However, this work does not represent well the phenomenological experience of individual motivation for collective action, which I describe as "group consciousness." Below, I review three social psychological theories that elaborate the phenomenological aspects of group consciousness and connections to collective action. The first, Gurin, Miller, and Gurin's (1980) theory of stratum consciousness, describes four critical elements necessary for the development of group consciousness. The second, Cross's (1971; Cross & Vandiver, 2001) theory of nigrescence, describes in detail the phenomenological experience involved in the individualized process of developing a stable politicized group identity. The third, Crosby's (1976) conceptualization of relative deprivation, describes in great detail the five elements necessary for the development of feelings of injustice, and also illuminates the individual level factors that might moderate the relationship of relative deprivation to collective action. The integration of these social psychological theories adds to our understanding of the phenomenological experience of motivation for collective action on an individual level.

Stratum Consciousness

Based in social identity theory (Tajfel & Turner, 1979), stratum consciousness was defined by Gurin and her colleagues (P. Gurin, 1985; Gurin et al., 1980) as composed of four elements: (1) *identification with a group*, that is, recognition of shared interests among the group or a sense of common fate; (2) *power discontent*, or belief that one's group is deprived of power and influence relative to a high-status group; (3) withdrawal or *rejection of legitimacy*, or belief that disparities based on group membership are illegitimate (also called system blame); and (4) *collective orientation*, or belief that group members should work together to eliminate those obstacles that affect them as a group. Gurin later added cognitive centrality to this model (Gurin & Markus, 1989).

This definition of stratum consciousness was used to describe the gender consciousness of women and men, age consciousness of older and younger people, race consciousness of African Americans and whites, and class consciousness of blue-collar and middle-class workers (P. Gurin, 1985; Gurin et al., 1980). They found that group identification was related to the other three elements of the model (power discontent, rejection of legitimacy, collective orientation). This conceptualization was also supported in the political science literature by Klein's (1984) description of the societal level elements of feminist consciousness.

The latter three elements of stratum consciousness (power discontent, rejection of legitimacy, and collective orientation) compose a political ideology, one that recognizes the group's position in a power hierarchy, rejects other groups' rationalizations of relative positioning, and embraces a collective solution to group problems. It is the combination of these three elements along with identification with a group that creates group consciousness on the individual level. Note that in this description of group consciousness, it is not necessary to identify with a social movement or as an activist (as it is in Simon and Klandermans's [2001] notion of politicized collective identity.) Rather, individual members of low-status groups will possess differing levels of each of Gurin et al.'s (1980) elements, and the higher they score on group identification, power discontent, rejection of legitimacy, and collective orientation, the more likely they are to be politically active (see Duncan, 1999; Duncan & Stewart, 2007).

As identifications with groups and individuals are a part of personal identity, Gurin's model provides us with a framework with which to explore the associations between group consciousness and personal identity. Similar to identifications with individuals (Freud, 1946), a group identification involves "the awareness of having ideas, feelings, and interests similar to others" (Gurin et al., 1980, p. 30). Group identifications, however, are based on shared "stratum" characteristics rather than personal characteristics. Stratum characteristics can be based on involuntary group memberships such as race, ethnicity, gender, age, generation, and class of origin as well as on voluntary group memberships, such as social movement organizations. The nature of group consciousness based on *voluntary*, or permeable group memberships differs qualitatively from one based on *involuntary*, or impermeable memberships. For example, if the personal cost of acting on a voluntary group identification gets too high, an individual can pass out of the group fairly easily. However, involuntary group members do not possess this option (see Andrews, 1991, for a discussion of this topic).

Tajfel's (1978) conceptualization of social identity posits that group identity is subsumed by personal identity. Social or group identity describes "that *part* of an individual's self-concept which derives from his knowledge of his membership of a social group (or groups) together with the value and emotional significance attached to that membership" (p. 63). Simply identifying with a group is not enough to create group consciousness; group identification must be *politicized* to produce group consciousness. Consider, for example, identification as a feminist; many women identify strongly as women without possessing a feminist consciousness, because identification with the group "women" is not necessarily accompanied by an assessment of the unequal position of women as a group (Henderson-King & Stewart, 1994).

In various situations, different identifications may become more salient than others and this salience may be related to awareness of oneself as a minority (Markus & Kunda, 1986). For example, being the only psychologist in a room full of physicists may make one very aware of one's professional identification. At a gay rights rally, sexual orientation would be salient for all participants, gay and straight. For gay people, the salience of sexual identity might be organized around feelings of power discontent or relative deprivation. For straight people, on the other hand, the privilege of their heterosexual sexual orientation might be more salient. For members of high-status groups, then, group consciousness may be organized around awareness of a privileged identity.

According to Markus (1990), aspects of the universe that are designated as parts of one's identity, or "me":

> become coordinates or frames of individual consciousness. Other "non-me" aspects can be made salient and focal, but those that are claimed as "me" have a durable salience. The "me" aspects are perpetually used as benchmarks for organizing and understanding the rest of the universe. (p. 183)

During the development of group consciousness, a group identification may take on a durable salience. For example, when race consciousness is developing, race becomes a benchmark against which information gleaned from the environment is judged and interpreted. Gurin and Markus (1989) showed that women who found gender to be salient endorsed more gender identity descriptors, made these endorsements more quickly, and expressed higher levels of confidence in these descriptors than women who found gender less salient, thus displaying the centrality of gender to the cognitive organization of information.

In addition, group identifications are organized in relation to each other. One's experiences as a man depend on other group characteristics; for example, whether one is a white man or a black man. Feminist scholars have termed this phenomenon *intersectionality* (Cole, 2009; Dill, 1983; Stewart & McDermott, 2004). The question of salience of identifications can become very complicated when identifications are understood in relation to each other. How identifications with groups and individuals become politicized is a complicated issue, and one that needs elaboration.

The Development of Politicized Group Identifications: The Example of Nigrescence
Cross's (1971; Cross & Vandiver, 2001) theory of nigrescence contributes to our understanding of

group consciousness by describing the process involved in politicizing a group identification. Although Cross's model was originally developed to describe the development of a politicized racial identification, his model has been adapted to describe the development of other types of group consciousness as well (e.g., ethnic consciousness, feminist consciousness, gay/lesbian consciousness; see Constantine, Watt, Gainor, & Warren, 2005, for a review). There are, of course, differences in the oppressive circumstances facing different low-status groups; thus the process of politicization may deviate more or less from Cross's description.

Cross's model involves five stages, and documents the development of new, low-status group politicized identities. Briefly, *preencounter* describes the worldview of a nonpoliticized individual as a person who views being a low-status group member as either irrelevant to daily life or as an obstacle, and seldom a symbol of culture and tradition. The *encounter* stage marks the awakening of the individual to the realities of the unequal position of her or his group in society, and often involves anger at society and high-status groups (similar to Gurin et al.'s, 1980, power discontent and rejection of legitimacy). The encounter stage begins the process of identity change to accommodate a new, collective ideology that interprets personal experiences of oppression as due to group membership rather than personal characteristics. *Immersion/emersion* involves a total rejection of dominant culture values, and an uncritical acceptance of those of the low-status group. Successful negotiation of this stage involves heavy reliance on the collective, where the individual finds companionship, solace, and models of "how to be" a good politicized group member. Cross's stage 4 involves *internalization* of the new identification, which describes the worldview of the newly politicized person. Individuals no longer rely on the collective for self-definition; they have internalized the meaning of their group identification and are ready to operate once again in the dominant culture. Finally, *internalization-commitment* is characterized by an active and continuing commitment to redressing injustices encountered by the group, and is not embraced by every person (Cross, 1991).

The models of race consciousness described by Cross and feminist consciousness described by Downing and Roush (1985) have been supported in several studies (Carter & Helms, 1987; Parham & Helms, 1981, 1985a, 1985b; Rickard, 1989, 1990). For example, Rickard (1989, 1990) showed

that college women categorized as possessing preencounter identifications were more likely to belong to conservative and traditional campus organizations (Right to Life and College Textiles and Clothing organizations), hold traditional views about dating, and endorse negative attitudes toward working women. College women categorized as having internalized politicized (feminist) identifications were more likely to belong to the National Organization of Women and the campus Gay/Lesbian Alliance, hold nontraditional views about dating, and feel more positively toward working women. More recent research is consistent in linking feminist identities to political activism in white and black women and men (Duncan, 1999; Duncan & Stewart, 2007; Liss, Crawford, & Popp, 2004; White, 2006).

In later modifications of Cross's theory, it was suggested that a stage model may not be appropriate to describe the ongoing process of politicizing a group identification; rather, it may be more useful to think of these stages as descriptors of experiences of group consciousness that occur in conjunction with one another, and not always in the same order (Parham, 1989; White, 2006; Worrell, Cross, & Vandiver, 2001). Nonetheless, Cross's original model of nigrescence discusses in detail some of the issues that individuals face when developing politicized group identifications. Once a politicized group identification is established (stages 2–5 of Cross's model), how might it get transformed into collective action?

Relative Deprivation Theory

Crosby's (1976) formulation of relative deprivation elaborates the power discontent and rejection of legitimacy aspects of the stratum consciousness model (Gurin et al., 1980). In addition, it provides a link between group consciousness and collective action. Relative deprivation describes the negative emotions experienced by individuals who feel unjustly deprived of something they desire (Crosby, 1976; J. Davis, 1959; Gurr, 1970; Runciman, 1966). According to Crosby's model, relative deprivation occurs when five preconditions are met. These five preconditions are necessary and sufficient to experience relative deprivation:

(1) see that other possesses X (some desired good),
(2) want X,
(3) feel that one deserves X,
(4) think it feasible to obtain X, and
(5) lack a sense of responsibility for failure to possess X.

Crosby (1976) reviewed a large body of empirical literature to support her model. In an expansion of Crosby's model, Crosby and Gonzalez-Intal (1984) included feelings of deprivation on the behalf of members of other groups ("ideological deprivation," Clayton & Crosby, 1992) and resentment over a third party's undeserved possession of goods. Jennings (1991) posited that these two extensions of relative deprivation theory might account for participation in social movements by members of groups who do not directly benefit from the achievement of the movement's goals (see, also, Iyer & Ryan, 2009).

In Crosby's early work, group identification, a central element of Gurin et al.'s (1980) model, was not mentioned as a necessary precondition for the experience of *personal* relative deprivation; in later work on fraternal (group) deprivation, Clayton and Crosby (1992) discussed the essential role of group identification. However, group identification has always been implicit in Crosby's (1976) notion of relative deprivation. For example, in preconditions 1 and 3 (see that other possesses X, feel that one deserves X), comparison between one's situation and that of another occurs, and this comparison may be based on an awareness that the two individuals belong to the *same* group or to *different* groups.

When the group comparison occurs at a political level, or the justification for the inequity is explicitly political, the relative deprivation that develops is very similar to Gurin et al.'s (1980) notion of stratum consciousness (except that Crosby does not assume a collective orientation). If a group identification becomes politicized through the process of group comparison (group identification), awareness of inequities (power discontent), and rejection of responsibility for these inequities using a political analysis (rejection of legitimacy), then relative deprivation and stratum consciousness look similar. For example, in Crosby's (1982) empirical examination of gender discrimination, men were paid more than women working the same jobs. In this study, women workers assumed that their salary levels were determined independent of gender, and so compared their salaries to both male and female employees. Because these women saw "workers" to be the relevant group within which to compare salaries, and not "women workers," their salaries were found to be deficient, and they developed politicized gender identifications.

Crosby (1976) outlined the possible outcomes for the individual and society after relative deprivation, identifying variables that could moderate the relationship between relative deprivation and its outcomes. Depending on personality and environmental factors, relative deprivation could lead either to nonviolent personal or social change or violence against the self or society. In group consciousness terms, personal and environmental conditions could moderate the relationship between group consciousness and personal or collective action, either by stymieing group consciousness or by channeling it into nonviolent or violent personal or collective action.

Crosby implicated two potential personality moderators in her analysis, intro/extrapunitiveness, and personal control. Specifically, she argued that after developing relative deprivation, individuals' tendency to turn their anger either inward (intropunitive) or outward toward society (extrapunitive) and whether they had high or low personal control would affect their future behaviors. The intro/extrapunitive dimension appears to be related to system blame. People who direct their anger outward should be more comfortable with systemic explanations for their group's low status.

Personal control is similar to political self-efficacy. An individual with low personal control "feels that he cannot change his lot nor affect society" (Crosby, 1976, p. 100). Crosby argued that for extrapunitive individuals with high personal control encountering open opportunities for change, constructive social change was a likely result of relative deprivation. On the other hand, if opportunities were blocked, or the individual had low control, violence against society might result. If the person were intropunitive, either stress symptoms (if low control or blocked opportunities) or self-improvement (if high control and open opportunities) were the likely results of relative deprivation.

For example, actions taken by activists in the U.S. South during the early civil rights movement focused attention on the unconstitutionality of segregation in schools, on buses, and in public spaces. Protesters were extrapunitive, had strong political self-efficacy, and sensed that opportunities were open for change. Peaceful social change resulted. On the other hand, during the late 1960s, when civil rights activists began working on desegregating housing in the northern United States, the target of their efforts was harder to pinpoint. Few laws were being broken, but the disparities between whites and blacks in housing conditions were extreme. Similar to the protesters in the early civil rights movement, these later protesters were extrapunitive and had strong political self-efficacy, but found that their efforts to change housing situations were ineffective (opportunities for change were blocked). Some activists turned to violent social protest as a result (see, Hampton, Fayer, & Flynn, 1990, for first-person accounts of the civil rights movement.)

Integration of Social Psychological Theories

Table 31.1 presents the central elements of the four theories I have discussed in order to illustrate their commonalities and differences. Central to all of the social psychological models is a sense of power discontent and rejection of individualistic explanations for these power differences—perhaps best summarized as feelings of relative deprivation (encompassing element 1 of SIMCA, all elements of relative deprivation theory, elements 2 and 3 of stratum consciousness theory, and element 2 of nigrescence theory). A sense of identification with a disenfranchised group is key to making these comparisons in the first place, for without the proper reference group, there is no feeling of relative deprivation. Element 2 of SIMCA, element 1 of stratum consciousness, and elements 2 and 3 of nigrescence theory explicitly recognize the importance of group identification.

The four theories differ in their articulation of the connections between these feelings of deprivation or consciousness and action orientation and behavior taken on behalf of the group. For example, stratum consciousness theory specifies that a collective (rather than individualistic) orientation toward action is required, and SIMCA specifies that group-based efficacy is important to produce collective action. Crosby's (1976) relative deprivation theory, on the other hand, does not explicitly consider collective versus individualistic action orientations, but emphasizes instead different outcomes for the self and society of individualistic versus systemic explanations for power differences. Nigrescence theory does not specify the nature of action but simply labels it as the ultimate achievement in demonstrating an integrated identity.

These theories are most useful in explaining why people might participate in collective action when taken in conjunction with each other. The injustice aspect of SIMCA and relative deprivation theories describe a negative emotional state and consequences for action of such emotions, but do not explicitly identify the sense of common fate (provided by the social identity element of SIMCA, stratum consciousness, and nigrescence theories) that is necessary for experiencing such emotion at the group level. The efficacy element of SIMCA and stratum consciousness theories include the collective element necessary for converting feelings of deprivation into collective action, but do not articulate an explicit connection to action or outline a process of how such consciousness might develop on an individual level. Nigrescence theory fills in the latter gap, providing a detailed description of how individuals can develop politicized group identifications. Thus, all four models are useful for understanding why some people—above and beyond their demographic characteristics—might participate in collective action.

Table 31.1 Key Elements of Four Social Psychological Theories Used to Explain Motivation for Participation in Collective Action

| | Group Consciousness Theories | | |
SIMCA (van Zomeren et al., 2008)	Relative Deprivation (Crosby, 1976)	Stratum Consciousness (Gurin et al. 1980)	Nigrescence (Cross, 1971; Cross & Vandiver, 2001)
1. Injustice	1. See others with X	1. Group identification	1. Preencounter
2. Identity	2. Want X	2. Power discontent	2. Encounter
3. Efficacy	3. Deserve X	3. System blame	3. Immersion/emersion
	4. Feasible to get X	4. Collective orientation	4. Internalization
	5. Not own fault don't have X		5. Internalization-commitment

Individual Differences, Group Consciousness, and Collective Action

The social psychological models described above are essential for understanding motivation for participation in collective action (Path B in Figure 31.1). However, the personality psychology approach to understanding participation in collective action has articulated the individual difference variables important to group consciousness (Path A) and collective action (Path C), and developed completely independently of the work in social psychology. Early work in personality psychology attempted to identify individual difference variables that distinguished 1960s student activists from nonactivists (e.g., Block, Haan, & Smith, 1973). Current work in personality has moved beyond these early efforts to document group differences. Instead, it dovetails nicely with the social psychological work on social identity, allowing us to identify personality correlates of group consciousness and collective action (e.g., Curtin, Stewart, & Duncan, 2010; Duncan, 1999, 2010; Duncan & Stewart, 2007).

The personality literature on collective action was largely empirically based, with no coherent unifying theory. In this section, then, I use the model described in Figure 31.1 to organize and review the personality literature related to group consciousness and collective action (Paths A and C). Throughout this section, I integrate the personality work with the social psychological theories of group consciousness and discuss evidence for how individual characteristics might be mediated or moderated by group consciousness. I consider individual differences in both life experiences (including family background characteristics, developmental stage, experiences with discrimination, low-status group memberships, resources, access to social movement organizations) and personality characteristics (including personal political salience, political self-efficacy, generativity, authoritarianism, cognitive flexibility, impulsivity, autonomy, openness to experience, optimism, and need to evaluate).

Typically, personality and social psychology are integrated in such a way as to consider the person x situation interaction (Higgins, 1990). In social psychological experiments, the situation is manipulated, and individual differences in personality characteristics are assumed to be randomly distributed across conditions. In personality psychology, the situation is assumed to be constant and the personality characteristics of individuals vary. However, in this review of the personality characteristics related to group consciousness and collective action, I treat situational variables (defined as naturally

occurring life experiences rather than experimental manipulations), as individual difference variables. That is, in the following discussion, I consider how variations in life experiences between individuals have differential effects on the development of group consciousness and collective action.

LIFE EXPERIENCES

Family Background Characteristics

Consistent with theories of generational continuity, studies of 1960s student activists found that early participants in 1960s social movements tended to come from *politically liberal families of origin* (Acock, 1984; Block, Haan, & Smith, 1969; Braungart & Braungart, 1990; Flacks, 1967; Glass, Bengtson, & Dunham, 1986; Jennings & Niemi, 1968, 1982; Middleton & Putney, 1963), and *liberal or nonreligious families* (A. Astin, 1968; H. Astin, 1969; Block et al., 1973; R. Braungart, 1969; Flacks, 1967; Geller & Howard, 1969; Heist, 1965; Lichter & Rothman, 1981–82; Solomon & Fishman, 1964; Watts, Lynch, & Whittaker, 1969; Watts & Whittaker, 1966). It is likely that liberal family background contributes to participation in collective action indirectly, by increasing the chance that individuals will be taught systemic explanations for social problems, thus increasing group consciousness (a mediated effect).

Research on the childrearing styles of the parents of student activists showed that these early activists came from relatively warm and permissive homes where discipline per se was not emphasized, where parents were likely to involve the child in family decisions, and where the environment was accepting and affirming (Block et al., 1973; Braungart & Braungart, 1990; Flacks, 1990). These characteristics, which differentiated early movement participants from nonparticipants, may have contributed indirectly to the development of group consciousness by allowing the activists the freedom to explore ideas encountered in the social environment, rather than directly influencing participation in collective action. Or, those politicized students with permissive parents might have been more likely to translate their group consciousness into action (a moderated effect). In addition, there is support for direct (modeling) effects as well. That is, some studies have found that parents' active commitment to collective action as a "way of doing" social change encourages children to do the same (Duncan & Stewart, 1995; Katz, 1968; Thomas, 1971).

Developmental Stage

Erikson's (1963) articulation of eight universal psychosocial stages suggests that there may be particular times in life when an individual is especially open to experiences that might lead to group consciousness. Stewart and Healy (1989) hypothesized that social events experienced in late adolescence and early adulthood affect perceptions of opportunities and life choices, which can be incorporated into personal identity (R. Braungart, 1975; Duncan & Agronick, 1995; Fitzgerald, 1988; Schuman & Scott, 1989; Stewart & Gold-Steinberg, 1990), and that events experienced in later (midlife) adulthood affect perceptions of new opportunities and choices, which can create opportunities for identity revision (Duncan & Agronick, 1995; Stewart & Healy, 1989; see also Stewart & Deaux, chapter 26, this volume). According to Stewart and Healy's (1989) theory, an individual is more likely to develop group consciousness during *early adulthood* or *midlife*, when identity formation or revision is apt to occur; this is true for both high-status and low-status group members. In addition, the likelihood of developing group consciousness should drastically increase if, during a "receptive" psychosocial stage, an individual experiences a social event focused on issues that resonate to a particular group membership. For example, research suggests that women who were young adults during the women's movement were more likely to develop feminist consciousness than women who were in early middle adulthood at the time of the movement, because the younger women were in a receptive developmental stage (Duncan & Agronick, 1995). Likewise, young adults growing up when there is no women's movement, or when there is a movement against gains for women, should be less likely to develop feminist consciousness (Duncan & Stewart, 2000; Zucker & Stewart, 2007). Thus, developmental stage may moderate the relationship between exposure to a social movement and the development of group consciousness and collective action.

Personal Experiences with Discrimination

Cross's (1971; Cross & Vandiver, 2001) encounter stage specifies that personal experiences with discrimination often lead to the process of politicizing a group identification. Members of low-status groups in society have been shown to be more aware of group memberships than are high-status group members, increasing the likelihood that they will identify with these groups, be exposed to a collective ideology, and develop group consciousness (Duncan, 1999; P. Gurin, 1985; Gurin et al., 1980; Lykes, 1985). There is also evidence that various gendered life experiences are related to the development of

feminist identities in women. For example, research has found that experiences of abortion (Stewart & Gold-Steinberg, 1990; Zucker, 1999), sexual victimization (Koss & Cleveland, 1997), and divorce (Fahs, 2007) are related to women's politicization, presumably because these experiences call into question the legal, social, and economic equality of women relative to men. Thus, they would be directly related to feelings of relative deprivation. Discrimination, then, is related to both identity and injustice, and probably is related indirectly to collective action, by increasing the probability that group consciousness will develop.

Low-Status Group Memberships

Politicization of low-status group identifications among people who are also high-status group members (e.g., feminist identification in *white* women and race identification in black *men*) may increase awareness of oppression in general, based on reflection about high-status group memberships. Lykes (1985) suggested that participating in social movements designed to challenge oppressive structures could lead members of high-status groups to embrace a collective orientation, and perhaps lead to group consciousness around low-status group memberships (Path C to reverse Path B).

Membership in multiple low-status groups may be related to higher levels of group consciousness because each low-status group membership increases the likelihood of recognizing any sort of structural oppression (Cole, 2009; Gurin et al., 1980; Lykes, 1985). At the same time, multiple low-status group membership may be related to lower levels of collective action around a particular group membership as the individual divides his or her time among multiple causes (Dill, 1983). Collective action around issues of specific concern to members of particular combinations of multiple low-status groups (e.g., working-class women) may alleviate the problem of division of time; however, many members of multiple low-status groups find themselves having to prioritize causes (Beale, 1970; Collins, 1989, 1991; hooks, 1981). Nonetheless, low-status group membership should contribute to group consciousness, which, in turn, might lead to collective action.

Material Resources

Resource mobilization theory (McCarthy & Zald, 1977) contends that social movements arise when enough economic and human resources are mobilized for a particular cause. Kerbo (1982) posited that this is especially true for movements of affluence or conscience; that is, social movements arising during economically stable time periods. On the individual level, one of the most consistent findings about both white and black student political activists is that they came from economically privileged family backgrounds (A. Astin, 1968; Block, Haan, & Smith, 1969; R. Braungart, 1969; Geller & Howard, 1969; Gurin & Epps, 1975; Orum & Orum, 1968; Pinkney, 1969; Searles & Williams, 1962). However, these relationships might be moderated by group consciousness; that is, politicized individuals with *higher incomes* may be more likely to participate in collective action, at least for movements of conscience. Ability to mobilize material resources is distinguished here from group-based efficacy. It is likely that resource mobilization acts to moderate relationships between group consciousness variables and collective action, whereas group-based efficacy (or the feeling that one's group can make change) mediates relationships between individual difference variables, identity, and collective action.

Education and Work Experience
Studies about the development of group consciousness in low-status group members have shown that education and work experience are related to higher levels of ethnic and gender consciousness (Caplan, 1970; Carroll, 1989; P. Gurin, 1987; Sears & McConahay, 1973). Thus, education may indirectly increase participation in collective action, by increasing group consciousness. Education specifically about a group's low-status position in society has also been shown to increase levels of group consciousness (e.g., Women's Studies courses increase feminist identifications; Bargad & Hyde, 1991; Henderson-King & Stewart, 1999).

Access to Social Movement Organizations
Social movement organizations often have at least two complementary goals: to increase group consciousness and organize collective action. Access to an organization where participants feel comfortable and accepted can thus facilitate participation in collective action in at least three different ways. First, by recruiting interested, but not necessarily politicized, individuals, social movement organizations can involve individuals in collective action directly (and perhaps also lead participants to develop group consciousness; Path C and reverse Path B). Klandermans and Oegema (1987) found that informal networks of friends and acquaintances active in the peace movement were important in motivating interested, but not necessarily politicized individuals

to attend an anti–nuclear arms rally. Second, by raising individuals' group consciousness, and then providing a cohesive plan for action, social movement organizations may increase participation in collective action indirectly (Paths A and B; Zurcher & Snow, 1992). Third, belonging to a social movement organization may also help sustain individual active commitment to a cause (Path C; Gerlach & Hine, 1970; Kanter, 1972; Wilson, 1973). Thus, participation in social movement organizations may have direct effects on collective action, as well as effects mediated or moderated by group consciousness.

PERSONALITY CHARACTERISTICS
Personal Political Salience
The tendency to attach personal meaning to the larger social world has been associated with political activism and responsiveness to social movements in college students and midlife women (Cole & Stewart, 1996; Cole, Zucker, & Ostrove, 1998; Curtin et al., 2010; Duncan, 1999; Duncan & Agronick, 1995; Duncan & Stewart, 1995, 2007). For example, in four samples of educated midlife women, group consciousness mediated the relationship between personal political salience and activism related to the politicized identity (after controlling for education and income). That is, for white women, feminist consciousness mediated the relationship between personal political salience and women's rights activism. Further, for white women, politicized racial identity mediated the relationship between personal political salience and civil rights activism (Duncan & Stewart, 2007). This represented some of the first evidence we have for the utility of group consciousness variables for predicting activism by high-status group members on behalf of low-status groups.

Political self-efficacy
The relationship between *political self-efficacy* and political participation is well documented (Cole & Stewart, 1996; Cole et al., 1998; Finkle, 1985; Verba & Nie, 1972). People high in political self-efficacy believe that their actions can effectively influence the political process, that what they do politically makes a difference (Renshon, 1974). High political self-efficacy probably interacts with Gurin et al.'s (1980) concept of collective orientation to produce collective action. Though typically considered a political variable, individual differences in political self-efficacy affect levels of activism. Individuals possessing both group consciousness and high political self-efficacy should be more likely

to act on their beliefs, whereas individuals possessing group consciousness but low political efficacy may choose not to act, believing their actions will be ineffectual (a moderated effect). It is likely that group-based efficacy operates by increasing individuals' sense that their political actions make a difference. Individuals act, certainly in conjunction and under the auspices of groups, but it is individual actors who make social change. In addition, some researchers have found that the combination of high efficacy and high political trust is related to conventional political participation, while high efficacy and low trust is associated with participation in forceful and unconventional social change (Crosby, 1976; Erikson, Luttbeg, & Tedin, 1988; Shingles, 1981). These relationships probably also moderate the relationship between group consciousness and collective action.

Generativity

Generativity, or the desire to contribute to future generations, can be expressed in work, family, and political domains (Erikson, 1963). Generative individuals, desiring to contribute to a better world, should display an interest in participating in social movements concerned with justice and equality. Higher scores on measures of generativity have been related to political activism in college-aged and midlife adults (Cole & Stewart, 1996; Hart, McAdams, Hirsch, & Bauer, 2001; Peterson & Duncan, 1999; Peterson & Klohnen, 1995; Peterson, Smirles, & Wentworth, 1997; Peterson & Stewart, 1996; Stewart & Gold-Steinberg, 1990). It is likely that group consciousness either mediates or moderates this relationship. It might be that generative individuals are drawn to ideologies that attribute social problems to systemic causes, which could lead to collective action. It is also likely that highly generative individuals with high group consciousness may be more likely to participate in collective action than either highly generative individuals with low group consciousness or politicized individuals scoring low on generativity.

Authoritarianism

In general, authoritarianism has been negatively associated with political activism, except in a few studies where it was positively related to pro-life activism. For example, right wing authoritarianism (RWA) was negatively associated with activism for women's rights (Duncan, 1999; Duncan, Peterson, & Winter, 1997) and antiwar activism (Duncan & Stewart, 1995), but Duncan et al. (1997) found a positive relationship between RWA and attending pro-life rallies. Peterson et al. (1997) found a positive relationship between RWA and petition signing, letter writing, and donating money for pro-life causes. In both of these cases, overall participation in pro-life causes was low, even though the samples were not particularly liberal ideologically. In terms of other conservative activism, Duncan and Stewart (1995) found no relationship between RWA and participation in Support Our Soldiers (SOS) rallies during the first Gulf War, and Peterson et al. (1997) found no relationship between RWA and activism for the Republican Party. In sum, it appears that authoritarianism is usually unrelated to political activity, but when authoritarians are active, it is for conservative causes. Finally, Duncan (1999) found that the relationship between low RWA and women's rights activism was mediated by feminist consciousness. Some sort of conservative group consciousness might mediate the relationship between RWA and participation in conservative causes, as well. Research on the psychology of conservative activists is sparse, and therefore an area ripe for research.

Other Personality Variables

Research showed that students politically active during the early to mid-1960s scored higher than nonactivists on three additional measures of personality: *cognitive flexibility*, *autonomy*, and *impulse expression* (Baird, 1970; Block et al., 1973; G. Gurin, 1971; Heist, 1965; Katz, 1968; Whittaker & Watts, 1971). It is likely that the relationship between collective action and cognitive flexibility and autonomy was mediated through group consciousness. That is, much of the student activism during the early to mid-1960s (when most of these studies were conducted) was based on ideologies and actions that were not widely endorsed at the time, and, in fact, often labeled "antiestablishment." Autonomous and flexible thinkers were probably more likely to be attracted to such unconventional ideologies, some of which may have led to group consciousness, which in turn may have led to collective action. On the other hand, group consciousness may have moderated the relationship between impulse expression and participation in collective action, as more impulsive students might have felt freer to act on their awareness of inequities than more cautious students.

Other personality variables that have been related to activism include *openness to experience* (Curtin et al., 2010), *optimism* (Galvin & Herzog, 1998; Greenberg & Schneider, 1997), and *need to evaluate* (Bizer, Krosnick, Holbrook, Wheeler, Rucker, &

Petty, 2004), all of which might be mediated or moderated through group consciousness. In six samples of young, middle-aged, and older adults, Curtin et al. found that *openness to experience* was related to activism. In the younger samples, there was both a direct and indirect effect, and in the older samples, the effects were mostly indirect. For the indirect effects, the relationship between openness to experience and activism was mediated by personal political salience, or the tendency to attach personal meaning to social events (Duncan, 2005). Curtin et al. argued that openness to experience may be a precursor to attaching personal meaning to social events, which is strongly related to activism, both directly and indirectly (through group consciousness).

In their study of 209 animal rights activists, Galvin and Herzog (1998) found that activists scored higher on a measure of dispositional *optimism* than two unrelated samples of college students and cardiac patients. They found a small but significant positive correlation between optimism and overall belief that the movement would be successful. Similarly, Greenberg and Schneider (1997) found that, compared to those who participated less, people who participated more in protecting their neighborhoods (through volunteering, attending meetings, contacting an elected official, or by calling the police) scored higher on dispositional optimism. Optimism might moderate the relationship between injustice and collective action, or be related to collective action indirectly through its effects on efficacy.

The *need to evaluate* is described as an individual difference variable that reflects an individual's propensity to create and hold attitudes about a variety of objects. In their analysis of 1998 and 2000 National Election Study data, Bizer et al. (2004) found that the need to evaluate was positively related to electoral activism (attending rallies, wearing buttons, encouraging others to vote, working for a candidate) and either voting, or saying that one planned to vote in an upcoming election. Need to evaluate, then, is related to political information seeking, which might lead to perceptions of injustice, a mediated effect.

Integrating Personality and Social Psychological Work on Group Consciousness and Collective Action

Table 31.2 brings together the personality research on individual difference variables with the social psychological models presented earlier. It summarizes

the individual difference variables, identifies the relevant aspects of group consciousness to which they are hypothesized to be related, and states whether effects on collective action might be mediated through group consciousness or moderate the effects of group consciousness on collective action. The left-hand column lists the individual difference variables reviewed in this chapter that are related to group consciousness and collective action. The middle column lists the elements of group consciousness related to collective action. For example, included in the injustice category are relative deprivation, power discontent, system blame, and encounter. Included under identity are group identification and nigrescence, and under efficacy, collective orientation. The right-hand column specifies whether the effects on collective action are hypothesized to be mediated by group consciousness variables or whether they moderate the relationship between group consciousness and collective action.

One way to use this table is to consider how various individual difference variables are related to collective action via the group consciousness variables. It was only by combining the personality and social psychological research on group consciousness and collective action that these relationships were possible to theorize. These could be mediated, moderated, or direct relationships, depending on the variables. For example, Duncan (1999; Duncan & Stewart, 2007) found that personal political salience (a personality variable) was related to collective action indirectly, through its effects on politicized group identifications (specifically through group consciousness). On the other hand, access to social movement organizations would most likely moderate the relationship between a politicized group identification and collective action. However, most of these relationships are only hypothesized, and need to be investigated. Another promising avenue for future research is to document which individual difference variables relate to particular group consciousness variables. Some possibilities are listed in Table 31.2. This table provides researchers with many potentially exciting possibilities for future research integrating the personality and social psychological models of collective action.

A Note About Terminology

One of the most difficult challenges involved in writing this chapter (and working in this area more generally) was reconciling differences in terminology and meaning by personality and social psychologists. The constructs discussed are closely related,

Table 31.2 Individual Difference Variables, Group Consciousness Variables, and Their Hypothesized Effects on Collective Action

Individual Difference Variables	Related Group Consciousness Variables	Hypothesized Effect on Collective Action
Life Experiences		
Liberal family of origin	Injustice	Mediation
Warm, permissive family	Injustice	Mediation, moderation
Modeling of activism	Efficacy	Moderation, direct
Developmental stage	Identity	Moderation
Discrimination	Injustice, identity	Mediation
Low-status group membership	Identity	Mediation
Material resources	Efficacy	Moderation
Education	Injustice, identity	Mediation
Access to social movement organizations	Injustice, identity, efficacy	Mediation, moderation, direct
Personality		
Personal political salience	Injustice, identity, efficacy	Mediation
Political self-efficacy	Efficacy	Moderation
Generativity	Injustice	Mediation, moderation
RWA	Injustice	Mediation
Cognitive flexibility	Injustice	Mediation
Autonomy	Injustice	Mediation
Impulsivity	Efficacy	Moderation
Openness to experience	Injustice (personal political salience)	Mediation
Optimism	Injustice, efficacy	Mediation, moderation
Need to evaluate	Injustice	Mediation

and yet a variety of terms have been used to describe them. The most important of these were related to the group consciousness variables. Starting with the earliest use, Gurin et al. (1980) used "stratum consciousness." Duncan (1995, 1999; Duncan & Stewart, 2007) used both "group consciousness" and "politicized group identifications." Simon and Klandermans (2001) used "politicized collective identities." These terms are very closely related but are not identical. Politicized collective identities implicated, as integral to their definition, collective action in a larger social context, whereas group consciousness was defined as an individual difference variable that could lead to behavioral outcomes, but did not include action as central to its definition. In addition, the definition of politicized collective identity was expanded to include identification with social movement organizations (Simon et al., 1998). To date, stratum and group consciousness have been used to describe the identities of members of particular demographic groups, rather than members of political organizations. Keeping the various group consciousness elements separate, as most of the social psychological research has done, allows for a fine-grained analysis of particular processes involved in motivating collective action. Combining these elements into a politicized group identification variable, as personality psychologists have done, has allowed the incorporation of additional, individual-level variables into analyses. Both approaches are valid, and the approach recommended for researchers depends on the research question.

Future Directions

The integration of the personality and social psychological research on motivation for collective action has made it clear that there are many potentially exciting and fruitful avenues for future research. Among the many different possible directions for future research to explore are the following: (1) mapping out the similarities and differences in volunteerism and collective action; (2) understanding collective action undertaken by allies, or members of groups who do not share an identity with the low-status group; (3) collective action based on voluntary (or hidden) group memberships; (4) complicating models of collective action with an understanding of intersectionality; (5) application of existing models of collective action to right-wing or conservative collective action; and (6) understanding how the manipulation of group consciousness components affects the likelihood of collective action. Each of these potential research topics is considered below.

Similarities and Differences in Volunteerism and Collective Action

Snyder and Omoto (2008) defined volunteering as "freely chosen and deliberate helping activities that extend over time, are engaged in without expectation of reward or other compensation and often through formal organizations, and that are performed on behalf of causes or individuals who desire assistance" (p. 3). Snyder and colleagues have conducted research on the importance of match between individual motivations for participation (e.g., affirming values, enhancing self-esteem, making friends, acquiring skills, community concern) and how well the volunteer activity fulfills those motivations. They found that match between motivation and volunteer opportunity led to positive outcomes (Clary & Snyder, 1991; Snyder & Omoto, 2000, 2001). This research fits into the tradition of relating personality variables to collective action, or Path C of Figure 31.1.

Snyder and Omoto (2008) argued that identity can play a part in motivating volunteerism, just as it motivates collective action for political causes. It is probably true, as well, that the motives for volunteer-

ing outlined by Snyder and colleagues could be applied to motivation for collective action. Both of these questions could be investigated in future research.

There are at least two ways that volunteer work and collective action differ, however: (1) volunteerism is usually concerned with helping needy individuals, without necessarily challenging political or social systems, whereas collective action is usually about challenging such systems (see, e.g., Simon & Klandermans, 2001); and (2) volunteerism does not usually require identification with the group of the individual one is helping, only empathy, whereas collective action usually entails politicizing a group identification.

For example, the definition of volunteering given above makes no mention of the "power struggle" between groups mentioned as critical for politicized collective identities (Simon & Klandermans, 2001; Subašić et al., 2008). In other words, although volunteer activities may be undertaken because of an ideological commitment to redressing injustice, such activities do not necessarily have to involve power discontent and rejection of legitimacy, to use Gurin et al.'s (1980) terms.

In addition, volunteerism can be undertaken on behalf of either members of one's ingroup or outgroup, and does not necessarily involve the politicization of a group identification. Research shows that dispositional empathy and liking are related to increased volunteering (Batson, 1998; M. Davis, 2005), with empathy being more closely linked to ingroup helping and liking linked to outgroup helping (Stürmer, Snyder, & Omoto, 2005; Stürmer, Snyder, Kropp, & Siem, 2006). However, as discussed above, most models of collective action recognize the central role played by politicized group identifications (Duncan, 1999; Simon & Klandermans, 2001; Stürmer & Simon, 2005; van Zomeren et al., 2008).

One avenue of future research could examine the links between volunteering and the development of group consciousness. That is, it would be useful to identify the characteristics of volunteer experiences that lead to the rejection of legitimacy of individualistic explanations for social problems. For example, it is possible to volunteer for a mentoring program for "at risk" youth (e.g., Big Brothers/Big Sisters) and have both mentor and mentee benefit on an individual level without any subsequent questioning of the circumstances that lead some children to be deemed "at risk." Other volunteers could do so in the context of a community-based learning class that involved learning about systemic reasons for the circumstances that lead to "at risk" youth. One might expect that the latter type of experience would be more likely to expose individual volunteers to ideologies that could then lead to group consciousness around the causes of social problems.

Collective Action Taken by Allies, or Outgroup Members

Another aspect of the volunteer-collective action relationship could be fruitfully studied by investigating collective action taken by high-status group members on behalf of low-status group members, or "allied" collective action (e.g., straight allies of lesbian, gay, bisexual, transgendered, and queer groups). Allied collective action is concerned with helping low-status group members by challenging the system, rather than by helping individuals. Such activism may require an identification with the low-status group, but it may be based more on a critical analysis of privilege, or with a more generalized ideology, rather than personal experience with discrimination (or anticipation of personal gain). Crosby and Gonzalez-Intal (1984) argued that feelings of deprivation on the behalf of members of other groups ("ideological deprivation") were rare, but Jennings (1991) posited that it might account for participation in social movements by members of groups that do not directly benefit from the achievement of the movement's goals. In fact, such ideological deprivation could be coupled with a superordinate group identification (Subašić et al., 2008) and collective orientation to create a politicized group identification, but one based on humanistic values (or identification with all humanity; McFarland, 2010). Recent research shows that identification with opinion-based groups is related to intentions to act collectively (Bliuc, McGarty, Reynolds, & Muntele, 2007; McGarty, Bliuc, Thomas, & Bongiorno, 2009; Musgrove & McGarty, 2008). Perhaps such identification is similar to ideological deprivation. Regardless, factors motivating allies to participate in collective action on behalf of low-status group members is an understudied area, and one ready for research.

Collective Action Based on Voluntary (or Hidden) Group Memberships

Much of the work identifying motivational antecedents to participation in collective action has been based on work with impermeable and stable group memberships (Tajfel, 1978). Although not generally mentioned, these group memberships are typically visible to outside observers. However, there are also instances of collective action that occur based on more permeable and unstable group memberships; for example, groups that form around solving a particular, temporary problem. Whether a politicized group identification is useful or necessary in these cases is an empirical question (McGarty et al., 2009).

A related, but also infrequently studied question revolves around the relationship of invisible low-status group memberships, or what researchers call "concealable stigmas" (Frable, Platt, & Hoey, 1998; Pachankis, 2007) to collective action. Research has shown that politicizing such group memberships (e.g., gay identity) is a powerful predictor of collective action (Stürmer & Simon, 2004, 2005). Research on people with concealable stigmas shows that the strain of having to "come out" in every new situation is related to negative mental health outcomes (Frable, Platt, & Hoey, 1998; Pachankis, 2007). Staying invisible, then, may be less preferable than visibly identifying with a low-status group. However, the factors that lead some members of groups with concealable stigmas to politicize their identities and some not to do so is understudied and an exciting potential avenue for future research.

Complicating Models of Collective Action with an Understanding of Intersectionality

In a recent article, Cole (2009) addressed the complexity of multiple group memberships for psychological research, and her insights are valuable for collective action researchers. She described intersectionality as "analytic approaches that simultaneously consider the meaning and consequences of identity, difference, and disadvantage" (p. 170). That is, all people possess multiple social identities, some of which are high-status and some of which are low-status. For example, white women are advantaged due to race and disadvantaged due to gender. Feminist theorists have discussed the dilemmas for collective action inherent in intersectional identities since the 1970s (e.g., Beale, 1970; Combahee River Collective, 1977/1995). Hurtado (1989) explicitly recognized that a low-status group's position relative to a high-status group could differ based on additional group memberships. In her case, Hurtado discussed the ways in which white women and women of color had different relationships to white men, and that those differences affected the type and form of their oppression. Cole (2009) provided specific recommendations for researchers interested in dealing with intersectional identities in the research process (see, also, Greenwood, 2008). The group consciousness models described in this article do not explicitly address intersectionality. However, attending to the complexities involved in people's negotiation of group memberships could deepen our understanding of motivation for collective action, and provide productive new possibilities for research.

Understanding Right-Wing or Conservative Collective Action

Another area crying out for research is understanding the antecedents of right-wing or conservative political activism. There is some, mostly qualitative, work produced by sociologists and political scientists; for example Ginsburg's (1998/1989) research on pro-choice and pro-life activists in Fargo, North Dakota, and Ezekiel's (1995) research on U.S. neo-Nazis and Ku Klux Klan members. In psychology, some researchers have examined the correlates of prowar activism (Duncan & Stewart, 1995), or looked at levels of right and left wing authoritarianism in radical left and radical right activists (Van Hiel, Duriez, & Kossowska, 2006). In Jost, Glaser, Kruglanski, and Sulloway's (2003) meta-analysis, they found that several psychological variables, including intolerance of ambiguity, death anxiety, low openness to experience, uncertainty intolerance, needs for order, structure and closure, low integrative complexity, and fear of threat and loss, were related to conservatism (see also, Van Hiel, Onraet, & De Pauw, 2010). They argued that conservative ideology was rooted in a psychological resistance to change and justification of inequality, and that the psychological variables mentioned above helped conservatives manage uncertainty and threat.

To my knowledge, no researcher has attempted to systematically apply group consciousness theories to understand conservative or right-wing activism. (However, see Duncan, 2010, for a case study using these theories to describe the activism of Ingo Hasselbach, a former Neo-Nazi). It would be useful to see if such models applied to activists on the right. Crosby and Gonzalez-Intal (1984) discussed the application of relative deprivation theory to explain backlash, or resentment over an outgroup's undeserved possession of goods. It is quite possible, even likely, that a politicized group identification can be developed from relative deprivation based on an assessment that a low-status group who had gained some absent rights (e.g., women gaining access to educational opportunities) was actually getting something they did not deserve, or that their gain of rights took away some previously enjoyed privilege of the high-status group. That is, it is possible that relative deprivation can develop in members of high-status groups based on erroneous perceptions of status. For example, in Klatch's (1987) qualitative analysis of conservative women activists, it was clear that these women had a strong (traditionally feminine) gender identification, possessed a sense of relative deprivation about how their conservative moral values were being represented in society, and organized collectively to protest injustices. Similarly, in her study of contemporary conservative women activists, Schreiber (2008) explicitly noted that these activists had appropriated from feminists the language of identity politics, and possessed politicized (traditionally feminine) gender identities. Exploring the group consciousness of conservative activists more systematically, and how relative deprivation based on false assessments of status can be sustained, are fascinating research questions (see, e.g., Duncan, 2010; Ezekiel, 1995).

Implications for Increasing or Decreasing Collective Action

Knowing the components that comprise group consciousness, relative deprivation, or politicized collective identities suggests ways in which societal structures can interfere with these elements to restrict the collective action of low-status group members. On the other hand, it also suggests strategies that can be used by social movement organizations to politicize potential recruits. One of the main ways in which the collective action of low-status groups is kept low in the United States is through limiting system blame or the relative deprivation precondition—"lack a sense of personal responsibility for not having X" (Crosby, 1976, p. 90). Belief in meritocracy is powerful in the United States, and there is very little serious discussion of structural impediments to individual achievement (Kluegel & Smith, 1986). Thus, when members of a particular group are relatively powerless, they mostly believe it is their own fault—that if they exerted enough effort they would succeed. Related to meritocracy beliefs is the profound belief in individualism in most capitalistic countries. Thus, even if a group member feels a sense of discontent, it is fairly unlikely that collective solutions will be embraced, unless the group has a history of collective action. Even in cultures where meritocracy beliefs and individualism are not as entrenched as in the United States, other aspects of relative deprivation may be limited.

Another powerful way in which the development of low-status group consciousness is hindered is by limiting groups' access to comparison groups that could lead to accusations of unfair treatment. For example, statistics from the U.S. government show that some of the lowest paying jobs are positions as child care workers, maids, and teacher assistants. They also happen to be female dominated jobs. In the case of teacher assistants, 89% of job holders are women (Weinberg, 2004). Women teacher assistants earn, on average, $15,000 a year, whereas men earn, on average, $20,000 a year in the same positions. Because there are so few men in this field, women do not have ready access to a relatively better paid comparison group that could lead to a sense of injustice, which could lead them to develop relative deprivation and group consciousness. (see, e.g., Alksnis, Desmarais, & Curtis, 2008; Major, 1989.) To solve the problem of lack of reasonable comparisons in gender segregated professions, comparable worth activists have tried to change the relevant comparison group from other women working in exactly the same profession to men working in jobs requiring equivalent levels of education and experience. Such comparisons usually show women at a disadvantage. One major purpose of social movement organizations is to provide individuals with the missing preconditions of relative deprivation, providing alternative, systemic explanations for group members' lack of power and influence, and encouraging and modeling collective action as a strategy for redressing power imbalances.

Research has shown that education about systemic causes of powerlessness in a particular group increases group consciousness and collective action. For example, Henderson-King and Stewart (1999) compared two groups of women who wanted to take Introduction to Women's Studies—one group was admitted to the class, the other was wait-listed. Before and after the semester-long class, Henderson-King and Stewart measured several different aspects of feminist identity. At the end of the semester, they found that the women who had taken the women's studies class scored higher than their wait-listed counterparts on feminist identification, power discontent, a composite of common fate and system blame, sensitivity to sexism, and feelings about feminists. Experimental studies focused around systematically removing and replacing Crosby's (1976) five relative deprivation preconditions could go a long way toward providing practical suggestions for social movement organizations looking to increase participation in their organizations.

Conclusion

In this chapter, I reviewed and integrated the personality and social psychological research on motivation for collective action. Using the model presented in Figure 31.1 allows us to fill in the gaps in both literatures to arrive at a more complete understanding of why some people develop group consciousness and get involved in collective action whereas similar others do not. The identity and injustice-based theories offered by social psychologists (Crosby, 1976; Cross, 1971; Cross & Vandiver, 2001; Gurin et al., 1980; van Zomeren et al., 2008) offer compelling motives for participation in collective action. However, these theories are not good at explaining individual variation in group consciousness and collective action. Personality psychologists, on the other hand, document which individual difference variables distinguish between activists and nonactivists, and how predictive of collective action each might be; however, they do not necessarily explain how these differences motivate collective action. Taken together, these research traditions in social and personality psychology can describe individual motivation for participation in collective action.

This integration of theories has pointed out several areas that need further elaboration and research. These include understanding the relationship between volunteerism and collective action; understanding collective action undertaken by allies and based on voluntary group memberships; complicating models of group consciousness and collective action with an understanding of intersectionality; applying existing models to understand right-wing or conservative activism; and understanding how manipulating aspects of group consciousness increases or decreases the likelihood of collective action. Each of these potential research topics is possible using a combination of experimental and survey research techniques.

Finally, the approach I have taken in this chapter, reconciling seemingly disparate, but similar, constructs by integrating them in a model that respects both individual and group level differences, is one that researchers studying other aspects of psychology might fruitfully employ. Using experimental methods to identify how a particular process works under controlled conditions is essential to understanding psychological phenomena. Equally important is understanding and respecting the variability within groups represented by personality psychology's study of individual difference variables. Only when these are taken together can we expect to gain a full understanding of human behavior.

References

Acock, A. C. (1984). Parents and their children: The study of inter-generational influence. *Sociology and Social Research, 69*, 151–171.

Agronick, G. S., & Duncan, L. E. (1998). Personality and social change: Individual differences, life path, and importance attributed to the women's movement. *Journal of Personality and Social Psychology, 74*, 1545–1555.

Alksnis, C., Desmarais, S., & Curtis, J. (2008). Workforce segregation and the gender wage gap: Is "women's" work valued as highly as "men's"? *Journal of Applied Social Psychology, 38*, 1416–1441.

Andrews, M. (1991). *Lifetimes of commitment: Aging, politics, psychology*. New York: Cambridge University Press.

Astin, A. W. (1968). Personal and environmental determinants of student activism. *Measurement and Evaluation in Guidance, 1*, 149–162.

Astin, H. S. (1969). *Themes and events of campus unrest in twenty-two colleges and universities*. Washington, DC: Bureau of Social Science Research.

Baird, L. L. (1970). Who protests: A study of student activists. In J. Foster & D. Long (Eds.), *Protests! Student activism in America* (123–133). New York: Morrow.

Bargad, A., & Hyde, J. S. (1991). Women's studies: A study of feminist identity development in women. *Psychology of Women Quarterly, 15*, 181–201.

Batson, C. D. (1998). Altruism and prosocial behavior. In D. T. Gilbert, S. T. Fiske, & G. Lindzey (Eds.), *The handbook of social psychology* (4th ed., Vol. 2, pp. 282–316). New York: McGraw-Hill.

Beale, F. (1970). Double jeopardy: To be black and female. In T. Cade (Ed.), *The black woman* (pp. 90-100). New York: Signet.

Bizer, G. Y., Krosnick, J. A., Holbrook, A. L., Wheeler, S. C., Rucker, D. D., & Petty, R. E. (2004). The impact of personality on cognitive, behavioral, and affective political processes: The effects of need to evaluate. *Journal of Personality, 72*, 995–1027.

Bliuc, A., McGarty, C., Reynolds, K., & Muntele, D. (2007). Opinion-based group membership as a predictor of commitment to political action. *European Journal of Social Psychology, 37*, 19–32.

Block, J. H., Haan, N., & Smith, M. B. (1969). Socialization correlates of student activism. *Journal of Social Issues, 4*, 143–177.

Block, J. H., Haan, N., & Smith, M. B. (1973). Activism and apathy in contemporary adolescents. In J. F. Adams (Ed.), *Understanding adolescence: Current developments in adolescent psychology* (pp. 168–205). Boston: Allyn & Bacon.

Braungart, M. M., & Braungart, R. G. (1990). The life-course development of left- and right-wing youth activist leaders from the 1960s. *Political Psychology, 11*, 243–282.

Braungart, R. G. (1969). Family status, socialization, and student politics: A multivariate analysis. *American Journal of Sociology, 77*, 108–130.

Braungart, R. G. (1975). Youth and social movements. In S. Dragastin & G. Elder (Eds.), *Adolescence in the life cycle* (pp. 255–290). Washington, DC: Hemisphere.

Caplan, N. (1970). The new ghetto man: A review of recent empirical studies. *Journal of Social Issues, 26*, 59–73.

Carroll, S. J. (1989). Gender politics and the socializing impact of the women's movement. In R. Sigel (Ed.), *Political learning in adulthood* (pp. 306–339). Chicago: University of Chicago Press.

Carter, R. T., & Helms, J. E. (1987). Relationship of black value orientations to racial identity attitudes. *Measurement and Evaluation in Counseling and Development, 19*, 185–195.

Clary, E. G., & Snyder, M. (1991). A functional analysis of altruism and prosocial behavior: The case of volunteerism. In M. Clark (Ed.), *Review of personality and social psychology* (Vol. 12, pp. 119–148). Thousand Oaks, CA: Sage.

Clayton, S. D., & Crosby, F. J. (1992). *Justice, gender, and affirmative action*. Ann Arbor: University of Michigan Press.

Cole, E. R. (2009). Intersectionality and research in psychology. *American Psychologist, 64*, 170–180.

Cole, E. R., & Stewart, A. J. (1996). Meanings of political participation among black and white women: Political identity and social responsibility. *Journal of Personality and Social Psychology, 71*, 130–140.

Cole, E. R., Zucker, A. N., & Ostrove, J. M. (1998). Political participation and feminist consciousness among women activists of the 1960s. *Political Psychology, 19*, 349–371.

Collins, P. H. (1989). The social construction of black feminist thought. *Signs, 14*, 745–773.

Collins, P. H. (1991). *Black feminist thought*. New York: Routledge.

Combahee River Collective (1995). Combahee River Collective statement. In B. Guy-Sheftall (Ed.), *Words of fire: An anthology of African American feminist thought* (pp. 232–240). New York: New Press. (Original work published 1977)

Constantine, M. G., Watt, S. K., Gainor, K. A., & Warren, A. K. (2005). The influence of Cross's initial black racial identity theory on other cultural identity conceptualizations. In R. T. Carter (Ed.), *Handbook of racial-cultural psychology and counseling: Vol. 1. Theory and research* (pp. 94–114). Hoboken, NJ: Wiley.

Corning, A. F., & Myers, D. J. (2002). Individual orientation toward engagement in social action. *Political Psychology, 23*, 703–729.

Crosby, F. J. (1976). A model of egoistical relative deprivation. *Psychological Review, 83*, 85–113.

Crosby, F. J. (1982). *Relative deprivation and working women*. New York: Oxford University Press.

Crosby, F. J., & Gonzalez-Intal, A. M. (1984). Relative deprivation and equity theories: Felt injustice and the undeserved benefits of others. In R. Folger (Ed.), *The sense of injustice* (pp. 141–166). New York: Plenum.

Cross, W. E., Jr. (1971). The Negro-to-black conversion experience: Toward a psychology of black liberation. *Black World, 20*, 13–27.

Cross, W. E., Jr. (1991). Shades of black: Diversity in African American identity. Philadelphia, PA: Temple University Press.

Cross, W. E., Jr., & Vandiver, B. J. (2001). Nigrescence theory and measurement: Introducing the Cross Racial Identity Scale (CRIS). In J. G. Ponterotto, J. M. Casas, L. A. Suzuki, & C. M. Alexander (Eds.), *Handbook of multicultural counseling* (2nd ed., pp. 371–393). Thousand Oaks, CA: Sage.

Curtin, N., Stewart, A. J., & Duncan, L. E. (2010). What makes the political personal? Openness, personal political salience, and activism. *Journal of Personality, 78*, 943–968.

Davis, J. A. (1959). A formal interpretation of the theory of relative deprivation. *Sociometry, 22*, 280–296.

Davis, M. H. (2005). Becoming (and remaining) a community volunteer: Does personality matter? In A. M. Omoto (Ed.), *Processes of community change and social action* (pp. 67–82). Mahwah, NJ: Erlbaum.

Dill, B. T. (1983). Race, class, and gender: Prospects for an all-inclusive sisterhood. *Feminist Studies, 9,* 131–150.

Downing, N. E., & Roush, K. L. (1985). From passive acceptance to active commitment: A model of feminist identity development for women. *The Counseling Psychologist, 13,* 695–709.

Drury, J., & Reicher, S. D. (2005). Explaining enduring empowerment: A comparative study of collective action and psychological outcomes. *European Journal of Social Psychology, 35,* 35–38.

Duncan, L. E. (1995). *Personality and life experiences: Sources of feminist consciousness and women's rights activism.* Unpublished doctoral dissertation, University of Michigan, Ann Arbor.

Duncan, L. E. (1999). Motivation for collective action: Group consciousness as mediator of personality, life experiences, and women's rights activism. *Political Psychology, 20,* 611–635.

Duncan, L. E. (2005). Personal political salience as a self-schema: Consequences for political information processing. *Political Psychology, 26,* 965–976.

Duncan, L. E. (2010). Using group consciousness theories to understand political activism: Case Studies of Barack Obama, Hillary Clinton, and Ingo Hasselbach. *Journal of Personality, 78,* 1601–1636.

Duncan, L. E., & Agronick, G. S. (1995). The intersection of life stage and social events: Personality and life outcomes. *Journal of Personality and Social Psychology, 69,* 558–568.

Duncan, L. E., Peterson, B. E., & Winter, D. G. (1997). Authoritarianism and gender roles: Toward a psychological analysis of hegemonic relationships. *Personality and Social Psychology Bulletin, 23,* 41–49.

Duncan, L. E., & Stewart, A. J. (1995). Still bringing the Vietnam war home: Sources of contemporary student activism. *Personality and Social Psychology Bulletin, 21,* 914–924.

Duncan, L. E., & Stewart, A. J. (2000). A generational analysis of women's rights activists. *Psychology of Women Quarterly, 24,* 297–308.

Duncan, L. E., & Stewart, A. J. (2007). Personal political salience: The role of personality in collective identity and action. *Political Psychology, 28,* 143–164.

Erikson, E. H. (1963). *Childhood and society.* New York: Norton.

Erikson, R. S., Luttbeg, N. R., & Tedin, K. L. (1988). *American public opinion.* New York: Macmillan.

Ezekiel, R. S. (1995). *The racist mind: Portraits of American Neo-Nazis and Klansmen.* New York: Penguin.

Fahs, B. (2007). Second shifts and political awakenings: Divorce and the political socialization of middle-aged women. *Journal of Divorce and Remarriage, 47,* 43–66.

Finkle, S. (1985). Reciprocal effects of participation and political efficacy: A panel analysis. *American Journal of Political Science, 29,* 891–911.

Fitzgerald, J. M. (1988). Vivid memories and the reminiscence phenomenon: The role of a self narrative. *Human Development, 31,* 261–273.

Flacks, R. (1967). The liberated generation: An exploration of the roots of student protest. *Journal of Social Issues, 23,* 52–75.

Flacks, R. (1990). Social bases of activist identity: Comment on Braungart article. *Political Psychology, 11,* 283–292.

Frable, D. E. S., Platt, L., & Hoey, S. (1998). Concealable stigmas and positive self-perceptions: Feeling better around similar others. *Journal of Personality and Social Psychology, 74,* 909–922.

Freud, A. (1946). *The ego and the mechanisms of defence.* New York: International Universities Press.

Galvin, S. L., & Herzog, H. A. (1998). Attitudes and dispositional optimism of animal rights demonstrators. *Society and Animals, 6,* 1–11.

Geller, J. D., & Howard, G. (1969). Some sociopsychological characteristics of student political activists. *Journal of Applied Social Psychology, 2,* 112–137.

Gerlach, P., & Hine, V. H. (1970). *People, power, change: Movements of social transformation.* Indianapolis: Bobbs-Merrill.

Gill, R., & Matheson, K. (2006). Responses to discrimination: The role of emotions and expectations of emotional regulation. *Personality and Social Psychology Bulletin, 32,* 149–161.

Ginsburg, F. D. (1998). *Contested lives: The abortion debate in an American community.* Berkeley: University of California Press. (Original work published 1989)

Glass, J., Bengtson, V. L., & Dunham, C. C. (1986). Attitude similarity in three-generation families: Socialization, status inheritance, or reciprocal influence? *American Sociological Review, 51,* 685–698.

Greenberg, M., & Schneider, D. (1997). Neighborhood quality, environmental hazards, personality traits, and resident actions. *Risk Analysis, 17,* 169–175.

Greenwood, R. M. (2008). Intersectional political consciousness: Appreciation for intragroup differences and solidarity in diverse groups. *Psychology of Women Quarterly, 32,* 36–47.

Gurin, G. (1971). *A study of students in a multiversity (Project 5-0901).* Ann Arbor: University of Michigan, Office of Education.

Gurin, P. (1985). Women's gender consciousness. *Public Opinion Quarterly, 49,* 143–163.

Gurin, P. (1987). The political implications of women's statuses. In F. J. Crosby (Ed.), *Spouse, parent, worker: On gender and multiple roles* (pp. 167–198). New Haven, CT: Yale University Press.

Gurin, P., & Epps, E. (1975). *Black consciousness, identity, and achievement.* New York: Wiley.

Gurin, P., & Markus, H. (1989). Cognitive consequences of gender identity. In S. Skevington & D. Baker (Eds.), *The social identity of women* (pp. 152–172). Newbury Park, CA: Sage.

Gurin, P., Miller, H., & Gurin, G. (1980). Stratum identification and consciousness. *Social Psychology Quarterly, 43,* 30–47.

Gurr, T. R. (1970). *Why men rebel.* Princeton, NJ: Princeton University Press.

Hampton, H., Fayer, S., & Flynn, S. (1990). *Voices of freedom: An oral history of the civil rights movement from the 1950s through the 1980s.* New York: Bantam Books.

Hart, H. M., McAdams, D. P., Hirsch, B. J., & Bauer, J. J. (2001). Generativity and social involvement among African Americans and white adults. *Journal of Research in Personality, 35,* 208–230.

Heist, P. (1965). Intellect and commitment: The faces of discontent. In O. A. Knorr & W. J. Minter (Eds.), *Order and freedom on the campus* (pp. 61–69). Boulder, CO: Western Interstate Commission for Higher Education.

Henderson-King, D. H., & Stewart, A. J. (1994). Women or feminists? Assessing women's group consciousness. *Sex Roles, 31,* 505–516.

Henderson-King, D., & Stewart, A. (1999). Educational experiences and shifts in group consciousness: Studying women. *Personality and Social Psychology Bulletin, 25,* 390–399.

Higgins, E. T. (1990). Personality, social psychology, and person-situation relations: Standards and knowledge activation as a common language. In L. A. Pervin (Ed.), *Handbook of personality: Theory and research* (pp. 301–338). New York: Guilford.

hooks, B. (1981). *Ain't I a woman? Black women and feminism.* Boston: South End.

Hurtado, A. (1989). Relating to privilege: Seduction and rejection in the subordination of white women and women of color. *Signs, 14,* 833–855.

Iyer, A., & Ryan, M. K. (2009). Why do men and women challenge gender discrimination in the workplace? The role of group status and in-group identification in predicting pathways to collective action. *Journal of Social Issues, 65,* 791–814.

Jennings, M. K. (1991). Thinking about social injustice. *Political Psychology, 12,* 187–204.

Jennings, M. K., & Niemi, R. G. (1968). The transmission of political values from parent to child. *American Political Science Review, 62,* 169–184.

Jennings, M. K., & Niemi, R. G. (1982). *Generations and politics: A panel study of young adults and their parents.* Princeton, NJ: Princeton University Press.

Jost, J. T., Glaser, J., Kruglanski, A. W., & Sulloway, F. J. (2003). Political conservatism as motivated social cognition. *Psychological Bulletin, 129,* 339–375.

Kanter, R. M. (1972). *Commitment and community* Cambridge, MA: Harvard University Press.

Katz, J. (1968). The activist revolution of 1964. In J. Katz & Associates (Eds.), *No time for youth* (pp. 386–414). San Francisco: Jossey-Bass.

Kawakami, K., & Dion, K. L. (1993). The impact of salient self-identities on relative deprivation and action intentions. *European Journal of Social Psychology, 23,* 525–540.

Kerbo, H. R. (1982). Movements of "crisis" and movement of "affluence": A critique of deprivation and resource mobilization theories. *Journal of Conflict Resolution, 26,* 645–663.

Klandermans, B. (1984). Mobilization and participation: Social-psychological expansions of resource mobilization theory. *American Sociological Review, 49,* 583–600.

Klandermans, B., & Oegema, D. (1987). Potentials, networks, motivations, and barriers: Steps towards participation in social movements. *American Sociological Review, 52,* 519–531.

Klatch, R. E. (1987). *Women of the New Right.* Philadelphia: Temple University Press.

Klein, E. (1984). *Gender politics: From consciousness to mass politics.* Cambridge, MA: Harvard University Press.

Kluegel, J. R., & Smith, E. R. (1986). *Beliefs about inequality: Americans' view of what is and what ought to be.* Hawthorne, NJ: Aldine de Gruyer.

Koss, M. P., & Cleveland, H. H. (1997). Stepping on toes: Social roots of date rape lead to intractability and politicization. In M. D. Schwartz (Ed.), *Researching sexual violence against women: Methodological and personal perspectives* (pp. 4–21). Thousand Oaks, CA: Sage.

Lichter, S. R., & Rothman, S. (1981–82). Jewish ethnicity and radical culture: A social psychological study of political activists. *Political Psychology, 3,* 116–157.

Liss, M., Crawford, M., & Popp, D. (2004). Predictors and correlates of collective action. *Sex Roles, 50,* 771–779.

Lykes, M. B. (1985). Gender and individualistic vs. collectivist bases for notions about the self. *Journal of Personality, 53,* 356–383.

Major, B. (1989). Gender differences in comparisons and entitlement: Implications for comparable worth. *Journal of Social Issues, 45,* 99–115.

Markus, H. (1990). On splitting the universe. *Psychological Science, 1,* 181–185.

Markus, H., & Kunda, Z. (1986). Stability and malleability of the self-concept. *Journal of Personality and Social Psychology, 51,* 858–866.

McCarthy, J., & Zald, M. (1977). Resource mobilization and social movements. *American Journal of Sociology, 82,* 1212–1241.

McFarland, S. (2010). Personality and support for universal human rights: A review and test of a structural model. *Journal of Personality, 78,* 1735–1764.

McGarty, C., Bliuc, A., Thomas, E. F., & Bongiorno, R. (2009). Collective action as the material expression of opinion-based group membership. *Journal of Social Issues, 65,* 839–857.

Middleton, R., & Putney, S. (1963). Student rebellion against parental political beliefs. *Social Forces, 41,* 377–383.

Mummendey, A., Kessler, T., Klink, A., & Mielke, R. (1999). Strategies to cope with negative social identity: Predictions by social identity theory and relative deprivation theory. *Journal of Personality and Social Psychology, 76,* 229–245.

Musgrove, L., & McGarty, C. (2008). Opinion-based group membership as a predictor of collective emotional responses and support for pro- and anti-war action. *Social Psychology, 39,* 37–47.

Orum, A. M., & Orum, A. W. (1968). The class and status bases of Negro student protest. *Social Science Quarterly, 49,* 521–533.

Pachankis, J. E. (2007). The psychological implications of concealing a stigma: A cognitive-affective-behavioral model. *Psychological Bulletin, 133,* 328–345.

Parham, T. (1989). Cycles of psychological Nigrescence. *The Counseling Psychologist, 17,* 187–226.

Parham, T. A., & Helms, J. E. (1981). Influence of a black student's racial identity attitudes on preference for counselor race. *Journal of Counseling Psychology, 28,* 250–257.

Parham, T. A., & Helms, J. E. (1985a). Relation of racial identity attitudes to self-actualization and affective states of black students. *Journal of Counseling Psychology, 32,* 431–440.

Parham, T. A., & Helms, J. E. (1985b). Attitudes of racial identity and self-esteem of black students: An exploratory investigation. *Journal of College Student Personnel, 26,* 143–146.

Peterson, B. E., & Duncan, L. E. (1999). Generative concern, political commitment, and charitable actions. *Journal of Adult Development, 6,* 105–118.

Peterson, B. E., & Klohnen, E. C. (1995). Realization of generativity in two samples of women at midlife. *Psychology and Aging, 10,* 20–29.

Peterson, B. E., Smirles, K. A., & Wentworth, P. A. (1997). Generativity and authoritarianism: Implications for personality, political involvement, and parenting. *Journal of Personality and Social Psychology, 72,* 1202–1216.

Peterson, B. E., & Stewart, A. J. (1996). Antecedents and contexts of generativity motivation at midlife. *Psychology and Aging, 11,* 21–33.

Pinkney, A. (1969). *The committed: White activists in the civil rights movement.* New Haven, CT: College and University Press.

Renshon, S. A. (1974). *Psychological needs and political behavior: A theory of personality and political efficacy.* New York: Free Press.

Rickard, K. M. (1989). The relationship of self-monitored dating behaviors to level of feminist identity on the Feminist Identity Scale. *Sex Roles, 20,* 213–226.

Rickard, K. M. (1990). The effect of feminist identity level on gender prejudice toward artists' illustrations. *Journal of Research in Personality, 24,* 145–162.

Runciman, W. G. (1966). *Relative deprivation and social justice.* Berkeley: University of California Press.

Schreiber, R. (2008). *Righting feminism: Conservative women and American politics.* New York: Oxford University Press.

Schuman, H., & Scott, J. (1989). Generations and collective memories. *American Sociological Review, 54,* 351–381.

Searles, R., & Williams, J. A. (1962). Negro college students' participation in sit-ins. *Social Forces, 40,* 215–220.

Sears, D. O., & McConahay, J. S. (1973). *The politics of violence: The new urban blacks and the Watts riots.* Boston: Houghton Mifflin.

Shingles, R. D. (1981). Black consciousness and political participation: The missing link. *American Political Science Review, 75,* 76–91.

Simon, B., & Klandermans, B. (2001). Politicized collective identity: A social psychological analysis. *American Psychologist, 56,* 319–331.

Simon, B., Loewy, M., Stürmer, S., Weber, U., Freytag, P., Habig, C., et al. (1998). Collective identification and social movement participation. *Journal of Personality and Social Psychology, 74,* 646–658.

Smith, H. J., & Ortiz, D. J. (2002). Is it just me? The different consequences of personal and group relative deprivation. In I. Walker & H. J. Smith (Eds.), *Relative deprivation: Specification, development, and integration* (pp. 91–115). Cambridge, UK: Cambridge University Press.

Snyder, M., & Omoto, A. M. (2000). Doing good for self and society: Volunteerism and the psychology of citizen participation. In M. Van Vugt, M. Snyder, T. Tyler, & A. Biel (Eds.), *Cooperation in modern society: Promoting the welfare of communities, states, and organizations* (pp. 127–141). London: Routledge.

Snyder, M., & Omoto, A. M. (2001). Basic research and practical problems: Volunteerism and the psychology of individual and collective action. In W. Wosinska, R. Cialdini, D. Barrett, & J. Reykowski (Eds.), *The practice of social influence in multiple cultures* (pp. 287–307). Mahwah, NJ: Erlbaum.

Snyder, M., & Omoto, A. M. (2008). Volunteerism: Social issues perspectives and social policy implications. *Social Issues and Policy Review, 2,* 1–36.

Solomon, F., & Fishman, J. R. (1964). Youth and peace: A psycho-social study of student peace demonstrators in Washington, D.C. *Journal of Social Issues, 20,* 54–73.

Stewart, A. J., & Gold-Steinberg, S. (1990). Midlife women's political consciousness. *Psychology of Women Quarterly, 14,* 543–566.

Stewart, A. J., & Healy, J. M., Jr. (1989). Linking individual development and social changes. *American Psychologist, 44,* 30–42.

Stewart, A. J., & McDermott, C. (2004). Gender in psychology. *Annual Review of Psychology, 55,* 519–544.

Stürmer, S., & Simon, B. (2004). The role of collective identification in social movement participations: A panel study in the context of the German gay movement. *Personality and Social Psychology Bulletin, 30,* 263–277

Stürmer, S., & Simon, B. (2005). Collective action: Towards a dual-pathway model. *European Review of Social Psychology, 15,* 59–99.

Stürmer, S., Snyder, M., Kropp, A., & Siem, B. (2006). Empathy-motivated helping: The moderating role of group membership. *Personality and Social Psychology Bulletin, 32,* 943–956.

Stürmer, S., Snyder, M., & Omoto, A. M. (2005). Prosocial emotions and helping: The moderating role of group membership. *Journal of Personality and Social Psychology, 88,* 532–546.

Subašić, E., Reynolds, K. J., & Turner, J. C. (2008). The political solidarity model of social change: Dynamics of self-categorization in intergroup power relations. *Personality and Social Psychology Review, 12,* 330–352.

Tajfel, H. (1978). Social categorization, social identity, and social comparison. In H. Tajfel (Ed.), *Differentiation between social groups.* New York: Academic.

Tajfel, H., & Turner, J. C. (1979). An integrative theory of intergroup conflict. In W. G. Austin & S. Worchel (Eds.), *The social psychology of inter-group relations* (pp. 33–47). Monterey, CA: Brooks/Cole.

Thomas, L. E. (1971). Political generation gap: A study of liberal and conservative activist and nonactivist students and their parents. *Journal of Social Psychology, 84,* 313–314.

Van Hiel, A., Duriez, B., & Kossowska, M. (2006). The presence of left-wing authoritarianism in western Europe and its relationship with conservative ideology. *Political Psychology, 27,* 769–793.

Van Hiel, A., Onraet, E. & De Pauw, S. (2010), The relationship between social-cultural attitudes and behavioral measures of cognitive style: A meta-analytic integration of studies. *Journal of Personality, 78,* 1765–1799.

van Zomeren, M., Postmes, T., & Spears, R. (2008). Toward an integrative social identity model of collective action: A quantitative research synthesis of three socio-psychological perspectives. *Psychological Bulletin, 134,* 504–535.

van Zomeren, M., Spears, R., Fischer, A. H., & Leach, C. W. (2004). Put your money where your mouth is!: Explaining collective action tendencies though group-based anger and group efficacy. *Journal of Personality and Social Psychology, 87,* 649–664.

Verba, S., & Nie, N. (1972). *Political participation in the United States.* New York: Harper & Row.

Watts, W. A., Lynch, S., & Whittaker, D. (1969). Alienation and activism in today's college-age youth: Socialization patterns and current family relationships. *Journal of Counseling Psychology, 16,* 1–7.

Watts, W. A., & Whittaker, D. (1966). Free speech advocates at Berkeley. *Journal of Applied Behavioral Science, 2,* 41–62.

Weinberg, D. H. (2004). *Evidence from Census 2000 about earnings by detailed occupation for men and women.* Washington, DC: U. S. Census Bureau.

Whittaker, D., & Watts, W. A. (1971). Personality characteristics associated with activism and disaffiliation in today's college youth. *Journal of Counseling Psychology, 18,* 200–206.

White, A. (2006). Racial and gender attitudes as predictors of feminist activism among self-identified African American feminists. *Journal of Black Psychology, 32,* 455–478.

Wilson, J. (1973). *Introduction to social movements.* New York: Basic Books.

Worrell, F. C., Cross, W. E., & Vandiver, B. J. (2001). Nigrescence theory: Current status and challenges for the future.

Journal of Multicultural Counseling and Development, 29, 201–213.

Yzerbyt, V. Y., Dumont, M., Wigboldus, D., & Gordijn, E. (2003). I feel for us: The impact of categorization and identification on emotions and action tendencies. *British Journal of Social Psychology, 42,* 533–549.

Zucker, A. N. (1999). The psychological impact of reproductive difficulties on women's lives. *Sex Roles, 40,* 767–786.

Zucker, A. N., & Stewart, A. J. (2007). Growing up and growing older: Feminism as a context for women's lives. *Psychology of Women Quarterly, 31,* 137–145.

Zurcher, L. A., & Snow, D. A. (1992). Collective behavior: social movements. In M. Rosenberg & R. H. Turner (Eds.), *Social psychology: Sociological perspectives* (pp. 447–482). New Brunswick, NJ: Transaction.

Social Policy
Barriers and Opportunities for Personality and Social Psychology

Allen M. Omoto

Abstract

This chapter explores some of the historical linkages between personality, social psychology, and social policy, and especially as exemplified in the action research tradition. It does not review specific policies or case examples, but instead focuses on conceptual issues in integrating personality and social psychology for social policy research, program development, and evaluation. The chapter describes general orientations in personality and social psychology and how they may produce different understandings and solutions for social problems. Some of the differences in orientation are proposed as hindering the integration of personality and social psychology, whereas others are framed as complementary and likely to enhance policy work. Illustrative examples are offered of ways to integrate personality and social psychology in policy-relevant research, and other possible levels and contexts for personality and social psychologists to engage in policy work are also noted. The chapter concludes by outlining several systemic influences on policy involvement by personality and social psychologists, with a call for training programs to "rediscover" emphases on social policy, and by encouraging personality and social psychology to more highly value and actively participate in social policy research and work of all types.

Keywords: policy, action research, social issues, social problems, Kurt Lewin, applied psychology

People make policies and policy decisions every day. The parent who decrees that there will be no cell phone use during family meals, the professor who does not permit makeup exams or who subtracts points from late assignments, the decision in employment settings to not allow food or drink in work areas are all examples of policies. They are decisions or practices that are made to correct a perceived problem or to avoid a potential future problem. As illustrated by these simple examples, policies can be corrective or preventive. Thus, the parent who bars cell phone use could be trying to correct a perceived problem in family interaction and attentiveness, whereas the classroom policies of the professor may have been adopted in order to avoid having to make judgments about "good" and "bad" reasons that students miss exams as well as to clearly outline consequences for late work. The prohibition

against food and drink in work spaces may have been adopted in response to past problems with spilled drinks damaging computers or other equipment, to avoid future problems of this sort, or simply in the interests of presenting a more professional work environment. Not only do people make policies every day, but stated and even implied policies regulate and guide a substantial proportion of their behaviors.

At still broader levels, policies are adopted by professional guilds and associations as well as by companies, foundations, and businesses of all stripes, and are used to communicate definitions and priorities, regulate behaviors (e.g., codes of practice or behavior), and to chart courses for the short and long term. Mission statements commonly express general policy orientations and purposes, and these may be further expanded on and operationalized in specific strategic plans, initiatives, and programs. Social policies and social programming are also designed, adopted, implemented, and evaluated by larger organizations and institutions, including government at many levels. Thus, in the United States, statewide policy mandates concerning educational testing and achievement trickle down to affect district-level guidelines and programs, if not school-specific instructional activities and policies. Similarly, public good policies, such as safety belt laws, smoking and alcohol regulations, drug-free workplace assurances, antidiscrimination protections, or diversity-aspirational benchmarks, cut across sectors and influence individual and collective behaviors at multiple levels and in a wide variety of contexts. Policies and programs at all levels can be adopted in response to specific and emergent problems (e.g., after-school activity programs for a growing population of "latchkey kids," curfews put in place to combat looting and nuisance activities, parking restrictions after heavy snowfall). Policies can be enacted in laws, but also can be instantiated as sets of operating procedures, required or recommended practices, or even mutually agreed on rules of engagement or interaction. Policies vary in their degree of formalness, to whom they apply, and also the consequences for compliance or noncompliance. Furthermore, they can be prescriptive or proscriptive in describing behaviors that are to be encouraged or behaviors to be avoided.

This is obviously a very broad swath. The focus of this chapter is on formal *social policies* most generally, or policies that impact the behaviors of individuals and groups, and that are not specific or idiosyncratic to some family, municipality, or company. Social policies focus on social issues and problems, and generally are concerned with improving the conditions or standards of people's lives, although there may be disagreement on what constitutes improvement and on the means to achieve any change. *Public policies* are policies adopted by governmental entities, and can include many social policies, although as used in this chapter, social policies need not be rooted in governmental bodies. Finally, there are, of course, many public policies that have little direct connection to social issues or problems (e.g., policies related to international aid, military readiness, and economic or fiscal conditions); these are beyond the scope of this chapter.

This chapter does not summarize research on social policy, and is not even organized around examples of social policy successes or failures for personality and social psychologists. Rather, it attempts to consider, and to speculate on, the ways in which personality and social psychology can more fully embrace social policy work. To this end, it considers the guiding orientations of personality and social psychologists, and some possible implications for how social problems and policies are constructed and understood. The starting point for this discussion is the assumption that personality and social psychologists are *not* as involved in social policy work as they once were or as they can be. And furthermore, that there are likely real benefits in terms of scientific progress and public acceptance and support that could be realized from greater involvement in social policy work (see Baron, Bazerman, & Shonk, 2006; Caplan & Nelson, 1973; Lorion, Iscoe, DeLeon, & VandenBos, 1996; Miller, 1969; Thaler & Sunstein, 2008). In keeping with the theme of this *Handbook*, these issues will be considered with reference to a rapprochement or integration of personality and social psychology.

Action Research and Social Policy Involvement

At the outset, it is also important to be clear that the perspective offered here is that personality and social psychologists *should* be interested in social policies and social programming. In fact, they should have more than an interest in policies; they should be actively working to inform, develop, study, and evaluate social policies. While this perspective guides the analysis to follow, it may not be shared by all contemporary personality and social psychologists. However, as direct intellectual descendents of Kurt Lewin, interest in social policy and change lurks somewhere in the DNA of personality and social psychologists. Lewin is perhaps most commonly quoted by personality and social psychologists for his conceptualization of behavior as a function of the person and environment (i.e., $B = f[P, E]$, Lewin, 1940/1997), with the important proviso that the person and environment are interdependent. And, indeed, this simple formula may help explain the yin and yang of personality and social psychology, or the symbiotic push-pull dialectic that has long existed between these areas.

However, Lewin also is well known for his commitment to "action research" (Chein, Cook, & Harding, 1948; Lewin 1946/1997; Sanford, 1970) and to social science that could make a difference in people's lives and be used for the betterment of society (see Pettigrew & Cherry, chapter 2, this volume). As Lewin famously stated in his discussion of action research, "research that produces nothing but books will not suffice" (Lewin, 1946/1997, p. 144). Lewin wrote about the necessary and close connections between theoretical and applied psychology, with the goals of the theorist and of the practitioner considered as coequal. In this view, to the extent that research is done carefully and appropriately, then answers to theoretical problems can be achieved at the same time that practical social problems are effectively addressed. In short, there should be a "close cooperation between theoretical and applied psychology," and in Lewin's words, this could be accomplished if "the theorist does not look toward applied problems with highbrow aversion or with a fear of social problems, and if the applied psychologist realizes that there is nothing so practical as a good theory" (Lewin, 1943–44/1997, p. 288).

In this action research tradition, therefore, science and scientific methods are used to inform and evaluate social programming, and theories can be used for practical benefit and application. At the same time, however, practically focused research is useful for developing and refining theory and methodology. This can include research in naturalistic settings, on pressing social problems, and even on specific and local programs and concerns (for some expansions on these ideas, see Cialdini, 1980; Omoto & Snyder, 1990).

In outlining processes of action research, Lewin (1946/1997) described a recurring spiral of planning, action, and fact-finding in which ideas and (even informal) theories lead to the implementation of action or programs that are then evaluated or for which effects are assessed through data collection, which leads to subsequent revision of the original plan. In short, there is mutually enhancing intertwining of conceptual concerns with data collection and practical program implementation. The overall result of this spiral is evolving and ever-more-refined scientific understanding and practical effectiveness. Following this lead, Chein et al. (1948) delineated four types of action research, each one potentially an end in itself but also able to build on other types in addressing social problems and advancing theory. What the different types of action research have in common is an orienting assumption that the problems to be broached grow out of community interests, and that they are explored by an action researcher who remains responsive to community input and priorities. So, for example, *diagnostic* and *participant* action research focus on diagnosing or gaining deeper understanding of a problem, with the latter type involving close collaboration with the people who are to take action and who will be most affected by the policies and actions of interest. The other two types of action research, *empirical* and *experimental*, stress the recording and analysis of the effects of actions taken, with experimental action research offering up the possibility of implementing alternative actions so as to be able to compare relative effectiveness. In this framework, the types of action research vary in the extent to which they involve stakeholders, practitioners, or individuals directly impacted by programs and social problems, involve implementation of different treatments or experimental conditions (generally in naturalistic settings), and include formal and systematic methods of data collection. One point to stress, however, is that research and action, much like person and environment, are interdependent and should not be considered separately. They strengthen each other so that severing the connection, while leaving viable entities, is far from ideal.

Personality psychologists and especially social psychologists have not been shy to study social issues and social problems of the day. There is a long history of research and theorizing on issues related to women's rights and intergroup relations (see, for example, Tropp & Molina, chapter 22, this volume), including racial prejudice and discrimination. In more recent times, personality and social psychologists have investigated a wide range of topics such as the psychological aspects of homelessness (e.g., Shinn & Weitzman, 1990; Toro, 2007); immigration (e.g., Deaux, 2006; Deaux, Esses, Lalonde, & Brown, 2010 ; Ryan & Casas, 2010); environmental issues (e.g., Vlek & Steg, 2007; Zelezny & Schultz, 2000); service learning and volunteerism (e.g., Snyder & Omoto, 2008; Stukas & Dunlap, 2002); lesbian, gay, bisexual, and transgender rights (e.g., Chamberlain, Miller, & Bornstein, 2008; Hatzenbuehler, 2010; Herek, 2007; health concerns, such as tobacco, obesity, and HIV infection (e.g., Gibson, 1997; Fisher, Kohut, Fisher, 2009; Krantz, 1978; Miller & Downey, 1999; Stroebe, 2008); and educational opportunities and diversity (e.g., Gurin, Dey, Hurtado, & Gurin, 2002; Niemann & Maruyama, 2005; Peck, Feinstein, & Eccles, 2008; Zirkel, 2008). It remains unclear, however, if applied research or even research on social issues is any longer at or near the heart of personality or social psychology. In fact, results of searches of the 2009 impact ratings as derived from Journal Citation Reports® Social Sciences Edition of journals using different key subject categories suggest they are not (Thomson Reuters, 2009). There were no journals with "applied" or "policy" in their titles among either the top ten journals in "personality" or in a search using the dual categories of "social" and "psychology." Shifting the focus to a search of the top ten journals categorized as "psychology" and "applied" likewise revealed no journals with "social" or "personality" in their titles.

However, even granting an enduring interest in social issues by personality and social psychologists, it can be argued that another part of the Lewin legacy—the focus on social programs, social experimentation, and social policy—has been largely lost or receded in prominence (Sanford, 1970). In their respective chases to be recognized as legitimate and rigorous sciences, the fields of personality and social psychology may have opted to emphasize the theoretical over the practical, thereby also forsaking policy involvement. And, as the multidisciplinary field of program evaluation has coalesced and grown in recent years (e.g., Donaldson & Scriven, 2003), it may have usurped or helped to excise those parts of personality and social psychology that traditionally have focused on social policy. At minimum, social policy work appears to play a less central role in the lives of academic personality and social psychologists today than in the past, and reports of this type of work are unlikely to be found in mainstream publication outlets in these fields.

While perhaps obvious to state, social programming and many applied concerns lend themselves to social policy research and development. What may be less obvious, however, is that policy work, at least at broader levels, involves commitment to a social issue or problem, theoretical frameworks, and the collection of data in helping to diagnose a problem and to test the effects of naturally occurring or implemented interventions. In short, social policy development and evaluation often goes beyond what is conventionally considered applied research while also encompassing more than "pure" or basic research. To be explicit, applied research may not have theoretical guides or implications; it is strictly problem-focused and even potentially limited to a specific concern in a particular context. Thus, it may not have any obvious connections or implications for broader social policies. Meanwhile, basic research may have little direct connection to social problems and issues, and especially because it typically aims to be abstract, generalizable, and to transcend the local. Theories and basic research may be suggestive of certain policies and programs, but purely theoretical work is not generally focused on policy concerns or programming.

The point here is that social policy work can and does incorporate the concerns of applied researchers as well as theorists and theoretical researchers, and it does so while extending beyond specific locations, populations, and problems. Thus, although applied research is sometimes equated with policy concerns, it is important to recognize the bridging role that psychologically based policy analyses and research can play between applied and basic research and goals. As will be explored later in this chapter, a renewed appreciation and investment in social policy might also help to reconnect personality and social psychology.

Policy-Relevant Differences Between Personality and Social Psychology

In general terms, policy work involves both the definition of a problem and working toward a solution to that problem and, for personality and social psychologists, it can involve two main prongs of activity: policy development and policy evaluation. That is, social problems can be socially constructed or understood in a variety of ways. In the political realm, or at least with respect to public discourse, this is similar to how the terms of debate are defined and who controls them. Political effectiveness often seems to flow from having effectively defined a problem or the terms of debate for a given audience (e.g., the general public or a particular constituency). Beyond problem definition, however, policy work clearly involves proposing potential solutions or interventions to problems and social issues. Having defined a problem in a particular way, policies must be responsive to the purported causes and also seek to remediate lasting damage.

Personality and social psychologists are unlikely to construct or to understand social problems in the same ways, and consequently, may propose different types of policy solutions. Their different orientations or orienting viewpoints of the causes of behavior, the extent to which conditions and solutions are mutable, time perspective, and even (implied) political ideologies may provide barriers for collaborative work on social policies or in policy contexts. At the same time, however, the possibility for better or closer integration of personality and social psychology also offers heretofore untapped opportunities for effective social policy involvement. In short, reconnecting personality and social psychology may not only serve the respective fields but also help to enlarge and embrace their efforts in the social policy realm, and to reclaim part of what may have been lost or diminished in terms of societal relevance.

Personality psychologists or those who adopt a general personality approach are interested in development, change, and regularities in behavior, all presumably driven by a latent characteristic, trait, or disposition. Their focus is on individual-to-individual variability and the development and acquisition of certain traits and characteristics, as well as how traits are manifested in overt behavior. That is, observable behavior is assumed to be caused by, and a relatively direct reflection of, something about the individual, with this something likely to manifest itself across multiple and even diverse situations. The explanatory mechanisms of preference in this approach include traits, motivations, and abilities, or more generally, latent characteristics that individuals carry with them across settings and circumstances.

Social psychologists, on the other hand, have historically paid relatively little attention to the development of characteristics and to within-person change, let alone between-person variation. In adopting a social psychological perspective, or a more extreme situational emphasis, circumstances determine behavior and any regularities in behavior are more likely the consequence of consistent pressures or similarities in situations rather than as determined by characteristics internal to individuals. The lessons of social psychology are more about "the power of situations," and explanatory mechanisms involve the construction and construal of current circumstances and environments. These situations, moreover, involve social (e.g., actual, imagine, and implied others; Allport, 1985) and nonsocial elements (e.g., ambient temperature, noise, time constraints).

Locus or Causes of Problems

With these lenses, then, personality and social psychologists, or at least people who adopt the traditional and stereotyped characterization of them, "see" the causes of social problems as emanating from different sources. For the personality adherent, the problem of pollution is likely to be wasteful individual habits and avarice, of unemployment to be laziness and self-indulgence, and of crime to be lack of self-control and antisocial tendencies. For a social psychologist, however, environmental degradation is more likely to be seen as caused by the miscoordination of behavior and unawareness of independencies between people and segments of society. Unemployment, meanwhile, results from social systems that undervalue certain skills and experiences while simultaneously overvaluing ones that are not equitably distributed across people, or perhaps more directly, to unequal opportunities between people. Causes of crime are likewise found in societal structures and situational constraints or affordances that are conducive to and reinforce legal transgressions or criminal behaviors. It is the power of the situation that drives bad behavior rather than inherent evil of perpetrators or callous disregard for others.

The simplest way to characterize these differences is in terms of differences in locus of causality (e.g., Heider, 1958; Jones et al., 1972; Weiner, 1985). The personality psychologist, in focusing on dispositional characteristics, emphasizes internal locus whereas the social psychologist, in focusing on situational causes, emphasizes external factors as causal determinants for problems. Of course, the fundamental attribution error, or the tendency to focus on persons rather than environments as causal agents for action, is well established across people who vary in experience, expertise, and knowledge (Gilbert, 1998; Jones & Harris, 1967; Jones & Nisbett, 1971; Ross, 1977), but may also differ by culture (see Miller, 1984). That is, psychologist or not, individuals are likely to be seen as the causes of their own problems more so than that their situations or structural differences are responsible for their problems, although explanations for one's own problems or successes may be influenced by differential availability of information and ego protective motivations (e.g., see Miller & Ross, 1975). The point is that, even in the face of the general tendency to blame individuals for their outcomes, there may be a relative difference in emphasis between personality and social psychologists by virtue of their habitual ways of explaining behaviors and the "causes" that are given primacy in their theorizing.

This same logic can and does apply to success. The personologist sees success, advantage, and achievement as individually caused; the person or even team or company has succeeded because of their intelligence, hard work, superior communication skills, and so on. For the social psychologist, however, success may be more a matter of time and place, of being in the right place at the right time or of being fortunate enough either to have been born into or to happen upon circumstances that offered a "sweet spot" for success and achievement.

In turning to an understanding of problem solutions, personality and social psychologists are likely to prefer different methods of amelioration. That is, their different diagnoses of the causes of the problem call for different methods of solution. To return to the examples above, a personality psychologist may advocate for individual incentives for curbing wasteful and polluting behaviors or training programs that teach people new skills that could help them to find a job. Criminals should be timed out through incarceration while at the same time, perhaps, provided opportunity to change or "better" themselves though rehabilitative services, education and training, and even empathy training.

From a social psychological perspective, however, the focus of intervention is likely to be on circumstances or societal structures that disconnect individuals from each other, that maintain inequities in access and resources, and that cause conditions of hardship or strife to be disproportionately experienced by people simply because of where they live, their gender, their racial or ethnic heritage, or other nonrelevant personal characteristics. Contingencies in the current environment need to be explicated or rearranged in order to support alternative and non-problematic behaviors. Thus, social psychologically inspired solutions to problems are likely to focus on broad-based programs that powerfully compel or persuade individuals to take appropriate and corrective action. To reduce waste and overconsumption of resources, then, community interdependencies should be outlined, and hefty taxes or penalties might be levied against individuals who violate clearly stated standards for consumption. To reduce crime, alternative routes for advancement and success, and ones incompatible with illegal actions, need to be developed and made salient in select social settings.

In integrating personality and social psychological perspectives, then, causal explanations or diagnoses for social problems become more complicated and involve variables at different levels of analysis. It is insufficient to attend only to individuals and to attempt to change them without simultaneously acknowledging the influence of and potentially intervening on the social circumstances and environments to which individuals have access and in which they live.

Essentialism and Social Constructionism

A related distinction can be seen in essentialist versus social constructionist explanations for behavioral consistency and attitudes. Essentialist perspectives emphasize characteristics or properties that must be possessed in order to fit in a category or class. These traits and characteristics are often viewed as in-born, relatively unchangeable, and universal. Essentialist beliefs (about, for example, sexual orientation or gender categories; e.g., Bohan, 1993; Haslam & Levy, 2006; Hegarty & Pratto, 2001; Prentice &

Miller, 2007; Wood & Eagly, 2002) can be contrasted with relatively more fluid, modifiable, and context-dependent constructionist perspectives that emphasize broad situational and cultural determinants of perceptions and action.

This distinction between essentialist beliefs and explanations and social constructionist accounts can be linked to differences between typical personality and social psychological orientations. Specifically, essentialist assumptions about social categories and people emphasize immutable and internal characteristics, and as such, appear to be well aligned with personality approaches that stress latent and relatively stable traits and dispositions as explanations for behavior. On the other hand, constructionist perspectives that assume historically bound and culturally rooted understandings of categories and behavioral tendencies are more consistent with social psychological emphases on determinants of behavior as found in current social environments.

To be sure, there are policy implications for adopting essentialist or constructionist views of human beings and social problems. For example, although essentialist beliefs may be multidimensional, to the extent that people believe that homosexuality is the result of nature rather than nurture or political choice, they report less prejudice toward gay and lesbian identified people (see Haslam & Levy, 2006). Consequently, they are less likely to support antigay legislation or ballot initiatives that discriminate against lesbian or gay individuals. In fact, in amicus curiae or friend of the court briefs filed by the American Psychological Association in court cases the point is often made that sexual orientation is generally not chosen and is resistant to change (American Psychological Association [APA], 2010). In addition, homosexuality is noted as a normal expression of human sexuality that is generally discussed (in scientific and lay circles) in categorical terms. It is unfair if not illegal to discriminate against individuals because of who they are, and especially if they cannot change their identity or personal characteristics.

A relatively more constructionist approach, on the other hand, stresses the social structural barriers and norms that restrict the behaviors of individuals and "force" particular modes of behavior on individuals who happen to possess certain characteristics (e.g., female sex) or inclinations. In this sense, individuals, their identities, and their behaviors, are products of their social settings, including the cultural and historical time period in which the person lives. As corollaries to these points, many policy debates and amicus curiae point to the stress and hardship that individuals must endure because of societal prejudice (APA, 2010; Herek, 2006). For example, research suggests that to the extent that people believe that homosexuality is a choice, they are likely to report less tolerance and more prejudice (Haslam & Levy, 2006).

Simply put, essentialist and constructionist assumptions run throughout many policy debates. They also are not new to personality and social psychology, including in assessments of the field as a whole and theorizing within it (e.g., Gergen, 1973; Schlenker, 1974). Adopting an essentialist (or relatively personality) perspective lends itself to certain types of arguments and ameliorative plans, whereas constructionist views suggest other targets for policies and change. If the "problem" is rooted in essentialist explanations, then efforts should be directed at identifying individuals likely to possess the problem (i.e., correct classification). Once identified, these individuals can be enrolled in programs, isolated from others, or otherwise intervened upon in attempting to change them. In complementary fashion, efforts can be directed at changing the causes of the problematic condition in the future. In short, the targets of prejudice are likely to be the focus of interventions.

If the "problem" results from specific societal constructions, however, then the target of intervention is societally based and efforts should be directed at changing beliefs, attitudes, and actions of broader collectives and cultures. So, for example, opinion change campaigns could be mounted in order to inform and persuade people or even simply to challenge the values and beliefs that they hold that cause them to respond negatively to others (e.g., Grube, Mayton, & Ball-Rokeach, 1994). The focus of policy programs are not the individuals who are victimized (i.e., the targets), but rather, the social climates that permit stigmatization and victimization to occur or the socially constructed, consensually held views or caricatures of the targets of prejudice. In social psychological terms, the group mind, norms, public opinion, or stereotypes need to be effectively addressed. In fact, there are some well-known and heavily researched topic areas, such as on the contact hypothesis (Pettigrew & Tropp, 2006, 2011; see also Tropp & Molina, chapter 22, this volume), that either implicitly or explicitly adopt this perspective. In simplistic terms, this perspective suggests that if people had more and authentic contact with different individuals, they would come to see the similarities across people and unfounded prejudice would be reduced.

Time Frame and Methodological Approaches

Another set of differences between personality and social psychologists relates to the time frame or scope of time considered in theorizing and research, as well as related correlational and experimental methodological propensities. For personality psychologists, in contrast to social psychologists, individual change and development are of central rather than secondary interest. By necessity, then, time is extended into the past as well as into the future, and theorizing takes seriously the socialization of individuals, maturational differences, and developmental processes (see Stewart & Deaux, chapter 26, this volume).

For social psychologists, on the other hand, contemporaneity is a key principle or assumption (e.g., Lewin, 1943/1997; Gold, 1992); that is, the causes of actions and events are in the here and now. The past and the future can be included as potential causes, but only as they are represented and construed contemporaneously. Even when individual differences are included in social psychological theorizing, in fact, they are typically assessed close to the time at which they are likely to be active or to influence behavior. There is relatively little emphasis placed on how individuals come to possess traits or dispositions in the first place or even how these regularities may be changed in response to social feedback, maturational processes, or new environmental contingencies.

Consistent with these differences in time perspective, the research methodologies that have come to be favored by personality and social psychologists are not the same, nor are they even consistent with each other (e.g., Tracy, Robins, & Sherman, 2009). Furthermore, they do not appear to be well matched or conducive to policy work. Personality psychologists tend to be relatively expert at longitudinal data collections, and to make use of correlational research designs and data analytic techniques. In attempting to assess the role played by personality traits or characteristics in overt behavior, they may observe individuals in multiple and different situations or even collect reports of behaviors from a variety of informants (Funder, 1999; Fast & Funder, 2008; Kolar, Funder, & Colvin, 1996). In addition, many personality psychologists focus on assessment and measurement concerns, and on developing more reliable and valid measures of personality traits or propensities. These measures can be used for diagnostic and categorization purposes, to be sure, but superior measurement qua measurement is unlikely to provide rationale or justification for social policies.

Following participants and collecting data over long stretches of time (e.g., the famous Terman study of gifted children, see Shurkin, 1992; Terman, 1959), and doing so with minimal intervention or interference, may be able to provide useful building blocks for policies and social programming. However, wide windows of time and natural history data may run counter to the goals of many social programs and policymakers: their goals are to develop and implement quick fixes to problems and to show demonstrable effects of programs.

Social psychologists, on the other hand, have evidenced a strong historical predilection for laboratory experimentation in which presumably key features of situations are manipulated and their effects on the behavior of participants reported or observed. The research designs are generally simple (as evidenced by the "classic" 2 × 2 design) and often lacking in mundane realism. Field experiments are not unknown in social psychology, but they may still involve the embedding of a situational manipulation in a naturally occurring context and often do not include more than a few different research conditions. Thus, for example, helping tendencies have been studied as a function of the number of bystanders present (Darley & Latané, 1968; Latané & Nida, 1981; Levine & Crowther, 2008) or the ostensible need of a victim (Piliavin & Piliavin, 1972), normative influence in the form of litter or messages on hotel room placards have been investigated as means of deterring littering or water conservation (Goldstein, Cialdini, & Griskevicius, 2008; Kallgren, Reno, & Cialdini, 2000; see also Keizer, Lindenberg, & Steg, 2008), and the impact of choice on the health of aging adults studied by introducing small changes in nursing home environments and routines (Langer & Rodin, 1976; Rodin & Langer, 1977). Nonetheless, the vast majority of research is not field-based, but instead occurs in the psychological laboratory (Sears, 1986). The benefits of being able to establish causality through experimentation are great, at least in the minds of social psychologists, and overshadow the limitations of these simple and relatively unrealistic research designs and settings.

The simplicity and elegance of experiments conducted in laboratory settings is easily defended, and especially to the extent that social psychologists seek to isolate singular causal mechanisms. What is less clear, though, is how this "context free" research maps onto policy considerations and social problems. To the extent that social psychological researchers also employ deception and create complicated scenarios to investigate relatively simple mechanisms, their research methodology veers farther from reality and becomes less accessible to nonexperts. Policymaking involves stakeholders and constituents, and contexts in which multiple and potentially interacting influences are at play. The individuals involved in these efforts are unlikely to appreciate the conceptual basis for social psychological experimentation and may be reluctant to base policy and social programs on research conducted in artificial settings (and in which participants have been duped in the process). Finally, the generally ahistorical nature of causal theories and research in social psychology (i.e., its contemporaneous focus) runs counter to many naive theories and beliefs about people's behaviors.

A common research practice among both personality and social psychologists that likely further limits the perceived usefulness of their work for social policies is the heavy reliance on data collection from student samples (e.g., Sears, 1986; but see Anderson, Lindsay, & Bushman, 1999). In fact, psychology, and especially personality and social psychology, has been criticized for its excessive reliance on WEIRD samples, or people from Western, Educated, Industrialized, Rich, and Democratic societies (Henrich, Heine, Norenzayan, 2010), with questions arising about the generalizability of research findings based on these samples. Clearly many social policies are important for these societies and samples, but even in the United States, only roughly 30% of the adult population possess college degrees (U.S. Census Bureau, 2011). To do policy-related research, and to do it in contexts and with populations for which policies matter most, therefore, will require personality and social psychologists to venture out of laboratories and away from student populations to a greater extent and to embrace a wider range of research contexts, populations, and problems. In short, stronger connections to the real world and to the lives of everyday people will likely be needed.

Thus, for both personality and social psychologists, the windows of time with which they concern themselves and the particular methods that they commonly utilize may place them at a disadvantage in interacting in the policy realm and with policymakers. If these perspectives and preferences could be better integrated in complementary fashion, then it is feasible that personality and social psychologists could make a stronger case for the policy-relevance of their research. To do so may also mean that integrated theorizing would place individuals in broader contexts, including ones focused on the choice of situations and reciprocal influences of individuals and situations (e.g., Snyder & Ickes, 1985) and also that take seriously psychological futures (e.g., Markus & Nurius, 1986) or prospects for individuals and their behaviors. In the policy realm, this might mean a reorientation so as to downplay immediate and quick solutions to problems in favor of greater recognition of the evolving nature of persons and social problems. A more fully integrated and policy-relevant personality and social psychology would model change and growth while also seeking to test longer-term effects of policies and interventions, including on collateral issues and concerns (that is, in complex systems rather than simple, single variable causal systems).

Ideological Congeniality

Another difference between personality and social psychology that has implications for policy involvement lies in the political ideologies with which each is most compatible or easily linked. As a psychological entity, an ideology is "a belief system of the individual that is typically shared with an identifiable group and that organizes, motivates, and gives meaning to political behavior broadly construed" (Jost, 2006, p. 653). As students of political processes can well attest, ideology can and does drive many policy debates and decisions. One of the great frustrations for social scientists is that their data are not necessarily used in social policy formulation (DeLeon, 1986, 1988; Miller, 1969). Rather, policies often flow from deeply entrenched ideologies or worldviews, and in fact, the data that do exist may be interpreted against the backdrop of these ideologies or even discounted prima facie because they are inconsistent with a prevailing ideological stance. Social scientists may not believe or want to acknowledge that ideologies are real or that their work could be used to support certain ideological positions. To deny the influence of ideologies, however, would be short-sighted and out of step with a growing body of evidence (see Jost, 2006).

As noted above, personality psychologists tend to emphasize internal locus and to explain actions in terms of individual traits and motivations rather than as due to the influences or accidents of situations. This orientation would seem to fit well with an ideological frame that emphasizes the justness of the world, a world in which bad people do bad things and reap punishment whereas good people commit positive acts and are likely to be socially and tangibly rewarded (Lerner, 1980). In this view, the reason that some people succeed and others fail is largely a consequence of differential internal characteristics such as ability or motivation, and the world is seen as functioning as a meritocracy. Thus, a woman's failure to advance in a male-dominated profession is because she lacks the appropriate disposition for success (e.g., Fiske, Bersoff, Borgida, Deaux, & Heilman, 1991). She is either too soft and fragile to compete, or her leadership characteristics are judged to be abrasive and off-putting in a woman (Eagly & Carli, 2007; Eagly & Karau, 2002).

In the United States, this is a politically conservative ideology that has come to be most often associated with the Republican Party. This is not to say that personality psychologists are likely to be politically conservative or registered Republicans (which are themselves empirical questions), but only that the types of explanations and causes that personality psychology tends to emphasize in explaining behavior seem to jibe nicely with more conservative ideologies (e.g., Carroll, Perkowitz, Lurigio, & Weaver, 1987; Skitka, Mullen, Griffin, Hutchinson, & Chamberlin, 2002; Skitka & Tetlock, 1993; but also see Morgan, Mullen, & Skitka, 2010).

For social psychologists, meanwhile, the causes of success and failure can be and are often hidden from view. The focus on individuals and their actions obscures how unequal social structures and environmental constraints overdetermine the outcomes of individuals and social groups. There is no assumption of social justice, but rather, a desire for justice. Thus, social psychological explanations seem most sympathetic to a worldview or ideology that stresses inherent injustice or unequalness, and where the success of a racer is determined less by natural talent, motivation, or persistence and more by how close that racer started to the finish line relative to other racers. In other words, systems are unequal and yet people create mythologies or scripts that permit them to see the systems as just, right, and given (e.g., Jost, Glaser, Kruglanski, & Sulloway, 2003; Jost, Banaji, & Nosek, 2004; Pratto et al. 2000; Sidanius & Pratto, 1999; Skitka et al., 2002). In short, and despite social psychologists' best advice and intentions, people fall prey to a form of the naturalistic fallacy in which the way things are is as they should be; what exists is right and good.

Returning to the example of the woman who does not advance in a male-dominated profession, a social psychologist would point to the stereotypes that pervade her work environment, to the lack of other successful women whose presence changes the social climate and who model appropriate behaviors, to the expectations and standards of the people evaluating her, and to the competing demands and stress that the woman is likely to face from nonworkplace responsibilities and roles (Fiske et al. 1991; Biernat, 2003, 2005; Marcus-Newhall, Halpern, & Tan, 2006). The glass ceiling that the woman hits is less about her and more about her social settings and the factors embedded in these settings that conspire to hinder her advancement. In the United States, this is a relatively politically liberal ideological stance that is more often associated with the Democratic Party, if not more extreme "left-wing" political parties. These parties tend to espouse redistributive social programs and policies, or ones in which attempts are made to level playing fields and histories of injustice are acknowledged if not (monetarily) redressed.

Thus, although psychologists are purported to be politically liberal and to marginalize conservative views (e.g., Redding, 2001), it would seem that the perspectives of personality and of social psychologists may be better matched to either relatively more conservative or more liberal political ideologies and policy arguments. This is obviously a speculative claim. However, as personality and social psychologists wade into policy waters, this apparent difference may warrant attention, and especially for situations in which research from one or the other perspective might unwittingly be used to support a certain political or ideological position.

It is unclear what implications an integration of personality and social psychology might have for this apparent difference in ideological congeniality. Perhaps integrated personality and social psychologists, at least in the United States, could work in a postpartisan manner, acknowledging and appreciating differing political viewpoints. Alternatively, they may be better suited to work for either main political party because they have the flexibility and approaches that are congenial to both. In this sense, then, there may be more opportunity for people who integrate personality and social psychology to involve themselves in politically partisan issues simply because they are not restricted to the right or the left, but can work with both sides of the aisle. Clearly, the United States has a unique political (and policy-setting) system, one in which a relatively clear distinction is made between Republicans and Democrats and their prevailing ideologies. In other countries, political ideologies are cast differently and there are political systems that require broader coalitions and more than two parties as well

as systems in which only one ideology and "party" dominate. The point remains, however, that personality and social psychology may better serve different ideological positions, and that integrating them may permit a wider spectrum of political and policy involvement than either perspective taken alone.

Conducting Policy-Relevant Research

If more personality and social psychologists involved themselves in policy work, what would be the consequence? What would psychologists who integrate personality and social psychological approaches bring to the policy table? As noted at the outset, the majority of this chapter is speculative, relies on stereotypes of personality and social psychologists, and is not supported by data or illustrative studies. Also taken as a starting point was the observation that personality and social psychologists play only minor roles in current policy work. Certainly, personality and social psychologists conduct research that is potentially relevant to social policies, and some have as the focus of their research rigorous analyses of social policies. However, policy research, at least in the Lewinian action research tradition, is no longer common in the mainstream of personality and social psychology; it may be being pursued, but it does not appear to be a major current in either field.

This observation invites the question, What might policy-related research that integrates personality and social psychology look like? Two brief and immodest examples will help illustrate possible ways in which personality and social psychology can be integrated in policy-relevant research. For a number of years, my colleagues and I have pursued a program of research on volunteerism, much of it focused on the specific context and issue of AIDS volunteerism (see Omoto & Snyder, 1995, 2010; Omoto et al., 2000; Snyder & Omoto, 2008; Snyder, Omoto, & Crain, 1999). There can be no denying that the HIV epidemic has been a critical social and public health issue worldwide for the past 30 years, and in our research, we have attempted to remain sensitive to the dynamic of this epidemic while trying to understand and enhance constructive citizen-based responses to it. Drawing from theories in personality and social psychology as well as the results of our empirical investigations, we have developed a conceptual model—the Volunteer Process Model—that organizes our understanding of volunteerism and that helps guide our research activities (e.g., Omoto & Snyder, 1995, 2002; Snyder, Omoto, & Smith, 2010).

In this model, volunteerism is conceptualized in terms of a process that unfolds over time and that engages concerns at multiple levels of analysis. At an *individual* level, the model calls attention to the activities and psychological processes of individual persons and the recipients or targets of volunteerism, including their personality characteristics and motivational tendencies. At more social psychological *interpersonal* and *group* levels of analysis, the model makes clear that volunteerism occurs in the context of or because of people's interpersonal relationships, may be enacted by groups and collectives, and may take place through community-based organizations and institutions. Volunteerism also is carried out for the purposes of improving the conditions of members of social groups. Finally, at a broader *societal* level, the model considers the linkages between individuals and their societies as well as cultural factors associated with the emergence and evolution of traditions of volunteerism, service, and community involvement. Volunteerism is not unique to HIV infection; it occurs in response to and on behalf of a number of social issues and throughout the world (e.g., Allik & Realo, 2004; Curtis, Grabb, & Baer, 1992; Van Vugt, Snyder, Tyler, & Biel, 2000). Thus, volunteerism and our model detailing its levels and processes have their own connections to social policies and programs even outside the HIV context (for more, see Snyder & Omoto, 2008).

Furthermore, volunteerism is conceptually and practically linked to a number of activities and behaviors in which individuals seek to address problems of society, often in coordinated fashion (e.g., Omoto, 2005; Omoto & Snyder, 2002; Snyder & Omoto, 2000, 2001; Van Vugt & Snyder, 2002). These activities, commonly referred to as civic engagement or citizenship behaviors, can all be considered forms of social action (key descriptive and explanatory features of social action are beyond the scope of this chapter and are described elsewhere; Snyder & Omoto, 2007). Suffice it to say, social action by individuals and groups can and does take many forms, including forms that are explicitly political and those that are not necessarily politically motivated or tinged. Importantly for personality and social psychology, social action varies between and within individuals and across social situations and cultures.

Extending our model beyond volunteerism to broader social action, the different emphases of personality and social psychologists can be seen in the different levels of analysis, but also in potential interactions between levels that are also highlighted in the model. So, for example, the model calls attention to features of persons that may lead them to engage in social action (including individual differences in personality, attitudes, values, and motivations), as well as features of the social circumstances and environments (including people's memberships in relationships, groups, and organizations), and the features of broader surrounding communities that promote or impede social action (including cultural conceptions of the nature of involvement and participation in society). In this way, then, the model, and a good deal of our empirical work, integrates personality and social psychological perspectives, if not actual operations and measures, in an attempt to predict and explain socially meaningful, policy-relevant action.

A substantial portion of this research on volunteerism has been conducted in close collaboration with community-based AIDS service organizations. That is, volunteers, clients, and staff in collaborating organizations assisted with planning the research, honing materials, and in the implementation of studies. Our goals were to test and extend scientific and theoretical concerns, but also to contribute to the policies and practices in these organizations by helping them fact-find about their current and potential volunteer recruitment plans and the support programs they provide. Thus, while integrating personality and social psychological perspectives, this research possesses many of the key features of action research.

In the first example, we combined a personality psychology focus on individual differences in motivation with a general social psychological message about the need for volunteers in attempting to address the real world policy concern of how to more effectively recruit volunteers for AIDS service organizations. To be sure, existing volunteer recruitment attempts for many types of organizations that utilize volunteers come from diverse sources situated at different levels. There are macro societal level persuasive message campaigns, community and organizational level efforts, and even individual-to-individual recruitment activities. The small-scale, individual-to-individual attempts to persuade may rely on idiosyncratic knowledge about potential volunteers and interpersonal connections to them, and in this way, they are consistent with approaches in personality psychology. Meanwhile, the efforts of organizations (such as volunteer service organizations, political parties, and social movements) to reach out and recruit people for participation, that engage consensus and normative processes, can be thought of as more social (or perhaps community) psychological in approach.

It is common practice for volunteer service organizations to publish notices in community newspapers or distribute brochures in community gathering places announcing their need for volunteers and informing prospective volunteers of how to get involved. These efforts do not typically engage individual difference or personality considerations, but instead, may be crafted in a one-size-fits-all mode. The apparent logic is that people simply need to be made aware of the need for volunteers and how to get involved; this information will move them to action. Building on theory and research that has identified a diversity of motivations for volunteering, and between-person differences in motivations, we examined whether messages that spoke directly to the motivations of certain people would be more effective in recruiting those people to volunteer (for related research, see Clary et al., 1998; Houle, Sagarin, & Kaplan, 2005; Omoto & Snyder, 1995). We reasoned that individual differences in motivation could be leveraged for recruitment: to the extent that prospective volunteers could see AIDS volunteerism as a way to satisfy important personal goals and motivations, then they should be more positively disposed to volunteer.

Based on this reasoning, we had volunteers at an AIDS service organization evaluate three newspaper-type advertisements encouraging AIDS volunteerism (Omoto, Snyder, & Smith, 1999). One ad contained a self-focused motivational appeal (e.g., "volunteer to feel better about yourself"), one contained an other-focused motivational appeal (e.g., "volunteer to help people in need"), and one ad contained no motivational appeal but simply made the need for volunteers known. In addition, these active volunteers completed an inventory that permitted us to assess the degree to which they possessed relatively self- and other-focused motivations for their volunteer work. We found that the ads with motivational appeals were generally preferred to the control (no motivation) ad. Further, preference for the other-focused motivation ad over the control ad was strongly predicted by volunteers' other-focused motivation and not by their self-focused motivation. Meanwhile, self-focused motivation, and not other-focused motivation, predicted volunteer preference for the self-focused motivation ad.

Having established differential appeal of the motivation ads, we next placed the ads in newspapers at two different universities, in reverse orders, to test whether they would be differentially effective in actually recruiting volunteers for AIDS service organizations (Smith, Omoto, & Snyder, 2001). Respondents who telephoned in response to an ad were sent a questionnaire to complete and return that assessed their self-focused and other-focused motivations. Across sites, more people called for information about volunteering in response to the motivational ads than to the control ad. The other-focused ad attracted the most respondents, with callers in response to this ad also more likely to follow through with their intent to pursue volunteerism than people who called in response to the control ad. Again, individual differences in measured motivation (taken from the follow-up questionnaires) mattered: people who responded to the other-focused ad were higher in other-focused motivation than people who responded to the comparison ads. For whatever reason, this individual difference x ad type matching pattern was not observed for the self-focused motivation ad (Smith, Omoto, & Snyder, 2001).

Taken together, these field-based studies support the use of specific motivational appeals in volunteer recruitment, with these appeals also especially likely to attract motivationally matched prospective volunteers. The point for this chapter, however, is that they provide illustration of one way of integrating personality and social psychological perspectives in policy relevant research. The personality or individual difference perspective is embodied in the assumption and measurement of specific personal motivations, whereas the social psychological perspective is seen in making clear the current need for volunteers as well as in comparing ads that simply state this need to ads that contain additional and persuasive content (motivational messaging). The research has the potential to advance conceptual issues related to helping behavior, motivations, and persuasion processes, but also to contribute to practical concerns related to volunteer recruitment and effective community-based responses to HIV disease.

The second example is a recently completed field-based experiment in which we attempted to intentionally foster psychological sense of community among volunteers, clients, and staff recruited through AIDS service organizations and who were previously unacquainted with each other (see Omoto & Snyder, 2010; Snyder & Omoto, 2011). Based on our multidimensional conceptual definition of psychological sense of community, we expected individuals exposed to an intervention focused on developing psychological sense of community with people affected by HIV and AIDS to subsequently have a heightened sense of community, but also to feel better about themselves, have greater optimism about their life circumstances, to take better care of themselves, and to be more likely to engage in community-enhancing activities such as volunteerism, activism, and broader social engagement.

The intervention was rooted in our psychological theorizing and research and implemented in successive waves in a series of workshop sessions conducted in small groups by trained facilitators. The facilitators introduced the group-based exercises by discussing and highlighting the facets of sense of community each exercise addressed, and closed each exercise by stressing the facets again and challenging participants to think about how they could instantiate them in their own life circumstances. Besides this key intervention condition, some participants in each wave were randomly assigned to a comparison intervention condition that consisted of workshop sessions of similar size and length focused on community education; these sessions did not include community-building activities but instead engaged participants in educational activities designed to increase their knowledge, skills, and confidence in negotiating the AIDS service system. Finally, one-third of participants in each wave were assigned to a control condition in which they did not take part in any workshops. To track the impact of participation, all participants completed an extensive self-report battery of attitudinal, behavior, and mental health measures at baseline (enrollment in the study), again soon after they completed their workshops, and again several months later, with the timing of control group assessments corresponding to the two intervention conditions.

Our analyses of the data collapsing over waves suggest that the community-building intervention did indeed enhance psychological sense of community both in comparison to the other conditions and between baseline and follow-up assessments. Participants who took part in the community-building intervention also reported less negative affect, more safer-sex and self-protective behaviors, greater intentions and reports of community-enhancing social action (e.g., giving money and goods to charity, joining community groups and organizations, participating in social activism), and increased intentions to help and educate others, at least as compared to participants in the no workshop control condition.

This is precisely the pattern of results that we predicted and it illustrates the power of a situational manipulation, in keeping with social psychological approaches, to impact subsequent attitudes, affect, and reports of behavior. Because we used an experimental design, again consistent with a good deal of traditional social psychological research, we have increased confidence that psychological sense of community is what caused people to take action benefiting themselves, others, and the broader social system. In this intervention study, sense of community was by design a broad and overarching construct that incorporated a number of more specific social psychological mechanisms—norms, expectations, belonging, social support—any of which alone or in combination could be responsible for the obtained effects.

What we also know, however, is that the benefits attributable to the sense of community intervention are associated with individual-level scores on a measure of psychological sense of community that we included in the questionnaire battery. That is, taking the perspective of a personality psychologist, we examined individual differences in a measure of psychological sense of community with people affected by HIV and AIDS concurrently and prospectively. Scores on this measure predicted the outcomes of interest. Thus, although this research started with what might be described as a social psychological approach, by incorporating an individual difference measure (as would be consistent with a personality perspective), we were able to make more refined predictions and better hone in on the likely explanatory variable. It is not necessarily uncommon for researchers to marry situational manipulations with corresponding individual difference measures of related constructs as one way to integrate personality and social psychology. This is typically done in a series of studies, some using a situational manipulation and some a measured variable approach. In our work, we have simply combined these approaches in a single study.

The results of this study have theoretical and practical implications. The study informs theorizing and research on sense of community, coping, help-seeking and help-giving, as well as broader social action. It also addresses practical considerations related to how to more effectively engage people in issues related to HIV disease, including care and advocacy, and especially for people who are HIV-infected. Related to this last point, the results of this study appear to hold even when examining data only for HIV-infected participants. And, it has clear practical implications for AIDS service organizations, as well as other types of organizations and institutions, that seek to mobilize people around causes and to encourage them to work on behalf of those causes and impacted communities.

Additional Contexts and Types of Policy Involvement

Together, these examples illustrate some possible ways that personality and social psychology can be integrated in policy-relevant research. There are many other forms this integration can take as well as policy topics and social problems that can be addressed. The studies described above reflect different ways of combining individual difference measures with a concomitant focus on situational influences. The examples also reflect different ways of conducting action research; what the studies have in common is that they involved people impacted by policies and programs in their planning and implementation, they built on and extended psychological theory, and they were conducted in field-based settings using rigorous social scientific methodologies (including experimentation). The studies themselves and their results also led to practical recommendations for policies and practices related to the specific problem of how society can more effectively respond to the HIV epidemic, but also to more general concerns about how to reverse declining citizen involvement in civic institutions and increase volunteerism and other forms of social action (e.g., Putnam, 2000). In short, the research connects personality and social psychology while also intertwining basic and applied foci and methodologies in the interests of theoretical advance and helping to solve pressing social problems.

Conducting (any version of) action research is extremely difficult, and may not be possible or advisable for everyone. Moreover, there are other avenues by which research in personality and social psychology can influence policymaking and policymakers. For example, psychologists of all types can be called on to provide expert testimony or to help prepare amicus curiae briefs in court cases, or to otherwise work in judicial settings (Borgida & Fiske, 2008; Tremper, 1987). Psychologists may serve as consultants to advocacy organizations or lobbyists, they can conduct polling and message framing analyses on candidates and issues, and they can assist or agitate at the grass roots (Wittig & Bettencourt, 1996; Wollman, Lobenstine, Foderaro, & Stose, 2005). Personality and social psychologists can participate in policy work in legislative contexts, including by participating in public hearings, paying visits to key elected officials, and even helping to draft legislation (e.g., Melton, 1995; Shinn, 2007). Closer to home, they can engage in policy development and evaluation in their own workplaces, institutions (e.g., churches, schools), and even professional associations; all of these bodies make and enforce policies that regulate behaviors. Furthermore, personality and social psychologists can attempt to influence policies, leaders, and the public by writing op-ed pieces for newspapers, blogging, or offering other forms of social commentary (see Epstein, 2006; Sommer, 2006). And, of course, they can seek leadership offices. Their expertise and training in personality and social psychology may not uniquely qualify them for these offices, unless of course they are within professional associations, but serving as a leader or chief officer is clearly another avenue for directly influencing or determining the form and adoption of many social policies.

Across these many different contexts and activities, it can be speculated that there may be social policy domains that better align with personality or social psychological orientations. In fact, it may be that personality and social psychologists will be differentially effective or perhaps differentially comfortable participating in policy work in different realms. For example, many policy decisions, or decisions with policy implications, are made in the judicial system. This is true in the United States as well as in other countries throughout the world. In most court cases, a decision is rendered about a single case. This case may test general legal conventions and understanding, or it may be seen as an exemplar of a class of individuals or cases. When a decision is rendered on a specific case, that decision often has implications for other similar cases or legal questions (e.g., as when a type of law or practice is struck down by a judicial decision). In these instances, broad policies flow from what might be characterized as an inductive process, going from a specific case to a general class. Of course, certain (sympathetic) cases are sometimes intentionally chosen by attorneys and advocacy groups to bring a policy issue to the fore, but the decision is still made about the case at hand and then generalized to include other similar or matching cases. This focus on idiographic, individual case information, reflective of what might be considered a case study approach, has the look and feel of a good deal of personality theorizing and research. Consequently, personality psychologists may find work in the judicial realm a comfortable fit, at least as compared to other policy contexts.

Another realm in which policies are developed and adopted, at least in democratic organizations and nation-states, are when votes are cast to determine outcomes. So, for example, citizen ballot initiatives, coalition government negotiations, and different versions of "majority rule," are all used to make decisions about adopting, modifying, or rejecting policies. Effectiveness in this policy realm hinges on convincing the most number of people or the most influential individuals to take a particular side or to adopt a specific policy or stance. In short, social psychological processes involving conformity, persuasion, norms, and consensus-building, if not illusions of all of these, play critical roles. A single case example can help to persuade a skeptical electorate, but the decision itself is made by the collective voice, as influenced by the context and current social climate. This focus on normative, group, or consensual processes would seem to be a good fit with social psychological theories and explanatory mechanisms. As such, electoral and legislative realms may be relatively easy for social psychologists to understand and in which to work.

Returning to one of the initial assumptions of this chapter, personality and social psychologists can and should be concerned with policy. They may not have the resources, interest, or wherewithal to conduct action research, but they can work on social policy in a number of different ways and in a wide variety of contexts in which policies are made and influence behavior. It is reasonable and understandable for psychologists to feel more comfortable and to be of greatest value when participating in policy work on topics on which they have expertise, such as when they offer expert opinion in an area in which they have conducted research. Regardless of issue expertise, though, it is reasonable to consider what psychologists who integrate personality and social psychology bring to any policy table in terms of perspective and commitment. Posed as a question, even if they do not conduct policy-relevant research themselves or do not have a wealth of topic-specific knowledge, how might the perspectives of these psychologists contribute to policy debates?

If there is any truth in some of the distinctions that have been outlined between personality and social psychologists, then integrating personality and social psychological perspectives should lead to relatively complex, nuanced, and postpartisan policies that are also well grounded in theory and rigorous research. That is, rather than set policies or develop programs for only those people afflicted by a disease, who are marked by a condition, or who

are currently in need of assistance, a personality perspective would call attention to the other end of the spectrum and to the people who are not currently affected and their trajectory or likelihood of being impacted in the future. Personality psychologists may have preferred traits or characteristics that they study, and even in ends of continua (e.g., narcissists, right wing authoritarians, extraverts), but analyses from this perspective also often consider the full range of manifestations or scores on traits or characteristics. Many social policies, however, focus only on a "high" or "low" end of a dimension, with that end also often being "problematized" (e.g., problems of illicit drug users, the personal and social consequences of homelessness, criminal tendencies of the socially deviant, or even educational needs of gifted children).

Social psychological analyses, on the other hand, are likely to emphasize the pressure of situations, social and normative influences, as well as structural inequities that give rise to conditions of disparity or social problems. The "fault" for problems would not necessarily be nested within individuals, but instead, in the life circumstances and current social contexts that are likely to produce problematic behavior in nearly any person. In keeping with this identified cause, proposed policy solutions would likely target systemic influences and broad-based social factors. Instead of targeting and fixing the person, a social psychological perspective would include careful analysis of operative situational pressures and efforts to change reward contingencies and salient causal factors in the problematic setting. It would also not be inconsistent for the social psychologist to note the uniqueness of local conditions and situations and to factor these into policy recommendations.

Thus, the integration of personality and social psychology should result in complex analyses of social issues, and probably relatively large and encompassing strategies for solution. Much as an interactionist perspective in research blends attention to personality or individual differences with systematic situational variation, an integrated psychologist who is also interested in social policy would want a dual focus on who is and is not impacted (the personality continuum) with situational vulnerabilities and affordances that give rise to the problem (the social psychological perspective). That is, the classic person x situation interaction could be framed either as a question about why certain people appear to manifest problems in a given setting while others do not, or as a question about how certain situations or circumstances seem to be conducive to particular (mis)behaviors among individuals from particular social strata, or who have specific political ideologies, or who possess certain traits or characteristics. Regardless of the framing of these problems, social policies are unlikely to be focused on only the people manifesting the problem in the current environment. To do so, and indeed as is often currently done, would be deemed a short-term fix for integrated psychologists. They might point out that other interventions or policies may be necessary for these same people in different settings, or for people who do not currently manifest the problem in this particular setting. With recognition of the dynamic and interdependent nature of the person and setting, social policies will likely need to be changed, tweaked, or disbanded as they take hold and affect people and their settings.

These integrated psychologists are also likely to offer broad-scale interventions and policy recommendations that cut across different levels of analysis or explanation. This may mean that they would offer policy recommendations that are more ambitious and far-reaching than policies typically considered. Many social policies are relatively simple at a conceptual level, but complicated in their implementation. They may aim to impact an entire class of people without regard to circumstance, or they are focused on changing circumstances so as to be the same for all people. A policy analysis that simultaneously considers differences between people and circumstances as espoused by an integrated personality and social psychologist is likely to look very different.

In addition to this broader perspective that is projected in time and across levels of analysis, the psychologist who integrates personality and social psychology in policy work may be able to speak to political conservatives and political liberals (at least as they are traditionally constructed in the United States) as they view the causes and solutions to many social problems. Although the social issues on which the individual is likely to weigh in may have a liberal bent, reflecting psychology's general affinity for liberal causes and viewpoints (Redding, 2001), politically conservative policymakers may be more likely to resonate to personality-based analyses whereas political liberals may be more likely to embrace a social psychological analysis and set of solutions. Building on these speculative differences, then, integrated personality and social psychologists may be able to converse with and convince a broader range of the political spectrum as compared to psychologists working from either perspective alone.

Finally, personality and social psychologists are likely to share a commitment to research and data. They are likely to be concerned about collecting data in order to accurately diagnose a problem as well as to evaluate the effectiveness of implemented policy programs or interventions. This commitment to empirical observation and data, to not being swayed by vivid case examples, and to being willing to look beyond if not disprove commonsense and intuition, can be of considerable value in many policy realms. The integrated personality and social psychologist has training and appreciation for research methodology in the social sciences and can easily discern rigor in research, including being able to judge what may be less reliable and valid conclusions on which to base policy decisions. This focus and commitment can help scientific psychologists in a policy realm because their arguments are grounded in observation and data rather than solely in opinion, values, and political ideology. That is, they may be less likely to be seen as politically motivated, they may enter the political fray from a more dispassionate stance than clear advocates or political "hacks," and it is possible that their contributions consequently may be less likely to be discounted. In short, the scientific mantel may offer respect and entrée that are not accorded to others. Certainly, there is no escaping the criticism that the "facts" of psychological science are inextricably linked to ideology and the worldviews of those who conduct the research. However, the attempt to push beyond these confines in order to see without the blinders of ideology, party affiliation, or moral judgment—that is, to base conclusions on empirical observations that are the result of agreed on rigorous scientific methods—is a scientific value that is decidedly not shared by all stakeholders in policy debates but that an integrated personality and social psychologist would likely bring to the policy table.

Systemic Influences on Policy Involvement

So far, this chapter has touched on some of the key points of the action research tradition (Lewin, 1946/1997) and its blueprint for combining basic, applied, and policy agendas in social science research. In addition, some of the distinctive features of personality and social psychology have been reviewed, including with speculation on possible implications for social policy work. Examples were presented of policy-relevant research that attempts to integrate personality and social psychological perspectives, and there was also discussion of alternative avenues and realms for policy involvement by personality and social psychologists. In the final sections of this chapter, a set of systemic barriers to policy involvement that confront personality and social psychology separately and together will be outlined along with suggestions for overcoming these barriers. Framed another way, it may be worth asking, given the great potential, what it is that seems to be keeping personality and social psychology from coming together and more actively engaging in social policy research, development, and evaluation?

The answer to this question is not likely to be easy, straightforward, or even testable. It should be pointed out, however, that some possible answers have already been uncovered: action research is difficult to do, many social policy domains and activities fall outside people's "comfort zones," and personality and social psychology may not see problems in the same way or speak with a single voice in identifying causes or in making policy recommendations for problem amelioration.

Professional Societies and Professional Socialization

Another possible answer harkens back to Lewin, who was not only concerned with the interdependence of persons and their environments, but also with formalization and the pursuit of psychological laws and theories (Lewin, 1940/1997). Although not speaking specifically about personality or social psychology but rather psychology in general (reflecting the state of the times), Lewin stressed the need for definitive and rather immediate steps toward formalization if psychology was to achieve status as "an acceptable science" (p. 171). He made numerous suggestions and offered words of warning about the nature and timing of formalization and theorizing too, but one of his main messages was that psychology as an empirical science needed to embrace theory and the possibility of general psychological laws and propositions.

This appears to be the message that has had considerable uptake among personality and social psychologists. Indeed, a wealth of narrow, even "midrange" theories have been proposed in personality and social psychology over the last half century, and so much so that there have been calls for greater theoretical integration and for the development of training tools and reward structures that encourage creative, integrative, and "bigger" theorizing (Kruglanski, 2001). Theoretical frameworks that better integrate personality and social psychological constructs could certainly fit this bill, and would

probably result in a more holistic view of human beings than is offered by many microlevel theories that focus on processes and mechanisms without regard to social context and integration.

In their excitement to pursue formalization and theoretical work as presaged by Lewin, however, personality and social psychologists may have inadvertently or intentionally turned away from each other and from engagement in policy topics and research. Possible evidence for this speculation can be found in an informal analysis of the self-descriptive statements of some of the professional associations relevant to personality and social psychology. As noted at the outset, professional associations and organizations can and do set policies that regulate the behaviors of their members (see also Deaux & Snyder, chapter 33, this volume). These policies can be explicitly stated or can be less conspicuously communicated through norms, priorities, mission statements, and practices. Thus, it is not unreasonable to look at mission statements and organizational descriptions in an attempt to get a handle on some of the priorities and barriers that impact work in personality and social psychology. This analysis reveals what appears to be a shared neglect of applied research as well as nonrecognition of policy work as within the purview of personality and social psychology.

Take, for example, the description statement for the largest current player in personality and social psychology, the Society for Personality and Social Psychology (SPSP). This society purports to have over 7,000 members and to be the largest organization of personality and social psychologists in the world. What is most telling for current purposes is that SPSP's description statement—what it publicly communicates about itself and the goals of personality and social psychology—makes no explicit mention either of social policy or of applications and applied research: "The Society promotes scientific research in personality and social psychology by publishing scientific journals, organizing an annual conference, sponsoring activities that foster professional development among students and faculty, and maintaining close ties with science advocacy offices" (Society for Personality and Social Psychology, 2011). It would appear that the primary goals of SPSP and its members are to support *scientific* research in personality and social psychology and communicating this work to fellow scientists. This statement does not mention the translation of findings into policies or practically oriented research on social policies or societal problems.

SPSP is not alone in this regard. The Society for Experimental Social Psychology (roughly 800 members) and the European Association for Social Psychology (approximately 1,000 members), two smaller associations of social psychologists, likewise stress their scientific base and share goals of advancing research in social psychology (European Association for Social Psychology, 2011; Society for Experimental Social Psychology, 2011). Neither of these organizations includes personality research in their missions, and there are no statements that refer to policy, application, or practical concerns. The relatively new Association for Research in Personality, founded in 2001, has a mission statement similar in form to SPSP's, emphasizing the scientific study of personality, and making no mention of social psychology or applied or policy research or analyses (Association for Research in Personality, 2011). The founders of this organization, many of whom were also active members of SPSP, apparently felt that the vibrancy and wealth of personality psychology was not being served within SPSP, and thus they formed a separate society. At the same time, however, they appear to have neglected to actively embrace policy involvement.

As revealed by this analysis, personality and social psychology seem to be moving apart and claiming more circumscribed territories, with neither choosing to annex the wilderness of social policy. It could be argued that policy-relevant research falls within the scope of the science each society aims to support. However, the failure of the society statements to mention policy along with the explicit focus on scientific audiences would seem to suggest otherwise. These societies reflect and influence the priorities of their fields and are also contexts for the professional socialization and development of newer scholars. As such, and as gauged by their mission statements, they may be creating systemic barriers to the integration of personality and social psychology as well as barriers to social policy research and involvement.

To be fair, there is at least one society, the Society for the Psychological Study of Social Issues (SPSSI), that espouses interest in social issues and policies. In its description statement, however, SPSSI claims no special allegiance to personality or social psychology: "SPSSI is an association of approximately 3000 psychologists, allied scientists, and others, who are interested in the application of research on the psychological aspects of important social issues to public policy solutions" (Society for the Psychological Study of Social Issues, 2011). SPSSI does publish journals focused on social issues and policy, with two different journals with the word "policy" in their titles begun just in the past decade (i.e., *Analyses of Social Issues and Public Policy* started in 2001, and *Social Issues and Policy Review* initiated in 2007). Thus, SPSSI would seem to be an ideal home for personality and social psychologists interested in applied and policy work, but it is relatively small and more broadly constituted than just personality and social psychologists or even just psychologists.

Policy work, although apparently relatively neglected by contemporary personality and social psychologists and their professional associations, ironically, might also offer an ideal opportunity for bringing them together. As has been noted, should they choose to enter the policy fray, personality and social psychologists are likely to come from different but complementary perspectives. Emphasizing a superordinate goal of improving and evaluating social policy may be one way of reducing the indifference if not enmity that seems to have developed between them. That is, principles for reducing group conflict or for finding a common ingroup identity (Gaertner & Dovidio, 2000; Dovidio, Gaertner, & Saguy, 2009) might reasonably be applied to personality and social psychologists. Thus, tackling common and superordinate problems, as in the case of policy concerns, might provide a venue for reducing prejudice and unease (e.g., Sherif, 1956). It might also provide impetus for further advancements in both fields, and to the extent that new and integrated policies are useful, help gain credibility and esteem from stakeholders and the public at large. In short, cooperation between personality and social psychologists as occasioned by policy involvement may be good for all concerned.

Training Programs

Obviously, though, this may be more difficult in practice than in concept. For successful integration and policy involvement, training programs will need to be revamped and refocused. Rather than a singular focus on personality or social psychology, or even a dual personality-social emphasis, a three-legged foundational stool that includes training in personality, social psychology, and policy will need to be developed and implemented. Among the topics policy training could reasonably include are applied research methods, participatory approaches, strategies for communicating with nonspecialists (including orally and in writing), policy and cost-benefit analyses, evaluation practices, with any or all of these supplemented with practical experiences and internships.

In addition, it is typical for policy problems to be approached with a variety of tools and even from multiple disciplinary angles. Within academic institutions and some funding agencies, there is a growing push to develop interdisciplinary research teams and to address theoretical and applied problems from a variety of perspectives. This integrated approach, not only across personality and social psychology, but across a number of social science disciplines, not incidentally, was also advocated by Lewin in his model of action research. To work effectively in many policy realms, therefore, personality and social psychologists not only will have to get along with each other, but to rub shoulders and learn from and with their brethren in other social sciences (e.g., Pettigrew, 1988).

It is not clear that such training programs or models currently exist. The Social Psychology Network is an electronic resource that purports to maintain a database of more than 300 social-personality graduate programs in psychology from 45 countries (Social Psychology Network, 2011a). One feature of this Web site is that it permits a search of graduate programs by keywords and displays results on a map of the world (Social Psychology Network, 2011b). A search using the keyword "policy" revealed a total of two PhD programs, one located in the United States and one in Finland, and no masters programs. Using the more general (but not synonymous) keyword "applied," rather than "policy," resulted in a total of 15 graduate programs worldwide, nine of which (all PhD) were located in North America. None of the programs that were identified in either search had "personality" in their titles; they were primarily described as programs in "Applied Social Psychology." As suggested by this exercise, the separation of personality and social psychology is less complete than the separation of either or both of these fields from policy and applied concerns, at least in terms of formal training models and degrees. If personality and social psychology are to be better integrated and also connected to social policy work, then training programs must be developed and also named in ways that make these connections obvious.

Reward Structures
Along with training models, reward structures are likely to require realignment so that engagement and dissemination outside the academy is valued. On this point it should be noted that greater involvement in policy work is consistent with emphases on the scholarship of engagement (e.g., Boyer, 1990, 1996) and the development of community-university partnerships. The scholarship of engagement, which in some quarters is known as outreach scholarship, public scholarship, community-based scholarship, or community-engaged scholarship, presents an integrated model for academics. There is considerable overlap and mutual reinforcement among teaching, research, and service activities, with these activities also providing benefit to the external (nonuniversity) community. In recent years, American universities have increasingly been asked to justify themselves and their practices and to prove their worth. The scholarship of engagement and direct policy involvement provide opportunities for universities and scholars to do just that.

Of course, there are many policy practitioners trained in personality and social psychology working outside of the academy. A challenge for professional societies and training programs, then, is to figure out ways to keep these individuals connected and visible, including encouraging them to publish in personality and social psychology outlets. There need to be benefits for them of continuing involvement and they need to be appreciated and valued in their disciplinary homes. Should personality and social psychology take up the challenge of more actively and intentionally engaging in policy work, then these potentially contentious issues will need to be addressed head-on.

Furthermore, as academic institutions continue to shrink and tenure-track faculty positions become rarer, pressure is likely to increase to find or develop alternative career opportunities outside academia, both for the viability of the field as a whole as well as for the survival of individuals within it. An obvious alternative at this point would appear to be policy work of many different types. Thus, there are several potential upsides to helping train and encourage policy work among personality and social psychologists. Doing so may lead to interdisciplinary collaboration and novel approaches to vexing theoretical and practical problems, it could lay the groundwork for increased respect and appreciation from nonacademic audiences, and it would enhance the marketability and career opportunities for newly trained or even seasoned personality and social psychologists.

Forward, with Caution
There are very real challenges to integrating personality and social psychology and engaging in policy work. However, there appear to be clear potential benefits to doing so. Having discussed some of the most obvious systemic influences on policy involvement, it

may be relatively easy to envision paths that, even if difficult, could take personality and social psychologists to a promised land of greater policy involvement. In moving forward, though, there are some points of caution to note. In particular, and briefly, personality and social psychologists embarking on the journey of policy involvement should: (1) beware academic and scientific hubris and remind themselves to work within their own limits, (2) recognize their own potential biases in terms of political leanings and ideological beliefs, and (3) take care not to overpromise on what they can deliver.

Psychologists, Not Policymakers

The first caution about engaging in policy work for personality and social psychologists is to remember that their expertise is in research methodology and psychological theory, and not in policy analyses or political processes. Policy work, including law-making and legislative processes, are said to be like making sausage. It may be unrealistic, therefore, to expect personality and social psychologists, even with the advantages of an integrated perspective, to be able to effectively navigate the political hurdles likely to be encountered in policy work. Ignorance of policy processes and pragmatic and political considerations are likely to frustrate well-meaning psychologists, and especially those armed with data who believe that the "truth" or "facts" that they possess should hold sway.

Related to this issue, and especially for personality and social psychologists who work in academic settings, is the simple observation that scientific or academic hubris can undermine effective work in many policy realms. Typically, psychologists will not be the policymakers (unless, of course, they are setting policy for their academic department, consulting agency, or professional society), and they must remain cognizant of their roles as well as the limits of their expertise and data (e.g., WEIRD samples). The high-minded scientist who merely deigns to partake in policy activities is likely to draw dislike and disdain from more experienced policymakers, and may elicit resistance or blatant reactance to their policy recommendations. In addition, a good deal of policy work depends on and is influenced by personal relationships, including relationships between policymakers, constituents, stakeholders, and other associates. Personality and social psychologists can offer their expertise in policy realms, but they will need to do so in a collaborative manner. They may do well, in fact, to follow some of what they know about interpersonal relationships, persuasion processes, and intergroup identities and relations in order to be more effective spokespersons for their science and perspectives.

In addition, the preferences and metabolism of research psychologists and policymakers are not necessarily compatible. Personality and social psychologists strive for scientific certainty, including reliable measurement, replicable results, and cross-validation of findings. They are methodical in their work, at least collectively if not individually, and this may mean that they work on a problem for years or even entire careers; the pace of work can be slow and deliberate, with small incremental increases in knowledge a reasonable benchmark for accomplishment. Policymakers, on the other hand, are often called on to make decisions in the face of uncertainty and in response to unforeseen circumstances and events. Certainty is a luxury that they cannot often afford. Similarly, policy decisions and program implementation often must be quick and decisive, either in response to immediate and pressing problems or at least before the next election cycle and the end of a term of office. To work effectively in policy contexts, then, personality and social psychologists may need to alter their own preferences and work styles, or even learn how to separate and respect their concerns from the priorities and goals of policymakers.

Political Ideology and Policy

Although it may go without saying, political and ideological views influence social policies. They also may influence topics, positions, approaches, and even conclusions drawn from data. And, they may complicate policy debates and policy formation, creating additional hurdles to overcome in arriving at (mutually agreeable) decisions. Psychology in general, has been branded as having a liberal bias, or at least as dominated by people with liberal political views (e.g., Redding, 2001; see Tierney, 2011, for discussion of a similar charge against social psychology). Consequently, personality and social psychologists interested in policy work may more naturally and easily work with or for liberal causes and with actors on the political left. People can hardly be faulted for working for causes in which they believe or about which they have strong opinions, and these personal commitments should not be assumed to diminish effectiveness. It can be argued, for example, that lobbyists are some of the most influential players in policy formulation and also some of the best sources of information on policy topics, and this is true *despite the fact* that their agendas are well known or easily discerned.

For some, the ostensible liberal bias of psychology contradicts the values of cultural diversity and inclusion that are embedded in the field, and has resulted in a general lack of sociopolitical diversity among psychologists. In this view, "conservatives and conservative views are vastly underrepresented in psychology" (Redding, 2001, p. 205), with a similar criticism recently having been leveled at personality and social psychology along with an explicit call for recruiting more political conservatives into professional societies (see Haidt, 2011; Tierney, 2011). In addition to offering several examples that he believes illustrate how liberal bias in psychology influences social policy research and the conclusions drawn from the research, Redding provides an analysis of articles published in the *American Psychologist* between 1990 and 1999 and the *Journal of Social Issues* (a SPSSI journal). He reports that over 95% of the articles published in both journals could be classified as expressing liberal political views.

Redding's article, regardless of whether its recommendations for more research from a conservative perspective is heeded, raises critical issues about how psychologists and their work are perceived by policymakers and also how psychology's liberal bent may work against effectiveness in a variety of policy and nonpolicy settings. The article goes on to suggest several strategies for increasing political diversity in psychology, including suggesting that advocacy be separated from psychological science. On this point the argument goes that a good deal of advocacy by and for psychology is based on specific liberal values and viewpoints and not on data. The concern is that psychologists trade on their professional status in pushing for liberal social policies even in the absence of sufficient data; this is intellectually dishonest and may undermine the field as a whole.

As provocative as these ideas may be, and indeed, they may offer proof of the health of American psychology and of personality and social psychology by the fact that they have received large stages on which to play, they actually say relatively little about how psychology intersects with the public and social policy work. As noted earlier, psychologists can engage in policy-relevant work in a variety of professional and nonprofessional contexts and on a wide range of topics and issues. Policy and policymakers are seldom value-free, so having a liberal (or conservative) viewpoint should not disqualify a person from policy involvement. What may be key in this regard is possessing the ability to clearly recognize and "own" a partisan point of view rather than

attempting to "pass" as unbiased or objective (see also Harris & Nicholson, 1998; Tetlock 1994). As personality and social psychologists increase their involvement in social policy work, therefore, they would do well to reflect on their political leanings and ideological stances, or perhaps even to consciously opt to work on only certain issues or causes.

Scale of Impact: Promises and Aspirations
Finally, personality and social psychologists should be careful not to overpromise constituents or to set their sights higher than can be reasonably achieved. That is, as integrated personality and social psychologists involve themselves in policy work to a greater extent, they may expect that their policies will have profound influence and lasting impact. They have a wealth of knowledge about human behavior, can see the nuance of social problems, and may be likely to advocate for complex and sweeping solutions; that is, they may gravitate toward supporting large interventions that will wipe away the problem forever. Moreover, to fail in this endeavor would be to fail humanity and also be a loud and negative statement about the value of an integrated personality and social psychology, or even psychology more generally, for social policy work.

Large-scale problems may in the end require large-scale solutions. However, an underappreciated and more realistic approach is to aim for small-scale solutions, including breaking down a large problem into more manageable and tractable component problems (Weick, 1984). Thus, to make progress addressing seeming intractable social problems, psychologists (or even policymakers and concerned citizens) need to focus on potential "small wins." The war against poverty, obesity, or terrorism is not likely to be won by a single reform or solution, but rather, by way of many incremental and small-scale victories. As suggested by Weick nearly a quarter century ago, appreciating the psychology of small wins can recalibrate expectations for success and aid in the plotting of strategies for creating greater change.

Thus, personality and social psychologists should not expect nor promise that they can solve a major policy problem from the get-go, but rather, they may be wise to be more circumspect in their aspirations and efforts. If psychologists judge their impact on social problems against a standard of eliminating or solving a problem, they likely will be disappointed. The field and its enthusiasm for policy work will suffer. To the extent that high expectations have been created for policymakers, the public, or other consumers, failure will also result in lost confidence and greater skepticism. Setting policy aspirations a little closer and smaller, at least at the outset, would be one way of helping to demonstrate success and build confidence in the approach being peddled. In keeping with the psychology of small wins, a series of small-scale successes may soften the ground for future success while also providing a more solid foundation on which to build larger scale interventions, policies, and even psychological theorizing.

Summary and Concluding Comments

This chapter has taken a long and winding road in covering selective biases, barriers, and opportunities for personality and social psychologists to be involved in social policy work of different types. At one time, personality and social psychology were closely and inextricably linked to each other, but also to social policy research and involvement. These linkages are perhaps most obviously seen in the action research tradition (Lewin, 1946/1997). It appears that since Lewin's time, personality and social psychology have advanced and matured as separate subdisciplines, linked by a common intellectual history, but not fully comfortable with their connection. As personality and social psychology have moved to distinguish themselves from each other, including by way of founding separate professional associations and journals, they seem to have followed parallel paths of focusing on scientific and theoretical advance more than on applied issues and concerns. It also appears that the commitment to fuller engagement with society has waned, including less active participation in social policy development and evaluation.

As this chapter has attempted to make clear, however, there is considerable potential for personality and social psychology, and personality and social psychologists, to contribute to policy work on a host of issues and in a variety of different contexts and realms. Currently, it would appear that only a small part of this potential is being realized, and what little of it there is, not necessarily enjoying a very high profile. There are meaningful and important differences between personality and social psychology that should not be discounted because they likely have implications for how social problems are understood and for the social policies offered to address these problems.

Nonetheless, it is possible to integrate personality and social psychology in policy-relevant research, as well as to see the perspectives as complementary rather than mutually exclusive in what they might bring to policy development and evaluation. A reorientation of the fields and some revamping of training programs may be necessary in order to realize more of the potential of an integrated personality and social psychology for social policy. By all indications, these efforts should be worthwhile and need to be encouraged. Reengagement in social policy is likely to have salutary effects for increasing public faith and esteem, for the pragmatic concern of creating employment opportunities for personality and social psychologists, for scientific advance in theory and methods, and for the practical and societal concern of creating effective solutions to pressing social problems.

References

Allik, J. & Realo, A. (2004). Individualism-collectivism and social capital. *Journal of Cross-Cultural Psychology, 35,* 29–49.

Allport, G. W. (1985). The historical background of social psychology. In G. Lindzey & E. Aronson (Eds.), *The handbook of social psychology* (3rd ed., Vol. 1, pp. 1–46). New York: Random House.

American Psychological Association (2010). Brief of *Amicus Curiae* Perry v. Schwarzenegger, US Court of Appeals for the Ninth Circuit. Washington, DC: Author.

Anderson, C. A., Lindsay, J. J., & Bushman, B. J. (1999). Research in the psychological laboratory: Truth or triviality? *Current Directions in Psychological Science, 8,* 3–9.

Association for Research in Personality (2011). *Association for Research in Personality*. Retrieved March 21, 2011, from http://www.personality-arp.org/index.htm.

Baron, J., Bazerman, M. H., & Shonk, K. (2006). Enlarging the societal pie through wise legislation: A psychological perspective. *Perspectives on Psychological Science, 1,* 123–132.

Biernat, M. (2003). Toward a broader view of social stereotyping. *American Psychologist, 58,* 1019–1027.

Biernat, M. (2005). *Standards and expectancies: Contrast and assimilation in judgments.* New York: Psychology Press/Taylor and Francis.

Bohan, J. S. (1993). Regarding gender: Essentialism, constructionism, and feminist psychology. *Psychology of Women Quarterly, 17,* 5–22.

Borgida, E., & Fiske, S. T. (2008). *Beyond common sense: Psychological science in the courtroom.* Malden, MA: Blackwell.

Boyer, E. (1990). *Scholarship reconsidered: Priorities of the professoriate.* Princeton, NJ: Carnegie Foundation for the Advancement of Teaching.

Boyer, E. (1996). The scholarship of engagement. *Journal of Public Service and Outreach, 1,* 11–20.

Caplan, N., & Nelson, S. D. (1973). On being useful: The nature and consequences of psychological research on social problems. *American Psychologist, 28,* 199–211.

Carroll, J., Perkowitz, W., Lurigio, A., & Weaver, K. (1987). Sentencing goals, causal attributions, and personality. *Journal of Personality and Social Psychology, 52,* 107-118.

Chamberlain, J., Miller, M. K., & Bornstein, B. H. (2008). The rights and responsibilities of gay and lesbian parents: Legal developments, psychological research, and policy implications. *Social Issues and Policy Review, 2,* 103–126.

Chein, I., Cook, S. W., & Harding, J. (1948). The field of action research. *American Psychologist, 3,* 43–50.

Cialdini, R. B. (1980). Full-cycle social psychology. In L. Bickman (Ed.), *Applied social psychology annual* (Vol. 1, pp. 21–47). Beverly Hills, CA: Sage.

Clary, E. G., Snyder, M., Ridge, R. D., Copeland, J. T., Stukas, A. A., Haugen, J. A., et al. (1998). Understanding and assessing the motivations of volunteers: A functional approach. *Journal of Personality and Social Psychology, 74,* 1516–1530.

Curtis, J. E., Grabb, E., & Baer, D. (1992). Voluntary association membership in fifteen countries: A comparative analysis. *American Sociological Review, 57,* 139–152.

Darley, J., & Latané, B (1968). Group inhibition of bystander intervention in emergencies. *Journal of Personality and Social Psychology, 10,* 215–221.

Deaux, K. (2006). *To be an immigrant.* New York: Russell Sage.

Deaux, K., Esses, V. M., Lalonde, R. N., & Brown, R. (Eds.). (2010). Immigrants and hosts: Perceptions, interactions, and transformations. *Journal of Social Issues,* (Vol. 66, No. 4). Hoboken, NJ: Wiley-Blackwell.

DeLeon, P. H. (1986). Increasing the societal contribution of organized psychology. *American Psychologist, 41,* 466–474.

DeLeon, P. H. (1988). Public policy and public service: Our professional duty. *American Psychologist, 43,* 309–315.

Donaldson, S. I. & Scriven, M. (2003). *Evaluating social programs and problems: Visions for the new millennium.* Mahwah, NJ: Erlbaum.

Dovidio, J. F., Gaertner, S. L., & Saguy, T. (2009). Commonality and the complexity of "we": Social attitudes and social change. *Personality and Social Psychology Review, 13,* 3–20.

Eagly, A. H., & Carli, L. L. (2007). *Through the labyrinth: The truth about how women become leaders.* Boston: Harvard Business School Press.

Eagly, A. H., & Karau, S. J. (2002). Role congruity theory of prejudice toward female leaders. *Psychological Review, 109,* 573–598.

Epstein, R. (2006). Giving psychology away: A personal journey. *Perspectives on Psychological Science, 1,* 389–400.

European Association for Social Psychology (2011). *European Association for Social Psychology.* Retrieved March 21, 2011, from http://www.easp.eu/

Fast, L. A., & Funder, D. C. (2008). Personality as manifest in word use: Correlations with self-report, acquaintance-report, and behavior. *Journal of Personality and Social Psychology, 94,* 334–346.

Fisher, W. A., Kohut, T., & Fisher, J. D. (2009). AIDS exceptionalism: On the social psychology of HIV prevention research. *Social Issues and Policy Review, 3,* 45–77.

Fiske, S. T., Bersoff, D. N., Borgida, E., Deaux, K., & Heilman, M. E. (1991). Social science research on trial: Use of sex stereotyping research in *Price Waterhouse v. Hopkins. American Psychologist, 46,* 1049–1060.

Funder, D. C. (1999). *Personality judgment: A realistic approach to person perception.* San Diego, CA: Academic.

Gaertner, S. L., & Dovidio, J. F. (2000). *Reducing intergroup bias: The common ingroup identity model.* Philadelphia: Psychology Press.

Gergen, K. J. (1973). Social psychology as history. *Journal of Personality and Social Psychology, 26,* 309–320.

Gibson, B. (Ed.). (1997). Social science perspectives on tobacco policy. *Journal of Social Issues.* (Vol. 53, No. 1)). Hoboken, NJ: Wiley-Blackwell.

Gilbert, D. T. (1998). Ordinary personology. In D. T. Gilbert, S. T. Fiske, & G. Lindzey (Eds.), *The handbook of social psychology* (4th ed., Vol. 2, pp. 89–150). Boston: McGraw-Hill.

Gold, M. (1992). Metatheory and field theory in social psychology: Relevance or elegance? *Journal of Social Issues, 48,* 67–78.

Goldstein, N. J., Cialdini, R. B., & Griskevicius, V. (2008). A room with a viewpoint: Using social norms to motivate environmental conservation in hotels. *Journal of Consumer Research, 35,* 472–482.

Grube, J. W., Mayton, D. M., II, & Ball-Rokeach, S. J. (1994). Inducing change in values, attitudes, and behaviors: Belief system theory and the method of value self-confrontation. *Journal of Social Issues, 50,* 153–174.

Gurin, P., Dey, E. L., Hurtado, S., & Gurin, G. (2002). Diversity and higher education: Theory and impact on educational outcomes. *Harvard Educational Review, 72,* 330–366.

Haidt, J. (2011). *The bright future of post-partisan social psychology.* Retrieved March 21, 2011, from http://www.edge.org/3rd_culture/haidt11/haidt11_index.html

Harris, B., & Nicholson, I. (1998). Toward a history of psychological expertise. *Journal of Social Issues, 54,* 1–5.

Haslam, N., & Levy, S. R. (2006). Essentialist beliefs about homosexuality: Structure and implications for prejudice. *Personality and Social Psychology Bulletin, 32,* 471–485.

Hatzenbuehler, M. L. (2010). Social factors as determinants of mental health disparities in LGB populations: Implications for public policy. *Social Issues and Policy Review, 4,* 31–62.

Hegarty, P., & Pratto, F. (2001). Sexual orientation beliefs: Their relationship to anti-gay attitudes and biological determinist arguments. *Journal of Homosexuality, 41,* 121–135.

Heider, F. (1958). *The psychology of interpersonal relations.* Hillsdale, NJ: Erlbaum.

Henrich, J., Heine, S. J., & Norenzayan, A. (2010). The weirdest people in the world? *Behavioral and Brain Sciences, 33,* 61–135.

Herek, G. M. (2007). Confronting sexual stigma and prejudice: Theory and practice. *Journal of Social Issues, 63,* 905–925.

Herek, G. M. (2006). Legal recognition of same-sex relationships in the United States: A social science perspective. *American Psychologist, 61,* 607–621.

Houle, B. J., Sagarin, B. J., & Kaplan, M. F. (2005). A functional approach to volunteerism: Do volunteer motives predict task preference? *Basic and Applied Social Psychology, 27,* 337–344.

Jones, E. E., & Harris, V. A. (1967). The attribution of attitudes. *Journal of Experimental Social Psychology, 3,* 1–24.

Jones, E. E., Kanouse, D. E., Kelley, H. H., Nisbett, R. E., Valins, S., & Weiner, B. (Eds.). (1972). *Attribution: Perceiving the causes of behavior.* Morristown, NJ: General Learning Press.

Jones, E. E., & Nisbett, R. E. (1971). *The actor and the observer: Divergent perceptions of the causes of behavior.* New York: General Learning Press.

Jost, J. T. (2006). The end of the end of ideology. *American Psychologist, 61,* 651–670.

Jost, J. T., Banaji, M. R., & Nosek, B. A. (2004). A decade of system justification theory: Accumulated evidence of conscious and unconscious bolstering of the status quo. *Political Psychology, 25,* 881–919.

Jost, J. T., Glaser, J., Kruglanski, A. W., & Sulloway, F. (2003). Political conservatism as motivated social cognition. *Psychological Bulletin, 129,* 339–375.

Kallgren, C. A., Reno, R. R., & Cialdini, R. B. (2000). A focus theory of normative conduct: When norms do and do not affect behavior. *Personality and Social Psychology Bulletin, 26,* 1002–1012.

Keizer, K., Lindenberg, L., & Steg, L. (2008). The spreading of disorder. *Science, 322,* 1681–1685.

Kolar, D., Funder, D. C., & Colvin, C. R. (1996). Comparing the accuracy of personality judgments by the self and knowledgeable others. *Journal of Personality, 64,* 313–337.

Krantz, D. S. (1978). The social context of obesity research: Another perspective on its place in the field of social psychology. *Personality and Social Psychology Bulletin, 4,* 177–184.

Kruglanski, A. W. (2001). That "vision thing": The state of theory in social and personality psychology at the edge of the new millennium. *Journal of Personality and Social Psychology, 80,* 871–875.

Langer, E. J., & Rodin, J. (1976). The effects of choice and enhanced personal responsibility for the aged: A field experiment in an institutional setting. *Journal of Personality and Social Psychology, 34,* 191–198.

Latané, B., & Nida, S. (1981). Ten years of research on group size and helping. *Psychological Bulletin, 89,* 308–332.

Lerner, M. J. (1980). *The belief in a just world: A fundamental delusion.* New York: Plenum.

Levine, M., & Crowther, S. (2008). The responsive bystander: How social group membership and group size can encourage as well as inhibit bystander intervention. *Journal of Personality and Social Psychology, 95,* 1429–1439.

Lewin, K. (1940/1997). Formalization and progress in psychology. In K. Lewin, *Resolving social conflicts and field theory in social science* (pp. 169–190). Washington, DC: American Psychological Association.

Lewin, K. (1943/1997). Defining the "Field at a given time." In K. Lewin, *Resolving social conflicts and field theory in social science* (pp. 200–211). Washington, DC: American Psychological Association.

Lewin, K. (1943–44/1997). Problems of research in social psychology. In K. Lewin, *Resolving social conflicts and field theory in social science* (pp. 279–288). Washington, DC: American Psychological Association.

Lewin, K. (1946/1997). Action research and minority problems. In K. Lewin, *Resolving social conflicts and field theory in social science* (pp. 143–152). Washington, DC: American Psychological Association.

Lorion, R. P., Iscoe, I., DeLeon, P. H., & VandenBos, G. R. (Eds.). (1996). *Psychology and public policy: Balancing public service and professional need.* Washington, DC: American Psychological Association.

Marcus-Newhall, A., Halpern, D. F., & Tan, S. J. (2006). *The changing realities of work and family: A multidisciplinary approach.* Malden, MA: Wiley-Blackwell.

Markus, H., & Nurius, P. 1986. Possible selves. *American Psychologist, 41,* 954–969.

Melton, G. B. (1995). Bringing psychology to Capitol Hill: Briefings on child and family policy. *American Psychologist, 50,* 766–770.

Miller, C. T., & Downey, K. T. (1999). A meta-analysis of heavyweight and self-esteem. *Personality and Social Psychology Review, 3,* 68–84.

Miller, D. T., & Ross, M. (1975). Self-serving biases in the attribution of causality: Fact or fiction? *Psychological Bulletin, 82,* 213–225.

Miller, G. A. (1969). Psychology as a means of promoting human welfare. *American Psychologist, 24,* 1063–1075.

Miller, J. G. (1984). Culture and the development of everyday social explanation. *Journal of Personality and Social Psychology, 46,* 961–978.

Morgan, G. S., Mullen, E., & Skitka, L. J. (2010). When values and attributions collide: Liberals' and conservatives' values motivate attributions for alleged misdeeds. *Personality and Social Psychology Bulletin, 36,* 1241–1254.

Niemann, Y. F., & Maruyama, G. (Eds.). (2005). Inequities in higher education: Issues and promising practice in a world ambivalent about affirmative action. *Journal of Social Issues* (Vol. 61, No. 3). Hoboken, NJ: Wiley-Blackwell.

Omoto, A. M. (Ed.). (2005). *Processes of community change and social action.* Mahwah, NJ: Erlbaum.

Omoto, A. M., & Snyder, M. (1990). Basic research in action: Volunteerism and society's response to AIDS. *Personality and Social Psychology Bulletin, 16,* 152–166.

Omoto, A. M., & Snyder, M. (1995). Sustained helping without obligation: Motivation, longevity of service, and perceived attitude change among AIDS volunteers. *Journal of Personality and Social Psychology, 68,* 671–686.

Omoto, A. M., & Snyder, M. (2002). Considerations of community: The context and process of volunteerism. *American Behavioral Scientist, 45,* 846–867.

Omoto, A. M., & Snyder, M. (2010). Influences of psychological sense of community on voluntary helping and prosocial action. In S. Stürmer & M. Snyder, (Eds.), *The psychology of prosocial behavior: Group processes, intergroup relations, and helping* (pp. 223–243). Oxford, UK: Blackwell.

Omoto, A. M., Snyder, M., & Martino, S. C. (2000). Volunteerism and the life course: Investigating age-related agendas for action. *Basic and Applied Social Psychology, 22,* 181–198.

Omoto, A. M., Snyder, M., & Smith, D. M. (1999). Newspaper study [Unpublished Data]. Lawrence: University of Kansas.

Peck, S. C., Feinstein, L., & Eccles, J. S. (Eds.). (2008). Unexpected educational pathways. *Journal of Social Issues* (Vol. 64, No. 1). Hoboken, NJ: Wiley-Blackwell.

Pettigrew, T. F. (1988). Influencing policy with social psychology. *Journal of Social Issues, 44,* 205–219.

Pettigrew, T., & Tropp, L. (2006). A meta-analytic test of intergroup contact theory. *Journal of Personality and Social Psychology, 90,* 751–783.

Pettigrew, T. F., & Tropp, L. M. (2011). *When groups meet: The dynamics of intergroup contact.* Philadelphia, PA: Psychology Press.

Piliavin, J. A., & Piliavin, I. M. (1972). The effects of blood on reactions to a victim. *Journal of Personality and Social Psychology, 23,* 253–261.

Pratto, F., Liu, J. H., Levin, S., Sidanius, J., Shih, M., Bachrach, H., et al. (2000). Social dominance and the legitimation of inequality across cultures. *Journal of Cross Cultural Psychology, 31,* 369–409.

Prentice, D. A., & Miller, D. T. (2007). Psychological essentialism of human categories. *Psychological Science, 16,* 202–206.

Putnam, R. D. (2000). *Bowling alone.* New York: Simon & Schuster.

Redding, R. E. (2001). Sociopolitical diversity in psychology: The case for pluralism. *American Psychologist, 56,* 205–215.

Rodin, J., & Langer, E. J. (1977). Long-term effects of a control-relevant intervention with the institutionalized aged. *Journal of Personality and Social Psychology, 35,* 897–902.

Ross, L. (1977). The intuitive psychologist and his shortcomings: Distortions in the attribution process. In L. Berkowitz (Ed.),

Advances in experimental social psychology (Vol. 10, pp. 173–220). New York: Academic.

Ryan, C. S., & Casas, J. F. (Eds.). (2010). Latinos and Latino immigrants in the United States. *Journal of Social Issues* (Vol. 66, No. 1). Hoboken, NJ: Wiley-Blackwell.

Sanford, N. (1970). Whatever happened to action research? *Journal of Social Issues, 26*, 3–23.

Schlenker, B. R. (1974). Social psychology and science. *Journal of Personality and Social Psychology, 29*, 1–15.

Sears, D. O. (1986). College sophomores in the laboratory: Influences of a narrow data base on social psychology's view of human nature. *Journal of Personality and Social Psychology, 51*, 515–530.

Sherif, M. (1956). Experiments in group conflict. *Scientific American, 195*, 54–58.

Shinn, M. (2007). Waltzing with a monster: Bringing research to bear on public policy. *Journal of Social Issues, 63*, 215–231.

Shinn, M., & Weitzman, B. C. (Eds.). (1990). Urban homelessness. *Journal of Social Issues* (Vol. 46, No. 4). Hoboken, NJ: Wiley-Blackwell.

Shurkin, Joel. (1992). *Terman's kids: The groundbreaking study of how the gifted grow up.* Boston: Little, Brown.

Sidanius, J., & Pratto, F. (1999). *Social dominance: An intergroup theory of social hierarchy and oppression.* New York: Cambridge University Press.

Skitka, L. J., Mullen, E., Griffin, T., Hutchinson, S., & Chamberlin, B. (2002). Dispositions, scripts, or motivated correction? Understanding ideological differences in explanations for social problems. *Journal of Personality and Social Psychology, 83*, 470–487.

Skitka, L. J., & Tetlock, P. E. (1993). Providing public assistance: Cognitive and motivational processes underlying liberal and conservative policy preferences. *Journal of Personality and Social Psychology, 65*, 1205–1223.

Smith, D. M., Omoto, A. M., & Snyder, M. (2001, June). *Motivation matching and recruitment of volunteers: A field study.* Presented at the annual meetings of the American Psychological Society, Toronto, Canada.

Snyder, M., & Ickes, W. (1985). Personality and social behavior. In G. Lindzey & E. Aronson (Eds.), *The handbook of social psychology* (3rd ed., Vol. 2, pp. 883–947). New York: Random House.

Snyder, M., & Omoto, A. M. (2001). Basic research and practical problems: Volunteerism and the psychology of individual and collective action. In W. Wosinska, R. Cialdini, D. Barrett, & J. Reykowski (Eds.), *The practice of social influence in multiple cultures* (pp. 287–307). Mahwah, NJ: Erlbaum.

Snyder, M., & Omoto, A. M. (2000). Doing good for self and society: Volunteerism and the psychology of citizen participation. In M. Van Vugt, M. Snyder, T. R. Tyler, & A. Biel (Eds.), *Cooperation in modern society: Promoting the welfare of communities, states, and organizations* (pp. 127–141). London: Routledge.

Snyder, M., & Omoto, A. M. (2007). Social action. In A. W. Kruglanski & E. T. Higgins (Eds.), *Social psychology: A handbook of basic principles* (2nd ed., pp. 940–961). New York: Guilford.

Snyder, M., & Omoto, A. M. (2008). Volunteerism: Social issues perspectives and social policy implications. *Social Issues and Policy Review, 2*, 1–36.

Snyder, M., & Omoto, A. M. (2010, June). *Caring, concern, and community connection: The psychology of social action.* Keynote

address presented at the meeting of the Society for the Psychological Study of Social Issues, New Orleans, LA.

Snyder, M., Omoto, A. M., & Crain, A. L. (1999). Punished for their good deeds: The stigmatization of AIDS volunteers. *American Behavioral Scientist, 42*, 1175–1192.

Snyder, M., Omoto, A. M., & Smith, D. M. (2010). The role of persuasion strategies in motivating individual and collective action. In E. Borgida, C. Federico, & J. Sullivan (Eds.), *The political psychology of democratic citizenship* (pp. 125–150). New York: Oxford University Press.

Social Psychology Network (2011a). *Social Psychology Network.* Retrieved March 21, 2011, from http://www.socialpsychology.org/

Social Psychology Network (2011b). *Map of Social-Personality Psychology Graduate Programs.* Retrieved March 21, 2011, from http://www.socialpsychology.org/maps/gradprograms/

Society for Experimental Social Psychology (2011). *Society for Experimental Social Psychology.* Retrieved March 21, 2011, from www.sesp.org/

Society for Personality and Social Psychology (2011). *Society for Personality and Social Psychology.* Retrieved March 21, 2011, from http://www.spsp.org/

Society for the Psychological Study of Social Issues (2011). *Society for the Psychological Study of Social Issues.* Retrieved March 21, 2011, from http://www.spssi.org/

Sommer, R. (2006). Dual dissemination: Writing for colleagues and the public. *American Psychologist, 61*, 955–958.

Stroebe, W. (2008). *Dieting, overweight and obesity: Self-regulation in a food-rich environment.* Washington, DC: American Psychological Association.

Stukas, A. A., & Dunlap, M. R. (Eds.). (2002). Community involvement, service-learning, and social activism. *Journal of Social Issues* (Vol. 58, No. 3). Hoboken, NJ: Wiley-Blackwell.

Terman, L. M. (Ed.). (1959). *The gifted group at mid-life.* Stanford, CA: Stanford University Press.

Tetlock, P. E. (1994). Political psychology or politicized psychology: Is the road to scientific hell pave with good moral intentions? *Political Psychology, 15*, 509–524.

Thaler, R. H., & Sunstein, C. R. (2008). *Nudge: Improving decisions about health, wealth, and happiness.* New Haven, CT: Yale University Press.

Thomson Reuters (2009). *2009 Journal Citation Reports® Social Science Edition.* New York: Author.

Tierney, J. (2011, February 7). Social scientist sees bias within. *New York Times.*

Toro, P. A. (Ed.). (2007). International perspectives on homelessness in developed nations. *Journal of Social Issues* (Vol. 63, No. 3). Hoboken, NJ: Wiley-Blackwell.

Tracy, J. L., Robins, R. W., & Sherman, J. W. (2009). The practice of psychological science: Searching for Cronbach's two streams in social-personality psychology. *Journal of Personality and Social Psychology, 96*, 1206–1225.

Tremper, C. R. (1987). Organized psychology's efforts to influence judicial policy making. *American Psychologist, 42*, 496–501.

U. S. Census Bureau (2011). *The 2011 Statistical Abstract* (Section 4: Education, p. 215–301). Retrieved March 21, 2011, from http://www.census.gov/compendia/statab/cats/education/educational_attainment.html

Van Vugt, M., & Snyder, M. (2002). Cooperation in the 21st Century: Fostering community action and civic participation. *American Behavioral Scientist, 45*, 761–918.

Van Vugt, M., Snyder, M., Tyler, T., & Biel, A. (Eds.). (2000). *Cooperation in modern society: Promoting the welfare of communities, states, and organizations.* London: Routledge.

Vlek, C., & Steg, L. (Eds.). (2007). Human behavior and environmental sustainability. *Journal of Social Issues* (Vol. 63, No. 1). Hoboken, NJ: Wiley-Blackwell.

Weick, K. E. (1984). Small wins: Redefining the scale of social problems. *American Psychologist, 39,* 40–49.

Weiner, B. (1985). An attributional theory of achievement motivation and emotion. *Psychological Review, 92,* 548–573.

Wittig, M. A., & Bettencourt, B. A. (Eds.). (1996). Social psychological perspectives on grassroots organizing. *Journal of Social Issues* (Vol. 52, No. 1). Hoboken, NJ: Wiley-Blackwell.

Wollman, N., Lobenstine, M., Foderaro, M., & Stose, S. (2005). *Principles for promoting social change: Effective strategies for influencing attitudes and behaviors* (2nd ed). Washington, DC: Society for the Psychological Study of Social Issues. Retrieved March 21, 2011, from http://www.spssi.org/_data/n_0001/resources/live/PPSC_2ndED_Apr2005_1.pdf

Wood, W., & Eagly, A. H. (2002). A cross-cultural analysis of the behavior of women and men: Implications for the origins of sex differences. *Psychological Bulletin, 128,* 699–727.

Zelezny, L. C., & Schultz, P. W. (Eds.). (2000). Promoting environmentalism. *Journal of Social Issues* (Vol. 56, No. 3). Hoboken, NJ: Wiley-Blackwell.

Zirkel, S. (2008). Creating more effective multiethnic schools. *Social Issues and Policy Review, 2,* 187–241.

Personality and Social Psychology
The State of the Union

Kay Deaux *and* Mark Snyder

Abstract

In this epilogue to the *Handbook of Personality and Social Psychology*, we reflect on how the contributions to the *Handbook* illustrate the ways in which personality and social psychology relate to and contribute to each other. Among the patterns of conjunction reflected in these contributions are bridges (joining distinct social and personality perspectives on a substantive area), combined territories (with relatively seamless mergers between fields), and ravines (where the distance between fields has been substantial but where developmental opportunities exist). We also assess the roles played by professional associations, scientific journals and edited collections, departmental structures, funding agencies, and educational and training programs as they facilitate or inhibit integrative work.

Keywords: integrative perspectives, bridges, combined territories, ravines, professional associations, scientific journals, departmental structures, funding agencies, educational programs

Few if any of you who are reading this closing statement will have taken the full journey through the volume that we as editors have taken. Much more likely you have selectively dipped into the volume, visiting topics with which you have considerable familiarity to see how a combined personality and social perspective is represented and perhaps also sampling some less familiar areas that pique your curiosity and invite you to become acquainted with new perspectives. As editors, however, we have had the opportunity (and of course, the obligation) to read every chapter and we emerge from the process with a greatly enlarged appreciation of how exciting and how necessary this volume is. Sometimes, it is easy to identify the separate contributions of personality and social psychologists to a research area; other times, the lines are much fuzzier and the boundaries highly permeable. Yet, in all cases we believe that the combined perspectives give us a sharper and more comprehensive understanding of the psychological processes at work.

Patterns of Personality and Social Conjunction

In the introductory chapter to this volume, we talked about the potential and the reality of bridges between the fields of personality and social psychology. The idea of a bridge, as we developed it in that chapter, presumes that there are strong foundations on both sides of the space to be spanned, and that traffic can move in either direction. In crossing the bridge, social and personality psychologists learn to appreciate and to use some of the concepts of others, integrating some perspectives while maintaining a solid foothold on one side or the other.

Now, having read the chapters that authors have given us, we find a need to expand our metaphorical categories. The idea of a *bridge* is a good representation of some of the chapters. But, we also encountered topics and discussions that seemed to be saying something else. For these alternative models, we use the terms "combined territories" and "ravines," representing areas in which the merger of fields is more seamless, on the one hand, or where the distance between fields has limited bridge-building activity.

Bridges

The concept of a bridge speaks to bidirectional travel between the fields of personality and social psychology. As discussed in the opening chapter to this volume, although there are varieties of interactionist models, one prominent approach formulates interactionism in statistical terms, as a P × S interaction in which person and situation variables are considered both as main effects and as potential moderators of each other in an interaction term.

Such a P × S interactionist approach has been particularly prevalent at the intersection of personality and social psychology and, indeed, can be found in many of the areas represented in this volume. In his analysis of individual and societal well-being, Oishi (chapter 24) illustrates this strategy with a specific consideration of the main effects of both personality and social factors and followed by a review of evidence for interactive effects. Within the area of attitudes, the theory of planned behavior described by Ajzen (chapter 15) includes both person factors (e.g., attitudes, intentions, and habits) and situational factors (e.g., perceived normative pressure). Similarly, the area of helping behavior, initially dominated by a situationist perspective, now readily incorporates both personality (e.g., dispositional empathy) and situational determinants (e.g., social norms) (see Nadler, chapter 16, this volume). Simpson and Winterheld (chapter 20) explicitly use a P × S framework to discuss various models of close relationships and highlight the ways in which situations elicit distinctive reactions in people with specifiable dispositional strengths or weaknesses.

An update of the ANOVA-based formulation of a P × S framework can be seen in the multilevel modeling approach detailed by Christ, Sibley, and Wagner (chapter 10 in this volume). Here the emphasis is on different levels of analysis (e.g., individual and group level data) that are assessed simultaneously, allowing the investigator to consider how the same psychological construct, such as psychological well-being, might show different patterns of association depending on the context in which it is being assessed. As an example, Christ et al. cite the work of Kuppens, Realo, and Diener (2008), who were interested in the relationship of life satisfaction to the frequency of positive and negative emotional experiences and found that life satisfaction was more strongly related to the presence of positive emotions than to the absence of negative emotions.

However, country-level variables moderated these relationships such that, for example, negative emotional experiences were more influential in individualistic than in collectivist nations. Here the joint contributions of personality and social factors are considered on a broader canvas, allowing us to consider multiple levels and moderating factors simultaneously.

Combined Territories

Another form of interactionist thinking, as discussed in the opening chapter, is less statistical and more dynamic in its conceptualization, emphasizing the mutual interplay between and reciprocal influences of personal and situational factors. This sense of interactionism falls more easily into the category that we are here calling *combined territories*. We use the term "combined territories" to describe those topical areas in which communication between personality and social psychologists has already been extensive and/or where the demarcation lines are not even drawn, as fields have developed in ways that eschew the language of separation between personality and social psychology.

The area of self and identity (see Crocker and Canevello, chapter 11) can readily be used as an example of the first circumstance, where investigators have frequently drawn from both subdisciplines to conceptualize their questions. Indeed, questions of self-definition, as influenced by both internal and external processes, are so fundamental that the area of self and identity is also one in which psychologists and sociologists frequently overlap and develop integrated theories that draw their key principles from both disciplines (see Deaux & Burke, 2010). Some of the earliest analysts of self, such as William James (1890) and George Herbert Mead (1934), found it impossible not to invoke both person and situation factors in their analysis of self processes. As Crocker and Canevello observe, however, differences between the emphases of personality and social psychologists can be noted. Both disciplines, for example, focus on self-esteem, but personality psychologists are more likely to think in terms of stable levels of and individual differences in self-esteem, while social psychologists are more likely to treat self-esteem as a malleable outcome of specific events. Yet even here, as Luhtanen and Crocker (1992) have shown, one can meaningfully distinguish between personal and collective self-esteem, both being components of a more inclusive notion of relatively stable self-regard. Similarly, one might be tempted to characterize the personality approach by pointing to the copious development of individual difference measures whose prefix is "self" (e.g., self-awareness, self-consciousness, self-discrepancy, self-efficacy, self-monitoring, self-regulatory focus), but many of these concepts have been used as both independent and dependent variables, considering the stable and malleable aspects of the same process. Further, as Crocker and Canevello argue, investigation of both aspects in a traditional P × S model, which assumes static and independent processes, might better yield to a more dynamic analysis of mutual influence and dynamic change.

Interpenetrating processes are fundamental to the analysis of Mendoza-Denton and Ayduk (chapter 18), who show how social relationships determine the development, structure, and expression of personality; their view of the personality system is necessarily shaped by culture and interpersonal encounters. Adams (chapter 8) also argues for interdependence as he analyzes the cultural constitution of personal experience and the psychological constitution of social worlds. In both of these discussions, it is considered impossible to consider the person without the social and vice versa.

A second version of the combined territory includes topic areas that have developed in ways that avoid a simple parsing of personality and social components. Both motivation (Norem, chapter 12) and emotion (Clore and Robinson, chapter 13) can serve as examples, where the investigative history of the field predates sharp divisions between personality and social psychology and researchers freely draw from both fields while developing concepts and research strategies that are uniquely suited to the questions at hand. In the case of motivation, questions of conscious and unconscious/nonconscious motivation have been the site of an intricate dance between personality and social psychology over the years, as emphasis and acceptance have ebbed and flowed in convergent or divergent streams. Processes such as regulatory focus and self-determination also illustrate what Norem terms the "increasingly porous" boundaries that separate the two fields. Similarly in the field of emotion, many of the key questions that continue to interest investigators were formulated prior to the development of social and personality as distinct fields, and contemporary successors often see themselves in more generalist terms, drawing freely not only from social and personality psychology but from biological and neuroscience sources as well.

Another example of combined territories is offered in the much newer field of neuroscience, as surveyed by Amodio and Harmon-Jones (chapter 6). Although neuroscience approaches are in many respects much newer than either personality or social psychological approaches, their origin outside of either field has made them beholden to neither. Certainly it is true that, as Amodio and Harmon-Jones detail, the widespread adoption of social cognition perspectives within contemporary social psychology has proved particularly receptive to neuroscience extensions. Yet, it is also true that the uncharted territory offered by social neuroscience research allows a rethinking and potentially a reformulation of the ways in which individual differences influence neurological patterns. More generally, Amodio and Harmon-Jones argue that neuroscience is "a field in which traditional boundaries between the person and the situation are reinterpreted as complex, dynamic, and inherently multilevel interactions" (p. 64 of ms.). In reviewing work on topics ranging from the self to intergroup relations, they illustrate the ways in which this new field of investigation is creating a new standard for disciplinary definition.

Ravines

We use the term "ravines" to describe those topic areas in which communication between personality and social psychologists has been quite limited. Our use of the term is not fatalistic, in that we do not believe that personality and social psychology have no common interests in these areas, or that their interests are irreconcilable. Indeed, a number of the authors in this volume have been masterful in their development of the common ground that might be established between personality and social psychology. Thus, the term "ravine" simply characterizes a field in which the future holds more promise than past work may have suggested.

In some cases, a field of study has been much more strongly associated with one discipline than with the other by virtue of how the field is defined. Group processes and intergroup relations, for example, have generally been associated with social psychology and not with personality psychology because of their emphasis on units of analysis larger than the individual. Psychology and law, as discussed by Kassin and Kovera (chapter 30), is an area in which situational variables have received most of the attention, in part because the goals of the investigation have been defined in terms of procedural interventions and changes that are inherently situational in nature. To the extent that one can identify practices that are likely to lead to fairer processes and more just outcomes within the legal system, the emphasis is likely to remain on specific situational variables rather than any individual variation among participants in the system. This tradition stands somewhat apart from a more clinically based forensics tradition, in which attention is more typically directed toward characteristics of the individual perpetrator or victim.

In other cases, both personality and social psychologists have been active in an area, but the research activity has tended to develop along separate trajectories. Van Knippenberg (chapter 27) describes such a pattern of separation in the domain of leadership research, but takes on the challenge of finding integrative space by proposing a person-in-situation model of leadership effectiveness. Similarly faced with two divergent literatures in the area of collective action, Duncan (chapter 31) offers a model that integrates the personality tradition with its emphasis on individual difference correlates of collective action with the social psychological work that stresses motivational causes.

In their chapter on personality, social psychology, and psychopathology, Costanzo, Hoyle, and Leary (chapter 23) argue strongly for bringing the study of normal and abnormal together on the same continua and by so doing, uniting not only personality and social psychological perspectives but also recognizing the essences that they share with the more extreme manifestations studied in the field of psychopathology. These authors remind us that the field defined by Morton Prince in the early days of the *Journal of Abnormal and Social Psychology* was one in which these various strands were woven together and they present a strong case for readoption of this shared perspective.

Our examples of bridges, combined territories, and ravines are obviously selective, chosen to illustrate the range of possibilities rather than to attempt an exhaustive categorization. In the hands of other editors, other exemplars might be chosen, and indeed, even from the present editors, the richness of the territory covered by all of the authors in this volume made any illustrative selection somewhat arbitrary. We also recognize that the three categories themselves are not sharply defined, but rather represent fuzzy sets in which a chapter might be fairly represented in more than one grouping. The key message, however, remains the same, namely that the conjunction of personality and social psychology can be represented in many different ways and that the goal of an integrated science will be attained through multiple pathways that are shaped by the past histories of the fields as well as their future potentials.

Living Conditions: The Infrastructure of Personality and Social Psychology

In any academic enterprise, intellectual pursuits are housed within social structures and larger systems. Although our authors for the most part have focused on the conceptual and empirical bases for analyzing the ways in which personality and social psychology encounter one another, a number of them have also pointed to historical circumstances that have fostered or discouraged the union. Pettigrew and Cherry (chapter 2), given their task to provide an historical account, address these issues most directly at the beginning of this *Handbook*, and we think it is appropriate to end with some consideration of the larger context as well. It seems particularly important, as we hope for a future in which personality and social psychology are not only good neighbors but united partners as well, to consider how well the infrastructure of our discipline supports and how it might encourage this joint state.

The relevant components of the system are numerous: they include the organizations to which we belong, the journals and handbooks we publish, the funding agencies that support our work, and the departments in which we reside. Further, as we look to the future, we also need to think about the ways that we teach our discipline to the next generations of scholars. In the following pages, we consider how each of these domains is critical to our enterprise.

Professional Organizations

Professional organizations that serve personality and social psychologists suggest a dual reality. On the one hand, the Society of Personality and Social Psychology (SPSP), established as a freestanding organization in 1974 while retaining affiliation with the American Psychological Association as Division 8, speaks to the combination and even integration of the fields of personality and social psychology. At the same time, single-discipline organizations such as the Association for Research in Personality, the Society for Personology, and the Society of Experimental Social Psychology exist and often thrive. Similarly in Europe, the European Association of Social Psychology and the European Association of Personality Psychology coexist but do not unite. The existence of these separate societies serves to reinforce separate identities as social or personality psychologists that, while they may coexist under the superordinate umbrella of an organization such as

SPSP, nonetheless represent different groups. These distinctions are maintained with the separate awards given by SPSP—a Donald Campbell award for social psychology and the Henry Murray and Jack Block awards for personality psychology.

It might also be worth noting that in both the United States and Europe, membership in the social psychology associations is larger than that in the personality associations (though, in each case, there are people who are members of both). This size differential has existed for a great many years and, at least from the perspective of those interested in social identity and intergroup relations, at times appears to influence the relationship between the two fields.

Are there ways to bring these professional groups closer together in the service of a more integrated agenda? Although joint meetings between groups may not always be feasible, possibilities for more integrative activities within each organization's convention should be possible. Convention programming in personality meetings might include invitations to social psychologists to talk about common domains, and vice versa. Given that a significant number of scholars are members of both a personality and a social psychology organization, those people could be asked to organize sessions that would specifically address crossover possibilities. None of these activities need dominate a convention program, but if some space were allotted to such activities at each meeting of the group, consciousness and a sense of possibility and potential could be raised.

Journals

Like the organizations from which they often originate, the journals in the field display both integration and separation. *Personality and Social Psychology Bulletin (PSPB)* began publication soon after SPSP became a freestanding organization, and was followed by *Personality and Social Psychology Review*. Both of these journals make no clear distinction between the two fields and the degree of integration in their pages primarily reflects the authors' proclivities and not explicit journal policy. The history of the leading journal in the field, the *Journal of Personality and Social Psychology (JPSP)*, reflects a more complicated development, as Costanzo, Hoyle, and Leary (chapter 23) describe. The *Journal of Abnormal and Social Psychology (JASP)* began in 1921 (with a minor revision of its name in 1925), succeeding the earlier *Journal of Abnormal Psychology*. *JASP* included articles representing a broad range of personality, social and abnormal psychology, with many studies freely crossing boundaries and combining insights from different perspectives. In 1965, a period characterized more by distinctions than by mergers, *JASP* was divided into two separate journals, the *Journal of Personality and Social Psychology* and the *Journal of Abnormal Psychology* (the latter reestablishing the distinctive position of abnormal psychology that Morton Prince had defined prior to the development of *JASP*). Although *JPSP* represented a united discipline on the cover, the inside of the journal established lines of demarcation, creating three distinct sections, the first two of which represented social psychological interests (Attitudes and Social Cognition; Interpersonal Relations and Group Processes) and the third covering Personality Processes and Individual Differences. European journals for the most part maintain the distinction between fields, as represented by the existence of both a *European Journal of Social Psychology* and a *European Journal of Personality*. In contrast, signaling a more ecumenical spirit, one of the most recent additions to the journal domain is *Social Psychology and Personality Science*, a venture sponsored jointly by a number of organizations in both Europe and the United States.

Another encouraging sign for those who favor creating conditions in which personality and social psychological approaches can more easily blend is the appearance of statements by analysts as well as editors that encourage rapprochement. In their recent analysis of the practice of psychological science, for example, Tracy, Robins, and Sherman suggested "that journal editors and reviewers make conscious efforts to bear in mind the potential benefits of an integrative approach" (2009, p. 1223). As if in response to this advice, upon assuming the editorship of *PSPB*, Kitayama stated his "commitment to the integrated nature of the field of personality and social psychology" (Kitayama, 2010, p. 3). Certainly statements alone do not change research practices. Yet, if at least some editors take seriously the mission, by encouraging submissions that reflect integration, by asking authors to consider literatures and perspectives whose relevance they may not have recognized, and by featuring articles that are positive exemplars of an integrated perspective, then progress will be made.

Funding Agencies

Funding agencies present a more complicated situation. Many of the funding sources within the United States are problem-oriented, most notably the National Institutes of Health, and their agenda are set less by discipline and more by a particular health concern. Even in units that are specifically targeted for social scientists, such as the Office of Behavioral and Social Science Research, the priorities are defined in terms such as "health disparities" or "health literacy." This nondisciplinary focus should allow projects that cross disciplinary boundaries to fare much better, to the extent that the proposals address the problem at hand. At the same time, the success of such proposals critically depends on the choice of reviewers and panel members, putting considerable power in the hands of the agency administrators, who may or may not see the integration of personality and social psychology as a major concern.

The National Science Foundation, in contrast, is structured along disciplinary lines. Within this structure, there is a Social Psychology panel that, although it includes "personality processes" in its definition of interests and funds proposals in both personality and social psychology, may by virtue of its name be seen as more hospitable to social psychologists and may attract (and ultimately fund) more social psychology proposals than personality proposals. Anecdotal evidence of this differential can be found in a Google search within the NSF data base: the term "social psychology" garners over 10,000 cites with nsf.gov funding appearing first on the list, while "personality" has only 1,500 cites and the first reference is to the personality of North American squirrels!

The role of funding agencies, both in the United States and elsewhere, is certainly too large and complicated a topic to develop here, given the wide variation in missions, agenda, and procedures for staffing and funding. Nonetheless, the influence of these agencies on shaping the directions and the degree of development of various scientific disciplines and subfields cannot be underestimated, and the integrative future of social and personality psychology is not immune to these influences.

Department Structures

Can personality and social psychology be integrated in educational institutions? Harvard's legendary Department of Social Relations, as described by Pettigrew and Cherry (chapter 2), stands out as an example of a program that eschewed disciplinary boundaries. Bridging more than just personality and social psychology, the department drew from sociology, anthropology, and clinical psychology as well, bringing together such luminaries as Gordon Allport, Henry Murray, Robert White, Talcott Parsons, Samuel Stouffer, and Clyde Kluckholm. Gordon Allport, of course, stands as a model of the integrating

scholar, making major contributions to both personality (e.g., Allport, 1937) and social psychology (Allport, 1954). However, among the members of the Department of Social Relations, as Pettigrew and Cherry note, personality and social psychologists were more likely to link to the nonpsychologists than to each other, as common theoretical interests trumped discipline. The Harvard experiment lasted 26 years, forming shortly after World War II (an event that had fostered interdisciplinary work on common goals) and terminating in 1972.

Few other departments made such ambitious attempts to cross disciplinary boundaries; rather, the trend for many years was in the direction of increasing specialization and distinctive identities. Personality and social psychology programs were often quite separate during this era. In at least one case, at Columbia University in the 1960s, social psychology established a freestanding department of its own, separate from all other versions of psychology and operating at only the graduate level. More recently, there is evidence that some more integrated programs have developed in many universities. A survey of social and personality psychology doctoral programs in the United States and Canada, conducted in 1992, explored the diversity of self-labels in doctoral programs (Uleman & Weary, 1995). Approximately 30% of the programs that responded considered themselves to be combined social-personality programs. On the separatist side of the ledger, 44% of the programs labeled themselves "social psychology," using that term either alone or with "experimental" or "applied" preceding it, while none of the programs that responded to this survey defined themselves as exclusively personality. (The remainder of the sample either reported that their department did not have separate programs or offered a label that was idiosyncratic and coded as "other.") (Uleman, personal communication, February 8, 2011).

The continuing development of joint personality-social psychology programs would surely foster the kinds of integrative thinking that we are advocating. The value-added features of such programs are stressed by Tracy et al. (2009) as well, who point out the benefits that are likely to accrue if both personality and social psychologists are regularly interacting and learning about each other's work. Such interdisciplinary contact not only can create friendships and create positive affect toward the other's field (see Tropp & Molina, chapter 22 in this volume), but can also lay the foundation for collaborative research projects that will further develop the integrative perspective.

Teaching Social/Personality Psychology

The development of combined social-personality programs does not guarantee that the two fields will be integrated in any meaningful way, as *JPSP*, with its unified title but partitioned sections, indicates. Data available from the Uleman and Weary (1995) survey suggest that both personality and social topics are included in the curricula of most programs, whatever their label. Exactly what balance exists between approaches, however, may be less easily discerned from these data, and the numerical advantage that social psychologists have in most departments suggests that course distribution could well be uneven. Further, the numbers alone do not determine the particular content that any course might take. Probably more important and less frequent than the presence of both personality and social psychology courses in a curriculum is the existence of courses that directly aim to combine the two perspectives within a single course (although both of the editors have taught such a course for years). We don't know how many such courses exist in graduate curricula, but some data suggest that in principle, an integrated syllabus might not be so hard to construct. In the Tracy et al. (2009) analysis of psychological practice, they found considerable overlap in the research topics that personality and social psychologists study (considerably more commonality than they found for choice of research design and statistical procedures). On a wide variety of topics varying from self-esteem and self-regulation to aggression and persuasion, personality and social psychologists did not differ in the likelihood that they would study the topic. Indeed, as some of the research areas exemplified in the discussion of bridges and combined territories, there is a long history of crosscurrents between the two disciplines.

On the basis of their analysis, Tracy and her colleagues make a strong recommendation for the curricular integration of social and personality psychology. They advocate giving exposure to a wide variety of methods and statistical procedures and highlighting the complementary values that the two perspectives bring to any research arena. Course syllabi that draw on the literature from both streams, textbooks that offer broader perspectives, and handbooks that join the fields together are all part of their recommended strategy for future training. Clearly we concur, especially with the latter suggestion, and we hope that this *Handbook* will be a crucial sourcebook for those who want to take the integrated path.

Epilogue

"The future is plump with promise," Maya Angelou once said. We feel that way about the prospects for the integration of personality and social psychology. The beliefs of possibility that we felt when we began this project have been so richly supported and strengthened by the work of the authors in this volume. They have discovered connections in the existent literature and they have pointed to exciting new paths for future investigation. Although obstacles exist, the potential benefits are far stronger, and we hope that this *Handbook* will serve as a springboard, energizing and inspiring the work of scholars in the future.

References

Allport, G. W. (1937). *Personality: A psychological interpretation.* New York: Holt.

Allport, G. W. (1954). *The nature of prejudice.* Reading, MA: Addison-Wesley.

Deaux, K., & Burke, P. (2010). Bridging identities. *Social Psychology Quarterly, 73*(4), 315–320.

James, W. (1890). Principles of *psychology.* H. Holt.

Kitayama, S. (2010). Editorial. *Personality and Social Psychology Bulletin, 36,* 3–4.

Kuppens, P., Realo, A., & Diener, E. (2008). The role of positive and negative emotions in life satisfaction judgement across nations. *Journal of Personality and Social Psychology, 95,* 66–75.

Luhtanen, R., & Crocker, J. (1992). A collective self-esteem scale: Self-evaluation of one's social identity. *Personality and Social Psychology Bulletin, 18,* 302–318.

Mead, G. H. (1934). *Mind, self, and society* (edited by C. W. Morris). Chicago: University of Chicago Press.

Tracy, J. L., Robins, R. W., & Sherman, J. W. (2009). The practice of psychological science: Searching for Cronbach's two streams in social-personality psychology. *Journal of Personality and Social Psychology, 96,* 1206–1225.

Uleman, J. S., & Weary, G. (1995). Survey of doctoral programs in personality and social psychology, 1992. *Personality and Social Psychology Bulletin, 21,* 245–255.

INDEX

16 Principle Factors (16 PF), personality inventory, 22, 526

A

Abilities
coalition partners, 165
domination, 200
Abnormal Psychology, White, 19
Abortion, attitudes, 372
Abstract properties, concrete vs., of situations, 71–72
Academics, multiculturalism, 639
Acceptance, personality and social psychology, 46–48
Accessibility
attitudes, 371
culture as, 329
dispositions, 368–375
emotion, 327
knowledge activation, 452
personality traits, 368–369
trait, and prediction of behavior, 370–371
Accomplishment striving, work, 708
Acculturation. *See also* Multiculturalism
bidimensional model of, 627
cross-national studies, 627–628
cultural frame-switching, 628–629
domains and levels, 629–630
individual vs. societal levels, 628
and multiculturalism, 627–630
Accuracy
eyewitness identification, 764–766
initial impressions, 348–351
research on, 338
stereotypes, 348–349
target, 352
trait judgments, 349
Achievement
leadership personality, 676–677
motives, beliefs and goals, 301
Action
downstream consequences of, 196–197
explanations, 340
upstream impacts on, 196
Action research. *See also* Social policy
diagnostic and participant, 806
empirical and experimental, 806
Lewin, 805–806
social policy involvement, 805–806

types of policy involvement, 817–819
Activation
cultural cognitive affective processing (C–CAPS), 452–453
person–in–situation, 683–685
Active facilitation, 342
Active ingredients
situations, 448, 450–451, 457, 459
term, 71
Activism, personality variables, 792–793
Actor effect, 217
Actor-partner interdependence model (APIM)
distinguishable dyads, 219–221
dyadic research, 217–221
group research, 230–232
indistinguishable dyads, 218–219
lagged APIM models for dyads, 225–227
multilevel strategy, 250
over-time standard APIM, 221, 223–225
Adaptationism
adaptation, 154
adaptiveness, 154
by-products, 155
evolutionary biologists identifying adaptation, 155–156
evolutionary psychology, 156–157
evolutionary quantitative genetics, 154–157
exaptation, 154–155
function, 154
secondary adaptation, 155
Adaptive contingent variation, social spheres, 172
Adaptiveness, adaptation, 154
Adaptive team leadership, 719
Adjustment
divorce, 652
multiculturalism, 638–639
Adolescents, attachment, 581
Adult, personality change, 39
Adult Attachment Interview (AAI), 508
Affect
construction of self, 186
distinguishing, and emotion, 325–326
emotion, 318
Affect, Cognition, and Stereotyping, 26

Affect-as-information hypothesis, emotion, 324, 328
Affect Balance Scale, well-being, 598
Affective empathy, description, 422
Affective events theory, work attitudes, 713
Affective priming, 345
Affective processing, personality and top-down factors, 329–330
Affective style
neuroscience, 137
resting frontal cortical asymmetry, 127–128
Affiliation, leadership personality, 676–677
Affordances, 182
cultural psychology, 182
interdependence theory, 79
model, 67
Person x Situation (P x S), 66
power of situation, 86–87
self-esteem, 504–505
selfways, 187
social world, 167–168
term, 67
African Americans
aggression reduction programs, 424–425
Boas and biological evolution, 17
civil rights movement, 660
divorce, 653
identity category, 194
interracial contact, 559
Jim Crow racism, 545–546
multiculturalism, 637
oppression, 16
race-based rejection sensitivity (RS-race), 458
African settings, interdependent constructions, 185–187, 189
Age
immigration and arrival, 658–659
war experiences, 665–666
Agency, human adaptation, 579
Agential behavior, helping, 395
Aggregation, multilevel analysis, 243–244
Aggression
alcohol consumption, 423
empathy and, 423–424
profile stability, 449
programs to reduce, 424–425

Aging, perceiver feature, 353
Agreeable-dominant (AD), interpersonal
   circumplex, 450
Agreeableness, helping, 411
Agreeable-submissive (AS), interpersonal
   circumplex, 450
AIDS
   empathic feelings, 431
   promoting empathy, 560
   volunteerism, 813–817
Alcohol consumption, aggression, 423
Aldorno, Theodor, 22
Alibi evidence, legal system, 760–761
Allies, collective action, 796
Allport, Floyd
   social psychology, 73
   Social Psychology, 18
Allport, Gordon, 4, 13, 18, 20, 23
Alternating biculturals, 632
Alternativism, personality, 42
Altruism
   help-giving, 399–400
   personality, 396, 398–399
   research, 395
   suffering, 409
American Psychological Association
   (APA), 26, 151, 809
American Psychologist, 824
American society, developments, 16–18
Amygdala, brain, 113
*Analyses of Social Issues and Public
   Policy*, 821
Analysis, behavior, 100–101
An Atlas of Interpersonal Situations,
   78–79, 80
Anchoring-and-adjustment model,
   biases, 356
Anger, asymmetric frontal cortical activity,
   128–129
Animalistic dehumanization, 341
ANOVA model
   data analysis, 210
   explanation, 354
   human beings as, 27
   P x S framework, 831
Anterior cingulate cortex (ACC), control
   activity, 117, 134
Anthropology, Yakima Native
   Americans, 17
Antisocial behavior
   dehumanization, 433–435
   disconnectedness, 421
   dispositional empathy and, 422–426
   empathy and offending, 425–426
   lacking empathy, 419–421
   person, situation, 421–422
Antiwar activism, 792
Anxiety
   intergroup, 136–137
   personality vulnerabilities, 586
   reduction through intergroup contact,
      558–560, 561
   sport-team, 527

Applicability, knowledge activation, 452
Appraisals, 165, 298
Approach-avoidance reactions, motives,
   289–290
Approach motivation, emotions, 323
AREA model (attention, reaction,
   explanation and adaptation), 607, 616
Army Air Force, pilots, 19
Aronson, Elliot, 27
Arrival conditions, immigration, 655–657
Artifacts, byproducts and settings,
   target, 352
Asian Americans, race-based rejection
   sensitivity (RS-race), 458
Asian immigrants, 656
Assessment. *See* Behavior assessment
Assimilation, 555–556, 626
Association for Psychological Science
   (APS), 27
Association for Research in Personality, 6,
   27, 833
Asymmetric frontal activity
   anger, 128–129
   state affect, 128
   trait affective style, 127–128
Attachment. *See also* Behavioral systems
   attachment behavioral system, 471–473
   behavioral system, 471–473
   caregiving behavioral system, 474–475
   children and adolescents, 581
   diathesis-stress and, styles, 507–510
   exploration behavioral system, 473
   helping relations and, 407–408
   measurement of individual differences
      in orientations, 477–478
   measuring individual differences in
      behavior, 478–480
   mental health, 481–482
   person-situation interactional
      framework, 470–471
   power behavioral system, 476–477,
      484–485
   sexual behavioral system, 475–476
   transmission gap, 487
Attachment theory
   interactional, 496, 502–503
   research, 467–468
   study of dispositions, 494
Attack of 9/11, impact, 667
Attention, impression formation, 345
Attentional adhesion, 345
Attitudes
   accessibility, 371
   affective and cognitive components,
      715
   behavior, 371–372
   changing implicit, 383–384
   compatibility principle, 714
   concept, 13, 24
   controlled/explicit responses, 372–373
   explicit, and persuasion, 380–381
   ideological, 426–428
   individual differences, 381–382

internal dispositions, 368
iterative processing model, 321
job, 710–715
neural assessments, 123–124
organizational commitment,
   711–712, 714
persuasion, 379–386
social psychology, 20, 40, 122–124
sociocultural influence, 192–194
theory of planned behavior, 376
Attitude strength, prediction of behavior,
   373–374
Attitudinal ambivalence, valence
   acquisition, 346–347
Attribution, help-giving, 400–401
Attribution effects, emotion, 328
Attribution principle, emotion, 327
Attribution theory, explanation, 354–355
Auditory cues, target, 352
Australia, multiculturalism, 625
Authoritarianism
   group behavior, 521
   group consciousness, 792
   research, 24
   social psychology, 22
Authoritarian parenting, 22
Authoritarian personality, 495, 548–549
The Authoritarian Personality,
   Aldorno, 22
Authority ranking, models of
   relationality, 186
Autocorrelation, 225
Automatic change processes, 383
Automaticity, learning and memory,
   116–117
Automatic processes, impression
   formation, 344–345, 347–348
Autonomy
   personality, 792
   self-determination theory, 296
Autonomy-oriented help, 405–406
Availability, knowledge activation, 452
The Averaged American, Igo, 15
Aversive-arousal reduction hypothesis,
   help-giving, 399
Aversive racism, 546
Avoidance, attachment, 478
Avoidant, attachment, 189408

B

B = *f*(P,E), Lewin's formula, 3, 6, 33, 74
Baby boomers, 660
Back, Kurt, 22
Back to the Future, McFly's personality,
   448, 462
Bales Interaction Process Analysis (IPA),
   100, 101
Ballew v. Georgia, 768
Banal dehumanization, 435
Barker, Roger, 22
Basis of control, situation dimensions,
   500, 501
Bavelas, Alex, 22

Behavior. *See also* Antisocial behavior; Behavior assessment; Life span
  assessing, 93–94, 96–106
  attachment, 581
  attitudes, 371–372
  attitudes and, 24–25
  attitude strength and prediction of, 373–374
  B = *f*(P,E) formula, 3, 6, 33, 74
  changing, 384–385
  compatibility, 375–379
  critical components of field, 578–579
  description, 94–96, 468–469
  dimensions, 95–96
  emotions affecting, 325–326
  empathic feelings, 431–432
  explanations, 354–356
  framework for Lewinian equation, 577–578
  human niche and social adaptations, 163–169
  "if–then" model, 77
  implicit attitudes and, 374–375
  individual, 369–370, 373
  integration into social and personality psychology, 106–107
  intentions, 378
  intergroup affect and stereotypes, 342
  low frequency, 96
  matching frames to perception of, 738
  measuring, 95–96
  nominal vs. psychological situations, 71
  novel vs. habitual, 96
  overt, 93, 94
  patterns of, 369, 372
  personality, 576–577
  personality dispositions, 378–379
  person x situation interactionism, 74–75
  persuasion, 379–386
  prediction of, 368–375
  recapitulation, 375, 379
  research and theory, 583
  situational context, 77–78
  situations and influence on, 84–85
  social context, 84–85
  socially undesirable, 96
  spontaneous inferences from, 347
  stability over life span, 649–651
  theory of planned, 376–377
  trait accessibility and prediction of, 370–371
  variability, 95
Behavioral activation system (BAS)
  attachment, 486
  health behavior, 739
  motivation, 290
  personality, 739
Behavioral approach sensitivity, anger, 128
Behavioral beliefs, term, 376
Behavioral control, theory of planned behavior, 377
Behavioral ecology, emotions, 322

Behavioral genetics, traits, 38–39
Behavioral inhibition system (BIS)
  attachment, 486
  health behavior, 739
  motivation, 290
  personality, 739
Behavioral observation
  assessing behavior, 96, 97–99
  selecting or developing system, 99–101
Behavioral signature model, interactionist, 75–78
Behavioral signatures, variability across situations, 450–451
Behavioral systems
  association with personality, 486
  attachment and emotion regulation, 480–481
  attachment and mental health, 481–482
  attachment and mental representations of self, 481
  attachment, 471–473
  attachment theory, 467–468, 470–471
  caregiving, 474–475
  concept of, 468–471
  evolution, 467
  exploration behavioral system, 473
  exploring psychological correlates, 482–483
  hyeractivation and deactivation scale items, 479
  individual-differences components, 469–470
  individual differences in, functioning, 480
  interrelations of, 483–486
  measurement of individual differences, 477–480
  normative parameters, 468–469
  origins of individual differences, 486–488
  personality structure of development, 483–488
  power, 476–477
  sexual, 475–476
Behavioral variability, stability in situations, 448–449
Behavior assessment
  behavioral observation, 97–99
  choosing task and setting, 101–102
  coder computer support systems, 105
  Electronically Activated Recorder (EAR), 104
  formulating research question, 99
  generalizability of system, 101
  Interaction Process Analysis (IPA), 100
  Internet, 104–105
  Leadership Trait Questionnaires (LTQ), 100
  level of analysis, 100–101
  methods, 96–97
  new technologies in, 103–105
  observation of personal living spaces (PLS), 105–106

  reliability, 102–103
  selecting observation system, 99–101
  social and personality psychology, 106–107
  stages of behavioral observation, 98
  strengths and weakness of behavior observation, 103
  surveillance monitors, 104–105
  training coders, 102–103
  virtual reality, 104
  webcams, 104–105
Behavior-in-situation approach, leadership, 674
Behaviorism, groups, 518–519
Behavior therapy
  cognitive, 576
  psychotherapy, 575
Beliefs, achievement, 301
Belongingness, help-giving and, 409–410
Benedict, Ruth, 17
Berscheid, Ellen, 21
BIAS map, (behaviors from intergroup affect and stereotypes), 342
Bicultural. *See also* Multiculturalism term, 625
Bicultural identity integration (BII)
  acculturation and multiculturalism, 632–636
  Chinese-American biculturals, 633, 635–636
  feelings and perceptions, 643n.6
  high vs. low levels of, 635
  multiracial experience, 643n.7
  version 2 of scale (BIIS), 634
Biculturalism
  adjustment, 638–639
  alternation, 632
  bicultural identity integration (BII), 632–636
  BII scale (BIIS) version 2, 634
  fusion, 632
  measurement, 638
  term, 641
  See also Multiculturalism
Bidimensional model, acculturation and multiculturalism, 627, 628, 630
Big Five
  accretion of processes, 55
  behavioral system and personality, 486
  cross-cultural validity of, 37
  hierarchical structure, 50
  important traits, 39
  judging targets, 339–340
  personality dimensions, 137–138
  personality trait, 18, 23
  person-in-situation and leadership, 685–688
  predicting group performance, 525–526
  predicting life outcomes, 38
  stereotype, 343
  taxonomy, 450
  trait hierarchy, 36–37

Big Five (*Contd.*)
  trait perspective, 675–678, 678–682
  traits, 523–524
  trait stability over time, 649
  two-step development of, 36
  variance, 174–175
  whole trait theory, 50–56
Bioenergetic view, emotions, 323
Biological evolution, Boas, 17
Biological psychology, 45
Biology, evolutionary, 157–158, 240
Biparental care, human adaptive
      complex, 161
Black exceptionalism hypothesis,
      intergroups, 555–556
Blended biculturals, 632
Blink, Gladwell, 94
Boas, Franz, environmentalism, 17
Borderline personality disorder (BPD), 45
Bottom-up approach, rejection
      sensitivity, 459
Bounded rationality model, 27
Brain
  amygdala (AMG), 113
  coronal slice through, 113
  empathy, 120–121
  human adaptive complex, 162
  intergroup emotion and, 136–137
  lateral aspect of right hemisphere, 116
  mechanism, 115
  medial aspect of left hemisphere, 113
  medial prefrontal cortex (mPFC), 113
  orbital frontal cortex (OFC), 113
  research on intergroup bias and,
      131–133
  social neuroscience approach, 112
Brain mapping
  neuroscience, 112–113, 125
  racial bias, 130–131
Brainstorming, group discussion, 528,
      538n.6
Bridges, personality and social psychology,
      830, 831
Bridgman, Percy, Vienna–Circle
      positivism, 21
Brigham, Carl, 16
Brown, Roger, 20
Buddhism, 15, 264–265
Burch v. Louisiana, 768
Buss–Derkee Hostility Inventory, 423
By-products, adaptation, 155
Bystander intervention, experiments, 94
Bystanders, help-giving, 396–397

C
California Psychology Inventory, 782
Canada
  immigration, 656
  multiculturalism, 625, 630
Capacity, coalition partners, 164
Caregiving behavioral system, 474–475,
      479, 484
Caribbean, immigration, 656–657

Carlsmith, Merrill, 27
Carlson, Rae, 24
Catastrophes
  attack of 9/11, 667
  earthquakes, 667
  general impact of war, 663–665
  Holocaust, 665–667
  Hurricane Katrina, 667
  internment of Japanese Americans,
      665–667
Categorical outcomes, multilevel
      modeling, 247
Categorization
  model of, 554
  motivation, 290–292
Categorization theory, leadership, 682
Cattell, Raymond, test analyses, 22
Causal effect, intentions and behavior, 378
Causal history of reasons, 355
Causality, social policy, 808–809
Causality orientations, self-determination
      theory, 296
Center for Epidemiological Studies
      Depression (CES-D) Scale,
      well-being, 601
Centering, multilevel modeling, 246
Central Intelligence Agency (CIA), 19
Certainty-oriented people (COs), 529
Change. *See* Life span
Charismatic leadership
  effectiveness, 677, 681, 690
  five-factor model, 685–686
  organization psychology, 717–718
  presidential, 675
Children. *See* Attachment
  attachment, 487, 581
  development, 18
  impact of divorce, 651, 652–654
  reducing aggression, 424–425
Chinese-Americans, biculturals,
      632–633, 635
Chinese immigrants, 656
Chronology. *See* Personality and social
      psychology
Civil rights. *See also* Prejudice
  activism, 660
  Medgar Evers, 545
  movement, 21, 787–788
Clinical psychology, 45
Closeness, social comparison, 166
Coaction phenomenon, groups,
      536–537
Coalitional psychology, humans, 165
Coalitional success, human adaptive
      complex, 162
Coalition partners
  abilities and appraisals, 165
  capacity, 164
  compatibility, 164–165
  psychology, 165
  reputations, 164–165
  trustworthiness, 164
Coder computer support systems, 105

Coder training, behavior assessment,
      102–103
Cognitive-affective mediating units
      (CAUs), 452–453, 458, 462, 497
Cognitive-affective personality system
      (CAPS)
  antisocial behavior, 421
  behavioral signature model, 75–78
  cultural CAPS (C-CAPS), 448, 451–452
  interactional theory, 496, 497–499,
      504–504
  knowledge acquisition and activation in
      C-CAPS, 452–453
  model, 26, 42, 50
  multilevel radical coefficient model
      (MRCM), 253
  personality triad, 87
  study of dispositions, 494
Cognitive capital, human adaptive
      complex, 161
Cognitive dissonance theory, Festinger, 27
Cognitive empathy, description, 422
Cognitive flexibility, personality, 792
Cognitive perspectives. *See also* Self
  person, 41–43, 57
  social psychology based, 42–43
Cognitive processes, well-being and self-
      reports, 604–605
*Cognitive Processes in Stereotyping and
      Intergroup Behavior*, 26
Cognitive psychology, 45
Cohesion, group maintenance, 531–532
Cohesiveness, group data, 212–214
Collaboration, personality and groups, 534
Collective action
  allies or outgroup members, 796
  authoritarianism, 792
  future directions, 795–798
  generativity, 792
  group consciousness, 782
  implications for increasing or
      decreasing, 797–798
  individual differences, group
      consciousness and, 789–793
  integrated model, 782
  intersectionality, 796–797
  life experiences, 789–791
  motivation for participation, 788
  nigrescence theory, 785–786
  participation, 781
  perceived efficacy, 783
  perceived injustice, 783
  personality and life experiences, 782
  personality and social psychology,
      781–782, 793, 794
  personality characteristics, 791–793
  personality variables, 792–793
  politicized group identity, 783–784
  politicized identifications, 785–786
  relative deprivation theory, 786–788
  social identity theories, 783–784
  social psychological models of group
      consciousness and, 782–788

stratum consciousness, 784–785
terminology, 793–795
understanding right–wing or
conservative, 797
voluntary group memberships, 796
volunteerism vs., 795–796
Collective leadership capacity, 719
Collective personality
organizational psychology, 709–710
theory borrowing, 706
Collective representations, psychology, 15
Collectivism-individualism, follower and
leadership, 680, 693–694
College Textiles and Clothing
organizations, 786
Colonial mentality, concept, 195
Combined territories, personality and
social psychology, 830, 831–832
Common-bond experience, constructions
of self, 186
Common goals, intergroups, 552–553
Common ingroup identity model, 433
Common sense, forensic psychology, 772
Communal sharing, models of
relationality, 186
Communication, group discussion,
527–528
Communism, political pressure by
McCarthy, 21
Community, volunteerism, 813–817
Compartmentalization, bicultural
identity integration scale (BIIS)-2,
633–636
Compatibility
attitude theory, 714
behavior, 375–379
coalition partners, 164–165
Competitive altruism hypothesis, 404
Competitive jungle, prejudice, 427
Competitors, group members, 162
Compilation, teamwork, 720
Compliance, confessions, 757–758
Composition, teamwork, 720
Comprehensive Quality of Life scale,
well-being, 599
Conceptual act model, emotions, 319
Conceptual distinguishability, dyadic
design, 216–217
Conceptualization
personality and social psychology,
48–49
social sphere, 167
Concrete properties, abstract vs., of
situations, 71–72
Conductance hypothesis, helping
relations, 401
Confessions
dispositional risk factors, 757–758
false evidence ploy, 758–759
Miranda rights, 757, 758, 760
phenomenology of innocence, 759–760
police interrogations, 756–760
situational risk factors, 758–759

Conflict
bicultural identity integration scale
(BIIS)-2, 633–636
groups and situations, 520–525
impact of divorce, 652–653
monitoring, 117
motive/goal systems, 304–305
realistic vs. symbolic threat, 551
resolution of relational conflict,
532–533
Conformity, group decision-making, 530
Confrontation, confessions, 757
Congruence, motive/goal systems,
304–305
Conjoint constructions, cultural-ecological
variation, 193
Conscious emotional experiences, 326
Conscious goal pursuit, 303–304
Conscious motives, person, 43
Consensus, group decision-making,
530–531
Conservatives
collective action, 797
ideology, 812–813
Consistency
eyewitness identification, 765
multilevel radical coefficient model
(MRCM), 251–252
similar situations, 75
traits, 40
Construal, personality, 42
Construal level theory (CLT), 354
Constructionism, social policy, 809–810
Construct validity concept, well-being,
599–600
Consumption, energy, by groups, 537
Content, goal, 298–299
Context in person
attitudes and dispositions, 192–194
cultural-ecological scaffolding of self,
187–190
dispositions, 183
independent constructions of self,
183–187
independent selfways, 187–188
interdependent constructions of self,
185–187
interdependent selfways, 188–189
personal identity, 191–192
propensities for prejudice, 194–195
selfways as habitus, 190
sociocultural bases of psychological
experience, 190–195
See also Cultural psychology
Contingencies, self-esteem, 269–270, 275
Continuity. See Life span
Control
detecting need for, 134
implementing, 134–135
intergroup bias, 133–135
personality vulnerabilities, 586
power behavioral system, 476–477
situation dimensions, 500, 501

Controlled processes
attitudes, 372–373
impression formation, 344, 347–348
Controversy, multiculturalism, 626
Cooley, Charles, environmentalism, 16
Cooperation, intergroups, 552–553
Coordination situations,
interdependence, 82
Correspondence
outcome, and interdependence,
81–82
situation dimensions, 500, 501
Corticospinal inhibition, ingroup and
outgroup pain, 428–429
Cortisol, psychological dispositions,
138–139
Cosmopolitan approach,
multiculturalism, 626
Cost-benefit modeling, evolutionary
economics, 156
Courts, forensic psychology, 772
Credibility, deception, 349–350
Criminal Interrogations and Confessions,
manual, 755
Cross-cultural variation
cultural psychology, 182
multilevel analysis, 242, 254–257
Cross-group
empathy, 433
helping relations, 405
intergroup contact, 556–558
potential for positive outcomes,
561–562
Crow, Jim, racism, 545–546
Cue utilization, target, 352
Cue validity, target, 352
Cultural activation, multiculturalism,
640–641
Cultural anthropology, attitude
assessment, 18
Cultural artifacts, 194
Cultural blendedness, bicultural identity
integration scale (BIIS)-2, 633–636
Cultural cognitive-affective processing
system (C-CAPS)
knowledge acquisition and activation,
452–453
organization, 453
social interaction, 448, 451–452
tying, to social interactions,
453–454
Cultural diversity, multiculturalism, 626
Cultural encapsulation, acculturation, 629
Cultural frame-switching (CFS),
acculturation, 628–629
Cultural harmony, bicultural identity
integration scale (BIIS)-2, 633–636
Cultural practices, 194
Cultural psychology
attitudes and dispositions, 192–194
beyond cultural variation, 190–195
beyond self-construal, 187–190
context in person, 183–195

Cultural psychology (*Contd.*)
cultural-ecological scaffolding of self, 187–190
downstream consequences of action, 196–197
dynamic construction of personal identity, 197–198
independent constructions of self, 183–187
independent selfways, 187–188
intentional worlds, 198–201
intentional worlds of domination, 199–201
interdependent constructions of self, 185–187
interdependent selfways, 188–189
personal identity, 191–192
person in context, 195–201
propensities for prejudice, 194–195
selfways as habitus, 190
selfways as intentional worlds, 199
social and personality psychology, 182–183, 201–202
sociocultural bases of species–typical tendencies, 190–191
upstream impacts on action, 196
well-being, 608
Cultural variation
cultural-ecological variation, 193
evolutionary perspective, 170–171
intentional worlds of domination, 199–201
Culture
accessibility, 329
emotion, 319
levels of analysis, 240
persons nested in, 250–251
situations, 85–86
Cummings, E. E., emotions, 320
Cumulative continuity, interaction, 26
Cyberspace, target, 352

D
Dangerous world, prejudice, 427
Darwin, Charles, 152–153
Darwinism, 153, 157
Data analysis, definitions, 211–212
Daubert v. Merrell Dow Pharmaceuticals, 772
Deactivation
attachment behavioral system, 472–473
attachment theory, 470
caregiving behavioral system, 475, 482–483
exploration behavioral system, 473
power behavioral system, 477
scale items for behavioral system, 479, 482
sexual behavioral system, 475–476
Debate, person-situation, 39–40
Decategorization processes, 554
Deception, perceiving, 349–350
Deception detection

evidence, 754–756
training, 755–756
Decision-making
achievement of consensus, 530–531
brainstorming, 528, 538n.6
conformity, 530
emotion and, 326
group discussion, 527–528
groups, 527–531
influence, 528–530
Defensive helping, 405
Defensive pessimism, self-regulation, 302
Defensive projection, perception, 350
Degree of interdependence, situation dimensions, 500, 501
Degree of uncertainty, situation dimensions, 500, 501
Dehumanization, us vs. them, 433–435
De La Beckwith, Byron, killing Evers, 545
Delay-of-gratification, situations, 82–83
Demands-abilities, person-job fit, 708
Democrats, ideology, 813
Density distributions, states, 52–53
Departments, personality and social psychology, 835
Dependency/risk regulation, person-by-situation approach, 503–505
Depression, Great, 19, 651
Depression, resting frontal asymmetric activity, 127–128
Descartes, emotion regulation, 129, 319, 326
Descriptive, whole trait theory, 51, 52–55
Descriptive approach, theory-driven vs., 72–73
Deutsch, Morton, 22
Developmental antecedents, help-giving, 398
Developmental stage, life experiences, 789–790
Developmental systems theory, evolution, 157–158
Dewey, John, 16, 73
Diagnostic action research, 806
Diagnostic and Statistical Manual (DSM), 69
Diagnostic and Statistical Manual, 5th edition (DSM–V), 38, 574
Digital recordings, behavior, 105
Dilthey, Wilhelm, 14
Disaggregation, multilevel analysis, 243–244
Disconnectedness, antisocial behavior, 421
Discrimination
empathy, 420
helping relations across racial boundaries, 406–407
personal experiences, 790
rejection, 589
stereotypes, 342
Discriminative facility, research, 459
Disguised egoism, help-giving, 399–400
Disjoint constructions, cultural-ecological variation, 193

Disorder-based perspectives, person, 35, 44–45
Dispositional empathy, 411, 426–428
Dispositions
accessibility of, 368–375
confessions, 757–758
habits and behaviors, 378–379
helping relations, 401, 403
internal, 367–368, 386–387
personality, 683, 694
recapitulation, 375, 379
sociocultural influence, 192–194
strategy, 65, 495
term, 36
See also Attitudes
Dissonance theory, 27
Distance, bicultural identity integration scale (BIIS)-2, 633, 634
Distinguishability, definition, 211–212
Distinguishable dyads, actor-partner independence model (APIM), 219–221
Distortions, motivated biases and, 350–351
Diversity, multiculturalism, 639–640
Division 8 of the American Psychological Association (APA), 26
Divorce
impact of, 652–654
influence on children, 651
no-fault, 652
Dominance
group influence, 529
status, 165–166
Dominating research themes, 24
Domination, intentional worlds, 199–201
Down-regulation, emotion, 129
Dual crises, 23–25
Dual-judgment model, 356
Durkheim, Emile, 15, 17–18
Dyads. *See also* Over-time dyadic models
accuracy, 233
actor-partner interdependence model (APIM), 217–221
definitions for data analysis, 211–212
design issues for studying, over time, 222–223
distinguishability, 211–212
lagged models for, 225–227
levels of analysis, 240
multilevel analysis, 242
multilevel modeling (MLM), 214–216
nonindependence, 211
over-time dyadic models, 221–230
over-time standard APIM, 223–225
overview of studies, 209–211
persons nested in, 250
social and personality psychology, 209
social interaction, 459
testing distinguishability with MLM, 216–217
Dynamic construction, personal identity, 197–198

Dynamic interaction, personality psychology, 25
Dynamic interactionism, person and situation, 5
Dynamic Theory of Personality, Lewin, 13
Dysfunction, sexual behavioral system, 475

E

Earthquakes, impact, 667
Ecological niche, concept, 159–160
Economics
  evolutionary, 156
  immigration, 656
  impact of divorce, 653–654
Economy of action, emotions, 322
Education
  communism and McCarthy, 21
  group consciousness and collective action, 798
  personality and social psychology, 836
  work experience, 791
Effort, emotions, 322–323
Ego-defensive function, 382
Egoism, help-giving, 399–400
Elaboration likelihood model (ELM), 379, 381, 382, 385
Elderly, attitudes toward, 429, 430, 432
Electroencephalography (EEG), neuroimaging, 115, 127
Electronically Activated Recorder (EAR), 104
Embodies cognitive capital, human adaptive complex, 161
Emergent leadership, study, 682
Emergent third culture, multiculturalism, 640
Emotional intelligence (EI), 353
Emotional suffering, dehumanization, 434–435
Emotions
  abilities and appraisals, 165
  affect, 318
  affecting behavior, 325–326
  approach motivation, 323
  attachment and, regulation, 480–481
  attitudes, 321
  construction of self, 186
  culture, 319
  decision-making, 326
  description, 317–319
  distinguishing affect and, 325
  early history, 315–317
  effort, 322–323
  empathy, 419–421
  energy, 323
  fear, 323
  fear processing, 125–126
  gratitude, 401
  influencing perception, 322–325
  interactive personality-social entity, 317
  motivation and, 124–125
  natural kinds, 318

personality and social psychology, 316–317, 329–331
  personality or social outcome, 330
  physiological reactions, 315
  prefrontal cortex (PFC) asymmetries, 127–129
  reactions, 319
  regulating thought, 326–329
  regulation, 129–130, 319–322
  sadness, 323
  sentiments, 341
  social resources, 324–325
Empathic Quotient, 423
Empathic Responsiveness Questionnaire (ERQ), 424
Empathy. *See also* Antisocial behavior
  affective, 422
  aggression, 423–424
  antisocial behavior, 419–421
  cognitive, 422
  cross-group friendship, 433
  dehumanization, 433–435
  description, 422
  dispositional, and antisocial behavior, 422–426
  dispositional, ideological attitudes and prejudice, 426–428
  empathic feelings, 431–432
  from lack of, to prejudice, 427–428
  gap, 356
  intergroup contact and intergroup bias, 432–433
  lack of "realistic," 435
  offending, 425–426
  promoting, through intergroup contact, 560–561
  role-playing and perspective-taking, 429–431
  self, 120–121
  social life, 419
  us vs. them, 428–435
Empathy-altruism hypothesis, help-giving, 399–400
Empirical action research, 806
Empirical distinguishability, dyadic design, 216–217
Employee engagement, work, 712
Energy, emotions, 323
Energy consumers, group, 537
Environment
  B = *f*(P,E) formula, 3, 6, 33, 74
  interpersonal rejection, 588–590
  person in, 586–587
  self-regulatory processes, 584–586
  vulnerability-inducing, 580–582
Environmentalism, replacing Social Darwinism, 17
Environmental issues, attitudes, 372
Equality matching, models of relationality, 184–185
Equal status, situation for intergroups, 552–553
Eriksen Flankers Task, 117

Erikson, Erik, 18–19, 23
Essentialism
  social policy, 809–810
  stereotypes, 341
Essentialist thinking, evolution theory, 153
Estrogen, human environment, 159
Ethnicity, personality and social psychology, 23–24
Ethnic minority groups
  immigration, 656–659
  multiculturalism, 625, 636–637
Ethnic nationalism, 242
European approach, groups, 519–520
European Association of Personality Psychology, 6, 27, 821, 833
European Association of Social Psychology, 6, 27, 821, 833
European Journal of Personality, 25, 834
European Journal of Social Psychology, 25, 834
European Review of Social Psychology, 25
Evaluative conditioning (EC), valence acquisition, 346
Evaluative priming, 345
Event-related potentials (ERPs), 115, 118–119
Evers, Medgar, civil rights, 545
Evidence. *See also* Forensic psychology; Jury trial
  alibi, 760–761
  deception detection, 754–756
  eyewitness identifications, 761–766
  inadmissible, 771
  police interrogations and confessions, 756–760
Evocation, term, 460
Evoked culture, 171
Evolutionary biologists, 154, 155–156
Evolutionary biology, evolution, 157–158
Evolutionary perspectives. *See also* Human niche
  adaptationism, 154–157
  adaptive contingent variation, 172
  Big Five, 174–175
  cost-benefit modeling, 156
  cultural variation, 170–171
  Darwin, 152–153
  developmental systems theory, 157–158
  ecological niche, 159–160
  evolutionary biology, 157–158
  evolutionary economics, 156
  evolutionary psychology, 156–157
  friendship, 168–169
  genetic variation in personality, 173–174
  individual differences, 171–172
  kinship, 170
  mating and pair-bonding, 169–170
  modern synthesis, 153
  negative frequency-dependent selection, 172–173
  norms and morality, 170
  personality and social psychology, 151–152
  phylogenetic analysis, 158–159

Evolutionary perspectives. (*Contd.*)
reflections, 175–176
social adaptations and human niche,
163–169
social behavior, 169
theory of evolution by natural selection,
152–153
variations in fitness, 173
Evolutionary processes, democratic
society, 16
Evolution-based theories, motive classes,
291–292
Exaptation, adaptation, 154–155
Exchange situations, interdependence, 82
Expectancy-value model, attitude, 376
Experiences in Close Relationships
inventory (ECR), 478
Experimental action research, 806
Experimental psychology, Harvard, 20
Experimental Psychology, Woodworth and
Schlosberg, 315
Experimental Social Psychology, Murphy
and Murphy, 13–14
Explanations
attribution theory, 354–355
self-referential perception of others,
355–356
simulation theory, 355–356
theory of mind, 355
Explanatory
processes, 53–54
whole trait theory, 51, 52–55
Explicit attitudes, persuasion, 380–381
Explicit impressions, term, 338
Explicit responses, attitudes, 372–373
Exploration behavioral system, 473, 479
Explorations in Personality, Murray, 19
Extensive cooperation, human adaptive
complex, 161–162
Extraversion, 529
Extrinsic motivation, self-determination
theory, 295–296
Eyewitness identifications. *See also*
Forensic psychology
accuracy and consistency of
descriptions, 765
estimator variables, 761–762
identification speed, 765–766
lineup administration, 764
lineup composition, 763
lineup instructions, 763
lineup presentation, 763–764
stress, 762
system variables, 763–764
weapons, 762
witness accuracy, 764–766
witness confidence, 765

F
Facebook, behavior, 105
Faces
affect and asymmetric frontal activity, 128
Asian, 132

attention, 345
Black vs. White, 130, 131–133
implicit motives, 293
impressions, 338
perception, 118–119
research on intergroup bias and brain,
131–133
seeing groups, 130
target features, 351
Facial Action Coding System (FACS),
100, 102
Facilitation, active and passive, 342
Factional influence, 529
Fairness, leadership, 691, 693–694
False consciousness, concept, 22
False evidence ploy, confession, 758–759
Family
background, and life experiences, 789
immigration and, dynamics, 654–659
impact of divorce, 652–654
kinship helping, 407
Fantasy realization theory, goals, 300
Fear
emotions, 323
neuroscience, 125–126
Feature utilization, 68
Felt security, attachment system, 471
Feminism
personality and social psychology,
23–24
women's movement, 661–663
Festinger, Leon, 22
Field theory, situation, 74
Fishing, human adaptive complex, 161–162
Fitness, variations in, 173
Follower, personality-in-situation,
692–694
Foragers, human adaptive complex,
161–162
Forensic psychology
alibi evidence, 760–761
behavior in legal system, 753–754
deception detection, 754–756
decision rule, 768–769
dispositional risk factors, 757–758
evidentiary issues, 769–770
eyewitness identifications, 761–766
Frye test, 772
inadmissible evidence, 771
jury nullification, 771–772
jury selection, 766–768
lineups, 763–764
nonevidentiary issues, 770–772
personality and social psychology,
753–754
phenomenology of innocence, 759–760
police interrogations and confessions,
756–760
postdictors of witness accuracy,
764–766
pretrial publicity, 770–771
procedural issues in jury decision-
making, 768–769

science, common sense and role of, in
courts, 772
situational risk factors, 758–759
system variables of lineups, 763–764
training to detect deception,
755–756
trial by jury, 766–772
witness accuracy, 764–766
wizards of lie detection, 756
Fragmented pluralism approach,
multiculturalism, 626–627
Frameworks, describing others, 343–344
Framing, message, for health, 738–740
Frankfurt School, Marxists, 22
Freedom House Ratings, multilevel
analysis, 255
Frenkel-Brunswik, Else, 22
Freud, Sigmund
attachment, 467
behavior, 468
emotion regulation, 129
personality layers, 15
Friendship
cross-group, in intergroup contact,
556–558
mutualism, 168–169
potential, 557
Frijda, Nico, 25
Frye test, expert testimony, 772
Function, adaptation, 154
Functional design, concept, 155
Functional leadership theory, team
leadership, 718
Functional magnetic resonance imaging
(fMRI), brain mapping, 112, 115, 124
Functional projection, perception, 350
Fundamental attribution error (FAE), 354
Funding agencies, personality and social
psychology, 834–835

G
Galton, Francis, social factors, 16
Gays and lesbians
empathic feelings, 431–432
social policy, 809–810
Gender
discrimination, 787
empathy and offending, 425
help-giving, 398
immigration, 659
mating motives, 291–292
personality and social psychology, 23–24
Gene-environment interaction, well-
being, 611
General Social Survey, multilevel
analysis, 254
Generation, divorce, 654
Generational analysis, immigration,
654–655
Generation-since-immigration, 654
Generativity
caregiving behavior, 474
collective action, 792

Genes
evolutionary biology, 157–158
evolution theory, 152–153
modern synthesis, 153
negative frequency-dependent selection, 172–173
roles in personality and social psychology, 137–138
Genetic determinism, Darwinism, 157
Genetic program, concept, 157
Genetics, traits, 38–39
Genetic variation, personality, 173–174
GenX, 660
Gestalt psychology, attitude assessment, 18
Gibsonian approach, perception of situations, 70–71
Global cultures, multiculturalism, 640
Globalization, multiculturalism and, 641–642
Global-local focus, emotions, 328–329
Global/local processing style model (GLOMO), 345
Goal orientation, leadership, 689–690
Goals
achievement situations, 301
appraisal, 298
automatic processes and implicit, 302–303
congruence and conflict, 304–305
conscious vs. nonconscious goal pursuit, 303–304
defensive pessimism, 302
definition, 297
fantasy realization theory, 300
intergroups, 552–553
mind-set theory of action phases, 299
personal, as personality, 301–302
personality systems interaction theory, 299
research, 288–289, 297–298
selection and commitment, 299–300
self-regulation, 300
structure and content, 298–299
Goddard, Henry, 16
Go/No-Go Associations Test (GNAT), 348
Go/No-Go task, 117
Google Scholar, 13, 26
Grant Study, well-being, 602
Gratification, ability to delay, 82–83
Gratitude, helping relations, 401
Great Depression, 19, 651
Greatest Generation, and Baby Boom, 660
Group consciousness. See also Collective action
individual differences, and collective action, 789–793
low-status, 798
personality and social psychology, 781–782, 793, 794
relative deprivation theory, 786–788
social psychological models of, and collective action, 782–788
Group decision-making

conformity, 530
consensus, 530–531
group discussion, 527–528
influence, 528–530
risk, 531
Group identification, self-categorization, 650
Group identities, social theories, 783–784
Group maintenance
cohesion, 531–532
integration of new members, 533
resolution of relational conflict, 532–533
Group mean, 234
Group membership
collective action based on voluntary, 796
low-status, 790
monitoring salience of, 553–558
Group mind, notions of, 17–18
Group-oriented collectivists, interdependent constructions, 186–187
Group personality composition (GPC), 525
Groups. See also Intergroup processes; Multiculturalism
actor-partner interdependence model (APIM) for, 230–232
authoritarianism, 521
Big Five predicting performance, 525–526
Big Five traits, 523–524
coaction phenomenon, 536–537
conflict situations, 520–525
decision-making, 527–531
definition, 521
definitions for data analysis, 211–212
distinguishability, 211–212
future research, 534–537
helping relations, 395
history of groups-individual differences interface, 518–520
individual differences, 517
individual-group discontinuity, 524
levels of analysis, 240
membership, 535–536
models for research, 230–235
multiculturalism, 625, 636–637
multilevel analysis, 242
multilevel modeling (MLM), 212–214
nature of personality in, 536–537
nonindependence, 211
one-with-many (OWM) design, 232–234
overview of studies, 209–211
persons nested in, 250
role of personality and behavior, 524–525
situations, 85–86
social and personality psychology, 209
social relations model (SRM), 234–235
social value orientation (SVO), 522–523
sports, 526–527

task-performing, 525–527
trust, 521–522, 526
understudied traits, 526
us vs. them, 428–435
Groups-individual differences
behaviorism, 518–519
discontinuity, 524
European approach, 519–520
history, 518–520
Mann review, 520
systematic approach, 519–520
Growth models, dyadic, 227–230
Guilford, J. P., 19
Guilt, emotion, 324
Gulf War, 792

H

Habits, personality dispositions, 378–379
Habitual behavior, novel vs., 96
Habitus, selfways as, 190
Handbook of Personality and Social Psychology, plan of action, 6–8
Handbook of Personality Psychology, 6, 24
Handbook of Social Psychology, 6, 26
Handbooks, 6
Harvard
dual crises, 23–25
personality and social psychology, 20
Social Relations Department, 20, 835
Harvard Psychological Clinic, 18
Health, personality, 41
Health behavior
implications for interventions, 735
interplay between moderators and mediators, 733, 734
intervention strategies, 729–730
linkages between personality and, 730–731
matching frames to perception of behavior, 738
matching frames to personality, 738–740
matching intervention strategies to people, 735–745
measurement-of-mediation approach, 737
mediated moderation, 732–734
mediation and moderation connection, 732–735, 745–747
message framing, 738–740
message tailoring, 740–741
moderated mediation, 734–735
morbidity and mortality rates, 729
patient x treatment matching, 742–744
person x intervention strategy (P x IS), 731, 736
person x situation (P x S) perspective, 731, 743
precaution adoption process model (PAPM), 730, 735, 741, 742, 746
principles in social and personality psychology, 730
processes underlying matching interventions, 744–745

Health behavior (*Contd.*)
  stage matching, 741–742
  theory of planned behavior (TPB), 731
  translation of theory into practice,
    747–748
  transtheoretical model (TTM), 730, 742
Health psychology, 46
Hedonic adaptation, well-being, 606–607
Hedonic treadmill theory, well-being,
  613–614
Help, characteristics of, 402
Helper
  characteristics of, 402
  consequences of help-giving, 403–404
Help-giving. *See also* Helping relations
  altruism or disguised egoism, 399–400
  altruistic personality, 398–399
  attribution, 400–401
  belongingness, 409–410
  consequences of, for helper, 403–404
  developmental antecedents, 398
  gender, 398
  helping relations and, 395–396
  motivation to help, 399–401
  normative influences, 397
  research, 396–401
  situational determinants, 396–397
  social responsibility, 397
  when people help, 396–397
  who helps?, 397–399
Helping
  research, 394–395
  social interaction, 394–396
  social psychology of, 411–412
Helping relations. *See also* Help-giving
  attachment and, 407–408
  characteristics of help, 402
  characteristics of helper, 402
  characteristics of recipient, 402–403
  disposition, 401
  gratitude, 401
  helper-recipient relations, 404
  help-giving and, 395–396
  help-giving for helper, 403–404
  intergroup, 404–407
  intergroup, between differentially
    advantaged groups, 405–406
  kin vs. non-kin, 407
  negative consequences, 401–403
  positive consequences, 401
  racial boundaries, 406–407
  recipient coping, 403
  self-categorization and cross-group, 405
  self-threat and self-support, 401–403
  social exclusion and helping, 408
  volunteering, 408–409
Herskovits, Melville, 17
Heuristic-systematic model, 379
Hidden profile effect, group discussion, 536
Historical generation, immigration, 654
Hitler, Adolf, personality evaluation, 19
HIV/AIDS, volunteerism, 813–817
Holidays, official, 194

Holistic tendencies, constructions of
  self, 185
Holocaust, catastrophe, 665–667
Homburger, Erik, 18
Hormones
  estrogen, 159
  psychological dispositions, 138–139
Human adaptation, behavior, 579
Human adaptive complex, 161–163
Human beings
  ANOVA model, 27
  capacity to conceive self, 263–264
  phylogenies, 159
  situations and behavior, 84–85
Human Development Index (HDI),
  United Nations, 254–255
Humanitarian intervention, poor, 16
Humanization, self, 121
Human niche
  alternative views of, 163
  coalition partners, 164–165
  coevolved components of human
    adaptive complex, 162–163
  ecological niche, 159–160
  hominin niches vs. ape niche, 160–161
  human adaptive complex, 161–162
  primate niches and evolution of
    Miocene apes, 160
  social adaptations, 163–169
Human sexuality, social constructionism,
  809–810
Hunting, human adaptive complex,
  161–162
Hurricane Katrina, impact, 667
Hyperactivation
  attachment behavioral system, 472–473
  attachment theory, 470
  caregiving behavioral system, 475,
    482–483
  exploration behavioral system, 473
  power behavioral system, 477, 485
  scale items for behavioral system, 479
  sexual behavioral system, 475–476
Hypothesis testing, social neuroscience,
  113–114
Hypothetical construct, subjective
  well-being, 600

I

Ickes, William, 26
Identity. *See* Multicultural identity; Self
Identity stories
  content of, 191–192
  dynamic construction of personal,
    197–198
  organization of, 192
  personal, 191–192
Ideological attitudes
  attachment, and prejudice, 427
  dispositional empathy, 426–428
Ideology, 548–549
  belief system, 812–813
  political, and policy, 823–824

Imagined community, collective self, 185
Immersive virtual environment
  technologies (IVET), 104
Immigration
  conditions of arrival, 655–657
  economic conditions, 656
  family dynamics, 654–659
  generational analysis, 654–655
  intersectional analysis of experience,
    657–659
  motivation to leave, 655
  social conditions, 656–657
Implicit Association Test (IAT), 43, 321,
  344, 384, 559
  Black–White IAT, 131, 132
  racial, 428–429
Implicit attitudes
  behavior, 374–375
  changing, 383–384
Implicit goals, automatic processes and,
  302–303
Implicit impressions, term, 338
Implicit motive theory
  motivation, 292–295
  profiles, 293–294
  relationships between implicit and
    explicit motives, 294–295
Implicit personality theories (IPT),
  339–340
Implicit responses, attitude, 374–375
Impressions
  accuracy of initial, 348–351
  attention, 345
  conceptions of traits, 340–341
  control and automatic processes,
    347–348
  deception, 349–350
  formation processes, 344–348
  frameworks describing others, 343–344
  lay descriptions of others, 338–344
  motivated biases and distortions,
    350–351
  perceiver features, 353
  perception, 338–339
  priming, 345–346
  relational features, 353–354
  social and personality psychology,
    337–338
  spontaneous inferences from
    behaviors, 347
  stereotypes, 341–343
  target features, 351–352
  terms, 338
  traits' relations to each other, 339–340
  types, 341
  valence acquisition, 346–347
Impulse expression, personality, 792
Incidental effects, adaptation, 155
Inclusive fitness hypothesis, 407
Independence, recipient of help,
  410–411
Independent constructions, self, 183–187
Indistinguishable, group members, 212

Indistinguishable dyads, actor-partner independence model (APIM), 218–219
Individual, discontinuity with groups, 524
Individual-collectivism, leadership, 680, 693–694
Individual differences, multilevel radical coefficient model (MRCM), 252
Individual level. acculturation and multiculturalism, 627, 628, 630
Individual well-being. See also Well-being measurement of, 598–599
term, 597–598
Industrial/organizational (I/O) psychology, 45–46
Infants. See also Attachment parent-child attachment, 487
Influence, group decision-making, 528–530
Informant report, assessing behavior, 96–97
Information, group discussion, 527–528
Information certainty, interdependence, 81, 83
Infrahumanization, dehumanization measure, 434
Ingroup love, vs. outgroup hate, 546
Ingroup members. See also Groups us vs. them, 428–435
Inhibition, person-in-situation, 683–685
Injustice, perceived, 783
Innocence
alibi evidence, 760–761
phenomenology of, 759–760
Input-process-output, team effectiveness, 720
Insecurity
attachment, 481
attachment behavioral system, 472–473
Institute for Social Research (ISR), University of Michigan, 20
Institute of Personality, Assessment and Research (IPAR), University of California, 20
Integration
emerging opportunities for, 56–57
levels between personality and social psychology, 47
likely routes of, 48–49
new members into groups, 533
opportunities for, 33–34
personality and social psychology, 46–48
whole trait theory, 49–56
Integrative approach, benefits for well-being, 614
Intelligence testing, developments, 16–17
Intentional behaviors, 340
Intentional worlds
cultural psychology, 198–201
domination, 199–201
selfways as, 199
Intentions
behavior, 378
changing, 385–386

implementation, 386
predicting, 378
Interactional continuity, style, 26
Interactional perspectives
attachment theory, 496, 502–503
cognitive-affective processing system (CAPS) model, 496, 497–499
dependency/risk regulation and self-esteem, 503–505
future directions, 510–513
interdependence theory, 496, 499–501
psychology, 494–496
situation dimensions, 500, 501
theories, 496–503
Interactional strategy, 65
Interactionism
integrated, dynamic and situated, 25
person x situation, 74–75
Interactionist views, persons and situations, 4–5
Interaction Process Analysis (IPA), behavior, 100, 101
Interactions, Person x Situation (P x S), 66
Interaction signatures, relationships, 499
Interactive pluralism approach, multiculturalism, 627
Interdependence theory (IT)
An Atlas of Interpersonal Situations, 78–79
basis of interdependence, 82
description, 78–79
groups, organizations and cultures, 85–86
interactional, 496, 499–501
mutuality of outcome interdependence, 81
outcome correspondence, 81–82
outcome interdependence, 81
person and situation, 79–80
situations, 70
study of dispositions, 494
taxonomy of situations, 80–81
temporal structure, 82–83
Interdependent constructions, self, 185–187
Intergroup
control and regulation of, bias, 133–135
empathy and, contact and bias, 432–433
helping relations, 404–407
intergroup helping as status relations model (IHSR), 405
situational conditions, 552
social-personality research, 131–133
Intergroup emotion
anxiety, 136–137
brain, 136–137
negative affect, 136
Intergroup processes, 130
anxiety reduction through, 558–560
cooperation and common goals, 552–553
cross-group friendship, 556–558
defining prejudice, 546–547
diverse societies, 552–562
equal status in situation, 552–553
institutional support, 553

potential for positive outcomes, 561–562
promoting empathy through, 560–561
recategorization and superordinate group identities, 555–556
relationship motivation and needs, 562
salience of group membership, 553–558
situational conditions for, contact, 552
specifying sources of prejudice, 547–552
Internal dispositions. See also Dispositions behavior, 367–368
theory and research, 386–387
Internalization, self-determination theory, 296
Internal working models, behavior, 469
International Social Survey Program (ISSP), 243
Internet, behavior, 104–105
Internment, Japanese Americans, 665–667
Interpersonal circle, 77
Interpersonal circumplex model, situation-behavior, 450
Interpersonal dimension, person-situation, 448
Interpersonal dynamics, self, 279–281
Interpersonal forces, behavioral field, 578
Interpersonal goals, dynamics of, 280–281
Interpersonal processes, social and personality psychology, 209
Interpersonal rejection
environmental vulnerabilities, 588–590
personality vulnerabilities, 590
P x E vulnerabilities, 587–590
Interpersonal Relations and Group Processes (IRGP), 209–210
Interpersonal situations, types, 458
Interpersonal theory (IT), groups, 518
Interpretation
emotion, 316
incorporating, and meaning, 48
Interpretative process, whole trait theory, 53, 54
Intersectional analysis, immigration experience, 657–659
Intersectionality
collective action, 796–797
phenomenon, 785
Intervention. See also Health behavior AIDS and volunteerism, 815–816
healthy behavior, 729–730
intervention challenge, 733, 735
matching to people, 735–745
moderator and mediators, 733, 735
theoretical challenge, 733–734, 735
well-being, 608–610
Intra-individual variation, well-being, 601–603
Intrinsic motivation, self-determination theory, 295–296
Invention of Society, Moscovici, 15
Isolation, confessions, 757
Item response theory (IRT), well-being, 600–601
Iterative processing model, attitudes, 321

J

James, William, 16, 315, 317
Japanese Americans, internment of, 665–667
Jews, dehumanization, 434
Job attitudes. *See also* Work
  organizational psychology, 710–715
  specific work attitudes, 711–712
Job involvement, work, 714
Job satisfaction, work, 713–714
Johnson v. Louisiana, 768
Journal of Abnormal and Social Psychology (JASP), 23, 574, 577, 833, 834
  creation, 575, 592
Journal of Abnormal Psychology (JAP), 23, 574
Journal of Applied Psychology, 715
Journal of Personality, 577
Journal of Personality and Social Psychology (JPSP), 23, 26, 574, 577, 715, 834
Journal of Research in Personality, 49
Journal of Social Issues, 24, 782, 824
Judging others, impression, 356
Judgmental biases, well-being, 606
Jung, Carl, 15
Jury trial. *See also* Forensic psychology
  bias in jury selection, 768
  decision rule, 768–769
  evidentiary issues, 769–770
  inadmissible evidence, 771
  jury nullification, 771–772
  jury selection, 766–768
  jury size, 768
  nonevidentiary issues, 770–772
  pretrial publicity, 770–771
  procedural issues, 768–769
  scientific jury selection, 767–768
Juvenile dependence, human adaptive complex, 161

K

Kagan, Jerome, 20
Kahneman, Daniel, Nobel Memorial Prize in Economics, 28
Kelley, Harold, ANOVA model, 27
Kelman, Herbert, 20
Kinship, 170, 407
Klineberg, Otto, 17
Kluckhohn, Clyde, 20
Knowledge acquisition, 452–453
Knowledge function, 382
Kroeber, Alfred, 17

L

Labor movement, activism, 659
Lagged models, dyads, 225–227
Language dominance, 528
Latent trait, well-being, 600–601
Late positive potential (LPP), oddball task, 123–124
Latino immigrants, social conditions, 656–657
Leader-follower relationship

follower personality-in-situation, 692–694
  leadership effectiveness, 674, 687
Leader-member exchange (LMX)
  leadership effectiveness, 674, 687
  organizational psychology, 716–717
Leadership
  Big Five, 678–682
  charismatic, 675, 677, 681, 690, 717–718
  collectivism-individualism, 680, 693–694
  fairness, 691, 693–694
  follower personality-in-situation, 692–694
  goal orientation, 689–690
  leader-follower relationship, 674, 687
  leader-member exchange (LMX), 674, 687, 716–717
  learning orientation, 687–688
  motivation, 680–681
  organizational psychology, 715–719
  personality and, 715–716
  personality and, effectiveness, 674–675
  person-in-situation, 674, 682–688, 691–692
  person x situation interactions, 691–692
  research, 673–674
  self-efficacy, 680–681
  self-regulatory focus, 689–690
  self-sacrificial, 717–718
  social groupings, 673
  social identity theory, 690–691
  team, 718–719
  trait activation theory, 684–685, 688–689
  trait perspective, 675–678
  transformational, 679–681, 685–686, 690, 691, 717–718
Leadership Behavior Description Questionnaire (LBDQ), 101
Leadership categorization theory, 690
Leadership Trait Questionnaires (LTQ), 100
Learning
  automaticity, 116–117
  leadership, 687–688
Least preferred coworker (LPC), leadership effectiveness, 677–678
LeBon, Gustave, 17–18
Legal system. *See* Forensic personality
Lesbians. *See* Gays and lesbians
Level, self-esteem, 266–268, 273–274
Levinson, Daniel, 22
Lewin, Kurt, 13, 511
  action research, 805–806
  B = *f*(P,E) formula, 3, 6, 33, 74, 805
  death, 22, 537n.2
  E term, 579
  field theory, 74, 493, 494
  framework for equation, 577–578
  laboratory experiments, 21
  methodological advances, 19
  Person term, 579
Lexical hypothesis, personality, 447

Lie detection
  evidence, 754–756
  situational influences, 756
  training, 755–756
  wizards, 756
Life experiences
  collective action, 794
  group consciousness, 794
  group consciousness and collective action, 789–791
  individual differences, 794
Life satisfaction, 608, 661
Life span
  behavior through life stages, 649–651
  catastrophes of human and natural origin, 663–667
  general impact of war, 663–665
  immigration and family dynamics, 654–659
  impact of divorce, 652–654
  life changes, 651
  person and social contexts, 651
  seeking social change, 659–663
  stages, 663
Lineups. *See* Eyewitness identifications
Lippitt, Ronald, 22
Low frequency behaviors, 96

M

McCarthy, Joseph, communism in education, 21
McDougall, William, 16
MacKinnon, Donald, Institute of Personality, Assessment and Research (ISAR), 20
Major histocompatibility complex (MHC), genes, 172–173
Mann review, groups, 520
Many-perceivers, one-target (MP1T) design, group, 232
Marital research, stability, 459
Market pricing, models of relationality, 184
Marriage
  impact of divorce, 652–654
  relationship commitment, 460–461
Martyr's behavior, 529
Marxists, Frankfurt School, 22
Maslow, Abraham, 23
Master identities, content of, 191
Matching interventions. *See also* Health behavior
  health behavior, 744–745
  message framing, 738–740
  message tailoring, 740–741
  patient x treatment, 742–744
Mating, evolutionary perspective, 169–170
Mead, George Herbert, 16
Mead, Margaret, 17
Meaning
  emotion, 316
  incorporating interpretation and, 48
Measurement
  behavior, 95–96

biculturalism, 638
individual well-being, 598–599
multicultural identity, 630–636
traits, 37, 49
Mechanism, brain, 115
Mechanistic dehumanization, 341
Medial prefrontal cortex (mPFC)
activity in, 114
brain, 113
significance of, 121–122
Mediation model, leadership, 681
Mediators and moderators. *See also* Health
behavior
health behavior, 732–735, 745–747
interplay between, 733, 734
mediated moderation, 732–734
moderated mediation, 734–735
Medical students, attitudes toward
elderly, 429
Members, integration of new, in
groups, 533
Membership, low-status group, 790
Memory, automaticity, 116–117
Mendelian gene theory, 153
Mental health, attachment and, 481–482
Mental interactions, 73
Mentalizing, theory of mind, 119–120
Mere exposure effect, 320, 346
Message framing
health, 738–740
perception of behavior, 738
personality, 738–740
Message tailoring, health, 740–741
Methodological integration, well-being,
610–612
Mexican Americans, immigration, 654–655
Mimicry, empathy, 420, 428
Mindfulness
goal pursuit, 303–304
self-esteem, 271–272
Mind-set theory of action, 299
Minimization, confessions, 757, 759
Minnesota Multiphasic Personality
Inventory (MMPI), 17, 601
Minority groups, multiculturalism, 625,
636–637
Miranda rights, 757, 758, 760
Mirror neurons, empathy, 121
Mischel, Walter, 26
Mission statements, social policy, 804–805
Model of ambivalence-induced discomfort
(MAID), 346–347
MODE model, attitude-behavior, 372
Moderators. *See* Mediators and
moderators
Monoculturalism, 626
Montagu, Ashley, 17
Mood effects, well-being, 605
Morale, social psychology, 20
Morality, evolutionary perspective, 170
Morbidity rates, health, 729
Mortality rates, health, 729
Mortality salience (MS)

impression, 350
social psychology, 581
Moscovici, Serge, 15
Mosteller, Frederick, 20
Motivated biases, distortions and, 350–351
Motivation
achievement, 301
approach and avoidance, 289–290
behavioral inhibition and activation
systems, 290
categorization of motives, 290–292
congruence and conflict, 304–305
emotion and, 124–125
emotions, 323
future directions, 303–305
help-giving, 399–401
historical influence, 289
immigration, 655
implicit motive theory, 292–295
intergroup relations, 562
leadership, 680–681, 690, 694
perception of relevance, 125
personality and social psychology,
287–289, 305–306
personality as, 706, 707–708
perspectives on person, 43–44, 57
prefrontal cortex (PFC) asymmetries,
127–129
promotion-focused tendencies, 184
regulatory focus theory (RFT), 290
self-determination theory, 295–297
social psychology, 44
study of, 287
Motivational process, whole trait theory, 53
Motive profile approach, leadership, 677
Motives, self-esteem, 270–271, 275–277
Multicultural, term, 625
Multicultural identity
bicultural identity integration (BII),
632–636
biculturalism, 630, 631
individual differences in, 631–636
measurement, 630–636
operationalization, 630–636
Multiculturalism
acculturation and, 627–630
Chinese-Americans, 633, 635–636, 640
cosmopolitan approach, 626
defining, 624–630
emergent third culture, 640
fragmented pluralism approach,
626–627
and globalization, 641–642
governments with, policies, 625, 630
group differences in, 636–637
identity, 624–625, 630–636
ideology and policies, 625
interactive pluralism approach, 627
minority groups, 625
new directions, 640–641
prevalence and importance, 623–624
psychological and societal
consequences, 637–640

societal and intergroup levels, 625–627
Multilevel modeling (MLM)
aggregation and disaggregation, 243–244
applications in personality and social
psychology, 251–256
cross-cultural research, 242
data analytic approach, 210
differences across persons, 241
dyadic data, 214–216
group data, 212–214
integrating personality and social
psychology, 239–240, 249–251,
256–257
levels of analysis, 240
national identification and
anti-immigrant prejudice, 243
persons nested in cultures or nations,
250–251
persons nested in dyads or groups, 250
persons nested within groups, 242
situations or contexts nested in persons,
249–250
testing distinguishability in dyadic
design, 216–217
when and why for analyses, 240–244
within-person variability, 241
Multilevel random coefficient model
(MRCM)
categorical outcomes, 247
centering, 246
cross-cultural research, 254–256
integrating personality and social
psychology, 249–251
introduction, 244–247
level 2 variables as outcome, 248–249
multilevel mediation, 247
multilevel structural equation modeling
(ML-SEM), 247–248
nonlinearity, 247
personality or within persons processes,
251–252
personality x situation, 253–254
person x situation, 253–254
statistical analysis, 240
Multilevel structural equation modeling
(ML–SEM), 247–248, 256
Multiple inference model, 355
Multistate-multitrait-multiconstruct
model, well-being, 600
Murder, antisocial behavior, 420
Murphy, Gardner, *Experimental Social
Psychology*, 13–14
Murray, Henry
academic psychology, 15
Explorations in Personality, 601
personality psychology, 18
stimulus situation, 73
Mutual acceptance, personality and social
psychology, 46–48
Mutual constitution
cultural psychology, 182
social interaction, 459
Mutual differentiation model, 433

Mutualism, friendship, 168–169
Mutuality of dependence, situation
    dimensions, 500, 501

N

Naive realism, 183
National Institutes of Health, 834
Nationalism, 242
Nationality, ethnic vs. civic, 243
National Science Foundation, 835
Nations
    levels of analysis, 240
    persons nested in, 250–251
Nativism, 626
Natural kinds, emotion, 318
Natural science, Allport, 18
Natural selection, 152–153, 155
The Nature of Prejudice, Allport, 13, 18
Needs, leadership personality, 676–677
Needs-supplies fit, person-job fit, 708
Negative affect (NA), 37, 136
Negative frequency-dependent selection,
    genes, 172–173
Negativity, person vs. situation, 24
Negotiation, social value orientation, 523
Nested data
    dyads, 250
    groups, 250
    multilevel analysis, 243
    multiple situations or contexts,
        249–250
Netherlands, multiculturalism, 625
Neural assessments, attitudes, 123–124
Neuroscience. *See also* Self
    affective style, 137
    amygdala (AMG), 113
    anger, 128–129
    asymmetric involvement of prefrontal
        cortex (PFC), 127–129
    attitudes, 122–123
    automaticity, 116–117
    brain mapping, 112–113
    brain mapping of racial bias, 130–131
    content areas, 115
    control, 116, 117
    control and regulation of intergroup
        bias, 133–135
    emotion and motivation, 124–125
    emotion regulation, 129–130
    empathy, 120–121
    fear processing, 125–126
    hormones and psychological
        dispositions, 138–139
    humanization, 121
    hypothesis testing, 113–114
    intergroup emotion and brain, 136–137
    intergroup processes, 130
    medial prefrontal cortex (mPFC), 113
    mentalizing and theory of mind,
        119–120
    methods of social and personality, 115
    neural assessments of attitudes,
        123–124

orbital frontal cortex (OFC), 113
perceiving faces, 118–119
perception of motivational relevance, 125
perception of self and others, 118–122
questions for analysis, 115
research of intergroup bias and brain,
    131–133
reverse inference, 114–115
reward processing, 126–127
roles of genes in personality and social
    psychology, 137–138
seeing groups, 130
self, 118
significance of mPFC, 121–122
social, approach, 112
social and personality psychology,
    111–112, 139
social cognition and self, 116–125
state affect, 128
stereotyping, 133
trait affective styles, 127–128
Neuroticism, group data, 212–214
New Orleans, Hurricane Katrina, 667
Nigrescence, politicized group
    identification, 785–786
Nobel Memorial Prize in Economics,
    Kahneman, 28
No-fault divorce, 652
Nominal situations vs. psychological, 71
Nonconscious goal pursuit, 303–304
Nonindependence, definition, 211
Nonlinearity, multilevel modeling, 247
Normative beliefs, term, 376
Normative parameters, behavioral systems,
    468–469
Norms
    evolutionary perspective, 170
    help-giving, 397
North American experimental
    psychology, 27
Novel behavior, vs. habitual, 96

O

Obama, Barack, multiculturalism, 623
Obedience, behavior, 94
Obedience experiments, affordance, 68
Obesity, health, 729
Objective features vs. perceived features of
    situations, 70–71
Observation
    assessing behavior, 96, 97–99
    personal living spaces, 105–106
    selecting or developing system, 99–101
    strengths and weakness of behavior, 103
Occupational psychology, 702
Offending, empathy and, 425–426
Office of Strategic Services (OSS), 19
Official holidays, 194
Olfaction and hormone effects, target, 352
One-perceiver, many-targets (1PMT)
    design, group, 232
One-with-many design (OWM), group
    research, 232–234

Operationalization, multicultural identity,
    630–636
Optimism, activism, 793
Orbital frontal cortex (OFC)
    brain, 113
    reward processing, 126–127
Orchestration, genetic program, 157
Organizational behavior, 702
Organizational commitment, attitude,
    711–712, 714
Organizational psychology. *See also* Work
    collective personality, 709–710
    definitions, 702–703
    job attitudes, 710–715
    leader-member exchange (LMX),
        716–717
    leadership, 715–719
    personality and social psychology and
        work attitudes, 712–715
    personality as motivation, 706,
        707–708
    personality as predictor, 706–707
    person-environment fit, 704–710
    team leadership, 718–719
    teams and teamwork, 719–722
    themes, 702
    theory borrowing, 703–704
    trait activation theory, 706, 708–709
Organizations
    levels of analysis, 240
    situations, 85–86
Outcomes
    interdependence, 81–82
    predicting important life, 38
Outgroup hate, ingroup love vs., 546
Outgroup members. *See also* Groups
    collective action, 796
    us vs. them, 428–435
Outliers, Gladwell, 94
Over-time dyadic models, 221–230
    design issues, 222–223
    growth models, 227–230
    lagged models for dyads, 225–227
    person-period data structure, 224
    standard actor-partner interdependence
        model (APIM), 223–225
    three-level nested vs. crossed
        depiction, 221

P

Pain matrix, 420, 428–429
Pair-bonding, evolutionary perspective,
    169–170
Parental divorce, influence on children, 651
Parents. *See* Attachment
Parsons, Talcott, 20
Participant action research, 806
Partner effect, 217
Passive facilitation, 342
Pathogens, evolutionary perspective, 171
Patient x treatment matching, health
    behavior, 742–744
Peace, Great Depression, 19

Perceived features, objective vs., of
  situations, 70–71
Perceived organizational support, work,
  712, 714
Perceiver effect, 234
Perceiver qualities, Big Five, 174–175
Perceiver variance, 235
Perception
  behavioral control, 377
  deception, 349–350
  emotions influencing, 322–325
  perceiver features, 353
Performance, 166, 200
Permeability, regions, 577
Persian Gulf War, 664–665
Person. *See also* Traits
  antisocial behavior, 421–422
  approaches to self, 279
  cognitive perspectives on, 41–43
  comparing perspectives, 45
  conceptions of, 7
  current knowledge about traits, 35
  disorder-based perspectives, 44–45
  environment, 586–587
  integrating perspectives, 56–57
  interaction with situations, 4–5
  interdependence theory, 79–80
  motivational perspectives, 43–44
  multilevel radical coefficient model
    (MRCM), 251–252
  nested in cultures or nations, 250–251
  nested in dyads and small groups, 250
  person-situation debate, 39–40
  person x situation interactionism, 74–75
  perspectives on, 34–35
  rapid growth and opportunities for
    integration, 33–34
  relationship of personality to social
    psychology fields, 45–49
  self-esteem, 265–266
  trait developments of decade, 36–41
  trait perspectives on, 35–41
Personal Data Sheet, Woodworth, 17
Personal identity, 191–192, 197–198
Personality
  adulthood personality change, 39
  affective processing, 329–330
  altruistic, in help-giving, 398–399
  antisocial behavior, 421–422
  authoritarian, 548–549
  Back to the Future movie character,
    448, 462
  behavior, 369
  behavioral systems and, 483–488
  behavioral systems association with, 486
  Big Five, 675
  characteristics, 791–793
  collective action, 794
  concept, 86
  construal and alternativism, 42
  defensive pessimism, 302
  definition, 649
  emotion, 330

five-factor model, 675
Freud, 15
genetics, 38–39
genetic variation in, 173–174
group behavior, 524–525
group consciousness and collective
  action, 791–793
groups research, 535–536
help-giving, 398–399
influence, 529
integrating perspectives within, 55–56
interpersonal and intergroup
  helping, 411
interpersonal theories, 446–447
Jung, 15
leader, and effectiveness, 688–692
leadership and, 715–716
leadership effectiveness, 674–675
levels of analysis, 240
linkages between health and, 730–731
matching frames to, 738–740
motivation, 706, 707–708
multilevel radical coefficient model
  (MRCM), 251–252, 253–254
nature of, in groups, 536–537
normal and abnormal behavior,
  576–577
personal goals as, 301–302
personal vulnerability, 582–583
persons and situations, 14
rejection sensitivity, 456–459
relational schemas, 454–455
relationship outcomes, 460–461
role of, 5
self-monitoring, 707
social identities, 650–651
social interaction, 446–451
states, 52
subjective well-being (SWB), 37–38
target and observer agreement, 39
transference and relational self, 455–456
understanding, within social
  interaction, 451–454
understanding by situation, 331
vulnerabilities, 586, 590
Personality: A Psychological Interpretation,
  Allport, 13, 17, 18
abnormal psychology, 591–592
advantages to integration of, 46
bridges, 830, 831
collective action, 781–782, 793, 794
combined territories, 830, 831–832
coming back together (1985–present),
  26–28
conceptions of self, 265
contributions to science of well-being,
  610–614
cultural psychology, 182–183, 201–202
department structures, 835
dual crises (1965–1985), 23–25
early developments (1920–1935), 16–18
emotions, 316–317, 318, 320, 322,
  329–331

evolutionary perspectives, 151–152
funding agencies, 834–835
future directions for well-being
  research, 614–615
health behavior, 730
impressions, 337–338
infrastructure, 833–836
integrating behavior into, 106–107
integration levels, 47
internal dispositions, 367–368
journals, 834
motivation, 287–289, 305–306
multiculturalism and globalization,
  641–642
multilevel modeling, 239–240,
  249–251, 256–257
mutual acceptance, 46–48
neuroscience, 111–112, 139
origins through World War I, 14–16
policy differences, 807–813
professional organizations, 833–834
psychopathology, 574
ravines, 830, 832–833
research and theory, 583
research of intergroup bias and brain,
  131–133
role of genes in, 137–138
social-cognitive theory, 51
structural differentiation and slow
  acceptance (1950–1965), 21–23
teaching, 836
war influences, 18–21
work attitude study, 712–715
Personality and Social Psychology Bulletin,
  26, 834
Personality and Social Psychology Review,
  26, 834
Personality at the Crossroads, 74
Personality development, study, 534–535
Personality disorders, characteristics, 35,
  44–45
Personality Inventory
  16 Principle Factors (16 PF), 22
  Bernreuter, 17
Personality Processes and Individual
  Differences (PPID), 209–210
Personality psychologists, 3
  Big Five, 174–175
  contributions to science of well-being,
    598, 599–604, 615
  definitions, 3–4
  group identification and self-
    categorization, 650
  individual characteristics, 14
  integration of, and social psychology, 46
  intergroup bias and the brain, 131–133
  mutual acceptance of social and, 46–48
  perceived crisis, 24
  perspectives on person, 34–35
  relationship to social psychology fields,
    45–49
  research, 4
  routes of integration, 48–49

Personality psychologists (*Contd.*)
    situations mattering in, 66–68
    social psychology venturing into, 5
    trait hierarchy, 36–37
    whole trait theory, 49–56
Personality signatures, 450
Personality systems interaction theory,
    goals, 299
Personality testing, developments, 16–17
Personality traits, accessibility, 368–369
Personal Living Space Cue Inventory
    (PLSCI), 105–106
Personal living spaces (PLSs), observation,
    105–106
Personal moderators, situations and
    behavior, 4
Personal norms, help-giving, 397
The Person and the Situation, 65
Person-by-situation. *See also* Interactional
    perspectives
    close relationships, 493–494
    future directions, 510–513
Person effects, situation effects vs., 25
Person-environment fit
    organizational psychology, 704–710
    personality as motivation, 706,
        707–708
    personality as predictor, 706–707
    trait activation theory, 706, 708–709
Person in context. *See also* Cultural
    psychology
    cultural worlds, 195–201
    downstream consequences of action,
        196–197
    dynamic construction of personal
        identity, 197–198
    intentional worlds, 198–201
    upstream impacts on action, 196
Person-in-situation
    activation, 683–685
    before the Big Five, 685
    Big Five and beyond, 685–688
    effectiveness, 683–685
    inhibition, 683–685
    leader personality and effectiveness,
        688–692
    leadership, 674, 682–688
    trait activation model, 683, 684–685,
        686–687
PERSON model, accuracy, 349
Person models, describing others, 343
Personology Society, Carlson, 24
Person-situation debate
    Person x Situation (P x S) interactions, 66
    term, 65
Person-situation interaction
    attachment theory, 470–471
    social psychology, 25
Person variables, term, 67
Person x intervention strategy (P x IS),
    health behavior, 731, 736
Person x situation (P x S) perspective,
    health behavior, 731, 743

Person x situation interactions
    approaches to self, 279
    self-esteem, 265–266, 278–279
Perspective-taking, empathy, 429–431
Persuasion
    attitudes research, 107
    automatic change processes, 383
    central processing, 381
    changing behavior, 384–385
    changing implicit attitudes, 383–384
    changing intentions, 385–386
    elaboration likelihood model (ELM),
        379, 381, 382, 385
    explicit attitudes and, 380–381
    implementation intentions, 386
    shallow/heuristic processing, 382–383
Pessimism, defensive, 302
Pettigrew, Thomas F., multilevel modeling,
    239–240
P-factor analysis, well-being, 602
Philadelphia Geriatric Center Morale
    Scale, well-being, 598–599
Philosophies of Human Nature scale, 522
Phylogenetic analysis, evolution, 158–159
Phylogenetic tree, 158
Phylogeny, 158
Police interrogations, confessions, 756–760
Policy. *See* Social policy
Political activism, seeking social change,
    659–663
Politicization, low-status group
    membership, 790
Population thinking, evolution theory, 153
Positive affect (PA), 37
Positive and Negative Affect Schedule
    (PANAS), well-being, 599
Positron emission tomography (PET),
    cerebral blood flow, 118
Post-traumatic stress disorder (PTSD)
    survivor syndrome, 665
    war, 664–665
Poverty, Great Depression, 19
Power
    behavioral system, 476–477, 479,
        484–485
    impression, 353–354
    leadership personality, 676–677
    social dominance theory, 549
    social identity, 784
"Power of the situation," 65–66, 86–87, 182
Pragmatic accuracy, 349
Pragmatic response, adaptation, 158
Precaution adoption process model
    (PAPM), behavior change, 730, 735,
        741, 742, 746
Precipitating situations, interactional
    strategy, 495, 496
Preformationism, 158
Prefrontal cortex (PFC)
    asymmetries associated with emotion
        and motivation, 127–129
    empathy, 420
    implementing control, 134–135

Prejudice. *See also* Intergroup processes
    antisocial behavior, 420
    attachment, ideological attitudes and, 427
    authoritarian personality, 548–549
    contemporary forms of, 546–547
    defining intergroup, 546–547
    definitions, 546
    dispositional empathy, ideological
        attitudes and, 426–428
    from lack of empathy to, 427–428
    Great Depression, 19
    human propensities for, 547–548
    individual and ideological bases of,
        548–550
    ingroup love vs. outgroup hate, 546
    intergroup contact, 433
    Jim Crow racism, 545–546
    propensities for, 194–195
    realistic vs. symbolic threat, 551
    rejection, 589
    self-categorization theory (SCT),
        547–548
    social and structural dynamics of,
        550–552
    social dominance theory (SDT), 549–550
    social identity theory (SIT), 547
    social integration vs. segregation,
        551–552
    specifying sources of, 547–552
    stereotypes, 342
    system justification theory (SJT), 550
Prestige, status, 165–166
Prevention-focused tendencies,
    construction of self, 186
Priming
    attachment, 472, 485
    impression formation, 345–346
Prisoner Dilemma Paradigm context, 432
Prisoners, dehumanization, 433–435
Prisoner's dilemma game, 529
Procedural priming, 345
Process dissociation procedure (PDP),
    347–348
Professional associations, personality and
    social psychology, 5–6
Professional societies, social policy,
    820–821
Promotion focus, power, 476
Prosocial behavior, helping, 394–395
Proximate causation, evolutionary
    psychology, 156–157
Psychological dispositions, hormones and,
    138–139
Psychological distance, impression, 354
Psychological immune systems,
    evolutionary perspective, 171
*Psychological Science in Court: Beyond
    Common Knowledge*, Borgida and
    Fiske, 772
Psychological situations, nominal vs., 71
Psychology. *See also* Personality and social
    psychology; Personality psychology;
    Social psychology

interactional perspectives in, 494–496
multiculturalism, 637–640
self-regulation and P x E vulnerabilities, 583–587
Psychopathology
meaning and purpose, 579–580
personality and social behavior, 574
research and theory, 583
social psychology and, 575
Psychotherapy, behavior therapy, 575
Public policies. *See also* Social policy
multiculturalism, 625, 630
Punishment, justification, 538n.5
Puppet Procedure, empathy, 423

Q

Quarrelsome-dominant (QD), interpersonal circumplex, 450
Quarrelsome-submissive (QS), interpersonal circumplex, 450

R

Race-based rejection sensitivity model (RS-race), 457–458, 460
Racial bias
brain mapping, 130–131
intergroup anxiety, 136–137
research on intergroup bias and brain, 131–133
role-playing, 430
Racial boundaries, helping relations across, 406–407
Racial segregation, 16, 130
Racism, Jim Crow, 545–546
Random error process, whole trait theory, 53
Ravines, personality and social psychology, 830, 832–833
Realistic accuracy model (RAM), 349
Realistic threat vs. symbolic threat, 551
Recapitulation, dispositions and behavior, 375, 379
Recategorization, intergroups, 555–556
Recipient
consequence of help for, coping, 403
helping relations, 402–403
independence and, of help, 410–411
Reciprocal altruism, 409
Reciprocal design, group, 232
Regulation
attachment and emotion, 480–481
emotion, 129–130, 321–322
intergroup bias, 133–135
risk, and self-esteem, 503–505
Regulatory focus theory (RFT)
close relationships, 505–506
motivation, 290
Regulatory forces, behavioral field, 578
Reid, John E., lie detection, 755
Rejection. *See also* Interpersonal rejection
P x E vulnerabilities and interpersonal, 587–590
word, 589
Rejection sensitivity

If ... then ... signatures, 456–457
personality, 456–459
race-based model (RS-race), 457–458
self-fulfilling prophecy, 460
social environment, 77
social identity, 457–459
Relational conflict, resolution of, 532–533
Relational features, impressions, 353–354
Relationality, independent construction of self, 184–185
Relational schemas, personality dynamics, 454–455
Relational self, transference and, 455–456
Relational signatures, attachment, 507
Relations. *See* Helping relations
Relationship effect, 234
Relationships. *See also* Dyads; Groups
affecting individual-level outcomes, 461
attachment, 488
Big Five factors and leadership, 678–682
close, and well-being, 607–608
dependency/risk regulation and self-esteem, 503–505
diathesis-stress and attachment styles, 507–510
dynamics of risk regulation, 280
future directions, 510–513
helping relations, 407–409
impact of divorce, 652–654
interactional approach, 494–496
interactional programs of research, 503–510
intergroup motivation and needs, 562
marriage, 460–461
multiculturalism and adjustment, 638–639
personality processes shaping, 460–461
person-by-situation perspectives on close, 493–494
regulatory focus and close, 505–506
social and personality psychology, 209
Relative deprivation theory, group consciousness and collective action, 786–788
Relevance, perception of motivational, 125
Reliability, training and behavior assessment, 102–103
Repetitive priming, 345
Republican Party, 792, 812, 813
Reputations
coalition partners, 164–165
target, 352
Research, personality and social psychology, 4
Research methodology, social policy, 810–812
Research question, behavior assessment, 99
Resolution, group maintenance, 532–533
Resource-holding power (RHP), 476
Resource mobilization theory, social movements, 790–791

Reverse inference, neuroscience, 114–115
Reward processing, neuroscience, 126–127
Reward structures, social policy, 822
Reynolds, Katherine, 25
Riesman, David, 20
Right to Life, organization, 786
Right wing authoritarianism (RWA)
group consciousness, 792
prejudice, 426–427
stereotype, 343
Right-wing conservative, collective action, 797
Risk, group decision-making, 531
Risk regulation
dynamics of, in relationships, 280
person-by-situation approach, 503–505
Riverside Behavioral Q-sort (RBQ), observation system, 100, 101, 102
Riverside Situational Q-Sort, 70
"Robbers Cave" study, outgroup competition, 82, 94
Rogers, Carl, 23
Role-playing, empathy, 429–431
Rorschach test, well-being, 601
Rosenberg Self-Esteem Inventory (RSEI), 266
Ross, Edward, 16
Rule interdependent, interdependence theory, 80

S

Sadness, emotions, 323
Safety, attachment behavioral system, 471–473
Salience, group membership in intergroup contact, 553–558
Sanford, Nevitt, 22
Sapir, Edward, 17
Satisfaction with Life Scale (SWLS), well-being, 599, 601
Scaffolding
cultural-ecological, of self, 187–190
selfways, 187
Scherer, Klaus, 25
Scholarly journals, 6
Science, forensic psychology, 772
Science and Human Behavior, Skinner, 519
Secondary adaptation, 155
Secondary strategies, attachment, 470
Second Step: A Violence Prevention Program, 424
Secure-base script, behavior, 469
Security
attachment, 484, 485
attachment behavioral system, 471–473
Seeing groups, social categories, 130
Segmented assimilation, 556
Segregation
cross-group friendship, 558
racism and social policy, 16
social integration vs., 551–552
Selective prediction, term, 735

Self. *See also* Self-esteem
attachment and mental representations of, 481
attitudes, 122–124
automatic and controlled processing, 116
automaticity, 116–117
behaviorism, 16
Buddhist philosophy, 264–265
capacity to conceive, 263–264
control, 117
cultural-ecological scaffolding of, 187–190
defining the, 264–265
emotion and motivation, 124–125
empathy, 120–121
humanization, 121
independent constructions of, 183–187
interdependent constructions of, 185–187
interpersonal and intrapersonal dynamics of, 279–281
limitations of person, situation and person x situation, 279
mentalizing and theory of mind, 119–120
perceiving faces, 118–119
perception of, 118–122
personality and social psychology conceptions of, 265
role of self-directed negative affect, 136
self-regulation, 305
significance of medial prefrontal cortex (mPFC), 121–122
social cognition and, 116–125
social interactions, 461
social-personality psychology, 118
social psychology, 43
Self-categorization
helping relations, 405
social identity and, 650
Self-categorization theory (SCT)
prejudice, 547–548
us vs. them, 428
Self-compassion, 272
Self-concept clarity, social interactions, 461
Self-determination theory
assumptions of universality, 296–297
causality orientations, 296
internalization, autonomy and self-regulation, 296
intrinsic vs. extrinsic motivation, 295–296
motivation, 295–297
Self determination theory (SDT), motivation and person, 43–44
Self-efficacy
leadership, 680–681, 685
manipulation, 377
political, 791–792
Self-esteem
contingencies of, 269–270, 275
dynamics of, 280–281
effects on state, 278–279

future directions, 273
individual differences, 266–273
level of, 266–268, 273–274
moderator of effects of situations, 278
motives, 270–271, 275–277
personality and social psychology, 831–832
person-by-situation approach, 503–505
person x situation interactions, 278–279
relationship outcome, 460
self-transcendence, 271–273, 277–278
situational variability, 273–278
stability of, 268–269, 274–275
terror management theory, 276–277
viewing through person, situation and person x situation, 265–266
well-being, 608
Self-monitoring
adaptive contingent variation, 172
group maintenance, 533
leadership, 681–682
personality, 707
Self-referential perception, simulation theory and, 355–356
Self-regulation
affect and, 300
cognitive-affective personality system (CAPS), 76
defensive pessimism, 302
environmental vulnerabilities, 584–586
leadership, 689–690, 693
person, 43–44
personality vulnerabilities, 586
P x E vulnerabilities, 583–587
self and, 305
self-determination theory, 296
strength, 300
Self-relevance, social comparison, 166–167
Self-reports
assessing behavior, 96–97
cognitive processes and well-being, 604–605
Self-sacrifice, leadership, 717–718
Self-selection, environment, 550
Self-support, helping relations, 401–403
Self-threat, helping relations, 401–403
Self-threats, 275–277
Self-transcendence, self-esteem, 271–273, 277–278
Self-views, personal vulnerability, 582–583
Selfways
as habitus, 190
independent, 187–188
intentional worlds, 199
interdependent, 188–189
scaffolding or affordances, 187
Self-worth, relationship-specific, 461
Semantic priming, 345
Sensitivity, caregiving behavior, 474
Sentiments, 341

Sexual behavioral system, 475–476, 479, 484
Sexual Behavioral System scale, 484
Sexual minorities
multiculturalism, 641
social constructionism, 809–810
Shared leadership, team, 718–719, 721
Shoda, Yuichi, 26
Signature, term, 76
Significant-other (S-O) schemas, 455–456
Silent Generation, 660
Silent majority, 784
Simmel, George, 15
Simulation theory, self-referential perception of others, 355–356
Situation. *See also* Person-in-situation
antisocial behavior, 421–422
approaches to self, 279
aspects of study, 84–85
behavioral signature model, 75–78
cognitive-affective personality system (CAPS), 75–78
concrete vs. abstract properties, 71–72
confession, 758–759
conflict, and groups, 520–525
definitions, 69–73
delay-of-gratification, 82–83
descriptive vs. theory-driven approaches, 72–73
early concepts, 73–83
equal status of intergroups, 552–553
extending to groups, organizations and cultures, 85–86
field theory, 74
"if-then" model, 77
incorporating, 48
interaction of persons and, 4–5
interdependence theory (IT), 78–83
leadership as person-in-, 674, 682–688
lie detection, 756
long-term consequences of, 49
mattering in personality psychology, 66–68
mattering in social psychology, 64–66
multilevel radical coefficient model (MRCM), 253–254
nominal vs. psychological, 71
objective vs. perceived features, 70–71
person-situation debate, 39–40
person x situation interactionism, 74–75
"power of the situation", 65–66, 86–87
searching for stability in behavioral inconsistency, 448–451
self-esteem, 265–266
social value orientation (SVO), 522–523
strength, 683, 689
strong vs. weak, 83–84
taxonomy, 68–73, 80–81
term, 64, 69
trait relevance, 683, 689
types of interpersonal, 458

Situational attributions, experience of self, 185
Situational context, behavior, 77–78
Situational determinants
  help-giving, 396–397
  interpersonal and intergroup helping, 411
Situationalism, social psychology, 14
Situational moderators, personality and social behavior, 4
Situational strategy, 65, 495–496
Situational variability, self-esteem, 273–278
Situation effects, person effects vs., 25
Situation interactions, personality by, 331
Snyder, Mark, 26
Social, definition, 15
Social adjustive function, 382
Social behavior
  interactional approach, 494
  situationist approach, 395
Social bonds, dynamics of self-esteem, 280
Social cognition theory, behavioral control, 377
Social-cognitive perspective
  strengths, 50
  trait perspective and, 50
  weaknesses, 50–51
Social cognitive transference, impressions, 346
Social comparisons, specialization, 166–167
Social conditions, immigration, 656–657
Social constructionism, social policy, 809–810
Social constructivist, personality, 447
Social coordination, situation and behavior, 84–85
Social Darwinism
  environmentalism replacing, 17
  moralism, 15–16
  social psychology, 16
Social dominance orientation (SDO)
  prejudice, 426–427, 549–550
  stereotype, 343
Social dominance theory (SDT), prejudice, 549–550
Social exchange model, conformity, 530
Social exclusion, helping, 408
Social experiences, behavior changing over, 469–470
Social identity
  personality, 650–651
  rejection sensitivity, 457–459
  self-categorization and, 650
Social identity theory (SIT)
  collective action, 783–784
  leadership, 690–691
  prejudice, 547
  stratum consciousness, 784–785
  Tajfel, 25
  us vs. them, 428
Social information processing, work attitudes, 712–713

Social integration vs. segregation, 551–552
Social interaction. *See also* Help-giving; Helping relations
  cultural cognitive-affective processing system (C-CAPS), 448, 451–452
  helping others, 394–396
  individual-level outcomes, 461
  local consistencies in if ... then ... patterning, 459
  personality, 446–451
  personality shaping relationships, 460–461
  understanding personality within, 451–454
Social Issues and Policy Review, 821
Socially undesirable behaviors, 96
Social movements
  access to, organizations, 791
  civil rights, 660
  generations, 660
  labor, 659
  personality and, experience, 659–663
  protest activism, 660–661
  resource mobilization theory, 790–791
  student participation, 659
  Vietnam War, 659
  women, 661–663
Social networking, behavior, 105
Social neuroscience. *See also* Neuroscience
  brain, 112
Social order, 15
Social outcome, emotion, 330
Social policy
  action research and, 805–807
  challenges and caution, 822–825
  conducting research, 813–817
  differences between personality and social psychology, 807–813
  essentialism and social constructionism, 809–810
  focus on issues and problems, 804–805
  ideological congeniality, 812–813
  influences on involvement, 819–822
  locus or causes of problems, 808–809
  mission statements, 804–805
  political ideology and, 823–824
  professional societies, 820–821
  promises and aspirations, 824–825
  public policies, 805
  reward structures, 822
  scale of impact, 824–825
  social issues, 806–807
  theory vs. policy work, 823
  time and methodological approaches, 810–812
  training programs, 821–822
  types of involvement, 817–819
Social problems. *See also* Social policy
  locus or causes of, 808–809
  See also Social policy
Social psychologists, 3
  attitudes, 40

cognitive perspectives on person, 42–43
contributions to science of well-being, 598, 604–610, 615
defining situation, 73
empathy-antisocial behavior, 421–422
integration of personality and, 46
integration of theories, 788–795
intergroup bias and the brain, 131–133
leadership, 674
morale and attitudes, 20
motivational perspectives, 44
mutual acceptance of personality and, 46–48
personality and behavior, 447
recognizing included concerns, 56
relationship of personality to, 45–49
research, 4
routes of integration, 48–49
situations mattering in, 64–66
trait perspectives, 41
vulnerability-inducing environments, 580–582
whole trait theory, 49–56
Social Psychology, Allport, 18
Social Psychology and Personality Science, 27, 834
Social Psychology Network, training, 822
The Social Psychology of Groups, 86
Social Relations Department
  Harvard, 20, 835
  interdisciplinary scholarship, 20–21
Social relations model (SRM)
  accuracy, 349
  group research, 234–235
Social resources, emotions, 324–325
Social responsibility, help-giving, 397
Social roles, describing others, 343–344
Social situation, persons and situations, 14
Social sphere
  adaptive contingent variation, 172
  affordances in, 167–168
Social value orientation (SVO), group behavior, 522–523
Social work, political bias, 21
Societal level, acculturation and multiculturalism, 627, 628, 630
Society
  multiculturalism, 637–640
  predicting well-being of, 599
Society for Personality and Social Psychology (SPSP), 6, 26, 820–821
Society for Personology, 833
Society for the Psychological Study of Social Issues (SPSSI), 19, 821
Society of Experimental Social Psychology, 6, 27, 833
Society of Personality and Social Psychology (SPSP), 833
Sociocultural bases
  attitudes and dispositions, 192–194
  content of identity stories, 191–192
  cultural-ecological variation, 193
  personal identity, 191–192

Sociocultural bases (*Contd.*)
  propensities for prejudice, 194–195
  sociocultural sources, 193–194
  species-typical tendencies, 190–191
Socratic effect, term, 380
Spandrels, adaptation, 155
Special design, concept, 155
Specialization, social comparisons and, 166–167
Spencer, Herbert, 16
Spontaneous inferences, behaviors, 347
Spontaneous responses, attitude, 374–375
Spontaneous trait inferences (STIs), 347
Spontaneous trait transference (STT), 347
Sport groups, task-performing, 526–527
Stability
  behavioral inconsistency across situations, 448–451
  self-esteem, 268–269, 274–275
  social interaction, 459
Stability-inducing process, whole trait theory, 53
Stage matching, behavior change, 741–742
State affect, asymmetric frontal activity, 128
States, density distributions of, 52–53
Statistical interactionism, person and situation, 5
Statistical tool, multilevel analysis, 256–257
Status
  dominance and prestige, 165–166
  helper-recipient relations, 404
Stereotype content model (SCM), 342
Stereotypes
  accuracy, 348–349
  African Americans, 431
  categories, 341–343
  essentialism, 341
  motivation, 291
  personality research, 534
  priming, 345–346
Stereotyping
  antisocial behavior, 420
  emotions, 328
  outgroup member, 430
  racial bias, 133
Stern, Wilhelm, holistic perspective, 18
Stimuli, emotions, 323
Stimulus situation, 73
Stouffer, Samuel, 20
Strange Situation, assessment procedure, 477
Strategic helping, 406
Stratum consciousness, definition, 784–785
Strength
  job attitude, 714–715
  situation, 683, 689
Strength model, regulatory control, 82–83
Stress, eyewitness identifications, 762
Strong situations
  interactional strategy, 495–496
  vs. weak, 83–84
Stroop color naming task, 117
Stroop task, control, 135

Stroop test, emotions, 323
Structural equation modeling (SEM), well-being, 600
Structure, goal, 298–299
Subjective norm, theory of planned behavior, 376–377
Subjective well-being. *See also* Well-being
  goals and motives, 603–604
  personality, 37–38
  term, 597–598
  value-as-a-moderator model, 612–613
Subjectivism, social psychology, 14
Suffering, 409, 434–435
Suggestibility, confessions, 757–758
Superordinate identities, intergroups, 555–556
Support Our Soldiers (SOS), 792
Surveillance monitors, behavior, 104–105
Survivor syndrome, 665
Sustained volunteering, 408–409
Symbolic threat, realistic vs., 551
SYMLOG (System for the Multiple Level Observation of Groups), 20, 100, 101
Sympathy, empathy and perspective-taking, 427
Systematic approach, groups, 519–520
System justification theory (SJT), group hierarchy, 550

T
Tailoring, message, for health, 740–741
Tajfel, Henri, social identity theory (SIT), 25
Taoism, 15
Target effect, 234
Targets
  features, 351–352
  impressions, 338–339
Target variance, 235
Task
  group, 525–527
  group data complexity, 212–214
Taxonomy, situations, 68–73, 80–81
Teaching, personality and social psychology, 836
Team leadership. *See also* Leadership; Organizational psychology
  collective underpinnings of, 720–721
  organizational psychology, 718–719
  team effectiveness, 719–720
  teams and teamwork, 719–722
Team mental models, teamwork, 720–721
Team transactive memory, teamwork, 721
Technologies, behavior assessment, 103–105
Temporal process, whole trait theory, 53
Temporal structure
  interdependence, 81, 82–83
  situation dimensions, 500, 501
Territories, combined, personality and social psychology, 830, 831–832
Terror management, social psychology, 581

Terror management theory, self-esteem, 276–277
Test gap, domination, 200
Thematic Apperception Test (TAT), 19, 293, 481, 601–602
Theoretical integrations, well-being, 612–614
Theoretic-empirical response, adaptation, 158
Theory borrowing
  collective underpinnings of, 720–721
  organizational psychology and practice of, 703–704
Theory-driven approaches, descriptive vs., 72–73
Theory of evolution, Darwin, 152–153
Theory of mind
  explanations, 355
  mentalizing and, 119–120
  traits, 340
Theory of planned behavior (TPB)
  attitude, 376
  health, 731
  intentions and behavior, 378
  perceived behavioral control, 377
  subjective norm, 376–377
Thibaut, John, 22
Third culture, emergent, 640
Thomas, W. I., personality and situation, 16
Thought
  emotion as trigger of, 326
  emotions regulating, 326–329
Threat, realistic vs. symbolic, 551
Time, social policy, 810–812
The Tipping Point, Gladwell, 94
Top-down approach, rejection sensitivity, 459
Trace measures, assessing behavior, 96–97
Training
  deception detection, 755–756
  programs for social policy, 821–822
  Social Psychology Network, 822
Trait activation
  leadership effectiveness, 684–685, 688–689
  person-in-situation, 683, 686–687
Trait activation theory, organizational psychology, 706, 708–709
Trait judgments, accuracy in, 349
Trait relevance, situation, 683, 689
Traits. *See also* Person
  accessibility of personality, 368–369
  adulthood personality change, 39
  behavioral genetics and genetics, 38–39
  Big Five, 523–524
  conceptions of, 340–341
  cross-cultural validity of Big Five, 37
  current knowledge about, 35
  explanatory and descriptive, 51
  hierarchy, 36–37

improving measurement, 37
person-situation debate, 39–40
perspectives on person, 35–41
predicting important life outcomes, 38
prediction of general outcomes, 38
processes and mechanisms underlying, 40–41
processes underlying, 54
relations to each other, 339–340
research developments, 36–41
resting frontal cortical asymmetry, 127–128
schematicity, 369
social psychology, 41
specific and important, 39
strengths and weaknesses, 50–51
subjective well-being, 37–38
target and observer agreement, 39
understudies, of groups, 526
whole trait theory, 49–56
Transference, relational self and, 455–456
Transfer of attitudes recursively (TAR) model, 347
Transformational leadership
effectiveness, 679–681, 690, 691
five-factor model, 685–686
organization psychology, 717–718
Transmission gap, attachment, 487
Transtheoretical model (TTM), 385, 730
Trigger of thought, emotion as, 326
Trust
coalition partners, 164
group behavior, 521–522
group performance, 526
Tversky, Amos, 28

U

Ultimate causation, evolutionary psychology, 156–157
Uncertainty orientation (UO), groups, 529
Unconscious motives, person, 43
Unintentional behaviors, 340
United Nations, Human Development Index (HDI), 254–255
United States
context of divorce, 652–653
funding agencies, 834–835
immigration, 654–655
personality psychology, 17
Universality, self-determination theory, 296–297
University of California at Berkeley, Institute of Personality, Assessment, and Research (IPAR), 20
University of Michigan
dual crises, 23–25
Institute for Social Research (ISR), 20
University of Minnesota, personality and social programs, 21
University of Virginia, psychology, 21
Us vs. them, empathy, 428–435
Utilitarian function, 382

V

Valence acquisition, impressions, 346–347
Valuation rules, interdependence theory, 79
Value-as-a-moderator mode, subjective well-being, 612–613
Value-expressive function, 382
Variability
behavior, 95
cross-situational, 448
Variance components, multilevel radical coefficient model (MRCM), 251–252
Vienna-circle positivism, operational definitions, 21
Vietnam War, opposition, 659
Violence, 425, 434
Virtual reality, behavior assessment, 104
Visual cues, target features, 351
Vogel, Ezra, 20
Volunteering, helping, 408–409
Volunteerism
AIDS/HIV, 813–817
collective action and, 795–796
Volunteer process model, 409
Vulnerability
complexity of P x E effects, 590–591
environments, 580–582, 584–586
personal, 582–583, 586–587
personality, 586, 590
P x E, and interpersonal rejection, 587–590
self-regulation and P x E, 583–587

W

Wainwright v. Witt, 768
War
general impact of, 663–665
Holocaust, 665–667
internment of Japanese Americans, 665–667
Persian Gulf War, 664–665
personality and social psychology, 18–21
World War II, 664
Watson, John, behaviorist manifesto, 17
Weak situations
interactional strategy, 495–496
strong vs., 83–84
Weapons, eyewitness identifications, 762
Webcams, behavior, 104–105
Weber, Max, 15
WEIRD (western, educated, industrialized, rich and Democratic societies), social policy, 811, 823
Well-being. *See also* Individual well-being; Subjective well-being
AREA model, 607, 616
benefits of integrative approach, 614
close relationships and, 607–608
cognitive processes underlying self-reports, 604–605
construct validity, 599–600
cultural psychology, 608
future directions for research, 614–615
gene-environment interaction, 611
goals and motives, 603–604
hedonic adaptation, 606–607
hedonic treadmill theory, 613–614
intervention studies, 608–610
intra-individual variation, 601–603
judgmental biases, 606
latent trait, 600–601
methodological integration, 610–612
mood effects, 605
personality and social psychology contributions, 610–614
personality psychology contributions, 598, 599–604
social psychology contributions, 598, 604–610
term, 597
theoretical integrations, 612–614
value-as-a-moderator model, 612–613
West India, migration, 657
White, Robert W., *Abnormal Psychology*, 19
Whole trait theory
complementary strengths, 50
complementary weaknesses, 50–51
Density Distributions approach, 52–53
descriptive and explanatory side, 51, 52–55
fitting two parts of traits together, 51
producing Big Five, 55
Williams v. Florida, 768
Windelband, Wilhelm, goals of scientific work, 14
Within-person variability, multilevel analysis, 241
Wizards, lie detection, 756
Women
activism of rights, 792
African American oppression and, 16
divorce, 652–654
Women's Movement, 782
Work. *See also* Organizational psychology
affective events theory, 713
education and, experience, 791
employee engagement, 712
job attitudes, 710–715
job involvement, 714
job satisfaction, 713–714
leadership, 715–719
perceived organization support, 712, 714
personality and social psychology, 712–715
role in lives, 701–702
social information processing theory, 712–713
specific work attitudes, 711–712
work psychology, 702
Working memory capacity (WMC), perceiver feature, 353
Working models, behavior, 469–470
World Values Scale, well-being, 598

World Values Survey, multilevel analysis, 254

Worldviews, 579, 582–583

World War I, 17

World War II, 651, 664

World wars, multilevel analysis, 255

Wundt, Wilhelm, natural science and human science, 14–15

Y

Yakima Native Americans, anthropology and psychology, 17

Youth, reducing aggression, 424–425

YouTube, behavior, 105

Z

Zander, Alvin, 22

Zero acquaintance, perception, 338